Children & Adolescents
Clinical Formulation & Treatment

Comprehensive Clinical Psychology

Volume 5

Children & Adolescents: Clinical Formulation & Treatment

Comprehensive Clinical Psychology

Volume 5

Editor
Thomas Ollendick
Virginia Tech, Blacksburg, VA, USA

Comprehensive Clinical Psychology Editors-in-Chief
Alan S. Bellack
The University of Maryland at Baltimore, MD, USA
Michel Hersen
Pacific University, Forest Grove, OR, USA

2001

AN IMPRINT OF ELSEVIER SCIENCE

AMSTERDAM—LONDON—NEW YORK—OXFORD—PARIS—SHANNON—TOKYO

Elsevier Science Ltd., The Boulevard, Langford Lane, Kidlington, Oxford, OX5 1GB, UK

First edition 1998
Paperback edition 2001

Library of Congress Cataloging-in-Publication Data
Comprehensive clinical psychology / editors-in-chief. Alan S. Bellack, Michel Hersen. —1st ed.
    p. cm.
    Includes indexes.
    Contents: v. 1. Foundations / volume editor, Eugene Walker — v. 2. Professional issues / volume editor, Arthur N. Wiens — v. 3. Research and Methods / volume editor, Nina R. Schooler — v. 4. Assessment / volume editor, Cecil R. Reynolds — v. 5. Children & adolescents / volume editor, Thomas Ollendick — v. 6. Adults / volume editor, Paul Salkovskis — v. 7. Clinical geropsychology / volume editor, Barry Edelstein — v. 8. Health psychology / volume editors, Derek W. Johnston and Marie Jonhston — v. 9. Applications in diverse populations / volume editor, Nirbhay N. Singh — v. 10. Sociocultural and individual differences / volume editor, Cynthia D. Belar — v. 11. Indexes.
    1. Clinical psychology. I. Bellack, Alan S. II. Hersen, Michel.
    [DNLM: 1. Psychology, Clinical. WM 105 C737 1998]
RC467.C597 1998
616.89--dc21
DNLM/DLC
for Library of Congress   97-50185
                                    CIP

British Library Cataloguing in Publication Data
A catalogue record for this book is available from the British Library.

ISBN 0-08-042707-3 (set : alk. paper)
ISBN 0-08-043144-5 (Volume 5)
ISBN 0-08-044020-7 (Volume 5 paperback)

Transferred to digital printing 2005

Contents

Contents

Introduction to *Comprehensive Clinical Psychology*

Co-Editors-in-Chief

Alan S. Bellack and Michel Hersen

Background

Clinical psychology is a relatively new field. While its roots can be traced back to at least the late nineteenth century, its evolution as a distinct academic discipline and profession dates only to the Second World War. The first 20 years of this postwar period saw steady, albeit nonspectacular, growth. Based substantially in the United States and Europe during this period, the study of clinical psychology developed as an alternative to medical school and psychiatry for many students interested in clinical service careers or the scientific study of human behavior. Postgraduate training was conducted exclusively in large university psychology departments within a strict scientist–practitioner model. The total number of Ph.D. candidates admitted to graduate school programs each year was relatively small; there were fewer than 50 accredited programs in the United States during much of this period, each admitting only 5–10 students. The number of new Ph.D.'s produced each year was substantially less, as many students failed to complete the rigorous scientific requirements of these elite programs. Career opportunities were similarly delimited, due in no small part to restraints on clinical practice imposed by psychiatrists and other physicians. The dominant form of psychotherapy was psychoanalysis, and psychologists were either excluded from psychoanalytic institutes or trained only as lay analysts who were proscribed from clinical practice. Few jurisdictions awarded licenses for independent practice, and psychologists generally were not reimbursed for their activities unless they worked under the direction of a physician. A sizable minority of clinical psychologists followed their mentors into university positions, teaching and conducting research. The majority, who were more interested in clinical service, opted for work in large psychiatric or Veterans Administration hospitals, where the modal activity was psychological testing; verbal psychotherapy was provided at the discretion of medical supervisors. A gradually increasing number of psychologists elected to be in private practice, where there was a greater professional autonomy. Medical hegemony over services for psychiatric disorders was even greater in Europe and Latin America.

The last 30 years has witnessed a massive change in the profession, stimulated by a number of scientific, clinical, and economic factors. Psychoanalysis gradually fell out of favor due to a dearth of data on its effectiveness and a desire for shorter term treatments that were not the primary purview of psychiatrists. First, client-centered therapy and then behavior therapy emerged as brief, highly effective alternatives. The former was entirely a product of clinical psychology, and was the intellectual and technical forebear of the current mandate for empirical evaluation of psychotherapies.

Carl Rogers, his colleagues, and students were the first to demonstrate the feasibility of careful, objective evaluation of the therapy process as well as outcome. While behavior therapy owes much of its legacy to psychiatrists such as Joseph Wolpe, it was substantially a product of academic psychologists searching for an approach with a strong scientific underpinning (in this case learning theory) that could be subjected to rigorous scientific scrutiny. Early behavior therapy emerged simultaneously in the UK and the US: in the UK psychologists such as Hans Eysenck based their work on Pavlov and classical conditioning, while in the US researchers were following Skinner and operant conditioning theories. The two schools merged with cognitive therapy, developed largely by Beck and Ellis through the 1960s, when the limitations of behavior therapy in isolation became apparent, particulary with depressed patients, and cognitive-behavior therapy is now widely practised.

Behavior therapy and cognitive-behavior therapy have not only proven themselves to be effective with a broad array of disorders, they have since been shown to be very successful alternatives to pharmacotherapy as well. Notably, behavior therapy was able to produce significant changes in populations that had previously been warehoused as untreatable, including people with physical and developmental disabilities and schizophrenia. Many of the most important contributions to the behavior therapies came from the UK, The Netherlands, South Africa, Australia, and Scandinavia, providing a tremendous stimulus for the development of clinical psychology globally. The availability of cost-effective, scientifically sound nonmedical treatments has decreased the medical monopoly of psychiatric/mental health services around the world and fostered the evolution of clinical psychology as a legally sanctioned helping profession, as well as a prestigious scientific discipline.

Scientific advances in our understanding of the brain and the role of psychosocial factors in physical health and illness have led to the development of two other rapidly growing subspecialties of clinical psychology: neuropsychology and health psychology. Novel assessment and treatment technologies in these two areas have created professional opportunities for clinical psychologists in medical schools, general medical hospitals, and other nonpsychiatric settings. Clinical psychologists can now be found conducting research and providing services in departments of neurology and neurosurgery, medicine, cardiac surgery, pediatrics, anesthesiology, oncology, and other medical specialty areas, as well as in the traditional psychiatric settings. They increasingly serve as directors of governmental agencies and service facilities. They comprise a large percentage of research grant recipients in the US, Canada, and the UK, and sit on prestigious government and foundation review boards. In fact the field has earned sufficient public recognition that it now has the somewhat dubious distinction of having clinical psychologists as lead characters on television shows and in cinema.

Stimulated, in part, by these exciting developments in scientific progress and clinical creativity, the field has grown geometrically in the past two decades. Psychology is now the second leading undergraduate major in the US and is increasingly popular elsewhere in the world as well. There are now more than 175 doctoral programs in the United States, each admitting many more students per annum than the 5–10 that has been typical of traditional scientist–practitioner Ph.D. programs over the past 25 years. Some of these schools have entering classes as large as 200 per year. Moreover, along with the professional school movement, which began in the 1970s, a new degree, the Psy.D. (or Doctorate in Psychology), is regularly being offered as an alternative to the Ph.D. Basically a professional rather than an academic degree, the Psy.D. is reflective of the local practitioner–scientist model rather than the scientist–practitioner.

Yet another trend in the field is the proliferation of master's level psychologists, specifically trained to carry out some of the more mundane functions formerly implemented by doctoral level psychologists. Indeed, each year in the United States alone 10 000 new master's level psychologists graduate from university programs. The financial and programmatic implication of such large numbers is obvious.

Statistics are not readily available about the size of the profession in all regions of the globe, but anecdotal evidence supports the hypothesis that the field is growing worldwide. As previously indicated, behavioral and cognitive-behavioral therapies owe a substantial debt to scientists and clinicians from Europe, Australia, and South Africa. There are now enough cognitive-behavior therapists to support national societies in most Western European countries, as well as Asia, Australia, and Latin America. Many of the most important developments in the psychosocial treatment of severe and persistent mental illness in the last decade have come from the United Kingdom, Australia, Switzerland, and Germany. Psychologists in Scandinavia, the United Kingdom, and the Netherlands have played a central role in the development of cognitive-behavioral treatments for anxiety and depression, and there have also been notable contributions from these regions to health psychology. As the hold of psychoanalytic therapies on psychiatric treatment in Europe continues its inevitable decline, there will be increasing opportunities for clinical psychologists to provide shorter term behavioral and cognitive-behavioral treatments. In addition, exciting developments are also emerging from Japan, China, and other countries in the Pacific rim. It seems likely that the global influence of regional approaches and thinking will lead to a more multicultural and universal psychology than has been the case in the past.

The scientific and clinical literatures have burgeoned along with the number of clinical psychologists in the world. This has been an era of rapid growth of knowledge and increasing specialization. General topics, such as psychological assessment, clinical child psychology, and psychotherapy, that used to merit only one or two graduate courses to establish expertise, have expanded and are subdivided to the extent that circumscribed specialty areas, such as neuropsychology, geropsychology, behavioral pediatrics, or cognitive-behavior therapy for depression can each require postdoctoral training. Consequently, hundreds of undergraduate, graduate, and professional level texts are published each year. Specialty journals abound. Where a few key generalist journals such as the *Journal of Consulting and Clinical Psychology* used to represent the entire field, each subdiscipline now has multiple journals, and there are both national journals (e.g., the *British Journal of Clinical Psychology*, the *British Journal of Health Psychology*, the *Australian Journal of Cognitive and Behavioral Therapy*) and journals representing specific populations or disorders (e.g., *Addictive Behaviors*, *Journal of Family Violence*, *Journal of Clinical Geropsychology*), or domains of practice (e.g., *Journal of Clinical Psychology in Medical Setting*). Specialization has made it difficult for professionals to keep abreast of developments within their immediate areas of expertise, and impossible for them to be conversant with the literature in other areas. Moreover, given the plethora of choices, it is also virtually impossible for either students or professionals to know where to find the most accurate, up-to-date information in most areas.

The combination of a large and increasing number of students and professionals, and rapidly growing scientific and clinical literature, makes this a particularly appropriate time for *Comprehensive Clinical Psychology*. This multivolume work encompasses the entire field, and represents a single source of information on the scientific status of clinical psychology and its subspecialties, on theory, and on clinical techniques. The work covers the history of the field, and current thinking about training, professional standards and practices, and sociocultural factors in mental health and illness.

Genesis of Comprehensive Clinical Psychology

Following preliminary conceptual discussions between Elsevier Science and Alan S. Bellack at several international conferences in 1994, Michel Hersen was asked to join as Co-Editor-in-Chief. The first official planning meeting for the project took place in June 1995. In addition to Elsevier Science staff, Alan S. Bellack and Michel Hersen invited Tom Ollendick, Nina Schooler, and Warren Tryon to serve as consultants. At that meeting, the philosophical and international scope of the project was agreed upon and established, with the scientific underpinnings of the field identified as the model. The objective here was to ensure that chapters reflect our core knowledge and that the material stand the test of time.

At that meeting, we also underscored that since clinical psychology was now an international discipline, the work should reflect contributions at the cross-cultural level, with chapters solicited from eminent psychologists worldwide. Although it was acknowledged that the United States was in the forefront of the field, the work could not simply represent the American perspective but to the extent possible would represent diversity at its best. Consistent with the international perspective, at the initial planning meeting, the importance of having an Honorary International Editorial Advisory Board comprised of international representatives was acknowledged, and the 10 specific volumes to comprise *Comprehensive Clinical Psychology* were identified. Preliminary outlines for each volume were developed and volumes editors were considered.

The international perspective was to be reflected at a tripartite level. First, diversity among editors and contributors for their respective volumes was selected as a goal. Second, chapters in each volume were designed to reflect diversity by providing the reader with worldwide examples, not simply the Anglo-Saxon view. Of course, where basic facts and principles were the same, there was no need to present regional diversity. Third, and related to the first two parts, the Honorary International Editorial Advisory Board provided us with an international perspective on overall organization and specifics for the individual volumes.

Between June and October 1995, Alan S. Bellack and Michel Hersen, in consultation with Elsevier Science, invited the ten volume editors to assume their positions, and a meeting of the Editors-in-Chief, the ten volume editors (C. Eugene Walker, Arthur N. Wiens, Nina R. Schooler, Cecil R. Reynolds, Thomas Ollendick, Paul Salkovskis, Barry Edelstein, Marie Johnston and Derek W. Johnston, Nirbhay N. Singh, and Cynthia D. Belar), and Elsevier Science staff was convened in October of that year. At that meeting, each of the volume editors presented his or her conception of the relevant volume, and the nature of coverage and particular contributors was discussed at length. Most of all the philosophical underpinnings of the work were stressed so as to insure intervolume consistency.

Subsequent to the October 1995 meeting, the enormous work to bring this project to fruition began, with potential authors invited to contribute, manuscripts reviewed, and then edited. Were it not for the wonders of electronic communication, a project of this scope would not have been possible, especially given the international aspects involved. A lengthy series of checks and balances was instituted to guarantee the quality and excellence of each contribution. The volume editor first approved each contributor's chapter outline, followed by editing and approval of the text. This process frequently required several revisions. The Co-Editor-in-Chief then reviewed each chapter for scope, level, and overlap, but only after the volume editor had first verified the accuracy of references cited. After the Co-Editor-in-Chief's labors, the manuscript was reviewed by Elsevier staff for format, writing style, reference checking, and other technical issues.

Aims and Scope

The final organization and contents of the work evolved over a series of discussions between the Editors-in-Chief, the volume editors, and Elsevier Science. It was comparatively easy to select the primary domains that needed to be covered: history, treatment, assessment, research, training, and professional issues. It was also comparatively easy to identify the first two-thirds, or so, of specific topics that required chapter-length coverage: treatment of the primary *DSM/ICD* disorders, basic research strategies, standard assessment techniques, etc. However, organizing the vast set of requisite topics into coherent volumes, determining which topics warranted independent chapters, and assigning page limits to individual chapters proved to be daunting. Two broad organizational themes immediately suggested themselves: a focus on core themes or techniques across populations vs. integrated coverage of populations. For example, the former would have entailed volumes on treatment modalities, such as behavior therapy, as they are applied to children and adults, while the latter would call for separate volumes on children and adults that covered diverse approaches. To complicate matters, some topics, such as Research Methods and Professional Issues, do not lend themselves to breakdown by population, and others, such as Behavioral Medicine, do not lend themselves to a breakdown by themes or techniques. Volume length was also an important factor, making some content-based solutions less practical than others. For example, we determined that treatment should receive more attention than assessment; a strict population-based solution would have led to separate short volumes on assessment of adults and children. Ultimately, we opted for an organizational structure that balanced practical considerations with our collective prediction about how the individual volumes would be used. While it was different earlier in the development of the field, we believe that the current trend is for people to be more organized around populations than techniques. Hence, more people are likely to pick up and cross-reference a single volume on children or the elderly than a volume on Behavior Therapy. Our strategy for identifying chapter length topics and associated page limits is more difficult to explain. Once again, we relied on our collective judgement, honed by negotiation. In rough order, priority was given to topics that had established empirical literatures, that were deemed to be "important," that had broad interest, and that were likely to be at least as important in the next decade. Page limits were determined substantially by estimates of the first two criteria. We began with an overall target for the entire work and minimums and maximums for volumes, and then worked backwards to divide up the allotted pages among the chapters designated for each volume. Given that no scheme will please everyone, we are confident that the organization of the work adequately reflects the field now and in the foreseeable future.

Under the careful aegis of the outstanding group of experts comprising the Honorary International Editorial Advisory Board, 10 leading international scholars were selected to edit the 10 specific volumes.

Volume 1 (*Foundations*), edited by C. Eugene Walker, provides a complete overview of the basic foundations of clinical psychology, with special emphasis on the relationship between clinical psychology and other fields of science. Beginning with a brief history of clinical psychology, as well as a look at its current scientific status, this informative volume covers such topics as the biological bases of clinical psychology, elucidating research in genetics, psychobiology, psychopharmacology, and the use of animal models in human mental health problems; clinical psychology in the behavioral sciences, including anthropology, epidemiology, sociology, and research psychology; and the major systems and theories that are used in clinical psychology. The volume also describes various techniques for library research and information retrieval in psychology.

Volume 2 (*Professional Issues*), edited by Arthur W. Wiens, focuses on the professional, legal, and ethical issues that are relevant to clinical psychology. The volume addresses the various educational and training programs available, such as doctoral study, internship training, and postdoctoral residency programs, and reviews the accreditation of these programs. Also highlighted are the various international government guidelines for registration, certification, and licensing, including a discussion of the advantages of specialty recognition and practice certificates. The volume concludes with a look at ethical and legal guidelines in the management of clinical psychology practices, national healthcare policies, and advocacy efforts for government support for practitioners.

Volume 3 (*Research and Methods*), edited by Nina R. Schooler, explores the function of research in clinical psychology. The volume begins with an in-depth look at research approaches, including the use of descriptive studies, single case designs, observational methods, and other methods of analysis. The volume goes on to explore a broad range of topics that have been the focus of research, such as test development and validation, personality assessment, clinical interventions, and service evaluations and outcomes. Finally, various statistical techniques are reviewed, including descriptive and inferential statistics, factor analysis, and sampling and generalizability.

Volume 4 (*Assessment*), edited by Cecil R. Reynolds, provides valuable information on the development and role of assessment in clinical practice, analyzing such topics as psychometrics; taxonomic, functional, and actuarial approaches to diagnosis; and specific instruments, techniques, and procedures. Chapters also review the range of assessment techniques and procedures used in clinical practice, with emphasis on intelligence, neuropsychological, personality, projective, computer-assisted, therapeutic, and forensic assessment. The volume concludes with a review of legal guidelines and regulations in the use of psychological testing.

Volume 5 (*Children & Adolescents: Clinical Formulation & Treatment*), edited by Thomas Ollendick, draws on the experience and research of leading scientists and clinicians from Australia, Canada, Israel, the United Kingdom, and the United States to present state-of-the-art information on all aspects of child psychology and psychiatry, with special attention given to the psychopathology, assessment, treatment, and prevention of childhood behavioral disorders. The volume highlights the developmental-contextual framework used in the clinical formulation of these disorders, as well as process and outcome issues in treatment. Various theoretical perspectives are also reviewed, including applied behavior analysis, family systems therapy, play therapy, and pharmacologic therapy. In the final section, all of the major childhood disorders found in the *DSM* and *ICD* are described, with information on their prevalence, etiology, assessment, and treatment. This section also analyzes the empirical status of the various therapies used for treatment of childhood disorders.

Volume 6 (Adults: Clinical Formulation & Treatment), edited by Paul Salkovskis, provides valuable insights into the basis of the psychological theories and interventions used for behavioral and emotional problems and reviews how to integrate clinical skills with these theories. Various treatment approaches are addressed, such as cognitive therapy, family therapy, and Humanistic/Rogerian/Gestalt approaches, as well as the issues related to treatments, including stress management, arousal reduction methods, suicidal behavior, and specific issues in working with groups. The final section details specific problem areas and disorders, ranging from such universally recognized problems as gambling and substance abuse to more specific disorders such as post-traumatic stress, depression, obsessive-compulsive, and the various phobias. Each chapter in the volume emphasizes approaches that have an empirical basis.

Volume 7 (Clinical Geropsychology), edited by Barry Edelstein, addresses the emerging field of clinical psychology in the aging population. The volume begins with a review of this area of research, presenting important epidemiological information. The volume then offers a detailed look at issues that range from analyzing physiological and cognitive aspects to cognitive changes and specific neurological disorders common among older adults. Specific topics covered include sexuality, bereavement, anxiety, substance abuse, and schizophrenia. Each chapter presents a summary of clinical research and its practical application. Voids in the knowledge base are also noted, along with recommendations for the direction of future investigations. The volume also addresses management problems, such as incontinence, wandering, and aggressive behavior, and reviews the various mental healthcare systems available in different countries.

Volume 8 (Health Psychology), edited by Derek W. Johnston and Marie Johnston, provides a comprehensive overview of the development and application of clinical health psychology. Beginning with a discussion of training, assessment, and measurement issues, this volume analyzes the key behaviors that either affect or are related to health. Topics covered include stress and disease, the experience of illness, and behavior that can affect the neuroendocrine, cardiovascular, and immune systems. The volume also provides a detailed analysis of specific clinical problems and their psychological aspects and interventions. These include cancer, diabetes, epilepsy, disfigurement, and smoking.

Volume 9 (Applications in Diverse Populations), edited by Nirbhay N. Singh, covers the broad spectrum of diverse issues that clinical psychologists typically face in their work. Four sections outline the various psychological aspects found in different populations, as well as methods for assessment, diagnostic information, and interventions useful with these different groups. Section I focuses on select child, adolescent, and adult populations, including those with developmental disorders, learning disabilities, and mental retardation. Section II is devoted to various types of families and their issues, including families of individuals with HIV or AIDS, families of alcoholics, and families of children with serious emotional disturbances. Section III covers victims of violence and abuse, including child sexual abuse. Section IV examines perpetrators of violence and abuse, including sex offenders and issues of domestic violence.

Volume 10 (Sociocultural and Individual Differences), edited by Cynthia D. Belar, covers cross-cultural psychopathology and interventions. Chapters examine such select topics as gender, sexual orientation, socioeconomic status, religions, and training for clinical psychologists. The volume also provides valuable insights into the use of clinical psychology in different parts of the world, as well as personality assessment across international settings.

Given the scope and detail of *Comprehensive Clinical Psychology*, Volume 11 is devoted to: (i) a Name Index, (ii) a Subject Index, (iii) a List of Contributors, and (iv) a list of the Contents of All Volumes. The Name Index is an accumulation of all the authors who are cited in text in the reference sections throughout the entire work. The Subject Index, consisting of more than 40 000 entries, is a consolidation of all the individual volume subject indexes. It is presented in word-by-word alphabetical sequence with a maximum of three levels of heading. Terminology in the index is based on standard internationally recognized sources. Cross-references are provided to assist the user to locate preferred terms and terms of related interest.

Acknowledgments

To produce a tome of this magnitude requires an enormous number of individuals with unique talents working in concert. To begin with, we applaud the herculean efforts of our driving force and friend at Elsevier Science, Barbara Barrett. We also gratefully acknowledge the efforts of two other publishing editors at Elsevier Science, Susan Hanscom and David Hoole, who provided guidance and encouragement along the way. We are particularly thankful for the exceptionally hard work of Angela Greenwell and her staff in Oxford, who made sure that all tasks were implemented reasonably on time and who orchestrated the day-to-day management of this huge undertaking. Next, we thank our eminent volume editors, who had the difficult job of soliciting, tracking, and editing manuscripts for their respective volumes. Similarly, we thank the Honorary International Editorial Advisory Board for their excellent input in developing the outline for the work and suggestions as to potential international contributors. Of course, we owe a great deal to the individual contributors who agreed to share their expertise with us in a timely fashion. Finally, we are most appreciative of our own editorial assistants, Sonia McQuarters and Burt G. Bolton, who repeatedly have provided us with the kind of support that makes all of this a possibility.

HONORARY INTERNATIONAL EDITORIAL ADVISORY BOARD

xiii

Preface

The study of child behavior disorders is of relatively recent origin; the systematic assessment and effective treatment of these disorders is of even more recent origin. Prior to the nineteenth and twentieth centuries, the study of psychopathology was concerned almost exclusively with adult behavior disorders. Child behavior disorders received little attention. In all probability, this state of affairs resulted from the prevailing viewpoints of children as miniature adults (Ollendick & Hersen, 1989, 1993, 1998). As such, children were thought to evince problems similar to adults and to benefit from reasoned advice much like their adult counterparts.

A variety of reasons have been put forth to account for the status of children in those times. The most plausible explanations appear to be related to societal forces and conditions. More specifically, infant mortality rates were exceedingly high and child labor laws were nonexistent. As noted by Bremmer (1970), "epidemics, malnutrition, and ordinary diseases of childhood and those contracted from mothers, especially tuberculosis, carried off hundreds in the earliest stages in life" (p. 15). It has been estimated that as many as two-thirds of all children died before they reached the age of four (Aries, 1962). Those who survived typically became valuable "economic commodities." Their economic value was ensured by an apprenticeship system that required them to work at the age of six, frequently under poor conditions and for prolonged periods of time. Inasmuch as they worked up to 14 hours a day in unhealthy and unsafe settings, it is little wonder that few children lived to adolescence (Brown, 1939). Those who managed to survive to the age of 12 were quickly ushered into marital contracts, arranged for them by their elders to ensure their ongoing economic value. Large families were required in a society characterized by early infant deaths and inappropriate and unsafe work settings for its children.

From this brief historical commentary, it is evident that children and adolescents were not viewed as important in their own right (i.e., as children). Rather, they were viewed similarly to slaves or, in the least, as valuable chattel who filled an important and vital economic role in society. They were expected to behave and work like an adult and yet did not possess privileges associated with adulthood. Their status was a precarious one indeed.

Aries (1962) suggests that changes in the prevailing viewpoint of children began to be evident in the late 1600s and early 1700s. This trend was first noted in upper socioeconomic families. In these families, perhaps because of increased leisure time, improved health practices, and the decreased necessity for children to work for their own survival, the status of childhood improved. Coincident with these developments, parents began to play with their children, to express affection toward them, and to enjoy them as children, not as miniature adults. As parents and other adults in society became more interested in children, concerns about their physical and emotional development surfaced as well. No longer viewed as economic necessities, children were viewed as little "persons" unto themselves and in need of adult guidance and moral support. Rousseau, writing in the mid-1700s, best captured the essence of childhood:

> We expect to find the man in the child without thinking what the child is before he is a man. Childhood has ways of seeing, thinking, feeling, peculiar to itself; nothing is more absurd than to wish to substitute ours in their places. (quoted in Brown, 1939, p. 11)

Based on the emerging philosophies of Rousseau and Locke, as well as other philosophers, the child began to be viewed as a *tabula rasa* (i.e., a blank slate) that could be affected by a variety of experiences. The duty of parents and other adults in society was to help "shape" children and to ensure their growth and development. This philosophical stance resulted in several advances: moral education, compulsory schooling, and improved healthcare for children. Moreover, it also served as the forerunner of early psychosocial theories and treatments for children and adolescents, including psychoanalysis and behavior therapy (Ollendick & Hersen, 1989).

Thus, after centuries of neglect, the importance and uniqueness of childhood was acknowledged. Of course, it took many years before Rousseau's philosophical notion of childhood was accepted by society and incorporated into ongoing parenting and educational practices. Some might argue that this notion still has not found total acceptance, even in highly civilized societies today. Child abuse and neglect are persistent even—somewhat surprisingly, these tragic events rank as one of the five leading causes of death in children in the US even to this day (along with accidents, cancer, congenital abnormalities, and pneumonia).

Because a psychology of childhood was largely nonexistent before the late 1600s and early 1700s, conceptions of child behavior disorders were necessarily limited and similar to those proposed for adult disorders. As is generally well know, early Greeks and Romans believed that behavior disorders were the result of biological or organic "imbalances." Hippocrates spoke of "humoral substances" that, when they became imbalanced, resulted in "mental" disorders. Given this organic disease perspective, children (as well as adults) with behavior disorders were viewed as defective and were treated as objects of scorn, ridicule, and persecution. In ancient Rome, for example, children who were severely impaired (e.g., mentally retarded and/or probably psychotic) were disposed of in the river Tiber by their parents to relieve themselves and society of the burden of caring for them (Rosen, Clark, & Kivitz, 1976). Less impaired children, such as enuretics, were treated with a variety of concoctions thought to relieve the "humoral imbalances" and to restore the child to an appropriate, balanced biological state. Glicklich (1951), in a fascinating account, traced some of the early treatments of enuresis: burning the crop of the cockerel and giving it to the child to drink in tepid water; shaving a hare's scrotum and placing it in wine for the child to drink; and giving the child the toasted seed of the wild rue to drink every third day!

As noted in our discussion of the emergence of childhood, conceptions of childhood as being distinct from adulthood began to emerge in the 1600s and early 1700s. Even with these developments, however, the behavior problems of childhood continued to be viewed much as were those of adults. At this time, the prevailing societal attitudes fostered a resurgence of the organic disease model, first introduced by Hippocrates. In contrast, however, the resurgence of the organic model was also characterized by a more humane attitude and concern for the child. As noted by Zilboorg and Henry (1941), this combined viewpoint was related to significant advances that were occurring in the fields of physiology, neurology, and general medicine, and to developing moral attitudes toward the "mentally ill." These moral attitudes were seen most clearly in Pinel's unchaining of the inmates when he became head of the Bicetre Hospital in Paris in 1792. Pinel stressed the natural causes (i.e., organic or biological) of "insanity" rather than demoniacal possession that had been in vogue; in his opinion, patients required moral treatment based on kindness and forbearance rather than ridicule and punishment. Implicit in the early moral treatment philosophies was the notion that "psychological" factors could beneficially affect the "insane" and improve their conditions. This notion was not completely incompatible with early organic theories, as organic changes were often attributed to psychological causes such as disappointment or bereavement (Achenbach, 1974). Thus, although the role of psychological factors was emerging, the prevailing viewpoint was a medical or organic one, with a humane attitude superimposed upon it.

During this same era, a second philosophical force was emerging, which was to usher in the view of psychopathology as determined by environmental causes in addition to biological ones (Rie, 1971). This view essentially reaffirmed the humanitarian attitude but also posited that behavior problems were caused by environmental factors. Most notable, sensory stimulation, or a lack of it, was viewed as a primary determinant of behavior. This philosophy, articulated most forcibly by Rousseau, laid the early foundation for the work of Itard and Seguin in the 1800s. In 1801, a young adolescent boy ("the wild boy of Aveyron") was found naked and wandering in the forest and was referred to Itard for treatment. Itard described the boy in the following way:

> What do we see? A disgustingly dirty child affected with spasmodic movements and often convulsions who swayed back and forth ceaselessly like certain animals in the menagerie, who bit and scratched those who opposed him, who showed no sign of affection for those who attended him; and who was, in short, indifferent to everything and attentive to nothing. (quoted in Harrison & McDermott, 1972, p. 727)

Here was Rousseau's "natural savage" awaiting intervention. Itard's treatment, based largely on the repetition of sensory stimulation, was designed to socialize and educate the child. Although Itard worked incessantly for five full years with this child, "Victor" acquired very few skills, and Itard concluded that he had been largely unsuccessful in his rehabilitative efforts. He asserted that the boy's "idiocy" (mental retardation) prevented successful intervention.

Despite Itard's failure, the principles underlying this approach were well entrenched and were introduced into America by Sequin in 1848. Thus, a view of psychopathology as being determined by organic and/or environmental causes was generally accepted in the mid-1800s. In the late 1800s and the early 1900s, a number of currents merged that appear to have provided the bedrock of child psychopathology as studied today. Many of these developments occurred concurrently, suggesting a *zeitgeist* that was conducive to change and an interaction that promoted progress (Achenbach, 1974; Ollendick

& Hersen, 1983). Among these developments were the discovery and care of the mentally retarded, the development of intelligence tests, the formulation of the basic principles of psychoanalysis and behaviorism, the child study movement, and the development of child guidance clinics. Whereas all of these factors may seem somewhat unrelated, they all appear to have focused attention on the growing child and on the developmental aspects of child psychopathology.

Currently, many issues remain and, consequently, the study of child psychopathology and its assessment and treatment remain vibrant and dynamic. Issues associated with the nature of child psychopathology, the models for conceptualizing child psychopathology, the classification and categorization of such psychopathology, etiological agents contributing to the onset and course of psychopathology, and viable strategies for the efficacious treatment all warrant further exploration. Moreover, the critical role of development remains to be systematically investigated as it pertains to each of these basic issues. Surely, a host of other issues await our attention as well.

This volume in *Comprehensive Clinical Psychology* addresses many of these issues in considerable detail. In Section I, the foundations for the conceptualization, assessment, and treatment of child psychopathology are examined. First, Richard Lerner and his colleagues articulate a developmental perspective of child psychopathology that pays close attention to the processes characteristic of childhood and to important developmental norms that guide us in determining which behaviors are problems and which are endemic to childhood and not necessarily of concern. Throughout this chapter, the relative plasticity of human development across the lifespan—a plasticity deriving from the dynamic interactions between the individual child and the context in which that child is embedded—is emphasized. In so doing, important issues of continuity and stability of child behavior disorders are addressed in detail. In the second chapter in Section I, Martin Herbert details the process of piecing together a clinical formulation of the child's problems and the contexts that surround them. Using the "craft of a potter" as the metaphor, he describes the art and science of clinical formulation. He further demonstrates how difficulties, indeed failures, in the treatment of children's behavior problems can frequently be traced back to a lack of precision during this crucial phase of assessment and intervention. He further asserts that the case study is the bedrock of clinical work, and an invaluable scientific method of inquiry. He reminds us that it provides us with an exemplar of that unique blending of idiographic and nomothetic approaches that have their parallels in the artistic and scientific facets of the practice of clinical psychology. Clinical formulation is richly detailed by this master clinician. In the remaining two chapters in Section I, Stephen Shirk and Robert Russell explore process issues and John Weisz examines outcome findings and related issues in child psychotherapy. Both of these chapters are state-of-the-art. As will be evident to the reader, process issues have been relatively ignored in the literature, and few studies have examined either child or therapist characteristics that might moderate treatment outcome. However, examination of process issues is critical to the future development of child psychotherapy. Shirk and Russell outline a research agenda related to process–outcome linkages and advise us to explore basic pathogenic mechanisms underlying various child behavior disorders which will help guide us in the search for critical change processes in child psychotherapy. Similarly, John Weisz points us to important social, developmental, and cultural contexts that characterize child psychopathology and the necessary conditions for evaluating the effectiveness of various treatments. Although we might think that we have many treatments that "work" with children and their families, Weisz dispels this myth and urges us to conduct more careful and systematic trials in real-world settings. All in all, these first four chapters set the stage for the remainder of the volume. Important developmental issues are highlighted, clinical formulation is explicated, and the processes and outcomes of child psychotherapy are articulated.

Section II of this volume reviews major theoretical approaches that have been used in the treatment of diverse child behavior disorders. Each chapter uses a similar format. The theoretical underpinnings of the approach are articulated first, followed by the history of the approach and its current status. Fascinating details about the early beginnings of the approaches and the proponents of the approaches are included. Next, assessment and clinical formulation specific to each approach are presented, followed by a description of the intervention procedures and the proposed mechanisms of change. Finally, each chapter provides research findings for the theoretical approach that is reviewed in that chapter and future directions for research and practice are indicated. In the first chapter in Section II, Alan Hudson provides insightful commentary on applied behavior analysis, whereas Philip Kendall and his colleagues present cognitive-behavioral therapy in rich detail in the chapter that follows. Considerable support is found for use of both of these learning-based approaches with a variety of child behavior problems. In the next chapter, Jose Szapocznik, James Alexander, and their colleagues detail the complexities and nuances of family systems therapy. They conclude that family systems therapy lacks a solid empirical base which demonstrates its efficacy; nonetheless, exciting work is occurring with this treatment modality and the future holds considerable promise for systems-based interventions. Considerably more support is evident for parent training procedures as detailed by Carolyn Webster-Stratton and Carole Hooven in the chapter that follows, especially with noncompliant and oppositional children. In fact, parent training appears to be the treatment of choice for such children. In the next two chapters in this section, Sandra Russ reviews the practice and efficacy of play therapy with children and Mary Target and Peter Fonagy explore the use and efficacy of psychodynamic therapy. Russ describes play therapy as in a state of transition. Although play-oriented therapy is the dominant and most enduring approach to child treatment, treatment outcome studies are few. Thus, we really know very little about how it works or if it works at all. Fortunately, the field appears to be undergoing critical examination and well-designed treatment studies are underway. A similar state might be said to characterize psychodynamic therapy for children. Long-practiced, controlled treatment outcome studies are rare. As with play therapy, however, critical clinical trials are underway. The next chapter in Section II examines the use of pharmacological therapies with children. Nirbhay Singh and Cynthia Willis provide a detailed review of major pharmacological agents, their effects and side effects, and the outcomes associated with their use. This chapter will serve as a trustworthy resource for those not trained in such interventions. Overall, these chapters review major interventions for working with children and critically examine the empirical support for each. Although differential efficacies can be said to exist, each of the procedures has some support. Nonetheless, it is evident that much more work needs to be undertaken before the routine use of any of these procedures can be more fully endorsed. In fact, some disorders of childhood seem resistant to all types of therapy. In the final chapter in Section II, Susan Spence examines the area of prevention of child and adolescent disorders. She concludes that it is now feasible to identify major risk and protective factors for the development of conduct disorders and internalizing problems (i.e., anxiety and affective disorders) in young people and that many of these problems are preventable through established interventions with high-risk samples. The value of prevention programs should not be underestimated. For many children whose problems persist, change is much more difficult. In sum, Section II presents exciting prevention and intervention strategies and provides rich commentary on their effectiveness.

Section III of this volume addresses major child psychopathologies, their assessment, and treatment. Utilizing a structured format, the first part of each chapter reviews the disorder under consideration, exploring its phenomenology, prevalence, etiology, and diagnostic features. This section is followed by a detailed examination of the conceptualization and clinical formulation of the disorder, its multimethod and multisource assessment, and, finally, its psychosocial and pharmacological treatment. Finally, each chapter concludes with a section on future directions for research and practice. Overall these chapters provide current and scholarly information about the various disorders, suggest assessment strategies that are developmentally sensitive and psychometrically sound, and provide a detailed evaluation of the empirical status of the various treatment strategies. The chapters are exciting and provide a glimpse into clinical practice that is both clinically sensitive and empirically supported.

More specifically, in the first four chapters of Section III, Mark Dadds, Paula Barrett, and Vanessa Cobham address childhood anxiety disorders; Golda Ginsburg and Wendy Silverman examine specific phobias; Derek Bolton reviews obsessive-compulsive disorder; and Sean Perrin, Patrick Smith, and William Yule explore post-traumatic stress disorder. Following these chapters, William Reynolds addresses childhood depression, and Anthony Spirito and Deidre Donaldson examine the special topic of suicide and suicide attempts in adolescents. Collectively, these six chapters provide rich detail on the major "internalizing" disorders and conclude that much progress has been made in their understanding, assessment, and treatment. Exciting and empirically supported treatments are available for these disorders. In the next three chapters, the "externalizing" disorders of childhood are presented. C. Keith Conners and Drew Erhardt review attention-deficit hyperactivity disorder, Ron Prinz explores oppositional defiant disorder and conduct disorder, and Holly Waldron addresses substance abuse disorders. As with the internalizing disorders, much is known about the externalizing disorders and we can conclude that effective treatments are on the horizon. In the final six chapters of Section III, elimination disorders (C. Eugene Walker), eating disorders (David Garner and Linda Myerholtz), sleep disorders (Avi Sadeh and Reut Gruber), somatoform disorders (Judy Garber), factitious disorders (Judith Libow), and schizophrenia in children and adolescents (Cindy Yee and Marian Sigman) are examined in detail. Although effective treatments have been identified for both elimination and eating disorders, such is not the case for sleep disorders, somatoform disorders, factitious disorders, and schizophrenia. The latter disorders represent disorders in need of considerable attention in the years ahead so that significant advances might be made. All in all, this volume presents current research and practices on the clinical formulation, assessment, and treatment of diverse child disorders. Although not exhaustive, it is intended to provide detail on the major disorders and the major issues attendant to them. It takes a clinical-research approach that is both developmentally sensitive and contextually embedded. Children are not miniature adults, rather they are growing, developing organisms who are richly embedded in diverse social contexts including the family, school, and communities in which they live. As such, they need to be viewed as distinct from adults and as important in their own right. Children have come of age. Hopefully, this volume will assist in their ongoing recognition and provide the reader with much information about assessment and treatment practices that are in their best interests.

In a volume such as this, many persons are to be recognized. Among the foremost are the distinguished, international contributors. Quite obviously, without them, the scholarly and sensitive treatment of each topic could hardly have been realized. I would also like to acknowledge the various professionals at Elsevier Science who have made such an undertaking possible. Their support through the conception and execution of the project has been invaluable. They kept me "on track," and I thank them for doing so. Of course, thanks are also extended to Alan Bellack and Michel Hersen who provided me the opportunity to edit this volume in the *Comprehensive Clinical Psychology* tome. Their trust and investment in me is greatly appreciated. In addition, I would like to give thanks to the many children and adolescents, including my own daughters (Laurie and Kathleen) who have, perhaps unwittingly and unknowingly, provided me a rich and exciting glimpse into their lives, both normal and abnormal. They have taught me much. To them, I dedicate this volume.

References

Achenbach, T. M. (1974). *Developmental psychopathology*. New York: Ronald Press.

Aries, P. (1962). *Centuries of childhood*. New York: Vintage Books.

Bremmer, R. H. (Ed.) (1970). *Children and youth in America: A documentary history, 1600–1865* (Vol. 1). Cambridge, MA: Harvard University Press.

Brown, F. J. (1939). *The sociology of childhood*. Englewoods Cliffs, NJ: Prentice-Hall.

Glicklich, L. B. (1951). An historical account of enuresis. *Pediatrics, 8*, 859–876.

Harrison, S. I., & McDermott, J. E. (Eds.) (1972). *Childhood psychopathology: An anthology of basic readings*. New York: International Universities Press.

Ollendick, T. H., & Hersen, M. (1983). *Handbook of child psychopathology*. New York: Plenum.

Ollendick, T. H., & Hersen, M. (1989). *Handbook of child psychopathology* (2nd ed.). New York: Plenum.

Ollendick, T. H., & Hersen, M. (1993). *Handbook of child and adolescent assessment*. Boston: Allyn & Bacon.

Ollendick, T. H., & Hersen, M. (1998). *Handbook of child psychopathology* (3rd ed.). New York: Plenum.

Rie, H. E. (Ed.) (1971). *Perspectives in child psychopathology*. Chicago: Aldine-Atherton.

Rosen, M., Clark, G. R., & Kivitz, M. S. (Eds.) (1976). *The history of mental retardation: Collected papers* (Vol. 1). Baltimore: University Park Press.

Zilboorg, G., & Henry, G. W. (1941). *History of medical psychology*. New York: Norton.

Contributors

Dr. J. F. Alexander
Social and Behavioral Sciences, University of Utah, Salt Lake City, UT 84121, USA

Dr. P. M. Barrett
School of Psychology, Griffith University, Goldcoast Campus, Queensland, Australia

Dr. D. Bolton
Department of Psychology, Institute of Psychiatry, De Crespigny Park, Denmark Hill, London,
SE5 8AF, UK

Dr. B. C. Chu
Department of Psychology, Temple University, Weiss Hall (265-66), Philadelphia, PA 19122, USA

Ms. V. E. Cobham
Department of Psychology, University of Queensland, Queensland 4072, Australia

Dr. C. K. Conners
Department of Psychiatry, Duke University Medical Center, Box 3362, Durham, NC 27710, USA

Professor M. R. Dadds
School of Applied Psychology, Griffith University, Nathan Campus, Queensland 4111, Australia

Dr. D. Donaldson
Child Psychiatry, Rhode Island Hospital and Brown University School of Medicine,
593 Eddy Street, Providence, RI 02903, USA

Dr. C. R. Ellis
Department of Pediatrics, Medical College of Virginia, Virginia Commonwealth University,
PO Box 980506, Richmond, VA 23298-0506, USA

Dr. D. Erhardt
Department of Psychology, Pepperdine University, Malibu, CA, USA

Dr. P. Fonagy
Department of Clinical Health Psychology, University College London, Gower Street, London, WC1E
6BT, UK

Dr. J. Garber
Department of Psychology, Vanderbilt University, Box 512 Peabody, Nashville, TN 37203, USA

Dr. D. M. Garner
Toledo Center for Eating Disorders, 7261 West Central Avenue, Toledo, OH 43617, USA
Department of Psychology, Bowling Green State University, Bowling Green, OH, USA
Women's Study Program, University of Toledo, Toledo, OH, USA

Dr. G. S. Ginsburg
Division of Applied Psychology & Quantitative Methods, University of Baltimore, 1420 North
Charles Street, Baltimore, MD 21204, USA

Ms. R. Gruber
The Laboratory for Children's Sleep and Arousal Disorders, Department of Psychology, Tel Aviv
University, Ramat Aviv, Tel Aviv, 69978 Israel

Professor M. Herbert
Department of Psychology, Washington Singer Laboratories, University of Exeter, Perry Road, Exeter,
EX4 4QG, UK

Dr. C. Hooven
Parenting Clinic, University of Washington, Seattle, WA 98195, USA

Dr. K. A. Howard
Center for Child, Family, and Community Partnerships, Boston College, Campion Hall,
140 Commonwealth Avenue, Chestnut Hill, MA 02167, USA

Professor A. Hudson
Department of Psychology and Intellectual Disability Studies, Royal Melbourne Institute of
Technology, PO Box 71, Bundoora, Victoria 3083, Australia

Dr. P. C. Kendall
Department of Psychology, Temple University, Weiss Hall (265-66), Philadelphia, PA 19122, USA

Dr. R. M. Lerner
Center for Child, Family, and Community Partnerships, Boston College, Campion Hall,
140 Commonwealth Avenue, Chestnut Hill, MA 02167, USA

Dr. J. A. Libow
Department of Psychiatry, Children's Hospital Oakland, 747 Fifty Second Street, Oakland,
CA 94609-1809, USA

Dr. A. L. Marrs
Department of Psychology, Temple University, Weiss Hall (265-66), Philadelphia, PA 19122, USA

Dr. J. Miller
Miami Institute of Professional Psychology, 8180 North West 36th Street, Miami, FL 33166, USA

Dr. L. E. Myerholtz
Department of Psychology, Bowling Green State University, Bowling Green, OH, USA

Dr. S. G. Perrin
Department of Psychology, Institute of Psychiatry, De Crespigny Park, Denmark Hill, London,
SE5 8AF, UK

Dr. R. J. Prinz
Department of Psychology, University of South Carolina, Columbia, SC 29208, USA

Dr. W. M. Reynolds
Department of Educational Psychology and Special Education, University of British Columbia,
2125 Main Mall, Vancouver, BC, Canada, V6T 1Z4
8036 Makah Road, Birch Way, WA 98230, USA

Dr. M. S. Robbins
Department of Psychology and Behavioral Sciences, University of Miami School of Medicine,
Center for Family Studies, 1425 North West 10th Avenue, 3rd Floor, Miami, FL 33136, USA

Dr. S. W. Russ
Psychology Department, Case Western Reserve University, Cleveland, OH 44106-7123, USA

Dr. R. L. Russell
Department of Psychology, Loyola University Chicago, 6525 North Sheridan Road, Chicago,
IL 60626, USA

Dr. A. Sadeh
The Laboratory for Children's Sleep and Arousal Disorders, Department of Psychology, Tel Aviv
University, Ramat Aviv, Tel Aviv, 69978 Israel

Dr. S. R. Shirk
Child Study Center, Department of Psychology, University of Denver, Denver, CO 80208, USA

Dr. M. D. Sigman
Department of Psychiatry and Biobehavioral Sciences, University of California, Los Angeles,
Neuropsychiatric Institute, Los Angeles, CA 90024-1759, USA

Dr. W. K. Silverman
Department of Psychology, Florida International University, University Park, Miami, FL 33199, USA

Dr. N. N. Singh
Department of Psychiatry, Medical College of Virginia, Virginia Commonwealth University,
PO Box 980489, Richmond, VA 23298-0489, USA

Mr. P. A. Smith
Department of Psychology, Institute of Psychiatry, De Crespigny Park, Denmark Hill, London
SE5 8AF, UK

Dr. S. H. Spence
Department of Psychology, University of Queensland, Brisbane, Qld 4072, Australia

Dr. A. Spirito
Child Psychiatry, Rhode Island Hospital and Brown University School of Medicine, 593 Eddy Street,
Providence, RI 02903, USA

Dr. J. Szapocznik
Department of Psychology and Behavioral Sciences, University of Miami School of Medicine,
Center for Family Studies, 1425 North West 10th Avenue, 3rd Floor, Miami, FL 33136, USA

Dr. M. Target
The Anna Freud Centre, 21 Maresfield Gardens, Hampstead, London, NW3 5SH, UK

Dr. H. B. Waldron
Department of Psychology, Logan Hall, The University of New Mexico, Albuquerque,
New Mexico 87131, USA

Dr. C. E. Walker
Department of Psychology & Behavioral Sciences, University of Oklahoma Health Sciences Center,
PO Box 26901, South Pavilion, 5th Floor, Room 217, Oklahoma City, OK 73190-3048, USA

Dr. M. E. Walsh
Center for Child, Family, and Community Partnerships, Boston College, Campion Hall,
140 Commonwealth Avenue, Chestnut Hill, MA 02167, USA

Dr. C. Webster-Stratton
Parenting Clinic, University of Washington, Seattle, WA 98195, USA

Dr. J. R. Weisz
Department of Psychology, Franz Hall, University of California, Los Angeles, 405 Hilgard Avenue,
Los Angeles, CA 90095-1563, USA

Dr. C. M. Yee-Bradbury
Department of Psychology, Franz Hall, University of California, Los Angeles, 405 Hilgard Avenue,
Los Angeles, CA 90095-1563, USA

Professor W. Yule
Department of Psychology, Institute of Psychiatry, De Crespigny Park, Denmark Hill, London,
SE5 8AF, UK

Comprehensive Clinical Psychology

This volume was previously published as part of the eleven-volume work *Comprehensive Clinical Psychology*, the contents of which are outlined here.

5.01

Developmental-contextual Considerations: Person–Context Relations as the Bases for Risk and Resiliency in Child and Adolescent Development

RICHARD M. LERNER, MARY E. WALSH, and KIMBERLY
A. HOWARD
Boston College, Chestnut Hill, MA, USA

5.01.1 INTRODUCTION

Neither behavioral and emotional problems of children and adolescents, nor instances of positive functioning and healthy development that occur for these age groups, arise from biogenic, psychogenic, or sociogenic sources acting independently on the individual

(Lerner, 1986, 1995; Lerner, Hess, & Nitz, 1990, 1991). Rather, both problematic and healthy instances of behavior and development during childhood and adolescence—and indeed across the entire life-span—arise from the dynamic interaction (Lerner, 1978) or fusion (Tobach & Greenberg, 1984) of variables from multiple levels of organization. These levels include the biological (e.g., the genetic or hormonal), psychological (e.g., the cognitive or personological), social (e.g., peer group and family relational), and societal (e.g., educational, political, or economic institutional); and also involve the cultural, the designed and natural physical ecological, and the historical levels (Bronfenbrenner, 1979, in preparation; Elder, Modell, & Parke, 1993; Ford & Lerner, 1992; Lerner, 1986, 1991, 1995).

Thus, both the emergence of behavioral and emotional problems, and the risk for development of such problems, lies in the changing relations among multiple levels of organization that comprise the context, or the ecology, of human life (Bronfenbrenner & Morris, 1998; Lerner, 1995; Lerner et al., 1990). Similarly, development of positive, healthy behaviors (i.e., behaviors that meet, or fit, the behavioral, physical, or social demands of the context, and are thus able to be construed as "adaptive," or adjusted; Lerner & Lerner, 1983), and resistance to, or resiliency from, threats to development of such behaviors lie in integrations across time of biological-through-historical levels of organization, that is, in the micro and macro systems comprising the ecology of human behavior and development (Bronfenbrenner, 1979).

Accordingly, any attempts to describe or explain the problematic vs. healthy status of behavior, and/or the bases or actualization of risk or resiliency in human life, require reference to the relations between individuals and the contexts of human development. Simply, then, behavior or health problems, and risks and resiliency, require integrated consideration of people and the context within which they develop (Lerner, 1991, 1995, 1997; Sameroff, 1989). A "developmental contextual" (Lerner, 1986; Lerner & Kaufmann, 1985) theoretical frame is needed to understand, appraise, and devise policies and programs that promote positive human behavior and development (Lerner, 1995).

5.01.1.1 The Role of Developmental Contextual Theory

Developmental contextualism is a theory of human development that has direct importance for understanding the bases, assessment, and

treatment of behavioral and emotional problems in childhood and adolescence (Lerner, 1986, 1995; Lerner et al., 1990, 1991). Behavioral/emotional problems involve the malfunctioning of the human psychosocial system (Magnusson & Öhman, 1987). Thus, development of behavioral/emotional problems involves the emergence of nonadaptive, nonfit, or inadequate characteristics in this psychosocial system. From a developmental contextual perspective, behavioral/emotional problems exist and develop when, and only when, an inadequate relation exists between psychological and social functioning, that is, between individuals and their context. It is a malfunctional person–context relation which defines problematic behavior and development; and it is from the changing nature of this relation—occurring normatively or through remedial, preventive, or enhancing interventions—that either healthy/positive or maladaptive, and hence negative, nonfit, or problematic behaviors develop (Sameroff, 1989).

We should emphasize that this relational, developmental contextual view is compatible with those of other developmentalists studying either clinical problems in childhood and adolescence and/or developmental psychopathology (e.g., Cicchetti, 1984, 1987; Magnusson, 1988; Magnusson & Öhman, 1987; Super, 1987; Wapner & Demick, 1988). To illustrate, Cicchetti (1987), writing about psychopathology during human infant development, notes that:

> it is inappropriate to focus on discrete symptomatology to infer the presence of nascent or incipient infant psychopathology. Rather, disorders in infancy are best conceptualized as relational psychopathologies, that is, as consequences of dysfunction in the parent–child–environment system. (p. 837)

A similar stress on the relational and developmental contextual character of psychopathology is made by Super (1987), who considers "disorders of development as a class of phenomena that reveal something of the nature of our children and also of the nature of the worlds we make for them" (p. 2). Indeed, he notes that:

> The settings, customs, and psychology of caretakers not only regulate the healthy emergence of human potential, they also shape the possibilities of disorder. At every stage of the etiology, expression, course, intervention, and final outcome of developmental problems, human culture structures the experience and adjusts the odds. (Super, 1987, p. 7)

In a corresponding vein, Öhman and Magnusson (1987) indicate that:

any disease must be understood as resulting from a multiplicity of causal events spanning observational levels from biochemistry to sociology. Thus, any single-factor, linear causal model is unrealistic for understanding disease in general, and mental disorders in particular. Instead, multiple interacting causal factors that often change in their effect over time must be postulated. (p. 18)

(see also Magnusson, 1988; Magnusson & Allen, 1983; Super & Harkness, 1982, 1986).

Given, then, the apparent prominence of ideas pertinent to a developmental contextual perspective for understanding development across the life-span and, for present purposes, the pertinence of this perspective for conceptualizing the developmental, contextual, and individual-ecological relational bases of child and adolescent problem behaviors, or resiliency to the emergence of such problems, it is useful to discuss the features of developmental contextualism.

5.01.2 AN OVERVIEW OF DEVELOPMENTAL CONTEXTUALISM

Children and adolescents, and their families, communities, and societies develop; they show systematic and successive changes over time (Lerner, 1986). These changes are interdependent. Changes within one level of organization, for example, developmental changes in personality or cognition within the individual, are reciprocally related to developmental changes within other levels, such as those involving changes in caregiving patterns or spousal relationships within the familial level of organization (e.g., Hetherington, Lerner, & Perlmutter, 1988; Lerner, 1984; Lerner & Spanier, 1978; Lewis, 1997; Lewis & Rosenblum, 1974).

Moreover, reciprocal changes among levels of organization are both products and producers of reciprocal changes within levels. For example, over time, parents' "styles" of behavior and of rearing influence children's personality and cognitive functioning and development; in turn, interactions between personality and cognition constitute an emergent "characteristic" of human individuality that affects parental behaviors and styles and the quality of family life (e.g., Baumrind, 1995; Lerner, 1978, 1982; Lerner & Busch-Rossnagel, 1981; Lerner, Castellino, Terry, Villarruel, & McKinney, 1995; Lewis, 1997; Lewis & Rosenblum, 1974).

Within developmental contextualism, levels are conceived of as integrative organizations. That is:

the concept of integrative levels recognizes as equally essential for the purpose of scientific analysis both the isolation of parts of a whole and their integration into the structure of the whole. It neither reduces phenomena of a higher level to those of a lower one, as in mechanism, or describes the higher level in vague nonmaterial terms which are but substitutes for understanding, as in vitalism. Unlike other "holistic" theories, it never leaves the firm ground of material reality ... The concept points to the need to study the organizational interrelationships of parts and whole. (Novikoff, 1945, p. 209)

Moreover, Tobach and Greenberg (1984) have stressed that:

the interdependence among levels is of great significance. The dialectic nature of the relationship among levels is one in which lower levels are subsumed in higher levels so that any particular level is an integration of preceding levels ... In the process of integration, or fusion, *new* levels with their own characteristics result. (p. 2)

The course of human development is the product of the processes involved in the "dynamic interactions" (Lerner, 1978, 1979, 1984) among integrative levels.

In emphasizing that systematic and successive change (i.e., development) is associated with alterations in the dynamic relations among structures from multiple levels of organization, developmental contextualism provides a scope for contemporary developmental research and intervention that is not limited by (or, perhaps better, confounded by an inextricable association with) a unidimensional portrayal of the developing person (e.g., the person seen from the vantage point of only cognitions, or emotions, or stimulus–response connections, or genetic imperatives; e.g., see Piaget, 1970; Freud, 1949; Bijou & Baer, 1961; and Rowe, 1994, respectively). Rather, the power of the stress in developmental contextualism on processes of dynamic person–context relations is the "design criteria" imposed on research, method, and intervention pertinent to the study of any content area or dimension of the developing person. This power is constituted by four interrelated assumptive dimensions of developmental contextual theory (Lerner, 1998). Accordingly, it is useful to discuss these dimensions in order to illuminate the key theoretical and methodological (e.g., research design and measurement) issues pertinent to understanding how biological, psychological, and contextual processes combine to promote either healthy or problematic behavior and development across the life-span and also within the periods of childhood and adolescence.

5.01.2.1 Change and Relative Plasticity

The central idea in developmental contextualism is that changing, reciprocal relations (or dynamic interactions) between individuals and the multiple contexts within which they live comprise the essential process of human development (Lerner, 1986; Lerner & Kauffman, 1985). Accordingly, developmental contextualism stresses that the focus of developmental understanding must be on systematic change (Ford & Lerner, 1992). This focus is required because of the belief that the potential for change exists across the life-span (e.g., Baltes, 1987). Although it is also assumed that systemic change is not limitless (e.g., it is constrained by both past developments and by contemporary contextual conditions), developmental contextualism stresses that relative plasticity exists across life (Lerner, 1984). The resilient behavior in children and adolescents provides a concrete instance of such plasticity (Masten, 1989; Werner, 1990, 1995).

There are important implications of relative plasticity for the application of development science to address problems of human behavior and development. For instance, the presence of relative plasticity legitimates a proactive search across the life-span for characteristics of people and of their contexts that, together, can influence the design of policies and programs promoting positive development (Birkel, Lerner, & Smyer, 1989; Fisher & Lerner, 1994; Lerner & Hood 1986).

5.01.2.2 Relationism and the Integration of Levels of Organization

From a developmental contextual perspective, human behavior is both biological and social (Featherman & Lerner, 1985; Tobach & Schneirla, 1968). In fact, no form of life as we know it comes into existence independent of other life. No animal lives in total isolation from others of its species across its entire life-span (Tobach, 1981; Tobach & Schneirla, 1968). Biological survival requires meeting demands of the environment or, as we note later, attaining a goodness of fit (Chess & Thomas, 1984; Lerner & Lerner, 1983, 1989; Thomas & Chess, 1977) with the context. Because this environment is populated by other members of one's species, adjustment to (or fit with) these other organisms

is a requirement of survival (Tobach & Schneirla, 1968).

Developmental contextualism emphasizes that the bases for change, and for both plasticity and constraints in development, lie in relations that exist among multiple levels of organization that comprise the substance of human life (Ford & Lerner, 1992; Schneirla, 1957; Tobach, 1981). These levels range from the inner biological level, through the individual/psychological level and the proximal social relational level (e.g., involving dyads, peer groups, and nuclear families), to the sociocultural level (including key macro-institutions such as educational, public policy, governmental, and economic systems) and the natural and designed physical ecologies of human development (Bronfenbrenner, 1979; Riegel, 1975). These levels are structurally and functionally integrated, thus requiring a systems view of the levels involved in human development (Ford & Lerner, 1992; Sameroff, 1983; Smith & Thelen, 1993; Thelen & Smith, 1994).

Developmental contextualism (Lerner, 1986, 1991, 1995) is one instance of such a developmental systems perspective and, as such, promotes a relational unit as a requisite for developmental analysis (Lerner, 1991): variables associated with any level of organization exist (are structured) in relation to variables from other levels; qualitative and quantitative dimensions of the function of any variable are also shaped by the relations that the variable has with variables from other levels. Unilevel units of analysis (or components of, or elements in, a relation) are not an adequate target of developmental analysis; rather, the relation itself—the interlevel linkage—should be the focus of such analysis (Lerner, 1991; Riegel, 1975).

Relationism and integration have a clear implication for unilevel theories of development and for approaches to intervention that emphasize a similarly unilevel (e.g., a psychogenic or biogenic) orientation to etiology or "treatment": at best, such approaches are severely limited, and inevitably provide a nonveridical depiction of development, due to their focus on what are essentially main effects embedded in higher order interactions (e.g., see Walsten, 1990); at worst, such approaches are neither valid nor useful. Accordingly, neither biogenic theories or interventions (e.g., ones based on genetic reductionistic conceptions such as behavioral genetics or sociobiology; Freedman, 1979; Plomin, 1986; Rowe, 1994; Wilson, 1975), psychogenic theories or interventions (e.g., behavioristic or functional analysis models; Baer, 1970, 1976; Bijou, 1976; Bijou & Baer, 1961; Skinner, 1938), nor sociogenic theories or interventions (e.g., "social mold" conceptions of socialization; e.g., Homans, 1961; and see Hartup, 1978, for a review) provide adequate frames for understanding or addressing problems of human development. Interventions based on such theories are insufficiently attentive to the potential plasticity that exists in the human development system, and thus the multiple levels of this system that provide "points of entry" for useful interventions (Birkel, Lerner, & Smyer, 1989; Lerner, 1984, 1995).

Developmental contextualism moves beyond simplistic division of sources of development into nature-related and nurture-related variables or processes. Instead, developmental contextualism sees multiple levels of organization that exist within the ecology of human development as part of an inextricably fused developmental system, one that affords formulation of a rich and multilevel array of strategies for developmental interventions into the life course (for example, see the chapters in Lerner, 1998).

5.01.2.3 Historical Embeddedness and Temporality

The relational units of analysis of concern in developmental contextualism are considered "change units" (Lerner, 1991). The change component of these units derives from the ideas that all levels of organization involved in human development are embedded in history, that is, they are integrated with historical change (Elder, 1980; Elder et al., 1993). Relationism and integration mean that no level of organization functions as a consequence of its own, isolated activity (Tobach, 1981; Tobach & Schneirla, 1968). Each level functions as a consequence of its structural integration with other levels (Tobach & Greenberg, 1984). History—change over time—is incessant and continuous, and it is a level of organization that is fused with all other levels. This linkage means that change is a necessary, an inevitable, feature of variables from all levels of organization (Baltes, 1987; Lerner, 1984); in addition, this linkage means that the structure, as well as the function, of variables changes over time.

The continuity of change that constitutes history can lead to both intra-individual (or, more generally, intralevel) continuity or discontinuity in development, depending on the rate, scope, and particular substantive component of the developmental system at which change is measured (Brim & Kagan, 1980; Lerner, 1986, 1988; Lerner & Tubman, 1989). Thus, continuity at one level of analysis may be coupled with discontinuity at another level;

quantitative continuity or discontinuity may be coupled with qualitative continuity or discontinuity within and across levels; and continuity or discontinuity can exist in regard to both the processes involved in (or "explanations" of) developmental change and in the features, depictions, or outcomes (i.e., the "descriptions") of these processes (Cairns & Hood, 1983; Lerner, 1986).

These patterns of within-person change pertinent to continuity and discontinuity can result in either constancy or variation in rates at which different individuals develop in regard to a particular substantive domain of development. Thus, any pattern of intra-individual change can be combined with any instance of interindividual differences in within-person change, that is, with any pattern of stability or instability (Lerner, 1986; Lerner & Tubman, 1989). In other words, continuity–discontinuity is a dimension of intra-individual change and is distinct from, and independent of, stability–instability, which involves between-person change, and is, therefore, a group, and not an individual, concept (Baltes & Nesselroade, 1973; Lerner, 1976, 1986).

In sum, since historical change is continuous, temporality is infused in all levels of organization. This infusion may be associated with different patterns of continuity and discontinuity across people. The potential array of such patterns has implications for understanding the importance of human diversity, and design and implementation of interventions into the course of human development.

5.01.2.4 The Limits of Generalizability, Diversity, and Individual Differences

The temporality of the changing relations among levels of organization means that changes that are seen within one historical period (or time of measurement), and/or with one set of instances of variables from the multiple levels of the ecology of human development, may not be seen at other points in time (Baltes, Reese, & Nesselroade, 1977; Bronfenbrenner, 1979; Valsiner, 1998). What is seen in one data set may be only an instance of what does or what could exist. Accordingly, developmental contextualism focuses on diversity: of people, of relations, of settings, and of times of measurement (Lerner, 1991, 1995, 1997).

Individual differences within and across all levels of organization are seen as having core, substantive significance in understanding human development (Baltes et al., 1977; Lerner, 1991, 1995, 1997) and for designing interventions that fit specific needs and characteristics of diverse groups toward which such efforts may be directed. Indeed, diversity is the exemplary illustration of the presence of relative plasticity in human development (Lerner, 1984). Moreover, by inferring that it is possible to generalize from across-person variation that exists within time to within-person variation across time, diversity constitutes the best evidence of the potential for change in the states and conditions of human life (Brim & Kagan, 1980). It underscores the belief that interventions can make a difference in human development.

Moreover, individual structural and functional characteristics constitute an important source of people's development (Lerner, 1982; Lerner & Busch-Rossnagel, 1981). The individuality of each person promotes variation in the fusions he or she has with the levels of organization within which the person is embedded. For instance, people's distinct actions or physical features promote differential actions (or reactions) in others toward them (Lerner, 1987). These differential actions, which constitute feedback to the person, shape, at least in part, further change in the person's characteristics of individuality (Lerner & Lerner, 1989; Schneirla, 1957). For example, the changing match, congruence, or goodness of fit between people's developmental characteristics and their context provide a basis for consonance or dissonance in their ecological milieu; the dynamic nature of this interaction constitutes a source of variation in positive and negative outcomes of developmental change (Lerner et al., 1990, 1991; Lerner & Lerner, 1983; Thomas & Chess, 1977; Thomas, Chess, Birch, Hertzig & Korn, 1963).

The major assumptive dimensions of developmental contextualism—systematic change and relative plasticity, relationism and integration, embeddedness and temporality, generalizability limits and diversity—are very much intertwined facets of a common conceptual core. And, as is also the case with levels of organization that are integrated to form the substance of developmental change, the assumptive dimensions reflect the essential features of superordinate developmental systems views of human development (Ford & Lerner, 1992). As is the case with the several defining features of the life-span developmental perspective, which—according to Baltes (1987)—need to be considered as an integrated whole, the assumptive dimensions of developmental contextualism need to be appreciated simultaneously. Such appreciation is required to understand the breadth, scope, and implications for research and application of this conceptual framework.

5.01.3 BASES AND IMPLICATIONS OF DEVELOPMENTAL CONTEXTUALISM AND CHILD AND ADOLESCENT DEVELOPMENT

Since the early 1970s the study of children and their contexts has evolved in at least three significant directions: changes in the conceptualization of the nature of the person; the emergence of a life-span perspective about human development; and stress on the contexts of development. These trends were both products and producers of developmental contextualism. This perspective has promoted a rationale for a synthesis of research and outreach; a synthesis focused on the diversity of children and on the contexts within which they develop.

Much of the history of the study of human development prior to the mid-1970s was predicated on either organismic or mechanistic (reductionistic) models (Overton & Reese, 1973, 1981; Reese & Overton, 1970). In turn, it is accurate to say that since the 1970s, developmental contextual conceptions have been increasingly prominent bases of scholarly advances in human development theory and methodology (Dixon & Lerner, 1992; Dixon, Lerner, & Hultsch 1991; Lerner, Hultsch, & Dixon, 1983; Riegel,   1975, 1976a, 1976b; Sameroff, 1975, 1983). Indeed, the three above-noted themes in the study of human development define the place of developmental contextualism in theory and research since the late 1970s. Accordingly, it is useful to discuss each of these themes in some detail.

5.01.3.1 Children's Influences on Their Own Development

Children have come to be understood as active producers of their own development (Bell, 1968; Lerner & Spanier, 1978; Lewis & Rosenblum, 1974; Thomas et al., 1963). These contributions primarily occur through the reciprocal relations individuals have with other significant people in their context: for example, children with family members, caregivers, teachers, and peers.

The content and functional significance of the influences that people have on others and, in turn, on themselves, occur in relation to people's characteristics of individuality (Schneirla, 1957). Individual differences in people evoke differential reactions in others, reactions which provide feedback to people and influence the individual character of their further development (Schneirla, 1957). Accordingly, individuality—diversity among people—is central in understanding the way in which any given person is an active agent in his or her own development (Lerner, 1982, 1991; Lerner & Busch-Rossnagel, 1981). Thus, as we have emphasized, diversity has core, substantive meaning and, as such, implications for all studies of human development.

To illustrate these points, it is useful to recall the old adage "the child is father of the man." This means simply that people's characteristics when they are children relate to their characteristics during adulthood. However, there is another way of interpreting this quotation: How we behave and think as adults—and perhaps especially as parents—is very much influenced by our experiences with our children. Our children rear us as much as we do them. Because we are parents, we are different adults than we would be if we were childless. But, more importantly, the specific and often special characteristics of a particular child influence us in unique ways. How we behave toward our children depends to a significant extent on how they have influenced us to behave. Such child influences are termed "child effects."

The presence of such child effects constitutes the basis of bidirectional relations between parents and children. This bidirectional relation continues when the child is an adolescent and an adult. Corresponding relations exist between people and siblings, friends, teachers, and indeed all other significant people in their life. Indeed, this child–other relation is the basic feature of the developmental contextual relations that characterize the social creature we call a human being.

Child effects emerge largely as a consequence of a child's individual distinctiveness. All children, with the exception of genetically identical (monozygotic) twins, have a unique genotype, that is, a unique genetic inheritance. Similarly, no two children, including monozygotic twins, experience precisely the same environment. All human characteristics, be they behavioral or physical, arise from an interrelation of genes and environment (Anastasi, 1958; Lerner, 1986). Given the uniqueness of each child's genetic inheritance and environment, the distinctiveness of each child is assured (Hirsch, 1970; Feldman & Lewontin, 1975). In other words, every child is unique and therefore individually different from every other child.

This individuality may be illustrated by drawing on the study of temperament (Chess & Thomas, 1984; Thomas & Chess, 1977; Thomas et al., 1963). Temperament is a characteristic of children's behavior that describes how they act. For instance, all children eat and sleep. Temperament is the style of eating or sleeping shown by the child; if the child eats

the same amount at every meal and/or gets hungry at the same time, then this child has, in regard to eating, a regular, or rhythmic, temperament. A child who gets hungry at different times of the day, or who may eat a lot or a little without any seeming predictability, would, in regard to eating, have an arrhythmic temperament. Similarly, obviously all children sleep. However, some children may sleep irregularly, that is, for seemingly unpredictable (at least to their parents) lengths of time, periods interspersed with wakeful periods of crying and fussing. Simply, one child may be an arrhythmic eater and sleeper, whereas another child might sleep and eat in a more regularly patterned way, and/or when awake may show more smiling than crying and fussing.

The importance of these individual differences arises when we recognize that, as a consequence of their individuality, children will present different stimulation to parents. Children with the above-noted temperamental styles present different stimuli to their parents as a consequence of their respective eating and sleep/wake patterns; the experience for a parent of having a pleasant, regularly sleeping child, who is predictable in regard to eating habits as well, is quite different from the experience for a parent who has a moody, irregularly sleeping and eating child. However, the effect of the child's stimulation of the parent depends in part on the parent's own characteristics of individuality. To explain this point it is useful to consider the second theme in the literature that helped crystallize the developmental contextual view of human development.

5.01.3.2 Development as a Life-span Phenomenon

The emergence of interest during the 1970s and 1980s in a life-span perspective about human development led to the understanding that development occurs in more than the childhood or adolescent years (Baltes, 1968, 1987; Block, 1971; Brim & Kagan, 1980; Elder, 1974, 1980; Featherman, 1983; Riley, 1979; Schaie, 1965). Parents as well as children develop as distinct individuals across life (Lerner & Spanier, 1978). Parents develop both as adults in general and, more specifically, in their familial and extrafamilial (for example, vocational or career) roles (Vondracek, Lerner, & Schulenberg, 1986). Indeed, the influence of children on their parents will depend in part on the prior experience the adult has had with the parental role and on the other roles in which the parent is engaged (e.g., worker, adult–child, and caregiver for an aged parent) (Hetherington &

Baltes, 1988). Thus, people's unique history of experiences and roles, as well as their unique biological (e.g., genetic) characteristics, combine to make them unique, and with time, given the accumulation of the influences of distinct roles and experiences, increasingly more so across the course of life (Lerner, 1988). This uniqueness is the basis of the specific feedback parents give to their individual children.

That is, parents who are stimulated differentially may be expected to differentially react to, or process (e.g., think and feel about) the stimulation provided by their child. A child with an irregular temperament might evoke feelings of frustration and exasperation and thoughts of concern in his or her parents (Brazelton, Koslowski, & Main, 1974; Lewis & Rosenblum, 1974). We might expect, however, that the parents of a child with a predictable and rhythmic style would be better rested than would the parents of an arrhythmic child. When the rhythmic child was awake, they would have a child with a more regularly positive mood, and this too would present less stress on them as parents and as spouses.

The individuality of parental reactions underscores the idea that parents are as individually distinct as their children. Not all parents of an irregularly eating and sleeping, moody child will react with concern and/or frustration. Similarly, some parents will be stressed by even the most regular, predictable, and positive of children. Such parental individuality makes child effects more complicated to study. However, at the same time, parental individuality underscores the uniqueness of each child's context. Simply, then, it may be expected that, as a consequence of the different stimulation received from their children, and in relation to their own characteristics of individuality, parents will provide differential feedback to their children.

Such differential feedback may take the form of different behavior shown to children by parents and/or of different emotional climates created in the home (Brazelton et al., 1974). For instance, parents of an irregular child might take steps to alter his or her eating and sleep/wake patterns. In regard to sleeping, they might try to cut naps short during the day in order that the child be more tired in the evening. In addition, during the time when they are appraising the success of their attempts to put the child on an imposed schedule a general sense of tenseness might pervade the household. "Will we have another sleepless night? Will we be too tired to be fully effective at work?" they might wonder.

The presence of differential feedback by parents of temperamentally distinct children becomes an important part of the child's experience, and this feedback is distinct in that it is based on the effect of the child's individuality on the parent. Thus, the feedback serves to promote the child's individuality further.

5.01.3.2.1 Circular functions and bidirectional socialization

The reciprocal child–parent relations involved in child effects constitute a circular function (Schneirla, 1957) in individual development: children stimulate differential reactions in their parents, and these reactions provide the basis of feedback to the children, that is, return stimulation which influences their further individual development. These circular functions underscore the point that children (and adolescents, and adults) are producers of their own development and that people's relations to their contexts involve bidirectional exchanges (Lerner, 1982; Lerner & Busch-Rossnagel, 1981). Parents shape their children, but part of what determines the way in which they do this is the children themselves.

Children shape their parents—as adults, as spouses, and of course as parents *per se*—and in so doing, children help organize feedback to themselves, feedback which contributes further to their individuality and thus the circular function starts all over again (that is, the child effects process returns to its first component). Characteristics of behavioral or personality individuality allow the child to contribute to this circular function. However, this idea of circular functions needs to be extended; that is, in and of itself the notion is silent regarding specific characteristics of the feedback (e.g., its positive or negative valence) children will receive as a consequence of their individuality. In other words, to account for the specific character of child–context relations the circular functions model needs to be supplemented; this is the contribution of the goodness-of-fit model.

5.01.3.2.2 The goodness-of-fit model

Just as children bring their characteristics of individuality to a particular social setting there are demands placed on them by virtue of the social and physical components of the setting. These demands may take the form of: (i) attitudes, values, or stereotypes that are held by others in the context regarding the person's attributes (either physical or behavioral characteristics); (ii) the attributes (usually behavioral) of others in the context with whom the child must coordinate, or fit, his or her attributes (also, in this case, usually behavioral) for adaptive interactions to exist; or, (iii) the physical characteristics of a setting (e.g., the presence or absence of access ramps for the motorically handicapped) which require the child to possess certain attributes (again, usually behavioral abilities) for the most efficient interaction within the setting to occur.

Children's individuality, in differentially meeting these demands, provides a basis for the specific feedback they get from the socializing environment. For example, considering the demand "domain" of attitudes, values, or stereotypes, teachers and parents may have relatively individual and distinct expectations about behaviors desired of their students and children, respectively. Teachers may want students who show little distractibility, but parents might desire their children to be moderately distractible, for example, when they require their children to move from television watching to dinner or to bed. Children whose behavioral individuality was either generally distractible or generally not distractible would thus differentially meet the demands of these two contexts. Problems of adjustment to school or to home might thus develop as a consequence of a child's lack of match (or goodness of fit) in either or both settings. In turn, interventions aimed at ameliorating or preventing such problems should focus on enhancing fit—on improving the child–context relation—and not on either child or context alone.

The importance of such an approach to intervention is underscored by the research of Thomas and Chess (1977, 1980, 1981) and Lerner and Lerner (1983, 1989). These researchers have found that if a child's characteristics of individuality provide a goodness of fit with demands of a particular setting, adaptive outcomes will accrue in that setting. Those children whose characteristics match most of the settings within which they exist receive supportive or positive feedback from the contexts and show evidence of the most adaptive behavioral development. In turn, of course, poorly fit, or mismatched, children—those whose characteristics are incongruent with one or most settings—appear to show alternative developmental outcomes.

In sum, then, the literature on child effects and on the life-span perspective promote a concern with individual differences; with variation in developmental pathways across life; and with the developmental contextual idea that changing relations (occurring "naturally" or through interventions) between people and their context provide the basis, across life, of the individual's unique repertoire of physical, psychological, and behavioral characteristics (Lerner, 1991). The recognition of this link between person and context was a product and a producer of the third theme emerging in the study of human development since the 1970s.

5.01.3.3 Development in its Ecological Context

The study of children and their parents became increasingly "contextualized," or placed within the broader "ecology of human development," during this period (Bronfenbrenner, 1977, 1979; Elder, 1974; Garbarino, 1992; Pepper, 1942). This focus has involved a concern with the "real life" situations within which children and families exist; it has also led to the study of the bidirectional relations between the family and other social settings within which children and parents function, for instance, the workplace, the welfare office, the day-care center, the Medicaid screening office, and the formal and the nonformal educational and recreational settings present in a neighborhood or a community (Lewis & Feiring, 1978; Lewis & Rosenblum, 1974). Thus, fit between youth and their contexts involves much more than relations between children and their parents and, as we have emphasized, interventions to enhance the congruence between person and context can involve any one or several levels within the ecology of human development.

To understand how the social context contributes to bidirectional person–context relations, we should reiterate that a child is not best thought of as merely similar to all other children, or as simply different from others with respect to only one, or even just a few, characteristics. Instead, individual differences exist with respect to numerous characteristics. We have illustrated how at least some of these changes occur through bidirectional relations children have with their parents. However, we have not yet stressed that parents too are made up of multiple dimensions of individuality which, as with the child, develop across time (e.g., see Baltes, 1987).

Another point not yet illustrated is that both the child and the parent have other social roles. These roles lead both children and parents into social relationships with other groups of people, that is, with other social networks. Parents are also spouses, adult children of their own parents, workers, and neighbors. Children also may be siblings and friends of other children; and as they progress through childhood and, later, adolescence, they become students and often at least part-time employees, respectively. The sorts of relationships in these other social networks in which children and parents engage when outside of their role of child or parent, respectively, can be expected to influence the parent–child relationship (Bronfenbrenner, 1977, 1979).

A child's poor performance at school may influence his or her behavior in the home, and especially, may alter the quality of the parent–

child relationship. In turn, a problematic home situation—as is experienced by children in families wherein parental abuse or neglect of the child occurs—will affect the child's relationships with peers, teachers, and other family members (Baca Zinn & Eitzen, 1993; Belsky, Lerner, & Spanier, 1984).

In regard to parents, strain in the spousal relationship can occur if adults spend too much energy in their parental caregiving role (J. V. Lerner, 1994). For instance, a child's unpredictable sleep pattern and negative mood when awake can severely tax a parents' energy. Energy and time needed for parents to be good spouses to each other therefore may not be available. In addition, the fatigue caused by the demands of parental roles can be expected to influence parents' performance in the workplace (J. V. Lerner, 1994). It is difficult for people who have been up all night caring for a crying infant to be at their best at work the next morning. In turn, of course, problems at work can be brought home. Parents whose energies are significantly depleted outside the home may not have the stamina during the evening to be attentive, patient parents to their children (or attentive, emotionally supportive spouses for their mates).

Thus, bidirectional relationships exist between child and parent (Bornstein & Tamis-LeMonda, 1990; Lerner & Lerner, 1987); and these relationships are in turn reciprocally related to other social networks within which the dyad exists and to the broader societal and cultural context. For example, studying mother–infant dyads in the United States, France, and Japan, Bornstein et al. (1992) found both culture-general and culture-specific patterns of maternal responsiveness to characteristics of infant individuality (e.g., in regard to activity level, exploration, and vocalization). In short, relationships among children, parents, and contexts constitute a complex state of affairs.

One approach to the conceptualization of these relations that we see as particularly useful has been proposed by Bronfenbrenner and his colleagues (e.g., Bronfenbrenner & Crouter, 1983; Bronfenbrenner & Morris, 1998; Garbarino, 1992). Bronfenbrenner's work has been a major catalyst in promoting the contextualization of human development, and in helping us understand why the study of development must move beyond its status during the 1970s, as "the science of the strange behavior of children in strange situations with strange adults for the briefest possible periods of time" (Bronfenbrenner, 1977, p. 513). Bronfenbrenner (1977, 1979, 1983) has argued that human development needs to be understood as it occurs in its real-world setting or "ecology." He believes that

this ecology of human development is composed of four distinct although interrelated systems, or types of settings.

The first, the "microsystem" is composed of "the complex of relations between the developing person and environment in an immediate setting containing the person" (Bronfenbrenner, 1977, p. 515). Furthermore, an infant's microsystems may be interrelated. What occurs in day care may affect what happens in the family, and vice versa. The second ecological stratum, termed the "mesosystem," is defined as "the interrelations among major settings containing the developing person at a particular point in his or her life" (e.g., the interaction between day care and family: Bronfenbrenner, 1977, p. 515).

Bronfenbrenner labels the third system as the "exosystem" and defines it as:

> an extension of the mesosystem embracing . . . specific social structures, both formal and informal, that do not themselves contain the developing person but impinge upon or encompass the immediate setting in which the person is found, and thereby delimit, influence, or even determine what goes on there [e.g., the parent's social role as "worker"]. (Bronfenbrenner, 1977, p. 515)

Finally, Bronfenbrenner notes that there exists a "macrosystem" within the ecology of human development. This system is composed of cultural values and beliefs as well as historical events (e.g., wars, floods, famines), both of which may affect other ecological systems.

In short, then, Bronfenbrenner's model of the ecology of human development allows us to devise a means to represent the idea that the bidirectional socialization which occurs between children and parents is embedded in a still more complex system of social networks and of societal, cultural, and historical influences. This system represents a rich set of "targets of opportunity" for the design, delivery, and sustainability of interventions into the course of human development.

5.01.3.3.1 Levels of embeddedness in the ecology of human development

The core idea in developmental contextualism is that the organism (organismic attributes or, most generally, biology) and context cannot be separated (Gottlieb, 1991, 1992; Lerner, 1984; Tobach, 1981). Both are fused across all of life, and thus across history. One way to illustrate just what is involved in this relation, even for one person, is to consider the diagram presented in Figure 1 (see Lerner, 1984, 1986).

It is important to indicate at this point that we may speak of dynamic interactions between

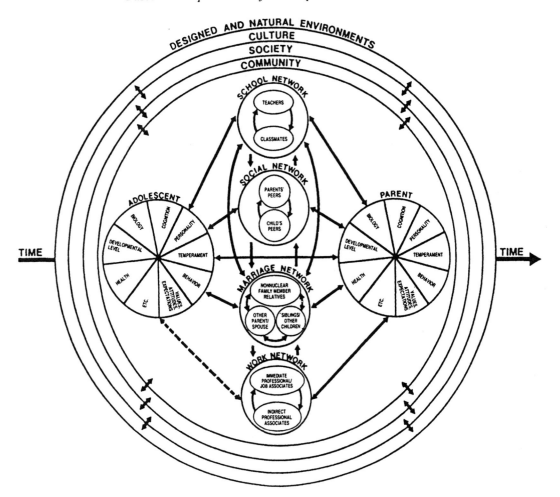

Figure 1 The developmental contextual view of human development: adolescent–child relations and interpersonal and institutional networks are embedded in and influenced by particular community, societal, cultural, and designed and natural environments, all changing across time (across history).

parent and child that pertain to either social or physical (for instance, biological or physiological) relations. For example, in regard to social relationships, the parent "demands" attention from the child, but the child does not show it; this "lights" the parent's "short fuse" of tolerance; the parent scolds the child, who then cries; this creates remorse in the parent and elicits soothing behaviors from him or her; the child is calmed, snuggles up to the parent, and now both parties in the relationship show positive emotions and are happy (see Tubman & Lerner, 1994, for data pertinent to such parent–child relationships).

In turn, we may also illustrate dynamic interactions which involve not only the exchange of "external" social behaviors but also involve biological or physiological processes. For example, parental religious practices, rearing practices, or financial status may influence the child's diet and nutritional status, health, and medical care. In turn, the contraction of an infectious disease by either parent or child can lead to the other member of the relationship contracting the disease. Moreover, the health and physical status of the child influences the parents' own feelings of well-being and thus hopes and aspirations regarding the child (Finkelstein, 1993).

Thus, Figure 1 illustrates that within and among each of the networks which is depicted, one may conceive of bidirectional relationships existing among the people populating the network. A child effect may function, in a sense, like a small pebble thrown into a quiet lake. It can prompt a large ripple. In turn, of course, the reverse of this possibility can occur. Events in settings lying far beyond the child–parent relationship can influence it. For instance, the resources in a community for child day care during the parent's working hours, the laws (e.g., regarding tax exemptions) or social programs available in a society supporting day care, and the cultural values regarding families who place their infants in day care, all exert an impact on the quality of the parent–child relationship.

Moreover, as we have just noted, the child–parent relationship, and the social networks in which it is located, are embedded in still larger community, societal, cultural, and historical levels of organization. These relations are illustrated also in Figure 1. Time (history) cuts through all the systems. This feature of the figure is introduced to remind us that, as with the people populating these social systems, change is always occurring. Diversity within time is created as change across time introduces variation into all levels of organization involved in the system depicted in Figure 1.

In other words, all changes are embedded in history (Baltes, 1987; Elder, 1974; Elder et al., 1993), that is, time "cuts through" all levels of organization. As such, the nature of parent–child relations, of family life and development, and of societal and cultural influences on the child–parent–family system are influenced by both normative and non-normative historical changes (Baltes, 1987) or, in other words, by "evolutionary" (i.e., gradual) and "revolutionary" (i.e., abrupt; Werner, 1957) historical changes. This system of multiple, interconnected, or "fused" (Tobach & Greenberg, 1984) levels comprises a complete depiction of the integrated organization involved in the developmental contextual view of human development (Lerner, 1986, 1991).

5.01.4 IMPLICATIONS FOR METHOD AND APPLICATION

In essence, (i) individuality (diversity); (ii) change, involving both the individual and the context; and, as a consequence; (iii) further individuality, are the essential features of human development within developmental contextualism. Given that the multiple levels of change involved in person–context relations may involve individuals at any point in their lives—whether they are infants or young children, on the one hand, or adults (and acting in roles such as parents, spouses, or teachers), on the other—it is possible to see why a developmental contextual perspective provides a useful frame for studying development across the life-span and a rich opportunity to design and implement both individual and group interventions into the course of human life.

The possibility that bidirectional relations exist across the life-span among all the levels shown in Figure 1 represents a formidable state of complexity, but one which behavioral and social science theory, research, and intervention must address. If the scholarship of research and application does not cope with this complexity, then neither research nor intervention will be adequate. That is, research inattentive to the complexity of person–context relations will be deficient in that either it will fail to appreciate the substantive nature of individual, familial, or relationship variation and/or it will mistakenly construe variation around some mean level as, at best, error variance (Lerner, 1991, 1997). In turn, applications—policies and/or intervention programs (that are at least ideally) derived from research (Lerner & Miller, 1993)—will insufficiently fit with the needs of the specific people intended to be served by these interventions, if it is the case that these activities are insufficiently informed by knowledge about the specific characteristics of individuality of these groups. However, developmental contextualism offers an alternative to this situation. It does so by stressing the importance of a focus on diversity and context for integrated research and application.

As we have emphasized, developmental contextualism stresses the bidirectional connections between individuals and the actual ("ecologically valid") settings within which they live. This emphasis has brought to the fore of concern in the social and behavioral sciences both "diversity" (individual differences) and "context" (of peoples and their sociocultural institutions). In addition, we have explained that developmental contextualism emphasizes the relation between individuals and their context, a focus that has resulted in the recognition that a synthesis of perspectives from multiple disciplines is needed to understand the multilevel (e.g., person, family, and community) integrations involved in human development. Furthermore, there has been a recognition that to understand the basic process of human development—the process involved in the changing relations between individuals and contexts—both descriptive and explanatory research must be conducted within the actual ecology of people's lives.

Descriptive research involves the depiction, or representation, of development as it exists for a given person or group, in one or more contexts, at one or more points in time. Explanatory research involves the introduction (through manipulation or statistical modeling) of variation into such person–context relations. These planned variations in the course of human life are predicated on: (i) theoretical ideas about the source of particular developmental phenomena (for specific combinations of people and contexts); or on (ii) theoretically guided interests about the extent to which a particular developmental phenomenon (e.g., cognitive development in the aged years) may show systematic change in structure and/or function, that is plasticity, across the life-span (Baltes, 1987; Lerner, 1984). In either of the above cases such researcher-introduced variation is an attempt to simulate the "natural" variation of life; if theoretical expectations are confirmed, the outcomes of such investigations provide an explanation of how developmental change occurs within a person or group.

Given the developmental contextual focus on studying person–context relations within the actual ecology of human development, explanatory investigations by their very nature constitute intervention research. In other words, the goal of developmental contextual explanatory research is to understand the ways in which variations in ecologically valid person–context relations account for the character of actual or potential trajectories of human development, that is, life paths enacted in the "natural laboratory" of the "real world." Therefore, to gain understanding of how theoretically relevant variations in such person–context relations may influence actual or to-be-actualized developmental trajectories, the researcher may introduce policies and/or programs as, if you will, "experimental manipulations" of the proximal and/or distal natural ecology. Evaluations of outcomes of such interventions become, then, a means to bring data to bear on theoretical issues pertinent to changing person–context relations and, more specifically, to the plasticity in human development that may exist, or that may be capitalized on, to enhance human life (Lerner, 1988). In other words, a key theoretical issue for explanatory research in human development is the extent to which changes—in the multiple, fused levels of organization comprising human life—can alter the structure and/or function of behavior and development.

Of course, independent of any researcher-imposed attempts to intervene in the course of human development, the naturally occurring events experienced by people constantly shape, texture, and help direct the course of their lives. That is, the accumulation of the specific roles and events a person experiences across life—involving normative age-graded events, normative history-graded events, and non-normative events (Baltes, 1987; Baltes, Reese, & Lipsitt, 1980)—alters each person's developmental trajectory in a manner that would not have occurred had another set of roles and events been experienced. The between-person differences in within-person change that exist as a consequence of these naturally occurring experiences attest to the magnitude of the systematic changes in structure and function—

the plasticity—that characterizes human life (Lerner, 1984).

Explanatory research is necessary, however, to understand what variables, from what levels of organization, are involved in particular instances of plasticity that have been seen to exist. In addition, such research is necessary to determine what instances of plasticity may be created by science or society. In other words, explanatory research is needed to ascertain the extent of human plasticity or, in turn, the limits of plasticity (Lerner, 1984). From a developmental contextual perspective, conduct of such research requires scientists to alter the natural ecology of the person or group they are studying. Such research may involve either proximal and/or distal variations in the context of human development (Lerner & Ryff, 1978); but, in any case, these manipulations constitute theoretically guided alterations of the roles and events a person or group experiences at, or over, a portion of the life-span.

These alterations are indeed, then, interventions: they are planned attempts to alter the system of person–context relations constituting the basic process of change; they are conducted in order to ascertain the specific bases of, or to test the limits of, particular instances of human plasticity (Baltes, Dittmann-Kohli, & Dixon, 1984; Baltes, Smith, & Staudinger, 1992). These interventions are a researcher's attempt to substitute designed person–context relations for naturally occurring ones, a substitution done in an attempt to understand the process of changing person–context relations providing the basis of human development. In short, then, basic research in human development is intervention research.

Accordingly, the cutting-edge of theory and research in human development lies in the application of the conceptual and methodological expertise of human development scientists to the "natural ontogenetic laboratory" of the real world. Multilevel—and hence, qualitatively and quantitatively multivariate—and longitudinal research methods must be used by scholars from multiple disciplines to derive, from theoretical models of person–context relations, programs of research that involve the design, delivery, and evaluation of interventions aimed at enhancing—through scientist-introduced variation—the course of human development.

In short, in developmental contextualism there is a stress on ontological (and on epistemological, we would add) relationism and contextualization. These emphases have brought to the fore of scientific, intervention, and policy concerns issues pertinent to the functional importance of diverse person–context interactions. Examples are studies of the effects of variations in maternal employment on infant, child, and young adolescent development; the importance of differences in quality day care for the immediate and long-term development in children of healthy physical, psychological, and social characteristics; and the effects of variations in marital role strain and in marital stability–instability on the healthy development of children and adolescents.

Diversity of people and their settings means that one cannot assume that general rules of development either exist for, or apply in the same way to, all children and families. Moreover, one cannot assume, even if only small portions of the total variance in human behavior and development reflect variance that is unique to an individual or group, that this nonshared variance is not the most salient information we have when attempting to understand or enhance the quality of the lives for the person or group.

5.01.4.1 Clinical Application

With its emphasis on the relations between the individual and the context, and on the diversity of people and settings, developmental contextualism has important implications for clinical practice, including: (i) a focus on the dynamic character of behavior and pathology, (ii) specification of the impact of context on behavior, (iii) recognition of the role of strengths and assets, and (iv) utilization of multiple levels of assessment and intervention.

The developmental contextualist framework challenges clinicians to shift from a static focus on classification of the symptoms of psychopathology to a more dynamic orientation in which psychopathology is viewed as a product of the relationship between development and specific environments. The dominant diagnostic system now used by most clinicians, *Diagnostic and statistical manual of mental disorders (4th ed.)* (*DSM-IV*) (American Psychiatric Association, 1994), classifies problem behavior in terms of characteristic features of disorders at a single point in time, accounting for neither the development of the disorder nor the context in which it occurs (Achenbach, 1990; Cowan, 1988).

A developmental perspective requires a consideration of the meaning of behaviors at different developmental periods. Behaviors that are "normal" at one age, may be "abnormal" at another (Campbell, 1989; Sroufe, 1990; Sroufe & Rutter, 1984). For instance, enuresis is not uncommon in three- and four-year-old children but is unusual for a 10 year old. Knowing the child's developmental period may aid one in

more thoroughly assessing the factors contributing to this behavior. Achenbach (1990) points out that:

> to improve our understanding of maladaptive behavior, it is helpful to view it in relation to normative sequences and achievements for particular ages. When this is done it is evident that many behavioral and emotional problems for which professional help is sought are not qualitatively different from those that most individuals display to some degree at some time in their lives. (p. 4)

A developmental perspective, therefore, encourages clinicians to consider not only what is abnormal behavior or development, but what is normal as well. An understanding of healthy development and the factors that influence both positive and negative outcomes contributes to our understanding of psychopathology (Cicchetti & Garmezy, 1993; Sroufe, 1990; Sroufe & Rutter, 1984).

The influence of development on the interpretation of behaviors is particularly evident in the area of cognitive development (Campbell, 1989). For example, if a five-year-old child whose grandfather has died says that he wants "to go where grandpa is," the clinician interprets the child's wish quite differently than a similar wish expressed by a 14 year old. The clinician recognizes that the 14 year old has a more mature concept of the meaning of death, requiring a different kind of clinical response. The behavior may look similar, but its meaning is very different at these two developmental periods. Similar characteristics displayed at various points in ontogeny may have different implications because they are embedded in a distinct developmental milieu. In short, the accurate assessment of behaviors requires an understanding of appropriate and inappropriate, adaptive and maladaptive, and expected and unexpected behaviors/skills/abilities throughout an individual's development.

An understanding of the development of a disorder, that is, how an individual found himself or herself on a particular developmental path, provides a more complete explanation of an individual's behaviors, thus allowing for a broader range of interventions. A developmental perspective provides guidance in the choice of interventions (Campbell, 1989). For instance, understanding the cognitive-developmental level of a four-year-old child, one would not be likely to use cognitive-behavioral reframing strategies during treatment. Clinicians must plan interventions that are appropriate for children at their current developmental level. Similarly, it is a widely understood phenomenon that older children can experience a greater number of differentiated emotions than a younger child. The child's developing ability to experience and identify emotions will guide practitioners in developing appropriate interventions.

A developmental contextualist framework involves not only a focus on development, but development in relation to context. The traditional *DSM-IV* approach to diagnosis/treatment does not view the behavior as the product of person–context relations. On the contrary, while it "does not claim that every category of disorder represents a mental illness, its classification system has its conceptual roots in the medical model of psychopathology, with its assumption that psychopathology is a disease located somewhere in the patient' (Cowan, 1988, p. 7). Within a developmental contextualist framework, the problem behavior is not located "within the child" (e.g., the child "has" a conduct disorder), but rather is viewed as a disturbance in the relationship or a lack of fit between the child and the settings which impact him or her. Rather than a focus on "fixing the child," developmental contextualism requires the clinician to address the fit or match between the child and the contexts which surround the child (e.g., family, school, community, culture, etc.). From this perspective, behavior is inexplicable when considered in isolation from the context in which it occurs. As an example, consider a five-year-old boy exhibiting behaviors characteristic of separation anxiety, that is, manifesting distress when away from his parents, worrying that he may get hurt if not with his parents, and refusing to sleep apart from his parents. An acontextual explanation may conclude that this behavior, while typical of a two-year-old child, is abnormal for a five-year-old child. However, if this child is living in a violent neighborhood where physical danger is a daily reality, the behaviors that he is exhibiting are not "abnormal," nor are they unexpected. To be understood appropriately and completely, this child's behavior would need to be considered as a function of his context. Spencer (1990), states that "the integration or consideration of culture and context should afford a better match between policy, practice, and positive family and child outcomes" (p. 269). From a developmental contextualist perspective, clinicians will be most effective when they understand and approach problem behavior in terms of a lack of fit between child and context.

A developmental contextual approach also acknowledges that behaviors that are adaptive in one context may be maladaptive in another context. For instance, a child's neighborhood environment may make aggressive behavior important to the child's survival, but this behavior may be maladaptive in the school environment. If one intervenes to change the maladaptive behavior witnessed at school without understanding the adaptability of this same behavior in the neighborhood, one could be doing this child a disservice. The child no longer exhibits aggressive behavior at school, but now is disadvantaged on the streets. An accurate assessment of children's difficulties requires an understanding of children within their contexts and their "problematic" behaviors within these contexts. In our example, the behavior of the child fits his neighborhood context, but does not fit well with his school context. The goodness-of-fit principle explained above implies that an intervention should work to enhance the fit of child and context. The problem does not lie solely in the environment or solely within the child. Problems result when there is a lack of fit between the individual and the context. Using a developmental contextual perspective, a clinician will gather information on the child's context to better understand the factors influencing and reinforcing the problem behavior.

Not only do children exist within their immediate contexts, but they also exist within a specific historical moment. The concept of temporality suggests that at different historical moments the person–context relation could have different meanings, that is, what is considered "normal" changes over time. For instance, a teacher living in the southern United States who is teaching poor black children to read would be viewed quite differently at different points in history. One hundred years ago such a teacher may have been viewed as a sociopath, as someone who goes against social conventions and social norms. Today that same teacher may be viewed as a dedicated, caring individual. The person–context relation not only exists in ontogenetic time, but in historical time as well.

The concept of temporality also argues for examining "tried and true" interventions such as individual counseling. Humans are embedded in the historical time in which they live. Not only do individuals change over time, but changes also occur in the wider society. Systems of assessment and intervention must be reevaluated to ensure that earlier models, developed in earlier historical moments, remain relevant and effective in the current time period. For example, the earlier exclusive reliance on individual psychotherapy has begun to give way to increased emphasis on prevention measures and group interventions. New models of treatment have begun to emerge, for example, group and family counseling and psychoeducational intervention. There is an increased emphasis on providing services through community schools. As our culture and needs change, so do our modes of intervention. In a similar manner, the types of problems presented to clinicians today are often different from those one would have found in past decades. While syndromes similar to what is now called Attention Deficit Hyperactivity Disorder have been discussed since the 1860s, the symptoms that have defined the syndrome have changed. In the 1960s, the emphasis was on hyperactivity, whereas today hyperactivity is only one aspect of the disorder; one that is not even necessary for diagnosis (Barkley, 1990).

The implicit suggestion in many of the above examples is that a child's context is not unidimensional. Children exist within a family, a peer group, a school system, a community, a culture, and a specific period in history. Similarly, their problems are not unidimensional. Their development is affected by experiences at the inner biological, the individual/ psychological, the social relational, the sociocultural, and the ecological levels of organization. Given these multiple levels, accurate assessment requires integrating information about the child from multiple perspectives. Achenbach (1990) suggests five axes that are relevant to the assessment of children. These comprise parent reports, teacher reports, cognitive assessment, physical assessment, and direct assessment of the child. The axes from which one gathers information will depend upon the relevance of each axis to the child's current situation.

A developmental contextual perspective requires not only multiple-level assessment but also multiple-level interventions. Within this framework, psychotherapeutic interventions are expanded to include multiple levels of organization (i.e., biological, sociohistorical, cultural, psychological, etc.). This results in a shift in the clinician's orientation from a typical unilevel approach to intervention strategies involving multiple levels of organization. A child's development does not occur at the same rate and in a parallel fashion at each of the levels of organization. Therefore, an unevenness in strengths and weaknesses may be observed. By focusing on weaknesses only, one falls into a deficit model that focuses only on children and their "abnormal" behaviors without considering contextual factors. A developmental-contextual approach considers children within their contexts and identifies strengths as well as deficits. This approach uses an optimization framework, focusing on and building on strengths to maximize a child's full development. The clinical intervention, then, will focus on the relationships among the levels of

organization and therefore will be multimodal. While a child may manifest a weakness at one level, for example, the inner-biological level, he or she may be functioning well at another level, for example, the social relational level. Intervention can occur at any level and, given the interconnectedness of the levels, will help to promote growth in other levels.

The implications of the interconnectedness of the levels (i.e., plasticity) are evident in the research on resilience. The resilience literature clearly demonstrates that children have "self-righting tendencies that move children toward normal development under all but the most persistent adverse circumstances" (Werner, 1990, p. 112). Werner (1990) identifies three areas of protective factors that may contribute to a child's resilience. These include:

> dispositional attributes of the child that elicit predominantly positive responses from the environment, such as physical robustness and vigor, an easy temperament, and intelligence; affectional ties and socialization practices within the family that encourage trust, autonomy and initiative; and external support systems that reinforce competence and provide children with a positive set of values. (p. 111)

These protective factors are found at various levels of organization, for example, dispositional attributes are characteristics of the child, and are, therefore, found at the individual/ psychological level, while affectional ties are located at the social relational level of organization. Behavioral change, then, is the result of the impact of both contextual and organismic characteristics on the individual's current functioning. However, as the literature on risk and prevention demonstrates, contextual and organismic factors do not interact in an additive or linear manner, but in a multiplicative way (Sameroff, 1996). It is therefore imperative that a clinician appreciate the complex and continually changing interplay between individuals and their contexts when engaging in clinical interventions.

In essence, plasticity implies that interventions are not fruitless endeavors and that poorly functioning individuals are not doomed to remain poorly functioning if an intervention can be developed that addresses a strength. While it is true that development may be constrained by past developments and current contextual conditions, plasticity implies that humans do have the potential for change across the life-span (Sroufe, 1990; Sroufe & Rutter, 1984). Clinicians can help to remove the constraining aspects of the child's context. To optimize the effects of an intervention, the clinician must address the contextual constraints at all levels of organization. For example, a homeless child who acts out in school requires a more complex diagnosis than that provided by the diagnostic label "conduct disorder," and a treatment plan more comprehensive than that offered by a unilevel intervention such as "insight-oriented therapy," or "pharmacological treatment" (Walsh, 1992; Walsh & Buckley, 1994). This broader view of assessment and intervention planning requires that a single practitioner, for example, a psychologist, take into account the various perspectives of the child's behavior offered by different professionals. Cowen (1984) argued compellingly for a more integrated approach to practice:

> Although most mental health professionals are knowledgeable about the nature and assessment of human adjustment, they are not Renaissance persons with exhaustive knowledge of complex feeder-domains such as education, sociology, environmental planning, economics, family relations, architecture, public health, epidemiology, and social ecology, which contain significant knowledge about factors that relate to human adjustment. The points to stress are that: (a) the potential generative base for primary prevention work is much broader than the mental health fields as classically designed, and (b) in the long run, accessing and harnessing important bodies of generative information calls both for new alliances between mental health professionals and members of the other disciplines and new types of training that cut across traditional disciplinary lines. (p. 487)

The concept of multiple levels of organization, then, implies not only multiple levels of assessment and intervention by clinicians, but also collaboration among professionals. For instance, in the example of the homeless child who acts out in school, one might have the school nurse assess their nutritional and physical needs, the teacher assess their educational needs, the school psychologist explore their emotional needs, and the parents report on their behavior outside of school and the social and economic stressors placed on them as a family. Such a collaboration would lead to a more holistic understanding of this boy's needs than would a simple diagnosis of "conduct disorder." Accordingly, the resulting intervention would also be holistic in nature, involving all of the collaborators.

In short, from a developmental contextual perspective, integrated multidisciplinary and developmental research devoted to the design of intervention programs for the person or group should be moved to the fore of scholarly concern. This integrative research and outreach must involve two other considerations: first, this research and outreach must involve collaborations among disciplines and between scholarly and community interests; and second, this research and outreach must be integrated with policies and programs.

5.01.4.2 The Need for Collaborative Research and Outreach

To be successful, these endeavors require more than collaboration across disciplines. In addition, two other types of collaboration are necessary. First, multiprofessional collaboration is essential. Colleagues in the research, policy, and intervention communities must plan and implement their activities in a synthesized manner in order to successfully develop and extend this vision. All components of this collaboration must be understood as equally valuable, indeed as equally essential. The collaborative activities of colleagues in university extension and outreach; in program design and delivery; in elementary, middle (or junior high), and high schools; in policy development and analysis; and in academic research are vital to the success of this new agenda for science and outreach for children, adolescents, parents, and their contexts, for example, their extended families, their schools, their workplaces, and their communities (Brabeck et al., 1997; Weissbourd, 1996).

Second, given the contextual embeddedness of these synthetic research and outreach activities, collaboration must occur with the people we are trying both to understand and to serve. Without incorporation of the perspective of the community into our work—without the community's sense of ownership, of value, and of meaning for these endeavors—research and outreach activities cannot be adequately integrated into the lives we are studying.

Thus, from a developmental contextual perspective, research that "parachutes" into the community from the heights of the academy (i.e., that is done in a community without collaboration with the members of the community) is flawed fatally in regard to its ability to understand the process of human development. This is the case because human development does not happen at the general level (Lerner, 1988, 1991); it does not occur in a manner necessarily generalizable across diverse people and contexts (Bibace & Walsh, 1979). Development happens in particular communities, and it involves the attempts of specific children and families to relate to the physical, personal, social, and institutional situations found in their communities. Without bringing the perspective of the community into the "plan" for research, then, scholars may fail to address the correct problems of human development, the ones involved in the actual lives of the people they are studying. And if the wrong problem is being addressed, any "answers" that are found are not likely to be relevant to the actual lives of people. Not surprisingly, these answers will be seen all too often (and quite appropriately) as irrelevant by the community.

In turn, however, if community members collaborate in the definition of the problems of development that they are confronting, and if they participate in the research process, then the obtained answers are more likely to be considered significant by the community members. This will increase the likelihood of these answers being used to build community-specific policies and programs. Moreover, community empowerment and capacity building occur by engaging in a collaborative process wherein the community places value and meaning on, and participates in, the research and outreach being conducted within its boundaries (Dryfoos, 1990, 1994; Schorr, 1988).

5.01.4.3 Implications for Policies and Programs

In order to be complete, the integrative research promoted by a developmental contextual view of human development must be synthesized with two other focuses. Research in human development that is concerned with one, or even a few, instances of individual and contextual diversity cannot be assumed to be useful for understanding the life course of all people. Similarly, policies and programs derived from such research, or associated with it in the context of a researcher's tests of ideas pertinent to human plasticity, cannot be assumed to be applicable, or equally appropriate and useful, in all contexts or for all individuals. Accordingly, developmental and individual differences-oriented policy development and program (intervention) design and delivery would need to be integrated fully with the new research base for which we are calling (Lerner & Miller, 1993; Lerner et al., 1994).

As emphasized in developmental contextualism, the variation in settings within which people live means that studying development in a standard (for example, a "controlled") environment does not provide information pertinent to the actual (ecologically valid), developing relations between individually distinct people and their specific contexts (for example, their particular families, schools, or

communities). This point underscores the need to conduct research in real-world settings, and highlights the ideas that: policies and programs constitute natural experiments, that is, planned interventions for people and institutions; and the evaluation of such activities becomes a central focus in the developmental contextual research agenda we have described.

In this view, then, policy and program endeavors do not constitute secondary work, or derivative applications, conducted after research evidence has been complied. Quite to the contrary, policy development and implementation, and program design and delivery, become integral components of this vision for research; the evaluation component of such policy and intervention work provides critical feedback about the adequacy of the conceptual frame from which this research agenda should derive (cf. Lanier, 1990). This conception of the integration of multidisciplinary research endeavors centrally aimed at diversity and context, with policies, programs, and evaluations is illustrated in Figure 2.

A vision of the integration between developmental research and policies and programs was articulated in the 1970s by Bronfenbrenner (1974), and more recently by Zigler (in press). Bronfenbrenner argued that engagement with social policy not only enhances developmental research but, consistent with the developmental contextual perspective, it also augments understanding of key theoretical issues pertinent to the nature of person–context relations. Bronfenbrenner (1974) noted that:

In discussions of the relation between science and social policy, the first axiom, at least among social scientists, is that social policy should be based on science. The proposition not only has logic on its side, but what is more important, it recognizes our proper and primary importance in the scheme of things. The policymakers should look to us, not only for truth, but for wisdom as well. In short, social policy needs science.

My thesis in this paper is the converse proposition, that, particularly in our field, science needs social policy—needs it not to guide our organizational activities, but to provide us with two elements essential for any scientific endeavor— vitality and validity ... I contend that the pursuit of [social policy] questions is essential for the further development of knowledge and theory on the process of human development. Why essential? ... [Because] issues of social policy [serve] as points of departure for the identification of significant theoretical and scientific questions concerning the development of the human organism as a function of interaction with its enduring environment—both actual and potential. (pp. 1–2,4)

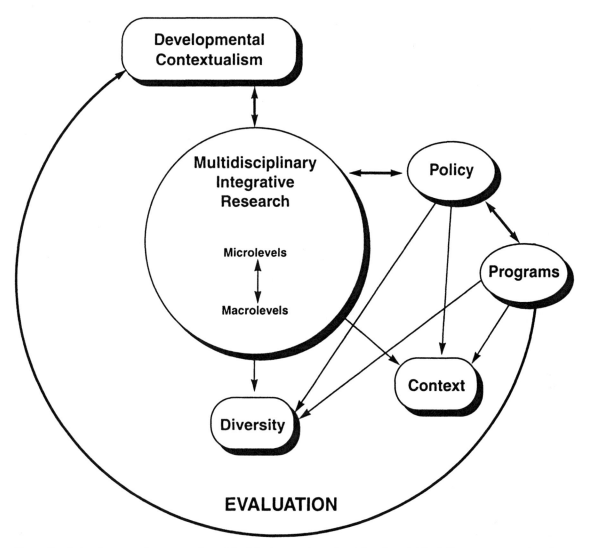

Figure 2 A developmental contextual model of the integration of multilevel, multidisciplinary research, aimed at diversity and context, with policies, programs, and evaluations.

In short, developmental research informs and is informed by social policy. It is our contention that policy development, program design and delivery, and developmental research need to be integrated fully to optimally benefit the recipients of social programs.

5.01.5 CONCLUSIONS AND FUTURE DIRECTIONS

Developmental contextualism and the research and intervention associated with it take an integrative approach to the multiple levels of organization presumed to comprise the nature of human life; that is, "fused" (Tobach & Greenberg, 1984) relations among biological, psychological, and social and physical contextual levels comprise the process of developmental change in human life. Rather than

approach variables from these levels of analysis in either a reductionistic or in a parallel-processing approach, developmental contextualism rests on the idea that variables from these levels of analysis are dynamically interactive: they are reciprocally influential over the course of human ontogeny (Lerner, 1986, 1991, 1995).

In turn, developmental contextualism provides an agenda not only for a developmental, dynamic, and systems approach to research about child and adolescent development. As well, such theory allows us to envision the possibility of promoting positive developmental trajectories in youth (Lerner, 1995). We, as clinicians, researchers, and policy makers, may actualize this vision if we remain assiduously committed to a developmental systems orientation; if we recognize the "double-edged sword" nature of plasticity that derives from the functioning of this system; and if we therefore create, through policies and programs, a "convoy of social support" (Kahn & Antonucci, 1980) across the life course of children and adolescents. Such a convoy would be a network encompassing the familial, community, institutional, and cultural components of the ecology that impacts people's behavior and development across their life.

The concepts of person, of context, and of the relations between the two found in a developmental contextual perspective are, as a set, quite complex, and impose formidable challenges on those who seek to understand the developmental bases of psychopathology and of nonpsychopathologic behavior, to derive feasible research from this perspective, and to use this conception and its associated research for the design and implementation of interventions. As we have argued, this developmental contextual perspective leads to an integrated, multilevel concept of development, one in which the focus of inquiry is the organism–environment dynamic interaction. Furthermore, such an orientation places an emphasis on the potential for intra-individual change in structure and function—for plasticity—across the life-span. Moreover, this perspective requires a temporal (historical)/longitudinal and a relational/comparative orientation to research and to intervention.

A major challenge of this perspective is the derivation and empirical testing of models reflecting the nature of dynamic, interlevel interactions across time. As we have indicated, one reasonably successful path we have taken involves the testing of the goodness-of-fit model of person–context relations. Of course, the goodness-of-fit model is not the only conception of person–context relations that may be derived from a developmental contextual orientation. There are perhaps an infinity of possible interlevel relations that may occur and a potentially similarly large array of ways to model them. Indeed, tests of other models derived from or consistent with a developmental contextual or life-span perspective have also found considerable empirical support (e.g., Baltes, 1987; Caspi & Elder, 1988; Featherman, 1985; Perlmutter, 1988).

The tests of such models will profit by triangulation of the constructs within each of the levels of analysis thought to interact dynamically within a given model. For instance, in regard to the biological/organismic-psychosocial interactions assessed within the goodness-of-fit model, biological changes could be simultaneously indexed both by more molecular (e.g., hormonal) changes, and by more molar, bodily measures. Similarly, contextual demands could be simultaneously appraised by assessing both attitudes/expectations about behavior held

by a person's significant other and actual behavioral exchanges between a person and these others. Such triangulation would not only provide convergent and discriminant validation information but also better insight would be gained about whether all modalities of functioning within a level of analysis are of similar import for the development of psychopathological or nonpsychopathological functioning in particular person–context interactions.

In sum, the relative plasticity of human development across the life-span—a plasticity deriving from the dynamic interactions between organism and context which characterize human functioning—is already well documented (Baltes, 1987; Brim & Kagan, 1980; Featherman, 1983; Hetherington, Lerner, & Perlmutter, 1988; Lerner, 1984; Sorensen, Weinert, & Sherrod, 1986). Thus, a future including the sorts of directions we suggest should enrich greatly our understanding of the precise conditions promoting and constraining the development of psychopathology. Given, then, the present literature, and the promise we see for tomorrow, we believe there is reason for great optimism about the future scientific and clinical use of the developmental contextual view of the biological and social contextual bases of, on the one hand, functional, adaptive behaviors and, on the other, malfunctional, psychopathological ones.

5.01.6 REFERENCES

Achenbach, T. M. (1990). Conceptualization of developmental psychopathology. In M. Lewis & S. M. Miller (Eds.), *Handbook of developmental psychopathology* (pp. 3–14). New York: Plenum.
American Psychiatric Association. (1994). *Diagnostic and statistical manual of mental disorders* (4th ed.). Washington, DC: Author.
Anastasi, A. (1958). Heredity, environment, and the question, "how?" *Psychological Review, 65,* 197–208.
Baca Zinn, M., & Eitzen D. S. (1993). *Diversity in families* (3rd ed.). New York: Harper Collins College.
Baer, D. M. (1970). An age-irrelevant concept of development. *Merrill Palmer Quarterly of Behavior and Development, 16,* 238–45.
Baer, D. M. (1976). The organism as host. *Human Development, 19,* 87–98.
Baltes, P. B. (1968). Longitudinal and cross-sectional sequences in the study of age and generation effects. *Human Development, 11,* 145–171.
Baltes, P. B. (1987). Theoretical propositions of life-span developmental psychology: On the dynamics between growth and decline. *Developmental Psychology, 23,* 611–626.
Baltes, P. B., Dittmann-Kohli, F., & Dixon, R. A. (1984). New perspectives on the development of intelligence in adulthood: Toward a dual-process conception and model of selective optimization with compensation. In P. B. Baltes & O. G. Brim, Jr. (Eds.), *Life-span development and behavior* (Vol. 6, pp. 33–76). New York: Academic Press.

Baltes, P. B., & Nesselroade, J. R. (1973). The developmental analysis of individual differences on multiple measures. In J. R. Nesselroade & H. W. Reese (Eds.), *Life-span developmental psychology: Introduction to research methodological issues* (pp. 219–251). New York: Academic Press.

Baltes, P. B., Reese, H. W., & Lipsitt, L. P. (1980). Life-span developmental psychology. *Annual Review of Psychology, 31,* 65–110.

Baltes, P. B., Reese, H. W., & Nesselroade, J. R. (1977). *Life-span developmental psychology: Introduction to research methods.* Monterey, CA: Brooks/Cole.

Baltes, P. B., Smith, J., & Staudinger, U. M. (1992). Wisdom and successful aging. In T. B. Sonderegger (Ed.), *Nebraska Symposium on Motivation* (Vol. 39, 123–167). Lincoln, NE: University of Nebraska Press.

Barkley, R. A. (1990). Attention deficit disorders: History, definition, and diagnosis. In M. Lewis & S. M. Miller (Eds.), *Handbook of developmental psychopathology* (pp. 3–14). New York: Plenum.

Baumrind, D. (1995). *Child maltreatment and optimal caregiving in social contexts* (MSU Series on Children, Youth, and Families). New York: Garland.

Bell, R. Q. (1968). A reinterpretation of the direction of effects in studies of socialization. *Psychological Review, 115,* 81–95.

Belsky, J., Lerner, R. M., & Spanier, G. B. (1984). *The child in the family.* Reading, MA: Addison-Wesley.

Bibace, R., & Walsh, M. (1979). Clinical developmental psychologists in family practice settings. *Professional Psychology, 10,* 441–450.

Bijou, S. W. (1976). *Child development: The basic stage of early childhood.* Englewood Cliffs, NJ: Prentice-Hall.

Bijou, S. W., & Baer, D. M. (Ed.) (1961). *Child development: A systematic and empirical theory.* New York: Appleton-Century-Crofts.

Birkel, R., Lerner, R. M., & Smyer, M. A. (1989). Applied developmental psychology as an implementation of a life-span view of human development. *Journal of Applied Developmental Psychology, 10,* 425–445.

Block, J. (1971). *Lives through time.* Berkeley, CA: Bancroft.

Bornstein, M. H., & Tamis-LeMonda, C. S. (1990). Activities and interactions of mothers and their firstborn infants in the first six months of life: Covariation, stability, continuity, correspondence, and prediction. *Child Development, 61,* 1206–1217.

Bornstein, M. H., Tamis-LeMonda, C. S., Tal, J., Ludemann, P., Toda, S., Rahn, C., Pecheux, M., Azuma, H., & Vardi, D. (1992). Maternal responsiveness to infants in three societies: The United States, France, and Japan. *Child Development, 63,* 808–821.

Brabeck, M., Cawthorne, J., Cochran-Smith, M., Gaspard, N., Green, C. H., Kenny, M., Krawczy, K. R., Lowery, C., Lykes, M. B., Minuskin, A. D., Mooney, J., Ross, C. J., Savage, J., Soifer, A., Smyer, M., Sparks, E., Tourse, R., Turillo, R. M., Waddock, S., Walsh, M., & Zollers, N. (1997). Changing the culture of the university to engage in outreach scholarship. In R. M. Lerner & L. A. K. Simon (Eds.), *Creating the new outreach university for America's youth and families: Building university–community collaborations for the twenty-first century (pp. 335–366).* New York: Garland Press.

Brazelton, T. B., Koslowski, B., & Main, M. (1974). The origins of reciprocity: The early mother–infant interaction. In M. Lewis & L. A. Rosenblum (Eds.), *The effect of the infant on its caregivers* (pp. 49–76). New York: Wiley.

Brim, O. G., Jr., & Kagan, J. (Eds.) (1980). *Constancy and change in human development.* Cambridge, MA: Harvard University Press.

Bronfenbrenner, U. (1974). Developmental research, public policy, and the ecology of childhood. *Child Development, 45,* 1–5.

Bronfenbrenner, U. (1977). Toward an experimental ecology of human development. *American Psychologist, 32,* 513–531.

Bronfenbrenner, U. (1979). *The ecology of human development.* Cambridge, MA: Harvard University Press.

Bronfenbrenner, U. (1983). The context of development and the development of context. In R. M. Lerner (Ed.), *Developmental psychology: Historical and philosophical perspectives* (pp. 39–83). Hillsdale, NJ: Erlbaum.

Bronfenbrenner, U. & Morris, P. A. (1998). The ecology of developmental processes. In R. M. Lerner (Ed.), *Theoretical models of human development.* Vol. 1. of the *Handbook of child psychology* (5th ed., pp. 993–1028). New York: Wiley.

Bronfenbrenner, U., & Crouter, A. C. (1983). The evolution of environmental models in developmental research. In W. Kersen (Ed.), *Handbook of child psychology, Vol 1: History, theories, and methods* (pp. 39–83). New York: Wiley.

Cairns, R. B., & Hood, K. E. (1983). Continuity in social development: A comparative perspective on individual difference prediction. In P. B. Baltes & O. G. Brim, Jr. (Eds.), *Life-span development and behavior* (Vol. 5, pp. 302–358). New York: Academic Press.

Campbell, S. B. (1989). Developmental perspectives. In T. H. Ollendick & M. Herson (Eds.), *Handbook of child psychopathology* (pp. 5–28). New York: Plenum.

Caspi, A., & Elder, G. H., Jr. (1988). Childhood precursors of the life course: Early personality and life disorganization. In E. M. Hetherington, R. M. Lerner, & M. Perlmutter (Eds.), *Child development in life-span perspective* (pp. 115–142). Hillsdale, NJ: Erlbaum.

Chess, S., & Thomas, A. (1984). *The origins and evolution of behavior disorders: Infancy to early adult life.* New York: Brunner/Mazel.

Cicchetti, D. (1984). The emergence of developmental psychopathology. *Child Development, 55,* 1–7.

Cicchetti, D. (1987). Developmental psychopathology in infancy: Illustration from the study of maltreated youngsters. *Journal of Consulting and Clinical Psychology, 55,* 837–845.

Cicchetti, D., & Garmezy, N. (1993). Prospects and promises in the study of resilience. *Development and Psychopathology, 5,* 497–502.

Cowan, P. A. (1988). Developmental psychopathology: A nine-cell map of the territory. In E. D. Nannis & P. A. Cowan (Eds.), *New Directions for Child Development, No. 39: Developmental psychopathology and its treatment* (pp. 5–29). San Francisco, CA: Jossey-Bass.

Cowen, E. L. (1984, April). A general structural model for primary prevention program development in mental health. *Personnel and Guidance Journal,* 485–490.

Dixon, R. A., & Lerner, R. M. (1992). A history of systems in developmental psychology. In M. H. Bornstein & M. E. Lamb (Eds.), *Developmental psychology: An advanced textbook* (3rd ed., pp. 3–58). Hillsdale, NJ: Erlbaum.

Dixon, R. A., Lerner, R. M., & Hultsch, D. F. (1991). The concept of development in individual and social change. In P. Van Geert & L. P. Mos (Eds.), *Annals of theoretical psychology,* (Vol. 7, pp. 279–323). New York: Plenum.

Dryfoos, J. G. (1990). *Adolescents at risk: Prevalence and prevention.* New York: Oxford University Press.

Dryfoos, J. G. (1994). *Full service schools: A revolution in health and social services of children, youth and families.* San Francisco: Jossey-Bass.

Elder, G. H., Jr. (1974). *Children of the Great Depression: Social change in life experiences.* Chicago: University of Chicago Press.

Elder, G. H., Jr. (1980). Adolescence in historical perspective. In J. Adelson (Ed.), *Handbooks of adolescent psychology* (pp. 3–46). New York: Wiley.

Elder, G. H., Jr., Modell, J., & Parke, R. D. (Eds.) (1993). *Children in time and place: Developmental and historical insights*. New York: Cambridge University Press.

Featherman, D. L. (1983). Life-span perspectives in social science research. In P. B. Baltes & O. G. Brim, Jr. (Eds.), *Life-span development and behavior* (Vol. 5, pp. 1–57). New York: Academic Press.

Featherman, D. L. (1985). Individual development and aging as a population process. In J. R. Nesselroade & A. von Eye (Eds.), *Individual development and social change: Explanatory analyses* (pp. 213–241). New York: Academic Press.

Featherman, D. L., & Lerner, R. M. (1985). Ontogenesis and sociogenesis: Problematics for theory about development across the lifespan. *American Sociological Review, 50*, 659–676.

Feldman, M. W., & Lewontin, R. C. (1975). The heritability hang-up. *Science, 190*, 1163–1168.

Finkelstein, J. W. (1993). Familial influences on adolescent health. In R. M. Lerner (Ed.), *Early adolescence: Perspectives on research, policy and intervention* (pp. 111–126). Hillsdale, NJ: Erlbaum.

Fisher, C. B., & Lerner, R. M. (Eds.). (1994). *Applied developmental psychology*. New York: McGraw-Hill.

Ford, D. L., & Lerner, R. M. (1992). *Developmental systems theory: An integrative approach*. Newbury Park, CA: Sage.

Freedman, D. G. (1979). *Human sociobiology: A holistic approach*. New York: Free Press.

Freud, S. (1949). *Outline of psychoanalysis*. New York: Norton.

Garbarino, J. (1992). *Children and families in the social environment* (2nd ed.). New York: Aldine de Gruyter.

Gottlieb, G. (1991). The experiential canalization of behavioral development: Theory. *Developmental Psychology, 27*, 4–13.

Gottlieb, G. (1992). *Individual development and evolution: The genesis of novel behavior*. New York: Oxford University Press.

Hartup, W. W. (1978). Perspectives on child and family interaction: Past, present, and future. In R. M. Lerner & G. B. Spanier (Eds.), *Child influences on marital and family interaction: A life-span perspective* (pp. 23–45). New York: Academic Press.

Hetherington, E. M., & Baltes, P. B. (1988). Child psychology and life-span development. In E. M. Hetherington, R. M. Lerner, & M. Perlmutter (Eds.), *Child development in life-span perspective* (pp. 1–19). Hillsdale, NJ: Erlbaum.

Hetherington, E. M., Lerner, R. M., & Perlmutter, M. (Ed.). (1988). *Child development in life-span perspective*. Hillsdale, NJ: Erlbaum.

Hirsch, J. (1970). Behavior-genetic analysis and its biosocial consequences. *Seminars in Psychiatry, 2*, 89–105.

Homans, G. C. (1961). *Social behavior: Its elementary forms*. New York: Harcourt, Brace, & World.

Kahn, R. L., & Antonucci, T. C. (1980). Convoys over the life course: Attachment, roles, and social support. In P. B. Baltes & O. G. Brim (Eds.), *Life-span development and behavior* (Vol. 3, pp. 253–286). Hillsdale, NJ: Erlbaum.

Lanier, J. E. (1990). *Report to focus group colleagues on "teaching," National Academy of Education study on the future of educational research*. East Lansing, MI: College of Education, Michigan State University.

Lerner, J. V. (1994). *Working women and their families*. Thousand Oaks, CA: Sage.

Lerner, R. M. (1976). *Concepts and theories of human development*. Reading, MA: Addison-Wesley.

Lerner, R. M. (1978). Nature, nurture, and dynamic interactionism. *Human Development, 21*, 1–20.

Lerner, R. M. (1979). A dynamic interactional concept of individual and social relationship development. In R. L.

Burgess & T. L. Huston (Eds.), *Social exchange in developing relationships* (pp. 271–305). New York: Academic Press.

Lerner, R. M. (1982). Children and adolescents as producers of their own development. *Developmental Review, 2*, 342–370.

Lerner, R. M. (1984). *On the nature of human plasticity*. New York: Cambridge University Press.

Lerner, R. M. (1986). *Concepts and theories of human development* (2nd ed.). New York: Random House.

Lerner, R. M. (1987). A life-span perspective for early adolescence. In R. M. Lerner & T. T. Foch (Eds.), *Biological-psychosocial interactions in early adolescence: A life-span perspective* (pp. 9–34). Hillsdale, NJ: Erlbaum.

Lerner, R. M. (1988). Personality development: A life-span perspective. In E. M. Hetherington, R. M. Lerner, & M. Perlmutter (Eds.), *Child development in life-span perspective* (pp. 21–46). Hillsdale, NJ: Erlbaum.

Lerner, R. M. (1991). Changing organism–context relations as the basic process of development: A developmental-contextual perspective. *Developmental Psychology, 27*, 27–32.

Lerner, R. M. (1995). *America's youth in crisis: Challenges and options for programs and policies*. Thousand Oaks, CA: Sage.

Lerner, R. M. (1997). Relative plasticity, integration, temporality, and diversity in human development: A developmental contextual perspective about theory, process, and method. *Developmental Psychology, 32*(4), 781–786.

Lerner, R. M. (Ed.) (1998). *Theoretical models of human development*. Volume 1 of *The Handbook of Child Psychology* (5th ed., pp. 1–24). New York: Wiley.

Lerner, R. M., & Busch-Rossnagel, N. A. (Eds.) (1981). *Individuals as producers of their development: A life-span perspective*. New York: Academic Press.

Lerner, R. M., Castellino, D. R., Terry, P. A., Villarruel, F. A., & McKinney, M. H. (1995). A developmental contextual perspective on parenting. In M. H. Bornstein (Ed.), *Handbook of parenting: Vol. 2. Biology and ecology of parenting* (pp. 285–309). Hillsdale, NJ: Erlbaum.

Lerner, R. M., Hess, L. E., & Nitz, K. (1990). A developmental perspective on psychopathology. In M. Hersen & C. G. Last (Eds.), *Handbook of child and adult psychopathology: A longitudinal perspective* (pp. 9–32). New York: Pergamon.

Lerner, R. M., Hess, L. E., & Nitz, K. (1991). Towards the integration of human developmental and therapeutic change: A developmental contextual perspective. In P. R. Martin (Ed.), *Handbook of behavior therapy and psychological science: An integrative approach* (pp. 13–34). New York: Pergamon.

Lerner, R. M., & Hood, K. E. (1986). Plasticity in development: Concepts and issues for intervention. *Journal of Applied Developmental Psychology, 7*, 139–152.

Lerner, R. M., Hultsch, D. F., & Dixon, R. A. (1983). Contextualism and the character of developmental psychology in the 1970s. *Annals of the New York Academy of Sciences, 412*, 101–128.

Lerner, R. M., & Kauffman, M. B. (1985). The concept of development in contextualism. *Developmental Review, 5*, 309–333.

Lerner, R. M., & Lerner, J. V. (1983). Temperament-intelligence reciprocities in early childhood: A contextual model. In M. Lewis (Ed.), *Origins of intelligence: Infancy and early childhood* (pp. 399–421). New York: Plenum.

Lerner, R. M., & Lerner, J. V. (1987). Children in their contexts: A goodness of fit model. In J. B. Lancaster, J. Altmann, A. S. Rossi, & L. R. Sherrod (Eds.), *Parenting across the lifespan: Biosocial dimensions* (pp. 377–404). Chicago: Aldine.

Lerner, R. M., & Lerner, J. V. (1989). Organismic and social contextual bases of development: The sample case of early adolescence. In W. Damon (Ed.), *Child development today and tomorrow* (pp. 69–85). San Francisco: Jossey-Bass.

Lerner, R. M., & Miller, J. R. (1993). Integrating human development research and intervention for America's children: The Michigan State University model. *Journal of Applied Developmental Psychology, 14*, 347–364.

Lerner, R. M., Miller, J. R., Knott, J.H., Corey, K. E., Bynum, T. S., Hoopfer, L. C., McKinney, M. H., Abrams, L. A., Hula, R. C., & Terry, P. A. (1994). Integrating scholarship and outreach in human development research, policy, and service: A developmental contextual perspective. In D. L. Featherman, R. M. Lerner, & M. Perlmutter (Eds.), *Life-span development and behavior*, (Vol. 12, pp. 249–273). Hillsdale, NJ: Erlbaum.

Lerner, R. M., & Ryff, C. D. (1978). Implementation of the life-span view of human development: The sample case of attachment. In P. B. Baltes (Ed.), *Life-span development and behavior* (Vol. 1, pp. 1–44). New York: Academic Press.

Lerner, R. M., & Spanier, G. B. (Eds.). (1978). *Child influences on marital and family interaction: A life-span perspective.* New York: Academic Press.

Lerner, R. M., & Tubman, J. (1989). Conceptual issues in studying continuity and discontinuity in personality development across life. *Journal of Personality, 57*, 343–373.

Lewis, M. (1997). *Altering fate.* New York: Guilford Press.

Lewis, M., & Feiring, C. (1978). A child's social world. In R.M. Lerner & G.B. Spanier (Eds.), *Child influences on marital and family interaction* (pp. 47–66). New York: Academic Press.

Lewis, M., & Rosenblum, L. A. (Ed.). (1974). *The effect of the infant on its caregivers.* New York: Wiley.

Magnusson, D. (1988). *Individual development from an interactional perspective: A longitudinal study.* Hillsdale, NJ: Erlbaum.

Magnusson, D., & Allen, V. L. (Ed.). (1983). *Human development: An interactional perspective.* New York: Academic Press

Magnusson, D., & Öhman, A. (Eds.). (1987). *Psychopathology: An interactional perspective.* Orlando, FL: Academic Press.

Masten, A. S. (1989). Resilience in development: Implications of the study of successful adaptation for developmental psychopathology. In D. Cicchetti (Ed.), *The emergence of a discipline: Vol. 1. Rochester symposium on developmental psychopathology* (pp. 261–294). Hillsdale, NJ: Erlbaum.

Novikoff, A. B. (1945). The concept of integrative levels of biology. *Science, 62*, 209–215.

Öhman, A., & Magnusson, D. (1987). An interactional paradigm for research on psychopathology. In D. Magnusson & A. Öhman (Eds.), *Psychopathology: An interactional perspective* (pp. 3–19). Orlando, FL: Academic Press.

Overton, W. F., & Reese, H. W. (1973). Models of development: Methodological implications. In J. R. Nesselroade & H. W. Reese (Eds.), *Life-span developmental psychology: Methodological issues* (pp. 65–86). New York: Academic Press.

Overton, W. F., & Reese, H. W. (1981). Conceptual prerequisites for an understanding of stability–change and continuity–discontinuity. *International Journal of Behavioral Development, 4*, 99–123.

Pepper, S.C. (1942). *World hypotheses.* Berkeley, CA: University of California.

Perlmutter, M. (1988). Cognitive development in life-span perspective: From description of differences to explanation of changes. In E. M. Hetherington, R. M. Lerner, &

M. Perlmutter (Eds.), *Child development in life-span perspective* (pp. 191–214). Hillsdale, NJ: Erlbaum.

Piaget, J. (1970). Piaget's theory. In P. H. Mussen (Ed.), *Carmichael's manual of child psychology* (Vol. 1, pp. 703–732). New York: Wiley.

Plomin, R. (1986). *Development, genetics, and psychology.* Hillsdale, NJ: Erlbaum.

Reese, H. W., & Overton, W. F. (1970). Models of development and theories of development. In L. R. Goulet & P. B. Baltes (Eds.), *Life-span developmental psychology: Research and theory* (pp. 115–145). New York: Academic Press.

Riegel, K. F. (1975). Toward a dialectical theory of development. *Human Development, 18*, 50–64.

Riegel, K. F. (1976a). The dialectics of human development. *American Psychologist, 31*, 689–700.

Riegel, K. F. (1976b). From traits and equilibrium toward developmental dialectics. In W. J. Arnold & J. K. Cole (Eds.), *Nebraska symposium on motivation* (pp. 348–408). Lincoln, NE: University of Nebraska Press.

Riley, M. W. (Ed.) (1979). *Aging from birth to death.* Washington, DC: American Association for the Advancement of Science.

Rowe, D. C. (1994). *The limits of family influence: Genes, experience, and behavior.* New York: Guilford Press.

Sameroff, A. (1975). Transactional models in early social relations. *Human Development, 18*, 65–79.

Sameroff, A. (1983). Developmental systems: Contexts and evolution. In W. Kessen (Ed.), *Handbook of child psychology* (Vol. 1, pp. 237–294). New York: Wiley.

Sameroff, A. (1989). Models of developmental regulation: The environtype. In D. Cicchetti (Ed.), *The emergence of a discipline* (Vol. 1, pp. 41–68). Hillsdale, NJ: Erlbaum.

Sameroff, A. (1996, Fall). Democratic and republican models of development: Paradigms and perspectives. *Developmental Psychology Newsletter*, 1–9.

Schaie, K. W. (1965). A general model for the study of developmental problems. *Psychological Bulletin, 64*, 92–107.

Schneirla, T. C. (1957). The concept of development in comparative psychology. In D. B. Harris (Ed.), *The concept of development* (pp. 78–108). Minneapolis, MN: University of Minnesota Press.

Schorr, L. B. (1988). *Within our reach: Breaking the cycle of disadvantage.* New York: Doubleday.

Skinner, B. F. (1938). *The behavior of organisms.* New York: Appleton.

Smith, L. B., & Thelen, E. (Eds.). (1993). *A dynamic systems approach to development: Applications.* Cambridge, MA: MIT Press.

Sorensen, B., Weinert, E., & Sherrod, L. R. (Ed.). (1986). *Human development and the life course: Multidisciplinary perspectives.* Hillsdale, NJ: Erlbaum.

Spencer, M. B. (1990). Development of minority children: An introduction. *Child Development, 61*, 267–269.

Sroufe, L. A. (1990). Considering normal and abnormal together: The essence of developmental psychopathology. *Development and Psychopathology, 2*, 335–347.

Sroufe, L. A., & Rutter, M. (1984). The domain of developmental psychopathology. *Child Development, 55*, 17–29.

Super, C. M. (1987). The role of culture in developmental disorder. In C. M. Super (Ed.), *The role of culture in developmental disorder* (pp. 2–7). San Diego, CA: Academic Press.

Super, C. M., & Harkness, S. (1982). The infant's niche in rural Kenya and metropolitan America. In L. L. Adler (Ed.), *Cross-cultural research at issue* (pp. 47–56). New York: Academic Press.

Super, C. M., & Harkness, S. (1986). The developmental niche: A conceptualization at the interface of child and culture. *International Journal of Behavioral Development, 9*, 1–25.

Thelen, E., & Smith, L. B. (1994). *A dynamic systems approach to the development of cognition and action.* Cambridge, MA: MIT Press.

Thomas, A., & Chess, S. (1977). *Temperament and development.* New York: Brunner/Mazel.

Thomas, A., & Chess, S. (1980). *The dynamics of psychological development.* New York: Brunner/Mazel.

Thomas, A., & Chess, S. (1981). The role of temperament in the contributions of individuals to their development. In R. M. Lerner & N. A. Busch-Rossnagel (Eds.), *Individuals as producers of their own development: A life-span perspective.* New York: Academic Press.

Thomas, A., Chess, S., Birch, H. G., Hertzig, M. E., & Korn, S. (1963). *Behavioral individuality in early childhood* (pp. 231–255). New York: New York University Press.

Tobach, E. (1981). Evolutionary aspects of the activity of the organism and its development. In R. M. Lerner & N. A. Busch-Rossnagel (Eds.), *Individuals as producers of their development: A life-span perspective* (pp. 37–68). New York: Academic Press.

Tobach, E., & Greenberg, G. (1984). The significance of T. C. Schneirla's contribution to the concept of levels of integration. In G. Greenberg & E. Tobach (Eds.), *Behavioral evolution and integrative levels* (pp. 1–7). Hillsdale, NJ: Erlbaum.

Tobach, E., & Schneirla, T. C. (1968). The biopsychology of social behavior of animals. In R. E. Cooke & S. Levin (Eds.), *Biologic basis of pediatric practice* (pp. 68–82). New York: McGraw-Hill.

Tubman, J. G., & Lerner, R. M. (1994). Affective experiences of parents and their children from adolescence to young adulthood: Stability of affective experiences. *Journal of Adolescence, 17,* 81–98.

Valsiner, J. (1988). The development of the concept of development: Historical and epistemological perspectives. In W. Damon (Ed.), *Handbook of child psychology* (5th ed., Vol.1, pp. 189–232). New York: Wiley.

Vondracek, F. W., Lerner, R. M., & Schulenberg, J. E. (1986). *Career development: A life-span developmental approach.* Hillsdale, NJ: Erlbaum.

Walsh, M. E. (1992). *"Moving to nowhere": Children's stories of homelessness.* Westport, CT: Auburn House.

Walsh, M. E., & Buckley, M. A. (1994). Children's experiences of homelessness: Implications for school counselors. *Elementary School Guidance and Counseling, 29*(1), 4–15.

Walsten, D. (1990). Insensitivity of the analysis of variance to heredity–environment interaction. *Behavioral and Brain Sciences, 13,* 109–120.

Wapner, S., & Demick, J. (1988, October 25–27). *Some relations between developmental and environmental psychology: An organismic-developmental systems perspective.* Paper presented at the "Visions of Development, the Environment, and Aesthetics: The Legacy of Joachim Wohlwill" conference, The Pennsylvania State University, University Park.

Weissbourd, R. (1996). *The vulnerable child: What really hurts America's children and what we can do about it.* Reading, MA: Addison-Wesley.

Werner, E. E. (1990). Protective factors and individual resilience. In S. Meisels & J. Shonkoff (Eds.), *Handbook of early childhood intervention* (pp. 97–116). New York: Cambridge University Press.

Werner, E. E. (1995). Resilience in development. *Current Directions in Psychological Science, 4*(3), 81–85.

Werner, H. (1957). The concept of development from a comparative and organismic point of view. In D. B. Harris (Ed.), *The concept of development* (pp. 125–148). Minneapolis, MN: University of Minnesota Press.

Wilson, E. O. (1975). *Sociobiology: The new synthesis.* Cambridge, MA: Harvard University Press.

Zigler, E. E. (in press). Child development and social policy. *Child Development.*

5.02
Clinical Formulation

MARTIN HERBERT
University of Exeter, UK

5.02.1 INTRODUCTION

The process of piecing together a clinical formulation lies at the very center of the practitioner's craft, bridging, as it does, the issues of assessment, etiology, and intervention which inform clinical work. The skills involved in specifying the nature of the presenting problem, formulating explanatory hypotheses, determining and evaluating a test of the formulation, and translating it into a treatment plan have their roots in psychological science and art.

The assertion that there is a place for art (imagination and lateral thinking) as well as science (empirical research) in the many complex activities that contribute to the final clinical formulation, might well be regarded as contentious. Indeed those who embrace a scientist-practitioner approach to clinical psychology practice may well see it as erroneous—a matter returned to later in this chapter. Generally speaking, the formulation is a means to an end, an intervention of some kind. However, it may be an end in itself: an expert report for the courts, or an assessment for the social, health, or educational services.

The way in which clinical formulations are conceptualized, and the consequent selection of data describing the client's problem, varies not only in terms of its purpose but also (as we shall see) in relation to the theoretical assumptions of the practitioner. The process usually involves four kinds of activity, summarized by the mnemonic ASPIRE (Sutton & Herbert, 1992), which represents the stages in working up a case study and, more specifically, a clinical formulation:

(i) *Stage 1, Assessment (AS)*:
  (a) focusing on the "What?" question—that is what is/are the problem(s)?
  (b) focusing on the "Which?" question—that is which of the problems are to be addressed, and in what order?
  (c) focusing on the "Why?" question—that is why have the problems arisen?

(ii) *Stage 2, Planning (P)*: focusing on the "How?" question—that is, how are we (practitioner and clients) going to address the problems?

(iii) *Stage 3, Implementation of the intervention (I)*

(iv) *Stage 4, Rigorous evaluation (RE)*.

This framework provides a process-guide which, like the experimental method it resembles, is well suited to problem-solving. It also serves as a means of organizing this chapter, which examines each of the stages: first within a theoretical and then within a practice-oriented context.

5.02.2 THE CLINICAL FORMULATION: THEORETICAL ISSUES

The process of formulating is, figuratively speaking, like the action of a funnel containing a series of filters which represent choice and decision points. They have the function of distilling a many-sided childhood problem into a relatively brief, formal statement about one's conclusions and recommendations. The resulting formulation may serve as an expert report of some kind, or as the groundplan for a hoped-for alleviation of the presenting difficulties. Whatever its purpose, it is likely to be an amalgam of analysis, explanation, and intentions that emerge at the end of the metaphorical funnel.

The broadly based strategic decisions will have been made at the opening to the funnel, namely the chosen ideological stance (e.g, scientist-practitioner or humanist) and the theoretical model (say, cognitive-behavioral, Rogerian, or psychodynamic) adopted for the casework. Of course, the choices may not be starkly either/or, as when an eclectic style of working is preferred.

5.02.2.1 Clinical Psychology as Applied Science

At the broad end of the figurative funnel referred to earlier, is a filter influencing the clinical information that is edited in (and out) of the formulation. It involves the choice or rejection of a science-based philosophy of clinical work.

Long and Hollin (1997) make the point that the history of the scientist-practitioner stance is marked by an enduring struggle between advocates and opponents of a research-based profession—which is to say, a practice that is based on an empirically based assessment of problems, and the application of validated treatment methods which are linked (through the formulation) to theoretically coherent causal hypotheses. The reliance of the "scientist-practitioner" on empirical methods generates a model for service provision that is competency based. For Gambrill (1983) this requires:

(i) a focus on the present, which may be related to events in the past, and requires clarification by an exploration of the past (e.g., the person's learning history, deeply rooted attributions and ideologies);

(ii) a focus on describing problems (assessing them by a process of surveying, selecting, and prioritizing difficulties) and operationalizing them by means of multidimensional measurable outcomes;

(iii) a focus on multiple response systems of an individual nature (e.g., cognition, affect, and physiology) and of an interactional kind (e.g., family, school, workplace);

(iv) a focus on positive behaviors and events;

(v) a focus on the relationship between behavior and events in the external environment that elicit or maintain it.

Criticisms of the validity of such an idealized model have centered, *inter alia*, on the inadequacies of positivist philosophies of science and experimental research methodology for addressing the complexities and subtleties of individual psychopathology, or the sheer irrelevance of research for clinical practice. An example would be the attitude to formulating held by psychologists in the tradition of Maslow (1954) and Rogers (1957) whose ideas have been seminal in humanist psychology. Individuals are viewed as having an inherent need to grow. This intrinsic motivation reveals itself in the process called self-actualization.

Such a positive, optimistic (critics might say romantic) view of human nature, has little in common with the kind of formulations which are so preoccupied with analyzing and cataloging the failures or deficiencies of parents and children that they neglect to see their strengths and potential for self-directed growth. Such analyses are regarded by the severest critics as mechanistic, demeaning, and dehumanizing.

This is a view that is strongly contested (e.g., Herbert, 1987a, 1987b) when it is used in an overinclusive manner to cover all science-based practice. For those clinical psychologists who see themselves as scientific practitioners, their appeal to science is not usually restricted to the results and methods of traditional experimentation alone. The limitations of experimental methods are well known in relation to the study of human behavior: its sensitivity to minor variations in sampling and procedure, leading to failures of replication (i.e., to findings which are not robust); its confusion of aggregate effects with generalized effects (i.e., tendency to confuse an aggregate statistical effect with a general or common effect); its tendency to prefer methodological rigor over conceptual or practical experience; its liability to experimenter effects and demand factors; its neglect of contextual factors; and finally, its presumption that the experimental method is superior to the other methods regardless of circumstance (see Bromley, 1986).

Bromley (1986), while acknowledging that the case study cannot replace other experimental methods, is of the opinion that certain problems, notably the issues faced by clinical psychologists, lend themselves to this method of investigation. He provides an invaluable guide to the effective use of the case study as a method of inquiry and formulation. He suggests that the

findings of scientific case studies depend, not so much on the logic of statistical inference, but rather on the logic of substantive reasoning. Case studies, he proposes, can generate and test abstract and general theories; when used systematically they are capable of combining basic and applied science—not only psychological, but also legal science. Bromley argues plausibly for the application of what he calls a quasi-judicial approach to clinical problems, drawing on the knowledge base of legal science for guidance on (among other things) rules of evidence. Some practical implications are studied later in this chapter.

With regard to the other criticisms of the irrelevance of research, Cohen's (1977, 1979) surveys indicated that 40% of mental health professionals thought there was no relevant research to inform clinical practice, while the other 60% were of the opinion that less than one-fifth of research articles had any applicability to professional settings. It is perhaps surprising that research and practice should be thought of by so many as mutually unhelpful or, at worst, incompatible, given that problem-solving is an essential ingredient of both of them (see for different sides of the argument, Meehl, 1971; Peterson, 1976; Shakow, 1978; Watzlawick, Weakland, & Fisch, 1974).

Long and Hollin (1997) point out that the growth in clinical research which was a concomitant of the burgeoning of learning-theory-based (behavioral) methods of intervention, from the 1950s onwards, led to the development of innovative and flexible research designs and methods (see Barlow & Hersen, 1984). This meant that practitioners could link more confidently, and in logical fashion, their application of particular therapeutic methods/ techniques to an empirically based theory of dysfunctional behavior. This relationship could then be clearly enunciated in a formulation and, furthermore, validated by means of $N = 1$ designs. It has to be said that by no means was everyone convinced by such confidence in the logical linkage between learning theory and its therapeutic methodology (e.g., Erwin, 1979; Power, 1991). Another development that broadened the appeal of the scientist-practitioner viewpoint was the growing sophistication and respectability of qualitative research methods (e.g., Marshall & Rossman, 1989). Certainly, it has gone some way to mitigate the accusations of triviality aimed at the kind of research that is narrowly or obsessively "quantiphrenic" in its definition of legitimate methodology.

Despite such developments, reservations about the validity of a scientist-practitioner approach to generating clinical formulations continues to inform debate on the appropriate model for practice and, thus, training in the profession (see Andrews, 1989; Gambrill, 1990; Pilgrim & Treacher, 1992, for discussions of these issues).

5.02.3 THE ASSESSMENT PROCESS

The filters mentioned above play a critical role in determining what information is pertinent in the investigation of the client's problems, and which assessment methods will generate the clinical data necessary for an intervention. As the funnel narrows, so does the focus of the questions: "What?," "Which?," "Why?," and "How?" that give direction to the assessment.

The final "How?" query leads to the strategic formulation of a precise treatment plan, and the tactical specification of methods/techniques for bringing about change.

5.02.3.1 The "What?" Question

Hepworth and Larsen(1990, p. 155) define this question in terms of "gathering, analyzing and synthesizing salient data." But what constitutes salient data? Answers to this question are likely to vary (alarmingly, some would say) according to the clinician's therapeutic model and its theoretical assumptions. At its most basic is the issue of what constitutes a priority in any clinical investigation: description or categorization—a debate centering on the concepts of assessment and diagnosis. Clinical psychologists tend to prefer the term "assessment" to "diagnosis"—a word that means to distinguish, and is essentially about classification. An assessment conveys the broader descriptive implications of an investigation or analysis of the causes or nature of a condition, situation, or problem. These implications are supposed to be neatly encapsulated within a diagnostic label, but, in reality, seldom are.

The differentiation of the "What?" and "Why?" questions is somewhat artifical as they tend to merge as the assessment progresses. When the collection of sufficient data allows for it, there is a formal explication: the formulation of a set of explanatory hypotheses describing the determinants, historical and current, of the problem. These, in turn, generate possible solutions to the client's difficulties.

5.02.3.2 The "Which?" Question

One of the clinicians' first choices is where to concentrate their attention in what may present itself as a welter of conflicting claims, complaints, and accusations. Some of the problems will reside mainly within an individual (e.g., fear) but even then they will have repercussions. The individual's parents (or partner) worry about his or her suffering. Or the problems put constraints on the activities of the family, as when holidays are not possible because (say) a mother is agoraphobic, feeling anxious about leaving the house, and panicky in a crowded shopping center.

Other problems arise from the relationships and interactions (such as the give-and-take transactions) between people. For example:

(i) mother–father: disagreements about the children, quarrels over decisions, other marital difficulties;

(ii) parent(s)–child: management difficulties, disappointments over the child's achievements or lack of them;

(iii) child–parent(s): resentments about being "babied," complaints about unfairness, or favoritism;

(iv) child–child: sibling rivalry, jealousy.

As the assessment proceeds, the client(s) may be one of these persons (a school-refusing child), two of them (the embattled parents), or all of them (the family). The practitioner might even have to work more widely in the neighborhood, at the school, or with other agencies in the community. Who the client is, is in fact a vexed question, as can be seen when examining systemic ideologies.

5.02.3.3 The "Why?" Question (Etiology)

Etiology—the study of causes of disease—has served physical medicine well. Research firmly rooted in scientific philosophy and methodology has led to an impressive armamentarium of rational treatments which have done much to reduce human suffering. Not surprisingly, psychologists and psychiatrists entertained high hopes of emulating their physician colleagues by endeavoring to work within a scientific and (notably, for psychiatrists) a medical framework. The complexity of psychiatric and psychological problems has led to great confusion in the analysis of causes (Herbert, 1994a). There is an all-too-human tendency to oversimplify and think of causality in linear, univariate terms: A causes B; B is the effect of A. However, there is no limit to the analysis of causes. One finds not a single antecedent, not even a chain of antecedents, but a whole interlacing network of them, as indicated by this complexity in Fielding's formulation of an adolescent patient's obsessional anxiety (Fielding, 1983) (see Figure 1).

One point of agreement that appears to emerge from the plethora of findings about problems like these is their multicausality. Mayer-Gross, Slater, and Roth (1955) make the point that in medicine it is necessary to deal with causes of all kinds, not just those that are

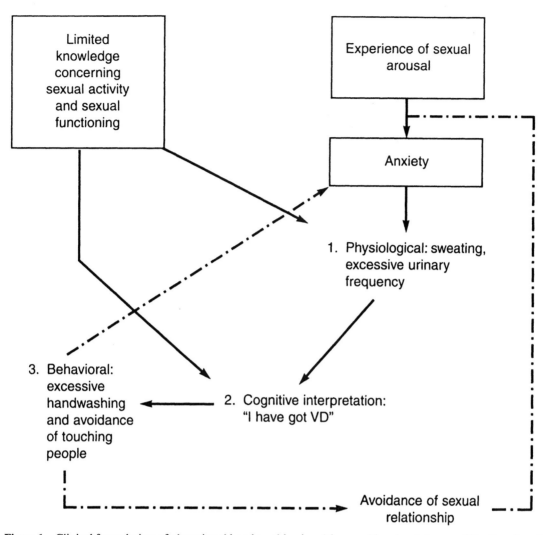

Figure 1 Clinical formulation of obsessional hand-washing in a 16-year-old male adolescent. (The Practice of Clinical Psychology in Great Britain, by D. Fielding (1993) Chichester: Wiley Copyright 1994 by Wiley. Reprinted with permission.)

both necessary and sufficient. In searching for a cause of some phenomenon, we are really searching for a quantitative relationship. If *A* is the necessary and sufficient cause of *B*, then there is a one-to-one relationship between *A* and *B*. If *A* is a necessary but not sufficient cause of *B*, then there is no *B* without *A*, but *A* may be combined with *X* or *Y*, instead of with *B*. If the variety of these *X*s and *Y*s is great, the causal relationship, though it still exists, is thereby attenuated. If *A* is neither necessary nor sufficient, then there are *A*s without *B*s and *B*s without *A*s, and the strength of the causation will depend on the proportionate relationship between *A/B* and *A* on the one hand and *B* on the other.

Mayer-Gross et al. (1955) observe that it is not difficult to founder in a causal network. We are less likely to do so if we take into account the quantitative aspect of causation. It is at this

point that so much psychological thinking loses cogency and direction. Quantitatively important causes are tangled in a knot of others with only a slight or entirely unknown quantitative relationship with the effects we are interested in.

The reality for psychologists and psychiatrists is the complex, multivariate nature of most of the phenomena they study. In their clinical formulations, they have to take into account both intrinsic (organismic) factors and extrinsic (environmental) influences. The latter may consist of direct (proximal) and indirect contemporary (contextual), as well as indirect predisposing (organismic) and historical (distal) determinants (see Figure 2).

The tendency for clinical child psychologists to work in multidisciplinary teams which include, *inter alia*, psychiatrists, speech therapists, and social workers, or in close collaboration with medical colleagues (e.g., GPs and

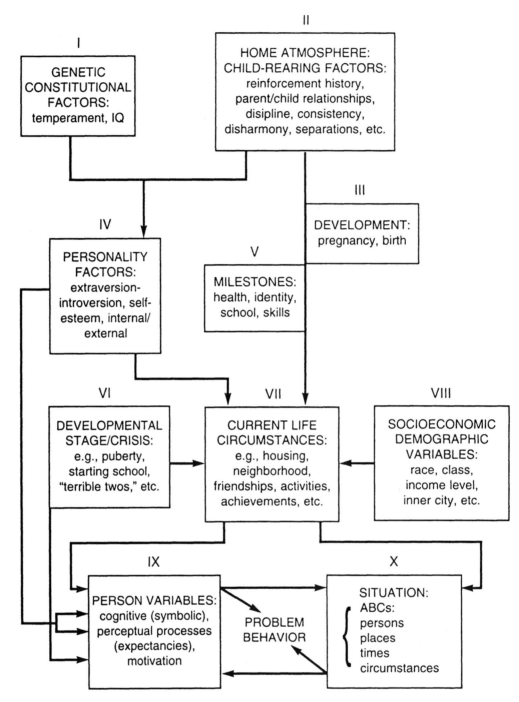

Figure 2 The 10-factor clinical formation of causation ("Psychology and crime," by R. G. V. Clarke, 1977; *Bulletin of the British Psychological Society, 30*, pp. 280–283. Copyright 1977 by the British Psychological Society. Reprinted with permission).

pediatricians) is understandable when we look at this complexity of physical, social, economic, and psychological influences on psychopathology. Behavior results from a very complex interaction of psychosocial and biological determinants (Herbert, 1991a). The important caveat in relation to clinical formulations is not to neglect, through a commitment to a psychogenic model or biogenic theory of

psychopathology, the possibility of complications from the other side of the causal equation.

The trouble with the search for causal reasons is that there are several levels of explanation which may apply to a particular problem. This is illustrated by a young child who has a learning problem which is affecting her ability to read. On top of this, she has certain behavioral problems, as constant failure is causing her morale to sink lower and lower. Diagnostic tests carried out by the psychologist show that she has a visual-perceptual handicap. Remedial treatment is available to help her overcome her reading problem. The remedial teacher could teach her to recognize words and their meanings through the medium of her other sensory modalities. Here, the visual handicap is one explanation of the reading difficulty. Some clinicians would rest content with this level of causal explanation—the so-called instrumental level of explanation. The explanation is sufficiently precise to be instrumental in planning some therapeutic measures to mitigate the cause–effect sequence of events. Or it may simply be instrumental in providing the individual with a satisfactory account of some event. It is sufficient in that it explains, and raises no further questions in his or her mind.

While this explanation provides an account of an important antecedent condition in the problem—in this case the visual-perceptual handicap—other clinicians might claim that the diagnostician should search for "original" or "deeper" causes. In this case they would feel it necessary to determine whether the visual problem is due to organic causes, perhaps resulting from complications during her birth or a genetic predisposition.

5.02.3.4 The "How?" Question

The assessment of causal influence should, in an ideal world, inform the choice of therapeutic strategy or some broader-based community intervention. Only too often the assessment data, like the occupants of Procrustes' bed, are made to fit the favored therapeutic model. There is an implied suggestion that a particular approach can be applied to all problems. Sadly, faith, rather than evidence, is mostly what is on offer to support the more Panglossian prospectuses. The most durable and popular of the psychological therapies for children have been relationship therapy, play therapy, child analysis, behavior therapy/modification, and the relative newcomers cognitive behavior therapy, behavioral and nonbehavioral family therapy, and behavioral parent training. There is some overlap in process (if not in name) between the various psychological therapies, but they are essentially different, not only in their outward and visible manifestations, their "technology," but also, as one would expect, in their underlying theoretical rationale and, consequently, their goals.

Although there is no one coherent theory of therapeutic change, there is some overlap in goals. For Kazdin (1987, 1988), the goals

consist of improving adjustment and functioning in both intrapersonal and interpersonal spheres and reducing maladaptive behaviors and various psychological (also physical) complaints. Even when there are differences of emphasis in therapeutic goals, all treatments share the objective of producing change.

Any form of therapy (be it psychotherapy or behavior therapy) involves psychological influence—implicit or explicit—deployed in the setting of a relationship between client and therapist. The dichotomy drawn between interpersonal and relationship factors on the one hand, and technique on the other, seems somewhat forced; indeed, it may be false, because it is doubtful whether these two major components in the therapeutic enterprise can ever be isolated in pure and separate cultures.

5.02.4 EXPLANATORY MODELS

One can say with confidence that there are considerable variations on the theoretical themes that inform similarly-named treatments. Different theories of family process generate different schools of family therapy (Herbert, 1997a; Vetere & Gale 1987). Play therapy also draws on different nuances of childhood "psychopathology" theory, and thus takes different forms (including active play therapy, release therapy, and the play interview) and is being applied on a dyadic, one-to-one basis (e.g., Axline's approach) or in a group format (e.g., Filial therapy).

Psychological therapies can be differentiated on two major dimensions:

(i) a passive vs. an active role on the part of the therapist;

(ii) the method (technique) vs. relationship as the main agent for change.

They can further be distinguished in terms of five attributes:

(i) the goals (or purpose) of therapy, for example, supportive, prescriptive, or exploratory;

(ii) the means by which goals are sought; this encompasses the theoretical rationale, for example, behavioral, cognitive, client-centered, or psychodynamic, (in child therapy these approaches may be mediated by talking to, playing with, rewarding the child or rehearsing skills with him or her);

(iii) the modality of therapy, for example, individual, group, couple or family;

(iv) the level of expertise of the therapist;

(v) the adoption of an expert or collaborative approach to clients.

The range of choices of individual psychotherapies—notably in the case of adolescents—constitutes a "menu" which almost rivals the feast available to adults: psychodynamic, client-centered, behaviorally oriented psychotherapy, communication, drama, role-construct, social system, multimodal, transactional, existential, gestalt, to mention a few. These are relatively broad approaches or perspectives. When we come down to techniques a conservative estimate suggests that there are more than 200 to choose from (Kazdin, 1988; Tuma, 1989).

What does such profusion mean? The sceptic might say that when so many treatments are in use, applied often to the same kinds of problem, it means that we lack a firm conceptual grasp of causation. In any event does it matter if the critics are correct in saying that psychotherapy has no adequate unifying theory? Why not simply consider treatment as a technology without recourse to any distinctive foundational theory? Erwin (1979) is of the opinion that we cannot afford to ignore the study of theoretical foundations. He states that an adequate theory might provide some important practical benefits. For example, if better clinical techniques are to be developed, it will be helpful to know exactly which features of the successful techniques are therapeutically productive and why, also which techniques have a greater antecedent likelihood of success than do others. This is a cue to look briefly at the major therapeutic models and the formulations which predicate their use.

5.02.4.1 The Medical Model—Diagnostic Formulations

Nowhere is the influence of medical ideologies in clinical child psychology more pronounced than in the reliance on classification and the diagnoses of children's psychological problems. Underlying the creation of classificatory systems (e.g., the *DSM-IV* (American Psychiatric Association, 1993) and *ICD-10* (World Health Organization, 1992) and taxonomies of "symptoms" is the assumption that specific syndromes (disease patterns) with identifiable and specific causes (etiologies) can be diagnosed. It might be added that the only justification for applying diagnostic categories to children is that not only should they imply reliable descriptive criteria and clear causal theories, but also that treatment implications should flow from the choice of label.

The particular issue of reliability in the assignment of diagnostic categories remains a contentious one (Zwick, 1983). This is a potentially major stumbling block as the validity of any system of measurement or classification depends, in large part, on its reliability. Achenbach and Edelbrock (1989) made the point that in order to be effective, formal diagnoses (and diagnostic formulations) require reliable taxonomic distinctions so that we can link cases that share useful similarities and to distinguish between cases that differ in important ways. The various *DSM* criteria for childhood psychopathology consist mainly of lists of behavioral-emotional problems rather than clearly identifiable physical abnormalities, and they are problems to be judged as present or absent. Unfortunately, as the authors state:

> most of these problems are not easily categorized as present or absent. Instead they vary with the child's age, situation, and interaction patterns. Whether the child is deemed to have a particular problem depends on when and how the child is assessed. Because many of the problems for which mental health services are sought occur outside the clinic setting, assessment typically requires information from people other than clinicians, such as parents and teachers. The different situations in which they see the child and the different roles they play with respect to the child are bound to affect what they report. (p. 55)

Achenbach, McConaughty, and Howell (1987) carried out a meta-analysis of 269 samples (in studies published from 1960 to 1986) of correlations between different informants (parents, teachers, trained observers, mental health workers, peers, and the children themselves) reporting children's behavioral-emotional problems. The mean correlations between informants playing similar roles with respect to the children, including pairs of parents, teachers, mental health workers, and trained observers ranged from 0.54 (mental health workers) to 0.64 (pairs of teachers) with an overall mean of 0.60. This substantial, although far from perfect, level of agreement dropped considerably when informants had different roles with the children. The mean correlations ranged from 0.24 (between parents and mental health workers) to 0.42 (between teachers and direct observers) with an overall mean of 0.28—statistically significant but low. With regard to the self-reports and others' reports of the same child, the mean correlation of 0.22 is statistically significant but even lower.

With regard to the face-validity of psychiatric categories for professionals, a survey of 1000 qualified or trainee American psychiatrists by Jampala, Sierles, and Taylor (1986) is of interest. A full 48% did not believe in the validity of the *DSM-III* criteria and 55% would have ceased to use it, had it not been required. They felt that the diagnostic categories failed to accommodate almost half of their patients. This is a serious indictment since the salient point about a classification-based formulation is that it needs to be comprehensive and to group individuals according to their distinguishing problematic behavioral, cognitive, and affective patterns. In the taxonomics of childhood disorder there is probably no better example of the difficulties, contradictions, and confusions than the criteria for attention deficit hyperactivity disorder and hyperkinesis provided in the *DSM-IV* and *ICD-10* systems, respectively.

Reviews of the literature suggest that despite interesting correlations between "problematic" childhood behaviors, the vast majority of "disorders" (it is difficult to avoid medical usage) cannot be conceptualized—except figuratively—as disease entities. Unlike many of the acute physical illnesses the structure of a presenting psychological problem, the etiology of the problem, and the implied treatment do not closely map on to each other (Sturmey, 1996). Achenbach and Edelbrock (1989) conclude a review of these issues by acknowledging that there is little agreement about the proper nature and role of diagnosis with respect to the psychopathology of children.

Whatever the reliability and validity of diagnostic schemes, there is an objection raised by many psychologists (and psychiatrists) to what they see as invidious "labeling" and stigmatizing of individuals by reducing complex "life problems" to a restrictive medical category. There is concern about how parents', teachers', and children's attributions, perceptions, and actions are affected by being told by an expert that the child has a disorder of some kind. Such reification may absolve parents from any sense that they can influence the difficulties. It may "tell" the child that they are different from other children, and furthermore, not in control of their actions—a pessimistic message to instill in someone at an impressionable stage of life. Most worring is the absence of a clear relationship between most global diagnostic classifications applied to particular children and any clear etiology or focused therapeutic/remedial program of action (Herbert, 1964).

The reality is that childhood signs of psychological abnormality are, by and large, manifestations of behavioral, cognitive, and emotional responses common to all children. Their quality of being dysfunctional lies in their inappropriate intensity, frequency, and persistence; most childhood disorders differ in degree, rather than kind, from normal behavior. The exceptions to this generalization are rare (see Herbert, 1994b). That generalization does, however, raise ethical problems for the practitioner. Leung (1975) observes that, whereas the

medical model provides a reasonably unambiguous ethical rationale for treatment by an *a priori* standards of "health" and "pathology," behavioral definitions tend to construe abnormality as not in itself different from normal behavior. If abnormal behavior is considered learned, therapists are involved in making, or at least concerning themselves with, value judgments that some other behavior would be preferable—a social, subjective, and therefore potentially prejudicial decision. This leads inexorably to the following questions, the answers to which have the status of ethical imperatives for the therapist as agent of change: "To whom is the behavior undesirable? Is it *really* in need of modification, and if so, to what must it reasonably change?"

Of course, the medical model has produced highly effective aids to the treatment of childhood psychopathology, but it also raises a moral dimension, particularly in the use of potentially harmful and/or addictive medication. As in the case of "owning" a diagnostic label, the attributions for a child's locus of control that follow from the regular use of drugs prescribed to make him or her "quieter" and "better behaved" are matters of concern.

A pitfall of using diagnostic classification in clinical formulations is the tempting but illusory impression it can give the practitioner of having explained the problem, when all it amounts to is a renaming process, and consequently a "thought-stopper." Take the boy who is always on the go, fidgets, is endlessly flitting from one activity to the next, and is very difficult to manage. The teacher who refers him to the clinic wishes to have an answer to the question: "Why does the child have such poor concentration, and why is he so disruptive—forever interfering and going "off task," defying my requests?" The report that comes back states that the child is ADHD (hyperactive). If asked to explain this diagnosis ("How do you conclude that the child is hyperactive?"), the clinician is quite likely to have to return to the observations they were asked to explain in the first place: "Because the child is inattentive, fidgety, overactive, and noncompliant." Many of the explanatory constructs in the mental health field are tautologies of this kind.

Ross (1968) finds parallels between the practitioner's preoccupation with classification and the fairy tale in which the opportunity for a princess to live her life happily ever after depends on her discovering the name of an ill-tempered creature. She goes to great lengths, and upon achieving her goal earns her salvation. Ross calls the preoccupation with seeking a name for a child's problem in order to "save" it, the "Rumpelstiltskin fixation." It should not be the primary task of psychologists, he admonishes, to identify a disease by its signs and symptoms, but rather to get on with their real job of describing children and their difficulties in terms adequate enough to bring effective interventions into play, and with them, positive outcomes.

In the real world, of course, the clinician does not always have the luxury to be too pedantic (or precious) about such matters. While there may be misgivings about labeling children, there may be compelling policy, planning, service development, resource mobilizing, and research reasons for doing so. For the private practitioner there is the consideration that insurance companies insist on formal diagnoses.

5.02.4.2 The Statistical Model—Multivariate Analyses

Statistical (and particularly factor analytic) methods have proved popular in the search for clusters of problems which might lend support to the classifications built upon clinical observation and experience. What is advocated is an empirical approach which involves a minimum of assumptions and constructs regarding the causation of behavioral disorders. Despite the range of instruments that is available and the number of dimensions measured by these instruments, two major dimensions emerge from most analyses: problems of an *undercontrolled* type (variously referred to as conduct disorder, aggressive, externalizing, acting out) and an *overcontrolled* type (emotional disturbance, personality disorder, inhibited, internalizing, anxious) (Quay, 1986).

There is some limited overlap between behavioral dimensions (obtained by psychological measurement and factor analysis) and *DSM* criteria (see Quay, 1986). Their limitations with regard to implying causation or generating individual treatment options are much the same, although Achenbach and Edelbrock (1989) have illustrated ways in which the Child Behavior Checklist and Child Behavior Profile can be put to practical use, by providing quantitative descriptions of behavioral competencies and problems at various levels.

5.02.4.3 The Psychoanalytic Model—Psychodynamic Formulations

The "psychodynamic approach" is a superordinate title for a variety of therapeutic developments which had their origins in Freudian psychoanalysis (Lee & Herbert, 1970; Rycroft, 1966; Tuma, 1989). The term encompasses theories of personality and thera-

pies which assume the existence of unconscious mental processes, and which concern themselves with the elucidation of motives and the transference relationship, that is, the transfer on to the therapist of attitudes, longings, and feelings attaching to significant others.

Farrell (1970), in his synoptic account of psychoanalytic doctrine, states that the classical Freudian theory is primarily a theory about mental energy. This takes two fundamental forms which, in the early and better-known version of the theory, are the sexual and the self-preservative; and this energy goes to determine the character of the stages (oral, anal, etc.) through which the mind develops. In the course of this development the mind becomes differentiated into the structures of id, ego, and superego, cut across by the critically important barrier separating the unconscious from the preconscious elements of the mind. The total balance and distribution of energy is controlled by the mechanisms of defense, such as repression, regression, displacement, and so on. Where this control had not been satisfactorily achieved in the past, the repression barrier keeping the unconscious instincts of the system at bay is apt to break down under frustration. The unconscious comes to the surface in the compromise form of neurotic or "acting out" symptoms.

The neo-Freudian ideas of Melanie Klein (1975) have a different emphasis. This is primarily a doctrine about the "object relations" an infant forms (especially with the objects of mother and her breast) and about the internal world of the infant's unconscious fantasies. From the outset, infants experience the anxieties of living and are faced, in particular, with the breast that both satisfies and frustrates them. They deal with these difficulties by means of the defenses of introjection, projection, and splitting. Thus, to begin with, infants introject the breast (i.e., incorporate it in fantasy) and split the good breast from the bad. The character of infants' object relations—their good or bad quality—and the extent to which they get through various early stages satisfactorily are all of crucial importance to them. Therefore, the liability of the grown-up man or woman to break down, and the character of his or her collapse when it comes, are critically dependent on what happens inside the infant during the first year of life.

Therapists working with a psychodynamic model give much more weight to intrapsychic events in their formulations than behavior therapists because their perspectives are characterized by different epistemologies. These differences are illustrated in case history formulations from the mid-1920s. Where Little

Hans, with his deeply symbolic fear of horses, became the much-quoted standard-bearer of the psychoanalytic paradigm, Little Peter (age 2 years 10 months at the beginning of his treatment for a fear of rabbits) became the exemplar of the behavioral paradigm (see Freud, 1926; Jones, 1924).

Freud was essentially a proponent of *verstehende* or "understanding" psychology; he wished to answer the "whys" of human conduct. Despite his training in medicine and research work in physiology he was not content with the "mere" observation of surface behavior or with the investigation of neurophysiology; he was determined to explain the mental mechanisms underlying complex sequences of behavior. He wished to account for the whole of human mentation at the psychological level of explanation—formulating the experience of the neurotic patient, in terms of the meaning of his/her symptoms.

Psychoanalytic formulations (whatever the present-day school of psychoanalysis) tend to be derived from extensive arrays of molar segments of self-report and verbal exchange with the therapist, collected (usually) over a considerable period of time. The records of the therapy would be copious. By way of contrast, the clinical child psychologist, in scientific mode, is concerned with a deliberately curtailed and simplified series of events in the life of his/her clients. Analysts see superficiality in such parsimony— a misdirection of "gaze" which will simply result, if only presenting "symptoms" are removed, in other symptoms (the outer and visible signs of the "real" underlying difficulties) coming to the surface. This is the disputed phenomenon called "symptom substitution."

There have been intense debates about the status of psychoanalysis and its many-faceted progeny, the "psychodynamic approach." It is difficult for the hermeneutic framework of the psychodynamic model to be integrated within that of the scientist-practitioner approach (see Farrell, 1970; Fisher & Green, 1996; Long & Hollin, 1996; Pumpian-Mindlin, 1952; Rachman, 1963; Wachtel, 1977; Webster, 1995). And yet Freud's aim was to establish a "scientific psychology," and his wish was to achieve this "metapsychology" by applying the same principles of causality as were at that time considered valid in physics and chemistry.

For Farrell (1966), the fact that no usable "correspondence rules" (i.e., operational definitions) had been constructed for any of the large numbers of concepts of psychoanalytic theory, was a major stumbling block in testing its validity. If patients ask what terms like "repression" mean or what phrases like Klein's "fantasized incorporation by the infant to the breast" indicate, there is likely in Farrell's words (p. 22) to be "elucidation by means of, in part, the concept of psychic energy ... an explanation *per obscurius*, or an abrupt plunge into psychological absurdity."

Rycroft (1966) maintains that what Freud was engaged in was not explaining the patient's symptoms causally, but understanding them in order to give them meaning. This was not the scientific procedure of elucidating causes, but the semantic one of making sense of them. He says it can be argued that much of Freud's work was discovering that neurotic symptoms are meaningful, disguised communications, but that owing to his scientific training and allegiance, he formulated his findings in the conceptual framework of the physical sciences.

Psychoanalytically-oriented psychotherapy or play therapy with children is a less ambitious and demanding form of psychoanalysis than the form used with adults. Here the relationship between child and analyst is a means whereby therapeutic goals are achieved. The child is helped, by means of play and therapeutic conversations:

> to undo the various repressions, distortions, displacements, condensations, etc., which had been brought about by the neurotic defence mechanisms, until, with the active help of the child, the unconscious content of the material is laid bare. (Anna Freud, 1946, p. 71)

5.02.4.4 The Personality Typology Model—Trait Formulations

The personality structure approach to assessment postulates personality dimensions, in part inherited, that influence what and how children learn as they grow up. It has been observed that every person is, in certain respects, like all other persons, like some other persons, and like no other person. The nomothetic disciplines which favor the philosophy and methods of the exact sciences have been applied to the study of the highly generalized personality attributes (types and traits), while idiographic methods have been used to explore the aspect of uniqueness and individuality. According to one theory, the possession of particular combinations of personality characteristics (e.g., extraversion/introversion and neuroticism) determine whether certain children are predisposed to acquire dysthymic or conduct disorders (Eysenck, 1967). Given an extreme position on the continuum toward introversion or extraversion (which has implications for the individual's conditionability) and a labile or reactive autonomic nervous system (a high rating on neuroticism), the child is thought to be particularly susceptible to acquiring phobic anxiety through ease of social conditioning, or a conduct disorder because of its relative failure.

There are several limitations to the use of personality typing in the formulating process. The situations sampled are restricted in range: for example, behavior at home or at school. Furthermore, assessment methods tend to emphasize verbal behavior such as interviews, self-reports, and questionnaires. In the applications of such methods of assessment, personality differences in behavior across settings are seen as error variance in an imperfect measurement system. Greatest weight is placed on the initial assessment and diagnosis rather than on repeated, ongoing assessments. In personality-type assessments the person's behavior is compared with statistical norms.

The practical implications of an assigned personality "diagnosis" or profile for a treatment plan are limited (Herbert, 1965; Moore, Bobblitt, & Wildman, 1968). The issue of situation specificity makes it difficult to make predictions or arrive at precise conclusions of an individual kind, on the basis of generalized constructs. On the other hand, the early assessment of temperament—the constitutional aspects of personality—into its major categories "difficult," "easy," or "slow to warm up" and its behavioral referents, may allow preventive clinical work to be planned (Thomas, Chess, & Birch, 1968). A mismatch between parental attributes and the child's temperamental style can result in an extended series of mutually unrewarding interactions which are foundational for later relationships. They can lead to depression in mothers (in particular) and faulty or incomplete socialization in children (see Iwaniec, 1995).

The idiographic disciplines, such as biography, literature, and history, endeavor to understand and illuminate some particular event. The use of idiosyncratic and subjective projective techniques is an example of this tradition in clinical work. The case study is an exemplar of what Allport (1937) believes is an ideal combining of the idiographic and nomothetic approaches for the fully rounded appreciation of the person and their situation. In the view of Bromley (1986) it is the bedrock of clinical investigation, and part of the scientist-practitioner's armamentarium.

5.02.4.5 The Systemic Model—Family Therapy Approaches

An individual in a family system is affected by the activities of other members of the family. Whereas the traditional treatment model tended to identify the nominated client or patient as the unit of attention (e.g., the child referred to the child guidance clinic), the focus of assessment in the light of this interactional frame of reference is far more broadly conceived. Thus the focus of help is not necessarily prejudged as only the child who was referred; rather, the unit of attention becomes the family (or one of its subsystems).

The systemic perspective is well-illustrated in family therapy, a fashionable approach to childhood psychological disorder. There is no one therapeutic entity under the rubric "family therapy," but several schools or paradigms. For example, there is the structural school of Minuchin and his colleagues (Minuchin, 1974). Strategic family therapy has its origins in the Palo Alto research group led by Bateson (e.g., Bateson, Jackson, Haley, & Weakland, 1956; Jackson, 1957). Humanistic, existential therapies of the 1960s, such as Gestalt therapy, psychodrama, client-centered therapy, and the encounter group movement, influenced the theory and methods of various experiential family therapies—challenging the positivist tenets of the more problem-focused schools of family therapy (e.g., Satir, 1967). Behavioral family therapy and cognitive-behavioral therapy have their intellectual roots in social learning theory (Patterson, 1982). Psychodynamic and object relations perspectives, derived from psychoanalytic theory, found an exponent in Ackerman (1958). The intergenerational perspective, which looks beyond the immediate family circle and enlists the cooperation of others in resolving the family's distress, is associated with the names of pioneers such as Bowen (Bowen, 1966). If this were not a daunting enough choice, the clinican could look to the Milan Systemic Approach, the McMaster Family Model, Problem-solving Therapy, Brief Family Therapy, or Social Network Therapy (see Herbert, 1997a). Piercy, Sprenkle, and associates (1986) describe 54 technique skills for the major family therapies.

As with other therapeutic models the paths on the journey toward making a formulation are many and not always clearly signposted. What does unite most family therapies as they engage in their divergent formulations and treatment strategies, although at a high level of abstraction, is a perspective which requires that children's problems be understood as the consequence of the pattern of recursive behavioral sequences that occur in dysfunctional family systems. The systems approach, as it translates to family work, embraces the concept of reciprocal/circular causation in which each action can be considered as the consequence of the action preceding it and the cause of the action following it. No single element in the sequence controls the operation of the sequence as a whole, because it is itself governed by the operation of other elements in the system. Thus, any individual in a family system is affected by the activities of other members of the family, activities which his or her actions or decisions (in turn) determine. This recursive element makes the formulation of what is cause and effect extremely complex.

Family therapists, whatever their methods and theoretical underpinnings, tend to believe that behavior problems in children are symptomatic (or, indeed, artifacts) of dysfunctional family life; the goal of treatment is therefore the improvement of family functioning. The members are encouraged, by a variety of therapeutic strategies and homework tasks, to understand the alliances, conflicts, and attachments that operate within the family unit and to look at themselves from a fresh perspective and to seek alternative solutions to their dilemmas.

The family, as a small group, can be observed and assessed on a variety of dimensions: patterns of communication, cohesion and processes of decision making (see Vetere & Gale, 1987). The major concepts for an assessment and formulation in family therapy are listed by Dare (1985) as follows:

(i) seeing the family as having an overall structure;

(ii) understanding the symptom as having a potential function;

(iii) understanding the location of the family on the life cycle;

(iv) understanding the intergenerational structure of the family;

(v) making an overall formulation linking the preceding four features;

(vi) linking the formulation to appropriate interventions.

Typically, an assessment by a family therapist (see Lask, 1987) might concern itself with whether there is:

(i) too great a distance between members of the family, leading potentially to emotional isolation and physical deprivation;

(ii) excessive closeness between members of the family, leading potentially to overidentification and loss of individuality;

(iii) an inability to work through conflicts, solve problems, or make decisions;

(iv) an inability on the part of parents to form a coalition and to work together, with detrimental effects on the marriage and/or the children;

(v) an alliance across the generations, disrupting family life, as when a grandparent interferes with the mother's child-rearing decisions;

(vi) poor communication between members;

(vii) a failure to respond appropriately to each other's feelings.

Some of the ways in which a child may contribute (wittingly or unwittingly) to a family's inability to cope with conflict have been described by Lask (1987):

(i) *parent–child coalition*, where one parent attacks the other, using one of the children as an ally;

(ii) *triangulation*, where both parents attempt to induce a child to take *their* side;

(iii) *go-between*, where a child is used to transmit messages and feelings;

(iv) *whipping-boy*, where one parent, instead of making a direct attack on the other, uses their child as a whipping-boy;

(v) *child as weapon*, where one parent attacks the other using the child as a weapon;

(vi) *sibling transfer*, where the children agree to divert the parents' arguing.

There are family therapists who neglect to assess the influence of wider social systems (e.g., school, neighborhood, sociocultural network). The social context is played down as a source of influence. It is an article of faith that the outward and visible signs of the family's problems, as manifested to a group of observers/commentators behind a one-way screen, represent reliably what is going wrong. How representative of a family's repertoire the samples of interaction (sometimes distorted by observer effects) are in reality, is a moot point.

Bronfenbrenner (1979) recommends the assessment of the following systems when producing a formulation:

(i) *microsystems*, which are the daily settings of the client (e.g., home, school, work), the physical environments, and the people within these settings with whom the client interacts;

(ii) *mesosystems:* the links between microsystems (i.e., the name and quality of connections between the environments);

(iii) *exosystems:* the situation (e.g., mother working full time) which may impact on the client's life, but in which he or she is not directly involved;

(iv) *macrosystems:* the broad institutional patterns and value systems of the culture which affect the meso- and exosystems.

Whiting (1963) points out that the most significant actions taken by parents, significant in the sense of having the most impact on children, have to do with their assignment of children to various niches or settings in a society, from crèches and nurseries/kindergartens to private schools, apprenticeships, helping sell produce in the market, or tending animals. Each of these settings has flow-on effects upon the people children encounter, their opportunities for play with peers, and their opportunities to acquire informal cognitive skills. These many and varied influences give the child his or her unique quality.

The individual client is also conceptualized in systemic terms. For example, Hepworth and Larsen (1990) make a formulation on the basis of describing (say) the child as a system composed of six intrapersonal dimensions:

(i) biophysical functioning (e.g., physical attributes, physical health, use and abuse of drugs and alcohol);

(ii) cognitive and perceptual functioning (e.g., cognitive level and flexibility, self-concept, judgment);

(iii) emotional functioning (e.g., emotional control, depression, anxiety);

(iv) behavioral functioning (e.g., deficits, excesses, patterns of concern);

(v) motivation (e.g., precipitating events);

(vi) culturally determined patterns (e.g., norms, values).

What we now have is an assessment process which may be focused on an individual (e.g., child), a group (e.g., family) or an organization (e.g., school). The first is sometimes neglected in family therapy formulations.

The family is thought of as dynamic in the sense that it is subject to continuous change. Like individuals, families are believed to pass through developmental life-cycle stages. Each life-cycle stage is believed to have its own accompanying set of tasks to be accomplished if families are to make successful transitions from one stage to the next (Carter & McGoldrick, 1988). A concept like that of life stages highlights a problem for practitioners assessing families. How do they adopt a standard by which to evaluate functional ("healthy") as opposed to dysfunctional ("unhealthy") patterns of family organization, transitions, boundaries, homeostatic (equilibrium-seeking) strategies, rules, roles, decision-making processes, communications, or any of the other attributes family therapists believe to be significant? Obviously, there are diverse cultural "norms" or values in these matters.

What is not always clear in clinical formulations which highlight the types of causal influence listed by Lask (above) is the precise mechanism whereby family patterns relate functionally to the day-to-day specificities (i.e., with regard to persons, places, times, or situations) of the referred problem. The majority of nonbehavioral family therapy processes are formulated in somewhat global terms and pitched at a high level of abstraction. It becomes very difficult to define operationally the key independent treatment variables at this level of strategy generality (de Kemp, 1995). At the

dependent variable end of the therapeutic equation, emphasis can be placed on symptom reduction/removal alone (called first-order change), or a more systemic level of family transformation (second-order change). Second-order change is empirically and conceptually difficult to identify and quantify.

The primary goals of family therapists, as defined by family therapists from several disciplines, tend to be divergent. Furthermore, there is little consensus about which factors constitute evidence of an efficacious outcome. A survey (*inter alia*) of family therapists' primary goals for therapy (Group for the Advancement of Psychiatry, 1970) elicited the following objectives expressed as percentages with regard to all families:

(i) improved communication (86%);

(ii) improved autonomy and individuation (56%);

(iii) improved empathy (56%);

(iv) more flexible leadership (34%);

(v) improved role agreement (32%);

(vi) reduced conflict (23%);

(vii) individual symptomatic improvement (23%);

(viii) improved individual task performance (12%).

Practitioners are not always clear about whether they are concerned with symptom reduction, family restructuring, or both.

Critical surveys (e.g., Herbert, 1987a; Kaslow, 1980; Reimers & Treacher, 1995) suggest that pragmatic, structured family therapies (i.e., those concerned principally with behavioral change) have produced the most convincing evidence of effective therapeutic outcome for the psychosocial problems of children. A particular criticism of the family therapy field is their antiempirical stance and consequent rejection of basic research (e.g., Watzlawick, Weakland, & Fisch, 1974).

5.02.4.5.1 Behavioral family therapy

The work of Patterson in Oregon was part of, and the inspiration for, a rapid growth in what might be called "behavioral family therapy" (see Alexander & Parsons, 1982; Griest & Wells, 1983; Herbert, 1994b; Patterson, 1982). This approach—sometimes also referred to as "systemic behavioral therapy"—is in large part concerned with the assessment of naturally occurring environmental influences, specifically those occurring within the family between parents, siblings, and child, in order to modify deviant behavior and teach new skills and behavior repertoires. It is an elaboration of learning-theory-based behavior therapy, and finds much of its intellectual sustenance in social learning theory. The basic level of formulation remains the functional analysis to which is turned to; it illustrates neatly the scientist-practitioner way of working, the approach of the applied psychologist.

5.02.4.6 The Behavioral Model—Functional Analysis

Haynes and O'Brien(1990) define functional analysis as: "the identification of important, controllable, causal, functional relationships applicable to a specified set of target behaviors for an individual client" (p. 654). In the behavioral canon, the formulation is directed towards the precise identification of the antecedent, outcome, and symbolic conditions which control the problem behavior. Behavior theorists often refer to their assessment—as a simple mnemonic for clients—in ABC terms (see Figure 3).

From a behavioral perspective, a child who indulges in frequent acts of defiance and outbursts of verbal abuse would be observed in order to determine the specific circumstances and conditions in which the unacceptable behaviors occur. Such conditions may involve antecedent organismic (O) and/or environmental stimulus events (A) which precipitate or set the scene as discriminative stimuli for the outbursts and the consequent events (C). The B term in the ABC analysis can stand for the behavior(s) being studied and the beliefs (attributions, perceptions, interpretations) of the child/parents about what is happening, why it is happening, and what the outcomes are likely to be.

The formulation involving an ABC linear analysis is, of necessity (given the complexity of behavior), elaborated into a recursive sequence such that Cs become As that generate new Cs, and so on. Learning occurs within a social nexus; rewards, punishments, and other events are mediated by human agents within attachment and social systems and are not simply the impersonal consequences of behavior. Children do not simply respond to stimuli; they interpret them. They are relating to, interacting with, and

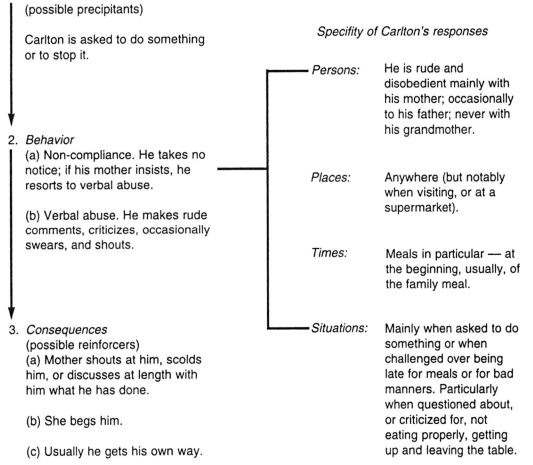

Figure 3 The ABC of behavoir.

learning from people who have meaning and value for them.

Bandura (1977) suggests that stimuli influence the likelihood of particular behaviors through their predictive function, not because they are automatically linked to responses by occurring together; contingent experiences create expectations rather than stimulus–response connections. Not surprisingly, behavioral work based on this premise is increasingly systemic, dealing with caregivers and nominated child "patients" in their own right as individuals, and analyzing their relationships to each other (as dyadic attachment subsystems). Also studied are their communications, interactions, boundaries, and perceptions of one another within a holistic and dynamic family system.

5.02.4.6.1 Behavioral formulations

In identifying controlling variables, the contemporary causes of problem behavior may exist in the client's environment or in his or her own thoughts, feelings, or bodily processes (organismic variables), and they may exert their influence as proximal (current) influences which are direct in their effects and close in time to the actions they influence. They are functionally related to behavior and can thus be tested in therapy—as hypotheses about causation—using single-case experimental designs. The formulation is directed toward the precise identification of the antecedent, outcome, and symbolic conditions that control the problematic behavior or beliefs (see Figure 4).

A distinction is made between the direct and vicarious learning experiences that contribute to the acquisition of problematic behavior and those contemporary influences which determine whether the client will perform the behavior he or she has acquired. For example, in the conduct disorders, some antisocial action which has been acquired by imitation or modelling may not be performed, either because appropriate instigating conditions do not occur or because its consequences are likely to be unrewarding or unpleasant. Maladaptive actions that are reinforced in terms of favorable consequences tend to be repeated. The reinforcement which strengthens an adolescent's disruptive behaviour—to take an increasingly typical example from the contemporary classroom—may be in terms of direct external reinforcement, vicarious or observed reinforcement, or self-reinforcement.

5.02.4.6.2 Distal consequences (Figure 4)

While it is true to say that clinicians delineate certain "symptoms" as pathognomonic of particular psychiatric disorders, the fact is that in the area of disorders of childhood it is mainly social rather than medical criteria of what is problematic that are dealt with. It is important to look not only at the immediate consequences of a client's behavior, but also at the longer-term implications (distal outcomes). What are the likely consequences of nonintervention in the problem for the person and his family? Problem behaviors are usually so called because they have a variety of unfavorable short-term and long-term outcomes. They are therefore referred to as maladaptive actions or dysfunctional thoughts and feelings; they are inappropriate in terms of several criteria which are assessed by the therapist.

Ultimately, the professional judgment of a client's behavioral/psychosocial/mental status is made in individual terms, taking into account his or her particular circumstances. It involves an estimate of the consequences that flow from the client's specific thoughts, feelings, and behaviors and general approach to life, with particular reference to their personal and emotional well-being, their ability to form and maintain social relationships, their ability to work effectively and (in the case of children) learn academically, and their accessibility to socialization (Figure 4, category 7). All are subject to disruption in emotional and behavioral disorders, and are gravely affected in the conduct disorders of childhood and adolescence (Herbert, 1987a). Other factors to be considered are youngsters' self-esteem and competence.

Social psychology can contribute to the overall assessment (Durkin, 1995). Take, for example, the socially isolated child: immature, self-centered children are not always able to manage the give-and-take of friendship. Exchange theory gives us pointers to why this should be so; it provides one method of evaluating friendships. Those theorists who employ "exchange theory" in analyzing aspects of social behavior and friendship view social interactions as a social exchange somewhat analogous to economic exchange. People are influenced (consciously and unconsciously) by the ratio of "rewards" to "costs" incurred in the interaction.

In the assessment of the implications for social relationships, it might be useful to draw up a balance sheet. On the debit side, the term "cost" is applied to deterrents that may be incurred in contacts with another person—such as hostility, anxiety, embarrassment, and the like. For attraction to a potential friend to occur the reward–cost outcome must be above the "comparison level," a standard against which satisfaction is judged.

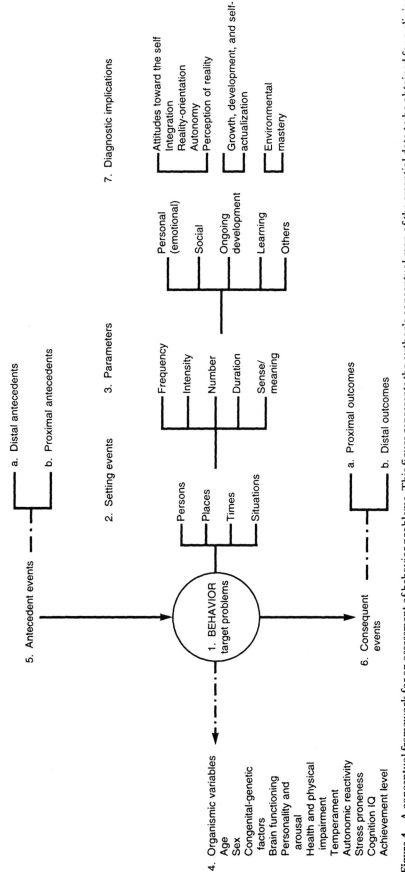

Figure 4 A conceptual framework for an assessment of behavior problems. This figure represents the author's conceptual map of the essential data to be obtained for a clinical formulation. It takes account of the client, significant others (e.g., interactions), behaviors and beliefs, current and historical events. It also provides diagnostic criteria by examining the longer-term implications of these behaviors and beliefs.

Organismic variables include individual differences produced by age, sex, genetic constitution, physiology, and by cognitive representations (schema, attributions, etc.) based on past learning (Figure 4, category 4). Behavior therapists tend to adopt a transactional position—the view that behavior results from a (still poorly understood) interaction of the current situation and individual differences (biological and psychosocial).

5.02.4.6.3 The formal assessment

Assessment in the behavioral mode involves a recursive process both in repeatedly testing and in revising the model of the person's behavior. It is also repeatedly used to monitor changes in the person's behavior across time and settings. Repeated evaluation is also essential to evaluate and modify treatment. The assessment procedure is idiographic and tailored very carefully to the person's own unique configuration of strengths and weaknesses. Behavior therapists insist on carefully monitored pretreatment assessments. They believe that the client—which may include adults (e.g., parents) as well as children—is best described and understood by determining what he or she thinks, feels, and does in particular life situations. The goal is eventually to help the clients to control their own behavior and achieve self-selected goals. It is crucial in behavioral assessment and treatment to reformulate these complaints and goals in operational terms, that is, in overt terms of what the client says and does, and in a manner that lends itself to quantifying the problem (Ollendick & Hersen, 1984).

Wilson and Evans (1983) studied the reliability of target behavior selection in behavioral assessment by asking 188 members of the Association for Advancement of Behavior Therapy to assess three written case descriptions of (i) fearfulness, (ii) conduct disorders, and (iii) social withdrawal in children. Subjects were posed four open-ended questions: (i) whether treatment was warranted; (ii) to describe the child's major difficulty; (iii) state treatment goals; and (iv) specify and rank order treatment targets. Granted that the means of assessment is somewhat artificial there was nevertheless a surprisingly low agreement (38%) between clinicians in selecting a first-priority behavior for treatment. There was considerable variability in selecting behaviors for intervention and, perhaps surprisingly, a substantial (22%) tendency to introduce psychodynamic and intrapsychic terminology such as "internalized hostility," "poor self-concept," and "insecure child." Only approximately 20% of responses referred to specific target behaviors. Psychody-

namic explanations were more likely in complex problems. This study is a matter of concern for advocates of functional analysis if its results are cross-validated. It indicates poor agreement between raters on the apparently simple task of identifying target behaviors.

Two questions regarding the validity of functional analysis are especially important: "What constitutes an adequate functional analysis?" and "When are the clinician's judgments valid during functional analysis?" Oliver and Head (1993, p. 14) reviewed published criteria for an adequate functional analysis and suggest that three criteria must be met: "that behavior (B) is considered in terms of the influence of events preceding the behavior, or its antecedents (A), and the events consequent (C) upon it...That the influences of antecedents and consequences should be empirically demonstrated...That all necessary and sufficient conditions for a behavior to occur should be considered."

Contemporary behavior analysts use and integrate many different assessment methods, including interviews with the client and third parties, psychometric assessments, idiographic self-reports, psychophysiological measures, and mini-experiments (Dougher, 1994; Sturmey, 1996). The purpose is to generate and evaluate hypotheses concerning the clinical problem. Information is collected which requires careful interpretation. At times this may be a highly inferential process. Although the functions of target behaviors may be readily apparent in some situations, this is not always the case.

Barrios (1988) notes that assessment, including behavioral assessments, may serve many different purposes. Behavioral assessment has been used in order to assist in diagnosis to evaluate treatment efficacy, to evaluate the most appropriate form of intervention for an individual client; also to assess whether clients are capable of change (e.g., in their parenting practices (Herbert, 1991b)).

5.02.4.7 Developmental-behavioral Formulations

"Development" is typically defined as a progressive series of orderly, coherent changes leading to the goal of maturity. This may be the grand design, but as many long-suffering parents and teachers know to their cost, children's progress through life is often disorderly and incoherent, and the changes (when change is not being resisted) are not always in the direction of maturity. Developmental frameworks for assessing individuals and families emerged from research and theory relating to their progress through life-cycle stages, and the therapeutic strategies they generate (e.g., Carter & McGoldrick, 1988). Several theorists (e.g. Achenbach, 1974, 1982; Cicchetti, 1984a, 1984b; Herbert, 1974) have urged the necessity for underpinning the study of child psychopathology with principles and findings from developmental psychology—an approach which has been referred to as the "developmental psychopathology movement" (Gelfand, Jensen, & Drew, 1988). This developmental framework has been applied to clinical practice in the form of a broad-based, interdisciplinary knowledge-base, incorporating works as diverse as that of ethologists, developmental neurologists, cognitive anthropologists, cognitive-development theorists, and social-learning theorists.

5.02.4.7.1 A developmental knowledge base

The difficulty for the clinician formulating his/her assessment within a developmental context is that there is no agreed, conceptually coherent theory of normal child development as a touchstone for understanding and assessing clinical abnormality, nor any single explanation of the processes of normal growth and development. Developmental theories range from the psychoanalytic (e.g., Freud's stages of psychosexual development), the ethological (e.g., Bowlby's attachment theory), behavioral (e.g., Bandura's social-learning theory) to the structural-developmental (e.g., Kohlberg's theory of moral development). Each of these theoretical perspectives provides a particular methodology and conceptual framework for viewing the specifics of developmental processes. Conceptions of individual characteristics also vary from those postulating stability to those assuming constant change. For example, trait theorists investigate nomothetically, relatively fixed relationships between characteristics (e.g., temperament, intelligence) across various ages, while those favoring an idiographic approach examine the individual's unique and dynamically changing organization of personality attributes.

A contemporary assessment framework leading to a formulation and treatment plan for childhood psychological disorders (see Herbert, 1987b; Ollendick & King, 1991) requires measures of behavioral, cognitive, and physiological responding as well as, notably, a determination of the developmental, social, and cultural context within which the problem occurs. The strategy is to begin with a broad-based assessment of the child and his or her environment (e.g., family, school, peers) and then to obtain information regarding specific stimulus features, response modes, antecedents, and consequences, severity, duration, and pervasiveness of the particular problems. The assessment utilizes a multimethod, problem-solving approach to obtain as complete a picture of the child and the family as is possible, one that generates in logical fashion, a treatment plan. The design of such treatment plans requires a multidimensional model in order to accommodate conceptually the different social contexts (home, school, and neighborhood) and the various levels of intervention that characterize child behavior therapy.

There are several key developmental questions to ask in formulating whether a problem merits serious concern:

(i) Do the child's problems interfere with the forward momentum and course of normal development?

(ii) Are they causing him/her to "regress," or slowing him/her down?

(iii) Do they represent a "cul-de-sac," taking him/her in the direction of a self-defeating lifestyle?

(iv) Is the child's adaptive behavior appropriate to his/her age, intelligence, and social situation?

(v) Is the environment making reasonable demands of the child?

(vi) Is the environment satisfying the crucial needs of the child, that is, the needs that are vital at his/her particular stage of development?

The family (or some other agent of socialization) may be dysfunctional. Thus, if the child's behavior is abnormal (unusual), troublesome, and self-defeating—and the answers to the last two questions are "No"—then you are still faced with a problem. However, it is more of a "problem situation" than an intrinsic disorder, or, more accurately, a systemic, interactional problem.

For Cicchetti and his colleagues (Cicchetti, Toth, & Bush, 1983) abnormal patterns of behavioral adaptation—as represented by clinical problems such as hyperactivity and failure-to-thrive—are most fruitfully construed and formulated as a series of stage—and age-related "tasks." The issue of "competence" is common to all of them and, as the child gets older, his or her self-esteem. If the child fails to develop skills and social competence, he or she is likely to suffer a sense of inadequacy which has spiralling ramifications. There is evidence, not only of the power of parents to facilitate the child's mastery of developmental tasks or hinder him or her, but to do this unwittingly (Cicchetti, Toth, & Bush, 1983). These matters become important themes in the final formulation.

The evaluation of normality and abnormality within a developmental framework requires a familiarity with general principles of development with particular reference to personality and behavior. It necessitates a comprehensive knowledge of children, how they think and talk, their skills and limitations at various ages, their typical repertoires of behavior, and the life-tasks and crises that they confront. Such a normative or comparative approach needs to be complemented by an idiographic assessment which takes into account biographical and social-contextual influences (Whiting, 1963).

The value of a developmental framework for clinical work does not cease after adolescence. We do not stop developing as adults. It is short-sighted to try to understand, say, an adolescent's misdemeanors without considering the preoccupations and attitudes characteristic of his or her parents' stage of life.

5.02.4.8 Social-learning Model—Cognitive-behavioral Approach

Behavior does not occur in a social vacuum, nor is its acquisition a passive process. Human beings are problem solvers and active explorers of their world. Cognitive-behavior therapists (e.g., Hollon & Beck, 1994) subscribe to a model of human behavior and cognition which goes beyond the earlier epistemological position of radical behaviorists and focuses on the active processing of expectations, hypotheses, and theories. These have been added to that other "ghost in the machine"—the self—with which most behavior therapists now happily (and others, uneasily) cohabit.

An important feature of the social learning model, within which cognitive-behavior therapy finds much of its theoretical rationale, is the acknowledgment of this active element in learning and the part played by *understanding*. Not all of a child's learning (e.g., to ride a bike) involves understanding, but much learning involves knowing rather than simply doing. Stimuli, notably social stimuli, have meaning for the child, who acquires knowledge of social situations which is used in adapting to them. The failure to comprehend these meanings—as seen, for example, in the child with a Semantic-Pragmatic Disorder—has a devastating effect.

The cognitive-behavior therapy approach does not lend itself to any one simple definition (see Fishman, Rodgers, & Franks, 1988; Guidano & Liotti, 1983). Its focus, however, on goal setting and self-directive behavior by the client, and on divergent thinking as a means to inventive solutions to life's problems, is congruent with the philosophy of much contemporary casework with children and their families. Therapists assess, as primary data, children's problematic behavior, but also the phenomenology of their problems: their verbal reports of internal representations of events, experiences, and opinions, such as attitudes towards self, parents, and school. These attitudes, like theories, have, *inter alia*, a knowledge function. They provide a frame of reference within which individuals make interpretations of their world, creating a model—a figurative set of "goggles"—through which they construe and make sense of people and life-events. This personal construct system (Kelly, 1955) is accessible to investigation by means of the Kelly Repertory Grid.

The constructs of parents, some developed in the bosom of their family of origin, others elaborated with more recent experiences of parenting, give meanings to their offspring's behavior and can facilitate mutually-satisfactory interactions. Sadly, some constructs, if distorted by ignorance, misunderstandings, or paranoia, can mislead parents into self-defeating confrontations with their children.

There is a wide range of cognitive-behavioral methods; they share a common assumption that children (and, indeed, their parents) can be helped to eliminate dysfunctional attitudes and behaviors and to learn more adaptive strategies and skills (e.g., self-control, effective communication, negotiation), by reinforcing prosocial and socially sensitive behavior, challenging irrational beliefs and faulty logic, and by self-instruction and positive self-statements as well as the more traditional behavioral change techniques (Herbert, 1987b, 1989, 1993, 1997b; Kendall & Braswell, 1985).

5.02.4.9 Integrative Models

Given that there is no grand, general psychological theory of human behavior on offer in academic psychology departments, but rather a number of poorly integrated middle-range theories (e.g., learning theory, cognitive science, etc.), it should not be surprising that clinical psychologists find few convincing overarching theories or integrative models to make sense of psychopathology in childhood or adulthood.

The Kendall and Lochman (1994, p. 844) description of the cognitive-behavioral therapies is in terms that suggest there is a broader convergence of concepts in their rationale than in most of the other approaches. They state that:

...they integrate cognitive, behavioral, affective, social and contextual strategies for change. The cognitive-behavioral model includes the relationships of cognition and behavior to the affective state of the organism and the functioning of the organism in the larger social context.

A rationale for many practitioners is that all therapies contain an element of *learning*, something about which psychologists have considerable knowledge and experience of workable applications. Goldstein, Heller, and Sechrest (1966, p. 63) propose the following definition of psychotherapy:

> Whatever else it is, psychotherapy must be considered a learning enterprise. We need not specify too narrowly just what is to be learned in psychotherapy; it may be specific behaviors or a whole new outlook on life, but it cannot be denied that the intended outcome of psychotherapy is a change in an individual that can only be termed a manifestation of learning.

In the author's opinion, what gives cognitive-behavioral therapy its present ethos of an informed rather than ragbag eclecticism, is its deep roots in empirical psychology, and a track record of encouragingly successful outcomes in a wide range of childhood behavior problems (Herbert, 1997a, 1997b; Kendall & Braswell, 1985; Kendall & Lochman, 1994).

5.02.5 THE CLINICAL FORMULATION—PRACTICE ISSUES

Rigorous assessment is the *sine qua non* of effective intervention. The formulation, which bridges these activities, depends upon the clinician's practice wisdom and skill in "mining" for the data with which it is constructed. The different stages of the ASPIRE process leading towards a formulation (described at the beginning of this chapter), involve a sometimes daunting array of practical choices, decisions, actions, and caveats. Not infrequently, incoming data—sometimes as far forward in client contact time as the intervention—demands a reformulation and possibly a "rethink" of the therapeutic program.

As any choice of key issues to discuss for their practice implications is likely to seems somewhat arbitary a few areas found to be important for clinical practice have been selected (see Tables 1 and 2).

5.02.6 CONDUCTING A FORMULATION

5.02.6.1 The Intake Interviews—Preparation

The interview is an essential method for gaining access to parents' and children's problems. It sounds deceptively simple and straightforward but requires careful preparation. The following questions illustrate some of the issues:

(i) What do I wish to find out (what are my objectives in this interview?)

(ii) Who do I need to speak to in order to fulfill my objectives? (All the family members; parents only; the child alone; his/her brothers and sisters?)

(iii) Do I invite them to meet me as a full family group? Do I speak to the mother first? Both parents together? Should the child be present initially?

(iv) How do I begin the interview?

(v) How do I introduce myself?

(vi) How do I let them know what to expect?

(vii) How do I best express some quite complex and potentially threatening ideas?

(viii) How do I reassure them about confidentiality?

(ix) What is the best way of eliciting reliable and relevant information?

(x) How do I deal with their tendency to digress or to set an agenda which avoids key issues?

(xi) Indeed, what *is* relevant (salient) information?

(xii) How do I terminate the interview, without leaving clients feeling "up in the air" or threatened?

5.02.6.2 Engaging the Clients

There is an important general consideration: the perspective, "style," or model of help to be adopted. In the expert model the professionals view themselves as very much in charge because of their monopoly (or near-monopoly) of expertise, responsibility, and, therefore, decision-making. The client is relatively passive as a recipient of advice, "prescriptions" (about health or how to behave), or possibly therapy of one kind or another. At the other extreme, clients (say parents) are viewed very much as consumers of the professionals' services, with the right to select what *they* believe is most appropriate to their needs. Decision-making is ultimately in the parents' control, with professionals acting as consultants, negotiation and discussion playing a large part in the client–practitioner relationship. The formulation is very much a self-directed, demystified process.

In between, lies the collaborative or partnership model. Here the professionals perceive themselves as having expertise but sharing it and imparting it to parents and other non- or paraprofessionals so that *they* facilitate much of the training/therapy of the child.

Cunningham and Davis (1985), in the context of work with mentally handicapped clients, devised a list of questions for estimating where one stands on the expert–consumer continuum vis-à-vis clients:

(i) Have I met the family?

(ii) Do I consider the child in the context of his/her family?

(iii) Do I have regular, two-way communication with the family?

(iv) Do I respect and value the child as a person?

(v) Do I respect and value the family?

(vi) Do I feel the family has strengths to help the child?

(vii) Have I identified the parents' abilities and resources?

(viii) Do I always act as honestly as possible?

(ix) Do I give them choices about what to do?

(x) Do I listen to them?

(xi) Have I identified their aims?

(xii) Do I negotiate with them?

(xiii) Do I adjust according to the joint conclusions?

(xiv) Do I assume they have some responsibility for what I do for their child?

(xv) Do I assume I have to earn their respect?

(xvi) Do I make the assumption that we might disagree about what is important?

(xvii) Do I believe they can change?

(xviii) Have I tried to identify the parents' perceptions of their child?

(A high proportion of "yes" responses suggests the generalized use of a consumer model; many "no" responses indicates an expert model).

5.02.6.3 The First Contact

The clinician conducts a guided conversation in which they ask questions and listen empathetically (with the "third ear" as it has been called)

to the answers and to spontaneous comments. A collaborative style comes into effect from the very first encounter if this is the approach of choice. The practitioner, after explaining their role and what lies ahead for the client(s), attempts to engage willingness to cooperate and possibly change, by entering the client's concerns, experience, and feelings. The construction of a family tree (genogram) is a useful means—especially with children—of establishing rapport and getting to know who significant members of the family and friends are (Herbert, 1991b).

Parents are invited to explain their coping and disciplinary strategies, as well as their theories regarding possible causes of the child's problems which they have had the opportunity to describe. Ideally, they come to feel that the clinician is making a genuine effort to understand their internal reality. Other matters for discussion are the child's assets, and the parents', and, if present, the child's hopes and goals for therapy (see Herbert, 1987a, 1987b; Webster-Stratton & Herbert, 1994, for detailed accounts).

5.02.6.4 The "What?" Question

A failure to define the client's problem in precise terms, or to bring the circumstances in which it occurs into sharp focus, leads to the premature formulation of cause–effect relationships. To discuss causal factors before the "to-be-explained" phenomenon is adequately specified and measured is a reversal of scientific problem-solving.

Table 1 Beginning an assessment.

Initial screening	Phase 1
Step 1	Explain how you intend to work. Foster a good working relationship
Step 2	Obtain a general statement of the problem(s)
Step 3	Specify the problem(s) more precisely
Step 4	Elicit the desired outcome(s).
Step 5	Construct a problem profile (Herbert, 1987b)
Step 6	Introduce the idea of behavior sequences by looking at your client(s) typical day(s)
Step 7	Establish problem priorities
Further assessment	Phase II
Step 8	Work out a family life map (Herbert, 1988)
Step 9	Make an estimate of your client's assets
Step 10	Ask your adult clients about their goals (e.g., for their children). Ask the child about his or her wishes and requirements
	Phase III
	Collect more detailed "baseline" data. Give clients homework tasks, for example, keeping diaries, frequency charts, etc . . .

Table 2   From planning to implementation.

Planning	*Phase 1*
Step 1	Consider informal and/or direct solutions
Step 2	Accentuate the positive
Step 3	Consider the wishes of those around the client
Step 4a	Begin with problems where success is likely
Step 4b	Select relevant areas of change
Step 5	Choose your intervention
Step 6	Monitor your client's progress
Implementation	*Phase II*
Step 7	Implement the intervention
Step 8	Review your intervention
Step 9	Gradually fade out the program
Follow-up	*Phase III*
Step 10	Conduct a follow-up exercise

This is not the place to consider the many aids to description and measurement for formulation purposes, that are available. (Useful guides to the psychometric and evaluative literature are available in Barkley, 1990, 1994; Berger, 1996; Ollendick & Hersen, 1984; Ollendick & King, 1991; Scott, 1996; Webster-Stratton & Herbert, 1994).

There are several "what" questions which, with others, generate precise hypotheses to explain the child's difficulties:

(i) What is the child doing and saying that is problematic?

(ii) Under what conditions are these behaviors emitted?

(iii) What tasks/problems is the child confronting in his/her life-situations?

(iv) What pro-social behaviors does the child emit?

(v) Under what conditions do these behaviors occur?

(vi) What situations are being avoided?

(vii) What are the implications for the child (and significant others) if s/he does not change?

(viii) What actions need to be encouraged and shaped up?

The preliminary information about the referral comes usually from parents. They tend to report their children's problems in terms of rather vague, global labels such as "aggressiveness," "tantrums," "defiance," or "rebelliousness." It is vital to encourage them to give descriptive examples of the problem, in other words to define what they mean in specific and observable terms. There follow two examples of a parent's complaint. The first is uninformative; the second provides a firm foundation for further assessment.

(i) Peter was playing with his cars when I asked him to get ready for school. Peter took no notice. I snatched away his toys and there was a scene. As a result, Peter had one of his tantrums and gave me a lot of abuse.

(ii) Peter was playing with his cars. I told him it was already 7.30 and time to get washed, dressed, and ready to leave for school. Peter did not answer or make a move. I told him the time again and repeated my instructions. Peter asked for a few minutes play. I said he was already late and told him to put the cars away. He now said "No!" just like that. I snatched his cars away. He lay down, screamed, and kicked his legs on the floor for a few minutes until I smacked him. He then went to change, muttering that he hated me and would leave home. I took no notice. His father took no interest in what went on; he ignored the entire thing.

After an initial report from parents (or teachers), the clinician needs to observe the child. It is important to confirm the parents' observations and especially those based on hearsay, for example, what she has heard about her child's behavior at school. A major source of error in the assessment and treatment of children in clinics or residential settings is the tendency to ascribe to the child properties which overemphasize the generality and invariance of personality traits and problem behavior. Such reification undermines effective formulating.

As an example, the problem could be a boy who bullies other children. The tendency is to make an entity of the bullying. It is done by describing the problem in the form of a noun or adjective ("there is a lot of violence in him"; "he is an aggressive boy"). The youngster is assessed in terms of what he is or has rather than in terms of what he does in particular situations. In the next stage the child is quite likely to be inferred to have "a need for aggression." From this point on, the distinction between what is observed and what is inferred, what is direct evidence and what is hearsay interpretation tends to become blurred. For all the popularity of trait theories, practitioners, as we have seen, make little use in therapy of the diagnostic information from personality typologies.

Behaviorally oriented psychologists tend to view behaviors with, say, aggressive or anxiety attributes as instances or samples of response classes rather than as the outward and visible signs of internal or underlying dispositions. They tend to avoid trait labels. Diverse attributes would be considered to be members of the same response class because it could be shown that such attributes enter into the same functional relationships with antecedent, concurrent, and consequent stimulus conditions, rather than because they coexist or covary in a group of persons.

5.02.6.5 Unpacking the Problem

In the case of complex problems it is helpful to have (or to construct) a conceptual framework—a guide to the factors that require investigation. Figure 5 presents an example of how, with a problem like school refusal, the clinician can unpack or unravel the processes underlying the problematic situation into their constituent elements, as an aid to the assessment and formulation. Thus with the school refusal problem the clinician might ask: "What does a young person have to do in order to go to school (successfully), remain at school, and then return home at the appropriate time?" "What incentives ('push–pull') or deterrent influences are operating in this child's situation?" The flow chart (Figure 5) illustrates the "push" and "pull" factors which function to impel or attract children to school, and hold them there, and the stages at which things can go wrong.

5.02.6.6 Communication

Young children tend to be talkative but may be limited in their ability to reflect insightfully about their experiences; adolescents are often introspective (reflective) but have a way of becoming monosyllabic when asked personal questions. This poses a problem for the would-be interviewer.

Children are not always very good at expressing their fears, frustrations, or uncertainties. They cannot always tell their parents, let alone a comparative stranger, how they feel, but they have a language that adults can learn to translate—the language of behavior and fantasy. What they do (in a direct sense in everyday life) and say (indirectly through play or story-telling) can be most revealing. The advantage of using projective techniques (which include play,

puppets, dramatic creations, completing stories or sentences) for assessment, is that they involve relatively unstructured tasks that permit an almost unlimited variety of responses. The client has to fall back on his or her own resources rather than stereotyped, socially desirable answers. The techniques (as psychometric instruments) do have their critics, but are invaluable if used cautiously as aids to communicating with children (Babiker & Herbert, 1996).

Where the child is too loyal, too frightened or ashamed, or too inarticulate to speak about feelings (or painful events in the family) it may be possible to express these emotions in play, drawing, drama (with puppets or miniatures), or stories. They are undoubtedly an invaluable adjunct to work with children and involve the empathic imagination and creativity referred to at the beginning of this chapter (see Herbert, 1988).

5.02.6.7 The "Which?" Question

An issue which arises early in a clinical assessment involves prioritizing problems. Clinicians with mandatory obligations have their own guidelines to follow. The practitioner's and parents' hierarchy of tasks might be influenced by the following considerations with regard to the problem(s):

(i) their annoyance value;
(ii) their actual/potential dangerousness;
(iii) their interference with the life of the family or its individual members;
(iv) their accessibility to change (improvement) and an intervention;
(v) their frequency, intensity, and magnitude;
(vi) their disabling implications;
(vii) the "costs" of change in terms of resources (time, money, etc.) and other people's well-being;
(viii) the ethical acceptability of the desired outcome;
(ix) the availability of the necessary helping skills or resources.

5.02.7 THE FORMULATION

The formal or main phase of assessment can be said to be over when the clinician has a reasonably clear picture of the clients' difficulties, strengths, history, social setting, and background. They should have a reasonably clear picture of why the problems developed and how they "look" against a framework of normal development. Relevant intrinsic attributes of the child have been assessed. The problem is

Has to → wake up on time	Get bathed, → dressed, breakfasted	Leave the → house on time	Make a → journey	Enter the → school gates	Go to → assembly	Stay in → the school	Go home → at appropriate time

(1) Does he wake on time? If not, why not? (2) Does he get enough sleep? If not, why not (going to bed late; lying in bed unable to sleep because of morbid pre-occupations, tense, depressed?)	(3) Anyone to structure his day at home, e.g. supervise his getting ready ("push")? (4) Is he sick/anxious/panicky? (5) Any reason he needs to be at home (care for a sick member of the family, parents keep him at home to look after siblings, etc.)? (6) Is he afraid to leave home because concerned about his mother's health, afraid of an accident befalling her (preoccupation with death, separation anxiety)? (7) Is he depressed, overwhelmed by apathy, helplessness, inertia?	(8) Is he teased/bullied on the way to, or at school? (9) Claustrophobia/clothing (adequate for school?)/homework (10) Is there anything to keep him at school (interests, friends, teacher)? (11) Deviant models (peer group) for truanting (12) Other "pull" factors absent? (Is he under-achieving grossly at school, bored?) (13) Does anyone really know him or take an interest in him at school?

Figure 5 "Push–pull" influences in a child's school attendance.

formulated usually in systemic terms, that is to say as it impinges on a family or school system rather than on an individual alone.

5.02.7.1 The "Why?" Question

The formulation provides a summary of the salient information collected; it is "formulated" in the sense that the practitioner puts forward an "explanatory story" (hopefully, a valid one) to impose meaning on the data collected. The formulation consists of a series of hypotheses which are statements about how the problem arose, when and where it occurs, and why it is maintained.

A particular skill is one of editing. It involves the identification of the important influences and controlling variables—among, potentially, so many—in order to plan an effective intervention. The principle of parsimony is helpful here; one invokes those causal factors that are sufficient to facilitate such an intervention. There is a balance to be struck between the wastefulness and risks of overinclusiveness (that is to say excessive complexity), on the one hand, and simplistic theorizing on the other.

Bromley (1986) describes the required steps for explication of the individual case.

(i) State clearly the problems and issues.

(ii) Collect background information as a context for understanding (i).

(iii) Put forward *prima facie* explanations (conjectures/hypotheses) and solutions (pro-

gram formulation) with regard to the client's personality and predicament—on the basis of information available at the time, and on the basis of the principle of parsimony. Examine the simple and obvious answers first. They may, of course, have to be rejected if they don't stand up to critical examination. This guides (iv).

(iv) Search for further/additional evidence. New hypotheses/explanations will have to be formulated and examined.

(v) Search again and admit for consideration, sufficient evidence to eliminate as many of the suggested explanations (hypotheses) as possible; the hope is that one of them will be so close to reality as to account for all the evidence and be contradicted by none of it. The evidence may be direct or indirect; but it is vital that it should be admissable, relevant, and obtained from competent and credible sources.

(vi) Enquire critically into the sources of evidence, as well as the evidence itself. Bromley (1986) makes the point that in the case of personal testimony, this is analogous to cross-examinations in a court of law; otherwise it amounts to checking the consistency and accuracy of all items of evidence.

(vii) Examine carefully the internal logic, coherence, and external validity of the entire network of associations and hypotheses formulated to explain the client's predicament and proposals to solve the problems.

(viii) Select the "most likely" interpretation, provided it is compatible with the evidence (some lines of argument will be obviously inadequate whereas others will be possible or even convincing).

(ix) Work out the implications of your explanations for intervention/treatment or some other action (or, indeed, inaction).

Always ask yourself about the implications (e.g., the risks involved) of making Type I as opposed to Type II errors in your assessment. Is it more damaging to your client if you risk Type I errors (i.e., asserting relationships falsely) than if you risk Type II errors, which deny relationships that actually exist? The academic psychologist tends to minimize errors of incautious assertion at the expense of relatively common Type II errors. The clinician often acts on the basis of weakly supported propositions because of the dangers of ignoring potentially significant associations. But of course there may also be some risks in presuming relationships which do not have any basis in reality. This step requires that you

(x) Work out the implications in specific terms.

Therapeutic change depends, *inter alia*, upon persuasion (providing reasons why the client should change his/her attitudes and behavior); teaching (all therapies, it might be said, involve new learning); and the provision of explanations (reframing; cognitive restructuring).

Insight is not rejected as a facilitative therapeutic agent. Yelloly (1972, p. 147) states that:

> Awareness can operate in a number of ways. The sheer provision of accurate information may correct a false and erroneous belief and bring about considerable change in behavior. Prejudice for instance, may be diminished by new information which challenges the prejudiced belief. And in human beings (pre-eminently capable of rational and purposive action) comprehension of a situation, knowledge of cause and effect sequences and of one's own behavior and its consequences, may have a dramatic effect on manifest behavior. Thus to ignore the role of insight is just as mistaken as to restrict attention wholly to it.

5.02.7.2 Explaining to Parents

The attempt to "make sense" of complicated problems for (say) parents and teachers, depends upon the particular circumstances of the case, but also on the ability of the practitioners to translate technical matters into plain, unpatronizing language. Although behavior therapy is not primarily an insight-based therapy, undoubtedly the understanding of its rationale and how it applies to the individual child facilitates the process of change, as mentioned above (Herbert, 1987b).

A functional analysis can be a rich source of insights for the client. A connotation of such an analysis is that the behaviors under consideration serve a purpose, that is, are functional (dysfunctional though they may appear to the professional eye) for the individual. Clinical psychology is full of examples of this kind of functionalism; therapists commonly talk of the secondary gains arising from clinical problems. Their implications for the individual's well-being and effective functioning provide a diagnostic guideline for the therapist and an insightful view of causation for the client. The meaning of the problems for the child and indeed for his or her family—the sense made of them and the payoff they provide—constitute a vital element of the formulation conveyed to the clients.

In behavioral work, in the author's opinion, explanations in terms of a functional analysis can operate at two levels. At its simplest, behavior is a function of certain contingent stimuli, originating in the person's internal and external environment. Here, the important questions are: "what triggers (elicits) the phobia?" or "what reinforcement does the child get for behaving in this antisocial way?" At a more interpretive level, the child's behavior may have the function of solving (or attempting to solve) a developmental or life problem. To make sense of it, one might ask (*inter alia*): "what immediate "solutions" (even if self-defeating in the longer term) do the child's actions provide for himself or herself?" Also, "what purpose does the child's behavior serve in terms of his or her family life and its psychological and social dynamics?"

A clinical formulation which is being explained to parents might sound something like this:

> Andrew has not yet learned to control his temper. He "lets go" in a frightening tantrum—banging his head, kicking, screaming, and yelling—when he cannot get his own way, also when you try to insist on his doing something, refuse his commands, or attend to people other than himself at a time when he wants your undivided attention. The result (usually) is that he achieves his goal, he coerces you both into giving way—a very rewarding state of affairs seen from his point of view; a very unrewarding (and sometimes humiliating) state of affairs seen from your perspective. Occasionally you stick to your guns which means that Andrew has been getting rather inconsistent messages; the consequences of his undesirable actions are not predictable. Sometimes (but rarely) you punish his unacceptable behavior, generally when there are visitors. Sometimes you ignore it, for example, at the supermarket. Generally you "reward" it and thus make it more likely to recur, by giving in to him. Andrew has learned to make this outcome

more likely by escalating the tantrums into very violent and therefore frightening episodes. It now has to be made quite clear to him that his bad behavior will have consequences that are not only unrewarding, but also unpleasant enough to make him relinquish his tantrum. You have tried smacking which you admit makes him worse and you miserable. A method called response-cost will be used—in essence, fining his tantrums. At the same time it will be made very beneficial for him to be more obedient, to ask nicely and to control his temper. His successes will be recorded on this chart and show him how he can earn treats when he has collected a certain number of stickers.

5.02.8 THE "HOW?" QUESTION— IMPLEMENTING AN INTERVENTION

Client commitment and resistance to change are among the most critical features to assess and manage when implementing a successful intervention of whatever kind. The collaborative approach as elaborated by Webster-Stratton and Herbert (1994) is designed, by means (*inter alia*) of self-empowering strategies, the use of relationship, respectful attention to clients' feelings and ideas, and the use of metaphor and humor, to stimulate their interest and incentive to change, and to overcome resistances. Herbert and Wookey (1997) have been able to confirm the effectiveness of such process variables in a succession of parent groups.

The self-empowering strategies are designed to enhance self-esteem and perceived self-efficacy. Perceived self-efficacy is a significant item in any formulation of the likely success of such an approach (see Webster-Stratton & Herbert, 1994). Bandura (1977) is of the opinion that human behavior is subject to two major categories of influence: efficacy expectations (the conviction that one can successfully carry out the behavior required to produce a given outcome) and outcome expectations (the estimate that one's behavior will lead to certain outcomes).

These constituent parts of this crucial notion of perceived self-efficacy are distinguished because a mother or father may believe that a particular course of action (e.g., a behavioral program) will produce certain outcomes, that is, an improvement in their child's behavior. However, they may have serious misgivings as to whether they have the wherewithal (e.g., patience and consistency) to bring about such a desirable outcome. All psychological procedures designed to bring about change, whatever the type, are thought (by some psychologists) to depend on beliefs about the level of skill required to bring about an outcome and the likely end result of a course of action.

Efficacy expectations are thought to be the most important component. The main effect on outcome expectations is through the strengthening of efficacy expectations ("I *am* able to do it!"). Successful helping thus depends, in this view, on the degree to which the interventions create or strengthen the client's expectations of personal efficacy. It appears that verbal persuasion has only relatively weak and short-lived effects on such expectations. Performance accomplishments, on the other hand, have the most powerful effects, hence the concentration on "doing" (e.g., behavior rehearsal, modeling, role-play, homework tasks) in behavioral parenting training (Webster-Stratton, & Herbert, 1994).

5.02.8.1 The Collaborative Approach

Webster-Stratton and Herbert (1993) are of the opinion that the collaborative approach to clinical work by empowering clients is highly effective in producing favorable outcomes with the conduct disorders (see Herbert, 1995; Herbert & Wookey, 1997; Patterson & Forgatch, 1985; Spitzer, Webster-Stratton, & Hollinsworth, 1991). In a collaborative relationship:

> ... the therapist works with parents by actively soliciting their ideas and feelings, understanding their cultural context, and involving them in the therapeutic experience by inviting them to share their experiences, discuss their ideas, and engage in problem-solving. The therapist does not set him/ herself up as the "expert" dispensing advice nor lectures to parents about how they should parent more effectively; rather, the therapist invites parents to help write the "script" for the intervention program. The therapist's role as collaborator, then, is to understand the parents' perspectives, to clarify issues, to summarize important ideas and themes raised by the parents.... (Webster-Stratton & Herbert, 1994, p. 108)

The partnership between clients and practitioner, it is suggested, has the effect of giving back dignity, respect, and self-control to parents who are often seeking help for their children's problems at a vulnerable time of low self-esteem, self-blame, guilt, and learned helplessness (Herbert & Wookey, 1997).

5.02.8.2 Rigorous Evaluation

Data collection begun in the baseline period continues throughout the intervention period. It is vital to keep a close watch on what happens in the early stages to ensure that the program is being followed correctly and any unforeseen problems that arise are dealt with quickly. This is the rigorous evaluation component of the ASPIRE process.

In the light of the data collected relating to the target behavior(s), or any other objective information, it may be necessary to reformulate one's previous conclusions and modify the intervention in some way. In the case of behavioral work the program is flexible and if the chosen target behavior is not changing after a reasonable period of time it becomes essential to review all aspects of the work.

The following questions may be useful.

(i) Are there powerful competing reinforcers or interfering factors in the client's environment operating against the program? Can these be modified?

(ii) Are the reinforcers well chosen and effective?

(iii) Is the parent working effectively and being reinforced for his or her participation?

(iv) Are the behavioral objectives realistic? Are they within the client's repertoire?

(v) Have you proceeded too quickly? Is it necessary to go back to an earlier stage in the intervention plan?

The time for the program to end depends upon the goals established at the beginning of treatment although new (or elaborated) goals may emerge during the intervention.

5.02.9 SUMMARY

This chapter begins by stating that the piecing together of a clinical formulation is central to the practitioner's craft. The choice of the word "craft" was deliberate. The craft of the potter is an apt metaphor for the many-faceted psychological skills applied to the task of analyzing and synthesizing, into a relatively brief statement—a formulation—about complex human problems. Potters are *applied scientists* when they draw upon an empirical knowledge base for the different clays and glazes they use, and the parameters for firing the products they make. But they become artists as well, when they design and decorate their creations, and when they bring to bear a delicacy, intricacy, and sureness of touch as they shape the clay.

Undoubtedly there is something called a "clinical art," especially in the ingenuity with which an assessment and intervention are put into effect. Nevertheless, in the opinion of this author, the major part of the clinical endeavor remains a scientific one. The balance of these emphases differs according to the basic assumptions of the theoretical model adopted and the clientele one works with. Certainly therapy with children demands a good deal of imagination and "artistry," especially if they are to remain well motivated.

The chapter demonstrates how difficulties and, indeed, failures in the treatment of children's behavior problems can frequently be traced back to a lack of precision during the crucial assessment phase of a clinical contact. A scientist-practitioner trying to explain a particular phenomenon will be at pains to bring that phenomenon into "sharp focus" by describing and measuring it in all its manifestations as objectively as possible. The analysis of a problematic situation and the planning of an intervention require as much knowledge and skill as any other aspect of the clinical psychologist's input, possibly more. The AS-PIRE procedures outlined for conducting such an assessment follow broadly the tried and tested scientific method of problem-solving.

The scientist-practitioner's science, however, is not, and because of the exigencies of clinical work cannot be, of the kind represented by what might be called "scientism"—a pharisaical insistence on the letter rather than the spirit of scientific method. There has to be room for intuition, insight, and creativity as long as they are checked and validated whenever possible by rigorous evaluation. It has been said that what cannot be measured cannot be changed, a proposition that has much merit as long as measurement does not generate into a sterile obsession with minutiae. The case study is the bedrock of clinical work, and an invaluable scientific method of enquiry. It provides us with an exemplar of that unique blending of idiographic and nomothetic approaches that have their parallels in the artistic and scientific facets of clinical psychology.

5.02.10 REFERENCES

Achenbach, T. M. (1974). *Developmental psychopathology.* New York: Ronald Press.
Achenbach, T. M. (1982). *Developmental psychopathology* (2nd ed.). New York: Wiley.
Achenbach, T. M., & Edelbrock, C. S. (1989). Diagnostic, taxonomic and assessment issues. In T. Ollendick & M. Hersen (Eds.), *Handbook of child psychopathology* (2nd ed.). New York: Plenum.
Achenbach, T.M., McConaughty, S. H., & Howell, C.T. (1987). Child/adolescent behavioral and emotional problems: implications of cross-informant correlations for situational specificity. *Psychological Bulletin, 101,* 213–232.
Ackerman, N. (1958). *The psychodynamics of family life.* New York: Basic Books.
Alexander, J. F., & Parsons, B. V. (1982). *Functional family therapy.* Monterey, CA: Brooks/Cole.
Allport, G. W. (1937). *Personality: A psychological interpretation.* London: Constable.
American Psychiatric Association (1993). *Diagnostic and statistical manual of mental disorders* (4th ed.) (*DSM-IV*). Washington, DC: American Psychiatric Association.
Andrews, D. A. (1989). Recidivism is predictable and can be influenced: using risk assessments to reduce recidivism. *Forums on Corrections Research, 1,* 11–18.

Axline, V. M. (1947). Play therapy procedures and results. *American Journal of Orthopsychiatry, 25,* 618–627.

Babiker, G., & Herbert, M. (1996). The role of psychological instruments in the assessment of child sexual abuse. *Child Abuse Review, 5,* 239–251.

Bandura, A. (1977). Self-efficacy: Toward a unifying theory of behavioral change. *Psychological Review, 84,* 191–215.

Barkley, R. A. (1990). *Attention-deficit hyperactivity disorder: A handbook for diagnosis and treatment.* New York: Guilford Press.

Barkley, R. A. (1994). *Taking charge of ADHD.* New York: Guilford Press.

Barlow, D., & Hersen, M. (1984). *Single case experimental designs: Strategies for studying behavior change.* New York: Pergamon.

Barrios, B. A. (1988). On the changing nature of behavioral assessment. In A. S. Bellack & M. Hersen (Eds.), *Behavioral Assessment: A practical handbook* (3rd ed.). New York: Pergamon.

Bateson, G., Jackson, D. D., Haley, J., & Weakland, J. (1956). Toward a theory of schizophrenia. *Behavioral Science, 1,* 251–264.

Berger, M. (1996). *Outcomes and effectiveness in clinical psychology practice.* Division of Clinical Psychology Occasional Paper, No. 1. Leicester: British Psychological Society.

Bowen, M. (1966). Theory in the practice of psychotherapy. In P. J. Guerin (Ed.), *Family therapy: Theory and practice.* New York: Gardner.

Bromley, D. (1986). *The case-study method in psychology and related disciplines.* Chichester, UK: Wiley.

Bronfenbrenner, U. (1979). *The ecology of human development: Experiments by nature and design.* Cambridge, MA: Harvard University Press.

Carter, B., & McGoldrick, M. (1988). *The changing family life cycle: A framework for therapy* (2nd ed.) New York: Gardner.

Cicchetti, D. (1984a). The emergence of developmental psychopathology. *Child Development, 55,* 1–7.

Cicchetti, D. (1984b). *Developmental psychopathology.* Chicago: University of Chicago Press.

Cicchetti, D., Toth, S., & Bush, M. (1983). Developmental psychopathology and incompetence in childhood: suggestions for intervention. In B. B. Lahey & A. E. Kazdin (Eds.), *Advances in clinical child psychology* (Vol. 11). New York: Plenum.

Clarke, R. G. V. (1977). Psychology and crime. *Bulletin of the British Psychological Society, 30,* 280–283.

Cohen, L. H. (1977). Factors affecting the utilisation of mental health evaluation and research findings. *Professional Psychology, 8,* 526–534.

Cohen, L. H. (1979). The research relationship and information source reliance of clinical psychologists. *Professional Psychology, 10,* 78–85.

Cunningham, C., & Davis, H. (1985). *Working with parents: Frameworks for collaboration.* Milton Keynes, UK: Open University Press.

Dare, C. (1985). Family therapy. In M. Rutter & L. Hersov (Eds.), *Child and adolescent psychiatry* (2nd ed.). Oxford: Blackwell Scientific.

de Kemp, R. (1995). *Interactions in family therapy: A process research.* Nijmeger, The Netherlands: Nederlands.

Dougher, M. J. (1994). Introduction. *The Behavior Analyst, 17,* 261.

Durkin, K. (1995). *Developmental social psychology: From infancy to old age.* Cambridge, MA: Blackwell.

Erwin, E. (1979). *Behavior therapy: scientific philosophical and moral foundations.* Cambridge: Cambridge University Press.

Eysenck, H. J. (1967). *The biological basis of personality.* Springfield, IL: C. C. Thomas.

Farrell, B. A. (1970). Psychoanalysis: The method. In S. G. Lee & M. Herbert (Eds.), *Freud and psychology.* Harmondsworth, UK: Penguin.

Fielding, D. (1983). Adolescent services. In A. Liddell (Ed.), *The practice of clinical psychology in Great Britain.* Chichester: Wiley/Leicester: British Psychological Society.

Fisher, S., & Green, R. (1996). *Freud scientifically reappraised: Testing the theories and the therapy.* Chichester, UK: Wiley.

Fishman, D. B., Rodgers, F., & Franks, C. M. (1988). *Paradigms in behavior therapy: Present and Past.* New York: Springer.

Freud, A. (1946). *The psychoanalytic treatment of children.* New York: International Universities Press.

Freud, S. (1926). *Inhibitions, symptoms and anxiety. Standard Edition* (Vol. 21, pp. 87–172). London: Hogarth Press (1959).

Gambrill, E. (1983). *Casework: A competency based approach.* Englewood Cliffs, NJ: Prentice-Hall.

Gambrill, E. (1990). *Critical thinking in clinical practice.* San Francisco: Jossey-Bass.

Gelfand, D. M., Jensen, W. R., & Drew, C. J. (1988). *Understanding childhood behavior disorders.* New York: Holt, Rinehart, and Winston.

Goldstein, A. P., Heller, H., & Sechrest, L. B. (1966). *Psychotherapy and the psychology of behavior change.* New York: Wiley.

Griest, D. L., & Wells, K. C. (1983). Behavioral family therapy with conduct disorders in children. *Behavior Therapy, 14,* 37–53.

Group for the Advancement of Psychiatry (GAP) (1970). *The field of family therapy.* New York: GAP.

Guidano, V. F., & Liotti, G. (1983). *Cognitive processes and emotional disorders.* New York: Guilford Press.

Haynes, S. N., & O'Brien, W. H. (1990). Functional analysis in behavior therapy. *Clinical Psychology Review,10,* 649–668.

Hepworth, D., & Larsen, J. (1990). *Direct social practice: Theory and skills* (3rd ed.). Belmont, CA: Wadsworth.

Herbert, M. (1964). The concept and testing of brain-damage in children: A review. *Journal of Child Psychology and Psychiatry,5,* 197–216.

Herbert, M. (1965). Personality factors and bronchial asthma. *Journal of Psychosomatic Research,8,* 353–356.

Herbert, M. (1974). *Emotional problems of development in children.* London: Academic Press.

Herbert, M. (1987a). *Conduct disorders of childhood and adolescence: A social learning perspective* (2nd ed.). Chichester, UK: Wiley.

Herbert, M. (1987b). *Behavioral treatment of children with problems.* London: Academic Press.

Herbert, M. (1988). *Working with children and their families.* Leicester: British Psychological Society/Routledge.

Herbert M. (1989). Aggressive and violent children. In K. Howells & C. R. Hollin (Eds.), *Clinical approaches to violence.* Chichester, UK: Wiley.

Herbert, M. (1991a). *Clinical child psychology: Social learning, development and behavior.* Chichester, UK: Wiley.

Herbert, M. (1991b). *Child care and the family: Resource pack.* Windsor, UK: National Foundation of Educational Research—Nelson.

Herbert, M. (1993). Foreword. In V. Varma (Ed.), *How and why children hate.* London: Jessica Kingsley.

Herbert, M. (1994a). Etiological considerations. In T. H. Ollendick, N. J. King, & W. Yule (Eds.), *International handbook of phobic and anxiety disorders in children and adolescents.* New York: Plenum.

Herbert, M. (1994b). Behavioral methods. In M. Rutter, E. Taylor, & L. Hersov (Eds.), *Child and adolescent psychiatry* (3rd ed.). Oxford: Blackwell Scientific.

Herbert, M. (1995). A collaborative model of training for parents of children with disruptive behavior disorders. *British Journal of Clinical Psychology,34,* 325–342.

Herbert M. (1997a) *Family treatment.* In T. H. Ollendick & M. Hersen (Eds.), *Handbook of child psychology* (3rd ed.). New York: Plenum.

Herbert, M. (1997b) *Cognitive-behavior therapy of adolescents with conduct disorders.* In P. Graham (Ed.), in press.

Herbert, M. & Wookey, J. A. (1997). *Child-wise parenting skills manual.* Exeter, UK: Impact Publications.

Hollon, S. D., & Beck, A. T. (1994). Cognitive and cognitive behavioural therapies. In A. E. Bergin & S. L. Garfield (Eds.), *Handbook of psychotherapy and behavior change* (4th ed.). New York: Wiley.

Iwaniec, D. (1995). *Emotional abuse and neglect.* Chichester, UK: Wiley.

Jackson, D. (1957). The question of family homeostasis. *Psychiatric Quarterly Supplement,31,* 79–80.

Jampala, V. C., Sierles, F. S., & Taylor, M. B. (1986). Consumers' views of DSM-III: Attitudes and practices of U.S. psychiatrists and 1984 graduating residents. *American Journal of Psychiatry,143,* 148–153.

Jones, M. C. (1924). The elimination of children's fear. *Journal of Counseling Psychology,7,* 383–390.

Kaslow, F. W. (1980). History of family therapy in the United States: A kaleidoscopic overview. *Marriage and Family Review,3,* 77–111.

Kazdin, A. E. (1987). Treatment of antisocial behaviour in children: current status and future directions. *Psychological Bulletin,102,* 187–203.

Kazdin, A. E. (1988). *Child psychotherapy: developing and identifying effective treatment.* New York: Pergamon.

Kelly, G. A. (1955). *The psychology of personal constructs.* New York: Norton.

Kendall, P. C., & Braswell, L. (1985). *Cognitive-behavioral therapy for impulsive children.* New York: Guilford Press.

Kendall, P. C., & Lochman, J. (1994). *Cognitive-behavioral therapies.* In M. Rutter, E. Taylor, & L. Hersov (Eds.), *Child and adolescent psychiatry* (3rd ed.). Oxford: Blackwell Scientific.

Klein, M. (1975). *The writings of Melanie Klein* (4 vols.). London: Hogarth Press.

Lask, B. (1987). Physical illness, the family and the setting. In A. Bentovim, G. Gorell-Barnes, & A. Cooklin (Eds.), *Family therapy.* London: Academic Press.

Lee, S. G., & Herbert, M. (1970). *Freud and psychology.* Harmondsworth, UK: Penguin.

Leung, F. L. (1975). The ethics and scope of behavior modification. *Bulletin of the British Psychological Society,28,* 376–379.

Long, C. G., & Hollin, C. R. (1997). The scientist-practitioner model in clinical psychology: a critique. *Clinical Psychology and Psychotherapy, 4,* 75–83.

Marshall, C., & Rossman, G. B. (1989). *Designing qualitative research.* Newbury Park, CA: Sage.

Maslow, A. H. (1954). *Motivation and personality.* New York: Harper & Row.

Mayer-Gross, W., Slater, L., & Roth, M. (1955). *Clinical psychiatry.* London: Cassell.

Meehl, P. B. (1971). A scientific, non-researched doctorate for clinical practitioners: Arguments pro and con. In R. R. Holt (Ed.), *New horizons for psychotherapy.* New York: International University Press.

Minuchin, S. (1974). *Families and family therapy.* Cambridge, MA: Harvard University Press.

Moore, C., Bobblitt, W., & Wildman, R. (1968). Psychiatric impressions of psychological reports. *Journal of Clinical Psychology, 24,* 373–376.

Ollendick, T. H., & Hersen, M. (Eds.) (1984). *Child behavioral assessment principles and procedures.* New York: Pergamon.

Ollendick, T. H., & King, N. J. (1991). Fears and phobias of childhood. In M. Herbert (Ed.), *Clinical child psychology: Social learning development and behaviour.* Chichester, UK: Wiley.

Oliver, C., & Head, D. (1993). Self-injurious behavior: Functional analyses and interventions. In R. S. P. Jones & C.B. Eyeres (Eds.), *Challenging behavior and intellectual disability: A psychological perspective.* Clevedon, UK: BILD Publications.

Patterson, G. (1982). *Coercive family process.* Eugene, OR: Castalia.

Patterson, G. R., & Forgatch, M. (1985). Therapist behavior as a determinant for client noncompliance: A paradox for the behavior modifier. *Journal of Consulting and Clinical Psychology, 53,* 846–851.

Peterson, D. R. (1976). Need for the doctor of psychology degree in professional psychology. *American Psychologist, 31,* 792–798.

Piercy, F. P., Sprenkle, D., & associates (1986). *Family therapy sourcebook.* New York: Guilford Press.

Pilgrim, D., & Treacher, A. (1992). *Clinical psychology observed.* London: Tavistock/Routledge.

Power, M. J. (1991). Cognitive science and behavioral psychotherapy: where behavior was there shall cognition be. *Behavioral Psychotherapy, 19,* 20–41.

Pumpian-Mindlin, E. (Ed.) (1952). *Psychoanalysis as science.* New York: Basic Books.

Quay, H. C. (1986). Classification. In H. C. Quay & J. S. Werry (Eds.), *Psychopathological disorders of childhood* (3rd ed.). New York: Wiley.

Rachman, S. (Ed.) (1963). *Critical essays on psychoanalysis.* Oxford: Pergamon.

Reimers, S., & Treacher, A. (1995). *Introducing user-friendly family therapy.* London: Routledge.

Rogers, C. R. (1957). *Client centered therapy.* Dallas, TX: Houghton Mifflin.

Ross, A. O. (1968). Conceptual issues in the evaluation of brain damage. In J. L. Khanna (Ed.), *Brain damage and mental retardation: a psychological evaluation.* Springfield, IL: C. C. Thomas.

Ross, R. R., & Gendreau, P. (1980). *Effective correctional treatment.* Toronto, Canada: Butterworth.

Rycroft, C. (1966). Causes and meaning. In C. Rycroft (Ed.), *Psychoanalysis observed.* London: Constable.

Satir, V. (1967). *Conjoint family therapy.* Palo Alto, CA: Science and Behavior Books.

Scott, S. (1996). Measuring oppositional and aggressive behaviour. *Child Psychology and Psychiatry Review, 1,* 104–109.

Shakow, D. (1978). Clinical psychology seen some 50 years later. *American Psychologist, 33,* 148–158.

Spitzer, A., Webster-Stratton, C., & Hollinsworth, T. (1991). Coping with conduct-problem children: Parents gaining knowledge and control. *Journal of Clinical Child Psychology, 20,* 413–427.

Sturmey, P. (1996). *Functional analysis in clinical psychology.* Chichester, UK: Wiley.

Sutton, C., & Herbert, M. (1992). *Mental health: A client support resource pack.* Windsor, UK: National Foundation of Educational Research—Nelson.

Thomas, A., Chess, S., & Birch, H. G. (1968). *Temperament and behavior disorders in children.* London: University of London Press.

Tuma. J. M. (1989). Traditional therapies with children. In T.H. Ollendick & M. Hersen (Eds.), *Handbook of child psychopathology* (2nd ed.). New York: Plenum.

Vetere, A., & Gale, A. (1987). *Ecological studies of family life.* Chichester, UK: Wiley.

Wachtel, P. L. (1977). *Psychoanalysis and behavior therapy.* New York: Basic Books.

Watzlawick, P., Weakland, J., & Fisch, R. (1974). *Changes: principles of problem formulation and problem resolution.* New York: Norton.

Webster, R. (1995). *Why Freud was wrong: Sin, science and psychoanalysis.* London: Harper Collins.

Webster-Stratton, C., & Herbert, M. (1993). What really happens in parent training? *Behavior Modification, 17,* 407–456.

Webster-Stratton, C., & Herbert, M. (1994). *Troubled families, problem children: Working with parents—a collaborative approach.* Chichester, UK: Wiley.

Whiting, B. (1963). *Six cultures: Studies of child rearing.* New York: Wiley.

Wilson, F. E., & Evans, J.M. (1983). The reliability of target-behavior selection in behavioral assessment. *Behavioral Assessment, 5,* 15–23.

World Health Organization (1992). *The ICD-10 classification of mental and behavioral disorders: Clinical descriptions and diagnostic guidelines.* Geneva, Switzerland: World Health Organization.

Yelloly, M. (1972). The concept of insight. In D. Jehu (Ed.), *Behavior modification in social work.* Chichester, UK: Wiley.

Zwick, R. (1983). Assessing the psychometric properties of psychodiagnostic systems: How do research diagnostic criteria measure up? *Journal of Consulting and Clinical Psychology, 51,* 117–131.

5.03
Process Issues in Child Psychotherapy

STEPHEN R. SHIRK
University of Denver, CO, USA

and

ROBERT L. RUSSELL
Loyola University Chicago, IL, USA

5.03.1 INTRODUCTION

According to Orlinsky and Howard (1986, pp. 311–312) the therapy process refers to "everything that can be observed to occur between and within the patient and therapist during their work together." This is indeed a broad domain of inquiry; nevertheless, research

on therapeutic transactions, patient and therapist characteristics, and change events during
treatment have been relatively neglected by
child therapy investigators. As Kazdin, Bass,
Ayers, and Rodgers (1990) have reported, less
than 3% of all child therapy studies have
investigated treatment processes, and few
studies have examined either child or therapist
characteristics that could moderate treatment
outcome. Although there is some evidence to
suggest increasing attention to these aspects of
child treatment since the 1980s (cf. Russell &
Shirk, in press; Shirk & Russell,1996), much of
the child therapy literature retains a restricted
focus on comparisons of treatment packages or,
to a lesser degree, on the evaluation of specific
techniques.

The relative neglect of child therapy processes
is puzzling for a number of reasons. First, from a
clinical perspective, the primary experience of
practicing therapists is the ongoing transactions
that comprise therapy sessions. In essence,
social and symbolic exchanges constitute the
principle phenomena of child psychotherapy.
Viewed from this perspective, one might expect
the study of process to be at the forefront of
child therapy research. In fact, Kazdin et al.
(1990) found that child practitioners regard
studies of process and its relation to outcome to
be a top research priority. Yet the investigation
of process remains in the background of child
therapy research. Second, growing evidence
from the adult psychotherapy literature has
shown that variation in processes within
sessions, as well as characteristics of therapists
and patients, have an important bearing on
treatment outcome (Orlinsky, Grawe, & Parks,
1994). Nevertheless, process research is "perhaps the area of work that is most discrepant
between child and adult therapy" (Kazdin,
1995, p. 268).

Given the restricted focus of child therapy
research, it is proposed to cast a broad net
across empirical literatures that could inform
understanding of child therapy processes. It has
been argued elsewhere (cf. Shirk & Russell,
1996) that much of the child psychotherapy
literature has evolved in isolation from basic
developmental research that entails important
implications for understanding therapeutic
processes. Therefore, the approach to process
issues in child psychotherapy is developmental
in two ways. First, child therapy, regardless of
treatment type, can be viewed as developmental
process. Psychotherapy process is fundamentally concerned with the course of change over
time. What makes this process developmental is
that the aim of therapeutic change involves the
progressive transformation of the child's basic
capacities to interact competently in the world.

Second, research on developmental processes in
everyday, nontherapeutic contexts can have an
important bearing on how the process of child
treatment is understood (Shirk, 1988; Shirk &
Russell, 1996). Consequently, the chapter is not
restincted to studies of child therapy process *per
se* but integrates research from the developmental literature where appropriate.

A number of models of therapeutic change
have been advanced in the adult therapy
literature (cf. Howard, Lueger, Mahling, &
Martinovich, 1993; Prochaska, DiClemente, &
Norcross, 1992). Common to these models is a
sequential perspective on the course of therapy
that delineates different phases of treatment
with characteristic treatment processes. Such a
framework has yet to be developed for child
treatment. As a start, this review of child
therapy process is organized around salient
phases of treatment. Specifically, this chapter
follows the "flow" of therapeutic interaction
from referral to termination. Along the way
factors that influence the referral process,
readiness or preparation for treatment, social
and symbolic exchanges in sessions, and the
relation between process and outcomes are
considered. The primary aim is to identify
critical process issues that have relevance for the
practice of child therapy and for the conduct of
future research.

5.03.2 REFERRAL TO CHILD PSYCHOTHERAPY

Unlike adults, children rarely refer themselves for psychological treatment. In fact, it is
not uncommon for others to be more distressed
by the child's problems than is the child.
Referral to child therapy typically involves
judgments and decisions by other people,
usually parents and teachers, in the child's life.
Thus, from the outset, the process of child
therapy is embedded in a social context that goes
beyond the transactions between patient and
therapist. In order to understand the referral
process in child therapy, it is essential to
examine the reactions of "referring" adults to
various forms of child problem behaviors. To
this end, investigators have begun to examine
factors that influence parent and teacher
decision making about referral to child treatment.

5.03.2.1 Parent and Teacher Perceptions of Problem Behaviors

One of the well-worn paths to the child
psychology clinic begins with the parent–
teacher conference. In this context, adult

perceptions and appraisals of child behavior problems influence decisions about referral. Because teachers are a primary referral source, a number of investigators have examined their evaluations of children's problem behaviors. Walker, Bettes, and Ceci (1984) asked preschool teachers to evaluate the severity, long-term outcome, stability, and need for referral of three vignettes that depicted children at two ages (3.5 and 5.5 years) who presented with aggression, hyperactivity, or withdrawal. The gender of the child was also varied. Among the central findings of the study, preschool teachers tended to view disruptive behavior problems as more severe, more stable, and portending poorer long-term outcomes than problems of withdrawal.

Consistent with these evaluations, teachers were more likely to agree that disruptive children should be referred for professional help than children showing signs of withdrawal. A similar pattern of results was obtained by Weisz et al. (1988), who found that elementary school teachers rated undercontrolled problems, relative to overcontrolled problems, as more serious, worrisome, and less likely to improve. Examination of referral problems in US clinics has revealed higher rates of undercontrolled problems than overcontrolled problems. Although it is likely such differences reflect variations in prevalence rates for the two broad classes of disorders, it is also possible that differences in problem appraisal among referring adults contributes to this difference.

One implication of this pattern—that undercontrolled problems are viewed as more serious than overcontrolled problems—is that children with symptoms of depression and anxiety may be under-referred for treatment because of beliefs that such problems are transient and will diminish over time. Research, however, has indicated that internalizing problems may be more persistent than once believed, and that untreated internalizing problems constitute a risk factor for future psychiatric disorders (Ollendick & King, 1994).

An alternative approach to evaluating the "referability" of various types of emotional and behavioral problems has been advanced by Weisz and Weiss (1991, p. 267), who operationalized referability as "the frequency with which a child problem is reported as a presenting complaint at mental health clinics, relative to the frequency of that problem in the general population." Epidemiological data were collected in both the USA and Thailand with a broad-band measure of child behavior problems. Clinic records from multiple sites were coded for specific presenting problems in both countries. Referability indices were computed

for specific behavioral problems for children between the ages of 6 and 11 years. Results from the US sample indicated that problems with serious implications for self or others, such as attacking other people or deliberately harming the self, were among the most referable problems. And like the results from the vignette studies, overcontrolled problems, such as perfectionism and self-consciousness, were among the least referable problems. This pattern of results suggests that the lower number of internalizing problems in clinics is not just a function of differences in problem prevalence but may reflect parental judgments about the prognosis for specific problems and the degree to which such problems can be remediated or tolerated in the home.

The foregoing studies suggest that problem type is an important contributor to decisions about clinic referral. Overall, undercontrolled problems appear to have the greatest capacity to elicit referral. Other factors, however, may influence parents' and teachers' referral decisions. A number of investigators have examined other child and family characteristics that could affect the referral process, including: child age, gender, and cultural background. In addition, numerous studies have suggested that parental characteristics, specifically parental psychopathology, are associated with perceptions of child behavior problems.

5.03.2.1.1 Child age and referral

Results from several studies have shown that younger children in the classroom are referred for mental health services at a higher rate than their older classmates (Drabman, Tarnowski, & Kelly, 1987; Tarnowski, Anderson, Drabman, & Kelly, 1990; Wisniewski, Andrews, & Mulick, 1995). Although one might expect these children to be less mature and possibly less advanced academically, Tarnowski et al. did not find significant differences in cognitive functioning or academic achievement between younger and other children in the same classroom. This pattern of findings was replicated and extended by Wisniewski et al., who also found a disproportionately high referral rate for younger children, and did not find group differences in indices of cognitive functioning or in levels of behavior problems. Thus, the disproportionate rate of referral did not seem to be attributable to "objective" age differences in the rate or severity of behavioral or academic problems.

The lack of a systematic relationship between referral and "objective" reasons for referral has suggested the possible contribution of teacher bias in the referral process. In their analysis of child characteristics associated with referral,

Wisniewski et al. (1995) found that as children deviated upward from the mean in height and weight, they were referred at disportionately higher rates. This tendency was particularly prominent among younger children in the classroom. As Wisniewski et al. observed, children's physical characteristics appear to be influencing teachers' referral decisions. Younger children who are relatively large for their age may be referred at a higher rate because they are misperceived to be similar to older children on academic dimensions. Thus, when these less mature children function at a level that is discrepant with teacher expectations for the average child in the class, but appropriate for their age level, they are viewed as needing remedial services (Wisniewski et al., 1995). In essence, perceived discrepancies based on non-academic factors (physical size) appear to contribute to teacher referral decisions. This interpretation is consistent with the formulation advanced by Masten and Braswell (in press), who propose that referral decisions are linked to judgments about discrepancies between age and the successful negotiation of specific developmental tasks. Teachers may have clear expectations for grade level, and expect all children at that level to complete specific tasks regardless of variation in age within the classroom.

5.03.2.1.2 Child gender and referral

Despite developmental evidence suggesting that parents monitor their daughters' behavior more closely than their sons', and tolerate less behavioral disruption from female children than males (Zahn-Waxler, 1993), boys are more often referred to clinics than girls. Several explanations can be offered for this apparent inconsistency. First, boys may simply evince higher rates of emotional and behavioral problems than girls (McDermott, 1996), consequently differences in prevalence rates may account for differences in referral rates. Second, although parents monitor their daughters' behavior more closely than their sons', differences in the types of problems expressed by males and females could affect referral. Given evidence for more disruptive behavior problems among males than females (McDermott, 1996), and evidence indicating that such problems are viewed as more serious by teachers and parents, gender differences in type of problem could account for gender differences in referral. Parents might conclude that disruptive, particularly aggressive, problems cannot be handled without professional help. On the other hand, the tendency to view internalizing problems as more transient and less severe may result in the underreferral of females who have been shown to express more internalizing problems, such as depression, particularly during adolescence (Nolen-Hoeksema, 1990).

In this context, the finding of Weisz and Weiss (1991) that problems are more referable for girls than for boys, at least in the USA, is somewhat surprising. Although gender did not affect the relative referability of specific problems for males and females, fighting, for example was highly referable for both genders; in general, problems were more referable for girls than boys. Thus, when girls show a specific problem, they are more likely to be referred than boys—although it is important to keep in mind that a number of problems characteristic of depression have low referability.

One area where this is particularly the case, are problems that load on the Sex Problems factor of the Child Behavior Checklist (Achenbach & Edelbrock, 1981). Although girls do not show an overall higher prevalence rate on these types of problems, when they do show such problems they are more likely to be referred than boys. Taken together, evidence for greater referability for females than males, but higher rates of male than female referral to clinics, suggests that higher rates of behavior problems, particularly undercontrolled problems, among young males relative to females account for their overrepresentation in clinics.

In summary, although parents and teachers do not report differences in the seriousness of problems when they evaluate males and females in vignettes (Walker et al., 1984; Weisz et al., 1988), differences in referability suggest that their actual referral decisions may be influenced by the child's gender, and possibly by different sex-typed expectations for boys and girls. The overrepresentation of males in clinics appears to follow from higher rates of undercontrolled behavior problems relative to females, and possibly to the under-referral of females with internalizing problems.

5.03.2.1.3 Referral and cultural background

A series of studies has revealed that culture plays an important role in adults' perceptions of child emotional and behavioral problems (Lambert, Weisz, & Knight, 1989; Lambert et al., 1992; Weisz et al., 1988; Weisz & Weiss, 1991). For example, in comparing the perceptions of American and Jamaican adults, Lambert et al. (1992) found that cultural background was related to evaluations of undercontrolled behaviors but not overcontrolled problems, such that Jamaicans seemed more concerned about disruptive problems than American adults. Cultural differences were also reported by Weisz et al., who found that Thai adults expressed less concern about both over- and undercontrolled behaviors than American adults. This pattern was also partially supported in the "referability" study of Weisz and Weiss. Undercontrolled problems, but not overcontrolled problems, were more referable in the USA than Thailand.

These findings suggest that culture may set a threshold for adult tolerance for distress about childhood problems, and that tolerance levels may vary by type of problem (Lambert et al., 1992). For example, Weisz and Weiss (1991) found that problems such as fighting, swearing, and threatening were more likely to prompt referral in the USA than Thailand, whereas the opposite was true for such problems as strange behavior, fears of school, and liking to be alone. Thus, one factor that may influence the degree to which problems are regarded as serious enough for referral is the cultural context in which they occur. It is likely that ethnic variation within the same society could exert a similar influence; however, such findings have yet to be reported. Clinical reports also have suggested that members of different ethnic groups vary in their interest or willingness to utilize professional services for child behavior problems (cf. Tharp 1991).

5.03.2.1.4 Referral and parental psychopathology

Parental accounts of child behavior problems are often presented with a strong affective valence. Consequently, parents, who are often entangled in their child's presenting problems, are not necessarily neutral reporters. This has raised concerns that parents' own affective states could bias their reports of child behavior problems. This clinical concern appears to be validated by a growing body of evidence that suggests that parental depression is associated with ratings of child behavior problems (cf. Schaughency & Lahey, 1985; Webster-Stratton, 1988). Specifically, the association between maternal depression and ratings of externalizing problems has been established in multiple studies, and has prompted some to conclude that "parent's depression rather than the child's behavior is a significant factor in the referral of these children for treatment" (Rickard, Forehand, Wells, Greist, & McMahon, 1981, p. 204).

From a process perspective, depression, or other forms of parental distress, may narrow the parent's tolerance for variation in child behavior such that minor behavioral deviations are misperceived as abnormal. Depressed parents, relative to their nondepressed counterparts, may become more distressed by typical child misbehavior, and amplify the severity of child problems in their behavioral reports. To the degree that referral is associated with parental judgments about the abnormality of behavior, the narrowed band of tolerance found among depressed parents would result in a lowered threshold for referral. In essence, referral is based on a distorted perception of child behavior problems.

In his review of research on the link between maternal depression and distorted perception of child behavior problems, Richters (1992) raised serious concerns about the existing evidence for this connection. Obviously, inferences about perceptual distortions do not directly follow from group differences in behavioral reports of depressed and nondepressed mothers. High rates of behavior problems could stem from problematic interactions in families with a depressed parent rather than from parental misperceptions. According to Richters, the distortion hypothesis requires (i) depression-related discrepancies with criterion ratings such that depressed mothers show less concordance with validated criterion than do nondepressed mothers, and (ii) evidence that the criterion rating is more reliable or accurate than maternal ratings, themselves. Based on a review of 17 studies that reported a depression–distortion link, Richters concluded that the vast majority fail to meet the foregoing criteria. Consequently, he concluded that "there appears to be no empirical foundation for the widespread belief that depressed mothers have distorted perceptions of their children's problems" (Richters, 1992, p. 496). However, as Richters wisely noted, the absence of evidence should not be confused with evidence for absence of distortion. Although existing research has revealed a relation between parental depression and child problem behaviors, the causal relationship and relative contribution of parental perceptions have not been clearly established.

Parents are in a unique position to evaluate the nature and severity of child problem behaviors, for example, they are aware of the child's behavior across contexts and over time; however, parents are often participants in or recipients of the child's problem behaviors. Consequently, parents' perceptions of their child's behavior could be influenced not just by their own affective state but by their role in their child's problem. Research in this area is virtually nonexistent; however, Reid, Kavanagh, and Baldwin (1987) have observed that abusive parents appear to view their children's behavior as more problematic than suggested by extensive behavioral observations. As Reid et al. have noted, the perception of child behavior as highly problematic may function to rationalize maltreatment by abusive parents. Such findings serve as a reminder that parents are participant-observers of their children's behavior, and that such a standpoint may contribute to biased perceptions or interpretations of child behavior.

5.03.2.2 Process Issues in Clinical Referral

Adult perceptions of child problems are an integral part of the clinical referral of children. Existing research has revealed that problem type, child age, gender, and cultural context are associated with adult perceptions of children's problems. Although there is evidence for a relationship between maternal depression and reports of child behavior problems, the accuracy of depressed mothers' perceptions has not been adequately addressed and awaits further investigation.

One of the major limitations of research on referral to child therapy is the absence of an explicit process model. Fragments of a model can be found across studies, but an integrated perspective on the relative contribution of specific judgments, for example, about the severity, abnormality, prognosis, and etiology of child problems, to referral decisions has not been advanced. As in all process research, the guiding question should be *how* do parents arrive at a decision to refer their children for treatment. For example, it is possible that referral involves the interplay between cognitive processes, such as judgments about abnormality (itself a function of social comparison processes), and emotional processes, such as demoralization following repeated failures at resolving the problem within the family. Future studies could manipulate these factors in case vignettes, for example, problem severity and intransigence, in order to evaluate their contribution to referral decisions. Other factors, such as the availability of services and parental perceptions of the efficacy of such services, are likely to contribute to the referral process as well.

5.03.3 READINESS AND PREPARATION FOR CHILD THERAPY

Treatments vary in the degree to which child participation is critical for successful outcome. Traditional child treatments such as psychodynamic, experiential, and play therapies, as well as cognitive and cognitive-behavioral therapies, require active child involvement in therapy. Although treatment tasks vary substantially across these therapies, they share the common assumption that children's active participation

is essential for successful outcomes. In contrast, some child treatments such as parent management training require only minimal, if any, participation by the child in therapy sessions. Instead, parent collaboration with treatment is critical for altering child behavior (Patterson & Chamberlain, 1994). It should be noted, however, that many child behavioral treatments, such as desensitization and social skills training, require high levels of child participation in sessions.

Research on adult psychotherapy has indicated that active participation in treatment is one of the best process predictors of treatment outcome (Frieswyk et al., 1986; Gomes-Schwartz, 1978). In this context it is interesting to note that research has indicated that nearly two-thirds of all children aged between 7 and 15 years would feel negatively if they were referred to see a psychologist (Sigelman & Mansfield, 1992). Given that children appear to be "reluctant consumers" of mental health services, it is surprising that few studies have addressed children's participation in treatment and its relation to outcome.

One of the few studies to address this issue, conducted by Braswell, Kendall, Braith, Carey, and Vye (1985), examined children's level of involvement in cognitive–behavioral therapy and found that a number of verbal indicators of active participation predicted therapeutic gains. Specifically, children's tendency to make spontaneous verbal elaborations about treatment tasks and therapists" encouragement and corrective feedback appeared to be among the best predictors of change in teacher ratings of self-control. Similarly, Colson et al. (1991) found that ratings of treatment difficulty, that is, the degree to which patients' were viewed as defiant and uncooperative in treatment, were negatively associated with ratings of patient progress in a sample of hospitalized adolescents. The findings of this study, although suggestive of a link between quality of participation and treatment outcome, are compromised by the absence of independent process and outcome ratings. Despite limited empirical findings on the relation between in-session participation and treatment outcome in the child literature, clinical theory and evidence from the adult therapy literature indicate that the study of treatment participation and the factors that promote or obstruct it represent a critical area for child psychotherapy process research.

5.03.3.1 Readiness for Therapy

Some years ago, Anna Freud (1965) recognized that a number of developmental factors could interfere with children's willingness to participate in therapy. A major obstacle, according to Freud, is the child's lack of awareness or acknowledgment of his or her own emotional or behavioral problems. As she noted, due to their immaturity, children often have "no insight into their abnormalities" and that, accordingly, "they do not develop the same wish to get well and the same type of treatment alliance" as adults (Freud, 1965, p. 28). In the absence of self-acknowledged emotional or behavioral problems, children do not experience a need for change, and, consequently, a need for treatment. Moreover, when problems are acknowledged, Freud observed that children typically locate the source of the problem in the external world and prefer environmental or situational solutions to their problems. This type of problem construal is incongruent with forms of therapy that focus on child-centered treatment processes such as altering affect regulation strategies, modifying cognitive patterns, or developing specific social skills. Furthermore, even when children recognize emotional or behavioral problems, and acknowledge a role in them, they do not necessarily view others as useful agents of change. Consequently, the degree to which children view interpersonal coping strategies as useful or effective could influence their willingness to utilize psychotherapy to deal with their difficulties. Given these potential obstacles, treatment engagement represents one of the major challenges of child therapy.

In an effort to integrate multiple processes that could influence children's willingness to participate in therapy, Shirk (Shirk, 1990; Shirk & Saiz, 1992) presented a developmental social-cognitive model of alliance formation. Elaborating on Anna Freud's clinical insights (Freud, 1965), Shirk hypothesized that developmental variations in children's cognitions about their own emotions and behaviors could contribute to their willingness to engage in the process of therapy.

5.03.3.1.1 Problem acknowledgment

The first source of social cognitive influence is hypothesized to be children's recognition and acknowledgment of emotional or behavioral problems. Children who do not acknowledge problems are expected to be more difficult to engage in a process that involves problem remediation. Moreover, from a developmental perspective, the ability to recognize one's emotional and behavioral difficulties should be related to the development of self-evaluative, especially social comparative, processes. Younger children, lacking in perspective-taking

ability, find it difficult to distinguish between wishful images of self and actual characteristics (Leahy & Huard, 1976). In fact, research by Harter (1988) has indicated that younger children, especially those of preschool age, overrate competencies and minimize difficulties. Furthermore, there is some evidence to suggest that this tendency is amplified in clinic populations (Vondra, Barnett, & Cicchetti, 1989; Zimet & Farley, 1986). In fact, it is not uncommon to find significant discrepancies between parent and child evaluations of problem behaviors and emotions (Achenbach, McConaughy, & Howell, 1987; Kazdin, French, & Unis, 1983).

In a study with a heterogeneous sample of psychiatrically hospitalized children, Shirk, Saiz, and Sarlin (1993) found that children's level of problem acknowledgment at admission was predictive of therapists'' ratings of the treatment alliance 3 weeks later. This finding is consistent with earlier research indicating that children's reluctance to participate in therapy is linked to problem denial (Taylor, Adelman, & Kaser-Boyd, 1985). Closer analysis of the alliance data indicated that problem acknowledgment predicted the affective quality of the therapeutic relationship but not children's level of collaboration with therapeutic tasks. The failure to find a relationship with task collaboration could be due to methodological limitations. First, task collaboration was narrowly defined as verbalization about problems and feelings; and, second, verbalization was assessed through global ratings by therapists. It is possible that specific coding of verbal interactions by observers would have yielded different results. In fact, research by Russell, Bryant, and Estrada (1996) has shown that child therapy sessions in which there is a positive therapeutic relationship are characterized by distinctive patterns of child–therapist discourse. However, the link between child problem acknowledgment and involvement in treatment processes, including verbal interaction, awaits further investigation.

5.03.3.1.2 Problem attributions

The second postulated source of social-cognitive influence involves children's attributions for their presenting problems. Research on adult psychotherapy has indicated that patients who view their problems as externally imposed are not likely to benefit from treatment (Kirtner & Cartwright, 1958; Salzman, Luetgert, Roth, Creasant, & Howard, 1976). Similarly, children may acknowledge the existence of problems but locate the source of their problems in the external environment. Although the child's attributions may be accurate in some cases, and consistent with certain forms of therapy, for example, family therapy, for child-centered treatments such an attributional pattern could undermine willingness to participate in child-focused interventions.

Developmental research indicates that children's understanding of the causes of behavior shows a general trend from external to internal attributions with increasing age (Shirk, 1988). As children acquire complex concepts of internal, psychological functioning, and develop the capacity to reflect on such processes, these concepts can be applied to observed behavior, including their own problematic behavior. As a result, internal attributions for behavior problems should increase with age during middle childhood. In fact, research on children's understanding of deviant behavior has revealed that children increasingly attribute such behavior to internal, psychological processes with increasing age (Coie & Pennington, 1976).

Two treatment outcome studies point to the potential relevance of children's attributions for treatment process. In the first, Bugental, Whalen, and Henker (1977) predicted that children's causal attributions for academic outcomes would moderate the effect of two types of treatment, a 6 week self-instructional training program (internal locus) or a 6 week social reinforcement program (external locus) for hyperactive boys. It was predicted that outcomes would be more positive for subjects with attribution-congruent treatments, for example, social contingency treatment for children with external attributions, than for those with incongruent treatments. Although the treatments did not produce changes in teacher ratings of disruptive behavior, subjects in the attribution-congruent treatments showed greater improvement on a measure of cognitive functioning. Thus, it appeared that treatment outcome was, in part, a function of the match between child attributional pattern and locus of treatment. It is possible that children in attribution-incongruent treatments were less engaged, or viewed the treatments as less acceptable, and therefore benefited less than children in congruent treatments; however, this process hypothesis was not evaluated.

Research by Weisz (1986) on the relationship between control-related beliefs and treatment outcome in child therapy carries implications for the link between problem attribution and treatment involvement. According to Weisz, children vary in the degree to which they view outcomes as contingent on their own behavior or efforts. In a therapeutic context, children who believe that problem resolution is contingent on

altering their own behavior should be more willing to engage in therapeutic problem solving than children who view problem solutions as independent of their efforts. As Weisz noted, individual differences in contingency beliefs could lead to corresponding differences in therapeutic involvement, thereby resulting in differential rates of change during treatment. In a study with 8–17 year olds referred for outpatient therapy, Weisz found a significant relationship between contingency beliefs, measured prior to treatment, and total problem reduction. Although these results are consistent with the view that attributions for problems promote or obstruct therapeutic engagement, the level of treatment involvement was not directly assessed in this study. Consequently, the link between pretreatment attributional patterns and therapy process has yet to be investigated.

5.03.3.1.3 Help-seeking expectations

A third source of social cognitive influence involves children's beliefs about the usefulness of other persons in resolving emotional or behavioral difficulties. From a developmental perspective, beliefs about the responsiveness and effectiveness of potential caregivers, including therapists, is likely to be rooted in early experiences of care (Shirk & Saiz, 1992). One of the basic tenets of attachment theory is that individuals develop internal working models of the self in relation to attachment figures that reflect the history of caregivers' reactions to the child's emotional needs and distress (Bowlby, 1988; Main, Kaplan, & Cassidy, 1985). Repetitions of infant–caregiver interactions are presumed to establish core beliefs about the availability and responsiveness of others.

Approach or avoidance patterns in times of distress are hypothesized to be linked to these core beliefs (Kobak & Sceery, 1988). Research on children's coping strategies has revealed significant individual differences in the degree to which children utilize others when confronted with psychological stressors (Garber, Braafladt, & Zeman, 1991). Among some groups of troubled children, for example, children displaying symptoms of depression, the use of others for coping with distress appears to be relatively limited (Garber et al., 1991). In fact, Garber, Braafladt, and Weiss (1995) have found that depressed girls rated mother-initiated affect regulation strategies as less effective than did nondepressed girls. Van Horn (1996) found that beliefs about the effectiveness of interpersonal coping strategies was associated with preadolescents perceptions of prior maternal care. Taken together, these results suggest that early experiences of care could shape children's expectations about the usefulness of other persons, including therapists, in helping them deal with emotional or behavioral difficulties.

Although there is growing interest in the relationship between attachment related beliefs and psychotherapy process and outcome among adults (cf. Dozier, Cue, & Barnett, 1994; Fonagy et al., 1996), this potentially fruitful area remains unexplored with children in treatment.

In addition to pretreatment social cognitions, other child characteristics could influence children's willingness to engage in therapy. For example, patterns of interpersonal problems, such as those that characterize oppositional–defiant disorder, are likely to carry over into therapeutic interactions and obstruct treatment participation. In this connection, Eltz, Shirk, and Sarlin (1995) found that the number of interpersonal problems reported prior to treatment was negatively related to the development of a working alliance among adolescent inpatients. In addition, characteristics associated with specific disorders could constitute impediments to treatment. For example, the relatively low levels of social competence and reflectiveness found among children with externalizing problems could interfere with their involvement in therapy. Surprisingly, children with externalizing symptoms do not show poorer outcomes than children with internalizing symptoms (Weisz, Weiss, Han, Granger, & Morton, 1995); however, this result could reflect the use of parent-centered interventions, for example, parent management training, rather than child-centered interventions with externalizing disorders. Among the internalizing disorders, symptoms of depression such as hopelessness, lack of energy, or social withdrawal could undermine participation in treatment (Stark et al., 1991).

In summary, studies of differential treatment responsiveness are beginning to consider pretreatment child characteristics (cf. Kazdin, 1995); however, few studies have examined these characteristics in relation to treatment process. What is needed are studies that examine relations among child characteristics that are hypothesized to promote or obstruct children's willingness to participate in treatment, specific dimensions of treatment process such as participation in treatment tasks, and variations in treatment outcome. Unlike comparisons of treatment packages, where individual patterns are typically ignored, such studies could potentially reveal patterns of "fit" between child characteristics and treatment processes that are associated with improved outcomes.

5.03.3.2 Preparation for Child Therapy

Evidence from both the adult and child psychotherapy literatures has indicated that discrepancies between client's expectations about the roles and processes of therapy and the reality they encounter in treatment can have a variety of negative effects, including willingness to sustain participation in treatment (Coleman & Kaplan, 1990; Day & Reznikoff, 1980; Frank, 1974; Strupp & Hadley, 1977). Studies with normative samples of children have shown that young children often have limited knowledge about psychologists' roles, practices, and the process of psychotherapy, but that knowledge and expectations become increasingly accurate with age (Bonner & Everett, 1982; Sigelman & Mansfield, 1992). Interestingly, there is some evidence to suggest that children's perceptions of psychologists' traits, such as smart or perceptive, become less positive with age (Sigelman & Mansfield, 1992), though overall attractiveness of a depicted therapist remains high among normative samples (Bonner & Everett, 1980). Furthermore, it has been shown that appropriateness of children's expectations are associated with accuracy of parental expectations (Day & Reznikoff, 1980). Of central importance, however, is a finding indicating that inappropriate expectations about therapy are related to premature termination from child treatment (Day & Reznikoff, 1980). This pattern of findings has prompted investigators to design preparation techniques that could counter inappropriate expectations and sustain or enhance children's participation in treatment.

A number of preparation techniques have been devised, including pretherapy preparation interviews during which the purpose, process, and roles of therapy are explained (Holmes & Urie, 1975), audiotape presentations in which a "radio announcer" and child interview a therapist about the structure, roles, and processes of therapy (Bonner & Everett, 1986), and videotape presentations in which child participants are interviewed about their experiences and/or simulated therapy process is modeled (Coleman & Kaplan, 1990; Weinstein, 1988).

One of the most consistent findings to emerge from studies of therapy preparation has been that prepared children and parents evince greater knowledge and understanding about the structure and process of therapy than their nonprepared counterparts (Bonner & Everett, 1986; Coleman & Kaplan, 1990; Day & Reznikoff, 1980; Weinstein, 1988). However, the impact of this increased knowledge and understanding on therapy process and outcome is less clear. Results are mixed with regard to preventing premature drop-out from therapy. For example, Holmes and Urie (1975) found that prepared clients were less likely to terminate therapy prematurely than nonprepared clients, whereas two other studies failed to demonstrate this effect (Day & Reznikoff, 1980; Weinstein, 1988). Day and Reznikoff did find that prepared families had fewer failed or cancelled appointments than nonprepared families. Thus, the impact of these preparatory interventions on maintaining participation in treatment has yet to be clearly established. In fairness, research in this area has been hampered by small, heterogeneous samples that may obscure preparatory effects. However, as Weinstein has noted, the modest impact of preparatory interventions may reflect the fact that most interventions have not been guided by conceptual models of treatment engagement.

Another aim of preparatory interventions has been to enhance children's active participation in therapy. Several studies have examined relations between therapy preparation and indices of treatment process. Unfortunately, the results have been disappointing. For example, Day and Reznikoff (1980) examined the relationship between preparation and child verbalization in therapy. Preparation consisted of videotaped modeling of children talking in therapy. Despite the close relation between the preparation technique and the measure of process, comparisons of verbal samples from three sessions failed to show an effect for preparation. In a related study, Weinstein (1988) examined the relation between preparation and children's ability to adapt to the client role. Adaptation to role was assessed by child and therapist questionnaires that tapped children's comfort with therapy and their communication with the therapist. Again the preparatory intervention involved children modeling active participation in treatment. There was also no effect for preparation on either the quality of the therapeutic relationship or the character of communication. In one of the only studies to examine preparation in relation to outcome, Coleman and Kaplan (1990) found that mothers in the prepared group reported a significantly greater decrease in problem behaviors by the fourth session than did nonprepared mothers. Unfortunately, no results were reported for post-treatment outcomes; consequently, it is not clear whether these short-term effects reflected transitory changes in perceptions or enduring, enhanced outcomes. Consistent with these findings, Bonner and Everett (1986) found that preparation increased parents' and children's expectations for positive treatment outcomes. Thus, it is possible that preparation influences parents' prognostic ex-

pectations which are reflected in more positive perceptions of their children's problems relative to pretreatment. Alternatively, changes in child and parent outcome expectations could have an immediate impact on child behavior problems that may or may not endure over the course of treatment. The fact that prepared children did not report greater behavioral improvement than nonprepared children favors the interpretation that preparation may influence maternal perceptions of child problems. Research in this area would be advanced by evaluating the durability of these effects, and by the assessment of change by sources who are blind to preparation condition.

In summary, despite consistent evidence showing that treatment preparation enhances parents' and children's understanding of therapy, evidence for the impact of improved understanding on therapy process is quite limited. It is possible that other therapist, child, and family characteristics exert a greater influence on treatment participation than general knowledge of and expectations for therapy. The goodness of fit between child and therapist or parent and therapist is likely to be a powerful determinant of treatment involvement and continuation; however, research on therapist–client matching in child treatment lags far behind the adult literature (cf. Beutler, 1991). In fairness, few studies have examined the relation between preparation and treatment process; consequently, it is probably premature to dismiss such interventions as ineffective. However, research on treatment preparation could be improved by a closer analysis of child and parent cognitions that interfere with treatment participation. Targeting specific "interfering" cognitions could prove to be more effective than interventions aimed at increasing general knowledge about the structure and process of therapy.

5.03.3.3 Process Issues in Readiness and Preparation for Therapy

Initiation of child therapy is complicated by the fact that children rarely seek psychological services on their own. Youngsters often enter therapy with considerable reluctance that is frequently associated with (i) negative perceptions of therapy, (ii) lack of problem acknowledgment, and (iii) lack of choice in the decision to seek help (Taylor et al., 1985). These findings suggest that children's cognitions about therapy and their own difficulties, as well as their control-related beliefs and help-seeking expectations, may impact their willingness to engage in treatment. Unfortunately, research on readiness and preparation for child therapy is marked by a number of major limitations.

First, and perhaps most striking, is the dearth of validated measures of child treatment participation. Before investigators can identify predictors of treatment involvement, conceptual and operational definitions of positive participation must be advanced and assessed. It should be noted that a few studies have produced promising leads. For example, research by Braswell et al. (1985) suggests that children's verbalizations in sessions can be used as markers of active involvement. Of course, given the fact that verbal activity in therapy varies with age (Lebo & Lebo, 1957), and that different forms of therapy rely on verbal interaction to varying degrees (Russell, Greenwald, & Shirk, 1991), a single index of verbal participation is not likely to be an adequate measure of involvement for different forms of treatment and for children at different developmental levels. In related research, Estrada, Russell, McGlinchey, and Hoffman (1994) developed an observational rating scale for identifying dimensions of participation in child therapy sessions. Factor analysis of ratings of child behavior produced three factors that the authors labeled therapeutic relationship, therapeutic work, and readiness. The therapeutic work factor was defined by high loadings on items assessing productivity, understanding, exploration of feelings, and engagement. Given that the work factor was derived from observations of psychodynamic therapy, it is not clear whether similar factors would emerge from ratings of other types of treatments, or if other indicators of active participation would be more relevant in other forms of child therapy.

Although these initial attempts to operationalize therapeutic participation appear promising, they raise two critical issues. The first is that the character of treatment participation is likely to vary across types of child therapies. Consequently, research in this area will benefit from decomposition of the stream of therapy process into specifiable tasks (Greenberg & Newman, 1996). Identification of therapy tasks and their component features will provide an anchor for operational definitions of active participation or therapeutic collaboration.

Second, treatment tasks are likely to vary according to children's developmental level (if therapists are gearing their interventions to children's capacities). Thus, a brand-name treatment, such as cognitive-behavioral therapy, may involve different tasks for children at different ages, or if it is developmentally sensitive the components of specific treatment tasks could vary developmentally, for example,

tasks such as self-instructional training might be simplified for younger children.

A second major limitation to research on readiness for therapy is that the conceptual and empirical focus has been restricted to the individual child. One of the distinctive features of child therapy is that it occurs in the context of ongoing relationships with other care-givers, typically parents. Research on parent management training, in which parents are the primary participants, has indicated that maternal depression and antisocial behavior predict initial resistance in therapy (Patterson & Chamberlain, 1994). Yet the contribution of parent or family factors to child treatment participation has been largely unexamined. In an exploratory study, Raney, Shirk, Sarlin, Kaplan, and During (1991) found that adolescent inpatients' perceptions of their parents' collaboration with the treatment team was associated with therapists' ratings of the individual treatment alliance later in treatment. Although preliminary, these results suggest that alliance formation in individual treatment may be influenced by the parents' relationship with the therapist, or at least by the child's or adolescent's perception of that relationship. Such potential effects are worth investigating, as they redirect attention to the broader social context of children's participation in treatment.

A final limitation is the virtual absence of studies of in-session transactions that could account for variation in child participation. Again, research on parent management training has revealed that pretreatment characteristics of parents account for initial levels of resistance, but that the nature of the transactions between parent and therapist predict changes in resistance (negative participation) over the course of treatment (Patterson & Chamberlain, 1994). Early 1970s child therapy research has shown that variation in therapist-offered levels of empathy, regard, and genuineness are associated with child verbal behavior in sessions (Siegel, 1972).

However, this type of research, linking therapist behavior with child involvement, has not developed up to 1997. Similarly, despite interest in child characteristics that predict participation in therapy, studies of therapist characteristics and their impact on child treatment participation are lacking. In the 1970s, Ricks (1974) demonstrated that child therapists trained in the same treatment orientation vary substantially in the way they relate to child patients, and that these differences are associated with differential treatment outcomes. Similarly, Alexander, Barton, Schiavo, and Parsons (1976) found that therapist relationship characteristics, such as warmth and humor, accounted for substantial variance (45%) in treatment outcome in functional family therapy. Despite these promising leads, research has remained focused on the evaluation of treatment packages while neglecting the therapist who delivers the treatments. Overall, then, research in this area should shift its focus from the individual child to encompass both child and therapist, and to the characteristics that define productive and unproductive therapeutic dyads.

5.03.4 IN-SESSION TRANSACTIONS IN CHILD THERAPY

A major focus of psychotherapy process research is on transactions that occur during face-to-face meetings between patient and therapist. Often these transactions are studied in their own right with the aim of discovering what actually comprises "therapy" of one type or another. Less frequently, aspects of transactions are measured and related to outcomes at the session or treatment level. Among the most salient aspects of child therapy transactions are interpersonal and symbolic exchanges between child and therapist. Both have been posited to contribute to variation in treatment outcome (cf. Shirk & Russell, 1996), and both have received some attention from child therapy investigators.

5.03.4.1 Interpersonal Transactions in Child Therapy

Child psychotherapy, regardless of treatment type, occurs in an interpersonal context. For some time, interpersonal processes have figured prominently in the adult psychotherapy literature, and reviews have indicated that characteristics of the relationship between patient and therapist are among the best process predictors of treatment outcome (Horvath & Luborsky, 1993). Although research on interpersonal processes in child psychotherapy is relatively limited, a review of child process reveals an enduring, but thin, line of inquiry on interpersonal processes in child treatment (cf. Russell & Shirk, in press). A review of this literature also indicates that interpersonal and relationship processes have been conceptualized in a number of ways.

Two basic models of the interpersonal processes in child treatment are prominent. The first conceptualizes relationship processes as a means to an end. The quality of the therapeutic relationship, and the transactions that contribute to relationship quality, are viewed as the foundation for the implementation of other (active) technical interventions. In essence, the relationship functions to promote or obstruct collaboration with treatment tasks that are posited as active change mechanisms. Interpersonal transactions that contribute to a positive relationship between child and therapist enable the child to work purposefully on resolving problems. This conceptualization is found in most models of the therapeutic alliance where a distinction is often made between the affective quality of the relationship and the quality of treatment collaboration (cf. Bordin, 1979; Horvath & Luborsky, 1993; Shirk & Saiz, 1992). Thus, despite substantial differences in the nature of treatment tasks, psychodynamic and cognitive-behavioral approaches appear to share this basic conceptualization of the therapeutic relationship. This conceptualization might be termed the indirect model of interpersonal process in child treatment. Although relationship processes are necessary for successful outcome, their influence on outcome is mediated through the child's active participation in treatment tasks. Relationship processes facilitate the operation of technical interventions, ranging from interpretation to practicing consequential thinking.

An alternative conceptualization views relationship processes as active change mechanisms. Thus, rather than positing an indirect relation between interpersonal processes and treatment effects, this perspective holds that interpersonal transactions have an unmediated impact on treatment outcome. This view might be termed the direct model of interpersonal process in child therapy, and takes its clearest form in treatments that emphasize "corrective relationship experiences."

Two child treatment approaches have emphasized the "corrective" nature of therapeutic transactions, but with somewhat different interpretations of the corrective process. The first can be found in client-centered models of child therapy. Here, the provision of a warm, accepting, and nonjudgmental relationship is viewed as a catalyst for self-propelled development (Axline, 1947). The second is found in psychodynamic, especially analytic, models that emphasize the role of transference in treatment process. A version of this perspective holds that children enter therapy with pathogenic beliefs that are "tested" in relation to the therapist (Gibbons & Foreman, 1990). Therapist actions in response to these interpersonal tests can either confirm or disconfirm the underlying pathogenic beliefs that prompt the behavior. The relationship serves a corrective function insofar as therapeutic transactions disconfirm pathogenic expectations. Although corrective processes are conceptualized differently in these two approaches, both assume that interpersonal processes are directly responsible for therapeutic change. It is interesting to note that in the adult literature, relationship processes have been shown to have a direct effect on treatment outcome even among treatments that emphasize technical operations, such as cognitive therapy (Burns & Nolen-Hoeksema, 1992). Thus, relationship processes might exert both direct and indirect effects on child outcomes, even among treatments that focus on collaboration with specific therapeutic tasks.

5.03.4.1.1 Research on interpersonal processes in child therapy

Although research on relationship processes is relatively limited, studies based, often implicitly, on either the direct or indirect model of interpersonal process can be found. One of the clearest examples of research based on the direct model comes from studies on the impact of variations in therapist-offered conditions of warmth, genuineness, and accurate empathy on treatment outcome. For example, Truax, Altman, Wright, and Mitchell (1973) compared the outcomes of a small sample of children described as mildly disturbed who received either relatively high or low levels of therapist-offered relationship conditions during treatment. Levels of therapist warmth, genuineness, and empathy were assessed during two sessions, and conditions were categorized by a median split. Outcomes, largely measures of adjustment, were assessed from multiple perspectives, including parent, therapist, and independent psychometrician. Regarding the impact of high or low levels of therapist conditions, the results were mixed. No group differences were found for psychometrist ratings; however, both therapist and parent ratings of overall change in adjustment showed significant effects for condition. Consistent with expectations, children who received high levels of therapist-offered conditions showed significantly greater benefits than their low-condition counterparts; in fact, children who received low levels of therapist-offered conditions showed deterioration on five times as many measures of specific outcomes as children receiving high levels. The authors interpreted these findings in a manner consistent with the direct model of interpersonal process, namely that relationship quality, or at least the type of relational response offered by the therapist, exerts a significant impact on treatment outcome. The study, however, was compromised in a number of ways. Children were not randomly assigned to therapists who were identified as high or low on the provision of warmth, genuineness, and regard prior to treatment. Consequently, differences in out-come might reflect unequal distributions of recalcitrant children across conditions. Furthermore, given that therapists were classified on the basis of their responses to treated children, difficult children might not have elicited high levels of therapist-offered warmth, genuineness, and empathy. Therapist-offered conditions, then, might be related to outcome, not because of children's differential responsiveness to variation in therapist-offered conditions but because children who are more or less difficult to change differentially elicit these conditions from therapists. Finally, it is important to note that interpersonal process is defined in terms of the behavior of only one of the interactants, that is, in terms of the type of therapist-offered relationship. The quality of the dyadic relationship as it develops between therapist and child, or even as it is experienced by the child, is not considered.

Many of these serious limitations are overcome in Kendall's (1994) randomized clinical trial for the treatment of anxiety disorders in children. As part of this manualized, cognitive-behavioral intervention, children's perceptions of the therapeutic relationship were assessed in order to examine possible relations with outcome. Items on the scale referred to children's feelings for the therapist and perceptions of the quality of their relationship with the therapist. In this controlled outcome study there was some, albeit limited, evidence for associations between perceived relationship quality and indices of treatment outcome. Approximately 30% of correlations between relationship quality and outcome were significant in the predicted direction; however, the majority of these involved shared source variance (child self-reports). The strongest pattern of results was between perceived relationship quality and child reports of changes in symptoms of anxiety and depression, with significant less improvement for those cases reporting poorer relationships than those reporting more positive relationships. Although the study did not provide strong evidence for the role of relationship factors, the tendency for most children to report positive relationships with their therapists may have limited variability and attenuated relationships with outcome.

Clearly, the study represents a significant advance over earlier work on relations between interpersonal process and outcome. Technical aspects of the treatment were controlled, children were randomly assigned to therapists who delivered the "same" treatment, and the quality of the relationship, rather than behaviors of one participant were assessed. With respect to interpersonal processes, however, the study is limited in several ways. The quality of the relationship was assessed from only one perspective which yielded limited variability, and relationship quality was assessed at only one point in time, at the end of treatment. Thus, it is possible that children's experience of symptom reduction could have contributed to their evaluation of the therapeutic relationship.

A study by Eltz et al. (1995) examined relationships among maltreatment experience, therapeutic relationship formation, and treatment outcome in a heterogeneous sample of psychiatrically hospitalized adolescents. Like the previous studies, this investigation is consistent with the direct model of interpersonal process; however, two advances are noteworthy. First, the quality of the therapeutic relationship was assessed from both therapists' and adolescents' perspectives; and, second, the relationship was measured at two points in time during the course of treatment. The latter enabled the investigators to examine patterns of relationship formation in a rudimentary manner. The study revealed that adolescents who showed more positive change in relationship quality, regardless of maltreatment status, evinced greater treatment gains across sources of outcome ratings relative to those showing less positive patterns of relationship development. These results suggest that changes in the pattern of relationship quality may be a better predictor of outcome than "one-shot" assessments. The more consistent pattern of associations between relationship quality and outcome in this study compared to Kendall's (1994) trial might reflect important differences in the types of children treated or in types of treatments delivered. In the latter study, patients were seriously disordered and showed marked variability in their capacity to form a therapeutic relationship. Furthermore, inpatient psychotherapy was not manualized, but instead focused on processing relationship issues. In this context, relationship quality may be the primary active ingredient of therapy, in contrast to treatments that rely on compliance with specific therapeutic tasks. Of course, the lack of control over the delivery of therapy raises the possibility that the association between relationship quality and outcome are confounded with unexamined technical differences across treatments.

In summary, these three studies provide relatively clear examples of existing research on interpersonal processes in child therapy based on the direct model. According to this perspective, the quality of the therapeutic relationship is assumed to have a direct bearing on variations in treatment outcome. Although progress can be detected across these studies, evidence for a direct relation between relationship quality and outcome in child treatment is rather limited.

Research on the indirect model of interpersonal process in child therapy is sparse. According to this perspective, relationship quality impacts outcome by promoting or obstructing treatment collaboration. Drawing on the work of Bordin (1979) and Luborsky (1976), Shirk and Saiz (1992) developed a measure of the therapeutic alliance for child therapy that distinguished between the affective quality of the relationship and collaboration with treatment tasks. Consistent with the indirect model, Shirk and Saiz hypothesized that a positive relationship between child and therapist would promote collaboration with therapy tasks. In a study with a diagnostically heterogeneous, hospitalized sample of 7–12 year old children who were seen in short-term dynamically oriented therapy, children and their therapists rated both dimensions of the working alliance. Reliabilities for both therapist and child ratings ranged from acceptable to excellent. Moreover, child and therapist perspectives on the affective quality of the relationship were moderately correlated. For both therapist and child reports, the affective quality of the relationship was positively associated with task collaboration, in this case, verbalization of feelings and problems. The results were consistent with the prediction that the affective quality of the relationship potentiates task collaboration. However, inferences of directionality are limited by the fact that the alliance was assessed at only one point in time; thus it is possible that children who establish a collaborative relationship feel positively about their relationship with their therapist, and are viewed by their therapist in a positive light. Confidence in the hypothesized relation between affective quality and task collaboration would be increased through the assessment of the alliance at multiple points in time, and by supplementing participant reports of task collaboration with independent observational ratings of involvement in specific therapeutic tasks. The major limitation of this study, however, was the absence of data on the relation between alliance and outcome; consequently, neither direct nor indirect effects could be assessed.

Along similar lines, Estrada et al. (1994) developed observational scales to assess dimensions of participation in child therapy. Factor analyses of 117 session segments revealed 3 therapist and 3 child factors. One of the child factors and one of the therapist factors concerned the quality of the therapeutic relationship. Items such as empathy, warmth, and positive relationship loaded on the therapist factor; and in a complementary manner items such as trust and openness loaded highly on the child relationship factor. There was significant covariation between independent ratings of child and therapist relationship quality. In addition, factors emerged for both child and therapist ratings that referred to involvement in the tasks of therapy, what Estrada et al. labeled therapeutic work. Again, child and therapist ratings were significantly correlated. Furthermore, in keeping with the indirect model, there was evidence to suggest that the quality of the relationship is associated with involvement in therapeutic work. Children with more positive relationships evinced higher levels of work than children who were rated as having less positive relationships. Moreover, ratings of technical lapses by the therapist, such as low responsiveness or inattentiveness, were negatively associated with the quality of the child's relationship with the therapist. These results suggest that relationship quality and task collaboration represent distinguishable aspects of the working alliance with children, and that they are associated in predictable ways. However, the directionality of this association remains ambiguous because process factors were assessed at the same point in time. In fact, the finding that therapist technical lapses are associated with the child's relationship factor is suggestive of an alternative account, namely that relationship quality is a function of the therapist's technical skill. For example, therapists who are adept at introducing treatment tasks and stimulating participation may be viewed quite positively by their child patients. Finally, like the Shirk and Saiz (1992) study, this investigation was aimed at scale development and not at evaluating process–outcome relations. As a result, the indirect model of interpersonal process has yet to be tested.

Other investigators have assessed aspects of the therapeutic relationship and/or involvement in treatment tasks. As mentioned, Braswell et al. (1985) have operationalized involvement in terms of child and therapist verbal behavior, but they did not examine this characteristic in connection with relationship quality. Smith-Acuna, Durlak, and Kaspar (1991) assessed both child and therapist experiences of therapy and found reliable dimensions corresponding to affective quality and interactive behavior; however, it was not clear that the latter dimension reflected therapeutic work. Moreover, no significant relations were found between therapist and child ratings of either dimension; however, associations within perspective were not reported. Finally, Patterson and his colleagues (Chamberlain, Patterson, Reid, Kavanagh, & Forgatch, 1984; Patterson & Chamberlain, 1994) have developed a microanalytic coding system to assess cooperative or resistant behavior by parents in parent management training. Although this line of research has yielded important findings on factors that influence resistance, and on the relation between resistance and outcome, as is discussed later in this chapter, quality of relationship is subsumed under resistant or cooperative behavior. As such, the parents' feelings about the therapist are not viewed as a separate component of the treatment relationship, although therapist behaviors that are often viewed as facilitators of relationship quality are examined separately.

In summary, research examining either the direct or indirect models of interpersonal process in child treatment is relatively sparse. One of the most glaring limitations in this area of investigation is the virtual absence of studies that have adequately assessed both process and outcome. Given the clinical emphasis on the importance of the therapeutic relationship for successful outcome across multiple types of treatments, research that addresses multiple dimensions of the relationship at multiple points in treatment, and relates these dimensions, not just with each other but with treatment outcome, is desperately needed.

5.03.4.2 Process Issues in Interpersonal Transactions

In addition to the virtual absence of research linking interpersonal processes with treatment outcome, a number of other limitations characterize this line of investigation. First, there has been a tendency to treat the therapeutic relationship as a static entity. Most studies evaluate the relationship at one point in time and fail to assess variations in relationship patterns over the course of treatment. There have been some noteworthy exceptions. For example, Siegel (1972) examined changes in child verbalizations as a function of high and low levels of therapist-offered conditions across multiple sessions of dynamically oriented therapy. But, like most studies in this area, relations with outcome were untested.

Second, almost no studies have conceptualized or assessed interpersonal processes as transactions consisting of linked sequences of exchanges between child and therapist. Instead, the focus has been on child or therapist experience of the relationship, an important aspect of interpersonal process, or on ratings of individual behavior. Interestingly, one of the earliest studies of child therapy process, conducted by Moustakas and Schalock (1955), examined contingencies, albeit in rudimentary way, between child and therapist behaviors. This approach to interpersonal process in child treatment remains underdeveloped.

Finally, child process investigators have largely failed to identify critical interpersonal change events or sequences that could be predictive of outcome. For example, sequences such as the "rupture and repair" of the therapeutic alliance (Safran & Muran, 1996, p. 447) or the resolution of therapeutic impasses (Diamond & Liddle, 1996) have been postulated as critical events that contribute to outcome. Close analyses of the interpersonal transactions that constitute these events could have important implications for the conduct of therapy.

5.03.4.2.1 Future directions for research

Programmatic research by Patterson and his colleagues on resistance in parent management training addresses many of the major limitations found in process studies of child-centered therapy, including the explication of a specific process model, the examination of interpersonal exchanges over multiple sessions, and the evaluation of process–outcome relations. Although this work focuses on parental resistance, and not on interactions between therapist and child, these studies constitute a research strategy that could be applied to interactional processes in child therapy. Among the many strengths found in this line of research are (i) the operationalization of a pivotal clinical construct, (ii) the development of a reliable coding system for tracking different types of resistant behavior in therapy, (iii) the systematic analysis of patterns of resistance over the course of therapy, (iv) the investigation of antecedents of resistance, including both client pretreatment characteristics and therapist actions, and (v) the analysis of the impact of resistance on treatment outcome. The approach also sets the stage for the study of therapeutic transactions, that is, patterns of interdependencies between therapist and client behavior over the course of treatment. Because this line of investigation goes beyond the scope of many studies of child therapy process, and could serve as a prototype for investigations in this area, this work will be reviewed in some detail.

As Patterson and Chamberlain (1994) note, resistance to change is a phenomenon acknowledged by virtually all the major therapeutic systems, yet relatively little empirical research has been conducted on this pivotal clinical problem. One difficulty has stemmed from the lack of a consensual definition of resistance and a corresponding method of operationalizing the concept. In many ways, resistance can be understood most simply as the inverse of the collaborative aspect of the therapeutic alliance. High levels of collaboration indicate that the client is working with the therapist on the specified tasks of therapy. Resistance, then, reflects the absence of this collaborative activity. This framework appears to be consistent with the conceptualization presented by Patterson and colleagues. Parent behavior in therapy is conceptualized as either cooperative or resistant. The former reflects a pattern of behavior that follows the direction set by the therapist, whereas the latter involves behavior that is oppositional, helpless, or tangential to the therapeutic task. Based on observations of treatment failures, five types of resistant responses were identified and reliably coded as part of the Client Resistance Coding System (Chamberlain et al., 1984). These included such behaviors as talking over or cutting off the therapist, expressing an unwillingness or an inability to follow the therapist's suggestions, challenging the therapist's qualifications, introducing new topics to shift the session away from the therapist's direction, and not tracking the therapist's verbalizations. Thus, unlike most of the previously reviewed studies, this approach to interpersonal process employed an observational system with well-defined behavioral markers. It is noteworthy that these markers of interpersonal process are most readily identified through parental language behavior. Given developmental differences in language use between children and adolescents, it is not clear if these markers would be as evident in child therapy.

Several studies have indicated that resistant behaviors in parent training sessions can be reliably coded (Chamberlain et al., 1984; Patterson & Forgatch, 1985), and that they cohere as a meaningful index of parental resistance. Correlational analyses suggest that there are two clusters of parental resistance, one characterized by challenging responses and the other by helpless responses, or what Patterson and Chamberlain (1994, p. 59) have dubbed, "I won't" or "I can't" patterns of resistance.

One advantage of conceptualizing resistance at the level of molecular events is that it allows for an analysis of patterns of resistance over the course of a session or across an entire treatment. It was hypothesized that a prototypical pattern of resistance would emerge in successful parent training cases (Chamberlain et al., 1984; Patterson & Forgatch, 1985). Resistance was expected to be low in the initial phase of treatment as the therapist attempts to build rapport and gather information about the presenting problem. Movement into the middle phase of treatment was expected to be marked by a rise in resistance as the therapist focused on parenting strategies and recommended changes in parenting behavior. During the final phase of treatment it was expected that resistance would decline as the therapist focused on consolidation of acquired skills. In essence, an explicit process model, labeled the "struggle hypothesis" (Patterson & Chamberlain, 1994), was formulated and tested.

Research by Chamberlain et al. (1984) confirmed this pattern, with parents showing the highest levels of resistance in the middle phase of treatment. Cases rated as more successful showed the expected decline in resistance between the middle and late phases of treatment. Parents who dropped out of treatment evinced higher levels of initial resistance to therapy than those that continued; however, among those completing therapy, initial levels of resistance were unrelated to ratings of treatment success. It should be noted that an important limitation of this study was the use of therapist ratings of success as the sole index of treatment outcome (although such ratings have subsequently been shown to be related to changes in child behavior). Nevertheless, the results of this study provide the foundation for two important hypotheses. First, the findings suggest that the pattern of resistance over the course of treatment may be a better predictor of treatment outcome than mean levels of resistance. Second, the results suggest that parental resistance is not exclusively the function of individual dispositional differences, but may be closely related to variations in therapist behavior. Both hypotheses represent significant departures from the type of questions typically addressed in studies of child therapy process. The former draws attention to patterns of change and the shape of trajectories over the course of treatment, and the latter underscores the importance of investigating process at the level of client–therapist exchanges where interpersonal interdependencies can be uncovered.

In an effort to understand the impact of therapist behavior on parent resistance, Patterson and Forgatch (1985) examined the covariation in therapist and client reaction sequences. They hypothesized that efforts to produce change would have an unintended "paradoxical" effect on clients by increasing levels of noncompliance. In the first study involving six therapist–client pairs, they predicted that therapist efforts to teach and confront would be associated with the greater conditional likelihood of resistant behavior compared to base rate levels. Conversely, therapist supportive and facilitative behaviors were expected to result in lower conditional probabilities of noncompliance relative to base rate levels. In order to evaluate covariation between therapist and client behavior, it was necessary to develop a therapist behavior coding system to complement the client codes. The Therapist Behavior Code includes seven mutually exclusive categories such as support, teach, and confront. Results indicated that in four of the six pairs, therapists' attempts to teach was associated with significantly higher than base rate levels of resistance, and in six of six pairs, confrontation, described as a "more intrusive effort to re-educate," were associated with higher levels than base rate. Supportive and facilitative therapist behaviors were consistently associated with lower than base rate probabilities of resistant behavior. As Patterson and Forgatch (1985) note, despite the fact that therapist behavior preceded the parent reaction, causality could not be inferred because of the possible operation of an unidentified third variable.

In order to address the causal issue, Patterson and Forgatch (1985) conducted an experimental manipulation of therapist behavior in a second study. Utilizing an ABAB design, they showed that systematic manipulation of therapist "teach" and "confront" behaviors resulted in corresponding changes in client resistant behavior. Increases in teaching and confronting were matched by increases in resistant behavior in B1 and B2, and a reduction of teaching and confronting in A2 produced a return to baseline in resistant behaviors. Taken together these results provide support for the hypothesis that variation in parental resistance is not merely a function of dispositional differences across parents, but is linked to what the therapist does during the session. This is not to say that pretreatment characteristics are unrelated to parental resistance. In fact, Patterson and Chamberlain (1994) report that stress, depression, and parental antisocial behavior contribute to initial levels of maternal resistance even after partialling out indices of social disadvantage. It is noteworthy that changes in level of resistance are not predicted by pretreatment characteristics, instead the pattern of resistance over the course of treatment appears to be determined by interactional processes in sessions.

Finally, evidence indicates that the pattern of resistance over the course of treatment is strongly predictive of outcome (Stoolmiller, Duncan, Bank, & Patterson, 1993). Patterson and Chamberlain (1994, p. 56) hypothesized that the prototypical pattern of resistance in successful cases follows and inverted V function, and have dubbed this pattern the "struggle hypothesis." Cases that show a rise in resistance during the instructional middle phase followed by a decline toward the baseline in the latter phase of treatment were expected to show positive outcomes. Utilizing growth curve analysis, Stoolmiller et al. showed that lack of negative curvature in resistance curves predicted child arrests over a 2 year period following treatment. In contrast, the more conventional approach to assessing process by measuring resistance early and late in treatment and then computing a change score failed to predict child treatment outcome. As Stoolmiller et al. (1993, p. 927) note, "what goes on in the therapy process appears to have better predictive validity than the assessed therapy endpoint or overall change from therapy initiation to therapy termination."

In summary, this line of process research provides a blueprint for future investigations of interpersonal processes in child therapy. Although such studies might examine other process dimensions, for example, patterns of emotion-regulating interactions, emulation of the programmatic character of research on parental resistance would increase the likelihood of useful results.

5.03.4.3 Symbolic Transactions in Child Psychotherapy

Much of what has been said about interpersonal transactions in child psychotherapy applies to symbolic transactions as well. In fact, strictly speaking, the symbolic character of communication processes *per se* suggests that interpersonal and other types of meaningful exchanges in child therapy are properly considered a subtype of symbolic transactions. Clearly, discourse, nonverbal gestures, and play are inherently symbolic, regardless of what their topical focus may be, and regardless of how they may differ in terms of their constitutive communication channel (e.g., verbal vs. nonverbal), their degree of rule-governedness, their type of referentiality (e.g., referring to actual vs. pretend worlds), and their degree of consequentiality (e.g., literal vs. play actions). In brief, child psychotherapy is a form of symbolic interaction, and to understand its processes and how they relate to outcomes, requires an understanding of what humans do most characteristically, namely communicate vis-à-vis symbolic exchange.

Although the above may seem painfully rudimentary, the field of psychotherapy research, child and adult alike, has, in the main, skirted the difficult tasks of studying symbolic processes during the therapeutic hour and of relating them to outcomes, often themselves different types of symbolic processes (e.g., social skills, academic performance, self-presentation,

etc.). This is odd indeed if it is true that symbolic construals of self, other, and the world significantly determine conduct, coalitions, and feelings. Who we are and how we adjust may boil down to what we communicate in our ongoing discourses with others. It should come as no surprise that our status as "*Homo symbolicus*" or "*Homo narrans*" exacts such a price, or, rather, confers such an awesome privilege. The history of research on child psychotherapy seems to have avoided dealing systematically with the consequences of this anthropological truism.

At a simpler level, the lack of a systematically developed research tradition on symbolic processes in child psychotherapy is no less surprising. Experiential, psychodynamic, and cognitive–behavioral theories of treatment each stress aspects of verbalization or symbolization (i.e., what is termed "discourse" in the more current idioms) as constitutive of curative processes. According to experiential theory, symbolizing warded-off prereflective experiences, helps to integrate the client's self, or alternatively, reintroduces the client to his or her experience and to the complete sphere of his or her phenomenal world. In early psychodynamic theory, fully and completely describing early trauma in affect-laden language was thought to serve a cathartic function, just as in later psychodynamic theory, redescribing one's autobiographical experience in action language is thought to promote self-transformation and empowerment. In cognitive theory, rescripting event expectations or transforming narrative schemas of important autobiographical episodes corrects faulty causal theories of the world and appraisals of self-worth and blame. Cognitive–behavioral approaches often focus on self-directed language in the form of self-instructions or verbal problem-solving strategies. As central as symbolic processes have been in the theories that have informed child therapy practice, empirical research on them has been peripheral and sporadic.

However, there have been isolated attempts to study symbolic processes in child psychotherapy. These attempts can be conveniently described as exemplifying two very different research paradigms. These can be dubbed the monological and the dialogical paradigms. Basically, the monological paradigm promotes research strategies that tend to excise the individual's or dyad's symbolic communication from the temporal parameters of discourse and situations in which they are embedded in order to characterize therapeutic communication in terms of its internal features. The dialogical paradigm promotes research strategies that tend to contextualize the individual's or dyad's symbolic communication in the temporal flow of discourse and situations in which they are embedded in order to characterize communication in terms of its relational features.

By noting whether a study focuses on an individual's or dyad's symbolic communication (i.e., its speaker scope), and whether it uses monological or dialogical research strategies, a 2 × 2 matrix describing four methods for studying symbolic processes in child psychotherapy is devised. Rudimentary examples of two of these four investigative strategies were contained in the very first study of the process of child therapy. In it, Landisberg and Snyder (1946) reported the frequencies of certain types of child and therapist speech acts. For example, 30% of the utterances in the sessions sampled were therapist nondirective statements. Here, the focus is on an individual, the therapist, and aspects of his discourse have been excerpted from the flow of conversation and tallied in relative isolation from the context in which it had been embedded. These authors also reported dependent relationships between aspects of therapist and client discourse. For example, they reported that therapist reflection of feelings were most often followed by client giving of information or taking some positive action. Here the focus is on the interactive dyad, and aspects of the therapist's and client's discourse are described in relation to each other. The same strategy was employed by Moustakas and Schalock (1955), but they described dependencies running from therapist to child discourse and from child to therapist discourse. The history of research in child and adult symbolic processes in therapy, however, has contained far more studies influenced by the former, monological strategy than the latter, dialogical strategy.

Note that the studies described above are exclusively focused on describing process and relations in it. They do not relate the frequencies of, or the extent of certain types of dependencies between, aspects of therapist or client discourse to outcomes. Truax et al. (1973) provide an example of the use of the monological approach to relate process to outcomes. They reported that children who received the highest levels of therapist-offered relationship conditions evidenced more improvement on a host of outcome measures than children receiving the lowest levels of therapist conditions. This study would seem to support the idea that there is a dose–response relationship between therapist conditions and child outcomes, although the findings are ambiguous insofar as the therapists' behavior could have resulted from variation in child responsiveness (see Russell (1994) for a discussion of this relationship).

The other two cells of the 4 × 4 matrix represent two kinds of hybrids of the monological and dialogical approach. For example, Truax and Wittmer (1973) tabulated the degree to which a certain type of therapist–client exchange occurred across sessions of child treatment, and related these frequencies to outcomes. Basically, the exchange that they tabulated consisted of pairs of child defense–therapist confrontation. The study is focused on aspects of the dyadic exchange (a feature common to the dialogical approach), but exchanges are excerpted from the temporal flow of interactive discourse, and their frequency related to outcomes (a feature common to the monological approach). Interestingly, the authors reported that those clients whose defenses were most often confronted achieved significantly better outcomes than those whose defenses were less often confronted.

In the 1980s and 1990s the other hybrid began to emerge in process studies. For example, Mook (1982a, 1982b) and Russell et al. (1996) applied methods (the P technique, a form of factor analysis applied to within-subject data matrices) that enabled them to describe the underlying structure of covariation of sets of variables used to rate either the therapist's or client's utterances. Here the focus is relational and contextual, as it describes how sets of utterance characteristics (e.g., degrees of information seeking, interpretation, confrontation, empathy) covary over the temporal course of sessions (a feature common to the dialogical approach). In these studies the context is restricted to the corpus of therapist or client utterances, not the interaction between both (a feature common to the monological approach). Together, these studies suggested that therapist participation in treatment discourse is structured around at least two underlying tasks—information seeking alternating with attentive listening, and the application of therapist techniques that help to sustain topical focus across utterances.

The studies reviewed above are minimal instantiations of the four types of process studies defined by crossing methodological strategy (monological vs. dialogical) and speaker scope (one or more dimensions). More sophisticated instantiations have begun to appear. For example, in Shirk and Russell (1996), a study by Estrada, Russell and colleagues is described in which the P technique is used to examine the underlying interactive structure of child therapist and client discourse. Here the focus is on context and relation as incorporated in the P technique, but now both child therapist and child client discourse are entered into the analyses, thus representing the first fully dialogical study undertaken in child therapy. The authors compared high- with low-quality child therapy sessions, and found that the high-quality sessions contained more P-technique factors that indicated systematic conversational exchange between therapist and client across at least two turns of talk than the low-quality sessions.

Obviously, there are other types of studies that can be conducted on symbolic processes in child therapy. For example, Russell et al. (1991) attempted to describe types of therapist discourse taken in their totality. Three types were sufficient to describe the bulk of treatment studies. Therapist discourse tended to be either conversational, instructional, or behavioral as in operant or counterconditioning treatments. The intent of this meta-analytic study was to relate these types of discourse on symbolic tasks such as reading, spelling, and verbal interaction. The authors reported that the effect size associated with conversational discourse was over 10 times as large as that associated with instructional discourse and over four times as large as that associated with behavioral discourse. In addition, there was a relatively strong dose–response relationship between the number of sessions of treatment and the effect size associated with language outcome variables.

The conclusions of Russell et al. (1991, p. 918) to their meta-analysis are worth repeating: (i) "A potentially rich and clinically significant area of child functioning has been only sporadically studied (i.e., only about 20 out of 105 outcome studies contained a language measure)"; (ii) "Ratings or categorization of the *in vivo* therapist and child language interaction are [nearly] uniformly missing"; and (iii) "This domain of functioning seems sensitive to the effects of child treatment, providing an additional, nonreactive dimension for the assessment of outcome." As we have seen, since 1991, there have been both calls for more child process research (Kazdin, 1995) and several attempts to devise and apply dialogically oriented research strategies (e.g., Russell et al., 1996). The field is ripe to more fully plumb the complexities of symbolic interaction in child treatments.

5.03.4.3.1 Future directions for research

Several directions for future research seem worth pursuing. One is suggested by trends in the child process literature itself, and is reinforced by similar but earlier achieved advances in the adult process research. Over the course research since the 1940s, there has been a trend, in child and in adult process research, away from disproportionate reliance on monological research strategies and toward the development of more dialogical research strategies. These developments should continue as we better understand the bi- or multi-directional causality underlying the patterning of human interaction. As suggested in Section 5.03.4.2.1 in interpersonal processes, changes in the patternings of child and therapist discourse may be the best process predictors of treatment progress and outcomes. Second, there has been a dearth of process and outcome measures cut from the same conceptual cloth. Symbolic processes, evident everywhere in human interaction, can provide a rich resource for defining process and outcome variables that share considerable family resemblances. For example, despite the importance of language competence in skillful social behavior, problem-solving, and self-regulation, few studies measure language change, such as pragmatic competence, as an outcome of child treatment. Third, when the symbolic character of child therapy is taken seriously, its study will require familiarization not only with advanced quantitative and qualitative techniques of data analysis, but with theories of discourse and language analysis that have been developed in other disciplines. Thus, we recommend cross-disciplinary training for process researchers. Finally, following developments in the adult process literature, we recommend intensive study of sets of change episodes rather than random samples or whole therapy sessions. Such a focus may enable us to draw a finer bead on the mechanisms responsible for therapeutic change.

5.03.5 THERAPEUTIC TRANSACTIONS AND TREATMENT OUTCOMES

As Orlinsky et al. (1994, p. 270) have observed, the investigation of process–outcome relations is guided by the core question "What is effectively therapeutic about psychotherapy?" Given the relevance of this question for the practice of psychotherapy, one would assume that the investigation of process–outcome relations would represent one of the most prominent strategies among psychotherapy researchers. In fact, in the adult psychotherapy literature there has been rapid growth in this approach to treatment research. In their review of the process–outcome literature, Orlinsky and colleagues uncovered over 2300 findings, with more than half of them appearing since 1985. Studies of the therapeutic relationship alone accounted for nearly 1000 findings. Most importantly, process–outcome investigations have yielded promising results; Orlinsky et al. identified 11 robust process–outcome links, including global therapeutic bond, patient cooperation vs. resistance, and patient expressiveness.

In stark contrast to the adult literature, remarkably few studies of child psychotherapy have examined process–outcome relations. The magnitude of discrepancy cannot be overstated. In their review of 223 child treatment studies, Kazdin et al. (1990) identified only 6 that examined treatment process in relation to outcome! Our own review (Russell & Shirk, in press) revealed some growth in process–outcome research during the 1990s, but even a doubling of the number of studies represents a small effort in absolute terms. Not surprisingly, then, "robust" findings, or, for that matter, replicated findings, remain elusive.

How is the paucity of research on process–outcome relations in child psychotherapy to be accounted for? Surely child clinicians and researchers are no less interested than their adult counterparts in what is "effectively therapeutic." One clue to this remarkable gap can be found in what has been done by child therapy researchers. As Kazdin (1994, p. 577) has noted, much of child therapy research has utilized either a "treatment package strategy" or a "dismantling strategy." In the former, effects of whole treatments are evaluated, and in the latter, treatments are dissected and components are varied across groups. Common to both of these strategies is the assumption that broad technical procedures, for example, social skills training or problem-solving training, constitute the "effectively therapeutic" components of treatment. Thus, by examining the presence or absence of these components in relation to outcome, either by use of a control or dismantling comparison, one attains some perspective on treatment process, at least at a molar level. Although this is a reasonable starting point, the limitations of this perspective are worth mentioning.

First, even if we assume that the active ingredients of therapy are technical procedures—be they problem-solving training or mutual story-telling exchanges—such procedures can be instantiated in treatment in a variety of ways. For example, problem-solving training typically involves some combination of didactic, modeling, and role play activities with varying degrees of emphasis on hypothetical or "live" situations. Moreover, research has shown that the "same" treatment procedure or component delivered in alternative ways can have a differential effect on treatment outcome. For example, Schleser, Meyers, and Cohen (1981) varied the manner in which self-instructional training was presented to children with self-control problems.

In the traditional condition, the therapist provided the child with direct examples of self-instructions, such as, "What is it that I need to do"; in the directed-discovery condition, children were induced to discover basic self-instructions through dialogue with the therapist. For example, the therapist might ask "What is the first thing you need to ask yourself when you start a task?" Variation in this dimension of process, in this case discourse patterns, resulted in differences in skill generalization among more mature children. Although all treated children received the same treatment component, self-instructional training, the manner in which it was presented had an impact on outcome.

Alternatively, other investigators have found that variation in presentation of specific treatment procedures do not produce differential outcomes. Instead, what matters is the quality of the child's involvement with the treatment procedure, regardless of how it is presented. For example, Milos and Reiss (1982) assigned children who evinced high levels of separation anxiety to one of three thematic play conditions: free play, directed play, and modeled play. All three conditions produced comparable reductions in anxiety despite substantial variation in the nature of play interactions, that is, despite differences in the instantiation of thematic play as a treatment technique. However, variation in outcome was related to quality of treated children's play. Children who benefitted most displayed high levels of mastery of oriented play, regardless of technical variations in play interventions. Thus, what was "effectively therapeutic" could not be attributed to specific play techniques but to variations in children's play activity.

The focus on treatment packages or dismantled components of whole therapies restricts the search for effective ingredients of therapy in a second way. As mentioned, these approaches share the assumption that technical procedures are primarily responsible for therapeutic change. At one level of analysis, such an assumption seems to be warranted. Meta-analytic findings suggest that behavioral treatments produce larger treatment effects than nonbehavioral treatments (Weisz et al., 1995), and most certainly these two broad classes of treatment entail substantially different types of technical interventions. However, comparisons of treatments at a more molecular level, for example, comparisons of different types of behavioral treatments such as parent training vs. cognitive-behavioral treatments, do not reveal differential treatment effects. Thus, despite important differences in treatment techniques across subtypes of child behavior therapy, variations in treatment effectiveness are not clearly evident. Such equivalence raises the possibility that other processes which are common across technically diverse treatments could have a significant impact on treatment outcome.

Research on treatment of adult depression is an interesting case in point. Here the central focus has been on comparisons of treatment packages, for example, cognitive-behavioral vs. interpersonal therapy. Despite important differences in component techniques, several treatments appear to be equally effective (Robinson, Berman, & Neimeyer, 1990). Moreover, emerging evidence suggests that other processes, aside from technical procedures, contribute to recovery from depression. For example, analyses of outcomes for depressed adults treated with cognitive-behavioral methods have revealed that therapeutic empathy has a moderate to large effect on recovery, even after controlling for initial level of depression and technical factors (Burns & Nolen-Hoeksema, 1992). Our point is not that relationship processes are the active ingredient of psychotherapy, but rather that such processes are often overlooked when researchers narrowly focus on the evaluation or comparison of treatment packages. As this example suggests, important change processes can be detected by an analysis of process–outcome relations within a well-defined form of therapy. Our understanding of "what is effectively therapeutic" in child therapy will be advanced by broadening the scope of inquiry to include other, "nontechnical" dimensions of therapy process.

5.03.5.1 Promising Directions for Process–Outcome Research

Few studies have actually examined treatment processes in relation to various outcomes, at either the treatment or session level. The absence of findings makes it tempting to turn to the adult process–outcome literature for direction. As Kazdin (1995) has noted, one virtue of such an approach is that continuities and discontinuities between adult and child therapy could be investigated. Alternatively, one could adopt a developmental perspective and consider some of the features of child therapy that represent unique challenges for practicing child clinicians. Thus, analogous to the change events paradigm of process research (Greenberg, 1991), in which predefined change events are examined as an alternative to sampling the full flow of events during sessions, aspects of therapy could be selected because of their developmental significance in child treatment.

One of the most developmentally salient, and at times most problematic, aspects of child therapy process involves the referral process. Children rarely refer themselves for treatment, and often do not acknowledge stress or distress. Consequently, it is likely that children and adolescents will vary considerably in their interest in and motivation for treatment. Variation in motivation could have direct effects on treatment outcome, or could influence outcome indirectly by affecting collaboration with treatment tasks. In one of the few studies of process–outcome relations in child therapy, Braswell et al. (1985) found that verbal markers of active involvement in treatment were predictive of gains in cognitive-behavioral therapy. Thus, one area that merits further investigation is the relation between treatment collaboration/resistance and treatment outcome with children.

Although treatment collaboration/resistance may be related to various child pretreatment characteristics, it is also likely that patterns of therapist–child interaction contribute to treatment involvement. One area that has been ignored by researchers involves the establishment of treatment goals with child patients. Such goals are often defined by parents, teachers, or others who are affected by the child's difficulties. But to the degree that the child is to be an active participant in treatment, a shared definition of a problem (or situation to be changed) may be critical for treatment involvement. The early exchanges that contribute to the definition of goals for therapy represent a developmentally critical aspect of child therapy process, and a therapy event that is likely to vary substantially across children at different developmental levels. Language processes are likely to be pivotal in this aspect of therapy. For example, discrepancies between child and therapist narratives about presenting problems could influence the development of a collaborative treatment relationship.

A related issue involves the role of parents in child therapy. The dependency of children on adult care-givers carries a number of important implications for process–outcome research. First, parents make decisions about initiation and continuation in treatment. There are few consistent findings on factors affecting attrition from child therapy (Armbruster & Kazdin, 1994), but research indicates that a substantial portion of parents elect not to continue after an initial evaluation (Weisz, Weiss, & Langmeyer, 1987). One possibility is that continuation in child therapy may be predicted from the strength of alliance the therapist forms, not just with the child, but with the parents as well.

If this is the case, collateral parent consultation that keeps the parents informed and involved may be critical for effective child treatment. Relatively little is known about the type of parental involvement that could facilitate child treatment.

A second issue involves the role of ongoing parent–child interactions in relation to in-session interactions. For example, therapists may attempt to facilitate emotion expression in the context of therapy, only to have such efforts counteracted by sanctions against expressive behavior in the family. From a treatment perspective, collateral work with the family would be clearly indicated. From a process perspective, the link between in-session processes and treatment outcomes is likely to be moderated by parental acceptance and support of therapeutic activities. It is possible that treatment acceptability (Kazdin, French, & Sherick, 1981) will exert a significant influence on the strength of process–outcome relations. Similarly, variation in parental participation in programs aimed at generalization of in-session activities will undoubtedly influence process–outcome relations. Thus, the study of process–outcome relations in child therapy will need to be contextualized in order to account for the impact of facilitative or corrosive parent–child interactions.

In summary, process–outcome relations in child therapy remains a relatively uncharted area. Although various aspects of process have been investigated in child therapy (cf. Shirk & Russell, 1996), remarkably few studies have related these processes to treatment outcomes. Consequently, this area of investigation has yet to find a meaningful starting point. It is our recommendation that investigators consider developmentally salient process issues, such as interactions aimed at defining mutual treatment goals, as they begin to examine process–outcome relations.

5.03.6 CONCLUSIONS

A review of child therapy process research reveals some promising leads but many substantial gaps in the existing literature. Most striking is the dearth of research linking treatment processes with treatment outcomes. Linkages among referral processes, treatment preparations, treatment transactions, and outcomes are virtually unexplored. Although one might expect such studies to be the centerpiece of process research, their absence undermines our ability to answer the core question: "What is effectively therapeutic about child psychotherapy?" It is the contention that progress in the field hinges on a shift in research focus to an examination of therapeutic processes in relation to treatment outcomes. In order for such a shift to be fruitful, however, a number of changes must occur in the conduct of child process research.

First, the notion of therapy process implies a temporal dimension. Static operationalizations of process fail to capture the flow of therapy. "One-shot" assessments of critical processes, such as the therapeutic alliance, are not as likely to contribute to our understanding treatment process as patterns of processes across sessions or whole treatments. Furthermore, the investigation of transactions, that is, sequences of exchange that occur over time, should complement detailed characterizations of process. Such research holds promise for identifying specific patterns of interaction that constitute broad constructs such as the alliance or treatment involvement. Furthermore, the identification of such patterns could provide useful information to practicing child clinicians.

Second, process research itself has had a restricted focus. Most studies have examined the activities of one individual in isolation. Child process research must redirect attention to therapeutic exchanges and contingencies between child and therapist behavior. Ironically, few studies have examined interaction *per se*, the hallmark of therapeutic process. Instead, frequencies of individual behavior are typically tabulated without reference to dependencies between behaviors. Alternatively, few efforts have been made to examine process at the level of the dyad. Just as a secure attachment describes a type of relationship, shifting the unit of analysis to the dyad could reveal process characteristics that are not captured at the individual level. Finally, relatively little attention has been directed toward the broader social context in which child therapy process is embedded. For example, the contribution of parents and peers to children's involvement in therapy is relatively unexplored.

Finally, most child process research has been descriptive in nature, and atheoretical in focus. Part of the problem stems from the fact that child process research has evolved in isolation from the field of developmental psychopathology (Shirk & Russell, 1996). Treatment processes attain relevance to the degree to which they are specifically related to pathogenic processes. Thus, child process research cannot be dissociated from investigations of pathogenic mechanisms that contribute to child dysfunction. Understanding of pathogenic mechanisms will guide the search for change processes in child psychotherapy.

5.03.7 REFERENCES

Achenbach, T. M., & Edelbrock, C. S. (1981). Behavior problems and competencies reported by parents of normal and disturbed children aged 4 through 16. *Monographs of Society for Research in Child Development, 46* (1, No. 188).

Achenbach, T., McConaughy, S., & Howell, C. (1987). Child/Adolescent behavioral and emotional problems: implications of cross-informant correlations for situational specificity. *Psychological Bulletin, 101,* 213–232.

Alexander, J., Barton, C., Schiavo, R., & Parsons, B. (1976). Systems–behavioral intervention with families of delinquents: therapist characteristics, family behavior, and outcome. *Journal of Consulting and Clinical Psychology, 44,* 656–664.

Armbruster, P., & Kazdin, A. (1994). Attrition in child psychotherapy. In T. Ollendick & R. Prinz (Eds.), *Advances in clinical child psychology* (Vol. 16, pp. 81–108). New York: Plenum.

Axline, V. (1947). *Play therapy.* New York: Ballantine.

Beutler, L. (1991). Have all won and must all have prizes? Revisiting Luborsky et al.'s verdict. *Journal of Consulting and Clinical Psychology, 59,* 226–232.

Bonner, B., & Everett, F. (1982). Influence of client preparation and therapist expectations on children's attitudes and expectations of psychotherapy. *Journal of Clinical Child Psychology, 11,* 202–208.

Bordin, E. S. (1979). The generalizability of the psychoanalytic concept of working alliance. *Psychotherapy: Theory, Research, and Practice, 16,* 252–260.

Bowlby, J. *A secure base: parent–child attachment and healthy human development.* New York: Basic Books.

Braswell, L., Kendall, P., Braith, J., Carey, M., & Vye, C. (1985). "Involvement" in cognitive-behavioral therapy with children: Process and its relationship to outcome. *Cognitive Therapy and Research, 9,* 611–630.

Bugental, D., Whalen, C., & Henker, B. (1977). Cognitive attributions of hyperactive children and motivational assumptions of two behavior change approaches: evidence for an interactionist position. *Child Development, 48,* 874–884.

Burns, D., & Nolen-Hoeksema, S. (1992). Therapeutic empathy and recovery from depression in cognitive-behavioral therapy: a structural equation model. *Journal of Consulting and Clinical Psychology, 60,* 441–449.

Chamberlain, P., Patterson, G., Reid, J., Kavanagh, K., & Forgatch, M. (1984). Observation of client resistance. *Behavior Therapy, 15,* 144–155.

Coie, J., & Pennington, B. (1976). Children's perception of deviance and disorder. *Child Development, 47,* 407–413.

Coleman, D., & Kaplan, M. (1990). Effects of pretherapy videotape preparation on child therapy outcomes. *Professional Psychology: Research and Practice, 21,* 199–203.

Colson, D., Cornsweet, C., Murphy, T., O'Malley, F., Hyland, P., McParland, M., & Coyne, L. (1991). Perceived treatment difficulty and therapeutic alliance on an adolescent psychiatric hospital unit. *American Journal of Orthopsychiatry, 61,* 221–229.

Day, L., & Reznikoff, M. (1980). Preparation of children and parents for treatment at a children's psychiatric clinic through videotaped modeling. *Journal of Consulting and Clinical Psychology, 48,* 303–304.

Diamond, G., & Liddle, H. (1996). Resolving a therapeutic impasse between parents and adolescents in multidimensional family therapy. *Journal of Consulting and Clinical Psychology, 64,* 481–488.

Dozier, M., Cue, K., & Barnett, L. (1994). Clinicians as caregivers: role of attachment organization in treatment. *Journal of Consulting and Clinical Psychology, 62,* 793–800.

Drabman, R., Tarnowski, K., & Kelly, P. (1987). Are younger children disproportionately referred for childhood academic and behavior problems? *Journal of Consulting and Clinical Psychology, 55,* 907–909.

Eltz, M., Shirk, S., & Sarlin, N. (1995). Alliance formation and treatment outcome among maltreated adolescents. *Child Abuse and Neglect, 19,* 419–431.

Estrada, A., Russell, R., McGlinchey, K., & Hoffman, L. (1994, October). *The development of child and child therapist psychotherapy scales.* Poster presented at Kansas Conference on Clinical Child Psychology, Lawrence, Kansas.

Fonagy, P., Leigh, T., Steele, M., Kennedy, R., Mattoon, G., Target, M., & Gerber, A. (1996). The relation of attachment status, psychiatric classification, and response to psychotherapy. *Journal of Consulting and Clinical Psychology, 64,* 22–31.

Frank, J. (1974). Therapeutic components of psychotherapy. *Journal of Nervous and Mental Disease, 159,* 325–342.

Freud, A. (1965). *Normality and pathology in childhood: Assessments of development.* New York: International Universities Press.

Frieswyk, S., Allen, J., Colson, D., Coyne, L., Gabbard, G., Horwitz, L., & Newsome, G. (1986). Therapeutic alliance: its place as a process and outcome variable in psychotherapy research. *Journal of Consulting and Clinical Psychology, 54,* 32–38.

Garber, J., Braatladt, N., & Weiss, B. (1995). Attach regulation in depressed and nondepressed children and young adolescents. *Development and Psychopathology, 7,* 93–115.

Garber, J., Braafledt, N., & Zeman, J. (1991). The regulation of sad affect: An information processing perspective. In J. Garber & K. Dodge (Eds.), *The development of emotion regulation and dysregulation* (pp. 208–242). New York: Cambridge University Press.

Gibbons, J., & Foreman, S. (1989, June). *Advances in child psychotherapy research using the Mt. Zion Psychotherapy Research Model.* Panel presented at meetings of Society for Psychotherapy Research, Wintergreen, VA.

Gomes-Schwartz, B. (1978). Effective ingredients in psychotherapy: Prediction of outcome from process variables. *Journal of Consulting and Clinical Psychology, 46,* 1023–1035.

Greenberg, L. (1991). Research in the process of change. *Psychotherapy Research, 1,* 14–24.

Greenberg, L., & Newman, F. (1996). An approach to psychotherapy change process research: introduction to the Special Section. *Journal of Consulting and Clinical Psychology, 64,* 435–438.

Harter, S. (1988). Developmental and dynamic changes in the nature of the self-concept: implications for child psychotherapy. In S. Shirk (Ed.), *Cognitive development and child psychotherapy* (pp. 119–160). New York: Plenum.

Holmes, D., & Urie, R. (1975). Effects of preparing children for psychotherapy. *Journal of Consulting and Clinical Psychology, 43,* 311–318.

Howard, K., Lueger, R., Mahling, M., Martinovich, Z. (1993). A phase model of psychotherapy outcome: causal mediation of change. *Journal of Consulting and Clinical Psychology, 61,* 678–685.

Horvath, A., & Luborsky, L. (1993). The role of the therapeutic alliance in psychotherapy. *Journal of Consulting and Clinical Psychology, 61,* 561–573.

Kazdin, A. (1994). Psychotherapy for children and adolescents. In A. Bergin & S. Garfield (Eds.), *Handbook of psychotherapy and behavior change* (pp. 543–596). New York: Wiley.

Kazdin, A. (1995). Bridging child, adolescent, and adult psychotherapy: directions for research. *Psychotherapy Research, 5,* 258–277.

Kazdin, A. E., Bass, D., Ayers, W. A., & Rodgers, A.

(1990). Empirical and clinical focus of child and adolescent psychotherapy research. *Journal of Consulting and Clinical Psychology, 58*(6), 729–740.

Kazdin, A., French, N., & Sherick, R. (1981). Acceptability of alternative treatments for children: evaluations by inpatient children, parents, and staff. *Journal of Consulting and Clinical Psychology, 49*, 900–907.

Kazdin, A., French, N., & Unis, A. (1983). Child, mother, father evaluations of depression in psychiatric inpatient children. *Journal of Abnormal Child Psychology, 11*, 167–180.

Kendall, P. (1994). Treating anxiety disorders in children: results of a randomized clinical trial. *Journal of Consulting and Clinical Psychology, 62*, 100–110.

Kirtner, W., & Cartwright, D. (1958). Success and failure in client-centered therapy as a function of initial in-therapy behavior. *Journal of Consulting Psychology, 22*, 267–281.

Kobak, R., & Sceery, A. (1988). Attachment in late adolescence: working models, affect regulation, and representations of self and other. *Child Development, 59*, 135–146.

Lambert, M., Weisz, J., & Knight, F. (1989). Over- and undercontrolled clinic referral problems of Jamaican and American children and adolescents: The cultural general and the culture specific. *Journal of Consulting and Clinical Psychology, 57*, 467–472.

Lambert, M., Weisz, J., Knight, F., Desrosiers, M., Overly, K., & Thesiger, C. (1992). Jamaican and American perspectives on child psychopathology: further explorations of the threshold model. *Journal of Consulting and Clinical Psychology, 60*, 146–149.

Landisberg, S., & Snyder, W. U. (1946). Non-directive play therapy. *Journal of Clinical Psychology, 2*, 203–213.

Leahy, R., & Huard, C. (1976). Role-taking and self-image disparity. *Developmental Psychology, 12*, 504–508.

Lebo, D., & Lebo, E. (1957). Aggression and age in relation to verbal expression in nondirective play therapy. *Psychological Monographs: General and Applied, 71*(20), 1–12.

Luborsky, L. (1976). Helping alliances in psychotherapy. In J. Cleghorn (Ed.), *Successful psychotherapy* (pp. 92–116). New York: Bruner/Mazel.

Main, M., Kaplan, N., & Cassidy, J. (1985). Security in infancy, childhood, and adulthood: A move to the level of representation. In I. Bretherton & E. Waters (Eds.), Growing points of attachment and research. *Monographs of the Society for Research in Child Development, 50*, (1–2, Serial No. 209).

Masten, A., & Braswell, L. (in press). Developmental psychopathology: An integrative framework for understanding behavior problems in children and adolescents. In P. Martin (Ed.), *Handbook of behavior therapy and psychological science: An integrative approach*. New York: Pergamon.

McDermott, P. (1996). A nationwide study of developmental and gender prevalence in psychopathology in childhood and adolescence. *Journal of Abnormal Child Psychology, 24*, 53–66.

Milos, M., & Reiss, S. (1982). Effects at three play conditions on separation anxiety in children. *Journal of Consulting and Clinical Psychology, 50*, 389–395.

Mook, B. (1982a). Analyses of therapist variables in a series of psychotherapy sessions with two child clients. *Journal of Clinical Psychology, 38*, 63–76.

Mook, B. (1982b). Analyses of client variables in a series of psychotherapy sessions with two child clients. *Journal of Clinical Psychology, 38*, 263–274.

Moustakas, C. E., & Schalock, H. D. (1955). An analysis of therapist–child interaction in play therapy. *Child Development, 26*(2), 143–157.

Nolen-Hoeksema, S. (1990). *Sex differences in depression.* Stanford, CA: Stanford University Press.

Ollendick, T., & King, N. (1994). Diagnosis, assessment, and treatment of internalizing problems in children: the role of longitudinal data. *Journal of Consulting and Clinical Psychology, 62*, 918–927.

Orlinsky, D., Grawe, K., & Parks, B. (1994). Process and outcome in psychotherapy—Noch einmal. In A. E. Bergin & S. L. Garfield (Eds.), *Handbook of psychotherapy and behavior change* (4th ed., pp. 477–502). New York: Guilford Press.

Orlinsky, D. E., & Howard, K. I. (1986). Process and outcome in psychotherapy. In S. L. Garfield & A. E. Bergin (Eds.), *Handbook of psychotherapy and behavior change* (pp. 311–381). New York: Wiley.

Patterson, G., & Chamberlain, P. (1994). A functional analysis of resistance during parent training therapy. *Clinical Psychology: Science and Practice, 1*, 53–70.

Patterson, G., & Forgatch, M. (1985). Therapist behavior as a determinant of client noncompliance: a paradox for the behavior modifier. *Journal of Consulting and Clinical Psychology, 53*, 846–851.

Prochaska, J., DiClemente, C., & Norcross, J. (1992). In search of how people change: applications to addictive behaviors. *American Psychologist, 47*, 1102–1114.

Raney, D., Shirk, S., Sarlin, N., Kaplan, D., & During, L. (1991, March). *Parent collaboration as a predictor of adolescent inpatient treatment process and progress.* Paper presented at meetings of the Society for Adolescent Medicine, Denver, CO.

Reid, J., Kavanagh, K., & Baldwin, D. (1987). Abusive parents' perceptions of child behavior problems: an example of parental bias. *Journal of Abnormal Child Psychology, 15*, 457–466.

Richters, J. (1992). Depressed mothers as informants about their children: a critical review of the evidence for distortion. *Psychological Bulletin, 112*, 485–499.

Rickard, K., Forehand, R., Wells, K., Greist, D., & McMahon, R. (1981). Factors in the referral of children for behavioral treatment: a comparison of mothers of clinic-referred deviant, clinic-referred nondeviant, and nonclinic children. *Behavior Research and Therapy, 19*, 201–205.

Ricks, D. (1974). Supershrink: Methods of a therapist judged successful on the basis of adult outcomes of adolescent patients. In D. Ricks, M. Rott, & A. Thomas (Eds.), *Life history research in psychopathology*, (Vol. 3, pp. 275–297). Minneapolis, MN: University of Minnesota Press.

Robinson, L., Berman, J., & Neimeyer, R. (1990). Psychotherapy for the treatment of depression: a comprehensive review of controlled outcome research. *Psychological Bulletin, 108*, 30–49.

Russell, R. (1994). *Empirical investigations of psychotherapeutic techniques: A critique of and prospects for language analysis.* Ann Arbor, MI: University Microfilms International.

Russell, R., Bryant, F., & Estrada, A. (1996). Confirmatory P-technique analyses of therapist discourse: High versus low quality child therapy sessions. *Journal of Consulting and Clinical Psychology, 64*, 1366–1377.

Russell, R. L., Greenwald, S., & Shirk, S. R. (1991). Language in child psychotherapy: a meta-analytic review. *Journal of Consulting and Clinical Psychology, 6*, 916–919.

Russell, R., & Shirk, S. (in press). Child psychotherapy process research. In T. Ollendick & R. Prinz (Eds.), *Advances in clinical child psychology* (Vol. 20). New York: Plenum.

Safran, J., & Muran, C. (1996). The resolution of ruptures in the therapeutic alliance. *Journal of Consulting and Clinical Psychology, 64*, 447–458.

Salzman, C., Luetgert, M., Roth, C., Creasant, J., & Howard, L. (1976). Formation of a therapeutic relationship: experiences during the initial phase of psychotherapy as predictors of treatment duration and outcome. *Journal of Consulting and Clinical Psychology, 44,* 546–555.

Schaughency, E., & Lahey, B. (1985). Mothers' and fathers' perception of child deviance: roles of child deviance, parental depression, and marital satisfaction. *Journal of Consulting and Clinical Psychology, 53,* 718–723

Schleser, R., Meyers, H., & Cohen, R. (1981). Generalization of self-instructions: effects of general versus specific content, active rehearsal, and cognitive level. *Child Development, 52,* 335–340.

Shirk, S. (Ed.) (1988). *Cognitive development and child psychotherapy,* New York: Plenum.

Shirk, S. (1990). Cognitive processes in child psychotherapy: where are the developmental limits? In J. Dewit, W. Slot, H. van Leeuwen, & M. Terwogt (Eds.), *Developmental psychopathology and clinical practice* (pp. 19–31). Amsterdam: Acco.

Shirk, S., & Russell, R. (1996). *Change processes in child psychotherapy: Revitalizing treatment and research.* New York: Guilford Press.

Shirk, S., & Saiz, C. (1992). Clinical, empirical, and developmental perspectives on the therapeutic relationship in child psychotherapy. *Development and Psychopathology, 4,* 713–728.

Shirk, S., Saiz, C., & Sarlin, N. (1993, June). *The therapeutic alliance in child and adolescent treatment: initial studies with inpatients.* Paper presented at meetings of the Society for Psychotherapy Research, Pittsburgh, PA.

Siegel, C. (1972). Changes in play therapy behavior over time as a function of differing levels of therapist-offered conditions. *Journal of Clinical Psychology, 28,* 235–236.

Sigelman, C., & Mansfield, K. (1992). Knowledge of and receptivity to psychological treatment in childhood and adolescence. *Journal of Clinical Child Psychology, 21,* 2–9.

Smith-Acuna, S., Durlak, J. A., & Kaspar, C. J. (1991). Development of child psychotherapy process measures. *Journal of Clinical Child Psychology, 20,* 126–131.

Stark, K., Rouse, L., & Livingston, R. (1991). Treatment of depression during childhood and adolescence: cognitive-behavioral procedures for the individual and the family. In P. Kendall (Ed.), *Child and adolescent therapy: Cognitive-behavioral procedures* (pp. 165–208). New York: Guilford Press.

Stoolmiller, M., Duncan, T., Bank, L., & Patterson, G. (1993). Some problems and solutions to the study of change: significant patterns in client resistance. *Journal of Consulting and Clinical Psychology, 61,* 920–928.

Strupp, H., & Hadley, S. (1977). A tripartite model of mental health and psychotherapy outcomes. *American Psychologist, 32,* 187–196.

Tarnowski, K., Anderson, D., Drabman, R., & Kelly, P. (1990). Disproportionate referrals for child academic/behavior problems: replication and extension. *Journal of Consulting and Clinical Psychology, 58,* 240–243.

Taylor, L., Adelman, H., & Kaser-Boyd, N. (1985). Exploring minors' reluctance and dissatisfaction with psychotherapy. *Professional Psychology: Research and Practice, 3,* 418–425.

Tharp, R. (1991). Cultural diversity and treatment of children. *Journal of Consulting and Clinical Psychology, 59,* 799–812.

Truax, C. B., Altman, H., Wright, L., & Mitchell, K. M. (1973). Effects of therapeutic conditions in child therapy. *Journal of Community Psychology, 1,* 313–318.

Truax, C. B., & Wittmer, J. (1973). The degree of therapist's focus on defense mechanisms and the effect on therapeutic outcome with institutionalized juvenile delinquents. *Journal of Community Psychology, 1,* 201–203.

Van Horn, M. (1996). *The relationship of interpersonal perceptions and depression to evaluations of supportive interactions and interpersonally-oriented coping strategies.* Unpublished doctoral dissertation, University of Denver, Denver, CO.

Vondra, J., Barnett, D., & Cicchetti, D. (1989). Perceived and actual competence among maltreated and comparison school children. *Development and Psychopathology, 1,* 237–255.

Walker, E., Bettes, B., & Ceci, S. (1984). Teachers' assumptions regarding the severity, causes, and outcomes of behavioral problems in preschoolers: implications for referral. *Journal of Consulting and Clinical Psychology, 52,* 899–902.

Webster-Stratton, C. (1988). Mothers' and fathers' perceptions of child deviance: role of parent and child behaviors and parent adjustment. *Journal of Consulting and Clinical Psychology, 56,* 909–915.

Weinstein, M. (1988). Preparation of children for psychotherapy through videotaped modeling. *Journal of Clinical Child Psychology, 17,* 131–136.

Weisz, J. (1986). Contingency and control beliefs as predictors of psychotherapy outcomes among children and adolescents. *Journal of Consulting and Clinical Psychology, 54,* 789–795.

Weisz, J., Suwanlert, S., Chaiyasit, W., Weiss, B., Walter, B., & Anderson, W. (1988). Thai and American perspectives on over- and undercontrolled child behavior problems: exploring the threshold model among parents, teachers, and psychologists. *Journal of Consulting and Clinical Psychology, 56,* 601–609.

Weisz, J., & Weiss, B. (1991). Studying the "referability" of child clinical problems. *Journal of Consulting and Clinical Psychology, 59,* 266–273.

Weisz, J., Weiss, B., Han, S., Granger, D., & Morton, T. (1995). Effects of psychotherapy with children and adolescents revisited: A meta-analysis of treatment outcome studies. *Psychological Bulletin, 117,* 450–468.

Weisz, J., Weiss, B., & Langmeyer, D. (1987). Giving up on child psychotherapy: who drops out? *Journal of Consulting and Clinical Psychology, 55,* 916–918.

Wisniewski, J., Andrews, T., & Mulick, J. (1995). Objective and subjective factors in the disproportionate referral of children for academic problems. *Journal of Consulting and Clinical Psychology, 63,* 1032–1036.

Zahn-Waxler, C. (1993). Warriors and worriers: gender and psychopathology. *Development and Psychopathology, 5,* 79–89.

Zimet, S., & Farley, G. (1986). Competence and self-esteem of emotionally-disturbed children beginning day treatment. *Journal of the American Academy of Child and Adolescent Psychiatry, 25,* 76–83.

5.04

Outcome Findings and Issues in Psychotherapy with Children and Adolescents

JOHN R. WEISZ

University of California, Los Angeles, CA, USA

5.04.1 INTRODUCTION

After decades of child treatment guided by psychology's grand theories and rarely subjected to rigorous test, we are moving into an era in which claims of success may have little credence in the absence of outcome research. The forces ushering in this new era are both scientific and fiscal. On the scientific front, both the American Psychological Association (APA) and the American Psychiatric Association are moving toward identification of research-based principles and practices for intervention with adults, adolescents, and children (see, e.g., Task Force, 1995). On the fiscal front, the advent of managed care has brought increased attention to the issue of outcomes, as companies seek to limit the cost of care. In the area of child and adolescent treatment, the body of relevant evidence is now growing fast, with more than 300 child and adolescent treatment outcome studies already published. This chapter summarizes some of the major findings of these studies, and then becomes critical, noting limitations of the available evidence and suggesting issues that will need attention in the future. Throughout the chapter, the term "children" is used to refer to the age period from early childhood through adolescence, except where it is necessary to draw a distinction between children and adolescents.

5.04.2 SOCIAL, DEVELOPMENTAL, AND CULTURAL CONTEXT OF CHILD ASSESSMENT AND THERAPY

Although clinical work with children bears obvious similarities to work with adults, some important differences warrant emphasis. First, because children rarely perceive themselves as "disturbed" or as candidates for therapy, most referrals for treatment, up until late adolescence, tend to be made by parents, teachers, or other adults. These adults may thus be construed as "clients" in the sense that they commission the therapy, pay for it, and identify some or all of the goals the therapist is to pursue. Children may or may not participate in identifying target problems or setting treatment goals, and even when they participate, the adult input may be weighted more heavily. With therapy commissioned by adults, and its goals heavily influenced by adults, it is understand-

able that children may enter the process with little motivation for treatment or personal change, or with different objectives than those shared by the adults involved.

Given marked developmental differences in the self-awareness, psychological mindedness, and expressive ability of their clientele, child therapists must rely heavily on adults for information about the youngsters they treat, and this can present problems of several types. First, parents' and teachers' reports may be inaccurate, based on distorted samples of child behavior, influenced by their own adult agendas, calculated to conceal their own failings as parents (including neglect or abuse), or even biased by their own pathologies (see e.g., Kazdin, 1989); and levels of agreement among different adult informants reporting on the same child tend to be low (Achenbach, McConaughy, & Howell, 1987). Bias and distortion aside, adult reports of child behavior and adult identification of referral concerns are both apt to reflect the values, practices, and social ideals of their cultural reference group (see Weisz, McCarty, Eastman, Chaiyasit, & Suwanlert, 1997; Weisz et al., 1988; Weisz & Weiss, 1991).

Finally, children tend to be captives of their externally engineered environments to a much greater extent than do adults; one consequence may be that the "pathology" the child therapist treats may reside as much in a disturbed environment from which the child cannot escape as in the child himself or herself. This may limit the impact of interventions involving the child as solo or primary participant, and it may argue for involvement of others from the child's social context, but such significant others are not always willing or cooperative. So, in a number of ways, the child therapist faces challenges that are rather different from those confronted by one who treats only adults.

5.04.3 PREVALENCE OF CHILD DYSFUNCTION AND CHILD TREATMENT

Notwithstanding the difficulties of child assessment and child treatment, both practices are widespread, in both clinical practice and research contexts. Systematic efforts at assessment in the general population suggest that large numbers of children suffer from significant levels of disturbance, at least as defined within the current taxonomic systems. Epidemiologic studies in the late 1980s (summarized by Costello, 1989) indicated that at least 17% of children in the general population met criteria for at least one diagnosis in the *Diagnostic and statistical manual of mental disorders, Third Edition* (*DSM-III*; American Psychiatric Association, 1980); preliminary findings point to higher prevalence rates for the most recent edition of the diagnostic manual (*DSM-IV*). Of course, these rates of formal diagnosis overlook the many children who have very significant problems that fall short of full diagnosability, but may well need help, nonetheless.

Each year, many troubled children receive intervention in the form of child psychotherapy, but precise figures on the extent and cost are difficult to find. Figures for the late 1980s indicated that about 2.5 million American children received treatment each year (Office of Technology Assessment, 1986), and that the annual cost was more than $1.5 billion (Institute of Medicine, 1989). These figures are apt to be underestimates, given the likelihood that much child treatment is either not formally labeled "psychotherapy" (e.g., counseling in school) or not formally reported to government agencies (e.g., private practice paid out of pocket). Of course, much has changed since the 1980s, with some forces (e.g., the rise of managed care, general reductions in duration of inpatient stays) discouraging growth, but other forces (e.g., increased public awareness, legislated entitlements for handicapped children) encouraging growth, so updated statistics on use and costs are clearly needed.

5.04.4 TYPES OF TREATMENT AND PROBLEMS TARGETED IN TREATMENT

The most common types of treatment used with children, and the most common child conditions addressed in treatment, are described in other chapters of this volume, but a few facts germane to outcome assessment warrant emphasis here. As Kazdin (1988) noted, there are more than 230 named psychotherapies, but most of these have not been subjected to controlled tests of outcome. In general, outcome research with children has focused on a distinct subset of the treatments that bears little apparent relation to frequency of use in clinical practice. Among the psychological interventions (i.e., excluding pharmacological therapies), psychodynamic and family therapies are among the most widely practiced by clinicians but among the least studied by outcome researchers. By contrast, behavioral and cognitive-behavioral interventions are emphasized in outcome research to a degree that far exceeds their use in clinical practice.

There is somewhat closer correspondence between practice patterns and the outcome research with respect to problems targeted in treatment, but the correspondence is less than perfect. Most of the types of child problems encompassed in Chapters 13–27, this volume, have been the focus of both clinical attention and some outcome research, although much of the research has addressed specific problems or clusters of problems rather than full-blown diagnostic categories; this may have been appropriate, given periodic changes in the taxonomy, but late 1990s trends incline toward formal diagnostic assessment of children in clinical trials. Of the diagnostic categories noted in this volume, the problems associated with conduct disorder (and oppositional defiant disorder), attention deficit hyperactivity disorder (ADHD), anxiety disorders (including particularly specific phobias), and possibly somatoform disorder (especially chronic headache) have been emphasized in clinical trials research, whereas other problems frequently treated by practitioners are less evident in clinical trials research.

5.04.5 WHO CARES ABOUT OUTCOMES OF CHILD TREATMENT?

Stakeholders with an interest in the outcome of child treatment are numerous. The treated child's need for help, not to mention his or her investment of time and energy in the process of treatment, arguably makes the child the major stakeholder. Add parents and other family members who seek relief for the child, and also frequently for the family. Teachers' interests, as well, may include both concern for the child and for the classroom of which the child is a part. Those who finance the child's treatment (e.g., family members, government agencies, insurance carriers) have a clear stake. And finally, the therapists, clinic staff, administrators, and others in the "provider" community have a clear interest in the outcomes of the care in which they invest their careers. All these parties to the process of treatment have a clear stake in the question, "How effective is child psychotherapy?"

5.04.6 APPROACHES TO ASSESSING TREATMENT EFFECTS

This question can be answered via several different methods, a few of which need to be noted here. The most widely recognized is the clinical trial, an outcome study in which the post-treatment adjustment of a group of children who received a candidate intervention is compared with that of one or more control groups who did not. It is these clinical trials studies that are most frequently pooled in reviews and meta-analyses (see below), and that thus constitute most of the evidence discussed in this chapter. However, in circumstances where all the children in a target group must receive an active treatment, multiple baseline designs, ABAB (sometimes called "reversal") designs, and simultaneous/alternating treatment designs are useful. Such approaches characterize much of the treatment research with ADHD youngsters (see, e.g., Pelham et al., 1993), for example, and they are frequently used in cases where an entire classroom is the target of an intervention (e.g., Wurtele & Drabman, 1984). These non-clinical trials designs can also be applied to cases (sometimes involving rare conditions) where only one or two children will be treated (e.g., McGrath, Dorsett, Calhoun, & Drabman, 1988; Tarnowski, Rosen, McGrath, & Drabman, 1987). These alternative outcome assessment designs have generated a rich body of data on treatment effects, data that await an enterprising reviewer. For now, though, the focus is on the clinical trials research, which has been reviewed rather thoroughly in the form of several meta-analyses, as described below.

5.04.7 POOLING OUTCOME STUDIES VIA META-ANALYSIS: METHODS AND ISSUES

Research findings on psychotherapy effects can be pooled via a technique called meta-analysis (see Mann, 1990; Smith, Glass, & Miller, 1980; but see also critiques, e.g., by Wilson, 1985). The building block of meta-analyses is the effect size (ES) statistic. The ES is an index of the size and direction of treatment effects. For typical clinical trials studies, ES is the difference between the post-treatment mean on an outcome measure for the treated group vs. the corresponding control group mean, with the difference divided by the SD of the outcome measure. Figure 1 is a guide to interpreting ES values. As the figure indicates, positive ES values indicate treatment benefit, and negative values indicate a harmful effect. Each ES value corresponds to a percentile standing of the average treated child on the outcome measure(s) if that child were placed in the control group after treatment; for example, an ES of 0.9 indicates that the average treated child scored better after treatment than 82% of the control

group. As an aid to interpretation, Cohen's (1992) guidelines suggest that an ES of 0.20 may be considered a "small" effect, 0.50 a "medium" effect, and 0.80 a "large" effect. By averaging across the outcome measures used, a meta-analyst may compute a single mean ES for each study (or each treatment group) in the collection being reviewed. This permits computation of an overall mean ES for the entire collection of studies; it also permits comparison of mean ES across studies differing in potentially important ways: for example, in the type of therapy employed, the target problem being treated, or the age or gender of the children involved.

Methods have been proposed for assessing the quality of studies considered for inclusion in meta-analyses (see, e.g., Chalmers et al., 1981), but most meta-analysts in the psychotherapy research area have aimed for rather broad, representative collections of outcome studies, accepting a range of methods, provided that certain basic standards of experimental design are satisfied. Weiss and Weisz (1990) carried out a meta-analysis to assess the extent to which methodological variations in child outcome studies might be associated with differences in ES. Findings indicated that nine commonly noted internal and external validity factors (e.g., whether subjects were randomly assigned to groups, whether subjects were analog cases or clinical cases who would have been treated independently of the study) together accounted for 7% of the variance in ES, over a sample of 105 outcome studies. They also found no evidence that inclusion of methodologically weaker studies in meta-analyses has led to overestimates of ES; on the contrary, increased experimental rigor in the studies they sampled was generally associated with *larger* ES. Thus, it is possible that the most inclusive meta-analyses may tend to underestimate the true effect of therapy, compared to meta-analyses that apply strict methodological criteria to candidate studies.

Meta-analysts must make myriad decisions as they carry out their work, and many of these decisions have an impact on the ultimate ES values that will emerge. For example, decisions must be made about whether to (i) compute ES by dividing the treatment–control group difference by standard deviation (SD) of the control group or of the pooled control plus treatment groups; (ii) compute an average ES across all outcome measures within a study or keep these separate for overall ES calculation; (iii) combine ES computation across various treatment conditions, compute separate ES values for each treatment group in a study, or use some amalgam of these two approaches; and (iv) weight all studies equally or adjust ES according

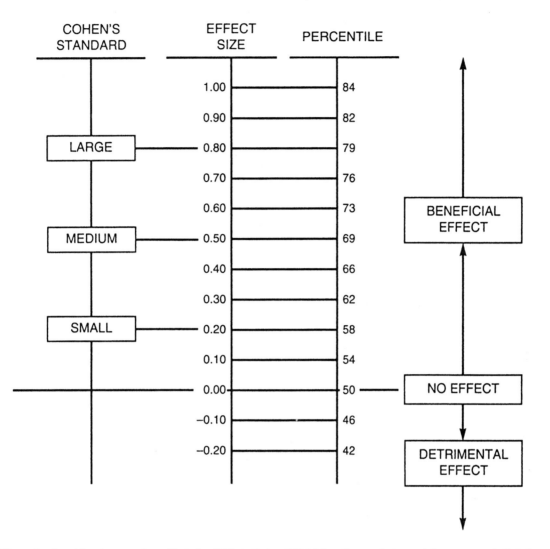

Figure 1 An aid to interpreting effect size (ES) statistics. ("Bridging the gap between laboratory and clinic in child and adolescent psychotherapy," by J. R. Weisz, G. R. Donenberg, S. S. Han, and B. Weiss, 1995, *Journal of Consulting and Clinical Psychology, 63,* pp. 688–701. Copyright 1995 by the American Psychological Association. Reprinted with permission.)

weight all studies equally or adjust ES according to sample size, ES variance, or some other leveling factor (for discussion of these and other decision-making issues, see Weisz & Weiss, 1993; Weisz, Weiss, Han, Granger, & Morton, 1995). Because scores of such decisions are made in any meta-analysis, it is essentially impossible that any two teams working independently will conduct their work in exactly the same way.

This fact, of course, highlights the need for caution in comparing findings across different meta-analyses, and thus in reading the results reported below. Differences in ES means across different meta-analyses may be influenced in part by differences in the ways the respective

meta-analysts compiled studies, pooled them, computed ES, or averaged ES within or across studies. To assist the reader in interpreting the meta-analytic findings reported below, the four issues noted in the preceding paragraph have been addressed in the following way: For each meta-analysis, only *exceptions* to the most common approach to each issue are noted. That is, unless otherwise noted, the meta-analysis being described involved the following modal procedures for child meta-analysis: (i) ES was calculated by dividing the treatment–control group difference by SD of the pooled control plus treatment groups; (ii) within each study, ES values are averaged across all outcome measures; (iii) within each study, separate ES means are maintained for each treatment vs. control group comparison; and (iv) ES values reported are unadjusted.

5.04.8 FINDINGS FROM META-ANALYSES

This section considers some of the findings of meta-analytic reviews, first covering overall effect sizes found in broad-based analyses, then noting findings of specially focused analyses, and finally identifying some heuristically useful findings on therapy, therapist, and child factors related to the magnitude of treatment effect.

5.04.8.1 Findings of Broad-based Meta-analyses

To date, there have been at least four broad-based child psychotherapy meta-analyses: that is, meta-analyses imposing minimal limits on treated problems or types of intervention to be included. In all, these four meta-analyses encompass more than 300 separate treatment outcome studies. In the earliest of these, Casey and Berman (1985) surveyed those outcome studies published between 1952 and 1983 that involved children aged 12 and younger. Mean ES was 0.71 for those studies that included treatment–control comparisons; in percentile terms, the average treated child scored better after treatment than 76% of control group children, averaging across outcome measures. In a second meta-analysis, Weisz, Weiss, Alicke, and Klotz (1987) reviewed outcome studies published between 1952 and 1983, with children aged 4–18. Mean ES (computed using control group SD) was 0.79; after treatment, the average treated child was at the 79th percentile of control group peers.

In a third broad-based meta-analysis, Kazdin, Bass, Ayers, and Rodgers (1990) included studies published between 1970 and 1988, with youngsters aged 4–18. Kazdin et al. included multiple types of studies, but for the subset that compared treatment groups and no-treatment control groups, mean ES was 0.88; the average treated child scored higher after treatment than 81% of the no-treatment comparison group. For studies comparing treatment groups to active control groups, mean ES was 0.77, indicating that the average treated child was functioning better, post-treatment, than 78% of the control group.

In the fourth broad-based meta-analysis, Weisz, Weiss, et al. (1995) included studies published between 1967 and 1993, involving children aged 2–18. ES values were calculated using control group SD (for rationale, see Weisz, Weiss, et al., p. 455), and using the conservative procedure of collapsing across treatment groups up to the level of analysis; for example, except for analyses comparing different types of therapy, ES values were averaged across treatment groups within a study. An overall mean ES of 0.71 indicated that, after treatment, the average treated child scored higher on the outcome measures than 76% of control group children. When ES values were weighted by the inverse of their variance, the overall ES mean dropped to 0.54. (For more detailed descriptions of the procedures and findings of these broad-based meta-analyses, see Weisz & Weiss, 1993.)

The findings of these four broad-based meta-analyses show rather consistent beneficial treatment effects; ES values ranged from 0.71 to 0.84 (0.84 is an estimated overall mean for the treatment–control comparison studies in Kazdin et al., 1990), near Cohen's (1988) "large effect" index of 0.80. (Note, though, that the Weisz, Weiss, et al. (1995) finding noted in the preceding paragraph suggest that true population ES means, adjusting for heterogeneity of variance, may be closer to "medium" effects.) For comparative purposes, Figure 2 shows findings of the four child meta-analyses together with findings of two of frequently cited meta-analyses with older groups, that is, Smith and Glass's (1977) meta-analysis of primarily adult psychotherapy outcome studies, and Shapiro and Shapiro's (1982) meta-analysis of exclusively adult outcome studies. As the figure indicates, effects found in the child meta-analyses fall roughly within the range of effects found in these two adult meta-analyses.

5.04.8.2 Findings of Specially Focused Meta-analyses

Beyond the findings of these broad-based meta-analyses, there is a good deal to be learned from focused meta-analyses addressing rather specific questions about child treatment effects. Three such projects have dealt with cognitive-behavioral therapy in particular. For example, Baer and Nietzel (1991), reviewing 36 outcome studies, found quite positive treatment effects for cognitive and/or cognitive-behavioral treatments addressing child impulsivity. Mean ES was 0.90, calculated with control group ES, pooling only across similar outcome measures, and without weighting; the mean dropped to 0.77 when ES was weighted by study sample size. Dush, Hirt, and Schroeder (1989) focused on 48 child outcome studies using the cognitive-behavioral technique of self-statement modification; pooling outcome measures to produce one ES mean per study, Dush et al. found a

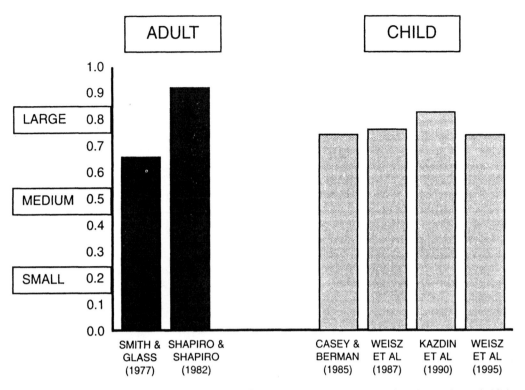

Figure 2 Mean effect sizes found in meta-analyses of psychotherapy outcome studies with adults and children. ("Bridging the gap between laboratory and clinic in child and adolescent psychotherapy," by J. R. Weisz, G. R. Donenberg, S. S. Han, & B. Weiss, 1995, *Journal of Consulting and Clinical Psychology*, *63*, pp. 688–701. Copyright 1995 by the American Psychological Association. Reprinted with permission.)

mean ES of 0.47. Durlak, Fuhrman, and Lampman (1991) surveyed 64 studies of cognitive-behavioral treatment with children, applied across a range of target problems. With ES values pooled within studies to produce a single mean ES per study, and weighting by study sample size, Durlak et al. found a mean ES of 0.56, averaging across all age levels. However, as these authors had hypothesized, the mean was considerably higher for older children (0.92 for ages 11–13) than for younger groups (0.57 for ages 5–7, 0.55 for ages 7–11), suggesting that these cognitively oriented treatments may be a better fit to more cognitively mature youth. In a worrisome finding, Durlak et al. noted a negligible correlation (–0.22) between cognitive changes and behavioral changes, thus raising an important question about a key assumption underlying cognitive-behavioral therapy, namely the notion that the technique brings about behavioral change by inducing cognitive change.

Family therapy has been the subject of two meta-analyses. Hazelrigg, Cooper, and Borduin (1987) reviewed 20 family therapy outcome studies, averaging across multiple effects within studies to produce a single mean ES per study. For the seven studies that met their methodological criteria and included outcome measures

of family interaction, the mean ES, weighted by study sample size, was 0.45; for the six methodologically appropriate studies that included behavior ratings of individual children in the family, the weighted mean ES was 0.50. Thus, although the number of relevant family therapy studies was small, Hazelrigg's meta-analysis pointed to beneficial effects. In another meta-analysis, Shadish et al. (1993) surveyed 101 studies involving family therapy (plus another 62 studies of marital therapy). Aggregating multiple ES values within studies to the study level, and weighting studies by the inverse of their sampling variance, Shadish et al. found a mean ES of 0.47 for the 44 family therapy studies that included treatment–control group comparisons. For comparison with the Hazelrigg et al. findings, Shadish also computed weighted ES means separately, for measures of family interaction and for ratings of individual family members' behavior; the family interaction ES was 0.31 (vs. 0.45 in Hazelrigg et al.), and the behavior rating ES was 0.66 (vs. 0.50 in Hazelrigg et al.).

Three additional meta-analyses illustrate the range of questions that can be addressed via this method of synthesis. Prout and DeMartino's (1986) meta-analysis, focused on psychotherapy in school settings, based ES computation on SD of the control groups, and pooled ES values only across groups of similar outcome measures; thus, 33 studies, involving 52 treatment–control comparisons, generated 119 individual ES values that were included in the analysis. The resulting (unadjusted) ES mean was 0.58. Russell, Greenwald, and Shirk (1991), computing ES using the control group SD in their meta-analysis of 18 child outcome studies, found that treatment was associated with significant improvement in children's language proficiency (unadjusted ES = 0.39). Treatments that emphasized spontaneous verbal interaction produced the biggest language improvements, compared to those involving more structured and constrained procedures. Finally, Saile, Burgmeier, and Schmidt (1988) carried out a meta-analysis of 75 controlled outcome studies involving psychological preparation of children for medical (including dental) procedures, ranging from minor procedures such as injections and drawing blood samples to such serious procedures as lumbar punctures. ES was computed using SD of study control groups. The overall mean ES was modest, 0.44, but there was considerable variation across types of intervention; for example, mean ES was only 0.22 for procedures in the "minor" category (e.g., injections) but 1.50 for procedures classified as "major" (e.g., cardiac catheterization). This report by Saile et al. (1988), like the article by Prout and DeMartino (1986), reminds us that a good deal of psychotherapy with children takes place in settings outside a therapist's office, and that evidence is needed on outcomes in these less traditional settings just as for office-based treatment.

5.04.8.3 Therapy, Therapist, and Child Factors Related to the Magnitude of Treatment Effects

In addition to overall mean ES values, meta-analyses can yield estimates of the impact of various therapy, therapist, and client factors on treatment outcome. Such estimates need to be interpreted with caution because of the confounding among factors (e.g., treatments and treated problems) that is common in meta-analyses. Some of the confounding can be addressed via statistical control and testing of interaction effects (see, e.g., Weisz et al., 1987; Weisz, Weiss, et al., 1995), although this is only a partial solution. In the two meta-analyses from the author's lab (Weisz et al., 1987; Weisz, Weiss, et al., 1995), studies involving behavioral treatments (e.g., behavioral contracting, modeling, cognitive-behavioral therapy) were found to produce larger effects than studies using

nonbehavioral treatments (e.g., insight-oriented therapy, client-centered counseling). The Casey–Berman (1985) meta-analyses showed the same effect, at $p = 0.06$; Kazdin et al. (1990) did not make this comparison; general superiority of behavioral methods was also reported in Prout and DeMartino's (1986) meta-analysis of school-based treatment studies, and in meta-analyses not specific to children, by Nicholson and Berman (1983) and Shadish et al. (1993). By contrast meta-analyses have generally not found treatment outcomes to differ reliably for different types of treated problems (e.g., internalizing vs. externalizing; for one exception, see Casey & Berman, 1985, pp. 392–393).

The relation between age and treatment outcome has varied across meta-analyses. However, the meta-analysis involving the most recent collection of studies (Weisz, Weiss, et al., 1995) found mean ES to be larger for adolescents than for children. This main effect was qualified by the age and gender interaction depicted in Figure 3; for samples of predominantly or exclusively adolescent girls, mean ES was twice as large as for adolescent boys and for children of both genders. Of course, adolescent girls may be more likely to be treated for internalizing problems than are younger children or adolescent boys; but we found no reliable difference in mean ES for internalizing vs. externalizing problems, nor was the age and gender interaction in Figure 3 qualified by type of treated problem (internalizing vs. externalizing), type of treatment (behavioral vs. nonbehavioral), or level of therapist training (professional vs. clinical trainee vs. paraprofessional). Perhaps there is something about the 1990s generation of treatments reflected in this 1995 meta-analytic collection of studies that fits the characteristics and needs of adolescent girls particularly well, but one is left to speculate about what that elusive quality may be.

Three additional findings illustrate other potentially useful contributions of meta-analytic data. First, meta-analysis can be used to assess the holding power of intervention effects. Findings in both the meta-analyses (Weisz et al., 1987; Weisz, Weiss, et al., 1995) indicated that treatment effects assessed immediately after treatment are quite similar to effects measured at follow-up assessments, which average about six months after treatment termination. This suggests that treatment benefits tend to be durable, at least within typical follow-up time frames (for similar conclusions derived from different kinds of outcome studies, see Durlak et al. (1991); Nicholson & Berman (1983); Shadish et al. (1993)). Second, individually administered treatments have tended to show larger effects than group treatments, although not always

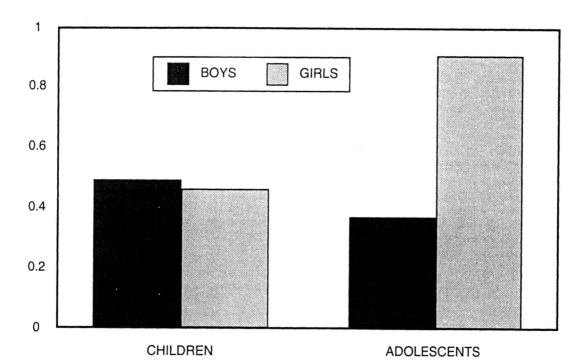

Figure 3 Mean effect size for samples of predominantly male and female children (11 years of age and younger) and adolescents (12 years and older). ("Effects of psychotherapy with children and adolescents revisited: A meta-analysis of treatment outcome studies," by J. R. Weisz, B. Weiss, S. S. Han, D. A. Granger, and T. Morton, 1995, *Psychological Bulletin, 117*, pp. 450–468. Copyright 1995 by the American Psychological Association. Reprinted with permission.)

significantly so (see Casey & Berman, 1985; Russell et al., 1991; Weisz et al., 1987; Weisz, Weiss, et al., 1995), and there is at least one exception in the area of cognitive-behavioral treatments for impulsivity (Baer & Nietzel, 1991).

A third finding (from Weisz, Weiss, et al., 1995) concerns the specificity of treatment effects. Obviously, children differ markedly from one another in the particular problems they manifest, and various therapies differ in the problems they are designed to address, but do these individual differences actually influence treatment outcome? Some (e.g., Frank, 1973) have proposed that psychotherapy has "nonspecific" effects, for example, helping people with diverse problems through such general means as promoting a feeling of being understood or encouraging an expectancy of relief. An alternative view is that therapies help in specific ways, having their strongest influence on the specific problems they are designed to address.

This controversy was addressed in Weisz, Weiss, et al. (1995) with a test of whether effects were larger for the specific problem domains targeted by a treatment than for other, more incidental domains. For example, we asked whether a treatment for anxiety produced bigger changes in anxiety than in related but more peripheral problems such as depression. Across multiple comparisons like these, we found that ES means were about twice as large for the specific problems addressed in treatment as for related problems that were not specifically addressed. This suggests that these psychotherapies were not merely producing global or nonspecific good feelings that influence diverse outcomes equally; instead, the treatments appeared to have rather precise, focused effects consistent with the particular objectives of the therapy.

In sum, evidence from broad-based meta-analyses of child psychotherapy outcome studies points to positive, problem-specific, and durable effects of mental health interventions for a variety of child problems. Clearly, child psychotherapy research is generating a number of encouraging findings. On the other hand, several conceptual and methodological issues require a good deal of attention in the future. Attention is now focused on some of these issues, and related suggestions for future research.

5.04.9 EXTERNAL VALIDITY AND RESEARCH THERAPY VS. CLINIC THERAPY

One issue is that of external validity. Most of the 300-plus studies in the meta-analyses reviewed above (particularly the recent and behavioral studies) involved participants, interventions, and/or treatment conditions that are actually not very representative of conventional clinical practice with referred children. In many of the studies, (i) children were recruited for treatment, were not actual clinic cases, and had lower levels of dysfunction than most referred children; (ii) child samples were homogenous, with therapy addressing only one or two focal problems (e.g., a specific phobia); (iii) therapists received considerable pretherapy training and session-by-session supervision in the specific intervention techniques they would use; and/or (iv) the therapy involved adherence to those specific techniques. In addition, (v) therapy was often highly structured and guided by a manual, with therapists monitored for fidelity to the treatment program.

These features of the outcome studies, although they are useful experimentally, tend to coalesce around an abstract category that the author and his colleagues (e.g., Weisz, Weiss, & Donenberg, 1992) have called research therapy, which we distinguish from conventional clinic therapy. Table 1 summarizes some illustrative differences between the two therapy genres. The two are best thought of as two poles of a multidimensional continuum; certainly no single feature shown in the table under Research therapy is present in all clinical trials studies, and few of the individual features listed under Clinic therapy are true of all clinic-based treatment. However, differences between child therapy in clinics and child therapy in clinical trials outcome studies are common enough for it to be reasonable to ask whether the positive outcomes generated in the research therapy studies, and summarized in the meta-analyses above, are representative of the outcomes achieved in actual clinical practice with children.

5.04.9.1 Evidence on the Effects of Clinic Therapy

To address this question, the author and colleagues carried out a search (described in Weisz, Donenberg, Han, & Weiss, 1995) for published outcome studies that focused on what might fairly be called clinic therapy. Studies were sought that involved (i) treatment of clinic-referred (i.e., not "analog" or recruited) youngsters, (ii) treatment in service-

Table 1 Some common characteristics of research therapy and clinic therapy.

Research therapy	Clinic therapy
Recruited cases (less severe, study volunteers)	Clinic-referred cases (more severe, some coerced into treatment)
Homogeneous groups	Heterogeneous groups
Narrow or single-problem focus	Broad, multiproblem focus
Treatment in lab, school settings	Treatment in clinic, hospital settings
Researchers as therapists	Professional career therapists
Very small caseloads	Very large caseloads
Heavy pretherapy preparation for therapists	Little/light pretherapy preparation for therapists
Preplanned, highly-structured treatment (manualized)	Flexible, adjustable treatment (no treatment manual)
Monitoring of therapist behavior	Little monitoring of therapist behavior
Behavioral methods (e.g., operant, respondent, modeling, CBT)	Nonbehavioral methods (e.g., psychodynamic, eclectic)

Source: Weisz, Donenberg, Han, & Weiss (1995). ("Bridging the gap between laboratory and clinic in child and adolescent psychotherapy," by J. R. Weisz, G. R. Donenberg, S. S. Han, & B. Weiss, 1995, *Journal of Consulting and Clinical Psychology, 63*, pp. 688–701. Copyright 1995 by the American Psychological Association. Reprinted with permission.)

oriented clinics or clinical agencies, not in research settings (e.g., not university labs or public schools), (iii) therapy carried out by practicing clinicians (as opposed to trained research assistants), and (iv) therapy that was part of the usual service provided by the clinic, not a special treatment program designed specifically for research. It was required that the studies involve direct comparison between youngsters who received treatment and a control group receiving no treatment or a placebo intervention.

One of the first lessons learned was this: clinic studies that meet the criteria outlined above are very rare. The author and colleagues had carried out one such study (Weisz & Weiss, 1989), but found only eight others that fit the criteria (Ashcroft, 1971; De Fries, Jenkins, & Williams, 1964; Jacob, Magnussen, & Kemler, 1972; Lehrman, Sirluck, Black, & Glick, 1949; Levitt, Beiser, & Robertson, 1959; Shepherd, Oppenheim, & Mitchell, 1966; Smyrnios & Kirkby, 1993; Witmer & Keller, 1942), and these spanned 50 years, most having been published many years earlier. Although the studies all compared treatment and control groups, they used several different methodologies (for details, see Weisz, Donenberg, Han, & Kauneckis, 1995). To facilitate comparison of these nine studies with the meta-analytic findings reviewed above, an ES or ES estimate was computed for each of the nine studies (using, where necessary, estimation procedures described by Smith et al., 1980, and Glass, McGaw, & Smith, 1981). As shown in Figure 4, ES ranged from −0.40 to + 0.29, with mean ES for the nine clinic studies (0.01) falling well below the mean ES of the four broad-based meta-analyses discussed earlier (0.77). Although these nine clinic studies provide only a very limited sample of clinical treatment, the disappointing findings certainly raise the possibility that outcomes of conventional clinical therapy may be less positive than the outcomes of research therapy.

It is useful to consider these findings in the light of evidence on "continuum of care" or "system of care" programs for children, that is, efforts to link multiple conventional mental health services for children with the services frequently organized and coordinated by individual child case managers (see, e.g., Stroul & Friedman, 1986). In one of the most recent (1995) and most ambitious of these efforts (see, Bickman, 1996; Bickman et al., 1995), the US Army spent $80 million to provide a continuum-of-care program for children of military personnel at Fort Bragg, NC; and to test the program's cost-effectiveness relative to more typical fragmented services in a matched comparison site. Considerable evidence indicates that the Fort Bragg program did produce a rich array of well-integrated mental health services (see details in Bickman et al., 1995). Indeed, the program was judged by the APA's section on Child Clinical Psychology and Division of Child, Youth, and Family Services Joint Task Force to be

> the most comprehensive program to date, integrating many of the approaches demonstrated by other service programs . . . integrated and flexibly constructed, yet comprehensive, [with] services available to be adapted to meet the needs of children and their families, rather than a simplistic application of a single approach. (Roberts, 1994, p. 215)

There is good evidence (see Bickman et al., 1995) that the program produced improved access to treatment, but it also cost more than services in the comparison site: $7777 per treated child vs. $4904. Unfortunately, despite the increased access to care and despite the increased costs, the Fort Bragg program produced clinical outcomes that were no better

than those in the matched comparison site. Fort Bragg children received more mental health intervention, at greater cost, but their mental health outcomes were not improved by the increase.

Similar null findings have emerged from other studies designed to alter, link, or improve delivery of conventional clinical services (see, e.g., Evans et al., 1994; Lehman, Postrado, Roth, McNary, & Goldman, 1994). A number of alternative interpretations of such findings may be plausible, but one possible interpretation is that the various treatments that are linked and coordinated in these continua of care are simply not very effective, individually or in combination. In fact, Bickman and colleagues (Bickman, 1996; Bickman et al., 1995) appear to favor such an interpretation, after having tested the major rival interpretations they could identify. Put simply, there is no indication that the individual interventions employed in these various continua of care have been shown to be effective in clinical trials (or approximations thereto); thus, it is possible that the various interventions are simply not very helpful to children. An array of ineffective services may not produce much true benefit regardless of the extent to which they are multiplied, coordinated, or organized into continua of care.

So, the evidence reviewed on representative clinical interventions with children points to two conclusions: Evidence on conventional clinical treatments provides little support for their effectiveness; evidence on effects of integrating conventional interventions into systems of care also shows little evidence of treatment benefit.

5.04.9.2 Research Challenges

The findings on clinic- and community-based interventions suggest useful directions for future research. First, it is clear that we need more information on outcomes of treatment under representative clinical conditions. Research in this genre—known as "effectiveness" studies, as opposed to controlled "efficacy" studies—is difficult but certainly not impossible, as the nine studies cited in Figure 4 demonstrate (for a discussion of the pros and cons of various relevant methods, see Weisz & Weiss, 1993). The base of information on psychotherapy effects in public clinics is quite thin, but the situation is even worse for other treatment contexts. As best as can be determined there is, up to 1997, no methodologically sound treatment–control study of outcomes in such now-common treatment configurations as individual and group private practice and health

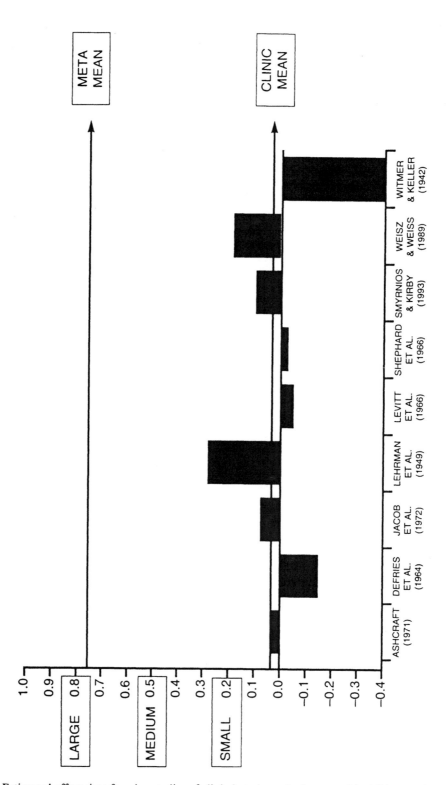

Figure 4 Estimated effect sizes for nine studies of clinic-based psychotherapy with children and adolescents. Horizontal arrows show mean effect size for four broad-based meta-analyses of laboratory outcome studies (top), and averaging across the nine clinic-based studies (bottom). ("Bridging the gap between laboratory and clinic in child and adolescent psychotherapy," by J. R. Weisz, G. R. Donenberg, S. S. Han, and B. Weiss, 1995, *Journal of Consulting and Clinical Psychology, 63*, pp. 688–701. Copyright 1995 by the American Psychological Association. Reprinted with permission.)

maintenance organized (HMOs). Evidence is needed on outcomes in these forms of practice to ascertain how practice effects in the 1990s compare to outcomes of laboratory interventions. Moreover, without such information, there is a lack of baseline data for tracking the impact of potentially critical changes in service patterns, such as the introduction of managed care, or implementation of empirically validated treatments (discussed below).

Second, assuming that further research continues to show poor effects of conventional clinical treatment, it is necessary to identify factors that explain why therapy in clinical trials experiments produces strong positive effects and therapy in clinics does not. The author and colleague have made two attempts to address this issue (Weisz, Donenberg, Han, & Kauneckis, 1995; Weisz, Donenberg, Han, & Weiss, 1995). In both, they used meta-analytic data sets to investigate which, if any, of the factors that distinguish research therapy from clinic therapy (e.g., of those shown in Table 1) might account for significant variance in outcome. In a 1995 effort, using the most complete sample (Weisz, Donenberg, Han, & Weiss, 1995), we examined eight potentially relevant factors (from the list shown in Table 1), and two were found that were significantly related to treatment outcome: First, behavioral treatments were associated with better outcomes than nonbehavioral treatments, and second, analog cases showed better outcomes than clinic-referred children. The first finding suggests the possibility that clinic-based treatment might be more effective if more behavioral treatments were used; nonbehavioral interventions are widely used in clinical practice, and it appears that behavioral therapies are not the first choice of most practitioners (see Kazdin, Siegel, & Bass, 1990). The second finding suggests that even lab-tested treatment methods may be less successful with truly clinic-referred children than with the less disturbed children who are so often the subjects in lab studies. This issue is discussed in the next section.

5.04.10 EXPORTABILITY OF EMPIRICALLY SUPPORTED TREATMENTS

At first, the array of findings presented above might appear to argue for incorporation of empirically supported treatments into clinical practice. The logic would be this: (i) evidence from clinical trials research with children shows positive effects of numerous treatments; (ii) evidence on conventional treatments in clinical settings shows generally modest-to-negligible effects; thus, (iii) to generate beneficial effects in clinical settings, one should identify those treatments that have been supported in clinical trials and export them to clinics. This logic may be appealing to many who support the efforts of the APA Task Forces (adult and child, see Task Force, 1995) on empirically validated treatments, and the logic may prove to be valid in the long term. However, it may be a mistake to assume that the empirically supported treatments are ready for export. The subjects and treatment conditions involved in tests of the empirically supported treatments tend to differ so much from everyday clinic cases and conditions that it is not clear how workable or effective the supported treatments will be in clinical settings. At the very least, the differences mean that treatment developers cannot simply drop their manuals at the clinic doorstep and assume that beneficial treatment effects will follow.

Table 1 offers several reasons for concern. As one example, the fact that empirically supported treatments have most often been supported with recruited or analog samples rather than referred children may be important. Indeed, in the analysis described above (Weisz, Donenberg, Han, & Weiss, 1995, p. 695) mean ES in even the clinical trials research was found to be significantly lower for studies using clinic-referred children than for those using analog samples. This raises a question as to whether treatments supported in clinical trials with subclinical samples recruited from schools would be equally effective with seriously disturbed children referred to clinics. As a second example, clinical trials studies frequently focus on homogeneous groups, selected for the presence of one or two target problems, and with exclusionary criteria eliminating children who have additional unwanted problems. One cannot be sure that treatments supported with such samples will be equally effective with the heterogeneous groups of multiproblem children frequently seen in clinical practice. As a third example from Table 1, the simple fact that most empirically supported treatments are behavioral (including cognitive-behavioral) may make them difficult to implement in clinics where most of the therapists are strongly psychodynamic, or are unfamiliar with, or even hostile toward, the behavioral perspective.

Beyond the issues suggested by Table 1, numerous practical problems arise. A simple example concerns the number of sessions needed to produce beneficial effects. The author's research in child mental health clinics (Weisz & Weiss, 1989; Weisz, 1996), has found that the average outpatient receives 5–10 sessions. By contrast, most of the manuals used to guide empirically supported treatments require more than a dozen sessions, and these are typically devoted to a single focal problem. Given the specificity of most manuals, children referred for three or four major problems may well be candidates for three or four manuals, each requiring more than 12 sessions. In an era of managed care in the private sector and modest capitated budgets in the public sector, strict session limits are apt to be the rule rather than the exception. Thus, it is fair to ask whether the kinds of manualized treatments that now prevail in the empirical literature can be made to work in clinics with prevailing session limits.

Before manualized treatments derived from the empirical literature are implemented in clinics and clinical training programs, a new genre of treatment outcome research may be needed that involves taking empirically supported treatments out of the laboratories where they were developed and studying them in the crucible of clinical practice. The purpose would be to find out what modifications are needed to make the treatments effective with the clientele, and the real-life constraints, of clinical practice. Several investigators have taken steps in this direction, for example, by treating truly disturbed children in university-based lab clinics (see, e.g., Kendall, 1994; Lovaas, 1987). However, more extensive attempts may be needed to incorporate lab-tested treatments into actual clinical practice, and test their effects, before it can be known just how exportable the experimentally derived treatments are, and what changes will be needed to make them work with seriously disturbed children.

5.04.11 CHILD PSYCHOTHERAPY AND DEVELOPMENTAL PSYCHOLOGY

A third issue that needs attention is the relative isolation of child psychotherapy research from the base of theory and evidence on human development. Despite clear overlap in their populations of interest, and despite their shared emphasis on the study of change, research on developmental psychology and on child psychotherapy have remained surprisingly separate, insular enterprises. Saile et al. (1988) have expressed a similar concern regarding treatments designed to prepare children for medical procedures. In introductions to journal articles on the various child treatments, it is surprisingly unusual to see either theories or empirical findings of developmental psychology cited as a basis for the treatment program. The Results sections of treatment outcome articles are frequently notable for relative inattention to developmental factors (even age!) that may relate to treatment effects.

One cause of this state of affairs may be the very success these relatively adevelopmental treatment efforts have had in producing positive effects. Such success may foster confidence that one is on the right track, and may thus undermine motivation to seek input from other subdisciplines. But treatment effects, although positive in most studies, might well be improved through closer ties to the study of development. Treatment benefit might well be enhanced to the extent that treatments fit developmental characteristics of the treated individuals; a knowledge of relevant developmental literature should enhance treatment planners' capacity to produce a good fit, and thus to test this notion.

In addition to treatment planning, developmental concerns may be relevant to outcome assessment. Because outcome research provides much of the feedback needed to guide the development and refinement of treatment procedures, outcome researchers may need to consider ways to attune such research to developmental questions, so as to stimulate clinical–developmental cross-pollination. Accordingly, this section addresses developmental issues that bear on both child treatment planning and outcome assessment.

5.04.11.1 Age

Most outcome researchers report the age range and mean for their samples, but few assess the potential moderating effect of age. Indeed, the Kazdin et al. (1990) survey of 223 child treatment outcome studies showed that only 7% examined any child, family, and therapist variables in relation to outcome. Age is one of the most easily accessible child characteristics, and within-study assessment of its moderating effects could be useful heuristically, generating promising developmental hypotheses. Broad-based meta-analyses like those described earlier can address the general relation between sample age and outcome, across studies; but this pooled approach lacks the precision and control of within-study analyses, or even more narrowly focused meta-analyses, such as Durlak et al.'s (1991) meta-analysis of cognitive-behavioral therapy outcome studies, discussed earlier. The Durlak et al. findings suggest the potential importance of testing for a moderating role of age in each individual outcome study. On the other hand, it must also be noted that the age variable is, at best, a rough summary index of multiple, diverse developmental factors—cognitive, social, and contextual—each warranting attention in its own right.

5.04.11.2 Cognitions About the Therapy Process and the Role of the Therapist

Adult clients frequently begin treatment with some understanding of the nature and purpose of psychotherapy and its purpose, and some sense of the therapist's role. Children, by contrast, may have little awareness of what therapy is, what a therapist does, or what their relationship with the therapist should be. The concepts children at various developmental levels apply to the process, the therapist, and the relationship, are apt to reflect their cognitive developmental level, in interaction with their previous relevant experience, which will differ markedly from one child to another. Our field needs basic inquiry into children's cognitions about these concepts, each of which could well influence their response to treatment and their ultimate treatment outcome.

5.04.11.3 Ability to "Decenter"

Piaget (e.g., 1929, 1962) wrote extensively about the development of "decentration," the ability to detach from one's own point of view and perceive objects or events from an alternate perspective. Early work on this theme dealt with visual perception, but the notion was eventually extended to social contexts and the ability to recognize the perspective of others on activities, events, and even oneself. A limited ability to decenter may set limits on the impact of treatments (e.g., cognitive-behavioral, psychodynamic) that involve role-playing or other efforts to help children see events, conditions, and even themselves from the perspective of others. Accordingly, research on this cognitive ability as it relates to child therapy could shed new light on how children respond to various perspective-taking intervention techniques.

5.04.11.4 Language Ability

Developmental variations in ability to encode and decode language may set limits on the success of therapy, particularly when it relies heavily on verbal interaction. Low level encoding skills may limit a child's ability to convey thoughts and feelings to the therapist, and thus limit the therapist's ability to tailor interventions to the child's inner state. As a simple example, both cognitive-behavioral and psychodynamic treatments for anxiety may require young clients to describe their anxious state in terms of both physiological arousal (e.g., "I feel tense, and I have a knot in my stomach") and psychological state (e.g., "It feels like everyone is staring at me; if I make a mistake, they'll think

I'm stupid"). Children who cannot generate such descriptions may not be able to help their therapist understand their anxious states fully enough to design appropriate interventions.

Limited ability to decode therapist comments may also be a problem, limiting how helpful those comments actually can be. Highly scripted, manual-driven therapies that are language-laden may fall outside the range of young clients' capabilities, thus limiting the impact of treatment. Assessment of children's language skills would facilitate detection of such problems.

Finally, considerable research, dating to the work of Piaget (1955/1923) and Vygotsky (1962/1934), points to developmental differences in the ability to use "private speech" or "inner speech" to inhibit or guide behavior (see also Kohlberg, Yaeger, & Hjertholm, 1968; and Zivin, 1979). Piaget and Vygotsky made different predictions about the developmental course of this phenomenon, and subsequent evidence has been equivocal and dependent on the specific type of inner speech involved (see, e.g., Meichenbaum & Goodman, 1979). However, it seems clear that developmental differences in the use of language to guide behavior may well foster differences in responsiveness to those therapies that stress language as a means of self-control. In cognitive-behavioral therapy, for example, children are taught to use "self-talk" to make themselves less impulsive, less anxious, less depressed, less aggressive, and/or more prosocial. Use of self-talk in these ways assumes a well-developed connection between language and action, an assumption that may need to be tested in child outcome research.

5.04.11.5 Comprehension of Concepts or "Lessons" of the Treatment Program

One cognitive phenomenon that cries out for attention in child psychotherapy research is the child's understanding of the conceptual content and central principles of the therapy program. Many child therapies are, in part, educational programs. For example, some treatment programs for depression are designed to teach children the basic components of depression, plus strategies for alleviating depressed mood; and some programs for anxiety try to teach the building blocks of anxiety (e.g., fear, physiological arousal, habitual avoidance, relief that rewards the avoidance), plus specific techniques for promoting exposure to the feared situation. Are there developmental differences in children's acquisition of these concepts and skills, and might such differences influence treatment outcome? For most child therapies, there is too little relevant evidence to provide an empirically respectable answer. Indeed, one of the most striking limitations of research in this field is the infrequency with which outcome researchers test which "lessons" of their treatment were actually learned. Beyond the value of such information for assessing goodness-of-fit between a treatment program to children at different developmental levels, the information would facilitate assessment of the extent to which grasping the various concepts and lessons is associated with clinical improvement.

5.04.11.6 Abstract Reasoning

Certain kinds of abstract thinking, including hypothetico-deductive reasoning, are consolidated in formal operations, typically in adolescence (Piaget, 1970). Yet some treatment programs for preadolescent children appear to require considerable abstract reasoning. For example, some social skills training programs ask children to generate hypothetical stressful social situations, think of various ways they might respond, envision ways that others might respond to their response, and imagine various possible outcomes of the hypothetical interactions that might ensue. As another example, some therapies for depression require movement from concrete instances to abstract categories when they try to teach children to recognize categories of depressogenic thinking such as overgeneralization and catastrophizing (see examples in Cicchetti, Rogosch, & Toth, in press). Developmentally sensitive investigators could help guide treatment developers, by assessing the extent to which children at various developmental levels can master such seemingly abstract reasoning.

5.04.11.7 Organization and the Orthogenetic Principle

The developmental theorist Heinz Werner (1957) proposed an *orthogenetic principle*, the notion that

> wherever development occurs it proceeds from a state of relative globality and lack of differentiation to a state of increasing differentiation, articulation, and hierarchic integration. (p. 126)

This principle overlaps partly with Piaget's (1970) concept of organization, the notion that the developing system integrates cognitive building blocks into an operating structure. In Piaget's view (supported by evidence), even memories of past experience can be reorganized to integrate such experience with newly developed cognitive structures. One implication of these two principles for child treatment re-

searchers is that some of the skills and information taught in a treatment program may be integrated into the developing child's cognitive system over the course of later development, not necessarily within the time frame of the typical child outcome study.

The implications of this notion could be profound. Perhaps, instead of construing child treatment as a direct induction of change, treatment programs should be seen as perturbations planted in the fertile soil of the individual's developing system and destined to interact with that system over time to produce structural changes in the ways the individual processes and responds to experience. Because the nature and timing of this interactive, unfolding process might be strongly influenced by the natural pace of development, our thinking about the objectives and the timing of outcome assessment might also need to be re-examined. Instead of focusing on proximal outcomes induced by their treatment programs alone and seen at the end of those 8–24 week programs, treatment researchers might focus on therapeutic-developmental exchanges, some effects of which might not be measurable until months or even years after treatment termination. Extending outcome research beyond the traditional follow-up periods (which are now rarely longer than six to nine months) might permit detection of slow-blooming changes or "sleeper effects," as the child's developing system integrates the lessons of therapy with other developmental inputs. Of course, extending follow-up assessments would also help researchers detect a falling off of treatment benefit over time, when that occurs.

5.04.11.8 Looking to the Future

This brief sampling of developmental issues suggests that there is much work to be done. Breaking down the traditional insularity of child psychotherapy research and developmental research, though difficult, may be useful to both enterprises. Benefits for those who study child psychotherapy may include richer and more fully informed models of child dysfunction, readiness for treatment, and intervention-to-child fit, and an expanded picture of how outcome assessment may be conducted and employed in the process of treatment development.

5.04.12 RELATION BETWEEN PROCESS AND OUTCOME

A fourth issue that needs attention is the relation between therapy process and outcome.

In Chapter 3, this volume, Stephen Shirk and Robert Russell describe the state of process research in the child area; the present chapter considers a few basic notions relevant to outcome assessment. The most general point concerns the importance of assessing process in relation to outcome. In the absence of process information, broadly construed, information about treatment outcomes is of limited value. When treatment works well, we need to know what processes were involved, so we can repeat them; and when treatment fails, we need to know what to stop doing. Relatively few child outcome studies provide clear measures of the "active ingredients" of their treatments. The typical clinical trial in the child area provides a rather global comparison of a control group to a treatment program involving multiple techniques. Significant global group differences at post-treatment and follow-up are indeed important elements of treatment validation, and for cost-effectiveness probably the most useful first step in treatment development. However, the lack of specificity regarding which elements of the treatment are producing which aspects of client change has led to calls for a more fine-grained analysis of the processes of child psychotherapy that mediate and/or moderate treatment outcome (Kendall & Morris, 1991; Kazdin, 1989), and other aspects of the therapeutic process deserve attention as well. Kazdin et al. (1990) reported that a fourth of their sample of 223 outcome studies varied some therapy components across groups, and only 2% evaluated outcome in relation to treatment processes; this suggests that there is room for growth in research on what factors over the course of the therapy process actually influence change. There are at least four ways of construing such research, each potentially useful.

5.04.12.1 Components of Treatment

In cases where well-replicated effects show a composite treatment program to be effective, a logical next step is to test the effects of various components of the program, in combinations that make sense theoretically and logically. At least two variations on this theme are well-recognized in the field. A dismantling approach involves breaking a program down into components and varying these across groups; an additive approach involves progressive addition of new components, or combining two or more treatments into one. In the Kazdin et al. (1990) analysis of 223 child treatment outcome studies, 26% involved the first approach, to some extent, and 19% involved the second approach. If these numbers seem surprisingly large, it

should be borne in mind that 60% of the Kazdin and co-workers' sample of studies involved comparison of two or more treatments, not necessarily with a no treatment or active control group. Nonetheless, the data suggests that research involving "unpacking" specific treatment components is underway in the child area.

5.04.12.2 Therapist Behavior

A second aspect of therapy process that deserves attention is the behavior and style of the therapist, independent of the specific components of an outline or manual. For example, a good deal of research has focused on therapist directness in communication with clients. In a series of studies, Patterson and his colleagues have noted that therapists' direct instructions to parents of antisocial children to change their parenting style are frequently met with noncompliance in session and resistance to change outside sessions (e.g., Patterson & Chamberlain, 1994; Patterson & Forgatch, 1985). On the other hand, Truax and Wittmer (1973) found evidence that directness by the therapist may have positive effects in confronting defense mechanisms in child therapy. As the findings of these two investigative teams suggest, any one aspect of therapist style or behavior may have differential effects depending on the content and objectives of the treatment; and, of course, therapist style may well interact with client style and personality to shape the ultimate effects. Despite the complexity of the task, and the infinite array of therapist style and behavior dimensions that might be addressed, research on this theme may be well worth the investment of time and intellectual resources it will require. Of all the research discussed in this chapter, it is among the most relevant to the task of training future therapists.

5.04.12.3 Child and Family Behavior

A third dimension of process that requires attention is the behavior of treated children and their families over the course of therapy. Research on this theme is illustrated by the work of Braswell, Kendall, Braith, Carey, and Vye (1985) and Gorin (1993) indicating that positive treatment outcomes are associated with clients' active participation in therapy. Causality is difficult to nail down in such research, and it is certainly possible that such client behavior as active participation may be either a cause of the ultimate treatment benefit, a signal that the treatment is resonating with the client and producing change, or both. But, causality aside, the identification of child and family behavior during therapy that can predict ultimate outcome can, in principle, provide a much-needed tool for therapists: a means of determining whether the treatment is working or not, and thus whether adjustments are needed, before the entire intervention program has ended.

5.04.12.4 Therapeutic Relationship

The therapeutic relationship, or working alliance, has been construed as involving two interrelated parts: the client's positive emotional connection to the therapist, and a shared conceptualization between the client and therapist of the tasks and goals of therapy (Bordin, 1979). In the adult literature, development of a therapeutic relationship has emerged as a particularly significant process correlate of positive outcome in several studies (Horowitz, Marmar, Weiss, DeWitt, & Rosenbaum, 1984; Luborsky, Crits-Christoph, Mintz, & Auerbach, 1988). Shirk and Saiz (1992) have argued that this process variable may be an even more significant contributor to outcome for children due to the "involuntary client" status of many children at the beginning of therapy, the nonverbal nature of many forms of client-centered and play therapy for children, and the social deficits that are hypothesized to be central in the development and maintenance of many serious child problems (e.g., aggression).

Child process researchers have studied the therapeutic relationship in play therapy (Howe & Silvern, 1981; Truax, Altmann, Wright, & Mitchell, 1973), family therapy (Friedlander, Wildman, Heatherington, & Skowron, 1994; Pinsoff & Catherall, 1986), individual psychodynamic therapy (Shirk & Saiz, 1992), cognitive-behavioral treatment (Kendall, 1994), child behavior therapy (Motta & Lynch, 1990; Motta & Tobin, 1992), and parent training (Webster-Stratton & Herbert, 1993). However, unlike the consistently positive findings in the adult process literature relating the working alliance to therapeutic success, evidence from child psychotherapy has been mixed, with Shirk & Saiz (1992) reporting positive associations between their measures of the therapeutic relationship and outcome in child psychodynamic psychotherapy, and both Kendall (1994) and Motta (Motta & Lynch, 1990; Motta & Tobin, 1992) finding no significant association between relationship quality and outcome with cognitive-behavioral treatment for anxiety and behavioral therapy for learning and disruptive behavior problems, respectively. The lack of agreement across studies is difficult to interpret, given the study-to-study differences in the way therapeutic

relationship is assessed. The field needs a well-validated set of measures for assessing the relationship. Developing such measures for child therapy will be a challenging task. Among the difficulties confronted, two are particularly notable: (i) the complexity of the relationship concepts involved relative to the limited verbal and conceptual facility of many of the children who will be the targets of the assessment; and (ii) the need to encompass not only the child–therapist dyad, but also the parents and possibly additional family members, whose relationship to therapist and child may be critical to the success of treatment.

5.04.13 CHILD AND FAMILY ETHNICITY AND CULTURE

A fifth issue is that of culture and ethnicity in relation to child treatments. In the great majority of child outcome studies, the samples appear to be predominantly Caucasian, although authors have frequently failed to be explicit about sample composition. In the Kazdin et al. (1990) survey of 223 child outcome studies, 80% failed to identify the ethnic composition of their sample. While mere reporting of the relevant numbers is rare, actual tests of ethnicity as a moderator of outcome are even rarer. Some have suggested that treatments tested primarily with mainstream samples may not necessarily be optimal for troubled members of ethnic minority groups (Gibbs & Huang, 1989; Rogler, Malgady, Costantino, & Blumenthal, 1987; Spurlock, 1985; Sue, 1977; Tharp, 1991). The treatments may not, for example, take into account the language, values, customs, child-rearing traditions, expectancies for child and parent behavior, and distinctive stressors and resources associated with different cultural groups. In the treatment setting, such cultural factors may lead to miscommunication and misunderstanding between the therapist and the client and family, thus increasing the likelihood of premature termination and poor treatment outcome (Ho, 1992; Sue & Zane, 1987). Tharp (1991) has also suggested that even the therapy modality requires attention, and that family and group interventions may be more appropriate than individual treatment for many minority youth, and more likely, as well, to generate information for the therapist on cultural issues relevant to the child, family, and community.

The literature on culture and psychotherapy is rich in recommendations for how to treat specific ethnic groups, but poor in controlled empirical assessment on these issues, with most recommendations based on anecdotal and experiential reports (see Gibbs & Huang, 1989; Ho, 1992). The array of hypotheses now available should provide fertile ground for experimentation in the future. For the present, though, a modest base of evidence is available to suggest trends that bear further study. Weisz, Huey, and Weersing (1996) identified 19 treatment outcome studies (most found in the meta-analytic collections from Weisz et al., 1987 and Weisz, Weiss, et al., 1995) in which the majority of the sample were ethnic minority children or families. A few of the findings of these studies are considered below, and four key questions are raised about treatment outcome and culture that need attention in future research.

5.04.13.1 How Effective are Tested Treatments with Ethnic Minority Children?

In general, children in the 19 studies improved significantly more than children in control conditions. Treatment showed a significant beneficial effect on externalizing problems in 79% of the group comparisons, and for internalizing problems the figure was 86%. On other outcomes, such as self-esteem, social skills, and family functioning, 46% of the comparisons showed significant treatment benefit. These figures appear somewhat more modest than the general trends seen in meta-analyses that apparently included predominantly Caucasian majority samples, but such a comparison is problematic because of numerous study-to-study differences in treated problems, types of treatment, and so forth. Direct comparison is far superior, but only one such comparison was identified in the 19 studies; Henggeler, Melton, and Smith (1992) found that African-American and Caucasian delinquents responded equally well to multisystemic treatment.

5.04.13.2 Is there Evidence of Treatment Type and Ethnic Group Interaction?

In a word, no. But this may be only because no complete test of such an interaction has been carried out. In the author's sample of 19 minority youth outcome studies, one study involved an initial step toward such a test. Szapocznik and colleagues (Szapocznik et al., 1989; Szapocznik, Kurtines, Santisteban, & Rio, 1990) tested the efficacy of structural family therapy (SFT) against individual psychodynamic child therapy (IPCT) with Hispanic families of boys with behavioral and emotional problems. Following treatment, SFT-treated children had fewer behavior

problems than IPCT children, but neither group differed significantly from children in a recreational control condition. At follow up, family functioning improved substantially following SFT relative to IPCT; indeed, with IPCT, family functioning actually worsened over time. The findings seem consistent with Tharp's (1991) contention that family-based therapies are more appropriate than individual treatment for minority children. However, Szapocznik et al. did not include comparison groups of non-Hispanic youth treated with SFT and IPCT. Thus, it appears that the field still awaits a full test of treatment type and ethnicity interaction.

5.04.13.3 Outcomes of Therapist–Client Matching for Ethnicity or Language

Although nine of the 19 studies in the collection involved some attempt at ethnicity and/or language match, none provided a direct test of the impact of the match, for example, by comparing matched and unmatched therapist–child pairs. Hayes, Cunningham, and Robinson (1977) reported that counselor race (African-American vs. Caucasian) did not appear to influence treatment outcomes with test anxiety and poor school motivation among African-American children, but they did not present substantiating analyses. In general, those studies in which some form of matching was carried out did not seem to show notably better success rates than the remainder of the 19. Again, such global comparison across studies lacks the precision of the direct, within-study tests that are most needed to address the "matching" question.

5.04.13.4 Outcomes of Adapting Therapies Specifically for Ethnic Minority Children

Ten of the 19 studies involved some sort of adaptation of the treatment program to cultural characteristics of the minority sample. The adaptations ranged from narrowly focused changes such as depicting minority figures in modeling tasks to such extensive change as essentially designing entire programs for a particular ethnic minority group. The fact that only one of the "unadapted" studies focused on internalizing problems ruled out comparisons on that dimension; however, the percentage of comparisons showing significant positive treatment effects was somewhat higher for externalizing problems (83% vs. 75%) and for problems in the "other" category (57% vs. 33%).

Direct comparisons of adapted and unadapted methods within the same study are difficult to find. A study by Constantino, Malgady, and Rogler (1986) did find that maladjusted Puerto Rican children in a culturally adapted modeling program involving cuento or folklore therapy showed less aggressive behavior following treatment than those in an art/play therapy control condition (APT). However, since APT subjects were even more aggressive than those in the no-therapy (NT) condition, the findings may reflect the ineffectiveness of APT as much as the superiority of cuento therapy. A more robust test of any culture-specific treatment approach would entail comparison with another empirically supported approach (e.g., social skills training for aggression). Where culture-calibrated changes have been made to a standard treatment program, it will be important to carry out direct comparison of outcomes for minority children receiving the altered program vs. outcome for minority children receiving the standard program.

Generalizing across the various themes and questions reviewed above, the state of affairs regarding culture and child psychotherapy can be summarized succinctly: there are intriguing hypotheses and important questions that need attention, but the numerous direct comparisons needed to test the hypotheses and answer the questions are lacking. With concern about culture and mental health growing steadily, it seems likely that the next generation of research will include increased attention to these matters.

5.04.14 CONTEXT SENSITIVITY OF TREATMENTS

A sixth issue arises because the interventions involved in most treatment research are rather removed from the contexts in which children live their lives. Most researchers would agree that children do not develop as solitary beings in a sterile environment, but rather as active participants in complex, multifaceted physical and social systems. Yet most treatment outcome research with children involves interactions with a single therapist, or sometimes with a small group of unfamiliar children, in the sterile environment of the therapist's office or therapy room. Pretherapy assessment and treatment planning typically involve very limited sampling of the child's life circumstances and behavior at home, at school, or with familiar peers. This may limit the capacity of the therapist to fit interventions precisely to conditions and context of the individual child's problems. In the worst cases, the problem may tilt treatment

development in the direction of "one-size-fits-all" or "cookie-cutter" therapies.

Numerous theorists and researchers (e.g., Bronfenbrenner, 1979, 1986; Masten, Best, & Garmezy, 1991) have emphasized the context boundedness of development, and discussed implications for adaptation and dysfunction. Others (e.g., Cicchetti & Toth, in press; Mash & Dozois, 1996) have noted the diverse ways in which the child's contexts and ecological systems can influence the development and expression of dysfunctional behavior and emotional states. Still others (e.g., Forehand, Lautenschlager, Faust, & Graziano, 1986; Kazdin, 1989) have noted that even what parents report (e.g., to assessors and therapists) regarding deviance and dysfunction in their children can be influenced by such diverse factors as parental psychopathology, marital discord, stress in the home, and even an intent to conceal harmful parental practices (e.g., abuse or neglect). Finally, it seems self-evident that the impact of psychotherapy with children may vary depending on the extent to which significant others in the child's contexts (e.g., parents, teachers) are involved and supportive of the process. The power of all the influences noted in this paragraph may be felt disproportionately in childhood, in part because children have such limited ability to select the contexts in which their development unfolds.

The message for treatment planners and treatment outcome researchers is that contextual factors and key individuals in the child's social environment (e.g., parents, teachers, siblings, peers) may need to figure significantly in pretreatment assessment, in treatment planning, in treatment delivery, and in outcome assessment. In general, these steps have only been taken in very limited and tentative ways in child psychotherapy research to date. There are some exceptions to this generalization, however, and noting a few of these may help illustrate what is possible in future child psychotherapy research.

In one approach, Lewinsohn and colleagues (see Lewinsohn, Clarke, Hops, & Andrews, 1990; Lewinsohn, Rohde, Clarke, Hops, & Seeley, 1994; Rohde, Lewinsohn, & Seeley, 1994) have created a parent counterpart to their Adolescent Coping with Depression group intervention. The objective is to promote parental understanding and acceptance of what is being taught to the adolescents, and to reduce family conflict by teaching parents some of the same communication and problem-solving skills their adolescents are learning. In another approach, such investigators as Szapocznik and colleagues (e.g., Szapocznik et al., 1989) treat problem behavior in Hispanic boys by means of structural family therapy. Webster-Stratton and colleagues (e.g., Webster-Stratton, Kolpacoff, & Hollinsworth, 1988) have developed a self-administered videotape therapy for families with conduct-problem children. Henggeler and colleagues (e.g., Henggeler, Melton, & Smith, 1992; Borduin et al., 1995), in perhaps the most context-sensitive approach yet developed, send therapists into the settings where juvenile offenders live their lives, working with them to develop treatments tailored to the strengths and limitations of their family, school, peer group, and neighborhood. Each of the intervention approaches cited here has shown positive effects relative to control groups, although Lewinsohn and colleagues have not yet found that adding parent training alone to their adolescent intervention improves benefits over and above treatment of adolescents only. Perhaps procedures that delve more deeply into the child's social systems are required to produce benefits greater than those of individually administered interventions.

Moving in the directions illustrated by these research teams certainly will complicate the work of treatment development and outcome assessment. On the other hand, such efforts seem essential if we are to assess the benefits of context-sensitive treatment. We need to find out what can be gained if we push beyond a narrow focus on child characteristics and toward a broader focus on potentiating and inhibiting forces in the social systems within which the child is growing up.

ACKNOWLEDGMENTS

The research program described in this chapter was supported through a Research Scientist Award (K05 MH01161) and research grants (R01 MH34210, R01 MH38450, R01 MH38240) from the National Institute of Mental Health, which I gratefully acknowledge. I also appreciate the important contributions made to this work by faculty and graduate student colleagues, clinic administrators and therapists, and the many children and parents who have participated in the research before, during, and after treatment.

5.04.15 REFERENCES

Achenbach, T. M., McConaughy, S. H., & Howell, C. T. (1987). Child/adolescent behavioral and emotional problems: Implications of cross-informant correlations for situational specificity. *Psychological Bulletin, 101*, 213–232.
American Psychiatric Association (1980). *Diagnostic and statistical manual of mental disorders* (3rd ed.). Washington, DC: American Psychiatric Association Press.
Ashcroft, C. W. (1971). The later school adjustment of treated and untreated emotionally handicapped children. *Journal of School Psychology, 9,* 338–342.
Baer, R. A., & Nietzel, M. T. (1991). Cognitive and behavioral treatment of impulsivity in children: A meta-analytic review of the outcome literature. *Journal of Clinical Child Psychology, 2,* 400–412.
Bickman, L. (1996). A continuum of care: More is not always better. *American Psychologist, 51,* 689–701.
Bickman, L., Guthrie, P. R., Foster, E. M., Lambert, E. W., Summerfelt, W.T., Breda, C. S., & Heflinger, C. A. (1995). *Evaluating managed mental health services: The Fort Bragg experiment.* New York: Plenum.
Bordin, E. S. (1979). The generalizability of the psychoanalytic concept of the working alliance. *Psychotherapy: Theory, Research, and Practice, 16,* 252–260.
Borduin, C.M., Mann, B. J., Cone, L. T., Henggeler, S. W., Fucci, B. R., Blaske, D., & Williams, R. A. (1995). Multisystemic treatment of serious juvenile offenders: Long-term prevention of criminality and violence. *Journal of Consulting and Clinical Psychology, 63,* 569–578.
Braswell, L., Kendall, P. C., Braith, J., Carey, M. P., & Vye, C. S. (1985). "Involvement" in cognitive-behavioral therapy with children: Process and its relationship to outcome. *Cognitive Therapy and Research, 9,* 611–630.
Bronfenbrenner, U. (1979). *The ecology of human development.* Cambridge, MA: Harvard University Press.
Bronfenbrenner, U. (1986). Ecology of the family as a context for human development. *Developmental Psychology, 22,* 723–742.
Casey, R. J., & Berman, J. S. (1985). The outcome of psychotherapy with children. *Psychological Bulletin, 98,* 388–400.
Chalmers, T. C., Smith, H., Blackburn, B., Silverman, B., Schroeder, B., Reitman, D., & Ambroz, A. (1981). A method for assessing the quality of a randomized clinical trial. *Controlled Clinical Trials, 2,* 31–49.
Cicchetti, D., & Toth, S. L. (in press). Transactional ecological systems in developmental psychopathology. In S. S. Luthar, J. A. Burack, D. Cicchetti, & J. R. Weisz (Eds.), *Developmental psychopathology: Perspectives on adjustment, risk, and disorder.* New York: Cambridge University Press.
Cicchetti, D., Rogosch, F. A., & Toth, S. L. (in press). Ontogenesis, depressotypic organization, and the depressive spectrum. In S. S. Luthar, J. A. Burack, D. Cicchetti, & J. R. Weisz (Eds.), *Developmental psychopathology: Perspectives on adjustment, risk, and disorder.* New York: Cambridge University Press.
Cohen, J. (1988). *Statistical power analysis for the behavioral sciences* (2nd ed.). Hillsdale, NJ: Erlbaum.
Cohen, J. (1992). A power primer. *Psychological Bulletin, 112,* 155–159.
Costantino, G., Malgady, R., & Rogler, L. (1986). Cuento therapy: a culturally sensitive modality for Puerto Rican children. *Journal of Consulting and Clinical Psychology, 54,* 639–645.
Costello, E. J. (1989). Developments in child psychiatric epidemiology. *Journal of the American Academy of Child and Adolescent Psychiatry, 28,* 836–841.
DeFries, Z., Jenkins, S., & Williams, E. C. (1964). Treatment of disturbed children in foster care. *American Journal of Orthopsychiatry, 34,* 615–624.
Durlak, J. A., Fuhrman, T., & Lampman, C. (1991). Effectiveness of cognitive-behavior therapy for maladapting children: A meta-analysis. *Psychological Bulletin, 110,* 204–214.
Dush, D. M., Hirt, M. L., & Schroeder, H. E. (1989). Self-statement modification in the treatment of child behaviour disorders: A meta-analysis. *Psychological Bulletin, 106,* 97–106.
Evans, M. E., Armstrong, M. I., Dollard, N., Kuppinger, A. D., Huz, S., & Wood, V. M. (1994). Development and

evaluation of treatment foster care and family-centered intensive case management in New York. *Journal of Emotional and Behavioral Disorders, 2,* 228–239.

Forehand, R., Lautenschlager, G. J., Faust, J., & Graziano, W. G. (1986). Parent perceptions and parent–child interactions in clinic-referred children: A preliminary investigation of the effects of maternal depressive moods. *Behavior Research and Therapy, 24,* 73–75.

Frank, J. D. (1973). *Persuasion and healing: A comparative study of psychotherapy.* Baltimore: Johns Hopkins University Press.

Friedlander, M. L., Wildman, J., Heatherington, L., & Skowron, E. A. (1994). What we do and don't know about the process of family therapy. *Journal of Family Psychology, 8,* 390–416.

Gibbs, J. T., & Huang, L. N. (1989). *Children of color: Psychological interventions with minority children.* San Francisco: Jossey-Bass.

Glass, G. V., McGaw, B., & Smith, M. L. (1981). *Meta-analysis in social research.* Beverly Hills, CA: Sage.

Gorin, S. S. (1993). The prediction of child psychotherapy outcome: Factors specific to treatment. *Psychotherapy, 30,* 152–158.

Hayes, E. J., Cunningham, G. K., Robinson, J. B. (1977). Counseling focus: Are parents necessary? *Elementary School Guidance and Counseling, 12,* 8–14.

Hazelrigg, M. D., Cooper, H. M., & Borduin, C. M. (1987). Evaluating the effectiveness of family therapies: An integrative review and analysis. *Psychological Bulletin, 101,* 428–442.

Henggeler, S. W., Melton, G. B., & Smith, L. A. (1992). Family preservation using multisystemic therapy: An effective alternative to incarcerating serious juvenile offenders. *Journal of Consulting and Clinical Psychology, 60,* 953–961.

Ho, M. K. (1992). *Minority children and adolescents in therapy.* Newbury Park, CA: Sage.

Horowitz, M. J., Marmar, C. R., Weiss, D. S., DeWitt, K. N., & Rosenbaum, R. L. (1984). Brief psychotherapy of bereavement reactions: The relationship of process to outcome. *Archives of General Psychiatry, 41,* 438–448.

Howe, P. A., & Silvern, L. E. (1981). Behavioral observation of children during play therapy: Preliminary development of a research instrument. *Journal of Personality Assessment, 45,* 168–182.

Institute of Medicine (1989). *Research on children and adolescents with mental, behavioral, and developmental disorders.* Washington, DC: National Academy Press.

Jacob, T., Magnussen, M. G., & Kemler, W. M. (1972). A follow-up of treatment terminators and remainers with short-term and long-term symptom duration. *Psychotherapy: Theory, Research, and Practice, 9,* 139–142.

Kazdin, A. E. (1988). *Child psychotherapy: Developing and identifying effective treatments.* Elmsford, NY: Pergamon.

Kazdin, A. E. (1989). Developmental psychopathology: Current research, issues, and directions. *American Psychologist, 44,* 180–187.

Kazdin, A. E., Bass, D., Ayers, W. A., & Rodgers, A. (1990). Empirical and clinical focus of child and adolescent psychotherapy research. *Journal of Consulting and Clinical Psychology, 58,* 729–740.

Kazdin, A. E., Siegel, T. C., & Bass, D. (1990). Drawing on clinical practice to inform research on child and adolescent psychotherapy: Survey of practitioners. *Professional Psychology: Research and Practice, 21,* 189–198.

Kendall, P. C. (1994). Treating anxiety disorders in children: Results of a randomized clinical trial. *Journal of Consulting and Clinical Psychology, 62,* 100–110.

Kendall, P. C., & Morris, R. J. (1991). Child therapy: Issues and recommendations. *Journal of Consulting and Clinical Psychology, 59,* 777–784.

Kohlberg, L., Yaeger, J., & Hjertholm, E. (1968). The development of private speech: Four studies and a review of theories. *Child Development, 39,* 691–736.

Lehman, A. E., Postrado, L. T., Roth, D., McNary, S. W., & Goldman, H. H. (1994). Continuity of care and client outcomes in the Robert Wood Johnson Foundation program on chronic mental illness. *Milbank Quarterly, 72,* 105–122.

Lehrman, L. J., Sirluck, Black, B. J., & Glick, S. J. (1949). *Success and failure of treatment of children in the child guidance clinics of the Jewish Board of Guardians, New York City.* Jewish Board of Guardians Research Monographs, No. 1.

Levitt, E. E., Beiser, H. R. & Robertson, R. E. (1959). A follow-up evaluation of cases treated at a community child guidance clinic. *American Journal of Orthopsychiatry, 29,* 337–347.

Lewinsohn, P. M., Clarke, G. N., Hops, H., & Andrews, J. A. (1990). Cognitive-behavioral treatment for depressed adolescents. *Behavior Therapy, 21,* 385–401.

Lewinsohn, P. M., Rohde, P., Clarke, G. N., Hops, H., & Seeley, J. R. (1994). *Cognitive-behavioral treatment for depressed adolescents: Treatment outcome and the role of parental involvement.* Unpublished manuscript. Eugene, OR: Oregon Research Institute.

Lovaas, O. I. (1987). Behavioral treatment and normal educational and intellectual functioning in young autistic children. *Journal of Consulting and Clinical Psychology, 55,* 3–9.

Luborsky, L., Crits-Christoph, P., Mintz, J., & Auerbach, A. (1988). *Who will benefit from psychotherapy?* New York: Basic Books.

Mann, C. (1990). Meta-analysis in the breech. *Science, 249,* 476–480.

Mash, E. J., & Dozois, D. J. A. (1996). Child psychopathology: A developmental-systems perspective. In E. J. Mash & R. A. Barkley (Eds.), *Child psychopathology* (pp. 3–60). New York: Guilford Press.

Masten, A., Best, K., & Garmezy, N. (1991). Resilience and development: Contributions from the study of children who overcome adversity. *Development and Psychopathology, 2,* 425–444.

McGrath, M. L., Dorsett, P. G., Calhoun, M. E., & Drabman, R. S. (1988). "Beat-the-buzzer": A method for decreasing parent–child morning conflicts. *Child and Family Behavior Therapy, 9,* 35–48.

Meichenbaum, D., & Goodman, S. (1979). Clinical use of private speech and critical questions about its study in natural settings. In G. Zivin (Ed.), *The development of self-regulation through private speech* (pp. 325–360). New York: Wiley.

Motta, R. W., & Lynch, C. (1990). Therapeutic techniques vs. therapeutic relationships in child behavior therapy. *Psychological Reports, 67,* 315–322.

Motta, R. W., & Tobin, M. I. (1992). The relative importance of specific and nonspecific factors in child behavior therapy. *Psychotherapy in Private Practice, 11,* 51–61.

Nicholson, R. A., & Berman, J. S. (1983). Is follow-up necessary in evaluating psychotherapy? *Psychological Bulletin, 93,* 261–278.

Office of Technology Assessment (1986). *Children's mental health: Problems and services—A background paper* (Publication No. OTA-BP-H-33). Washington, DC: US Government Printing Office.

Patterson, G. R., & Chamberlain, P. (1994). A functional analysis of resistance during parent training therapy. *Clinical Psychology: Science and Practice, 1,* 53–70.

Patterson, G. R., & Forgatch, M. S. (1985). Therapist behavior as a determinant for client noncompliance: A paradox for the behavior modifier. *Journal of Consulting and Clinical Psychology, 53,* 846–851.

Pelham, W. E., Carlson, C., Sams, S., Vallano, G., Dixon,

J., & Hoza, B. (1993). Separate and combined effects of methylphenidate and behavior modification on boys with attention-deficit-hyperactivity disorder in the classroom. *Journal of Consulting and Clinical Psychology, 55,* 76–85.

Piaget, J. (1929). *The child's conception of the world.* Totowa, NJ: Littlefield, Adams.

Piaget, J. (1955). *The language and thought of the child.* New York: Meridian. (Originally published 1923).

Piaget, J. (1962). *Play, dreams, and imitation.* New York: Norton.

Piaget, J. (1970). Piaget's theory. In P. H. Mussen (Ed.), *Carmichael's manual of child psychology* (Vol. 1, pp. 703–32). New York: Wiley.

Pinsoff, W. M., & Catherall, D. R. (1986). The integrative psychotherapy alliance: Family, couple, and individual therapy scales. *Journal of Marital and Family Therapy, 12,* 137–151.

Prout, H. T., & DeMartino, R. A. (1986). A meta-analysis of school-based studies of psychotherapy. *Journal of School Psychology, 24,* 285–292.

Roberts, M. C. (1994). Models for service delivery in children's mental health: Common characteristics. *Journal of Clinical Child Psychology, 23,* 212–219.

Rogler, L. H., Malgady, R. G., Costantino, G., & Blumenthal, R. (1987). What do culturally sensitive mental health services mean?: The case of Hispanics. *American Psychologist, 42*(6), 565–575.

Rohde, P., Lewinsohn, P. M., & Seeley, J. R. (1994). Responses of depressed adolescents to cognitive-behavioral treatment: Do differences in initial severity clarify the comparison of treatments? *Journal of Consulting and Clinical Psychology, 62,* 851–854.

Russell, R. L., Greenwald, S., & Shirk, S. R. (1991). Language change in child psychotherapy: A meta-analytic review. *Journal of Consulting and Clinical Psychology, 59,* 916–919.

Saile, H., Burgmeier, R., & Schmidt, L. R. (1988). A meta-analysis of studies on psychological preparation of children facing medical procedures. *Psychology and Health, 2,* 107–132.

Shadish, W. R., Montgomery, L. M., Wilson, P., Wilson, M. R., Bright, I, & Okwumabua, T. (1993). Effects of family and marital psychotherapies: A meta-analysis. *Journal of Consulting and Clinical Psychology, 61,* 992–1002.

Shapiro, D. A., & Shapiro, D. (1982). Meta-analysis of comparative therapy outcome studies: A replication and refinement. *Psychological Bulletin, 92,* 581–604.

Shepherd, M., Oppenheim, A. N., & Mitchell, S. (1966). Childhood behavior disorders and the child-guidance clinic: An epidemiological study. *Journal of Child Psychology and Psychiatry, 1,* 39–52.

Shirk, S. R., & Saiz, C. S. (1992). Clinical, empirical, and developmental perspectives on the therapeutic relationship in child psychotherapy. *Development and Psychopathology, 4,* 713–728.

Smith, M. L., & Glass, G. V. (1977). Meta-analysis of psychotherapy outcome studies. *American Psychologist, 32,* 752–760.

Smith, M. L., Glass, G. V., & Miller, T. L. (1980). *Benefits of psychotherapy.* Baltimore: Johns Hopkins University Press.

Smyrnios, K. X., & Kirkby, R. J. (1993). Long-term comparison of brief versus unlimited treatments with children and their parents. *Journal of Consulting and Clinical Psychology, 61,* 1020–1027.

Spurlock, J. (1985). Assessment and therapeutic intervention of Black children. *Journal of the American Academy of Child Psychiatry, 24*(2), 168–174.

Stroul, B. A., & Friedman, R. (1986). *A system of care for children and youth with severe emotional disturbances* (Rev. ed.). Washington, DC: Georgetown University

Child Development Center, CASSP Technical Assistance Center.

Sue, S. (1977). Community mental health services to minority groups: Some optimism, some pessimism. *American Psychologist, 32,* 616–624.

Sue, S., & Zane, N. (1987). The role of culture and cultural techniques in psychotherapy: A critique and reformulation. *American Psychologist, 42*(1), 37–45.

Szapocznik, J., Kurtines, W., Santisteban, D. A., & Rio, A. T. (1990). Interplay of advances between theory, research, and application in treatment interventions aimed at behavior problem children and adolescents. *Journal of Consulting and Clinical Psychology, 58,* 696–703.

Szapocznik, J., Rio, A., Murray, E., Cohen, R., Scopetta, M., Rivas-Vasquez, A., Hervis, O., Posada, V., & Kurtines, W. (1989). Structural family vs. psychodynamic child therapy for problematic Hispanic boys. *Journal of Consulting and Clinical Psychology, 57,* 571–578.

Tarnowski, K. J., Rosen, L. A., McGrath, M. L., & Drabman, R. S. (1987). A modified habit reversal procedure in a recalcitrant case of trichotillomania. *Journal of Behavior Therapy and Experimental Psychiatry, 18,* 157–163.

Task Force on Promotion and Dissemination of Psychological Procedures, Division of Clinical Psychology, American Psychological Association (1995, Winter). Training in and dissemination of empirically validated psychological treatments: Report and Recommendations. *The Clinical Psychologist, 48,* 3–24.

Tharp, R. G. (1991). Cultural diversity and treatment of children. *Journal of Consulting and Clinical Psychology, 59*(6), 799–812.

Truax, C. B., Altmann, H., Wright, L., & Mitchell, K. M. (1973). Effects of therapeutic conditions in child therapy. *Journal of Community Psychology, 1,* 313–318.

Truax, C. B., & Wittmer, J. (1973). The degree of therapist focus on defense mechanisms and the effect on therapeutic outcome with Institutionalized juvenile delinquents. *Journal of Community Psychology, 1,* 201–203.

Vygotsky, L. (1962). *Thought and language.* Cambridge, MA: MIT Press. (Originally published 1934).

Webster-Stratton, C., & Herbert, M. (1993). "What really happens in parent training?" *Behavior Modification, 17,* 407–456.

Webster-Stratton, C., Kolpacoff, M., & Hollinsworth, T. (1988). Self-administered videotape therapy for families with conduct-problem children: Comparison with two cost-effective treatments and a control group. *Journal of Consulting and Clinical Psychology, 56,* 558–566.

Weiss, B., & Weisz, J. R. (1990). The impact of methodological factors on child psychotherapy outcome research: A meta-analysis for researchers. *Journal of Abnormal Child Psychology, 18,* 639–670.

Weisz, J. R. (1996, in progress). *Studying clinic-based child mental health care.* Ongoing research project, University of California at Los Angeles.

Weisz, J. R., Donenberg, G. R., Han, S. S., & Kauneckis, D. (1995). Child and adolescent psychotherapy outcomes in experiments vs. clinics: Why the disparity? *Journal of Abnormal Child Psychology, 23,* 83–106.

Weisz, J. R., Donenberg, G. R., Han, S. S., & Weiss, B. (1995). Bridging the gap between lab and clinic in child and adolescent psychotherapy. *Journal of Consulting and Clinical Psychology, 63*(5), 688–701.

Weisz, J. R., Huey, S. J., & Weersing, V. R. (in press). *Psychotherapy outcome research with children and adolescents.* In T. H. Ollendick & R. J. Prinz (Eds.), *Advances in Clinical Child Psychology.* New York: Plenum.

Weisz, J. R., McCarty, C. A., Eastman, K. L., Chaiyasit,

W., & Suwanlert, S. (1997). Developmental psychopathology and culture: Ten lessons from Thailand. In S. S. Luthar, J. Burack, D. Cicchetti, & J. R. Weisz (Eds.), *Developmental psychopathology: Perspectives on adjustment, risk, and disorder* (pp. 568–592). New York: Cambridge University Press.

Weisz, J. R., Suwanlert, S., Chaiyasit, W., Weiss, B., Walter, B. R., & Anderson, W. (1988). Thai and American perspectives on over- and undercontrolled child behavior problems: Exploring the threshold model among parents, teachers, and psychologists. *Journal of Consulting and Clinical Psychology, 56,* 601–609.

Weisz, J. R., & Weiss, B. (1989). Assessing the effects of clinic-based psychotherapy with children and adolescents. *Journal of Consulting and Clinical Psychology, 57,* 741–746.

Weisz, J. R., & Weiss, B. (1991). Studying the referability of child clinical problems. *Journal of Consulting and Clinical Psychology, 59,* 266–273.

Weisz, J. R., & Weiss, B. (1993). *Effects of psychotherapy with children and adolescents.* Newbury Park, CA: Sage.

Weisz, J. R., Weiss, B., Alicke, M. D., & Klotz, M. L. (1987). Effectiveness of psychotherapy with children and adolescents: A meta-analysis for clinicians. *Journal of Consulting and Clinical Psychology, 55,* 542–549.

Weisz, J. R., Weiss, B., & Donenberg, G. R. (1992). The lab vs. the clinic: Effects of child and adolescent psychotherapy. *American Psychologist, 47,* 1578–1585.

Weisz, J. R., Weiss, B., Han, S. S., Granger, D. A., & Morton, T. (1995). Effects of psychotherapy with children and adolescents revisited: A meta-analysis of treatment outcome studies. *Psychological Bulletin, 117,* 450–468.

Werner, H. (1957). The concept of development from a comparative and organismic point of view. In D. Harris (Ed.), *The concept of development.* Minneapolis: University of Minnesota Press.

Wilson, G. T. (1985). Limitations of meta-analysis in the evaluation of the effects of psychological therapy. *Clinical Psychology Review, 5,* 35–47.

Witmer, H. L., & Keller, J. (1942). Outgrowing childhood problems: A study of the value of child guidance treatment. *Smith College Studies in Social Work, 13,* 74–90.

Wurtele, S. K., & Drabman, R. S. (1984). "/Beat-the-buzzer" for classroom dawdling: A one-year trial. *Behavior Therapy, 15,* 403–409.

Zivin, G. (Ed.) (1979). *The development of self-regulation through private speech.* New York: Wiley.

5.05
Applied Behavior Analysis

ALAN HUDSON

Royal Melbourne Institute of Technology, Bundoora, Vic, Australia

5.05.1 THEORETICAL UNDERPINNINGS

Applied behavior analysis (ABA) has it roots in the various learning theories of psychology. The theories of Pavlov, Watson, Thorndike, and Hull (Bry, 1975) provided the early impetus for the development of modern day ABA. Despite the substantial contributions of these scholars, the pre-eminent theorist in the field has clearly been Burrhus Frederick Skinner. The theoretical work by Skinner (1938, 1953, 1957, 1969) on operant conditioning has been the foundation on which ABA has been established. Skinner developed his early theoretical formulations of operant conditioning from research in laboratories with rats and pigeons. His later writings moved more toward applications of the theory with humans. One of his most read works, *Walden Two* (Skinner, 1948), was a novel about the ways in which operant conditioning could be used to create a human utopia.

Although operant conditioning is the foundation of ABA procedures, it is important to indicate that this does not mean that ABA clinicians are of the view that all problem behavior of human beings is the product of operant conditioning. On the contrary, ABA clinicians see all human behavior as resulting from the complex interaction of a number of variables. A useful conceptualization of the determinants of behavior has been offered by Ross (1976), who argued that the variables that effect an individual's behavior are (i) long-term genetic/constitutional factors, (ii) past learning history, (iii) current physiological state, and (iv) current environmental factors. The first three of these, often referred to as organismic variables (Ollendick & Cerny, 1981), are seen as being important but not easily manipulated to effect behavior change. In contrast, environmental factors that effect behavior are more amenable to change. It is the manipulation of these environmental variables, primarily in accordance with the principles of operant conditioning, that is the basis of ABA interventions in clinical psychology.

The fundamental elements in the theory of operant conditioning are the behaviors that people engage in and the antecedents and consequences of those behaviors. In regard to the relationship between behaviors and their consequences, the future occurrence of behaviors is dependent upon the current consequences of those behaviors. Behaviors that are followed by reinforcement will increase in frequency. Reinforcement can occur in two conceptually different ways. First, it can involve the contingent presentation of a "pleasant" stimulus, called a positive reinforcer, with the process being termed positive reinforcement. Alternatively it can involve the contingent removal of an "unpleasant" stimulus, called a negative reinforcer, with this process termed negative reinforcement. It is important to note that the property of a stimulus being a positive reinforcer is defined purely in terms of the effect of that stimulus when it is presented contingent upon the occurrence of the behavior. If contingent presentation leads to an increase in the frequency of the behavior, the stimulus is a positive reinforcer. In a similar fashion, a negative reinforcer is defined in terms of its capacity to increase behavior when it is removed contingent upon the occurrence of the behavior.

Behaviors that are followed by punishment will decrease in frequency. In a similar manner to reinforcement, punishment can occur in two ways: by the contingent presentation of a negative reinforcer (in these circumstances the term "punisher" may be used), or the contingent removal of a positive reinforcer. It might be expected that these processes would be called positive and negative punishment. This has not been the practice. Some authors refer to them as type 1 and type 2 punishment. Others use the term "punishment" only for the presentation of a negative reinforcer (punisher), and use the term response cost for the contingent removal of a positive reinforcer.

Finally, behaviors that are followed neither by reinforcement nor punishment will decrease in frequency, with this phenomenon being known as extinction.

A substantial amount of early operant conditioning research examined ways in which variations in the delivery of reinforcement effected the behavior it was contingent upon. For example, it was found that reinforcement delivered immediately after the occurrence of the behavior is more effective in increasing the rate of the behavior than reinforcement which is delayed for a short period of time. Of particular interest in regard to variation in delivery of reinforcement was the effect of not providing reinforcement for every occurrence of the behavior. Providing reinforcement for every occurrence became known as using a continuous schedule of reinforcement, whereas some variation of this is referred to as an intermittent schedule of reinforcement. The effects of various intermittent schedules on the rate of increase of behavior and subsequent extinction of the behavior were studied. Initial variations were made in the ratio of reinforcement (the number of responses that had to be emitted before reinforcement was provided), and the interval of reinforcement (the period of time that would be allowed to elapse before reinforcement was provided for the next response emitted). Ratio schedules could be fixed, in that reinforcement was provided after a set number of responses, or could be variable, in that reinforcement was provided after a varying number of responses. Similarly, interval schedules could involve a fixed or variable period of time. The effects of all types of schedules have been well documented in the literature, but one important finding for the ABA field is that to teach new behaviors it is better to begin with a continuous schedule. When the behavior is established, however, it is advisable to move to variable schedules as they are more resistant to extinction once learning has taken place.

As has been described, the effects of consequences on the future occurrence of behavior is a central component of the theory of operant conditioning. In addition, however, events or stimuli that precede the occurrence of the behavior are also important. These are usually referred to as the antecedents of the behavior. Antecedents go with the behavior and its consequences to make up the antecedent–behavior–consequence sequence that is so important in the use of ABA in applied settings.

One way in which antecedent stimuli are important in operant conditioning is that they can act as a signal that a behavior will be reinforced if the behavior is emitted. A young child might find that if he asks his mother for some candy, the answer will be no. If, however, he asks his father, the answer is yes. The child quickly learns to ask the father and not the mother. In these circumstances, discrimination learning has taken place, and the father is the discriminative stimulus for the behavior of asking for candy. The systematic reinforcement of a behavior under some stimulus conditions but not others is used to promote discrimination, and is referred to a discrimination training. Such training is an important component of many interventions based on ABA.

Traditionally, operant conditioning theory focused only on those antecedents and consequences that were temporally contiguous with the behavior. These are referred to as proximal antecedents and consequences. It became clear, however, that antecedents and consequences that are temporally removed from the behavior can also be important. These are referred to as distal antecedents and consequences.

In regard to distal consequences, they may exert more influence on a particular behavior than those that are more immediate. A student, for example, may engage in long hours of study during the weekend, resulting in fatigue and the missing of social activities (immediate punishers), for the sake of completing an assignment due on Monday morning (a powerful reinforcer).

Distal antecedents that are gaining increased attention in the use of ABA are referred to as setting events (Wahler & Fox, 1981). These are events that alter the probability that a proximal antecedent will be discriminative for the occurrence of a particular behavior. By way of example, a child at school may usually respond to a request from the teacher in a cheerful and compliant manner. However, on the days following domestic disruptions at home, the child is moody and non-compliant. Here the domestic disruptions act as a setting event that alters the probability of the child responding positively to the teacher.

An important point in relation to the antecedent–behavior–consequence sequence is that a single behavior may be associated with more than one antecedent and/or more than one consequence. For example, the behavior of one child hitting another child could be occasioned by the other child calling her a name, the other child having a toy that is wanted, or in response to a dare from a third child. Similarly, the aggressive behavior could have many consequences, for example the other child cries, the aggressive child gains the coveted toy, and also receives attention from an adult, all of which could be reinforcing.

One area of operant theory that is often not given much prominence in basic texts on ABA is that of rule-governed behavior. To illustrate this concept, let us take the example of a child who is usually slow with his work at school. One day the frustrated teacher tells him that if he completes all his mathematics problems in class, he will be permitted to go to play early. The child completes the problems and goes to play early. The behavior of completing the problems was not established by contingent reinforcement, but is an example of rule-governed behavior. Skinner defined a rule as a verbal statement that specifies the conditions under which a behavior is to occur, the behavior itself, and the consequence that will follow the behavior. The child in our example followed the rule "If you complete all problems in class, you will get to go to play early." However, such rule-governed behavior will occur only if certain conditions are met. First, the child must possess sufficient language skill to understand the rule. Second, the general response class of following similar rules must have been established. In this case, the child's learning history must be such that he has been contingently reinforced for following such rules in the past.

Skinner distinguished between two types of rules, one he called a command and the other advice. The word "command" is used when the person stating the rule controls the availability of the reinforcer. The situation given above is an example of a command rule. The teacher controlled the availability of early access to play. The word "advice" is used for those situations in which the person stating the rule does not control the availability of the reinforcer, but is aware of the contingency. An example of such a rule would be a parent telling her child "If you poke that stick into the electricity outlet, you will get a shock." A knowledge of the method of establishing or changing rule-governed behavior is progressively becoming more important in clinical applications of ABA.

It is critical that practitioners using ABA procedures in applied settings be thoroughly familiar with the fundamental theoretical concepts. A sound understanding of them is not only necessary for the development of effective treatment programs, it is impossible to effectively "trouble shoot" intervention programs if the clinician does not have mastery of the theory underlying the design of the program.

5.05.2 HISTORY OF THE APPROACH

As indicated in Section 5.05.1, ABA has derived primarily from the principles of learning, particularly operant conditioning. The refinement of these principles was effected through experimental research with animals, and was published through eminent journals such as the *Journal of the Experimental Analysis of Behavior*.

The application of ABA procedures with humans did not begin in any substantial way until the 1950s, when learning-theory-based approaches to intervention in human problems became a serious competitor to the traditional psychodynamic approaches derived from Freud and other psychoanalysts. Proponents of learning-theory-based approaches were dissatisfied with three major aspects of traditional approaches. The first was the heavy reliance on the use of putative intrapsychic constructs to explain behavior. Learning theorists preferred to study the behavior directly. The second was a propensity to explain abnormal behavior in terms of a medical or illness model. Learning theorists saw abnormality as being at the end of the continuum of normal development, and hence as being quantitatively, not qualitatively, different from normal behavior. The final point of dissatisfaction was with what was seen as unsubstantiated claims for success of traditional psychodynamic approaches. Hence, learning theorists placed great emphasis on experimental demonstrations of treatment efficacy.

Despite these common concerns with traditional therapies, learning-theory-based therapy did not emerge as a single entity. In the early days, two relatively different approaches were developed. ABA was one of these, and as indicated earlier, grew out of the operant conditioning work of Skinner. The other approach was founded more on classical conditioning, particularly the work of Pavlov (1927) and Hull (1943). Development of this approach for work with humans can probably be attributed to Eysenck (1959) and Wolpe (1958). A major difference between the two approaches was the importance placed on private or covert events within humans, such as thinking and feeling. Although Skinner recognized the existence of private events, he considered that there were serious limitations in being able to study them scientifically, and hence ABA clinicians initially focused on overt, observable behavior. In contrast, proponents of the other approach were quite comfortable working with constructs such as anxiety and fear. They considered that these processes were governed by the same principles of learning as were overt behaviors (Agras, Kazdin, & Wilson, 1979).

As time passed, further approaches developed within the framework of learning theory approaches to therapy. The 1960s and 1970s saw the evolution of what became known as cognitive behavior therapies. Perhaps the first of these was social learning theory. The principal theoretician in the development of social learning theory was Bandura (1969, 1977), who argued that cognitive processes played a mediational role between the antecedent and consequent stimuli that impinged on humans. Bandura's experimental work on observational learning has been particularly useful in explaining the acquisition of many human behaviors, but also is an important theoretical component of therapeutic modeling. Bandura's construct of self-efficacy has also proven to be popular in clinical practice. He argued that the knowledge by a person that a particular behavior would be reinforced was not necessarily enough to motivate the person to perform that behavior. What also was necessary was the person's belief that he or she had the ability to perform that behavior.

Other theoreticians who have contributed to the field of cognitive behavior therapy are Ellis (1979), Mahoney (1974), and Meichenbaum (1977). While the final products that they have developed are all a little different from each other, a key element that runs through all of them is what is referred to a cognitive restructuring. This process essentially involves teaching individuals to change their behavior by changing the ways in which they think about their behavior and its consequences.

While all of these developments within the framework of learning theory approaches to therapy have been important, the focus in this chapter is on ABA, although much of what is described as being the application of ABA incorporates elements from the other approaches.

Before moving on to the assessment and clinical formulation of the ABA approach, some comments about its applications could be informative. Because ABA first emerged as the application of principles derived from laboratory research to the resolution of human problems (Baer, Wolf, & Risley, 1968), many early applications of ABA were with psychiatrically and developmentally disabled people. The research by Ayllon and Michael (1959) on teaching psychiatric nurses to be behavioral engineers has been seen as the first publication in the emergence of ABA. The first issue of the *Journal of Applied Behavior Analysis (JABA)* in 1968 is probably a better-recognized marker of the beginning of the widespread usage of the approach. Many of the early *JABA* articles were in the disability field. As time has progressed, the principles of ABA have begun to be used in wide variety of fields. Engelmann and Carnine (1982) used ABA as a major plank in the development of their theory of instruction that is now the basis of many educational programs (Kameenui & Simmonds, 1990). Sulzer-Azaroff (1982) has used ABA in the promotion of better practices in the field of occupational health and safety, and there are many examples of the use of ABA in the organizational behavior and management literature (e.g., Brethower, 1972; Connellan, 1978). Finally, Biglan, Metzler, and Ary (1994) report on the use of ABA procedures to change behavior on a community-wide basis. In the remainder of this chapter, the focus will be on the use of ABA in the treatment of clinical problems of children and adolescents.

5.05.3 ASSESSMENT AND CLINICAL FORMULATION

There are several excellent texts available that give a full description of assessment and intervention procedures in ABA. To mention just a few authors, there is Cooper, Heron, and Heward (1987), Grant and Evans (1994), Martin and Pear (1996), and Sulzer-Azaroff and Mayer (1991). This chapter summarizes procedures that are more fully covered in these texts.

There are three steps involved in assessment and clinical formulation using the procedures of ABA: specification of the behavior, measurement of the behavior, and assessment of the function of the behavior.

5.05.3.1 Specification of Behavior

The first step in assessment and clinical formulation is the specification or description of the behavior of interest. It is essential that this specification be as precise as possible so that any confusion about what is meant is minimized. Terms such as "aggressive" or "self-injurious" are useful only as general descriptors of classes of behavior. They are not used in an ABA assessment as they can be interpreted in many different ways by observers. What is necessary is an accurate description of the behavior of interest; for example, the child "punches other children," or "slaps himself in the face." It is only when a precise description of the behavior is formulated that measurement, the second step in the formulation, can be reliably carried out.

5.05.3.2 Measurement of Behavior

Several methods of measuring behavior have been developed, the most commonly used being frequency counts, duration measures, counting of permanent products, and time sampling procedures, although other measures such as intensity and latency can be useful.

A frequency count involves, as the name suggests, counting the number of times the behavior occurs in a given time period, for example, during the course of one day. A duration measure involves measuring the total time the child spends engaged in the behavior of interest, again usually during the course of a day. The choice of measurement method is based on a consideration of which method will "give the best picture" of what is actually happening. To illustrate this, consider a child who punches other children. Each punch is quite discrete, and a frequency count will give an accurate assessment of the extent of the problem. In contrast, consider the child who sucks his thumb so much that physical damage is occurring. If this child puts his thumb in his mouth after breakfast and only takes it out to have lunch, a frequency count would record only one instance for that morning, not really reflecting the extent of the problem. A duration measure would clearly be better in this case.

Many behaviors result in relatively permanent products that can be counted, with the resulting sum being the measure of the occurrence of the behavior. The mathematics output of a child at school can be measured by the number of problems completed. A person who is trying to give up smoking could measure the amount of smoking by counting cigarette butts in an ashtray at the end of the day.

Time sampling is more complex than the frequency, duration, and permanent product methods, and involves breaking the observation period into relatively short time intervals (e.g., 15 seconds), and then noting whether or not the behavior occurs during that interval. There are variations of time sampling referred to as total interval, partial interval, and momentary time sampling. The term "total interval" is used when the behavior of interest has to occur for the complete duration of the time interval for it to be scored as an occurrence. "Partial interval" is used when the behavior only has to occur at some time during the interval, and not for the total interval. The term "momentary" is used when a behavior is scored only if it occurs at a particular instant in the interval, usually the end of the interval. While time sampling procedures are more labor-intensive than frequency or duration methods, they have some advantages in that several behaviors of several children can be observed simultaneously. The particular type of time sampling procedure used will depend on matters such as the type of behaviors being assessed and the time available to the observer.

Sometimes clinicians will be interested not only in how often or for how long a behavior occurs but also how strong or intense it is, and hence would introduce an intensity measure. A clinician treating a child who inappropriately calls out in public places might be interested in the volume of the calling out. Volume would be important if the objective of intervention was not to eliminate public conversation, but to reduce it to a socially acceptable level.

A final measure that might be used in assessing a behavior is that of latency, or the time that elapses between some important event and the onset of the behavior by the child. Latency measures are often used when the behavior of interest is compliance by the child with some instruction given by a parent or other caregiver.

There are two reasons why clinicians need to take precise measurements of the behaviors of interest as part of the assessment process. The first is related to making a decision about whether subsequent intervention is actually warranted. For example, take the case of a child who is referred by her parents because of a "low" level of compliance to instructions given by them. An initial assessment of the child's rate of compliance might indicate that her compliance is typical for a child of her developmental level. Under these circumstances, intervention to improve the child's compliance would not be indicated. Instead, the parents need assistance with improving their knowledge of child development, and perhaps some help with accepting the child as she is.

In most cases of the application of ABA, the initial measurement of the behavior of interest does indicate that some intervention is warranted. On some occasions, the measurement will show that the behavior is occurring more often than considered appropriate. This is referred to as having a behavioral excess, and hence the objective of intervention will be to reduce the occurrence of the behavior (weaken it), perhaps even to totally eliminate it. On other occasions, the measurement will show that behavior is not occurring as often as considered appropriate. This is referred to as having a behavioral deficit, and the objective of intervention will be to increase its occurrence (strengthen it). Once a behavior has been identified as being in need of either strengthening or weakening, it is referred to as a target behavior.

The second reason for taking precise measurements of the behaviors of interest is related to the need to evaluate the efficacy of any intervention that is proceeded with. Under these circumstances, the initial measurements form the baseline against which intervention efforts are evaluated. This means, of course, that measurement of the behaviors must continue during intervention. The issue of determining the efficacy of ABA intervention is dealt with more fully in Section 5.05.5.1.

5.05.3.3 Assessment of the Function of Behavior

The third step in clinical formulation is the assessment of the function of the target behavior, that is, to identify the antecedents and consequences which are functionally related to the behavior. Before a fuller discussion of this element is possible, a distinction needs to be made between the topography of a behavior and the function of a behavior. The topography of a behavior is what the person does, and can be readily seen by an observer. The function of the behavior is the purpose of the behavior, and this is much less obvious to the observer.

The distinction between topography and function is a very important one in ABA because the relationship between a behavior and its antecedents and consequences is to do with the function of the behavior, not the topography. To illustrate this, two scenarios can be considered.

The first considers two developmentally-delayed children who frequently slap their faces to the extent that physical damage is caused. One may do it, having learned that it is an effective way of getting attention from other people, that is, the behavior is being maintained by positive reinforcement. The second child may do it having learned that people who are making demands, stop it and go away, that is, the behavior is being maintained by negative reinforcement. The behaviors of both children may have exactly the same topography, but they have quite different functions. Hence, despite the similarity of the topography of the behaviors, the intervention programs will need to be very different and be based on the analysis of function of the behaviors.

In the second scenario, again consider two developmentally delayed children. Like the first child in the other scenario, one slaps his face because he has learned that it gains adult attention. The second child frequently takes his clothes off because he has found that this gains attention from other people. In both cases, the behaviors which are quite different topographically are performing the same function. Here, the intervention programs are likely to be quite similar.

A quite common mistake made by clinicians not skilled in ABA is that they design intervention programs around behavior topographies. Such an approach may achieve an occasional success, but in general it will produce failure.

In order to adequately identify the antecedents and consequences that are functionally related to the target behavior, information about the child and behavior must be gathered from an extensive range of sources. The most commonly used methods of information collection include the use of interviews, completion of written materials, and direct observation of the target behavior and its antecedents and consequences.

5.05.3.3.1 Interviews

When working with young children or children with developmental delay, the person initially interviewed is the child's caregiver, usually the parent. Protocols for the conduct of such interviews have been published (Table 1; Murphy et al., 1985; Webster-Stratton & Herbert, 1994). One focus of the interview is to gather as much information about the target behavior as possible. This will include the precise specification of the behavior, estimates of the occurrence of the behavior, and suggestions about potential antecedents and consequences that are functionally related to it. In addition, however, other information needs to be gleaned from parents about the skill levels of the child and the child's preferences (potential reinforcers). These could be important in the design of an intervention program. Another

issue to be discussed is what treatments have been tried in the past, presumably ineffectively. Such information is critical to the detail of what is included in an intervention program. It is usual that all of these matters are discussed at an initial interview with caregivers, the final part of which typically involves the establishment of procedures to collect baseline data.

When working with older children and adolescents, an interview might be conducted with them. Additionally, interviews might be conducted with significant others in the child's life, for example, teachers. Many of the same issues are covered in these interviews as those with caregivers. These interviews do, of course, allow the clinician to hear a different, and probably useful, perspective on the issues.

5.05.3.3.2 Written materials

In addition to the use of interviews, information can be gathered using a range of written materials. These would typically include standardized checklists about the child, for example, the Child Behavior Checklist (Achenbach & Edelbrock, 1983). If relevant, they may also include checklists about the functioning of other members, for example, measures of parental relationships or affective status.

Such written material can be of value for several reasons. First, it often includes normative data and can provide information on the occurrence of the behavior of interest relative to the general population. This information should be relevant in deciding whether or not to try to change the behavior of interest. Second, the use of standardized checklists might bring the clinician's attention to some relevant matters that have not been mentioned in any interviews conducted. Finally, if an intervention is carried out, the checklist can also be administered after intervention, and hence add to other information collected to evaluate the efficacy of the intervention.

5.05.3.3.3 Direct observation of the behavior

The final general source of information is that provided by direct observation of the behavior. Mostly, this is done by caregivers who collect data on the target behavior using frequency counts or duration measures. Obtaining good-quality data from caregivers is not always an easy task. It is important for clinicians to realize that for this part of the exercise it is the caregiver's recording behavior that is important, and attention must be paid to the antecedents and consequences of that behavior. First, the clinician needs to provide structured data collection sheets, clear instructions, and

Table 1   An interview schedule for use in the behavioral assessment of children's problems.

The "client" referred to below is a significant person in the referred child's life, for example, a parent

1. The establishment

(i)   Introduce yourself to the client (name and profession; how you like to be addressed; introduce any observer or colleague—name and role)
(ii) Engage in "small talk" to put the client at ease
(iii) Direct client to an appropriate chair if the interview is in an office (have chairs and furniture prearranged to facilitate communication, etc.)

Remember that this period is critical to the development of a good client–therapist relationship. Such a relationship is essential for therapeutic success

2. General

(i) State purpose(s) of interview
The client should be given a general statement on the purpose of the interview. This is important because some clients expect an immediate answer to their problem. Over the course of the interview it may be necessary to remind the client that management advice is not possible at this stage

(ii) Seek permission for note taking, etc.
Permission should be obtained from the client for note taking. Usually this is not a problem in terms of client permission. Should audio- or video-recording be thought to be an advantage, seek additional prior permission

(iii) Seek client's perception of problem
At this stage it is helpful to ask the client about the nature of the problem. This is simply to prompt clients to give their perception of why they have come to see you. The description given may not be satisfactory to you or the client at this stage, but continued exploration about the nature of the problem will follow later on in the interview. The idea of asking the question here is partially to set the stage for the next step, gathering general background information. Terminate this step by saying that you will come back to talking about the problem later, but first you want to obtain some other information about the child

(iv) Determine referral agency
Obtain or check details of the referring agency (professional's name, agency, phone number, etc.). Remember that good liaison with other agencies in the community is essential, but also that dual management can be wasteful, confusing, or deleterious

3. General background information

(i) Biographical information of child

   (a) name,
   (b) age (including date of birth),
   (c) address, and
   (d) telephone number

(ii) Family background

Here the interviewer collects information about:
   (a) whether the mother and father (or others filling these roles) are present in the household,
   (b) what employment, if any, parents (or other caretakers) have,
   (c) number and ages of siblings in the family,
   (d) any unusual family organizational pattern, such as an aunty or cousin living with the family, and
   (e) quality of relationship between the target child and other family or household members

(iii) Educational background

Here careful detail of the child's educational background is recorded, including:
   (a) number and type of schools attended,
   (b) general progress at school including any grades repeated,
   (c) any history of conflict with teachers,
   (d) current teacher's name, and
   (e) relationships with peers

(iv) Medical background

Here the interviewer lists any information regarding the child's medical background, particularly anything that is slightly out of the ordinary. Remember to question regarding:
   (a) general development milestones and behavior patterns,
   (b) childhood illnesses, and
   (c) any medication the child is currently on

Table 1 (continued)

If the behavioral interviewer is unsure about "normal" developmental rates of infants and children, standardized developmental checklists should be used

The above areas need to be explored because (a) most clients receiving clinical service expect such areas to be addressed, and (b) the information helps the clinician to appreciate the context of the problem, assists the clinician's choice of target behaviors, guides selection of assessment devices to be used, and identifies possible barriers to particular treatment programs

4. Specific information build-up

(i) Investigate the precise nature of the problem
Here the interviewer seeks to have the client state precisely what the nature of the problem is. Some clients may need extra time to articulate the problem, and some may need prompting to be specific

(ii) Investigate the extent of the problem
Here the interviewer seeks to obtain some estimate from the client about the frequency or the duration of the previously described behavior(s). At this point, self-report information is relied upon; at a later stage, more objective methods of assessment will need to be introduced

(iii) Investigate the apparent antecedents and consequences of the problem
Here the interviewer seeks to draw from the client a rough idea of what he or she perceives to be the antecedents and consequences associated with the particular behavior(s)
Choice of language on the part of the clinician is very important. Phrases like "what happens before," "events that trigger" (antecedents), and "what happens during and after" (consequences) are better for most clients

(iv) Determine what has previously been tried
Clients should be assisted to state previous attempts to handle the problem, and advice received from other agencies previously or currently involved

5. Clarification of expectations

(i) Establish agreement on the goal of treatment
Here the interviewer needs to come to agreement with the client regarding the goal of treatment. The goal must be stated in specific terms

(ii) Determine suitability of agency
State whether or not this agency is suitable for helping to achieve that goal, and if not, give client referral options

(iii) Establish realistic timeline for improvement
Ensure that the client is aware that the therapist does not have a magic wand to wave over the problem child and be able to immediately convert him or her from being a problem to no problem at all

(iv) Involvement of client
Impress upon the client the need for him or her to be actively involved in the intervention program, and if they decide to proceed that this will necessarily require active participation by the client

6. Setting of homework (if feasible at this stage)

The interviewer here needs to set very precise homework for the client to carry out during the subsequent period of time. Usually 1 week elapses between the first and second interviews. The specific instructions would usually require the collection of baseline data and the identification of the antecedents and consequences associated with the target behavior. Appropriate antecedent stimulus control of the client's behavior is usually best achieved through the handing out of very structured sheets that client has to fill in during the week and return at the next interview. It is important at the conclusion of the interview to make sure that the client is able to repeat precisely what is expected of him or her by the interviewer. (In many cases this homework setting can take up to 1 hour, so a separate interview for this purpose may be necessary)

7. Scheduling of next appointment

8. Termination of interview

Again remember the importance of a good client–therapist relationship

Source: reproduced with permission from Murphy, Hudson, King, and Remenyi (1985).

perhaps some role play practice at filling in the sheets. Although baseline data are usually collected for a period of two weeks, many clinicians find that a check-up phone call 2 days into data collection is important. Such a call will help overcome any difficulties encountered in the first days and increase the probability that the caregiver will return with useful data. These are all examples of establishing antecedent stimulus control over the data-collecting behavior of the caregivers. As ongoing data collection is important for evaluating interventions, the behavior of the caregivers needs to be reinforced by the clinician.

Older children and adolescents might also participate in collecting direct observation data on their own behavior. This would be absolutely necessary if the target behavior was covert; for example, having obsessive thoughts.

The final way in which direct observation data can be collected is by the use of independent observers who enter into the natural environment of the child. A potential difficulty to be addressed here is the extent to which the presence of an outsider is reactive and has an influence on the behavior being observed. The use of independent observers in standard clinical practice is often a luxury which cannot be afforded, and hence their use is often restricted to research settings.

5.05.3.3.4 Developing a hypothesis regarding the function of the behavior

When a broad set of information has been collected by the various methods described above, the clinician is in a position to formulate hypotheses about the functions of target behaviors. This task is a little like putting together a jigsaw puzzle. Some relevant information will be gathered from interviews, some more will result from written material, and even more from direct observations. Not always will the information from different sources be consistent. When the clinician stands back, as it were, a picture will emerge that suggests a potential functional relationship between the target behavior and its antecedents and consequences.

The extent to which this hypothesized relationship is correct can only be tested by manipulation of those antecedents and consequences via a carefully designed intervention program, and the ongoing measurement of the target behavior. If the behavior changes in the desired direction, the hypothesis has been supported (perhaps not proven, but this matter will be discussed further in Section 5.05.5.1). If the program has been implemented as intended and the behavior does not change in the desired direction, the hypothesis is not supported, and the clinician needs to go back to the drawing board. The introduction of the intervention tests the hypothesis. This hypothesis-testing process is a defining feature of the ABA approach to clinical intervention.

5.05.4 DESCRIPTION OF INTERVENTION PROCEDURES AND PROPOSED MECHANISMS OF CHANGE

As has been described earlier, the logical outcome of the completion of an ABA assessment is the development of an intervention program that is designed to strengthen or weaken the target behavior. Such a program will involve the use of procedures developed from the basic principles of operant conditioning described earlier. It is important to point out that a comprehensive intervention program for a given child may involve more than one target behavior, and hence involve the simultaneous application of more than one procedure. For purposes of clarity, however, each procedure will be described separately here. First, there will be coverage of the relatively specific procedures used to strengthen behavior. Then there will be a discussion of the procedures for weakening behavior. Finally, there will be a discussion of complex procedures for strengthening and weakening behaviors.

5.05.4.1 Procedures for Strengthening Behavior

The most commonly used procedures for strengthening behavior are the systematic use of reinforcement, prompting, shaping, chaining, and modeling.

5.05.4.1.1 Systematic use of reinforcement

The most straightforward procedure for strengthening behavior is simply to wait for the behavior to occur, and then to reinforce it. However, there are some important issues related to this seemingly straightforward process. Perhaps the most important of these is to select an appropriate reinforcer. It must be remembered that a reinforcer is defined in terms of its effect on the behavior it is contingent upon. Clinicians can err in what they think will be reinforcing for particular children. The information collected in the assessment phase is critical for the right choice of an effective reinforcer, and this is not always an easy task. Some clinicians develop what are termed reinforcement menus, or lists of things that are potentially reinforcing, and then have the child or caregiver select from the menu. Another very helpful hint is to use what is known as the Premack principle. Premack (1959) noted that the activities children chose to engage in during their free time could be used to reinforce other, less-preferred activities. He technically defined this as using higher-probability behaviors to reinforce lower-probability behaviors. The importance of the principle is that if you are having trouble identifying what is reinforcing for children, observe what they do in their free time.

Reinforcers vary in nature and can be classified in a number of ways. One of the earliest distinctions made was between primary and secondary reinforcers. A primary reinforcer, sometimes referred to as an unconditioned reinforcer, is one that does not depend on learning to have taken place for it to develop its reinforcing properties. Food, water, and warmth are examples of such primary reinforcers. In contrast, learning has been involved in secondary or conditioned reinforcers developing their reinforcing properties. For example, some children find playing games on a computer to be very reinforcing. For this to have happened, some learning about the computer and the particular game must have taken place. It can be argued that there is limited clinical usefulness in the distinction between primary and secondary reinforcers as ethical considerations dictate that children have a fundamental right to unrestricted access to most primary reinforcers, and hence they should not be used in ABA programs. It is the case, however, that edible reinforcers such as candy have been used successfully to motivate children who do not respond to secondary reinforcers.

A second distinction that is made in regard to types of reinforcers is that between naturally occurring and artificial reinforcers. A naturally occurring reinforcer is one that is readily available and typically used in the setting in which the ABA program is being conducted. In most homes, reinforcers such as parent attention, pocket money, and access to television are available to children. Unfortunately, these reinforcers are often given to the children in an unsystematic or unplanned manner. An artificial reinforcer is one that is not usually available in the setting, but is brought in for the purposes of the program. Candy is not usually used as a reinforcer in most classrooms but could be introduced for use in a program for a special purpose. It is generally advisable for clinicians to use artificial reinforcers only when absolutely necessary, as the fading of such reinforcers can be more difficult than is the case for naturally occurring reinforcers.

A third distinction that is made is between extrinsic and intrinsic reinforcers. An extrinsic reinforcer is one that is quite separate from the behavior that it is reinforcing in that the behavior could occur and not be followed by the reinforcer. If a clinician is using praise to reinforce a child's behavior, the behavior can be allowed to occur without the reinforcement being administered. An intrinsic reinforcer can be viewed as one that is actually part of the behavior. The behavior is reinforcing by itself and does not need an extrinsic reinforcer to maintain it. Most children do not need to be extrinsically reinforced for watching their favorite show on television. They do it because they like it. The distinction between intrinsic and extrinsic reinforcement can be clinically important. Some behaviors, for example reading, may initially need to be extrinsically reinforced to get them going, but once established, can be maintained by their own intrinsic reinforcement.

Yet another way of distinguishing among reinforcers is to classify them based on the broad type of reinforcer. The types listed can vary among authors in the field, but a common list includes social, food, activity, and token reinforcers. Social reinforcers include praise, hugs, or attention from another person. As the name suggests, food reinforcers are things the child can eat. Rather than being basic food requirements, which, as mentioned earlier, are problematical from an ethical viewpoint, they are special treats that the child does not have regular access to. Activity reinforcers are those things that the child likes to do, for example, playing games and watching television. Finally, token reinforcers do not have value in themselves but derive their value from what they can be exchanged for. Many classroom teachers have children earning points for completion of academic work, and then allow the children to exchange those points for back-up reinforcers such as extra time at recess or reduced homework. Money is certainly the most frequently used token reinforcer.

A final point to be made in regard to the systematic use of reinforcement to strengthen a target behavior is that the fundamental principles derived from learning theory need to be adhered to. Reinforcement usually needs to be immediate, particularly with children at a low developmental level. If another behavior occurs between the target behavior and the delivery of the reinforcement, the more recent behavior might be the one that is strengthened. The second behavior under these circumstances is usually referred to as superstitious behavior. Also, attention needs to be paid to what is known about schedules of reinforcement. A continuous schedule needs to be used to maximize the rate of development of the new behavior, and then there should be a move to an intermittent schedule, referred to as a thinning of the reinforcement, to make the behavior more resistant to extinction.

5.05.4.1.2 Prompting

The use of systematic reinforcement to strengthen a behavior can only be effective if the behavior occurs in the first place. If it is not occurring, it needs to be prompted in some way, and it can then be reinforced. Prompts can take a variety of forms, but can be categorized as being physical, verbal, or visual prompts.

A physical prompt is one in which the child is given some physical assistance to perform the required response. Many parents use physical prompts to teach their children to learn feeding and dressing tasks. Care needs to be taken in determining the precise manner of using physical prompts. For example, when teaching a child to use a spoon, it is better to stand behind the child with the assisting hand over the child's hand. Such placement minimizes distraction for the child and allows for co-active movement of adult and child from the bowl to the mouth. As with all prompts, this prompt will need to be faded as the behavior becomes established over several trials, and this can be done by movement of the adult hand slowly up the arm of the child.

A verbal prompt is one that involves the use of spoken words or sounds to help the child perform the behavior. A boy learning to dress himself might be prompted to "hold your shorts in front of you, now put one leg in, etc.," or a child learning to read but stumbles on a word might be prompted to "say the sound of the first letter."

As the name suggests, a visual prompt is something the child sees that helps with the response. If a child is sorting blocks according to shape, the teacher might prompt by pointing to the correct container. This is often referred to as a gestural prompt. A picture placed on the refrigerator to remind a child to empty the trash would also be a visual prompt. Written notes can also be considered to be visual prompts, although some authors consider these to be verbal prompts.

All prompts need to be faded as the target behavior becomes stronger. The way in which this is done will vary depending upon the task in question, but in general the procedure is to start with a strong prompt and weaken it progressively, but not so fast that the target behavior is lost. It must be remembered that the purpose of prompting is to get the behavior to occur so that it can be reinforced, and reinforcement should not usually be thinned until the prompt is removed.

5.05.4.1.3 Shaping

Some behaviors are so complex that no amount of prompting will elicit the desired final form of it, resulting in no reinforcement, and hence no behavior change. Under these circumstances, a decision is made to reinforce only some approximation to the desired behavior. Progressively, closer approximations to the behavior are required before reinforcement is forthcoming, and eventually the final behavior will have been totally shaped.

5.05.4.1.4 Chaining

Many behaviors that are of interest to clinicians are complex behaviors consisting of a number of smaller behaviors linked together to form a behavior chain. Each link of the chain can be conceptualized within the usual antecedent–behavior–consequence sequence, and is taught using the procedures described thus far. Additionally, however, the completion of one link is viewed as the antecedent stimulus occasioning the performance of the next link, which in turn becomes the stimulus for the occurrence of the next. The process of developing the final chain can be of three types, forward chaining, backward chaining, and total task training.

When using forward chaining, the initial link of the chain is the first taught, then the second, then the third, and so on until the complete chain has been learned. Prompting, shaping, and reinforcing could all be used in the teaching of each separate link. While learning each link, the child is usually helped through all of the remaining links so that task completion can be reinforced. Teaching a child to put on a pair of trousers might be a typical skill taught by using forward chaining.

When using backward chaining (sometimes called reverse chaining) it is the final link in the chain that is taught first, then the others are proceeded with working in reverse order. The initial link thus becomes the last taught. This approach is considered desirable when the complex behavior leads to some naturally occurring reinforcer being available, for example a child learning to use a spoon might start with the final link of placing the food in his mouth. This contiguity of naturally occurring reinforcement and task completion is considered to provide better motivation to learn the earlier links in the chain.

Whereas forward and backward chaining are typically used when a child has mastered few if any of the separate behavioral links, total task training is more efficient for situations in which the child has mastered most or all of the links. A child who has mastered simple addition, subtraction, multiplication, and division would typically be taught the behavioral chain involved in completing a long division by using a total task method.

5.05.4.1.5 Modeling

Modeling is sometimes described as being an example of visual prompting, but modeling used properly as a therapeutic technique involves more than just a prompt. Modeling as a technique depends to a large extent on the fact that people can and do learn much from imitating others. Children often engage in incidental imitation of others, and, much to the chagrin of parents, they often pick up behaviors other than those preferred by parents. Imitation is important but is only one of the many components of therapeutic modeling. As Bandura (1969) has pointed out, modeling involves attentional, retentional, motor reproduction, and motivational components. In practical terms, the full modeling procedure includes the following steps:

(i) Explanation to the learner to pay attention to the relevant aspects of the behavior to be modeled (e.g., "Look at how the model does . . .").

(ii) Recall by the learner of the aspects of the behaviors to be observed.

(iii) Reinforcement of this recall and corrective feedback by the clinician as necessary.

(iv) The demonstration of the desired behavior by the clinician.

(v) Recall by the learner of what was observed.

(vi) Reinforcement of this recall and corrective feedback by the clinician as necessary.

(vii) Performance of the behavior by the learner.

(viii) Reinforcement of this performance and corrective feedback by the clinician as necessary.

(ix) Repeat of the above steps as necessary.

This procedure will vary depending on the particular case. The model can be live or on film.

5.05.4.2 Procedures for Weakening Behavior

The most commonly used procedures for weakening behavior are differential reinforcement of incompatible behavior (DRI), differential reinforcement of alternate behavior (DRA), differential reinforcement of other behavior (DRO), extinction, timeout, overcorrection, and punishment. As can be seen in

Sections 5.05.4.2.1–5.05.4.2.3, several of these procedures for weakening behavior involve a concurrent strengthening of a nontarget behavior.

5.05.4.2.1 Differential reinforcement of incompatible behavior

Differential reinforcement of incompatible behavior (DRI) is a weakening procedure that is based on reinforcement. The behavior that is reinforced is not the target behavior, as this would clearly strengthen it, but rather is a behavior that is both desirable and topographically incompatible with the target behavior. The rationale is that the child cannot simultaneously engage in two incompatible behaviors, so as one is strengthened, the other must be weakened.

A DRI procedure could be used to intervene with a child who is continually out of his seat in the classroom. A desirable behavior that is topographically incompatible with roaming around the classroom is that of completing academic work. The teacher therefore could reduce the out-of-seat behavior by systematically reinforcing the child for completion of work. Another example of a behavior that could be treated with DRI is that of a young child who, while watching television, continually "twiddles" with her hair to the extent that bald patches are appearing. Such hair "twiddling" could be reduced by reinforcing the child for cuddling a teddy bear.

The big advantage of DRI is that the focus is on doing something positive, and not simply the removal of an unwanted behavior. It is for this reason that DRI is sometimes referred to as a constructional approach to weakening behavior. One potential procedural difficulty with DRI is that it is not always easy to find an appropriate behavior that is topographically incompatible with the target behavior. Another potential difficulty is that the child must be able to engage in the incompatible behavior for all of the time he would normally engage in the target behavior. This is usually referred to as complying with the 100% rule. Reinforcing piano playing could be used to treat the preschool child who hits other children, but the child could not be expected to play the piano for the total time in attendance at preschool.

It is important to note that when using DRI, some thought must to be given to what will be done if the target behavior does occur. There will be a need for a systematic response to that occurrence. The options will include strategies such as extinction, timeout, and punishment, all of which are discussed below.

5.05.4.2.2 Differential reinforcement of alternative behavior

In a similar fashion to DRI, the differential reinforcement of alternate behavior, or DRA, is a procedure that weakens the target behavior by reinforcing some specific other behavior. This is sometimes referred to as ALT-R. In contrast to DRI, the other behavior in DRA is not topographically incompatible with the target behavior. It is technically possible for the child to simultaneously engage in both the target behavior and the behavior being reinforced, but the expectation is that the reinforcement available for the new behavior will be of such strength that it will be preferred over the target behavior.

DRA also has the advantage of being a constructional approach to behavior reduction, and avoids the DRI difficulty of having to identify a topographically incompatible behavior.

As with DRI, when using DRA the target behavior can occur, and some systematic method of responding needs to be planned for.

5.05.4.2.3 Differential reinforcement of other behavior

Like DRI and DRA, the differential reinforcement of other behavior, or DRO, is a reinforcement-based procedure. Unlike the other procedures which reinforce some specific other behavior, DRO involves the reinforcement of any other behavior, that is, any behavior other than the target behavior. In effect, the DRO procedure translates into reinforcement being delivered for the absence of the target behavior for a predetermined period of time. Sometimes DRO is referred to as omission training. If DRO was being used to treat an aggressive behavior such as hitting other children, reinforcement would be delivered to the child after a set period time during which the child refrained from hitting.

There are many procedural variations of DRO (Vollmer & Iwata, 1992). First, there can be variations in the DRO time interval. The selection of this time is somewhat arbitrary, but it needs to be short enough to give the child a reasonable chance of securing the reinforcement. The time interval can be fixed or variable, but most commonly it is fixed for ease of implementation. One method of selecting the time is to make it the mean of the time intervals elapsing between responses during the collection of baseline data. This has been termed the inter-response time (IRT). Often in the use of DRO, a short time interval is started with, but this is progressively increased in length over

time. This procedure allows the gradual fading of the use of the reinforcement.

Another procedural variation is to do with what is termed interval resetting when the target behavior occurs. One option is to reset the clock at zero, so if the target behavior occurs after 2 minutes of a 3 minute interval, the child has to abstain from that behavior for a further 3 minutes before reinforcement is forthcoming. A second option is to allow the current interval to finish (with no reinforcement), and then require another full interval to elapse before reinforcement. In the case above, the child would have to wait 4 minutes for reinforcement. This second option has some advantages in settings such as classrooms where it is easier for a teacher to attend to a child at set times, for example every 15 minutes. A potential problem with this method of resetting is that a "smart" child who transgresses during a set interval may realize that there is effectively no penalty for further transgressions during the remainder of that period, and take advantage of this. The reset to zero approach can also encounter some difficulties with the smart child. Take, for example, a child on a DRO intervention for hitting other children. Immediately following the receipt of reinforcement for abstaining from hitting, she may realize that now is the time to "get in a few good ones," as the effect of this is to delay the next reinforcement for only a few seconds. Clinicians have combated this by making the reinforcement available after successive intervals free of target behavior greater than that available after just one interval.

A final point in regard to the use of DRO, just as is the case with DRI and DRA, is that the target behavior can occur when using DRO, and some systematic method of responding (e.g., extinction, timeout, punishment) needs to be planned for.

5.05.4.2.4 Extinction

Extinction as a weakening procedure in clinical settings is based directly on the operant conditioning principle that a behavior which is never reinforced will decrease in frequency. It relies on the successful identification, during the functional assessment of the target behavior, of the reinforcers that are maintaining that behavior. Once identified, the contingent delivery of the reinforcers is stopped, and the behavior will eventually disappear.

On the face of it, extinction appears to be a straightforward procedure to implement. However, there are many procedural difficulties that need to be considered in developing an extinction-based intervention. First, extinction can only be used for behaviors that are extrinsically reinforced. It is simply not possible to remove intrinsic reinforcement. Unfortunately, many undesirable behaviors of children and adolescents are engaged in because they are fun.

The second procedural problem is related to the fact that the implementation of an extinction procedure is often followed by a rapid escalation in the target behavior, aptly called the extinction burst, before the behavior eventually weakens. It is critical that this burst is able to be tolerated. If extinction was being used to reduce the self-injurious behavior of a developmentally disabled child, considerable damage could be caused during the burst, making extinction a contraindicated treatment. Similarly, although extinction is very effective in treating night-time crying of children, there are some parents who become so anxious during the burst that the treatment is aborted.

A third procedural problem associated with extinction results from the fact that a given target behavior might be maintained by several reinforcers. If extinction is to be effective, all sources of reinforcement must be terminated. Take, for example, the situation where the target behavior is that of a preschool child hitting other children. The functional analysis of this behavior might show, *inter alia*, that this happens when the child wants a toy from the second child, and that the hit results in the toy being given up, hence reinforcing the behavior. A hastily conceived extinction program could dictate that whenever this happens the preschool teacher should admonish the offender and return the toy to the second child, hence cutting off that source of reinforcement. It might be, however, that the offending child finds adult attention to be very reinforcing, and this will still be readily available when an aggressive incident takes place. Additionally, incidents such as these attract attention from other children, which is also potentially reinforcing. To be effective, an extinction program needs to remove all sources of reinforcement from the target behavior. Some, such as teacher attention, might be relatively easy to remove, whereas others, for example, peer attention, can be more of a problem.

The final procedural problem associated with extinction is that the source of reinforcement needs to be removed on all, not just some or even most, of the occasions on which the behavior occurs. We know from basic operant conditioning principles that behaviors can be maintained on very thin schedules of reinforcement, particularly if the schedule is variable. Consider the parents who deems that their attention is maintaining the tantrums being engaged in by their toddler. They decide to use extinction to remove the tantrums, and ignore them for almost all of the time. Occasionally, they are a little stressed, cannot ignore the child's behavior, and pay attention to him. Here the parents have in fact placed the child, not on an extinction schedule, but on a thin variable schedule of reinforcement. Sadly, as is also know from operant principles, such a schedule makes behavior resistant to extinction.

5.05.4.2.5 *Timeout*

Timeout is perhaps the most misunderstood concept in ABA. Technically it refers to time out from reinforcement, literally meaning that reinforcement is not available for any behavior. Given that it is probably impossible to create an environment that is totally devoid of all sources of reinforcement, the term "timeout" is used to refer to the situation in which the reinforcement available in the environment is reduced whenever the target behavior occurs. The reduction is usually for a relatively brief period of time such as a few minutes. The contingent use of timeout leads to a weakening of the target behavior.

Frequently, timeout is taken to mean removal of the child from the environment she is in to another environment. If the new environment has less reinforcement available than the former, then this is timeout. If, however, as is often the case, the new environment has more reinforcement available, it is not timeout. It is not uncommon for children in schools to be taken from their classrooms and placed in "timeout" in the corridor, perhaps outside the principal's office. Under these circumstances there is likely to be more reinforcement available in the corridor than in the classroom. For a start, aversive work requirements are removed. And other activities such as chatting to children moving through the corridor are available. Under these circumstances, the use of "timeout" is unlikely to weaken the target behavior. In reality, it is "timein," and likely to strengthen the target behavior.

There are several procedural variations of timeout. First, there is the distinction between exclusionary and nonexclusionary timeout. Exclusionary timeout refers to the actual removal of the child to another location which is less reinforcing. Nonexclusionary timeout refers to making the current environment less reinforcing. This can be done, for example, by stopping interaction with other people in the room, or restricting access to certain activities in the room, or even using a special timeout chair. As with exclusionary timeout, the period of time of implementation is brief.

The amount of minimum time that is associated with timeout varies with the clinician, although it is usually related to the age of children. One useful rule of thumb is to begin with 2 minutes for 2 year olds, and then add a minute for each year of age to 10 minutes.

An important issue to do with timeout is related to what the child is doing when the time period is up. Let us take the example of a 3 year old child who has been placed in exclusionary timeout, but screams, shouts, and bangs on the door for the entire 3 minutes. If he is then permitted to leave timeout, it is possible that screaming and shouting will be reinforced and be more likely to occur the next time the child is placed in timeout. This, of course, would be counterproductive, and most clinicians require a period of quiet time before timeout is terminated, resulting in the timeout period potentially being longer than the established minimum. The length of the extension varies from clinician to clinician, some require only 15 seconds of quiet time, while others require a period equivalent to the established minimum. In practice, while some children will initially engage in resistive behaviors, after a few systematic trials they learn that resistive behaviors simply increase the length of the timeout and are quickly dropped.

Timeout has clearly proven to be one of the more powerful ABA procedures, and is widely applicable. The major limitation to its use is the availability of a timeout environment. In terms of nonexclusionary timeout, it is sometimes difficult to make the current environment less reinforcing. For exclusionary timeout, it may be difficult to access a suitable venue. An additional potential problem with exclusionary timeout relates to the child refusing to go. A small child can be carried, but a child who is large compared to the adult might successfully resist. Problems such as these would be contraindicative of the use of timeout.

A final comment on exclusionary timeout relates to its use in settings where there are policies regarding seclusion of children. Clinicians need to be thoroughly familiar with such matters. Additionally, regardless of statutory requirements, ethical considerations demand that the timeout venue meets minimum standards of warmth, light, and physical comfort. It is also a good idea for a record to be kept of the frequency of use and duration of each application of timeout. Such records are important for demonstrating that timeout is being used as a therapeutic technique, and not just a method for isolating a difficult child.

5.05.4.2.6 Overcorrection

The use of overcorrection to weaken a target behavior typically involves two components,

restitution and positive practice. The restitution component involves the child in making good any damage caused by the target behavior. The positive practice component involves the child in repeatedly practising an alternative, acceptable behavior. Consider the use of overcorrection to treat disruptive behavior of children in the classroom. On entering the classroom, the child rushes down the aisle, knocks books off desks as he goes, and finally launches at a seat, pushing it across the classroom. The restitution component of overcorrection would require the child to return the scattered books to their desks and replace the chair to its proper place. The positive practice component would then require the child to leave the classroom, enter in an orderly fashion, and sit gently on the chair. Typically, several repetitions of the positive practice component would be required.

Overcorrection has had extensive use in treating disruptive behaviors, particularly those of children with a developmental disability, although its popularity does seem to have waned in recent years. This could be due the fact that the positive practice trials often involved physically forcing the child to engage in the behavior, and this has been seen as being unnecessarily aversive.

5.05.4.2.7 Punishment

Punishment as a therapeutic procedure has had two separate forms, the first involving the contingent removal of a positive reinforcer and the second involving the contingent delivery of a negative reinforcer.

The removal of a positive reinforcer is often referred to as response cost. The reinforcer would typically be one that is naturally occurring in the child's environment. Many families, for example, routinely restrict access to television or a favorite toy as punishment for a misdemeanor. Such use of punishment has rarely been controversial, provided that the reinforcers removed are viewed as privileges and not rights.

The negative reinforcer used in the second type of punishment is usually referred to as an aversive stimulus, and the use of such punishment procedures has been quite controversial. The controversy has centered not so much on the efficacy of such punishment, as there are well-documented examples of its successful use with seemingly intransigent behaviors such as self-injurious behavior exhibited by some people with developmental disabilities, but on ethical grounds, and the objections focus on the issue of whether punishment is ever really necessary. This matter will be addressed again in the discussion of the principle of the least restrictive alternative.

5.05.4.2.8 *The principle of the least restrictive alternative*

The procedures discussed for weakening behavior have been described with a particular order in mind. First covered were the differential reinforcement procedures, where the emphasis is on weakening the target behavior by strengthening other behaviors. These are generally considered to be minimally restrictive or intrusive for the child involved. At the other end of the spectrum was punishment using aversive stimuli, clearly a very intrusive procedure. It is generally accepted that clinicians should use interventions that are as minimally restrictive as possible, and this is referred to as the application of the principle of the least restrictive alternative (Turnbull, 1981).

While there is agreement that this principle ought be adhered to, what there is not agreement about is whether it is necessary to use aversive procedures at all. Some argue that all problematic behavior can be successfully treated if procedures such as the differential reinforcement procedures are used well. Others argue that there are not yet enough data available to warrant this conclusion, particularly in regard to behaviors such as the chronic self-injury exhibited by some people with developmental disabilities. An excellent selection of papers on this topic are included in Repp and Singh (1990).

5.05.4.3 Complex Procedures for Changing Behavior

The procedures described above are relatively specific, and are designed for either strengthening or weakening particular target behaviors. Sometimes the clinician is faced with a situation in which more generalized behavior change is required. In such situations, more complex procedures for changing behavior are appropriate. Examples of these are token systems, behavioral contracting procedures, and problem solving training.

5.05.4.3.1 *Token economies*

A token economy is a specifically constructed system in which desirable behaviors are reinforced with tokens and undesirable behaviors are punished by loss of tokens. Periodically, tokens can be exchanged for back-up reinforcers. Detailed planning is necessary for the successful establishment of a token economy. Care needs to be taken to ensure that back-up

reinforcers are only available through the system, and circumvention of the contingencies through theft is not possible.

5.05.4.3.2 *Behavioral contracting*

Behavioral contracting involves the entering of a formal agreement with the child about what behaviors are required of him and what reinforcers will be consequently available. Contracts are usually written, and need to be constructed with a careful eye to specificity. From a theoretical perspective, behavioral contracts are a particular example of establishing rule-governed behavior in the child (Martin & Pear, 1996).

5.05.4.3.3 *Problem solving training*

The aim of this overall process is not to solve a particular problem for the child but to teach a general strategy that can be implemented for a variety of presenting problems. To do this, however, problems must be dealt with on an individual basis. This procedure involves selecting an individual problem and directively leading the child through a series of steps to solve it. The steps followed typically include (i) specification of the problem, (ii) generation of possible courses of action, (iii) selection of a course of action, and (iv) trying out the selected option. When one problem has been successfully dealt with, others are handled in turn, but with the clinician playing a less directive role on each subsequent problem. From a theoretical perspective, problem solving training, like contracting, is related to the establishment of rule governed behavior (Martin & Pear, 1996). However, unlike in contracting where the rules are command rules in that the clinician controls the reinforcers, in problem solving training the rules are more advice rules as the clinician is unlikely to control the relevant reinforcers.

5.05.4.4 The Triadic Model in ABA with Children and Adolescents

As has been indicated, a fundamental tenet of ABA is that the environment plays a major role in the development and maintenance of all behavior. From a clinical perspective, the reinforcers and punishers that naturally occur in the environment are essential to the maintenance of the problem behaviors. For children, the major sources of these reinforcers and punishers are the significant adults in the child's environment, that is, people such as parents, teachers, or child care personnel. It is quite logical, therefore, that intervention for the clinical problems of children is mediated through these significant others. The systematic manipulation of reinforcers and/or punishers that must be implemented to change the child's behavior is effected by changing the behavior of these significant others. Hence, the application of ABA procedures with children is often referred to as the triadic model, as it involves three persons, that is, the clinician, the significant other, and the child (Herbert, 1991; Tharp & Wetzel, 1969).

The implication of this requirement to change the contingencies of the child's behavior by altering the adult's behavior is that the adult's behavior becomes the focus of the intervention. For example, noncompliance in young children is treated by teaching the parents to give clear instructions and to reinforce differentially child compliance (Forehand & McMahon, 1981). In these situations, the clinician must think about the ways in which the antecedents and consequences of the parents' behavior can be changed in order to alter that behavior. Modeling might be used to teach the parents new child management skills, and then social reinforcement used contingent upon applying these skills in the home.

5.05.5 RESEARCH FINDINGS

5.05.5.1 Efficacy

A trademark of ABA is the systematic collection of data on the behaviors that are targeted for change. These data are then graphed to display the impact of the intervention in changing the baseline rates of the behaviors. Time series research designs such as reversal designs and multiple baseline designs are typically used to examine the functional relationship between the intervention and the target behavior (Hersen & Barlow, 1984; Kazdin, 1982). While designs such as these have respectable internal validity and are necessary to demonstrate a functional relationship between the treatment and the observed changes in target behaviors, they are not always used in standard clinical practice. Most practitioners rely upon the simple AB (baseline–treatment) design, hopefully with some form of follow-up. While this design is weak in terms of internal validity in that other plausible hypotheses might be offered to account for the behavior change, it is much easier to implement in standard clinical settings. The design will tell the clinician if the behavior has changed in the desired direction, it is just that the clinician cannot be absolutely certain that the behavior change was caused by the intervention. While demonstrations of functional control can only

be demonstrated in individual interventions by the better-quality designs, some authors (Harris & Jensen, 1985) have argued that several replications of AB designs will produce the same strength of evidence of functional control as the more elaborate designs.

Regardless of the type of design, the traditional method for determining the existence of a treatment effect was that of visually analyzing the graphs constructed from the data collection. However, some authors (e.g., Crosbie, 1993) have warned against possible errors with this method, and have argued for the use of time series statistical analyses.

One point that supporters of visual analysis of data have made is that a statistically significant change might occur in the occurrence of the target behavior, but that the change might not be large enough to make a difference to the client's everyday functioning, that is, it might not be clinically significant. This issue of clinical significance of outcomes is part of a general construct that has become known as the social validity of the intervention (Kazdin, 1977; Wolf, 1978). Social validity is considered to have three components. The first of these is the social significance of the goals of the intervention, that is, have the right behaviors been selected as targets of change. The second is the social appropriateness of the intervention strategies, that is, if they are socially acceptable. The third is the social importance of the outcomes, that is, if the outcomes are clinically significant.

Notwithstanding the debate about the relative merits of visual and statistical analysis of data, ABA has been used either exclusively or in combination with other procedures to treat a broad range of clinical problems of children. These have included both externalizing disorders such as conduct disorders (Kazdin, 1987) and attention deficit hyperactivity disorder (Barkley, 1990), and internalizing disorders such as anxiety disorders (Siegel & Ridley-Johnson, 1985) and depression (Kazdin, 1990).

One matter that has received substantial attention in the use of ABA is the extent to which clinical effects are generalized. In order to examine generalization more fully, Drabman, Hammer, and Rosenbaum (1979) developed what they referred to as the generalization map. First, they discriminated among four basic types of generalization, namely generalization across settings, behaviors, subjects, and time. Setting generalization was considered to have occurred if there was change in the target behavior in a setting other than the one in which it was treated. Behavior generalization was considered to have occurred if a behavior not targeted changed along with the target behavior. Subject generalization was said to have occurred if the target behavior changed in an individual other than the child on whom treatment was focused. Finally, time generalization was said to have occurred if a change effected in the target behavior was still in place at a later time. In regard to generalization across time, a distinction is sometimes made between those occasions on which the treatment has been terminated and those on which it is still in place. Time generalization is used when the intervention has ceased, but the term maintenance is used if the treatment is still in place.

Each of the four basic types of generalization could occur alone or in combination with another. For example, generalization across settings and behavior would be said to occur when a nontargeted behavior changed in a setting other than the treatment setting. The four basic types can be combined in sets of two, three, or four to produce a map of 16 classes of generalization. Allen, Tarnowski, Simonian, Elliot, and Drabman (1991) reviewed 904 studies published in 28 journals over a 10 year period and found that only about half reported generalization data.

It may be the case that a lack of generalization is not a problem. Take the case of a child who exhibits problem behaviors in the home, but only at home. If an intervention strategy is put in place at home, and this successfully eliminates the behaviors, the issue of setting generalization is not relevant. If some form of generalization is required, however, it needs to be planned for. The intervention program should incorporate elements that promote the likelihood of generalization occurring. The need to actively program for generalization was initially called for by Stokes and Baer (1977), and more recently Stokes and Osnes (1989) presented a description of several programming tactics grouped into three general categories.

They described the first general category as the exploitation of current functional contingencies. This included tactics such as using naturally occurring reinforcers (and punishers) in the program. New behaviors may have to be taught, but, once learned, they will be maintained by the naturally occurring reinforcers. This will help with the fostering of time generalization. Another tactic in this category is to use naturally occurring reinforcers to systematically reinforce any examples of generalization that occur. If a child is on a program to improve behavior at home, reinforcement of better behavior at school by a teacher will promote setting generalization.

The second of Stokes and Osnes's categories was called training loosely. This refers to designing intervention programs that may begin by being tightly constrained, but move over time to being more diverse. An important tactic in such training is the use of what is referred to as multiple exemplars. A child learning a concept such as dog will be better ably to correctly identify all dogs if taught using a large range of examples of a "dog." A child undergoing compliance training will display better generalized compliance if taught using a range of instruction types and is reinforced using a range of reinforcement types.

The third of Stokes and Osnes's categories was referred to as the incorporation of functional mediators. A good example of a tactic in this category is seen in social skills training programs for children and adolescents. To increase the probability that skills learned in a clinical setting will be implemented in the community, the child carries a cue card which prompts the critical elements of the response required for a particular social situation.

As was indicated earlier, ABA interventions with children typically involve the triadic model in that behavior change in the child is effected through behavior change in a significant adult in the child's environment. When thinking from within the framework of the triadic model, the issue of generalization is complex because consideration must be given not only to generalization of the child's behavior but also to that of the adult. Sanders and James (1983) identified types of generalization that were relevant to parent behavior when training parents to implement intervention programs with their children. They referred to these as generalization across settings, behaviors, children, and time. Generalization across settings refers to the parent's ability to use the child management skills learned in one setting (e.g., the clinic) in a second setting (e.g., the home). Generalization across behaviors refers to the ability of the parent to use skills learned for one child behavior with a second behavior of the child. Generalization across children refers to the ability of the parent to use skills learned for managing one child for the management of a second child. Generalization across time refers to the parent's ability to continue to use learned skills after the training program has been concluded. These types of generalization of parent behavior are clearly an extension of the types of generalization cited by Drabman et al. (1979) in relation to child behavior.

Within the triadic model of treating children's clinical problems, it must be remembered that generalization of the behavior of the significant other in the child's environment must be planned for. The suggestions offered by Stokes and Osnes (1989) for promotion of generalization apply equally to the behavior of the adults as they do to the children who are the target of intervention. Sanders and Dadds (1993) provide an excellent set of suggestions for promoting the generalization of skills learned by parents in child management training programs.

5.05.5.2 Effectiveness

A distinction between efficacy and effectiveness is offered by Hoagwood, Hibbs, Brent, and Jensen (1995). Efficacy is considered to have been demonstrated when positive results are found in tightly controlled clinical trials. Effectiveness, however, is only demonstrated when efficacious procedures are successfully implemented with heterogeneous samples in natural settings (health clinics, homes, or schools) by practitioners other than research therapists. To assist in attempts to move from studies of efficacy to studies of effectiveness, Hoagwood et al. propose a three dimensional model, with the dimensions being labelled validity, intervention, and outcome.

For increased external validity, researchers are encouraged to conduct efficacy studies in more naturalistic settings. Because a fundamental premise of ABA is that the environment is a major determinant of behavior, most ABA interventions do occur in homes, or schools, and, as such, many of the reported studies already meet this requirement. The treatment of the presenting problem in the venue in which it occurs reduces the need to build in procedures for generalization across settings. Additionally, most ABA interventions with children involve the triadic model in which a significant other in the child's environment (parent or teacher) actually implements the intervention program. This training of the significant other to do this adds further to the validity of the intervention.

For improved performance on the outcome dimension, researchers are encouraged to broaden the range of outcome measures to include variables other than defining symptoms. ABA practitioners have taken substantial steps in this regard with the search for improved generalization across behaviors, and hence a variety of areas of child functioning are measured. Also, in a desire to achieve social validity of interventions, practitioners are assessing aspects such as consumer satisfaction with the outcomes of intervention.

For improved performance on the intervention dimension, researchers are urged to use less highly structured and manualized interventions to allow more access by practitioners in the field. However, as indicated by Hoagwood et al. (1995), care needs to be taken not to sacrifice treatment integrity. The move from high to low structure without loss of treatment integrity can only be achieved with highly trained practitioners. As indicated earlier, a thorough knowledge of the principles and procedures of ABA are necessary if a practitioner is to successfully implement, and potentially "trouble shoot," intervention programs.

5.05.6 FUTURE DIRECTIONS FOR RESEARCH AND PRACTICE

ABA is now well accepted as a sound model for the treatment of the clinical problems of children and adolescents. As was mentioned earlier, generalization of behavior change was a major issue in ABA. The acceptance of the need to actively program for generalization and the development of tactics for this (Stokes & Baer, 1977; Stokes & Osnes, 1989; Sulzer-Azaroff & Mayer, 1991) has made it less of an issue. Where to from here? While efficacious and effective treatment models are important, it would be generally accepted that prevention of clinical problems is always a better option than cure. It is in the sphere of prevention that ABA has much to offer.

Caplan's (1964) distinction among primary, secondary, and tertiary prevention of mental health problems is useful for a discussion of a future role of ABA. Primary prevention is absolute prevention as commonly understood. Secondary prevention refers to early identification of a problem and intervening in a manner to restrict development of it and to ameliorate any long-term effects. Tertiary prevention is intervention with fully developed mental health problems. Most of the applications of ABA up to 1997 have been in the realm of tertiary prevention. A child presents with a clinical problem and an ABA intervention is developed and implemented. There have been some excellent examples of ABA being used in secondary prevention. The work of Lovaas with autistic children is very relevant here. The long-term intensive use of ABA with young children diagnosed as autistic led to improvement in all of them, some to the extent that they could not be discriminated from typically developing children (McEachin, Smith, & Lovaas, 1993).

Researchers such as Loeber (1990, 1991) have studied the developmental pathways of conduct disorders and have identified the key risk factors associated with the development of such disorders. FAST Track is a long-term program aimed at providing intensive family- and school-based interventions for young children identified as being at risk for the development of conduct disorder (Conduct Problems Research Group, 1992; McMahon et al., 1995). It is a multicomponent program being implemented in four different locations in the USA and involves 500 high-risk children in elementary school. In addition, there are 800 high-risk or normal comparison children. All children are followed through eight years of school.

The real challenge is to have the principles and procedures of ABA adopted in mainstream family, health, and educational services with a view to the promotion of sound mental health. A useful model for conceptualizing interventions with families has been provided by Sanders and Dadds (1993), who identify five levels of intervention in families. These are described as (i) written advice only, (ii) written advice plus minimal therapist contact, (iii) written advice plus active parent training, (iv) intensive behavioral parent training, and (v) behavioral family intervention. These levels reflect differing intensities of intervention. The parent training referred to is the behavioral parent training that has been used extensively and successfully (Forehand & McMahon, 1981; Sanders & Dadds, 1993). At level (iii) it is relatively focused and helps parents manage specific problems with their children. At level (iv) it is more general and helps parents deal with a broader range of presenting problems. At level (v), the behavioral family intervention includes the training of level (iv), but addresses other matters such as marital problems or parental anxiety or depression. The interventions of levels (iii)–(v) are conducted by mental health specialists, and are examples of Caplan's tertiary prevention procedures. Interventions at levels (i) and (ii), however, are much closer to primary and secondary prevention.

Work by Sanders and his colleagues at the University of Queensland in Australia involves the development of an extensive range of written material that is available to families via level (i) and (ii) interventions. The materials, known as "tip sheets," provide advice to parents on fostering healthy development in their children. The tip sheets focus on specific parenting issues such as the management of feeding, sleeping, and compliance problems in their children. They are available to the public through a wide variety of primary care service agencies such as child health nurses, local doctors, and kindergartens. The advice given in the tip sheets is based on extensive empirical research.

The development of broad-scale, community-based, preventative interventions, such as those being developed by Sanders, is the challenge for the future use of ABA with children and adolescents.

5.05.7 SUMMARY

Clinical interventions based on the ABA approach have their roots in learning theory, particularly operant conditioning. Clinical problems are conceptualized as specific behaviors occurring too often (behavioral excesses) or too infrequently (behavioral deficits). The focus of intervention is on increasing behavioral deficits or weakening behavioral excesses. This is effected by manipulation of the antecedents and consequences that are functionally associated with those behaviors.

An important feature of ABA is its strong commitment to systematic data collection and evaluation of the success of interventions. A corollary of this commitment to data-based evaluation is that ABA is a hypothesis-testing approach. Once a target behavior has been identified for change, a hypothesis is formulated about the antecedents and consequences that are functionally related to the behavior. If success in not achieved by a manipulation of these antecedents and consequences, a new hypothesis needs to be considered.

Interventions derived from ABA have been used for the successful treatment of a range of clinical problems of children and adolescents. Early applications were in the field of mental retardation, but there is now a substantial record of success in the use of ABA for treating the broad spectrum of externalizing and internalizing disorders.

The challenge for the future use of ABA is in the realm of prevention. The learning principles which form the foundation of ABA apply to all children. The opportunity is at hand, therefore, to use these principles to construct community-based programs that either prevent the development of clinical problems (primary prevention), or that involve the early identification and treatment of clinical problems before they become major difficulties (secondary prevention).

ACKNOWLEDGMENTS

Thank you to my colleagues Jay Birnbrauer, Jan Matthews, and Roger Miller for their valuable comments on an early draft of this chapter.

5.05.8 REFERENCES

Achenbach, T. M., & Edelbrock, C. S. (1983). *Manual for the Child Behavior Checklist and Revised Child Behavior Profile.* Burlington, CT: University Associates in Psychiatry.

Agras, W. S., Kazdin, A. E., & Wilson, G. T. (1979). *Behavior therapy: toward an applied clinical science.* San Francisco, CA: Freeman.

Allen, J. S., Tarnowski, J. K., Simonian, S. J., Elliot, D., & Drabman, R. S. (1991). The generalization map revisited: assessment of generalized treatment effects in child and adolescent behavior therapy. *Behavior Therapy, 22,* 393–405.

Ayllon, T., & Michael, J. (1959). The psychiatric nurse as a behavioral engineer. *Journal of the Experimental Analysis of Behavior, 1,* 323–334.

Baer, D. M., Wolf, M. M., & Risley, T. R. (1968). Some current dimensions of applied behavior analysis. *Journal of Applied Behavior Analysis, 1,* 91–97.

Bandura, A. (1969). *Principles of behavior modification.* New York: Holt, Rinehart, & Winston.

Bandura, A. (1977). *Social learning theory.* Englewood Cliffs, NJ: Prentice-Hall.

Barkley, R. A. (1990). *Attention-deficit hyperactivity disorder: a handbook for diagnosis and treatment.* New York: Guilford Press.

Biglan, A., Metzler, C. W., & Ary, D. V. (1994). Increasing the prevalence of successful children: the case for community intervention research. *The Behavior Analyst, 17,* 335–351.

Brethower, D. M. (1972). *Behavior analysis in business and industry: a total performance system.* Kalamazoo, MI: Behaviordelia.

Bry, A. (1975). *A primer of behavioral psychology.* New York: New American Library.

Caplan, G. (1964). *Principles of preventative psychiatry.* New York: Basic Books

Conduct Problems Prevention Reseach Group (1992). A developmental and clinical model for the prevention of conduct disorders: The FAST Track Program. *Development and Psychopathology, 4,* 509–527.

Connellan, T. K. (1978). *How to improve human performance: behaviorism in business and industry.* New York: Harper and Row.

Cooper, J., Heron, T., & Heward, W. (1987). *Applied behavior analysis.* Columbus, OH: Merrill.

Crosbie, J. (1993). Interrupted time-series analysis with single-subject data. *Journal of Consulting and Clinical Psychology, 61,* 966–974.

Drabman, R. S., Hammer, D. A., & Rosenbaum, M. S. (1979). Assessing generalization in behavior modification with children: the generalization map. *Behavioral Assessment, 1,* 203–219.

Ellis, A. (1979). Rational-emotive therapy as a new theory of personality and therapy. In A. Ellis & J. M. Whitely (Eds.), *Theoretical and empirical foundations of rational-emotive therapy.* Monterey, CA: Brookes/Cole.

Engelmann, S. & Carnine, D. (1982). *Theory of instruction: principles and applications.* New York: Irvington.

Eysenck, H. J. (1959). Learning theory and behavior therapy. *Journal of Mental Science, 195,* 61–75.

Forehand, R., & McMahon, R. (1981). *The noncompliant child.* New York: Guilford Press.

Grant, L., & Evans, A. (1994). *Principles of behavior analysis.* New York: Harper Collins.

Harris, F. N., & Jensen, W. R. (1985). Comparisons of multiple-baseline across person designs with AB designs with replication: issues and confusions. *Behavioral Assessment, 7,* 121–127.

Herbert, M. (1991). *Clinical child psychology: social learning, development, and behavior.* Chichester, UK: Wiley.

Hersen, M., & Barlow, D. (1984). *Single case experimental designs: Strategies for studying behavior change* (2nd ed.). New York: Pergamon.

Hoagwood, K., Hibbs, E., Brent, D., & Jensen, P. (1995). Introduction to the special edition: efficacy and effectiveness in studies of child and adolescent psychotherapy. *Journal of Consulting and Clinical Psychology, 63,* 683–687.

Hull, C. L. (1943). *Principles of behavior.* New York: Appleton Century Crofts.

Kameenui, E., & Simmons, D. (1990). *Designing instructional strategies: the prevention of academic and learning problems.* Columbus, OH: Merrill.

Kazdin, A. E. (1977). Assessing the clinical or applied importance of behavior change through social validation. *Behavior Modification, 1,* 427–451.

Kazdin, A. E. (1982). *Single-case research designs: methods for clinical and research settings.* New York: Oxford University Press.

Kazdin, A. E. (1987). *Conduct disorder in children and adolescents.* Newbury Park, CA: Sage.

Kazdin, A. E. (1990). Childhood depression. *Journal of Child Psychology and Psychiatry, 31,* 121–160.

Loeber, R. (1990). Development and risk factors of juvenile antisocial behavior and delinquency. *Clinical Psychology Review, 10,* 1–41.

Loeber, R. (1991). Antisocial behavior: more enduring than changeable? *Journal of American Child and Adolescent Psychiatry, 30,* 393–397.

McEachin, J. H., Smith, T., & Lovaas, O. I. (1993). Long term outcome for children with autism who received early intensive behavioral treatment. *American Journal of Mental Retardation, 97,* 359–372.

McMahon, R. J., Bierman, K., Cole, J., Dodge, K., Greenberg, M., & Lochman, J. (1995, July). *The prevention of conduct disorders in school-aged children: The FAST Track Project.* Paper presented at the World Congress of Behavioral and Cognitive Therapies, Denmark.

Mahoney, M. J. (1974). *Cognition and behavior modification.* Cambridge, MA: Ballinger.

Martin, G., & Pear, J. (1996). *Behavior modification: what it is and how to do it* (5th ed.). Englewood Cliffs, NJ: Prentice-Hall.

Mahoney, M. J. (1974). *Cognition and behavior modification.* Cambridge, MA: Ballinger.

Meichenbaum, D. (1977). *Cognitive behavior modification: an integrative approach.* New York: Plenum.

Murphy, G. C., Hudson, A. M., King, N. J., & Remenyi, A. (1985). An interview schedule for use in the behavioural assessment of children's problems. *Behaviour Change, 2,* 6–12.

Ollendick, T. H., & Cerny, J. A. (1981). *Clinical behavior therapy with children.* New York: Plenum.

Pavlov, I. P. (1927). *Conditioned reflexes.* London: Oxford University Press.

Premack, D. (1959). Toward empirical behavioral laws. 1: positive reinforcement. *Psychological Review, 66,* 219–233.

Repp, A. C., & Singh, N. N. (Eds.) (1990). *Current perspectives on the use of nonaversive and aversive interventions for persons with developmental disabilities.* New York: Sycamore.

Ross, A. O. (1976). *Psychological disorders of children: a behavioral approach.* New York: McGraw-Hill.

Sanders, M. R., & Dadds, M. R. (1993). *Behavioral family intervention.* Needham Heights, MA: Allyn & Bacon.

Sanders, M. R., & James, J. E. (1983). The modification of parent behavior: a review of generalization and maintenance. *Behavior Modification, 7,* 3–27.

Skinner, B. F. (1938). *The behavior of organisms.* New York: Appleton-Century-Crofts.

Skinner, B. F. (1948) *Walden two.* New York: Macmillan.

Skinner, B. F. (1953). *Science and human behavior.* New York: Macmillan.

Skinner, B. F. (1957). *Verbal behavior.* New York: Macmillan.

Skinner, B. F. (1969). *Contingencies of reinforcement: a theoretical analysis.* New York: Appleton-Century-Crofts.

Siegel, L. J., & Ridley-Johnson, R. (1985). Anxiety disorders of childhood and adolescence. In P. H. Bornstein & A. E. Kazdin (Eds.), *Handbook of clinical behavior therapy with children* (pp. 266–308). Homewood, IL: Dorsey Press.

Stokes, T. F., & Baer, D. M. (1977). An implicit technology of generalization. *Journal of Applied Behavior Analysis, 10,* 349–367.

Stokes, T. F., & Osnes, P. G. (1989). An operant pursuit of generalization. *Behavior Therapy, 20,* 337–355.

Sulzer-Azaroff, B. (1982). Behavioral approaches to occupational safety and health. In L. Frederiksen (Ed.), *Handbook of organizational behavior management* (pp. 505–538). New York: Wiley.

Sulzer-Azaroff, B., & Mayer, G. R. (1991). *Behavior analysis for lasting change.* New York: Holt, Rinehart, & Winston.

Tharp, R. G., & Wetzel, R. J. (1969). *Behavior modification in the natural environment.* New York: Academic Press.

Turnbull, H. R. III (Ed.) (1981). *The least restrictive alternative: principles and practice.* Washington, DC: American Association on Mental Deficiency.

Vollmer, T. R., & Iwata, B. A. (1992). Differential reinforcement as treatment for behavior disorders: procedural and functional variations. *Research in Developmental Disabilities, 13,* 393–417.

Wahler, R. G., & Fox, J. J. (1981). Setting events in applied behavior analysis: Toward a conceptual and methodological expansion. *Journal of Applied Behavior Analysis, 14,* 327–338.

Webster-Stratton, C., & Herbert, M. (1994). *Troubled families—problem children: working with parents a collaborative process.* New York: Wiley.

Wolf, M. M. (1978). Social validity: The case for subjective measurement or how applied behavior analysis is finding its heart. *Journal of Applied Behavior Analysis, 11,* 203–214.

Wolpe, J. (1958). *Psychotherapy by reciprocal inhibition.* Stanford, CA: Stanford University Press.

5.06
Cognitive-behavioral Therapy

PHILIP C. KENDALL, ABBE L. MARRS, and BRIAN C. CHU
Temple University, Philadelphia, PA, USA

5.06.1 THEORETICAL UNDERPINNINGS

Cognitive-behavioral therapy (CBT) with children and adolescents, relative to other theoretical approaches to psychological therapy, is a young but quickly developing area of clinical psychology. In a survey published in 1982, it was found that 40% of the new faculty in clinical psychology programs approved by the American Psychological Assoication identified themselves as cognitive-behaviorally oriented with an additional 18% identifying themselves as behaviorally oriented (Kleges, Sanchez, & Stanton, 1982). The combination of these two groups represents a majority of those surveyed. Given this presence in the training programs for the field, it is reasonable to expect that this orientation will continue to flourish and expand in the future. More importantly, however, the continued development of CBT in children and adolescents will be determined by evaluation of outcomes applied to the wide variety of psychological problems in youth (e.g., Kendall, 1991).

The achievements of CBT may be attributed to an intelligent integration of several theoretical perspectives: most notably, learning theory (behavior therapy) and cognitive theory (and therapy). CBT combines the paradigms of learning theory with an understanding of, and attention, to the cognitive activities of the client. Greatest emphasis is placed on the learning process and the influence of contingencies and models in the environment, while still reserving a central role for the individual's mediating/information processing style in understanding the development and remediation of psychological distress (Kendall, 1985).

5.06.1.1 Key Features of CBT

In addition to defining CBT as a rational integration of behavioral and cognitive theories and therapies, it may also be useful to distinguish this approach from others by examining its key features. Following a cognitive prototypes construct (e.g., Rosch, 1973, 1975) from experimental cognitive psychology, the degree to which a category member is "related" to the category in general depends on the number of features that the member shares with the category. In this case, given a list, such as the one below, of potential features of the cognitive-behavioral (CB) approach, one can determine the degree to which one would classify any given example as cognitive-behaviorally oriented. Aside from the first two features listed, none of the other elements is required for an intervention to be considered cognitive-behavioral. The first two features in the following list from Ingram, Kendall, and Chen (1991) represent core characteristics of the approach.

(i) Cognitive variables are assumed to be important causal and maintaining mechanisms. This statement does not rule out that other causal mechanisms may be operating as well, but rather that cognitive variables are important in conceptualizing the onset and course of a disorder.

(ii) Given that cognitive variables can be causal and maintaining agents, at least some of the treatment methods and strategies are aimed at cognitive targets.

(iii) A functional analysis of the variables maintaining the disorder is undertaken. This analysis may include examination of cognitive, behavioral and affective variables.

(iv) Both cognitive and behavioral therapeutic strategies are employed. As evidenced by Beck's (Beck, Rush, Shaw, & Emery, 1979) approach to the treatment of adult depression, as well as Stark and Kendall's (1996) approach with depressed youth, this combination may involve using behavioral strategies to target cognitive objectives as well as cognitive strategies to effect behavioral change.

(v) Empirical verification is sought and emphasized in at least three different ways. First, empirical research is used to examine the effects of the therapeutic procedures and to study the causal mechanisms of the changes observed.

Second, the use of objective assessment during therapy provides a means of assessing therapeutic progress. Third, clients are taught how to gather data to test their assumptions and/or beliefs.

(vi) Typically, interventions are time-limited. Booster and maintenance sessions may be applied as necessary.

(vii) The client and therapist operate in a collaborative relationship, working together toward the goal of alleviating dysfunctional thinking and behavior.

(viii) CB therapists are active and offer to help evaluate suggestions rather than being passive and nondirective.

(ix) Educating the client about the CB model of dysfunction, the role of their thinking in the maintenance of dysfunction, and the need to modify dysfunctional cognition and behavior is deemed important.

(x) CB therapists serve as coping models, providing demonstrations in role-plays of ways to manage dysfunction and different situations.

A few words on what CBT is not. Unlike the psychodynamic perspective which concerns itself in part with efforts to uncover unconscious early experiences and trauma, CBT focuses more on the present, but acknowledges that early experiences are influential in learning behavior patterns and cognitive styles. Similarly, CBT does not focus on biological, neurological, or genetic aspects although again it acknowledges that they play a role, to varying degrees, in several disorders.

5.06.1.2 Behavior and Cognition in Context

Although it is clear from the listed features that CBT places major emphasis on both the learning process and mediating/information-processing factors, CBT also considers the relationship of cognition and behavior to affective state and functioning in the larger social context. This aspect of CBT is especially important in the treatment of children and adolescents because of the centrality of the social context in the developmental trajectory of children. Specifically, adequate relations with peers is a crucial component of successful adjustment, and consequently an approach which is sensitive to these issues both during the assessment and intervention phases of treatment is favored.

Equally, if not more, important, in considering children in context, is an understanding of the family. Many of the rules and roles for later social interaction are first introduced in this social microcosm. Consideration of the modeling and reinforcement practices parents use with their child can provide clues to the therapist about factors that may be maintaining the targeted behavior. For example, a parent who has perfectionistic expectations of their child, and who only rewards the child for flawless performance, may be a contributing factor in the maintenance of the child's anxiety in testing situations or in the child's overly harsh criticisms of themselves. Additionally, parents may prove to be a valuable resource as diagnostic and therapeutic collaborators: first, by providing information about the nature of the problem as it manifests itself outside the clinic, and second, by reinforcing at home lessons taught and gains made in therapy.

5.06.1.3 The Nature of Cognition

Given the centrality of cognition, an account of CBT requires a discussion of the more detailed features of cognition: cognitive structures, cognitive content, cognitive processes, and cognitive products (Ingram & Kendall, 1986; Kendall, 1993; Kendall & Ingram, 1987, 1989). Cognitive structures can be thought of as mental templates that are based on an accumulation of experiences in memory which act to guide and filter the understanding of new experiences. Cognitive content refers to ongoing self-talk, as well as the information that is stored and organized in memory. Self-talk or internal speech are examples of surface cognitive content. Cognitive structures serve to trigger automatic cognitive content and information processing. Cognitive processes are the procedures by which the cognitive system operates—how we go about perceiving, recalling, and interpreting experience. Search and storage mechanisms and inferential and retrieval processes are examples of cognitive processes. Cognitive products are the end result of the operations of the system. These are the thoughts that an individual experiences as a result of the interacting content, process, and structure, and can be illustrated by causal attributions

Psychopathology (and psychological therapy) may be related to problems (and corrections) in any or all of the above areas of cognition, and the understanding of specific disorders and their treatment benefits from consideration of each of these factors for each client. For example, an anxiety-disordered youth who has a schema for threat (cognitive structure) about danger (evaluative and physical) would have automatic thoughts (questions) and an internal dialogue (cognitive content) that would be consistent with that schema (worry). The cognitive process that this individual engaged in would be influenced by the cognitive

structures and would therefore be likely to consist of selective attention to cues for evaluation and risks of negative outcomes. Consequently, the individual would be predisposed to see danger in events and to hold demanding expectancies about the future.

Cognition can be divided further. Just as child behavior disorders can be broken down into internalizing and externalizing varieties where internalizing behavioral disorders involve problems within the self and externalizing disorders pertain to conflict with the outside world (Achenbach, 1906), so too can dysfunctional cognitions be subdivided. Two separate categories for cognitive dysfunctions have been described (Kendall, 1985, 1993): cognitive deficiencies and cognitive distortions. Deficiencies refers to an absence of thinking where it would be beneficial (i.e., acting before thinking). Children and adolescents with these deficits in information processing fail to engage in forethought and planning. Conversely, children and adolescents who have distorted cognition are not failing to engage in information processing but are rather doing so in a dysfunctional, "crooked" manner. On a historical note, the distinction between deficient and distorted cognition highlights the differences between the forerunners of adult CBT which focused primarily on distorted thinking, and early child CBT which was mainly intent upon remediation of cognitive deficits in children (Kendall, 1977; Meichenbaum & Goodman, 1971).

Although the distinction between distorted and deficient cognition often runs parallel to the distinction between internalizing and externalizing behavior (i.e., disorders associated with distorted cognition also tend to be associated with internalizing behavior, anxiety, and depression; and deficient cognition with externalizing disorders, attention-deficit hyperactivity disorder (ADHD), tend to group together), the associations are not perfect (Kendall & MacDonald, 1993). For example, aggressive behavior (externalizing) entails cognitive deficiencies and cognitive distortions (e.g., Dodge, 1980; Dodge & Frame, 1982; Lochman, 1987).

Some consider the frontier in current CBT conceptualizations of cognition to be the constructivist narrative. Proponents of this view (e.g., Epstein & Erskine, 1983; Guidano & Liotti, 1983; Harvey, Weber, & Orbach, 1990; Mahoney & Lyddon, 1988; McNamee & Gergen, 1992; Meichenbaum & Fitzpatrick, 1993; Neimeyer, 1993; Neimeyer & Feixas, 1990; White & Epston, 1990) see the human mind as a product of constructive symbolic activity and see reality as a product of personal meanings that individuals create. In contrast to a solely information-processing view of cognition, this perspective holds that there are many realities, and thus the distortion of a universal reality can no longer be seen as a viable metaphor for explaining the existence of psychopathology. This evolving CB approach maintains instead that some realities are more functional than others for given individuals in given circumstances. A goal of the therapist then becomes one of helping clients become aware of how they create their realities and the ensuing consequences of those constructions.

5.06.1.4 Developmental Sensitivity

CBT does *not* subscribe to what Kendall (1984) described as "the developmental uniformity myth." Rather, children are not homogeneous and CBT acknowledges that treatment may be differentially effective as a function of a child's developmental level. This developmental sensitivity also implies that each individual child is not "constant" from pre- to post-treatment. Relatedly, one must note that children with the same behaviors but of different ages are not necessarily alike. Avoiding the developmental uniformity myth means giving adequate consideration to age (age groups or developmental groups) as a potential moderator variable of treatment effects, and creating interventions which are intentionally geared specifically to the child's age or level of cognitive development. This issue is considered further in Sections 5.06.3 and 5.06.5.

5.06.1.5 Role(s) of the CB Therapist

Elsewhere, Kendall (1993) used the terms "consultant," "diagnostician," and "educator" to refer to the therapeutic posture of the therapist. As a consultant (collaborator), the therapist is viewed as having ideas worthy of trying but not as the one who has all of the answers. A goal is to give the client the opportunity to try new ways of thinking and behaving and to help them make sense of the experiences and the results. The therapist intentionally acts as a problem-solving model as one way of encouraging the client to become an independent and mature problem solver. As a diagnostician, the therapist integrates data gathered from many sources: synthesizing new information with knowledge about psychopathology, normal development, and psychologically healthy environments. The outcomes of this process are well reasoned decisions about the nature of the problem and the optimal strategy for its treatment. As an educator, the therapist attempts to present the information of therapy in a manner which facilitates the client's

learning-specific behaviors, cognitive skills, and emotional development. Helping clients to think for themselves is an ultimate goal. Thinking for oneself may provide the maximum possibility for the generalization of skills learned in therapy to other problematic areas which may or may not be present at the time of treatment. In this way, although CBT is not aimed at providing a cure *per se* for a client's problems (Kendall, 1989), the changes produced by the intervention can be used in the management of psychopathology in areas beyond those where they were initially applied.

5.06.1.6 Realistic Goals for Therapy

In helping a client cope with problems (rather than striving to cure the problem), CBT provides the client with realistic expectations about potential outcomes. Psychological change is not linear, and lapses/relapses are likely. CBT prepares clients for the fact that booster sessions may be necessary and helps them view lapse in a constructive manner rather than as a failure. Implicit in this idea is the notion that all forms of psychopathology are not equally responsive to psychological interventions. This realistic appraisal helps the client and therapist focus on doable change that is likely to occur.

Although little written attention has been devoted to factors such as trust, respect, and relationship as part of the CBT process, this should not be taken as an indication that they are not important elements of this treatment. Our discussion has focused on elements of treatment that are specific to CBT and because those factors are essential elements of all forms of treatment, it was not deemed necessary to discuss them specifically here.

5.06.2 HISTORY OF THE APPROACH

Consideration of the origins of CBT is helpful in setting the current features of the approach in their proper context. However, all accounts of historical information can only represent a limited perspective on the events of the past. This account of the history of CBT with children was shaped in large part by the work of Meichenbaum (1995) and Meyers and Craighead (1984).

In some senses Witmer (1907) could be credited with the earliest example of contemporary behavior therapy. His psychological clinic, established in 1896, was the first of its kind. His interventions with childhood academic and mental health problems had many of the hallmarks of current CB approaches: they were directive, educational, based on principles from perception and learning, and empirically evaluated for effectiveness.

More traditional accounts of the birth of behavior therapy with children, however, usually begin with the work of Watson (1924) and his colleagues Rayner (Watson & Rayner, 1920) and Jones (1924a, 1924b). Together these pioneers in behavior therapy with children studied the effects of conditioning on the development and amelioration of fears. Somewhat later, although equally durable to the effects of time is the "bell-and-pad" procedure originally introduced by the Mowrers (Mowrer & Mowrer, 1938) for the treatment of enuresis.

These early endeavors were all but ignored until the 1960s, however, due to the prevalence of the psychoanalytic treatment of psychological problems at that time. When the psychoanalytic era waned, it was Rogers' (1951) client-centered therapy which emerged as an approach that was especially embraced by school psychologists. By the late 1950s and early 1960s, most psychologists, psychiatrists, social workers, and school psychologists were either using psychoanalytic or client-centered techniques with their child clients.

The therapeutic effectiveness of the prevailing approaches began to be questioned: in child-clinical circles, the critiques of psychodynamic psychotherapy (Levitt, 1957, 1963) were based on the lack of data to support the effectiveness of the psychodynamic approach. Early inroads by behavior therapists were seen in the treatment of severely disordered children. Perhaps because of the level of difficulty associated with treating these clients with the traditional methods of the time and perhaps because of the appropriateness of the behavioral approach, these early applications of behavior therapy to clinical cases were welcomed and successful. The majority of clinical applications of behavioral principles during this time focused on the application of operant procedures, with some ancillary use of modeling and systematic desensitization used specifically for anxiety and phobic disorders.

Fueled by empirical literature, clinical behaviorism took hold. The potential to predict and modify abnormal behavior through the study of the stimulus–response links thought to account for its occurrence created much excitement and anticipation in the field. The boom of behavior therapy was further bolstered by the creation of several scholarly journals (e.g., the *Journal of Applied Behavior Analysis*, created in 1968) and professional associations which specialized in behavior therapy and applied behavior analysis (e.g., the Association for the Advancement of Behavior Therapy).

Experimental and developmental psychologists were among the first to reconsider cognitive constructs and models as possible moderators of behavior. Clinical and social psychology also began to incorporate theories of cognition into what had previously been strictly behavioral models. Although the shift away from strict behavior therapy toward cognitive behavior therapy was marked by more than a few bumps in the road, this process should be considered more of an evolution than a revolution (Meichenbaum, 1995). According to Meyers and Craighead (1984), the shift toward CBT with children was influenced by three primary factors: cognitive psychology, self-control clinical interventions, and cognitive therapy.

5.06.2.1 The Impact of Cognitive Psychology

Cognitive psychology influenced behavior therapy with children in several ways. First, social learning theorists (e.g., Bandura, 1969; Kanfer & Phillips, 1970; Mischel, 1973; Rotter, 1966) and others provided explanations of phenomena which had previously been explained solely by behavioral principles. Perhaps the most long-lived of these has been the account of modeling effects. Bandura suggested that in addition to being explained by the principles of learning, observational learning was also influenced by the processes of attention, retention, motor reproduction, and incentive and motivation. Not only was this expansion into cognitive concepts, such as attention and retention, innovative and groundbreaking in its own right, but it also set the stage for more flexible and expansive theorizing than was previously the case under strict behaviorism.

A second avenue of impact for cognitive psychology came from research findings on the inferential and decision-making processes of individuals (e.g. Kahnemann, Slovic, & Tversky, 1982; Nisbett & Ross, 1980; Tversky & Kahnemann, 1974). These researchers and others drew the field's attention to the fact that individuals are often biased, inefficient, and incompetent information processors, with poor decision-making abilities. They mounted evidence for the fact that decision making was often influenced by habits of thinking, or mental heuristics, rather than being based on real events. This information provided a much needed metaphor for understanding psychopathology from a cognitive perspective.

Problem-solving and coping skills interventions were developed to put findings from cognitive psychology to work in clinical practice (e.g., D'Zurilla, 1986; D'Zurilla & Goldfried, 1971; Meichenbaum, 1985; Spivack & Shure, 1974). Programs were designed to teach and evaluate social problem-solving thinking: alternative thinking—generating multiple potential solutions to interpersonal problems; means–end thinking—considering the step-by-step process necessary to reach a desired goal; and, consequential thinking—focusing on the consequences that occur as a result of choosing a particular behavioral response (Spivak & Shure, 1974). The early success in teaching children problem-solving skills has led to much work in this area.

Based on the work of the cognitive developmental psychologists Vygotsky (1978) and Luria (1976), Meichenbaum and Goodman (1971) developed a self-instruction program to teach impulsive children how to control their behavior. Vygotsky and Luria suggested that during development, children's behavior is first under the verbal control of the social environment (most often by adults), and then gradually under personal control through overt speech and then slowly through covert speech. Applying these principles, Meichenbaum and Goodman's procedure entailed having an experimenter model overt behavior and associated self-statements for the impulsive child. The success of this early trial of self-instruction training has led to its application in a wide variety of other child and some adult psychopathology fields (e.g., Craighead, Wilcoxon-Craighead, & Meyers, 1978; Kendall & Williams, 1981; Meichenbaum, 1977).

5.06.2.2 Self-control Clinical Interventions

Self-control interventions, like many other influences on strict behavior therapy, were originally explained by the same operant models which formed the core of behavior therapy. During the late 1960s, however, cognitive explanations for self-control procedures began to develop and to spark researchers to think about changing internal thought processes as a means of teaching the individual self-control (e.g. Mahoney, 1974; Kendall & Braswell, 1982; Kanfer & Karoly, 1972; Craighead, Brownell, & Horan, 1981).

5.06.2.3 Cognitive Therapy

Unlike self-control programs, cognitive therapy developed outside and separate from the realm of behavior therapy. Working almost exclusively in the clinic as opposed to in the laboratory, Ellis and Beck, two major leaders in the development of cognitive therapy, were

separately developing interventions aimed specifically at altering maladaptive cognitive processes. Ellis' (1962) rational-emotive therapy focused on the idea that individuals behave maladaptively because of irrational and illogical thought processes. It is what individuals think about the things they say and do that has the potential to upset them. Beck's (1976) approach to cognitive therapy also saw maladaptive cognitions as a culprit in the etiology of psychopathology. Beck argued that these maladaptive thought processes were a reflection of an individual's assumptions and beliefs about themselves and the world. Cognitive therapy focuses on modifying the fundamental assumptions and beliefs on which the maladaptive thoughts are based. In both cases, the success of these approaches in treating adults has greatly influenced the development of CBT.

5.06.3 ASSESSMENT AND CLINICAL FORMULATION OF THIS APPROACH

CBT's approach to assessment has two foci. First, the assessment process is viewed as a hypothesis-testing endeavor. These hypotheses then guide the process of understanding a given child in their social context so that appropriate treatment strategies can be implemented to ameliorate the child's current difficulties (Ollendick & Hersen, 1993). Unlike more traditional assessment methods which are focused on searching for underlying personality characteristics or traits that are assumed to be causal factors in current distress, the hypothesis-generating process places primary importance on clearly describing current behavior, thought patterns, affective understanding, and environmental conditions which are thought to be related to the presence and maintenance of the child or adolescent's distress. Also, in contrast to traditional assessment techniques, CBT assessment strives to take a sampling as opposed to a symbolic approach to choosing and interpreting the results of testing. That is to say, CBT assessment techniques, being based on observable behaviors and reliably measured cognitive and environmental variables require little inferential work. More traditional assessment procedures, in contrast, rely on viewing the testing results as an indirect manifestation of underlying personality traits which are thought to be causing the presenting problems. Accurate sampling of behavior and cognition which are similar if not identical to the behavior and cognition which are targeted by the intervention is therefore a cornerstone of the CB assessment process.

Second, CBT views the assessment process as a means of evaluating the effectiveness of specific intervention procedures. Given the importance CBT places on the empirical evaluation of its treatment procedures, this is an essential part of the assessment process. Being able to report that a given behavior or cognition changes from pretreatment to post-treatment requires careful measurement of these elements at both time periods. Establishing that the observed changes are due to the intervention and not to some other confounding variable, however, requires additional consideration and controls.

5.06.3.1 Developmental Sensitivity Revisited

In child and adolescent treatment, a potential threat to the internal validity of the treatment is the effects of maturation. Children and adolescents are changing organisms who may simply "grow out of" their original presenting problems. To assert that the observed changes from pre- to post-treatment are due to the intervention and not to maturation, one must not only accurately measure the target constructs at pre- and post-treatment, but one must also know what norms are appropriate for comparison purposes at each time. The norms used prior to treatment may no longer be appropriate following treatment. CBT assessment procedures strive to be developmentally sensitive by using age-appropriate data on which decisions about the efficacy of treatment will be based.

A method for treatment evaluation might be to use the "normative comparisons" approach to clinical significance (Kendall & Grove, 1988). In addition to using statistically significant changes as a barometer of effectiveness, this approach also evaluates interventions based on the child's level of functioning in comparison to a meaningful and representative nondisturbed reference group. Because of maturational factors, it is essential that normative reference groups match clients on age. When a client, after statistically meaningful treatment effects, has returned to symptom levels indistinguishable from normals, then the normative comparison method can be said to have provided evidence of clinically significant change.

CBT assessments are geared to be developmentally sensitive because, in deciding if treatment is needed for a given problem or in deciding what aspects of a child's presenting picture are outside of the normal range, a clinician needs to be aware of the appropriate group with which to compare a child's behavior and cognition. For example, it is more acceptable for a six-year-old to exhibit mild features of separation anxiety than for a 14-year-old to exhibit the same pattern.

A further challenge to the accurate assessment of children and adolescents is that manifested symptoms of a given disorder may vary with developmental level. This complicates the diagnostic picture for youth because the behavior and cognition targeted by a certain intervention may vary and other symptoms of the same problem may take their place. It is analogous to trying to hit a moving target. For instance, Strauss, Lease, Last, and Francis (1988) reported that the American Psychiatric Association's *Diagnostic and statistical manual of mental disorders (third edition, revised) (DSM-III-R)* category of overanxious disorder was most often typified by unrealistic worry about the appropriateness of past behavior and comorbidity with major depression and simple phobia in children and adolescents aged 12–19; in contrast, in children aged 5–11 this type of worry was often not endorsed and comorbidity was more often seen with separation anxiety and ADHD.

It is somewhat unclear whether the observed differences in symptom manifestation across developmental levels are due to changes in comprehension and/or expression abilities or in some other factor which changes with developmental stage. This being so, it is important for classification systems used to diagnose children to be sensitive to these issues. For this reason, among others, the practice of simply scaling down adult syndromes to be applied to youth is not considered appropriate or desirable. While our current system of classifying childhood psychopathology takes into account the fact that children possess the same capacities as adults in terms of: influencing others through social interaction; processing and interpreting information in their environments; and, making choices that shape their worlds; it has also evolved to include specific diagnostic categories which may be unique to childhood, and may be more congruent with how a child or adolescent would present with a given difficulty. Diagnostic systems need to continue to develop as more data about the reliability and validity of the childhood diagnostic categories become available (Callahan, Panichelli-Mindel, & Kendall, 1996).

The challenge of collecting assessment data from children and adolescents is formidable. One facet of this issue is that assessment instruments are created by adults, and although some progress has been made in developing assessment tools that are geared for younger clients, this is still an area in need of attention. For example, a very common way of assessing the degree to which someone experiences a specific symptom is through a rating scale with approximately five anchor points ranging from "never" to "always." Evans and Nelson (1986) presented data that call into question a young child's ability to make the fine-grain distinctions which are required by these five-point scales. Some investigators (e.g., Finch & Montgomery, 1973; Sheslow, Bondy, & Nelson, 1982) have used pictorial assessment instruments instead of verbal ones to address this problem.

To increase the likelihood of obtaining assessment data that is reliable and valid, CB theorists agree with the suggestion to use multiple modes of assessment. Typically, paper-and-pencil questionnaires, structured interviews, and behavioral observations are cornerstones of CB assessments. No single approach perfectly captures the complexity that is involved in developing a case profile for a child or an adolescent, but the hope is that through using multiple methods one can begin to triangulate on the truth. It is important to emphasize, however, that this combination of assessment modalities is only as strong as its weakest link, and therefore the compilation of multiple methods does not excuse the assessor from considering reliability and validity data for each assessment tool used.

Another consideration when attempting to formulate a treatment plan for a child or adolescent is that youth rarely refer themselves for treatment. Usually a concerned adult (teacher, parent, or other adult figure in the child's life) brings the child to treatment. This may mean that the child or adolescent does not acknowledge that they have a problem requiring treatment and either from obstinacy or ignorance may not be able to provide the assessor with enough information on which to formulate the case. With some disorders, the child or adolescent's inability to provide the needed information may be directly related to the presenting problem. For example, an anxious child with perfectionism and need for social acceptance may be especially apprehensive about sharing their problems with the assessor because of a fear of being perceived negatively.

For the parent or referring adult's part as well, there may be reasons not to rely solely on the information provided. For instance, consistent with Harris and Ferrari (1983), it has been speculated that parents cannot consistently evaluate their child's behavior objectively; they may hold distorted perceptions and/or unrealistic expectations for their child. This inaccuracy may be related to something as simple as unfamiliarity with what is appropriate behavior for children of certain ages or it may be related to issues and problems that the parent is experiencing. CB theorists do not believe that a child's behavior is entirely caused by underlying personality traits that are constant across situations, so it also stands to reason that a parent or teacher who is observing a child in only a limited number of environments could not be expected to provide complete information about the nature of a child's difficulties. Therefore, whether through lack of information or inappropriate expectations, assessment of children and adolescents is best when drawn from many sources. Typically these include self-, parent-, and teacher-reports, and shared experiences with the therapist.

5.06.4 THE EFFICACY AND EFFECTIVENESS OF COGNITIVE-BEHAVIORAL TREATMENTS

Two terms have appeared for evaluating a treatment's success: efficacy and effectiveness. Efficacy and effectiveness studies can be distinguished by the amount of control exerted by the experimenter in the study. Hoagwood, Hibbs, Brent, and Jensen (1995, p. 683) defined efficacy studies as those in which "considerable control has been exercised by the investigator over sample selection (usually recruited samples), over delivery of the intervention, and over the conditions under which the intervention or treatment occurred." The typical example of an efficacy study is a randomized clinical trial in a structured university clinic setting. An intervention's effectiveness is typically tested using a more heterogeneous sample of clients or a more naturalistic setting (e.g., home, school, or more general medical setting), or by having treatment provided by real-world practitioners rather than research therapists (Hoagwood et al., 1995). The primary purpose of effectiveness studies is to evaluate how viable, or how transportable, an efficacious treatment is in real-world settings which often include a wide array of environmental factors that may impact treatment success.

Randomized clinical trials of psychological therapy for children and adolescents have been scant in comparison to studies of adults. Nevertheless, compared to other child treatment modalities, CBT is one of the more frequently and rigorously evaluated therapeutic interventions. In one study, analyzing the characteristics of child and adolescent research from 1970 to 1988, behavior modification was found to be the focus of 49.5% of all therapy studies and cognitive-behavioral approaches the focus of 22.1% (Kazdin, Bass, Ayers, & Rodgers, 1990). The majority of the studies surveyed were conducted in research-oriented clinics. Recently, the transportability of treatment from well-controlled research experimentation to more real-world practicing clinical settings has become a research question (Hoagwood et al., 1995; Kendall & Southam-Gerow, 1995). Among the differences between clinical research and clinical practice, clients seen in research settings are thought to present with a restricted range of disorders with less severe symptomatology (though this has not been the case in recent research), due to exclusion criteria set by the experimenter. Therapy in research clinics is also often conducted by specially trained therapists with small caseloads in well-controlled environments (Weisz, Weiss, & Donenberg, 1992). These differential specifications and conditions under which treatment is provided can be a source of concern when considering evaluations of treatment methods and processes.

A growing list of well-controlled therapy outcome studies has contributed to establishing the efficacy of CBT for children. CB interventions designed for children with depression have produced reductions in self-reports and clinical ratings of depressive symptoms in comparison to waitlist controls (Reynolds & Coats, 1986; Stark, Reynolds, & Kaslow, 1987), accompanied by reductions in anxiety and improvement in academic self-concept (Reynolds & Coats, 1986). Similarly, in a comparison of CBT with and without parental involvement, Lewinsohn et al. (1990) found that compared to a waitlist condition, both treatment conditions resulted in greater reductions in depressive symptomatology and percentage of clients meeting diagnostic criteria for major depressive disorder (MDD) (i.e., 57.1% of children in individual treatment, and 52.4% of individual plus parent treatment met criteria for depression at post-treatment, vs. 94.7% of waitlist). CBT has also demonstrated some superiority over traditional counseling modalities. For example, Stark, Rouse, and Livingston (1991), in a direct comparison of CBT to a traditional counseling program (duration of 24–26 sessions), found that CBT led to greater improvements in depression and reductions in depressive thinking (see also Stark & Kendall, 1996; Stark et al., 1996).

With regard to long-term treatment effects for children with depression, treatment gains have been maintained over short-term follow-up periods of 5–8 weeks (Reynolds & Coats, 1986; Stark, Reynolds, & Kaslow, 1987). However, longer-term follow-up evaluations have yielded more inconsistent results. For example, Stark et al. (1991) noted that some treatment gains were not maintained at seven-month follow-up. Conversely, Lewinsohn et al. (1990) found that depressed adolescents who had received CBT treatment continued to show increased recovery rates over a 2-year follow-up period, with only 17% still meeting *DSM* criteria for MDD at 6, 12, and 24 months.

Cognitive-behavioral interventions with anxiety-disordered youth, a clinical population often overlooked because their behavior may be less disruptive than children with externalizing disorders, have received empirical support (Kendall, 1994; Kendall et al., in press). In comparison to an eight-week waitlist control, a 16-week CB intervention (see Kendall, Kane, Howard, & Siqueland, 1990) produced both statistically and clinically significant improvements on parent-, child-, and teacher-reported measures for 47 children diagnosed with a primary anxiety disorder (Kendall, 1994). These improvements were evident on measures of anxiety, internalizing behavior problems, and depressive symptomatology. Nearly two-thirds of participants no longer met diagnostic criteria for their primary anxiety disorder following treatment. Children participating in the CBT group showed clinically significant gains by returning to within nondeviant limits on many of these measures. Gains seen at post-treatment were also maintained at one-year (Kendall, 1994) and longer-term (3.35-year) follow-ups (Kendall & Southam-Gerow 1996). In a second randomized clinical trial, Kendall et al. (in press) replicated the efficacy of this protocol with 94 anxiety-disordered children. In addition to demonstrating similar treatment gains as the previous trial (Kendall, 1994), comorbid status was not shown to moderate outcome. The program was effective when applied with families (Howard & Kendall, 1996), and work done in Australia, using a modified version of this program (Barrett, Dadds, & Rapee, 1996), provides a cross-cultural and independent replication of favorable treatment outcomes.

CBT has been applied with children exhibiting aggression and antisocial behavior. In a randomized clinical trial of 112 children (aged 7–13) exhibiting antisocial behavior, Kazdin, Bass, Siegel, and Thomas (1989) found significantly greater therapeutic effects for two forms of CBT in comparison to relationship therapy (RT). The two CBT interventions were a problem-solving skills training (PSST) and a problem-solving skills training with *in vivo* practice (PSST-P). At post-treatment, outcome measures revealed significant treatment effects for parent-, teacher-, and child-completed measures. Although all three treatment groups led to some improvements over the course of treatment, the magnitude of the improvements and breadth across measures were greater for children in the PSST and PSST-P groups than for those in the RT group. The improvements of the two PSST groups were particularly superior to those of the RT group in the areas of prosocial measures (social competence and global adjustment) and on diverse scales that reflect problem behavior at school. In this study, the practice component appeared to enhance PSST. In another study (Kazdin, Siegel, & Bass 1992), a parent management component enhanced therapeutic effects over PSST in child and parent functioning and placed a greater proportion of youth within normative levels of functioning.

Other studies have found that CB therapeutic effects may lead to improvement in social-cognitive processes associated with aggressive behaviors (e.g., disciplining for fighting) or improvements in interpersonal skills, but may not lead to change on ratings on teacher reports (Baum, Clark, McCarthy, Sandler, & Carpenter, 1986; Kettlewell & Kausch, 1983; Lochman, White, & Wayland, 1991). The success of CBT in the treatment of aggressive youth is also tempered by difficulties with generalization of treatment effects and persistently elevated levels of disruptive behaviors in normative comparisons. For example, long-term follow-up assessments suggest that decreases in aggressive or delinquent behaviors are often not maintained over time (Kazdin, 1987; Kendall & Braswell, 1982; Lochman, 1992), or are not generalized across situations, for example, classroom behaviors (Baum et al., 1986; Lochman, Burch, Curry, & Lampson, 1984).

To aggregate findings across studies, researchers have used meta-analysis. Meta-analysis, with reference to therapy outcomes, provides a format for quantitatively assessing the effects of particular treatments across studies. In general, behavioral and CB therapies have compared favorably to other theoretical approaches. In meta-analyses including only controlled studies, the mean effect sizes for CBT have ranged from 0.56 to 0.81, for behavioral therapies (including studies of CBT) from 0.88 to 0.91, and for nonbehavioral therapies (including client-centered and psychodynamic therapies) from 0.40 to 0.44 (Casey & Berman, 1985; Durlak, Furhman, & Lampman, 1991; Weisz, Weiss, Alicke, & Klotz, 1987). In general, findings have supported the importance of the behavioral component of CBT (Durlak et al., 1991; Weisz et al., 1987). A meta-analysis that compared controlled outcome studies conducted in both research and practicing clinics found that only the use of behavioral interventions and the treatability of clients (severity of symptoms and presence of comorbidity) predicted treatment outcome (Weisz, Donenberg, Han, & Weiss, 1995).

One meta-analysis focused specifically on CBT. Durlak et al. (1991) reviewed 64 reports of controlled CBT studies conducted between the years of 1970 and 1987 involving children between the ages of five and 13. The overall effect size (ES) for CBT was 0.56. This overall ES represents a moderately beneficial treatment effect, but it should be noted that children who had reached the cognitive stage of formal operations (ages 11 to 13), displayed a large treatment effect (ES = 0.92) in response to CBT. The ES in older children was twice as large as that for children in less advanced cognitive stages (0.57 for ages five to seven; 0.55 for ages eight to 11). The analyses provided data that are consistent with two assumptions of CBT: first, that cognitive developmental level is a factor in a client's response to treatment; and second, that activating cognitive processes may be one of the specific treatment components of CBT.

Durlak et al.'s (1991) review also demonstrated that children undergoing CBT exhibited clinically meaningful gains. In studies comparing treated groups to normative samples, (see also normative comparisons; Kendall & Grove, 1988), treated children displayed clinically meaningful gains (i.e., changed from being beyond normal limits at pretest to being well within normal limits at post-treatment) on measures of personality functioning and cognitive tempo. Contrary to expectations, clinically significant changes were not obtained on behaviorally oriented measures in children who underwent treatment. Although scores on behavioral measurements did decrease in the predicted direction, they did not decrease enough to return youths to within normal ranges. In general, after age was taken into account, no other factors were significant in moderating treatment outcome.

A challenge facing "effectiveness" researchers is finding ways to employ interventions in a fashion that will reach wider populations without sacrificing treatment integrity. Clinical research has traditionally placed internal validity (the extent to which the treatment works) in a position of primary importance above external validity (a treatment's generalizability). This is not unreasonable because many interventions have yet to be empirically supported (Kazdin, 1988). Issues of internal and external validity are of interest to the effectiveness researcher.

Psychological treatment conducted with children in practicing-clinical settings has traditionally enjoyed less success than psychological interventions performed in research-based clinics (Weisz & Weiss, 1989). In Weisz et al.'s (1995) analysis of this discrepancy between research and clinical interventions, it was demonstrated that improvement differences could be accounted for by the use of behavioral interventions and the relative treatability of the client population (severity of symptoms, less presence of comorbidity) in research clinics. Thus, two possibilities for improvement in interventions in clinical settings might be to employ more behavioral techniques, and to specialize clinics so that treatment can focus on circumscribed problems. Research clinics must also progress towards developing interventions that lend themselves better to real-world clinical practice. This may include developing interventions capable of addressing multiple problems sequentially or simultaneously.

5.06.5 PROCEDURES AND PROPOSED MECHANISMS OF CHANGE

Cognitive-behavioral therapy is an active, structured approach to treatment that aims to produce change in an individual's dysfunctional cognition and maladaptive behavior. Its procedures are based on the assumption that cognitive variables are important causal and maintaining mechanisms in the onset and course of a disorder, but that affective and behavioral variables are interrelated and influential as well. Specifically, CBT has been defined as those sets of therapeutic procedures that: (i) place primary importance on the causal/maintaining role of cognitive processes; (ii) use at least some therapeutic procedures aimed at altering aspects of cognition; (iii) examine cognitive, behavioral, and affective variables maintaining the disorder; (iv) may use both behavioral and cognitive techniques to target cognitive objectives, (v) emphasize empirical verification in research, assessment, and treatment; (vi) tend to be time-limited with the possibility of maintenance sessions; (vii) promote a collaborative relationship between client and therapist; and (viii) recommend active therapist participation during sessions (Ingram, et al., 1991).

Given this framework, one therapeutic pathway lies in remedying the identified dysfunction, focusing on the provision of skills and opportunities to practice these skills, and beginning new learning trajectories. One strategy for reaching this goal is the "consultative" role (also called "collaborative empiricism"; Hollon & Beck, 1979), in which the client and therapist work together as active collaborators in the identification of problems, the design and execution of tests of specific hypotheses, and the reanalysis of beliefs (Kendall, Vitousek, & Kane, 1991). As therapy progresses, the client learns to become an active and skeptical social scientist who has the ability to evaluate critically their own ideas, beliefs, and resulting behavior. Cognitive-behavioral theorists believe that data

generated by the client in unbiased experiments, more than a therapist's credibility, persuasiveness, or authenticity, are the instigators of change. Treatment emphasizes inductive strategies for the modification of beliefs, operating from the assumption that "an actual demonstration of a belief's invalidity will go further to change a belief than will a discussion with the therapist" (Piasecki & Hollon, 1987, p.123).

A second therapeutic pathway lies in changing the valence of the child's self-talk. In one study of the treatment of youth with anxiety disorders (Treadwell & Kendall, 1996), negative self-talk was found to play a role in both predicting anxiety, and mediating treatment gains. It was hypothesized that negative self-talk, as opposed to positive self-talk, is predictive of maladjustment (Kendall, 1985). The results (Treadwell & Kendall, 1996) indicated that higher functioning was linked to fewer negative self-statements, but not to greater positive self-talk. Moreover, as children reduced their anxious distress, the accompanying negative self-talk became less frequent. The reduction of negative self-talk was found to mediate gains from CBT.

Procedures used by many CBTs include: affective education, relaxation training, social problem-solving, cognitive restructuring/attribution retraining, contingent reinforcement, modeling, role plays, and training workbooks. The behavioral component of CBT (e.g., modeling, role plays) is designed to illustrate the connection between mood and behavior and to provide practice opportunities for new skill-building. The cognitive component (e.g., cognitive restructuring, problem solving) is designed to teach the child to identify, re-evaluate, and replace maladaptive thoughts. Some techniques necessarily draw from both behavioral and cognitive concepts emphasizing the connection between thought, affect, and action.

Affective education teaches the child to recognize, label, and self-monitor physiological and emotional cues and, eventually, control behavioral reactions that accompany these cues. It focuses on gaining a greater understanding of one's outward manifestations of emotions to become aware of the situations that pose particular difficulties. Relaxation training, which is often tied to affective education, may be considered a first line of defense for children against increased levels of arousal. An objective in relaxation training is to teach the child to manage the physiological responses to emotionally stressful situations. The tandem of affective education and relaxation training free the child from the initial distress of a stressful situation and allow them to process information in a more reasoned and less dysfunctional manner.

Cognitive restructuring consists of strategies aimed at altering cognitive distortions or teaching skills to overcome cognitive deficiencies. The child practices identifying and testing the legitimacy of their own self-talk, or automatic thoughts, and changing self-talk to see the behavioral consequences. Attribution retraining is similar in that it teaches the child to be aware of the nature of their explanations for positive and negative outcomes. Reward and reinforcement can be used as either a method of motivating behavioral activity and teaching cognitive flexibility (as in children with internalizing disorders) or as a way of suppressing behavioral activity (as in children with externalizing disorders).

Modeling and role-playing are two techniques in which a therapist demonstrates to a child how to analyze and evaluate affect, cognition, and behavior. In coping modeling, the therapist describes a situation and relates how they might react in such a situation. The therapist would verbally proceed through the steps of identifying the problem, gathering and isolating key pieces of information, devising alternative actions, and thinking through and acting out conclusions. By modeling the entire scenario, the therapist illustrates to the child that effective problem solving involves a step-by-step process. Role plays enable the child and therapist to learn to be prepared for problems before they arise, and provide practice in the skills learned in sessions before attempting them in real-life situations.

Generally, CBT protocols have two portions. The first portion of the treatment plan focuses on educating the child in the above skills so that the child will be prepared ahead of time when difficult or challenging situations arise. The second half of the treatment plan generally is used to provide the child with opportunities to practice the skills which he or she has just learned. This is accomplished by having the clinician set up a number of manageable scenarios in the real world and allowing the child to confront the ensuing problems on their own.

Not all of the strategies are used identically in every case. Rather, the therapist uses judgment in adjusting strategies to be best suited to the child's developmental sophistication, presenting problem, and extra-therapy environment. Assuming that all children or all therapists are the same, or that all outcomes will be of a uniform type, would be to fall prey to the "uniformity myths" (Kiesler, 1966).

When designing a treatment strategy it is important that the plan includes training for generalization across skills and settings (Kendall, 1989). That is, the therapist must be mindful that mastery of a skill within the confines of the therapy room does not necessa-

rily translate into successful application in the child's natural environment. A child who has demonstrated competence in giving a speech in front of a group may still have a fear of attending a party. To facilitate generalization, therapy can focus on "training diversely" (i.e., exposing the child to a variety of scenarios) so that the child will not be caught off-guard by novel situations (Stokes & Baer, 1977). The therapist can be mindful of current functional contingencies in the child's natural environment: for instance, if a child has difficulties asserting themself, the therapist, under the assumption that most teachers would provide positively reinforcing experiences, might set up an experience where the child must ask the teacher for help. The goal of generalization is to make the child aware that the skills learned in session are not unique to any individual setting, but useful across settings.

5.06.5.1 Proposed Mechanisms of Change

As mentioned previously, childhood disorders can be broken down into internalizing and externalizing varieties, each with cognitive dysfunctions (e.g., deficiencies, distortions). Children who exhibit externalizing behavior tend to display impulsivity and deficits in thinking whereas children with internalizing disorders tend to show overcontrol and distortions in thought. Because of these differences, it is reasonable that the strategies used in treatment accommodate to the specific cognitive needs of the child. Likewise, our notions regarding the active mechanisms involved in change reflect our conceptualization of the client within these categories.

Children with ADHD, for example, characteristically exhibit heightened motor activity, impulsivity, deficits in attention, and deficits in rule-governed behavior (Barkley, 1990). Treatment for children with ADHD tends to involve response-cost contingencies within a context of social reward to reduce unwanted behavior and increase the rates of desirable behavior. The primary goal of the CB therapist is to help the impulsive child internalize steps that can guide effective problem solving: identifying the problem, reflecting on solutions, making a decision, and taking action (Kendall, Kortlander, Chansky, & Brady, 1992). Therapy operates on the idea that the child is deficient in a particular cognitive skill (e.g., rule-governed and linguistically guided behavior) and that training can provide the necessary information to shape more positive behavioral trajectories.

On the other hand, modifying existing cognitive distortions is a primary component and proposed instigator of change in children with internalizing disorders, such as anxiety. Clinically anxious children may have excessive concerns about separation from their caregivers, as in separation anxiety, or they may excessively fear evaluation or rejection by their peers, as in social phobia. Such anxiety manifests in physiological (e.g., excess perspiration, or blushing), behavioral (e.g., avoidance, tremors), and cognitive (e.g., self-doubt, misperceptions of environmental demands) symptoms and can lead to severe interference in the child's daily activities. These distorted misperceptions of the demands in the environment, along with distorted underestimates of personal ability, exacerbate unwanted anxious arousal. The strategies used in treating anxious children may resemble those used with externalizing populations (e.g., social problem solving, modeling, positive reinforcement) but, with internalizing children, the process is focused on altering dysfunctional thinking (distortions) and changing related maladaptive behavior. Thus, the anxious child is taught to evaluate the legitimacy of anxiety-producing automatic thoughts ("If I go to the party, I'll just embarrass myself") and to reconsider less disturbing ways of looking at the world. The therapist helps the child develop a coping template that involves correcting misinterpretations, and viewing events and the environment through an alternative lens based on coping.

In aggression, both cognitive deficiencies and distortions may be present (Kendall, Ronan, & Epps, 1991). This combination requires multifaceted treatment. Also, with comorbidity being the rule rather than the exception, therapists must often combine strategies. In such cases, therapy has the dual function of filling in the gaps where information was needed and aiding the child in constructing a coping template which promotes alternative, healthy ways of thinking. Both components are viewed as essential if the child is to successfully overcome the challenges of adjustment.

In returning to the client as a social scientist, we can conceptualize CBT as any therapy which involves teaching the client strategies that will help them to: (i) formulate specific predictions relevant to their dysfunctional beliefs; (ii) design and carry out extratherapy experiments that bear on these predictions; and (iii) re-evaluate their original hypotheses with respect to the data that are obtained. This formulation might also include the act of supplying a client with any information that would facilitate the process of hypothesis testing (e.g. teaching the problem-solving steps to an impulsive child).

The reader is reminded that the CBT model does not propose to provide a cure for child-hood disorders. Rather, it imparts, and promotes through practice, the ingredients essential for successful coping. The ultimate goal of CBT is not to eradicate the disorder, but to provide the child with multiple lines of defense so that they will have a sense of competence and control when confronted with stress and emotional arousal.

5.06.6 FUTURE DIRECTIONS FOR RESEARCH AND PRACTICE

With a rapidly growing proportion of researchers studying CBT (Kazdin et al., 1990; Klesges et al., 1982) and an expanding list of successful applications of CB to childhood disorders (see Kendall, 1993), there is reason to suggest that CBT will continue to undergo expansion. Attention to some key issues will assure the field's continued development. These issues include: (i) a growing need for development and study of standardized treatment manuals; (ii) an expanding emphasis on research aimed at understanding the active components of CBT, as well as understanding the underlying mechanisms maintaining childhood disorders; (iii) an increasing concern for the transportability of interventions from the research clinic to real-world service clinics; and (iv) a need for further study in the comparative and facilitative effects of pharmacological treatments.

Several randomized clinical trials evaluating CBT attest to its efficacy with some childhood disorders (e.g., anxiety, depression). More work needs to be done with disorders that have not been fully studied with CB protocols. The development and evaluation of manualized treatments, and the study of the role of flexibility in the use of manuals, deserves emphasis.

Demonstrating the efficacy of an intervention is a first step. Understanding the underlying behavioral and cognitive processes causing and maintaining a disorder as well as understanding the specific effects of therapeutic techniques is the second step. Which components are necessary? Which are helpful? Which are harmful? More clinical trials with active control groups (e.g., relationship therapy) may help examine the role of nonspecific factors of treatment. Such studies would allow us to begin to separate gains unique to the intervention from gains resulting from more general therapeutic factors.

Research is needed to determine the degree to which research clinic procedures can be transported to service clinics (Hoagwood et al., 1995; Kendall & Southam-Gerow, 1995). Are there client or therapist factors that contribute to differential outcomes? How are treatment-outcome studies received? Practicing clinicians may incorporate findings into their daily work, but research journals are not the practitioner's preferred method of receiving knowledge (Beutler, Williams, Wakefield, & Entwhistle, 1995). The transportability of research clinic interventions would benefit from progress on two fronts: first, research interventions should be tested in service clinics and any moderators of treatment should be examined; second, there needs to be more collaboration among research clinicians and service practitioners. Collaboration may help inform scientists on which areas of research are most relevant to practitioners and in what ways transportability could be improved. Such collaboration may help practitioners appreciate the value of data-supported interventions and inform practitioners how best to utilize findings from research clinics.

The recent pharmacological trend in treating mental health problems dictates that professionals within the field keep abreast regarding the usage and efficacy of pharmacological agents in treatment. Medications used in adult treatment are sometimes prescribed to children presenting similar symptoms but without the benefit of controlled, experimental evaluations. For example, in the treatment of depressed children and adolescents, various tricyclic antidepressants (TCA) (e.g., imipramine, desipramine, amitriptyline, and nortriptyline) and serotonin-specific reuptake inhibitors (SSRIs; e.g., fluoxetine, sertraline, paroxetine, and fluvoxamine) are commonly prescribed. However, despite what appears to be widespread general use of TCAs and SSRIs with children and adolescents, neither category of medication has consistently been demonstrated to be superior to a placebo (Jain et al., 1992; Simeon et al., 1990; Sommers-Flanagan & Sommers-Flanagan, 1996). Future research with pharmacological treatments with children needs to be directed toward determining the efficacy of the pharmacological agent alone or in combination with psychological interventions. Research addressing the comparative and facilitative effects of pharmacotherapy with youth is also required.

Much work remains in the application of CBT to childhood disorders. Applications of CBT for some disorders need to be developed, whereas in other disorders (e.g., anxiety, depression) research might focus on underlying cognitive processes and mechanisms of change. What aspects of cognitive processes and self-talk differentiate depressive from anxious self-talk? Which behaviors and cognitive processes show the greatest correlation with therapeutic change? Further research can also be done to enhance the transportability of CB interventions to practicing clinics. What are the factors that moderate outcome outside the research clinic's walls? What are the comparative and facilitative benefits of pharmacological treatments used in combination with CBT with children? Although CBT with youth is itself a relatively young approach, it has matured and continues to enjoy much activity and growth.

5.06.7 REFERENCES

Achenbach, T. M. (1966). The classification of children's psychiatric symptoms: A factor analytic study. *Psycological Monographs, 80* (whole No. 615).

Bandura, A. (1969). Social-learning theory of identification processes. In D. Goslin (Ed.), *Handbook of socialization theory and research* (pp. 213–262). Chicago: Rand McNally.

Barkley, R. (1990). *Attention-deficit hyperactivity disorder. A handbook for diagnosis and treatment.* New York: Guilford Press.

Barrett, P., Dadds, M., & Rapee, R. (1996). Family treatment of child anxiety: A controlled trial. *Journal of Consulting and Clinical Psychology, 64,* 333–342.

Baum, J. G., Clark, H. B., McCarthy, W., Sandler, J., & Carpenter, R. (1986). An analysis of the acquisition and generalization of social skills in troubled youths: Combining social skills training, cognitive self-talk, and relaxation procedures. *Child and Family Behavior Therapy, 8,* 1–27.

Beck, A. T. (1976). *Cognitive therapy and the emotional disorders.* New York: International Universities Press.

Beck, A. T., Rush, A. J., Shaw, B. F., & Emery, G. (1979). *Cognitive therapy of depression.* New York: Guilford.

Beutler, L. E., Williams, R. E., Wakefield, P. J., & Entwhistle, S. R. (1995). Bridging scientist and practitioner perspectives in clinical psychology. *American Psychologist, 50,* 984–994.

Callahan, S. A., Panichelli-Mindel, S., & Kendall, P. C. (1996). DSM-IV and internalizing disorders: Modifications, limitations, and utility. *School Psychology Review, 25,* 298–308.

Casey, R. J., & Berman, J. S. (1985). The outcome of psychotherapy with children. *Psychological Bulletin, 98,* 388–400.

Craighead, W. E., Brownell, K. D., & Horan, J. J. (1981). Behavioral interventions for weight restriction and smoking cessation. In W. E. Craighead, A. E. Kazdin, & M. J. Mahoney (Eds.), *Behavior modification: Principles, issues, and applications* (2nd ed., pp. 288–312). Boston: Houghton Mifflin.

Craighead, W. E., Wilcoxon-Craighead, L. W., & Meyers, A. W. (1978). New directions in behavior modification with children. In M. Hersen, R. M. Eisler, & P. M. Miller (Eds.), *Progress in behavior modification* (Vol. 6, pp. 159–201). New York: Academic Press.

Dodge, K. A. (1980). Social cognition and children's aggressive behavior. *Child Development, 51,* 162–170.

Dodge, K. A., & Frame, C. L. (1982). Social cognitive biases and deficits in aggressive boys. *Child Development, 53,* 620–635.

Durlak, J. A., Furhman, T., Lampman, C. (1991). Effectiveness of cognitive-behavior therapy for maladapting children: A meta-analysis. *Psychological Bulletin, 110,* 204–214.

D'Zurilla, T. (1986). *Problem-solving therapy: A social competence approach to clinical intervention.* New York: Springer.

D'Zurilla, T., & Goldfried, M. (1971). Problem solving and

behavior modification. *Journal of Abnormal Psychology, 78,* 107–126.

Ellis, A. (1962). *Reason and emotion in psychotherapy.* New York: Lyle Stuart.

Epstein, S., & Erskine, N. (1983). The development of personal theories of reality. In D. Magnusson & V. Allens (Eds.), *Human development: An interactional perspective.* New York: Academic Press.

Evans, I. M., & Nelson, R. O. (1986). Assessment of children. In A. R. Ciminero, K. S. Calhoun, & H. E. Adams (Eds.), *Handbook of behavioral assessment* (2nd ed., pp. 601–630). New York: Wiley.

Finch, A. J., & Montgomery, L. E. (1973). Reflection-impulsivity and information seeking in emotionally disturbed children. *Journal of Abnormal Child Psychology, 1,* 358–362.

Guidano, V. F., & Liotti, G. (1983). Cognition in processes and emotional disorders. New York: Guilford Press.

Harris, S. L., & Ferrari, M. (1983). Developmental factors in child behavior therapy. *Behavior Therapy, 14,* 54–72.

Harvey, J. H., Weber, A. L., & Orbach, T. L. (1990). *Interpersonal accounts: A social psychological perspective.* Oxford, UK: Blackwell.

Hoagwood, K., Hibbs, E., Brent, D., & Jensen, P. (1995). Introduction to the special section: Efficacy and effectiveness in studies of child and adolescent psychotherapy. *Journal of Consulting and Clinical Psychology, 63,* 683–687.

Hollon, S., & Beck, A. T. (1979). Cognitive therapy of depression. In P. C. Kendall and S. Hollon (Eds.), *Cognitive-behavioral interventions: Theory, research, and procedures* (pp. 153–204). New York: Academic Press.

Howard, B., & Kendall, P. C. (1996). Cognitive-behavioral family therapy for anxiety-disordered children: A multiple-baseline evaluation. *Cognitive Therapy and Research, 20,* 423–444.

Ingram, R. E., & Kendall, P. (1986). Cognitive clinical psychology: Implications of an information processing perspective. In R. Ingram (Ed.), *Information processing approaches to clinical psychology* (pp. 3–22) New York: Academic Press.

Ingram, R. E., Kendall, P. C., & Chen, A. H. (1991). Cognitive-behavioral interventions. In C. R. Snyder & D. R. Forsyth (Eds.), *Handbook of social and clinical psychology: The health perspective* (pp. 509–522). New York: Pergamon.

Jain, U., Birmaher, B., Garcia, M., et al. (1992). Fluoxetine in children and adolescents with mood disorders: A chart review of efficacy and adverse effects. *Journal of Child and Adolescent Psychopharmacology, 2,* 259–265.

Jones, M. C. (1924a). The elimination of children's fears. *Journal of Experimental Psychology, 7,* 382–390.

Jones, M. C. (1924b). A laboratory study of fear: The case of Peter. *Journal of Genetic Psychology, 31,* 308–315.

Kahnemann, D., Slovic, P., & Tversky, A. (1982). *Judgement under uncertainty: Heuristics and biases.* Cambridge, UK: Cambridge University Press.

Kanfer, F. H., & Karoly, P. (1972). Self-control: A behavioristic excursion into the lion's den. *Behavior Therapy, 3,* 398–416.

Kanfer, F., & Phillips, J. (1970). *Learning foundations of behavior therapy.* New York: Wiley.

Kazdin, A. E. (1987). *Conduct disorder in childhood and adolescence.* Beverly Hills, CA: Sage.

Kazdin, A. E. (1988). *Child psychotherapy: Developing and identifying effective treatments.* Elmsford, NY: Pergamon.

Kazdin, A. E., Bass, D., Ayers, W. A., & Rodgers, A. (1990). Empirical and clinical focus of child and adolescent psychotherapy research. *Journal of Consulting and Clinical Psychology, 58,* 729–740.

Kazdin, A. E., Bass, D., Siegel, T., & Thomas, C. (1989). Cognitive-behavioral therapy and relationship therapy in the treatment of children referred for antisocial behavior. *Journal of Consulting and Clinical Psychology, 57,* 522–535.

Kazdin, A. E., Siegel, T., & Bass, D. (1992). Cognitive problem-solving skills training and parent management training in the treatment of antisocial behavior in children. *Journal of Consulting and Clinical Psychology, 60,* 733–747.

Kendall, P. C. (1977). On the efficacious use of verbal self-instructions with children. *Cognitive Therapy and Research, 1,* 331–341.

Kendall, P. C. (1984). Social cognition and problem-solving: A developmental and child-clinical interface. In B. Gholson & T. Rosenthal (Eds.), *Applications of cognitive developmental theory* (pp. 115–148). New York: Academic Press.

Kendall, P. C. (1985). Toward a cognitive-behavioral model of child psychopathology and a critique of related interventions. *Journal of Abnormal Child Psychology, 13,* 357–372.

Kendall, P. C. (1989). The generalization and maintenance of behavior change: Comments, considerations, and the "no-cure" criticism. *Behavior Therapy, 20,* 357–364.

Kendall, P. C. (1991). Guiding theory for treating children and adolescents. In P. C. Kendall (Ed.), *Child and adolescent therapy: Cognitive-behavioral procedures* (pp. 3–24). New York: Guilford Press.

Kendall, P. C. (1993). Cognitive-behavioral therapies with youth: Guiding theory, current status, and emerging developments. *Journal of Consulting and Clincial Psychology, 61,* 235–247.

Kendall, P. C. (1994). Treating anxiety disorders in children: Results of a randomized clinical trial. *Journal of Consulting and Clinical Psychology, 62,* 100–110.

Kendall, P. C., & Braswell, L. (1982). Cognitive-behavioral self-control therapy for children: A components analysis. *Journal of Consulting and Clinical Psychology, 50,* 672–690.

Kendall, P. C., Flannery-Schroeder, E., Panichelli-Mindel, S. M., Southam-Gerow, M. A., Henin, A., & Warman, M. (in press). Therapy for anxiety-disordered youth: A randomized clinical trial and the effects of comorbidity and treatment segments. *Journal of Consulting and Clinical Psychology.*

Kendall, P. C., & Grove, W. M. (1988). Normative comparisons in therapy outcome. *Behavioral Assessment, 10,* 147–158.

Kendall, P. C., & Ingram, R. E. (1987). The future of the cognitive assessment of anxiety: Let's get specific. In L. Michelson & M. Ascher (Eds.), *Anxiety and stress disorders: Cognitive-behavioral assessment and treatment* (pp. 89–104). New York: Guilford Press.

Kendall, P. C., & Ingram, R. E. (1989). Cognitive-behavioral perspectives: Theory and research on depression and anxiety. In P. C. Kendall & D. Watson (Eds.), *Anxiety and depression: Distinctive and overlapping features.* New York: Academic Press.

Kendall, P. C., Kane, M., Howard, B., & Siqueland, L. (1990). *Cognitive-behavioral therapy for anxious children: Treatment manual.* Ardmore, PA: Workbook.

Kendall, P. C., Kortlander, E., Chansky, T. E., & Brady, E. U. (1992). Comorbidity of anxiety and depression in youth: Treatment implications. *Journal of Consulting and Clinical Psychology, 60,* 869–880.

Kendall, P. C., & MacDonald, J. P. (1993). Cognition in the psychopathology of youth and implications for treatment. In K. S. Dobson and P. C. Kendall (Eds.), *Psychopathology and cognition* (pp. 387–430). San Diego, CA: Academic Press.

Kendall, P. C., Ronan, K. R., & Epps, J. (1991). Aggression in children/adolescents: Cognitive-behavioral treatment perspective. In D. J. Pepler & K. H. Rubin (Eds.), *The development and treatment of childhood aggression* (pp. 341–360). Hillsdale, NJ: Erlbaum.

Kendall, P. C., & Southam-Gerow, M. A. (1995). Issues in the transportability of treatment. The case of anxiety disorders in youths. *Journal of Consulting and Clinical Psychology, 63,* 702–708.

Kendall, P. C., & Southam-Gerow, M. A. (1996) Long-term follow-up of a cognitive-behavioral therapy for anxiety-disordered youth. *Journal of Consulting and Clinical Psychology, 64,* 724–730.

Kendall, P. C., Vitousek, K. B., & Kane, M. (1991). Thought and action in psychotherapy: Cognitive-behavioral approaches. In M. Hersen, A. Kazdin, & A. Bellack (Eds.), *Clinical psychology handbook* (pp. 596–626). New York: Pergamon.

Kendall, P. C., & Williams, C. L. (1981). Behavioral and cognitive behavioral approaches to outpatient treatment with children. In W. E. Craighead, A. E. Kazdin, & M. J. Mahoney (Eds.), *Behavior modification: Principles, issues, and applications* (2nd ed., pp. 402–417). Boston: Houghton Mifflin.

Kettlewell, P. W., & Kausch, D. F. (1983). The generalization of the effects of a cognitive-behavioral treatment program for aggressive children. *Journal of Abnormal Child Psychology, 11,* 101–114.

Kiesler, D. J. (1966). Some myths of psychotherapy research and the search for a paradigm. *Psychological Bulletin, 65,* 110–136.

Klesges, R. C., Sanchez, V. C., & Stanton, A. L., (1982). Obtaining employment in academia: The hiring process and characteristics of successful applicants. *Professional Psychology, 13,* 577–586.

Levitt, E. (1957). The results of psychotherapy with children: An evaluation. *Journal of Consulting Psychology, 21,* 189–196.

Levitt, E. (1963). Psychotherapy with children: A further evaluation. *Behaviour Research and Therapy, 1,* 45–51.

Lewinsohn, P. M., Clarke, G. N., Hops, H., & Andrews, J. (1990). Cognitive-behavioral treatment for depressed adolescents. *Behavior Therapy, 21,* 385–401.

Lochman, J. E. (1987). Self- and peer perceptions and attributional biases of aggressive and nonaggressive boys in dyadic interactions. *Journal of Consulting and Clinical Psychology, 55,* 404–410.

Lochman, J. E. (1992). Cognitive-behavioral interventions with aggressive boys: Three-year follow-up and preventive effects. *Journal of Consulting and Clinical Psychology, 60,* 426–432.

Lochman, J. E., Burch, P. R., Curry, J. F., & Lampron, L. B. (1984). Treatment and generalization effects of cognitive-behavioral and goal-setting interventions with aggressive boys. *Journal of Consulting and Clinical Psychology, 52,* 915–916.

Lochman, J. E., White, K. J., & Wayland, K. K. (1991). Cognitive-behavioral assessment and treatment with aggressive children. In P. C. Kendall, (Ed.), *Child and adolescent therapy: Cognitive-behavioral procedures* (pp. 25–65). New York: Guilford Press.

Luria, A. R. (1976). *Cognitive development: Its cultural and social foundations.* Cambridge, MA: Harvard University Press.

Mahoney, M. J. (1974). *Cognition and behavior modification.* Cambridge, MA: Ballinger.

Mahoney, M. J., & Lyddon, W. J. (1988). Recent developments in cognitive approaches to counseling and psychotherapy. *The Counseling Psychologist, 16,* 190–234.

McNamee, S., & Gergen, K. J. (Eds.) (1992). *Therapy as social construction.* London: Sage.

Meichenbaum, D. (1977). *Cognitive-behavior modification: An integrative approach.* New York: Plenum.

Meichenbaum, D. (1985). *Stress inoculation training.* Elmsford, NY: Pergamon.

Meichenbaum, D. (1995). Cognitive-behavioral therapy in historical perspective. In B. Bongar & L. E. Beutler (Eds.), *Comprehensive textbook of psychotherapy* (pp. 140–158). New York: Oxford University Press.

Meichenbaum, D., & Fitzpatrick, D. (1993). A constructivist narrative perspective of stress and coping: Stress inoculation applications. In L. Goldberger & S. Breznitz (Eds.), *Handbook of stress* (pp. 706–723). New York: Free Press.

Meichenbaum. D. H., & Goodman, J. (1971). Training impulsive children to talk to themselves: A means of developing self-control. *Journal of Abnormal Psychology, 77,* 115–126.

Meyers, A. W., & Craighead, W. E. (1984). Cognitive behavior therapy with children: A historical, conceptual, and organizational overview. In A. W. Meyers & W. E. Craighead (Eds.), *Cognitive behavior therapy with children* (pp. 1–17). New York: Plenum.

Mischel, W. (1973). Toward a cognitive social learning reconceptualization of personality. *Psychological Review, 80,* 221–234.

Mowrer, O. H., & Mowrer, W. M. (1938). Enuresis—A method for its study and treatment. *American Journal of Orthopsychiatry, 8,* 730–738.

Neimeyer, R. A. (1993). An appraisal of constructivist psychotherapies. *Journal of Consulting and Clinical Psychology, 61,* 221–234.

Neimeyer, R. A., & Feixas, G. (1990). Constructivist contributions to psychotherapy integration. *Journal of Integrative and Eclectic Psychotherapy, 9,* 4–20.

Nisbett, R., & Ross, L. (1980). *Human inference: Strategies and shortcomings of social judgement.* Englewood Cliffs, NJ: Prentice-Hall.

Ollendick, T. H., & Hersen, M. (1993). Child and adolescent behavioral assessment. In T. H. Ollendick & M. Hersen (Eds.), *Handbook of child and adolescent assessment* (pp. 3–14). Boston: Allyn & Bacon.

Piaseki, J., & Hollon, S. D. (1987). Cognitive therapy for depression: Unexplicated schemata and scripts. In N.S. Jacobson (Ed.), *Psychotherapists in clinical practice: Cognitive and behavioral perspectives* (pp. 121–152). New York: Guilford Press.

Reynolds, W. M., & Coats, K. I. (1986). A comparison of cognitive-behavioral therapy and relaxation training for the treatment of depression in adolescents. *Journal of Consulting and Clinical Psychology, 54,* 653–660.

Rogers, C. R. (1951). *Client-centered therapy.* Boston: Houghton Mifflin.

Rosch, E. (1973). On the internal structure of perceptual and semantic categories. In T. M. More (Ed.), *Cognitive development and the acquisition of language* (pp. 111–144). New York: Academic Press.

Rosch, E. (1975). Cognitive representations of semantic categories. *Journal of Experimental Psychology: General, 104,* 192–233.

Rotter, J. (1966). Generalized expectancies for internal versus external control of reinforcement. *Psychological Monographs, 85.*

Sheslow, D. V., Bondy, A. S., & Nelson, R. O. (1982). A comparison of graduated exposure, verbal coping skills and their combination in the treatment of children's fear of the dark. *Child and Family Behavior Therapy, 4,* 33–45.

Simeon, J. G., Dinicola, V. F., Ferguson, B. H., et al. (1990). Adolescent depression: A placebo-controlled fluoxetine study and follow-up. *Progress in Neuro-Psychopharmacology and Biological Psychiatry, 14,* 791–795.

Sommers-Flanagan, J., & Sommers-Flanagan, R. (1996). Efficacy of antidepressant medication with depressed youth: What psychologists should know. *Professional Psychology: Research and Practice, 27,* 145–153.

Spivack, G., & Shure, M. B. (1974). *Social adjustment of young children: A cognitive approach to solving real-life problems*. San Franscico: Jossey-Bass.

Stark, K. D., & Kendall, P. C. (1996). *Treating depressed children: Therapist manual for "ACTION."* Ardmore, PA: Workbook.

Stark, K., Kendall, P. C., McCarthy, M., Stafford, M., Barron, R., & Thomeer, M. (1996). *ACTION: A workbook for overcoming depression.* Ardmore, PA: Workbook.

Stark, K. D., Reynolds, W. M., & Kaslow, N. J. (1987). A comparison of the relative efficacy of self-control therapy and a behavioral problem-solving therapy for depression in children. *Journal of Abnormal Child Psychology, 15,* 91–113.

Stark, K. D., Rouse, L. W., & Livingston, R. (1991). Treatment of depression during childhood and adolescence: Cognitive-behavioral procedures for the individual and family. In P. C. Kendall (Ed.), *Child and adolescent therapy: Cognitive-behavioral procedures* (pp. 165–206). New York: Guilford Press.

Stokes, T. F., & Baer, D. M. (1977). An implicit technology of generalization. *Journal of Applied Behavior Analysis, 10,* 349–367.

Strauss, C. C., Lease, C. A., Last, C. G., & Francis, G. (1988). Overanxious disorder: An examination of developmental differences. *Journal of Abnormal Child Psychology, 16,* 433–443.

Treadwell, K. R. H., & Kendall, P. C. (1996). Self-talk with anxiety disorders: States of mind, content specificity, and treatment outcome. *Journal of Consulting and Clinical Psychology, 64,* 941–950.

Tversky, A., & Kahnemann, D. (1974). Judgement under uncertainty: Heuristics and biases. *Science, 185,* 1124–1131.

Vygotsky, L. S. (1978). *Mind in society: The development of higher psychological processes.* Cambridge, MA: Harvard University Press.

Watson, J. B. (1924). *Behaviorism.* Chicago: University of Chicago Press.

Watson, J. B. & Rayner, R. (1920). Conditioned emotional reactions. *Journal of Experimental Psychology, 3,* 1–14.

Weisz, J. R., Donenberg, G. R., Han, S. S., & Weiss, B. (1995). Bridging the gap between laboratory and clinic in child and adolescent psychotherapy. *Journal of Consulting and Clinical Psychology, 63,* 688–701.

Weisz, J. R., & Weiss, B. (1989). Assessing the effects of clinic-based psychotherapy with children and adolescents. *Journal of Consulting and Clinical Psychology, 57,* 741–746.

Weisz, J. R., Weiss, B., Alicke, M. D., & Klotz, M. L. (1987). Effectiveness of psychotherapy with children and adolescents: A meta-analysis for clinicians. *Journal of Consulting and Clinical Psychology, 55,* 542–549.

Weisz, J. R., Weiss, B., & Donenberg, G. R. (1992). The lab versus the clinic: Effects of child and adolescent psychotherapy. *American Psychologist, 7,* 1578–1585.

White, M., & Epston, D. (1990). *Narrative means to therapeutic ends.* New York: Norton.

Witmer, L. (1907). Clinical Psychology. *Psychological Clinic, 1,* 1–9.

5.07

Family Systems Therapy with Children and Adolescents

MICHAEL S. ROBBINS and JOSÉ SZAPOCZNIK
University of Miami, FL, USA
JAMES F. ALEXANDER
University of Utah, Salt Lake City, UT, USA
and
JAMIE MILLER
Miami Institute of Professional Psychology, FL, USA

5.07.1 INTRODUCTION

Family systems therapy has emerged as a viable treatment for certain child and adolescent problems. In fact, for some clinical populations of youth, family systems therapy has been acknowledged as the "treatment of choice" (Gordon, Arbruthnot, Gustafson, & McGreen, 1988; Kazdin, 1993, 1994a; Liddle & Dakof, 1995a, 1995b). Despite its rapid growth in clinical and research settings, some continue to view family systems therapy as merely an adjunct to traditional individual modalities.

Family systems therapy, however, represents a "whole new way of conceptualizing human problems, of understanding behavior, the development of symptoms, and their resolution" (Sluzki, 1978, p. 366) in which the transformation of family interactions is its defining feature. Because interactions are viewed as pivotal in the etiology and maintenance of psychopathology, interactions are the ultimate target of intervention in family systems therapy.

Interactions are defined as the complex and interdependent patterns of behaviors and responses within the family. A fundamental assumption in family systems theory is that an individual's behavior is quite different from what it would be if it were possible for that individual to act in isolation. That is, the behaviors of individual family members are linked in an interdependent fashion, and each family member is viewed as being responsible for contributing to, maintaining, or changing the system's interactions (Szapocznik & Kurtines, 1989). The interdependent or linked behaviors among individuals tend to repeat, and ultimately become patterns of interaction that characterize the family system. It is these repetitive patterns of interaction that are the focus of family systems therapy.

While the family is at the core of the intervention strategy, family systems therapy appreciates the full range of systemic influences that affect the individual. For example, family systems therapy acknowledges the important influence of peers (Boivin & Begin, 1989; Dishion, French, & Patterson, 1995; Parker & Asher, 1987), school (Rutter, 1983), and the neighborhood (Brooks-Gunn, Duncan, Klebanov, & Sealand, 1993) on children and their families. A fuller appreciation of the range of systems that influence children and their families also includes biological processes (i.e., genetics) as well as individual psychological processes (i.e., cognitions). However, although the interface between the family and its context is acknowledged (Alexander, Barton, Waldron, & Mas, 1983; Szapocznik & Kurtines, 1993), it is the interactions that occur within the family that are the primary focus of intervention.

It is important to note that there is considerable heterogeneity within the field of family systems therapy in how different models of systemic intervention conceptualize and treat psychopathology. Some models focus relatively more on intrapersonal (i.e., psychodynamic, cognitive) processes, while others focus more on interpersonal (i.e., behavioral, multisystemic/ contextual) processes. Such differential foci, however, tend to be a matter of emphasis rather than epistemology, and most models contain both intrapersonal as well as interpersonal elements. What cuts across family systems models, however, is a focus on patterns of interactions within the family. Thus, in this chapter, it is our intention to highlight the interactive and interdependent nature of family interactions that is ubiquitous to family systems intervention, rather than to draw attention to differences (often subtle) between the various systemic interventions.

In this chapter we present an overview of the development and current state of the science in family systems therapy with children and adolescents. By family systems therapy, we refer to clinical models that postulate underlying mechanisms which are based on the fundamental tenets of systems theory. To be included in this review, the intervention model had to contain a specific focus on processes (i.e., patterns of interaction) of the family system. By family, we refer to nuclear, blended, or other types of family arrangement. Intervention models more strongly rooted in behavioral theory are not reviewed in this chapter (for a review of these see Estrada & Pinsof, 1995).

5.07.2 THEORETICAL UNDERPINNINGS OF FAMILY SYSTEMS THERAPY

Considerable research indicates that social/contextual factors profoundly influence a child's developmental trajectory (Bronfenbrenner, 1995). Within the social context, the family has undoubtedly the most fundamental influence, having been referred to as the "bedrock" of child development (Bronfenbrenner, 1979; 1986; Szapocznik & Coatsworth, submitted for publication). The family system serves a critically important socialization influence for children and adolescents (Rutter & Cox, 1985); consequently, problems within the family system can dramatically influence youth. In fact, research has consistently demonstrated that problems within the family system are associated with a variety of psychological and behavioral problems in children and adolescents (Forehand, 1993; Kazdin & Kolko, 1986; Rutter & Garmezy, 1983).

So, what is the family system? How does it influence the child's development, including the development of psychological and behavioral problems? Is the family system amenable to change? And, if so, are these changes associated with improvements in the child's behavior? To answer these questions, it is important to understand some of the basic processes that underly the family system. In this section, some of the basic tenets of family systems theory are presented.

5.07.2.1 The Family System

The fundamental epistemology underlying family systems therapy is that of general systems theory (von Bertalanffy, 1968). In fact, the core assumption in family systems therapy is that the family operates according to basic rules and processes that govern all types of systems. From this perspective, a system is defined as a:

circumscribed complex of relatively bounded phenomena, which, within these bounds, retains a

relatively stationary pattern of structure in space or of sequential configuration in time in spite of a high degree of variability in the details of distribution and interrelations among its constituent units of lower order. (The system) responds to alterations of the environment by an adaptive redirection of its component processes in such a manner as to counter the external change in the direction of optimum preservation of its systemic integrity. (Weiss, 1969, pp. 11–12)

Chaos theory (Briggs & Peat, 1989; Gleik, 1987) can be used to explain the apparent paradox that a high degree of variability in the details of the behaviors of individual family members, in the context of the family, emerge as relatively stationary patterns of interaction over time and space. At the core of family systems theory is the notion that the family is a dynamic, self-regulating system comprised of interdependent parts that interact with one another in a somewhat predictable manner. The family system is dynamic in that it is comprised of individuals that interact and mutually influence one another (and their environment) continuously. And, it is self-regulating in that these interactions strive to maintain the integrity of the system. Integrity or self-preservation, however, are not equivalent to adaptive functioning. By maintaining integrity, we refer to the system's ability to maintain its characteristic organization regardless of whether this organization is adaptive or maladaptive.

The most important systemic principle that dominates family systems theory is that of interdependence. Interdependence refers to the complex connections and mutual influence of individual parts within a system. In families, interactions between and among family members are the primary means through which interdependence is defined. Understanding interactions—and consequently, interdependence—requires an understanding of the basic principles of systems theory. The following section briefly reviews some of the systemic principles that are critically relevant for assessment and intervention in the family context. This review is not exhaustive. For a more thorough review of systems principles see Broderick (1993), Buckley (1968), Goldenberg and Goldenberg (1996), Hanson (1995) and Steinglass (1987).

5.07.2.1.1 *Wholeness: the whole is more than the sum of its parts*

Basic to family systems theory is the assumption that the family is a dynamic system that can only be understood by overtly recognizing the complex interplay among all of its constituent parts. One cannot break the system down to its molecular parts, and then put the parts back together again to understand how the family operates. That is, achieving some level of understanding about an individual's internal (e.g., psychological) dynamics or a single aspect of family functioning (e.g., marital conflict) is useful, but it does not necessarily help the therapist predict (or even understand) how the family comes together and interacts as a system. It is only by examining the unique way in which the parts interact and reciprocally influence each other that the family system can be understood. This philosophy is represented in the systemic assumption that "the whole is more than the sum of its parts."

This is not to say that the individual parts of the family system are not important. In fact, we support attempts at formally integrating intrapersonal factors into family systems treatment (Breunlin, Schwartz, & Kune-Karrer, 1992; Liddle, 1994), and believe that future family systems model building must continue to build on such attempts to take into account the individual characteristics of family members. What we are trying to convey here, however, is that molecular examinations of the family do not capture the true complexity of the family system. And that even though "there is no phenomenon in a living system that is not molecular ... there is none that is only molecular, either" (Weiss, 1969, pp. 10–11). In other words, it is useful to understand how an individual family member interprets/processes information and how this processing influences their behavior; however, to understand the mutual influence and interdependent nature of family interactions such information must then be incorporated at the level of the family. Thoughts, feelings, and individual behaviors are thus considered to contribute to the interpersonal context of the family, but are not considered to be the defining features of the family. In family systems therapy, assessment and intervention occurs at both the molecular and molar levels. The therapist attends to the internal realities of individual family members and specific aspects of family relations (e.g., marital conflict), but also examines the unique way in which these aspects come together and influence the adaptive and maladaptive behaviors of the youth.

The essence of the concept of wholeness exists in the reality that although the family is comprised of multiple individuals with different emotions, beliefs, and behavioral repertoires, the family system develops its own unique identity that is not fully explained by these individual characteristics. As suggested in the biological sciences, the patterned processes that

occur within systems do not occur because of some "prearranged, absolutely stereotyped mosaic of singletracked component performances" (Weiss, 1969, p. 9). Rather, these repetitive processes occur as individual parts in the system submit to the organizing rules of the system. In the family system, for example, although individual family members are capable of exhibiting an infinite number of interactions, they tend to interact in a manner that "fits" or is "consistent with" the governing rules of the family system.

The concept of "wholeness" has critical implications for treatment. For example, while individual family members' values, beliefs, and emotions, as well as particular relationships within the family (e.g., sibling, parent, parent–child) are considered to be important, systemic treatment must involve assessment and intervention at the level of the family as a whole. The family therapist is thus interested in changing the family's unique pattern of interaction. For example, an intervention designed to promote healthy connectedness between a parent and an adolescent must also take into account the impact that such an increase in connectedness will have on other aspects of the parent–adolescent relationship as well as on other individuals in the family. As is evident in this example, family systems therapists often target individuals or specific relationships within the family, but they do so with an explicit understanding of the potential reverberations that such interventions will have throughout the family system. It should also be noted that these interventions are typically utilized as a means to an end, and are often implemented as one aspect of a larger treatment plan that addresses changes in complex patterns of interaction at the level of the family system. Thus, in the scenario presented above, improving parent–adolescent connectedness may serve as a springboard for improving the parents' monitoring of the adolescent's behaviors. Moreover, this improved parent–adolescent bond may result in the formation of a new leadership subsystem (comprised of parent and adolescent) in which the adolescent is supported in taking over some of the developmentally appropriate leadership responsibilities within the family.

It is important to note that the concept of wholeness explains current family interactions, but does not explain why the family adopts one particular pattern of interaction over another. In fact, most family systems theories focus more on present interactions than on their historical antecedents. Many factors are likely to contribute to the emergence of specific patterns of interaction within the family, including individuals' predispositions (e.g., biological, personality) and personal history (e.g., family of origin, interpersonal relationships) as well as major developmental milestones (e.g., marriage, birth of children) and contextual factors (e.g., deteriorating conditions in neighborhoods, parent's loss of job).

When individuals first come together to form a relationship, their unique individual qualities probably define the possible range of interactions that may occur. Although there are an infinite number of possibilities that may occur within this range, specific patterns emerge and become relatively stable. As noted, the emergence of one pattern over another is probably influenced by many factors. While the relationship is partly determined by the persons involved, it cannot be predicted from the individual predispositions of each of its participants. The individuals involved in the interaction define the range of possibilities that may occur, but the specific pattern that emerges cannot be predicted from knowledge of each individual's potential.

Initially specific patterns may become repeated because they are personally gratifying to one or both of the participants or because it serves an important function in the relationship. As a particular interaction is repeated, it becomes increasingly stable and predictable, and, over time, may persist even if it no longer serves the important function it once served.

5.07.2.1.2 Boundaries: individuals, subsystems, and the environment

The systemic concept of "boundary" is a prominent aspect of family systems therapy. Conventionally, boundaries have been seen as the metaphorical "walls" that separate people, denoting where one person or group of persons ends and where the next begins. However, family systems theorists (Szapocznik & Coatsworth, submitted for publication) have recognized that just as boundaries signify separateness, they also denote connectedness. For example, the parent–child boundary not only signifies the distinction between the parenting subsystem and the child subsystem, but it also signifies the precise point at which they come together to interact as parent and child. Take for example an analogy from biology. Initially a cell membrane was viewed as a "wall" that helped contain the contents of the cell, and that separated the inside of the cell from the outside of the cell. This view provided the membrane with a certain "concreteness." A more contemporary view of a cell membrane, however, reveals that the "wall" is constantly negotiating transfer of biological components

from inside to outside and vice versa. Thus, the cell membrane represents the cell's systematic mechanism for regulating transactions with its environment. This dynamic view of "boundaries" is reflected in the family systemic focus on the reciprocal process of interactions within the family, and between the family and its environment (Bronfenbrenner, 1979, 1986; Magnusson, 1995; Szapocznik & Coatsworth, submitted for publication). In families, boundaries are established by rules, both those that are discussed as well as those that are never discussed, but which everyone understands. Four important boundaries in family systems therapy are presented below.

The *family–environment boundary* denotes the separation/connectedness between the family and the environment. The simplest way of differentiating (or defining the family–environment boundary) a family from the environment is by examining biological relationships, or by examining who lives together and shares daily household responsibilities (Greenwood, Hervis, Mitrani, Taylor, & Szapocznik, 1995). Beyond these important distinguishing qualities, the family system is also characterized by its relatively stationary and unique pattern of interactions.

The boundary between the family and the environment is more or less permeable. That is, much like the membrane of a cell, this boundary regulates communication between the family and environment, and represents the precise point at which they intersect and reciprocally influence each other. (Note: Although we do not focus on it in this section, information also flows to and from the environment to specific individuals within the family. That is, individuals within the family also interact directly with the environment.)

The family–environment boundary may be critically related to the family's functioning, and is frequently an indication of potential problems in the family's ability to function adaptively. For example, Alexander (1988) notes that in families in which there is incest, the boundary between the family and environment is often rigid, resulting in increased insularity of the family, and an inability of the family to receive and respond adaptively to "feedback" from the environment.

The internal *family subsystem boundary* separates/connects subsystems within the family. The family system divides itself into various alliances to distribute its many roles and functions. These alliances are referred to as subsystems. Subsystems are typically organized by age or function. For example, the parental subsystem consists of the parents or, in single-parent families, the parent and another adult figure or an older child. The child subsystem consists of the siblings in the family (typically grouped together by age or gender). Subsystems are often utilized as the vehicle for completing the various roles and functions of the family.

The most important subsystem boundary in family systems therapy is the parent–child subsystem boundary. This boundary regulates the extent to which parents (or a parent and an older child, extended family member, or other parental adult) are able to work together as a unit to carry out the family's rules and responsibilities. Implementing rules, however, is only one way in which the parental subsystem interacts with the child subsystem. The parental subsystem is also responsible for caring, nurturing, and providing guidance to the youth. It should also be noted that influences at the parental subsystem and child subsystem are bidirectional. The child subsystem also influences the parents. Take the case of a behavior problem youth as an example. The behaviors of these youths are frequently very intense and disruptive, and often elicit controlling responses by the parent(s). In fact, over time parents of behavior problem youth are likely to utilize many different strategies to attempt to manage or cope with their child's disruptive behaviors. This bidirectional influence is not limited to maladaptive interactions; in fact, in every family (beginning with the birth of children), children and parents continuously influence the behaviors of one another.

The *interpersonal boundary* separates/connects individual family members. This boundary represents the amount of separation/connection in each of the dyadic relationships in the family. At one extreme, this interpersonal boundary can be extremely rigid or impermeable (e.g., nothing gets through the boundary). When boundaries are so impermeable, the emotional and psychological distance between people is great. One strength in relationships in which there is an impermeable boundary is that individuals are often very autonomous and independent. However, a weakness in these relationships is that individuals do not benefit from supportive relationships, and they are more likely to experience existential crises and feelings of loneliness.

At the other extreme, the boundary can be far too tenuous. When boundaries are so tenuous, the emotional and psychological closeness between people is great. Individuals in relationships with highly permeable boundaries benefit from the supportive ties they have with other individuals. It is not uncommon for individuals in these relationships, however, to have difficulty establishing their own unique identity separate from other family members.

It is important to note that for any individual, the boundary separating/connecting them to other family members is unique to each particular relationship. For example, a father and his daughter may have a relatively permeable boundary in which there is a consistent, unobstructed flow of information. However, in the same family, there may be a rigid boundary between father and son in which communication is virtually nonexistent. Thus, the interpersonal boundary between individual family members is uniquely defined for each relationship in the family. In this sense, boundaries are considered to be characteristics of relationships rather than trait-like characteristics of individuals. (It should be noted that the interpersonal boundary is not unique to family relationships. Any relationship involves the continuous flow of information between its participants.)

The *interpersonal–intrapersonal boundary* represents the point at which interactions influence an individual's internal (i.e., psychological) world, and the point at which these internal processes influence the interaction. In family systems theory, the boundary between family interactions (interpersonal) and intrapersonal functioning is emphasized because of the family's profound influence on an individual's emotional and behavioral adjustment. All interpersonal relationships include emotional and cognitive intrapersonal components. These intrapersonal components influence the interpretation of information as well as the individual's behavioral response. Thus, the interpersonal–intrapersonal boundary regulates the flow of information from interactions with family members into the intrapersonal realm of the individual, where it is processed, and then ultimately influences the behavioral reactions of individual family members involved in the interaction.

5.07.2.1.3 *Homeostasis, feedback, and change*

As mentioned above, every system has built in mechanisms for ensuring its survival. The struggle for the survival of the system involves balancing between maintaining stability within the system and adapting to meet changing internal and external demands. Thus, there are two ways a system can function to maintain its viability. The first involves the process by which the system continuously monitors the activities of the family, and provides corrective feedback (information flow) to family members when they behave in ways that are not consistent with the family's rules. Such feedback operates to restore the family's equilibrium. This process, homeostasis, is critical for maintaining consistency and stability within the family over time.

However, because families are always in flux (e.g., children and parents' development, changing environmental conditions), there must also be mechanisms for ensuring that the family system adjust to meet the changing needs of its members or its environmental context. Similar to the processes involved in maintaining homeostasis, the process of change requires continuous feedback about the consequences of interactions within and outside of the family. As information is fed back to the system, the family is able to change those interactions that may have become obsolete or are leading towards the dissolution of the family. This process of the family system changing to meet changing internal or external demands is called recalibration.

A common example of how the recalibration process works and how it often goes awry in families is evident in the changing demands that are encountered as children mature during adolescence. The "task oriented" leadership style that may have worked when children were young often does not work when issues of autonomy and independence surface during adolescence. Parents must adjust their parenting style to fit the needs of the developing adolescent. Many parents continue to be very authoritarian (Baumrind, 1991a, 1991b) despite the fact that it is not working and that their child now requires a more flexible, negotiating parental style.

As the above example suggests, flexibility is a critical component in the recalibration process. That is, families must have the flexibility to adapt to changing internal and external circumstances. Flexibility is a measure of the system's ability to change and reorganize to meet changing needs. Flexibility also refers to the system's ability to adjust to the various situations confronting its members on a daily basis. To the extent that the system rigidly adheres to one pattern of interaction, the more likely it is that problems will arise. Thus, in a sense, flexibility refers to the inherent capabilities of the system and its ability to adaptively utilize a repertoire of interactions. More flexible systems are able to engage in a broader range of behaviors and are able to alter their patterns of interaction to meet the unique challenges they face on a continuous basis. Adaptive family functioning requires a balance between homeostasis and flexibility. Too much emphasis on stability prevents necessary adaptability, but excessive flexibility leads to chaotic family functioning (Minuchin & Fishman, 1981).

5.07.2.1.4 Complementarity

Family systems theory suggests that behaviors in an interaction are complementary (Minuchin & Fishman, 1981; Szapocznik & Kurtines, 1989), like a hand and glove are complementary: they fit together perfectly well. Thus, in addition to being inextricably linked to one another, family members' behaviors occur together as perfect counterparts. The basic assumption is that family members' behaviors mutually influence one another; consequently, any symptomatic behavior must be connected to other behaviors within the family. The principle of complementarity flows logically from the concept of interdependence (i.e., the connectedness and mutual influence of persons within the system). Thus, if a youth is using drugs, the question becomes: What are the complementary behaviors; that is, the behaviors that allow or encourage the youth to behave in this way? In other words, what are the social interconnections between family members that are conducive to drug use?

In addition to the complementary relationships among family members, family systems therapists are also concerned with the complementary interactions at the interface ("boundary") between the family and its social environment. For example, Steinberg and colleagues have shown that an authoritative parenting style is more strongly associated with academic achievement than nonauthoritative parenting style (Steinberg, Mounts, Lamborn, & Dornbush, 1991; Steinberg, Darling, Fletcher, Brown, & Dornbush, 1995). Thus, authoritative parenting behaviors are associated with/ complement the child's academic achievement. However, this relationship appears to be moderated by ethnicity and peer group membership. European and Hispanic-American adolescents benefit more from authoritative parenting than African- or Asian-American adolescents (Steinberg et al., 1991; see also Florsheim, Tolan, & Gorman-Smith, in press). In part, this appears to be due to the nature of the peer groups with whom they affiliate. While in general adolescents from authoritative homes tend to associate with competent peers, for some ethnic groups it appears that the choice of which peer group one can associate with is restricted due to the neighborhood in which the child lives. Steinberg, Dornbush, and Brown (1992) found that Asian-Americans tended to associate with peers who support academic achievement, while the opposite was true for African-American adolescents in inner city neighborhoods. What these results suggest is that the nature of the peer group constrains the relationship between parenting style and academic achievement. It is also possible that parents may have an impact on the peer group. Thus, to fully understand the cross domain complementary (parent–peer) links associated with problem behaviors it is essential to consider the full range of intrafamily, adolescent–peer, and family–peer interactions that directly and indirectly influence the child's behaviors.

5.07.2.1.5 Reciprocal vs. linear causality

Family systems theory assumes reciprocal as opposed to linear causal explanations. Linear causality is based on the traditional stimulus–response behavioral view that one event "A" causes some response "B." This type of reductionistic thinking fails to capture the interdependence of individuals in any system. While it may be appropriate to highlight microanalytic sequences within the family (e.g., parents allow their adolescent daughter to stay out after curfew to avoid a confrontation with her), limiting our focus on these sequences fails to capture the true complexity of family interactions.

Circular causality assumes that any behavior in an interaction is simultaneously influenced by and influential on other behaviors in the interaction. In other words, causality is bidirectional. Thus, in the example of parents allowing their daughter to stay out after curfew to avoid a confrontation, a circular view of this sequence would begin with a recognition that the parent's behavior (e.g., avoiding confrontation) not only influenced the daughter's immediate likelihood of not being angry, but it also influenced the probability of her staying out beyond curfew in the future. Such a parental response may be the result of previous interactions in which the daughter responded with intense anger to the parent's confrontation. As a result, the parents' avoidance of confrontation in the current interaction may also influence the likelihood that the daughter will respond with intense anger to future parental confrontations of the daughter's behavior.

As is evident from this description, circular causality is informed by combinations of sequences of behavior. In this example only one particular sequence was highlighted. From a systemic perspective, however, it is not possible to understand a sequence outside of the context in which it occurs. Thus, to fully understand the mutual influence of parents and the adolescent in this example, the family systems therapist must also address other factors within the family (i.e., the parent's may not agree on basic rules within the house; consequently, they are unable to present a unified front to their daughter) or outside the family (i.e., the daughter may be associating with friends that foster an attitude of parental disrespect).

5.07.2.1.6 Process vs. content

Process can refer to the behaviors which are involved in an interaction; what and how things happen; as well as to the messages which are communicated by the nature of interactions or by the style of communication, including all that is communicated nonverbally such as feelings, tone, and power.

Content refers to the specific and concrete facts used in the communication. Content includes such things as the reasons that family members offer for a given interaction. For example, when a depressed mother says that her child is an obstacle to her completing school, it is important to attend both to the content (the specific issue raised) as well as to the process (the child being identified as the sole source of all of the family's problems).

Process and content may sometimes be contradictory. For example, an adolescent might say "I want help for my depression," while her behavior is that she disappears from home at the time agreed for family therapy sessions.

An emphasis on process (as opposed to content) is a predominate theme across family systems therapy models. The emphasis is on identifying the nature of the interactions in the family (diagnosis) and in changing those interactions that are maladaptive. Content is not ignored, particularly content that is emotionally valenced. However, the focus of therapy is on changing patterns of interaction. The therapist who responds primarily to content and loses sight of the process, will be unable to implement the kinds of family changes required to alleviate the problems experienced by the child.

5.07.3 HISTORY OF FAMILY SYSTEMS THERAPY

Most reviews cite the period directly following World War II as the most influential time in the evolution of family systems therapy (Goldenberg & Goldenberg, 1983). A variety of factors, including difficulties in the reunification process, the "baby boom," and changing social mores about familial roles and responsibilities created a large need for the development of a new wave of intervention that directly addressed family factors (Goldenberg & Goldenberg, 1983; Nichols & Schwartz, 1995). As a result of the large personal and societal demands, psychosocial interventions, including family therapy, flourished.

There are many excellent reviews that trace the development of family systems therapy, including landmark reviews by Guerin (1976), Goldenberg and Goldenberg (1983) Kaslow (1980), Nichols (1984), and Nichols and Schwartz (1995). Rather than summarize the work of these authors, this section focuses on those developments that directly contributed to our current conceptions of interactions, the cornerstone of the family systems approach. This review is not intended to be exhaustive. Our intention here is to chronicle the evolution of some of the critical events that led to our current conceptualization of the role of family interactions in the etiology and treatment of child and adolescent psychological problems.

5.07.3.1 The Family's Role in the Etiology of Schizophrenia

The 1950s was a critical decade in the development of the family systems approach. Four independent research groups proved to be the most influential in developing systemic theories of family functioning. Each of these groups were developing family theories about the development of schizophrenia.

5.07.3.1.1 Bateson and the Palo Alto Group

Bateson and his colleagues, the Palo Alto Group, were interested in developing a communication theory, which applies basic cybernetic principles within the family system, to explain the etiology of schizophrenia. The combined work of the Palo Alto Group provided the underpinnings for many of the current systemic theories of family functioning and family therapy. In particular, their systemic conceptualization of homoestasis, identified patienthood, and process vs. content is recognized in contemporary family systemic treatment models.

According to Bateson and colleagues (1972), whenever the integrity of the system is at stake, its natural tendency is to maintain homeostasis. One way in which the family system restores equilibrium is through a process in which one person becomes the symptom bearer. For example, an adolescent becomes severely depressed and suicidal whenever there is marital conflict, forcing the parents to stop fighting by refocusing on their child's depression. This process by which the child refocuses the problematic experience/event onto themselves labeled "identified patienthood," represented a

shift in focus away from a purely intrapsychic conceptualization of the etiology of psychopathology towards a more interactional understanding of the onset of psychological problems.

Perhaps the greatest contribution of the Palo Alto Group to family systems theory was their conceptualization of the etiology of schizophrenia from a communication theory perspective. Bateson, Jackson, Haley, & Weakland (1956) introduced the concept of the double-bind communication as evidence of the family's role in the etiology of schizophrenia. It was their assumption that schizophrenia is caused by confusing communications within the family. In examining family conditions that precipitated schizophrenic episodes, they discovered that communication patterns in families with schizophrenic patients were characterized by confusion and contradiction. In particular, they noted that these communications occurred in the context of an important relationship, they contained two or more related but contradictory messages that also contained a threat (or perception of threat), and that the schizophrenic patient was forced to respond to these contradictory messages. For example, Bateson et al. (1956, p. 259) present the case of a young schizophrenic patient who was visited by his mother in the hospital. When she arrived, he put his arm around her and she stiffened. Sensing her discomfort he immediately withdrew his arm, and she responded by asking, "Don't you love me anymore?" The patient then blushed, prompting his mother to respond, "Dear, you must not be so easily embarrassed and afraid of your feelings." Following his mother's visit, the patient relapsed.

The concept of double-bind communications has influenced the development of several modern day family systemic concepts. For example, the concept of double-bind was the earliest articulation of the importance of process. Although content was critical in determining whether or not contradictory messages were in fact present, the primary emphasis was on the interactive process that was viewed as conducive to the development of schizophrenic symptomatology. For example, to engender schizophrenic behaviors, double-bind communications had to be a repetitive and stable characteristic of family interactions.

5.07.3.1.2 Lidz: the role of the marital relationship

Lidz may have been the first scientist interested in examining the role of the family in the etiology of schizophrenia. Lidz was strongly rooted in psychoanalytical therapy, and his primary interest was in understanding the way in which parents influenced the internal processes of identification and incorporation in their offspring (c.f. Nichols, 1984). However, through his intensive study of the families of schizophrenic patients, he developed a family theory of the origins of schizophrenia that brought together psychoanalytic theories about the important influence of parental personality on child development, and modern family systems theory.

In 1949, Lidz challenged Fromm-Reichmann's (1948) belief that a cold, domineering, and guilt-inducing mother ("schizophrenogenic mother") was responsible for the etiology of schizophrenia. In particular, Lidz documented the important contributions of fathers and—more importantly—the marital relationship, to the development of schizophrenia (Lidz & Lidz, 1949; Lidz, Cornelison, Fleck, & Terry, 1957; Lidz, Parker, & Cornelison, 1956). This transition from the individual to dyad to triadic relationships is a remarkable contribution to family systems theory.

Lidz is most recognized for his articulation of two types of marital relationships which contribute to the onset of schizophrenia. The first, "marital schism," involves a chronic failure in the marital relationship. In marital schism, spouses are in constant conflict and frequently undermine each other, openly competing for the loyalty of their children, and behaving in ways which fail to complement the behaviors of their partner. Quite often one partner, typically the father, is emotionally or physically disengaged from the family.

The second pattern, "marital skew," is characterized by severe psychopathology in one of the spouses. Spouses assume complementary roles which are pathological. One is dominant while the other is submissive. The dominant partner is typically the one with the serious psychopathology. Thus, even though on the surface they may appear strong and capable, their ability to provide direction and leadership within the family is severely compromised. The weaker partner goes along with and even supports the pathological tendencies of the superior parent.

Lidz et al., (1957) provided a complex rationale about the way in which "marital schism" and "marital skew" led to schizophrenia in girls and boys. What is important here, however, is his articulation of the relationship between family processes and the development of serious psychopathology. His observations and research went beyond the prominent linear cause–effect theories of the time, and prompted the development of a new wave of research and clinical development.

5.07.3.1.3 Wynne: the family unit

Wynne's theories of the role of the family in the development of schizophrenia profoundly influenced current family systemic theories' conceptualization of boundaries and alliances. According to Wynne (Wynne, Rycoff, Day, & Hirsch, 1958), interactions in families with schizophrenic members were characterized by two processes: pseudomutuality and pseudohostility.

Pseudomutuality is defined as interactions that give the impression that the family is functioning adaptively, but hide the fact that there are serious problems in the family. Boundaries in these families are very blurred, and individual autonomy and outside relationships are discouraged. He describes the boundary between the family and its environment as a "rubber fence" that stretches to allow some contact, but that is essentially impermeable. Thus, outside forces rarely precipitate a restructuring of family responsibilities; and, even if conflict between the family and its environment does emerge, the family responds by becoming even more insular.

Pseudohostility is similar to pseudomutuality, but involves a dramatic expression of conflict in response to minor disruptions in family alliances. Since the family is preoccupied with maintaining togetherness, a dramatic amplification of a minor problem actually operates as a "feedback" mechanism for the family. Family members move in quickly to repair the minor split and restore the system's togetherness.

Wynne's theories were critical in articulating the importance of boundaries and feedback mechanisms in the family system. His explanation of how a disturbance in family boundaries influences the development of major psychopathology represents one of the earliest structural interpretations of family functioning.

5.07.3.1.4 Bowen: multigenerational influences and the development of family systems therapy

Similar to Lidz, Bowen focused on disturbances in parental interactions, and their relationship to schizophrenia. In particular, Bowen (1960) coined the term "emotional divorce" to point out the emotional distance between the parents of schizophrenics. He claimed that children were often the only area in which these parents shared any common interest or were able to collaborate. Perhaps his most well-known contribution to the study of the family's role in the development of schizophrenia is his "three generation hypothesis."

According to Bowen (1960), the parents of schizophrenics are typically very disturbed individuals, who have themselves experienced serious problems with their parents which they are now replaying with their own children.

Bowen's work, however, goes well beyond his contributions regarding schizophrenic patients. In fact, Bowen is recognized as the father of family systems therapy (Papero, 1990). His theories influenced our current focus on triangulational, multigenerational interactions, and the sibling subsystem. He was also influential in adapting his family theories into a clinical model of family systems therapy. According to Bowen, family systems therapy is phasic, consisting of evaluation and intervention. To assist in the evaluative process, he developed the "genogram" as a method of depicting multigenerational patterns and influences (Papero, 1990).

5.07.3.1.5 About schizophrenia

Research of the family's role in the onset of schizophrenia was not merely coincidental. At this time, psychosocial interventions with schizophrenia were virtually ineffective and psychotropic medications were virtually non-existent. The medical treatments that did exist (e.g., electroconvulsive therapy and lobotomy) were associated with severe side effects. There was obviously a strong demand for identifying causal pathways to the disease, and perhaps an even greater need for identifying effective interventions. Many of the assumptions of these early family theorists about the relationship between schizophrenia and pathological family relationships have since been refuted by contemporary theories and research of schizophrenia. Perhaps the error in these early theories about family process and schizophrenia was to not consider the possible impact of the child's schizophrenic functioning on parents' behaviors over the course of the child's development. Nevertheless, research with schizophrenia proved to be fertile ground for family therapy theorists to take their first steps.

5.07.3.2 Other Major Theoretical Figures in Family Systems Therapy

Among the most influential figures in the systemic movement were John Bell; Don Jackson—the founder of the Mental Research Institute—who was later joined by Virginia Satir, Jay Haley, John Weakland, Paul Watzlawick, Arthur Bordin, and Richard Fisch; Nathan Ackerman; Carl Whittaker; Ivan Boszormenyi-Nagy; Gerald Zuk; James Framo;

Salvador Minuchin—the founder of the Philadelphia Child Guidance Clinic—who worked closely with Braulio Montalvo and Bernice Rosman; and Mara Selvini-Palazzoli at the Institute for Family Studies in Milan.

It is impossible to document all of the important contributions made by each of these leaders. Excellent reviews are found elsewhere (Guerin, 1976; Goldenberg & Goldenberg, 1983; Kaslow, 1980; Nichols, 1984; Nichols & Schwartz, 1995). Suffice it to say that nearly every current model of family therapy has strong theoretical ties to the work of one—and sometimes many—of these family theorists. These individuals were critical in bringing basic research and theory about family interactions to life in the clinical setting. They proliferated new theories about the family system and developed innovative techniques to modify family interactions. The seminal work of these investigators carried over into the 1970s as family therapists developed a new wave of techniques to change family interactions (Goldenberg & Goldenberg, 1983), including working with families at their home (Speck, 1964) and working in the community with extended family members, friends, neighbors and other persons (Speck & Attneave, 1973).

It is unfortunate, however, that the rush towards clinical practice was so profound that research into basic family processes and into the efficacy and effectiveness of family systems interventions was delegated to a lesser role. For example, in one comprehensive review of the literature Wells & Dezen (1978) identified only 20 well designed studies that examined the efficacy or effectiveness of family systems interventions. In the following section, we review evidence for the efficacy and effectiveness of family therapy models that have been influenced by the theoretical and clinical work of these early family systems theorists.

5.07.4 EFFICACY AND EFFECTIVENESS RESEARCH OF FAMILY SYSTEMS THERAPY

In reviewing the current empirical status of family systems therapy, our primary strategy involved identifying groups of studies or programs of research within a particular target population (e.g., depression, conduct disorder). Individual studies and case studies were excluded. The studies reported here are organized along three broad clinical domains: (i) mood disorders; (ii) psychosomatic disorders; and (iii) conduct disorders. Most of the studies cited here included randomization procedures for assigning cases to treatment, an appropriate comparison condition, and clear inclusion/ exclusion criteria specifying a "clinical" child/ adolescent population. Some of the effectiveness studies included in this review did not have a formal comparison group, but did have some degree of methodological rigor (e.g., pre–post assessments, procedures for monitoring of the delivery of intervention).

Although it was our intention to address the breadth of contexts in which family systems therapy has been applied, we attempted to identify those family models with rich empirical as well as clinical histories. It is our assertion that in a review chapter such as this it is important to include family interventions that have some level of empirical justification. We do not wish to downplay the potential utility of applying family systems therapy to a variety of clinical populations. However, we do wish to convey the importance of the interplay between theory, research, and clinical model building. Table 1 contains relevant information from selected studies in this review.

5.07.4.1 Mood Disorders

Similar to reviews by Kazdin (1994), Alexander, Holtzworth-Munroe, and Jameson (1994), and Estrada and Pinsof (1995), our review of the literature noted a lack of research on the efficacy and effectiveness of family systems therapy for internalizing disorders with children and adolescents. This section reviews the sparse research that does exist, and attempts to highlight promising programs underway at the time of writing.

5.07.4.1.1 Depression

We were not able to identify a single study that examined the efficacy of family systems therapy with depressed youth. In our discussions with family systems therapists and researchers, we were able to identify two significant depression studies. First, Brent and colleagues at Western Psychiatric Institute have made a large efficacy study (funded by the National Institutes of Mental Health) comparing the effects of different psychotherapy models, including family systems therapy, with depressed youth (Brent, personal communication February 8, 1997).

Second, Diamond (Philadelphia Child Guidance Center and Medical School of the University of Pennsylvania) and Siqueland (Medical School of the University of Pennsylvania) have adapted structural family therapy for treating depressed adolescents (Diamond & Siqueland, 1995). This approach integrates structural family therapy (Minuchin, 1974;

Minuchin & Fishman, 1981; Stanton et al., 1982) and multidimensional family therapy principles (Liddle, 1991; Liddle, Dakof, & Diamond, 1991) as well as research on attachment. Therapy focuses on: (i) re-establishing or strengthening the parent–adolescent relationship to provide both structure and emotional support for the adolescent; (ii) decreasing marital or parent–adolescent conflict, and improving negotiation and communication within the family; and (iii) decreasing parental hostility and criticism. Diamond and Siqueland (1996) re port important changes in depressive symptoms, attachment, and family interaction in pilot cases. This model is under formal development (funded by the National Institute on Mental Health) at the Philadelphia Child Guidance Center.

5.07.4.1.2 Youth with Other Mood Related Symptoms

Henggeler and colleagues (in press) compared the effectiveness of multisystemic therapy (MST) to hospitalization for youth who presented with suicidal ideation, homicidal ideation, or threat of harm to self or others due to mental illness. MST (discussed further in Section 5.07.4.3.1), is a family-based, contextual approach that addresses the complexity of factors (family and environmental) that influence the youth's psychological and behavioral adjustment. In this pilot investigation, youth in multisystemic therapy showed a greater decrease in internalizing and externalizing symptoms than youth who had been hospitalized. MST was effective in reducing rates of hospitalization and total days hospitalized.

In a study conducted by Gutstein, Rudd, Graham, and Rayha (1988) a systemic crisis intervention was implemented with suicidal, depressed, or behavior problem youth who presented with an immediate crisis. The crisis intervention involved stabilizing family members' anxiety surrounding the crisis, mobilizing extended family members to become involved around the crisis, and restructuring family and extended family relationships to provide long-term solutions to the current crisis. Results demonstrate the effectiveness of the systemic crisis intervention in ameliorating family members' sense of crisis, limiting future suicidal attempts, and improving family functioning over time.

5.07.4.2 Psychosomatic Disorders

There are promising finding on the effectiveness of structural (e.g., Minuchin et al., 1975, 1978) and strategic (e.g., Palazzoli–Selvini,

Table 1 Review of selected publications.

Reference	Model	Population	Design	Finding
Mood disorders				
Diamond & Siqueland (1995)	Structural/ Multidimensional/ Attachment principles	Depression	Pilot data for 10 families participating in a treatment development study. Pre–post assessments of emotional problems, and intensive assessments of therapeutic processes included	Changes in depressive symptoms, attachment, and family interaction were noted
Henggeler et al. (in press)	Multisystemic (MST)	Suicidal or homicidal ideation, or psychosis	Participants (n = 64) were randomly assigned to MST or hospitalization, and completed assessments of emotional and behavioral problems at five time points. Monthly interviews monitoring utilization of mental health and juvenile justice services were also conducted	MST showed a greater decrease in internalizing and externalizing scores, and reduced rates of out-of-home placements and total days of stay
Gutstein et al. (1988)	Systemic crisis intervention (SCI)	Suicidal ideation or attempt, depression, violent behavior, or serious behavior problems	All participants (n = 75) received a brief systemic intervention (< 20 hours), and completed four assessments of emotional and behavioral problems and family functioning	SCI effective in resolving crisis that precipitated treatment and decrease family dependence on institution
Psychosomatic disorders				
Minuchin et al. (1978)	Structural (SFT)	Anorexia	Participants (n = 53) were the first 53 anorectic patients treated. Data were gathered on the presenting characteristics of patients, the course of treatment, and follow-up data (approximately 2 years)	At follow-up, 86% of participants were rated as "recovered" from anorexia and its psychosocial components
Dare et al. (1990); Russell et al. (1987); Szmukler et al. (1985)	Structural/ strategic (SSFT)	Anorexia or bulimia	Participants (n = 80) were randomly assigned to SSFT or invidual therapy (IT), and completed assessments at intake and follow-up	SSFT and IT effective; however, SSFT was more effective when age of onset was before 18
Conduct disorder				
Alexander & Parsons (1973)	Functional (FFT)	Delinquent	Participants (n = 86) were randomly assigned to FFT, group therapy, psychodynamic family therapy, or control. Recidivism rates were obtained for 6–18 months following treatment	FFT more effective than other conditions in reducing recidivism rates

Table 1 continued

Reference	Model	Population	Design	Finding
Klein, Alexander, & Parsons (1977)	FFT	Siblings of youth in Alexander & Parsons (1973)	Arrests rates of the siblings of the delinquent youth in the original sample were compared at $2^1/_2$ year follow-up	Siblings of youth in FFT had lower rates of court involvement than siblings in other conditions
Barton et al. (1985)	FFT	Delinquent	Participants ($n = 74$) were referred to FFT or alternative treatment. Youth in the alternative treatment were selected to match youth in FFT. Number of arrests and recidivism rates were obtained for the 15 month period following incarceration	Youth in FFT were less likely to commit subsequent offenses than youth in alternative treatment. Youth in FFT also committed fewer offenses
Gordon et al. (1988); Gordon, Graves, & Arbuthnot (1995)	FFT	Delinquent	Participants ($n = 54$) received FFT or probation only. Recidivism rates were obtained for the 2–3 year period following intervention. In a follow-up study with these youth (now adults), court records from the next 3 years (5–6 years post intervention) were obtained	FFT reduced recidivism rates in the 2–3 year period following intervention (11% vs. 68%). Follow-up data show an arrest rate of 9% for FFT cases compared to 41% for the probation cases
Borduin et al. (1995)	Multisystemic (MST)	Delinquent	Participants ($n = 176$) were randomly assigned to MST or individual therapy. Assessments were administered at pre- and post-treatment	MST improved family functioning and adjustment, and prevented future arrests (4-year follow-up)
Henggeler, Melton, & Smith (1992)	MST	Delinquent	Participants ($n = 96$) were randomly assigned to MST or treatment as usual. Pre- and post-treatment assessments conducted, and criminal behavior and incarceration for 15 months following referral was obtained	MST reduced arrests and days incarcerated, and improved family functioning and peer relations
Henggeler et al. (1986)	MST	Delinquent	Participants ($n = 124$) received MST or treatment at a community agency. Participants were matched on important demographic characteristic. A nondeviant comparison group was included. Pre–post treatment assessments were completed	MST more effective in improving conduct, anxious-withdrawn behaviors, and family and peer relations
Szapocznik et al. (1989)	Structural (SFT)	Conduct disorder	Participants ($n = 69$) were randomly assigned to SFT, individual child dynamic psychotherapy (IT), or a no treatment control group. Assessments of behavior problems, family functioning, and individual dynamics were conducted at pre-, post-, and 1-year follow-up	SFT and IT reduced behavior problems. IT effective in improving individual dynamic functioning, but associated with a deterioration in family functioning, SFT effective in maintaining family functioning

Table 1 continued

Substance abuse

Study	Treatment	Population	Design	Results
Santisteban et al. (in preparation)	Structural (SFT)	Behavior problem (at risk) youth	Participants (n = 79) were randomly assigned to SFT or a control condition administered in group format (CG). Assessments were conducted at pre-, post-, and at 1-year follow-up	SFT more effective than CG in improving behavior problems and in maintaining family functioning. Exploratory analyses suggest that improvements in family functioning may mediated treatment outcome in SFT; however, only in those cases identified as "poor family functioning" at intake
Szapocznik et al. (1983) Szapocznik, Kurtines et al. (1989)	One person family therapy (OPFT)	Behavior problem (at risk) youth	Participants (n = 75; pooled sample) were randomly assigned to OPFT (individual sessions) or SFT (conjoint sessions). Assessments of behavior problems and family functioning were conducted at pre-, post- and follow-up	OPFT as effective as SFT in reducing behaviors problems and drug use, and in improving family functioning. Results demonstrate that a focus on family interactions in an individual treatment context yields results similar to those found in conjoint family sessions
Szapocznik et al. (1988)	Strategic structural systems engagement (SSSE)	Behavior problem (at risk) youth	Participants (n = 108) were randomly assigned to SSSE or engagement as usual (EAU). EAU was designed to resemble community standards in engaging behavior problem youth in treatment. Treatment was monitored to ensure differential level of engagement interventions in the SSSE and EAU groups	SSSE was more effective than EAU in engaging families and youth into treatment. Participants in SSSE were also more likely to complete treatment than participants in EAU
Santisteban et al. (1996)	SSSE	Behavior problem (at risk) youth	Participants (n = 193) were randomly assigned to engagement family therapy (SSSE + SFT), family therapy (SFT only), and group therapy (GT only). Treatment was monitored to ensure differential levels of engagement interventions across treatment groups	Results demonstrate the effectiveness of SSSE in engaging participants into treatment. Further analyses shed light on variables moderating the effectiveness of the specialized engagement interventions
Liddle et al. (1997)	MDFT	Substance abuse	Participants (n = 95) were randomly assigned to MDFT, adolescent group therapy, and multifamily educational intervention. Assessments were conducted at intake, termination, and at 6 and 12 month follow-up	MDFT demonstrated lower drug use and higher grades at termination than the alternative treatments. Results were maintained at 12 month follow-up

Boscolo, Cecchin, & Prata, 1974) family systems therapy in the treatment of psychosomatic disorders (e.g., eating disorders, diabetes, asthma). Much of this work is represented in the widespread publication of numerous case studies demonstrating the positive effects of family therapy with psychosomatic youth. However, a solid empirical base for family systems therapy is also emerging.

Family systems intervention with psychosomatic youth is traced directly to the work of Minuchin and colleagues at the Philadelphia Child Guidance Center. In their initial work, Minuchin et al. (1978) described five characteristics of "psychosomatic families": (i) enmeshed subsystem boundaries; (ii) overprotectiveness; (iii) rigidity; (iv) lack of conflict resolution; and (v) the child's involvement in parental conflict. In an initial study of structural family therapy, Minuchin et al. reported an 86% recovery rate.

There is considerable controversy, however, about the notion of whether there is such an entity as the "psychosomatic family." Coyne and Anderson (1989) assert that over-protection and enmeshment may be adequate responses of a system to the crisis of the patients. Moreover, other researchers (Garfinke & Garner, 1982; Grigg & Friesen, 1989; Marcus & Wiener, 1989) have found no unique pattern of family interaction that characterizes these families. This controversy is further fueled by the fact that Minuchin's impressive findings have never been replicated in subsequent studies (Kog, Vandereycken, & Vertommen, 1989).

Nevertheless, family therapy appears to be beneficial for patients with eating disorders (e.g., Kog & Vandereycken, 1989). For example, in what is perhaps the best designed study in this area, Dare and his colleagues (Dare, Eisler, Russell, & Szmukler, 1990; Russell, Szmukler, Dare, & Eisler, 1987; Szmukler, Eisler, Russell, & Dare, 1985) compared the efficacy of structural/strategic family therapy and individual therapy with anorectic and bulimic patients. Results demonstrate that both family and individual therapy are effective treatments with anorexic and bulimic patients. However, certain pretreatment patient attributes interacted with treatment. For example, family therapy was more effective than individual therapy when the patient's age of onset for the eating disorder was below 18.

Taken together, these results suggest that family systems therapy may be a promising treatment for adolescents with eating disorders. Although there is considerable controversy about whether or not there is a distinct entity called the "psychosomatic family," the overall results of treatment research in this area are encouraging. However, further research is needed to investigate the assumed theoretical mechanisms of action: the potential mediating role that changes in family interaction may have on treatment outcome with psychosomatic youth.

5.07.4.3 Conduct Disorders

In contrast to research with internalizing disorders, there is a large body of treatment research on the efficacy and effectiveness of family systems therapy with conduct disorders. Reviews of the treatment outcome research literature have consistently documented the efficacy and effectiveness of family-based approaches with problem behavior youth (e.g., Alexander et al., 1994; Chamberlain & Rosicky, 1995; Gurman, Kniskern, & Pinsof, 1986; Kazdin, 1993, 1994; Liddle & Dakof, 1995a, 1995b; Nichols & Schwartz, 1995; Tolan, Cromwell, & Brasswell, 1986). In this section, we review family systems interventions for youth with delinquency and substance abuse.

5.07.4.3.1 Delinquency

Family systems therapy has received extensive support with delinquent and behavior problem adolescents. Two programs of research have emerged for working with these youth: Functional family therapy and multisystemic family therapy.

Alexander and colleagues at the University of Utah have developed, refined, and evaluated the effectiveness and efficacy of functional family therapy (FFT; Alexander & Parsons, 1982; Barton & Alexander, 1981) with delinquent youth. FFT is based upon early family systemic (e.g., Haley, 1976) and behavioral (e.g., Patterson, 1971) frameworks, and has clearly identified and manualized specific phases of treatment (Alexander & Parsons, 1982; Morris, Alexander, & Waldron, 1988). Each phase includes a specific description of goals, requisite therapist characteristics, and techniques (Alexander et al., 1983).

In the initial phase of treatment, the introduction phase, the focus is on therapist characteristics that enhance the family's expectations about therapy. Empathy, compassion, and professionalism are all critical features of this phase. The key feature of this phase is that the therapist attempts to maximize the likelihood that the family will return for additional sessions with "hope" that family therapy can be beneficial.

In the second phase of treatment, the assessment phase (described below, see Section 5.07.5.2.1), the main therapeutic task is to identify the interpersonal relatedness needs (i.e., functions) of family members, and the maladaptive interactions and behaviors that family members implement to meet these needs.

In the third phase of treatment, the therapy phase, the main goal of the therapist is to create a motivational context that is conducive for long-term changes to occur. As in the introduction phase, basic therapist relational skills are a requisite for this phase; however, to meet the goals of this phase, these skills include the extensive use of therapist reframing to disrupt negative, defensive family interactions.

In phase four, the behavior change phase, FFT prescribes a greater emphasis on therapist structuring characteristics. Although relational skills are still important, therapists utilize a battery of behavioral techniques to promote behavior change within the family (Alexander et al., 1983). Techniques fall into three major classes: communication training, assignment of specific activities, and use of technical aids. FFT further emphasizes that these specific techniques must be tailored to the unique characteristics of each family, and must be consistent with the capabilities and interpersonal relatedness needs of each family member (Alexander et al., 1994; Barton & Alexander, 1981). Resistance to behavior change is redefined as the failure of the therapist to adequately motivate family members to change, an inappropriate assessment of interpersonal needs (i.e., functions), or the implementation of behavior change techniques that are not consistent with the functional needs of individual family members. Hence, resistance is moved from an intrapersonal or intrafamilial to a therapeutic holon.

Finally, in phase five, the generalization phase, the therapist is focused on generalizing the gains made in therapy to real world settings. Problematic interactions in other systems are identified and targeted for change, and potential future problems are anticipated and strategies are generated to deal with these problems.

In their initial investigations (Alexander & Parsons, 1973; Parsons & Alexander, 1973), FFT was shown to be superior to client-centered group therapy, psychodynamic family therapy, placebo treatment condition, and no-treatment control groups in reducing recidivism with primarily "status" offending adolescents. In a two and a half year follow-up (Klein, Alexander, & Parsons, 1977), siblings of youth in the FFT condition had significantly lower rates of court involvement than siblings from youth in the other conditions. In a subsequent investigation, Barton et al. (1985) further demonstrated the effectiveness of FFT by extending these findings to multiply offending delinquents. Independent researchers have also documented

the efficacy and effectiveness of FFT with behavior problem youth (Friedman, 1989; Gordon, Arbuthnot, Gustafson, & McGreen, 1988). In one investigation, examination of arrest rates during the three years following intervention, reveals that FFT cases (now adults) have an arrest rate of 9% for criminal offenses, compared to a 41% arrest rate for youth who had received probation services only (Gordon, Graves, & Arbuthnot, 1995).

Henggeler and colleagues' MST (Henggeler & Borduin, 1990) has also received extensive recognition for its effectiveness with delinquent youth. MST was developed for working with youth with severe delinquency and behavior problems. In MST, interactions in the family are critical; however, interactions with other important systems are also targeted. In particular, MST addresses interactions with school, peers, and juvenile justice. MST borrows from many models of family systems intervention to facilitate changes in the family system, and does not articulate a unique family systems component. MST has been shown to be effective in reducing delinquency, substance use, and other behavioral problems in several well-controlled randomized investigations (Borduin, Henggeler, Blaske, & Stein, 1990; Henggeler, Melton, & Smith, 1992; Henggeler et al., 1986). Perhaps more than any other family therapy model with adolescents, MST is having an impact at the policy level, as reflected by its adoption for public funding.

5.07.4.3.2 Substance abuse

Family systems therapy (FST) is also gaining recognition as an effective alternative for treating adolescent substance abuse. Liddle and Dakof (1995a, 1995b) note that a number of studies have been conducted since the mid-1980s examining the efficacy and effectiveness of FST with this clinical population (Azrin, Donohue, Besalel, Kogan, & Acierno, 1994; Friedman, 1989; Henggeler et al., 1991; Joanning, Thomas, Quinn, & Mullen, 1992; Lewis, Piercy, Sprenkle, & Trepper, 1990; Liddle & Dakof, 1994; Liddle et al., in press).

Liddle and Dakof (1995a, 1995b) also highlight Szapocznik and colleagues' program of research examining the efficacy of structural family therapy (SFT) with substance abusing youth (Szapocznik, Kurtines, Foote, Perez-Vidal, & Hervis, 1983, 1986; Szapocznik et al., 1988). This program of research has attempted to identify the needs of minority families and to develop, demonstrate, and investigate intervention strategies for substance abusing, behavior problem youth. The version of SFT that has emerged from this research

(Szapocznik & Kurtines, 1989) draws from structural (Minuchin, 1974; Minuchin & Fishman, 1981; Minuchin, Rosman, & Baker, 1978) and strategic (Haley 1976; Madanes, 1981) traditions in family therapy theory as well as from a rich clinical and research history working with inner city minority families.

Central to SFT theory is the concept that dysfunctional family structures (i.e., repetitive patterns of family interaction that characterize the interdependence of family members) give rise to or maintain the youth's problems (Minuchin Montalvo, Guerney, Rosman, & Schumer, 1967; Minuchin, 1974; Minuchin & Fishman, 1981; Szapocznik & Kurtines, 1989; Szapocznik & COSSMHO, 1994). Thus, the focus in SFT is on diagnosing and correcting repetitive patterns of interaction.

The three basic techniques in SFT are joining, diagnosing, and restructuring (Minuchin & Fishman, 1981; Szapocznik & Kurtines, 1989; Kurtines & Szapocznik, 1996). "Joining" refers to establishing a therapeutic relationship, in which the therapist is both a member and the leader, and that includes all family members. Joining, in addition to establishing rapport with each family member, requires identifying interactional patterns that guide family functioning; respecting such interactional patterns; and, entering the family by utilizing its established structure. As described in more detail below (see Section 5.07.5.2.2), diagnosis occurs along five dimensions: (i) structure, (ii) resonance, (iii) developmental stage, (iv) identified patienthood, and (v) conflict resolution.

"Restructuring" defines the broad range of interventions that the therapist undertakes to change maladaptive interactional patterns identified in the diagnostic process. These techniques represent a set of complementary tools that are not intended to be independent of each other, and include:

(i) *Working in the present*—the active ingredient is transforming family interactions in the here and now, which is distinguished from the typical use of "here and now" that refers to the intrapersonal process of experiencing feelings in the present. This present orientation is defined in terms of a focus on the process of family interactions, rather than on their content, or individual processes.

(ii) *Reframing*—represents a strategy of cognitive restructuring that promotes a new understanding or meaning for the family which in turn permits new and more adaptive interactions to emerge.

(iii) *Shifting boundaries and alliances*—involves breaking inappropriate alliances between family members and creating more adaptive and flexible alliances. For example, a common problem in families with a drug using adolescent is the tendency of parent figures to deflect dyadic conflict by involving the problem adolescent in the conflict. This process, labeled triangulation, often occurs when a lopsided alliance is formed between one parent figure and the problem youth against the other parent figure. By better balancing the overly strong and overly weak parent–youth alliances, and the overly weak parental alliance, more direct/uninterrupted communication between the parent figures gives rise to a new and stronger boundary around the parents.

(iv) *Redirecting communications*—involves promoting direct and specific communication between dyads, which sometimes requires blocking the interference of family members that do not permit such communications to occur.

In their initial investigations, Szapocznik and colleagues demonstrated that a family approach was effective with Hispanic families (Scopetta et al., 1977), and that family psychoeducational interventions rich with cultural content and aimed at transforming family interactional patterns could produce results as strong as family therapy (Szapocznik, Santisteban et al., 1986). In a subsequent study, combining a family approach with a cultural intervention, they demonstrated significant improvements in children's problem behaviors and family functioning (Szapocznik, Santisteban et al., 1989). In separate investigations, the efficacy of SFT with substance abusing and at risk adolescents was compared to a group therapy control condition (Santisteban et al., 1996, 1997) and individual dynamic psychotherapy (Szapocznik, Rio et al., 1989). In the former investigation, SFT produced significantly greater improvements in behavior problems than group counseling. Moreover, analyses of clinically significant change revealed that a substantially larger proportion of family therapy cases demonstrated reliable clinical improvement in behavior problems than did group cases. In the latter study, both SFT and the individual dynamic psychotherapy condition demonstrated significant improvements in behavioral problems (as compared to a no-treatment control group). However, SFT resulted in one-year follow-up improvements in family functioning, while individual dynamic psychotherapy resulted in a one-year follow-up deterioration in family functioning.

Szapocznik and colleagues have also developed and investigated two unique applications of SFT. The first application, one person family therapy (OPFT), is an intervention that is designed to target changes in maladaptive family interactions, but that attempts to do so without the whole family present in therapy (Szapocznik & Kurtines, 1989; Szapocznik, Kurtines, Perez-Vidal, Hervis, & Foote, 1989). OPFT has been shown to be as effective as the conjoint family approach in bringing about and maintaining significant improvements in: (i) behavior problems and drug use in youth, and (ii) family functioning (Szapocznik, et al, 1983; Szapocznik, Kurtines et al., 1986). For one-person interventions to produce desired changes in family interactions they had to explicitly target family change (Szapocznik, Rio et al., 1989).

The second application, strategic structural systems engagement (SSSE; Szapocznik & Kurtines, 1989; Szapocznik, Perez-Vidal, Hervis, Brickman, & Kurtines, 1989), was designed to more effectively engage adolescent drug users and their families in treatment. This approach was designed to overcome resistance by restructuring the interactions that permit resistance to occur. A core assumption in SSSE is that resistance is interaction-based; and consequently, therapists can strategically alter their behaviors to change the interactions that are interfering with the engagement process. In separate investigations with drug using Hispanic youth (Santisteban et al., 1996; Szapocznik et al., 1988), SSSE was significantly more effective than conventional engagement procedures in engaging in youth and their families into treatment. Moreover, the dropout rates in therapy were up to three times lower for families that had received the SSSE intervention than for those families that had not received this intervention.

Liddle and colleagues have developed and refined multidimensional family therapy (MDFT; Liddle; 1992, 1995) for inner city adolescent substance abusers. MDFT is an integrative family-based intervention that draws from structural family therapy, social learning theory, developmental theory, attachment theory, and empirical work (Liddle, 1994) to guide assessment and intervention within four interacting systems: (i) family system; (ii) parent–adolescent relations; (iii) parent subsystem—the self of the parent (parent as a parent and an individual adult); and (iv) adolescent subsystem—the self of the adolescent (adolescent as a son or daughter and as a member of a peer culture). Preliminary evidence for the efficacy of MDFT has been demonstrated in a controlled randomized clinical trial study comparing MDFT to adolescent group therapy and a multifamily educational intervention condition (Liddle et al., in press). Results demonstrated MDFT's superiority in reducing drug use and improving grades. The results from this study are currently in preparation. Data are currently being collected in a second National Institute on Drug Abuse funded controlled clinical trial study which compares MDFT to an individual-based cognitive therapy condition.

5.07.5 ASSESSMENT AND CLINICAL FORMULATION

The presenting problem or symptom exhibited by the child or adolescent (e.g., depression, substance abuse) is the family's ticket to coming to therapy. Family members typically enter therapy with the explicit goal of wanting to change the youth, and have minimal awareness of their own contribution to the problems experienced by the youth. For the family systems therapist, however, family interactions are the primary focus of treatment. The key to effective intervention thus begins with an accurate assessment and clinical formulation of family interactions that are related to the youth's problems. Assessment and clinical formulation (and ultimately intervention) always consider the general nature of family functioning as well as the specific relationship between the presenting problem and general family functioning.

Assessment and clinical formulation involves identifying strengths and weaknesses within the family. Weaknesses (i.e., problematic interactions) are presumed to be directly linked to the problem presented by the child. For example, parental conflict, parent–child relationship, triangulation, and a lack of subsystem differentiation, may all be related to the problem experienced by the child or adolescent. Family systems interventions reflect this focus on problematic interactions.

It is important to note, however, that the therapist's assessment of the family's strengths is perhaps as important as identifying weaknesses. Strengths refer to adaptive family interactions as well as to the particular capabilities of individual family members. This focus on strengths is not merely "lip service" or a reaction to "pathology-based" intervention models. Because the majority of family systems interventions are brief and problem-focused, therapists must utilize the family's resources to maximize their impact on the family. Although treatment does involve some skills building, it is not the primary focus of intervention. Rather, the primary focus is on utilizing the family's strengths to achieve the goals of treatment.

At a microlevel (moment by moment) in treatment, the therapist looks for intrapersonal and interpersonal strengths. Some examples of intrapersonal strengths include positive features such as love, commitment, and a desire to make things better. Interpersonal strengths include open and direct communication between family members, positive expressions of support, and the healthy expression of differences of opinion. These strengths are contrasted with microlevel intrapersonal and interpersonal weaknesses. Intrapersonal weaknesses at this level include hopelessness, anger (at worst, hate, or contempt), and negative attributions about self or other. Interpersonal weakness include the expression of contempt (as opposed to appropriate disagreements), intense and escalating levels of negativity, vague and indirect communication, developmentally inappropriate parent or child behavior, and conflict between parent figures.

At a molar level (assessment and clinical formulation of the family system), the strengths and weaknesses of complex patterns of interaction are considered. Some examples of strengths at this level include the family's flexibility to respond to changing internal (within family) and external conditions, their ability to negotiate and resolve their differences of opinion, and their ability to recognize that their problems are multifaceted as opposed to residing within one family member. Weaknesses at the molar level include a lack of parental cooperation in setting and enforcing rules, overly connected or disconnected interpersonal boundaries, the centralization of one family member, and the consistent denial, avoidance, or diffusion of family conflict.

5.07.5.1 Conducting Assessments in Family Systems Therapy

Family therapists are active and directive. They gather information about family interactions by asking directive questions about family interactions and by encouraging family members to interact in the treatment context. The process of assessment and clinical formulation, however, varies across family systems models. Thus, there is no standard, universally accepted procedure for conducting assessments and clinical formulation. Nevertheless, some of the strategies for assessing interactions are similar across models. In this section, we describe two general strategies for conducting assessments in family systems theory: (i) the family genogram, and (ii) enactments.

5.07.5.1.1 Family genogram

The genogram is a frequently used method for identifying who is in the family, and what

role important family members play with respect to one another. The conventional genogram includes biological family; however, genograms may also include individuals based on the function they serve within the family. For example, in our own work with inner city African-American families (Greenwood, Herves et al., 1995; Greenwood, Samuels, et al., 1995), defining "family" solely through biological relationships fails to represent the complex family/kinship network of these families. What is required is a more flexible approach to identifying family/kin that examines: (i) blood relation and/or extended kinship; (ii) perceived strength and duration of relationships; and (iii) perceived support—in either direction—(including financial, emotional, and instrumental help, e.g., who provides transportation, child care, and other types of assistance). In our experience, "family" often includes all individuals living within a household (except for roommates and transient "live-ins") as well as other important significant others who may or may not be biologically related to one another.

The genogram is like a family tree in that it depicts all of the important relationships within the family. One of the most important reasons for constructing a genogram is to obtain a more complete picture of the family constellation. The genogram is a tool for systematically identifying who is in the family—getting around the common problem of some families not letting therapists know about key but conflicted or undesirable relations. Thus, the genogram can also be useful in helping the therapist depict adaptive and maladaptive family interactions (e.g., conflicted or supportive relations may be depicted using a jagged line or straight line).

There are many strategies for conducting genograms, and various symbols are used to denote meaningful relationships and/or roles within the family. Regardless of the strategy or symbols used, the genogram is an excellent method for organizing the complex interconnections between family members in a coherent, organized manner. The drawback of the genogram is that it is a "snapshot" of the family, and as such yields relatively little information about family interactions. In other words, the genogram tends to be static rather than dynamic. Genograms represent the first stage of the assessment process, and are often used to establish rapport and gather information about who are the potentially critical "players" in the youth's life. This information provides the context for further assessment into the dynamic interaction patterns that characterize the family members identified in the genogram.

5.07.5.1.2 Assessment through direct observation of family interactions: enactments

Minuchin and colleagues (Minuchin, 1974; Minuchin & Fishman, 1981) were the first to emphasize the importance of enactments in FST. In fact, they describe enactments as the primary vehicle through which interactions are identified and changed in therapy. Enactments are defined as family interactions in the treatment context that reflect the family's characteristic manner of interacting outside of therapy. That is, enactments reflect the family's overlearned behaviors that are present in most situations. Enactments allow the therapist to directly observe family interactions, and are thus critical for assessment and clinical formulation. The basic philosophy is that family members will enact "real world" interactions through their enactments in the treatment. Thus, by observing these enactments in therapy, the therapist can directly assess strengths and weaknesses within the family, including important changes in family interaction that occur as therapy progresses.

Enactments are promoted by a therapeutic focus of encouraging, helping, or allowing family members to behave/interact in their characteristic manner, that is, as they would naturally behave if the therapist were not present (Szapocznik & Kurtines, 1989). Very frequently family members will spontaneously enact in their typical way when they fight, interrupt, or criticize one another. However, because of the nature of therapy, it is not uncommon for family members to centralize therapists, in which case, the therapist will need to be more active in facilitating direct communication between family members (i.e., enactments). To facilitate enactments, the therapist systematically redirects communications to encourage interactions between family members.

Enactments permit the therapist to view the family directly as it really is, with its overlearned, rigidly repetitive patterns of interaction. In this case, the therapist observes problems directly and does not have to rely on stories about what typically happens when the therapist is not present. By doing so, the therapist gathers information about family functioning directly by facilitating family interactions in therapy. We believe that there can be considerable discrepancies between what individuals report and how they actually behave (enact) in the family context. Moreover, family reports tend to be influenced by attributions; whereas, observations of enactments permit the identification of circular/systemic processes.

5.07.5.2 The Underlying Nature of Family Interactions

In clinical work, there is a range of theory driven information that is obtained through assessment. In this section, we present assessment information from two theory driven interventions for which there is also considerable efficacy research.

5.07.5.2.1 Functional family therapy

In FFT, the therapist's assessment is designed to identify the "functions" of each family member in relation to one another. Functions represent a short-hand term for the relational needs, whether they be inborn or learned, that underly individuals' apparent motivations for distance/autonomy and connectedness/interdependency with others (Alexander & Parsons, 1982). These patterns become evident over time in relationships, and often differ for a given individual in different relationships. Thus, unlike the intrapersonal concept of "personality" which presumes a core underlying motivational structure, a functional family therapist's assessment of functions often identifies important motivational differences within one person. A parent, for example, may have a "favorite" child (with whom they might even be "enmeshed"), while at the same time have another child whom they reject and may even attempt to expel from the household. In such situations it is inappropriate to think of the parent in a unitary fashion (enmeshed or disengaged). Instead the functional family therapist understands that the motivational needs of the parent, and perhaps the children, with respect to each other are markedly different. As a result, behaviors that would be syntonic for the parent with respect to the "close" child could be quite dystonic with respect to the "distanced" child. Additional complexity occurs when the motivational structure differs for members of a dyad—for example, a parent retains strong affiliation (connectedness needs) towards a youth, while the youth is "emancipating" (distancing from the parent) and developing much stronger connectedness needs outside the family. In FFT, neither the parent's functional need with respect to the child or the child's functional need with respect to the parent are pathologized. Rather, the therapist identifies the maladaptive behaviors that a person is using to meet their functional needs. For example, adolescents who sneak out of the house after curfew to hang out with friends may be considered to have an interpersonal (i.e., functional) need for distance from their parents. However, the manner in which they are fulfilling this need is considered to be inappropriate (e.g., sneaking out of the house). In FFT, the goal of assessment and clinical formulation is to identify each family members' functional needs with respect to other family members, and to understand the adaptive and maladaptive behaviors that are being utilized by family members to maintain these interpersonal needs.

5.07.5.2.2 Structural family therapy

A different strategy for assessing family interactions is found in the work of Szapocznik and colleagues (Hervis, Szapocznik, Mitrani, Rio, & Kurtines, 1991; Szapocznik & Kurtines, 1989; Szapocznik et al., 1991). The core of assessment and diagnosis in SFT involves identifying repetitive interactional patterns within the family along five interrelated dimensions: structure, resonance, developmental stage, identified patienthood, and conflict resolution.

(i) Structure

This refers to the organizational aspects of the repetitive patterns of interaction within the family. Three specific categories of family organization are examined: leadership, subsystem organization, and communication flow.

Leadership assesses the distribution of authority and responsibility within the family. This category includes (i) hierarchy (Who takes charge of the family's directorship? Is leadership in the appropriate hands? Is it shared? Is hierarchy appropriate with respect to age, role and function?); (ii) behavior control (Who keeps order, if anyone? Are attempts to keep order successful or ignored?); and (iii) guidance (Who provides advice and suggestions? Does the advice provided have an impact on family interaction?).

Subsystem organization is concerned with the formal and informal organization of the family system, including (i) alliances (Who supports whom? Are dyad members closer to each other than to the rest of the family? Are alliances appropriate?); (ii) triangulations defined as an interference by family member C in a conflict between family members A and B, where C acts as an intermediary between A and B and where such interference causes a detour away from the original conflict; and (iii) subsystem membership (Who is a member of which subsystem? Are subsystems comprised appropriately with respect to age and function? Are subsystem boundaries clearly defined?).

Communication flow is concerned with communication flow within the family. The following aspects of the quality, quantity, and direction of communication are assessed: (i) directness of communication (Do individuals communicate directly with each other?); (ii) gatekeepers—switchboard operators (Is there a gatekeeper who controls, directs, or channels communication flow?); and (iii) spokesperson (Is there a family member who speaks for others in the family or for the whole family?).

(ii) Resonance

This is a measure of subsystem differentiation which takes into account the threshold of each family member's sensitivity to one another. At one extreme, boundaries can be either extremely rigid or impermeable (lack of connectedness). At the opposite extreme, they can be too overinvolved. Both of these extremes are considered maladaptive. (This view may be contrasted with functional family therapy in which the interpersonal relatedness needs, i.e., functions, are not considered to be maladaptive.) Ideally, there is a midpoint which allows for permeability, such that interaction and communication are possible at appropriate times, while retaining adequate differentiation and separateness.

In assessing resonance, allowances must be made for the cultural background of the family (Kurtines & Szapocznik, 1996). However, when behaviors result in symptoms, they are considered problematic whether or not they are culturally sanctioned. For example, some families or relationships may be characterized by machismo, manifested as an uncertainty of a man's feelings towards his wife and a nonverbal expression that replaces communication in the form of sexually forcing himself onto his wife. In this extreme and stereotyped example of machismo, even if machismo is cultural, this pattern of behavior would clearly be viewed as maladaptive.

(iii) Developmental stage

This refers to the appropriateness of family members' interactions with respect to roles and tasks assigned to various family members, taking into consideration their age and position within the family. The following sets of roles and tasks are considered in examining this dimension. Parenting roles and tasks: Are parents parenting at a level consistent with the age of the children? For example, are controlling and nurturant functions in accordance with child's age and stage of psychological development?

Spousal roles and tasks: Are spouses parenting at cooperative and equal levels of development? Child/sibling roles and tasks: Do the children function competently for their age and have appropriate rights and responsibilities? Extended family member's roles and tasks: In extended families, are parents able to assume proper parental position relative to their children in light of the role of their own parents and other relatives?

It is noteworthy that the major flare-ups in family stress and conflict are likely to emerge at times when developmental milestones are reached, because these occasions expose the families to unexpected demands which stress the family. Frequently, as the family responds in old ways to the new emergent situation represented by a developmental milestone, crises at the interface between homeostasis and flexibility often propel the family to seek help.

(iv) Identified patienthood

Identified patienthood (IPhood) refers to the extent to which the family is convinced that their primary problem is all the fault of the person exhibiting the symptom. Thus, IPhood refers to the extent to which the family places the identified patient (IP) and the patient's identified problem to be the sole problem of the family and uses that IPhood as a means of maintaining family homeostasis. There are five signs indicative of strong IPhood: (i) negativity about the IP—statements to the effect that the IP is seen as the sole cause of family pain and unhappiness; (ii) IP centrality—the IP is frequently the center of attention and topic of conversation and interactions; (iii) overprotection of the IPhood—family avoids confrontation with IP dysfunction by excusing it, explaining it away, minimizing it, or feeling that there is nothing that can be done about it ("That's just the way they are."); (iv) nurturance of IPhood—the IP dysfunction is supported or abetted by other family members, for example, a sibling does the homework for an IP who skips school; and (v) denial of other problems—statements implying that the IP is causing problems and pain coupled with statements that there are no other family problems ("We would be a happy family if it wasn't for the IP's problem.")

(v) Conflict resolution

This is a measure of the family's style in managing disagreements. It is important to observe the handling of differences and disagreements in a variety of situations since various situations, differing in the level of inherent conflict or level of emotionality, may be handled differently. There are five conflict resolution styles identified: (i) denial—disagreements are not allowed to emerge and situations are structured to prevent different opinions or critical opinions, or redefined to prevent the emergence of conflict; (ii) avoidance—disagreement begins to emerge but is stopped, masked, or strongly inhibited in some way, for example, "Let's not have a fight now," "You're so cute when you're mad," "That's not really important"; (iii) diffusion—moving from one disagreement to another without letting any emerge fully or making personal attacks which are not part of the conflict issue; (iv) emergence without resolution—separate accounts and opinions regarding one disagreement are clearly expressed but no solution is negotiated; and (v) emergence with resolution—separate accounts and opinions regarding a single disagreement are clearly expressed and a single final version or solution acceptable to all family members is negotiated.

There is considerable debate as to which of these conflict resolution styles is most adaptive and successful. From a family systems, communication theory, and psychoanalytic point of view, it might be possible to order these conflict resolution styles from least to most healthy as follows: denial, avoidance, diffusion, emergence without resolution, and emergence with resolution. However, from a more strategic perspective, it can be suggested that different styles may be adaptive at certain times. As demonstrated by Greenwood et al. (submitted for publication; see also Szapocznik & Kurtines, 1989), considerable judgement is recommended in determining what is an appropriate mode of conflict resolution given the overall circumstances confronted.

5.07.5.3 Clinical Formulation in Family Systems Therapy

"Assessment" refers to the process of conducting a systematic review of the molecular aspects of family interaction to identify specific qualities in the patterns of interaction of each family. That is, assessment identifies the strengths and weaknesses of family interactions. In contrast, clinical formulation refers to the process of integrating the information obtained through assessment into molar processes that characterize the family's interactions (c.f., Szapocznik & Kurtines, 1989). In individual psychodiagnostics, clinical formulation explains the presenting symptom in relationship to the individual's psychodynamics. Similarly, clinical formulation in family systems, therapy explains the presenting symptom in relationship to the family's characteristic patterns of interaction.

In FST therapy, assessment and clinical formulation are essential components of the intervention model, and are thus guided by a unitary clinical theory. For this reason, the way in which the information gathered from assessments is combined differs across systemic approaches. This means that, depending on the treatment model, certain aspects of family interaction will receive extensive consideration and other aspects will receive less attention. For example, in FFT, the therapist's clinical formulation will always include a description of the way in which the youth's problem behaviors are meeting interpersonal relatedness needs; whereas, in SFT the therapist's clinical formulation will always include an articulation of the way in which disturbances in family interactions (i.e., structure, resonance, etc.) give rise to, or maintain, problem behaviors.

A variety of factors influence clinical formulation. Although not included in the assessment, information that can help contextualize family interactions is required for clinical formulation. For example, in assessment the appropriateness of each family member's developmental level is evaluated. However, in clinical formulation, information on major family developmental transitions or events that occur within or outside the family are also considered because they help to explain why a symptom may bring a family into treatment at a particular time. Also important to clinical formulation is the chronicity of the patterns encountered, or conversely, the family's flexibility in adapting to internal or external changes. Such flexibility is an important indicator of the level of effort that will be required to bring about changes in the family system.

Individual as well as external systemic factors must also be considered in the clinical formulation. At the individual level, psychological factors such as beliefs, attitudes, intelligence, and psychopathology, as well as biological factors must be considered when evaluating the impact of family interactions on the problems experienced by the youth. Moreover, other systems may have a profound impact on the family, and consequently, must be considered in the clinical formulation (Dishion et al., 1995; Szapocznik, Kurtines et al., 1997; Tolan, Guerra, & Kendall, 1995). For example, the youth's interactions at school or with peers, or the nature of the neighborhood may serve as a powerful risk or protective factor. In addition, parents' extended family, friends, or work may serve as a source of strength or stress that may or may not contribute to the problems experienced by the youth (Szapocznik & Coatsworth, submitted for publication).

5.07.6 MEDIATORS OF CHANGE: MECHANISMS OF ACTION IN FAMILY THERAPY WITH ACTING-OUT YOUTH

One of the most interesting contemporary theoretical and research questions in FST, and psychotherapy research in general, is "what makes therapy effective?" It is of considerable interest that across the various models reviewed there appear to be certain common ingredients that contribute to their efficacy/effectiveness. This section highlights these common ingredients by reviewing existing in-session family therapy process research on the "mechanisms of action" involved in the successful treatment of behavior problem youth. In particular, the primary goal is to identify specific therapist and family processes that contribute to outcome.

In this review, we focus on existing empirical research rather than on theoretical articulations of the therapeutic process. Unfortunately, only a handful of studies have been conducted to identify the critical processes that are essential to effective family therapy. Because so much of this work has been conducted with problem behavior adolescents, this section is organized to present the presumed mediators of successful and unsuccessful outcomes with behavior problem adolescents. Whenever possible, however, we have attempted to integrate research and clinical theory from other work with children and adolescents.

Process research findings from three important domains of family systems therapy are presented in this section: (i) establishing a therapeutic alliance with adolescents and their family members, (ii) managing highly conflicted family interactions; and (iii) changing parent–adolescent and family interactions. Table 2 summarizes this research, and includes clinical recommendations to family systems therapists working with behavior problem youth and their families.

5.07.6.1 The Critical Role of the Therapeutic Alliance in Family Therapy

It is now generally recognized that the therapeutic alliance is an important variable in psychotherapy research and a strong

Table 2 Clinical recommendations for family systems therapy with behavior problem youth.

Clinical recommendation	Reference	Future research questions
Building alliance with behavior problem youth Present as an ally by showing support and by demonstrating ways in which you can assist in helping the adolescent meet her/his treatment (or personal) goals Collaborate with adolescent to formulate personally meaningful treatment goals Attend to the adolescent's experiences by reflecting their thoughts and feelings	Diamond & Liddle (1996)	(i) What strategies are most effective in building alliances with parent figures and other family members? (ii) Are individual or conjoint sessions more effective in building alliances with adolescents (or parent figures)? (iii) How does the alliance change over the course of therapy? (iv) What is the relationship between the adolescent alliance, the parent alliance, and changes in behavioral outcomes?
Reducing within-family negativity Selectively respond to family member negativity by asking questions about exceptions to negative attributions or statements Reframe negative attributions and expectations in a positive manner Reframe in the context of negative family interactions to minimize the escalation of negativity in the session In conjoint sessions, direct statements that orient family to treatment toward parent figures	Melidonis & Bry (1995) Robbins, Alexander, Newell, & Turner (1996); Robbins, Alexander & Turner (1996)	(i) What is the relationship between negativity in the treatment context and changes in family functioning or behavioral outcomes? (ii) Does reframing improve the therapeutic alliance? (iii) Does reframing produce similar results over the course of therapy? (iv) What is the relationship between intrapersonal (i.e., attributional) changes and interpersonal (i.e., interactions) changes?
Handling resistance Approach resistance as interaction based, and adjust interventions during the engagement phase by using structural family therapy principles to overcome resistance to treatment Manage resistance by minimizing teaching or confrontive interventions, and by facilitating and supporting family members Resolve therapeutic impasse by blocking and working through negative affect, and by amplifying thoughts and feelings that promote constructive dialogue	Szapocznik et al. (1989); Santisteban et al. (1996) Patterson & Forgatch (1985) Diamond & Liddle (1996)	(i) What is the relationship between level of resistance and short-term (i.e., dropout) and long-term (i.e., behavioral changes) outcomes? (ii) Do different family members respond in a similar manner to therapist attempts to manage resistance? (iii) What are the therapist's structural maneuvers that encourage or discourage the family's (and specific family members') involvement in therapy?
Changing parent–adolescent interactions Focus on improving parental leadership, family subsystem organization, and communication flow Focus on facilitating the expression and resolution of within-family disagreements Focus on improving parenting practices, including positive discipline, monitoring, limit setting and communication, and consistency between parents	Robbins, Mitrani et al. (1996) Schmidt et al. (1996)	(i) What therapist interventions are most effective in changing parent–adolescent interactions? (ii) Are individual sessions with parent figures or the adolescent necessary to facilitate changes in parent–adolescent interactions? (iii) What is the relationship between the therapeutic alliance and changes in family interaction?

predictor of therapeutic outcome (Bordin, 1979; Dierick & Lietaer, 1990; Gaston, 1990; Hatcher, Barends, Hansell, & Gutfreund, 1995; Horvath & Luborsky, 1993; Lambert, Shapiro, & Bergin, 1986; Luborsky, Barber, & Crits-Christoph, 1990; Safran, Crocker, McMain, & Murray, 1990; Waterhouse & Strupp, 1984; Weinberger, 1995). While most conceptualizations of common factors in psychotherapy suggest that the therapeutic bond is important in all psychotherapies (Orlinsky, Grawe, & Parks, 1994), most of the research on alliance to date has focused on individual therapy. The individual psychotherapy literature indicates that the alliance itself has a direct therapeutic effect (Henry, Strupp, Schacht & Gaston, 1994; Lambert, 1992; Strupp & Hadley, 1979) in both long and short-term therapies, and appears to operate within treatments from many therapeutic orientations, including the more behavioral therapies in which the alliance is not as likely as in analytic therapies to be overtly mentioned as a therapeutic goal (Eaton, Abeles, & Gutfreund, 1988; Gaston, Marmar, Gallagher, & Thompson, 1991; Gomes-Schwartz, 1978; Horvath & Symonds, 1991; Koss & Shiang, 1994; Krupnick, Sotsky, Simmens, & Moyer, 1992; Muran et al., 1995).

The therapeutic alliance also appears to be an important predictor of the outcome of clients in non-individual treatment modalities (Gaston & Schneider, 1992; Henry et al., 1994; Pinsof & Catherall, 1986). In specific reference to family therapy, Gurman & Kniskern (1978) concluded that "the ability of the therapist to establish a positive relationship ... receives the most consistent support as an important outcome-related therapist factor in marital and family therapy" (p. 875). In their review of family therapy research, Friedlander, Wildman, Heatherington, and Skowrow (1994) assert that components of alliance in family therapy have been predictive of session effectiveness, continuation in treatment, and therapeutic outcome. Although these reviews assert that the therapeutic alliance is critical in family therapy, few studies have been specifically designed to examine the impact of alliance in family therapy. In fact, DiGiuseppe, Linscott, and Jilton (1996) note that process research on the therapeutic alliance in therapy with youth in general is alarmingly scarce.

5.07.6.1.1 Building an alliance with behavior problem youth: specific recommendations

Diamond and Liddle (1996) examined the relationship between specific therapist engage-

ment interventions and the strength of the therapist–adolescent alliance in multidimensional family therapy with drug using adolescents. In this study, therapist interventions and family alliance were rated in first and third sessions of five cases that showed the most improvement in alliance and five cases showing the least improvement in alliance. Results indicate that differences between the improved and unimproved groups do not appear until the third session of therapy. In session one, therapists try equally hard to engage reluctant adolescents. By session three, however, therapists in the improved alliance group were "formulating goals" "presenting themselves as an ally," and "attending to the adolescent's experience" significantly more than therapists in the unimproved group. Therapists in the unimproved group were "orienting adolescents to the collaborative nature of therapy" more than therapists in the improved group, though in both groups this intervention decreased over the first three sessions. These results are consistent with the assertions of other researchers who assert that although these factors are important, adolescents are particularly concerned with being involved in establishing the goals and tasks of therapy (DiGiuseppe, et al., (1996).

5.07.6.2 Reducing Within-family Negativity

Negativity, in the context of family functioning, has been heavily implicated in adolescent drug use and behavior problems. Research has shown that high levels of negativity interfere with effective problem solving and communication within the family (Alexander, Waldron, Barton, & Mas, 1989; Margolin, Burman, & John, 1989). These processes appear to play a similar role in the process of therapy itself, with numerous examples linking negativity in the therapy session to poor therapy outcome. Alexander, Barton, Schiavo, and Parsons (1976), for example, found that the ratio of negative to supportive statements was significantly higher in cases that dropped out of therapy than among cases that completed treatment. In turn, premature termination predicted recidivism in adolescents. In the same study, among the families that completed therapy, a reduction in family member negative behaviors during treatment was associated with positive outcome. Greater rates of within family disagreements have also been shown to be characteristic of noncompleters in structural-strategic family therapy (Shields, Sprenkle, & Constantine, 1991). A comprehensive review of the process of family therapy concluded that, in general, negativity may be predictive of premature termination (Friedlander et al., 1994).

5.07.6.2.1 *Examining the impact of therapist interventions on within family negativity*

Melidonis & Bry (1995) examined the effects of therapist questions about exceptions to family member statements on rates of blaming and positive statements in four families seen in a crisis unit for disruptive adolescent problem behaviors. They demonstrated that the therapist's use of exceptions questions was associated with a decline in blaming statements and an increase in positive statements.

Robbins, Alexander, Newell, & Turner (1996) examined the impact of specific types of therapist intervention (e.g., reframing, reflection, and organizational) on family members' negative attitude during the initial session of family therapy with a delinquent adolescent. Results revealed that: (i) across all therapist's interventions, adolescents were significantly more negative than mother's following therapist behaviors, but (ii) adolescents' attitudes improved from negative to neutral following therapist reframes but not other therapist interventions.

In a follow-up investigation, Robbins, Alexander, & Turner (submitted for publication) further examined the impact of therapist interventions on family processes. Similar to the previous study, the immediate effects of therapist reframing, reflection, and structuring interventions on family member behaviors were compared; however, only those therapist interventions that followed family member negative statements were included in the analysis. Results demonstrate that for this sample: (i) reframing is more effective than reflection and structuring statements in reducing family member negative behaviors; (ii) the results expanded the previous finding that adolescents respond more favorably to reframes than do mothers and fathers, now providing evidence of the effectiveness of reframing interventions for all family members; and (iii) adolescents responded more favorably to therapists (regardless of intervention) than did family members during negative exchanges.

These results demonstrate that highly negative and conflicted family interactions may be modified by therapist interventions in the treatment context. In particular, in the context of highly conflicted interactions, interventions that are positive and nonblaming appear to have a powerful effect on negative family interactions. These results are particularly evident for the adolescents in these samples, which is particularly promising given their highly negative and oppositional style when interacting with other family members and the therapist. Future research must attempt to link these changes in in-session conflict and negativity to other therapeutic changes and to the ultimate outcome of therapy.

5.07.6.3 Changing Parent–Adolescent Interactions

One of the core factors that consistently emerges in most etiological explanations of adolescent behavior problems is poor parenting and/or parent–child relationships. Aspects of the parent–child relationship that increase vulnerability to adolescent behavior problems include: lack of warmth and involvement, poor communication, lack of support, emotional distance, rejection, and lack of parental management (Kazdin, 1993, 1995; Kumpfer, 1989; Rutter & Guller, 1983; Werner & Smith, 1992; Widom, 1989). Research has also demonstrated that other parent and family factors, such as a lack of parental monitoring (Baumrind, 1991a, 1991b; Patterson & Dishion, 1985), harsh discipline, observed marital conflict, reciprocated negative communications, chronic parent–child conflict, and intense and frequent negative emotional expression (Alexander, 1973; Block, Block, & Keyes, 1988; Kandel, Kessler, & Margulies, 1978; Krinsley & Bry, 1991; Liddle & Dakof, 1995b; Rutter, 1980), play an important role in placing adolescents at risk for behavior problems (Hawkins, Catalano, & Miller, 1992; Jessor, 1976; Patterson, 1982; Simcha-Fagan, Gersten, & Langer, 1986). There is also an extensive literature indicating that changes in parenting practices positively impacts children's problem behaviors (for review see Estrada & Pinsof, 1995).

Support for the utility of interventions targeting the parent–child relationship in the context of family therapy comes from several sources. Parsons and Alexander (1973) found that positive modifications in parent–adolescent communications were associated with reduced recidivism (Alexander & Parsons, 1973) as well as a marked reduction in future offending by siblings (Alexander et al., 1976). In one study, Schmidt, Liddle, and Dakof (1996) linked improvements in parenting to reductions in drug abuse and behavior problems.

5.07.6.3.1 *Changes in family interactions in successful and unsuccessful outcome cases*

Robbins, Mitrani, Zarate, Coatsworth, & Szapocznik (1996) examined family interactions over the course of therapy in successful and unsuccessful cases to determine if changes in theoretically meaningful family interactions mediated treatment outcome. Four cases were selected that met the following criteria: case 1 showed improvement on measures of conduct disorder and had "good" pretreatment family functioning; case 2 showed improvement in conduct disorder and had "poor" pretreatment family functioning; case 3 showed no improvement and had "good" pretreatment family functioning; and case 4 showed no improvement and had "poor" pretreatment family functioning.

Results indicate that for families that showed improvement on measures of conduct disorder (cases 1 and 2), regardless of pretreatment family functioning, positive changes in family interaction were observed over the course of treatment; while for families that showed no improvement (cases 3 and 4), family functioning did not change, or worsened, over the course of treatment. These results provide limited but important support for the family therapy tenet that changes in family interaction mediate outcome. Moreover, these results highlight the importance of examining the therapeutic processes to understand those factors that contribute to successful therapy.

5.07.6.3.2 *Family members' resistance to change*

The results presented above suggest that family interactions play a critical mediating role in therapy with substance abusing, behavior problem youth. Attempts to change family interactions are often met with considerable resistance in therapy. For example, therapists appear to encounter the most "resistance" during the phase of treatment in which they are attempting to restructure family interactions (Chamberlain, Patterson, Reid, Kavanagh, & Forgatch, 1984). Therapists must successfully negotiate in-session "resistance" to achieve positive treatment outcomes.

Several important therapy traditions have viewed the therapeutic system's role in resistance and examined what therapists can do to prevent or manage resistance in family therapy. Resistance can be considered as a family characteristic or as a family response to an interaction with the therapist (Szapocznik & Kurtines, 1989; Szapocznik et al., 1989). Hence, at least in family systems thinking, the term "family resistance" fails to capture the systemic nature of the therapist–family relationship (Santisteban et al., 1996). This theoretical work and the empirical research of Patterson and colleagues, Alexander and colleagues, and Szapocznik and colleagues clearly demonstrate that so called family "resistant" behaviors appear to be elicited in interactions with the therapist, and as a result can be modified by altering the therapist's behaviors. For example, Patterson and Forgatch (1985) examined the immediate impact of therapist interventions on client noncompliance in families with a conduct disorder youth. The results of this study showed that therapist teach and confront were associated with increased noncompliance, whereas therapist facilitate and support were associated with decreased noncompliance. Reframing yielded mixed results.

Diamond and Liddle (1996) examined patterns of therapist's interventions and family interactions necessary to resolve therapeutic impasse in multidimensional family therapy with substance abusing youth. Impasse was defined as negative exchanges that thwart the therapist's attempts to facilitate parent–adolescent negotiations. This study demonstrated that families (in general) declined in functioning from the impasse phase to the intervention phase; however, families who successfully resolved the impasse improved their level of functioning following the impasse. Unsuccessful families, on the other hand, were initially more conflicted and pessimistic than successful families, and declined in functioning after the impasse. Results also indicated that therapists played a critical role in resolving parent–adolescent impasses. In successful resolutions, therapists were able to create an emotional treaty among family members by blocking and working through families' negative affect, and by amplifying thoughts and feelings that promoted constructive dialogue. Finally, adolescents became more cooperative and engaged in therapy when parents shifted from trying to control them to trying to understand them.

Taken together these results provide specific recommendations for handling "resistant" behaviors in family therapy. In particular, resistant behaviors must first be reconceptualized as part of an interaction with the therapist. Adopting this view permits the therapist to examine their own contribution to resistance and opens up possibilities for strategically altering their own behavior to influence family members. Therapist facilitative, supportive, and reframing interventions may be particularly useful when "working through" so-called resistant interactions. Likewise, therapist interventions that block negative affect and/or promote constructive dialogue appear to decrease resistant interactions in family therapy.

5.07.6.3.3 *The relationship between changes in parenting behaviors and adolescent behavioral outcomes*

Schmidt et al. (1996) examined in-session processes in multidimensional family therapy to determine: (i) the nature and extent of change in the behavioral, affective, and cognitive features of parenting; and (ii) the link between parental subsystem changes, and reduction in adolescent substance use and behavior problems. Results demonstrated significant decreases in negative parenting practices and significant increases in positive parenting features. Analyses with adolescent drug use and behavior problem scores indicated a significant relationship between parent improvement and reduction in drug use and acting out. These results demonstrate that not only are parenting behaviors amenable to therapist interventions, but that changes in parenting behaviors in family therapy are associated with changes in relevant adolescent behavioral outcomes. In fact, this relationship was evident in almost 60% of the families in this sample.

5.07.7 SUMMARY AND FUTURE DIRECTIONS

Although FST has emerged as a treatment of choice in the treatment of some child and adolescent clinical populations, the field lacks a solid empirical base demonstrating the efficacy and effectiveness of family systems interventions for a variety of clinical disorders of youth. With the exception of work with behavior problem youth, including substance abuse, family systems treatments have flourished in clinical rather than research settings. Thus, there is an obvious need to bridge the clinical–research gap in FST with childhood disorders.

Research also must be conducted to elucidate the important mechanisms of action in FST. At a molar level, this research should examine universal processes across theoretical models and clinical populations to shed light on what may be the "core" ingredients of FST. However, at a micro level, research must also provide therapists with specific clinical recommendations about how to work with youth and their families. That is, because therapists must respond to family members in the context of their present interactions in therapy, process research can assist clinical model developers in generating or testing the positive or negative

impact of particular therapeutic interventions on immediate and long-term outcomes. With respect to immediate and long-term outcomes, such research can also help describe the shape or trajectory of change in FST. The development of new statistical procedures, such as hierarchical linear modeling (Bryk & Raudenbush, 1992; Raudenbush, 1993) and latent growth curve analysis (see Burchinal, Bailey, & Snyder, 1994; Speer & Greenbaum, 1995), will permit research to examine complex clinical theories about the nature of change.

Other challenges face family systems theorists and researchers. For example, family systems therapists are increasingly acknowledging the interface between the family and the environment, and the complexity of factors that influence individual development (Dishion et al., 1995; Henggeler & Borduin, 1990; Szapocznik et al., 1997; Tolan et al., 1995). This recognition has led to the development of a new wave of multisystemic/ecosystemic interventions targeting interactions in (and between) many systems. The fact that most of these interventions have emerged in inner city contexts has illuminated a variety of other challenges that family systems therapists and researchers must address, such as: (i) working with ethnically diverse and the urban poor populations, (ii) confronting the deteriorating neighborhoods in which these families reside, and (iii) challenging conventional methods of service delivery (e.g., location of treatment). Such challenges will require considerable perseverance and ingenuity from the therapists who work in these contexts, and for the researchers who must attempt to shed light on the efficacy and effectiveness of this work and to understand how the change process unfolds.

A final challenge involves the considerable clinical skill and sophistication that is required to implement FST. It should be apparent from the discussion of FST in this chapter, that the therapist is required to recognize the nature of the interactions at every moment in therapy—and to track the evolving process as it unfolds. Moreover, the therapist must be able to intervene by strategically selecting, from a complex set of interventions, the intervention that will most effectively move the family toward the therapeutic goal of the intervention model at that point in time (e.g., engaging, building alliances, reducing negativity, or changing parenting). Traditionally, it has not been fully recognized that the teaching and learning of FST is a rather laborious process that requires education about the key concepts of the family process paradigm and the complex interpersonal skills required to facilitate change in the FST context. Moreover, training also requires an extensive apprenticeship in which new therapists can see families under intensive supervision. Recognition of the challenge of training and learning FST is critical if we will ever be able to transfer research findings into clinical practice. One of the great factors impeding this research to practice translation has been the lack of recognition of the considerable work involved when training and supervising therapists who participate in research projects; training which must be replicated at the service level if we are ever to translate our promising research findings into widespread clinical practice.

ACKNOWLEDGMENTS

This work supported by grants from the National Institute on Drug Abuse (# 1RO1 DA 10574) and the National Institute of Mental Health (# 1RO1 MH 55795) to José Szapocznik, Principal Investigator.

5.07.8 REFERENCES

Alexander, J. F. (1973). Defensive and supportive communications in family systems. *Journal of Marriage and the Family, 35*(4), 613–617.
Alexander, J. F. (1988). Phases of family therapy process: A framework for clinicians and researchers. In L. Wynne (Ed.), *The state of the art in family therapy and research: Controversies and recommendations* (pp. 175–187). New York: Family Process Press.
Alexander, J. F., Barton, C., Schiavo, R. S., & Parsons, B. V. (1976). Systems-behavioral intervention with families of delinquents: Therapist characteristics, family behaviors, and outcome. *Journal of Consulting and Clinical Psychology, 44*, 656–664.
Alexander, J. F., Barton, C., Waldron, H. B., & Mas, C. H. (1983). Beyond the technology of family therapy: The anatomy of intervention model. In K. D. Craig & R. J. McMahon (Eds.), *Advances in clinical behavior therapy* (pp. 48–63). New York: Brunner/Mazel.
Alexander, J. F., Holtzworth-Munroe, A., & Jameson, P. B. (1994). Research on the process and outcome of marriage and family therapy. In A. E. Bergin & S. L. Garfield (Eds.), *Handbook of psychotherapy and behavior change* (4th ed., pp. 595–630). New York: Wiley.
Alexander, J. F., & Parsons, B. V. (1973). Short-term behavioral intervention with delinquent families: Impact on family process and recidivism. *Journal of Abnormal Psychology, 81*, 219–225.
Alexander, J. F., & Parsons, B. V. (1982). *Functional family therapy*. Monterey, CA: Brooks/Cole.
Alexander, J. F., Waldron, H. B., Barton, C., & Mas, C. H. (1989). Minimizing blaming attributions and behaviors in delinquent families. *Special series on marital and family disorders. Journal of Consulting and Clinical Psychology, 57*(1), 19–24.
Alexander, P. C. (1985). A systems theory conceptualization of incest. *Family Process, 24*, 79–88.
Azrin, N. H., Donohue, B., Besalel, V. A., Kogan, E. S., & Acierno, R. (1994). Youth drug abuse treatment: A controlled outcome study. *Journal of Child and Adolescent Substance Abuse, 3*, 1–16.
Barton, C., & Alexander, J. F. (1981). Functional family therapy. In A. Gurman & D. Kniskern (Eds.), *Handbook*

of family therapy (pp. 403–443). New York: Brunner/Mazel.
Barton, C., Alexander, J. F., Waldron, H., Turner, C. W., & Warburton, J. (1985). Generalizing treatment effects of functional family therapy: Three replications. *The American Journal of Family Therapy, 13*(3), 16–26.
Bateson, G. (1972). *Steps to an ecology of mind*. New York Dutton.
Bateson, G., Jackson, D. D., Haley, J., & Weakland, J. H. (1956). Toward a theory of schizophrenia. *Behavioral Science, 1*, 251–264.
Baumrind, D. (1991a) Effective parenting during the early adolescent transition. In P. A. Cowan & M. Heatherington (Eds.). *Family transitions* (pp. 111–163). Hillsdale, NJ: Erlbaum.
Baumrind, D. (1991b). The influence of parenting style on adolescent competency and substance abuse. *Journal of Early Adolescence, 11*(1), 56–95.
Block, J., Block, J. H., & Keyes, S. (1988). Longitudinally foretelling drug usage in adolescence: Early childhood personality and environmental precursors. *Child Development, 59*, 336–355.
Boivin, M., & Begin, G. (1989). Peer status and self-perception among early elementary school children: The case of the rejected children. *Child Development, 60*, 591–596.
Bordin, E. S. (1979). The generalizability of the psychoanalytic concept of the working alliance. *Psychotherapy, 16*, 252–260.
Borduin, C. M., Henggeler, S. W., Blaske, D. M., & Stein, R. J. (1990). Multisystemic treatment of adolescent sexual offenders. *International Journal of Offender Therapy and Comparative Criminology, 34*(2), 105–113.
Bowen, M. A. (1960). A family concept of schizophrenia. In D. D. Jackson (Ed.), *The etiology of schizophrenia* (pp. 341–372). New York: Basic Books.
Breunlin, D. C., Schwartz, R. C., & Kune-Karrer, B. M. (1992). *Transcending the models of family therapy*. San Francisco: Jossey-Bass.
Briggs, J., & David Peat F. (1989). Turbulent mirror: An illustrated guide to chaos theory and the science of wholeness. New York: Harper and Row.
Broderick, C. B. (1993). *Understanding family process: Basics of family systems theory*. Newbury Park, CA: Sage.
Bronfenbrenner, U. (1979). *The ecology of human development*. Cambridge, MA: Harvard University Press.
Bronfenbrenner, U. (1986). The ecology of the family as a context for human development. *Developmental Psychology, 22*, 723–742.
Bronfenbrenner, U. (1995). Developmental ecology through space and time: A future perspective. In P. Moen, G. H. Elder, & K. Luscher (Eds.), *Examining lives in context: Perspectives on the ecology of human development* (pp. 619–647). Washington, DC: American Psychological Association.
Brooks-Gunn, J., Duncan, G. J., Klebanov, P. K., & Sealand, N. (1993). Do neighborhoods influence child and adolescent development? *American Journal of Sociology, 99*, 353–395.
Bryk, A. S., Raudenbush, S. W. (1992). *Hierarchical linear models: applications and data analysis methods*. Newbury Park, CA: Sage.
Buckley, W. (Ed.) (1968). *Modern systems research for the behavioral scientist*. Chicago: Aldine.
Burchinal, M. R., Bailey, D. B., & Snyder, P. (1994). Using growth curve analysis to evaluate child change in longitudinal investigations. *Journal of Early Intervention, 18*, 403–423.
Chamberlain, P., Patterson, G. R., Reid, J. B., Kavanagh, K., & Forgatch, M. S. (1984). Observation of client resistance. *Behavior Therapy, 15*, 144–155.
Chamberlain, P., & Rosicky, J. G. (1995). The effectiveness

of family therapy in the treatment of adolescents with conduct disorders and delinquency. *Journal of Marital and Family Therapy, 21*(4), 441–460.

Coyne, J. C., & Anderson, B. J. (1989). The "psychosomatic family" reconsidered II: Recalling a defective model and looking ahead. *Journal of Marital and Family Therapy, 15,* 139–148.

Dare, C., Eisler, I., Russell, G. F. M., & Szmukler, G. I. (1990). The clinical and theoretical impact of a controlled trial of family therapy in anorexia nervosa. *Journal of Marital and Family Therapy, 16,* 39–57.

Diamond, G., & Liddle, H. A. (1996). Resolving a therapeutic impasse between a parent and an adolescent in family therapy. *Journal of Consulting and Clinical Psychology, 64*(3), 481–488.

Diamond, G., & Siqueland, L. (1995). Family therapy for the treatment of depressed adolescents. *Psychotherapy, 32*(1), 77–90.

Diamond, G. M., & Siqueland, L. (1996, June). *A family based treatment approach for adolescent major depression: Model and pilot results.* Paper presented at the 27th annual meeting of the Society for Psychotherapy Research, Amelia Island, FL.

Dierick, P., & Lietaer, G. (1990). Member and therapist perceptions of therapeutic factors in therapy and growth groups: Comments on a category system. In G. Lietaer, J. Rombauts, & R. Van Balen (Eds.), *Client-centered and experiential psychotherapy in the nineties* (p. 741–770). Leuven, Belgium: Leuven University Press.

DiGiuseppe, R., Linscott, J., & Jilton, R. (1996). Developing the therapeutic alliance in child–adolescent psychotherapy. *Applied & Preventive Psychology, 5*(2), 85–100.

Dishion, T. J., French, D. C., & Patterson, G. R. (1995). The development and ecology of antisocial behavior. In D. Cicchetti & D. J. Cohen (Eds.), *Developmental psychopathology. Vol. 2: Risk, disorder and adaptation* (pp. 421–471). New York: Wiley.

Eaton, T. T., Abeles, N., & Gutfreund, M. J. (1988). Therapeutic alliance and outcome: Impact of treatment length and pretreatment symptomatology. *Psychotherapy, 25,* 536–542.

Estrada, A. U., & Pinsof, W. M. (1995). The effectiveness of family therapies for selected behavioral disorders of childhood. *Journal of Marital and Family Therapy, 21*(4), 403–440.

Florsheim, P., Tolan, P. H., & Gorman-Smith, D. (In press). Family processes and risk for externalizing behavior problems among African-American and Hispanic boys. Submitted to *Journal of Consulting and Clinical Psychology.*

Forehand, R. (1993). Family psychopathology and child functioning. *Journal of Child and Family Studies, 2,* 79–85.

Friedlander, M. L., Wildman, J., Heatherington, L., & Skowrow, E. A. (1994). What we do and don't know about the process of family therapy. *Journal of Family Psychology, 8,* 390–416.

Friedman, A. S. (1989). Family therapy vs. parent groups: Effect on adolescent drug abusers. *The American Journal of Family Therapy, 17,* 335–347.

Fromm-Reichmann, F. (1948). Notes on the development of treatment of schizophrenics by psychoanalytic psychotherapy. *Psychiatry, 11,* 263–274.

Garfinkel, P. E., & Garner, D. M. (1982). *Anorexia nervosa: A multidimensional perspective.* New York: Brunner/Mazel.

Gaston, L. (1990). The concept of the alliance and its role in psychotherapy: Theoretical and empirical considerations. *Psychotherapy, 27,* 143–153.

Gaston, L., Marmar, C. R., Gallagher, D., & Thompson, L. W. (1991). Alliance prediction of outcome beyond in-treatment symptomatic change as psychotherapy processes. *Psychotherapy Research, 1,* 104–113.

Gaston, L., & Schneider, J. (1992, August). *The Alliance in Group Psychotherapy.* Paper presented at the meeting of the International Association of Group Psychotherapy, Montreal, Canada.

Gleick, J. (1987). *Chaos: making a new science.* New York: Viking.

Goldenberg, I., & Goldenberg, H. (1983). Historical roots of contemporary family therapy. In B. B. Wolman & G. Stricker (Eds.), *Handbook of family and marital therapy* (pp. 77–89). New York: Plenum.

Goldenberg, I. & Goldenberg, H. (1996). *Family therapy: An overview* (4th ed.). Pacific Grove, CA: Brooks/Cole.

Gomes-Schwartz, B. (1978). Effective ingredients in psychotherapy: Prediction of outcome from process variables. *Journal of Consulting and Clinical Psychology, 46,* 1023–1035.

Gordon, D. A., Arbuthnot, J., Gustafson, K. E., & McGreen, P. (1988). Home-based behavioral-systems family therapy with disadvantaged juvenile delinquents. *The American Journal of Family Therapy, 16*(3), 243–255.

Gordon, D. A., Graves, K., & Arbuthnot, J. (1995). The effect of functional family therapy for delinquents on adult criminal behavior. *Criminal Justice & Behavior, 22*(1), 60–73.

Greenwood, D., Hervis, O. E., Mitrani, V. B., Taylor, D., & Szapocznik, J. (1995, August). *Family definition in low income, HIV-1 seropositive African American women.* Paper presented at the meeting of the American Psychological Association, APA 103rd Annual Convention, New York.

Greenwood, D., Robbins, M. S., Tejeda, M., Samuels, D., Ironson, G., Antoni, M., & Szapocznik, J., (submitted for publication). Family functioning and social support moderate and relationship between average monthly CD4 cell change and psychological distress in HIV-positive African American women. *Journal of Consulting and Clinical Psychology.*

Greenwood, D., Samuels, D., Sorhaindo, L., McIntosh, S., Ironson, G., Antoni, M., Blake, R., & Szapocznik, J. (1995, February). *Social support networks and satisfaction in African American, post-partum, HIV positive women.* Paper presented at the First National Scientific Meeting on HIV infection in Adult and Adolescent Women, Washington, DC.

Grigg, D. N., & Friesen, J. D. (1989). Family patterns associated with anorexia nervosa. *Journal of Marital and Family Therapy, 15,* 29–42.

Guerin, P. J. (1976). Family therapy: The first twenty-five years. In P. J. Guerin (Ed.), *Family therapy: Theory and practice* (pp. 2–22). New York: Gardner.

Gurman, A. S., & Kniskern, D. P. (1978). Research on marital and family therapy: Progress, perspective and prospect. In S. L. Garfield & A. E. Bergin (Eds.), *Handbook of psychotherapy and behavior change: An empirical analysis* (2nd ed., pp. 817–902). New York: Wiley.

Gurman, A. S., Kniskern, D. P., & Pinsof, W. M. (1986). Research on the process and outcome of marital and family therapy. In S. L. Garfield & A. E. Bergin (Eds.), *Handbook of psychotherapy and behavior change* (3rd ed., pp. 565–624). New York: Wiley.

Gutstein, S. E., Rudd, M. D., Graham, J. C. & Rayha, L. L. (1988). Systemtic crisis intervention as a response to adolescent crises: An outcome study. *Family Process, 27,* 201–211.

Haley, J. (1976). Development of theory: A history of a research project. In C. E. Sluzki & D. C. Ransom (Eds.), *Double bind: The foundation of a communications approach to the family.* New York: Grune & Stratton.

Hanson, B. G. (1995) *General systems theory: Beginning with wholes.* Washington, DC: Taylor & Francis.

Hatcher, R. L., Barends, A., Hansell, J., & Gutfreund, M.

J. (1995). Patients' and therapists' shared and unique views of the therapeutic alliance: An investigation using confirmatory factor analysis in a nested design. *Journal of Consulting and Clinical Psychology, 63,* 636–643.

Hawkins, J. D., Catalano, R. F., & Miller, J. Y. (1992). Risk and protective factors for alcohol and other drug problems in adolescence and early adulthood: Implications for substance abuse prevention. *Psychological Bulletin, 112,* 64–105.

Henggeler, S. W., & Borduin, C. W. (1990). *Family therapy and beyond: A multisystemic approach to treating the behavior problems of children and adolescents.* Pacific Grove, CA: Brooks/Cole.

Henggeler, S. W., Borduin, C. M., Melton, G. B., Mann, B. J., Smith, L. A., Hall, J. A., Cone, L., & Fucci, B. R. (1991). Effects of multisystemic therapy on drug use and abuse in serious juvenile offenders: A progress report from two outcome studies. *Family Dynamics Addiction Quarterly, 1,* 40–51.

Henggeler, S. W., Melton, G. M., & Smith, L. A. (1992). Family preservation using multisystemic therapy: An effective alternative to incarcerating serious juvenile offenders. *Journal of Consulting and Clinical Psychology, 60,* 953–961.

Henggeler, S. W., Rodick, J. D., Borduin, C. M., Hanson, C. L., Watson, S. M., & Urey, J. R. (1986). Multisystemic treatment of juvenile offenders: Effects on adolescent behavior and family interaction. *Developmental Psychology, 22,* 132–141.

Henggeler, S. W., Rowland, M. D., Pickrel, S. G., Miller, S. L., Cunningham, P. B., Santos, A. B., Schoenwold, S. K., Randall, E., & Edwards, J. E. (in press). Investigating family based alternatives to institution-based mental health services for youth. Lessons learned from a pilot study of a randomized field trial.

Henry, W. P., Strupp, H. H., Schacht, T. E., & Gaston, L. (1994). Psychodynamic approaches. In A. E. Bergin & S. L. Garfield (Eds.), *Handbook of psychotherapy and behavior change* (4th ed., pp. 467–508). New York: Wiley.

Hervis, O. E., Szapocznik, J., Mitrani, V. B., Rio, A. T., Kurtines, W. (1991). *Structural family sytstems ratings: a revised manual.* Unpublished document. Miami, FL: University of Miami, Spanish Family Guidance Center, Department of Psychiatry and Behavioral Sciences.

Horvath, A. O., & Luborsky, L. (1993). The role of the therapeutic alliance in psychotherapy. *Journal of Consulting and Clinical Psychology, 64,* 561–573.

Horvath, A. O., & Symonds, D. B. (1991). Relationship between working alliance and outcome in psychotherapy: A meta-analysis. *Journal of Counseling Psychology, 38,* 139–149.

Jessor, R. (1976). Predicting time of onset of marijuana use: A developmental study of high school youth. *Journal of Consulting and Clinical Psychology, 44,* 125–134.

Joanning, H., Thomas, F., Quinn, W., & Mullen, R. (1992). Treating adolescent drug abuse: A comparison of family systems therapy, group therapy, and family drug education. *Journal of Marital and Family Therapy, 18,* 345–356.

Kandel, D., Kessler, R., & Margulies, R. (1978). Antecedents of adolescent initiation into stages of drug use: A developmental analysis. *Journal of Youth and Adolescents, 7,* 13–40.

Kaslow, F. W. (1980). History of family therapy in the United States: A kaleidoscopic overview. *Marriage and Family Review, 3,* 77–111.

Kazdin, A. E. (1993). Treatment of conduct disorder: Progress and directions in psychotherapy research. *Development and Psychopathology, 5,* 277–310.

Kazdin, A. E. (1994a). Psychotherapy for children and adolescents. In A. E. Bergin & S. L. Garfield (Eds.), *Handbook of psychotherapy and behavior change*

(4th ed., pp. 543–594). New York: Wiley.

Kazdin, A. E. (1995). *Conduct disorders in childhood and adolescence* (2nd ed.). Thousand Oaks, CA: Sage.

Kazdin, A. E., & Kolko, D. J. (1986). Parent psychopathology and family functioning among childhood firesetters. *Journal of Abnormal Child Psychology, 14,* 315–329.

Kazdin, A. E., Stolar, M. J., & Marciano, P. L. (1995). Risk factors for dropping out of treatment among white and black families. *Journal of Family Psychology, 9*(4), 402–417.

Klein, N. C., Alexander, J. F., & Parsons, B. V. (1977). Impact of family systems intervention on recidivism and sibling delinquency: Preliminary findings. *Journal of Consulting and Clinical Psychology, 45,* 469–474.

Kog, E., & Vandereycken, W. (1989) The facts: A review of research data on eating disorder families. In W. Vandereycken, E. Kog, & J. Vanderlinden (Eds.), *The family approach to eating disorders.* New York: PMA.

Kog, E., Vandereycken, W., & Vertommen, H. (1989). Multimethod investigation of eating disorder families. In W. Vandereycken, E. Kog, & J. Vanderlinden (Eds.), *The family approach to eating disorders.* New York: PMA.

Koss, M. P., & Shiang, J. (1994). Research on brief psychotherapy. In A. E. Bergin & S. L. Garfield (Eds.), *Handbook of psychotherapy and behavior change* (4th ed., pp. 664–700). New York: Wiley.

Kinsley, K., & Bry, B. H. (1991). Sequential analyses of adolescent, mother, and father behaviors in distressed and nondistressed families. *Child and Family Behavior Therapy, 13*(4), 45–62.

Krupnick, J., Sotsky, S., Simmens, S., & Moyer, J. (1992, June). *The role of the therapeutic alliance in psychotherapy and pharmacotherapy outcome: Findings from the NIMH Treatment of Depression Collaborative Research Program.* Paper presented at the annual meeting of the Society for Psychotherapy Research, Berkeley, CA.

Kumpfer, K. L. (1989). Family function factors associated with delinquency. In K. L. Kumpfer (Ed.), *Literature review of effective parenting projects: Strategies for high risk youth and families.* (Research Report No. 2). Washington, DC: Office of Juvenile Justice Delinquency Prevention.

Kurtines, W. & Szapocznik, J. (1996). Family interaction patterns: Structural family therapy within contexts of cultural diversity. In E. D. Hibbs & P. S. Jensen (Eds.), *Psychosocial treatments for child and adolescent disorders: Empirically based strategies for clinical practice.* Washington, DC: American Psychological Association.

Lambert, M. J. (1992). Implications of outcome research for psychotherapy integration. In J. C. Norcross & M. R. Goldstein (Eds.), *Handbook of psychotherapy integration.* New York: Basic Books.

Lambert, M. J., Shapiro, D. A., & Bergin, A. E. (1986). The effectiveness of psychotherapy. In S. L. Garfield & A. E. Bergin (Eds.), *Handbook of psychotherapy and behavior change* (3rd ed., pp. 157–211). New York: Wiley.

Lewis, R. A., Piercy, F. P., Sprenkle, D. H., & Trepper, T. S. (1990). Family based interventions for helping drug-abusing adolescents. *Journal of Adolescent Research, 5,* 82–95.

Liddle, H. A. (1991). Empirical values and the culture of family therapy. *Journal of Marital and Family Therapy, 17,* 327–348.

Liddle, H. A. (1992). A multidimensional model for the adolescent who is abusing drugs and alcohol. In W. Snyder & T. Ooms (Eds.), *Empowering families, helping adolescents: Family-centers treatment of adolescents with alcohol, drug and other mental health problems.* Washington, DC: U.S. Public Health Service, U.S. Government Printing Office.

Liddle, H. A. (1994). The anatomy of emotions in family

therapy with adolescents. *Journal of Adolescent Research, 9,* 120–157.

Liddle, H. A. (1995). Conceptual and clinical dimensions of a multidimensional, multisystems engagement strategy in family-based adolescent treatment (Special issue: Adolescent Psychotherapy). *Psychotherapy: Theory, Research and Practice, 32,* 39–58.

Liddle, H. A., & Dakof, G. A. (1994, February). *Effectiveness of family-based treatments for adolescent substance abuse.* Paper presented at the 1994 Society for Psychotherapy Research Conference, Santa Fe, NM.

Liddle, H. A., & Dakof. G. A. (1995a). Efficacy of family therapy for drug abuse: Promising but not definitive. *Journal of Marital and Family Therapy, 21*(4), 511–544.

Liddle, H. A., & Dakof, G. A. (1995b). Family-based treatment for adolescent drug use: State of the science. In E. Rahdert & D. Czechowicz (Eds.), *Adolescent drug abuse: Clinical assessment and therapeutic interventions* (pp. 218–254). NIDA Research Monograph No. 156, NIH Publication No. 95-3908. Rockville, MD: National Institute on Drug Abuse.

Liddle, H. A., Dakof, G. A., & Diamond, G. (1991). Multidimensional family therapy with adolescent substance abuse. In E. Kaufman & P. Kaufman (Eds.), *Family therapy with drug and alcohol abuse* (pp. 120–178). Boston: Allyn & Bacon.

Liddle, H. A., Dakof, G. A., Parker, K., Diamond, G. S., Barrett, K., & Tejeda, M. (in press). Multidimensional family therapy of adolescent substance abuse.

Lidz, T., Cornelison, A., Fleck, S., & Terry, D. (1957). Intrafamilial environment of the schizophrenic patient. I: The father. *Psychiatry, 20,* 329–342.

Lidz, R. W., & Lidz, T. (1949). The family environment of schizophrenic patients. *American Journal of Psychiatry, 106,* 332–345.

Lidz, T., Parker, B., & Cornelison, A. R. (1956). The role of the father in the family environment of the schizophrenic patient. *American Journal of Psychiatry, 113,* 126–132.

Luborsky, L., Barber, J., & Crits-Christoph, P. (1990). Theory-based research for understanding the process of dynamic psychotherapy. *Journal of Consulting and Clinical Psychology, 58,* 281–287.

Magnusson, D. (1995). Individual development: A holistic, integrated model. In P. Moen, G. H. Elder, & K. Luscher (Eds.) *Examining lives in context,* (pp. 19–61). Washington, DC: American Psychological Association.

Madanes, C. (1981). *Strategic family therapy.* San Francisco: Jossey-Bass.

Marcus, M. A., & Wiener, M. (1989). Anorexia nervosa reconceptualized from a psychosocial transactional perspective. *American Journal of Orthopsychiatry, 59,* 346–354.

Margolin, G., Burman, B., & John, R. S. (1989). Home observations of married couples reenacting naturalistic conflicts. Special issue: Coding marital interaction. *Behavioral Assessment, 11*(1), 101–118.

Melidonis, G. G., & Bry, B. H. (1995). Effects of therapist exceptions questions on blaming and positive statements in families with adolescent behavior problems. *Journal of Family Psychology, 9*(4), 451–457.

Minuchin, S. (1974). *Families and family therapy.* Cambridge, MA: Harvard University Press.

Minuchin, S., Baker, L., Rosman, B. L., Liebman, R., Milman, L., & Todd, T. C. (1975). A conceptual model of psychosomatic illness in children. *Archives of General Psychiatry, 32,* 1031–1038.

Minuchin, S., & Fishman, H. C. (1981). *Family therapy techniques.* Cambridge, MA: Harvard University Press.

Minuchin, S., Montalvo, B., Guerney, B. G., Rosman, B. L., & Schumer, F. (1967). *Families of the slums.* New York: Basic Books.

Minuchin, S., Rosman, B. L., & Baker, L. (1978). *Psychosomatic families: Anorexia nervosa in context.* Cambridge, MA: Harvard University Press.

Morris, S., Alexander, J. F., & Waldron, H. (1988). Functional family therapy: Issues in clinical practice. In I. R. H. Falloon (Ed.), *Handbook of behavioral therapy* (pp. 109–127). New York: Guilford.

Muran, J. C., Gorman, B. S., Safran, J. D., Twining, L., Samstag, L. W., & Winston, A. (1995). Linking in-session change to overall outcome in short-term cognitive therapy. *Journal of Consulting and Clinical Psychology, 63,* 651–657.

Nichols, M. P. (1984). *Family therapy: Concepts and methods.* New York: Gardner.

Nichols, M. P., & Schwartz, R. C. (1995). *Family therapy: Concepts and methods* (3rd ed.). Boston: Allyn & Bacon.

Orlinsky, D. E., Grawe, K., & Parks, B. K. (1994). Process and outcome in therapy—noch einmal. In A. E. Bergin & S. L. Garfield (Eds.), *Handbook of psychotherapy and behavior change* (4th ed., pp. 270–376). New York: Wiley.

Palazzoli-Selvini, M., Boscolo, L., Cecchin, G. F., & Prata, G. (1974). The treatment of children through brief therapy of their parents. *Family Process, 13,* 429–442.

Papero, D. V. (1990). *Bowen family systems theory.* Boston: Allyn & Bacon.

Parker, J. G., & Asher, S. R. (1987). Peer relations and later personal adjustment: Are low-accepted children at risk? *Psychological Bulletin, 102,* 357–389.

Parsons, B. V., & Alexander, J. J. (1973). Short-term family intervention: A therapy outcome study. *Journal of Consulting and Clinical Psychology, 41,* 195–201.

Patterson, G. R. (1971). *Families: Applications of social learning to family life.* Champaign, IL: Research Press.

Patterson, G. R. (1982). *Coercive family process.* Eugene, OR: Castalia Publishing.

Patterson, G. R., & Dishion, T. J. (1985). Contributions of families and peers to delinquency. *Criminology, 23,* 63–79.

Patterson, G. R., & Forgatch, M. (1985). Therapist behavior as a determinant for client non-compliance: A paradox for the behavior modifier. *Journal of Consulting and Clinical Psychology, 53*(6), 846–851.

Pinsof, W. M., & Catherall, D. R. (1986). The integrative psychotherapy alliance: Family, couple, and individual therapy scales. *Journal of Marital and Family Therapy, 12,* 137–151.

Raudenbush, S. W. (1993). Hierarchical linear models and experimental data. In L. Edwards (Ed.), *Applied analysis of variance in behavioral sciences* (pp. 459–496). New York: Marcel Dekker.

Robbins, M. S., Alexander, J. F., Newell, R. M., & Turner, C. W. (1996). The immediate effect of reframing on client attitude in family therapy. *Journal of Family Psychology, 10*(1), 28–34.

Robbins, M. S., Alexander, J. F., & Turner, C. W. (submitted for publication). The impact of therapist reframing on reciprocal pejorative family member interactions in family therapy with delinquent youth.

Robbins, M. S., Mitrani, V., Zarate, M., Coatsworth, D., & Szapocznik, J. (1996, June). *Linking process to outcome in structural family therapy with drug using youth: An examination of the process of family therapy in successful and unsuccessful outcome cases.* Paper presented at the 27th Annual meeting of the Society for Psychotherapy Research, Amelia Island, FL.

Russell, G. F. M., Szmukler, G. I., Dare, C., & Eisler, I. (1987). An evaluation of family therapy in anorexia nervosa and bulimia nervosa. *Archives of General Psychiatry, 44,* 1047–1056.

Rutter, M. (1980). *Changing youth in a changing society.* Cambridge, MA: Harvard University Press.

Rutter, M. (1983). School effects on pupils progress: Research findings and policy implications. *Child Development, 54,* 1–29.

Rutter, M., & Cox, A. (1985). Other family influences. In M. Rutter & L. Hersov (Eds.), *Child and adolescent psychiatry.* Boston: Blackwell Scientific Publication.

Rutter, M., & Garmezy, N. (1983). Developmental psychopathology. In P. H. Mussen (Ed.) *Handbook of child psychology* (Vol. IV). New York: Wiley.

Rutter, M., & Guilier, H. (1983). *Juvenile delinquency: Trends and perspectives.* New York: Penguin.

Safran, J., Crocker, P., McMain, S., & Murray, P. (1990). Therapeutic alliance rupture as therapy event for empirical investigation. *Psychotherapy, 27,* 154–165.

Santisteban, D. A., Coatsworth, J. D., Perez-Vidal, A., Mitroni, V. B., Jean-Gilles, M., & Szapocznik, J. (1997). Brief structural strategic family therapy with African American and Hispanic high risk youth: A report of outcome. *Journal of Community Psychology, 25*(5), 453–471.

Santisteban, D. A., Szapocznik, J., Perez-Vidal, A., Kurtines, W. M., Coatsworth, J. D., LaPerriere, A., & Lyons-Howie, E. (1996). *The efficacy of brief strategic/structural family therapy in modifying behavior problems and an exploration of the role that family functioning plays in behavior change.*

Schmidt, S., Liddle, H. A., & Dakof, G. (1996). Changes in parenting practices and adolescent drug abuse during multidimensional family therapy. *Journal of Family Psychology, 10*(1), 12–27.

Scopetta, M. A., Szapocznik, J., King, O. E., Ladner, R., Alegre, C., & Tillman, W. S. (1977). *The Spanish Drug Rehabilitation Research Project* (Final Report to NIDA Grant No. H81 DA 01696-03). Miami, FL: University of Miami Spanish Family Guidance Center.

Shields, C. G., Sprenkle, D. G., & Constantine, J. A. (1991). Anatomy of an initial interview: The importance of joining and structuring skills. *The American Journal of Family Therapy, 19*(1), 3–18.

Simcha-Fagan, O., Gersten, J. C., & Langner, T. S. (1986). Early precursors and concurrent correlates of patterns of illicit drug use in adolescence. *Journal of Drug Issues, 16,* 7–28.

Sluzki, C. E. (1978). Marital therapy from a systems theory perspective. In T. J. Paolino & B. S. McCrady (Eds.), *Marriage and marital therapy.* New York: Brunner/Mazel.

Speck, R. V. (1964). Family therapy in the home. *Journal of Marriage and the Family, 26,* 72–76.

Speck, R. V., & Attneave, C. (1973). *Family networks: Rehabilitation and healing.* New York: Pantheon.

Speer, D. C., & Greenbaum, P. E. (1995). Five methods for computing significant individual client change and improvement rates: support for an individual growth curve approach. *Journal of Consulting and Clinical Psychology, 63*(6), 1044–1048.

Stanton, M. D., Todd, T. C., and associates. (1982). *The family therapy of drug abuse and addiction.* New York: Guilford.

Steinberg, L., Darling, N., Fletcher, A. C., Brown, B. B. & Dornbush, S. M. (1995). Authoritative parenting and adolescent adjustment: An ecological journey. In P. Moen, G. H. Elder & K. Luscher (Eds.) *Examining lives in context* Washington, DC: American Psychological Association.

Steinberg, L., Dornbush, S. M., & Brown, B. B. (1992). Ethnic differences in adolescent achievement: An ecological perspective. *American Psychologist, 47,* 723–729.

Steinberg, L. Mounts, N., Lamborn, S. & Dornbusch, S. (1991). Authoritative parenting and adolescent adjustment across varied ecological niches. *Journal of Research on Adolescence, 1*(1), 19–36.

Steinglass, P. (1987). A systems view of family interaction and psychopathology. In T. Jacob (Ed.), *Family interaction and psychopathology: Theories, methods, and findings,* (pp. 25–65). New York: Plenum.

Strupp, H. H., & Hadley, S. W. (1979). Specific versus nonspecific factors in psychotherapy: A controlled study of outcome. *Archives of General Psychiatry, 36,* 1125–1136.

Szapocznik, J., & Coatsworth, J. D. (submitted for publication). Structural ecosystems theory: An ecodevelopmental framework for organizing risk and protection for drug abuse. *American Psychologist.*

Szapocznik, J., & COSSMHO (1994). Structural family therapy. In J. Szapocznik (Ed.), *A Hispanic/Latino family approach to substance abuse prevention* (pp. 41–74). Rockville, MD: Center for Substance Abuse Prevention.

Szapocznik, J., & Kurtines, W. M. (1989). *Breakthroughs in family therapy with drug abusing and problem youth.* New York: Springer.

Szapocznik, J., & Kurtines, W. M. (1993). Family psychology and cultural diversity: Opportunities for theory, research and application. [Invited Article] *American Psychologist, 48*(4), 400–407.

Szapocznik, J., Kurtines, W. M., Foote, F., Perez-Vidal, A., & Hervis, O. E. (1983). Conjoint versus one person family therapy: Some evidence for effectiveness of conducting family therapy through one person. *Journal of Consulting and Clinical Psychology, 51,* 881–899.

Szapocznik, J., Kurtines, W. M., Foote, F., Perez-Vidal, A., & Hervis, O. E. (1986). Conjoint versus one person family therapy: Further evidence for the effectiveness of conducting family therapy through one person. *Journal of Consulting and Clinical Psychology, 54*(3), 395–397.

Szapocznik, J., Kurtines, W. M., Perez-Vidal, A., Hervis, O. E., & Foote, F. (1989). One person family therapy. In R. A. Wells & V. J. Gianetti (Eds.), *Handbook of brief psychotherapies* (pp. 493–510). New York: Plenum.

Szapocznik, J., Kurtines, W., Santisteban, D. A., Pantin, H., Scopetta, M., Mancilla, Y., Aisenberg, S., McIntosh, S., Perez-Vidal, A., & Coatsworth, J. D. (1997). The evolution of structural ecosystemic theory for working with Latino families. In J. Garcia & M. C. Zea (Eds.) *Psychological interventions and research with Latino populations* (pp. 166–189). Boston: Allyn & Bacon.

Szapocznik, J., Perez-Vidal, A., Brickman, A. L., Foote, F. H., Santisteban, D., Hervis, O. & Kurtines, W. M. (1988). Engaging adolescent drug abusers and their families in treatment: A strategic structural systems approach. *Journal of Consulting and Clinical Psychology, 56,* 552–557.

Szapocznik, J., Perez-Vidal, A.., Hervis, O. E., Brickman, A. L., & Kurtines, W. M. (1989). Innovations in family therapy: Strategies for overcoming resistance to treatment. In R. A. Wells & V. J. Giannetti (Eds.), *Handbook of brief psychotherapies* (pp. 93–114). New York: Plenum.

Szapocznik, J., Rio, A. T., Hervis, O. E., Mitrani, V. B., Kurtines, W. M., & Faraci, A. M. (1991). Assessing change in family functioning as a result of treatment: The Structural Family Systems Rating Scale (SFSR). *Journal of Marital and Family Therapy, 17*(3), 295–310.

Szapocznik, J., Rio, A. T., Murray, E., Cohen, R., Scopetta, M. A., Rivas-Vasquez, A., Hervis, O. E., & Posada, V. (1989). Structural family versus psychodynamic child therapy for problematic Hispanic boys. *Journal of Consulting and Clinical Psychology, 57*(5), 571–578.

Szapocznik, J., Santisteban, D., Rio, A., Perez-Vidal, A., & Kurtines, W. M. (1989). Family Effectiveness Training: An intervention to prevent drug abuse and problem behavior in Hispanic adolescents. *Hispanic Journal of Behavioral Sciences, 11*(1), 3–27.

Szapocznik, J., Santisteban, D., Rio, A., Perez-Vidal, A.,

Kurtines, W. M., & Hervis, O. E. (1986). Bicultural effectiveness training (BET): An intervention modality for families experiencing intergenerational/intercultural conflict. *Hispanic Journal of Behavioral Sciences, 6*(4), 303–330.

Szmukler, G. I., Eisler, I., Russell, G. F. M., & Dare, C. (1985). Anorexia nervosa, parental "expressed emotion" and dropping out of treatment. *British Journal of Psychiatry, 147,* 265–271.

Tolan, P. H., Cromwell, R. E., & Brasswell, M. (1986). Family therapy with delinquents: A critical review of the literature. *Family Process, 25,* 619–650.

Tolan, P. H., Guerra, N. G., & Kendall, P. C. (1995). A developmental-ecological perspective on antisocial behavior in children and adolescents: Toward a unified risk and intervention framework. *Journal of Consulting and Clinical Psychology, 63,* 579–584.

Von Bertalanffy, L. (1968). *General systems theory.* New York: Braziller.

Waterhouse, G. J., & Strupp, H. H. (1984). The patient–therapist relationship: Research from the psychodynamic perspective. *Clinical Psychology Review, 4,* 77–92.

Weinberger, J. (1995). Common factors aren't so common: The common factors dilemma. *Clinical Psychology: Science and Practice, 2,* 45–69.

Weiss, P. A. (1969). The living system: Determinism stratified. In A. Koestler & J. R. Smythies (Eds.), *Beyond reductionism* (pp. 3–42). Boston. Beacom Press.

Wells, R. A., & Dezen, A. E. (1978). The results of family therapy revisited: The nonbehavioral methods. *Family Process, 17,* 251–274.

Werner, E. E., & Smith, R. S. (1992). *Overcoming the odds: High risk children from birth to adulthood.* Ithaca, NY: Cornell University Press.

Widom, C. S. (1989). Does violence beget violence? A critical examination of the literature. *Psychological Bulletin, 106,* 3–28.

Wynne, J. C., Ryckoff, I., Day, J., & Hirsch, S. I. (1958). Pseudo-mutuality in the family relationships of schizophrenics. *Psychiatry, 21,* 205–220.

5.08
Parent Training for Child Conduct Problems

CAROLYN WEBSTER-STRATTON and CAROLE HOOVEN
University of Washington, Seattle, WA, USA

5.08.1 INTRODUCTION

Prior to 1965, most attempts to treat childhood behavior problems focused exclusively on the child. Approaches included outpatient play therapy and inpatient child therapy. Since the mid-1970s, however, there has been a shift in treatment philosophy for child conduct problems from an exclusive focus on the child to recognition of the primary social context in which the child lives—that is, the family. As a result, parent training (PT) has become an integral part of services for many childhood disorders including autism and developmental disabilities (Schreibman, Kaneko, & Koegel, 1991); academic, learning and language delays (Laski, Charlop, & Schreibman, 1988); externalizing problems such as attention deficit disorder (Anastopoulos, Barkley, & Sheldon, 1996); oppositional and conduct disorders (Forehand, Steffe, Furey, & Walley, 1983; Patterson, Chamberlain, & Reid, 1982; Webster-Stratton, Kolpacoff, & Hollinsworth, 1988); and internalizing disorders such as fears and anxiety disorders (Barrett, Dadds, & Rapee, 1993). PT is also widely used with abused and neglected children as a component of a multifaceted intervention (Lutzker, 1992), as well as for maritally distressed parents (Dadds, Schwartz, & Sanders, 1987) and for parents who are divorced (Grych & Finchman, 1992). This extensive empirical base supports the hypothesis that when parents are trained to implement behavior change strategies, there is a corresponding improvement in their parenting interactions, which in turn results in improvements in children's social and emotional adjustment.

PT is a generic term used herein to refer to forms of intervention for child behavior problems in which parents are trained to work with their children. In this approach parents are not only included in the therapeutic process, they are utilized as cotherapists working under the guidance of the therapist to invoke change in their child's behavior. The training focuses on altering parents' perceptions, attributions, affect, and parenting behaviors toward their children. The term "parent training" is used here in preference to other terms such as "family management training," "parent–child interactional training," or "functional family therapy" to more accurately reflect the fact that in PT it is the parents who are the targets of the treatment and prevention efforts. PT is an empirically supported, therapeutic process based on the twin assumptions that, since parents are the primary socializing agents in their children's lives, parenting practices are important— sometimes the critical determinants—in the

development and maintenance of many maladaptive child behaviors and, more importantly, that positive parenting practices are the key to facilitating and maintaining positive changes in child behavior.

There are many versions of PT, but they all share several characteristics in common. First, it is the parents who are trained; there is no direct intervention with the children. Second, parents are taught to identify, observe and define behaviors they want to increase or decrease. Third, parents learn social learning principles including positive reinforcement (e.g., praise and incentive programs) and discipline strategies (e.g., ignoring, loss of privileges, time out). Fourth, they are taught these approaches by means of interactive discussion, modeling, role playing, videotape demonstrations, home assignments, and direct feedback.

A number of theories about the socialization of behavior and emotion have shaped the specific methods, goals, content, and therapeutic process of different PT programs. A parent's function may be formulated as a teacher, coach, model, relational partner, attachment figure, or proximal gatekeeper for the larger environmental conditions; and each shift in emphasis brings a somewhat different focus for PT. Moreover, as current theories of child psychopathology have become more developmental in perspective and ecological in scope, PT has drawn from and integrated a number of theoretical perspectives, from general theories of learning and development to specific research areas and agendas. The evolution of PT from an operant behavioral approach to a model which includes relational, affective, and even broader ecological factors has brought a broader theoretical base, one that incorporates multiple theoretical approaches.

5.08.1.1 General Theoretical Underpinnings

PT draws from and includes theories of learning, theories of therapeutic change, and theories of child social and emotional development. The theoretical mainstays of PT can be, and often have been, subsumed under three general areas: (i) social learning theory, which includes behavioral and cognitive-behavioral views; (ii) "relational theories" such as attachment and psychodynamic theories; and (iii) a family systems perspective which includes the parent–child and other familial relationships. In addition, extensive research in child development has provided PT programs with a framework of empirically-based models of normal and pathological child development.

5.08.1.2 Contributions from Social Learning Theory

Contemporary PT has its roots in applied behavior analysis, models of operant behavior (Baer, Wolf, & Risely, 1968), and social learning theory (Bandura, 1977). A key assumption is that children's behaviors are learned from their interactions with significant persons in their lives, particularly their parents. Child problem behaviors—be they internalizing problems, such as fears and anxieties, or externalizing problems, such as defiance and aggression—are thought to be maintained by environmental reinforcements. The focus of PT from this perspective is on changing maladaptive child behaviors by changing the environmental contingencies which maintain these problem behaviors. For example, to take an internalizing problem such as a social phobia or separation anxiety, research has suggested that family interactions play a role in the development and maintenance of these fears (Kendall, 1992); parents may inadvertently reward anxious behavior by their attention as well as by removing aversive stimuli such as household chores or permitting a child to stay home from school (King, Hamilton, & Ollendick, 1988).

Therefore, this approach emphasized the importance of parents as "behavior change agents" for their children (Patterson, 1982; Patterson, Cobb, & Ray, 1973; Wahler, 1976). Parents were taught specific parenting strategies such as child-directed play, praise and tangible reinforcement, and discipline approaches such as ignoring misbehavior, time out and response cost. These parenting behaviors and strategies helped parents avoid negative reinforcement traps and coercive interactions with their children (Patterson, 1982, pp. 27, 28) as well as positive reinforcement traps (Wahler, 1975) which were thought to lead to escalating child behavior problems. Likewise, this conceptualization has been particularly useful and relevant for child externalizing problems. Research has demonstrated that parents of antisocial children do engage in particular parenting practices which promote aggressive behavior (through attention and compliance to child coercive strategies) and suppress prosocial behavior (by ignoring or even providing aversive consequences) (Hinshaw & Anderson, 1996; Patterson, 1982, 1986).

Social learning theory (Bandura, 1977) posits that behavior is learned not only by experiencing the direct consequences of those behaviors, but also by observing similar behavior and its consequences. Thus, Bandura emphasized the importance of parents "modeling" appropriate social interactions for their children, since children learn by watching their parents interact (with each other and with others), and not just by their responses to the child's own behaviors. Behavioral models are particularly potent when they are persons of higher social status, such as parents, teachers, and older peers, and when their acts are perceived to be rewarded or accepted (Bandura, 1977). Again, the research supports this modeling theory in studies which have shown that children with high levels of fears and anxieties are more likely than nonfearful children to have anxious or fearful parents (Kendall, 1992), as well as studies showing that aggressive children are more likely than nonaggressive children to have parents who use aggressive discipline or who are antisocial themselves (Patterson, DeBaryshe, & Ramsey, 1989).

In accordance with this social learning model, then, PT programs are aimed at helping parents identify and isolate their children's prosocial (or appropriate) and maladaptive (or inappropriate) behaviors, change the reinforcement contingencies, and implement rewards for positive behavior and sanctions for negative behavior. The general purpose of PT from this perspective is to alter the interactions between parents and children so that prosocial behavior rather than coercive behavior is modeled and reinforced by parents (Kazdin, 1987). Social learning theory informs PT's methods as well as content, using live and videotape modeling, role play and rehearsal of new skills, home practice assignments, and direct reinforcement (social and tangible) of parents for their achievements during training.

5.08.1.3 Contributions from Cognitive Psychology

Other theoretical perspectives helped expand our understanding of not only the importance of training parents to change their behavior responses to children but also the importance of influencing parents' perceptions, affect, and cognitions about their children. Cognitive psychology, in particular, focuses on the meanings we make of life events, and how those meanings influence our motivation, behavior, and ability to change. Cognitive events such as attributional biases, self-efficacy beliefs, and negative self-statements influence the course of psychopathology as well as the ability to parent effectively. Bandura proposed that central to parents' ability to change their behavior is their belief about their own self-efficacy (Bandura, 1982)—that is, their belief about the degree to which they can be successful with their children. Attribution theory (Smith & O'Leary, 1995) and learned helplessness theory (Abramson, Seligman, & Teasdale, 1978; Folkman & Lazarus, 1988; Seligman, 1975) are other cognitive theories that posit the importance of beliefs and expectations in influencing parents' interactions with their children.

These expanded theoretical perspectives led to a blending of cognitive and behavioral theories and a concomitant shift in PT known as the cognitive-social learning approach. The cognitive-social learning approach treats cognitions as covert behaviors, subject to the same laws of change as more overt behaviors, and hence appropriately examined, isolated, and differentially reinforced (Meichenbaum & Turk, 1987) as part of the PT process. For example, if parents perceive their children as more powerful than themselves, as motivated and able to hurt them, perhaps even predicting when their child is young that their child will become a juvenile delinquent, those parents are less likely to respond to their child's misbehavior in a positive and consistent manner. Furthermore, parents' negative expectations for a child may become a self-fulfilling prophesy, influencing the child's own self-perceptions and expectations. Parents are often unaware of how their beliefs about their own powerlessness relative to their child can undermine their parenting interactions—resulting in poor limit setting, withdrawal from conflict, lack of structure, and further loss of control. Out of this school of thought have come adjuncts to PT including training for parents in coping via self-statements, problem-solving techniques, stress management, and self-reinforcement strategies.

5.08.1.4 Contributions from Relational Theories

In the category of relational theories attachment theory and psychoanalytic theory are included because of their central concern with emotion, affective processes, and the quality of relationships. Although a more positive parent–child relationship is expected to result from improved parenting strategies, an articulated relational theory did not initially inform PT. Qualitative aspects of parent–child interactions were only indirectly acknowledged. For instance, even in those few behavioral programs which did include training for parents in child-directed play skills, the purpose of this training was to increase the reinforcing power of parental attention; improving relationships was merely a secondary benefit (Forehand & McMahon, 1981). However, as PT expanded beyond its operant focus, child-directed play therapy became a technique and a source of

theory concerning the affective and relational aspects of parenting (Eyberg & Boggs, 1989), as separate from behavioral management. Within a relational focus, PT aims to increase parent–child bonding by teaching parents techniques for increasing their positive interactions with their child—as a goal in itself. The emphasis is on increased expression and communication of positive affect, including love, affection, acceptance, enjoyment, and empathy as well as increasing parents' pleasure in their children and enjoyment of play with them. Another aspect to PT that grows out of relational theory is training parents in how to respond to children's expression of emotions as well as how to manage their own emotions. This renewed interest in affective processes reflects a growing recognition from the research that a parent's emotional expression and regulation are likely to affect the quality of their children's emotional language, which in turn affects the quality of their social relationships and ability to self-regulate in the face of conflict.

5.08.1.5 Contributions from Family Systems Theory

Current PT programs have also been influenced by family systems theory. In this theoretical perspective, family factors are recognized as the larger context for parent–child interactions. From a family systems perspective, this means the focus of concern in PT is enlarged to include such factors as family roles, rules, and communication patterns, and those factors are conceptualized as family structures (Minuchin, 1974) and processes (Haley, 1976). A family systems perspective emphasizes the impact of these structures and processes on the parent–child relationship and behaviors. Inherent in the treatment of families from the systems perspective is an understanding of how family dysfunction (e.g., marital conflict) impacts both parent and child functioning, and PT targets not just parenting behaviors but family interaction patterns (including parent–child, marital, and sibling relationships), family perceptions of individual members, as well as parents' memories of their family of origin and what they learned from that experience.

5.08.1.6 Emerging Perspectives

More recently, in the early 1990s, functional contextualism (Biglan, 1993) has led to our understanding of how social environment—such as stressful life events, socioeconomic status, racism, lack of support systems—influence parents' ability to maintain behavior change. At this point the influence of this perspective on PT programs is still slight, but therapists are beginning to consider factors such as these when designing programs for socio-economically deprived families and families experiencing considerable life stress.

5.08.2 CHILD CONDUCT PROBLEMS

Despite some evidence suggesting that PT may be a useful treatment for children's internalizing disorders (see Sanders, 1996 for review), this chapter focuses on PT as a treatment approach for young preschool and school-age children with oppositional defiant disorder (ODD) and conduct disorder (CD), defined generically in this paper as conduct problems. We have confined our review of PT to the treatment of conduct problems because there exists a large body of programmatic research regarding the etiology and treatment of conduct problems and because comparatively less is known about the causes of internalizing disorders. Conduct problems frequently co-occur with other disorders such as attention deficit disorder, learning disabilities, language delays, and internalizing problems such as anxiety and somatization. Moreover, children with conduct problems frequently come from families who are experiencing considerable marital discord, depression, and distress. What we know about PT as an intervention for children with conduct problems may provide a paradigm for other less well-researched child-hood disorders, including internalizing disorders.

5.08.2.1 Prevalence

Childhood conduct problems are the most frequently occurring disorder in both clinic-referred and general populations (Quay, 1986). Results of epidemiological studies have indicated that the percentage of young children meeting the criteria for the clinical diagnoses of ODD and CD ranges from 7% to 25%, with the prevalence varying according to the population surveyed (Campbell, 1995; Landy & Peters, 1991; Richman, Stevenson, & Graham, 1982). Even for preschoolers, relatively high proportions of parents complain of noncompliance, limited self-control, aggression, and poor relations with siblings and peers (Richman et al., 1982). In a study involving over 400 high-risk families in Seattle, Washington, Webster-Stratton (1995) reported that more than 25% of children scored above the 90th percentile for aggressive behaviors as reported by their mothers. In a large-scale screening study of

day-care attendees (2–4 years old) in rural Vermont, Crowther, Bond, and Rolf (1981) found that at least 20% of the children exhibited high frequencies of aggressive and disruptive behaviors, with the greatest severity observed among preschool boys. Boys are two to three times more likely than girls to manifest conduct problems (Quay, 1986).

"Externalizing" behavior problems are characterized by high rates of hyperactivity, aggression, impulsivity, defiance, and noncompliance (Campbell, 1995; Campbell & Ewing, 1990; Robins, 1981). The greatest stability in preschool child behavior problems occurs among externalizing problems in contrast to internalizing disorders, which are age-specific and usually but not always remit over the course of development (Fisher, Rolf, Hasazi, & Cummings, 1984). A variety of studies have shown high continuity between behavior problems in the early preschool years and conduct disorders in adolescence (Egeland, Kalkoske, Gottesman, & Erickson, 1990; Richman et al., 1982; Rose, Rose, & Feldman, 1989). Campbell's (1991) review of a series of longitudinal studies of hard-to-manage preschoolers reveals a surprising convergence of findings. At least 50% of preschool children with moderate to severe externalizing problems continued to show some degree of disturbance at school age, with boys doing more poorly than girls. Of those with continuing behavior problems, 67% met diagnostic criteria for attention deficit hyperactivity disorder (ADHD), ODD, or CD at age 9. Moreover, Eyberg (1992) points out that this percentage may be an underestimate, since many of the most dysfunctional families were lost to follow-up.

Developmental theorists have suggested that there may be two developmental pathways related to conduct disorders: the "early-onset" vs. "late-onset" pathways (Patterson et al., 1989). The hypothesized "early-onset" pathway begins formally with the emergence of aggressive and oppositional disorders (ODD) in the early preschool period, progresses to aggressive (e.g., fighting) and nonaggressive (e.g., lying and stealing) symptoms of conduct disorders in middle childhood, and then develops into the most serious symptoms by adolescence, including interpersonal violence and property violations (Lahey, Loeber, Quay, Frick, & Grimm, 1992). In addition, there is an expansion of the settings in which the problem behaviors occur, from home to daycare or preschool, then to school, and finally to the broader community. For "late-onset" (adolescent-onset) conduct disorders, the prognosis seems more favorable. Adolescents who are most likely to be chronically antisocial are those who first evidenced symptoms of aggressive behaviors in the pre-school years, followed by early-onset ODD or CD (White & Bailey, 1990). Children with early-onset ODD also account for a disproportionate share of delinquency in adolescence. Thus ODD is a sensitive predictor of subsequent CD, and the primary developmental pathway for serious conduct disorders in adolescence and adulthood appears to be established in the preschool period (Loeber, 1991).

The next section discusses theories regarding the etiology of conduct problems. These are important in terms of their implications for intervention, including PT.

5.08.2.2 Etiological Models

Theories regarding the causes of child conduct problems posit five different types of influence on child behavior: biological, attachment, family and parent–child interactions, sociocognitive, and environmental. Due to space limitations we will focus primarily on parental and familial models because of their clear implications for PT. However, it should be clear that by limiting our discussion of the biological, attachment, and sociocognitive models we do not mean these should be ignored and should not be enlisted when appropriate nor do we mean to imply that these are necessarily competing models. For instance, research indicates that biological and environmental factors are interrelated and transactional (Caspi & Moffitt, 1995). A more complete review of these models is available from the first author.

5.08.2.2.1 Biological model

Psychobiological research on child conduct disorders has lagged behind similar work on adult criminality and antisocial behavior, but is gaining recognition—particularly research concerning the temperamental, psychophysiological, and neurophysiological aspects of externalizing disorders. Still, many studies suffer from small or incompletely specified samples, lack of diagnostic specificity, and lack of longitudinal follow-up; there is a need for replication and cross-validation. The biological model argues that some abnormal aspect of the child's internal organization at the physiological, neurological, and/or neuropsychological level (which may be genetically transmitted) is at least partially responsible for the development of conduct problems. The most overt evidence for a biological component for children with ODD/CD includes the disproportion of boys to girls and the apparent heritability of antisocial traits, based on the high number of criminals in

some families (Hutchings & Mednick, 1977). Adherents of this view have proceeded somewhat cautiously, lest they appear to be endorsing biological determinism. However, since the late 1980s a substantial body of research has been accumulating which supports the inclusion of biological factors in models of development and maintenance of conduct disorder (see Hinshaw & Anderson, 1996 for a review).

Biological explanations for antisocial behavior need not imply that an antisocial personality is biologically predetermined. Even biology is hypothesized to be subject to environmental impact. Biology in itself is only suggestive of a vulnerability to other risk factors (e.g., parental socialization influences) for antisocial behaviors. Furthermore, biological markers of antisocial behavior have thus far been isolated only for subsets of children with more extreme deficits, such as undersocialized aggressive conduct disorder, who are often doubly impaired with ADHD. We do not know what, if anything, biology has to contribute to our understanding of milder deficits. Lahey, Hart, Pliszka, Applegate, and McBurnett (1993) state clearly that investigation of biological variables such as neurotransmitters, brain imaging techniques, skin conductance, or hormonal influences does not imply that psychosocial factors have no role in the maintenance of childhood conduct problems. On the contrary, they postulate "that a socio-environmental event (e.g., abnormal infant experience) could be one of the causes of aggression, but that the effect of this experience on aggression is mediated by alterations in neurotransmitter activity" (Lahey et al., 1993, p. 142). Indeed, the amount of variance accounted for by biological factors appears to be relatively small. Factors such as family support, quality of parent management strategies and socioeconomic status appear to interact with the child's biology or temperament to influence outcome, again suggesting the mediating role of the child's microsystems.

The research findings regarding children with conduct problems who have such difficulties as low autonomic reactivity (Quay, 1993) have implications for how biological deficits may be amplified over time and for how parenting can exacerbate or minimize inherent deficits. For example, children with biological deficits are not as responsive to their parents' normal efforts to praise, reward, set limits, and impose negative consequences; they may even appear to their parents to be indifferent to their discipline attempts. This lack of responsiveness on the part of the child not only makes the child less reinforcing to the parent but also leads parents to feel the effects of their parenting approaches are unpredictable. As parents continue to experience a lack of success in parenting, they develop a low sense of self-efficacy, become more inconsistent in their parenting responses and sometimes resort to increased use of spanking and harsh punishment.

This theory suggests the need for PT programs which help parents understand their children's biological deficits (their unresponsiveness to aversive stimuli and heightened interest in novelty), and support parents in their use of effective parenting approaches so that they can continue to be positive and provide consistent responses. Parents who are concerned that their child is not responsive to praise or appears not to care about consequences can learn that this apparent invulnerability is a coping response for dealing with negative feedback about his or her behavior. The data regarding autonomic underarousal theory suggests that these children will require over teaching (i.e., repeated learning trials) in order to learn to inhibit undesirable behaviors and to manage emotion. They will need consistent, clear, specific limit setting that utilizes simple language and concrete cues and reminders. Their parents will need to rely on tangible reinforcement and novel reward systems, rather than punishment, and will need to help their children anticipate possible consequences. The research regarding these children's possible language and reading delays suggests the need to train parents in ways to help their children with verbal skills such as self-talk management, problem solving, and communication, as well as reading skills.

5.08.2.2.2 Attachment model

Bowlby's (1980) observations of neglected infants introduced us to a new way of understanding children's emotional development. Both his method and thinking have led to attachment theory as a model for describing and accounting for the effects of parent–child relationships. Studies of attachment relationships have focused on mothers and infants; young school-age children have been studied much less frequently. Rarely has the research concerned itself with father/child attachment relationships. Specific research regarding the connections between children's attachment status and the development of conduct problems is very much in its infancy.

Since the late 1980s, methods of measuring attachment beyond toddlerhood have been developed, with two new attachment paradigms targeted for preschool and early primary age children (Cassidy & Marvin, 1992; Main & Cassidy, 1987). Several studies utilizing those

measures of attachment with young children have found relationships between insecure attachment and child aggressive behaviors (Greenberg, Speltz, & DeKlyen, 1993). However, attachment status on its own probably does not directly relate to conduct disorder, nor to any specific psychological disorder. The differences between high- and low-risk samples suggest that secure attachment serves as a protective factor in the presence of other risk factors for conduct problems (Dishion, French, & Patterson, 1995).

Finally, in postulating an association between early attachment and psychopathology, one must exercise caution. For attachment status interacts not only with parenting practices, but also emerges as a result of reciprocal interactions with other risk factors such as child biology and temperament, parent psychopathology and social stress. For example, an interaction of biology and attachment may operate as follows: for a certain subset of children with early-onset conduct problems, biology—that is, a difficult temperament—may underlie their difficulties in social learning and communication, both of which may influence mutual acceptance, leading to negative affect and attachment difficulties. In addition, parental depression has been shown to be linked to child attachment status (Radke-Yarrow, 1991; Speiker & Booth, 1988). Furthermore, both attachment and depression are related to parents' parenting skills. For example, in one study both insecurely attached mothers and depressed mothers were likely to retreat when their attempts to limit set with their children were met with resistance; they also showed more inappropriate use of affection. Finally, severe maternal depression, like other severe stressors, appears to be related to disorganized attachment status (Teti, Gelfand, & Messinger, 1995).

The concept of internal working models is helpful for PT programs because it focuses attention on the quality of parent–child relationships and the need for security and predictability in relationships. In the case of the insecurely attached child and parent, the model suggests the need for a more complex PT program involving a focus on relationship building, communications skills, cognitive techniques, and affect management skills. Along with parenting techniques, the insecurely attached parent will need to learn to control negative affect in the parent–child relationship and to communicate positive emotion such as empathy; beyond that, the parent may need help developing empathy and positive feelings for the child. PT can work with parents' perceptions of their child so that parents can recognize how their responses to their child's behavior may in a large part be based on their own past relationships with their parents and not on the child himself (Stroufe & Fleeson, 1986). The therapist's frequent articulation and expression of empathy during training for the parent and child as well as education about child development—specifically, the needs of difficult children—can help parents to understand their child's point of view. This change in perspective can ultimately lead to change in the parents' internal working model of the child, which can then lead to changes in the internal working model of the relationship for both the parent and child. PT for the insecurely attached child must also involve training the parent in attachment-promoting interactions, such as "child-directed play," a method of play which involves listening, following the child's lead, describing and reflecting on the child's actions, and praising and encouraging the child's ideas and behaviors. Daily child-directed play sessions influence the child's working model of the parent as well as the parent's working model of the child. Finally, the attachment perspective on PT suggests that the therapist's role is to provide a secure base for parents who are exploring new perspectives and models of relationships. By being consistent, predictable, empathic, accepting, and reinforcing, the therapist can provide the parent with a new working model, namely that of a supportive relationship.

5.08.2.2.3 Family functioning

Research findings have provided the impetus to expand our models to include other family and contextual variables, reflecting a broader systems view of family influences on children's behavior. Clear connections have been established between parental psychopathology (including antisocial behavior and depression), marital conflict and parenting interactions and child conduct problems.

(i) Antisocial behavior

Intergenerational linkages with respect to criminal behavior have been established for some time (Frick & Jackson, 1993), and there is considerable evidence associating certain types of parental psychopathology with childhood aggression and conduct problems (Patterson, 1982). Specifically, depression in the mother, alcoholism and substance abuse in the father (Frick et al., 1992), and antisocial and aggressive behavior in either the mother or the father (Faraone, Biederman, Keenan, & Tsuang, 1991; Frick, Kuper, Silverthorn, & Cotter, 1995) have been implicated as risk factors. An association has also been found between children's aggres-

sion and their parents' aggression at the same age (Huesmann, Eron, Lefkowitz, & Walder, 1984). In a prospective study of 171 clinic boys, parental antisocial personality disorder (APD) was a significant correlate of conduct problems, but the interaction of parental APD and the boys' verbal intelligence predicted the persistence of conduct problems over time (Lahey, Loeber, Hart, & Frick, 1995).

(ii) Depression

Depression—maternal depression in particular—has received a great deal of attention in terms of its influence on child adjustment. Children of depressed parents have been shown to be at increased risk for conduct problems (Downey & Coyne, 1990). Clinic mothers of children with conduct problems consistently rate themselves as more depressed (on the Beck Depression Inventory) than nonclinic mothers of typically developing children, suggesting a relationship between maternal depression and reported child behavior problems (Griest & Wells, 1983; Webster-Stratton & Hammond, 1988). Studies have suggested that depressed mothers make more negative appraisals of their children's behaviors (Schaughency & Lahey, 1985) than their spouses or nondepressed mothers (Webster-Stratton & Hammond, 1988). However, research (using direct observation) evaluating the relationship between depressed and nondepressed mothers' parenting behavior and their children's behavior has yielded conflicting conclusions. Some researchers (Hops et al., 1987; Rickard, Forehand, Wells, Griest, & McMahon, 1981) have found that depressed mothers of clinic-referred children use not more but fewer commands and criticisms than nondepressed mothers, while others have found maternal depression to be related to increased criticisms, spankings, and unsupportive or inconsistent parenting (Cunningham, Bennes, & Siegel, 1988; Webster-Stratton & Hammond, 1988). Still others have found no relationship between maternal depression and parenting behavior (Rogers & Forehand, 1983). Furthermore, the possible linkage between fathers' depression, parenting behaviors, and child conduct problems has not been explored in the research. Finally, it is important to recognize that depression is associated with other stress variables such as poverty, marital distress, and negative life events, making it difficult to determine what effects are attributable to depression *per se.*

The relationship between maternal depression and conduct problems has been conceptualized as follows: maternal depression results in negative appraisals of the child's behavior and contributes to a mother's negative responses (increased irritability, hostility, and punishment) to her child's misbehavior (Patterson, 1982). It has also been theorized that in response to an increase in maternal criticisms, the child displays an increase in noncompliance and other misbehaviors (McMahon & Forehand, 1984; Webster-Stratton & Hammond, 1988). These child misbehaviors further exacerbate the mother's depression, negative appraisals of the child and negative parenting behavior. Not only does the mother reinforce the child's misbehavior (through her negative attention), but the child learns more hostile and irritable behaviors through modeling the behavior of the depressed mother (Downey & Coyne, 1990). It has also been argued that depression contributes to the "coercive" cycle by resulting in decreased maternal attention for positive behaviors, decreased positive reinforcement, and lack of consistent supervision. In other words, depression results in the mother being emotionally unavailable and inattentive to the child. Thus maternal depression may indirectly lead to conduct problems as a result of negative reinforcement of inappropriate child behaviors, inconsistent limit setting, and emotional unavailability.

However, the association between maternal depression and child conduct problems is not adequate justification for concluding that depression "causes" child conduct problems. An alternative model could be postulated reversing the directionality—that is, the child's difficult and unpredictable negative behaviors are minimally reinforcing the mother's efforts, resulting in inconsistent and negative parenting responses; as the mother fails in her efforts to control the child's behavior, she becomes increasingly depressed. The research finding that maternal depression can improve with PT programs suggests that there is a three-way reciprocal interaction between the child's conduct problems, negative parenting style, and maternal depression. And as noted earlier it is highly probable that depression is linked to attachment status and that these two factors operate in some kind of synergy.

(iii) Marital conflict

In addition to depression in the parents, another family characteristic that has been found associated with the development of conduct problems is interparental conflict and divorce (Kazdin, 1987). In particular, boys appear to be more apt to show significant increases in antisocial behavior following divorce. However, some single parents and

their children appear to do relatively well over time postseparation, whereas others are chronically depressed and report increased stress levels. Once researchers began to differentiate between parental divorce, separation, and conflict, they began to understand that it was not divorce *per se* that was the critical factor in the child's subsequent behavior and socioemotional development, but rather the degree and intensity of parental conflict (O'Leary & Emery, 1982). For example, children whose parents divorce but whose homes are conflict-free are less likely to have problems than children whose parents stay together but experience a great deal of conflict (McCord, McCord, & Thurber, 1962). Children whose parents divorce and continue to have conflict have more problems than children whose parents experience conflict-free divorce (Hetherington, Cox, & Cox, 1982) Moreover, intact families who seek help for child behavior problems commonly present high levels of marital strife (Johnson & Lovitz, 1974; Oltmanns, Broderick, & O'Leary, 1977). In Webster-Stratton's studies of over 400 families with conduct problem children, 75% of the parents reported having been divorced at least once and/or described their current marriage as distressed; half of the married couples reported experiences with spouse abuse and violence. (Webster-Stratton, 1996b). These findings highlight the role of parents' marital conflict and spousal aggression as key factors influencing children's behavior problems. This is corroborated by the earlier work of Rutter et al. (1974), who reported that marriages characterized by tension and hostility were more closely associated with children's behavior disturbances than marriages characterized as apathetic and indifferent.

The role played by marital conflict, as well as parents' expression of negative affect, is further emphasized in studies of couples with children in laboratory situations requiring interpersonal negotiation or conflict resolution (Grych & Fincham, 1990). Studies suggest that factors such as children's exposure to marital conflict (Grych & Fincham, 1990; Porter & O'Leary, 1980), spousal physical aggression (Jouriles et al., 1991; Jouriles, Murphy, & O'Leary, 1989), and child-rearing disagreements (Dadds et al., 1987) account for variance beyond that of general marital stress in a control sample. Katz and Gottman (1994) found an association between high levels of "mutual contempt" or belligerence in couples' relationships and high levels of anger, physical aggression, and noncompliance in the children of those couples. Cummings and his colleagues have demonstrated that exposure to verbal anger and violence between adults is associated with anger and physical aggression in children (J. S. Cummings, Pellegrinia, Notarius, & E. M. Cummings, 1989). When children become sensitized to conflict as a result of repeated exposure to their parents' fights, they are more prone to emotional and behavioral dysregulation (i.e., greater distress and anger) (Cummings & Zahn-Waxler, 1992). These studies indicate the importance of moving beyond the study of individual risk factors (such as marital dissatisfaction and conflict) to the study of risk mechanisms—that is, the underlying processes that cause the risk factor to lead to conduct problems. The important questions then become: which aspect of conflict carries the risk? and, can it be mediated by an affectionate relationship between parent and child or by enlightened parenting?

However, like depression, marital variables appear to interact reciprocally in complex ways with other family and biological factors. For example, the effects of marital conflict and hostility on conduct problems appear to be mediated by the quality of parenting and degree of parental availability (Cummings, Simpson, & Wilson, 1993). Furthermore, Lahey et al. (1988) discovered that the effects of divorce on conduct problems were almost entirely related to parental diagnosis of antisocial personality disorder. Rutter (1986) has called attention to the relationship between marital discord and parental depression, and the possible causal role of marital discord in child behavioral outcomes. One possible hypothesis is that parents' depression affects their children by influencing marital functioning (increasing marital distress); marital functioning, in turn, affects parenting behaviors and parent–child interactions. An alternative hypothesis is that marital distress increases the likelihood of ineffective parenting; this contributes to child conduct problems, which in turn contribute to parental depression and further marital distress.

Certainly, the data suggest that parental depression covaries with marital distress and anger (Hay, Zahn-Waxler, Cummings, & Iannotti, 1992). Both overt and covert anger between parents are more frequent in homes of depressed parents. Depressed mothers have been shown to have more difficulty resolving conflicts than nondepressed mothers (Kochansaka, Kuczynski, Radke-Yarrow, & Welsh, 1987). Instead of attempting to reach compromises as a means of ending conflicts, depressed mothers have been reported to withdraw. However, impaired conflict resolution skills are not limited to the depressed mother. High levels of negative affect and hostility in mothers

or fathers certainly can disrupt a couple's ability to resolve conflicts. Moreover, it is further hypothesized that a couple's chronic failure to resolve conflicts leads to increasing negative affect in both parents, which may well contribute to escalating anger in parenting as well as marital interactions. In turn, children who are repeatedly exposed to their parents' negative affect and inability to resolve issues are said to be sensitized, whereby their negative reactions are intensified (E. M. Cummings & Davies, 1994).

A number of investigators are postulating that marital distress (conflict, hostility, etc.) is the primary mediator in the transmission of conduct problems, rather than depression *per se* (Cox, Puckering, Pound, & Mills, 1987). On the basis of their extensive review of the literature on children with depressed parents, Downey and Coyne (1990, p. 68) concluded that "marital discord is a viable alternative explanation for the general adjustment difficulties of children with a depressed parent" (see also Cummings & Davies, 1994). Nonetheless, the precise mechanisms underlying the relationship between marital conflict, depression, parenting, and child adjustment have been little investigated and are poorly understood. This is partially due to the fact that research has consisted largely of global self-report measures of marital satisfaction (or of depression) rather than measures of specific areas of disagreement and close observation of communication and affect. The prediction of child outcomes may be improved substantially by greater specification of how conflict is expressed within families. In a study of 120 families involving detailed observation of marital communication and problem-solving as well as observation of children's interactions with a best friend, Webster-Stratton (1996b) reported a correlation between, on the one hand, high levels of collaboration, engagement, and positive communication in couples and, on the other hand, lower levels of child noncompliance and externalizing problems at home, as well as a correlation between higher levels of positive social skills and conflict management skills and lower levels of negative interactions with peers. Alternatively, negative marital communication, low levels of communication, and poor parental problem-solving between couples were correlated with children's conduct problems at home and their poor conflict management skills with peers. These data provide some support for the notion that a couple's communication patterns in general— and their conflict-resolution style in particular—may be a key variable in the development of their child's conduct problems and peer relationships. This dovetails with the work of Cummings and colleagues (Cummings, Ballard, El-Sheikh, & Lake, 1991; Cummings & Davies, 1994), who found that helping families resolve their conflicts and providing children with explanations of their conflicts (i.e., absolving children from any blame) is helpful for children's emotional adjustment. They conclude that parents' successful resolution of conflicts results in a significant reduction in their children's anger and distress.

(iv) Parenting interactions

Parenting interactions are clearly the most well-researched and most important proximal cause of conduct problems. Research has indicated that parents of children diagnosed as ODD/CD lack certain fundamental parenting or behavior management skills. For example, those parents have been reported to exhibit fewer positive behaviors, to be more violent and critical in their use of discipline, to be more permissive, erratic, and inconsistent, to be more likely to fail to monitor or supervise their children's behaviors, and to be more likely to reinforce inappropriate behaviors and to ignore or punish prosocial behaviors (Patterson, 1982). The most influential developmental model for describing the family dynamics that underlie early antisocial behavior is Patterson's theory of the "coercive process" (Patterson, 1982), a process whereby children learn to escape or avoid parental criticism by escalating their negative behaviors, which in turn leads to increasingly aversive parent interactions. These negative responses, in turn, directly reinforce the child's deviant behaviors. Such mutual training in aversive responding intensifies both the child's aggressive behavior and the parents' hostile, nonresponsive behavior. These findings point also to the importance of the affective nature of the parent–child relationship. There is considerable evidence that a warm, positive bond between parent and child leads to more positive communication and parenting strategies and a more socially competent child (Baumrind, 1971).

Research on family socialization related to aggression increasingly recognizes the bi-directionality of child and parent behavior (Lytton, 1990). It is conceivable that negative parenting behavior is in part a reaction to difficult, oppositional, aggressive child behavior. In a study by Anderson, Lytton, and Romney (1986), mothers of boys with CD were compared with another group of mothers interacting with their own sons, with another boy who had a diagnosis of CD, and with a boy who had no diagnosis of CD. Mothers in both groups were more negative when interacting with the boys with CD, supporting the child-to-parent model. However, mothers of sons with CD were the most negative, suggesting that a history of negative interactions plays an important role (Anderson et al., 1986). The most conclusive evidence for the causal role of parenting interactions in promoting aggressive behavior arises from the research on PT interventions designed to decrease negative parenting behavior. Randomized studies have consistently shown that the risk for conduct problems decreases in groups of parents who received training in more effective parenting skills. These studies will be reviewed in a subsequent section of this paper.

This research regarding family functioning and parent–child interactions argues for parent training programs which attend not only to parenting skills but also to the other interpersonal and relational difficulties of family members. While positive parenting may buffer some of the effects of marital conflict, antisocial behavior, and depression, it would seem logical that if the intervention could also address parental psychopathology and reduce marital conflict, then there might be a greater likelihood for longer-lasting results from intervention.

5.08.2.2.4 Sociocognitive model

One way in which biological and family factors may exert effects on children's behavior problems is through the child's perceptions and evaluations of his or her social circumstances. The seminal work of Dodge and his colleagues has been extraordinarily helpful in suggesting ways in which children process and encode their social experiences (Crick & Dodge, 1994). A series of studies has revealed that aggressive children display deficits in social problem-solving skills (Asarnov & Callan, 1985), define problems in hostile ways, seek less information, generate fewer alternative solutions to social problems, and anticipate fewer consequences for aggression (Rubin & Krasnor, 1986; Slaby & Guerra, 1988). Aggressive behavior in children is correlated with their low empathy for others across a wide age range (Feshbach, 1989). It has also been suggested that children with conduct disorders distort social cues during peer interactions (Milich & Dodge, 1984), including attributing hostile intent to neutral situations. Aggressive children search for fewer cues or facts (i.e., they underutilize cues) when determining another's intentions (Dodge & Newman, 1981) and focus more on aggressive cues (Goutz, 1981). There is also a suggestion in the literature that attributional distortions and underutilization of cues pertain specifically to the subgroup of aggressive children with comorbid ADHD (Milich & Dodge, 1984). It is theorized that the impulsive cognitive style of these children limits their scanning of pertinent social cues before responding, so that they have difficulty perceiving or understanding another person's point of view and are unable to interpret interpersonal situations accurately. This would explain both their lack of social competence and their antisocial behavior. Negative exchanges with peers or with parents then contribute to rejection, further negative responses, and further negative attributions.

These findings argue for the need for PT programs to include ways that parents can teach their children more appropriate social skills as well as how to problem-solve, to control angry responses, and to anticipate negative consequences of aggression. They need to help their children learn to reframe negative appraisals, to detect and express their feelings appropriately, and to learn to take the perspective of another—i.e., develop empathy skills. Parents also need help finding ways to foster more positive peer relationships for their children, such as by inviting friends over and setting up structured home activities, by enrolling them in appropriate community programs, and so forth. These data also suggest the need for PT to be combined with child training (CT), a process whereby children are directly trained in social skills and problem-solving by teachers, school counselors, and parents.

5.08.2.2.5 Environmental model

(i) Insularity and lack of support

Parents' relationships with others outside the family have also been linked to child conduct problems. Studies have assessed both the quantity and quality of maternal contacts outside the home in clinic-referred families of children with conduct problems. Wahler (1980) has used the term "insular," defined as "a specific pattern of social contacts within the community that are characterized by a high level of negatively perceived social interchanges with relatives and/or helping agency representatives and by a low level of positively perceived supported interchanges with friends" (Wahler & Dumas, 1984), to characterize a subgroup of mothers of children with conduct problems. These mothers have been observed to be more aversive and use more aversive consequences with their children than "noninsular" mothers (Webster-Stratton, 1985a, 1985b). Wahler found that on days when mothers reported a high number of contacts with friends (days we

might characterize as "noninsular"), maternal aversive behavior and oppositional child behavior was consistently lower than on days when the number of contacts with friends was low (Wahler, 1980).

"Insular" families feel isolated not only from other parents in their communities, but also from their children's schools. They report frequent negative encounters with teachers concerning their children's behavior problems. Such encounters only add to parents' feelings of incompetence, their sense of helplessness regarding appropriate strategies to solve the problems, and their alienation from the school. Parents' inability to collaborate successfully with teachers (and thereby to reinforce them) contributes to teachers' perceptions of parents as uninterested or uncaring in regard to their children's problems. Such blaming attitudes on the part of teachers further escalates parents' sense of isolation and stigmatization regarding their child's problems. The child, in turn, is constantly observing his or her parents' mounting frustration and inability to communicate, as well as his or her teachers' lack of commitment to his family and his learning. This spiraling pattern of child negative behavior, parent demoralization and withdrawal, and teacher reactivity disrupts the connection between home and school and produces a dissonance between the socialization activities of the school and home, further contributing to the child's disengagement from the teacher and from school, and making eventual school drop out a likelihood.

(ii) Socioeconomic disadvantage

Isolation covaries with other important environmental factors that adversely affect family functioning, including economic disadvantage and an aggregate of related risk factors: unemployment, perceived stress, low education, and number of stressful life events. These have been shown to have negative effects on parenting, including the development of abusive disciplinary practices, and on child behavior, including early-onset conduct problems (Hawkins, Catalano, & Miller, 1992; Kazdin & Kolko, 1986; Rutter & Giller, 1983). Low-income parents are more at risk than are middle-income parents for high levels of psychological stress (Gecas, 1979), "power assertive" (i.e., coercive) discipline strategies (Daro, 1988; Trickett, Aber, Carlson, & Cicchetti, 1991), and a tendency to rationalize as legitimate even inappropriate parenting decisions (Hoffman, 1984). It has been argued that "negative parenting behavior is the primary pathway through which poverty undermines children's socioemotional functioning" (McLoyd, 1990). Clearly, child abuse occurs at all income levels; however, there is a higher incidence of physical abuse in families below the poverty line (Straus & Gelles, 1986), even when reporting bias is taken into account. Offord and colleagues found that low income was one of the most significant risk factors for conduct disorder, but that it had its effect on young children, not on adolescents (Offord, Alder, & Boyle, 1986). Moreover, they showed that rates of conduct disorder were significantly higher for children from low-income welfare families than for children from low-income nonwelfare families (Offord, Boyle, & Szatmari, 1987).

Families of children with conduct problems report major life stressors at a rate two to four times greater than families with "normal" children (Webster-Stratton, 1990b). Moreover, parents of children with conduct problems indicate that they experience more day-to-day difficulties than nonclinic families. An accumulation of minor but chronic day-to-day stressors appears to disrupt parenting behaviors and leads to increased rates of coercive behavior and irritability in parents' interactions with their children (Forgatch, Patterson, & Skinner, 1988). Additionally, parents who are depressed, stressed, or demoralized are less likely to be able to provide the cognitive stimulation, emotional support, and social learning necessary to foster a child's positive behavior. Wahler and Sansbury (1990) proposed that highly stressed mothers are less able to screen out extraneous information (e.g., negative interchanges with neighbors or spouse), causing them to react inconsistently or indiscriminately to their children's behavior.

A key issue is whether these environmental factors directly contribute to child behavior problems or whether their effects are mediated by variables such as parenting skills. A synthesis by Capaldi and Patterson (1994) examined a wide array of factors for their predictive relationships to conduct disorders, testing for direct and indirect effects. They found that unemployment, low socioeconomic status, multiple transitions, and high levels of family adversity were related to early-onset conduct problems, but not to late-onset; however, the relationship was less strong when parenting variables were taken into account. The direct effects of low socioeconomic status, in particular, were erased when parenting variables were included; the roles of family transitions, stress, and unemployment also appeared to be indirect. They proposed that environmental variables were related to conduct disorders in a "chain reaction" fashion, whereby unemploy-

ment, for example, increased the family stress and the numbers of family transitions, which in turn decreased parental involvement and monitoring and increased the amount of "coercive" parenting. In another study, it was shown that family variables served as a protective factor against risk incurred by high-frequency encounters with significant violence in the neighborhood (Richters & Martinez, 1993). Thus it would seem that the effects of environmental factors on conduct problems are primarily indirect, not direct. However, this is not to discount their importance in explaining the development of conduct problems or their potential impact on parents' ability to sustain consistent and positive parenting.

Again, we see the powerful buffering effects of parenting even in situations of poverty and high levels of stress. But these data also seem to suggest that PT programs which help parents cope with environmental stressors will be more effective and far reaching.

This discussion of etiology relating to conduct problems is concluded by arguing for a complex theoretical model which considers the strong likelihood of transactional, reciprocal relationships among the biological, psychological, familial, sociocognitive, and environmental factors influencing child behavior. In all likelihood, antisocial behavior is not the sum of a certain number of risk factors, but the result of the interaction of multiple risk factors (Hinshaw & Anderson, 1996). Indeed some variables, for example, depression, may be consequences rather than precursors of conduct problems. Furthermore, the interplay of risk is particularly potent for "early-onset" conduct disorder, the course of which leads to more serious delinquency (Quay, 1986). Such a complex model will necessitate a family intervention which takes into consideration all of these intertwining factors.

5.08.3 DESCRIPTION OF INTERVENTION PROCEDURES AND PROPOSED MECHANISMS OF CHANGE

This review, emphasizes interventions geared towards younger preschool and school-aged children (as opposed to adolescents) because of the emerging evidence that children who begin antisocial behavior early are at significantly greater risk than those who become antisocial later, both for chronic offending during adolescence and for careers as antisocial adults (Patterson et al., 1989). The following discussion highlights several PT programs which were selected on the basis of their widespread availability, detailed descriptions of training procedures, and extensive evaluation of both the short-term and long-term effectiveness of the intervention.

The most highly influential PT program was developed by Patterson, Reid, and their colleagues at the Oregon Social Learning Center (Patterson et al., 1982; Patterson, Reid, Jones, & Conger, 1975). Spanning two decades of research with more than 200 families, their work provides an exemplary model for outcome research with conduct-problem children. Although directed toward parents of preadolescent and adolescent children who were engaged in overt conduct disorders, their program will be described here because it has provided the foundation for numerous other PT programs.

The program starts with having parents read a programmed text, either *Living with children* (Patterson, 1976) or *Families* (Patterson, 1975). Afterwards, they complete a test on the reading material. The therapist then works with each parent individually in a step-by-step approach wherein each newly learned skill forms the foundation for the next new skill. Five behavior management practices form the core content of the program. First, parents are taught to pinpoint the problem behaviors of concern and to track them at home (e.g., compliance versus noncompliance). Second, they are taught how to use social and tangible reinforcement techniques (e.g., praise, point systems, privileges, treats) and to shift from tangible to social reinforcers over time. Third, they are taught discipline procedures: 5-minute time-outs, short-term privilege removal, response cost, and work chores. Fourth, they are taught to "monitor"—that is, to provide close supervision for their children even when the children are away from home. This involves parents knowing where their children are at all times, what they are doing, and when they will be home. In the final phase of treatment, parents are taught problem-solving and negotiation strategies and become increasingly responsible for designing their own programs. The treatment content has been described in a manual by Patterson (1975) and elaborated upon by Reid (1987).

Like all PT programs, this intervention is based on a model which posits the primacy of ineffective parenting skills in the development of conduct problems: parents inadvertently teach their children noncompliance and aggression by modeling and reinforcing those behaviors in their daily interactions with their children. Here, the focus of intervention is the particular parent behaviors which support the child's negative behaviors. For example, instead of backing down (and rewarding) their child's coercive response to commands, or using harsh punitive parenting to gain compliance, parents are taught to follow through with commands in a reasonable and consistent manner. Instead of ignoring prosocial efforts and attending to negative behaviors, they are taught to reward appropriate behavior that they had hitherto overlooked.

Another influential PT program was developed originally by Hanf (1970) at the University of Oregon Medical School and later modified and evaluated extensively by McMahon and Forehand (1984). It was designed to treat noncompliance in young children, ages 3–8 years. As described by Forehand and McMahon (1981) in their book, *Helping the noncompliant child,* the first phase of this comprehensive PT program involves teaching parents how to play with their children in a nondirective way and how to identify and reward children's prosocial behaviors through praise and attention. The objective is for parents to learn to break the coercive cycle by increasing their social rewards and attention for positive behaviors and reducing their commands, questions, and criticisms. Parents also learn to use social and tangible rewards for child compliance and to ignore inappropriate behaviors. The second phase of the program involves teaching parents how to give direct commands in such a way as to gain more compliance and how to use 3-minute time-outs for noncompliance. Progression to each new skill in the treatment program is contingent on the parent's achieving an acceptable degree of competence in the previously presented skill.

The program is conducted in a clinic setting where the therapist works with individual parents and children together. Treatment methods include role-playing, modeling, and coaching. The clinic utilizes a playroom equipped with one-way mirrors for observation and "bug-in-the-ear" devices through which the therapist can prompt and give feedback to parents while they play with their child. Homework is assigned in the form of daily 10-minute play sessions with the child using the strategies learned in the clinic.

In this intervention the focus is on the reinforcement value of parental attention. Parents are taught to use "descriptive commenting" with appropriate behaviors—that is, to describe their children's behavior when they are acting in appropriate, positive ways—and to praise those behaviors. Parental attention reinforces and thus promotes the replacement behaviors, the positive behaviors which serve to replace the negative behaviors. Only after mastering the use of positive attention are parents taught discipline techniques to limit negative behavior. Reorienting the pattern of parent–child interactions from negative to positive reinforcement is presumed to interrupt the overlearned negative cycles in which many parents of noncompliant children find themselves, and which only promote further noncompliance.

The emphasis of this parent training (Hanf, 1970) on the relational aspects is also found in the intervention developed by Eyberg (1988) called "parent–child interaction therapy" (Hembree-Kigin & McNeil, 1995). While the emphasis on behavior management is maintained, the skills for child-directed play are elaborated in great detail, composed of "DRIP skills": describe, reflect, imitate, praise. Eyberg (1988) presents this program as an integration of traditional play skill values and current behavioral thinking about child management (Eyberg & Boggs, 1989). It is felt that parents' nondirective play with their children improves children's frustration tolerance, helps reduce the anger level of oppositional children, and offers more opportunities for prosocial behavior to occur (Hembree-Kigin & McNeil, 1995). Moreover, engaging in play with their children helps parents recognize their children's positive qualities. As parents learn nondirective play skills, they learn how to respond in a sensitive and genuine manner, how to relate to their child's level of development, and how to stimulate their learning. The primary goal of this training is to strengthen attachment and establish a warm, loving relationship between the parent and child.

Another example of a PT program for young children with conduct problems was developed by Webster-Stratton (1981b, 1982a, 1982b, 1984). Based on the early theoretical work of Patterson (1975) and Hanf (1970) regarding key parenting and relationship skills and behavioral principles to be learned in order to reduce conduct problems, the program utilizes videotape modeling methods. The content of the BASIC program incorporates Patterson's (1982) nonviolent discipline components concerning time-out, logical and natural consequences, and monitoring, components of Hanf's (1970) "child-directed play" approaches and the strategic use of differential-attention, encouragement and praise, and effective use of commands. This content has been embedded in a relational framework including parent group support, mutual problem-solving, self-management, and a collaborative relationship with the therapist. This approach is designed to promote parental self-efficacy and engagement with the program and to reduce parental resistance and drop-out (Webster-Stratton & Hancock, in press). Parents are taught to examine and alter the irrational thinking which derails their implementation of effective parenting. The

ADVANCE PT program includes content on problem-solving, communication (D'Zurilla & Nezu, 1982; Spivak, Platt, & Shure, 1976), and self-control techniques. In 1990, another new program was developed, entitled *Supporting your child's education*, to address risk factors related to children's poor academic readiness and weak home/school connection (Webster-Stratton, 1992b). In this program, parents learn how to prepare their preschool children so they can be successful in school. (Webster-Stratton and colleagues have developed a videotape program for teachers based on the same principles; teachers are trained in strategies for managing classroom behavior and for working collaboratively with parents.)

This program of research has been concerned with methods of presenting the parenting program—that is, developing the most cost-effective, widely applicable, and sustaining methods for training parents. Based on Bandura's (1982) modeling theory, the program utilizes videotape-modeling methods. The series of 10 videotape programs of modeled parenting skills (250 vignettes, each of which lasts approximately 1–2 minutes) are shown by a therapist to groups of parents (8–12 parents per group) in 13 sessions (26 hours). The vignettes show parent models in natural situations (unrehearsed) with their children "doing it right" and "doing it wrong" in order to demystify the notion that there is "perfect parenting" and to illustrate how one can learn from one's mistakes. After each vignette, the therapist leads a group discussion of the relevant interactions and encourages parents' ideas. Vignettes of parenting mistakes provide a wonderful opportunity to engage parents in analyses and critical thinking about what makes one technique effective while another is not. Group discussion provides a way for parents to gain acknowledgment for their thoughts and experiences. It also provides a safe forum for disclosure of past mistakes as well as fears, regrets, misgivings, etc. Therapists have the opportunity to model positive self-talk as they discuss vignettes or relate similar experiences, and such talk encourages parents to refrain from self-blame about their own parenting mistakes, and instead to believe in their future successes. Efforts are made to promote the modeling effects for parents by encouraging identification with the models shown on the videotapes; the videotapes show parents of differing sexes, ages, cultures, socioeconomic backgrounds, and temperaments demonstrating different levels of parenting skill, so that parents will perceive the models as similar to themselves and their children. Home activities are given out each week which include daily practice exercises as well as a weekly chapter to read or listen to on audiotape from the book, *The incredible years: A trouble-shooting guide for parents* (Webster-Stratton, 1992a).

The group discussion and collaborative format were chosen to ensure that the intervention would be sensitive to individual cultural differences and personal values, as well as to enhance parents' commitment to parental self-management. The program is also designed to help parents understand and learn to accept normal variation in children's developmental abilities, emotional reactions, and temperament style. The self-management aspect of the program is emphasized by asking each parent to identify the particular positive behaviors they want to see more of in their children and the negative behaviors they want to decrease. These targeted behaviors then become the focus for them to apply the "parenting principles" which they learn in the program. In this sense the program is "tailored" to each family's individual needs and goals as well as to each child's abilities.

The program utilizes group process not only because it is more cost effective but also because it addresses an important family risk factor—namely, the family's sense of isolation and stigmatization. The parent groups enhance and promote parent support networks and mutual collaboration (Webster-Stratton & Herbert, 1993, 1994). This support is also extended during the week by means of weekly assignments which include "buddy calls," a process whereby parents call each other to share their experiences regarding the assignments. However, the program has also been given to over 80 parents of conduct problem children as a completely self-administered intervention—that is, parents view the videotapes and complete the homework assignments without therapist feedback or group support.

5.08.4 RESEARCH FINDINGS REGARDING TRADITIONAL PARENT TRAINING

5.08.4.1 Short- and Long-term Follow-up and Program Generalizeability

The use of PT as an intervention for child conduct problems has been extensively researched, and there are a number of excellent reviews (Henggler, Borduin, & Mann, 1993; Kazdin, 1987; Miller & Prinz, 1990; Patterson, Dishion, & Chamberlain, 1993). Programs have reported high parental ratings of acceptability and consumer satisfaction (Cross Calvert & McMahon, 1987; McMahon & Forehand, 1984; Webster-Stratton, 1989). The success of short-

term treatment outcome has been verified by significant changes in parents' and children's behavior and in parental perceptions of child adjustment (Kazdin, 1985; McMahon & Forehand, 1984; Patterson & Reid, 1973; Webster-Stratton, 1981a, 1982a, 1984, 1990a; Webster-Stratton, Hollinsworth, & Kolpacoff, 1989) in comparison to waiting-list control families. Home observations have indicated that parents who have undergone training have been successful in reducing children's levels of aggression by 20–60% (Patterson et al., 1982; Webster-Stratton, 1985b). While the majority of studies have been conducted with Caucasian mothers, there is some evidence that parent training is also effective with fathers (Webster-Stratton, 1985a, 1990a) and with ethnic minorities (Strayhorn & Weidman, 1989; Webster-Stratton, 1995).

Generalization of behavior improvements has been demonstrated from the clinic setting to the home (Patterson & Fleischman, 1979; Peed, Roberts, & Forehand, 1977; Webster-Stratton, 1984) over reasonable follow-up periods (1–4 years) and to untreated child behaviors (Arnold, Levine, & Patterson, 1975; Fleischman, 1981; Forehand & Long, 1986; Webster-Stratton, 1982a; Webster-Stratton & Hammond, 1990). A 14 year follow-up of parents who attended the Forehand and McMahon program indicated that treated families were performing comparably to non-referred "normative" samples on measures of internalizing and externalizing behaviors, social competence, relationship with parents and academic progress. Unfortunately, the data are mixed regarding generalization of child behavior improvements from the home to the school setting.

Several studies have found that even when a child's behavior improved at home, his or her teacher did not necessarily report improvements in conduct problems and peer relationships in the classroom (Breiner & Forehand, 1982; Forehand, Breiner, McMahon, & Davies, 1981; Forehand, Rogers, McMahon, Wells, & Griest, 1981; Forehand et al., 1979). The Webster-Stratton (1981a) program found significant improvements in child adjustment at school as reported by teachers immediately post-treatment, but a year later these were not maintained. In another randomized study of 43 aggressive boys (grades 2–6), when treatment families were compared with a waiting-list control group, they showed significant increases in family cohesion, empathy, problem-solving efficiency, total family relationships, and positive child behaviors at home and school, with corresponding decreases in family conflict and negative/aggressive child behaviors at home and at school (Sayger, Horne, Walker, & Passmore, 1988). In a follow-up study of this sample, Sayger, Horne, and Glaser (1993) found that these positive changes in behavior at school, in marital satisfaction, in maternal depression, and in family relationships in general were maintained.

5.08.4.2 Comparison of PT with Other Types of Family Therapy

A few studies have compared the basic PT approach with other forms of family therapy. Patterson compared families randomly assigned to his PT program with those who received treatment from various clinicians in the community representing a range of therapeutic approaches. Results indicated the superiority of PT in producing reductions in child deviance (Patterson et al., 1982). In a subsequent study, Patterson and Chamberlain (1988) randomly assigned parents to their PT program or to a community agency employing eclectic family therapy. Findings indicated significant reductions in child deviant behaviors for PT, but no significant reductions for children in the family therapy condition. Wells and Egan (1988) also evaluated a study comparing PT with family systems therapy. Results indicated that their program was more effective than family systems therapy based on observations of parent and child behaviors, but both programs showed significant decreases in child problem behaviors as reported by parents.

In 1996, Taylor, Schmidt, and Hodgins (1996) reported on a study where they randomly assigned 110 families to a waiting-list control group, to Webster-Stratton's PT program (videotape modeling therapist-led group approach), or to a children's mental health center whose usual treatment approach to conduct problems was eclective, based on individual intervention tailored according to the therapist's personal assessment of a family's needs. Results indicated that the PT program was superior to eclectic treatment in terms of mother's reports of child improvements at home, mothers' confidence levels, and overall consumer satisfaction.

In addition to comparing PT with other forms of family therapy, there have been some attempts to determine which aspects of PT account for the improvements resulting from treatment. For example, to what extent is therapeutic change accounted for by the content, the therapy methods (i.e., videotape modeling), the group support, or the therapist's interpersonal skills? In this vein, Webster-Stratton and colleagues have attempted to

determine which methods of PT are most effective. In their first randomized study, they showed that the therapist-led group discussion videotape modeling method (GDVM) was equally good if not more effective than a PT method based on the highly individualized one-to-one "bug-in-the-ear" approach involving direct coaching of the parent and child (Webster-Stratton, 1984). Next they showed that PT based on the GDVM approach was somewhat more effective than either PT based on a therapist-led group discussion approach—without videotape modeling (GD)—or a completely self-administered videotape modeling approach—without therapist feedback or group discussion (IVM) (Webster-Stratton et al., 1988, 1989). All three approaches showed significant improvements in comparison to the waiting-list control condition—even the self-administered videotape modeling program had better treatment adherence than the group discussion approach without videotape modeling. At 3 year follow-up, the improvements in conduct problems (as reported by parents) were maintained only in the group trained by GDVM. In contrast, parents in both the IVM and GD conditions reported significant increases in their children's conduct problems from the 1 year to 3 year follow-up (although still below baseline levels). This component analysis of PT methods seems to suggest that PT methods based on videotape modeling plus parent group discussion and support will produce more sustained and long-term effects than programs which do not use videotape modeling or group discussion and mutual support methods. Moreover, the group approach represents a cost-effective alternative to conventional family therapy (i.e., individual therapy with a single family).

5.08.4.3 Factors Contributing to Program Success or Failure

Despite the general overall success of these programs in producing statistically significant changes in parent and child behaviors, there is also evidence that some families do not respond to treatment; these children continue to have clinically significant behavior problems after treatment (Eyberg & Johnson, 1974). In long-term follow-up studies, 30–40% of treated parents and 25% of teachers report children to have behavior problems in the deviant or clinical range (Forehand, Furey, & McMahon, 1984; Schmaling & Jacobson, 1987; Webster-Stratton, 1990a; Webster-Stratton & Hammond, 1990). In the Forehand and Long (1986) review, according to behavior observation measures, 4 of the 12 programs failed to produce changes in behavior that were maintained over time; and follow-ups were beset with high attrition rates (50%). In an effort to account for these treatment failures, researchers have focused on identifying variables other than parenting skills which may be directly or indirectly related to the continuation of conduct problems. In particular, there is an emerging literature concerned with family variables such as parents' personal problems, marital relationships, and relationships with others outside the family. Parent and family characteristics such as parental depression, marital conflict, spouse abuse, lack of a supportive partner, poor problem-solving skills, and high life stress have been shown to be associated with fewer treatment gains (Forehand et al., 1984; Forgatch, 1989; Webster-Stratton, 1985b).

5.08.4.3.1 Parental depression

There are somewhat conflicting results regarding the influence of depression on parents' ability to benefit from PT (Forehand et al., 1984; Wahler, 1980; Webster-Stratton, 1988; Webster-Stratton & Hammond, 1988). Researchers have long noted that pretreatment levels of maternal depression (self-reported symptoms, not formal diagnosis) are significant predictors of attrition rates during PT (McMahon, Forehand, Griest, & Wells, 1981) and failure to take part in follow-up assessments. However, research has rarely evaluated paternal depression as a predictor of treatment outcome. In the only study to be found concerning the role of fathers' depression, Webster-Stratton and Hammond (1990) evaluated the relative contribution of maternal and paternal depression (along with other variables related to parents' mental and emotional states) to short-term and long-term treatment outcome for 101 families who had been treated for their children's conduct problems via PT. They found that pretreatment levels of maternal and paternal depression (as measured by the Beck Depression Inventory) were significant predictors of maternal and paternal reports of their children's maladjustment (i.e., failure to fall into the normal range on standardized parent report measures) immediately post-treatment; however, reported depression was not related to clinically significant behavioral improvements following treatment—either in parenting behaviors (i.e., a 30% drop in criticisms from baseline) or in the child's interactions with mothers or fathers (i.e., a 30% drop in total negative behaviors from baseline)

(Webster-Stratton, 1994). At 1 year follow-up, pretreatment levels of depression still predicted mother and father reports of child adjustment, but again were not related to parent and child behavioral improvements at home (as independently observed) or to child behavior at school (as reported by teachers). On the other hand, marital status and socioeconomic status for mothers were strong predictors of continuation of mothers' critical behaviors and child conduct problems post-treatment, while marital dissatisfaction and negative life events were strong predictors of fathers' critical behaviors and child conduct problems at follow-up. This study confirmed an earlier study by Forehand and Furey (1985) which found an association between marital satisfaction and parent and child behaviors, and an association between depression and mothers' perceptions or attributions concerning their children, but not mothers' behaviors.

Studies have also shown that maternal depression significantly improves following PT when subjects are compared with waiting-list control mothers (Forehand, Wells, & Griest, 1980). In a study involving 85 families of children with conduct problems, Webster-Stratton (1994) reported that both mothers and fathers showed significant reductions in depressive symptoms immediately after PT, levels which were maintained 2 years later. Of the total sample, 31.2% of mothers and 22.4% of fathers indicated depressive symptoms in the mild to moderate range pretreatment; after PT, 54.2% of the depressed mothers and 83.3% of the depressed fathers had changed into the normal range. Further analysis indicated that those mothers who showed significant improvements in their depression scores (into the normal range) reported more significant improvements in child adjustment than mothers whose depression scores remained abnormal, and their children showed a higher ratio of positive to negative social skills (30% increase) than children of mothers with abnormal depression scores. For fathers, no significant relationships were found between an improvement in depression level and improvements in child behavior. These data suggest that the best predictor of long-term treatment outcome for children may be mothers' post-treatment levels of depression, rather than pretreatment levels.

5.08.4.3.2 Marital conflict

Next, consider the impact of marital conflict on treatment outcome (Grych & Fincham, 1990). Earlier it was noted that the relationship between the intensity of marital conflict and levels of childhood behavior problems (Fantuzzo et al., 1991). Unfortunately, only a few studies have examined the relationship of marital variables to treatment outcome for parents of children with conduct disorders. Some of the early studies (Oltmanns et al., 1977) found no relationship between pretreatment levels of marital adjustment and treatment outcome, and found no changes in marital satisfaction following treatment. However, others have found marital distress to be an important predictor of treatment failure (Dadds et al., 1987; Webster-Stratton, 1994). Dadds found that marital conflict was predictive of poor treatment outcome assessed at 6 month follow-up (Dadds & McHugh, 1992). In Webster-Stratton and Hammond's (1990) study, marital status and marital conflict (for mothers and fathers, respectively) were factors that made the greatest contribution to the prediction of child behavior problems immediately post-treatment. One year later, marital status was the strongest predictor of treatment outcome as measured by teachers' reports of child behavior; single-parent families accounted for significantly more nonresponders to treatment (Webster-Stratton, 1990a). Mothers of children classified as nonresponders also reported significantly lower income and more depression than mothers of children classified as responders. However, at 1 year follow-up there were no significant differences in levels of marital conflict reported by parents of children classified as responders and parents of non-responders. Moreover, Webster-Stratton found that marital conflict did not improve as a result of PT, unlike mothers' depression. Consequently, it appears that while PT can improve parent–child interactions and maternal depression, it has no impact on marital satisfaction or conflict; conversely, marital conflict and marital satisfaction do appear to have an impact on the outcome of PT.

These findings suggest a model in which the key causal factor behind child conduct problems is not lack of parenting skills *per se*, but rather parents' lack of conflict management skills. Parents who have more difficulties with communication, conflict resolution, and affect regulation find it harder to cope with life stressors, marital disagreements, and common child misbehaviors. As a result, not only do they fall into the negative reinforcement trap when parenting, but they also model their troubled communication and affective patterns for their children, thereby further contributing to their children's difficulties with peer relationships including poor communication and poor problem-solving, as well as escalating anger and aggression.

5.08.4.3.3 Insularity and socioeconomic disadvantage

How do insularity, family socioeconomic disadvantage, and high levels of life stress contribute to treatment success or failure? Recruitment rates for PT interventions with low-income families of conduct-disordered children are low (Spoth & Redmond, 1995). Families who are socioeconomically disadvantaged have often been reported to be more likely to drop out of treatment (Eyberg, 1992) and more likely to relapse or fail to make clinically significant improvements following treatment or to maintain treatment effects over time (Dumas & Wahler, 1983; Wahler & Afton, 1980; Wahler & Dumas, 1984; Wahler & Fox, 1982; Webster-Stratton, 1985b). In a study of 257 clinic children and their families who initiated treatment for aggressive behavior, it was shown that parental stress (total stress and life events) predicted early drop-out from treatment but not late drop-out (Kazdin & Mazurick, 1994). Wahler (1980) found that mothers who reported having had negative interactions with their community before treatment were less likely to maintain treatment effects over time.

Socioeconomic disadvantage coupled with social isolation or insularity resulted in a steady increase in the probability of PT treatment failure (Dumas & Wahler, 1983). Finally, in another study it was shown that those clinic families who had a partner or father involved in treatment (presumably providing more support) were more likely to sustain treatment effects 2–3 years later (Webster-Stratton, 1985a). A family's ability to maintain treatment effects at one year follow-up has been correlated with their degree of negative life crisis and environmental stresses (e.g., move to new neighborhood, death in family, unemployment), degree of insularity or support, and poverty (Webster-Stratton, 1985b).

All of these findings taken together suggest that PT programs need to be broadened to emphasize partner involvement (see earlier discussion regarding marital support and communication training), parent support, marital communication, problem-solving and coping skills. Moreover, the failure of many programs to result in child behavior improvements which generalize to school settings suggests the need for some form of training that equips parents to collaborate with teachers in order to improve their children's behavior at school as well as at home. This broadened view of PT will more accurately reflect the more complex model concerning the etiology of conduct problems.

5.08.4.3.4 Child characteristics

With respect to child characteristics, such as the nature of the child conduct problems, the child's age, sex, race, and particular biology, there is a lack of information concerning the important child predictors of long-term treatment outcome. Outcome studies rarely separate results for preschoolers from results for school-aged children. However, there is a suggestion from several follow-up studies of PT programs for parents of children with conduct disorders that the younger the child at the age of treatment, the more positive the child's behavioral adjustment at home and at school (Strain, Steele, Ellis, & Timm, 1982). Dishion, Patterson, and Kavanagh (1992) reported that children aged 2–6 years had the most significant improvements. Neither sex nor race have predicted outcome, although there is a suggestion in the literature that there may be different etiological factors leading to ODD/CD for girls and boys (Webster-Stratton, 1996a). There is scant research concerning how child biological factors affect PT outcome, although it has been suggested that the prognosis is worse for children with conduct problems combined with ADHD (unless medication is added) (Barkley, 1996; Walker, Lahey, Hynd, & Frame, 1987). Nonetheless, this research was carried out with older children, leaving it unclear how child biological factors influence PT for young children. Webster-Stratton's studies did not find that child age, sex, or hyperactivity predicted treatment success; instead, it was family factors such as life stress, socioeconomic status, and marital conflict that predicted long-term outcome in terms of the continuation of child antisocial behavior following her PT program (Webster-Stratton, 1985b; Webster-Stratton & Hammond, 1990).

5.08.4.3.5 Therapy characteristics

It is clear that not all PT programs are equally effective. Therapy factors, such as the format and methods of training, the dose and length of treatment received, and therapist characteristics, undoubtedly play an important role in predicting treatment outcome. However, these therapy factors have rarely been evaluated. For example, length of treatment has rarely been assessed as an independent variable. Kazdin (1987) has suggested that PT programs less than 10 hours in duration are less likely to be effective with conduct-disordered children. Certainly the programs which we have highlighted above have been lengthy, ranging from 20 to 45 hours. Related to the length of the treatment program is the dose of therapy which the family actually

received. There is some suggestion in the literature that families who attend more sessions (greater than 50%) have a more successful outcome than families with poor attendance (Strain et al., 1982). However, this finding has not been reported by other researchers (Dumas & Albin, 1986). Another factor related to treatment dose is whether the father (or some other family member) participated in the training along with the mother. In one study, it was shown that those clinic families who had a partner or father involved in treatment (presumably providing more support) were more likely to sustain treatment effects 2–3 years later (Webster-Stratton, 1985a). The existing evidence would suggest that the involvement of another supportive family member leads to better generalization and maintenance of treatment effects over time (Webster-Stratton, 1985a; Webster-Stratton et al., 1988). Finally, Webster-Stratton's studies suggest that treatment methods such as group support and videotape modeling add substantially to the long-term effectiveness of PT programs (Webster-Stratton, 1984, 1990a).

5.08.4.3.6 Therapist characteristics

There is even less research concerning the role of the therapist and the therapeutic process in predicting treatment outcome. Webster-Stratton and Herbert c(1993, 1994) have described their PT programs as based on a collaborative or partnership model, whereby the therapist works *with* parents by actively soliciting their ideas and jointly involving them in the process of problem-solving, sharing, discussing, and debating ideas and solutions (also see Webster-Stratton & Herbert, 1994). It is suggested that this approach empowers parents by giving back dignity, respect, and self-control to parents who are often seeking help for their children's problems at a vulnerable time of low self-confidence and intense feelings of guilt and self-blame (Spitzer, Webster-Stratton, & Hollinsworth, 1991). On the other hand, some behavioral PT programs seem to be based on an "expert" or hierarchical model, whereby the therapist is more directive—suggesting solutions and dispensing advice for the parents. To this author's knowledge, there has been no research comparing PT programs in terms of their different helping models and different sets of assumptions about the cause of family problems.

While there are no comparison studies, one of the most comprehensive microsocial analyses of therapist–client interchanges was conducted by Patterson and Forgatch (1985). They showed that directive therapist behaviors such as "teach" and "confront" increased the likelihood of parental resistance and noncooperativeness in a session. On the other hand, therapist behaviors such as "facilitate" and "support" led to reliable decreases in client noncompliance. Patterson and Chamberlain (1988) have proposed a therapy model which postulates that therapist behaviors play a secondary role to extrafamilial, interpersonal, and child factors in predicting parent response to the early stages of treatment, but play a primary role in predicting client noncompliance in the later stages of therapy. In another study, Alexander and Parsons (1973) examined the role of therapist characteristics in predicting outcome (as defined by completion of treatment and recidivism rate) for families that participated in family functioning therapy (FFT). They found that relationship characteristics (affect, warmth, humor) accounted for 45% of the variance in predicting outcome, whereas structuring characteristics (directiveness and self-confidence) only accounted for an additional 15% of the variance.

5.08.4.4 Limitations of Studies Related to Treatment Outcome

The research regarding treatment outcome is beset with methodological problems. First, there is a lack of unanimity as to what is meant by "successful" treatment or "improvement" in conduct problems. Different studies have utilized different criteria for evaluating treatment outcome as well as different measures of those criteria. Because of the expense involved in observational methods, some studies have used mothers' reports of improvement in the child's behaviors as the definitive outcome criterion; however, global ratings by parents may reflect how they feel about themselves and their child, rather than any real change in child behavior. Further, it appears that the validity of raters' evaluations varies according to characteristics of the raters. For example, Patterson has shown that the more deviant or socially disadvantaged the parents, the less convergence there is between their ratings and teacher ratings or observational ratings (Patterson et al., 1993). Studies of clinical samples have shown maternal ratings of problem children to be correlated more highly with their self-ratings of depression than with the observed behavior of their children (Forehand et al., 1984; Griest, Forehand, Wells, & McMahon, 1980). Patterson and Narrett (1990) have suggested that mothers' ratings of child behavior reflect improvement even when there is no

treatment—resulting in the impression that anything and everything works! On the other hand, neither is independent observation of behavior a wholly unbiased method of evaluating change, though it appears to be less susceptible to some of the problems of self-report measures.

Even when researchers agree on the criterion for evaluating treatment outcome, there may be no agreement on what variable represents that criterion. For instance, if observable behavior is the criterion, the question then becomes whether the relevant outcome variable is parent behavior or child behavior. Whether one expects parent and child behavior to change simultaneously depends on one's theoretical model. Those who ascribe to the PT model believe that changes in parenting behavior (the most proximal variable being influenced by the treatment) eventually will cause changes in child behaviors (the more distal variable), which implies that the appropriate criterion for evaluating the success of PT is, at least for the short term, parenting behavior. Support for this theory is found in one study which showed that the magnitude of changes in parental discipline correlated significantly with changes in antisocial behavior (Dishion et al., 1992). Patterson and Forgatch (1995) examined separately the contributions of baseline, termination, and change scores from parent and teacher reports, as well as observations and process variables to determine their validity as predictors of future child outcomes. The results indicated that termination scores for parents' behaviors post-treatment and the amount of change in parental practices (i.e., positive problem-solving) were powerful predictors of long-term outcome for children, defined as future arrests or removal from home. Neither termination ratings nor change ratings of teacher or parent reports nor termination scores of child adjustment immediately post-treatment predicted future child arrests or out-of-home placements. This study supports the use of parent behavior as predictors of child outcomes—and yet there is no consensus that child arrests or out-of-home placements are criteria for treatment success.

Another issue regarding treatment outcome is: how much change constitutes significant improvement? Often observational measures lack normative data on comparable nonclinic samples with which to compare our clinic samples. As a result, researchers typically utilize percentage improvement from baseline to indicate clinically significant change. But there is no consensus regarding the degree of improvement—the percentage of change—that is necessary to declare behavior "improved." Moreover, in a case where a child does show a 30% or even a 50% reduction in aggressive or noncompliant behaviors from baseline, but is still in the clinical range, is he or she defined as improved or not?

The next limitation to existing research concerns risk factors. As can be seen, in this review, studies typically have analyzed a single risk factor by means of global measures (such as depression, marital satisfaction, family insularity, or life stress) and correlated it with some aspect of treatment outcome. Just as there is a problem with the use of global self-report measures of treatment outcome, there is a problem with the use of global self-report measures as predictors. Global reports do not elucidate the precise aspects of, say marital distress or depression, nor the mechanisms by which these problems maintain the problem behaviors—i.e., contribute to the failure of treatment. In addition to this problem, most studies have been based on short-term results of treatment; they have told us little about the more important concern, namely how these family processes influence long-term treatment outcome. Moreover, very few studies have compared the relative weight or contribution of individual risk factors (such as depression in combination with marital distress) with treatment outcome. In comparison to the large number of individual treatment outcome studies, there is a paucity of studies containing any information about predictors of treatment success, in most cases because the study sample size was too small to form any meaningful conclusions.

Another problem with the research on risk factors is that those studies which have looked at predictors of treatment outcome in terms of children's conduct problems have tended to combine both boys and girls in their samples. It is highly probable that the predictors will be different for boys and girls. Webster-Stratton (1996a) found not only that the predictors differed depending on whether the outcome variable assessed was child externalizing problems at home (according to independent observations) or at school (according to teachers), but also that there were gender differences in predictors: mother negativity and depression and father negativity and life stress significantly predicted girls' externalizing problems 2 years post-treatment and accounted for 49% of the variance, whereas for boys no parenting or family variables emerged as predictors—rather independent observations of externalizing behaviors at baseline were the best predictors of boys' continuing externalizing problems at home 2 years later.

5.08.5 BROADENING THE FOCUS OF PT

Despite the limitations in research studies and differences in outcome measures employed, there has been remarkable consistency in the findings and they seem to hold true even in the face of these problems. Research results regarding the characteristics of families who failed to respond to PT pointed to the necessity of expanding our etiological models as well as broadening our PT focus. Since the mid-1980s, efforts have been made to improve the effectiveness of PT by adding other therapy components to the basic programs: training in social learning principles, problem-solving, self-control and emotional regulation, marital communication, anger management skills, "synthesis training," and ways to give and get support. These components include more sophisticated affective and cognitive skill training. Evaluation of the effectiveness of these adjuncts to PT helps test models regarding the important factors contributing to the maintenance of conduct problems.

5.08.5.1 PT with Marital and Other Parent-focused Adjuncts

Based on the studies indicating associations between marital conflict and poor child-treatment outcomes, a number of investigators have evaluated the effects of adding specific marital treatment components to standard PT. Greist et al. (1982) compared PT with a program which combined PT with a focus on marital adjustment and extrafamilial relationships. The combined program showed greater improvements in terms of child deviance at short-term follow-up. Dadds et al. (1987) examined the specific effects of a brief marital communication intervention, partner-supported training, as an adjunct to PT for parents with a child who had conduct problems. Results indicated that the adjunctive marital component led to enhanced treatment outcomes for couples experiencing discord (but not for maritally satisfied couples) compared with the couples experiencing discord who received only PT (Dadds & McHugh, 1992; Dadds et al., 1987).

Two other consistently documented factors related to treatment failure or drop-out and failure to maintain change following treatment are social disadvantage and isolation (Dumas & Albin, 1986; Webster-Stratton, 1985b). A number of studies have developed PT programs addressing these issues. Wahler (1980) and Wahler and Dumas (1989) defined "insular" parents as those who experience low levels of positively perceived social interactions and high levels of negatively perceived coercive exchanges within the community. They hypothesize that insular mothers have disruptions in their monitoring processes which interfere with their ability to adequately monitor their children and result in indiscriminate responding. Consequently, these researchers developed an adjunct treatment called "synthesis training" whereby parents are taught how their external events or circumstances influence their parenting behavior in order to help them be more effective at monitoring and providing discriminate responses. Synthesis training has been evaluated with multistressed mothers of children with conduct problems (Wahler, Cartor, Fleischman, & Lambert, 1993) and compared with PT alone, and with PT plus friendship liaison. Results indicated that parents who received the synthesis training had reductions in their indiscriminate parenting and their children demonstrated behavioral improvements. Mothers in the basic PT did not change their behavior, nor did their children.

Dadds and McHugh (1992) assessed the role of social support in the outcome of PT for single parents of conduct problem children and assessed the impact of "adjunctive ally support" training (AST) on treatment outcome. Single parents with children diagnosed with ODD or CD were randomly assigned to PT or PT plus AST. Improvements were found in both groups, but AST produced no extra gains. However, responders from both groups were more likely than nonresponders to report high levels of social support from friends, a finding which is consistent with that mentioned earlier regarding father involvement in the PT (Webster-Stratton, 1985a).

In an attempt to address a number of family issues including social support, marital issues and maternal depression, Webster-Stratton (1994) developed a lengthy, 14 week adjunct program (ADVANCE) involving therapist-led group discussions of videotape vignettes on all the following topics: strengthening social support and self-care, personal self-control, family communication skills, problem-solving between adults (and with teachers), and teaching children to problem-solve. Emotional communication is a major emphasis of this advanced program. This is an important skill for families who have until recently felt overwhelmed by negative affect, and who may have indirectly or directly communicated to their children that negative emotions are too frightening or too aversive to share. Parents learn to talk to children about emotion and to respond to their children's emotions appropriately and contingently as a way of increasing their children's emotional regulation (Denham, 1989; Denham, Zoller, & Couchold, 1994).

Families of children with conduct problems were randomly assigned to either the basic PT (GDVM) or GDVM plus ADVANCE. Results immediately post-treatment showed significant improvements in parents' problem-solving, communication and collaboration skills, as well as in children's problem-solving, for families in the combined treatment. Both mothers and fathers from the combined program reported increased consumer satisfaction, and there were no drop-outs from the ADVANCE program, suggesting the perceived usefulness of the skills taught in this program. Moreover, fathers who showed improvements in marital communication and problem-solving post-treatment also showed significantly greater improvements in parenting skills (specifically, reduced hostility and criticisms with children). However, children of ADVANCE parents failed to show significantly enhanced improvements over the children of GDVM parents in terms of child deviance. Both groups of children showed significant reductions in child deviance at home. It was hypothesized that the effects of the ADVANCE parents' improved communication and problem-solving skills may have been delayed, as children need to be exposed to repeated modeling over a sustained period of time. This suggests the need for longer-term follow-up of the two groups.

In summary, studies which have investigated the potential contribution of adjuncts to the standard PT intervention have generally indicated that components which address the social context of families, marital issues, and parental depression can improve the short- and long-term outcomes over and above basic PT (Dadds et al., 1987; Griest et al., 1982; Webster-Stratton, 1994 1997b).

5.08.5.2 PT with Child Training Adjuncts

Studies have indicated that children with ODD/CD may have some sociocognitive deficits in social problem-solving, self-control, and perceptions; these may be of biological origin, may be the result of parental modeling, or some combination of the two. This has led to a few studies evaluating the effects of combining child training (CT) with PT. Kazdin, Siegel, and Bass (1992) compared three interventions: PT, problem-solving skills training for children (PSST), and PT combined with PSST. Each treatment reduced overall child conduct problems and increased social competence. However, the combined treatment led to more durable changes in child behavior, placing a higher proportion of children in the range of normal functioning. The combined treatment also resulted in greater changes in parent functioning, including reductions in parental stress, depression, and overall symptoms. These results were maintained at 1 year follow-up. In another study, Baum, Reyna-McGlone and Ollendick (1986) compared three different interventions: PT, PT combined with child self-control training, and a control condition in which parent discussion was combined with a child attention control condition (control). Results indicated that the PT intervention (with or without the CT component) was superior to the control condition and, for the most part, the two treatment conditions did not differ from each other immediately post-treatment. However, at follow-up the combined treatment (PT plus child self-control training) was superior to PT alone and to the control condition on observational measures of child deviant behavior and on child and mother reports of adjustment.

Finally, Webster-Stratton (1997b) compared four conditions: PT, CT, CT + PT, and a waiting-list control group. Post-treatment assessments indicated that all three treatment conditions had resulted in significant improvements in comparison with controls, as measured by mother and father reports, daily observations of targeted behaviors at home and laboratory observations of interactions with a best friend. Comparisons of the three treatment conditions indicated that CT and CT + PT children showed significant improvements in problem solving as well as conflict management skills, as measured by observations of their interactions with a best friend; differences among treatment conditions on these measures consistently favored the CT condition over the PT condition. As for parent and child behavior at home, PT and CT + PT parents and children had significantly more positive interactions in comparison with CT parents and children. One year follow-up assessments indicated that all the significant changes noted immediately post-treatment were maintained over time. Moreover, child conduct problems at home had significantly lessened over time. Analyses of the clinical significance of the results suggested that the combined CT + PT condition produced the most significant improvements in child behavior at 1 year follow-up.

In summary, these studies on child adjuncts to PT support the hypothesis that supplementing PT with a component that addresses the child directly increases the efficacy of PT. Additionally, these data point to the necessity for long-term assessment of interventions, since the benefits of the adjunct treatment often were not evident until the follow-up evaluation.

5.08.5.3 Future Directions for Research and for Practice

Our review of the research regarding PT has focused on programs for children with ODD/CD because this area comprises the largest body of research regarding PT. Second, we have focused on programs that target preschool and school-age children rather than adolescents because we feel adolescent conduct disorders necessitate other interventions such as individual therapy in addition to or alongside PT. We have not reviewed PT programs specifically targeted at other childhood disorders such as autism, anxiety disorders, learning disabilities, and ADHD.

Despite the limitations of existing research, the evidence appears to support a more comprehensive, multisystem-based model in which conduct problems are not seen merely as evidence of inept parenting skills which need to be changed via treatment, but instead where parenting behavior is seen to be impacted by the events and conditions within and outside the family. We believe the findings to date argue for broader-based treatments which address multiple risk factors and strengthen multiple protective factors such as parenting skills, support networks, and problem-solving and communication as a means of preventing early-onset conduct problems. By strengthening parenting skills and problem-solving strategies and ensuring adequate support (through broader-based family training support groups) for families of young children with conduct problems, we can help families buffer some of the potentially disruptive effects of ongoing depression, marital conflict, negative life stress, and poverty on children's adjustment. Indeed, initial studies of broader-based interventions suggest they promote more enduring child improvements which generalize across settings and over time, as well as fewer treatment drop-outs. Combining PT with CT appears to lead to even greater maintenance of improvements in parent and child behaviors.

Nonetheless, the original formulation of Patterson et al. (1975) is still compelling, particularly as it relates to young children with conduct problems: parenting skills are the most important proximal cause of early-onset conduct problems, because parents are still the primary agents of socialization of the child at this age. Given that this formulation is correct, the success of treatment programs in changing the parenting behavior of parents of young children should predict the child's future adjustment. For children aged 3–7 years, peer rejection, deviant peer groups, academic failure, and negative reputations have not stabilized, whereas for the older school-age child these factors play a key role in maintaining the conduct problems and must be taken into account in intervention. Moreover, parents of younger children are still hopeful and their patterns of parenting are more malleable than those parents who have spent years of coping unsuccessfully with an oppositional child at home. Support for this idea comes from studies which have suggested that PT is more effective in improving both parenting skills and child adjustment when offered to parents of younger children versus older school-age children and adolescents (where presumably more will be required in terms of direct intervention with the child and his or her peer group) (Strain et al., 1982). Further support for the importance of developing comprehensive interventions that can strengthen parenting skills and thereby influence the long-term outcome for children's adjustment is provided by Patterson and Forgatch's (1995) study.

5.08.5.4 Expansion Across Multiple Settings

Nonetheless, while PT holds much promise for treating children with conduct problems, there are several important limitations to this approach. The first important limitation is the inability of this approach to consistently produce child behavior improvements which generalize beyond the home to day-care or school settings and to peer relationships. While the majority of children improve their social behavior at home, 30–50% continue to have significant school problems such as social acceptance, conduct problems, and academic underachievement. Intervening with children's teachers as well as their parents would seem to offer far better possibilities of generalizing improved social skills from the home to preschool and school settings. In particular, schools may enhance the effects of PT by providing teachers not only with classroom behavior management training, but also with the curriculum and support to directly offer training in social skills and problem-solving.

A second limitation is that, despite the documented links between academic underachievement, language delays, reading and learning disabilities, ADHD, and conduct disorders, PT programs rarely, if ever, have included an academic skills enhancement program for parents. Parents need to know not only how to help their children with their antisocial problems but also how to teach and support them regarding their academic difficulties. They need to know how to work with teachers and schools in order to foster a supportive relation-ship between the home and school settings. Parents and teachers alike need to understand how to collaborate with one another, to build supportive teams to help these children both academically and socially. Such a coordinated effort between the home and school regarding social and academic goals will offer the possibility for more consistent generalization of child improvements across settings. There is little or no research comparing PT with PT offered in conjunction with teacher training or, more generally, evaluation of intervention efforts to span home and school. Research which evaluates the added effects of combining teacher training and parents' academic skills training to our traditional PT approaches should be encouraged.

5.08.5.5 Teachers and Other Professionals

Since preschoolers living in more dysfunctional or disrupted family environments or in poverty are at particular risk for persistent problems, the need for strong educational and therapeutic preschool programs with nurturing and well-qualified teachers is critical. This means preschool teachers and child care workers should be well trained in child development and behavior management skills. Stable and nurturing caregivers may be able to buffer the effects of parental unavailability or psychopathology, at least for some children. However, all too often these are the very children who are spending large amounts of time in the least adequate facilities with untrained caregivers, where child-to-caretaker ratios make it impossible to provide the attention, affection, and emotional support they need. Finally, since parents bring their first questions about common developmental issues and problem behaviors to their pediatrician or family physician, these professionals also need training that allows them to understand parental perspectives within a developmental framework—so that they neither pathologize common problems nor minimize parents' concerns.

5.08.5.6 Addressing Extrafamilial Change

Interventions which have focused on adjuncts to PT reflect a paradigm shift from individual change (i.e., parenting skills) to within-family change (i.e., marital communication and problem-solving skills). But there has been no further shift to what might be called extra-familial or interfamilial change, such as a family's need to form stronger and more supportive connections with other families and with the community in general. We theorize that, particularly for low-income families, there is an urgent need to broaden PT programs so as to focus on building community and parent support networks. Indeed there is evidence from the "buffering" interpretation of social support (Cohen & Willis, 1985) that particularly for low-income families, the greater the number of people parents felt they could rely on for informal assistance and the more satisfied they felt with their social support, the more likely they were to be nurturing and positive in their parenting interactions and the less likely they were to report problematic behavior (Hashima & Amato, 1994) compared with low-income mothers who felt isolated and dissatisfied with their social support (Jennings, Stagg, & Conners, 1991).

Many interventions have been based on the individual one-to-one counseling model which fosters reliance on the therapist. Those programs which have used a group approach (Webster-Stratton, 1994) have suggested that fostering supportive social networks was a primary purpose of the group approach. The therapeutic group can decrease families' isolation, promote a feeling of support and involvement, and build a sense of community. However, little reference is made to the specific therapeutic strategies used to achieve this goal. Indeed, compared with our well-developed research methods of measuring parent behavior change, few studies report outcome measures having to do with change in social networks, parents' sense of support, or their involvement in their communities (including their children's school) as a result of PT. If we are going to develop more effective interventions targeting these factors, we will need suitable outcome measures (Webster-Stratton, 1997a).

5.08.5.7 Engaging Low-income Families, Understanding Obstacles and the Importance of Culture

The PT literature has suggested that PT is less effective with disadvantaged parents— particularly low-income single mothers (Wahler, 1980). Such families have been described as unmotivated, resistant, unreliable, disengaged, chaotic, in denial, disorganized, uncaring, dysfunctional, and unlikely candidates for this kind of treatment—in short, "unreachable." However, these families might well describe traditional clinic-based programs as "unreachable." Clinical programs are often too far away from home, too expensive, insensitive, distant, inflexible in terms of scheduling and content, foreign in terms of language (literally or figuratively), blaming or critical of their lifestyle. A cost–benefit analysis would, in all likelihood, reveal that the costs to these families of receiving treatment far outweigh the potential benefits—even though they do genuinely want to do what is best for their children. Perhaps this population has been "unreachable" not because of their own characteristics, but because of the characteristics and obstacles of the interventions they have been offered.

The paradox is that while, on the one hand, we decry the lack of efficacy of therapy (i.e., PT) with economically disadvantaged families, on the other hand, we also maintain the belief that if we could just do *more psychodynamic therapy* focusing more broadly (i.e., on family dysfunction and parental psychopathology), we would be more effective. But we believe the problem may not lie in the focus of the therapy (i.e., parenting skills vs. family dynamics), but rather in the therapeutic model or approach—namely, a traditional clinic-based model of PT. Before abandoning PT as an intervention with this population, we should examine alternative models of delivering PT which take the broader social context into consideration. If PT is offered in nonstigmatizing locations (as opposed to mental heath centers) and made readily available in communities through churches, schools, and community centers, the programs might well attract more families. PT programs which provide for transportation, day care, meals, flexible scheduling, and attend to some of the obstacles for families getting to and staying involved with programs are likely to be more successful. More research is needed on how programs can be made culturally sensitive and tailored to the specific needs and priorities of the particular parents involved. In general, much more research is needed on ways to promote parental involvement and engagement in PT programs.

Socioeconomically disadvantaged families and rural families are less likely to seek mental health services for children's behavioral problems. This may be due to psychological obstacles such as the stigma associated with seeking assistance for psychological problems. Or it may be due to differences in priorities, or to cultural differences in how behavior problems are viewed and solved within a family. For example, in some cultures there is shame attached to disclosing family problems outside the family which extends to the entire family, relatives, and ancestors. Or it may be the result of an attitude that little can be done about the problem. As we noted earlier, failure to access such services may result from structural obstacles such as difficulty accessing and paying for services, lack of transportation, the distance involved in getting to the service, lack of baby-sitting for other children, inflexible clinic hours, etc. It is necessary to understand the obstacles that disadvantaged groups experience when accessing services and to develop more effective ways of reaching these families and attracting them to such programs.

The growing ethnic diversity among families in the United States also makes it imperative that we not only recognize and understand different cultural attitudes and practices regarding parenting, but more importantly develop interventions that are culturally informed and appropriate for different ethnic groups. It is important to be cautious about generalizations regarding specific cultural groups, for every parent is different and has his or her own unique history. Nevertheless, it is essential to understand the cultural values and historical factors that are the context for parenting, influencing parents' behavior with their children (Harkness & Super, 1995). For example, parents from certain cultural groups may put a high priority on their children developing habits of obedience, humility, respect for the elders, reliance on family networks, and family interdependence, while parents from other groups may value creativity, personal self-control, and emotional independence. In some cultural groups communication styles are open, volatile, and expressive, while in other groups communication is more indirect and infrequent. Attitudes toward discipline range from strict discipline practices of cultures which value obedience to authority to the permissive discipline practices of cultures which place emphasis on personal autonomy and self-respect. PT research encompassing cultural issues is almost nonexistent (Forehand & Kotchick, 1996). Apart from anecdotal information, we do not know whether certain behavior management strategies (e.g., play, time out, ignoring) are more easily accepted in some cultural groups than others or if a certain therapeutic style would be more effective than another. Finally, mistrust of the majority culture by ethnic minorities can be a barrier to PT. Ethnic minorities walk a fine line between maintaining their cultural history and traditions and adopting the strategies of the European–American culture that are typically associated with success (Coughlin, 1995). This is yet another reason why parenting programs which are collaborative are more likely to be accepted by parents: because parents set their own goals for therapy based on their personal values. Collaborative therapy is inherently more accommodating of cultural differences, whereas noncollaborative therapies are more likely to be shaped by the cultural values and norms of the therapist.

Webster-Stratton has conducted a randomized study to evaluate a prevention program for a multiethnic group of 250 Head Start families, 90% of whom were on welfare. This 9 week, 2 hour parenting program was community-based (held in housing units, churches, and schools) and addressed many of the issues of economically disadvantaged families by providing transportation, day care, dinners, afternoon and evening groups, and parent group support. Since a major theme of the program (in addition to learning parent management skills) was to decrease family isolation by learning effective ways to give and get support (inside and outside the family), parents were paired up to make weekly "buddy" calls. Group leaders called parents weekly. Teachers were also trained in the program and encouraged to provide extra support to families. Visits to classrooms were arranged as well as helping parents write positive notes to teachers.

Preliminary results are promising, with over 85% of those who participated attending over two-thirds of the sessions. In comparison with mothers in the Head Start centers which did not offer this program, mothers made significantly fewer critical remarks, used less physically negative discipline, and were more positive, appropriate, and consistent in their discipline style. Intervention mothers perceived their family service workers as more supportive than did comparison mothers; furthermore, teachers reported that intervention mothers were more involved in their children's education than nonintervention mothers. In turn, intervention children were observed at home to exhibit significantly fewer negative behaviors, less noncompliance, more positive affect, and more prosocial behaviors than children in Head Start centers which did not offer the parent intervention.

Consumer satisfaction with the program was high, with 89% reporting "positive" to "very positive" overall satisfaction, 91% reporting they expected positive results, and 95% saying they would "highly recommend" the program to others. Over 85% of the parents in the intervention condition wanted the program to be longer and to continue into the kindergarten year (Webster-Stratton, 1995). While it cannot be determined precisely what the active ingredient of this intervention was because there was no comparison PT intervention, the data are suggestive of the value of directly targeting social support both within and outside the family as well as eliminating barriers regarding transportation, day care, and food for low-income families.

In another randomized study (Cunningham, Bremner, & Boyle, 1995), families were randomly assigned to either a 12 week clinic-based individual PT (Clinic/Individual) or a 12 week community-based large group PT (Community/Group) or a waiting-list control condition. Families who were significantly more likely to enroll in the Community/Groups were characterized as immigrant families, those using English as a second language, and parents of children with severe behavior problems. Parents in Community/Groups reported greater improvements in behavior problems at home and better maintenance of these gains at 6 month follow-ups. Moreover, Community/Group interventions were six times more cost effective than Clinic/Individual training. This important study suggests the potential for group community PT programs as a valuable resource which may reduce the cultural, linguistic, and family barriers which prevent participation in clinic-based programs.

5.08.5.8 More Complex Models

It has become evident that the etiology of and treatment model for young children's conduct problems are complex and transactional and must involve not only attention to family functioning and parent–child mechanisms but also the other domains of influence we have mentioned—namely, child biological and sociocognitive factors, attachment issues, and the wider contextual influences (Caspi & Moffitt, 1995). While there have been some efforts to study the interrelationship between various types of PT and family contextual factors, there is comparatively little research looking at the interrelationships between PT and child biology, sociocognitive factors, and parent–child attachment.

These interrelationships are important to understand, for the length, breadth, setting, and focus of training needs to be matched to the risk domains affecting the child's problems. For example, if a child has biological and sociocognitive risk factors as well as insecure attachment with his or her parent, and lives in a stressful family environment, he or she will need a far more comprehensive intervention (involving parent and child training as well as teacher training to alter the peer context in the classroom) than a child who has no biological or family risk factors and has not yet developed pervasive conduct problems which have generalized from home to school. The child who has no biological factors and nonpervasive conduct problems (that is, setting specific) may be adequately treated with a basic PT program. On the other hand, the child coming from a family where there are family problems and

social context factors such as drug abuse, marital distress, depression, and attachment problems but who has no biological factors will need an intervention that focuses on family interpersonal problems as well as parenting skills. Depending on the parents' willingness and/or ability to benefit from such a comprehensive family intervention, we may need to supplement the family intervention with teacher training and child training. We should undertake research where we identify risk groups and then evaluate levels of intervention—ranging from relatively basic PT programs to more comprehensive programs involving parent, teacher, and child training.

5.08.5.9 Understanding Therapeutic Process Variables

It is clear that there is a need for research evaluating competing models regarding the etiology of childhood conduct problems. There is a further need for research regarding the critical therapeutic change processes (e.g., comparing interventions which focus on promoting parent–child attachment, interpersonal relationships, and the collaborative process vs. those which are more parent behavior skill-based). While PT research in recent years has focused on expanding the content for PT to include broader family issues, it has largely ignored the role of variables having to do with the therapeutic process itself. Yet these variables affect a family's level of engagement in therapy, their level of resistance and the acceptability of parenting strategies by different cultural and ethnic groups. For example, in one of the earliest studies of therapeutic process, Patterson and Forgatch (1985) have highlighted the critical importance of the manner in which the therapist deals with resistance. They showed that when therapists met parent resistance with confrontation and teaching, there was an increase in parental resistance; when the therapist was nonconfrontive, supportive, and nondirective, the resistance decreased. These findings are important, since parental resistance is a major cause of parental drop-out from therapy and failure to make changes. In another study, Patterson and Forgatch (1995) showed a relationship between fathers' confrontational behavior in therapy and lack of change in mothers' discipline strategies, and a relationship between mothers' hopeless and defending behavior and fathers' discipline strategies. In addition, Alexander and his colleagues have examined the influences of therapist characteristics (e.g., gender) and processes on family behavior (Alexander, Waldron, Newberry, &

Liddle, 1988). They have provided extensive work on the notion of therapist "reframing," suggesting that it is a more effective therapeutic process than therapist teaching and reflecting for reducing defensiveness in parents and adolescents (Robbins, Alexander, Newell, & Turner, 1996). Webster-Stratton and Herbert (1994) have emphasized the importance of a collaborative relationship and interpersonal process with parents and a group approach to PT. This collaboration encompasses 10 domains of therapist skills: (i) building supportive and caring relationships; (ii) empowering parents through behaviors such as reinforcing and validating parental insights; (iii) using active teaching skills (e.g., videotape modeling, role-play, rehearsal, parent group and therapist feedback, home assignments); (iv) interpreting (analogies and metaphors), reframing, and persuading; (v) leading and challenging; (vi) prophesizing (anticipating set-backs and successes); (vii) individualizing, generalizing, and contextualizing; (viii) preparing for the long-term; (ix) fostering PT groups as support systems; and (x) building parent support outside the group. Further research regarding the use of these therapy skills is worth pursuing, in order to understand their relationship to parent engagement in PT and to compare their effects with PT programs which do not utilize these strategies.

Patterson and Forgatch (1995) showed that parental social disadvantage, antisocial behavior, and depression were associated with increased parental resistance throughout PT. They proposed that parental resistance could result from four factors: (i) a history of failure in discipline attempts with the child; (ii) parental psychopathology, depression, and antisocial behavior; (iii) stress and social disadvantage; and (iv) the therapist's clinical skills in teaching and confronting parents. These findings suggest the complex interplay between family, contextual, and therapy process factors.

5.08.6 SUMMARY

Despite the evidence concerning the stability of conduct problems stemming from preschool into later life and the effectiveness of family intervention programs, there is an appalling lack of availability of comprehensive training programs for parents of young children with behavior problems. While funds are available for various mental health screening programs for preschoolers, they are rarely available to provide intervention once children with conduct problems are identified. These children have largely been neglected by the mental health community, which has targeted school-age and adolescence for intervention efforts. Preschoolers are offered help primarily if they have more serious cognitive or developmental delays such as mental retardation, or marked psychosocial disadvantage. When young children with conduct problems come to the attention of professionals, they are frequently ineligible for programs or their problems are dismissed as age-appropriate behaviors which are likely to be outgrown.

Not only are there few programs available, even when children have been identified as having ODD or CD, but there are even fewer prevention programs designed to identify high-risk families and to offer training and support when children are toddlers, before conduct problems develop. Gross, Fogg and Tucker (1995) evaluated the 10 week Webster-Stratton basic parenting program with parents of toddlers judged by their parents as behaviorally difficult. Results suggested that PT led to significant increases in maternal self-efficacy, decreases in maternal stress, and improvements in the quality of mother–toddler interactions. Improvements were maintained 1 year later.

Because it is clear that relatively marked behavior problems in preschoolers have long-term developmental consequences for some proportion of children and their families, the need for early intervention programs is obvious—and pressing. Although comprehensive treatment programs for preschoolers may seem costly in the current economic climate, reducing conduct problems in young children will ultimately decrease the need for mental health and educational services later on. The cost of not treating such early problems far outweighs the cost of instituting appropriately targeted intervention programs when children are young.

5.08.7 ACKNOWLEDGMENTS

This research was supported by the NIH National Center for Nursing Research Grant #5 RO1 NR01075–10 and Research Scientist Development Award MH00988–05 from NIMH.

5.08.8 REFERENCES

Abramson, L. Y., Seligman, M. E. P., & Teasdale, J. D. (1978). Learned helplessness in humans: Critique and reformulation. *Journal of Abnormal Psychology, 87,* 49–74.
Alexander, J. F., & Parsons, B. V. (1973). Short-term behavioral intervention with delinquent families: Impact on family process and recidivism. *Journal of Abnormal Psychology, 1,* 219–225.
Alexander, J. F., Waldron, H., Newberry, A. M., & Liddle,

N. (1988). Family approaches to treating adolescents. In F. M. Cox, C. Chilman, & E. Nunnally (Eds.), *Families in trouble.* New York: Sage.

Anastopoulos, A. D., Barkley, R. A., & Sheldon, T. L. (1996). Family based treatment: Psychosocial intervention for children and adolescents with attention deficit hyperactivity disorder. In E. D. Hibbs & P. S. Jensen (Eds.), *Psychosocial treatments for child and adolescent disorders: Empirically based strategies for clinical practice* (pp. 267–285). Washington, DC: American Psychological Association.

Anderson, K. E., Lytton, H., & Romney, D. M. (1986). Mothers' interactions with normal and conduct-disordered boys: Who affects whom? *Developmental Psychology, 22,* 604–609.

Arnold, J. E., Levine, A. G., & Patterson, G. R. (1975). Changes in sibling behavior following family intervention. *Journal of Consulting and Clinical Psychology, 43,* 683–688.

Asarnov, J. R., & Callan, J. W. (1985). Boys with peer adjustment problems: Social cognitive processes. *Journal of Consulting and Clinical Psychology, 53,* 80–87.

Baer, D. M., Wolf, M. M., & Risely, T. R. (1968). Some current dimensions of applied behavior analyses. *Journal of Applied Behavior Analyses, 1,* 91–97.

Bandura, A. (1977). *Social learning theory.* Englewood Cliffs, NJ: Prentice-Hall.

Bandura, A. (1982). Self-efficacy mechanisms in human agency. *American Psychologist, 84,* 191–215.

Barkley, R. A. (1996). Attention deficit/hyperactivity disorder. In E. J. Mash & R. A. Barkley (Eds.), *Child psychopathology* (pp. 63–112). New York: Guilford Press.

Barrett, P. M., Dadds, M. R., & Rapee, R. M. (1993). *Family Intervention for Childhood Anxiety: A Controlled Trial.* Paper presented at the 27th Annual Convention of the Association for Advancement of Behavior Therapy, Atlanta, GA.

Baum, C. G., Reyna-McGlone, C. L., & Ollendick, T. H. (1986). *The efficacy of behavioral parent training: Behavioral Parent Training Plus Clinical Self-control Training, and a Modified STEP Program for Children Referred with Noncompliance.* Paper presented at the meeting of the Association for Advancement of Behavior Therapy, Chicago.

Baumrind, D. (1971). Current patterns of parental authority. *Psychology Monographs, 1,* 1–102.

Biglan, A. (1993). *A functional contextualist framework for community intervention.* Reno, NV: Context Press.

Bowlby, J. (1980). *Attachment and loss: Loss, sadness, and depression.* New York: Basic Books.

Breiner, J., & Forehand, R. (1982). Mother–child interactions: A comparison of a clinic-referred developmentally delayed group and two non-delayed groups. *Applied Research in Mental Retardation, 3*(2), 175–183.

Campbell, S. (1995). Behavior problems in preschool children: A review of recent research. *Journal of Child Psychology and Psychiatry & Allied Disciplines, 36*(1), 113–149.

Campbell, S. B. (1991). Longitudinal studies of active and aggressive preschoolers: Individual differences in early behavior and outcome. In D. Cichetti & S. L. Toth (Eds.), *Rochester symposium on developmental psychopathology* (pp. 57–90). Hillsdale, NJ: Erlbaum.

Campbell, S. B., & Ewing, L. J. (1990). Follow-up of hard-to-manage preschoolers: Adjustment at age 9 and predictors of continuing symptoms. *Journal of Child Psychology and Psychiatry, 31*(6), 871–889.

Capaldi, D. M., & Patterson, G. R. (1994). Interrelated influences of contextual factors on antisocial behavior in childhood and adolescence for males. In D. C. Fowles, P. Sutker, & S. H. Goodman (Eds.), *Progress in experimental personality and psychopathology research*

(pp. 165–198). New York: Springer.

Caspi, A., & Moffitt, T. E. (1995). The continuity of maladaptive behavior: From description to understanding in the study of antisocial behavior. In D. Cicchetti & D. J. Cohen (Eds.), *Developmental psychopathology* (Vol. 2, pp. 472–511). New York: Wiley.

Cassidy, J., & Marvin, R. S. (1992). *Attachment organization in preschool children: Procedures and coding manual.* Unpublished manuscript.

Cohen, S., & Willis, T. A. (1985). Stress, social support, and the buffering hypothesis. *Psychological Bulletin, 98,* 310–357.

Coughlin, E. K. (1995). American's dilemma. *The Chronicle of Higher Education, 42*(2), 10–11.

Cox, A. D., Puckering, C., Pound, A., & Mills, M. (1987). The impact of maternal depression in young people. *Journal of Child Psychology and Psychiatry, 28,* 917–928.

Crick, N. R., & Dodge, K. A. (1994). A review and reformulation of social information processing mechanisms in children's social adjustment. *Psychological Bulletin, 115,* 74–101.

Cross Calvert, S., & McMahon, R. J. (1987). The treatment acceptability of a behavioral parent training program and its components. *Behavior Therapy, 18,* 165–179.

Crowther, J. K., Bond, L. A., & Rolf, J. E. (1981). The incidence, prevalence, and severity of behavior disorders among preschool-aged children in day care. *Journal of Abnormal Child Psychology, 9,* 23–42.

Cummings, E. M., Ballard, M., El-Sheikh, M., & Lake, M. (1991). Resolution and children's responses to interadult anger. *Developmental Psychology, 27,* 462–470.

Cummings, E. M., & Davies, P. (1994). *Children and marital conflict.* New York: Guilford Press.

Cummings, E. M., Simpson, K. S., & Wilson, A. (1993). Children's responses to interadult anger as a function of information about resolution. *Developmental Psychology, 29,* 978–985.

Cummings, E. M., & Zahn-Waxler, C. (1992). *Emotions and the socialization of aggression: Adults' angry behavior and children's arousal and aggression.* New York: Springer.

Cummings, J. S., Pellegrinia, D. S., Notarius, C. I., & Cummings, E. M. (1989). Children's responses to angry adult behavior as a function of marital distress and history of interparent hositility. *Child Development, 60,* 1035–1043.

Cunningham, C. E., Bennes, B. B., & Siegel, L. (1988). Family functioning, time allocation, and parental depression in families of normal and ADDH children. *Journal of Clinical Child Psychology, 17,* 169–179.

Cunningham, C. E., Bremner, R., & Boyle, M. (1995). Large group community-based parenting programs for families of preschoolers at risk for disruptive behaviour disorders: Utilization, cost effectiveness, and outcome. *Journal of Child Psychology and Psychiatry, 36,* 1141–1159.

Dadds, M. R., & McHugh, T. (1992). Social support and treatment outcome in behavioral family therapy for child conduct problems. *Journal of Consulting and Clinical Psychology, 60,* 252–259.

Dadds, M. R., Schwartz, M. R., & Sanders, M. R. (1987). Marital discord and treatment outcome in behavioral treatment of child conduct disorders. *Journal of Consulting and Clinical Psychology, 16,* 192–203.

Daro, D. (1988). *Confronting child abuse: Research for effective program design.* London: Free Press.

Denham, S. A. (1989). Maternal affect and child's social emotional competence. *American Journal of Orthopsychiatry, 59,* 368–376.

Denham, S. A., Zoller, D., & Couchold, E. A. (1994). Socialization of preschoolers' emotion understanding. *Developmental Psychology, 30,* 928–936.

Dishion, T. J., French, D. C., & Patterson, G. R. (1995).

The development and ecology of antisocial behavior. In D. Cicchetti & D. J. Cohen (Eds.), *Developmental psychopathology. Vol 2: Risk disorder and adaptation* (pp. 421–471). New York: Wiley.

Dishion, T. J., Patterson, G. R., & Kavanagh, K. (1992). *An experimental test of the coercion model: Linking theory, measurement, and intervention.* New York: Guilford Press.

Dodge, K. A., & Newman, J. P. (1981). Biased decision-making processes in aggressive boys. *Journal of Abnormal Psychology, 90*(4), 375–379.

Downey, G., & Coyne, J. C. (1990). Children of depressed parents: An integrated review. *Psychological Bulletin, 108,* 50–76.

Dumas, J. E., & Albin, J. B. (1986). Parent training outcome: Does active parental involvement matter? *Behavior Research and Therapy, 24*(2), 227–230.

Dumas, J. E., & Wahler, R. G. (1983). Predictors of treatment outcome in parent training: Mother insularity and socioeconomic disadvantage. *Behavioral Assessment, 5,* 301–313.

D'Zurilla, T. J., & Nezu, A. (1982). Social problem-solving in adults. In P. C. Kendall (Ed.), *Advances in cognitive behavioral research and therapy* (Vol. 1). New York: Academic Press.

Egeland, B., Kalkoske, M., Gottesman, N., & Erickson, M. F. (1990). Preschool behavior problems: Stability and factors accounting for change. *Journal of Child Psychology and Psychiatry, 31,* 891–909.

Eyberg, S. M. (1988). Parent–child interaction therapy: Integration of traditional and behavioral concerns. *Child and Family Behavior Therapy, 10,* 33–46.

Eyberg, S. M. (1992). Assessing therapy outcome with preschool children: Progress and Problems. *Journal of Clinical Child Psychology, 21*(3), 306–311.

Eyberg, S.M., & Boggs, S. R. (1989). Parent training for oppositional-defiant preschoolers. In C. E. Schaeffer & J. M. Brienmeister (Eds.), *Handbook of parent training* (pp. 105–132). New York: Wiley.

Eyberg, S. M., & Johnson, S. M. (1974). Multiple assessment of behavior modification with families. *Journal of Consulting and Clinical Psychology, 42,* 594–606.

Fantuzzo, J. W., DePaola, L. M., Lambert, L., Martino, T., Anderson, G., & Sutton, S. (1991). Effects of interpersonal violence on the psychological adjustment and competencies of young children. *Journal of Consulting and Clinical Psychology, 59,* 258–265.

Faraone, S. V., Biederman, J., Keenan, K., & Tsuang, M. T. (1991). Separation of *DSM-III* attention deficit disorder and conduct disorder: Evidence from a family genetic study of American child psychiatry patients. *Psychological Medicine, 21,* 1091–1121.

Feshbach, N. (1989). The construct of empathy and the phenomenon of physical maltreatment of children. In D. Cicchetti & V. Carlson (Eds.), *Child maltreatment: Theory and research on the causes and consequences of child abuse and neglect* (pp. 349–373). Cambridge, MA: Cambridge University Press.

Fisher, M., Rolf, J. E., Hasazi, J. E., & Cummings, L. (1984). Follow-up of a preschool epidemiological sample: Cross-age continuities and predictions of later adjustment with internalizing and externalizing dimensions of behavior. *Child Development, 55,* 137–150.

Fleischman, M. J. (1981). A replication of Patterson's "Intervention for boys with conduct problems." *Journal of Consulting and Clinical Psychology, 49,* 342–351.

Folkman, S., & Lazarus, R. S. (1988). Coping as a mediator of emotion. *Journal of personality and Social Psychology, 54*(3), 466–475.

Forehand, R., Breiner, J., McMahon, R. J., & Davies, G. (1981). Predictors of cross setting behavior change in the treatment of child problems. *Journal of Behavior Therapy*

and Experimental Psychiatry, 12(4), 311–313.

Forehand, R., & Furey, W. M. (1985). Predictors of depressive mood in mothers of clinic-referred children. *Behavior Research and Therapy, 23*(4), 415–421.

Forehand, R., Furey, W. M., & McMahon, R. J. (1984). The role of maternal distress in a parent training program to modify child noncompliance. *Behavioral Psychotherapy, 12,* 93–108.

Forehand, R., & Kotchick, B. A. (1996). Cultural diversity: a wake -up call for parent training. *Behavior Therapy, 27,*187–206.

Forehand, R., & Long, N. (1986). *A long-term follow-up of parent training participants.* Unpublished conference proceedings, Chicago.

Forehand, R. L., & McMahon, R. J. (1981). *Helping the noncompliant child: A clinician's guide to parent training.* New York: Guilford Press.

Forehand, R., Rogers, T., McMahon, R. J., Wells, K. C., & Griest, D. L. (1981). Teaching parents to modify child behavior problems: An examination of some follow-up data. *Journal of Pediatric Psychology, 6*(3), 313–322.

Forehand, R., Steffe, M. A., Furey, W. A., & Walley, P. B. (1983). Mother's evaluation of a parent training program completed three and one-half years earlier. *Journal of Behavior Therapy and Experimental Psychiatry, 14,* 339–342.

Forehand, R., Sturgis, E. T., McMahon, R. J., Aguar, D., Green, K., Wells, K., & Breiner, J. (1979). Parent behavioral training to modify child noncompliance: Treatment generalization across time and from home to school. *Behavior Modification, 3,* 3–25.

Forehand, R., Wells, K., & Griest, D. L. (1980). An examination of the social validity of a parent training program. *Behavior Therapy, 11,* 488–502.

Forgatch, M. (1989). Patterns and outcome in family problem solving: The disrupting effect of negative emotion. *Journal of Marriage and the Family, 5*(1), 115–124.

Forgatch, M., Patterson, G., & Skinner, M. (1988). A mediational model for the effect of divorce in antisocial behavior in boys. In E. M. Hetherington & J. D. Arasteh (Eds.), *The impact of divorce, single parenting and stepparenting on children* (pp. 135–154). Hillsdale, NJ: Lawrence Erlbaum Associates.

Frick, P. J., & Jackson, Y. K. (1993). Family functioning and childhood antisocial behavior: Yet another reinterpretation. *Journal of Clinical Child Psychology, 22,* 410–419.

Frick, P. J., Kuper, K., Silverthorn, P., & Cotter, M. (1995). Antisocial behavior, somatization, and sensation-seeking behavior in mothers of clinic-referred children. *Journal of American Academy of Child and Adolescent Psychiatry, 34*(6), 805–812.

Frick, P. J., Lahey, B. B., Loeber, R., Stouthamer-Loeber, M., Christ, M. A., & Hanson, K. (1992). Familial risk factors to oppositional defiant disorder and conduct disorder: Parental psychopathology and maternal parenting. *Journal of Consulting and Clinical Psychology, 60,* 49–55.

Gecas, V. (1979). The influence of social class on socialization. In W. Bum (Ed.), *Contemporary theories about the family.* New York: Free Press.

Goutz, K. (1981). Children's initial aggression level and the effectiveness of intervention strategies in moderating television effects on aggression. In K. R. Goutz (Ed.), *Attention and social problem-solving as correlates of aggression in preschool males* (pp. 181–197).

Greenberg, M. T., Speltz, M. L., & DeKlyen, M. (1993). The role of attachment in the early development of disruptive behavior problems. *Development and Psychopathology, 5,* 191–213.

Griest, D. L., Forehand, R., Rogers, T., Breiner, J., Furey, W., & Williams, C. A. (1982). Effects of parent enhancement therapy on the treatment of outcome and generalization of a parent training program. *Behaviour Research and Therapy, 20*(5), 429–436.

Griest, D. L., Forehand, R., Wells, K. C., & McMahon, R. J. (1980). An examination of differences between nonclinic and behavior-problem clinic-referred children and their mothers. *Journal of Abnormal Psychology, 89*(3), 497–500.

Griest, D. L., & Wells, K. C. (1983). Behavioral family therapy with conduct disorders in children. *Behavior Therapy, 14,* 37–53.

Gross, D., Fogg, L., & Tucker, S. (1995). The efficacy of parent training for promoting positive parent–toddler relationships. *Research in Nursing and Health, 18,* 489–499.

Grych, J. H., & Finchman, F. D. (1990). Marital conflict and children's adjustment: A cognitive contextual framework. *Psychological Bulletin, 108,* 267–290.

Grych, J. H., & Finchman, F. D. (1992). Interventions for children of divorce: Toward greater integration of research and action. *Psychological Bulletin, 111,* 434–454.

Haley, J. (1976). *Problem-solving therapy.* New York: Colophon Books.

Hanf, C. (1970). *Shaping mothers to shape their children's behavior.* Portland, OR: University of Oregon Medical School.

Harkness, S., & Super, C. M. (1995). Culture and parenting. In M.H. Bornstein (Ed.), *Handbook of parenting: Biology and ecology of parenting* (Vol. 2, pp. 211–234). Mahwah, NJ: Lawrence Erlbaum.

Hashima, P. Y., & Amato, P. R. (1994). Poverty, social support, and parental behavior. *Child Development, 65,* 394–403.

Hawkins, J. D., Catalano, R. F., & Miller, Y. (1992). Risk and protective factors for alcohol and other drug problems in adolescence and early adulthood: Implications for substance abuse prevention. *Psychological Bulletin, 112,* 64–105.

Hay, D. F., Zahn-Waxler, C., Cummings, E. M., & Iannotti, R. J. (1992). Young children's views about conflict with peers: A comparison of the daughters and sons of depressed and well women. *Journal of Child Psychology and Psychiatry, 33,* 669–684.

Hembree-Kigin, T. L., & McNeil, C. B. (1995). *Parent–child interaction therapy.* New York: Plenum.

Henggler, S. W., Borduin, C. M., & Mann, B. J. (1993). Advances in family therapy: Empirical foundations. *Advances in Clinical Child Psychology, 15,* 207–241.

Hetherington, E. M., Cox, M., & Cox, R. (1982). *Effects of divorce on parents and children.* Hillsdale, NJ: Erlbaum.

Hinshaw, S. P., & Anderson, C. A. (1996). Conduct and oppositional defiant disorders. In E.J. Mash & R.A. Barkley (Eds.), *Child Psychopathology.* New York: Guilford Press.

Hoffman, L. W. (1984). Work, family, and socialization of the child. In R. Parke, R. Emde, H. McAdoo, & G. Sackett (Eds.), *Review of child development research: The family,* (Vol. 7). Chicago: University of Chicago Press.

Hops, H., Biglan, A., Sherman, L., Arthur, J., Friedman, L., & Osteen, R. (1987). Home observations of family interactions of depressed women. *Journal of Consulting and Clinical Psychology, 55,* 341–346.

Huesmann, L. R., Eron, L. D., Lefkowitz, M. M., & Walder, L. O. (1984). Stability of aggression over time and generations. *Developmental Psychology, 20,* 1120–1134.

Hutchings, B., & Mednick, S.A. (1977). Criminality in adoptees and their adoptive and biological parents: A pilot study. In S. A. Mednick & K. O. Christiansen (Eds.), *Biosocial bases of criminal behavior.* New York: Gardner Press.

Jennings, K. D., Stagg, V., & Conners, R. E. (1991). Social networks and mother interactions with their preschool children. *Child Development, 62,* 966–978.

Johnson, S. M., & Lovitz, G. K. (1974). The personal and marital adjustment of parents as related to observed child deviance and parenting behaviors. *Journal of Abnormal Child Psychology, 2,* 193–207.

Jouriles, E. N., Murphy, C. M., Farris, A. M., Smith, D. A., Richters, J. E., & Waters, E. (1991). Marital adjustment, parental disagreements about child rearing, and behavior problems in boys: Increasing the specificity of the marital assessment. *Child Development, 62,* 1424–1433.

Jouriles, E. N., Murphy, C. M., & O'Leary, K. D. (1989). Interspousal aggression, marital discord, and child problems. *Journal of Consulting and Clinical Psychology, 57*(3), 453–455.

Katz, L. F., & Gottman, J. M. (1994). Patterns of marital interaction and children's emotional development. In R. D. Parke & S. G. Kellam (Eds.), *Exploring family relationships with other social contexts* (pp. 49–74). Hillsdale, NJ: Lawrence Erlbaum.

Kazdin, A. (1985). *Treatment of antisocial behavior in children and adolescents.* Homewood, IL: Dorsey Press.

Kazdin, A. E. (1987). Treatment of antisocial behavior in children: Current status and future directions. *Psychological Bulletin, 102*(2), 187–203.

Kazdin, A. E., & Kolko, D. J. (1986). Parent psychopathology and family functioning among childhood firesetters. *Journal of Abnormal Child Psychology, 14*(2), 315–329.

Kazdin, A., & Mazurick, J. L. (1994). Dropping out of child psychotherapy: Distinguishing early and late dropouts over the course of treatment. *Journal of Consulting and Clinical Psychology, 62,* 1069–1074.

Kazdin, A. E., Siegel, J. C., & Bass, D. (1992). Cognitive problem-solving skills training and parent management training in the treatment of antisocial behavior in children. *Journal of Consulting and Clinical Psychology, 60,* 733–747.

Kendall, P. C. (1992). Childhood coping: Avoiding a lifetime of anxiety. *Behavior Change, 3,* 70–73.

King, N. J., Hamilton, D. I., & Ollendick, T. H. (1988). *Children's fears and phobias: A behavioral perspective.* Chichester, UK: Wiley.

Kochansaka, G., Kuczynski, L., Radke-Yarrow, M., & Welsh, J. D. (1987). Resolution of control episodes between well and affectively ill mothers and their young child. *Journal of Abnormal Child Psychology, 15,* 441–456.

Lahey, B. B., Hart, E. L., Pliszka, S., Applegate, B., & McBurnett, K. (1993). Neurophysiological correlates of conduct disorder: A rationale and review of current research. *Journal of Clinical Child Psychology, 22,* 141–153.

Lahey, B. B., Hartdagen, W. E., Frick, P. J., McBurnett, K., Connor, R., & Hynd, G. W. (1988). Conduct disorder: Parsing the confounded relationship between parental divorce and antisocial personality. *Journal of Abnormal Psychology, 97,* 334–337.

Lahey, B. B., Loeber, R., Hart, E., & Frick, P. J. (1995). Four-year longitudinal study of conduct disorder in boys: Patterns and predictors of persistence. *Journal of Abnormal Psychology, 104*(1), 83–89.

Lahey, B. B., Loeber, R. L., Quay, H. C., Frick, P. J., & Grimm, J. (1992). Oppositional defiant and conduct disorders: Issue to be resolved for DSM-IV. *Journal of the American Academy of Child and Adolescent Psychiatry, 31*(3).

Landy, S., & Peters, R. D. (1991). Understanding and treating the hyperaggressive toddler. *Zero to Three, February,* 22–31.

Laski, K., Charlop, M. H., & Schreibman, L. (1988). Training parents to use the natural language paradigm to increase their autistic children's speech. *Journal of Applied Behavioral Analyses, 21,* 391–400.

Loeber, R. (1991). Antisocial behavior: More enduring than changeable? *Journal of the American Academy of Child and Adolescent Psychiatry, 30,* 393–397.

Lutzker, J. R. (1992). Developmental disabilities and child abuse and neglect: The ecobehavioral imperative. *Behavior Change, 9,* 149–156.

Lytton, H. (1990). Child and parent effects in boys' conduct disorder: A reinterpretation. *Developmental Psychology, 26,* 683–697.

Main, M., & Cassidy, J. (1987). *Reuion-based classifications of child–parent attachment organization at six-years of age.* Unpublished manuscript, University of California at Berkley.

McCord, J., McCord, W., & Thurber, E. (1962). Some effects of paternal absence on male children. *Journal of Abnormal and Social Psychology, 64,* 361–369.

McLoyd, V. C. (1990). The impact of economic hardship on black families and children: Psychological distress, parenting, and socioemotional development. *Child Development, 61,* 311–346.

McMahon, R. J., & Forehand, R. (1984). Parent training for the noncompliant child: Treatment outcome, generalization, and adjunctive therapy procedures. In R. F. Dangel & R. A. Polster (Eds.), *Parent training: Foundations of research and practice* (pp. 298–328). New York: Guilford Press.

McMahon, R. J., Forehand, R., Griest, D. L., & Wells, K. (1981). Who drops out of treatment during parent behavioral training? *Behavioral Counseling Quarterly, 1,* 79–85.

Meichenbaum, D., & Turk, D. (1987). *Facilitating treatment adherence: A practitioner's guidebook.* New York: Plenum.

Milich, R., & Dodge, K. A. (1984). Social information processing in child psychiatric populations. *Journal of Abnormal Child Psychology, 12*(3), 471–489.

Miller, G. E., & Prinz, R. J. (1990). Enhancement of social learning family interventions for childhood conduct disorder. *Psychological Bulletin, 108,* 291–307.

Minuchin, S. (1974). *Families and family therapy.* Cambridge, MA: Harvard University Press.

Offord, D. R., Alder, R. J., & Boyle, M. H. (1986). Prevalence and sociodemographic correlates of conduct disorder. *American Journal of Social Psychiatry, 6,* 272–278.

Offord, D. R., Boyle, M. H., & Szatmari, P. (1987). Ontario Child Health Study II: Six month prevalence of disorder and rates of service utilization. *Archives of General Psychiatry, 44,* 832–836.

O'Leary, K. D., & Emery, R. E. (1982). Marital discord and child behavior problems. In M. D. Levine & P. Satz (Eds.), *Middle childhood: Developmental variation and dysfunction* (pp. 345–364). New York: Academic Press.

Oltmanns, T. F., Broderick, J. E., & O'Leary, K. D. (1977). Marital adjustment and the efficacy of behavior therapy with children. *Journal of Consulting and Clinical Psychology, 45,* 724–729.

Patterson, G. R. (1975). *Families: Applications of social learning to family life.* Champaign, IL: Research Press.

Patterson, G. R. (1976). *Living with children: New methods for parents and teachers.* Champaign, IL: Research Press.

Patterson, G. R. (1982). *Coercive family process.* Eugene, OR: Castalia.

Patterson, G. R. (1986). Performance models for antisocial boys. *American Psychologist, 41*(4), 432–444.

Patterson, G. R., & Chamberlain, P. (1988). Treatment process: A problem at three levels. In L. C. Wynne (Ed.), *The state of art in family therapy research: Controversies and recommendations* (pp. 189–223). New York: Family Process Press.

Patterson, G. R., Chamberlain, P., & Reid, J. B. (1982). A comparative evaluation of a parent training program. *Behavior Therapy, 13,* 638–650.

Patterson, G. R., Cobb, J. A., & Ray, R. S. (1973). A social engineering technology for retraining the families of aggressive boys. In H. E. Adams & I. P. Unike (Eds.), *Issues and trends in behavior therapy* (pp. 139–210). Springfield, IL: Thomas.

Patterson, G. R., DeBaryshe, B. D., & Ramsey, E. (1989). A developmental perspective on antisocial behavior. *American Psychologist, 44*(2), 329–335.

Patterson, G. R., Dishion, T. J., & Chamberlain, P. (1993). *Outcomes and methodological issues relating to the treatment of antisocial children.* New York: Plenum.

Patterson, G. R., & Fleischman, M. J. (1979). Maintenance of treatment effects: Some considerations concerning family systems and follow-up data. *Behavior Therapy, 10,* 168–185.

Patterson, G. R., & Forgatch, M. S. (1985). Therapist behavior as a determinant for client noncompliance: A paradox for the behavior modifier. *Journal of Consulting and Clinical Psychology, 53*(6), 846–851.

Patterson, G. R., & Forgatch, M. S. (1995). Predicting future clinical adjustment from treatment outcome and process variables. *Psychological Assessment, 7*(2), 275–285.

Patterson, G. R., & Narrett, C. M. (1990). The development of a reliable and valid treatment programs for aggressive young children. *International Journal of Mental Health, 19,* 19–26.

Patterson, G. R., & Reid, J. B. (1973). Intervention for families of aggressive boys: A replication study. *Behaviour Research and Therapy, 11,* 383–394.

Patterson, G. R., Reid, J. B., Jones, R. R., & Conger, R. W. (1975). *A social learning approach to family intervention* (Vol. 1). Eugene, OR: Castalia.

Peed, S., Roberts, M., & Forehand, R. (1977). Evaluations of the effectiveness of a standardized parent training program in altering the interaction of mothers and their noncompliant children. *Behavior Modification, 1,* 323–350.

Porter, B., & O'Leary, K. D. (1980). Marital discord and childhood behavior problems. *Journal of Abnormal Child Psychology, 16,* 97–109.

Quay, H. C. (1986). Conduct disorders. In H. C. Quay & J. S. Werry (Eds.), *Psychopathological disorders of childhood* (pp. 35–72). New York: Wiley.

Quay, H. C. (1993). The psychopathology of undersocialized aggressive conduct disorder: A theoretical perspective. *Development and Psychopathology, 5,* 165–180.

Radke-Yarrow, M. (1991). Attachment patterns in children of depressed mothers. In C. M. Parke, J. Stevenson-Hinde, & P. Marris (Eds.), *Attachment across the life cycle.* London: Routledge.

Reid, J. B. (1987). *Therapeutic interventions in the families of aggressive children and adolescents,* Paper presented at the meeting of the Oreganizzato dalle Cattedre di Psicologia Clinica e delle Teorie di Personalita dell'Universita di Roma, Rome.

Richman, N., Stevenson, L., & Graham, P. J. (1982). *Preschool to school: A behavioural study.* London: Academic Press.

Richters, J. E., & Martinez, P. E. (1993). Violent communities, family choices, and children's chances: An algorithm for improving the odds. *Development and Psychopathology, 5,* 609–627.

Rickard, K. M., Forehand, R., Wells, K. C., Griest, D. L., & McMahon, R. J. (1981). Factors in the referral of children for behavioral treatment: A comparison of mothers of clinic-referred deviant, clinic-referred non-deviant and non-clinic children. *Behavior Research and Therapy, 19*(3), 201–205.

Robbins, M. S., Alexander, J. F., Newell, R. M., & Turner,

C. W. (1996). The immediate effect of reframing on client attitude in family therapy. *Journal of Family Psychology, 10*(1), 28–34.

Robins, L. N. (1981). Epidemiological approaches to natural history research: Antisocial disorders in children. *Journal of the American Academy of Child Psychiatry, 20,* 566–580.

Rogers, T. R., & Forehand, R. (1983). The role of depression in interactions between mothers and their clinic-referred children. *Cognitive Therapy and Research, 46,* 315–324.

Rose, S. L., Rose, S. A., & Feldman, J. (1989). Stability of behavior problems in very young children. *Development and Psychopathology, 1,* 5–20.

Rubin, K. H., & Krasnor, L. R. (1986). Social-cognitive and social behavioral perspectives on problem-solving. In M. Perlmutter (Ed.), *Cognitive perspectives on children's social and behavioral development, The Minnesota Symposia on Child Psychology* (Vol. 18, pp. 1–68). Hillsdale, NJ: Lawrence Erlbaum Associates.

Rutter, M. (1986). *The developmental psychopathology of depression: Issues and perspectives.* New York: Guilford Press.

Rutter, M., & Giller, H. (1983). *Juvenile delinquency: Trends and perspectives.* Harmondsworth, UK: Penguin.

Rutter, M., Yule, B., Quinton, D., Rowlands, O., Yule, W., & Berger, M. (1974). Attainment and adjustment in two geographic areas: Some factors accounting for area differences. *British Journal of Psychiatry, 126,* 520–533.

Sanders, M. R. (1996). New directions in behavioral family intervention with children. In T. H. Ollendick & R. J. Prinz (Eds.), *Advances in clinical child psychology* (Vol. 18, pp. 283–320). New York: Plenum Press.

Sayger, T. V., Horne, A. M., & Glaser, B. A. (1993). Marital satisfaction and social learning family therapy for child conduct problems: Generalization of treatment effects. *Journal of Marital and Family Therapy, 19,* 393–402.

Sayger, T. V., Horne, A. M., Walker, J. M., & Passmore, J. L. (1988). Social learning family therapy with aggressive children: Treatment outcome and maintenance. *Journal of Family Psychology, 1,* 261–285.

Schaughency, E. A., & Lahey, B. B. (1985). Mothers' and fathers' perceptions of child deviance: Roles of child behavior, parental depression, and marital satisfaction. *Journal of Consulting and Clinical Psychology, 53,* 718–723.

Schmaling, K. B., & Jacobson, N. S. (1987). *The clinical significance of treatment gains resulting from parent training interventions for children with conduct problems: An analysis of outcome data.* Paper presented at the meeting of the Association for the Advancement of Behavior Therapy, Boston.

Schreibman, L., Kaneko, W. M., & Koegel, R. L. (1991). Positive effects of parents of autistic children: A comparison across two teaching techniques. *Behavior Therapy, 22,* 479–490.

Seligman, M. E. P. (1975). *Helplessness.* San Francisco: Freeman.

Slaby, R., & Guerra, N. (1988). Cognitive mediators of aggression in adolescent offenders: 1. Assessment. *Development Psychology, 24,* 580–588.

Smith, A. M., & O'Leary, S. G. (1995). Attributions and arousal as predictors of maternal discipline. *Cognitive Therapy and Research, 19*(4), 459–471..

Speiker, S. J., & Booth, C. L. (1988). Maternal antecedants of attachment quality. In J. Belsky & T. Nnezworski (Eds.), *Clinical implications of attachment* (pp. 95–134). Hillsdale, NJ: Erlbaum.

Spitzer, A., Webster-Stratton, C., & Hollinsworth, T. (1991). Coping with conduct-problem children: Parents gaining knowledge and control. *Journal of Clinical Child Psychology, 20,* 413–427.

Spivak, G., Platt, J. J., & Shure, M. B. (1976). *The problem solving approach to adjustment.* San Francisco: Jossey-Bass.

Spoth, R., & Redmond, C. (1995). Parent motivation to enroll in parenting skills programs: A model of family context and health belief predictors. *Journal of Family Psychology, 9,* 294–310.

Strain, P. S., Steele, P., Ellis, T., & Timm, M. A. (1982). Long-term effects of oppositional child treatment with mothers as therapists and therapist trainers. *Journal of Applied Behavior Analysis, 15,* 1163–1169.

Straus, M. A., & Gelles, R. (1986). Societal change and change in family violence from 1975–1985 as revealed by two national surveys. *Journal of Marriage and the Family, 48,* 465–479.

Strayhorn, J. M., & Weidman, C. S. (1989). Reduction of attention deficit and internalizing symptoms in pre-schoolers through parent–child interaction training. *Journal of the American Academy of Child and Adolescent Psychiatry, 28,* 888–896.

Stroufe, L. A., & Fleeson, J. (1986). Attachment and the construction of relationships. In W. Hartup & Z. Rubin (Eds.), *Relationships and development* (pp. 51–71). Hillsdale, NJ: Erlbaum.

Taylor, T. K., Schmidt, F., & Hodgins, C. (1996). *A comparison of two treatments on young conduct problem children.* Paper presented at the American Psychological Association, Toronto, Canada.

Teti, D. M., Gelfand, D. M., & Messinger, D. S. (1995). *Developmental Psychology, 31,* 364–376.

Trickett, P. K., Aber, J. L., Carlson, V., & Cicchetti, D. (1991). Relationship of socioeconomic status to the etiology and developmental sequelae of physical child abuse. *Developmental Psychology, 27,* 148–158.

Wahler, R. G. (1975). Some structural aspects of deviant child behavior. *Journal of Applied Behavioral Analysis, 8,* 27–42.

Wahler, R. G. (1976). Deviant child behavior within the family: Developmental speculations and behavior change strategies. In H. Leitenberg (Ed.), *Handbook of behavior modification and behavior therapy.* Englewood Cliffs, NJ: Prentice-Hall.

Wahler, R. G. (1980). The insular mother: Her problems in parent–child treatment. *Journal of Applied Behavior Analysis, 13*(2), 207–219.

Wahler, R. G., & Afton, A. D. (1980). Attentional processes in insular and noninsular Mothers. *Child Behavior Therapy, 2,* 25–41.

Wahler, R. G., Cartor, P. G., Fleischman, J., & Lambert, W. (1993). The impact of synthesis teaching and parent training with mothers of conduct disordered children. *Journal of Abnormal Child Psychology, 12,* 425–440.

Wahler, R. G., & Dumas, J. E. (1984). Changing the observational coding styles of insular and noninsular mothers: A step toward maintenance of parent training effects. In R. F. Dangel & R. A. Polster (Eds.), *Parent training: Foundations of research and practice* (pp. 379–416). New York: Guilford Press.

Wahler, R. G., & Dumas, J. E. (1989). Attentional problems in dysfunctional mother–child interactions: An interbehavioral model. *Psychological Bulletin, 105,* 116–130.

Wahler, R. G., & Fox, J. J. (1982). Response structure in deviant child–parent relationships: Implications for family therapy. *Nebraska Symposium on Motivation, 29*(1), 1–46.

Wahler, R. G., & Sansbury, L. E. (1990). The monitoring skills of troubled mothers: Their problems in defining child deviance. *Journal of Abnormal Child Psychology, 18*(5), 577–589.

Walker, J. L., Lahey, B. B., Hynd, G. W., & Frame, C. L. (1987). Comparison of specific patterns of antisocial behavior in children with conduct disorder with or without coexisting hyperactivity. *Journal of Consulting and Clinical Psychology, 55*(6), 910–913.

Webster-Stratton, C. (1981a). Modification of mothers' behaviors and attitudes through videotape modeling group discussion program. *Behavior Therapy, 12,* 634–642.

Webster-Stratton, C. (1981b). Videotape modeling: A method of parent education. *Journal of Clinical Child Psychology, 10*(2), 93–98.

Webster-Stratton, C. (1982a). The long term effects of a videotape modeling parent training program: Comparison of immediate and 1-year followup results. *Behavior Therapy, 13,* 702–714.

Webster-Stratton, C. (1982b). Teaching mothers through videotape modeling to change their children's behaviors. *Journal of Pediatric Psychology, 7*(3), 279–294.

Webster-Stratton, C. (1984). Randomized trial of two parent-training programs for families with conduct-disordered children. *Journal of Consulting and Clinical Psychology, 52*(4), 666–678.

Webster-Stratton, C. (1985a). The effects of father involvement in parent training for conduct problem children. *Journal of Child Psychology and Psychiatry, 26*(5), 801–810.

Webster-Stratton, C. (1985b). Predictors of treatment outcome in parent training for conduct disordered children. *Behavior Therapy, 16,* 223–243.

Webster-Stratton, C. (1988). Mothers' and fathers' perceptions of child deviance: Roles of parent and child behaviors and parent adjustment. *Journal of Consulting and Clinical Psychology, 56*(6), 909–915.

Webster-Stratton, C. (1989). Systematic comparison of consumer satisfaction of three cost-effective parent training programs for conduct problem children. *Behavior Therapy, 20,* 103–115.

Webster-Stratton, C. (1990a). Long-term follow-up of families with young conduct problem children: From preschool to grade school. *Journal of Clinical Child Psychology, 19*(2), 144–149.

Webster-Stratton, C. (1990b). Stress: A potential disruptor of parent perceptions and family interactions. *Journal of Clinical Child Psychology, 19*(4), 302–312.

Webster-Stratton, C. (1992a). *The incredible years: A trouble-shooting guide for parents of children ages 3–8 years.* Toronto, Canada: Umbrella Press.

Webster-Stratton, C. (1992b). Supporting your child's education: parents and children videotape—program 8. Seth Enterprises, Seattle, WA.

Webster-Stratton, C. (1994). Advancing videotape parent training: A comparison study. *Journal of Consulting and Clinical Psychology, 62*(3), 583–593.

Webster-Stratton, C. (1995). *Preventing conduct problems in Head Start children: Preliminary short term results.*

Paper presented at the Society for Research in Child Development, Indianapolis, IN.

Webster-Stratton, C. (1996a). Early onset conduct problems: Does gender make a difference? *Journal of Consulting and Clinical Psychology, 64,* 540–551.

Webster-Stratton, C. (1996b). *Relationship between marital problem-solving and communication skills and child behaviors.* Unpublished manuscript, University of Washington, Seattle.

Webster-Stratton, C. (1997a). From parent training to community building. *Journal of Contemporary Services, 78,* 156–171.

Webster-Stratton, C. (1997b). Treating children with early-onset conduct problems: A comparison of child and parent training interventions. *Journal of Consulting and Clinical Psychology, 65*(1), 93–109.

Webster-Stratton, C., & Hammond, M. (1988). Maternal depression and its relationship to life stress, perceptions of child behavior problems, parenting behaviors and child conduct problems. *Journal of Abnormal Child Psychology, 16*(3), 299–315.

Webster-Stratton, C., & Hammond, M. (1990). Predictors of treatment outcome in parent training for families with conduct problem children. *Behavior Therapy, 21,* 319–337.

Webster-Stratton, C., & Hancock, L. (in press). Parent training: Content, methods and processes. In E. Schaefer (Ed.), *Parent training.* New York: Wiley.

Webster-Stratton, C., & Herbert, M. (1993). What really happens in parent training? *Behavior Modification, 17*(4), 407–456.

Webster-Stratton, C., & Herbert, M. (1994). *Troubled families—Problem children: Working with parents: A collaborative process.* Chichester, UK: Wiley.

Webster-Stratton, C., Hollinsworth, T., & Kolpacoff, M. (1989). The long-term effectiveness and clinical significance of three cost-effective training programs for families with conduct-problem children. *Journal of Consulting and Clinical Psychology, 57*(4), 550–553.

Webster-Stratton, C., Kolpacoff, M., & Hollinsworth, T. (1988). Self-administered videotape therapy for families with conduct-problem children: Comparison with two cost-effective treatments and a control group. *Journal of Consulting and Clinical Psychology, 56*(4), 558–566.

Wells, K. C., & Egan, J. (1988). Social learning and systems family therapy for childhood oppositional disorder: Comparative treatment outcome. *Comprehensive Psychiatry, 29*(2), 138–146.

White, A. G., & Bailey, J. S. (1990). Reducing disruptive behaviors of elementary physical education students with sit and watch. *Journal of Applied Behavior Analyses, 23*(3), 353–359.

5.09
Play Therapy

SANDRA W. RUSS
Case Western Reserve University, Cleveland, OH, USA

5.09.1 INTRODUCTION

Play therapy is in a state of transition. Play has been a part of therapy with children since Melanie Klein (1927) and Anna Freud (1927) first began using play techniques in child therapy in the 1930s. As of 1992, play in some form was used in child therapy by a majority of clinicians, as reported by Koocher and D'Angelo (1992). They stated that "play-oriented therapy remains the dominant and most enduring approach to child treatment ... practiced by clinicians" (p. 458). At the same time, play therapy is being increasingly criticized, along with many types of child therapy, for not having demonstrated treatment efficacy. In truth, there is not a strong empirical base for the effectiveness of play therapy (Phillips, 1985).

Suffice it to state, the empirical base of play therapy has not grown along with the clinical application of play therapy.

Nevertheless, there is an empirical literature in various areas of child psychology that supports the importance of play in child development. Play is involved in the development of many cognitive, affective, and personality processes that are important for adaptive functioning. Unfortunately, the field has not yet learned how to apply this accumulating knowledge base to play therapy. We know much about the role of play in child development, but have not utilized this knowledge in developing intervention and prevention programs that can be evaluated empirically. Research programs need to be developed that expand our knowledge about how play effects change and how we can facilitate play. The main point in this chapter is the thesis that play is an extremely worthwhile intervention approach with children and should be extensively investigated so that we can help children utilize this resource more effectively.

5.09.2 THEORETICAL UNDERPINNINGS

The theoretical underpinnings of play therapy come from two different sources. The first is the theory from the child psychotherapy literature. The second source is the theory and empirical work from the child development literature.

5.09.2.1 Conceptualizations from Child Therapy

In the child therapy literature, three broad functions of play emerge as important in therapy. First, play is a natural form of expression in children. Chethik (1989) refers to the language of play. Children use play to express feelings and thoughts. Chethik states that play emerges from the child's internal life and reflects the child's internal world. Therefore, children use play to express affect and fantasy and, in therapy, to express troubling and conflict-laden feelings. The expression of feelings itself, sometimes termed catharsis, is thought to be therapeutic (Axline, 1947; A. Freud, 1965; Moustakas, 1953). The therapist facilitates this process by giving permission for feelings to be expressed and by labeling the affect. By labeling the affect, the therapist helps to make the feeling less overwhelming and more understandable. In addition, the child feels more accepted as a whole person by the therapist and, in turn, is thought to become more self-accepting.

The child also uses this language of play to communicate with the therapist. It is essential that the therapist understand these communications, so that the therapeutic relationship can develop (Chethik, 1989). The therapist actively labels, empathizes and interprets the play, which in turn, helps the child feel understood (Russ, 1995). For many children, this feeling of empathy from the therapist facilitates change in their interpersonal representations and interpersonal functioning. The importance of expression through play and communication with the therapist is thought to be important by both psychodynamic and client-centered or person-centered approaches.

A second major function of play is as a vehicle for the occurrence of insight and working through. The conceptualization of this function of play is a psychodynamic one. Psychodynamic theory views the emotional resolution of conflict or trauma as a major mechanism of change in child therapy. Children reexperience major developmental conflicts or situational traumas in therapy. Many of these conflicts are expressed in play. The play process itself has been thought of as a form of conflict resolution. For example, Waelder (1933) has described the play process as one in which the child repeats an unpleasant experience over and over until it becomes manageable.

Freedheim and Russ (1992) described the slow process of gaining access to conflict-laden material and playing it out until the conflict is resolved. Erickson (1963) presented the concept of mastery, in which the child uses play to gain mastery over traumatic events and everyday conflicts. During this process, the therapist labels and interprets the play. Although there is controversy in the psychodynamic literature about how much interpretation should occur (Klein, 1955; A. Freud, 1966/1937), there is general agreement that working through and mastery are important mechanisms of change in play therapy.

A third major function of play in therapy is that of providing opportunities to practice with a variety of ideas, behaviors, interpersonal behaviors, and verbal expressions. Because play is occurring in a safe environment, in a pretend world, with a permissive, nonjudgmental adult, the child can try out a variety of expressions and behaviors without concern about real-life consequences. In some forms of play therapy, the therapist is quite directive in guiding the child to try new behaviors. For example, Knell (1993) developed a cognitive behavioral play therapy approach that actively uses modeling techniques and a variety of cognitive behavioral techniques.

It is important to point out that although these three major functions of play occur in normal play situations, the therapist builds on these normal functions by enhancing the play experience. The therapist creates a safe environment, gives permission for play to occur, actively facilitates play, and labels the thoughts and feelings expressed. For the psychodynamic therapist, interpretation specifically aids conflict-resolution. Because there are so many individual differences in play skills and abilities in children, there are many different kinds of play therapy techniques that are utilized.

5.09.2.2 Conceptualizations from Child Development

Conceptualizations from child development theory and research are relevant to the area of play therapy. Play is thought to facilitate both cognitive and emotional development. Children's play is related to a number of cognitive and affective processes that are important in child development (Russ, 1995). There is evidence that play facilitates cognitive and emotional development (see D. Singer & J. L. Singer, 1990, and Russ, 1993, 1995 for reviews). In play therapy, the therapy process uses these change processes, although not yet in any kind of systematic fashion. Research in this area is reviewed later in this chapter.

Play has been linked to the development of cognitive processes important in logical problem solving and in creative problem solving (Singer & Singer, 1990). For example, play has been related to and has facilitated insight ability (Vandenberg, 1980) and divergent thinking ability (Dansky, 1980; Russ & Grossman-McKee, 1990). Both cognitive and affective processes, important in creative thinking, are facilitated through play (Russ, 1993, 1995). In therapy, as both types of problem solving abilities develop, problem solving in everyday life can be enhanced.

Play is also thought to be related to general adjustment. Again, both cognitive and affective processes, important in adjustment, are developed in play. Play helps children learn to express and regulate their emotions. Play helps develop cognitive structures that, in turn, help children to integrate and modulate their emotions.

Children also use play to practice with and try out various coping strategies for different situations (Christiano & Russ, 1996). Children role play different scenarios and generate different solutions to everyday problems and stressful situations. For example, a child might try out different ways to handle teasing from other children or prepare for a frightening situation. In the Christiano and Russ (1996) study, the ability to express emotion and use good fantasy in play was related to the amount and variety of coping efforts children made in a

dental situation. Good players also reported less distress.

Traditionally, the play therapist has utilized all of these conceptualizations and mechanisms of change in working with children. The choice of specific techniques and mechanisms of change has depended upon the conceptualization of the case. What is needed for the future are play intervention strategies based on research that are matched to specific types of child populations.

5.09.3 HISTORY OF PLAY THERAPY

The history of play therapy is intertwined with the history of child therapy, and play has been used in different ways in different theoretical approaches (Kessler, 1988). Play was first used in child therapy by therapists in the psychoanalytic tradition. Tuma and Russ (1993) reviewed the psychoanalytic literature in detail. Psychoanalytic techniques were adapted to children by Hug-Hellmuth (1921, 1924), A. Freud (1927), and Burlingham (1932). Play was used to substitute for free association. In addition, the therapist was more responsive and gratifying to the child than the therapist would be with adults, and the child therapist actively worked to develop a positive attachment (A. Freud, 1946). Melanie Klein saw the importance of the communication value of play. She suggested that play for the child was the same as free association for the adult. She advocated active and direct interpretation of the unconscious processes expressed in play. Therefore, the therapist would continually interpret the child's play. A. Freud (1966/1937) also viewed play as a direct expression of fantasy and instincts in a less disguised and more accessible form than in adults. A. Freud was more cautious in her interpretations of the meaning of the child's play. She was also more respectful of the child's defenses than was Klein, and encouraged greater participation by the child. She thought that it was important that therapy be a positive experience for the child and that the child want to come to therapy.

The psychoanalytic approach has evolved into the psychodynamic approach. Psychodynamic therapists base their interventions and techniques on psychoanalytic principles, but therapy is shorter, less frequent (once a week rather than 4 or 5 times a week), has more focused and immediate goals, and is more flexible in incorporating a variety of therapeutic techniques (Tuma & Russ, 1993). Play remains a core part of the therapy process. The use of play in therapy and in child development is a great legacy of the psychoanalytic tradition.

The client-centered and relationship approaches to child treatment also utilized play. Axline (1947), in her nondirective approach, has the therapist focus on play as a major form of communication for and with the child. The therapist strives to understand and empathize with the child's issues. Interpretation of underlying dynamics or impulses is rare, however. The therapist trusts the child's developmental process and striving for self-development. A wonderful introduction to the use of play in child therapy, for beginning therapists of any theoretical perspective, is Axline's *Dibbs in Search of Self* (1964). Moustakas (1953) was another lending theorist in this area who stressed the importance of expression of feelings in play and the importance of the relationship between the child and therapist. Moustakas discussed the importance of the child and therapist experiencing each other (Moustakas, 1992). Genuineness in the relationship is an important aspect of therapy for Moustakas.

Although not usually associated with cognitive behavior therapy approaches, play has been used as a tool within that framework (Kessler, 1988). Meichenbaum (1974) thought that imagery and fantasy could be used to teach children self-control. Knell (1993) has developed cognitive behavioral play therapy techniques that use principles of modeling and reinforcement.

In addition, play techniques have been used in a variety of more specific approaches, such as Gardener's (1971) mutual story-telling techniques and Levy's (1938) release therapy for children who have experience trauma.

Today, as Koocher and D'Angelo (1992) stated, play approaches are the dominant treatment approaches in working with children. Play is used with a variety of child populations, in short-term and long-term approaches, and by a variety of theoretical approaches. Trends in child psychotherapy apply to play therapy as well. Therapy is becoming more specific, more focused, more active, and more theoretically integrated (Freedheim & Russ, 1992).

5.09.4 ASSESSMENT AND CLINICAL FORMULATION

One purpose of psychological assessment is to obtain a developmental picture of the child in specific areas of cognitive and personality functioning. Assessment determines how the child is functioning in areas of basic cognitive processes, object relations, capacity for empathy, internalized conflicts, capacity for delay of gratification, self-esteem, and coping resources (Russ, in press). Ultimately, assessment should help with choosing the optimal form of intervention. Play is frequently a part of the assessment process.

When one has the luxury of time, a battery of psychological tests combined with a play or interview session will usually give the fullest view of a child. Of course, information from the individual assessment of the child should be combined with multiple sources of information from the parents, school, and community. Because managed care has resulted in pressures to move more quickly in clinical practice, one must select carefully which assessment methods to use. Only the most reliable and empirically validated measures should be used.

The fact that most child psychologists use tests that tap different psychological processes is reflected in the results of different surveys of child practitioners. Tuma and Pratt (1982) found that most psychologists in their survey used intelligence tests (primarily the Wechsler Intelligence Scales), achievement measures, and projective tests such as the Rorschach, TAT, and drawings. Archer, Maruish, Imhof, and Piatrowski (1991), in a survey focusing on psychological assessment of adolescents, found that the most frequently used tests were the Wechsler Intelligence Scales, the Rorschach (ranked second overall), Bender-Gestalt, TAT, Sentence Completion, and the MMPI. Of those respondents who used a standard assessment battery (139 of 165), the most frequently used measures were the Wechsler, Rorschach, and TAT.

When using a standard battery, different processes are measured by different tests (Tuma & Russ, 1993). Measures of intelligence and perceptual motor functioning (such as the Bender-Gestalt) give information about basic cognitive functioning. Even if there is not a specific question about school performance, the intelligence test is valuable because it assesses how well the child is functioning in a variety of cognitive and perceptual areas. Intelligence tests provide an anchor for a developmental assessment.

Projective tests give information about the personality structure and personality dynamics of the child. Play and interview information are useful for this purpose as well. Frequently, the Rorschach and a story-telling projective technique (e.g., the TAT, Children's Apperception Test or CAT, and Roberts Apperception Test for Children) will be used together.

The Rorschach is especially valuable in describing personality structure (Exner, 1986). Exner discussed how the Rorschach reveals the organizing principles that the individual uses to deal with the world. This is true of children as well as adults. The Rorschach assesses reality testing, the capacity to perceive what is commonly perceived in situations, and how affect influences cognitive functioning. It also assess how the child experiences the world in terms of availability of affect, capacity to experience negative affects, and internal representations of other people.

Projective tests that involve telling stories complement the Rorschach by assessing personality dynamics. The child's wishes, fears, conflicts, and specific areas of emotional distress can emerge. Increasingly available are projective tests containing stimuli appropriate for younger children and ethnic minorities. Drawings and fantasy play can also be used as diagnostic instruments which are especially valuable in revealing personality dynamics.

Projective tests are being rediscovered with the growing focus on the development of object relations as a key element in a child's development. Projective tests are especially suited to assessing object relations. In a review of the literature, Stricker and Healey (1990) defined object relations as concerning "the cognitive, affective, and emotional processes that mediate interpersonal functioning in close relationships" (p. 219). Understanding the developmental level of the child's object relations gives clues to the interpersonal world of the child and offers a framework for explaining interpersonal difficulties the child may be having. Stricker and Healey (1990) also reviewed the major Rorschach-based and TAT-based object relations scales. These scales are relatively new and are still being validated. Interpersonal content has always been part of projective tests, but these new scales and the growing theoretical literature on object relations enable us to develop a more comprehensive understanding of this area by means of a more systematic evaluation of this variable.

Projective tests have been criticized for their lack of demonstrated validity (Dawes, 1994). However, a growing body of construct validity studies on the Rorschach (Weiner, 1996) and story-telling techniques (Westen, 1991) are available and should serve as a guide for when projective tests are appropriate.

Observer rating scales and self-report instruments round out the picture by offering well-validated diagnostic information about the child, compared with their same-aged peers.

5.09.4.1 Assessing Children's Play

Assessing children's play is a valuable addition to a standard test battery. Although many young children cannot readily engage in an interview, they can engage in play. Until the early 1990s there were very few standardized measures of children's play available. Schaefer, Gitlen, and Sangrund (1991) have reviewed the growing number of current play measures. As these play measures become better known and as their reliability and validity is ascertained, we can begin to assess play in a systematic way prior to, during, and after treatment. The development of play assessment instruments is an important step for the field. A formal assessment of play could tell us how well the child plays; assess how well the child could use play in therapy; identify the important conflict areas; assess how well affect is expressed and is regulated; determine how constricted the child's fantasy is; assess the development of internal representations; and assess the child's overall cognitive organization. Some of the information would supplement other test information and some would be unique. For example, the best way to determine how well a child can use play in therapy is to observe the child at play.

One possible instrument for assessing play is the Affect in Play Scale (Russ, 1987, 1993). In order to study affect in play and its correlate the Affect in Play Scale was developed by Russ and her students. This scale consists of a standardized puppet play task and specific criteria for a rating scale. The play task utilizes two neutral looking puppets, one boy and one girl and three small blocks that are laid out on a table. It is administered individually to the child. The play task is appropriate for children from 5 to 10 years of age. The instructions ask the child to play with the puppets any way he or she likes for five minutes. The play is videotaped. The instructions can be altered to pull for specific affective themes such as aggression or happiness. An extensive manual has been developed for rating the play. The Affect in Play Scale measures the amount of affect, type of affect, variety of affect, intensity of affect, comfort, quality of fantasy, imagination, and affective integration in the play. There are 11 possible affective categories: Happiness/Pleasure; Anxiety/Fear; Sadness/Hurt; Frustration/Displeasure; Nurturance/Affection; Aggression; Oral; Oral Aggression; Anal; Sexual; and Competition. Any verbal or physical expression between the puppets that reflects an affective category is rated as one affective unit. For example, if one puppet says to the other "I don't like you" it would be scored for one unit of aggressive content.

The Affect in Play Scale has good interater reliability, internal consistency, and good stability of scores across different samples of children. The scale has been used with public school, parochial school, middle-class suburban and inner city populations and has a growing body of validity studies. A review of the Affect in Play Scale and the manual can be found in Russ (1993). This scale could also be used as a measure of change in play intervention research and in play psychotherapy.

It is important to note that for many of the play measures available, including the Affect in Play Scale, play does not relate to traditional IQ measures (Russ & Grossman-McKee, 1990; Singer, 1973). Most of this research has been with children of normal intelligence. Children with major cognitive deficits should also show serious deficits in play skills. Nevertheless, it is important to have measures of children's fantasy and cognitive organization that are relatively independent of intelligence.

Play assessment is well-suited to a repeated measure design, (Russ, in press-b). Changes in the quality of play or the themes in play should occur during therapy. Different types of changes should occur for different types of children. For example, the constricted child should express more affect in play after therapy. The acting-out child should show better modulation of affect in play after treatment. Play measures should be sensitive to change processes in psychotherapy. Shirk and Russell (1996) have stressed the importance of developing measures that are sensitive to specific processes that are being addressed in psychotherapy. Play assessment can focus on cognitive, affective, and interpersonal processes important in psychotherapy.

The general assessment process should help the therapist formulate a diagnostic picture and assess the child's motivation for treatment, capacity to establish a good relationship, and ability to use play and/or verbalization. It should help decide what type of intervention to use, what specific process or symptom should be targeted, and treatment goals. Major mechanisms of change and techniques to bring about those changes should be identified. This leads to the discussion of intervention procedures and mechanisms of change.

5.09.5 INTERVENTION PROCEDURES AND PROPOSED MECHANISMS OF CHANGE

The concept of play psychotherapy is a bit of a misnomer because most psychotherapy with children is a mix of play and talk (Russ, 1995). Play is a tool which can be used in therapy for a variety of purposes. If and how play is used with a particular child in therapy depends upon the child's ability to use play, developmental level, age, ability to verbalize, and the overall treatment approach. In general, play therapy occurs within the context of the overall treatment plan.

In most forms of play therapy, the child and therapist meet individually once a week for 45–50 minute sessions. The mutual agreement between the child and the therapist is that the therapist is there to help the child express feelings and thoughts, understand causes of behavior, and form a relationship with the therapist (Freedheim & Russ, 1992). Traditionally, in both psychodynamic and client-centered approaches, the child structures the therapeutic hour by choosing the topics, forms of play, and setting the pace of therapy. In most cases, individual work with the child is only one part of the treatment program. Parent guidance and education, family sessions, and work with the school usually occur simultaneously with individual child therapy.

5.09.5.1 Issues in Using Play in Therapy

A number of practical issues arise in working with children in play therapy. Ideally, a psychological assessment will have been carried out so that the therapist has identified treatment goals and has developed a treatment plan. The therapist should have determined how much play will be utilized in the therapy, as well as the nature of the play to be encouraged. Usually, play approaches should be considered for children from 4 to 10 years of age.

5.09.5.1.1 How to get started

Many children need help initiating the play process. The therapist usually starts by telling the child that they can play or talk, and shows the child the toys and play materials that are available. Although many children go right to it, many others are reticent. The therapist might tell the child to pick one thing, and start with that or the therapist could pick something for the child. Clay and drawing material are good starters. As a last resort, the therapist might start with something themselves, and have the child join in.

5.09.5.1.2 Kinds of play materials

Most therapists agree that unstructured play materials that can encourage the use of fantasy and imagination are ideal. Toys that leave much room for individual expression are most appropriate for play therapy. Examples of relatively unstructured toys and material are: clay, crayons, cars, trucks, puppets, dolls, doll houses, and legos. Games such as checkers do not encourage free expression, and are not ideal for traditional play therapy. The child is often asked for suggestions of other toys that might be useful and encouraged to bring toys in from home. Different children use different media for expression and it is important to have a variety of items and to individually tailor what is available.

5.09.5.1.3 How much to engage in play

One recurring dilemma is how much the therapist should engage in the child's play. The amount of direction and activity by the therapist depends upon the general theoretical approach. In more traditional client-centered and psychodynamic approaches, the therapist tries not to play with the child, but rather to observe and comment on the child's play. Many children will eventually become comfortable playing in this way. Some children need more engagement by the therapist. With those children, the therapist tries to follow the lead of the child. The therapist might put on one of the puppets and play, but follow the lead of the child in choosing the topic and setting the dialogue.

In more directive approaches, such as cognitive-behavioral play therapy (Knell, 1993), the therapist will play in a very directive fashion. The therapist might put on a play, modeling adaptive coping strategies for an issue that the child is dealing with.

5.09.5.1.4 How much to interpret

An optimal amount of interpretation of the child's play would facilitate the play process and help the child understand his or her thoughts, feelings, and behavior. Too much interpretation will stop the play process. Most therapists today would agree with A. Freud (1976) that the child's defenses should be respected. Timing of interpretations is as important in child therapy as in adult therapy.

5.09.5.1.5 How to set limits

For play to be a safe mode of expression, limits about how to play are essential. If rules need to be set, then they should be set. Toys cannot be broken and the therapist cannot be a target for affective expression. Alternative modes of expression through play should be facilitated. For example, the child can be encouraged to verbalize anger at the therapist or to have the puppets fight it out in a pretend mode.

5.09.5.2 Mechanisms of Change in Therapy

How one uses play in the therapy depends upon how one conceptualizes the specific mechanisms of change to be used in the therapy. Freedheim and Russ (1983, 1992) identified six major mechanisms of change that occur in individual child psychotherapy. These mechanisms were based on those identified by Applebaum (1978) and Garfield (1980) in the adult literature. Different mechanisms of change are utilized in different types of psychodynamic psychotherapy with different types of childhood disorders. However, there is rarely a pure type of psychotherapy and frequently all of these mechanisms may occur in any one case. These mechanisms of change are thought to be universal and to cut across various theoretical approaches to psychotherapy. The specific role of play in these mechanisms was discussed by Russ (1995).

(i) *Catharsis and Labeling of Feeling.* Through talk and play, children express feelings and release emotion. This release of emotion has long been thought to be therapeutic (Axline, 1947, A. Freud, 1965; Moustakas, 1953). In addition, by labeling affect, the therapist helps to make the feeling less overwhelming and more understandable. Often, the labeling of affect occurs during pretend play. By saying to the child that the puppet is feeling angry, the therapist connects a label to a feeling state. Words help to put feelings into a context for the child, thus making the feelings less overwhelming.

(ii) *Corrective Emotional Experience.* The therapist accepts the child's feeling and thoughts. Often, the child's learned expectations are not met and a corrective emotional experience occurs (Kessler, 1966). For example, the automatic connection between the child's angry feelings towards father and resultant anxiety should gradually decrease as the therapist helps the child accept the feeling and understand the reasons for the anger. The therapist is not punitive, and is accepting of the child's having angry feelings. Often, these feelings are expressed through play.

(iii) *Insight and Working Through.* The emotional resolution of conflict or trauma is a major mechanism of change in play psychotherapy. One goal of the therapist when utilizing this mechanism of change is to help the child reexperience major developmental conflicts or situational traumas in therapy. Frequently, play is the vehicle for this working through process. Cognitive insight into origins of feelings and conflicts, causes of symptoms, links between thoughts, feelings, and actions is a goal of psychotherapy when underlying conflicts are a major issue (Sandler, Kennedy, & Tyson, 1980; Shirk & Russell, 1996). Verbal labeling of unconscious impulses, conflicts, and causes of behavior helps lend higher order reasoning skills to understanding problems. However, in many cases, especially with young children, cognitive insight does not occur. Rather, emotional reexperiencing, emotional working through, and mastery do occur and result in symptom reduction and healthy adjustment. This is an important point and is an often overlooked mechanism of change in child treatment. Messer and Warren (1995) also state that the goal of making the unconscious conscious needs to be modified in child play therapy with many children. In Erikson's (1963) concept of mastery, the child uses play to gain mastery over traumatic events and everyday conflicts. Resolving conflicts through play is part of normal child development. Waelder (1933) described the play process as one in which the child repeats an unpleasant experience over and over until it becomes manageable. As he puts it, the child "digests" the event. Freedheim and Russ (1992) describe the slow process of gaining access to conflict-laden material and playing it out until the conflict is resolved. The therapist helps guide the play, labels thoughts, feelings, and events, and makes interpretations to facilitate conflict resolution and the working through process. Because cognitive insight is not necessary for conflict resolution to occur, the amount of interpretation should be carefully considered by the therapist. This is especially true of interpretation of symbols in the play or of deeply forbidden wishes. Mild interpretations that link feelings and thoughts to behavior and that spell out cause and effect are especially helpful.

(iv) *Learning Alternative Problem-Solving Techniques and Coping Strategies.* The therapist, in a more directive approach, helps the child think about alternative ways of viewing a situation and generate problem-solving strategies. Role-playing and modeling of coping strategies are used. Practice with a variety of verbal expressions and interpersonal behaviors can occur in a safe, pretend play situation. For example, D. Singer (1993) gives examples of modeling techniques during therapy. Knell (1993) teaches the child new strategies for coping with feelings and situations.

(v) *Development of Internal Structure.* Many children have structural deficits that result in problems with self/object differentiation, interpersonal functioning, self-esteem regulation, impulse control, object constancy, and separation of fantasy from reality. In these children, there are major deficits in underlying cognitive, affective, and interpersonal processes. Structure-building approaches are based upon conceptualizations by Mahler (1968) and Kohut (1977) and view the therapist as being a stable, predictable, caring and empathic figure. Development of good object relations is a major goal of play therapy with these children. Gilpin

(1976) stressed that the role of the therapist is to become an internalized object. The relationship between the therapist and child is probably the most important aspect of therapy in helping this process to occur. Genuine understanding and expression of empathy by the therapist is a major technique that enables the child to develop. Play is important here as a form of communication in that the therapist can empathize with the child's expressions. The major change that occurs is through the relationship with the therapist that facilitates developing interpersonal representations in the child.

(vi) *Nonspecific Variables.* Nonspecific variables function in child therapy as they do in adult therapy. Expectation of change, hope, awareness of parental concern, no longer feeling so alone, are all factors that contribute to change in therapy.

5.09.5.3 Mechanisms of Change in Different Types of Therapy

5.09.5.3.1 *Psychodynamic play therapy*

Different types of therapy emphasize different mechanisms of change. Different techniques are used to foster the different mechanisms. The form of therapy most associated with the psychodynamic approach is insight-oriented therapy, and it is most appropriate for the child with anxiety and internalized conflicts (Tuma & Russ, 1993). This approach is appropriate for children who have age-appropriate ego development, show evidence of internal conflicts, have the ability to trust adults, have some degree of psychological-mindedness, and can use play effectively. Insight-oriented therapy is most often recommended for internalizing disorders including many of the anxiety disorders and depressive disorders. Children with internalizing disorders often experience internal conflicts and have good ego development and good object relations. An insight-oriented approach with a focus on conflict resolution is most appropriate for internalizing disorders. Many children in this broad category are good players and can easily engage in play in the therapy situation.

The goals of insight-oriented therapy are to help the child resolve internal conflicts and master developmental tasks. The major mechanism of change is insight and working through. Through the use of play and interpretation from the therapist, the child "calls forth forbidden fantasy and feelings, works through and masters developmental problems, and resolves conflicts" (Freedheim & Russ, 1983). Active interpretation of the child's play, expressions, and resistances is a major technique. For example, the therapist might interpret a child's stealing from mother's purse as an expression of anger at feeling neglected by her after the birth of a baby brother.

Insight and working through can also be helpful for a child with good inner resources who has experienced a specific trauma (such as the loss of as a parent). Altschul (1988) described the use of psychoanalytic approaches in helping children to mourn the loss of as a parent. In this application, Webber (1988) stressed that the therapist must first address the question of whether the child can do his or her own psychological work. If not, therapy can be a major aid in the mourning process.

A second major form of psychotherapy is the structure-building approach, which is used with children with structural deficits and major problems in developing good object relations. For children with impaired object relations, self/other boundary disturbances, and difficulty distinguishing fantasy from reality, the therapist uses techniques that foster the development of object permanence, self/other differentiation, and modulation of affect. The major mechanism of change is the building of internal structure such as object relations. Anna Freud (1965) described the development of object relations through a continual process of separation from the significant adult, usually the mother. Mahler (1975) elaborated on the separation-individuation process and described the development of object constancy and object representations. As Blank and Blank (1986) stressed, Mahler's concept of separation-individuation represented a new organizing principle to development. Object relations is not just another ego function, but plays a major role in the organization of intrapsychic processes.

The growing theory on the development of object relations is a new phase in psychoanalytic theory construction (Tuma & Russ, 1993). Good object relations involve well-developed object representations. The child must invest in the mental representation of the loved external object. Children who have inadequately developed object relations have structural deficits that impair a variety of functions. This impairment is evident with psychotic and characterological disorders. Children with severely impaired object relations, such as borderline children, have early developmental problems with a mix of severe dysfunction in the family and in the case of borderline children, perhaps a genetic predisposition. These children require a structure-building psychotherapeutic approach.

In this approach, empathy on the part of the therapist (as a general relationship factor) (Kohut & Wolfe, 1978) is a much more important intervention than is interpretation (Russ, 1995). Chethik (1989) provided an excellent discussion of psychotherapy with borderline children and narcissistically disturbed children. He pointed out that many of the therapeutic techniques are supportive in that they "shore up" defenses. The problems characteristic of borderline and narcissistic children are early developmental problems usually stemming from severe disturbance in the parent-child interaction. Kohut and Wolfe (1978) discussed the failure of empathy from the parent that is a major issue in the faulty parent-child interaction. Because of the frequency of this defect in parent-child relations, empathy from the therapist around the history of empathic failure becomes an important part of therapy. Frequently, help with problem solving and coping is also used with these children. Therapy with these children is usually long-term (one to two years) to be effective.

A third form of psychodynamic therapy is supportive psychotherapy, most appropriate for children with externalizing disorders. These children frequently act-out, have antisocial tendencies, and are impulse-ridden. The broad syndrome of externalizing disorders includes labels of acting-out, antisocial, character disorders, attention deficit disorders, and conduct disorders. Theoretically, psychodynamic theory views these children as having major developmental problems. These children have not yet adequately developed the processes necessary for delay of gratification. In addition, these children are frequently egocentric, demonstrate an absence of shame and guilt, and their ability to empathize with others is impaired. Kessler (1988) has recommended that structured, supportive therapy is more helpful to these children than any other kind of psychodynamic therapy. Therapy focuses on the here and now and on the development of problem-solving skills and coping resources. For example, the therapist might role-play with the child about how to handle teasing at school or how to be assertive with parents.

At this point, given the effectiveness of behavioral and cognitive-behavioral approaches in working with externalizing disorders, it appears that supportive psychodynamic psychotherapy is not the treatment of choice (Russ, 1995). It should only be used as a supplement to other treatment approaches in order to work on a specific issue.

Chethik (1989) has a thorough discussion of the use of play within the psychodynamic approach. As reviewed by Tuma and Russ (1993), he describes four stages of play development within psychotherapy (see Chethik, 1989, pp. 48–66 for a more detailed description).

(i) Initial period of nonengagement. Setting the stage-developing expectations, structure, and limits. The therapist first defines how play will be used for communication and how the child's internal life combined with play materials will express and replay the child's internal life for them both. "Meaningful play" must be developed, sometimes by varying the structure. This means that the overinstinctualized child (e.g., impulsive, fast to react) may require more structure, whereas the underinstinctualized child (e.g., obsessive, slow to react) may need to be encouraged to express instinctual life in play.

(ii) Early phase of affective engagement. As play develops, the therapist begins to share metaphors that emerge, and the child becomes attached to both the process and the therapist. When this happens, the therapist can then permit regressions by becoming a player in the play (by doing what the child asks him or her to do). The child can then express his or her instinctual life more freely because he or she identifies with the therapist and the therapist's sanctions. The safety the child feels in expressions are further ensured by imposing boundaries (e.g., by keeping forbidden expression in the room or having clean-up time). The unstructured quality, the accepting attitudes, and the boundaries all foster early "regression in the service of the ego." As the child feels more comfortable and masters anxiety, his or her play becomes more open. Those expressions at first defensively avoided are now displayed in full view of the therapist.

(iii) Emergence of central fantasies. As the process intensifies, the child elaborates highly invested fantasies in play. Repetitive play (characterized by the "compulsion to repeat") begins to deal with past traumatic and difficult situations. In the therapy process, however, the past has a changed outcome: acceptance of the play and interpretations by the therapist permit new solutions, either verbally or through play. Now the situation is in the control of the child.

(iv) Period of working through. Specific symptoms or behaviors often have more than one meaning. A working through period is necessary where a series and variety of interpretations are made to bring about change in a symptom. Symptoms are discussed in different contexts until all the meanings are worked out.

5.09.5.3.2 Cognitive-behavioural play therapy

Principles of cognitive-behavioral therapy and play therapy have been integrated into one approach. Knell (1993) introduced the concept of Cognitive-behavioral play therapy (CBPT) in which cognitive and behavioral

interventions are incorporated within a play therapy paradigm. Play itself is used to resolve problems.

Knell (1993) identified six properties of CBPT:

(i) The child is involved in the treatment through play.

(ii) CBPT focuses on the child's thoughts, fantasies, and environment.

(iii) CBPT provides a strategy or strategies for developing more adaptive thoughts and behaviors. The child is taught coping strategies for feelings and for situations.

(iv) CBPT is structured, directive, and goal oriented, rather than open-ended.

(v) CBPT incorporates empirically demonstrated techniques, such as modeling.

(vi) CBPT allows for an empirical examination of treatment.

Knell (1993) also identified similarities and differences between CBPT and more traditional psychodynamic or client-centered approaches. Similarities included: the importance of the therapeutic relationship; communications occur through play; therapy is a safe place; and play provides "clues" to understanding the child.

Differences suggested that in CBPT therapy is more directed and goal oriented; the therapist is involved in choosing play materials; play is used to teach skills and alternative behaviors; interpretations are given by the therapist (similar to psychodynamic but different from client-centered) and praise is a crucial component. It is also more empirically based.

These similarities and differences are true for the "classic" forms of psychodynamic play therapy. However, new forms of psychodynamic play therapy are also being developed that are more goal oriented. For example, Chethik's (1989) focal therapy is focused on specific problems and is of short duration. Messer and Warren (1995) have called for psychodynamic approaches to be adapted to short-term goal oriented frameworks. They state that short-term therapy is a frequent form of psychodynamic intervention and that play is a good vehicle for change. Still, Knell's (1993) approach is a thoughtful integration of different theoretical approaches and techniques and is an excellent model for how to integrate treatment approaches.

Bodiford-McNeil, Hembree-Kigin, and Eyberg (1996) have developed a CBPT approach that is focused on a specific population of children. Their short-term play therapy for disruptive children utilizes the principles of CBPT but tailors the approach for disruptive children. Their approach is also set for 12 sessions with very specific goals and objectives per session. For most of the 12 sessions, the first half of the session is task-oriented and the second half is child-directed play. The therapist uses a variety of techniques such as praise, reflection, imitation of play, questions, interpretation, reinforcement, and contingent attention. The therapist follows the child's lead in the play, but also tries to move it as quickly as possible. By the eighth session, the parent is included in the process and is coached to facilitate the child's play. Parents practice their play sessions at home with the child. Parents are taught most of the play facilitation skills, but not that of interpretation, which belongs in the domain of psychotherapy. Bodiford-McNeil et al.'s approach integrates techniques from a variety of theoretical approaches and chooses those that are most effective for a specific population, that is disruptive children. It is a good example of developing an integrated approach for a specific population.

5.09.5.4 Change Processes in Play in Child Development

Play facilitates change and growth in a variety of cognitive, affective, and personality processes. Play fosters growth in these areas in normal child development. These change mechanisms are thought to operate in the play therapy process, although not usually in a targeted and systematic fashion. The empirical literature in the play and child development area is relevant to the play psychotherapy literature. Russ (in press) has a more detailed review of the play and child development literature, with a specific focus on creativity.

5.09.5.4.1 Play and cognitive processes

Research has supported a relationship between play and creative cognitive processes (Dansky, 1980; Fein, 1981; Russ, in press-a). Saltz, Dixon, and Johnson (1977) found that fantasy play facilitated cognitive functioning on a variety of measures. They theorized that fantasy play is related to cognitive development because of the involvement of representational skills and concept formation. Singer and Singer (1976) concluded that the capacity for imaginative play is positively related to divergent thinking, verbal fluency, and cognitive functioning in general.

Early research on play and creative problem solving investigated play and insight ability. In a series of studies, Sylva, Bruner, and Genova (1976) concluded that play in children 3–5 years of age facilitated insight in a problem solving task. In one study, they had three groups of children. One group played with the objects which were later used in the problem-solving task. A second group observed the experimenter solve the problem. A third group was exposed to the materials. Significantly more children in the play and observation groups solved the problem than in the control group. The play group was more goal oriented in their efforts on the task and was more likely to piece together the solution than the other groups.

Vandenberg (1978) refined the experimental methodology of the Sylva et al. studies and used a wider age group, 4–10 years of age. The experimental group played with the materials to be used in the problem solving task and the control group was asked questions about the material. Children were also given hints as to the solution. The play group did significantly better on one of the two insight tasks following the intervention. Six and seven-year-olds benefited most from the play experience. Vandenberg concluded that the relationship between play and insightful tool-use was mediated by age and task characteristics. In a review of the insight and play studies, Vandenberg (1980) concluded that all studies in the area had the consistent finding that play facilitated insightful tool use and enhanced motivated task activity.

There is a substantial body of studies that has found a relationship between play and divergent thinking. Divergent thinking is the generation of a variety of ideas and alternative solutions to problems (Guilford, 1968). Divergent thinking is especially important in creativity. Singer and Singer (1990) viewed play as a way of practicing divergent thinking ability. Singer and Rummo (1973) found a relationship between play and divergent thinking in kindergarten boys. Pepler and Ross (1981) found that play was related to divergent thinking. Feitelson and Ross (1973) found that thematic play facilitated creative thinking. Experience with a divergent thinking task facilitated performance on divergent thinking tasks in a study by Pepler (1979). In that study, performance on the divergent thinking task could be predicted from the expression of symbolic and representational play. Hughes (1987) studied four- and five-year-olds and reported that manipulative play with objects facilitated divergent thinking, but only for the number of nonstandard responses on the Alternate Uses Test.

Wallach (1970) stressed the importance of the relationship between divergent thinking and fantasy. Subjects who scored well on divergent thinking tests produced novel stories on the TAT (Maddi, 1965) and engaged in daydreaming activity (Singer, 1973). Wallach (1970) proposed that breadth-of-attention deployment is the underlying variable involved in divergent thinking tasks. As Kogan (1983) pointed out, breadth-of-attention deployment refers to a scanning of the environment and memory in an associational manner. Both creativity and fantasy may share breadth-of-attention deployment. From a cognitive perspective, this variable could also account for the play-creativity link.

In several important studies, play facilitated divergent thinking in preschool children (Dansky, 1980; Dansky & Silverman, 1973). In particular, Dansky and Silverman found that children who played with objects during a play period gave significantly more uses for those objects than did control subjects. In a later study, Dansky (1980) found that make-believe play was the mediator of the relationship between play and divergent thinking. Free play facilitated divergent thinking, but only for children who engaged in make-believe play. Also, in this second study, play had a generalized effect in that the objects in the play period were different from those in the test period. These two studies are important because they are experimental studies that show a direct effect of play on divergent thinking.

Dansky's (1980) theoretical rationale for hypothesizing that play would facilitate divergent thinking was that the process of free combination of objects and ideas involved in play is similar to the elements involved in creative thinking. Dansky (1980) speculated that the free symbolic transformations inherent in pretend play helped create a temporary cognitive set toward the loosening of old associations. These ideas are consistent with the work of Sutton-Smith (1966, 1992) who stressed the role of play in the development of flexibility in problem solving. Play provides the opportunity to explore new combinations of ideas and to develop new associations for old objects. The object transformations that occur in play help to develop the capacity to see old objects in new ways. The capacity to see old objects and ideas in new ways should also aid in developing transformation abilities (i.e., the ability to break out of an old set and see a new solution to a problem). Kogan (1983) also suggested that children's play behavior involves a search for alternate modes of relating to the object, a process similar to searching for alternate uses for objects in divergent thinking tasks.

Pellegrini (1992) also identified flexibility as one link between play and creativity. In a study of third and fifth grade boys, flexibility in rough and tumble play was predictive of a variety of prosocial problem solving responses. Pellegrini proposed that in play, children recombine behaviors and develop flexible strategies. A varied problem solving repertoire aids in social competence. Saracho (1992) obtained results that also support a link between play and flexibility. She found that field independent children engaged more in play than did field dependent children and concluded, from observing the children's play, that the field independent children were exhibiting cognitive flexibility.

Until 15 years ago, the research on play and creativity had focused on cognitive variables as the explanatory mechanisms underlying the observed relationship. As discussed, explanations have included practice with divergent thinking, the recombination of objects and ideas, symbolic transformations, breadth-of-attention deployment, and the loosening of old cognitive sets or cognitive flexibility.

5.09.5.4.2 Play and affective processes

Play also facilitates affective development. Affect may also be involved in the link between play and creative problem solving. Play and affective processes are just beginning to be studied, mainly because of the difficulty in measuring affective processes in play. In general, the empirical study of affective expression in children is a young area (Masters, Felleman, & Barden, 1981). The theoretical explanations for the links between affect, play, and creativity have been in existence for some time, although research that tests theory is relatively recent.

The first major theoretical explanation for the relationship between affect and creativity was that of psychoanalytic theory, which proposed that controlled access to primary process thinking facilitated creativity. Primary process thinking was first conceptualized by S. Freud (1915/1958) as an early, primitive system of thought that was drive-laden and not subject to rules of logic or oriented to reality. Another way to view primary process thought is as affect-laden cognition. Russ (1987, 1993, 1996) proposed that primary process thought is a subtype of affect in cognition. Primary process content is material around which the child had experienced early intense feeling states (oral, anal, aggressive, etc.) According to psychoanalytic theory, primary process thinking facilitates creativity (Kris, 1952). Children and adults who have controlled access to primary process thinking should have a broader range of associations and be better divergent thinkers than individuals with less access to primary process. S. Freud's (1926/1959) formulation that repression of "dangerous" drive-laden content leads to a more general intellectual restriction predicts that individuals with less access to affect-laden cognitions would have fewer associations in general. Thus, children who are more expressive of and open to affective content would develop a richer, more complex store of affect-laden memories. This richer store of memories would facilitate divergent thinking and transformation abilities because it provides a broader range of associations and more flexible manipulation of images and ideas.

Primary process content can be expressed in play. As Waelder (1933) has noted, play is a "leave of absence from reality" (p. 222), and is a place to let primary process thinking occur. Play can be important in the development of primary process thought and, in turn, foster creative thinking.

Primary process theory is consistent with Bower's (1981) conceptualization of affect and memory processes (see Russ, 1993). The work on mood and memory suggests that the search process for associations is broadened by the involvement of emotion. Russ (1993) proposed that if primary process is thought of as mood-relevant cognition, then it could fit into a mood and memory theoretical framework. When stirred, primary process content could trigger a broad associative network. Primary process content was stored into the memory system when emotion was present. Access to this primary process content would activate emotion nodes and associations, thus broadening the search process.

Fein (1987) views affect as intertwined with pretend play and creativity. Fein (1987) viewed play as a natural form of creativity. She studied 15 children who were master players and concluded that good pretend play consists of five characteristics.

(i) *referential freedom*. The "as if," concept is important in that one object is treated as if it were another, one person functions as if they were another, time and place is as if it were different. Object substitutions and transformations occur.

(ii) *denotative license*. The child takes a divergent stance with respect to actual experience. There are pretend events, not just object substitution in an accurate account of events.

(iii) *affective relations*. Symbolic units represent affective relationships such as "fear of, love for, anger at." Fein proposed an affective symbol system that represents real or imagined experience at a general level. These affective units constitute affect-binding representational templates which store salient information about affect-laden events. The units are "manipulated, interpreted, coordinated and elaborated in a way that makes affective sense to the players" (p. 292). These affective units are a key part of pretend play and are especially important for creative thinking. Fein stated further that divergent thinking abilities like daydreams,

pretend play, or drawing can activate the affective symbol system.

(iv) *sequential uncertainty*. The sequence of events in pretend play has a nonlinear quality.

(v) *self-mirroring*. Children are aware of the pretend, nonreal quality of the play. The self is observed from a distance through the play.

One of Fein's (1987) major conclusions is that creative processes cannot be studied independently of an affective symbol system An affective symbol system is activated in pretend play and is probably facilitated through pretend play. The concept of affective symbols is consistent with the concept of primary process. Primary process content is proposed to be stored in the affect symbol system.

Vygotsky (1930/1967) is also a major theoretician in the area of affect, play, and creativity. He presented a rich conceptualization of play and creativity. Smolucha (1992) has translated and integrated Vygotsky's major papers on the topic of creativity. From her review of his work, a major premise in Vygotsky's theory is that imagination develops out of children's play. He stated: "The child's play activity is not simply a recollection of past experience but a creative reworking that combines impressions and constructs from them new realities addressing the needs of the child" (1930/1967, p. 7). Through play, children develop combinatory imagination (i.e., the ability to combine elements of experience into new situations and new behaviors). Combinatory imagination is significant because it can contribute to artistic and scientific creativity.

Morrison (1988) placed cognitive-affective development within an interpersonal framework. The cognitive integration of affect occurs within safe interactions with parents. Representations of self and others are fused with affect. In play, the child reconstructs past experience and explores definitions of the self. Old metaphors are constantly reworked. In this way, the child develops reflective thought. Conflicts from early interpersonal experience can be a major source of creative thinking in that the metaphors of early experience are reworked in creative acts. Santostefono (1988) also stressed the importance of play in metaphor construction. The process of constructing and negotiating metaphors is creative and can lead to later creativity.

Russ (1993) reviewed the affect and creativity literature and proposed five categories of affect that emerged as important in the creative process: access to affect-laden thoughts; openness to affect states; affective pleasure in challenge; affective pleasure in problem solving; and cognitive integration and modulation of affect. The question of whether or not these five categories are truly separate dimensions of affect needs to be investigated systematically. In Russ' model of affect and creativity, these affective processes are related to specific creative cognitive processes. The links between the processes are based on theory and the empirical literature. Two broad affective processes are access to affect-laden thoughts and openness to affect states.

Access to affect-laden thoughts is the ability to think about thoughts and images that contain emotional content. Affective fantasy in daydreams and in play are examples of affect-laden thoughts. Thoughts involving emotional themes such as aggressive and sexual ideation illustrate this kind of blending of affect and cognition. The psychoanalytic concept of primary process thinking is also an example of emotion-laden thinking (see Kris, 1952; Dudek, 1980; Rothenberg, 1990).

Openness to affect states is the ability to feel the affect itself. Comfort with intense affect, the ability to experience and tolerate anxiety, and passionate involvement in a task are examples of openness to affect states.

Two other more specific affective processes important in creativity are affective pleasure in challenge and affective pleasure in problem solving. The capacity to enjoy the excitement and tension in the challenge (Runco, 1994) and the capacity to take deep pleasure in problem solving (Amabile, 1990) are important in the creative process.

Finally, cognitive integration and modulation of affect is important in producing good and adaptive products. Cognitive control of affect is essential for the critical evaluation of ideas and products (Arieti, 1976; Kris, 1952).

There is a growing body of research that supports the link between play, affect, and creativity. Lieberman's (1977) work supports a relationship between affect in play and divergent thinking. She focused on the variable of playfulness which included the affective components of spontaneity and joy. She found that playful kindergarten children did better on divergent thinking tasks than nonplayful children. Singer and Singer (1990) reported that positive affect was related to imaginative play. Christie and Johnson (1983) also concluded that there is a relationship between playfulness and creativity. Singer and Singer (1981) found that preschoolers related as high imagination players showed significantly more themes of danger and power than children with low imagination.

In a series of studies by Russ and her colleagues using the Affect in Play Scale (APS), affect in play was found to be related to creativity. Russ and Grossman-McKee (1990) investigated the relationship among the APS and divergent thinking and primary process thinking on the Rorschach in 60 first and second grade children. As predicted, affective expression in play was significantly positively related to divergent thinking, as measured by the Alternate Uses Test. All major scores on the APS were significantly correlated with divergent thinking, with correlations ranging from 0.23 between comfort and divergent thinking to 0.42 between frequency of affective expression and divergent thinking. All correlations remained significant when IQ was partialed out; IQ had low correlations with the APS. The fact that intelligence did not relate to any of the play scores is consistent with the theoretical model for the development of the scale and is similar to the results of Singer (1973). Also, there were no gender differences in the pattern of correlations between the APS and divergent thinking.

The finding of a relationship between affect in play and divergent thinking (Russ & Grossman-McKee, 1990) was replicated by Russ and Peterson (1990; Russ, 1993) who used a larger sample of 121 first and second grade children. Once again, all of the APS scores were significantly and positively related to the Alternate Uses Test, independent of intelligence. Again, there were no gender differences in the correlations. Thus, with this replication, more confidence in the robustness of the relationship between affect in pretend play and creativity in young children is possible.

An important question about the APS is whether it is indeed measuring two separate dimensions of play—an affective dimension and a cognitive dimension—or is measuring one dimension an affect in fantasy dimension. The results of two separate factor analyses with the scale suggest two separate dimensions. Russ and Peterson (1990) carried out a principal component analysis with oblique rotation. It yielded two separate factors as the best solution. The first and dominant factor appeared to be a cognitive factor. Imagination, organization, quality of fantasy, and comfort loaded on this first factor. The second factor appeared to be an affective factor. Frequency of affective expression, variety of affect categories, and intensity of affect loaded on this second factor. Although separate factors, there was a significant amount of shared variance ($r = 0.76$), suggesting that the factors overlapped. A study by D'Angelo (1995) replicated the finding of two factors, one cognitive and one affective, with a sample of 95 first, second, and third grade children. This is an important finding because it lends support to the idea that cognitive expression and affective expression in play are related, but separate processes. Future studies with the play scale should use factor scores on the cognitive and affective factors as predictors of creativity.

Another interesting finding in D'Angelo's study (1995) was a significant relationship between the APS and Singer's (1973) imaginative play predisposition interview. Good players on the APS reported that they preferred activities that required using imagination.

A 1995 study (Russ, Robins, & Christiano, 1995), was a follow-up study of the first and second graders in the 1990 investigation of Russ and Peterson (1990). Fifth and sixth grade children were used for the follow-up. Thirty-one children agreed to participate in the follow-up study. This was a longitudinal study that explored the ability of the APS to predict creativity over a four year period (five years in some cases because the study took two years to complete). The major finding of the study was that quality of fantasy and imagination on the APS was predictive of divergent thinking over a four year period. However, the correlation between variety of affect and divergent thinking did not reach significance possibly due to the small sample size. In this study, an adapted version of the play task was administered to the older children. The instructions were altered so that the children were asked to put on a play with the puppets. The task was then scored based on the scoring criteria for the APS. Good stability was found in the dimensions being measured by the APS. For example, the size of the correlation between the two frequency of affect scores was $r = 0.33$, between the two variety of affect scores was $r = 0.38$, and between the two frequency of positive affect scores was $r = 0.51$. In general, the size of the correlations is respectable for a period of four and five years and lends support for enduring, stable constructs of affective expression in fantasy that are predictive over time of creative thinking. These findings also suggest an enduring quality to the affective and cognitive dimensions of the APS over a five year period.

5.09.5.4.3 Play and adjustment

There is some empirical work that suggest that play is related to adjustment. Singer and Singer (1990) concluded that imaginative play in children is related to academic adjustment and flexibility of thought. They also found that toddlers and preschoolers who engage in make-believe play are better adjusted across different situations. Burstein and Meichenbaum (1979) found that children who voluntarily played with stress-related toys prior to surgery demonstrated less distress and anxiety following surgery than children who avoided the toys. One might speculate that those children were

accustomed to using play to deal with stress and problems. In a study of 4 to 11 year olds, Kenealy (1989) investigated strategies that children use when they are feeling depressed and found that 50% of the children's responses included play strategies. Also, indirectly, if play facilitates flexible problem solving, there is evidence that flexible problem solving, in turn, aids the coping process (Follick & Turk, 1978).

In a study of urban children from 4 to 5 years of age, Rosenberg (1984) found that the quality of fantasy play for children playing in dyads was positively related to measures of social competence and ego resilience (Block-Q sort). Frequency of positive themes and relationship themes in the play was also related to ego resilience and social competence. In general, children with behavior problems and attachment problems had fewer positive and negative themes in play, with the exception of diffuse hostility.

Grossman-McKee (1990) found, using the APS with first- and second-grade boys, that boys who expressed more affect in play had fewer pain complaints than boys with less affect in play. Good players were also less anxious on the State-Trait Anxiety Inventory for Children (Spielberger, 1973).

In a study of 7 to 9 year olds, Christiano and Russ (1996) found a positive relationship between play and coping, and a negative relationships between play and distress. Children who were "good" players on the APS implemented a greater number and variety of cognitive coping strategies (correlations ranging from 0.52 to 0.55) during an invasive dental procedure. In addition, good players reported less distress during the procedure than children who expressed less affect and fantasy in play.

5.09.5.4.4 Meta-analysis

Fisher (1992) conducted a meta-analysis of 46 studies in the play and child development area up to 1987. He investigated the impact of play on cognitive, affective-social, and linguistic processes. Both correlational and experimental studies were included. He found a mean effect size of 0.347 which is of low to modest size. He concluded that the major finding was that play does result in moderately large to noteworthy improvements on children's development. He made special note of the larger effect size for divergent thinking and perspective taking criteria.

In summary, play helps the child to:
(i) Practice with the free flow of associations that is important in divergent thinking.
(ii) Practice with symbol substitution, re-combining of ideas, and manipulation of object

representations. These processes are important in developing insight abilities.

(iii) Express and experience both positive and negative affect.

(iv) Express and think about affect themes in fantasy. Emotional content and primary process content is permitted to surface and be expressed through play. Over time, the child develops a variety of memories and associations. This broad repertoire of associations helps in creative problem solving. Fein's (1987) affective symbol system could be developed in this way.

(v) Resolve conflicts and master the traumas of daily life.

(vi) Develop cognitive structure that could help the child contain and modulate affect.

(vii) Practice with a variety of coping skills and interpersonal behavior important in everyday life.

5.09.6 RESEARCH FINDINGS

Russ (1995) reviewed the current state of play therapy research. In that review, a distinction between psychotherapy outcome research in general and play intervention research was made. The broad category of psychotherapy outcome research makes sense because most of those studies did not focus specifically on play. Play is frequently embedded in the therapy intervention. Therefore, the results of those studies provide an important context in which to think about play.

5.09.6.1 Psychotherapy Outcome Research

In general, the early reviews of child therapy outcome studies concluded that there was little or no support for child therapy. More recent work has concluded that there is support for the effectiveness of child psychotherapy if the research is well designed.

A classic early review by Levitt (1957) concluded that the mean improvement rate for children was not significantly better than the baseline improvement rate of 72.5% for untreated controls. In later work, in a review of 47 reports of outcome studies, Levitt (1963, 1971) concluded that approximately two-thirds of treated children in therapy were improved, but again treated children were no better off than untreated controls. Levitt's conclusions were taken seriously by the field of child psychotherapy.

A number of researchers responded to Levitt's conclusions (Halpern, 1968; Heinicke & Goldman, 1960; Hood-Williams, 1960). One of the major methodological issues was that so

many of the untreated controls were defectors from treatment. Defectors were children who were evaluated and recommended for treatment but who had not entered treatment. Therefore, there may have been a number of confounding variables operating here to account for the results.

Barrett, Hanpe, and Miller (1978) and Hartmann, Roger, and Gelsand (1977) took a closer look at Levitt's reviews and at the research literature in general. They concluded that there was still no solid empirical evidence for the effectiveness of psychotherapy. Barrett et al. (1978) stated that the global nature of the research was a major problem and concluded that most of the research studies were not specific enough or focused enough to enable research questions to be answered. There was too much of a mix of populations, therapeutic approaches, and interventions in these studies. Often, the outcome measures were unrefined or nonexistent. This led to their often quoted conclusion that the question in psychotherapy research should not be "Does psychotherapy work?" but rather "Which set of procedures is effective when applied to what kinds of patients with which sets of problems and practiced by which sorts of therapists?" (p. 428)

A number of other methodological issues important for research in the child therapy area have been identified: namely, the importance of classification according to developmental level (Heinicke & Strassman, 1975); controlling for maturational effects (Koocher & Broskowski, 1977); the need for homogeneous treatment groups (Achenbach, 1978; Hartmann et al., 1977); the need to control for sex and age variables (Cass & Thomas, 1979); and the need for adequate outcome measures given at appropriate intervals (Kazdin, 1990, 1993b).

The field of child therapy research has followed these research guidelines and the research studies have become more focused and methodologically sophisticated. In addition, the technique of meta-analysis has enabled the field to arrive at a more systematic evaluation of outcome studies. As Weisz and Weiss (1993) noted, meta-analysis is a technique that enables the pooling and statistical summarizing of the results of outcome studies. The effect size (ES) is the statistical summary of the treatment efficacy across studies. Use of this systematic procedure helps avoid reviewer subjectivity in coming to conclusions.

Weisz and Weiss (1993) reviewed the major meta-analytic studies in the field of child psychotherapy. Casey and Berman (1985) calculated the effect of psychotherapy across 64 studies and found a mean effect size of 0.71. A slightly higher effect size of 0.79 was found by

Weisz, Weiss, Alicke, and Klotz (1987) in a review of 163 treatment-control comparisons. Both studies concluded that the average treated child functioned better after treatment than three-fourths of the untreated controls. In the Casey and Berman review, effect sizes did not differ as a function of whether play was used. In a meta-analyses by Kazdin, Bass, Ayers, and Rodgers (1990), for 64 studies involving treatment vs. no-treatment comparisons, the mean effect size was 0.88. Weisz and Weiss (1993) concluded that "the mean effect sizes reported in child meta-analyses are quite comparable to those of adult meta-analyses and that findings in both categories point to quite positive effects of therapy" (p. 46).

As Kazdin (1990) has pointed out, the results of these meta-analyses have contributed to the field in that they offer evidence that psychotherapy is more effective than no treatment with children. This conclusion is more encouraging than the conclusions based on the reviews in the 1950s, 1960s, and 1970s. Although these child therapy outcome studies did not focus on play *per se*, one might infer that play is an effective form of treatment since it is so frequently part of the therapy process. The Casey and Berman (1985) review found no difference in effectiveness between those studies that used play and those that did not.

Weisz and Weiss (1989, 1993) pointed out that most of the research studies in the meta-analyses involved controlled laboratory interventions. In many of these studies children were recruited for treatment and were not clinic-referred; samples were homogeneous; there was a focal problem; therapy focused on the target problem; therapists were trained in the specific treatment approaches to be used; and the therapy relied primarily on those techniques. In essence, this was good research that followed many of the methodological guidelines for adequate research design. On the other hand, Weisz and Weiss (1993) cautioned that the evidence for the effectiveness of psychotherapy is based on studies that are not typical of conventional clinical practice. Thus the findings may not be generalizable to real clinical work.

The results of the meta-analysis point to the need for specificity and precision. Weisz and Weiss (1993) concluded that the studies that showed positive results tended to "zoom in" on a specific problem with careful planning of the intervention. Freedheim and Russ (1983, 1992) stated that we needed to become very specific and ask "Which specific interventions affect which specific cognitive, personality, and affective processes? How are these processes related to behavior and practical clinical criteria?" (1983, p. 988). Shirk and Russell (1996) also call

for the targeting of specific cognitive, affective, and interpersonal processes in child therapy.

In a review of the play therapy research, Phillips (1985) also called for a systematic program of research with well-controlled studies. He concluded that the play therapy research that found positive results were those studies of a cognitive-behavioral nature that were carefully designed. Phillips speculated that the specificity of treatment goals and focused methods of the cognitive-behavioral studies partially account for the positive results. He recommended that all forms of play therapy be investigated with the precision of the cognitive-behavioral studies. In general there are not many play therapy studies in the literature and little exploration of variables that leads to change (Faust & Burns, 1991).

It should be relatively easy to apply the principles of specificity and focus to the play area. Play interventions and the cognitive and affective processes that they effect can be broken down into discrete units in controlled conditions. The large body of research in the play and child development literature offers a wealth of ideas and research lines that could be followed.

5.09.6.2 Play Intervention Research

As Russ has reviewed (1995), studies exist that have investigated the effect of play on specific types of problems and in specific populations. These studies are a good bridge between empirical laboratory studies of play and specific processes, like creativity, and more global clinical practice outcome studies. These studies have been labeled play intervention rather than play therapy, because the focus is highly specific. Usually, they involve only a few sessions with no emphasis on forming a "relationship" with a therapist. On the other hand, these studies differ from specific process research in child development in that they are problem focused and are not as fine-tuned as they would be in laboratory research. These play intervention research studies seem to fit some of Weisz and Weiss's (1993) criteria by including children who are not clinic-referred, by having homogeneous samples, and by having a focal problem that the therapy focused on.

Phillips (1985) reviewed two studies that would fall into this play intervention research category. Both involved the use of puppet play to reduce anxiety in children facing surgery. Johnson and Stockdale (1975) measured Palmer Sweat Index level before and after surgery. Puppet play in this study involved playing out the surgery. Johnson and Stockdale found less anxiety for the puppet-play group before and after surgery. The one exception was immediately before surgery, when the increased information may have elevated their anxiety. Cassell (1965) used puppets with children undergoing cardiac catheterization and found that anxiety was reduced before surgery for the puppet-play group compared with the no treatment control. There were no differences after surgery. The treatment group was less disturbed during the cardiac catheterization and expressed more willingness to return to the hospital for further treatment. Rae, Worchel, Upchurch, Sanner, and Daniel (1989) investigated the effects of play on the adjustment of 46 children hospitalized for acute illness. Children were randomly assigned to one of four experimental groups:

(i) Therapeutic play condition in which the child was encouraged to play with medical and nonmedical materials. Verbal support, reflection, and interpretation of feelings were expressed by the research assistant.

(ii) A diversionary play condition in which children were allowed to play with toys but fantasy play was discouraged. The toys provided did not facilitate fantasy, nor did the research assistant.

(iii) A verbally oriented support condition in which children were encouraged to talk about feelings and anxieties. The research assistant was directive in bringing up related topics and would ask about procedures.

(iv) A control condition in which the research assistant had no contact with the child.

All treatment conditions consisted of two 30-minute sessions. The main result of this study was that children in the therapeutic play group showed significantly more reduction in self-reported hospital-related fears than children in the other three groups. There were no differences among the groups for parent ratings.

Another specific problem area that lends itself to focused intervention research is that of separation anxiety. In an excellent example of a well-designed play intervention study, Milos and Reiss (1982) used play therapy for preschoolers who were dealing with separation anxiety. They identified 64 children who were rated as high-separation-anxious children by their teachers. The children were randomly assigned to one of four groups. Three play groups were theme related: the free-play group had appropriate toys; the directed-play group had the scene set with a mother doll bringing the child to school; the modeling group had the experimenter playing out a separation scene. A control group also used play with toys irrelevant to separation themes (blocks, puzzles, crayons). All children received three individual 10 minute play sessions on different days. Quality of play

was rated. The results showed that all three thematic play conditions were effective in reducing anxiety around separation themes when compared to the control group. An interesting finding was that, when the free-play and directed-play groups were combined, the quality of play ratings were significantly negatively related ($r = -0.37$) to a posttest anxiety measure. High-quality play was defined as play that showed more separation themes and attempts to resolve conflicts. One might speculate that the children who were already good players used the intervention to master their separation anxiety. Milos and Reiss concluded that their results support the underlying assumption of play therapy, that play can reduce anxiety associated with psychological problems. The finding that quality of play was related to effectiveness of the intervention is consistent with the finding of Dansky (1980); that free play facilitated creativity only for those children who used make-believe well.

A well-designed study by Barnett (1984) also looked at separation anxiety and expanded upon work by Barnett and Storn (1981) in which free play was found to reduce distress in children following a conflict situation. In the 1984 study, a natural stressor, the first day of school, was used. Seventy-four preschool children were observed separating from their mothers and were rated anxious or nonanxious. These two groups were further divided into play or no play conditions. The play condition was a free play condition. The no-play condition was a story-listening condition. For half of the play condition, play was solitary. For the other half, peers were present. The story condition was also split into solitary and peers present segments. Play was rated by observers and categorized in terms of types of play. Play significantly reduced anxiety in the high-anxious group. Anxiety was measured by the Palmer Sweat Index. There was no effect for low-anxious children. For the anxious children, solitary play was best in reducing anxiety. High-anxious children spent more time in fantasy play than did low-anxious children, who showed more functional and manipulative play. They engaged more in fantasy play when no other children were present. Barnett interpreted these results to mean that play was used to cope with a distressing situation. The findings supported her idea that it is not social play that is essential to conflict resolution, but rather imaginative play qualities that the child introduces into playful behavior. Actually, the presence of peers increased anxiety in the high-anxious group.

These play intervention studies are a few examples of the kind of studies that tell us about how play can be helpful in dealing with specific problems. The results of these studies suggest that play helps children deal with fears and reduce anxiety and that something about play itself is important and serves as a vehicle for change. The play experience is separate from the experience of a supportive and empathic adult. Results also suggest that children who are already good players are more able to use play opportunities to resolve problems when these opportunities arise. Teaching children good play skills would provide children with a resource for future coping.

5.09.7 FUTURE DIRECTIONS FOR RESEARCH AND PRACTICE

The main tasks of the next 10 years, up to 2007, in the play therapy area are to: (i) apply the body of knowledge from the play and child development research literature to play intervention and (ii) carry out well-designed play intervention studies with specific populations of children. These are major tasks that require a coordinated set of research studies and programs.

Play therapy itself will become more focused with specific populations of children. This is already occurring. For example, Chethik (1989) described "focal therapy" as therapy that focuses on a specific problem and is of short duration. Play is frequently used in this therapy. Focal stress events such as death in the family, divorce, hospitalization, or illness are examples of problems that would be dealt with Chethik stated that focal therapy is effective when the child has accomplished normal developmental tasks before the stressful event occurs.

Mann and McDermott (1983) discussed play therapy with abused and neglected children. Often, these children must be taught how to play. Gil (1991) provided a good review and discussion of post-traumatic play. An active approach in which she brings in outside material and events is often necessary. Gil stressed the importance of the therapist being an active participant in the play with abused children. If the child is a disorganized player, the therapist must focus the play choices in a relatively restricted setting. If the child has been under-stimulated and cannot play well, then the therapist should bring in appropriate toys and model play. For many abused children, the therapist needs to actively facilitate self-expression by such techniques as presenting the child with cartoon figures in different situations with the child filling in their words or pulling secrets from a "secrets" bag. For many children post-traumatic play is repetitive, devoid of pleasure, and can remain fixed (Gil, 1991). Gil attempts to intervene in this repetitive play by making

verbal statements, having the child take a specific role, or encouraging the child to differentiate between the traumatic event and current reality in terms of safety and what has been learned. Gil stated that the goal of interrupting the play is to generate alternatives that can lead to a sense of control, help feelings be expressed and orient the child toward the future. Gil's work illustrates how specific play techniques need to be developed for specific populations.

D. Singer (1993) described the active use of modeling, imagery techniques, and teaching adaptive skills within the play therapy context. Along with traditional play therapy techniques, she utilizes imagery techniques that help the child visualize people, conflicts, and resolutions. She also incorporates behavior modification techniques that reinforce positive behavior and lead to self-reward. Knell's (1993) cognitive-behavior play therapy and Bodiford-McNeil et al's. (1996) short-term play therapy are examples of focused therapies with a very active therapist.

Play therapy will also need to integrate a variety of theoretical approaches and techniques. As it becomes evident that a variety of theoretical approaches can use play in therapy, a larger variety of play techniques will become available. If we can combine this increased repertoire of play techniques with good research then the field of play therapy will move forward.

Short-term play intervention modules may evolve as effective interventions. Kazdin (1993a) discussed the possibility of having different modules of intervention for different problems. This concept would work for the play therapy area. 6–12 week play modules could be developed for different types of problems. Bodiford-McNeil et al. (1996) are already doing this with disruptive children. Children who have experienced trauma might benefit from the opportunity to play-out the issues in a focused approach. Constricted children could benefit from play modules directed at increasing affective expression. Play assessment could identify what types of play experiences could be most beneficial.

Research programs in play therapy need to be at both the micro and macro levels. First, laboratory research on play and cognitive and affective processes must continue. Concurrent, longitudinal, and experimental studies on specific dimensions of play and specific cognitive, affective, and personality processes need to be carried out in a systematic fashion. We especially need to identify what dimensions of play most relate to specific processes. For example, does affect expression increase divergent thinking? Does positive affect have a different effect than negative affect? Are there different effects with different age groups and different populations of children?

Second research needs to be carried out with focused play interventions. Russ (1995) outlined different types of play intervention research.

(i) Specific Play Interventions with Specific Populations and Specific Situations. The Barnett (1984) study with children who were experiencing the first day of school is a good example of this type of study. There are a variety of natural stressors that could be used to investigate play intervention. Divorce, natural disasters, dental visits, presurgery, and loss of a parent are all situations in which play intervention is used. We need to develop an empirical base for play intervention in these situations.

(ii) Refining Specific Play Techniques. The general question of what kinds of intervention by the therapist best facilitate play needs to be studied empirically. There are many guidelines in the clinical literature about how to facilitate play, but few are based on empirical work. How do we best encourage affect in play? When is modeling more effective than a less directive approach.? When is it less effective? For example, Gil (1991) pointed out that it is frequently important with sexually abused children to be nondirective, so that the child does not feel intruded upon. What kinds of intervention most enhance the working-through process and conflict resolution? These kinds of research questions can be posed in well-controlled experimental studies and in psychotherapy-process research.

Third, dissemination of research results should inform clinical practice and prevention programs. For example, guidelines about how to best facilitate affective expression in play could be better incorporated into play therapy. Treatment manuals using these guidelines can and should be developed.

In the future, large scale play training and prevention programs could reach large numbers of children. Play centers in schools might be one way to reach children (Russ, 1993). Smilanksy (1968) has demonstrated that play skills can effectively be taught to children by teachers in a relatively short time. More training groups for parents on how to help children play at home, perhaps through Head Start programs would also be worthwhile. Play preparation for hospital procedures might increase. Teaching children to use play as a major coping resource might be a trend of the future.

One thing is certain, children will continue to play. Above all else, it is fun and reinforcing. Children naturally use play for a variety of purposes. It is up to us to learn how children use play and to help them use play more effectively.

5.09.8 REFERENCES

Achenbach, T. (1978). Psychopathology of childhood: Research problems and issues. *Journal of Consulting and Clinical Psychology, 46,* 759–776.
Amabile, T. (1990). Within you, without you: The social psychology of creativity and beyond. In M. Runco & R. Albert (Eds.), *Theories of creativity* (pp. 61–69). Newbury Park, CA: Sage.
Applebaum, S. (1978). Pathways to change in psychoanalytic therapy. *Bulletin of Menniger Clinic, 42,* 239–251.
Archer, R., Maruish, M., Imhof, E., & Piatrowski, C. (1991). Psychological test usage with adolescent clients: 1990 survey findings. *Professional Psychology Research and Practice, 22,* 247–252.
Arieti, S. (1976). *Creativity: The magic synthesis.* New York: Basic Books.
Axline, V. M. (1947). *Play therapy.* Boston: Houghton-Mifflin.
Axline, V. M. (1964). *Dibs: In search of self: Personality development in play therapy.* Boston: Houghton Miffllin.
Barnett, I. (1984). Research note: Young children's resolution of distress through play. *Journal of Child Psychology and Psychiatry, 25,* 477–483.
Barnett, I., & Storn, B. (1981). Play, pleasure and pain: The reduction of anxiety through play. *Leisure Science, 4,* 161–175.
Barrett, C., Hampe, T. E., & Miller, L. (1978). Research on child psychotherapy. In S. Garfield & A. Bergin (Eds.), *Handbook of psychotherapy and behavior change* (pp. 411–435). New York: Wiley.
Blank, R., & Blank, G. (1986). *Beyond ego psychology: Developmental object relations theory.* New York: Columbia University Press.
Bodiford-McNeil, C., Hembree-Kigin, T. L., & Eyberg, S. (1996). *Short-term play therapy for disruptive children.* King of Prussia, PA: The Center for Applied Psychology.
Bower, G. H. (1981). Mood and memory. *American Psychologist, 36,* 129–148.
Burlingham, D. (1932). Child analysis and the mother. *Psychoanalytic Quarterly, 4,* 69–92.
Burstein, S., & Meichenbaum, D. (1979). The work of worrying in children undergoing surgery. *Journal of Abnormal Child Psychology, 7,* 121–132.
Casey, R. J., & Berman, J. S. (1985). The outcome of psychotherapy with children. *Psychological Bulletin, 98,* 388–400.
Cass, L., & Thomas, C. (1979). *Childhood pathology and later adjustment.* New York: Wiley.
Cassell, S. (1965). Effect of brief puppet therapy upon the emotional response of children undergoing cardiac catheterization. *Journal of Consulting Psychology, 29,* 1–8.
Chethik, M. (1989). *Techniques of child therapy: Psychodynamic strategies.* New York: Guilford.
Christiano, B., & Russ, S. (1996). Play as a predictor of coping and distress in children during an invasive dental procedure. *Journal of Clinical Child Psychology, 25,* 130–138.
Christie, J., & Johnson, E. (1983). The role of play in social-intellectual development. *Review of Educational Research, 53,* 93–115.
D'Angelo, L. (1995). Child's play: The relationship between the use of play and adjustment styles. Unpublished dissertation. Case Western Reserve University, Cleveland, OH.
Dansky, I. (1980). Make-believe: A mediator of the relationship between play and associative fluency. *Child Development, 15,* 576–579.
Dansky, J., & Silverman, F. (1973). Effects of play on associative fluency in preschool-aged children. *Developmental Psychology, 9,* 38–43.

Dawes, R. (1994). *House of cards: Psychology and psychotherapy, truth or myth.* New York: Free Press.

Dudek, S. (1980). Primary process ideation. In R. H. Woody (Ed.), *Encyclopedia of clinical assessment* (Vol. 1, pp. 520–539). San Francisco: Jossey-Bass.

Erikson, E. N. (1963). *Childhood and society.* New York: Norton.

Exner, J. (1986). *The Rorschach: A comprehensive system* (Vol. 1, 2nd ed). New York: Wiley.

Faust, J., & Burns, W. (1991). Coding therapist and child interaction: Progress and outcome in play therapy. In C. Schaefer, K. Gitlin, & A. Sandgrund (Eds.), *Play diagnosis and assessment* (pp. 663–689), New York: Wiley.

Fein, G. (1981). Pretend play in childhood: An integrative review. *Child Development, 52,* 1095–1118.

Fein, G. (1987). Pretend play: Creativity and consciousness. In P. Gorlitz & J. Wohlwill (Eds.), *Curiosity, imagination, and play* (pp. 231–304). Hillsdale, NJ: Erlbaum.

Feitelson, D., & Ross, G. (1973). The neglected factor-play. *Human Development, 16,* 202–223.

Fisher, E. (1992). The impact of play on development: A meta-analysis. *Play and Culture, 5,* 159–181.

Follick, M., & Turk, D. (1978). *Problem specification by ostomy patients.* Paper presented at the 12th Annual Convention for the Advancement of Behavior Therapy. Chicago, IL.

Freedheim, D. K., & Russ, S. W. (1983). Psychotherapy with children. In C. E. Walker & M. E. Roberts (Eds.), *Handbook of clinical child psychology* (2nd ed., pp. 978–994). New York: Wiley.

Freedheim, D. K., & Russ, S. W. (1992). Psychotherapy with children. In E. Walker & M. Roberts (Eds.), *Handbook of clinical child psychology* (2nd ed., pp. 765–780). New York: Wiley.

Freud, A. (1927). Four lectures on child analysis. In *The Writings of Anna Freud* (Vol. 1, pp. 3–69). New York: International Universities Press.

Freud, A. (1946). *The psychoanalytic treatment of children.* New York: International Universities Press.

Freud, A. (1966). The ego and the mechanisms of defense. In *The Writings of Anna Freud* (Vol. 2). New York: International Universities Press.

Freud, A. (1965). Normality and pathology in childhood: Assessments of development. In *The Writings of Anna Freud* (Vol. 6). New York: International Universities Press.

Freud, A. (1976). Changes in psychoanalytic practice and experience. In *The Writings of Anna Freud* (Vol. 7, pp. 176–185). New York: International Universities Press.

Freud, S. (1958). The unconscious. In S. Strachey (Ed. and Trans.), *The standard edition of the complete psychological works of Sigmund Freud* (Vol. 14, pp. 159–215). London: Hogarth Press (original work published 1915).

Freud, S. (1959). Inhibition symptoms, and anxiety. In J. Strachey (Ed. and Trans.), *The standard edition of the complete psychological works of Sigmund Freud* (Vol. 20, pp. 87–172). London: Hogarth Press (original work published 1926).

Garfield, W. (1980). *Psychotherapy: An eclectic approach.* New York: Wiley.

Gardner, R. (1971). *Therapeutic communication with children: The mutual storytelling technique.* New York: Aronson.

Gil, E. (1991). *The healing power of play.* New York: Guilford.

Gilpin, D. (1976). Psychotherapy of borderline psychotic children. *American Journal of Psychotherapy, 30,* 483–496.

Grossman-McKee, A. (1990). The relationship between affective expression in fantasy play and pain complaints in first and second grade children. *Dissertation Abstracts International, 50–09B,* 4219.

Guilford, J.P. (1968). *Intelligence, creativity and their educational implications.* San Diego, CA: Knapp.

Heinicke, C. & Goldman, A. (1960). Research on psychotherapy with children: A review and suggestions for further study. *American Journal of Orthopsychiatry, 30,* 483–494.

Heinicke, C. & Strassman, L. (1975). Toward more effective research on child psychotherapy. *Journal of Child Psychiatry, 14,* 561–588.

Hood-Williams, J. (1960). The results of psychotherapy with children. *Journal of Consulting Psychology, 24,* 84–88.

Hug-Hellmuth, H. (1921). On the technique of child-analysis. *International Journal of Psychoanalysis, 2,* 287–305.

Hug-Hellmuth, H. (1924). *New paths to the understanding of youth.* Leipzig-Wien, Germany: Franz Deuticki.

Hughes, M. (1987). The relationship between symbolic and manipulative (object) play. In D. Gorlitz & J. Wohwill (Eds.), *Curiosity, imagination, and play* (pp. 247–257). Hillsdale, NJ: Erlbaum.

Johnson, P. A., & Stockdale, D. E. (1975). Effects of puppet therapy on palmar sweating of hospitalized children. *Johns Hopkins Medical Journal, 137,* 1–5.

Kazdin, A. E. (1990). Psychotherapy for children and adolescents. In M. R. Rosenweig & L. W. Porter (Eds.), *Annual review of psychology* (pp. 21–54). Palo Alto, CA: Annual Review.

Kazdin, A. (1993a, August). Child and adolescent psychotherapy: Models for identifying and developing effective treatments. In S. Eyberg (Chair), *Psychotherapy for children and adolescents.* Symposium conducted at the meeting of the American Psychological Association, Toronto.

Kazdin, A. (1993b). Evaluation in clinical practice: Clinically sensitive and systematic methods of treatment delivery. *Behavior Therapy, 24,* 11–45.

Kazdin, A. Bass, D., Ayers, W., & Rodgers, A. (1990). Empirical and clinical focus of child and adolescent psychotherapy research. *Journal of Consulting and Clinical Psychology, 58,* 729–740.

Kenealy, P. (1989). Children's strategies for coping with depression. *Behavior Research Therapy, 27,* 27–34.

Kessler, J. (1966). *Psychopathology of childhood.* Englewood Cliffs, NJ: Prentice-Hall.

Kessler, J. (1988). *Psychopathology of childhood* (2nd ed.). Englewood Cliffs, NJ: Prentice-Hall.

Klein, M. (1927). Symposium on child analysis. *International Journal of Psychoanalysis, 8,* 339–370.

Klein, M. (1955). The psychoanalytic play technique. *American Journal of Orthopsychiatry, 25,* 223–237.

Knell, S. (1993). *Cognitive-behavioral play therapy.* Northvale, NJ: Aronson.

Kogan, N. (1983). Stylistic variation in childhood and adolescence: Creativity, metaphor, and cognitive styles. In P. Mussen (Ed.), *Handbook of child psychology* (Vol. 3, pp. 631–706). New York: Wiley.

Kohut, H. (1977). *The restoration of the self.* New York: International Universities Press.

Kohut, H., & Wolfe, E. R. (1978). The disorders of the self and their treatment: An outline. *International Journal of Psychoanalysis, 59,* 413–424.

Koocher, G., & Broskowski, A. (1977). Issues in the evaluation of mental health services for children. *Professional Psychology, 8,* 583–592.

Koocher, G., & D'Angelo, E. J. (1992). Evolution of practice in child psychotherapy. In. D. K. Freedheim (Ed.), *History of psychotherapy* (pp. 457–492). Washington, DC: American Psychological Association.

Kris, E. (1952). *Psychoanalytic exploration in art.* New York: International Universities Press.

Lieberman, J. N. (1977). *Playfulness: Its relationship to imagination and creativity.* New York: Academic Press.

Levitt, E. E. (1957). The results of psychotherapy with children: An evaluation. *Journal of Consulting Psychology, 21,* 189–196.

Levitt, E. E. (1963). Psychotherapy with children: A further evaluation. *Behavior Research and Therapy, 1,* 45–51.

Levitt, E. E. (1971). Research in psychotherapy with children. In A. E. Bergin & S. L. Garfield (Eds.), *Handbook of psychotherapy and behavior change: An empirical analysis* (pp. 474–484). New York: Wiley.

Levy, D. (1938). Release therapy in young children. *Psychiatry, 1,* 387–390.

Maddi, S. (1965). Motivational aspects of creativity. *Journal of Personality, 33,* 330–347.

Mahler, M. S. (1968). *On human symbiosis and the vicissitudes of individuation.* New York: International Universities Press.

Mahler, M. S. (1975). On human symbiosis and the vicissitudes of individuation. *Journal of American Psychoanalytic Association, 23,* 740–763.

Mann, E., & McDermott, J. (1983). Play therapy for victims of child abuse and neglect. In C. E. Schaefer & K. J. O'Connor (Eds.), *Handbook of play therapy* (pp. 283–307). New York: Wiley.

Masters, J., Felleman, E., & Barden, R. (1981). Experimental studies of affective states in children. In B. Lahey & A. Kazdin (Eds.), *Advances in clinical child psychology* (pp. 91–118). New York: Plenum.

Meichenbaum, D. (1974). *Cognitive-behavior modification.* New York: Plenum.

Messer, S. B., & Warren, C. S. (1995). Models of brief psychodynamic therapy. New York: Guilford.

Milos, M., & Reiss, S. (1982). Effects of three play conditions on separation anxiety in young children. *Journal of Consulting and Clinical Psychology, 50,* 389–395.

Morrison, D. (1988). The child's fist ways of knowing. In D. Morrison (Ed.), *Organizing early experience: Imagination and cognition in childhood* (pp. 3–14). Amityville NY: Baywood.

Moustakas, C. (1953). *Children in play therapy.* New York: McGraw-Hill.

Moustakas, C. (1992). *Psychotherapy with children: The living relationship.* Greeley, CO: Carron (original work published 1959).

Pelligrini, A. (1992). Rough and tumble play and social problem solving flexibility. *Creativity Research Journal, 5,* 13–26.

Pepler, D. (1979). Effects of convergent and divergent play experience on preschoolers problem-solving behaviors. Unpublished doctoral dissertation, University of Waterloo.

Pepler, D., & Ross, H. (1981). The effects of play on convergent and divergent problem solving. *Child Development, 52,* 1202–1210.

Phillips, R. (1985). Whistling in the dark?: A review of play therapy research. *Psychotherapy, 22,* 752–760.

Rae, W., Worchel, F., Upchurch, J., Sanner, J., & Daniel, C. (1989). The psychosocial impact of play on hospitalized children. *Journal of Pediatric Psychology, 14,* 617–627.

Rosenberg, D. (1984). *The quality and content of preschool fantasy play: Correlates in concurrent social-personality function and early mother-child attachment relationships.* Unpublished dissertation, University of Minnesota, Minneapolis.

Rothenberg, A. (1990). Creativity, mental health, and alcoholism. *Creativity Research Journal, 3,* 179–201.

Runco, M. A. (1994). Creativity and its discontents. In M. Shaw & M. A. Runco (Eds.), *Creativity and affect* (pp. 102–123). Norwood, NJ: Ablex.

Russ, S. W. (1987). Assessment of cognitive affective

interaction in children: Creativity, fantasy and play research. In J. E. Butcher & C. Spielberger (Eds.), *Advances in personality assessment* (Vol. 6, pp. 141–155). Hillsdale, NJ: Erlbaum.

Russ, S. (1996). Psychoanalytic theory and creativity: Cognition and affect revisited. In J. Masling & R. Bornstein (Eds.), *Psychoanalytic perspectives on developmental psychology* (pp. 69–103) Washington DC: APA Books.

Russ, S. (in press-a) Creativity and play. In M. Runco (Ed.), *Creativity research handbook* (Vol. 3). Creskill, NJ: Hampton Press.

Russ, S. (in press-b). Teaching child assessment from a developmental-psychodynamic perspective. In L. Handler & M. Hilsenroth (Eds.), *Teaching and learning personality assessment.* Hilldale, NJ: Erlbaum.

Russ, S. W. (1993). *Affect and Creativity: The role of affect and play in the creative process.* A Volume in The Personality Assessment Series. Hillsdale, NJ: Erlbaum.

Russ, S. W. (1995). Play psychotherapy research: State of the Science. In T. Ollendick & R. Prinz (Eds.), *Advances in clinical child psychology, 17* (pp. 365–391). New York: Plenum.

Russ, S. W., & Grossman-McKee, A. (1990). Affective expression in children's fantasy play, primary process thinking on the Rorschach, and divergent thinking, *Journal of Personality Assessment, 54,* 756–771.

Russ, S. W., & Peterson, N. (1990). *The Affect in Play Scale: Predicting creativity and and coping in children.* Manuscript submitted for publication.

Russ, S., Robins, D., & Christiano, B. (1995, March). The Affect in Play Scale: Longitudinal Predication. Paper presented at the meeting of the Society for Personality Assessment, Atlanta.

Saltz, E., Dixon, D., & Johnson, J. (1977). Training disadvantaged preschoolers on various fantasy activities: Effects on cognitive functioning and impulse control. *Child Development, 48,* 367–380.

Sandler, J., Kennedy, H., & Tyson, R. L. (1980). *The technique of child psychoanalysis: Discussion with Anna Freud.* Cambridge, MA: Harvard University Press.

Santostefano, S. (1988). Process and change in child therapy and development: The concept of metaphor. In D. Morrison (Ed.), *Organizing early experience: Imagination and cognition in childhood* (pp. 139–172). Amityville NY: Baywood.

Saracho, O. (1992). Preschool children's cognitive style and play and implications for creativity. *Creativity Research Journal, 5,* 35–47.

Schaefer, C., Gitlin, K., & Sandgrund, A. (1991). *Play diagnoses and assessment.* New York: Wiley.

Shirk, S. R., & Russell, R. (1996). *Change processes in child psychotherapy: Revitalizing treatment and research.* New York: Guilford.

Singer, D. (1993). *Playing for their lives.* New York: Free Press.

Singer, D. L., & Rummo, J. (1973). Ideational creativity and behavioral style in kindergarten-age children. *Developmental Psychology, 8,* 154–161.

Singer, D. & Singer, J. L. (1990). *The house of make-believe.* Cambridge, MA: Harvard University Press.

Singer, J. L. (1973). *Child's world of make-believe.* New York: Academic Press.

Singer, J. L., & Singer, D. L. (1976). Imaginative play and pretending in early childhood: Some experimental approaches. In A. Davids (Ed.), *Child personality and psychopathology* (Vol. 3, pp. 69–112). New York: Wiley.

Singer, J. L., & Singer, D. L. (1981). *Television, imagination, and aggression.* Hillsdale, NJ: Erlbaum.

Smilansky, S. (1968). *The effects of sociodramatic play on disadvantaged preschool children.* New York: Wiley.

Smolucha, F. (1992). A reconstructiion of Vygotsky's

theory of creativity. *Creativity Research Journal, 5,* 49–67.

Spielberger, C. D. (1973). *State-trait anxiety inventory for children.* Palo Alto, CA: Consulting Psychological Press.

Stricker, G., & Healey B. (1990). Projective assessment of object relations: A review of the empirical literature. *Psychological Assessment: A Journal of Consulting and Clinical Psychology, 2,* 219–230.

Sutton-Smith, B. (1966). Piaget on play—a critique. *Psychological Review, 73,* 104–110.

Sutton-Smith, B. (1992). The role of toys in the investigation of playful creativity. *Creativity Research Journal, 5,* 3–11.

Sylva, K., Bruner, J., & Genova, P. (1976). The role of play in the problem solving of children 3–5 years old. In J. Bruner, A. Jolly, & K. Sylva (Eds.), *Play.* New York: Basic Books.

Tuma, J., & Pratt (1982). Clinical child psychology practice and training: A survey. *Journal of Clinical Child Psychology, 11,* 27–34.

Tuma, J., & Russ, S.W. (1993). Psychoanalytic psychotherapy with children. In T. Kratochwill & R. Morris (Eds.), *Handbook of psychotherapy with children and adolescents* (pp. 131–161). Boston: Allyn & Bacon.

Vandenberg, B. (1978). The role of play in the development of insightful tool-using abilities. Paper presented at the American Psychological Association Meeting, Toronto.

Vandenberg, B. (1980). Play, problem-solving, and creativity. *New Directions for Child Development, 9,* 49–68.

Vandenberg, B. (1988). The realities of play. In D. Morrison (Ed.), *Organizing early experience: Imagination and cognition in childhood* (pp. 198–209). Amityville, NY: Baywood.

Vygotsky, L.S. (1967). Vaobraszeniye I tvorchestvo v deskom voraste [Imagination and creativity in childhood]. Moscow: Prosvescheniye. Original work published 1930.

Waelder, R. (1933). Psychoanalytic theory of play. *Psychoanalytic Quarterly, 2,* 208–224.

Wallach, M. (1970). Creativity. In P. Mussen (Ed.), *Carmichael's manual of child psychology* (Vol. 1, pp. 1211–1272). New York: Wiley.

Webber, (1988). Diagnostic intervention with children at risk. In S. Altschul (Ed.), *Childhood bereavement and its aftermath* (pp. 77–105). Madison, WI: International Universities Press.

Weiner, I.C. (1996). Some observations on the validity of the Rorschach Inkblot Method. *Psychological Assessment, 8,* 206–213.

Weisz, J.R., & Weiss, B. (1989). Assessing the effects of clinical-based psychotherapy with children and adolescents. *Journal of Consulting and Clinical Psychology, 57,* 741–746.

Weisz, J., & Weiss, B. (1993). *Effects of psychotherapy with children and adolescents.* Newbury Park, CA: Sage.

Weisz, J.R., Weiss, B., Alick, M.D., & Klotz, M.L. (1987). Effectiveness of psychotherapy with children and adolescents: A meta-analysis for clinicians. *Journal of Consulting and Clinical Psychology, 55,* 542–549.

Westen, D. (1991). Social cognitions and object relations. *Psychological Bulletin, 109,* 429–455.

5.10

Psychodynamic Therapy

MARY TARGET and PETER FONAGY
University College London, UK

5.10.1 THE PSYCHOANALYTIC ROOTS OF PSYCHODYNAMIC THERAPY

5.10.1.1 Definition of Psychodynamic Therapy

The term psychodynamic therapy covers psychotherapeutic approaches which share the assumption that psychological disorders are rooted in conflicting motivational states, often unconscious, which the individual responds to with a variety of habitual strategies (psychiatric symptoms). Most psychodynamic formulations specify that such conflict is "intrapsychic" (e.g., Brenner, 1982); others include interpersonal conflict, but even there the implication remains that conflict occurs between an internal state and the internal meaning of an external situation (Sullivan, 1953). Psychological intervention is conceived of as assisting individuals to use and develop their inherent capacities for understanding, learning, and emotional responsiveness, in response to the therapeutic relationship and especially the therapist's interpretations of the patient's motivations and strategies, to arrive at more adaptive resolutions. There is no fixed set of techniques to be used in this task, and different therapeutic orientations emphasize different, although substantively overlapping, procedures. Distinctions between types of psychodynamic therapy can be made along several lines; for example, we distinguish psychodynamic individual therapy from group therapy (Rose, 1972) or family approaches (Selvini Palazzoli, Boscolo, Cecchin, & Prata, 1978), expressive from supportive techniques (Luborsky, 1984), Freudian from Kleinian psychoanalytic orientation (King & Steiner, 1991), and therapies may be distinguished according to the relative emphasis of adjuncts such as play (Schaefer & Cangelosi, 1993), art (Simon, 1992), or drama (Johnson, 1982).

This chapter will principally concern itself with individual psychodynamic psychotherapy, using the verbal or play technique.

5.10.1.2 Historical Overview of Psychodynamic Developmental Theory

We will briefly summarize psychoanalytic theories of development, which are considered in more depth Chapter 14, Volume 1.

Freud was the first to give meaning to mental disorder by linking it to childhood experiences (S. Freud & Breuer, 1895), and to the vicissitudes of the developmental process (S. Freud, 1900). One of S. Freud's significant contributions was undoubtedly the recognition of childhood sexuality (S. Freud, 1905). Few, inside or outside psychoanalysis, now doubt that children experience sexual feelings from the earliest days (Green, 1985). S. Freud's discoveries radically altered our perception of the child from one of somewhat idealized naïveté and innocence to that of a human being struggling to adapt his biological, constitutional characteristics to social circumstances. S. Freud's image of the child is of a person in turmoil (S. Freud, 1933), struggling to achieve control over their biological needs, and make them acceptable to society at large through the microcosm of their family (S. Freud, 1930).

Ego psychologists balanced this view by focusing on the evolution of children's adaptive capacities (Hartmann, 1939), which they bring to bear on the struggle with their biological needs. Hartmann's model (Hartmann, 1939) attempted to take a wider view of the developmental process, to link drives and ego functions, and show how negative interpersonal experiences beyond the expectable range could jeopardize evolution of the psychic structures essential to adaptation. He also showed that the reactivation of earlier structures (regression) was the most important component of psychopathology. Hartmann (1995, p. 221) was also among the first to point to the complexity of the developmental process, stating that the reasons for the persistence of particular behavior are likely to be different from the reasons for the original appearance of the behavior, earlier in development. Among the great contributions of ego psychologists are the identification of the ubiquitous nature of intrapsychic conflict throughout development (Brenner, 1982), and the recognition that genetic endowment, as well as interpersonal experiences, may be critical in determining the child's developmental path. The latter idea has echoes in the epidemiological concept of resilience (Garmezy & Masten, 1991; Rutter & Quinton, 1984).

Child analysts (e.g., Fraiberg, 1969, 1980; Anna Freud, 1965) taught us that symptomatology is not a fixed formation, but rather a dynamic entity superimposed upon, and intertwined with, an underlying developmental process. A. Freud's study of symptomatic and asymptomatic children under great social stress led her to formulate a relatively comprehensive developmental theory, where the child's emotional maturity could be identified independently of diagnosable pathology. Particularly in her early work in the war nurseries (A. Freud, 1941–1945), she identified many of the characteristics which later research linked to the so-called resilient child (Rutter, 1990). For example, her observations spoke eloquently of the importance of social support which children could give one another in situations of extreme stress (concentration camps), which could ensure their physical and psychological survival. More recent research on youngsters experiencing trauma has confirmed her assertion of the protective power of sound social support (Garmezy, 1983; MacFarlane, 1987; O'Grady & Metz, 1987; Werner, 1989). Anna Freud's work stayed so close to the external reality of the child that it lent itself to a number of important applications (Goldstein, Freud, & Solnit, 1973, 1979).

A. Freud was also a pioneer in identifying the importance of an equilibrium between developmental processes (A. Freud, 1965). Her work is particularly relevant in explaining why children, deprived of certain capacities by environment or constitution, appear to be at greater risk of psychological disturbance. Epidemiological studies substantiate that harmonious development is threatened by constitutionally acquired weaknesses. Anna Freud's work is remarkable in that she was the first psychoanalyst to place the process and mechanisms of development at the center-stage of psychoanalytic thinking. Her approach is truly one of developmental psychopathology, insofar as she defines abnormal functioning in terms of its deviation from normal development, while at the same time using the understanding gained from clinical cases to illuminate us about the ontogenetic progress of the normal child (Cicchetti, 1990a; Sroufe, 1990).

Mahler (1968) drew attention to the paradox of self-development, that a separate identity implies the giving up of a highly gratifying closeness with the caregiver. Her observations of the "ambitendency" of children in their second year of life were helpful in understanding individuals with chronic problems of consolidating their individuality. Mahler's framework highlights the importance of the caregiver in facilitating separation, and helps explain the difficulties experienced by children whose parents fail to perform a social referencing function for the child, evaluating for them the realistic danger associated with unfamiliar environments (Feinman, 1991; Hornik & Gunnar, 1988). A traumatized, troubled parent may hinder rather than help a child's adaptation (Terr, 1983). An abusive parent may altogether inhibit the process of social referencing (Cicchetti, 1990b; Hesse & Cicchetti, 1982). The pathogenic potential of the withdrawing object, when confronted with the child's wish for separateness, was further elaborated by Masterson (1972) and Rinsley (1977), and is helpful in accounting for the transgenerational aspects of psychological disturbance (see Baron, Gruen, & Asnis, 1985; Links, Steiner, & Huxley, 1988; Loranger, Oldham, & Tullis, 1982).

Sandler's development of Anna Freud's and Jacobson's work (e.g., Sandler & Rosenblatt, 1962) is a coherent integration of the developmental perspective with psychoanalytic theory. His comprehensive psychoanalytic model has permitted developmental researchers (Emde, 1983, 1988a, 1988b; Stern, 1985) to integrate their findings with a psychoanalytic formulation, which clinicians have also been able to use. At the core of Sandler's formulation lies the representational structure which contains both reality and distortion, and is the driving force of psychic life. A further important component of his model is the notion of the background of safety (Sandler, 1987), closely tied to Bowlby's concept of secure attachment.

Klein and her followers constructed a developmental model (Klein, Heimann, Isaacs, & Riviere, 1946) which at the time met great opposition because of the apparently extravagant assumptions these workers were ready to make about the cognitive capacities of infants. However, developmental research appears to be consistent with many of Klein's claims concerning the perception of causality (Bower, 1989) and causal reasoning (Golinkoff, Hardig, Carlson, & Sexton, 1984). Kleinian developmental concepts have become popular because they provide helpful descriptions of the clinical interaction between both child and adult patient and analyst. For example, projective identification depicts the close control that primitive mental function can exert over the analyst's mind. Modern Kleinian psychoanalysts (Bion, 1962, 1963; Rosenfeld, 1971) have been particularly helpful in underscoring the potential impact of emotional conflict on the development of cognitive capacities.

The early relationship with the caregiver emerged as a critical aspect of development from studies of severe character disorders by psychoanalysts in Britain. Fairbairn's focus on the individual's need for the other (Fairbairn, 1952) helped shift psychoanalytic attention from structure to content, and profoundly influenced both British and North American psychoanalytic thinking. As a consequence of this development, the self as a central part of the psychoanalytic model emerged in the work of Balint (1937, 1968) and Winnicott (1971). The concept of the caretaker or false self, as a defensive structure created to master trauma in a context of total dependency, has become an essential developmental construct. Winnicott's (1965) notions of primary maternal preoccupation, transitional phenomena, the holding environment, and the mirroring function of the caregiver, provided a clear research focus for developmentalists interested in individual differences in the development of self-structure. The significance of the parent–child relationship is consistently borne out by developmental studies of psychopathology. These studies in many respects support Winnicott's assertions concerning the traumatic effects of early maternal failure, particularly maternal depression (see Cummings & Davis, 1994), and the importance of maternal sensitivity for the establishment of a secure relationship (Ainsworth, Blehar, Waters, & Wall, 1978; Belsky, Rovine, & Taylor, 1984; Bus & Van IJzendoorn, 1992; Grossmann, Spangler, Suess, & Unzer, 1985).

The central developmental idea of Kohut's formulation (Kohut, 1971, 1977, 1984) was the need for an understanding caretaker to counteract the infant's sense of helplessness in face of biological striving for mastery. Kohut emphasizes the need for such understanding objects throughout life and these notions are consistent with accumulating evidence for the powerful protective influence of social support identified across a wide range of epidemiological investigations (Brown & Harris, 1978; Brown, Harris, & Bifulco, 1986). The mirroring object becomes a "self-object," and the need for empathy drives development, which culminates in the attainment of a cohesive self. Drive theory becomes secondary to self-theory, in that the failure to attain an integrated self-structure both leaves room for, and in itself generates, both aggression and isolated sexual fixation. However, the self remains problematic as a construct; in Kohut's model, it is both the person (the patient) and the agent which is assumed to drive the person (Stolorow, Brandchaft, & Atwood, 1987). However, Kohut's descriptions of the narcissistic personality have been powerful and influential examples of the use of developmental theory in psychoanalytic understanding. Kohut's focus on self-esteem has been shown by empirical research to be appropriate and somewhat lacking in previous psychoanalytic formulations.

Kernberg's systematic integration of structural theory and object relations theory (Kernberg, 1976, 1982, 1987) is probably the most frequently used psychoanalytic model, particularly in relation to personality disorders. His model of psychopathology is developmental, in the sense that personality disturbance is seen to reflect the limited capacities of the young child to address intrapsychic conflict. Neurotic object relations show much less defensive disintegration of the representation of self and objects into libidinally invested part–object relations. In personality disorder, part–object relations are formed under the impact of diffuse, overwhelming emotional states, ecstatic, or of an equally overwhelming but terrifying and painful nature which signals the activation of aggressive or persecutory relations between self and object. Kernberg's models are particularly useful because of their level of detail and his determination to operationalize his ideas far more than has been traditional in psychoanalytic writing.

Bowlby's (1969, 1973, 1980) work on separation and loss also focused developmentalists' attention on the importance of the security (safety and predictability) of the earliest relationships. His cognitive-systems model of the internalization of interpersonal relationships (internal working models), consistent with object relations theory (Fairbairn, 1952; Kernberg, 1975) and elaborated by other attachment theorists (Bretherton, 1985; Crittenden, 1990; Main, Kaplan, & Cassidy, 1985), has been particularly influential.

According to Bowlby, the child develops expectations regarding a caregiver's behavior and the child's own behavior.These expectations are based on the child's understanding of experiences of previous interaction, and are helpful in organizing the child's behavior with the attachment figure and (through a process of extrapolation with others) with others. The concept has had very broad application. Bowlby's developmental model highlights the transgenerational nature of internal working models: our view of ourselves depends upon the working model of relationships which characterized our caregivers. Empirical research which places this intergenerational model under systematic scrutiny has begun, and the robustness of the findings is encouraging. There is an accumulating body of data which confirms that there is some kind of intergenerational transmission of attachment security and insecurity (see review by van IJzendoorn, 1995) and that parental mental representations pertinent to this process may be assessed before the birth of the first child (e.g., Fonagy, Steele, Moran, Steele, & Higgitt, 1991a; Fonagy, Steele, & Steele, 1991b; Ward & Carlson, 1995).

Stern's (1985) work represents a milestone in psychoanalytic theories of development. His work is remarkable within psychoanalysis for being normative rather than pathomorphic, and prospective rather than retrospective. His focus is the reorganization of subjective perspectives on self and other as these occur with the emergence of new maturational capacities. He is perhaps closest to Sandler in his psychoanalytic model of the mind, but his formulation of object relations also has much in common with those of Bowlby and Kernberg.

5.10.1.3 Evolution of the Psychodynamic Technique with Children

Specific therapeutic techniques which could help psychoanalysts in addressing psychiatric problems of childhood did not appear until the 1920s. Application of the insights gained from psychoanalytic treatment of adults to the treatment of children was prepared by Freud's observations concerning the psychology of young children. The most notable ones include Anna Freud's wishful dream for strawberries (S. Freud, 1900), and his grandson's separation game (S. Freud, 1920). Best known is S. Freud's case study of Hans (S. Freud, 1909), a five-year-old with an animal phobia, whose treatment by his physician father was supervised by S. Freud. All these observations were used by S. Freud principally to confirm his assumptions about infantile instinctual life through the direct observation of children and to prevent him (and other adult psychoanalysts) from making false developmental assumptions (S. Freud, 1926, p. 215).

Hug-Helmuth (1920, 1921) was the first clinician to introduce play therapy into the psychoanalyst's armamentarium. Her pioneering work, which is now largely forgotten, combined an insight-oriented technique, focused primarily on the child's unconscious sexual fantasies, with a powerful developmental perspective, whereby she saw the young person as needing to be "strengthened" in the mental capacities needed for his developmental tasks. This latter emphasis has echoes in present-day cognitive therapy and psychoanalytic approaches. Up to that point, most analysts shared the Hungarian analyst Ferenczi's skepticism about offering psychoanalysis to children who do not wish to be analyzed as they solely wish to play (see Group for the Advancement of Psychiatry, 1982, for a comprehensive history of the field).

The other great pioneers of the field, A. Freud (1946) and Klein (1932), independently (but frequently with reference to one another), evolved techniques to enable clinicians to take a psychoanalytic therapeutic approach to children. Klein's approach, working under the influence of Abraham, a Berlin based psychoanalyst, was to regard children's play as essentially the same as the free association of adults, motivated by unconscious fantasy activated principally by the relationship with the analyst and requiring verbalization (interpretation) if the child's anxiety was to be adequately addressed. Interpretation of the child's deep anxieties concerning destructive and sadistic impulses was the principal focus of child analytic work. She advocated that therapists establish an interpretative relationship, even with preschool children, from the beginning. The emphasis placed on the relationship with the analyst meant that work with parents and other adults in the child's life (e.g., teachers) was not seen as central.

Direct interpretation of the projective processes was seen by Klein as critical. In *Notes on some schizoid mechanisms* (Klein, 1946) and in her paper on *The origins of transference* (Klein, 1952), Klein discussed the importance of the common childhood unconscious fantasy of placing part of the self into another person and perceiving unwanted qualities in them rather than oneself in order to relieve oneself of unwanted feelings (such as greed or envy). This form of fragmentation of the sense of self was regarded by her as part of normal infantile development but when persisting beyond infancy was the cause of pathology and the key focus for interpretation. She assumed that while projective identification was distressing to the child it was also helpful in creating the fantasy, not only that others were the "containers" of the child's own unwelcome traits, but also that (as these unattractive attributes still partly belonged to the self) the child could control the other person (object). The clinician's understanding was enriched by the assumption that a child's perception of the clinician gave clues about conflictual aspects of the child's experience of his self. Bion (1959) showed how such projective experiences could be expected to have an impact on "the container" and how the capacity of that individual to "metabolize" (understand and accept) the projection may be critical in development as well as in the success of therapy. Thus, the therapist's subjective experience (countertransference) could be a clue to the child's unconscious fantasies, and her capacity to understand and tolerate these, the key component of successful treatment.

Modern Kleinians (e.g., DeFolch, 1988; O'Shaughnessy, 1988) have, to some degree, modified the classical Kleinian position; early interpretations of assumed deeply unconscious material are less frequently offered, and there is greater attention to defensive qualities of many

manifestations of the child's nonconscious processes. The immediate interaction with the analyst, however, remains the core focus of therapeutic work, and the underlying conceptualization remains based on the notion of fragmentation of the self-representational structure which may be undone through verbalization and interpretation. The countertransference experience of the therapist is the central guide.

Drawing on the work of Klein, Winnicott (1965, 1971) reinforced Klein's emphasis on the influence of early life on childhood pathology while introducing additional techniques into child analysis. For example, specific drawing techniques were used, while Winnicott also emphasized nonverbal aspects of the therapist's stance, in particular the importance of a "holding" environment and the central role of play. One of his major contributions was the concept of a transitional area between self and object where the subjective object and the truly objective object are simultaneously recognized (Winnicott, 1971). This insight was critical in developing an appreciation of the interpersonal nature of therapeutic interaction in child analysis (Altman, 1994).

By contrast, A. Freud's approach placed more emphasis on the child's developmental struggle with adaptation to a social as well as an intrapsychic environment. Her training as a nursery school teacher led her to be very concerned with the child's actual external circumstances, as well as their unconscious world. She made fewer assumptions concerning the meaning of the child's play, approached therapeutic work far more gradually, recommended working in collaboration with parents and teachers (particularly in communicating understanding derived from the therapy), and focused far more on the complications and conflicts arising from the child's libidinal (sexual) impulses than on innate aggression. Her focus was on the child's wish to protect their fragile internal world from conflict by adopting psychological strategies (mechanisms of defense, A. Freud, 1936) such as denial, repression, or identification with the aggressor. The focus of her technique therefore was the interpretation of defenses and through this, the anxieties which motivated them.

The Anna Freudian approach to child analysis invariably takes into consideration the limitations upon the child's "ego functioning" imposed by development, and has as its primary focus the support of the development of the ego and the restoration of the child to a normal developmental path. Pine (1985) stressed that the analyst, like the parent, creates a supportive environment for the child's incompletely developed ego. He saw such techniques as mutative in their own right and considered interpretations in the context of support to be qualitatively different from interpretations in the context of abstinence, as is recommended by Kleinian child analysts. The pressure for the analyst to be an active and "real" participant in the therapeutic situation has thus been growing apace (see also Altman, 1992; Warshaw, 1992). However, many of these reconceptualizations lack coherent theoretical rationale and specific technical recommendations as to how departures from abstinence may be put to good therapeutic effect.

Anna Freudian child psychoanalysis became popular as a treatment in the US in the first half of the twentieth century, and was systematically described by A. Freud and her colleagues (Sandler, Kennedy, & Tyson, 1980); it has also influenced many forms of psychodynamic treatment of children and families. Individual child psychodynamic psychotherapy, based on these principles, has been shown to be a form of treatment frequently used and highly regarded among child psychiatrists and psychologists in the US (Kazdin, Bass, Siegel, & Thomas, 1990a). In the UK, as well as in Latin America, Klein's model proved to be more popular.

5.10.1.4 The Common Assumptions of Psychodynamic Therapy

Psychodynamic child psychotherapy shares many of its basic assumptions with adult psychoanalysis. Numerous summaries of these are available (see Chapter 14, Volume 1, Fonagy, Target, Steele, & Gerber, 1995; Gabbard, 1994, 1995; Kernberg, 1995; Summers, 1994, for more comprehensive accounts) and here we shall only provide a brief overview.

Psychodynamically oriented child therapists assume that mental disturbance may be usefully studied at the level of *psychological causation*, that the representation of past experience, its interpretation, and meaning, largely unconscious, determine the child's reaction to his external world and capacity to adapt to it. The emphasis on psychic causation does not imply either a lack of respect for or inattention to other levels of analysis of childhood psychiatric problems such as the biological, the family, or broader social factors. Nevertheless, psychiatric problems, whether at the root genetic, constitutional, or socially caused, are seen by the psychodynamically oriented child clinician also as the meaningful consequence of the child's unconscious beliefs, thoughts, and feelings, and therefore, potentially accessible in psychotherapy.

Complex unconscious mental processes are assumed to be responsible for the content of thinking and behavior. In particular, unconscious fantasies associated with wishes for instinctual pleasure or safety (Sandler, 1987) motivate the child's behavior, affect regulation, and the ability to cope with the social environment.

The experience of the self with others is internalized and leads to representational structures of interpersonal interactions which, at the simplest level, determine expectations of others and more elaborately determine the "shape" of self and other representations, and the nature of the internal world of the child. This general idea is formulated somewhat differently by psychodynamic clinicians from different traditions. Bowlby's concept of "internal working models" of self–other relationships based on the infant–mother relationship is perhaps the closest to formulations from other areas of clinical psychology (Bowlby, 1973, 1980). In essence, all so-called "object-relations" theories posit that the emotional life of the child (and adult) is organized around mental representations, however partial, of the self in relation to an important figure, imbued with a specific affect (e.g., Kernberg, 1976).

It is assumed that psychic conflict is ubiquitous and a cause of suffering (or a felt lack of safety) (Brenner, 1982). Adverse environments of childhood may create intrapsychic conflicts of overwhelming intensity and/or fail to equip the child adequately to deal with conflicts within the normal range of early experience (Winnicott, 1965). Trauma (such as loss of a caregiver) or long-term abuse thus undermine personality development by intensifying incompatible wishes or reducing the child's capacity to resolve conflicts through mental work.

The child is predisposed to modify unacceptable unconscious wishes through a range of mental mechanisms aimed at reducing the sense of conflict. Defense mechanisms form a developmental hierarchy which reflects the degree of pathology experienced by the individual; developmentally early defenses, such as splitting, or projective identification, are normally associated with more severe disturbances. A neurotic symptom, such as phobic anxiety, may be understood as a result of displacement of fear from the representation of one model of interaction (e.g., father–child) to another (e.g., teacher–child). Considerably more resistant to therapy is the more primitive defense of splitting of affect, whereby a child alternately derogates and idealizes the caregiving figure. Immature or early defenses are assumed to reflect the absence of higher level, integrative capacities (Pine, 1985).

Psychodynamic therapists assume that the child's communication in the session has meaning beyond that intended by the child and, by analogous mechanisms, that the child's symptoms carry multiple meanings and reflect the nature of internal representations of others and their relationship to the child as the child perceives it. The therapist is able to bring the child's attention to aspects of his behavior which are ego-dystonic and hard to understand, and by making appropriate links illustrates to the child that they may be seen as rational in terms of unconscious mental experience and psychic causation (Sandler et al., 1980).

The relationship to the therapist has primacy, in that it provides a window on the child's expectations of others and can come to be a vehicle for the unwanted and disowned aspects of the child's thoughts and feelings. Transference displacement may include such aspects of past relationships or past fantasies about these as well as conflictual aspects of current relationships to parents, siblings, or important others. The child's verbal and nonverbal behavior (re-enactments) have an impact on the clinician, and through exploring the role he or she has been placed in by the child, the therapist is able to achieve a better understanding of the child's representation of role relationships and feelings about them (Tyson & Tyson, 1986).

Modern psychodynamic child psychotherapy emphasizes the current state of the child in relation to his environment, history of past relationships, and adaptations to these. Psychotherapists generally recognize that the therapy they offer has an important holding or containing function in the child's life which, beyond interpretation and consequent insight, creates the possibility of a reintegration or reorganization of the child's internal world that in turn facilitates the child's adaptive development. The child therapist takes a "whole person" perspective, encompassing all aspects of the child's unfolding concerns (biological, environmental, intrapsychic). The establishment of a relationship with an adult which is as far as possible open and nonexploitative may serve as the basis of new internalizations, bringing about a healthier resolution of pathogenic experiences.

5.10.2 CONTEMPORARY TECHNIQUE OF PSYCHODYNAMIC PSYCHOTHERAPY WITH CHILDREN

5.10.2.1 Indications

There has been general agreement on the ideal indications for child psychotherapy (Dowling & Naegele, 1995). These have traditionally included: (i) good intelligence and capacity to verbalize; (ii) a relatively supportive environment; (iii) diagnostic assessment indicating the primacy of internal conflict underlying symptomatology; (iv) the absence of gross interferences between parents and child (indicating adequate internal–external object relations); (v) the presence of anxiety; and (vi) the absence of pervasive developmental disorder, psychosis, major deficiencies in psychological capacities, or family constellations likely to interfere with treatment (chaotic environments and uncooperative parents). Although there have always been a number of child psychotherapists who have attempted to work with psychotic and autistic children (e.g., Alvarez, 1993; Klein, 1936), the majority have felt that they cannot help these children using psychoanalytically oriented work.

Child therapists have also addressed other disorders, often called borderline (Rosenfeld & Sprince, 1963). This group has been described on the basis of records at the Anna Freud Centre (Fonagy & Target, 1996a, 1996b). Others have taken a more traditional, descriptive approach and arrived at very similar characterizations (Cohen, Towbin, Mayes, & Volkmar, 1994; Towbin, Dykens, Pearson, & Cohen, 1993). These children appear to suffer from a variety of deficiencies of psychological capacities, shown by, for instance, lack of control over affect, lack of stable self- and other-representations, and diffusion of the sense of identity. As we shall see, such children require substantial modifications of traditional technique (Fonagy & Moran, 1991). Whereas the less severe, so-called neurotic, cases are well-served by a therapeutic process aimed at addressing distortions in their mental representations of others or of their relationships to them, we have suggested that the more severely disturbed group of patients require developmental therapy which can strengthen and support their adaptive defenses, and assist them in labeling and verbalizing their thoughts and feelings (Fonagy & Target, 1996a). This distinction is most readily conceptualized psychologically in terms of the classical distinction between mental representations and the mental processes which generate them. Whereas so-called classical technique has its main effect on the organization and "shape" of the child's mental representations (Sandler & Rosenblatt, 1962), developmental therapy aims to help develop mental processes which have been inhibited during early development (Fonagy, Moran, Edgcumbe, Kennedy, & Target, 1993).

5.10.2.2 Forms of Intervention for Neurotic Children

Psychodynamic child psychotherapy involves the elaboration and correction of distorted, and often unconscious mental representations. The therapist, on the bases of the child's verbalization, nonverbal play, and other behaviors, attempts to construct a model of the child's conscious and unconscious thoughts and feelings and, using this model, helps the child obtain insight into why they may seem irrational and inappropriate. Such understanding may result in the integration of developmentally earlier modes of thinking into a more mature, age-appropriate framework.

This treatment involves the use of toys, games, and other devices to engage children in a process of self-exploration with an adult who is friendly but tries, within a trusting relationship, to draw attention to the unconscious determinants of the child's behavior. The therapist uses the child's fantasy, games, and associations in conjunction with other sources of data from the family, school etc., to construct a hypothetical picture of the child's unconscious mental life and current emotional concerns. In this way the therapist aims to help the child to understand his emotional responses, confusions, concerns about his body, the unconscious meaning of his presenting symptoms for the child, anxieties about unconscious aggressive or sexual impulses, and worries about his relationships with caregivers, siblings, and peers.

The techniques used by psychodynamic child therapists have been systematized, on the basis of empirical observation, by P. Kernberg (1995). In her studies, she was able to reliably distinguish a number of interventions on the part of the therapist, in addition to interpretive work, which may facilitate change in the patient's mental representations. In particular, she has delineated supportive interventions aimed at allaying the child's anxiety, and increasing a sense of competence and mastery through information, suggestions, reassurance, and empathy. In addition, she has observed facilitative statements which enhance and maintain therapeutic exchange with the child, when the therapist reviews, summarizes, or paraphrases the child's communication to that point. Related to this are clarifications aiming to either prepare the child for an interpretation, or direct his attention to noticeable aspects of his behavior. Although these are important distinctions, they are not placed within a theoretical context, and the therapeutic impact of the process is still seen as chiefly related to interpretations.

Analysts consider a number of aspects of a child's material when they try to interpret it. These include: (i) the main things the child talks about, especially what they say about themself, others, and the analyst, and the nature of the relationship these suggest between themself and objects in their mind; (ii) what is left out, such as not referring to arguments between the parents, to school, or to other important events in the child's life of which the analyst is aware; (iii) their nonverbal behavior, such as infantile gestures, unusual levels of activity, or avoiding entering the consulting room; (iv) their play, including roles assigned to the child, analyst, or play figures; (v) signs of the child's emotional state; and (vi) dreams that the child tells the analyst about.

The analyst is informed by, but does not necessarily mention, the child's past history and the contents of the previous sessions. While the analyst may often be able to make important connections between the child's analytic material and their past experiences, interpretations early on are generally restricted to the current conflicts which the child seems to be experiencing, in the immediate context through which the child brings these into the analysis. However, ultimately the analyst will aim to help the child develop an emotionally meaningful understanding of the connections between past experience and current conflict.

Kernberg (1995) distinguishes between three aspects of interpretations: interpretations of defenses show children how the therapist thinks they protect themselves from unacceptable thoughts, feelings, and actions. For instance, the therapist might suggest to the child "You often say that you are no good at things, perhaps because you are worried that people will think that you are big headed." Drawing the child's attention to these serves a dual function in that what is defended against is brought into awareness and, by implication, the child is also prompted to consider alternative strategies for coping with or expressing the ideas, impulses, or feelings previously warded off.

A second class of interpretation may address the child's wishes, which the therapist thinks may underlie his behavior. Most frequently, these two classes of interpretation are offered together, with the therapist leading the patient to see the unconscious wish by showing the child how he protects himself from it. The therapist might say "I think you secretly wish to feel much better than everyone else, and that is why you are frightened of seeming to be big-headed."

Some child therapists address the child's past experience as part of a causal account of the child's current state of mind. These reconstructions may be helpful, although few psychodynamic child therapists would nowadays feel that the actual past experience needs to be uncovered in order for the child's problems to be adequately addressed. More commonly, interpretations may make reference to current experience, particularly in relation to the therapist. The latter, so-called transference interpretations aim to identify the role in which the therapist experiences being placed by the child. The analyst further assumes that this role corresponds to an internal representation of a relationship in the child's mind. Thus, for example, a child who places the therapist in the role of a critic is assumed to be externalizing an internal representation of a figure who constantly undermines the self, and bombards it with disparagement and criticism. "I think you are so worried about me criticizing you because there is a terrible voice inside your head which says that you are such a naughty child that nobody could love you." It is important to note that analysts do not assume that such a figure actually exists in the child's life; an "internal object" may be a separated off part of the child's self-representation, which has been felt to be too destructive and aggressive for the child to be able to like himself. Interpretation eventually addresses this facet as well, by showing the child how unacceptable he finds the small amount of residual envy or destructiveness which has remained part of the self-structure, and through this gradually modifies the child's internal standards, allowing it to experience his destructiveness as less catastrophic.

Whether the content of the interpretation concerns defenses, wishes, or past or current experience, the underlying structure of child analytic interpretations is largely similar. The analyst focuses on the child's anxiety in relation to the above domains, in particular the emotional states they generate. Thus, destructive impulses are most likely to be taken up in terms of the anxiety the child feels about his angry feelings. A further important focus is explicit recognition that the child is actively struggling against certain wishes, and that aspects of current and past experience have necessitated the use of defenses. In psychoanalytic shorthand, this is referred to as "interpreting the conflict." Thus, rather than saying "You seem to be feeling very angry with me today," an analyst might say "You seem anxious, maybe because you feel angry." Naturally, this could be an inappropriate interpretation if the child was consciously aware of feeling angry, and not in conflict about this. However, in this case too, the analyst attempts to find the source of any current anxiety, for

example, that the anger might destroy the otherwise valued relationship with the analyst.

The middle phase of analysis focuses particularly on the systematic use of transference interpretations to begin the "working through" process.

Transference is facilitated by: (i) the therapist's implicit offer of help and relatedness coupled with a basic stance of acceptance, encouragement to express thoughts and feelings, attention to resistances, and attunement to the child's predicaments; and (ii) a therapeutic structure that emphasizes regularity, consistency, and the specialness of the sessions (Chethik, 1989). Every action of the therapist conveys to the child that this time and space is set aside to better understand what bothers the child.

Signs of readiness for termination of the therapy are found both within and outside the sessions. Of course, sustained symptomatic improvement is important. Improvements in family and peer relationships are noted. The child's ability to make use of parents, teachers, and other people as sources of help and advice, and as models for identification, suggests that the analysis is becoming less necessary. Perhaps the most important indication for termination is evidence that the child is able to take advantage of normal developmental opportunities, to cope more effectively with stress and conflict, and to respond with greater freedom and mastery to demands for adaptation, coming from inside and outside.

Kernberg (1995) proposed the following specific features as showing readiness to end the therapy: (i) the child's statements about the therapist during the session convey an internalization of the analytic function, for example, comments about their sense of having been listened to or helped to make connections; (ii) the therapist finds more opportunities for interpretation, as opposed to clarifications or confrontations; (iii) the child introduces more material from current reality, suggesting a healthy decrease of investment in the analysis; (iv) there is more reflectiveness and capacity to use interpretations and resolve conflicts; (v) greater freedom, expressiveness, and pleasure in play; (vi) increased modulation of feelings, which permits discussion of experiences of sadness, concern, and gratitude; (vii) evidence of new adaptive interests; (viii) insight, humor, and a healthy capacity in the child to laugh at himself; (ix) flexible and adaptive coping and defensive operations, permitting the child to assume responsibility for their own actions; and (x) predominance of age-appropriate behavior, posture, and appearance.

5.10.2.3 Treatment Technique with Non-neurotic Disorders

More recently, the psychodynamic approach has been extended to apply not only to so-called neurotic disorders, but also to the understanding and treatment of borderline, narcissistic, delinquent, and conduct disordered youngsters (Bleiberg, 1987, 1994a, 1994b; Marohn, 1991; O'Brien, 1992; Rinsley, 1989), as well as schizoid and even psychotic children (e.g., Cantor & Kestenbaum, 1986). Clinical work with these more severely disturbed children quickly highlights the limitations of the "classical" analytic strategy. For example, the child's anxiety may not be accessible to awareness, and referring to it simply leaves the child confused. Also, there may be little evidence that the child is "struggling" against wishes, even when these are clearly socially unacceptable. In other children, defenses, as normally conceived, may be hard to identify. All these cases remind us of the need to reconsider child psychoanalytic techniques.

Bleiberg, Fonagy, and Target (1997) identify two clusters of youngsters who may be regarded as suitable for modified psychodynamic therapy, notwithstanding the severity of their disorder. They suggest that these clusters have in common the presence of at least one emotional disorder, for example, depression, dysthymia, generalized anxiety disorder (GAD), separation anxiety disorder, and social phobia; however, these symptoms must be seen in the context of a broader disturbance of social and emotional development, including marked impairment of peer relationships, affect regulation, frustration tolerance, and poor self-esteem.

One subgroup, designated cluster A, are characterized by fragile reality contact and thought organization, idiosyncratic magical thinking, ideas of reference, suspiciousness, and deep discomfort in social situations. They can neither make full sense of the social world, nor communicate adequately their internal states. They resemble the cluster A *DSM-IV* personality disorder diagnoses for adults and children described by Cohen et al. (1994), and Towbin et al. (1993) as multiplex personality disorder. By contrast, cluster B children show (if referred below school age) a hunger for social response, intense often dramatic affect, clinginess, hyperactivity, and temper tantrums. School-age children may meet axis 1 criteria for attention deficit hyperactivity disorder (ADHD), conduct disorder, or mood disorder, but their lack of adequate affect regulation is the major feature of the picture: a sense of elation and blissful merger with others close to the child seems to alternate with rage and self-hatred.

They have been linked to adult "dramatic" personality disorders (cluster B), and have been described by Bleiberg (1994a, 1994b) and by Petti and Vela (1990). We have linked both clusters to an impairment of reflective function (Bleiberg et al., 1997; Fonagy & Target, 1996a). As psychodynamic therapists have extended the scope of their work to include these groups of patients, their therapeutic approaches have increasingly emphasized aspects of interaction between child and therapist which promote opportunities for playing with ideas. To some degree, this is a shift of emphasis within existing therapeutic techniques, at the same time as including some new techniques which have previously been systematically excluded from psychodynamic work with neurotic children, because of the expected interference with therapeutic neutrality. All these strategies have in common an emphasis on the therapeutic value of play, not just in the sense of pretending, but of creating a safe opportunity for playing with alternative meanings of the child's experiences.

The main forms of intervention include: (i) enhancing reflective processes by encouraging the observation and verbalization of what it is the child is feeling, focusing on somatic and psychological experiences in the immediate situation; (ii) enhancing impulse control, by looking for ways of channeling impulses into socially acceptable forms of behavior, and increasing control over expression of feeling in action; (iii) enhancing cognitive self-regulation, both through strategies involving symbolization or metaphor, and through demonstrating the therapist's own capacities for reflection and moderation of experience through thinking and talking, rather than physical action or coercion; (iv) encouraging awareness of the feelings and thoughts of others, often initially focusing on the child's perceptions of the therapist's mental states, as a precursor to self-reflection; and (v) developing play, perhaps first with objects, then another person, ultimately with ideas, with the aim of showing the child that habitual thoughts and feelings are not the only way of seeing things, or necessarily the way that others see the world, and that not all adults relate to them as they may have been related to before.

Techniques with developmental disturbances does not involve working with the transference in the sense of expecting the child to "transfer" their thoughts and feelings about their parents onto the analyst. However, the child's feelings about the therapist remain central, because the clarification of the child's feelings about themselves and about the therapist is sometimes the most effective route towards acquiring mentalizing capacity. This requires the therapist to convey that the child's affect can be understood and managed by another person, rather than compounding what might have been the child's original experience, of a parent who has to twist or cut off emotional contact with the child to make the closeness of an intensive relationship more bearable. Late in the therapy with a developmentally disturbed child, it may also become helpful to make interpretations of neurotic conflict, which would previously have been experienced as meaningless or invasive.

The approach described is based on the assumption that reflective or mentalizing function is a key, biologically prepared human capacity triggered by specific aspects of normal parenting. A number of children—which we group into two developmental and clinical clusters—suffer from combinations of constitutional vulnerability and environmental disadvantage that create significant deficits in their ability to grasp mental states and find symbolic meaning in human behavior. This crucial deficit, as we have described, generates a host of problems in subsequent development and adjustment, including difficulties in relationships, impulse control, self-esteem, and overall difficulty in taking advantage of life's opportunities for growth.

We propose for these children a systematic psychodynamic psychotherapeutic approach aimed at enhancing the capacity to mentalize. While achieving such a goal is a by-product of traditional child psychoanalytic technique—and "psychological mindedness" is considered a precondition for child analysis proper—we suggest that a well-defined and deliberate focus on enhancing mentalization can lead to more effective and more specifically tailored approaches for a broad range of children with serious disturbances.

A therapeutic focus on mentalization, of course, does not preclude a variety of other therapeutic approaches, such as pharmacotherapy, family therapy, and cognitive-behavioral treatment. In effect, we propose that a psychoanalytic approach which promotes mentalization provides a conceptual glue to hold together a variety of interventions in a coherent treatment plan of greater clinical effectiveness (Bleiberg, 1994a, 1994b; O'Brien, Pilowsky, & Lewis, 1992).

Recasting psychoanalytic child therapy, from a predominantly insight-oriented, conflict-solving modality to a developmentally-based, mentalization-enhancing approach, brings it closer to the mainstream of contemporary developmental research and other, more empirically supported therapies. In particular, commonalities—and differences—between the approach described here and cognitive therapy warrant brief discussion. Both cognitive therapy and this approach aim at effecting a change in the ways people organize and structure experiences. Cognitive therapy, however, is both more "active" and directive and more narrowly focused on specific maladaptive cognitive schemas, for example, the particular cognitions underlying low self-esteem. By contrast, enhancing mentalization—while more targeted and "active" than traditional child psychoanalyses—aims at promoting a broad set of capacities, or mental processes, rather than correcting specific cognitive distortions.

The most important differences between the two approaches arise from the psychoanalytic origins of the psychotherapeutic strategy described in this chapter.

(i) These approaches are based on the assumption that the child's symptoms, and the entire organization of their subjective world, primarily represents an unconscious adaptation to the child's perceptions of reality. Child analysts therefore anticipate that children will try to resist the therapist's efforts, and the possibility of change: both of these, though well intentioned, threaten the child's best effort at adaptation thus far.

(ii) Child analysts have been trained to look for, respect, and address the child's deepest anxieties, which are likely to include anxiety about exercising the particular capacity that the treatment aims to promote, the recognition of mental experiences, and habitually thinking in terms of these to give the social world meaning and predictability.

(iii) Psychoanalytic training, supervision, and personal treatment should have helped the therapist to use her own thoughts and feelings to understand and empathize with the child's inner world, without getting stuck in response to the child's "concrete" ways of relating to themselves and others.

5.10.2.4 Working with the Parents

Regardless of the child's predominant disturbance, it is generally helpful for the therapist to have meetings with the parents or other caregivers, aiming to enhance their sensitivity to the child's worries, limitations, and needs. This may involve work on aspects of the child's environment or family which seem to impinge on the child's development, and the exploration of ways of freeing the child from avoidable stresses. Sometimes this involves offering parents therapy for themselves, but much more often it is enough to help the parent to think more objectively and productively about the child, and to find together ways of overcoming obstacles to the child's positive development. Interventions range from concrete suggestions and strategies to helping the parents to be more understanding of their child's thoughts and feelings. The analyst may show the parent distortions affecting the relationship, for instance, where the mother identifies her son with her husband, and then unconsciously expresses the anger she feels towards her husband to the child, generally an easier and more available target.

Discussion of the child's symptoms aims to help the parents to develop more awareness of the nature of the child's difficulties and feelings, and (often) insight into possible reasons for these to have arisen and become entrenched. Parents may tend to minimize the difficulties facing the child. For example, in one family the parents needed to be helped to recognize their child's distress when they compared the child's ability to make friends with that of his much brighter and more attractive brother; the parents had felt that this comparison would encourage the child to try harder, not understanding that the child's difficulty went far beyond what could be corrected by greater effort. This sort of discussion may be combined with thinking about better ways of managing practical problems, for instance, major tantrums in response to separation. The parents can also be shown connections between external events and stresses and symptoms, whether somatic, emotional, or behavioral. Some stresses (e.g., an inappropriate school setting) can be removed, while others (such as having a physically handicapped sibling) of course cannot, but even here ways of limiting pressure and damage may be found.

5.10.3 THE OUTCOME OF PSYCHODYNAMIC TREATMENT FOR CHILDREN AND ADOLESCENTS

Research in the field of child therapies has very much lagged behind the adult literature, in terms of both number of studies and quality of design (e.g., Barnett, Docherty, & Frommelt, 1991). This lag has been greater still in the area of psychodynamic therapies, partly because of a traditional antagonism among psychodynamic clinicians towards empirical evaluation, but also because of specific methodological difficulties in the design of studies of long-term, intensive treatments, where choosing a suitable control group poses practical and ethical problems, and the treatment goals are relatively difficult to operationalize (usually what is sought is a

change in unconscious psychic structure shown through subtle but pervasive personality changes, as opposed to change in more specific symptoms). For these reasons, evaluations of nonbehavioral therapies for children have most often been conducted by behaviorally-oriented clinicians, as a comparison condition for a trial of behavior or cognitive-behavior therapy (Shirk & Russell, 1992); they have also generally been administered in the form of brief, group therapy (to maintain comparability with the other treatment being evaluated) rather than longer-term, individual sessions as would be used in clinical practice (Kazdin, Siegel, & Bass, 1990b; Silver & Silver, 1983).

5.10.3.1 Reviews and Meta-analyses of Studies of Efficacy

Possibly partly for the reasons given above, meta-analyses of child therapy outcome studies have found psychodynamic and interpersonal therapies to be less effective than behaviourally-oriented techniques (Casey & Berman, 1985; Weisz, Weiss, Alicke, & Klotz, 1987). Weisz et al. (1987), for example, found an effect size exactly twice as great for behavioral therapies (0.88 vs. 0.44, $p < 0.05$). A further factor contributing to the difference has been identified by the authors of these meta-analyses, who found in both cases that the difference was reduced to nonsignificance once outcome measures very close to techniques practiced in the behavior therapy sessions were excluded from the comparison. Nevertheless, it remains a challenging fact that across the three studies which included some variant of brief, psychodynamic therapy, the mean effect size was negligible (0.01). If this were due to the use of therapeutic procedures in research studies which would never be expected to be effective in clinical practice, as persuasively argued by Shirk and Russell (1992), then it is imperative that the superior effectiveness of the procedures which would be used clinically be demonstrated. Thus far, the evidence from reviews of routine clinical work is dispiriting for psychodynamic therapy, as it is for child therapies of all orientations (see below), but the very small number of studies of outcome for this sort of therapy in a research setting which *do* use normal clinical procedures give more reason to be optimistic (see Section 5.10.3.3).

5.10.3.2 Review of Effectiveness in the Clinic

Serious doubt has been cast on the generalizablility of the lab-based studies of all forms of child treatment included in meta-analyses.

Weisz and Weiss (1989) observed that the meta-analyses to date had involved studies which did not represent normal clinic populations or practices. In particular, subjects were recruited rather than referred, samples were chosen for specific problems (e.g., phobias) on which the therapy was focused, therapists were specially and recently trained in the techniques to be evaluated. It was therefore felt necessary to see whether the good outcomes reported in these studies were also seen in the clinic.

The strategy was to compare 93 referred children who had received at least five sessions of therapy with 60 dropouts from the same clinics who had been offered treatment but did not attend. There were no significant differences on demographic or clinical variables between these groups when referred. The findings were very negative. There were no differences in outcome between treated and untreated children; both improved to an extent equivalent to the improvement found in untreated controls in other studies.

This first study of clinic-based treatment has generated increasing interest in the problem of applying research findings to clinical practice (see, for example, Hoagwood, Hibbs, Brent, & Jensen, 1995; Kendall & Southam-Gerow, 1995; Weisz, Weiss, Morton, Granger, & Han, 1992). Weisz, Donenberg, Han, and Weiss (1995) have reviewed evidence relating to the gulf between efficacy (in lab studies) and effectiveness (in clinic settings) in an attempt to disentangle the reasons behind the difference. The clinic-based studies included in their survey were few (only nine could be found in a thorough search, three of them carried out before 1960) and methodologically very limited, and one important point made by the authors is that well-designed effectiveness studies are desperately needed. They then attempted to test eight plausible reasons for the much larger effect sizes found in lab-based outcome studies, by conducting comparisons between over 100 of these studies, according to the presence or absence of possible mediating factors. They found that two did appear to be relevant (greater severity of clinical problems in clinic samples and greater likelihood of behavioral approach in lab studies). This, then, clearly suggests that the structured approach of behaviorally-oriented treatment tends to lead to greater effectiveness, and while it is clear that better-quality studies of the nonbehavioral therapies are badly needed, it may also be appropriate for psychodynamic clinicians to be considering whether their therapies can be made more focused on explicit goals, although these are likely to be formulated in terms of unconscious, intrapsychic structure and mechanisms.

5.10.3.3 Individual Studies of Outcome of Psychodynamic or Interpersonal Therapies

There have been very few studies of intensive, long-term psychoanalytic psychotherapy for children and adolescents.

A chart review of the outcome of 763 cases in child psychoanalysis has been carried out at the Anna Freud Centre in London (Fonagy & Target, 1994, 1995b; Target & Fonagy, 1994a, 1994b). While this retrospective methodology has severe limitations, the study reached a number of robust conclusions which need to be explored further in controlled, prospective investigations. The main findings were as follows.

(i) Attrition was low compared to reports of other treatment approaches. Overall, 18% of patients withdrew from treatment within six months, and as this made it unlikely that an analytic process would have been established and resolved, these children were excluded from the following analyses (further studies of attrition were, however, carried out).

(ii) Children with pervasive developmental disorders (e.g., autism) or mental retardation did not do well, even with prolonged, intensive treatment. Children with serious disruptive disorders also had relatively poor outcomes.

(iii) Younger children improved significantly more during psychodynamic treatment, and gained additional benefit from four to five times weekly sessions.

(iv) Anxiety disorders, particularly specific rather than pervasive symptoms, were associated with a good prognosis, even if the primary diagnosis was of a different type (e.g., disruptive disorder).

(v) Among children with emotional disorders, severe or pervasive symptomatology responded very well to intensive treatment (four to five sessions per week), but did not show satisfactory rates of improvement in nonintensive psychotherapy.

(vi) Predictors of improvement varied considerably between subgroups of the full sample, and by subdividing the sample according to diagnostic group and developmental level, it was possible to predict a majority of the variance in outcome within the subgroups.

We will now turn to smaller-scale, but prospective studies of psychoanalytic psychotherapy with children, beginning with the earliest systematic studies in the 1960s. After that, we will look at evidence on the efficacy of some forms of intervention based on modifications of psychodynamic psychotherapy.

Heinicke (1965) reported a study of a group of children aged 7–10 with developmental reading disorders linked to emotional symptoms. These children received psychoanalytic psychotherapy, either one or four sessions per week for two years. Greater improvement was found in the group receiving more frequent therapy. Heinicke and Ramsey-Klee (1986) extended this study, hoping to maximize the impacts of different treatment frequencies. They added a third group, matched to the first two, who received therapy once a week for the first year and four times a week for the second. Outcome was measured in terms of the referral problem (reading level) and general academic performance, together with a standardized psychodynamic diagnostic profile. At termination of therapy, there were no significant differences between the three treatment conditions, but at one-year follow-up, the groups which had received either four times a week treatment throughout, or once a week followed by four times a week, showed continued improvements on all measures, greater than those of the once a week group. It therefore seemed that more intensive treatment in the second year of treatment had a beneficial effect.

This study attempted to do three important things: (i) to evaluate the effectiveness of intensive and nonintensive psychodynamic therapy for emotional and learning disturbances; (ii) to isolate the impact of treatment frequency, which is of interest in a variety of therapies, and particularly—for practical and theoretical reasons—in psychodynamic treatment; and (iii) to measure change in both objective, service relevant ways, and ways consistent with the theoretical perspective. In all these respects, the study was innovative. There were difficulties with it, reflecting the methods prevalent in all outcome research 30 years ago when the basic design was planned. Thus, diagnostic characteristics of the sample were poorly described, the projective tests and diagnostic interview were of unknown reliability, and the therapy was not described in full detail, just being stated to be analytically oriented. The study does, however, clearly raise the possibility that for certain children, perhaps those with comorbid emotional and developmental disorders, intensive psychotherapy may offer more profound benefits than the same type of treatment offered once a week.

Moran and Fonagy have carried out a series of studies which overcame the problems of diagnosis and outcome measurement by choosing a group of physically ill children where difficulty in treating the medical condition was thought to be due to severely self-destructive behavior, sabotaging the treatment. The group chosen suffered from so-called brittle diabetes, and the studies assessed the effectiveness of adding psychoanalytic treatment to the existing medical care.

The first study (Moran & Fonagy, 1987) explored the relationship between metabolic control and the content of psychoanalytic sessions, in a single case study of an adolescent girl. Process reports were rated for the presence of psychodynamic themes; the association of certain themes with subsequent improvement, demonstrated through independent measures of diabetic control, was shown using time-series analysis. The second study by these authors (Moran, Fonagy, Kurtz, Bolton, & Brook, 1991) compared two matched groups of 11 diabetic children with highly abnormal blood glucose profiles and histories of regular admissions to the hospital. All patients were offered inpatient treatment, for the treatment group 15 weeks of intensive (three to four sessions per week) psychoanalytic psychotherapy was added. The children in the treatment group showed considerable improvements in diabetic control, maintained at one year follow-up; those in the comparison group had returned to pretreatment levels of metabolic control within three months of discharge from the hospital.

The third study (Fonagy & Moran, 1990) involved of a series of experimental single case investigations. The effect of brief psychoanalytic treatment on growth rate (measured by changes in height and bone age) was examined in three children whose height had fallen below the fifth percentile for age. In each case, treatment was linked to accelerated growth and a substantial increase in predicted adult height.

A different, ongoing study should be mentioned, in spite of methodological drawbacks, because of its attempt to assess outcome in clinically meaningful ways, and for its attention to a particularly needy (and costly) group. Lush, Boston, and Grainger (1991) compared 35 children in psychotherapy who were fostered or adopted with 13 similar children for whom psychotherapy had been recommended but did not start. The children were aged 2–18 years, and they mostly received weekly sessions for at least one year. For ethical reasons, children could not be randomly allocated to treated and untreated groups; the study was naturalistic. A further drawback was that, because no measures suitable for the assessment of psychodynamic change existed, measures were developed specially for the study and used without prior evidence of reliability or validity. However, there are indications that the therapy did benefit these deprived children. Preliminary results have been reported on the first 20 children to be treated. Sixteen cases made "good progress," as judged by therapists ratings and generally confirmed by parents' and external clinicians' opinions. An informal comparison was made with seven similar (but not matched) control children; none of these had improved during the same period.

Smyrnios and Kirkby (1993) have reported a comparison between 12 sessions of focal psychodynamic psychotherapy, and open-ended, nonfocused psychodynamic treatment with children aged 5–9 years. The mean number of child sessions was 10 for the time-limited condition and 27 for the unlimited condition. The parents of children in each treatment group were seen by a different therapist for guidance intended to support the child's treatment within a psychodynamic/family systems orientation. As with the individual therapy for the children, this parent work was much more focused on the identified problems and goals in the brief therapy condition. A further, minimal contact control condition involved assessment and feedback sessions only, with encouragement to the families to work at the goals by themselves. The groups were small, beginning with 10 children per condition, which had fallen to between six and eight by the time of the four year follow-up. The authors report that although pre- to post-treatment gains were significant for each condition, by follow-up, children in the time-unlimited condition no longer showed a significant improvement over the pretreatment levels of symptomatology as rated by the parents. Goals were found to be equally well attained at post-treatment and at follow-up in each of the conditions. Teachers' ratings of social adjustment did not show significant improvement for children in any condition, either at post-treatment or follow-up (there were trends towards improvement for all conditions, and the insignificant results may well reflect the small numbers involved). Essentially, children in the minimal contact control group showed improvements almost as great as those in the two treatment groups, and on one measure the time-limited treatment group did better than the open-ended one. The authors conclude that it may be most cost-effective to offer assessment and feedback rather than treatment to children such as those in this study.

There are several points that need to be made in interpreting the results of this study, some acknowledged by the authors.

The time-limited and minimal contact groups were both treated or assessed by one therapist, while the time-unlimited group were treated by a different therapist. This may well mean that therapist skill or commitment was not equal in the different conditions.

Although the assessments at pre- and post-treatment were carried out by an independent clinician, assessments at the four year follow-up were carried out by one of the authors who had also been the therapist for the time-limited and minimal treatment conditions. This would be likely to introduce a bias in favor of finding greater improvement in those conditions, not only because of therapist expectations, but also because parents interviewed by their child's therapist might be more likely to be positive than those seen by a stranger. Follow-up assessments by the children's teachers did not confirm the differences between groups found by the clinician interviewer.

It is mentioned that families in the minimal contact condition were in fact offered regular therapy sessions (presumably for child and parents separately, as for the other families) after a 12-week wait, although we are not told how many took this up. Thus, although the authors make an attractive argument that assessment only may be the most useful form of intervention, it seems unsafe to regard this group as untreated. In addition, it is stated that the majority of families across conditions sought further treatment during the follow-up period, which obscures the pattern of findings at follow-up.

The small sample size (down to an average of seven per group at follow-up) is unfortunate in that it casts doubt on generalizability and may have prevented certain trends from reaching statistical significance.

Despite these cautions, the study is a useful attempt to examine highly important questions, of whether evaluation alone may be as helpful as treatment, and whether offering more treatment produces better outcome. Although the authors intended to investigate the importance of the number of treatment sessions, it may be that the goal-oriented approach of both the time-limited and the minimal contact groups was helpful, and was the major difference between these groups and the open-ended one. It may also be, as the authors suggest, that the minimal contact condition inadvertently mobilized a useful sense of agency in the children and parents by helping them to clarify their goals and then encouraging the family to work towards them themselves. The open-ended treatment group therefore not only had a different therapist from the other two, but also had a far less focused and enabling approach.

5.10.3.4 Evaluation of Modifications of Psychodynamic Therapy

We will now more briefly survey some studies which have included forms of therapy related to psychodynamic therapies, or which have found some evidence of efficacy when it has been included as a control condition. Again, we will start with the earlier studies.

The pioneering study of Kolvin et al. (1981) will be included for what it can tell us about the amenability of different groups of children to treatment, with its careful design and relatively large sample size, even though it concerned therapy delivered through the school, and therefore difficult to apply directly in clinical psychology practice.

The study compared four forms of school intervention for nearly 600 children, found to be showing either neurotic or disruptive behavioral problems. These children were selected by screening 4300 children. The aim was to assess ways of helping maladjusted children within school, without recourse to psychiatric referral. The children were dichotomized in two major ways: younger vs. older (either 7–8 or 11–12 years old), emotional vs. disruptive disorders. These disorders were not defined by psychiatric diagnosis, but by extreme scores on measures of psychological adjustment in school, personality functioning, and peer acceptance. Children were randomly assigned to one of the four treatment conditions: (i) parent counseling—teacher consultation (three terms): social workers offered casework to parents and consultation to teacher; (ii) psychodynamic group therapy (one term only): the younger group played and were encouraged to reflect on feelings, while the older children discussed emotional issues; (iii) (a) behavior modification, for the older children only (two terms): attempted to alter behavior through systematic reinforcement, working towards specified individual goals; (b) nurture work, for younger children only (five terms): enrichment of social experience in small group with leader selected for warmth and motherliness, some shaping of desirable behavior; (iv) no treatment control condition. There were between 60 and 90 children in each age × treatment group.

Outcome was assessed at 18 months after the beginning of treatment, and at three years. In line with other intervention studies, children with emotional disorders were found to have significantly better outcome on the whole than those with disruptive behavior, irrespective of age and treatment type. It was also found that girls had significantly better outcome across groups. Generally, psychodynamic group therapy had the best outcome, and behavior modification was also helpful for the older children. Both were significantly more effective than counseling parents and teachers, or no treatment. Interestingly and unexpectedly, these differences between treatment and control groups widened over time, so that the effect

of intervention appeared to be increasingly evident, even two years after it had ended. As Kolvin et al. (1981) note, the most effective interventions were in fact the briefest, and therefore easily the most cost-effective.

Psychodynamic group therapy was carried out over just one term, but the effects were very clear two and a half years later. This was a surprising finding, and it is not clear to what extent it might have been specific to the school setting; the intervention might not have had the same impact in a different context. School is a very important and familiar social context for children, one which may be able to facilitate and sustain considerable therapeutic impact. Similarly encouraging results have been reported in other smaller scale, more recent studies (e.g., Lochman, Coie, Underwood, & Terry, 1993). It is also unfortunate that the length of treatment was not consistent across the conditions; it is just conceivable that the briefer treatments were more effective because they were briefer, certainly this is a factor which needs to be considered more seriously in research on the impact of psychotherapies for children, as Smyrnios and Kirkby (1993) have indicated.

Another study in which psychodynamic therapy has been used as a comparison treatment has been reported by Szapocznik et al. (1989), who treated disruptive adolescent boys from Hispanic families, using either structural family therapy or individual psychodynamic therapy, compared with a recreational control group. All groups were seen for 12–24 sessions over up to six months. On parent-rated measures of child behavior, child psychodynamic functioning and family functioning, both family therapy and individual psychodynamic treatment led to significant gains, and these gains were not significantly different from each other. However, at one-year follow-up, although child behavior was still improved in both treatment groups, family functioning had deteriorated in the individual therapy group, continued to improve in the family therapy group, and stayed the same in the control group. If this finding proved to be generalizable beyond Hispanic families with conduct-disordered adolescent boys, then it would point to a very important problem in using individual psychodynamic therapy with children or adolescents, that although the child might get better, even sustaining the improvement a year later, the family might function less well over time.

Another study, which like the Kolvin report found a supportive psychotherapy group to be unexpectedly beneficial, was carried out by Fine, Forth, Gilbert, and Haley (1991). They were interested in evaluating the efficacy of social skills training in the treatment of major depression or dysthymia. The patients were 47 adolescents who had been referred for psychiatric treatment, and were assigned to a 12-week therapy group using either supportive therapy or social skills training. Forty-one percent of the patients were receiving concurrent treatment, either psychotherapy, medication, or both. Against expectations, adolescents in the therapeutic support group were significantly less likely than those given social skills training to be diagnosed as depressed following treatment ($p < 0.03$), and had significantly lower scores on the Child Depression Inventory (CDI) self-report measure of depression ($p < 0.05$). These group differences were no longer significant at follow-up, but this appeared to be a result of diminishing sample size rather than a change in relative rates of depression.

As the authors point out, in the absence of an untreated control group, it is not possible to be confident that the two treatments improved on the spontaneous remission rate; 68% of adolescents in the study were no longer diagnosable at nine months follow-up, and in Kovacs, Gatsonis, Paulauskas, and Richards (1989) study the median time to recovery was 9.5 months. This suggests some beneficial impact of therapy, but it is difficult to be sure how comparable the samples in the different studies were. The high proportion of adolescents receiving other treatments in the study by Fine and co-workers also raises a major problem of interpretation. Nevertheless, the authors acknowledge the unexpected superiority of the therapeutic support group over the "active" treatment, and provide an interesting discussion of this. There were indications from process measures that adolescents in the social skills training group were considerably less engaged and more avoidant. The authors suggest that social skills training may be too demanding for clinically depressed adolescents, but that they may become able to use this approach as they become less depressed. They suggest that a fruitful approach might be to offer therapeutic support which introduces social skills training at a later stage.

This is reminiscent of some other studies where a behaviorally-oriented treatment has apparently been perceived by children in clinical samples as less acceptable. For instance, Apter Bernhaut, and Tyano (1984) reported that hospitalized adolescent patients with obsessive compulsive disorder (OCD) refused to cooperate with behavioral treatment, but did accept and improve with supportive psychotherapy. Given that most outcome studies with children and adolescents have used nonreferred, convenience samples, this introduces a note of caution into the common conclusion that cognitive-behavioral treatment is more effective; if it were less likely to be accepted by children with a clinical level of disorder, then there would probably be a higher rate of attrition, and a lower overall improvement rate than the outcome research would suggest. This probably underlines the need for the development of cognitive behavior therapy (CBT) manuals appropriate to referred children rather than to the milder and/or less complex cases recruited for many outcome studies. Some such manuals have been written and successfully tested for clinical samples (Kendall, 1994; March, Mulle, & Herbel, 1994).

An important development in the area of relatively brief, manualized but nonbehavioral therapies for children and adolescents is Interpersonal Psychotherapy for Adolescents (IPT-A: Moreau, Mufson, Weissman, & Klerman, 1991). This is an adaptation of a treatment approach developed for depressed adult patients (IPT: Klerman, Weissman, Ronsaville-Chevron, & Chevrones, 1984), which focuses on a specified range of interpersonal problems which may underlie the individual's affective state. Although those who have developed this treatment approach distinguish it clearly from psychodynamic therapy, in its focus on interpersonal as opposed to intrapsychic difficulties, and its model of depression as rooted primarily in disrupted attachments rather than aggression (see Mufson, Moreau, Weissman, & Klerman, 1993), the contrast they make applies more to classical than to contemporary psychoanalytic thinking, and we include IPT-A here as an approach closely related to certain strong trends in psychodynamic work.

IPT for adults has been tested in several clinical trials, notably the National Institute of Mental Health collaborative study of the treatment of depression (Elkin et al., 1989). This adult therapy was tested for a group of 38 adolescent in-patients diagnosed as suffering from major depression in an open trial (Robbins, Alessi, & Colfer, 1989). Robbins and co-workers reported that 47% of patients showed clinically significant improvement with IPT alone. (Lack of response was associated with dexamethasone nonsuppression and "melancholic subtype.") The nonresponders were then treated with a combination of tricyclic antidepressant and this version of IPT; 92% then responded. Unfortunately, since there appears to have been a 50% placebo response rate (see Mufson et al., 1993), the 47% improvement is not impressive, the approach obviously needs further evaluation, and there is a strong case for introducing modifications to the adult manual, as have the developers of IPT-A (Moreau et al., 1991). The authors of the adapted treatment approach have conducted an open trial using this modified, manualized approach with 14 adolescents (Mufson et al., 1993). By week 3 of the 12 week trial, two of the 14 patients had dropped out and one had been excluded for noncompliance. Of the remaining 11, 9 showed a significant decrease in depressive symptomatology, and 10 no longer met criteria for major depression. One could therefore regard this as a 71% success rate, which is encouraging. A randomized controlled trial is now in progress.

5.10.4 LIMITATIONS OF PSYCHODYNAMIC APPROACHES

A series of limitations render psychodynamic approaches vulnerable to being seen as impractical, unscientific, and uneconomical.

(i) Little operationalization in most descriptions of the treatment, whose value is attested to largely by selected material from individual cases.

(ii) Little attention to what forms of technique may be appropriate for children with a particular diagnosis or psychodynamic formulation.

(a) Very limited evidence of efficacy, especially support from randomized controlled trials.

(b) A prolonged treatment, with rather vague or global goals, raising considerable doubts about cost-effectiveness.

Psychodynamic child psychotherapists are therefore facing great challenges to their convictions and, as managed care restricts payment for such lengthy and poorly supported treatments, to their professional survival. Nevertheless, we hope to have indicated in this chapter that these real and legitimate challenges are now being fully recognized and actively addressed by psychoanalytically-oriented child therapists.

5.10.5 REFERENCES

Ainsworth, M. D. S., Blehar, M. C., Waters, E., & Wall, S. (1978). *Patterns of attachment: A psychological study of the Strange Situation.* Hillsdale, NJ: Erlbaum.
Altman, N. (1992). Relational perspectives on child psychoanalytic psychotherapy. In N. J. Skolnick & S. C. Warshaw (Eds.), *Relational perspectives in psychoanalysis* (pp. 175–194). Hillsdale, NJ: Analytic Press.
Altman, N. (1994). The recognition of relational theory and technique in child treatment. Special Issue: Child analytic work. *Psychoanalytic Psychology, 11,* 383–395.
Alvarez, A. (1993). *Live company.* London: Routledge.
Apter, A., Bernhout, E., & Tyano, S. (1984). Severe obsessive compulsive disorder in adolescence: A report of eight cases. *Journal of Adolescence, 7,* 349–358.
Balint, M. (1937/1965). Early developmental states of the ego, primary object of love. *Primary love and psycho-*

analytic technique (pp. 90–108). London: Tavistock.
Balint, M. (1968). *The basic fault.* London: Tavistock.
Barnett, R. J., Docherty, J. P., & Frommelt, G. M. (1991). A review of psychotherapy research since 1963. *Journal of the American Academy of Child and Adolescent Psychiatry, 30,* 1–14.
Baron, J., Gruen, R., & Asnis, L. (1985). Familial transmission of schizotypal and borderline personality disorders. *American Journal of Psychiatry, 142,* 927–934.
Belsky, J., Rovine, M., & Taylor, D. G. (1984). The Pennsylvania Infant and Family Development Project. III: The origins of individual differences in infant-mother attachment: Maternal and infant contributions. *Child Development, 55,* 718–728.
Bion, W. R. (1959). Attacks on linking. *International Journal of Psycho-Analysis, 40,* 308–315.
Bion, W. R. (1962/1967). A theory of thinking. *Second thoughts* (pp. 110–119). London: Heinemann.
Bion, W. R. (1963). *Elements of psycho-analysis.* London: Heinemann.
Bleiberg, E. (1987). Stages in the treatment of narcissistic children and adolescents. *Bulletin of the Menninger Clinic, 51,* 296–313.
Bleiberg, E. (1994a). Borderline disorders in children and adolescents: The concept, the diagnosis, and the controversies. *Bulletin of the Menninger Clinic, 58,* 169–196.
Bleiberg, E. (1994b). Neurosis and conduct disorders. In J. M. Oldham, & M. B. Riba (Eds.), *American Psychiatric Press Review of Psychiatry* (Vol. 13, pp. 493–518). Washington, DC: Psychiatric Press.
Bleiberg, E., Fonagy, P., & Target, M. (1997). Child psychoanalysis: Critical overview and a proposed reconsideration. *Psychiatric Clinics of North America, 6,* 1–38.
Bower, T. R. (1989). *The rational infant: Learning in infancy.* New York: Freeman.
Bowlby, J. (1969). *Attachment and loss* (Vol. 1). London: Hogarth Press and the Institute of Psycho-Analysis.
Bowlby, J. (1973). *Attachment and loss* (Vol. 2). London: Hogarth Press and Institute of Psycho-Analysis.
Bowlby, J. (1980). *Attachment and loss* (Vol. 3). London: Hogarth Press and Institute of Psycho-Analysis.
Brenner, C. (1982). *The mind in conflict.* New York: International University Press.
Bretherton, I. (1985). Attachment theory: Retrospect and prospect. In I. Bretherton & E. Waters (Eds.), *Growing points of attachment theory and research. Monographs of the Society for Research in Child Development* (Vol. 50, pp. 3–35). Chicago: University of Chicago Press.
Brown, G. W., & Harris, T. O. (1978). *Social origins of depression: A study of psychiatric disorders in women.* London: Tavistock.
Brown, G. W., Harris, T. O., & Bifulco, A. (1986). Long-term effects of early loss of parent. In M. Rutter, C. E. Izard, & P. B. Read (Eds.), *Depression in young people: Developmental and clinical perspectives* (pp. 251–296). New York: Guilford Press.
Bus, A. G., & Van IJzendoorn, M. H. (1992). Patterns of attachment in frequently and infrequently reading mother–child dyads. *Journal of Genetic Psychology, 153,* 395–403.
Cantor, S., & Kestenbaum, C. (1986). Psychotherapy with schizophrenic children. *Journal of the American Academy of Child Psychiatry, 25,* 623–630.
Casey, R. J., & Berman, J. S. (1985). The outcome of psychotherapy with children. *Psychological Bulletin, 98,* 388–400.
Chethik, M. (1989). *Techniques of child therapy: Psychodynamic strategies.* New York: Guilford Press.
Cicchetti, D. (1990a). An historical perspective on the discipline of developmental psychopathology. In J. Rolf, A. Masten, D. Cicchetti, & S. Weintraub (Eds.), *Risk and protective factors in the development of psychopathology*

(pp. 2–28). New York: Cambridge University Press.

Cicchetti, D. (1990b). The organization and coherence of socioemotional, cognitive, and representational development: Illustrations through a developmental psychopathology perspective on Down syndrome and child maltreatment. In R. Thompson (Ed.), *Socioemotional development. Nebraska symposium on motivation* (pp. 259–279). Lincoln, NE: University of Nebraska Press.

Cohen, D. J., Towbin, K. E., Mayes, L., & Volkmar, F. (1994). Developmental psychopathology of multiplex developmental disorder. In S. L. Friedman & H. C. Haywood (Eds.), *Developmental follow-up: Concepts, domains and methods* (pp. 155–182). New York: Academic Press.

Crittenden, P. M. (1990). Internal representational models of attachment relationships. *Journal of Infant Mental Health, 11,* 259–277.

Cummings, E. M., & Davies, P. T. (1994). Maternal depression and child development. *Journal of Child Psychology and Psychiatry, 35,* 73–112.

DeFolch, T. E. (1988). Guilt bearable or unbearable: A problem for the child in analysis. Special Issue: Psychoanalysis of children. *International Review of Psycho-Analysis, 15,* 13–24.

Dowling, A. S., & Naegele, J. (1995). Child and adolescent psychoanalysis. In B. E. Moore & B. D. Fine (Eds.), *Psychoanalysis: The major concepts* (pp. 26–44). New Haven, CT: Yale University Press.

Elkin, I., Shea, M. T., Watkins, J. T., Imber, S. D., Sotsky, S. M., Collins, J. F., Glass, D. R., Pilkonis, P. A., Lever, W. R., Docherty, J. P., Fiester, S. J., & Parloff, M.B. (1989). National Institute of Mental Health Treatment of Depression Collaborative Research Program: General effectiveness of treatment. *Archives of General Psychiatry, 46,* 971–982.

Emde, R. N. (1983). Pre-representational self and its affective core. *The Psychoanalytic Study of the Child, 38,* 165–192.

Emde, R. N. (1988a). Development terminable and interminable. I. Innate and motivational factors from infancy. *International Journal of Psycho-Analysis, 69,* 23–42.

Emde, R. N. (1988b). Development terminable and interminable. II. Recent psychoanalytic theory and therapeutic considerations. *International Journal of Psycho-Analysis, 69,* 283–286.

Fairbairn, W. R. D. (1952). *An object-relations theory of the personality.* New York: Basic Books.

Feinman, S. (1991). *Social referencing and the social construction of reality in infancy.* New York: Plenum.

Fine, S., Forth, A., Gilbert, M., & Haley, G. (1991). Group therapy for adolescent depressive disorder: A comparison of social skills and therapeutic support. *Journal of the American Academy of Child and Adolescent Psychiatry, 30,* 79–85.

Fonagy, P., & Moran, G. S. (1990). Studies on the efficacy of child psychoanalysis. *Journal of Consulting and Clinical Psychology, 58,* 684–695.

Fonagy, P., & Moran, G. S. (1991). Understanding psychic change in child analysis. *International Journal of Psycho-Analysis, 72,* 15–22.

Fonagy, P., Moran, G. S., Edgcumbe, R., Kennedy, H., & Target, M. (1993). The roles of mental representations and mental processes in therapeutic action. *The Psychoanalytic Study of the Child, 48,* 9–48.

Fonagy, P., Steele, H., Moran, G., Steele, M., & Higgitt, A. (1991a). The capacity for understanding mental states: the reflective self in parent and child and its significance for security of attachment. *Infant Mental Health Journal, 13,* 200–217.

Fonagy, P., Steele, H., & Steele, M. (1991b). Maternal representations of attachment during pregnancy predict the organization of infant–mother attachment at one year of age. *Child Development, 62,* 891–905.

Fonagy, P., & Target, M. (1994). The efficacy of psychoanalysis for children with disruptive disorders. *Journal of the American Academy of Child and Adolescent Psychiatry, 33,* 45–55.

Fonagy, P., & Target, M. (1996a). A contemporary psychoanalytical perspective: Psychodynamic developmental therapy. In E. Hibbs & P. Jensen (Eds.), *Psychosocial treatments for child and adolescent disorders: Empirically based approaches* (pp. 619–638). Washington, DC: American Psychological Association and National Institute of Health.

Fonagy, P., & Target, M. (1996b). Predictors of outcome in child psychoanalysis: a retrospective study of 763 cases at the Anna Freud Centre. *Journal of the American Psychoanalytic Association, 44,* 27–77.

Fonagy, P., Target, M., Steele, M., & Gerber, A. (1995). Psychoanalytic perspectives on developmental psychopathology. In D. Cicchetti & D. J. Cohen (Eds.), *Developmental psychopathology* (Vol. 1, pp. 504–554). New York: Wiley.

Fraiberg, S. (1969). Libidinal object constancy and mental representation. *The Psychoanalytic Study of the Child, 24,* 9–47.

Fraiberg, S. (1980). *Clinical studies in infant mental health.* New York: Basic Books.

Freud, A. (1936/1946). *The ego and the mechanisms of defense.* New York: International Universities Press.

Freud, A. (1941–1945/1974). Reports on the Hampstead Nurseries. In *The writings of Anna Freud.* New York: International Universities Press.

Freud, A. (1946). *The psychoanalytic treatment of children.* London: Imago Publishing.

Freud, A. (1965). *Normality and pathology in childhood.* Harmondsworth: Penguin .

Freud, S. (1900). The interpretation of dreams. In J. Strachey (Ed.), *The standard edition of the complete psychological works of Sigmund Freud* (Vols. 4 and 5, pp. 1–715). London: Hogarth Press.

Freud, S. (1905). Three essays on the theory of sexuality. In J. Strachey (Ed.), *The standard edition of the complete psychological works of Sigmund Freud* (Vol. 7, pp. 123–230). London: Hogarth Press.

Freud, S. (1909). Analysis of a phobia in a five-year-old boy. In J. Strachey (Ed.), *The standard edition of the complete psychological works of Sigmund Freud* (Vol. 10, pp. 1–147). London: Hogarth Press.

Freud, S. (1920). Beyond the pleasure principle. In J. Strachey (Ed.), *The standard edition of the complete psychological works of Sigmund Freud* (Vol. 18, pp. 1–64). London: Hogarth Press.

Freud, S. (1926). The question of lay analysis. In J. Strachey (Ed.), *The standard edition of the complete psychological works of Sigmund Freud* (Vol. 20, pp. 77–172). London: Hogarth Press.

Freud, S. (1930). Civilization and its discontents. In J. Strachey (Ed.), *The standard edition of the complete psychological works of Sigmund Freud* (Vol. 21, pp. 57–146). London: Hogarth Press.

Freud, S. (1933). New introductory lectures on psychoanalysis. In J. Strachey (Ed.), *The standard edition of the complete psychological works of Sigmund Freud* (Vol. 22, pp. 1–182). London: Hogarth Press.

Freud, S., & Breuer, J. (1895). Studies on hysteria. In J. Strachey (Ed.), *The standard edition of the complete psychological works of Sigmund Freud* (Vol. 2, pp. 1–305). London: Hogarth Press.

Gabbard, G. O. (Ed.). (1994). *Psychodynamic psychiatry in clinical practice: The DSM-IV edition.* Washington, DC: American Psychiatric Press.

Gabbard, G. O. (1995). Psychoanalysis. In H. I. Kaplan & B. J. Sadock (Eds.), *Comprehensive textbook of psychia-*

try (6th ed., pp. 431–478). Baltimore, MD: Williams & Wilkins.

Garmezy, N. (1983). Stressors of childhood. In N. Garmezy & M. Rutter (Eds.), *Stress, coping, and development in children* (pp. 43–84). Baltimore, MD: Johns Hopkins University Press.

Garmezy, N., & Masten, A. (1991). The protective role of competence indicators in children at risk. In E. M. Cummings, A. L. Greene, & K. K. Karraker (Eds.), *Life-span developmental psychology: Perspectives on stress and coping* (pp. 151–174). Hillsdale, NJ: Erlbaum.

Goldstein, J., Freud, A., & Solnit, A. J. (1973). *Beyond the best interests of the child.* New York: Free Press.

Goldstein, J., Freud, A., & Solnit, A. J. (1979). *Before the best interests of the child.* New York: Free Press.

Golinkoff, R. M., Hardig, C. B., Carlson, V., & Sexton, M. E. (1984). The infant's perception of causal events: The distinction between animate and inanimate objects. In L. P. Lipsitt & C. Rovee-Collier (Eds.), *Advances in infancy research.* Norwood, NJ: Ablex.

Green, R. (1985). Atypical psychosexual development. In M. Rutter & L. Hersov (Eds.), *Child and adolescent psychiatry: Modern approaches* (pp. 638–649). Oxford: Blackwell.

Grossmann, K. E., Spangler, G., Suess, G., & Unzer, L. (1985). Maternal sensitivity and newborn orienting responses as related to quality of attachment in Northern Germany. In I. Bretherton & E. Waters (Eds.), *Growing points in attachment theory and research. Monographs of the Society for Research in Child Development* (Vol. 50, pp. 233–256). Chicago: University of Chicago Press.

Group for the Advancement of Psychiatry. (1982). *The process of child therapy (GAP Report 111).* New York: Brunner/Mazell.

Hartmann, H. (1939/1958). *Ego psychology and the problem of adaptation.* New York: International Universities Press.

Hartmann, H. (1955/1964). Notes on the theory of sublimation. *Essays on ego psychology* (pp. 215–240). New York: International University Press.

Heinicke, C. M. (1965). Frequency of psychotherapeutic session as a factor affecting the child's developmental status. *The Psychoanalytic Study of the Child, 20,* 42–98.

Heinicke, C. M., & Ramsey-Klee, D. M. (1986). Outcome of child psychotherapy as a function of frequency of sessions. *Journal of the American Academy of Child Psychiatry, 25,* 247–253.

Hesse, P., & Cicchetti, D. (1982). Perspectives on an integrated theory of emotional development. *New Directions for Child Development, 16,* 3–48.

Hoagwood, K., Hibbs, E., Brent, D., & Jensen, P. (1995). Introduction to the special section: Efficacy and effectiveness in studies of child and adolescent psychotherapy. *Journal of Consulting and Clinical Psychology, 63,* 683–687.

Hornik, R., & Gunnar, M. R. (1988). A descriptive analysis of infant social referencing. *Child Development, 59,* 626–634.

Hug-Helmuth, H. (1920). Child psychology and education. *International Journal of Psycho-Analysis, 1,* 316–323.

Hug-Helmuth, H. (1921). On the technique of child analysis. *International Journal of Psycho-Analysis, 2,* 287–303.

Johnson, E. (1982). Principles and techniques in drama therapy. *International Journal of Arts and Psychotherapy, 9,* 83–90.

Kazdin, A. E., Bass, D., Siegel, T., & Thomas, C. (1990a). Cognitive behavioral treatment and relationship therapy in the treatment of children referred for antisocial behavior. *Journal of Consulting and Clinical Psychology, 58,* 76–85.

Kazdin, A. E., Siegel, T. C., & Bass, D. (1990b). Drawing

upon clinical practice to inform research on child and adolescent psychotherapy: A survey of practitioners. *Professional Psychology: Research and Practice, 21,* 189–198.

Kendall, P. C. (1994). Treating anxiety disorders in children: Results of a randomized clinical trial. *Journal of Consulting and Clinical Psychology, 62,* 100–110.

Kendall, P. C., & Southam-Gerow, M. A. (1995). Issues in the transportability of treatment: The case of anxiety disorders in youths. *Journal of Consulting and Clinical Psychology, 63,* 702–708.

Kernberg, O. F. (1975). *Borderline conditions and pathological narcissism.* New York: Aronson.

Kernberg, O. F. (1976). *Object relations theory and clinical psychoanalysis.* New York: Aronson.

Kernberg, O. F. (1982). Self, ego, affects and drives. *Journal of the American Psychoanalytic Association, 30,* 893–917.

Kernberg, O. F. (1987). An ego psychology-object relations theory approach to the transference. *Psychoanalytic Quarterly, 51,* 197–221.

Kernberg, P. F. (1995). Child psychiatry: Individual psychotherapy. In H. I. Kaplan & B. J. Sadock (Eds.), *Comprehensive textbook of psychiatry* (6th ed., pp. 2399–2412). Baltimore, MD: Williams & Wilkins.

King, P., & Steiner, R. (1991). *The Freud–Klein controversies.* London: Routledge.

Klein, M. (1932). *The psycho-analysis of children.* London: Hogarth Press.

Klein, M. (1936/1964). The psychotherapy of the psychoses, In *Contributions to psychoanalysis, 1921–1945.* New York: McGraw-Hill.

Klein, M. (1946). Notes on some schizoid mechanisms. In M. Klein, P. Heimann, S. Isaacs, & J. Riviere (Eds.), *Developments in psychoanalysis* (pp. 292–320). London: Hogarth Press.

Klein, M. (1952/1975). The origins of transference, *The Writings of Melanie Klein* (pp. 48–56). London: Hogarth Press.

Klein, M., Heimann, P., Isaacs, S., & Riviere, J. (Eds.) (1946). *Developments in psychoanalysis.* London: Hogarth Press.

Klerman, G. F., Weissman, M. M., Ronsaville-Chevron, B., & Chevrones, J. (1984). *Interpersonal psychotherapy of depression.* New York: Basic Books.

Kohut, H. (1971). *The analysis of the self.* New York: International Universities Press.

Kohut, H. (1977). *The restoration of the self.* New York: International Universities Press.

Kohut, H. (1984). *How does analysis cure?* Chicago: University of Chicago Press.

Kolvin, I., Garside, R. F., Nicol, A. E., MacMillan, A., Wolstenhome, F., & Leitch, I. M. (1981). *Help starts here: The maladjusted child in the ordinary school.* London: Tavistock.

Kovacs, M., Gatsonis, C., Paulauskas, S. L., & Richards, C. (1989). Depressive disorders in childhood IV. A longitudinal study of comorbidity with and risk for anxiety disorders. *Archives of General Psychiatry, 46,* 776–782.

Links, P. S., Steiner, M., & Huxley, G. (1988). The occurrence of borderline personality disorder in the families of borderline patients. *Journal of the Personality Disorders, 2,* 14–20.

Lochman, J. E., Coie, J. D., Underwood, M. K., & Terry, R. (1993). Effectiveness of a social relations intervention program for aggressive and nonaggressive, rejected children. *Journal of Consulting and Clinical Psychology, 61,* 1053–1058.

Loranger, A., Oldham, J., & Tullis, E. (1982). Familial transmission of DSM-III borderline personality disorder. *Archives of General Psychiatry, 39,* 795–799.

Luborsky, L. (1984). *Principles of psychoanalytic psy-*

chotherapy: A manual for Supportive-Expressive (SE) treatment. New York: Basic Books.

Lush, D., Boston, M., & Grainger, E. (1991). Evaluation of psychoanalytic psychotherapy with children: Therapists' assessments and predictions. *Psychoanalytic Psychotherapy, 5,* 191–234.

MacFarlane, A. C. (1987). Post-traumatic phenomena in a longitudinal study of children following a natural disaster. *Journal of the American Academy of Child and Adolescent Psychiatry, 28,* 764–769.

Mahler, M. (1968). *On human symbiosis and the vicissitudes of individuation.* New York: International Universities Press.

Main, M., Kaplan, N., & Cassidy, J. (1985). Security in infancy, childhood, and adulthood: A move to the level of representation. In I. Bretherton & E. Waters (Eds.), *Growing points in attachment theory and research. Monographs of the Society for Research in Child Development* (Vol. 50, pp. 66–104). Chicago: University of Chicago Press.

March, J. S., Mulle, K., & Herbel, B. (1994). Behavioral psychotherapy for children and adolescents with obsessive-compulsive disorder: An open trial of a new protocol-driven treatment package. *Journal of the American Academy of Child and Adolescent Psychiatry, 33,* 333–341.

Marohn, R. C. (1991). Psychotherapy of adolescents with behavioral disorders. In M. Slomowitz (Ed.), *Adolescent psychotherapy* (pp. 145–161). Washington, DC: American Psychiatric Press.

Masterson, J. F. (1972). *Treatment of the borderline adolescent: A developmental approach.* New York: Wiley Interscience.

Moran, G. S., & Fonagy, P. (1987). Psychoanalysis and diabetic control: A single case study. *British Journal of Medical Psychology, 60,* 357–372.

Moran, G. S., Fonagy, P., Kurtz, A., Bolton, A. M., & Brook, C. (1991). A controlled study of the psychoanalytic treatment of brittle diabetes. *Journal of the American Academy of Child Psychiatry, 30,* 241–257.

Moreau, D., Mufson, L., Weissman, M. M., & Klerman, G. L. (1991). Interpersonal psychotherapy for adolescent depression: Description of modification and preliminary application. *Journal of the American Academy of Child and Adolescent Psychiatry, 30,* 642–651.

Mufson, L., Moreau, D., Weissman, M. M., & Klerman, G. L. (1993). *Interpersonal psychotherapy for depressed adolescents.* New York: Guilford Press.

O'Brien, J. (1992). Children with attention-deficit hyperactivity disorder and their parents. In J. O'Brien, D. Pilowsky, & O. Lewis (Eds.), *Psychotherapies with children and adolescents: Adapting the psychodynamic process* (pp. 109–124). Washington, DC: American Psychiatric Press.

O'Brien, J., Pilowsky, D. J., & Lewis, O. (Eds.) (1992). *Psychotherapies with children and adolescents: Adapting the psychodynamic process.* Washington, DC: American Psychiatric Press.

O'Grady, D., & Metz, J. R. (1987). Resilience in children at high risk for psychological disorder. *Journal of Pediatric Psychology, 12,* 3–23.

O'Shaughnessy, E. (1988). W. R. Bion's theory of thinking and new techniques in child analysis. In E. B. Spillius (Ed.), *Melanie Klein today: Developments in theory and practice.* (Vol. 2, pp. 177–190). London: Routledge.

Petti, T. A., & Vela, R. M. (1990). Borderline disorders of childhood: An overview. *Journal of the American Academy of Child and Adolescent Psychiatry, 29,* 327–337.

Pine, F. (1985). *Developmental theory and clinical process.* New Haven, CT: Yale University Press.

Rinsley, D. B. (1977). An object relations view of borderline personality. In P. Hartocollis (Ed.), *Borderline personality disorders: The concept, the syndrome, the patient* (pp. 47–70). New York: International Universities Press.

Rinsley, D. B. (1989). Notes on the developmental pathogenesis of narcissistic personality disorder. *Psychiatric Clinics of North America, 12,* 695–707.

Robbins, D. R., Alessi, N. E., & Colfer, M. V. (1989). Treatment of adolescents with major depression: Implications of the DST and the melancholic clinical subtype. *Journal of Affective Disorders, 17,* 99–104.

Rose, S. D. (1972). *Treating children in groups.* London: Jossey-Bass.

Rosenfeld, H. (1971/1988). Contribution to the psychopathology of psychotic states: The importance of projective identification in the ego structure and object relations of the psychotic patient. In E. B. Spillius (Ed.), *Melanie Klein today* (pp. 117–137). London: Routledge.

Rosenfeld, S., & Sprince, M. (1963). An attempt to formulate the meaning of the concept borderline. *The Psychoanalytic Study of the Child, 18,* 603–635.

Rutter, M. (1990). Psychosocial resilience and protective mechanisms. In J. Rolf, A. S. Masten, D. Cicchetti, & S. Weintraub (Eds.), *Risk and protective factors in the development of psychopathology.* New York: Cambridge University Press.

Rutter, M., & Quinton, D. (1984). Long-term follow-up of women institutionalized in childhood: Factors promoting good functioning in adult life. *British Journal of Developmental Psychology, 18,* 225–234.

Sandler, J. (1987). *From safety to the superego: Selected papers of Joseph Sandler.* New York: Guilford Press.

Sandler, J., Kennedy, H., & Tyson, R. (1980). *The technique of child analysis: Discussions with Anna Freud.* London: Hogarth Press.

Sandler, J., & Rosenblatt, B. (1962). The concept of the representational world. *The Psychoanalytic Study of the Child, 17,* 128–145.

Schaefer, C. E., & Cangelosi, D. M. (Eds.) (1993). *Play therapy techniques.* Northway, NJ: Aronson.

Selvini Palazzoli, M., Boscolo, L., Cecchin, G., & Prata, G. (1978). *Paradox and counter-paradox.* New York: Aronson.

Shirk, S. R., & Russell, R. L. (1992). A reevaluation of estimates of child therapy effectiveness. *Journal of the American Academy of Child Adolescent Psychiatry, 31,* 703-709.

Silver, L., & Silver, B. (1983). Clinical practice of child psychiatry: A survey. *Journal of the American Academy of Child Psychiatry, 22,* 573–579.

Simon, M. R. (1992). *The symbolism of style: Art as therapy.* London: Routledge.

Smyrnios, K. X., & Kirkby, R. J. (1993). Long-term comparison of brief versus unlimited psychodynamic treatments with children and their parents. *Journal of Consulting and Clinical Psychology, 61,* 1020–1027.

Sroufe, L. A. (1990). An organizational perspective on the self. In D. Cicchetti & M. Beeghly (Eds.), *The self in transition: Infancy to childhood* (pp. 281–307). Chicago: University of Chicago Press.

Stern, D. N. (1985). *The interpersonal world of the infant: A view from psychoanalysis and developmental psychology.* New York: Basic Books.

Stolorow, R., Brandchaft, B., & Atwood, G. (1987). *Psychoanalytic treatment: An intersubjective approach.* Hillsdale, NJ: Analytic Press.

Sullivan, H. S. (1953). *The interpersonal theory of psychiatry.* New York: Norton.

Summers, F. (1994). *Object relations theories and psychopathology: A comprehensive text.* Hillsdale, NJ: Analytic Press.

Szapocznik, J., Rio, A., Murray, E., Cohen, R., Scopetta, M., Rivas-Vazquez, A., Hervis, O., & Posada, V. (1989). Structural family versus psychodynamic child therapy for problematic Hispanic boys. *Journal of Consulting and Clinical Psychology, 57,* 571–578.

Target, M., & Fonagy, P. (1994a). The efficacy of psychoanalysis for children with emotional disorders. *Journal of the American Academy of Child and Adolescent Psychiatry, 33,* 361–371.

Target, M., & Fonagy, P. (1994b). The efficacy of psychoanalysis for children: Prediction of outcome in a developmental context. *Journal of the American Academy of Child and Adolescent Psychiatry, 33,* 1134–1144.

Terr, L. C. (1983). Chowchilla revisited: The effects of psychic trauma four years after a school-bus kidnapping. *American Journal of Psychiatry, 140,* 1543–1550.

Towbin, K. E., Dykens, E. M., Pearson, G. S., & Cohen, D. J. (1993). Conceptualizing "borderline syndrome of childhood" and "childhood schizophrenia" as a developmental disorder. *Journal of the American Academy Child and Adolescent Psychiatry, 32,* 775–782.

Tyson, R. L., & Tyson, P. (1986). The concept of transference in child psychoanalysis. *Journal of the American Academy of Child Psychiatry, 25,* 30–39.

van IJzendoorn, M. H. (1995). Adult attachment representations, parental responsiveness, and infant attachment: A meta-analysis on the predictive validity of the Adult Attachment Interview. *Psychological Bulletin, 117,* 387–403.

Ward, M. J., & Carlson, E. A. (1995). Associations among Adult Attachment representations, maternal sensitivity, and infant–mother attachment in a sample of adolescent mothers. *Child Development, 66,* 69–79.

Warshaw, S. C. (1992). Mutative factors in child psychoanalysis: A comparison of diverse relational perspectives. In N. J. Skolnick & S. C. Warshaw (Eds.), *Relational perspectives in psychoanalysis* (pp. 141–173). Hillsdale, NJ: Analytic Press.

Weisz, J. R., Donenberg, G. R., Han, S. S., & Weiss, B. (1995). Bridging the gap between laboratory and clinic in child and adolescent psychotherapy. *Journal of Consulting and Clinical Psychology, 63,* 688–701.

Weisz, J. R., & Weiss, B. (1989). Assessing the effects of clinic-based psychotherapy with children and adolescents. *Journal of Consulting and Clinical Psychology, 57,* 741–746.

Weisz, J. R., Weiss, B., Alicke, M. D., & Klotz, M. L. (1987). Effectiveness of psychotherapy with children and adolescents: Meta-analytic findings for clinicians. *Journal of Consulting and Clinical Psychology, 55,* 542–549.

Weisz, J. R., Weiss, B., Morton, Granger, D., & Han, S. (1992). *Meta-analysis of psychotherapy outcome research with children and adolescents.* Los Angeles: University of California.

Werner, E. E. (1989). Children of the garden island. *Scientific American, April,* 106–111.

Winnicott, D. W. (1965). *The maturational process and the facilitating environment.* London: Hogarth Press.

Winnicott, D. W. (1971). *Playing and reality.* London: Tavistock.

5.11
Pharmacological Therapies

NIRBHAY N. SINGH and CYNTHIA R. ELLIS
Virginia Commonwealth University, Richmond, VA, USA

5.11.1 INTRODUCTION

Psychopharmacology as a treatment modality for children and adolescents is a relatively young discipline that is based more on the collective experiences of clinicians than on empirical verification of the effects of various classes of psychoactive medications on childhood disorders. This is one of the reasons why, until the mid-1990s, pharmacological therapy was seen as the treatment of last resort. Indeed, it was rarely considered during initial treatment formulation until all other treatment modalities, such as psychoanalytic and psychosocial interventions, had been exhausted. Child and adolescent psychiatrists followed two simple guidelines when considering the use of medication. First, because the rationale for using psychotropic medication for specific disorders was not well established in children, they were concerned that they may actually do more harm than good in prescribing medication before trying other therapies. Thus, they were adhering to one of the fundamental principles of medicine: *prima non nocere* ("first do no harm"). Of course, in some cases, appropriate use of medication may have been withheld for several weeks or months while alternative, but eventually ineffective, therapies were used. Second, they followed another principle of medicine: when in doubt, don't. In so doing, they may have actually not prescribed medication to some children who would have benefited from it. Even as late as in the 1970s, few child and adolescent psychiatrists prescribed medication for childhood disorders (Towbin, 1995) and, when they did, it was typically for an early variant of what is now called attention-deficit hyperactivity disorder (ADHD).

Few would argue that the situation is vastly different today. Although there is still a paucity of empirically based studies on the use of psychotropic drugs in the treatment of childhood disorders, medication is considered, along with other treatment modalities, an integral part of a treatment plan (Kaplan, Simms, & Busner, 1994; Olfson, Pincus, & Sabshin, 1994). Given our current understanding that medication alone is rarely sufficient in the treatment of a childhood disorder, pharmacotherapy is now considered an important, and often necessary, part of a multimodal treatment plan. Modern child and adolescent psychiatrists who espouse the biopsychosocial model of childhood disorders understand that psychopharmacology, like any other single modality treatment, is limited in scope because it focuses on only one aspect of the child. Given that children develop in an interactional biological, social, and cultural matrix, effective interventions must be multimodal, multifocused, and multidisciplinary in nature (Singh, Parmelee, Sood, & Katz, 1993; Werry, 1993).

Undoubtedly, psychopharmacology is a major component in the treatment of childhood disorders and, as more research is conducted on its use, it is likely to solidify its role as the cornerstone of a comprehensive treatment for childhood disorders. Approximately 12–22% of American children (i.e., up to 14 million children) have a diagnosable mental illness, and it is very likely that many of these children may benefit from psychopharmacologic treatment (Institute of Medicine, 1990). This means that unless all professionals who treat childhood disorders have a working knowledge of psychopharmacology, they will not be able to make informed judgements about a necessary and important component of treatment for many children.

Although we often assume that psychiatric treatment and the prescription of psychotropic medication is solely in the domain of psychiatrists, the fact is that the majority of prescriptions for psychotropic medication written for psychiatric disorders are by family practice and primary care physicians who have limited training in mental health (Beardsley, Gardocki, Larsen, & Hidalgo, 1988). Psychologists assume a major role in the baseline assessment of the child and his family and contribute to the case formulation. In addition, they are often responsible for monitoring the child's response to medication (Ellis, Singh, & Singh, 1997). Because they are the primary therapist for the child's psychosocial treatment, psychologists are in an ideal position to monitor symptomatic improvement, observe the emergence of side effects, and check for medication compliance. Having a good knowledge of psychopharmacology enables the psychologist to play an active collaborative role in recommending medication and dosage changes to the child's physician.

In this chapter, we begin with a brief historical introduction to child psychopharmacology, followed by sections on the prevalence of psychopharmacology of childhood disorders, general principles of pharmacotherapy, factors that affect the outcome of psychopharmacologic treatment, assessment and clinical formulation, and psychopharmacologic treatment of childhood disorders. Finally, we present our view of future directions for research and practice. We use the term psychotropic drug in this chapter to refer to any pharmacological agent that is prescribed for the explicit purpose of bringing about behavioral, cognitive, or emotional changes in the child. The term psychoactive drug is used in a more general sense to refer to any pharmacological agent that may have these effects regardless of the physician's intent when prescribing this type of medication. We use the term child to include children and adolescents, and he or his in a generic sense to include reference to boys and girls.

5.11.2 HISTORY OF PEDIATRIC PSYCHOPHARMACOLOGY

Pediatric psychopharmacology began with Bradley's (1937) serendipitous finding that benzedrine affected the behavior disorders of children. However, little progress was made in the general field of psychopharmacology until the biological revolution in adult psychiatry began in the early 1950s. While conducting animal experiments, the Australian psychiatrist Cade (1949) noted that lithium carbonate made the animals lethargic, prompting him to use the drug with agitated psychiatric patients for its sedative effects. This led to the search for other drugs that could be used with adult psychiatric patients. The explosive growth of psychotherapeutic drugs in the 1950s changed the nature of American psychiatry and psychopharmacology became the mainstay of psychiatric treatment, especially for patients with severe mental illness.

The findings in adult psychopharmacology were extrapolated for use in child and adolescent psychiatry. From the 1950s, and especially during the 1960s, case reports and experimental studies began to appear that reported the effects of antipsychotic, antidepressant, "minor tranquilizer," and stimulant medications for a number of childhood psychiatric disorders. While these case reports and studies had serious methodological flaws, often being devoid of any experimental controls, soft evidence accumu-

lated on the effects of certain drugs for specific disorders. For example, stimulants were generally found to be effective with many children with hyperactivity, imipramine (an antidepressant) was found to be effective for treating enuresis, and several antipsychotic medications were found to be effective for psychosis and aggressive behaviors.

The 1970s heralded an increasing interest in the scientific evaluation of existing drugs as well as in the development of related compounds in each drug class. Several advances were made in this period, including: (i) the development of diagnostic criteria for psychiatric disorders (e.g., research diagnostic criteria, *DSM*) so that the same disorders could be targeted across drug studies; (ii) increasingly sophisticated methodologies for drug evaluation studies; (iii) development of reliable and valid instruments sensitive to drug effects; (iv) increasing knowledge of pharmacokinetics of psychiatric drugs used with both children and adults; and (v) increasing monitoring of intended and adverse effects of drugs, both in the short- and long-term. Further, children were found to be drug responsive to a number of conditions that had previously not been the focus of pharmacotherapy, including eating disorders, aggressive conduct disorders, separation anxiety disorders (school phobia), bipolar disorders, depressive disorders, and Tourette's syndrome.

New drugs were added during this period of explosive growth in the use of pharmacotherapy. For example, anticonvulsant medications (e.g., carbamazepine, valproate) were found to be effective not only for seizure disorders but also for treating some children with bipolar disorder. The selective serotonin reuptake inhibitors (e.g., fluoxetine, sertraline, paroxetine) and the serotonergic-specific tricyclic drug, clomipramine, were found to be useful for a number of conditions, particularly depression and anxiety disorders, including obsessive-compulsive disorder. Further, dopamine receptor antagonists (e.g., clozapine, risperidone, olanzapine) that have far fewer neurological adverse effects than the traditional neuroleptics (e.g., chlorpromazine, thioridazine), and two new antidepressants (i.e., venlafaxine, nefazodone) were added to our pharmacotherapeutic armamentarium. Indeed, the search for new drugs that are more effective and have a better adverse effects profile than those currently available is one of the most vigorous and exciting areas of research in child psychiatry today.

Two other developments that occurred during this period should be noted. First, there was an increasing sophistication in the research methodology used to assess drug effects.

According to Werry (1993), because child psychiatry was preoccupied with psychoanalytic theory until the late 1970s, there was a lack of research in pediatric psychopharmacology. To a large extent, this void was filled by experimental and clinical psychologists who had better training than child psychiatrists in research methodology. They brought to the field of pediatric psychopharmacology experimental designs that could be used for clinical trials, and they were able to undertake complex statistical analyses of the data from experimental studies. Further, and in contrast to adult psychiatry, they emphasized the use of reliable and valid measures, including laboratory measures and rating scales, and the need for assessing the effects of medication on behavior, learning, and academic performance. However, one of the consequences of psychologists being more active than psychiatrists in psychopharmacological research was that they emphasized psychosocial rather than biological variables.

Second, beginning in the late 1980s, there was much negative media attention given to the use of Ritalin for the treatment of hyperactivity and attention deficit disorder (ADD: Brotman, 1992) and this negative attention is evident even in the late 1990s. One of the problems noted by the media was that this drug was prescribed excessively and probably inappropriately for many children. For example, Safer and Krager (1992) found that in Baltimore County, MD, the use of Ritalin increased fivefold from 1981 through 1987—far faster than one would have predicted from the figures on the prevalence of ADD in children. The media and litigation blitz which lasted about two years had a major effect on the prescribing practices of physicians in this particular county. Although the prescriptions for Ritalin decreased by 40% during this period, Safer and Krager reported that 36% of the children who discontinued Ritalin experienced major academic problems (i.e., failing grades, suspension from school) and another 47% had mild to moderate academic problems (e.g., lower grades, in-school detention). Further, as the number of prescriptions for Ritalin decreased during this period, there was concurrent fourfold increase in the number of prescriptions for tricyclic antidepressants among children with ADD. As the tricyclics have more troublesome side effects than Ritalin, the outcome for these children was not positive at all.

More recently, consumer groups and the Church of Scientology have attacked the use of fluoxetine (Prozac) on the basis of a report by Teicher, Glod, and Cole (1990) which reported the (re)emergence of severe suicidal preoccupation in six patients with severe depressive disorders following treatment with Prozac. However, none of the six patients actually attempted suicide while being treated with this drug. Further, studies have shown that Prozac is no more likely to induce suicidal feelings than any other antidepressant (Fava & Rosenbaum, 1991) and, at least in one study, it was found that the incidence of suicidal ideations was greater in patients treated with imipramine (a tricyclic antidepressant) or placebo than with Prozac (Beasley & Dornseif, 1991). Because research shows that the risk of Prozac-induced suicide is extremely low and that the suicide rate in untreated major depression is as high as 15%, the Federal Drug Administration (FDA) did not support the contentions of consumer groups or the Church of Scientology and refused to withdraw Prozac from the market (Burton, 1991). Although this controversy is related to adults, fluoxetine is also used with adolescents in the treatment of major depressive disorders, obsessive-compulsive disorder, and anxiety disorders (Popper, 1995). The effects of such controversies will affect the use of this drug with adolescents in the future.

Finally, the contribution of psychopharmacological research in developmental disabilities to the general field of child and adolescent psychopharmacology needs to be mentioned. From the mid-1960s until the 1980s, most child psychiatrists had an overwhelming interest in hyperactivity and ADHD and focused their research on the effects of stimulants on this disorder. Their interest in other disorders and other classes of drugs was minimal during this period. However, spurred by the methodological review of Sprague and Werry (1971), psychologists began testing the effectiveness of neuroleptics and other classes of drugs that were the mainstay of psychopharmacological treatment in developmental disabilities, especially for treating aggressive, self-injurious, and stereotypic behaviors (Aman & Singh, 1988; Singh, Ellis, & Singh, 1994; Singh, Guernsey, & Ellis, 1992; Singh & Winton, 1989). Much of the research on the psychopharmacology of the developmental disabilities since the mid-1970s has been methodologically innovative and experimentally rigorous. What we have learned from this endeavor has contributed much to the development of high-quality research in the psychopharmacology of child and adolescent disorders generally.

Since the 1980s, there has been an exponential growth in the number of studies published on the effects of medication in childhood disorders. The field of psychopharmacology of childhood disorders is rapidly achieving respectability and scientific credibility, and the launching of a specialist journal in 1990 (*Journal of Child and*

Adolescent Psychopharmacology) is an indication of the coming of age of this field.

5.11.3 PREVALENCE OF PSYCHOPHARMACOLOGY

Prevalence studies of pharmacotherapy for childhood disorders tell us something about the nature and patterns of drug usage in the treatment of psychiatric disorders in this population. Prevalence figures can also be useful in determining whether medication is being overused for certain disorders, or whether given drugs or classes of drugs are being overused for given symptoms or disorders. For example, the continuing debate about the excessive use of Ritalin is based in part on the number of prescriptions written each year for children with ADHD (Safer & Krager, 1992). Further, prevalence data also provide a useful guide to the way specific drugs are prescribed, evaluated, and monitored in clinical practice (Kaplan et al., 1994). As we have observed in the field of developmental disabilities (Ellis et al., 1997), prevalence studies are useful for examining the nature of the variables that are associated with drug use. These include, but are not limited to, characteristics of the child, physicians prescribing the medication (e.g., child psychiatrists, primary care physicians), the cultural and social milieu of the child, and psychosocial variables associated with drug use. Thus, prevalence studies provide us with a global picture of the patterns of psychopharmacological treatment for childhood disorders in general, and specific disorders in particular.

5.11.3.1 Developmental Disabilities

The best prevalence studies of pharmacotherapy have been published in the field of developmental disabilities (see Singh, Ellis, & Wechsler, in press). Following the seminal work of Lipman (1970) on the use of psychotropic drugs in residential facilities, a large number of prevalence studies have investigated the use of psychoactive medication in residential and community facilities for individuals with developmental disabilities. Overall, institutional surveys show that psychotropic drug usage ranges from a low of 19% to a high of 86%, with the majority of studies reporting prevalence rates between 30% and 50%. The use of seizure medication in institutions ranges from a low of 24% to a high of 56%, although typically it is between 25% and 45%. Together, psychotropic and antiepileptic medication usage in institutions ranges from 50% to 70%, with some individuals being prescribed both types of drugs concurrently.

Overall, there are fewer community surveys and these show that psychotropic drug usage with children ranges from 2% to 7%, and for adults it ranges from 14% to 36%. The use of seizure medication in community settings ranges from 12% to 31% for children and from 18% to 24% for adults. The combined prevalence of psychotropic and antiepileptic medications ranges from 19% to 33% for children and from 36% to 48% for adults.

Singh et al. (in press) have noted that various factors influence psychotropic drug use in individuals with developmental disabilities. For example, increasing dosages have been found to correlate highly with increasing age and decreasing intellectual impairment. There is a strong relationship between the type of residential facility and the use of medication to control behavior problems, with more medication being used in larger facilities and in facilities with very restrictive environments. Further, there is a strong positive correlation between the number and severity of an individual's behavior and psychiatric problems and the use of medication (Aman & Singh, 1988). For example, those who exhibit aggression, hyperactivity, self-injury, screaming, or anxiety are more likely to receive drug treatment than those who exhibit milder and less disruptive problems, such as noncompliance.

5.11.3.2 Attention-deficit Hyperactivity Disorder

Since the late 1960s, there has been increasing interest in the use of psychotropic drugs, especially psychostimulants, in the treatment of attention-deficit hyperactivity disorder (ADHD). Most of the early estimates came from the media rather than from scientific prevalence studies. For example, it was reported in the media that between 5% and 10% of students in Omaha public schools in 1970 were receiving stimulant medication for hyperactivity (Maynard, 1970), although later it was found that these figures actually were for children with learning disabilities. In any case, media estimates of the use of stimulants have continued to be published because of the concern that stimulant medication is prescribed for children who may not actually have ADHD and is being used in lieu of effective academic instruction (e.g., Gates, 1987; Hancock, 1996; Johnson, 1988; Landry, 1996).

In one of the earliest prevalence studies, Stephen, Sprague, and Werry (1973) estimated that 2–4% of school children in the Chicago area were receiving medication for hyperactivity in the 1970–1971 school year. Gadow's (1981) review of the use of drug treatment for hyperactivity suggested that the prevalence rate was between 1% and 2%, with considerable variability across geographic regions. Safer and Krager's (1988) longitudinal community surveys in Baltimore County, MD, showed that the prevalence of drug prescriptions doubled every 4–7 years, with about 6% of children in public elementary schools in this county receiving medication for hyperactivity by 1987. Further, almost all the prescriptions (99%) were for stimulants (93% methylphenidate, 4% pemoline, and 3% dextroamphetamine), and the ratio of boys to girls receiving the medication was 5:1. Sherman and Hertzig (1991) reviewed the state prescription records in 1986 and found that 0.4% of all 3–17 year olds in Suffolk County (Long Island, NY) received at least one prescription for methylphenidate for hyperactivity. The medication was typically prescribed by local pediatricians, and the ratio of boys to girls receiving methylphenidate was 6:1.

5.11.3.3 Serious Emotional Disturbance

Children with serious emotional disturbance (SED) typically have comorbid psychiatric disorders for which psychotropic medication is often indicated. They are prescribed more psychotropic medication than their peers without SED, regardless of whether the mental health services are provided in a psychiatric hospital (Singh, Landrum, Donatelli, Hampton, & Ellis, 1994) or in the community (Landrum, Singh, Nemil, Ellis, & Best, 1995). Further, the prevalence of psychotropic medication used with children with SED receiving inpatient psychiatric services or community-based services is much higher when compared to the 11% usage in school-identified students with SED (Cullinan, Epstein, & Sabornie, 1992; Cullinan, Gadow, & Epstein, 1987). For example, Silver et al. (1992) reported 43%, Epstein, Cullinan, Quinn, and Cumbald (1994) and Epstein, Cullinan, Quinn, and Cumbald (1995) reported 27% and 30%, respectively, and Barber, Rosenblatt, Harris, and Attkisson (1992) reported a prevalence of 34% for just antipsychotic medication. Singh et al. (1994) reported that 64% of the children with SED at a psychiatric hospital received at least one psychotropic medication.

5.11.3.4 Other Disorders

There is a paucity of prevalence data on the use of medication for children with other psychiatric disorders. The best data we have on individuals with autism comes from a large study by Aman, Van Bourgondien, Wolford,

and Sarphare (1995). The mean age of their sample of 859 individuals with autism was about 16 years. Of this sample, about 34% were taking some psychotropic medication or vitamin for autism or associated behavioral/psychiatric problems. Although about 19% reported having epilepsy, only 13% were actually taking anticonvulsant drugs. In total, over 50% of the sample were on psychoactive medication. There are no recent studies on the prevalence of psychopharmacological studies of children with depression. In two studies using selected samples of children being treated for depression, Kovacs, Feinberg, Crouse-Novak, Paulauskas, and Finkelstein (1984) reported that of the 65 children in their study, only two were on antidepressants, and another was treated with an antianxiety agent. In the other study, Keller, Lavori, Beardslee, Wunder (1991) reported that only one of 38 adolescents diagnosed as having an episode of major depression was treated with medication, in this case an antianxiety agent. As for enuresis, Foxman, Valdez, and Brook (1986) reported that 2% of a sample of 1724 5–13 year olds received medication (typically imipramine) for bedwetting. Although no drug prevalence data on children with Tourette's syndrome are available, one study in which a majority of the individuals with Tourette's syndrome were under 20 years of age reported that 71% of 1034 individuals had taken medication for Tourette's syndrome at some time, and 43% were taking medication at the time of the survey (Stefl, Bornstein, & Hammond, 1988). There are no reliable estimates of the use of medication in other childhood disorders.

These data provide a general view of the use of psychotropic and antiepileptic medication in a number of childhood disorders. However, many of the prevalence studies were poorly controlled, using ill-defined variables, small and selected samples, and so on, thus limiting the usefulness of the data that were reported. It is likely that the current use of medication in all childhood disorders is actually increasing because we have better-controlled studies than in the past indicating the effectiveness of newer medications, such as the selective serotonin reuptake inhibitors (SSRIs), with a number of these disorders. Obviously, there is a need for better controlled studies that examine the prevalence and patterns of drug use in children with various childhood disorders.

5.11.4 GENERAL PRINCIPLES OF PHARMACOLOGY

Psychopharmacology is a rapidly evolving area in child and adolescent psychiatry and it is important for clinicians working with children with psychiatric disorders to remain current with the research literature in this field. While we do not think that it is critical for nonmedical clinicians to be experts in the pharmacology of psychiatric drugs, it may be helpful for them to have a working knowledge of basic concepts in the field so that their collaboration with physicians can be more meaningful. For example, it may help them to better understand the theoretical bases of the choices made by a psychiatrist in the selection of specific agents for treating single or multiple childhood disorders. We will briefly mention three areas that are important for clinical psychologists as well as other nonmedical clinicians to be familiar with. However, we emphasize that this is a very complex, technical, and specialized field that cannot be adequately covered here, and we suggest that interested readers begin with general overviews (e.g., Clein & Riddle, 1995; Paxton & Dragunow, 1993) before delving deeper into the field.

5.11.4.1 Pharmacokinetics

Pharmacokinetics describes the time course and effects of drugs and their metabolites on the body. Thus, it describes what the body does to a drug. The most important pharmacokinetic factors that affect the time course and the effects of drugs on patients include: (i) absorption, which is the process that determines how a drug travels from the site of administration to the site of measurement (e.g., plasma, whole blood); (ii) first-pass effect, which is the hepatic extraction of orally administered drugs before they reach the systemic circulation; (iii) distribution, which indicates how much of a drug is distributed to the various organs or sites of action throughout the body; (iv) steady-state concentration, which indicates the concentration of the drug when the amount administered is equal to the amount eliminated per unit time; (v) half-life, which is the time required for the concentration of the drug in plasma or whole blood to fall by one-half; (vi) elimination rate constant, which is the proportion of the drug in the body that is eliminated per unit time; (vii) clearance, which provides a measure of elimination of the drug from the body and is calculated by multiplying the amount of drug in the body by the elimination rate constant; (viii) first-order kinetics, which occurs when the amount of the drug eliminated per unit time is directly proportional to its plasma concentration; and (ix) zero-order kinetics, which occurs only when a fixed amount of the drug is eliminated per unit time regardless of plasma concentration. Data

on these factors can be used to draw a unique kinetic profile of a given drug.

Together with pharmacodynamics, pharmacokinetics provides the bases for understanding the relationship of drug concentrations to clinical effects in children. Since the 1950s pharmacologists have developed the theoretical pharmacokinetic bases for most types of dosage regimens and have identified the therapeutic plasma concentration ranges for a number of psychotropic drugs that are currently used to derive rational dosage regimens (Evans, Schentag, & Jusko, 1986). Indeed, child psychiatrists rely on pharmacokinetic principles to optimize the effects of pharmacotherapy in children (Clein & Riddle, 1995; Greenblatt & Shader, 1987).

5.11.4.2 Pharmacodynamics

Pharmacodynamics deals with the relationship between drug dosage or concentration in the body and its drug effects, both desirable and undesirable. Thus, it deals with the mechanism(s) of drug action and generally describes what a drug does to the body. The most important pharmacodynamic considerations include: (i) receptor mechanism, which describes how the drug binds at the cellular level and initiates its pharmacodynamic effects; (ii) dose–response curve, which provides a plot of the drug concentration against the effects of the drug and allows comparison of the efficacy and potency of drugs; (iii) therapeutic index, which provides a relative measure of the toxicity and safety of a drug, and is calculated by dividing the median toxic dose by the median effective dose; (iv) lag time, which is the time taken for the full therapeutic effects of a given drug to appear, and the reasons for a delay in effects may be pharmacokinetic, pharmacodynamic, or both; and (v) tolerance, which refers to the responsiveness of a child to a particular drug as it is administered over time.

Children differ widely in terms of the drug dose that produces a given effect. Thus, clinicians must have a good knowledge of current pharmacodynamic principles to understand a child's response to psychotropic drugs (Dingemanse, Danhof, & Breimer, 1988; Paxton & Dragunow, 1993).

5.11.4.3 Pharmacogenetics

Pharmacogenetics deals with idiosyncratic or unusual drug responses that have a hereditary basis (Kalow, 1990). Responses to psychotropic and other drugs in children are modulated by their genetic predisposition. This is because "genes encoding enzymes or proteins that play a role in the drug response differ in some respect from one individual to the next" (Nebert & Weber, 1990, p. 469). When all other variables are held constant, the individual's pharmacogenetic response reflects a genetic difference in the metabolic rate when compared to that of a control subject. For example, Zhou, Koshakji, Silberstein, Wilkinson, and Wood (1989) compared the physiologic effects and the pharmacologic disposition of propranolol in a group of Caucasian Americans and a group of Chinese Orientals. They reported that the Chinese subjects were more responsive to the drug, displaying a larger reduction in the heart rate and blood pressure, because they metabolized the drug more efficiently than the subjects in the Caucasian group. According to Nebert and Weber (1990, p. 473), idiosyncratic drug responses that may be due to genetic variation in any of the subcellular steps involved in pharmacokinetics include the following mechanisms: (i) transport (absorption, plasma protein binding); (ii) transducer mechanism (receptors, enzyme induction, or inhibition); (iii) biotransformation; and (iv) excretory mechanisms (renal and biliary transport). Typically, clinical observations, family or twin studies, protein polymorphisms, animal modeling, and DNA polymorphism characterizations are methods used to discover new atypical drug responses that may have a pharmacogenetic basis. The clinical import of pharmacogenetics is that clinicians should be aware of the possibility of differences in drug response and dose requirements among children from various ethnic and racial groups.

5.11.5 FACTORS AFFECTING THE OUTCOME OF PHARMACOTHERAPY

The effects of psychotropic drugs are seldom determined solely by their pharmacological properties, such as those discussed above. Indeed, psychotropic medication is prescribed and used within a transactional system between the child, his family, physician and other clinicians, as well as others (e.g., teachers, peers) who are significant in the life of the child (Moerman, 1979; Singh & Aman, 1990). Of course, we must remember that children rarely, if ever, seek assistance from physicians directly; their parents and other caretakers do and, almost always, without asking for input from the child. The child's views of the treatment process, the child–physician therapeutic alliance, and the child's attributions of the effects of medication are also important and may be responsible for at least some of the effects of pharmacotherapy (Towbin, 1995). Further,

other factors, such as compliance, placebo effects, and sociocultural and ecobehavioral factors, are important in treatment outcome. However, the majority of studies in child psychopharmacology have focused on biological variables (e.g., pharmacokinetics, pharmacodynamics, and pharmacogenetics) to the exclusion of virtually all others.

Singh and Aman (1990) noted that our knowledge of the intended effects of psychotropic medication in children is often based on an assessment of the changes in the target behavior, symptoms, and syndrome as a result of a controlled trial of a given drug. They criticized this approach on the grounds that it does not include the study of environment × behavior × drug interactions and inter-relationships. The majority of current psychopharmacological research in general focuses on the consequences of specific drugs or drug combinations on the target behavior or diagnosis, without regard to the setting events or contextual variables that may influence the effects of the medication. A transactional analysis would require that the effects of pharmacotherapy be explained in terms of the relevant contextual variables that transact to determine treatment outcome.

There are a large number of contextual variables that may contribute to the outcome of psychopharmacotherapy. While all variables cannot be covered here, we present diverse examples to show that assessment of treatment outcome is much more complex than has hitherto been noted in psychopharmacological research.

5.11.5.1 Behavioral Teratogenesis

Girls of child-bearing age are always cautioned about the potential interaction between pregnancy and nursing, the course of a psychiatric disorder, and psychotropic treatment (Coyle, Wayner, & Singer, 1976; Schou, 1990). With some drugs (e.g., lithium, valproic acid), there is a real possibility of a drug × pregnancy interaction which increases the risk of malformations in the unborn child and the potential for later developmental anomalies. For example lithium may increase the risk of fetal macrosomia, premature delivery, and perinatal mortality (Schou, 1990), and the teratogenic effects of valproic acid on exposed fetuses includes a 1–2% incidence of spina bifida (Centers for Disease Control, 1983)

5.11.5.2 Behavioral Toxicity

Behavioral toxicity refers to the undesirable effects of essentially therapeutic levels of medication clinically indicated for a given disorder (DiMascio, Soltys, & Shader, 1970). These undesirable effects may include anticholinergic effects, alpha-adrenergic blockade, and dopaminergic effects, among others. In behavioral terms, behavioral toxicity can be classified as a concurrent stimulus event that affects the ongoing interactions of the child. For example, take the case of a child who is on medication for a seizure disorder. The drowsiness produced by his anticonvulsant medication (e.g., phenobarbital) may cause him to function more poorly than he might in its absence. Thus, in this case, behavioral toxicity may operate concurrently with classroom instruction or activities at home. In assessing the effects of psychopharmacotherapy, clinicians should include measures of behavioral toxicity because it will assist the child's treatment team to arrive at risk-to-benefit treatment decisions on the basis of data.

5.11.5.3 Compliance

Compliance is the degree to which a child adheres to the recommended treatment plan of the treating physician. In children, compliance with medication is typically partial because they tend to take medication irregularly or less often than is prescribed. The reasons for medication noncompliance can be categorized as "rational, capricious, absolute refusal, confusion, or iatrogenic" (Janicak, Davis, Preskorn, & Ayd, 1993). Often, noncompliance occurs because of unpleasant side effects of the medication and the perceived stigma associated with taking medication in school. Some children believe that taking medication somehow lessens their control of their lives, or that the medication determines what they do. Medication compliance in children can be increased by: (i) having the child actively participate in treatment planning; (ii) explaining to the child before treatment begins the expected side effects of the medication; (iii) emphasizing the positive aspects of taking the medication as prescribed, and (iv) having the simplest drug regimen (e.g., taking medication once a day for long-acting drugs). Further, compliance can be increased by involving the family in the treatment process. Clearly, these psychosocial factors associated with medication compliance affect the outcome of psychopharmacologic treatment.

5.11.5.4 Comorbidity

Comorbidity, which is the presence of disorders other than the one targeted for treatment, affects treatment outcome because the additional disorders change the simple drug $\times$ disorder $\times$ environment interaction to a more complex drug $\times$ disorder$_1$ $\times$ environment $\times$ disorder$_2$ interaction, if there is just one comorbid disorder. This interaction may mean that a second treatment, which could be pharmacotherapy or an alternative, is necessary to control a comorbid disorder, resulting in drug$_1$ $\times$ disorder$_1$ $\times$ environment $\times$ drug$_2$ $\times$ disorder$_2$ interaction. Of course, other interactions may also occur, such as drug$_1$ $\times$ drug$_2$ interaction, and changes in the physiologically determined susceptibilities of the drugs to interact with the environment to produce certain unintended, positive or adverse effects (i.e., side effects). This scenario suggests that the child must be adequately assessed not only for the target symptoms, syndrome, or disorder but also for comorbid disorders. Further, the interactive effects of treatments $\times$ environments $\times$ disorders must be assessed during clinical treatment and under baseline, placebo, and treatment in research protocols. This is a critical consideration for many childhood disorders. For example, comorbid axis I psychiatric disorders are commonly associated with childhood depression and ADHD (Kye & Ryan, 1995). The clinical import of this variable is that comorbidity may contribute to differential response to psychopharmacologic treatment.

5.11.5.5 Placebo Effects

The placebo effect in pharmacology is the phenomenon that is observed when a child exhibits a clinically significant response to a physiologically inert substance. This is not a rare phenomenon as it may account for 30–70% of the therapeutic responses observed in psychopharmacologic treatment (White, Tursky, & Schwartz, 1995). The placebo response is not due to the psychopharmacological properties of the drug; that is, the outcome is not due to the effects of the prescribed intervention. It results from purely psychological effects as a consequence of expectancy of an outcome from the treatment. While a majority of the placebo effects are established simply by asking the child if he is feeling better or by having the child complete a rating scale that provides a measure of his subjective well-being, often placebo effects can also be measured objectively. For example, individuals given placebo treatment for anxiety disorder often show less autonomic nervous system arousal (e.g., decrease in heart rate, lower blood pressure). Although there is some evidence of sustained placebo response in adults, children relapse fairly rapidly, suggesting that continued monitoring of a placebo response is absolutely necessary in this population.

5.11.5.6 Reciprocal Interactions

In behavioral terms, reciprocal interactions are concurrent stimulus–response contexts that set the occasion for further interactions. This is an important variable that affects the course of psychopharmacotherapy because the initial effects of drugs on a child may also have an effect on the reactions of others who interact with him. This phenomenon was clearly illustrated in the stimulant treatment of children with ADHD in which (i) the drug increased a child's compliance with parent demands, and (ii) the parents, in turn, reduced their commands and disciplinary behaviors, while increasing their positive interactions with the child (Barkley & Cunningham, 1979; Cunningham & Barkley, 1978). This highlights the importance of assessing drug effects on reciprocal interactions of the child with significant others in his environment (e.g., parents, siblings, peers, teachers).

Although we have selectively discussed some factors that affect the outcome of psychopharmacologic treatment, there are many factors that should be monitored for their impact on the outcome of pharmacologic intervention.

5.11.6 ASSESSMENT AND CLINICAL FORMULATION

5.11.6.1 Comprehensive Assessment

A comprehensive psychiatric assessment is necessary before a child is given pharmacotherapy. The clinician's goal is to understand the child's presenting problems or symptoms within the context of the highest level of diagnostic sophistication that can be reached on the basis of a comprehensive multidisciplinary assessment. There are four levels of diagnostic sophistication: (i) symptomatic, which includes isolated symptoms (e.g., auditory hallucinations) that provide an indication of a possible diagnosis (e.g., psychosis, not otherwise specified); (ii) syndromic, which includes a constellation of signs and symptoms that have been present for a given time, and standardized inclusionary and exclusionary criteria can be used to derive a diagnosis (e.g., depression); (iii) pathophysiologic, which includes structural or biochemical changes (e.g., elevated thyroid function tests, lowered thyroid-stimulating hormone) that indicate the diagnosis (e.g., hyperthyroidism); and (iv) etiologic in which

the diagnosis is based on known causative factors (Janicak et al., 1993). With children, most of the psychiatric diagnoses are at the syndromic level of sophistication because we do not currently have a good understanding of the etiologies of many childhood disorders. Thus, it is not uncommon to find wide variability in treatment outcome in children diagnosed with the same syndrome because they have similar presentations but with substantially different underlying mechanisms. This means that sometimes we treat children's behavioral symptoms or psychiatric disorders without fully appreciating their biological and genetic underpinnings or how these factors transact with the children's physical and cultural environment.

5.11.6.2 Baseline Assessments

A baseline assessment provides the basis for determining the child's psychopathological condition, indications for treatment, and the nature of the proposed treatment. It is multidimensional and multidisciplinary, incorporating assessments of the child's symptoms and functioning across multiple domains, as well as an evaluation of his family history and his physical and cultural environment. Typically, a baseline assessment includes: (i) source and the reason for referral, including the target symptoms that may be the focus of treatment; (ii) history of the presenting symptoms; (iii) psychiatric history and current mental status; (iv) developmental and medical history; (v) family and education/school history; and (vi) cultural context of the family (e.g., determine if there are any specific religious or cultural beliefs of the family that may interact with the child's psychiatric treatment in general, and psychopharmacological treatment in particular). Different mental health professionals may take the lead role in obtaining the baseline assessment data. Because of their broad-based training, child psychiatrists and clinical psychologists often assume a major role in these assessments, obtaining information on the child through structured interviews, behavioral observations, and standardized rating scales.

5.11.6.3 Disorder-specific Assessment Algorithms

Typically, clinicians develop a working hypothesis regarding the child's diagnosis during the initial assessments, or the child may be referred by another clinician for treatment of a specific disorder, such as ADHD. In such cases, clinicians may use an assessment algorithm designed to confirm the diagnosis and to provide data that can be used as the baseline for assessing treatment effects. For example, Table 1 presents the standard algorithm for screening children with ADHD at our clinic (see Garfinkel & Amrami, 1992). Assessment algorithms provide a distillation of current knowledge from multiple sources and disciplines regarding the assessment of a specific disorder. Further, they provide a useful framework for interdisciplinary assessments.

5.11.6.4 Baseline Assessments Specifically for Psychopharmacologic Treatment

The initial assessments can be used to determine the psychiatric diagnosis of the child, as well as to identify target symptoms best treated with pharmacotherapy (Sood & Singh, 1996). If a child is referred specifically for psychopharmacological treatment, he will need a baseline psychiatric assessment prior to initiation of medication. Premedication work-up typically includes a complete medical history, and physical and neurological examinations. Further, if data from initial baseline assessments are unavailable, other data may have to be gathered prior to formulating a treatment plan.

A psychiatric interview with the child, alone and together with his parents, is undertaken to determine a psychiatric diagnosis or diagnoses for which medication may be indicated. Further, this assessment enables the clinician to identify the target symptoms for treatment. While it is often thought that medication is prescribed for a target disorder (e.g., bipolar disorder, ADHD), in reality this is not the case. The clinician targets specific symptoms that serve as markers for the underlying psychopathology and the changes in these symptoms over the course of treatment are used to evaluate the effects of medication. Multiple symptoms are used as markers because some may respond to medication before others. For example, if we take a child with bipolar disorder, his sleep and appetite disturbances will improve earlier than his mood. Further, the clinician is careful to determine the phase of the child's illness (i.e., acute, relapse, recurrence) because of its importance in clinical decision making with regard to initial treatment as well as the need for and duration of maintenance and prophylactic therapy. Information on the temporal patterns

---

Table 1 Screening algorithm for attention-deficit hyperactivity disorder.

Initial referral may be either from school or home
Begin teacher–parent–child observational rating scale (e.g., Conners)
Refer to pediatrician or child psychiatrist or both:
    Complete physical examination, including:
        screen for lead toxicity and iron-deficiency anemia
        screen for other nutritional deficiencies
        detailed neurologic assessment, including perceptual motor tests to rule out focal
            neurological deficit
        thyroid panel (if indicated)
    Complete history, including:
        antenatal and perinatal history
        developmental milestones
        sleep history
        social and family history
        school history utilizing school records, grade-level screening medical history,
            especially trauma, infection, neurologic history, and allergies
    Use cognitive testing to assess intelligence and learning disabilities and organic
        brain syndromes
        Wechsler Intelligence Scale for Children-III
        Woodcock–Johnson
        Other tests, as indicated
    Psychometric testing
        Gordon diagnostic system
        Continuous performance test
    Evaluation of home situation
        If the evaluation is consistent with ADHD, a trial of sympathomimetic
            medication may be initiated
        Evaluation to monitor side effects, effectiveness of medication, four times yearly;
            alternative pharmaceutical or other therapies may be considered

of drug response and the phase of a child's illness is critical in the overall pharmacologic management of the child (Janicak et al., 1993).

5.11.6.4.1 Physical examination

The standard physical examination includes recording the child's temperature, pulse rate, respiratory rate, blood pressure, height, and weight. Because drugs may have adverse effects on the developing fetus, girls of childbearing age should be given a pregnancy test.

5.11.6.4.2 Laboratory tests and diagnostic procedures

Many of these tests would have been done during the baseline medical evaluation and need not be repeated. According to Green (1995, p. 26), standard laboratory tests for a premedication work-up may include the following:

(i) Complete blood cell count (CBC), differential, and hematocrit.

(ii) Urinanalysis.

(iii) Blood urea nitrogen (BUN) level.

(iv) Serum electrolyte levels for sodium (Na^+), potassium (K^+), chloride (Cl^-), calcium (Ca^{2+}), and phosphate (PO_4^{3-}) and carbon dioxide content (CO_2).

(v) Liver function tests: aspartate aminotransferase (AST) or serum glutamic oxaloacetic transaminase (SGOT), alanine aminotransferase (ALT) or serum glutamic pyruvic transaminase (SGPT), alkaline phosphatase, lactic dehydrogenase (LDH), and bilirubin (total and direct).

(vi) Serum lead level determination in children under seven years of age and in older children, when indicated.

In addition, other laboratory tests may be indicated prior to using specific psychoactive medications. For example, thyroid function tests are recommended prior to using tricyclic antidepressants and lithium; kidney function tests prior to using lithium carbonate; baseline and periodic electrocardiogram (ECG) for tricyclic antidepressants and lithium; an electroencephalogram (EEG) for antipsychotics, tricyclic antidepressants, or lithium for those who "have a history of seizure disorder, who are on an antiepileptic drug for a seizure disorder, or who may be at risk for seizures" (Green, 1995, p. 27).

5.11.6.4.3 Behavioral observations and rating scales

Except in emergency situations (e.g., violent, explosive behavior), a child is observed for 7–10 days for patterns in his general behavior as well as the target symptoms before initiating pharmacotherapy. In addition to the psychiatrist, clinical psychologists are in the best position to provide valid and reliable observation data on the child's behavior from multiple settings. These observations are useful in determining the stability of the child's problems as well as the need for medication, should the child's condition improve substantially during the observation period.

Behavioral observations are labor-intensive and often impractical in clinical practice. Fortunately, there are various rating scales that can be used to obtain reliable data on a child across multiple settings and by multiple raters (Sood and Singh, 1996). For example, the child behavior checklist (Achenbach, 1991a) is used widely for initial assessment of children and adolescents referred for psychiatric assessment, and the various Conners rating scales are used extensively with children with ADHD (Conners, (1990). Interested readers should consult Aman (1993) and Sood and Singh (1996) who have reviewed an extensive array of rating scales that can be used for this purpose.

5.11.6.5 Clinical Formulation

The diagnostic formulation follows the standard biopsychosocial model, which means that biological, psychological, and social factors are taken into account in developing a comprehensive framework for understanding the child's symptomatic presentation. Once the relevant data are gathered, the clinician synthesizes the information and reaches a working diagnosis. However, before a psychiatric diagnosis is reached, any general medical condition that may account for the child's problems are ruled out. In addition, it is critical that deviation from the normal range of development is considered. Further, a child may have symptoms of multiple conditions and all relevant diagnoses need to be considered (e.g, ADHD and learning disorders).

In the diagnostic formulation for psychopharmacological interventions, the clinician pays particular attention to signs and symptoms associated with psychiatric disorders that have a biological basis. These disorders have the potential for being responsive to psychoactive agents. Much of this information is obtained from the clinician's use of a descriptive, phenomenological assessment of the child's feelings, emotions, and behaviors because it provides important insights into the child's disorder(s). Information on the clinical course helps the clinician to place the disorder in a specific context because many pharmacologically responsive disorders have "characteristic beginnings, occur during particular stages of development, or are associated with particular sequelae" (Walkup, 1995, p. 26). For example, attention and concentration difficulties at age 5 or 6 years may be related to ADHD but at age 15 or 16 years, these symptoms are more likely to be associated with a mood disorder (Walkup, 1995). Detailed family history is also useful in diagnostic formulation for a number of reasons, such as providing additional support for the clinician's working hypothesis. The clinician uses all of this information to formulate a treatment plan that includes pharmacotherapy as well as some type of educational and psychosocial intervention because pharmacotherapy alone is rarely sufficient for complete recovery.

5.11.7 PSYCHOTROPIC MEDICATION IN CHILDHOOD DISORDERS

The main psychopharmacologic agents used in children are presented in Table 2 by class, generic name, and trade name. What follows in each section is a discussion of a given class of medication, mechanism of action, indications, dosing, and adverse effects. Only general principles and procedures of psychopharmacologic therapies are covered because applications of this treatment modality to specific psychopathologies are discussed elsewhere. However, as a general rule, it must be remembered that psychopharmacologic treatment is typically used as one component of a broad therapeutic approach to help alleviate psychiatric symptoms in children. Medication provides symptomatic relief, allowing the child to function more fully at school and at home, and in his community. Further, medication usually relieves the child's symptoms of psychiatric illness but it does not remove vulnerability to its recurrence because the environmental and constitutional stressors that gave rise to the illness are not affected by the medication.

5.11.7.1 Antipsychotics

The antipsychotics have been called major tranquilizers because of an early observation that chlorpromazine, the prototypical drug in this class, produced somnolence and relaxation. This led to the mistaken belief that the major action of antipsychotics was sedative. Antipsychotics have also been called neuroleptics because they are noted for producing signs of neurological dysfunction, principally Parkinson's syndrome, and other extrapyramidal reactions. Typically, drugs that produce both antipsychotic and extrapyramidal effects are called neuroleptic drugs. While the term neuroleptic continues to be used interchangeably with antipsychotic, the discovery of clozapine, an antipsychotic that is not a neuroleptic, means that this practice may now be inappropriate.

The antipsychotics consist of a group of eight classes of drugs, including phenothiazines (e.g., chlorpromazine [Thorazin], fluphenazine [Prolixin], thioridazine [Mellaril]), thioxanthenes (e.g., thiothixene [Navane]), dibenzoxazepines (e.g., loxapine [Loxitane]), dihydroindoles (e.g., molindone [Moban]), butyrophenones (e.g., haloperidol [Haldol], droperidol [Inapsine]), diphenylbutylpiperidines (e.g., pimozide [Orap]), benzamides (e.g., sulpiride [Dogmatil]), and benzisoxazole (e.g., risperidone [Risperdal]). Pharmacologically, the major classes of antipsychotics are remarkably similar and, when given in equivalent doses, they produce comparable benefits and induce a similar range of adverse effects (see Table 3).

5.11.7.1.1 Mechanism of action

The antipsychotics produce their therapeutic effects by blocking the D_2 subtype of dopamine receptors, although some of them may block the D_1 receptors as well. Blockade of the dopamine receptors is also responsible for most of the neurological and endocrinological adverse effects of antipsychotics. The difference in the adverse effects profiles of the antipsychotics is due to the fact that some of the antipsychotics also block noradrenergic, cholinergic, and histaminergic receptors. For example, blocking of the alpha-noradrenergic receptors by some antipsychotics probably accounts for their hypotensive action. When compared to the low potency antipsychotics (e.g., chlorpromazine, thioridazine), those with high potency (e.g., haloperidol, pimozide) are typically less sedating, produce less hypotension, and they generally have less effect on seizure threshold, fewer anticholinergic effects, less cardiovascular toxicity, less weight gain, and minimal effect on bone marrow and liver. Risperidone, a new antipsychotic medication, has D_2 as well as serotonergic (5-HT2) antagonist properties and lacks the acute extrapyramidal adverse effects of the traditional antipsychotics. Clozapine, an atypical antipsychotic, has weak D_2 antagonist properties but a high affinity for D_4 dopamine receptors, as well as a relatively strong antagonistic interaction with central alpha$_1$-adrenergic, cholinergic, histaminic (H1), and serotonergic (5-HT2) receptors (Baldessarini & Frankenburg, 1991; Lieberman, Kane, & Johns, 1989). Like risperidone, clozapine also lacks acute extrapyramidal adverse effects.

Pharmacological Therapies

Table 2 Psychoactive and psychotropic drugs by class.

Drug class/subclass	Generic name	Trade name
A. Antipsychotics		
Phenothiazines	chlorpromazine	Thorazine
	fluphenazine	Prolixin, Modecate
	mesoridazine	Serentil
	perphenazine	Trilafon
	thioridazine	Mellaril
	trifluoperazine	Stelazine
Thioxanthenes	chlorprothixene	Taractan
	thiothixene	Navane
Butyrophenones	haloperidol	Haldol
	pipamperon	Dipiperon
Rauwolfia alkaloids	reserpine	Rauloydin, Reserpoid, Sandril
Other antipsychotics	clozapine	Clozaril
	loxapine	Loxitane
	risperidone	Risperdal
	olanzapine	Zyprexa
B. Antidepressants		
Tricyclics	amitriptyline	Elavil, Amitril, Endep
	clomipramine	Anafranil
	desipramine	Norpramin, Pertofrane
	doxepin	Sinequan, Adapin
	imipramine	Tofranil
	nortriptyline	Pamelor
Monoamine oxidase inhibitors	isocarboxazid	Marplan
	phenelzine	Nardil
	tranylcypromine	Parnate
Selective serotonin reuptake inhibitors	fluoxetine	Prozac
	fluvoxamine	Luvox
	paroxetine	Paxil
	sertraline	Zoloft
Other antidepressants	bupropion	Wellbutrin
	trazodone	Desyrel
	venlafaxine	Effexor
C. Antimanics		
	lithium carbonate	Eskalith, Lithane, Lithobid
D. Anxiolytics		
Benzodiazepines	alprazolam	Xanax
	chlordiazepoxide	Librium
	diazepam	Valium
	lorazepam	Ativan
	oxazepam	Serax
	prazepam	Verstran
	temazepam	Restoril
	triazolam	Halcion
Antihistamines	diphenhydramine	Benadryl
	hydroxyzine	Atarax
	promethazine	Phenergan
Atypical anxiolytics	buspirone	BuSpar
E. Stimulants		
	amphetamine sulfate	Benzedrine
	dextroamphetamine	Dexedrine

Table 2 (continued)

Drug class/subclass	Generic name	Trade name
	methamphetamine	Desoxyn
	methylphenidate	Ritalin
	pemoline	Cylert
	mixed salts product[a]	Adderall
F. Antiepileptics		
	carbamazepine	Tegretol
	clonazepam	Klonopin
	diazepam	Valium
	ethosuximide	Zarontin
	felbamate	Felbatol
	gabapentin	Neurontin
	phenobarbital	Luminal, Gardenal
	phenytoin	Dilantin
	primidone	Mysoline
	sodium valproate	Depakene, Depakote, Epilim
	sulthiame	Ospolot
G. Others		
Beta-blockers	propranolol	Inderal
Alpha-2 blockers (nonspecific)	clonidine	Catapres
Alpha-2A blockers (selective)	guanfacine	Tenex
Opioid antagonists	naloxone	Narcan
	naltrexone	Trexan
Sympathomimetic amines	fenfluramine	Pondimin, Ponderax
Anticholinergics	benztropine	Cogentin
	biperiden	Akineton
	ethopropazine	Parsidol
	procyclidine	Kemadrin
	trihexyphendiyl	Artane

[a] Combination of dextroamphetamine sulfate, dextroamphetamine saccharate, amphetamine sulfate, and amphetamine aspartate.

5.11.7.1.2 Indications

In children, the antipsychotics are used mainly in the treatment of psychotic disorders, typically the positive symptoms, as well as other behavioral symptoms, such as agitation, aggression, tics, and stereotypies (Green, 1995; Kutcher, 1997). The positive symptoms include hallucinations, delusions, thought disorder (i.e., incoherency), and catatonic symptoms (e.g., stupor, negativism, rigidity, excitement, and posturing) or bizzare affect. The negative symptoms, which include affective blunting, poverty of speech and thought, apathy, anhedonia, and poor social functioning, respond well to the atypical antipsychotics (e.g., clozapine, risperidone). Among the antipsychotics, haloperidol and pimozide are the drugs of choice for treating children with Tourette's disorder. The low-potency drugs (e.g., chlorpromazine, thioridazine) are used to treat mania and, as a last resort, to treat aggressive behavior and severe agitation in children. The high-potency drugs (e.g., fluphenazine, perphenazine) are used for severe insomnia and severe self-injury. Clozapine is useful in treating refractory psychosis in adolescence, and risperidone is useful in treating both positive and negative symptoms of psychosis, as well as some symptoms associated with pervasive developmental disorder. Until recently, antipsychotics have been used widely in the treatment of self-injury, aggression, and agitation in children with developmental disorders (Ellis et al., 1997).

In terms of effects, there is little data to support the use of one antipsychotic drug over another because the action of these drugs is related to their structural similarities (Janicak et al., 1993). Thus, clinicians typically base their choice of one antipsychotic over another with regard to the adverse effect profile of the drugs.

Table 3 Antipsychotic drugs, trade names, potencies, and potential adverse effects.

Antipsychotic drug	Trade name(s)[a]	Potency[b]	Potential adverse effects profile			
			Sedation	Anticholinergic	Hypotension	Extrapyramidal
Chlorpromazine	Thorazine, Largactil	100 (low)	strong	strong	strong	weak
Fluphenazine	Prolixin, Modecate	1.5–3 (high)	moderate	weak	weak	strong
Haloperidol	Haldol	2–5 (high)	weak	weak	weak	strong
Loxapine	Loxitane	10–15 (medium)	moderate	moderate	moderate	strong
Mesoridazine	Serentil	50 (low)	moderate	strong	moderate	moderate
Molindone	Moban	6–10 (medium)	moderate	moderate	weak	strong
Perphenazine	Trilafon	10 (medium)	weak	weak	weak	strong
Pimozide	Orap	1 (high)	weak	weak	weak	strong
Risperidone	Risperdal	2–3 (low)	weak	weak	weak–moderate	weak
Thioridazine	Mellaril	97 (low)	strong	strong	strong	weak
Thiothixene	Navane	2–5 (high)	weak	weak	weak	weak
Trifluoperazine	Stelazine	3–5 (high)	moderate	weak	weak	strong
Triflupromazine	Vesprin	25–50 (low)	strong	moderate	strong	moderate

[a] Not all drugs are approved for use in children or in all countries.   [b] mg of drug equivalent to 100 mg chlorpromazine.

For example, because children should maintain a relatively high level of activity for their developmental and psychological well-being, the clinician may choose haloperidol (which has fewer sedative and cardiovascular effects) over chlorpromazine (which has fewer extrapyramidal complications). Further, our history of clinical experience suggests that some children do in fact respond to one antipsychotic but not to another. It may be that this is due to differences between the drugs in terms of absorption, distribution, accumulation at receptor sites, pharmacodynamic actions, metabolism of their derivatives, and adverse cognitive effects (e.g., as a result of sedation). In addition, the drugs may appear to act differentially if their effects are not compared at optimum dosages for the child.

5.11.7.1.3 Dosing and adverse effects

The recommended doses for antipsychotic drugs typically used with children are presented in Table 4. In general, oral dosage of the low-potency antipsychotics range between 3.0 and 6.0 mg/kg/day. On average, the dosage of high-potency antipsychotics range between 0.1 and 0.5 mg/kg/day, although dosages up to 1.0 mg/kg/day are not uncommon. The dosage of risperidone is about 1–3 mg/day or up to 85 μg/kg/day, the dosage for clozapine is between 3.0 and 5.0 mg/kg (Spencer, Wilens, & Biederman, 1995). The side effects of the antipsychotics are presented in Table 5.

5.11.7.2 Antidepressants

As the name implies, antidepressants are used to treat depression in children and adults. The serendipitous finding that iproniazid, a drug used to treat tuberculosis, had mood-elevating properties and inhibited the enzyme monoamine oxidase led to the development of a class of antidepressants called the monoamine oxidase inhibitors (MAOIs). Some years later, the drug imipramine (Tofranil) was developed, followed by a number of others with a similar structure—the tricyclic antidepressants. A new generation of antidepressants have become available, with some of them (e.g., fluoxetine) enjoying remarkable clinical success in the treatment of depression.

5.11.7.2.1 Mechanisms of action

The different classes of antidepressants can be categorized according to their structure and/or presumed mechanism of action. For example, Janicak et al. (1993, p. 242) categorized them as follows:

(i) Heterocyclics (HCAs, e.g., imipramine, Tofranil), which block the neuronal reuptake of norepinephrine and/or serotonin.

(ii) Selective serotonin reuptake inhibitors (SSRIs, e.g., fluoxetine [Prozac]), which modify serotonin neurotransmission by inhibiting the reuptake carrier.

(iii) Monoamine oxidase inhibitors (MAOIs; e.g., isocarboxazid [Marplan]), which increase the concentration of several biogenic amines.

(iv) Aminoketones (e.g., bupropion [Wellbutrin]), whose most potent known effect is neuronal dopamine reuptake blockade, but whose mechanism of action is unknown.

(v) Triazolopyridines (e.g., trazodone [Desyrel]), which have mixed effects on the serotonin system, with the predominant effect being 5-HT2 receptor blockade.

(vi) 5-HT_{1A} receptor partial agonists (e.g., buspirone [BuSpar]), marketed as anxiolytics, but which also have proven antidepressant properties, especially with higher doses.

Although the different classes of antidepressants have specific mechanisms of action, in general, the antidepressants block the reuptake of one or more catecholamines (i.e., norepinephrine, serotonin, and dopamine), thereby decreasing or downregulating the number of postsynaptic receptors. The MAOIs have a different mechanism of action; they increase the availability of catecholamines by blocking the enzyme monoamine oxidase.

5.11.7.2.2 Indications

In general, the antidepressants are used with children to treat ADHD, obsessive–compulsive disorder (OCD), enuresis, depression, anxiety, and tic disorders. The tricyclic antidepressants (e.g., imipramine, desipramine, nortriptyline) are used to treat major depressive disorders (MDD), enuresis, ADHD, tic disorders, and anxiety disorders. Clomipramine has been found to be effective with OCD. The SSRIs (e.g., fluoxetine, sertraline, paroxetine, fluvoxamine) are used to treat MDD, OCD, and anxiety disorders. Bupropion is used to treat ADHD and MDD; trazodone for MDD, aggression, and insomnia; and venlafaxine for MDD, OCD, and anxiety disorders. The MAOIs are now rarely used with children because of potential problems with medication compliance and adverse effects in this population (Viesselman, Yaylayan, Weller, & Weller, 1993).

Table 4 Recommended doses for the various classes of psychotropic drugs.

Drug	Average daily dose	
	Children	*Adolescents*
A. Antipsychotics		
Chlorpromazine	30–200 mg	40–400 mg
(>6 months of age)[a]	(2.5–6 mg/kg/day)	(3–6 mg/kg/day)
Thioridazine	75–200 mg	10–200 + mg
(>2 years of age)[a]	(0.5–3 mg/kg/day)	
Trifluoperazine	1–15 mg	1–20 mg
(>6 years of age)[a]		
Thiothixene	2–10 mg	5–30 mg
(>12 years of age)[a]		
Haloperidol	0.5–4 mg	2–16 mg
(>3 years of age)[a]	(0.05–0.15 mg/kg/day)	
Reserpine	0.02–0.25 mg	0.1–1.0 mg
Clozapine		50–200 mg
(>16 years of age)[a]		(3–5 mg/kg/day)
Loxapine	5–50 mg	20–100 mg
(>16 years of age)[a]		
B. Antidepressants		
Amitriptyline	30–100 mg	50–100 mg
(>12 years of age)[a]	(1–5 mg/kg/day)	(1–5 mg/kg/day)
Bupropion	25–150 mg	75–300 mg
(>18 years of age)[a]		(3–6 mg/kg/day)
Clomipramine	25–100 mg	50–150 mg
(>10 years of age)[a]		(2–3 mg/kg/day)
Desipramine	10–150 mg	50–150 mg
(>12 years of age)[a]	(1–5 mg/kg/day)	(1–5 mg/kg/day)
Fluoxetine	5–20 mg	10–60 mg
(>18 years of age)[a]		(0.5–1 mg/kg/day)
Fluvoxamine	25–200 mg	50–300 mg
(>8 years of age)[a]		
Imipramine	10–150 mg	50–200 mg
(>6 years of age)[a]	(1–5 mg/kg/day)	(1–5 mg/kg/day)
Notriptyline	10–100 mg	50–100 mg
(>12 years of age)[a]		(1–3 mg/kg/day)
Phenelzine		15–45 mg
(>16 years of age)[a]		(0.5–1 mg/kg/day)
Sertraline	25–100 mg	50–200 mg
(not in children)[a]		(1.5–3 mg/kg/day)
C. Antimanics		
Lithium carbonate[b]	300–900 mg	900–1200 mg
(>12 years of age)[a]		(10–30 mg/kg/day)
D. Anxiolytics		
Alprazolam	0.25–2 mg	0.75–5 mg
(>18 years of age)[a]		(0.02–0.06 mg/kg/day)
Chlordiazepoxide	10–30 mg	20–60 mg
(>6 years of age)[a]		
Diazepam	1–10 mg	2–20 mg
(>6 months of age)[a]		(max 0.8 mg/kg/day)
Lorazepam	0.25–3 mg	0.05–6 mg
(>12 years of age)[a]		(0.04–0.09 mg/kg/day)
Diphenhydramine	25–200 mg	50–300 mg
		(1–5 mg/kg/day)
Hydroxyzine	25–100 mg	40–150 mg
		(2 mg/kg/day)
Buspirone	2.5–15 mg	5–30 mg
(>18 years of age)[a]		(0.2–0.6 mg/kg/day)

Table 4 (continued)

Drug	Average daily dose	
	Children	Adolescents
E. Stimulants		
Dextroamphetamine	2.5–15 mg	5–40 mg
(>3 years of age)[a]	(0.15–0.5 mg/kg/dose)	(0.15–0.5 mg/kg/dose)
Methylphenidate	2.5–30 mg	10–60 mg
(>6 years of age)[a]	(0.3–1 mg/kg/dose)	(0.3–1 mg/kg/dose)
Pemoline	18.75–75 mg	37.5–112.5 mg
(>6 years of age)[a]	(1–3 mg/kg/day)	(1–3 mg/kg/day)
Mixed salts[c]	2.5–30 mg	5–40 mg
(>3 years of age)[a]		
F. Antiepileptics		
Carbamazepine[b]	200–800 mg	400–1000 mg
(>6 years of age)[a]	(5–20 mg/kg/day)	(10–30 mg/kg/day; max dose 1000 mg/day)
Ethosuximide[b]	250–800 mg	500–1500 mg
	(20–30 mg/kg/day)	(20–40 mg/kg/day)
Phenobarbital[b]	<250 mg	75–250 mg
	(4–8 mg/kg/day)	(1–3 mg/kg/day)
Phenytoin[b]	<300 mg	300–500 mg
	(7.5–9 mg/kg/day)	(6–7 mg/kg/day)
Primidone[b]	150–750 mg	750–1500 mg
Sodium valproate[b]	250–1000 mg	500–2000 mg
G. Others		
Propranolol	5–80 mg	20–140 mg (max 2 mg/kg/day)
Clonidine	0.25–0.3 mg	0.3–0.4 mg
(not in children)[a]	(3–6 µg/kg/day)	(3–6 µg/kg/day)
Naltrexone	10–50 mg	40–120 mg
(>18 years of age)[a]	(0.5–1.5 mg/kg/day)	(1–2 mg/kg/day)
Fenfluramine	30–60 mg	40–100 mg
(>12 years of age)[a]		(1–2 mg/kg/day)
Benztropine	0.5–4 mg	0.5–6 mg
(>3 years of age)[a]		(43–86 µg/kg/day)

[a] Recommended US Food and Drug Administration guidelines. [b] Dosage titrated by serum levels. [c] Combination of dextroamphetamine sulfate, dextroamphetamine saccharate, amphetamine sulfate, and amphetamine aspartate.

5.11.7.2.3 Dosing and adverse effects

The recommended doses for antidepressant drugs typically used with children are presented in Table 4. The dose of antidepressant drugs for children has to be individualized because of interchild variability in metabolism and elimination. In general, the typical dose for tricyclic antidepressants in children ranges from 2.0 to 5.0 mg/kg, with 1.0–3.0 mg/kg for nortriptyline. The potential cardiotoxic effects of the tricyclic antidepressants, and particularly the reports of sudden death associated with desipramine therapy (Riddle et al., 1991), have reduced the use of tricyclic antidepressants by some clinicians. The suggested daily dose for fluoxetine is 0.5–1.0 mg/kg; for paroxetine 0.25–0.70 mg/kg, for sertraline 1.5–3.0 mg/kg; and for bupropion 4.0–6.0 mg/kg/day in divided doses.

The side effects of the antidepressants are presented in Table 5.

5.11.7.3 Antimanics

Lithium carbonate is the main antimanic drug used to treat children who have bipolar disorder, with the anticonvulsants, carbamazepine (Ballenger & Post, 1980), and valproic acid (McElroy, Keck, & Pope, 1987) being used as alternative antimanic agents.

5.11.7.3.1 Mechanism of action

Little research has been done on the use of these antimanic agents with children, and their therapeutic mechanism(s) is virtually unknown.

Table 5 Psychiatric and behavioral indications and side effects of various classes of drugs.

A. Antipsychotics

Indications: Psychotic states, schizophrenia (exacerbations and maintenance); mania (in conjunction with lithium); behavior disorders with severe agitation, aggressivity, and self-injury; and dyskinetic movement disorders (e.g., Tourette's disorder and juvenile Huntington's disease)

Side effects: Anticholinergic effects, including dry mouth, constipation, blurred vision, and urinary retention (most common with low-potency phenothiazines); extrapyramidal reactions, including acute dystonia, akathisia, and tremor (particularly with high-potency phenothiazines); neuroleptic malignant syndrome; tardive dyskinesia (lower risk with clozapine and risperidone); other central nervous system effects, including sedation, fatigue, cognitive blunting, psychotic symptoms, confusion, and excitement; orthostatic hypotension and cardiac conduction abnormalities; endocrine disturbances (e.g., menstrual irregularities and weight gain); gastrointestinal distress; skin photosensitivity; granulocytopenia and agranulocytosis (clozapine); and allergic reactions.

B. Antidepressants

Indications: Enuresis; attention-deficit/hyperactivity disorder; major depressive disorder; and anxiety disorders (including school phobia, separation anxiety disorder, panic disorder, and obsessive-compulsive disorder)

Side effects: *Tricyclics:* Anticholinergic effects, including dry mouth, constipation, blurred vision, and urinary retention; cardiac conduction slowing (treatment requires EKG monitoring), mild increases and/or irregularity in pulse rate, and mild decreases or increases in blood pressure; confusion or the induction of psychosis; seizures; rash; and endocrine abnormalities
Monoamine oxidase inhibitors: Mild decreases or increases in blood pressure; drowsiness; weight gain; insomnia; and hypertensive crisis with nonadherance to dietary restrictions (necessary to eliminate high tyramine foods from diet) or with certain drugs
Selective serotonin reuptake inhibitors: Irritability; gastrointestinal distress; headaches; and insomnia
Other antidepressants: Irritability (bupropion, venlafaxine); insomnia (bupropion, venlafaxine); drug-induced seizures (bupropion, with high doses); changes in blood pressure (trazodone, venlafaxine); priapism (trazodone); sedation and sleepiness (trazodone, venlafaxine); gastrointestinal distress (venlafaxine); and headache (venlafaxine)

C. Antimanics

Indications: Manic episodes of bipolar disorder; unipolar depression/adjunct treatment in major depressive disorder; and behavior disorders with extreme aggression

Side effects: Kidney abnormalities leading to increased urination and thirst; gastrointestinal distress; fine hand tremor, weakness, and ataxia; possible thyroid abnormalities (with long-term use), weight gain, and electrolyte imbalances; sedation, confusion, slurred speech, irritability, headache, and subtle cogwheel rigidity; skin abnormalities; orthostatic hypotension and pulse rate irregularities; and allergic reactions

D. Anxiolytics

Indications: Anxiety disorders; seizure control; night terrors; sleepwalking; insomnia and acute management of severe agitation; adjunct treatment in mania and refractory psychosis; and Tourette's disorder

Side effects: Headache, sedation, and decreased cognitive performance; behavioral disinhibition, including overexcitement, hyperactivity, increased aggressivity, and irritability; gastrointestinal distress; central nervous system disinhibition resulting in hallucinations, psychotic-like behavior, and depression; physical and psychological dependence (particularly with long-acting benzodiazepines); rebound or withdrawal reactions (particularly with short-acting benzodiazepines); blood abnormalities; anticholinergic effects, including dry mouth, constipation, and blurred vision (antihistamines); and allergic reactions

E. Stimulants

Indications: Attention-deficit/hyperactivity disorder (including those with mental retardation, fragile X syndrome, Tourette's disorder, head trauma, pervasive developmental disorder, or other comorbid disorders); narcolepsy; and adjunctive treatment in refractory depression

Table 5 (continued)

Side effects:	Decreased appetite; weight loss; abdominal pain; headache, insomnia, irritability, sadness and depression; mild increases in pulse rate and blood pressure; possible temporary suppression of growth (with long-term use); choreoathetosis (pemoline) and, rarely, tic disorders; and elevated liver functions tests (pemoline)

F. Antiepileptics

Indications:	Seizure control; bipolar disorder; adjunct treatment in major depressive disorder; and severe behavior problems (e.g., aggression and self-injury)
Side effects:	Sedation, weakness, dizziness, disturbances of coordination and vision, hallucinations, confusion, abnormal movements, nystagmus, slurred speech, and depression; blood abnormalities; gastrointestinal distress; skin rashes, alterations in pigmentation, and photosensitivity reactions; increased or decreased blood pressure and congestive heart failure; abnormalities of liver functions (sodium valproate, carbamazepine – rare); genitourinary tract dysfunction; coarsening of facial features, enlargement of the lips, gingival hyperplasia, and excessive hair growth (phenytoin); and bone marrow suppression (carbamazepine, sodium valproate)

G. Others

Propranolol

Indications:	Behavior disorders with severe aggression, self-injury, or agitation; Tourette's disorder; and akathisia
Side effects:	Decreased heart rate, peripheral circulation, and blood pressure; fatigue, weakness, insomnia, nightmares, dizziness, hallucinations, and mild symptoms of depression; shortness of breath and wheezing (especially in patients with asthma); gastrointestinal distress; and rebound hypertension on abrupt withdrawal

Clonidine

Indications:	Attention-deficit/hyperactivity disorder; Tourette's disorder; behavior disorders with severe aggression, self-injury, or agitation; adjunct treatment of schizophrenia and mania; and possible use in anxiety disorders
Side effects:	Sedation; decrease in blood pressure; rebound hypertension; dry mouth; confusion (with high doses); and depression

Guanfacine

Indications:	Attention-deficit/hyperactivity disorder and Tourette's disorder
Side effects:	Sedation (less than with clonidine); decrease in blood pressure (less than with clonidine); rebound hypertension; dry mouth; confusion (with high doses); and depression

Opioid antagonists

Indications:	Self-injury and reversal of narcotic depression
Side effects:	Drowsiness; dizziness, dry mouth, sweating; nausea, abdominal pain; and loss of energy

Fenfluramine

Indications:	Management of obesity and possible use in the control of some behavior problems in pervasive developmental disorder
Side effects:	Anorexia, weight loss; drowsiness, dizziness, confusion, headache, and incoordination; mood alterations, anxiety, insomnia, weakness, agitation, and slurred speech; gastrointestinal distress; increased or decreased blood pressure and palpitations; skin rashes; dry mouth; eye irritation; and muscle aches

Anticholinergics

Indications:	Treatment of extrapyramidal reactions (dystonia, rigidity, tremor, and akathisia); sleep disorders; and agitation
Side effects:	Sedation; cognitive impairment; and anticholinergic effects, including dry mouth, constipation, and blurred vision

What we know is that they interact with various neurotransmitters, such as the catecholaminergic, indolaminergic, cholinergic, and γ-aminobutyric acid systems. It is likely that they affect both the pre- and postneuronal receptors as well as the postreceptor activity of these neurotransmitters.

5.11.7.3.2 Indications

Lithium is currently indicated for the treatment of bipolar disorder, aggression, impulsivity, and temper tantrums in children (Alessi, Naylor, Ghaziuddin, & Zubieta, 1994). The drug works reasonably well in children with behavior problems which are characterized by impulsivity, aggressiveness, rage, or emotional lability (Popper, 1995). However, clinicians are cautioned that most of this understanding comes from clinical experience and not from double-blind, placebo-controlled studies. Carbamazepine and valproic acid are indicated for bipolar disorder and as an adjunct treatment in refractory MDD.

5.11.7.3.3 Dosing and adverse effects

The recommended starting dosage for lithium ranges from 10 to 30 mg/kg in divided doses once or twice a day. Although there are no empirical data on this, Spencer et al. (1995) suggest serum levels of $0.8–1.5$ mEq/L^{-1} for acute episodes of mania and $0.6–0.8$ mEq/L^{-1} for maintenance therapy. The dosage and serum level needs to be individualized for optimum effectiveness. Given the approximately 18 h elimination half-life, lithium may take 5–7 days to reach steady state (Alessi et al., 1994). Daily carbamazepine dose in children ranges between 10 and 20 mg/kg, given twice a day. The recommended starting dose of valproic acid is 15 mg/kg/day, which can be gradually titrated up to 60 mg/kg/day, given three times a daily.

The side effects of the antimanics are presented in Table 5.

5.11.7.4 Anxiolytics

The anxiolytics are used to treat pathological anxiety states. Two general classes of drugs, antidepressants (mainly the tricyclics and the MAOIs) and the antianxiety agents (most notably the benzodiazepines), are used to treat the various anxiety disorders seen in children (e.g., separation anxiety disorder, panic disorder, agoraphobia, school phobia, and generalized anxiety disorder). The benzodiazepines are also known as sedative-hypnotics because they act as hypnotics in high doses, as anxiolytics at moderate doses, and as sedatives in low doses. In general, the sedatives reduce daytime activity, temper excitement, and generally calm the child, and hypnotics produce drowsiness and facilitate the onset and maintenance of sleep. The following benzodiazepine drugs are currently labeled as antianxiety agents for use in the United States: chlordiazepoxide (Librium); clorazepate (Tranxene); diazepam (Valium); lorazepam (Ativan); oxazepam (Serax); prazepam (Centrax); halazepam (Paxipam); and alprazolam (Xanax). Flurazepam (Dalmante) and temazepam (Restoril) are two other benzodiazepine drugs but these are marketed for insomnia. Buspirone, a nonbenzodiazepine anxiolytic, is an azaspirodecanedione that lacks sedative, anticonvulsant, or muscle relaxant properties.

5.11.7.4.1 Mechanism of action

The benzodiazepines are closely associated with γ-aminobutyric acid (GABA), the most prevalent inhibitory neurotransmitter system in the brain (Zorumski & Isenberg, 1991). The recognition sites for GABA are coupled to chloride ion channels, and when GABA binds to its receptors, these channels open, thereby increasing the flow of chloride ions into the neurons. There are two subtypes of central nervous system benzodiazepine receptors, BZ_1 and BZ_2. The BZ_1 receptors are involved in the mediation of sleep, and the BZ_2 receptors are involved in cognition, memory, and motor control. Theoretically, a benzodiazepine hypnotic can have more affinity for one or the other receptor, thereby producing differential response.

The mechanism of action of buspirone does not involve interaction with a benzodiazepine-GABA receptor. It interacts with presynaptic dopamine receptors and with postsynaptic $5-HT_{1A}$ (serotonin) receptors, for which it is a partial agonist. However, despite its affinity for dopamine receptors, buspirone is not a neuroleptic and it does not have adverse effects or risk profile of neuroleptics.

5.11.7.4.2 Indications

The high-potency benzodiazepines (e.g., clonazepam [Klonopin], alprazolam [Xanax], lorazepam [Ativan]) are used in the treatment of anxiety disorders, as an adjunct in the treatment of refractory psychosis and mania, severe agitation, Tourette's disorder, severe insomnia, and major depressive disorder with anxiety. The atypical anxiolytic, buspirone (BuSpar), is also used for anxiety disorders and as an adjunct in the treatment of refractory OCD. It is also used the treatment of refractory OCD. It is also used for treating aggressive behaviors in children with mental retardation and autism.

5.11.7.4.3 Dosing and adverse effects

The recommended dosage for the long-acting, high-potency benzodiazepine (i.e., clonazepam) is a one to three times a day administration of a total daily dose of 0.01–0.04 mg/kg (Spencer et al., 1995). The short-/intermediate-acting, high-potency benzodiazepines are given three to four times a day because they present a higher risk for rebound and withdrawal reactions. In terms of total daily doses, alprazolam is 0.02–0.06 mg/kg, lorazepam is 0.04–0.09 mg/kg, and oxazepam is 0.05–1.7 mg/kg (Spencer et al., 1995). The total daily dose of buspirone ranges from 0.3 to 0.6 mg/kg.

The side effects of the anxiolytics are presented in Table 5.

5.11.7.5 Stimulants

Stimulants are probably the most widely used psychotropic drugs with children. They are sympathomimetic drugs that are structurally similar to the endogenous catecholamines. The most commonly used stimulants include dextroamphetamine (Dexedrine), methylphenidate (Ritalin), and magnesium pemoline (Cylert).

5.11.7.5.1 Mechanism of action

The stimulants act in the central as well as in the peripheral nervous system by blocking the reuptake of catecholamines into the presynaptic nerve endings and by blocking degradation of the nerve endings by the monamine oxidase enzyme. It is likely that each of the stimulants has a distinct mode of action and therefore have differential clinical effects. Indeed, the precise mechanism of action of these compounds is still poorly understood.

5.11.7.5.2 Indications

The stimulants are indicated for ADHD, ADHD with comorbid disorders, ADHD in children with developmental disabilities, and as adjunctive therapy for refractory depression. Generally, stimulants are effective in controlling the symptoms of ADHD, especially hyperactivity, impulsivity, distraction, and inattention (Barkley, DuPaul, & Costello, 1993). Further, they are effective in improving parent–child interactions, peer relationships, academic productivity, and classroom behavior (Barkley, 1990). However, academic achievement is minimally affected by the stimulants but they do enhance performance on measures of vigilance, impulse control, fine motor coordination, and reaction time.

5.11.7.5.3 Dosing and adverse effects

For the short-acting stimulants, the recommended daily dosage is 0.3–1.5 mg/kg for dextroamphetamine and 1.0–2.0 mg/kg for methylphenidate. The onset of action for these compounds is within 30–60 min, with peak clinical effect being evident for up to three hours. The longer-acting magnesium pemoline is given in a single daily dose of 1–3 mg/kg. At therapeutic doses, the onset of action for this drug is very rapid, producing a clinical response almost immediately. Generally, the stimulants are given with or after meals because of their anorexigenic effects. Because of increased risk of liver toxicity with pemoline, it is generally not considered a first-line stimulant medication.

The side effects of the stimulants are presented in Table 5.

5.11.7.6 Antiepileptics

There is increasing indication that carbamazepine, clonazepam, and valproic acid are being used alone and in combination with standard psychotropic medications to treat adults with various psychiatric disorders, such as mania, depression, treatment-resistant or atypical panic disorder, and bulimia, among others (Post, 1987). As discussed in Section, Au:X-ref.OK?, carbamazepine and valproic acid are used as alternative mood-stabilizing antimanic agents in children with bipolar disorders. Case reports and uncontrolled trials suggest that carbamazepine may be useful in treating ADHD, intermittent explosive disorder, aggressive disorders, conduct disorder, and some mood disorders in children (Carpenter & Vining, 1993). However, there are few well-controlled studies attesting to the efficacy of carbamazepine in childhood disorders (Evans, Clay, & Gualtieri, 1987; Remschmidt, 1976), and it has not been approved by the Food and Drug Administration for neuropsychiatric indications in children.

Antiepileptics have a history of use in the developmental disabilities, especially for controlling intractable behavior problems. The primary psychiatric use of antiepileptics in children with developmental disabilities is for affective disorders, such as mania, bipolar disorder, or schizoaffective disorder, particularly if these disturbances have been resistant to standard psychotropic medication. Early studies strongly suggested that phenytoin

(Dilantin) may have some behavioral effects on individuals with developmental disabilities, but these claims have not been validated in well-controlled studies (see Aman & Singh, 1991). Carbamazepine, valproic acid, and, to a much lesser extent, clonazepam are currently being used for this purpose (Ellis et al., 1997). Much remains to be done with regard to establishing the efficacy of the antiepileptics in childhood psychiatric disorders, their mechanism(s) of action, dosage, and adverse effects.

5.11.8 FUTURE DIRECTIONS FOR RESEARCH AND PRACTICE

It is clear that we have come far since Bradley's serendipitous finding of the effects of benzedrine on the behavior of children. For several decades, psychopharmacology of childhood disorders was a neglected area of clinical practice because of a lack of knowledge. Research in the field was almost nonexistent because of a shortage of well-trained researchers as well as a lack of adequate scientific methodologies for studying drug effects in children. Indeed, for many decades, our information on drugs and dosage was derived from the adult literature even though we knew that children are not miniature adults. Indeed, studies showing that, unlike adults, adolescents do not reliably respond better to tricyclic antidepressants than to placebo attests to the fact that we cannot ever again assume that the clinical and research findings with adults will also be true for adolescents. That this assumption is passé has been endorsed by the FDA which now requires that all drugs intended for children to be tested with children so that the effects of these drugs and dosages can be appropriately determined.

Since the mid-1980s, child and adolescent psychopharmacology has achieved the status of a field worthy of scientific study in its own right. Yet much remains to be achieved. In general, virtually every area of psychopharmacology of childhood disorders needs further research. Indeed, we know so very little about the pharmacokinetics and pharmacodynamics of most major psychoactive medications as they pertain to children. Because developmental factors play such an important role in the outcome of pharmacotherapy, we need research that takes into account the interaction between the child's developmental level, environment, and different classes of drugs.

As for pharmacogenetics, we know little about the effects of hereditary factors on drug response with regard to adult populations and almost nothing in children (Nebert & Weber,

1990). For example, most of our knowledge of drug effects is with white populations, yet the majority of the world's population is of other ethnic origins and there is very little data on the interaction between ethnicity and psychotropic drugs. Current research strongly suggests that, at least in adults, ethnicity accounts for some of the interindividual variations in drug response to many psychotropic and other drugs (Lin, Poland, & Nakasaki, 1993). It is timely for us to consider ethnic differences in pharmacokinetics and pharmacodynamics in child populations. Other factors that impact drug outcome, such as compliance and placebo effects, are also influenced by cultural beliefs and expectations. Because these sociocultural determinants of treatment outcome are also an important factor in psychological therapy, this provides clinical psychologists a unique opportunity to study the effects of these variables in both psychological and psychopharmacologic treatment.

A majority of children with mental health problems have comorbid psychiatric disorders (Achenbach, 1991b). Comorbidity presents interesting challenges to clinicians because not only does it have important implications for pharmacologic treatment, it also has implications for other therapies. Of interest is the use of targeted combined psychotropic drugs for comorbid disorders in children. While we have traditionally eschewed the use of polypharmacy, especially intraclass polypharmacy, our current thinking is that there is indeed a place for combined psychotropic treatments. However, much of this thinking is based on clinical experience and not on well-controlled outcome studies. Further, given that psychopharmacologic treatment is only one component of a treatment regimen that includes psychosocial as well as educational intervention, more research is needed to assess the individual, combined, and interactive effects of these treatments.

In terms of clinical practice, there has been growing interest in individualizing care within standardized treatment protocols. For example, clinicians and researchers have been developing psychopharmacologic treatment algorithms for the various childhood disorders (Vitiello, 1997; Walkup, 1995). These algorithms are based mainly on our clinical experience and take into account children with comorbid disorders as well as interindividual variations in drug response. Because these algorithms have been developed on the basis of global characteristics of children with specific disorders, it assumes that the physician will use good clinical judgement with individual cases based on thorough baseline assessments. Further, because these algorithms are multistep procedures, an empirical evaluation of a particular algorithm for a specific disorder will necessitate the evaluation of the entire algorithm rather than its component steps. This is an exciting development in child psychopharmacology as it integrates clinical practice and research, where the clinical concerns of the child drives the research protocol.

5.11.9 SUMMARY

Psychopharmacology of childhood disorders is a growing area of clinical practice and research. For most of its 60 years, childhood psychopharmacology has played second fiddle to adult psychopharmacology but this is rapidly changing. The biological revolution has affected both child and adult psychiatry equally. Further, experimental and clinical psychologists have brought to this field useful research methodologies that have anchored psychopharmacological research in the context of the child's life rather than just on the child's biology. However, much of our current knowledge is still based on experience rather than on science. While child psychopharmacology is both a science and an art, we are well short on the science.

5.11.10 REFERENCES

Achenbach, T. M. (1991a). *Manual for the CBCL/4-18 and profile.* Burlington, VT: Department of Psychiatry, University of Vermont.
Achenbach, T. M. (1991b). Comorbidity in child and adolescent psychiatry: Categorical and quantitative perspectives. *Journal of Child and Adolescent Psychopharmacology, 1,* 271–278.
Alessi, N., Naylor, M. W., Ghaziuddin, M., & Zubieta, J. K. (1994). Update on lithium carbonate therapy in children and adolescents. *Journal of the American Academy of Child and Adolescent Psychiatry, 33,* 291–304.
Aman, M. G. (1993). Monitoring and measuring drug effects. II. Behavioral, emotional, and cognitive effects. In J. S. Werry & M. G. Aman (Eds.), *Practitioner's guide to psychoactive drugs for children and adolescents* (pp. 99–159). New York: Plenum.
Aman, M. G., & Singh, N. N. (1988). *Psychopharmacology of the developmental disabilities.* New York: Springer-Verlag.
Aman, M. G., & Singh, N. N. (1991). Psychopharmacological intervention. In J. L. Matson & J. A. Mulick (Eds.), *Handbook of mental retardation* (2nd ed., pp. 347–372). New York: Pergamon.
Aman, M. G., Van Bourgondien, M. E., Wolford, P. L., & Sarphare, G. (1995). Psychotropic and anticonvulsant drugs in subjects with autism: Prevalence and patterns of use. *Journal of the American Academy of Child & Adolescent Psychiatry, 34,* 1672–1681.
Baldessarini, R., & Frankenburg, F. R. (1991). Clozapine: A novel antipsychotic agent. *New England Journal of Medicine, 324,* 746–754.
Ballenger, J. C., & Post, R. M. (1980). Carbamazepine in manic-depressive illness: A new treatment. *American Journal of Psychiatry, 137,* 782–790.
Barber, C. C., Rosenblatt, A., Harris, L. M., & Attkisson,

C. C. (1992). Use of mental health services among severely emotionally disturbed children and adolescents in San Francisco. *Journal of Child and Family Studies, 1,* 183–207.
Barkley, R. A. (1990). *Attention deficit hyperactivity disorder: A handbook for diagnosis and treatment.* New York: Guilford Press.
Barkley, R. A., DuPaul, G. J., & Costello, A. (1993). Stimulants. In J. S. Werry & M. G. Aman (Eds.), *Practitioner's guide to psychoactive drugs for children and adolescents* (pp. 205–237). New York: Plenum.
Barkley, R. A., & Cunningham, C. (1979). The effects of Ritalin on the mother–child interactions of hyperactive children. *Archives of General Psychiatry, 36,* 201–208.
Beardsley, R. S., Gardocki, G. J., Larsen, D. B., & Hidalgo, J. (1988). Prescribing of psychotropic medication by primary care physicians and psychiatrists. *Archives of General Psychiatry, 45,* 1117–1119.
Beasley, C. M., & Dornseif, B. E. (1991). Fluoxetine and suicide: A meta-analysis of controlled trials of treatment of depression. *British Medical Journal, 303,* 685–692.
Bradley, C. (1937). The behavior of children receiving benzedrine. *American Journal of Orthopsychiatry, 9,* 577–585.
Brotman, A. (1992). *Practical reviews in psychiatry.* Birmingham, AL: Educational Reviews.
Burton, T. M. (1991). Antidepressant drug of Eli Lilly loses sales after attack by sect. *Wall Street Journal, April 19,* A1–A2.
Cade, J. (1949). Lithium salts in the treatment of psychotic excitement. *Medical Journal of Australia, 36,* 349.
Carpenter, R. O., & Vining, E. P. G. (1993). Antiepileptics (anticonvulsants). In J. S. Werry & M. G. Aman (Eds.), *Practitioner's guide to psychoactive drugs for children and adolescents* (pp. 321–346). New York: Plenum.
Centers for Disease Control (1983). Valproate: A new cause of birth defects—Report from Italy and follow-up from France. *MMWR, 32,* 438–439.
Clein, P. D, & Riddle, M. A. (1995). Pharmacokinetics in children and adolescents. *Child and Adolescent Psychiatric Clinics of North America, 4,* 59–75.
Conners, C. K (1990). *Conners' rating scales manual, Conners' teacher rating scales, Conners parent rating scales. Instruments for use with children and adolescents.* North Tonawanda, NY: Multi-Health Systems.
Coyle, I., Wayner, M. J., & Singer, G. (1976). Behavioral teratogenesis: A critical evaluation. *Pharmacology, Biochemistry and Behavior, 4,* 191–200.
Cullinan, D., Epstein, M. H., & Sabornie, E. J. (1992). Selected characteristics of a national sample of seriously emotionally disturbed adolescents. *Behavioral Disorders, 17,* 273–280.
Cullinan, D., Gadow, K. D., & Epstein, M. H. (1987). Psychotropic drug treatment among learning-disabled, educable mentally retarded, and seriously emotionally disturbed students. *Journal of Abnormal Child Psychology, 15,* 469–477.
Cunningham, C., & Barkley, R. (1978). The effects of methylphenidate on the mother–child interactions of hyperactive identical twins. *Developmental Medicine and Child Neurology, 20,* 634–642.
DiMascio, A., Soltys, J. J., & Shader, R. I. (1970). Psychotropic drug side effect in children. In R. I. Shader & A. DiMascio (Eds.), *Psychotropic drug side effects* (pp. 235–269). Baltimore: Williams and Wilkins.
Dingemanse, J., Danhof, M., & Breimer, D. D. (1988). Pharmacokinetic-pharmacodynamic modeling of CNS drug effects: An overview. *Pharmacology and Therapeutics, 38,* 1–52.
Ellis, C. R., Singh, Y. N., & Singh, N. N. (1997). Use of behavior-modifying drugs. In N. N. Singh (Ed.), *Prevention and treatment of severe behavior problems: Models and methods in developmental disabilities*

(pp. 149–176). Pacific Grove, CA: Brooks/Cole Publishing Co.

Epstein, M. H., Cullinan, D., Quinn, K. P., & Cumbald, C. (1994). Characteristics of children with emotional and behavioral disorders in community-based programs designed to prevent placement in residential facilities. *Journal of Emotional and Behavioral Disorders, 2,* 51–57.

Epstein, M. H., Cullinan, D., Quinn, K. P., & Cumbald, C. (1995). Personal, family, and service use characteristics of young people served by an interagency community-based system of care. *Journal of Emotional and Behavioral Disorders, 3,* 55–64.

Evans, R. W., Clay, T. H., & Gualtieri, C. T. (1987). Carbamazepine in pediatric psychiatry. *Journal of the American Academy of Child and Adolescent Psychiatry, 26,* 2–8.

Evans, W. E., Schentag, J. J., & Jusko, W. J. (1986). *Applied pharmacokinetic principles of therapeutic drug monitoring* (2nd ed.). San Francisco: Applied Therapeutics.

Fava, M., & Rosenbaum, J. F. (1991). Suicidality and fluoxetine: Is there a relationship? *Journal of Clinical Psychiatry, 52,* 108–111.

Foxman, B., Valdez, R. B., & Brook, R. H. (1986). Childhood enuresis: Prevalence, perceived impact, and prescribed treatments. *Pediatrics, 77,* 482–487.

Gadow, K. D. (1981). Prevalence of drug treatment for hyperactivity and other childhood behavior disorders. In K. D. Gadow & J. Loney (Eds.), *Psychosocial aspects of drug treatment for hyperactivity* (pp. 13–76). Boulder, CO: Westview Press.

Garfinkel, B. D., & Amrami, K. K. (1992). Assessment and differential diagnosis of attention-deficit hyperactivity disorder. *Child and Adolescent Psychiatry Clinics of North America, 1,* 311–324.

Gates, D. (1987). Just saying no to Ritalin. *Newsweek, November 23,* 6.

Green, W. H (1995). *Child and adolescent clinical psychopharmacology* (2nd ed.). Baltimore: Williams and Wilkins.

Greenblatt, D. J., & Shader, R. I. (1987). Introduction: pharmacokinetics in clinical psychiatry and psychopharmacology. In H. Y. Meltzer (Ed.), *Psychopharmacology: The third generation of progress* (p. 1339). New York: Raven Press.

Hancock, L. (1996). Mother's little helper. *Newsweek March 18,* pp. 51–56.

Institute of Medicine (1990). *Research on children and adolescents with mental, behavioral, and developmental disorders.* Bethesda, MD: National Institutes of Mental Health.

Janicak, P. G., Davis, J. M., Preskorn, S. H., & Ayd, F. J. (1993). *Principles and practice of psychopharmacology.* Baltimore: Williams and Wilkins.

Johnson, P. (1988). Family: Remedy led to "hell." *USA Today, April 27.*

Kalow, W. (1990). Pharmacogenetics: Past and future. *Life Sciences, 47,* 1385–1397.

Kaplan, S. L., Simms, R. M., & Busner, J. (1994). Prescribing practices of outpatient child psychiatrists. *Journal of the American Academy of Child and Adolescent Psychiatry, 33,* 35–44.

Keller, M. B., Lavori, P. W., Beardslee, W. R., & Wunder, J. (1991). Depression in children and adolescents: New data on "undertreatment" and a literature review on the efficacy of available treatments. *Journal of Affective Disorders, 21,* 163–171.

Kovacs, M., Feinberg, T. L., Crouse-Novak, M. A., Paulauskas, S. L., & Finkelstein, R. (1984). Depressive disorders in childhood: A longitudinal prospective study of characteristics and recovery. *Archives of General Psychiatry, 41,* 229–237.

Kutcher, S. P. (1997). *Child and adolescent psychopharma-*

cology. Philadelphia: W. B. Saunders.

Kye, C., & Ryan, N. (1995). Pharmacologic treatment of child and adolescent depression. *Child and Adolescent Psychiatric Clinics of North America, 4,* 261–281.

Landrum, T. J., Singh, N. N., Nemil, M. S., Ellis, C. R., & Best, A. M. (1995). Characteristics of children and adolescents with serious emotional disturbance in systems of care. Part II: Community-based services. *Journal of Emotional and Behavioral Disorders, 3,* 141–149.

Landry, S. (1996). Uncertainty grows over use of Ritalin. *Richmond Times-Dispatch, March 28,* A2.

Lieberman, J. A., Kane, J. M., & Johns, C. A. (1989). Clozapine: Guidelines for clinical management. *Journal of Clinical Psychiatry, 50,* 329–338.

Lin, K. M., Poland, R. E., & Nakasaki, G. (1993). *Psychopharmacology and psychobiology of ethnicity.* Washington, DC: American Psychiatric Press.

Lipman, R. S. (1970). The use of psychopharmacological agents in residential facilities for the retarded. In F. J. Menolascino (Ed.), *Psychiatric approaches to mental retardation* (pp. 387–398). New York: Basic Books.

Maynard, R. (1970). Omaha pupils given "behavior" drugs. *Washington Post, June 29.*

McElroy, S. L., Keck, P., & Pope, H. G. (1987). Sodium valproate: Its use in primary psychiatric disorders. *Journal of Clinical Psychopharmacology, 7,* 16–24.

Moerman, D. E. (1979). Anthropology of symbolic healing. *Currents in Anthropology, 20,* 59–80.

Nebert, D. W., & Weber, W. W. (1990). Pharmacogenetics. In W. B. Pratt & P. Taylor (Eds.), *Principles of drug action* (pp. 469–531). New York: Churchill Livingstone.

Olfson, M., Pincus, H. A., & Sabshin, M. (1994). Pharmacotherapy in outpatient psychiatric practice. *American Journal of Psychiatry, 151,* 580–585.

Paxton, J. W., & Dragunow, M. (1993). Pharmacology. In J. S. Werry & M. G. Aman (Eds.), *Practitioner's guide to psychoactive drugs for children and adolescents* (pp. 23–55). New York: Plenum.

Popper, C. W. (1995). Balancing knowledge and judgement: A clinician looks at new developments in child and adolescent psychopharmacology. *Child and Adolescent Psychiatric Clinics of North America, 4,* 483–513.

Post, R. M. (1987). Mechanisms of action of carbamazepine and related anticonvulsants in affective illness. In H. Y. Meltzer (Ed.), *Psychopharmacology: The third generation of progress* (pp. 567–594). New York: Raven Press.

Remschmidt, H. (1976). The psychotropic effects of carbamazepine in non-epileptic patients, with particular reference to problems posed by clinical studies in children with behavioral disorders. In W. Birkmayer (Ed.), *Epileptic seizures, behavior, pain* (pp. 253–258). Bern: Hans Huber.

Riddle, M. A., Nelson, J. C., Kleinman, C. S., Rasmusson. A., Leckman, J. F., King, R. A., & Cohen, D. J. (1991). Sudden death in children receiving Norpramin: A review of three reported cases and commentary. *Journal of the American Academy of Child and Adolescent Psychiatry, 30,* 104–108.

Safer, D. J., & Krager, J. M. (1988). A survey of medication treatment for hyperactive/inattentive children. *Journal of the American Medical Association, 260,* 2256–2258.

Safer, D. J., & Krager, J. M. (1992). Effect of a media blitz and a threatened lawsuit on stimulant treatment. *Journal of the American Medical Association, 268,* 1004–1007.

Schou, M. (1990). Lithium treatment during pregnancy, delivery, and lactation: An update. *Journal of Clinical Psychiatry, 51,* 410–412.

Sherman, M., & Hertzig, M. (1991). Prescribing practices of Ritalin: The Suffolk County, New York study. In L. L. Greenhill & B. B. Osman (Eds.), *Ritalin: Theory and patient management* (pp. 187–193). New York: Mary Ann Liebert.

Silver, S. E., Duchnowski, A. J., Kutash, K., Friedman, R. M., Eisen, M., Prange, M. E., Brandenburg, N. A., & Greenbaum, P. E. (1992). A comparison of children with serious emotional disturbance served in residential and school settings. *Journal of Child and Family Studies, 1,* 43–59.

Singh, N. N., & Aman, M. G. (1990). Ecobehavioral assessment of pharmacotherapy. In S. Schroeder (Ed.), *Ecobehavioral analysis in developmental disabilities* (pp. 182–200). New York: Springer-Verlag.

Singh, N. N., Ellis, C. R., & Singh, Y. N. (1994). Medication management. In E. Cipani & F. Spooner ·(Eds.), *Curricular and instructional approaches for persons with severe handicaps* (pp. 403–423). Boston: Allyn & Bacon.

Singh, N. N., Ellis, C. R., & Wechsler, H. A. (in press). Psychopharmacoepidemiology in mental retardation. *Journal of Child and Adolescent Psychopharmacology.*

Singh, N. N., Guernsey, T. F., & Ellis, C. R. (1992). Drug therapy for persons with developmental disabilities: Legislation and litigation. *Clinical Psychology Review, 12,* 665–679.

Singh, N. N., Landrum, T. J., Donatelli, L., Hampton, C., & Ellis, C. R. (1994). Characteristics of children and adolescents with serious emotional disturbance in systems of care. Part 1: Partial hospitalization and inpatient psychiatric services. *Journal of Emotional and Behavioral Disorders, 2,* 13–20.

Singh, N. N., Parmelee, D. X., Sood, A., & Katz, R. C. (1993). Collaboration of disciplines. In J. L. Matson (Ed.), *Handbook of hyperactivity in children* (pp. 305–322). Boston, MA: Allyn & Bacon.

Singh, N. N., & Winton, A. S. W. (1989). Behavioral pharmacology. In J. K. Luiselli (Ed.), *Behavioral medicine and developmental disabilities* (pp. 152–179). New York: Springer-Verlag.

Sood, A., & Singh, N. N. (1996). Diagnostic instruments. In D. X. Parmelee (Ed.), *Child and adolescent psychiatry* (pp. 19–31). St. Louis, MO: Mosby.

Spencer, T., Wilens, T., & Biederman, J. (1995). Psychotropic medication for children and adolescents. *Child and Adolescent Psychiatric Clinics of North America, 4,* 97–121.

Sprague, R. L., & Werry, J. S. (1971). Methodology of psychopharmacological studies in the retarded. *International Review of Research in Mental Retardation, 5,* 147–219.

Stefl, M. E., Bornstein, R. A., & Hammond, L. (1988). *The 1987 Ohio Tourette survey.* Milford, OH: Tourette Syndrome Association of Ohio.

Stephen, K., Sprague, R. L., & Werry, J. (1973). *Drug treatment of hyperactive children in Chicago.* Urbana, IL: Children's Research Center.

Teicher, M. H., Glod, C., & Cole, J. O. (1990). Emergence of intense suicidal preoccupation during fluoxetine treatment. *American Journal of Psychiatry, 147,* 207–210.

Towbin, K. E. (1995). Evaluation, establishing the treatment alliance, and informed consent. *Child and Adolescent Psychiatric Clinics of North America, 4,* 1–14.

Viesselman, J. O., Yaylayan, S., Weller, E. B., & Weller, R. A. (1993). Antidysthymic drugs (antidepressants and antimanics). In J. S. Werry & M. G. Aman (Eds.), *Practitioner's guide to psychoactive drugs for children and adolescents* (pp. 239–268). New York: Plenum.

Vitiello, B. (1997). Treatment algorithms in child psychopharmacology research. *Journal of Child and Adolescent Psychopharmacology, 7,* 3–8.

Walkup, J. T. (1995). Clinical decision making in child and adolescent psychopharmacology. *Child and Adolescent Psychiatric Clinics of North America, 4,* 23–40.

Werry, J. S. (1993). Introduction: A guide for practitioners, professionals, and public. In J. S. Werry & M. G. Aman (Eds.), *Practitioner's guide to psychoactive drugs for children and adolescents* (pp. 3–21). New York: Plenum.

White, L. Tursky, B., & Schwartz, G. E. (1995). *Placebo: Theory, research and mechanisms.* New York: Guilford Press.

Zhou, H. H., Koshakji, R. P., Silberstein, D. J., Wilkinson, G. P., & Wood, A. J. (1989). Racial differences in drug response: Altered sensitivity to and clearance of propranolol in men of Chinese descent as compared with American whites. *New England Journal of Medicine, 320,* 565

5.12
Preventive Interventions

SUSAN H. SPENCE
University of Queensland, Brisbane, Qld, Australia

5.12.1 INTRODUCTION

The past decade has seen rapid developments in the area of prevention of psychopathology. Mental health policymakers and planners have gradually come to recognize the value of prevention rather than intervention after problems have become well established. The prevention of psychological problems is typically emphasized as a target of many mental health policies across the world (Spence, 1996a). The increased focus upon prevention is reflected in the numerous published studies that describe preventive programs in many parts of the world. The literature reveals a wide spectrum of preventive efforts, ranging from generic attempts to enhance psychological well-being to those that focus on prevention of specific psychological disorders or a particular high-risk group. Nevertheless, the funds spent by health care providers on prevention of psychopathology represent a very small proportion of the total mental health budget (Mrazek & Haggerty, 1994; Spence, 1996a). In consequence, the vast majority of mental health professionals focus their work upon the treatment of existing psychopathology, rather than upon its prevention.

There are many reasons why prevention of psychopathology makes sense. Although estimates vary considerably, epidemiological studies suggest that, in any given year, around 20–30% of adults (Robins & Regier, 1991) and 10–15% of children and adolescents (Department of Health and Human Services, 1991; Institute of Medicine, 1989) will exhibit a psychological problem of sufficient magnitude to interfere significantly in daily functioning and that meets diagnostic criteria for a clinical disorder. The cost to the community of psychological disorders is enormous. For example, in 1993 the cost of psychological disorders in Australia (with a population of around 17 million) was estimated as being between A$3 and A$6 billion per annum (Human Rights and Equal Opportunity Commission, 1993, p. 835). This figure included the cost of consultations with mental health professionals, hospitalization, medications, housing, and pension payments. Estimating the annual cost of mental illness, drug and alcohol abuse in the USA for 1990, Eisenberg (1995) and Mrazek and Haggerty (1994) cite evidence to suggest an overall cost to the community of US$212 billion. Thus, successful prevention of mental health problems would produce huge economic savings to the community, over and above the obvious benefits of reduced personal suffering.

5.12.2 APPROACHES TO PREVENTION

Before proceeding, it is important to discuss the various approaches to prevention and the terminology used to describe these methods. Traditionally, three levels of prevention were described, namely primary, secondary, and tertiary (Caplan, 1964). The first level of primary prevention referred to efforts to reduce the incidence of new cases through intervention before disorders occur. Secondary prevention referred to interventions that aimed to reduce the prevalence of disorders through early identification of established cases. Tertiary prevention referred to efforts to reduce the duration and degree of disability associated with an existing disorder, through treatment and prevention of relapse.

The disadvantage of the primary, secondary, and tertiary distinction was that it could be said that secondary and tertiary levels related more to treatment than to prevention. Only the primary level related specifically to intervention prior to the development of a disorder, but the term provided minimal information about the

type of intervention being used. More recently, the prevention literature adopted an alternative approach to classifying preventive efforts that provides more detail about the type of prevention approach (Gordon, 1987). Gordon proposed three types of preventive approaches based on the presence and extent of risk factors related to the development of the disorder of concern among individuals who did not already manifest a disorder. These approaches were labeled universal, selective, and indicated. Universal preventive interventions are those that are provided to entire populations. Selective prevention is targeted to those individuals who are members of a group, the membership of which places them at increased risk for the development of a mental disorders. Indicated prevention focuses on asymptomatic but high-risk individuals who are found to manifest a risk factor, condition, or abnormality that identifies them as being at high risk for the future development of psychopathology (Gordon, 1987).

Although the universal, selective, and indicated distinction represented an advance upon the primary, secondary, and tertiary approach, this method of categorization is still subject to criticism. Such an approach assumes that psychological disorders are discrete, present–absent phenomena. In reality, most forms of psychopathology lie on a continuum from mild or few symptoms to more severe and/or numerous symptoms. The decision to classify a person as experiencing a mental disorder depends on meeting some arbitrary cut-off for the number and severity of symptoms. Furthermore, early, mild symptomatology is a risk factor for later development of many forms of psychopathology. For example, conduct disorder in young people tends to develop along a trajectory in which early symptoms are predictive of later development of more severe symptomatology (Farrington, 1995). Once on this trajectory, many children show increasing levels of symptomatology with increasing age. Thus, indicated prevention must also target those individuals who show early, mild symptomatology that represents a risk factor for later development of a more serious psychological disorder. Any method of categorizing preventive interventions needs to take into account the continuum of psychological difficulties and the trajectory in the development of many disorders. Implicit in Gordon's (1987) approach to prevention is the assumption that evidence is available regarding risk factors for the development of mental disorders. Risk factors refer to biological, environmental, and psychological factors that increase the probability of development of a psychological problem. Effective prevention requires not only that we are able to identify risk factors for particular forms of psychopathology, but also that we have reliable and valid methods of identifying those individuals who manifest these risk features and that we have effective means of altering these variables. As described below, there is now considerable evidence regarding those factors that increase the risk of development of psychological problems. Similarly, evidence has shown that many of these variables can be changed effectively.

One further development that should be mentioned in the area of prevention is the focus not only on identification and alteration of risk variables but also on protective factors. Protective factors refer to those variables that produce a resilience to the development of psychological difficulties in the face of adverse risk factors. Clearly there are many young people who emerge from the face of adversity relatively well-adjusted and unaffected by the risk factors to which they have been exposed. Increasingly, research has focused on identifying variables associated with resilience which buffer the impact of risk factors. This shift in emphasis is important, as there are many risk factors that cannot be easily altered or removed, and an alternative or additional strategy for prevention is to build up protective factors.

5.12.3 RISK FACTORS

Efforts to identify causal factors relating to the development of child and adolescent psychopathology have yielded a great deal of information concerning risk and protective factors. This knowledge has emerged from longitudinal studies that allow us to entangle some of the interrelationships between psychopathology and the myriad of correlated variables that are associated with psychological disorders. Although we are a long way from fully understanding the etiological factors in child psychopathology, the evidence is sufficiently well developed to allow us to draw some tentative conclusions. These points are discussed in more detail below but can be summarized as follows:

(i) It is clear that child psychopathology results from a complex interaction of numerous environmental and intrinsic child variables.

(ii) There are many different sources of influence and no one factor is sufficient to account for any specific emotional and behavioral disorder.

(iii) Risk factors appear to have a multiplicative, not just additive effect so that the probability of developing a behavioral or emotional disorder increases considerably as the number of risk factors affecting a child increases.

(iv) Some risk factors are common to a wide range of emotional and behavioral disorders, whereas others have a more specific influence upon particular forms of psychopathology.

5.12.3.1 Genetic and Biological Factors

It is well established that parents with psychopathology are more likely than parents without psychopathology to have children who exhibit emotional and behavioral problems. Similarly, children with psychiatric disorders are more likely than their well-adjusted peers to have parents who meet diagnostic criteria for a mental disorder. These familial factors hold for internalizing and externalizing disorders alike (Rutter et al., 1990). However, such results tell us little about the relative contribution of genetic and family environmental factors to the development of psychopathology. Parental psychopathology is frequently associated with greater family stress, financial difficulties, marital discord, and poor parenting skills. Thus, in addition to genetic contributions, we must also consider the environmental influences that accompany parental psychopathology. Although strong familial associations are evident for childhood depression, anxiety, conduct disorder, and attention deficit disorder, the evidence has not yet clarified the degree to which these reflect genetic or environmental influences (Rutter et al.). It is only for disorders such as autism, multiple tics, Tourette's syndrome, bipolar disorder, and schizophrenia that strong genetic influences have been clearly established.

Research into the heritability of disorders such as depression, anxiety, and disruptive behavior problems have produced more conflicting results. Where genetic influences have been implicated for these disorders, it appears that heritability relates to a genetic predisposition to develop a range of psychological problems, rather than the heritability of a specific disorder such as anxiety or depression. Furthermore, where strong heritability influences have been found, it is not clear what is inherited. For example, it is possible that children inherit a particular temperament style or other intrinsic characteristics (e.g., learning disability) that predisposes them to develop a range of psychological problems.

In addition to genetic influences, there are a range of biological factors that are associated with increased prevalence of child psychopathology. These include prenatal, birth, and early childhood influences, such as poor pre- natal health care (including smoking and drug–alcohol abuse), preterm delivery, birth delivery complications, and toxins. Again the mechanism of action of these biological vari- ables is unclear. It is possible that these biological factors impact upon child psycho- pathology through their role in the development of learning disabilities, or irritable, difficult temperament style. Alternatively, it is possible that the crucial variables associated with the development of child psychopathology are correlates of the biological factors, rather than biological factors *per se*. For example, it is feasible that parents who engage in high-risk prenatal behaviors, and who are therefore at greater risk of premature births, are more likely to be those parents who subsequently show poor parenting skills. Thus, the causal factor in the development of child psychopathology could be poor parenting skills rather than premature birth. Researchers are still in the process of unraveling these complex causal relationships.

Although the evidence indicates genetic and biological influences upon many forms of child psychopathology, it is important to note that many children with a strong family history of mental disorder or exposure to biological risk factors do not proceed to develop psycho- pathology. Similarly, many children without a family history of psychopathology or exposure to biological trauma do develop emotional and behavioral disorders. Thus, we need to examine the other characteristics of family environments and individuals that may increase or decrease the risk of developing child psychopathology.

5.12.3.2 Family Environment

There are many family environment factors that increase the chance of developing emo- tional or behavioral problems. Many of these factors appear to increase the chance of developing a wide variety of psychological disorders, rather than any one form of psycho- pathology. This may explain the high level of comorbidity between behavioral disorders of children and adolescents. For example, one of the most frequently noted correlates of many forms of child psychopathology is socioeco- nomic disadvantage. However, in trying to identify risk factors, it is often difficult to determine whether a particular variable has a direct effect upon the development of psycho- logical problems or is simply correlated with some other variable that impacts upon psycho- pathology. We know that socioeconomic dis- advantage is associated with many factors such as poor housing conditions, poor educational

resources, unemployment, single-parent status, increased financial stress, parental psycho- pathology (particularly depression and drug– alcohol abuse), residential areas with increased crime rates and impoverished social and recreational facilities. These variables are, in turn, all associated with elevated rates of child psychopathology (Dodge, Pettit, & Bates, 1994). Efforts to control for these variables in longitudinal research suggest that economic disadvantage, unemployment and single–parent status while being correlates of child psycho- pathology may not have direct effects. Rather, evidence suggests that factors such as parental psychopathology and poor parenting skills are likely to be the mechanism through which societal factors have their influence upon emotional and behavioral problems of child- hood (Dodge et al., 1994; Patterson, 1996). Thus, many children from poor, unemployed, or single-parent families may emerge as rela- tively well-adjusted young people if the parents are mentally healthy and have strong parenting skills.

Parental anxiety, depression, and alcohol abuse have been shown to be associated with a range of child and adolescent mental health problems (Rutter et al., 1990). Typically, the association between these forms of parent disorder and child psychopathology is not limited to a specific disorder across generations. Rather, parental anxiety, depression, and sub- stance abuse is linked to a range of psycholo- gical problems in the offspring. It is important, therefore, that we determine the mechanisms through which parental psychopathology has its action. There is a complex interrelationship between the factors of parental psychopathol- ogy, marital discord, lack of partner support, divorce and separation, single-parent status, increased exposure to life stressors (e.g., financial hardship), poor parenting skills, and negative patterns of communication within the family. All these variables have been identified as risk factors for the development of child psychopathology (Mrazek & Haggerty, 1994; Spence, 1996a). It is difficult to tease apart these interrelationships. Parental psychopathology is likely to increase marital difficulties, and similarly marital problems may increase dis- orders such as depression, anxiety, and sub- stance abuse. Effective parenting is likely to decline when parents experience emotional problems, and the rate of negative communica- tions between parents and children is likely to increase (Dadds, in press). Marital conflict may lead to divorce and separation, and the financial and emotional stress that frequently accom- panies single-parent status. Such stressors place an additional strain upon effective parenting, and may also exacerbate parental psychopathology. Overall, a complex interplay between risk factors operates to increase the chance that a child will develop psychological difficulties. Evidence suggests that the crucial variables in this network are the parenting skills and communication patterns between parent and child which play a mediating role in determining the influence of parental psychopathology upon child behavior problems (Harnish et al., 1995).

The variables of poor parenting skills and negative family communication patterns have been associated with a range of child and adolescent problems, including conduct disorder (Dadds, in press), depression (Kaslow & Racusin, 1994), attention deficit disorder (Barkley, 1989), and anxiety disorders (Dadds, Barrett, & Rapee, 1996). For some families, poor parenting skills and negative communication patterns may reflect long-term skill deficits, rather than a response to life circumstances. In either case, preventive interventions should ensure the development and use of effective parenting skills and positive family communication patterns. It is important to note, however, that the direction of causality is not always a simple one in which aversive parental communication patterns cause problematic child behavior. There is some evidence that the relationship may be a reciprocal one in which difficult child behavior may trigger negative parenting responses (Barkley, 1989). Thus we need to take into account the reciprocal nature of influences between parent and child behavior.

Much of the research relating to parental behavior and child psychopathology has focused upon the development of conduct disorder. However, recent studies have also demonstrated that parental behavior is probably an important contributing factor in the development of children's anxiety and depression (Sanders, Dadds, & Barrett, 1995). To date, these studies have been cross-sectional or have involved retrospective reports from anxious or depressed adults about their parent's behavior. Thus, it is not possible to draw firm conclusions about the direction of causality. However, the evidence points towards a significant role of parental factors in the development of childhood anxiety and depression. Rapee (1997), in a recent review of the literature, concluded that anxiety in children was associated with over-controlling/overprotective parenting styles which inhibit the development of problem-solving skills in children and limits their developing sense of self efficacy. Faced with stressful or novel situations, these children are then more likely to experience anxiety. In contrast, Rapee (1997) concluded that depression in children is associated with excessively critical and negative communications from parents.

5.12.3.3 Negative Life Events

There have been many studies investigating the impact of negative and traumatic life events in children. The results have tended to produce conflicting findings. Generally, the evidence suggests that higher rates of emotional and behavioral difficulties are associated with exposure to major negative life events (Goodyer & Altham, 1991). However, many young people who experience major trauma, such as death of a parent, family break up, war, and disasters, do not go on to develop clinically significant psychopathology. For example, children vary markedly in their adjustment following parental divorce, with many children coping well with the transition (Amata & Keith, 1991; Forehand, 1992). In contrast, some children experience considerable adjustment problems, particularly if the postdivorce environment is characterized by ongoing fighting between parents (Hess & Camara, 1979). Thus, negative life events clearly do not, on their own, provide an adequate explanation for the development of child psychopathology. Rather, it appears that the impact of negative life events depends on the characteristics of the child and the additional impact of other negative environmental factors. Furthermore, we need to understand more about the mechanisms and processes through which negative life events influence child psychopathology. Factors which appear to reduce the negative impact of aversive life events on children include social support and problem-focused coping strategies of the child (Compas, 1987). We also need to consider the impact of negative life events, such as parental divorce or death of a parent, upon the parenting style of the major caretaker. Traumatic life events may set in place a sequence of changes which culminate in ineffective parenting behavior and impaired family communication patterns. Thus, the relationship between negative life events and child psychopathology may be mediated by parenting behavior of the child's caretaker. There is some evidence to support this proposition from studies of children who experience significant trauma. McFarlane (1987) demonstrated that a strong predictor of children's adjustment following a severe bushfire was the mother's level of overprotective parenting.

In some instances, factors may interact to exacerbate or trigger the negative impact of adverse life events. For example Rutter (1987) described the interaction effect of maternal loss combined with other major, negative life events. Maternal loss on its own did not produce an increased risk of psychopathology, but when combined with some other major negative life event, the combined factors produced a three-fold increase in the chance of developing depression, far exceeding the impact of major negative life events alone. These results also demonstrated the delayed impact of maternal loss, in that this factor created vulnerability to psychiatric disorder only later in life and only when combined with other direct risk variables.

5.12.3.4 Intrinsic Child Characteristics

In addition to the environmental risk factors of child psychopathology, it is important to consider the intrinsic characteristics of the child that place him or her at greater risk (Coie et al., 1993). Child temperament and intellectual functioning have been shown in many studies to be risk factors for the development of child psychopathology. An early childhood temperament characterized by irritability, high levels of crying, irregular sleep, and eating problems is predictive of externalizing behavior problems in later childhood (Prior, 1992). Temperament influences can also be identified for internalizing disorders. The work of Kagan and colleagues (Kagan, Reznick, & Gibbons, 1989; Kagan & Snidman, 1991) has been influential in identifying a relatively stable temperament style which they term "behavioral inhibition." The characteristic features of behavioral inhibition include initial timidity, shyness, withdrawal, distress, and emotional restraint when exposed to unfamiliar people, places, or contexts (Asendorpf, 1993). This behavioral pattern is associated with elevated physiological indices of arousal and has been shown to have a strong genetic component (Plomin & Stocker, 1989). Children who show a stable temperament style of behavioral inhibition are more likely to develop anxious behavior and anxiety disorders during childhood (Biederman et al., 1993; Hirshfeld et al., 1992; Rosenbaum et al., 1993).

Although the evidence points to a significant contribution of early childhood temperament to the development of psychopathology, Prior (1992) pointed out that not all children who show these temperament patterns will progress to show behavioral difficulties later in childhood. Thus, we need to explain how childhood temperament interacts with other personal and environmental characteristics to determine the occurrence of psychopathology. In particular, it is important to identify those parenting patterns which buffer the impact of a difficult early childhood temperament and those parenting factors which may exacerbate the influence of high-risk temperament characteristics.

Low IQ and learning difficulties have also been linked to the greater prevalence of a wide range of emotional and behavioral problems in children, including conduct disorder, attention deficit–hyperactivity disorder, and depression (Farrington, 1995). The mechanisms by which low IQ and learning difficulties have an impact upon psychopathology is unclear. It is possible that school failure and negative school experiences set in train a trajectory towards conduct problems, low self-esteem, and depression. Alternatively, the biological factors that underlie low IQ and learning difficulties could also be responsible for attention problems, impulsivity and "difficult" temperament for some children. A further possible explanation could lie in heritable characteristics through which the parents of children who have low IQ and learning problems may have restricted cognitive abilities and consequently poor parenting skills. Much more research is needed to determine the mechanisms by which low IQ and learning difficulties impact upon child psychopathology. Meanwhile, these variables should be regarded as risk factors towards which preventive interventions should be directed.

Children's cognitive style is a further intrinsic child characteristic that has been found to predict later psychopathology, with particular patterns and styles being associated with specific forms of psychopathology. For example, a pessimistic cognitive style for interpreting information has been shown to predict later depression in children (Jaycox, Reivich, Gillham, & Seligman, 1994). Although longitudinal studies have yet to be completed, cross-sectional studies have shown an association between a cognitive style characterized by increased attention to and interpretation of threat stimuli among clinically anxious children (Kendall, 1991). Similarly, aggressive children are characterized by a bias towards processing information in a confronting and threatening manner (Lochman & Dodge, 1994).

Early childhood behaviors that represent mild symptomatology have also been found to significantly predict later clinical levels of psychopathology. For example, many studies have shown that early aggressive behavior is the best single predictor of risk for later aggression and delinquency (Guerra, Huesmann, Tolan, & Van Acker, 1995; Loeber, 1990). Therefore, within the "high-risk" category of young people to whom preventive interventions could be directed, we must include children who show early behavior problems.

To summarize, there are clearly a wide range of environmental and intrinsic child characteristics that interact as risk factors to increase the chance of developing emotional and behavioral problems. The challenge for researchers is how to identify clusters of risk factors that collectively increase the chance of the development of psychological problems. Kazdin and Kagan (1994) pointed out that individual risk factors may have only a minimal effect on their own, but may have a multiplicative, interactive influence upon psychopathology. It is also important to determine why some individuals who experience particular risk factors do not progress to show psychological difficulties. For example, not all children who manifest a stable temperament of behavioral inhibition proceed to develop an anxiety disorder. Similarly, not all children who show a "difficult" irritable early temperament style go on to show disruptive behavior problems. Thus, it is likely that certain childhood temperaments interact with particular parenting practices to increase the chance of psychological difficulties. In the case of children with a temperament style of behavioral inhibition, it may be only those children whose parents are overprotective and overcontrolling who go on to show anxiety problems. Those initially behaviorally inhibited youngsters whose parents encourage them to experience new situations, and who model a calm, problem-focused coping style, may be less likely to show anxious, fearful behavior as they grow older (Spencer, 1996b). Therefore, future research needs to clarify the way in which risk factors interact to elevate the risk of developing child psychopathology.

5.12.4 PROTECTIVE FACTORS

Although we now have a great deal of knowledge concerning the risk factors for the development of psychopathology, many of these factors are extremely hard to change. High levels of family stress, bereavements, family break-ups, parental psychopathology, single-parent status, and socioeconomic disadvantage, while important targets for reduction, are likely to continue to occur with relatively high frequency in our communities. Thus, it is important to identify those factors that protect children from the adverse consequences of such risk factors. We do know that many children emerge from high-risk environments without showing emotional and behavioral disorders. However, only recently have researchers started to investigate systematically those protective influences that produce a resilience against adverse risk factors. Moreover, Rutter (1987)

discussed confusion within the literature regarding what is meant by protective or resilience factors. He pointed out that many of the variables that had been proposed as protective factors merely represented the opposite end of continuum of a risk factor. For example, generally a high level of parenting skills, high intellectual functioning, and high socioeconomic status have been found to be associated with low levels of risk. Rutter proposed that protective factors do not refer to these opposite poles of risk factors, but rather they relate to variables that reduce the impact of a risk factor upon the development of psychopathology, instead of or in addition to having a direct effect of its own. Protective factors also include events which produce a turning point in a trajectory in the development of psychopathology towards a more adaptive long-term outcome.

Although the research is in its infancy, we can make some tentative suggestions about protective factors. Within the family, secure and harmonious parent–child relationships, social support from elders and peers, and a structured, coherent family environment have been shown to buffer the negative impact of social adversity (Rutter, 1987). Parental supervision and regulation of childrens' peer group activities outside the home have also been identified as factors that reduce the risk of delinquency for children reared in a high-risk environment (Patterson & Stouthamer-Loeber, 1984).

There are also intrinsic child characteristics that appear to serve a protective function against the development of a wide variety of emotional and behavioral problems. These include positive self-concept and a range of skills (problem solving, planning, skills to remove oneself from the risk environment, social skills), and academic success (Rutter, 1987; Werner, 1987). In a recent study, O'Donnell, Hawkins, and Abbott (1995) identified several factors that appeared to inhibit the risk of subsequent involvement in serious delinquency in a sample of boys who were identified as aggressive by teacher report at ages 10–11 years. Measures were taken at ages 12–13 years of prosocial skills, school achievement and bonding, norms against substance abuse, and interaction with adults and peers who were involved in antisocial behavior. These factors significantly discriminated between boys who were and were not involved in serious delinquent behavior one year later.

If we are able to identify protective factors, it is important that we examine the processes through which these variables modify the impact of risk factors. Again, the research is in its infancy, but we can speculate about likely mechanisms. For example, Rutter (1987) reported that children with "easy" temperaments are less likely to be scapegoated or become the targets for parental criticism and negative communication, thereby reducing the negative impact of risk factors such as parental depression or marital discord. Similarly, adolescents with strong planning skills were less likely to have teenage pregnancies nor to enter into marriage with a dysfunctional partner, thereby reducing the negative impact of early institutional care (Rutter, 1987). We can also speculate that children with good social skills are more likely to develop positive relationships with supportive parents, teachers, and peers, providing a buffer against a range of risk factors.

5.12.5 IMPLICATIONS FOR PREVENTION

Our knowledge regarding risk and protective factors for the development of psychopathology provides an indication as to the variables that should be targeted in preventive interventions. Effective prevention of child psychopathology requires not only that we are aware of risk and protective factors, but that effective methods are available for producing change in these variables. The evidence regarding risk and protective factors suggests that there are some variables that impact upon the development of a wide range of emotional and behavioral problems. However, many of these factors are difficult to change. For example, current technology does not permit alteration of genetic influences. Similarly, many children in our society will continue to be exposed to situations that place them at increased risk of psychopathology, such as parental mental illness, divorce, abuse, marital conflict, death of a parent, and other negative life events. Although an important goal for prevention is to reduce children's exposure to such high-risk situations, inevitably a significant number of children will still experience these adverse life circumstances. For these children, the aim of prevention must be to reduce the impact of risk factors by increasing childrens' coping skills and enhancing parenting skills.

There are many practical difficulties that lie in the way of the implementation of preventive programs. Frequently the families who could most benefit from preventive interventions are those who are most difficult to access in terms of willingness and ability to participate in the program. The children most at risk are likely to be living within impoverished life circumstances or within families who are experiencing significant stress (e.g., parental psychopathology, bereavements, single-parent status, and family

break-up). The evidence reviewed above suggests that two crucial factors that mediate the impact of environmental risk factors upon many forms of child psychopathology are parenting skills and parent–child communication patterns. Thus, it makes sense to suggest that training in parenting and family communication skills should be fundamental components of effective prevention. One of the goals of preventive programs must therefore be to identify ways of engaging parents from high-risk groups. The evidence also suggests that there are a range of intrinsic child variables that may mediate or moderate the impact of risk factors in the development of child psychopathology. A further approach to prevention may therefore be to focus on the development of protective factors in children. For example, programs could focus on the teaching of problem solving, planning, social, coping, and academic skills, all of which have been identified as protective factors. Similarly, it may be feasible to develop positive, supportive social networks with other key adults in the child's life, as a further protective factor.

The evidence regarding risk factors also suggested that the probability of developing psychological problems increases markedly as the number of risk factors increased. Indeed, there is some indication that this is not simply an additive effect, but rather the probability of developing psychopathology increases multiplicatively with increasing numbers of risk factors (Coie et al., 1993). This suggests that children most at risk will be those who experience multiple risk factors. Policymakers and mental health planners need to decide where best to invest funds in preventive programs. So far, there are many unanswered questions.

(i) Is it more cost-effective to focus preventive efforts on the few children with multiple risk factors, or upon a larger number of children with only one or two risk factors?

(ii) For children with multiple risk factors, are intensive interventions that tackle multiple etiologies required in order to prevent psychopathology, or can prevention with these children be achieved by tackling only one or two risk or preventive factors?

(iii) Should children be singled out for prevention programs through some process of assessment or identification, or should prevention be applied to whole populations in order to avoid specific targeting and potential effects of labeling?

(iv) Should preventive funds be invested in efforts to minimize one single disorder or, given the many common etiologies across disorders, into broad-spectrum projects that aim to prevent multiple forms of psychopathology?

(v) Are prevention programs best geared towards efforts to minimize environmental risk factors, or to providing children with the skills to cope with adverse life circumstances?

(vi) To which age group should preventive efforts be directed; to older children who are more able to understand the concepts being taught, or to younger children who have been exposed to risk factors for a shorter period of time?

Certainly, there are more questions than answers.

5.12.6 THE EFFECTIVENESS OF PREVENTIVE PROGRAMS

Prevention programs come in many forms and evaluative studies have suffered from a wide range of methodological limitations, making it difficult to draw general conclusions about their effectiveness. Some programs have taken a broad population approach, whereas others have targeted a specific high-risk group. The goal of prevention for some interventions has been general enhancement of mental health, whereas others have aimed to prevent some specific disorder. It is beyond the scope of this chapter to provide extensive descriptions of the many preventive interventions that have been reported in the literature and interested readers are referred to Mrazek and Haggerty (1994) for a more detailed review. What follows is a summary of some of the major preventive studies, as a means of illustrating some of the key points within the prevention area. In keeping with current methods of categorization, the following review will divide preventive interventions into three main types: universal, selective, and indicated approaches. The literature describing preventive interventions varies markedly in terms of the methodological rigor of evaluation methods. Some studies are simply descriptive or report case illustrations. Others have used quasi-experimental designs, with weak control procedures and/or lack of random assignment to conditions. We also need to bear in mind that selective publishing is likely to occur, with studies that produce positive, significant findings possibly being more likely to reach publication status. Nevertheless, there is convincing evidence within the literature to suggest that some interventions have been effective in preventing, or at least attenuating, the development of child psychopathology.

5.12.6.1 Universal Preventive Interventions

Universal interventions are those that are applied to whole populations. In some in-

stances, universal preventive interventions have been designed to enhance general mental health, whereas others have targeted one specific disorder such as conduct disorders, anxiety, depression, or substance abuse. The majority of universal preventive projects have been applied within school settings. For example, Kellam and Rebok (1992) described two classroom-based interventions that were designed to enhance children's reading skills and prosocial behavior as a means of preventing subsequent conduct and substance abuse problems. Preparatory research had identified reciprocal relationships between children's academic achievement and shy, depressive, and aggressive behavior. The first intervention involved a Mastery Learning curriculum for the enhancement of reading skills. The second intervention was based on the Good Behavior Game that consisted of a team-based, behavior management approach targeted at reducing aggressive behavior. In trials across 19 schools in Baltimore, Kellam, Rebok, Ialongo, and Mayer (1994) reported that the Good Behavior Game had a short-term impact upon aggression, but no direct or indirect impact upon academic achievement. In contrast, the Mastery Learning approach had a direct effect upon enhanced academic achievement, but also produced an indirect reduction in aggressive behavior. The longer term results from first grade intervention upon behavior at sixth grade revealed interesting results. Although there were no overall significant benefits of the Good Behavior Game in comparison to control children, a differential response was found for different groups of children. For males, those who showed the highest rates of aggression in first grade showed the greatest benefit from the Good Behavior Game at sixth grade follow-up. However, the approach was not effective in preventing children who were not aggressive in first grade from subsequently developing problems of aggression. These findings suggest that classroom-based behavior management approaches may offer promise in the prevention of aggressive behavior in children who manifest early disruptive behavior problems.

Reductions in conduct disorder and substance abuse are also goals of the Seattle Social Development Project. This intervention is based on the theoretical premise that strong bonds to family and school serve as protective factors against delinquency and drug abuse. Increases in feelings of attachment, commitment, and beliefs regarding participation in undesirable behavior are considered to be important aspects of the protective process. The project involves a multicomponent, universal preventive intervention that includes teacher training in classroom management and instructional methods, class-based interpersonal problem solving skills, training sessions, and a parent training component (Hawkins et al. 1992). The effects of the program were evaluated in schools within high crime areas. Those children who received the intervention were less likely to have initiated delinquent behavior and alcohol use, and showed higher school achievement four years after participating in the project, in comparison to children from schools or classrooms that did not receive the intervention.

Not all universal preventive studies have focused on conduct disorder as the outcome goal. In some instances the aim has been to prevent the onset of internalizing problems such as depression. For example, Clarke, Hawkins, Murphy, and Sheeber (1993) described two very brief preventive interventions for adolescent depression, neither of which produced significant benefits. Both interventions were conducted with a large number of youngsters within the context of regular classroom education. The first intervention involved three, 50 minute sessions of educational intervention, over three consecutive days, covering the nature of depression, its treatment, the benefits of seeking treatment when needed, and the need to increase pleasant events. No specific behavioral skills were trained. The intervention group was compared with a group of youngsters attending the usual health education class. The intervention had little impact on depressive symptoms for girls, and boys showed a small short-term improvement which was not maintained at 12 week follow-up. In the second intervention, Clarke et al. (1993) altered the program so that it involved five, 50 minute sessions. The first session included a shortened educational component covering the symptoms, causes, and treatments of depression. The remaining four sessions involved a behavioral program to increase participation in pleasant events. No significant benefits were found for either the sample as a whole, or for those adolescents with initial high levels of depression.

The poor results of these programs may make us pessimistic about the value of universal interventions in the prevention of depression among adolescents. However, such a conclusion may be premature. Clarke et al. (1993) criticized their own programs for failing to include a skills training component to rectify those skills deficits (e.g., social skills deficits) associated with depression in young people. In addition, the studies were excessively brief and the follow-up period of 12 weeks was too short to detect long-term benefits. Clarke et al. (1993) proposed that future prevention studies should focus on those factors that have been demonstrated to be

risk factors for the development of depression, such as poor social and interpersonal problem-solving skills, overly critical self-evaluation, low rates of self-reinforcement, and pessimistic thinking style.

Drug and alcohol abuse have been the targets of several preventive interventions. Price (1995) provided a valuable outline of the issues facing researchers and practitioners working in this area. Price discussed a variety of approaches to prevent substance abuse, including school-based, family-focused, and media-based programs. The prevention of substance abuse highlights the many different perspectives that can be taken. For example, substance use is influenced by economic factors such as the availability and price of drugs and alcohol. One approach to reducing substance abuse is therefore to manipulate the supply and cost of substances. Of course, this action could also produce negative side effects relating to criminal activities that may act as a means of obtaining money to purchase drugs. Thus, no simple solutions are presented. Although we are still a long way from finding solutions to the prevention of substance abuse in young people, preliminary studies of universal interventions are emerging that provide some encouraging findings relating to the prevention of early stage substance use, such as tobacco smoking (e.g. Caplan et al., 1992; Ellickson & Bell, 1990; Perry et al., 1989).

5.12.6.2 Selective Preventive Interventions

Selective prevention efforts are applied to those individuals who are members of a group, the membership of which places them at increased risk for the development of mental disorders. Over the past 20 years preventive interventions have been applied to a wide range of high-risk groups, focusing on parents and families who are dealing with major life transitions and/or high-risk situations. These include groups characterized by parental psychopathology, premature births, single parents, socioeconomic deprivation, teenage pregnancies, divorce, bereavement of a close family member, exposure to trauma and school transitions.

5.12.6.2.1 Children exposed to socioeconomic deprivation

Several preventive programs have been targeted towards children from high-risk geographical areas with elevated levels of poverty and societal risk factors. In some instances these studies have used random assignment and control groups in order to determine the long-term efficacy of the interventions. For example, Olds, Henderson, Tatelbaum, and Chamberlin (1988) described the Prenatal/Early Infancy Project which aimed to reduce mothers' health-damaging prenatal behaviors (i.e., diet and substance abuse), enhance parenting skills, and provide social support, assistance with continuing education, and contraceptive counseling. Women who received home nurse visitation during pregnancy and until the child was two years old showed significant reductions in preterm births and verified cases of child abuse in comparison to women who did not receive such an active intervention. A home visiting approach was also beneficial in the Early Intervention for Preterm Infants project (Field, Widmayer, Stringer, & Ingatoff, 1980) in enhancing physical and cognitive development among preterm babies born to young, single mothers from low socioeconomic backgrounds. This program focused on teaching mothers about caretaking practices and enhancing parent–infant interactions. Home visiting plus preschool developmental activities have also produced positive results in terms of physical and cognitive development of low birth weight babies (Kraemer & Fendt, 1990).

Some programs have included a wider spectrum of intervention approaches, of which home visiting is just one component. Lally, Mangione, Honig, and Wittner (1988), in a quasi-experimental design, demonstrated that a home visiting approach, in association with child care and early educational enrichment was associated with significant reductions in delinquent behavior at 10 year follow-up. This project involved primarily low-income, single mothers who participated in the intervention from the last trimester of pregnancy through to age five of the child. Home visiting is also an important focus within the recently established Better Beginnings, Better Futures Project in Ontario, Canada, that is aimed at families in socioeconomically disadvantaged areas. This project involves a series of programs, some of which include home visiting as a component. Other aspects of the project include classroom enrichment for teaching of academic and social skills, child care enrichment, parent training, parent support groups, and increasing community resources (Peters & Russell, 1994). The Healthy Start in Hawaii service is also worth mentioning here (US Advisory Board on Child Abuse and Neglect, 1990, cited in Mrazek & Haggerty, 1994). This service was not established as a research study but as a community intervention to reduce child abuse and neglect. The program is designed to identify at-risk children in the first three months of life and aims

to screen around 90% of the total population. Following early identification, families are allocated a lay-person home visitor, linkage to a primary health care service, parent education, and child care services. Since the establishment of the Healthy Start program, there has been a gradual decrease in child abuse and neglect cases in Hawaii, although it must be noted that there are no empirical control groups with which to compare the current rates of abuse and neglect of those families who received the intervention.

There are many other programs that have included home visiting as part of their intervention. Other components of multifaceted interventions have included parent education classes, preschool/nursery school facilities to promote social and academic skills, and home-based social and cognitive skills training (e.g., Houston Parent–Child Development Center, Johnson, 1991; Mother–Child Program of Verbal Interaction, Levenstein, 1992). These studies demonstrated that preventive interventions can be effective in enhancing the social and cognitive skills of children from socioeconomically deprived backgrounds. One of the most well-known, preventive projects is the Perry Preschool Program that combined home visiting and intensive preschool education. This selective intervention focused on children and their families who experienced severe poverty and included daily preschool attendance for two years and weekly home visiting by a trained teacher. Long-term follow-ups showed superior academic performance and social adjustment and lower rates of delinquent behavior through to late adolescence, compared to the randomly assigned control group (Berruteta-Clement, Schweinhart, Barnett, Epstein, & Weikart, 1984; Schweinhart, 1987).

Some studies have focused preventive efforts upon school-based interventions, with minimal involvement of parents. For example, Shure and Spivack (1980, 1982, 1988) reported the benefits of an interpersonal problem-solving program that was delivered to small groups of preschool children from economically deprived families. The curriculum ran over approximately three months, and involved several lessons per week to teach problem-solving skills. Children who received the intervention were reported to show enhanced social competence and lower rates of behavior problems in comparison to untrained control children. However, whether preschool interventions of this sort will be beneficial in producing long-term improvements through to adolescence remains to be demonstrated.

In summary, there are now a wide range of evaluative studies demonstrating that preventive interventions can be effective in enhancing social adjustment and decreasing psychopathology (particularly conduct disorder) in children from socioeconomically impoverished backgrounds. However, it is important to note that many of these studies involved relatively small numbers of families and very large numbers of intervention hours. Some studies required a very large investment of time from parents which precluded inclusion of those who were in employment. Furthermore, many studies do not report the cost of the intervention per family. Clearly, the cost of providing weekly home visits for 3–5 years, in addition to daily preschool facilities with low staff–child ratios, is enormous. Thus, although these interventions can clearly produce significant benefits, it remains to be determined whether it is feasible in financial and practical terms to apply such intensive interventions on a large-scale basis. A further problem in existing studies is the relatively high drop-out rate that is often reported, particularly from families with high levels of mobility. Thus, it is important to take into account the drop-out problem in interpreting the results of existing studies, and that efforts are put in place to maximize retention rates in future interventions.

5.12.6.2.2 *Assisting children to deal with school transition*

Children are required to deal with many changes throughout their lives, but the transition to a new school is suggested to be one of the most stressful (Soussignan, Koch, & Montagner, 1988). Children are required to adapt to different physical, social, and academic environments, with new sets of rules and regulations. Not surprisingly, many children find the transition very difficult and a variety of behavior problems have been linked with school transitions. These include peer relationship difficulties, school refusal, somatic complaints, academic failure, increased substance abuse, delinquency, and school drop-out (Hightower & Braden, 1991).

As a means of preventing adjustment problems associated with transition to secondary school, Felner and Adan (1988) developed the School Transition Environment Project (STEP). The STEP program consists of three components. The first organizes the physical plan of the school into units with home rooms in order to facilitate familiarity with the school environment. Children allocated to the program attend core academic subjects together in these home rooms. This process is suggested to make the school transition less overwhelming and stressful to incoming students. The second aspect of STEP includes a "home room" staff

member who has the responsibility for taking the daily attendance list, following up non-attendances, and counseling of pupils regarding academic or school adjustment problems. The final component involves a coordinated liaison between teaching and school counseling staff. The overall aims of the program are to increase personal relationships between pupils and staff and to create subenvironments within the overall large school environment.

Evaluations of the STEP approach have demonstrated that children who participated in the program showed greater improvements in academic performance and self-esteem, better school attendance, and lower school drop-out rates compared to control children who did not take part (Felner & Adan, 1988). Furthermore, the benefits have been replicated in a variety of different school settings with children from various social backgrounds. Overall, the approach appears to be a valuable method of reducing problems associated with school transition and provides a model which could be routinely adopted by school authorities.

5.12.6.2.3 *Children of parents with psychiatric disorders*

Given the convincing evidence that parental psychopathology is a risk factor for the development of psychological problems among children and adolescents, it is not surprising that researchers and practitioners are beginning to examine the value of applying preventive interventions with children of mentally ill parents. To date, however, there are few controlled evaluations to determine the effectiveness of such efforts. There is a strong theoretical case to suggest that preventive efforts should be directed towards the children of parents who experience chronic problems of depression, anxiety or psychosis. In particular, it is important that these parents are taught to use positive parenting skills and that support mechanisms are put in place to increase the chance that parents will continue to use these skills during episodes of psychological problems. However, we must also acknowledge that the children who live with a mentally ill parent may also need to learn coping and survival skills to assist them in dealing with traumatic life circumstances and phases of poor parenting. In one of the few experimental evaluations of a prevention program with children of severely depressed parents, Beardslee, Salt, Porterfield, and Rothberg (1993) reported positive results for two approaches. The first intervention involved a clinician-led psychoeducational method, whereas the second approach was lecture-based. However, as the study did not include a no-intervention comparison group, it is difficult to draw firm conclusions about the benefits of the interventions. Clearly, there is an urgent need for methodologically rigorous examinations of preventive efforts with children of mentally ill parents.

5.12.6.2.4 Children who have experienced trauma

Some aversive events occur unexpectedly and are of sufficient magnitude that they constitute a traumatic experience to children. Such traumas include environmental disasters (e.g., earthquakes, war, storms, or fires), serious accidents, and death of a close family member. Family break-up through parental separations and divorce could also be regarded as a traumatic event, although this area is covered separately below. There is now considerable evidence that children who experience traumatic events are at increased risk of developing emotional and behavioral problems. For example, following trauma, children show increased levels of fears relating to stimuli associated with the traumatic event, avoidance behaviors, somatic complaints, depression, sleep disturbance, and intrusive thoughts and images (Dollinger, 1986; Dollinger, O'Donnell, & Staley, 1984; Terr, 1981; Yule & Williams, 1990). Although such problems ameliorate relatively quickly for most children, a significant proportion of children show persistent anxiety symptoms for many months after the trauma (Terr, 1981). There is therefore a strong case for rapid intervention following trauma in order to prevent the development of persistent psychological problems.

Although much has been written about the need for interventions to prevent long-term psychological difficulties following trauma in children, we still have very little empirical evidence to permit us to determine the most effective approaches to prevention. Sugar (1989) emphasized the need for initial interventions with the parents of children who experience a traumatic event, given the evidence that parent reaction plays a highly significant role in determining child response (McFarlane, 1987). In large-scale disasters which affect whole communities, Sugar (1989) also stressed the need for community counseling and crisis-oriented group approaches in order to provide mutual support, decrease isolation and provide a larger perspective for the individual. Sugar pointed out, however, that the cornerstone of therapy should be individual counseling with children, which takes into account their developmental level and specific details of the traumatic situation experienced. The approach

taken to intervention should therefore be tailored to the needs of each child.

A variety of approaches have been used in what is commonly termed the "debriefing" of trauma victims. Yule (1991) suggested that this procedure should commence somewhere between 7 and 14 days following the event, with most survivors being too numb to benefit from counseling prior to this time. Nevertheless, Yule acknowledged that there is a lack of data to validate this proposal and we really do not know what type of intervention should best be used nor at what time after the occurrence of a traumatic event. Yule (1991) proposed a theory-driven approach to trauma counseling with children, based on Rachman's (1980) model of emotional processing which emphasized the need for vivid and prolonged exposure to disaster-related cues in order to facilitate emotional processing. Children may be trained in relaxation skills and gradually exposed to stimuli and memories relating to the trauma event. They are encouraged to describe their reactions and given reassurance that such reactions are understood and are a normal response to an abnormal experience.

To date, there is a lack of controlled experimental evaluations to enable us to identify the most effective means of preventing child psychopathology following trauma. There are many case studies and descriptive reports in the literature, but we now need carefully designed experimental evaluations.

5.12.6.2.5 Children whose parents separate or divorce

Parental divorce has been suggested to represent one of the most common and severe life stressors that confront children and adolescents (Hightower & Braden, 1991; Hodges, 1991). For some children, the emotional consequences may include depression, anger, disruptive behavior, anxiety and/or withdrawal, particularly in the first two years following the divorce or separation (Hess & Camara, 1979). Fortunately, evidence suggests that many children adapt well following family break-ups (Amata & Keith, 1991; Forehand, 1992). To a large extent, the adverse emotional consequences of parental separation and divorce are influenced by the quality of the relationships of the family members involved (Hess & Camara, 1979). Hess and Camara (1979), for example, reported that the negative effects of divorce were considerably less when positive relationships between the parents were maintained. Positive relationships between the child and both the custodial and the noncustodial parents were also found to be important in protecting the child from the negative effects of divorce. This study highlighted the importance of government and social service policies that facilitate positive relationships between ex-partners following separation and divorce. Mediation may be beneficial in reducing disputes between parents regarding custody, access, and property settlements.

We need to be able to identify those children who are most at risk of developing adverse reactions to parental divorce and separation and target preventative programs in their direction. Several programs have been developed for use with children whose parents have recently divorced (e.g., Hodges, 1991; Pedro-Carroll & Cowen, 1985). Pedro-Carroll and Cowen outlined the Children of Divorce Intervention Project (CODIP) which was developed for use on a small group basis within schools. The project aimed to prevent or ameliorate academic, behavioral, and emotional problems that children often experience during or after their parents' divorce. Components of the program included: (i) development of a supportive group environment; (ii) facilitation of the identification and expression of divorce related feelings; (iii) promotion of understanding of divorce-related concepts and rectifying misconceptions; (iv) teaching of coping skills, including social problem-solving skills; and (v) enhancement of children's positive perceptions of themselves and their families. The program involved 12–16 sessions, with methods including discussion, role-play, skills training, and home-based tasks.

Evaluations of the program demonstrated its effectiveness in producing reductions in anxiety, fewer behavioral problems, greater gains in school competencies, decreased feelings of self-blame, and better ability to solve divorce-related problems in comparison to children of divorce who did not participate in the project. Follow-up information suggested that the benefits were maintained for the majority of children at two years follow-up, although only around half the children continued to show the gains they had made over the comparison group at three year follow-up. Although independent replications using this approach are required, the CODIP program appears to offer promise in the prevention of adverse psychological consequences in children following parental divorce.

5.12.6.2.6 Children who show multiple risk factors

In view of the convincing evidence that risk factors have a multiplicative effect, not just an additive one, there is a strong case for focusing preventive efforts on young people who show a combination of risk factors. For example, Dishion and Andrews (1995) reported a study designed to prevent conduct disorder and substance abuse among "high-risk" adolescents who showed at least four risk factors. These risk factors concerned a range of factors such as poor parent–child relationships, lack of school engagement, problem behavior, early substance use, family substance use, and stressful life events. A parent management program involving 12, 90 minute, weekly sessions was beneficial in reducing family conflict and behavioral problems at school in comparison to the no-intervention group. There was also a trend towards longer-term reduction in substance use for the parent management group. Interestingly, the two comparison interventions that included grouping of high-risk youths together in sessions actually showed evidence of negative influence upon school behavior problems and substance use. This problem is discussed further below.

5.12.6.3 Indicated Preventive Interventions

As defined above, indicated prevention approaches are those that are applied to individuals who, on examination, are found to manifest a risk factor, condition, or abnormality that identifies them as being at high risk for the future development of psychopathology. The main distinction between selective and indicated prevention refers to the degree to which the risk factor is intrinsic to the individual rather than the group. Thus, selective interventions target persons who are judged to be at risk as the result of being a member of some group, the membership of which is known to be a risk factor for the development of psychopathology. In contrast, indicated prevention targets persons who possess some characteristic intrinsic to the individual that places them at risk for the development of psychopathology. Given our knowledge of early, mild symptomatology as a risk factor for later clinically significant psychopathology, programs that target mild psychopathology (alternatively known as early intervention) will be regarded as a form of indicated prevention. These approaches aim to identify early symptoms of emotional and behavioral disorders through screening programs, usually during early childhood. Such programs aim to break the trajectory typically involved in the development of many forms of psychopathology, including conduct disorder, depression, anxiety, and psychotic episodes.

5.12.6.3.1 Early intervention to prevent conduct disorder

Several programs have been developed for early identification with children who show subclinical levels of conduct disorder and aggression. A variety of approaches have been used in attempts to break the progression from early disruptive behavior problems to a full-blown conduct disorder. These have included parent training approaches, child-focused interventions, and multicomponent programs that involve a variety of parent- and child-focused methods. The rationale behind these interventions is the proposition that poor parenting skills, academic failure, and poor social skills are risk factors for the development of conduct disorder. Thus preventive interventions have focused on enhancing factors such as parenting, social, and academic skills.

For example, Tremblay et al. (1991, 1992, 1995) examined the outcome of a program designed to prevent serious conduct problems among a group of disruptive kindergarten boys from inner-city, low socioeconomic neighborhood schools. One hundred and seventy two boys, who were identified at the end of preschool as showing high levels of disruptive behavior, were randomly assigned to a preventive intervention, observational control, or no contact. The preventive intervention was conducted over a two-year period and involved parent and child interventions. The parent component involved up to 46 individualized home-based training sessions, with a mean number of 17.4 sessions focusing on monitoring of children's behavior, use of behavioral parenting methods, and crisis management techniques. The child-focused component included small group prosocial skills training, problem-solving, and self-control methods. These sessions were conducted over two school years, and included a small number of prosocial peers within each group.

Up to age 12, the boys who had earlier received the intervention showed better school attendance, were rated by their teachers as less disruptive in the classroom, and were less likely to have required special education experiences (Tremblay et al., 1992). However, the longer-term results reported by Tremblay et al. (1995) are extremely interesting. By age 15, the difference between preventive intervention and control boys had disappeared in terms of school placements and behavior in the classroom. Generally, there was a trend for behavior problems to decline with age for boys, irrespective of whether they participated in the preventive program. Juvenile court records also showed no significant differences between the intervention and control groups in terms of official court sanctions between ages 12 and 15. Furthermore, there were no differences between groups in terms of the boys' perceptions of their parents' punishment behavior, although the boys in the preventive group perceived their parents as engaging in a higher level of supervision than did the control group. Thus, despite a costly intervention over a two-year period, the long-term results of this study were disappointing. Positive benefits were noted in terms of classroom behavior and academic performance throughout elementary school, but the impact had largely disappeared by age 15. Tremblay et al. (1995) proposed that future studies should include booster sessions for boys and parents in order to maintain the benefits that are evident during elementary school years. They suggested that booster units are needed that focus on problem-solving skills, life skills, study skills, conflict resolution, self-control, and academic skills during early adolescence.

The value of the Tremblay et al. (1995) results is that they highlight the importance of extensive long-term follow-up. It will be several years before many of the recently established early intervention studies for the prevention of conduct disorders obtain adequate follow-up data to permit valid conclusions to be drawn about their long-term efficacy. For example, the FAST Track Project (Conduct Problems Research Group, 1992) is being conducted in multiple sites across the USA. Participants are preschoolers and their families where the youngsters have been identified as showing high levels of noncompliance and aggression at age four and therefore are considered to be at risk for future development of conduct disorders. The intervention continues over several years, with components focusing on the training of social skills, increasing peer acceptance, remedial educational tuition, and parent training. Parents are paid a small amount to attend the sessions and transport and child care is provided for the sessions. The long-term effectiveness of this approach is yet to be determined.

Lochman, Coie, Underwood, and Terry (1993) reported a controlled evaluation of a program targeted at fourth grade children who were identified as socially rejected and aggressive at school. The intervention included social skills training, anger management, and cognitively-based components to teach interpersonal problem solving and appropriate perception and interpretation of interpersonal cues. The school-based curriculum included small group and individual sessions over 12–18 sessions. By one year follow-up, there was a problem of drop out which restricts the conclusions that can be drawn. However, of those children who were both aggressive and rejected and who remained in the study at one year follow-up, those who received the intervention were rated by their teachers as being significantly less aggressive than those in the randomly assigned control condition. Whether these benefits are maintained at 5–10 year follow-ups remains to be demonstrated.

An alternative approach to early intervention with children who show disruptive and aggressive behavior during preschool years is the Triple P (Positive Parenting of Preschoolers) program described by Sanders and Markie-Dadds (1996). This project involves a multilevel approach in which the intensity of the intervention is tailored to the severity of the presenting problems of the child and family. Level 1 involves a community-based self-help approach involving tip sheets for parents and a manualized program concerning parenting skills for commonly occurring behavior problems. The Level 2 intervention includes minimal contact with a therapist by telephone in addition to the written self-help materials. Active training in parenting skills is then included at Levels 3 and 4, being applied to those families for whom the child behavior problems are not complicated by additional family problems such as marital discord or parental depression. In Level 5, intensive behavioral parent training is enhanced with treatments to reduce parental depression and marital discord. Short-term results suggest that this approach appears to offer promise in reducing subsequent conduct problems. However, it is not yet clear how effective the multilevel intervention strategy will be in producing long-term benefits through to adolescence, nor when applied on a large-scale, community basis.

5.12.6.3.2 Early intervention to prevent anxiety and depression

Recently, researchers have started to examine the benefits of preventive interventions with children who show mild depressive symptoms, again trying to break the trajectory in the development of clinical depression in later adolescence. Clarke et al. (1995) reported the results of a preventive program with high school adolescents who were assessed as showing elevated depressive symptomatology. These youngsters were randomly assigned to a 15-session cognitive group intervention or a "usual care" control condition. Survival analyses indicated a significant 12-month advantage for the prevention program, with affective

disorder total incidence rates of 14.5% for the active intervention and 25.7% for the control condition. Jaycox, Reivich, Gillham, and Seligman (1994) also reported positive findings in the prevention of depression of primary school children who reported mild symptoms of depression and parental conflict in the home. The intervention program involved teaching children to shift their cognitive style to more optimistic, rather than pessimistic, interpretations and training in interpersonal skills. At six-month follow-up, the preventive intervention group reported fewer symptoms of depression compared to a nonintervention control group, an effect that was still evident at two-year follow-up (Gillham, Reivich, Jaycox, & Seligman, 1995).

An early identification and intervention approach is also being trialed in the prevention of anxiety disorders in children and adolescents. Dadds, Spence, Holland, Barrett, and Laurens (1997) described an intervention for children who were identified as being at risk for the development of anxiety disorders by virtue of showing mild levels of anxiety and fearfulness. The aim of the project is to reduce symptoms of anxiety and enhance protective factors, such as child coping skills and appropriate parenting skills, in order to reduce the later development of anxiety disorders. After recruitment and diagnostic interviews with 1786 7–14 year olds, 128 children were selected and assigned to a 10-week school-based child and parent-focused psychosocial intervention, or a monitoring group.

At postintervention, approximately 10% of children in both groups had developed a full *DSM-IV* anxiety diagnosis, with no significant differences between groups. However, at six months follow-up, 54% of the children in the monitoring group had developed an anxiety disorder, compared with 16% in the intervention group (Dadds et al., 1997). The finding that over half of the children in the monitoring group who were "at risk" only, progressed into a formal anxiety disorder at the six month monitoring period, highlights the importance of late childhood and early adolescence as a critical time in the development of anxiety disorders (Spence & Dadds, 1996). The long-term benefits of this preventive intervention are still being examined.

To date, research into the prevention of anxiety and depressive disorders in children who manifest early symptomatology in these areas is only in an embryonic state. However, the results so far are encouraging and justify continued investigation of methods to interrupt the trajectory from preclinical symptomatology to clinical depression and anxiety.

5.12.6.3.3 *Early intervention to prevent psychotic episodes*

One of the most exciting developments in the area of indicated prevention concerns early intervention with individuals who show early signs of psychosis. For example, the Early Psychosis Prevention and Intervention Centre (Jackson, McGorry, Edwards, & Hulbert, 1996) provides early intervention for 16–30 year olds with an emerging psychosis. A cognitively-oriented psychotherapy approach is taken in the multiphase program. Intervention methods include development of a sense of hope, identifying personal strengths, developing coping mechanisms, education about psychosis, and establishment of social support networks. Preliminary results suggest that participants with first episode psychosis show lower negative symptoms and reduced disability scores compared to those who refused to participate or dropped out of the program. Although the lack of random assignment to groups represents a methodological limitation, the preliminary results suggest that early detection and intervention programs for psychosis warrant further empirical examination. The program is also limited to individuals who have already experienced their first episode of psychosis. Some interesting research reported by Birchwood (1995) suggested that prodromal signs (such as loss of mental agility, racing thoughts, disjointed thinking and confusion, feelings of derealization and heightened perception) can reliably predict the imminent onset of new episodes of psychosis. Birchwood used case studies to illustrate how cognitive–behavioral interventions and/or medication can be used to prevent subsequent episodes of psychosis in young people who manifest these prodromal signs. The programs described by Birchwood (1995) and Jackson et al. (1996) involved individuals who have already manifested their first episode of psychosis. Monitoring and identification of prodromal signs is used to cue the use of techniques to prevent the onset of subsequent episodes of psychosis. However, there is also some tentative evidence that it may be possible to prevent first episode by early detection of presymptoms of psychosis and intervention with adolescents and young adults (e.g. Falloon, 1992).

5.12.7 DIFFICULTIES AND CHALLENGES

There are an enormous number of practical difficulties in implementing preventive interventions and in evaluating their efficacy. The following section attempts to outline just a few of these issues for consideration. For example, it is important to bear in mind the possibility that preventive efforts may, in some instances, be counterproductive. We need to consider the possible detrimental effects of labeling individuals as being "at risk" of developing psychopathology. Any preventive efforts must ensure that the intervention does not produce changes in the behavior of significant others, such as peers, teachers, or family members that further increases the chance that the young person will develop emotional or behavioral difficulties. Similarly, preventive efforts must be cautious about the potential negative side effects of bringing together children who share common risk patterns. This is particularly relevant to programs that bring together adolescents who share risk factors relating to the development of substance abuse or severe conduct disorder. In some instances, the aggregation of high-risk youths has produced an iatrogenic effect. For example, Dishion and Andrews (1995) found that interventions that aggregated high-risk youths into groups produced escalations in tobacco use and problem behavior at school. This effect was not evident in the intervention that focused on parenting skills training and did not include group attendance by the adolescents.

A second issue for preventive interventions is to whom should preventive efforts be targeted in order to produce the most cost-effective benefits. One of the most significant areas of research for the future will be identification of combinations of risk factors that accurately predict the development of psychopathology and for which there are effective methods of change. This will enable us to target preventive efforts more specifically to those at greatest risk. Lochman et al. (1995) proposed that the most useful risk markers for a prevention program are those that are potentially modifiable as a result of intervention, or those that are markers for other changeable processes that mediate negative outcome Lochman et al. (1995) described how a multiple gating procedure can be used to identify children at risk of developing conduct problems. This study showed how parent ratings of early childhood behavior made a significant contribution over and above teacher ratings of child behavior in the prediction of subsequent conduct problems at school. Studies of this type will be valuable in steering future directions for prevention research and policy.

Although it may make sense to suggest that limited funds for prevention should be spent on those children most at risk rather than upon universal interventions, we do not have the evidence to back up this assumption. We need to determine whether universal interventions applied to whole populations can produce sufficiently strong results to impact upon the development of psychopathology among children with multiple risk factors. Given the relatively disappointing long-term effects of those intensive interventions that have been focused upon the prevention of behavior problems among children with mild symptomatology (e.g., Tremblay et al., 1995), it seems unlikely that a universal intervention could produce significant long-term benefits for these children. Nevertheless, this possibility warrants examination. An alternative approach is to follow the multilevel example outlined by Sanders and Markie-Dadds (1996). This system requires an assessment and prevention strategy that provides relatively cheap community-based initiatives that are likely to be helpful to the majority of families. More intensive approaches are reserved for those families and children who show persistent behavior problems or multiple risk factors. These multilevel preventive strategies require that systems are in place to identify those families who are in need of more complex interventions than those available at a community, universal level.

A third area of concern is the need to provide cost–benefit analyses, in terms of the cost of the preventive intervention vs. the reduction in costs of treatment of psychopathology. If mental health policymakers and planners are to be convinced that there is a case for investing large amounts of funding in preventive efforts, they need to be shown evidence of the likely economic benefits to the community. In the area of physical health it is easier to provide estimates regarding the cost savings of prevention programs. For example, it has been estimated that the cost–benefit ratio of the mumps–measles–rubella vaccine program in the USA is 14:1. For example, the 1983 immunization scheme produced cost savings of US$1.4 billion (White, Koplan, & Orenstein, 1985). The benefits of prevention in mental health are much harder to estimate. However, it should be possible to determine the cost of preventive interventions compared to the cost of long-term treatment of full-blown clinical cases through indicators such as the cost of mental health consultations, time off work, hospitalization, and pension payments.

5.12.8 CONCLUSIONS

Considerable advances have been made over the past 20 years in the area of prevention of child and adolescent psychopathology. The evidence presented in the present chapter suggests that we have made considerable

progress in identifying risk and protective factors relating to the development of child and adolescent psychopathology. It is now feasible to identify major risk and protective factors for the development of conduct disorders and internalizing problems in young people and many of these are potentially modifiable through psychological interventions. There have now been many studies of universal, selective, and indicated preventive interventions that have reported positive effects in reducing the risk for development of emotional and behavioral problems. However, most of the published papers relating to the efficacy of prevention of psychopathology are limited by relatively short follow-up periods or have failed to include a valid comparison group against which to compare changes over time. It is important therefore to bear these limitations in mind when interpreting the literature. There are still many unanswered questions. A great deal more research is needed before we can draw firm conclusions about which psychological problems can be prevented, what methods are most effective in preventing specific mental health problems, to whom should preventive programs be directed, and whether prevention is best directed at whole populations, or those with specific risk factors. Many methodologically rigorous and theoretically sound preventive studies are currently underway and the next decade should provide answers to many of these questions.

5.12.9 REFERENCES

Amata, P. R., & Keith, B. (1991). Parental divorce and the well-being of children: A meta analysis. *Psychological Bulletin, 110,* 26–46.
Asendorpf, J. B. (1993). Beyond temperament: A two-factor coping model of the development of behavioral inhibition during childhood. In K. H. Rubin & J. B. Asendorpf (Eds.), *Social withdrawal, inhibition and shyness in childhood* (pp. 265–269). Hillsdale, NJ: Lawrence Erlbaum Associates.
Barkley, R. A. (1989). Hyperactive girls and boys: Stimulant drug effects on mother–child interactions. *Journal of Child Psychology and Psychiatry, 30,* 379–390.
Beardslee, W. R., Salt, P., Porterfield, K., & Rothberg, P. C. (1993). Comparison of preventive interventions for families with parental affective disorder. *Journal of the American Academy of Child and Adolescent Psychiatry, 32,* 254–263.
Berrueta-Clement, J. R., Schweinhart, L. J., Barnett, W. S., Epstein, A. S., & Weikart, D. P. (1984). *Changed lives: The effects of the Perry Preschool Program on youths through age 19* (High/Scope Educational Research Foundation, Monograph 8). Pysilanti, MI: High/Scope Press.
Biederman, J., Rosenbaum, J. F., Bolduc-Murphy, E. A., Faraone, S. V., Chaloff, J., Hirshfeld, D. R., & Kagan, J. (1993). A 3-year follow-up of children with and without behavioral inhibition. *Journal of the American Academy of Child and Adolescent Psychiatry, 32*(4), 814–821.
Birchwood, M. (1995). Early intervention in psychotic

relapse: Cognitive approaches to detection and management. *Behaviour Change, 12*, 2–19.

Caplan, G. (1964). *Principles of preventive psychiatry*. New York: Basic Books.

Caplan, M., Weissberg, R. P., Grober, J. S., Sivo, P. J., Grady, K., & Jacoby, C. (1992). Social competence promotion with inner-city and suburban young adolescents: Effects on social adjustment and alcohol use. *Journal of Consulting and Clinical Psychology, 60*, 56–63.

Clarke, G. N., Hawkins, W., Murphy, M., & Sheeber, L. (1993). School-based primary prevention of depressive symptomatology in adolescents: Findings from two studies. *Journal of Adolescent Research, 8*, 183–204.

Clarke, G. N., Hawkins, W., Murphy, M., Sheeber, L., Lewinsohn, P., & Seeley, J. R. (1995). Targeted prevention of unipolar depressive disorder in an at-risk sample of high school adolescents: A randomized trial of group cognitive intervention. *Journal of the American Academy of Child and Adolescent Psychiatry, 34*, 312–321.

Coie, J. D., Watt, N. F., West, S. G., Hawkins, J. D., Asarnow, J. R., Markman, H. J., Ramey, S. L., Shure, M. B., & Long, B. (1993). The science of prevention: A conceptual framework and some directions for a National Research Program. *American Psychologist, 48*, 1013–1022.

Compas, B. (1987). Coping with stress during childhood and adolescence. *Psychological Bulletin, 101*, 393–403.

Conduct Problems Research Group. (1992). A developmental and clinical model for the prevention of conduct disorder: The FAST Track Program. *Development and Psychopathology, 4*, 509–527.

Dadds, M. R. (in press). Conduct disorder. In R. T. Ammerman & M. Hersen (Eds.), *Handbook of prevention and treatment of children and adolescents: Interventions in the real world context*. New York: Wiley .

Dadds, M. R., Barrett, P. M., & Rapee, R. M. (1996). Family process and child anxiety and aggression: An observational analysis. *Journal of Abnormal Child Psychology, 24*, 715–734.

Dadds, M. R., Spence, S. H., Holland, D. E., Barrett, P. M., & Laurens, K. R. (1997). Prevention and early intervention for anxiety disorders: A controlled trial. *Journal of Consulting and Clinical Psychology, 65*, 627–635.

DHHS (Department of Health and Human Services) (1991). *Healthy People 2000*. Washington, DC: Government Printing Office; DHHS Pub. No. (PHS) 91–50212.

Dishion, T. J., & Andrews, D. W. (1995). Preventing escalation in problem behaviors with high-risk young adolescents: Immediate and 1-year outcomes. *Journal of Consulting and Clinical Psychology, 63*, 538–548.

Dodge, K. A., Pettit, G. S., & Bates, J. E. (1994). Socialization mediators of the relation between socioeconomic status and child conduct problems. Special Issue: Children and poverty. *Child Development, 65*, 649–665.

Dollinger, S. J. (1986). The measurement of children's sleep disturbances and somatic complaints following a disaster. *Child Psychiatry and Human Development, 16*, 148–153.

Dollinger, S. J., O'Donnell, J. P., & Staley, A. A. (1984). Lightning-strike disaster: Effects on children's fears and worries. *Journal of Consulting and Clinical Psychology, 52*, 1028–1038.

Eisenberg, L. (1995). Social policy and the reality of prevention. In B. Raphael & G. D. Burrows (Eds.), *Handbook of studies on preventive psychiatry* (pp. 31–50). Amsterdam: Elsevier Science.

Ellickson, P. L., & Bell, R. M. (1990). Drug prevention in junior high: A multi-site longitudinal test. *Science, 247*, 1299–1305.

Falloon, I. R. (1992). Early intervention for first episode schizophrenia: A preliminary exploration. *Psychiatry, 55*, 4–15.

Farrington, D. P. (1995). The challenge of teenage antisocial behavior. In M. Rutter (Ed.), *Psychosocial disturbances in young people: challenges for prevention* (pp. 83–130). New York: Cambridge University Press.

Felner, R. D., & Adan, A. M. (1988). The School Transition Environment Project: An ecological intervention and evaluation. In R. H. Price, E. L. Cowen, R. P. Lorion, & J. Ramos-McKay (Eds.), *Fourteen ounces of prevention: A case book for practitioners* (pp. 111–122). Washington DC: American Psychological Association.

Field, T. M., Widmayer, S. J., Stringer, S., & Ignatoff, E. (1980). Teenage, lower-class, black mothers and their preterm infants: An intervention and developmental follow-up. *Child Development, 51*, 426–436.

Forehand, R. (1992). Parental divorce and adolescent maladjustment. *Behaviour Research and Therapy, 30*, 319–327.

Gillham, J. E., Reivich, K. J., Jaycox, L. H., & Seligman, M. E. P. (1995) Prevention of depressive symptoms in school children: Two year follow-up. *Psychological Science, 6*, 343–351.

Goodyer, I. M., & Altham, P. M. (1991). Lifetime exit events and recent social and family adversities in anxious and depressed school-aged children. *Journal of Affective Disorders, 21*, 219–228.

Gordon, R. (1987). An operational classification of disease prevention. In J. A. Steinberg & M. M. Silverman (Eds.), *Preventing mental disorders* (pp. 20–26). Rockville, MD: Department of Health and Human Services.

Guerra, N. G., Huesmann, L. R., Tolan, P. H., & Van Acker, R. (1995). Stressful events and individual beliefs as correlates of economic disadvantage and aggression among urban children. *Journal of Consulting and Clinical Psychology, 63*, 518–528.

Harnish, J. D., Dodge, K. A., Valente, E., & Conduct Problems Prevention Research Group (1995). Mother–child interaction quality as a partial mediator of the roles of maternal depressive symptomatology and socioeconomic status in the development of child behavior problems. *Child Development, 66*, 739–753.

Hawkins, J. D., Catalano, R. F., Morrison, D. M., O'Donnell, J., Abbott, R. D., & Day, L. E. (1992). The Seattle Social Development Project: Effects of the first four years on protective factors and problem behaviors. In J. McCord & R. Tremblay (Eds.), *The prevention of antisocial behavior in children* (pp. 139–161). New York: Guilford Press.

Hess, R. D., & Camara, K. A. (1979). Post-divorce family relationships as mediating factors in the consequences of divorce for children. *Journal of Social Issues, 35*, 70–95.

Hightower, A. D., & Braden, J. (1991). Prevention. In T. R. Kratochwill & R. J. Morris (Eds.), *The practice of child therapy* (pp. 410–440). New York: Pergamon.

Hirshfeld, D. R., Rosenbaum, J. F., Biederman, J., Bolduc, E. A., Faraone, S. V., Snidman, N., Reznick, J. S., & Kagan, J. (1992). Stable behavioral inhibition and its association with anxiety disorder. *Journal of American Academy of Child and Adolescent Psychiatry, 31*, 103–111.

Hodges, W. F. (1991). *Interventions for children of divorce*. New York: Wiley.

Human Rights and Equal Opportunity Commission (1993). *Human rights and mental illness: report of the national inquiry into the human rights of people with mental illness*. Canberra: Australian Government Publishing Service.

IOM (Institute of Medicine) (1989). *Research on children and adolescents with mental, behavioral, and developmental disorders*. Washington, DC: National Academy Press.

Jackson, H. J., McGorry, P. D., Edwards, J., & Hulbert, C. 1996). Cognitively oriented psychotherapy for early psychosis (COPE). In P. Cotton & H. Jackson (Eds.), *Early intervention and prevention in mental health* (pp. 131–154). Melbourne: The Australian Psychological Society.

Jaycox, L. H., Reivich, K. J., Gillham, J., & Seligman, M. E. P. (1994). Prevention of depressive symptoms in school children. *Behaviour Research and Therapy, 32,* 801–816.

Johnson, D. L. (1991). Primary prevention of behavior problems in young children: The Houston Parent–Child Development Center. In R. Price, E. L. Cowen, R. P. Lorion, & J. Ramos-McKay (Eds.), *Fourteen ounces of prevention: A casebook for practitioners* (pp. 44–52). Washington, DC: American Psychological Association.

Kagan, J., Reznick, J. S., & Gibbons, J. (1989). Inhibited and uninhibited types of children. *Child Development, 60,* 838–845.

Kagan, J., & Snidman, N. (1991). Infant predictors of inhibited and uninhibited profiles. *Psychological Science, 2,* 40–43.

Kaslow, N. J., & Racusin, G. R. (1994). Family therapy for depression in young people. In W. M. Reynolds & H. F. Johnston (Eds.), *Handbook of depression in children and adolescents* (pp. 345–363). New York: Plenum .

Kazdin, A. E., & Kagan, J. (1994). Models of dysfunction in developmental psychopathology. *Clinical Psychology: Science and Practice, 1,* 35–52.

Kellam, S. G., & Rebok, G. W. (1992). Building developmental and etiological theory through epidemiologically based preventive intervention trials. In J. McCord & R. E. Tremblay (Eds.), *Preventing antisocial behavior: interventions from birth through adolescence* (pp. 162–195). New York: Guilford Press.

Kellam, S. G., Rebok, G. W., Ialongo, N., & Mayer, L. S. (1994). The course and malleability of aggressive behavior from early first grade into middle school: Results of a developmental epidemiologically-based preventive trial. *Journal of Child Psychology and Psychiatry, 35,* 259–281.

Kendall, P. C. (1991). Considering cognition in anxiety-disordered children. Special Issue: Assessment of childhood anxiety disorders. *Journal of Anxiety Disorder, 5,* 167–185.

Kraemer, H. C., & Fendt, K. H. (1990). Random assignment in clinical trials: Issues in planning. *Journal of Clinical Epidemiology, 43,* 1157–1167.

Lally, J. R., Mangione, P. L., Honig, A. S., & Wittner, D. S. (1988). More pride, less delinquency: Findings from the ten-year follow-up study of the Syracuse University Family Development Research Program. *Zero to three, 8*(4) 13–18.

Levenstein, P. (1992). The Mother–Child Home Program: Research methodology and the real world. In J. McCord & R. C. Tremblay (Eds.), *Preventing antisocial behavior: Interventions from birth through adolescence* (pp. 43–66). New York: Guilford Press.

Lochman, J. E., Coie, J. D., Underwood, M. K., & Terry, R. (1993). Effectiveness of a social relations intervention program for aggressive and nonaggressive, rejected children. *Journal of Consulting and Clinical Psychology, 6,* 1053–1058.

Lochman, J. E., & Dodge, K. A. (1994). Social-cognitive processes of severely violent, moderately aggressive, and nonaggressive boys. *Journal of Consulting and Clinical Psychology, 62,* 366–374.

Lochman, J. E. & The Conduct Problems Prevention Research Group (1995). Screening of child behavior problems at school entry. *Journal of Consulting and Clinical Psychology, 63,* 549–559.

Loeber, R. (1990). Development and risk factors of juvenile antisocial behavior and delinquency. *Clinical Psychology Review, 10,* 1–41.

McFarlane, A. C. (1987). Posttraumatic phenomena in a longitudinal study of children following a natural disaster. *Journal of the American Academy of Child and Adolescent Psychiatry, 26,* 764–769.

Mrazek, P. J., & Haggerty, R. J. (Eds.) (1994). *Reducing the risks for mental disorders: Frontiers for preventive intervention research.* Washington, DC: National Academy Press.

O'Donnell, J., Hawkins, J. D., & Abbott, R. D. (1995). Predicting serious delinquency and substance use among aggressive boys. Special section: Prediction and prevention of child and adolescent antisocial behavior. *Journal of Consulting and Clinical Psychology, 63*(4), 529–537.

Olds, D. L, Henderson, C. R., Tatelbaum, R., Chamberlin, R. (1988). Improving the life-course development of socially disadvantaged mothers: A randomized trial of nurse home visitation. *American Journal of Public Health, 78,* 1436–1445.

Patterson, G. R. (1996). Some characteristics of a developmental theory for early-onset delinquency. In M. F. Lenzenweger & J. J. Haugaard (Eds.), *Frontiers of developmental psychopathology* (pp. 59–71). New York: Oxford University Press.

Patterson, G. R, & Stouthamer-Loeber, M. (1984). The correlation of family management practices and delinquency. *Child Development, 55,* 1299–1307.

Pedro-Carroll, J. L., & Cowen, E. L. (1985). The Children of Divorce Intervention Program: An investigation of the efficacy of a school-based prevention program. *Journal of Consulting and Clinical Psychology, 53,* 603–611.

Perry, C. L., Grant, M., Ernberg, G., Florenzano, R. U., Langdon, M. C., Myeni, A. D., Waahlberg, R., Berg, S., Anderson, K., Fisher, K. J., Bla-Temple, D., Cross, D., Saunders, B., Jacobs, D. R., & Schmid, T. (1989). WHO Collaborative Study on Alcohol Education and Young People: Outcomes of a four-country pilot study. *The International Journal of the Addictions, 24,* 1145–1171.

Peters, R. D., & Russell, C. C. (1994). *Better Beginnings, Better Futures Project: Model, program and research overview.* Ontario: Queen's Printer for Ontario.

Plomin, R., & Stocker, C. (1989). Behavioral genetics of emotionality. In S. Reznick (Ed.), *Perspectives on behavioral inhibition* (pp. 219–240). Chicago, IL: University of Chicago Press.

Price, J. (1995). Substance abuse: Risks and opportunities for prevention. In B. Raphael & G. D. Burrows (Eds.), *Handbook of studies on preventive psychiatry* (pp. 531–548). Amsterdam: Elsevier Science.

Prior, M. (1992). Childhood temperament. *Journal of Child Psychology and Psychiatry, 33,* 249–281.

Rachman S. J. (1980). Emotional processing. *Behaviour Research and Therapy, 18,* 51–60.

Rapee, R. M. (1997). The potential role of childrearing practices in the development of anxiety and depression. *Clinical Psychology Review, 17,* 47–67.

Robins, L. H., & Regier, D. A. (1991). *Psychiatric disorders in America: The Epidemiological Catchment Area Study.* New York: The Free Press.

Rosenbaum, J. F., Biederman, J., Bolduc-Murphy, E. A., Faraone, S. V., Chaloff, J., Hirshfeld, D. R., & Kagan, J. (1993). Behavioral inhibition in childhood: A risk factor for anxiety disorders. *Harvard Review of Psychiatry, May/June,* 2–6.

Rutter, M. (1987). Psychosocial resilience and protective mechanisms. *American Journal of Orthopsychiatry, 57,* 316–331.

Rutter, M., Macdonald, H., Le Couteur, A., Harrington, R., Bolton, P., & Bailey, A. (1990). Genetic factors in child psychiatric disorders–II. Empirical findings. *Journal of Child Psychology and Psychiatry, 31,* 39–83.

Sanders, M. R., Dadds, M. R., & Barrett, P. M. (1995). The prevention of anxiety and stress related disorders in children. In B. Raphael & G. D. Burrows (Eds.),

Handbook of studies on preventive psychiatry (pp. 399–421). Amsterdam: Elsevier Science.

Sanders, M. R., & Markie-Dadds, C. (1996). Triple P: A multilevel family intervention program for children with disruptive behavior disorders. In P. Cotton & H. Jackson (Eds.), *Early intervention and prevention in mental health* (pp. 59–85). Melbourne: The Australian Psychological Society.

Shure, M. B., & Spivack, G. (1980). Interpersonal problem solving as a mediator of behavioral adjustment in preschool and kindergarten children. *Journal of Applied Developmental Psychology, 1*, 29–44.

Shure, M. B., & Spivack, G. (1982). Interpersonal problem-solving in young children: A cognitive approach to prevention. *American Journal of Community Psychology, 10*, 341–356.

Shure, M. B., & Spivack, G. (1988). Interpersonal cognitive problem solving. In R. H. Price, E. L. Cowen, R. P. Lorion, & J. Ramos-McKay (Eds.), *Fourteen ounces of prevention: A casebook for practitioners* (pp. 69–82). Washingon, DC: American Psychological Association.

Soussignan, R., Koch, P., & Montagner, H. (1988). Behavioral and cardiovascular changes in children moving from kindergarten to primary school. *Journal of Child Psychology and Psychiatry, 29*, 321–333.

Spence, S. H. (1996a). A case for prevention. In P. Cotton & H. Jackson (Eds.), *Early intervention and prevention in mental health* (pp. 1–19). Melbourne: The Australian Psychological Society.

Spence, S. H. (1996b). The prevention of anxiety disorders in childhood. In P. Cotton & H. Jackson (Eds.), *Early intervention and prevention in mental health* (pp. 87–107). Melbourne: The Australian Psychological Society.

Spence, S. H., & Dadds, M. R. (1996). Preventing childhood anxiety disorders. *Behaviour Change, 13*, 241–249.

Sugar, M. (1989). Children in a disaster: An overview. *Child Psychiatry and Human Development, 19*, 163–179.

Terr, L. C. (1981). Psychic trauma in children: Observa-tions following the Chowchilla school-bus kidnapping. *American Journal of Psychiatry, 138*, 14–19.

Tremblay, R. E., Bitaro, F., Bertrand, L., LeBlanc, M., Beauchesne, H., Boileau, H., & David, L. (1992). Parent and child training to prevent early onset of delinquency: The Montreal Longitudinal-Experimental study. In J. McCord & R. Tremblay (Eds.), *Preventing antisocial behavior: Interventions from birth through adolescence* (pp. 117–138). New York: Guilford Press.

Tremblay, R. D., McCord, J., Boileau, H., Charlebois, P., Gagnon, C., LeBlanc, M., & Larivee, S. (1991). Can disruptive boys be helped to become competent? *Psychiatry, 54*, 148–161.

Tremblay, R. E., Pagani-Kurtz, L., Vitaro, F., Masse, L. C., & Pihl, R. O. (1995). A bimodal preventive intervention for disruptive kindergarten boys: Its impact through mid-adolescence. *Journal of Consulting and Clinical Psychology, 63*, 560–568.

US Advisory Board on Child Abuse and Neglect. (1990). *Child abuse and neglect: Critical first steps in response to a national emergence.* Washington DC: Government Printing Office.

Werner, E. E. (1987). Vulnerability and resiliency in children at risk for delinquency: A longitudinal study from birth to young adulthood. In J. D. Burchard & S. N. Burchard (Eds.), *Prevention of delinquent behavior* (pp. 16–43). Beverly Hills, CA: Sage.

White, C. C., Koplan, J. P., & Orenstein, W. A. (1985). Benefits, risks, and costs of immunization for measles, mumps, and rubella. *American Journal of Public Health, 75*, 739–744.

Yule, W. (1991). Work with children following disasters. In M. Herbert (Ed.), *Clinical child psychology: A social learning approach to theory and practice* (pp. 223–241). Chichester, UK: Wiley.

Yule, W. & Williams, R. (1990). Post-traumatic stress reactions in children. *Journal of Traumatic Stress, 3*, 279–295.

5.13
Anxiety Disorders

MARK R. DADDS and PAULA M. BARRETT
Griffith University, Qld, Australia

and

VANESSA E. COBHAM
University of Queensland, Australia

5.13.1 INTRODUCTION

Since Freud's description of separation fears in Little Hans at the turn of the century, anxiety disorders in children have received scarce but increasing attention from clinical researchers. Only recently, however, have controlled studies into the epidemiology, development, and treatment of these children gathered momentum.

There are a number of reasons for this neglect. Across most classes of psychopathology, children receive less attention than adults (Kazdin, 1985), and children with anxiety disorders often do not attract the attention of mental health services because their behavior may be relatively cooperative and unobtrusive compared with disruptive peers. Despite this, there is evidence to suggest that some forms of childhood anxiety are severely debilitating and predictive of chronic mental health problems.

Through this century, a number of critical issues regarding anxiety in children have emerged. Because far more research has been conducted into anxiety in adults, there has been a tendency for child researchers to borrow conceptual models and treatment techniques from the adult literature. The value of this has been assumed rather than supported by hard data and thus the field is becoming increasingly careful to incorporate and evaluate developmental factors into its borrowed models. Other issues are common to most forms of child psychopathology. The reliability, validity, and clinical utility of diagnostic systems remain controversial issues despite much effort to refine the various categorical systems currently in use. While this is true for all forms of psychopathology, the use of formal diagnoses with children has many unique problems raised by the rapid changes children go through and the diversity of stakeholders such as the child, parents, and teachers that are involved in the child's well-being. Further, the childhood anxiety disorders continue to elude attempts to find discrete categories, with overlap and comorbidity being the rule rather than the exception.

The relative importance and interaction of temperamental vs. learned factors has moved beyond simplistic nature–nuture debates to models that emphasize multiple causal variables that interact in predictable development sequences. Thus, a disorder is seen as taking a developmental trajectory through predictable changes and stable phases. For conduct disorder in children, much progress has been made in mapping common trajectories; for anxiety disorders, relatively little is known. Thus, the links between child and adult anxiety remain an area of speculation. The twentieth century has also heralded the growth of behavioral and cognitive sciences and family therapies as major clinical and scientific movements. Both are important to anxiety in children. Contemporary conceptual and treatment models emphasize the interactions of learning factors, cognitive style, and family process. Recently, exciting and important work has shown that these can be studied under controlled conditions and used with great effect to bring about clinically significant improvements in anxious children.

The aim of this chapter is to review current knowledge of the nature, development, and treatment of the major classes of childhood anxiety. Specifically, it will focus on the more general forms of anxiety disorder such as separation anxiety, social fears, and generalized

anxiety states. Simple phobias, obsessive compulsive disorder, and traumatic stress disorder are covered elsewhere in this volume.

5.13.2 ANXIETY DISORDERS

5.13.2.1 Phenomenology

Marks (1969) described fear as "a normal response to active or imagined threat in higher animals ... (comprising) an outer behavioral expression, an inner feeling, and accompanying physiological changes" (p. 1). Anxiety, a closely related construct, has been defined as "a dysphoric, aversive feeling similar to fear that arises without an obvious external threat" (Miller, 1983, p. 338) and "apprehension, tension, or uneasiness related to the expectation of danger, whether internal or external" (Kendall et al., 1992, p. 1). Although distinctions are typically made between the two constructs, the prevailing diagnostic classification system, the *Diagnostic and statistical manual of mental disorders* (*DSM*) (American Psychiatric Association [APA], 1994), conceptualizes both fear and anxiety as being manifested in very similar physiological, cognitive, and affective patterns (Kashani, Dandoy, & Orvaschel, 1991). Based on Lang's (1968) tripartite model, anxiety is typically viewed as a multidimensional construct involving physiological, behavioral, and cognitive components or symptoms.

Fear and anxiety are common, typically transitory, and, in many situations, adaptive in that they protect the individual from harm. This being the case, anxiety and anxiety disorders are typically conceptualized as varying quantitatively along a continuum, with the degree of distress, impairment in functioning, and/or interference with daily life, discriminating between what is "normal" and adaptive and what is problematic. The difficulty, of course, comes in deciding where normal anxiety ends, and clinical anxiety begins. This difficulty is especially marked in work with children owing to developmental considerations that must be taken into account. Given that the rate of development is far greater during childhood and adolescence than at any time in life, knowledge of what are "normal" fears and anxieties at each developmental stage is vital when attempting to ascertain whether or not a child suffers from clinical anxiety. A fear that is normative for a preschool-aged child may be maladaptive if experienced by an adolescent.

As a consequence of children's developmental experiences and increasing cognitive abilities, the content of their fears and anxieties changes over time, with the focus generally moving with age from concrete, external fears to increasingly internalized and abstract anxieties. Thus, infants tend to fear strangers, loud noises, and strange and unexpected objects (Jersild & Holmes, 1935), while children of one and two years of age fear separation from their parents, loud noises, animals, the dark, and the toilet (Miller, Barrett, & Hampe, 1974). Of these, fears about animals, the dark, and separation from parents frequently persist into a child's fifth year. Between the ages of four and six, predominant fears focus on kidnappers and robbers and supernatural beings, such as ghosts and monsters. At the age of approximately six years, fears of bodily injury, death, and achievement develop (Bauer, 1976; Croake & Knox, 1973), and for many children, these continue into early adolescence. The final developmental stage appears to begin at approximately 10 or 11 years of age, when fears regarding social comparison, physical appearance, personal conduct, and school examinations predominate (Croake, 1969; Miller, Barrett, Hampe, & Noble, 1972). Factor analyses have provided additional information regarding the organization of the content of childhood fears, with the most commonly accepted solution yielding five factors consisting of fear of: failure and criticism, the unknown, injury and small animals, danger and death, and medical procedures (Ollendick, Matson, & Helsel, 1985).

McFarlane, Allen, and Honzik (1954), for instance, reported that 90% of the normal children aged two to 14 years in their sample reported at least one specific fear. The vast majority of children report experiencing multiple fears, and although the number of self-reported fears appears to decline with age, this reduction does not seem to be as great as might be expected. Thus, Ollendick et al. (1985) reported an average of 14.2 fears in children aged seven to nine years and an average of 11.6 fears in their sample of 16 to 18-year-olds. Another consistent finding is that girls typically report more fears than boys (although whether this is due to actual gender differences or sociocultural factors remains unclear). King et al. (1989) reported the average numbers of fears for males and females aged between eight and 16 years to be 10 and 18, respectively. Across cultures, total scores on the Revised Fear Survey Schedule for Children (Ollendick, 1983) appear to be similar for children and adolescents in English-speaking countries (Ollendick, King, & Frary, 1989; Yule, Udwin, & Murdoch, 1990), although Dutch children have been found to score comparatively lower (Oosterlaan, Prins, & Sergeant, 1992) and Portuguese children to score comparatively

higher (Fonseca, 1993) than their American, Australian, and English counterparts. The most common fears reported by children and adolescents, however, appear to be stable across different countries and cultures.

In summary, fears and anxieties are common in children and adolescents and in the majority of cases, they are age-appropriate, mild, frequently adaptive, and transitory. Unfortunately, for some children the reverse is the case. The fear and anxiety they experience is so severe and/or pervasive that it can cause intense distress, functional impairment, and interference. It is upon this group that the remainder of this chapter will focus.

5.13.2.2 Diagnostic Features/Differential Diagnosis

The revised third edition of the *DSM* (*DSM-III-R*) (APA, 1987) listed three anxiety disorders that typically begin in childhood or adolescence. These were:

(i) Separation anxiety disorder, defined as undue anxiety regarding separation from significant figures in the child's life. The child's reaction to such separations is beyond that expected for his or her developmental level, and may at times approach the level of panic (Gittelman-Klein, 1988).

(ii) Avoidant disorder, defined, as extreme withdrawal from and/or avoidance of, contact with unfamiliar people. In order to meet diagnostic criteria for avoidant disorder, a child must manifest anxiety regarding new people and situations that is sufficiently severe to interfere with social functioning, while at the same time demonstrating a desire and a capacity for warm and close relationships with familiar people (such as family members).

(iii) Overanxious disorder, defined as exaggerated or undue anxiety or worry. This diagnostic category is characterized by generalized anxiety that may include: self-consciousness; excessive worry about future events (e.g., going to see a doctor), or about past events (e.g., something the child said that may have been taken the wrong way); and anxiety about performance and competence.

In addition to these three anxiety disorders of childhood and adolescence, children could also be diagnosed with anxiety disorders of "adulthood." These included agoraphobia, panic disorder with or without agoraphobia, specific or simple phobia, social phobia, obsessive compulsive disorder, post-traumatic stress disorder, acute stress disorder, generalized anxiety disorder, anxiety disorder due to a general medical condition, substance-induced anxiety disorder, and anxiety disorder not otherwise specified.

With the introduction of the *DSM-IV* (APA, 1994), categories have been changed so that only one anxiety disorder of childhood or adolescence remains—separation anxiety disorder. Avoidant disorder and overanxious disorder have been effectively subsumed into the diagnoses of social phobia and generalized anxiety disorder respectively. In addition, a child may still be diagnosed as suffering from any of the anxiety disorders of adulthood.

As it pertains to childhood anxiety, the classification system used in the *10th edition of the international classification of disorders (ICD-10)* (World Health Organization, 1992) is very similar to that used in *DSM-IV*. The differences between the *DSM-IV* and the *ICD-10* adult anxiety categories are minor and insignificant. For the childhood disorders, as is the case in *DSM-IV*, all anxiety diagnoses are grouped together in a single category, which is then split into a number of subcategories. In *ICD-10* these include: separation anxiety disorder; phobic anxiety disorder; social anxiety disorder of childhood; sibling rivalry disorder; and other childhood emotional disorders (including identity disorder and overanxious disorder).

It is important to note that very little empirical research has been conducted to validate the diagnostic categories for child anxiety disorders (Silverman, 1992; Werry, 1994). Although successive versions of the *DSM* have placed increasing emphasis on empirical research, Werry contended that, as yet, the major field trials aimed at validating the childhood anxiety disorders have not been undertaken. However, as Spence (1996) notes, the little evidence that has been available has typically been utilized effectively in developing the *DSM* system. For example, the diagnostic category of avoidant disorder was omitted from *DSM-IV* after research indicated that it did not differ sufficiently from the category of social phobia to justify its inclusion (Francis, Last, & Strauss, 1992). In a similar way, overanxious disorder was subsumed by generalized anxiety disorder on the basis of empirical research (Beidel, 1991).

The controversy over whether the childhood anxiety disorders are indeed distinct clinical entities is further fueled by the overlap in diagnostic criteria across the disorders (for instance, fears of poor performance and negative evaluation are common among children with both social phobia and generalized anxiety disorder), and by the consistent failure of research to differentiate between the different childhood anxiety disorders in terms of etiology.

Further, comorbidity among the childhood anxiety disorders is common, much as it is for adults (Sanderson, Di Nardo, Rapee, & Barlow, 1990). Klein and Last (1989) report that almost all anxiety disorder children meet criteria for at least one other anxiety disorder, most commonly overanxious disorder. Similarly, over 50% of children diagnosed with overanxious disorder report comorbid anxiety disorders.

Depression is also commonly reported as a concomitant condition in the childhood anxiety disorders (Brady & Kendall, 1992). The precise figures have varied somewhat, with two small studies reporting either no anxious children meeting criteria for depression (Hershberg, Carlson, Cantwell, & Strober, 1982) or over 80% meeting criteria (Bernstein & Garfinkel, 1986). These discrepancies may be due to a confound with age since older children with overanxious disorder or social anxiety disorder have been found to be more likely to meet criteria for comorbid depression than younger children (Last, Hersen, Kazdin, Finkelstein, & Strauss, 1989; Strauss, Lease, Last, & Francis, 1988). Last et al. (1987) reported that approximately 33% of their population of overanxious disorder and social anxiety disorder children also met criteria for major depression, a figure more in line with the adult literature (Sanderson et al., 1990).

Recently, research has been conducted that provides some support for the *DSM* classification of anxiety disorders. Spence (1996) employed confirmatory factor analysis to test whether the pattern of anxiety symptoms among a community sample of children is in keeping with the *DSM-IV* classification. Using two samples of 698 children aged between eight and 12 years, a model comprising six discrete but correlated factors (reflecting the areas of panic/agoraphobia, social phobia, separation anxiety, obsessive-compulsive problems, generalized anxiety, and physical fears) provided an impressive fit of the data, while the high correlations among latent factors were more than adequately explained by a higher-order model in which each of the six first-order factors loaded on a single, second-order factor (Spence, 1996). Thus, Spence concluded that the *DSM-IV* diagnostic categories of anxiety disorders in children have validity in terms of a strong second-order factor related to anxiety in general, within which the specific categories of anxiety can be identified.

A number of studies have assessed inter-diagnostician reliability with childhood anxiety disorders. Two issues related to reliability are important. First, there is the issue of the degree of agreement between two interviewers who have information from the same source. Second, given that children rarely go for treatment without the urging of a guardian, there is the issue of the degree of agreement between two different sources of information, most commonly, parent and child.

Looking first at the issue of agreement between two interviewers, a number of studies have been conducted showing somewhat mixed results, with kappas ranging from 0.22 to 1.00 (see Silverman, 1991, for a review). Many of these differences are likely to be a result of methodological issues so that data are currently inconclusive with respect to the reliability of childhood anxiety disorders (Silverman, 1991). Nevertheless, some suggestions can possibly be made. First, it seems that the use of structured clinical interviews can greatly enhance reliability (Last, 1988). Second, reliability appears to be considerably better when the second rating is based on a recording of the first, rather than having two clinicians separately interviewing the same source (Silverman, 1991). This latter finding suggests that while the criteria for childhood anxiety diagnoses may be quite reliable, the informants are not.

Rapee, Barrett, Dadds, and Evans (1994) compared inter-rater reliability using the Anxiety Disorders Interview for Children (ADIS), parent and child versions (Silverman & Nelles, 1988), to assess the diagnostic status of 161 children referred to an anxiety disorders clinic. It should be noted that Rapee et al. (1994) reported difficulties in differentiating social phobia from avoidant disorder and so these were grouped together as social phobia. First, interviewers were provided with either live or videotaped information from both parents and the child, yielding kappa coefficients of 0.63–0.82 across the different anxiety disorders. Similar agreement levels were found based on either parent interviews or child interviews alone. However, the agreement levels calculated by comparing diagnoses based on parent interviews with diagnoses based on child interviews were low, especially for overanxious disorder which was much more frequently reported by parents than children. Overall, the results indicate that the use of a structured interview can produce moderately to highly reliable diagnoses using the *DSM-III-R* system for childhood anxiety disorders, and that utilizing different sources of information is important in reaching an accurate final consensus diagnosis. Other research investigating the agreement between different sources has indicated that information derived about the child from the parents is often quite different from that reported by the child (see Klein, 1991, for a review) and different again from teachers' reports (Stavrakaki, Vargo, Roberts, & Boo-

doosingh, 1987). At present there is no evidence to indicate that one source of evidence is any more valid than another, thus the recommendation is that multiple informants are used in the diagnosis of childhood disorders.

5.13.2.3 Prevalence

The results of recently conducted epidemiological studies indicate that anxiety disorders are probably the most common category of childhood and adolescent disorders (Bernstein & Borchardt, 1991). In a large epidemiological study employing a semistructured diagnostic interview schedule, Kashani and Orvaschel (1990) found that anxiety disorders were the most common form of psychopathology reported by a community sample of children and adolescents across three age groups (eight, 12, and 17 years). These researchers reported that 25.7% of the eight-year-old children, 15.7% of the 12-year-olds, and 21.4% of the 17-year-olds met diagnostic criteria for an anxiety disorder. It is important to note, however, that the estimates reported in this study are typically criticized as being excessively high relative to those figures reported in other epidemiological investigations. For instance, in a general sample of nearly 800 pediatric patients aged seven to 11 years, Costello (1989) found that 8.9% met diagnostic criteria for at least one anxiety disorder, while Kashani and Orvaschel (1988) found that in a representative sample of 150 adolescents aged 14 to 16 years, 17.3% met diagnostic criteria for at least one anxiety disorder, and 8.7% met diagnostic criteria *and* exhibited dysfunction warranting treatment. In another major epidemiological study, conducted in New Zealand, McGee et al. (1990) reported the prevalence rate of any anxiety disorder among their sample of almost 1000 adolescents was 12.6%, making anxiety disorders the most prevalent disorder for this age group.

With respect to specific diagnoses, Kashani and Orvaschel (1990) reported that 12.9% of all children and adolescents in their nonreferred community sample met diagnostic criteria for separation anxiety disorder. Across the three age groups, the prevalence rates were: 18.6% of the eight-year-olds, 8.6% of the 12-year-olds, and 11.4% of the 17-year-olds. Costello (1989) found that approximately 4% of children aged seven to 11 met criteria for separation anxiety disorder, and Anderson, Williams, McGee, and Silva (1987) reported a prevalence rate of 3.5% for the 11-year-olds in their sample. In a follow-up of this same sample four years later, McGee et al. (1990) found that 2% of 15-year-olds met diagnostic criteria for separation anxiety disorder, while Kashani and Orvaschel (1988) reported a rate of 0.7% for the adolescents in their sample. Within a sample of children referred to an anxiety disorders clinic, separation anxiety disorder was the most common primary diagnosis, with a prevalence rate of approximately 33% (Last et al., 1987). Within this diagnosis, females tend to be overrepresented (across their three age groups, Kashani and Orvashel (1990) reported that 21.0% of girls, compared with 4.8% of boys, met diagnostic criteria for separation anxiety disorder), as do younger children, and Caucasian children from lower socioeconomic backgrounds. Further, an epidemiological study conducted by Velez, Johnson, and Cohen (1989) identified lower socioeconomic status as a risk factor for the development of separation anxiety disorder.

Prevalence rates for avoidant disorder tend to be somewhat lower than for either of the other two anxiety diagnoses of childhood and adolescence. Costello (1989), for instance, reported that 1.6% of children aged seven to 11 met diagnostic criteria for avoidant disorder. Also relevant here are prevalence rates for social phobia, which replaces avoidant disorder in *DSM-IV*. Kashani and Orvaschel (1990) reported that 1.0% of their total sample met criteria for this diagnosis. Across the three age groups, the rates were as follows: 0.0% of the 8-year-olds, 1.4% of the 12-year-olds, and 1.4% of the 17-year-olds. These authors also reported an even gender ratio for the diagnosis of social phobia—across the three age groups, 1.0% of boys and 1.0% of girls met criteria.

For overanxious disorder in children, the prevalence rates range from 2.9% (Anderson et al., 1987) to 4.6% (Costello, 1989), while 7% of adolescents have been reported to meet criteria for the diagnosis (Kashani & Orvaschel, 1988). Kashani and Orvaschel (1990) reported that 12.4% of their total sample met criteria for overanxious disorder, with the age breakdown being as follows: 8.6% of eight-year-olds, 11.4% of 12-year-olds, and 17.1% of 17-year-olds. As can be seen from these figures, this disorder seems to occur more frequently in older children. Within a clinically anxious sample, approximately 15% had a primary diagnosis of overanxious disorder (Last et al., 1987). In terms of the gender ratio, males and females appear to be equally represented within this diagnosis, until adolescence when there is female predominance (Werry, 1991). Finally, it appears that Caucasian children from middle and upper class families may be overrepresented in overanxious disorder (Last et al.), although this finding may well reflect referrals rather than prevalence.

Thus, while available data on the prevalence of anxiety disorders are somewhat discrepant in terms of specific rates of the various subcategories of anxiety disorders, they are unanimous in pointing to ubiquity and significance of anxiety problems in general throughout childhood and adolescence. Clearly, anxiety problems emerge as the most common form of psychological distress when the children and adolescents are asked themselves.

5.13.2.4 Etiology

It would be impossible to review all theories of all types of childhood anxiety in this chapter. Thus, we limit the scope in order to cover the major etiological positions that have been translated into contemporary clinical practice. These include psychodynamic, social learning, family systems, and biological theories of anxiety.

5.13.2.4.1 Psychodynamic

Freud's (1909) description of a phobic disorder in a five-year-old boy was the first time psychoanalysis was applied to a childhood disorder, and remains a seminal documentation of the psychodynamic approach to anxiety disorders. The child had phobias of horses and of leaving the family home and Freud interpreted these as stemming from Oedipal conflicts. The boy had witnessed a horse fall violently in the street. To Freud, the horse's violent struggles brought the boy's unconscious wishes to be violent toward his father to the conscious mind, thus provoking considerable anxiety. Thus, in the psychoanalytic approach the feared stimuli are seen as being secondary to the internal stimuli that they represent. Any number of unconscious conflicts can be associated with anxiety problems; the Oedipal conflict is but one example. The common element is that anxiety results from the conscious mind being overwhelmed by uncontrollable, threatening stimuli. While these stimuli can emanate from external sources, these rarely cause clinical anxiety states. Anxiety that arises from uncontrollable, threatening stimuli coming from the unconscious mind is more likely to cause disabling clinical anxiety states. For the child, focusing on external stimuli as feared objects is seen as functional in eliminating the true source of the anxiety from consciousness.

Uncontrolled case studies have claimed effectiveness using psychodynamic methods with anxious children (e.g., Le Roy & Derdeyn, 1976). However, controlled studies have produced equivocal results (e.g., Milos & Reiss, 1982) and, overall, these methods have received little empirical support. Other problems with the psychodynamic approach have been thoroughly discussed elsewhere (e.g., King, Hamilton, & Ollendick, 1988) including difficulty evaluating theories and therapies because of a lack of specificity of definitional constructs, and the length of time needed to implement treatments. Notwithstanding, there are aspects of psychodynamic theories of anxiety that warrant recognition and further attention. First, they alert us to the common developmental aspects of fear. That is, certain fears and anxieties come to the forefront of experience at specific biologically determined phases of life. For example, separation from caregivers is one of the first fear-provoking situations that both children and parents must successfully negotiate. Second, many contemporary psychodynamic models emphasize the role of interpersonal processes in the development and maintenance of anxiety states. For example, Kohut's (1971) and Mahler's (1968) work on object–self relations emphasize the importance of early parent–child relationships in the development of stable and robust self structures that promote psychological health. Bowlby's work on attachment processes provides a well-developed theoretical and methodological model describing attachment/separation processes throughout life development, and will be discussed later in this chapter. Third, in terms of processes of internalization leading to healthy self structures, contemporary psychodynamic models share much in common with modern information-processing models of anxiety in their emphasis on intrapsychic, even unconscious, processes that lead the sufferer to attend to and overinterpret threat stimuli, both internal (e.g., physiological arousal, dangerous thoughts) and in the external environment (e.g., criticism) (see Brewin, 1987).

5.13.2.4.2 Biological

A good deal is known about the neurophysiology and endocrinology of immediate "fight or flight" reactions to noxious stimuli (Gray, (1988). However, very little is known about the biological mechanisms involved in anxiety states that are more diffuse over stimulus conditions and time. At present, there are several lines of inquiry that may shed light on possible biological bases of anxiety. A recent review by Rutter et al. (1990) of genetic transmission studies indicated that a familial loading is evident for adult anxiety disorders. However, it is impossible to discern from available evidence whether the transmission is via genetic or environmental factors. For childhood anxiety disorders, the picture is even less clear and less adequately researched. While there appears to be a familial transmission of anxiety disorders in children, it is not clearly a genetic phenomenon and it does not show disorder specificity. That is, anxious children often have parents with a range of psychiatric disturbance, and anxiety problems in parents are associated with a similarly broad range of disturbance in their children (Rutter et al.).

Research has indicated that vulnerability to anxiety varies across individuals and is stable across time. With rhesus monkeys, Suomi (1986) has shown that certain individuals are more likely than others to respond to "challenge" situations with fear and behavioral inhibition. This vulnerability appears to be traitlike, existing at relatively high frequencies in genetic as opposed to environmental (adopted) siblings, and stable over time. Further, Suomi, Seaman, Lewis, Delizio, and McKinney (1978) demonstrated that imipramine reduces these fear reactions in vulnerable individuals during separation from parental figures. Similarly, Kagan, Reznick, and Snidman (1988) have shown that the traits of "behaviorally inhibited" infants are stable over time and consistently emerge when the infant is placed in a stressful situation. More recently, Biederman et al. (1990) compared two samples of children who had been classified as either inhibited or not inhibited/uninhibited, with a view to investigating whether behavioral inhibition is associated with anxiety in children. The results indicated that a wide range of internalizing and externalizing disorders were more prevalent in inhibited children compared with the not inhibited and healthy control children. Although this study was exploratory, the data suggest that behavioral inhibition to the unfamiliar may be one of the multiple risk factors implicated in the development of childhood anxiety disorders. More recent research has examined factors that may determine which behaviorally inhibited children are at risk of developing childhood anxiety disorders. Hirshfield et al. (1992), for instance, demonstrated that the association between childhood anxiety disorders and behavioral inhibition appears to be accounted for by those children who have stable behavioral inhibition (i.e., children who remained behaviourally inhibited at each of the follow-up points). More specifically, Rosenbaum et al. (1992) reported that greater anxiety loading in the parents increased the risk for anxiety disorders in behaviorally inhibited children.

A number of theories of anxiety that attempt to bridge behavioral and biological dimensions have been put forward, particularly with regard to inherited autonomic reactivity and conditionability (e.g., Gray, 1988); however the nature and function of biological mechanisms underlying anxiety disorders remain elusive and controversial. Further research cooperation between biologists and behaviorists is sorely needed.

5.13.2.4.3 Learning mechanisms

Modern behavioral conceptions of anxiety disorders emphasize conditioning and social learning processing in both the origins and maintenance of anxiety (Davey, 1992; Graziano, De Giovanni, & Garcia, 1979; King et al., 1988; Morris & Kratochwill, 1983; Mowrer, 1960; Thyer & Sowers-Hoag, 1988). Classical conditioning processes are invoked to explain how previously neutral stimuli (e.g., public transport) become threatening through association with unconditioned aversive stimuli (e.g., being lost, abandoned, fainting, or dying). Avoidance behavior, which is negatively reinforced by the reduction in anxiety it produces, maintains the fear by not allowing any natural extinction of the fear response to occur. Operant factors, such as reinforcement from significant others and avoidance of unpleasant responsibilities may also help maintain the fear. Such learning can be direct or vicarious, that is, acquired simply by observing the person's experience of fear, and is cognitively mediated. Cues that elicit fear can be regarded as information that is processed by individuals. Thus, cognitive processing mechanisms can be seen as an important link in the fear response. In adults, measures of cognitive processing of threat information discriminate between people with anxiety disorders and others (Rapee, 1991), and more recent research has indicated similar findings with anxious children (Barrett, Rapee, Dadds, & Ryan, 1996; Vasey, 1993). Anxiety disorders, especially the social types, may be in part maintained by social skills deficits in the child. If social interactions are repeatedly unsuccessful or unpleasant for the child, they are increasingly likely to avoid or to feel anxious in such situations. Hence, social skills interventions have become an important part of behavioral approaches to child anxiety (Graziano et al., 1979; King et al., 1988).

5.13.2.4.4 Stressful events

Anxiety states in children can be associated with exposure to both acute and chronic stressors such as loss of a parent, divorce, school failure, sexual and physical abuse, and physical illness. However, the increased occurrence of environmental stressors appear to precede the onset of nearly all psychiatric disorders and even physical illness (Goodyer, 1990). Much of the effect of environmental stressors are mediated through their effects on parent–child relations. For example, many of the deleterious effects of divorce on children are associated with changes in daily routine, discipline practices, and parent–child communication (Emery, 1982). While it is clear that stressors can produce anxiety in children (e.g., Dadds & Powell, 1991) it is not clear whether this also applies to clinically significant anxiety disorders in children who already had some vulnerability or disturbance predating the stressor (Goodyer, 1990).

5.13.2.4.5 Family processes

In research up until the 1970s, reviewed by Hetherington and Martin (1979), mothers of anxious children were consistently described as domineering, overprotective, and overinvolved with the child. However, as Hetherington and Martin also noted, this image of the overprotective mother and the highly structured family system were based on "rather indirect sources of data" (p. 61). Empirical studies were more limited in the support they provided for family factors, but included elevated levels of anxiety in the parents of anxious children (Bernstein & Borchardt, 1991), and marital conflict as a correlate of anxiety in nonclinic children (Dadds & Powell, 1991). However, more recent samples of anxious children found they were not different from other groups on marital conflict or dimensions of family functioning measured by the FACES scale (emeshment, adapatability). Further, Green, Loeber, and Lahey (1992) found no evidence for the presence of deviant family hierarchies, as predicted by family systems theory (Haley, 1976; Minuchin, 1974), in the families of overanxious boys. A study by Stark, Humphrey, Crook, and Levis (1990) showed that anxious children saw their families as less supportive, less sociable, more conflictual, and more enmeshed than nonclinic children. However, the results were even more striking for depressed and mixed depressed/anxious children and so these factors are unlikely to be specific correlates of childhood anxiety.

More impressive data has come from direct observational studies of social learning processes. Krohne and Hock (1993) argued that a child's competencies are related to the parents' tendency to help the child develop problem-solving and coping skills, and, inversely, to overly control the child (restriction). The idea of parental overcontrol has often been related to anxiety problems in children. Solyom, Silberfeld, and Solyom (1976) reported that mothers of agoraphobic patients scored significantly higher on measures of maternal control than mothers of normals. Krohne and Hock (1991) found that the mothers of high-anxious girls were judged by independent observers to be more restrictive than mothers of low-anxious girls during a common problem-solving task. Similarly, Dumas, LaFreniere, and Serketich (1995) observed parent interactions among aggressive, anxious, and nondistressed dyads. The anxious dyads were characterized by high parental control and aversiveness. According to Krohne and Hock, consequence expectancies on the other hand are related to the consistency of positive and negative feedback from parents. Kohlmann, Schumacher, and Streit (1988) found significant positive associations between parental inconsistency and trait anxiety in the child.

A more recent study has indicated that parents of anxious children may differ from other parents in terms of the way they teach their children to interpret and respond to ambiguous threat cues. Barrett et al. (1996) demonstrated that anxious children and their parents make relatively high numbers of threat interpretations and, hence, choose avoidant solutions when faced with ambiguous hypothetical social problems. As part of their experimental procedure, Barrett et al. also asked the families of anxious, aggressive, and nonclinic children to discuss how their child should deal with these ambiguous situations. For anxious children only, the likelihood that the child would devise an avoidant solution increased after the family discussion. It appears as if the family process can facilitate expression of the child's vulnerabilities. In a follow-up paper, Dadds, Barrett, Rapee, and Ryan (1996) analyzed the contingent stream of family behaviors that had been videotaped in the family discussions in the Barrett et al. study. Results showed that parents of anxious children were more likely to reciprocate avoidant solutions and less likely to encourage prosocial solutions to ambiguous social situations, than parents of nonclinic and aggressive children.

5.13.2.4.6 Recent studies of attachment processes

Attachment refers to the establishment of early intimate relationships and the internalization of these relationships as stable cognitive representations of the relation of the self to intimates throughout the lifespan (Bowlby, 1969). In the late twentieth century a number of strategies for operationalizing attachment processes have been developed, including observational measures of parent–infant bonds (Ainsworth, 1989), and self-report and structured interview measures of current adult relationships and past relationships to parents (Main, 1996). A number of manifestations of insecure attachment have been described and empirically verified, including dismissive (or avoidant, e.g., avoiding or failing to seek out intimate contact) and preoccupied (or anxious/ambivalent styles, e.g., showing distress at separation, clinging, failure to show independent exploration). Using various methods of categorizing attachment, numerous studies have been published showing that different attachment processes characterize psychologically healthy versus distressed adults and children. Clinic-referred samples of children and adults show relatively low rates of secure attachment, that is, intimate relationships marked by predictable, stable, and generous levels of care and support, compared with nonclinic samples (Main).

In general, however, it has been difficult to find specific relationships between particular forms of psychopathology and specific types of insecure attachment (see van Ijzendoom & Bakermans-Kranenburg, 1996, for a meta-analytic review). Recent improvements in the design of studies may overcome this lack of specificity. For example, Rosenstein and Horowitz (1996) found that psychiatrically hospitalized adolescents with a "preoccupied" attachment style were much more likely to have anxiety and depression problems than those with a dismissive style, who tended to show conduct problems. Clearly these results are encouraging and careful research is worth pursuing in this area. It should be noted, however, that the area still tends to be characterized by reliance on global typology categories and absence of specific descriptions of behavioral processes mediating attachment and psychopathology. This is highlighted by the DeKlyen (1996) study which showed that maternal attachment added no predictive power to the child's behavioral problems once direct observational measures of parent–child interactions were considered. Gender effects also need to be considered and more effort is needed to include fathers in this area. Cowan, Cohn, Pape-Cowan, and Pearson (1996), for example, found that mothers' and fathers' attachment styles were differentially related to internalizing vs. externalizing problems in their children. Further, few treatment developments from an attachment perspective have been subjected to controlled outcome and process studies.

5.13.2.4.7 Family systems theories

While there are several varieties of theoretical approaches that fall under the general banner of family systems theory, the common thread is the notion that the family system can be viewed as a functional or homeostatic unit. Disturbance in one family member (the "identified patient") is seen as part of a disturbed family system (Barnes, 1985). At extremes, the identified patient's problems are seen as a symptom that serves to maintain homoeostatic balance in an otherwise dysfunctional family. As an example, a child's separation anxiety may be seen as providing a parent with the feeling that they are needed, thereby reducing the likelihood that marital conflict will erupt over a distant, nonintimate marital relationship. Family systems theories have been quickly translated into clinical practice and have arguably been the "boom" therapy in the late twentieth century. Unfortunately, research into the conceptual validity and treatment efficacy of these approaches has lagged dramatically behind their enthusiastic translation into clinical practice. Despite repeated calls for these approaches to be evaluated, very little empirical work has been undertaken, and thus it is difficult to support any further expansion of these family systems models at this time.

5.13.2.5 Developmental Course

As already noted, for the majority of children and adolescents, fears and anxieties are typically common, functional, and transitory. For this reason, both clinicians and parents often view childhood anxiety as a passing complaint (Keller et al., 1992). Unfortunately, for a significant proportion of all children and adolescents, this is not the case and the prognosis, if they do not receive treatment, is much less encouraging than has previously been thought. For instance, in one study, 70.6% of children aged six to 12 years who had been diagnosed with overanxious disorder were found to have retained this diagnosis at two-year follow-ups (Pfeffer, Lipkins, Plutchik, & Mizruchi, 1988). Keller et al. assessed past and present psychopathology in 275 children and adolescents aged six to 19 years who had been recruited as part of a risk study. Fourteen percent of the children were found to have a history of an anxiety disorder, and of these children only 34% were anxiety diagnosis-free

at the time of the assessment. The average duration of the disorder to the time of interview was four years, but the Kaplan-Meier estimates indicated that 46% of the children with an anxiety disorder would still be ill eight years after the onset of the disorder. Keller et al. concluded by noting that "anxiety disorders in childhood may be more chronic than previously believed . . . anxiety disorders in children may be severe and enduring" (p. 598).

The chronicity of childhood anxiety would seem to be due, at least in part, to the tendency of anxiety to be associated with general social problems such as negative self-image, dependency on adults in social situations, comparatively poor problem-solving skills, unpopularity, and low rates of interaction with peers (Kashani & Orvaschel, 1990; Messer & Beidel, 1994; Panella & Henggeler, 1986; Rubin & Clark, 1983; Strauss, Frame, & Forehand, 1987). In clinical samples, anxious children are less successful in peer relationships than their nonreferred counterparts (Edelbrock, 1985; Puig-Antich et al., 1985; Strauss, Lahey, Frick, Frame, & Hynd, 1988). As a whole, this research indicates that anxiety in children and adolescents (in both clinical and nonreferred samples) is associated with significant psychosocial difficulties. Regardless of the casual direction of the relationship between anxiety and its psychosocial correlates, it makes sense to hypothesize that for many anxious children and adolescents, this relationship is one in which anxiety continually strengthens the psychological factors and vice versa, thus contributing to the chronicity of anxiety in children and adolescents who have not received treatment.

A final point worth making in this section is that although the connection between childhood and adult anxiety is not yet clearly understood, evidence from a variety of studies indicates that vulnerability to adult anxiety may manifest itself in childhood. In support of this contention, there is increasing empirical evidence that many adult anxiety disorders originally began in childhood or adolescence (Rapee & Barlow, 1992). Retrospective accounts of adult anxiety patients frequently describe the onset of anxious symptomatology in late childhood or adolescence (Gittelman, 1984; Mattison, 1992; Thyer, Parrish, & Curtis, 1985). Klein (1964), for instance, reported that at least half of a sample of severely impaired adult agoraphobic patients had had separation anxiety and difficulty adjusting to school during childhood, while Gittelman found that a notable proportion of hospitalized agoraphobic adults reported an early history of severe separation anxiety.

5.13.3 CONCEPTUALIZATION AND CLINICAL FORMULATION

5.13.3.1 Multimodal Assessment

Available assessment procedures in childhood anxiety disorders include the use of structured clinical interviews, self-report measures, direct behavioral observations, self-monitoring of behaviors and accompanying cognitions, and physiological assessment.

The structured clinical interview used most commonly with anxious children is the ADIS (Silverman & Nelles, 1988), with a form to be used for the child and a parallel form for the parents (ADIS-C and ADIS-P). The ADIS has questions relevant to the latest *DSM* categories and facilitates acceptable inter-rater reliability of anxiety diagnoses in children (see Rapee et al., 1994; Silverman, 1991). Many other structured interviews are available (see Silverman, 1991 for a review). It should be noted that the reliability achieved from these interviews varies considerably according to the source of the information, the skills of the interviewers, the age of the interviewees, the base rate of the target disorder, and other factors. Silverman (1991), in recognizing the variability of inter-rater reliability, advises researchers to speak of reliability levels in terms specific to particular cohorts rather than as a characteristic of particular disorders or interviews. With regard to the validity of diagnoses achieved from structured interviews, there is some evidence that convergence is acceptable with standardized checklists such as the CBCL (see below). Generally, however, little research has systematically addressed the many ways in which validity can be assessed, and, at present, the validity of the interviews must be considered unknown (Silverman, 1991).

A variety of self-report measures is available. The ones that have been most utilized both in research and clinical work include the Revised Children's Manifest Anxiety Scale (RCMAS) (Reynolds & Paget, 1981), the Revised Fear Survey Schedule for Children (FSSC-R) (Ollendick, 1983), the modified State-trait Anxiety Inventory for Children (STAIC) (Fox & Houston, 1983), and parent/teacher/child ratings of general adjustment across multiple dimensions of dysfunction on screening checklists such as the CBCL (Achenbach & Edelbroch, 1991). None of the anxiety checklists produces data that correspond to the current *DSM* or *ICD* categories. The FSSC-R is used for assessing the content and spread of children's fears, the RCMAS and the STAIC produce measures of felt anxiety symptoms (e.g., physiological, worry). While the reliability of these checklists is generally good, recent research has questioned their discriminative validity. That is, they cannot discriminate reliably between different groups of clinically referred children and the differentiation of anxious and attention deficit children seems particularly problematic (Perrin & Last, 1992). Further development of self-report measures is needed, exemplified by Spence's (1996) recent attempts to develop a self-report measure with symptom domains that correspond to current diagnostic categories.

It is possible to measure fear/anxiety indirectly by measuring the behaviors that people typically engage in when faced with specific threat-related stimuli. For example, measuring the amount of time a child spends at school will provide an indirect estimate of fear of school. Used under controlled conditions, these measures are usually referred to as behavioral avoidance or approach tests (BAT). The aim of the BAT is to collect objective information about how the person reacts (dependent variable) to fear stimuli (independent variable). For example, a person who has a crippling fear of dogs may be asked to approach and stroke a dog under controlled conditions (the dog is restrained). A range of dependent measures can be taken including proximity to the dog and other behaviors hypothesized to reflect the anxiety level. BATs can be standardized or individualized. The former are most commonly used for research purposes and involve a standard series of tasks to which all subjects are exposed. In an individualized BAT, the stimuli to which each child is exposed are selected on the basis of the child's own specific fears. Naturally, this would be more useful in a clinical situation but it is also valuable in research since it would maximize the fear ratings achieved.

There are many variations on the possible uses of BATs and we present a sample to give some indication of the adaptability of these tests in their use with children. Lang and Lazovic (1963) asked subjects to approach a harmless caged snake in a laboratory and scored the subject's behavior on a three-point scale corresponding to looking, touching, and holding behavior. In other studies, the subject was asked to remain still while the feared stimulus was brought closer in graded steps by an experimenter (Murphy & Bootzin, 1973). In these tests, the dependent measure is usually the distance from the child before the child conveys that he or she does not want the feared stimulus to come any closer. Although the child is always given the power to terminate these tests, active BATs are usually preferred owing to the unpleasantness and artificiality of asking a fearful child to remain passive while another person controls the feared stimulus, and to the advantages of practicing approach behavior that comes with the use of active BATs.

While most BATs have been used with animal phobias, other creative uses have been reported, including fear of blood (Van Hasselt, Hersen, Bellack, Rosenblum, & Lamparski, 1979), the dark (e.g., Giebenhain & O'Dell, 1984; Kelley, 1976), heights (Van Hasselt et al., 1979), medical procedures (Freeman, Roy, & Hemmick, 1976), water (Lewis, 1974), and strangers (Matson, 1981). In social fears and generalized anxiety conditions, it is difficult to specify the phobic stimuli in such a way as to allow their manipulation under controlled conditions. For example, a child may avoid school owing due to a fear of having to interact with large groups of unsupervised children as would be found in a school playground. Children with generalized anxiety are fearful of new events in their lives such as taking tests, going to camps, changing classes, or having to perform, which are all difficult to operationalize for use with BATs. This limitation is important and should be the attention of creative thinking and research. In the late twentieth century, anxiety research with both adults and children has increasingly focused on the more generalized forms of anxiety disorder (generalized anxiety, overanxious disorder, panic, social fear) rather than the simple of specific phobias. Owing to the difficulty of operationizing the objects of these fears, the salience of BATs in the research literature has decreased and progress in the development and refinement of these measurement strategies has slowed to a crawl.

A number of variables may affect the validity of BATs (Borkovec, Weert, & Bernstein, 1977). Clinicians and researchers rarely use existing procedures, and thus, comparison across studies is difficult. Furthermore, a BAT is a social situation in which many variables can influence the child's behavior and yet, very little research has been conducted into the role of contextual variables (cf., Kelley, 1976; Sheslow, Bondy, & Nelson, 1982). More attention needs to be given to contextual factors in childrens' performance in fearful settings. This should be done not just so we can control these as unwanted influences. Rather, we should try to understand the role of contextual factors as a means of further understanding the developmental origins of fear itself. The BAT, as well as being used as a standardized procedure for producing fear responses, could be used for assessing the role of social influences, such as the family, on childrens' anxiety.

Direct observations of childrens' anxiety have typically been designed to record discrete child behaviors in natural settings that elicit anxiety such as during medical procedures, public speaking, or school exams. Detailed reviews of these systems can be obtained from Barrios and Hartmann (1988), Dadds, Rapee, and Barrett (1994), and King et al. (1988). The Observer Rating Scale of Anxiety (Melamed & Siegel, 1975) was designed for observing children undergoing surgery and consists of 28 discrete child behaviors which the observer scores for frequency of occurrence. These include behaviors such as "trembling hands" and "clings to mother," as well as more general distress behaviors such as "crying" and "kicks." Similarly, the Behavior Profile Rating Scale (BPRS) (Melamed, Yurcheson, Fleece, Hutcherson, & Hawes, 1978) contains 27 behaviors for use in dental settings and, thus, includes relevant behaviors such as refusing to open one's mouth. For both systems, the frequency of discrete behaviors can be combined into an overall anxiety score, although it should be noted that the overall score reflects distress and noncompliant behavior as well as anxious behavior. Further, the BPRS contains items that are scored according to the dentist's behavior, for example, the "dentist uses loud voice." Reliability and discriminative validity data have been collected and are supportive of the systems. Another observational system that has been applied to stressful medical procedures and undergone extensive development and evaluation is the Procedure Behavioral Rating Scale and its derivatives (Jay & Elliott, 1984; Jay, Ozolins, Elliott, & Caldwell, 1983; Katz, Kellerman, & Siegel, 1980; Le Baron & Zeltzer, 1984). These systems involve an observer rating the frequency of a number of child fear and distress behaviors during bone marrow procedures.

Glennon and Weisz (1978) developed a system for observing anxiety in preschool children. Their main rationale was to develop a measurement system for use with young children that avoided problems of self-report and global adult ratings. The Preschool Observation Scale of Anxiety (POSA) contains 30 behaviors that were selected to reflect fearful behavior in young children. These include both direct signs of fear ("child complains of being afraid," "trembling," "fearful facial expression"), indirect signs of fear ("cry," "gratuitous movement," "nail biting"), and other behavior selected to reflect fear in this population ("masturbation," "silence," "rigid body posture"). Glennon and Weisz evaluated the POSA in observations of preschool children's behavior during a forced separation from their mothers at their regular preschool. However, the system could be used in any setting. Inter-rater reliabilities ranged from quite low to very high, as did the frequency of the observed behaviors themselves, and further work may be required to refine the sample of 30 behaviors. The POSA represents one of the few attempts to operationalize child anxiety into an observation system that can be used in a range of natural settings. Milos and Reiss (1982) used an observation system that scores the frequency of a single global behavior as a reflection of anxiety during separation. Neisworth, Madel, and Goeke (1975) designed a system that measures the duration of crying and screaming in preschoolers during their daily preschool routine.

By far the most research and theorizing that has occurred with regard to separation anxiety has occurred within the social attachment literature. The original impetus for this area came from the intensive observations of Harry and Margaret Harlow, using infant rhesus monkeys (Harlow & Harlow, 1962), Bowlby's (1973) observations of orphaned children, and Ainsworth's observations of separated infants (Ainsworth, Blehar, Waters, & Wall, 1978). Typically, the child is observed during separation from the mother, exposure to an unfamiliar adult, and reuniting with the mother (Ainsworth et al., 1978). Research by Kagan and colleagues has shown that the infant's behavior during such challenges is predictive of the later development of anxiety and social withdrawal problems. Specifically, infants that show "behavioral inhibition" (long latency to interact with and retreat from unfamiliar adults, cessation of play and clinging to the mother) are more likely to develop social anxiety and withdrawal later in childhood (Kagan, Reznick, & Snidman, 1988).

A number of systems have also been designed to observe children's responses to test performance and public speaking. For example, Wine (1979) developed an observational system that comprises 22 discrete behaviors that are recorded over a 15-minute interval immediately preceding a classroom examination. The behaviors are grouped into attending, task-related, activity, communication, and interactional behaviors. Few of these are directly reflective of the expression of anxiety but rather focus on the indirect effects of anxiety on the child's ongoing activities. Paul's (1966) timed behavior checklist was designed to measure the presence of overt anxiety in adolescents in public-speaking situations. It has been adapted for use with younger children's reactions to public speaking (Fox & Houston, 1981) and darkness (Giebenhain & O'Dell, 1994). The original contains 20 items that are recorded for occurrence or nonoccurrence over a series of observational intervals and can be reduced to an overall anxiety score for the observation session.

Another method for measuring anxiety is to have observers use global rating scales. As examples, an observer may be asked to observe a child for a five-minute period and then rate the child's level of anxiety on a five-point scale; and, a parent of a child with fear of school may be asked to provide a similar rating every minute for the 30-minute period at home immediately prior to leaving for school. These systems are generally easy to use, but have specific advantages and disadvantages. First, research has indicated that people are generally very consistent in their observations and descriptions of the effect in other people. Even across different cultures, people tend to agree on the facial expressions that signal fear (Ekman, 1980). Thus, inter-rater reliability is generally quite high for global ratings of anxiety. A number of studies of anxious children have used such global ratings and the reader is referred to the reviews by Barrios and Hartmann (1988) and King et al. (1988). The problem with global ratings is that it is not clear exactly what is being measured and thus they generally have little to contribute to our understanding of anxiety. This restricts their use to situations in which an inexpensive and simple measure of anxiety is needed, and as with all single measures, they should be used as part of a more comprehensive assessment package (King et al., 1988).

The development of observational strategies for measuring child anxiety mostly took place in the 1960s and 1970s and, since that initial burst of activity, little has occurred in terms of the development and refinement of these methodologies. Most existing observational strategies focus solely on the child. Creative attempts to operationalize the social context of the child's anxiety and examine its functional relationship to the development of anxiety are sorely needed. Questions remain unanswered about the validity of these systems in terms of the content of the behavioral categories used. With children, most of the observational systems contain a mix of direct expressions of anxiety as an effect, as well as protest behaviors that are thought to result from anxiety. Using observation systems that lump all effect and protesting behaviors together to produce one overall "anxiety" score will not differentiate between these children. More work is needed to examine whether it is psychometrically and conceptually sound to treat these various components as unitary reflections of anxiety; quite possibly they are functionally very different when one considers how they affect and are affected by their social context. The discriminative validity of these observational systems remain unclear. Very little evidence is available to indicate that these systems can differentiate anxious from nonanxious children. Further, there is no evidence to show that children with different types of anxiety problems can be differentiated. Finally, the targets of these systems are mainly restricted to simple fears that are expressed in highly structured settings. Little work has been done attempting to use observational measures with children with complex, generalized anxiety.

We believe that there is enormous unrealized potential in the use of direct observations of anxiety in young children. Two major areas for development suggest themselves. There is the need to understand the child's anxiety in terms of its social context. Thus, observation systems that score both the child's anxiety as well as other antecedent and consequent stimuli need to be developed. Also, observations need to be designed and used in a way that allows for conceptual integration with other aspects of anxiety such as cognitive processing style, family interaction, and physiological reactivity. For example, much progress is currently being made in understanding the way anxious people process information about threat in their environment (e.g., Butler & Mathews, 1983). That is, anxious people show an exaggerated tendency to perceive, attend to, and respond to threat in their environments. We may ask whether this processing style is learned through interaction with significant others, namely anxious parents. A methodology that integrates information processing and direct observation of the child in interaction with others may yield important insights into this process. The work by Krohne and colleagues (Krohne, 1992; Krohne & Hock, 1991) and Barrett et al. (1996), reviewed above, are examples of fruitful attempts in this direction.

5.13.3.2 Treatment Formulation

The treatment formulation represents the integration of the theory of etiology, a theoretically guided and multimodal assessment of the individual case, and the existing literature on the efficacy of available intervention strategies. While this will in part depend on the skills and theoretical approach of the particular clinician, a number of guiding principles can be extracted from existing knowledge.

The conceptualization of the case should include a diagnostic formulation in terms of current *DSM* or ICD systems with particular reference to the developmental and cultural characteristics of the child and the normative expression of fears and anxieties that exist in all children. As well as the normative and cultural aspects of fear, preliminary formulations should consider the likelihood that the child's fears and anxieties are realistic in context. We have

assessed a number of cases of "separation" and "social" fears in which the referred child was being exposed on a daily basis to threats of removal from the family home, and bullying at school, respectively. As previously stated, multiple informants should be used in gathering these data.

Factors hypothesized to be implicated in the development and maintenance of the anxiety problem should include a thorough examination of the following:

(i) Social learning factors: the extent to which the child experienced a learning history predictive of conditioned or traumatic responses to previously neutral stimuli, and what operant factors are currently maintaining a pattern of avoidance and anxious responding.

(ii) Cognitive factors: the extent to which the child shows a pattern of negative competency and outcome expectancies, low self-esteem, and over- or selective attention to potential threat in the environment.

(iii) Physiological factors: the extent to which the child exhibits physiological arousal (muscle tension, problem breathing) associated with avoidance and anxiety.

(iv) Family factors: the extent to which the child has stable, nurturing family relationships, and the extent to which the other family members have anxiety problems.

(v) Peers and social skills: the extent to which the child has the skills and opportunities to develop appropriate and pleasing peer relationships.

Using an assessment and therapy procedure that empowers the child and family in terms of acquired knowledge, skills, and decision making, the above factors should be summarized into a concise formulation and treatment plan that clearly prioritizes and addresses the relevant causal factors. The treatment plan will thus usually involve some combination of social learning interventions such as: exposure, modeling, and reinforcement for overcoming avoidance; cognitive skills for the child such as positive self-talk, developing positive expectancies, attention to nonthreat stimuli, and reinforcing oneself for success; relaxation, breathing retraining, and other skills for overcoming uncontrollable and unpleasant physiological arousal; a family intervention to establish other family members as positive models of courage and social competence, as sources of stable care and nurturance, and sources of reinforcement for success; and social skills and school interventions to facilitate positive peer relationships and remove any sources of (realistic) fear from the school setting.

The treatment formulation should specify clear goals for improvement that are graduated from easy to difficult so the child has early success and a growing sense of mastery. The active involvement of family members is important, especially for children in the preteenage years.

5.13.4 TREATMENT

5.13.4.1 Psychosocial Treatments

Psychodynamic and systemic therapies have been used in the treatment of childhood anxiety disorders; however, the lack of controlled studies prohibits conclusions about their usefulness. However, there have been some preliminary studies of psychodynamic treatments for childhood disorders. For example, although the studies by Milos and Reiss (1982) and Target and Fonagy (1994) do not allow conclusions about differential efficacy, they offer some hope for the use of empirical procedures with psychodynamic therapies. Hopefully, the early years of the twenty-first century will see these methods come under the scrutiny of careful research designs. In the following, we focus on cognitive-behavioral, family, and pharmacological treatments that have been evaluated, followed by a review of the main treatment outcome studies related to specific diagnostic groups.

In terms of cognitive-behavioral interventions, King et al. (1988) and Ollendick and Francis (1988) recommend an integrative treatment approach, encompassing exposure variants, modeling, operant, and cognitive-based procedures. Exposure techniques include the use of systematic desensitization proper (imaginal representation of the fear producing stimuli and the use of muscular relaxation as the competing inhibiting response), *in vivo* and imaginal exposure, and emotive imagery (the imagery component is used as the fear-inhibiting agent). An advantage in using these techniques is the clarity of procedural guidelines available to the therapist. Still controversial is the issue of what underlying mechanisms account for the success of exposure-based procedures. Originally, Wolpe (1958) explained it as reciprocal inhibition of anxiety through relaxation. However, numerous case studies have been reported wherein the relaxation had little effect on treatment outcome. More recent views conceptualize the changes during exposure treatments in terms of information-processing changes (Foa & Kozak, 1986). Implosion and flooding-type treatments are not usually used with children owing to the potential aversiveness of the procedures involved.

Modeling procedures include the use of films, *in vivo*, or participant-modeling variants. The child is prompted to imitate the performance of the model who is demonstrating nonfearful behaviors and is reinforced for closer approximation to the coping behavior. Modeling can provide an opportunity for both the vicarious extinction of a child's anxiety, and an acquisition of more accurate information and effective coping skills relative to the anxiety-provoking situation. The efficacy of modeling procedures in the treatment of childhood phobias and in the preparation of children for stressful events has been clearly documented (Ollendick & Francis, 1988).

Operant-based programs (based on contingency management principles) have been especially successful in the treatment of school refusal, socially avoidant children, and specific phobias (King & Ollendick, 1989). Operant procedures are based on the premise that fear and anxiety will reduce when nonfearful behaviors are reinforced and fearful behaviors are placed on an extinction schedule. Within this approach, it would not be considered necessary to use methods such as relaxation to reduce anxiety directly. The child is simply reinforced for approaching the feared stimuli and rewards for fearful behaviors (e.g., parental comforting, substitution of aversive activities by pleasant play time) are removed. The evidence for the efficacy of operant programs comes mainly from case studies with phobic children, and in general therapeutic success is enhanced when operant procedures are combined with other techniques (King et al. 1988; Ollendick & Francis, 1988).

Self-instruction training is the most commonly used cognitive-based procedure in the treatment of childhood anxiety (Graziano & Mooney, 1980; Meichenbaum & Genest, 1980; Meichenbaum & Goodman, 1971). It is aimed at changing the child's self-talk on the premise that self-doubting and negativistic self-talk increases anxiety and inhibits appropriate responses to feared stimuli. Basically, the child is taught to use competence-mediating statements in the presence of the anxiety-provoking stimuli. However, cognitive procedures alone are often not effective in overcoming anxiety reactions in children owing to the multiplicity of factors involved, such as environmental contingencies, skills competencies, individual developmental factors regarding awareness and identification of self-statements, and the strong physiological component of anxiety disorders.

The integration of cognitive and behavioral procedures in the treatment of childhood anxiety disorders seems to be largely supported in the literature. However, most of the studies previously described have focused on the treatment of specific phobias using single case designs. Evaluative studies on the treatment of separation anxiety, avoidant, and overanxious disorders were less evident. However, in recent years, a number of controlled trials have demonstrated the effectiveness of protocol-based psychosocial interventions that are applicable across various categories of child and adolescent anxiety disorders. Blagg and Yule (1984), working with a total of 66 children presenting with fear of school and separation from parents, examined treatment outcome associated with behavioral therapy, hospitalization, and psychotherapy plus home schooling. The behavior therapy program incorporated exposure to the school setting and contingency management implemented by both parents and teachers. Both at post-treatment and one year follow-up, separation anxiety symptomatology was absent in the behavioral therapy group but still present in the hospitalized (33.3%) and psychotherapy (94%) groups. Average duration of treatment was two weeks for behavior therapy, 45 weeks for hospitalization, and 72 weeks for psychotherapy plus homeschooling.

In the first controlled trial for mixed groups of anxious children, Kendall (1994) evaluated the effectiveness of a 16-session cognitive-behavioral therapy (CBT) program for a group of children with overanxious, separation, and social anxiety problems. The treatment centers around having the child develop an individualized FEAR plan: F, for feeling good by learning to relax; E, for expecting bad vs. good things to happen through positive self-talk; A, for approaching actions to take in the face of fear; and R, for rewarding oneself for efforts to overcome fear or worry. Compared with a waitlist control, the treated children showed clinically significant gains that were maintained at one year follow-up. Follow-up studies have replicated these positive outcomes (Kendall et al., in press) and shown that the treatment effects were maintained to follow-up assessments conducted an average of 3.5 years after treatment (Kendall & Southam-Gerow, 1996).

An issue raised by Kendall (1994) concerned the role of the family in these CBT programs. His recommendation was that active parental involvement is useful for positive child outcomes. More family systemic and psychodynamic theorists would argue that change in the family system would be critical to real change in the child's problem and, at extremes, that solely changing anxiety symptoms in the child without focusing on underlying family dynamics, would be counterproductive. This issue was addressed by Heard, Dadds, and Conrad

(1992) in a study researching the effects of a cognitive-behavioral intervention for childhood anxiety on family variables. They treated three adolescents presenting with simple phobias using contingency management, exposure, and self-instructional training. A multiple baseline design across subjects was used. Results showed marked improvement (at post-treatment and three months follow-up) in anxiety both at overbehavioral and cognitive levels for all three adolescents. Despite sole focus on the child's anxiety symptoms, no negative or compensatory effects on family process, or individual or dyadic adjustment in other family members were observed. Thus, they found no evidence for the family systems hypothesis that treating anxious children using solely child-focused behavioral techniques leads to negative consequences for the rest of the family system.

A recent controlled trial assessed the efficacy of involving parents of anxious children in a CBT program. Barrett, Dadds, and Rapee (1996) compared a CBT intervention based on Kendall's (1990) anxiety management program to an intervention that included the CBT intervention plus a family intervention, again for a mixed group of overanxious, separation anxiety, and socially phobic nine to 14-year-olds. Parental sessions introduced parents-to-child management skills (reinforcement skills, planned ignoring, giving, and backing up clear instructions) and how to use these skills to manage their child's anxiety, explained what the children were learning in the CBT program and illustrated how parents could model and encourage the use of strategies learned in the session, and showed parents how they could use the same strategies, that is, Kendall's FEAR plan, to manage their own anxiety. Evaluation of the program at the end of treatment revealed that 61% of children in the CBT group no longer met a *DSM-III-R* diagnosis, compared with 88% in the combined treatment. Less than 30% were diagnosis free in the waitlist control group. At 12 months follow-up, the relative superiority of the CBT plus family condition was maintained. Thus, it appears that the modification of parental skills can have a significant effect on anxiety in children when combined with a CBT program for the child. However, it is not clear whether a change in parental skills on its own will result in an improvement in child behavior, and it is not clear which aspect of the parental intervention was associated with the extra improvements.

Barrett (1995) showed that similar success rates could be achieved by presenting the combined CBT-family treatment in a group format to anxious children and their parents, thereby significantly reducing costs of intervention. Cobham and Dadds (1995) used the same group intervention to assess the role of parental anxiety in treatment outcome, and the extent to which the second component of Barrett et al.'s (1996) family treatment (parents skills for managing their own anxiety) could alleviate putative poorer treatment outcomes associated with high parental anxiety. Results indicated that high parental anxiety was a risk factor for poorer treatment outcomes for anxious children, and that specifically targeting parental anxiety for intervention could overcome this risk factor in the context of a cognitive-behavioral program for the child.

The above brief review indicates that anxiety disorders in late childhood and early adolescence can be effectively treated in the majority of referred cases. However, early intervention and prevention programs aimed at larger cohorts of children have the potential to be even more cost effective in reducing the incidence of childhood disorders and their cost to the community. A number of authors (e.g., King, Hamilton, & Murphy, 1983; Spence, 1994) have discussed the potential of such programs for children at risk for anxiety disorders. The Queensland Early Intervention and Prevention of Anxiety Project (Dadds, Spence, Holland, Barrett, & Laurens, 1997) utilized a school-based sample of 1786 seven- to 14-years olds. 9.7% of children were identified by teachers as having anxiety problems. A separate group (10.5%) scored 20 or above on the RCMAS. Only 2.0% were both nominated by teachers and scored above 19 on the RCMAS. *Post hoc* analyses showed that the low convergence between teachers' and children's reports may have been due in part to the tendency of some children not to report their anxiety, possibly owing to social desirability factors.

At the conclusion of a diagnostic interview, those children who fell within the "at risk" selection criteria were allocated to the intervention or monitoring condition on the basis of treratment vs. monitoring schools. The intervention was based on the Barrett study (1995) except that it was presented in group format in 10 sessions. On average, children attended over eight of the 10 child intervention sessions, mothers attended 1.7, and fathers 0.63 of three parent sessions. At pretreatment, approximately 75% of children interviewed met criteria for an anxiety diagnosis. At postintervention, improvement was noted for both intervention and monitoring groups. However, children who received the intervention emerged with lower rates of anxiety disorder at six months follow-up compared with those who were monitored only. Of those who had features of disorder, but no full disorder at pretreatment, 54% progressed to a diagnosable disorder at six months follow-up in the monitoring group compared with 16% in the intervention group. These results indicated that the intervention was successful in reducing rates of disorder in children with mild to moderate anxiety disorders, as well as preventing the onset of anxiety disorders in children with early features of a disorder.

5.13.4.2 Pharmacological Treatments

Medication is rarely used as the sole treatment for anxiety disorders in children and adolescents, but instead is typically one part of a treatment program (Allen, Leonard, & Swedo, 1995; Bernstein, 1994). Psychopharmacological interventions tend to be implemented more commonly with older children and adolescents, and also in cases where anxiety symptoms are particularly severe and resistant to other forms of treatment. Unfortunately, there are comparatively few studies that have attempted to evaluate the efficacy of psychopharmacological interventions with anxious children and adolescents. In addition, methodological shortcomings often make results equivocal or difficult to interpret, including small sample sizes, use of samples with mixed diagnoses based on noncurrent diagnostic systems (McDaniel, 1986), concurrent treatments which are not controlled, absence of placebo control groups, and inadequate medication dosages (Bernstein, 1994). These limitations must be kept in mind when evaluating outcome studies for each class of anxiolytics to be reviewed below.

A number of studies have suggested the possible benefit of benzodiazepines in the treatment of anxiety in children and adolescents. Simeon and Ferguson (1987) found that seven of 12 participants (aged eight to 16 years) with a diagnosis of avoidant and/or overanxious disorder manifested at least moderate improvements in terms of clinician-rated symptomatology when they received between 0.5 and 1.5 mg alprazolam (tradename Xanax) per day over a four-week period. Self-report, however, did not depict any improvement in anxiety symptoms. A subsequent, four week, double-blind, placebo-controlled study with a group of 30 children and adolescents (aged eight to 16 years) diagnosed with either avoidant or overanxious disorder and treated with a mean dose of 1.6 mg alprazolam found greater improvement on global improvement ratings compared with participants in a placebo group, although these results were not statistically significant (Simeon et al., 1992). More recently, Graae, Milner, Rizzotto, and Klein (1994) conducted a double-blind crossover trial with 12 children (aged seven to 13 years) with various anxiety diagnoses, in which four weeks of placebo were compared with four weeks of clonazepam (tradename Clonopin; up to 2 mg per day). Although 50% of the children no longer met diagnostic criteria at the end of the trial, clonazepam was not found to produce superior results to the placebo on clinical rating scales completed at the end of the study. In other uncontrolled studies, benzodiazepine treatments have been associated with a decrease in the frequency and/or intensity of symptomatology in children and adolescents with panic disorder (Kutcher & MacKenzie, 1988), and pediatric cancer patients prior to anxiety-provoking medical procedures (Pfefferbaum et al., 1987).

Clearly, the limited research that has examined the efficacy of benzodiazepine treatment of childhood anxiety is difficult to interpret. Less equivocal is the research on side effects related to this class of anxiolytics. The consensus in clinical studies appears to be that benzodiazepines are tolerated by children with minimal side effects (Bernstein, Garfinkel, & Borchardt, 1990; Biederman, 1987; Pfefferbaum et al., 1987; Simeon & Ferguson, 1987; Simeon et al., 1992), and that when side effects do occur, they tend to be dose-related (Kutcher, Reiter, Gardner, & Klein, 1992).

Reported side effects include: ataxia (unsteady gait), diplopia (blurred/double vision), reduced mental acuity, sedation, slurred speech, tremor, drowsiness (Biederman, 1991; Kutcher et al.), and behavioral disinhibition as evidenced by oppositional behavior, liability, and irritability (Graae et al., 1994). Although this class of medication seems to be comparatively safe in overdose (Kutcher et al.), as Biederman (1991) notes, the risks associated with tolerance and dependence in children treated with benzodiazepines are unknown at this time.

As is the case with the benzodiazepines, studies of the efficacy of tricyclic antidepressants with anxious children have produced conflicting results. Four placebo-controlled studies have investigated the outcome of tricyclic antidepressant interventions in the treatment of separation anxiety or school refusal associated with separation anxiety. In the first of these, Gittelman-Klein and Klein (1971, 1973) conducted a six-week trial in which 45 children were assigned randomly to either 100–200 mg of imipramine (tradename Tofranil) per day or a placebo group. Both groups also received behaviorally oriented psychotherapy. Compared with the placebo group, the imipramine group was superior—both in terms of the number of children returning to school and symptom improvement. Using an average dose of 153 mg of imipramine per day, Klein, Koplewicz, and Kanner (1992) were unsuccessful in their attempt to replicate these results in 20 children (aged six to 15 years) with separation anxiety. In another recent study, Bernstein et al. (1990) reported that there were no significant differences among groups of children and adolescents (aged seven to 17 years) who received either alprazolam (mean dosage of 1.8 mg per day), imipramine (mean dosage of 164.3 mg per day), or a placebo. Similarly disappointing results have been reported for the use of clomipramine (tradename Anafranil) in facilitating either a return to school or a reduction in anxious symptomatology with 51 anxious children and adolescents aged nine to 15 years (Berney et al., 1981). Although only one of the four studies reviewed above provides support for the efficacy of the tricyclic antidepressants in the treatment of separation anxiety (with or without school refusal), as Bernstein (1994) notes, one of the three negative studies used an arguably subtherapeutic medication dosage (Berney et al.), while the remaining two had very small sample sizes (Bernstein et al.; Klein et al.).

The most frequent side effects of using tricyclic antidepressants with children and adolescents include blurred vision, sedation, orthostatic-induced lightheadedness, dry mouth, urinary retention, and constipation. More uncommon side effects include jaundice, agitation, lethargy, heart rhythm problems, sleep disturbance, and allergic reactions. An additional problem associated with use of the tricyclic antidepressants is that overdosage may result in severe medical complications, including delirium, seizures, and heart rhythm problems.

Recently, there has been some suggestive evidence that buspirone (tradename Buspar) may be effective in the treatment of generalized anxiety in children and adolescents. In an uncontrolled case study, Kranzler (1988) reported that a 13-year-old boy with overanxious disorder and associated school refusal was successfully treated with 10 mg per day of buspirone. More recently, however, Kutcher et al. (1992), in a study of adolescents, diagnosed with either overanxious or generalized anxiety disorder, reported that following six weeks of buspirone therapy (between 15 mg and 30 mg per day), the adolescents' ratings of anxiety on self-report measures had decreased significantly. On the basis of these studies, Allen et al. (1995) suggested that controlled trials of buspirone with this clinical group may be merited. In addition to this suggestive evidence regarding its possible efficacy in the treatment of anxious children and adolescents, buspirone is also noteworthy for its lack of major side effects, its limited potential for abuse, and its low probability of producing withdrawal symptoms following cessation (Kutcher et al.).

Fluoxetine (tradename Prozac) has shown promise in the treatment of childhood obsessive compulsive disorder (Riddle, Hardin, King, Scahill, & Woolston, 1990; Riddle et al., 1992). More recently, however, an open study examining the efficacy and safety of fluoxetine in the treatment of more generalized anxiety in children has been conducted by Birmaher et al. (1994). Twenty-one treatment-resistant children and adolescents aged 11–17 years with diagnoses of overanxious disorder, separation anxiety disorder, or social phobia received a mean fluoxetine dose of 25.7 mg per day for an average of 10 months. At the end of the trial, 17 of the 21 subjects (81%) showed moderate to marked improvement in their anxiety symptoms. Combined with the fact that there were no significant side effects, these results prompted the authors to suggest that fluoxetine may have potential with nondepressed children and adolescents with anxiety disorders other than obsessive compulsive disorder and panic disorder (Birmaher et al., 1994)

As Coffey (1990) notes, the efficacy of beta-blockers in children and adolescents suffering from anxiety has yet to be clearly established, and as a consequence, this class of drug is not commonly used with children. There is, however, some evidence that beta-blockers may be effective in blocking the physiological symptoms of arousal typically associated with anxiety disorders. Famularo, Kinscherf, and Fenton (1988) conducted a four-week trial of propranolol (tradename Inderal; target dosage of 2.5 mg kg[1] per day) with 11 children (mean age of 8.5 years) with post-traumatic stress disorder. The results indicated that compared with a placebo, the active medication condition was associated with a significant improvement in symptoms, and that this improvement disappeared when the medication was discontinued. Side effects of the beta-blockers include constipation, sedation, nausea, hypotension, diarrhoea, bradycardia, increased airway resistance, vomiting, and depression. Kutcher et al. (1992) caution that this class of anxiolytics should be used only with treatment-resistant patients who are experiencing situational anxiety, and that if the beta-blockers are to be considered for use, the child or adolescent for whom they have been prescribed should be strictly monitored by medical staff.

Overall there is a lack of well-controlled and well-conducted research study into psychopharmacological interventions, and there is little support for them as sole treatments for anxiety disorders in children and adolescents. There may be a place for them in the treatment of this clinical population as an adjunct to other programs (such as behavioral, cognitive-behavioral, or psychotherapeutic interventions) but more research is needed. Of the various classes of anxiolytics reviewed here, the benzodiazepines have received the most empirical support, thus warranting their position as the medication most commonly prescribed for anxiety-disordered children and adolescents.

5.13.5 FUTURE DIRECTIONS FOR RESEARCH AND PRACTICE

So much needs to be done in the area of childhood anxiety disorders that we will limit our suggestions to a few broad areas. First, the relationship between child development and anxiety disorders remains relatively unexplored and the developmental course of anxiety problems needs to be clarified using longitudinal studies of large cohorts. Second, the validity of current diagnostic systems is uncertain and this makes definitive research into etiology and prognosis difficult. Third, measures that can clearly differentiate between anxiety and other childhood disorders, and between different types of child anxiety disorder are sorely needed. Fourth, experimental studies that integrate different putative causal mechanisms are needed. That is, studies need to measure social learning, cognitive, interpersonal, and biological aspects of anxiety concurrently before more comprehensive models of etiology can be developed and tested. Each of these aspects of anxiety seems important, but with researchers only considering one or two at a time, it is difficult to discern their relative and interactive importance in etiology. Fifth, evidence is emerging that psychosocial treatments are quite efficacious with clinically referred anxious children. Further, a recent study indicated that such treatments have the potential to be used in school settings as preventive interventions. Further research is needed to explore the effectiveness of these treatments across a range of clinical and community settings. Sixth, existing research into pharmacological interventions is scarce, poorly controlled, and rarely assessed concurrently with psychosocial interventions. Their efficacy needs to be assessed as does their community effectiveness and social validity.

Finally, as noted earlier three theoretical models of the development of anxiety disorders have credible explanatory power and at least limited empirical support: social learning theory (SLT), attachment theory (AT), and biological models such as Kagan's inhibition model. There may be a number of potential benefits to be made by contrasting and possibility integrating their complementary strengths and weaknesses. For example, in its purest forms, SLT takes all stimuli as equal in potential to elicit fear and has little to say about the biological and development relevance of various stimulus settings. By contrast, AT recognizes that particular settings may be potent for learning fear vs. courage, such as the parents' and child's first experiences of separation and reunion. Conversely, AT places little emphasis on the microprocesses that establish and maintain behaviors, or the methodologies by which these microprocesses can be examined under controlled conditions. SLT has a rich and successful history in these domains. The two models make predictions that are seemingly contradictory, at least in terms of our current understanding with respect to the development and expression of fear. For example, SLT would predict that contingent parental soothing should reinforce fear displays, and punishment of fear responses should suppress them. By contrast, AT predicts that parental soothing will facilitate the child's skills in self-soothing, leading to a decrease in future fear displays, whereas punishment of fear responses will lead to an insecure attachment and an increase in fear behavior. This raises the exciting possibility that critical experiments could be designed to compare and contrast these predictions. Attempts at integration have potential beyond simply watering down each model to find facile similarities between the two. Interesting attempts in this direction have already begun: for example, Brewin's (1987) argument that Bowlby's attachment model is complementary to contemporary cognitive models of how self-structures are internalized in anxiety and depressive disorders appears fruitful.

5.13.6 SUMMARY

Humans have an inherent capacity to react to threat stimuli with fear and anxiety. The strength of this reaction varies across individuals and with the nature of the stimulus. Important aspects of anxiety disorders include developmental factors, in that normal developmental tasks predispose humans to different anxieties at different times of life. Within this developmental framework, considerable explanatory power is afforded by classical, operant, and social learning processes in both the origins

and maintenance of child anxiety; and by variability in individual's susceptibility to react to stressful challenges with behavioral inhibition, anxiety and fear vs. disinhibition, impulsivity and aggression. The latter appear to be reasonably stable traits; however, the genetic and/or biological mechanisms underlying these processes are not understood. Recent developments in cognitive theory and research have shown that anxious people may process information in a way that increases the salience of threatening cues and catastrophic implications in their environment, but most of this work has been conducted with adults. With children, social contexts may be especially important to adjustment, and converging evidence suggests that high levels of control, restriction, attention to social threat, and endorsement of avoidant coping strategies are characteristic of families of anxious children.

Epidemiological studies indicate that anxiety disorders are the most common form of child and adolescent psychological problem. More tentative evidence indicates that these problems may, in their severest forms, be disabling and chronic and may have some continuity with adult anxiety problems. Anxiety is a very difficult phenomenon to measure in ecologically meaningful ways. To operationalize a person's ability to approach a snake in a laboratory is reasonably simple. However, to operationalize more complex forms of anxiety, such as generalized anxiety and panic, and then measure them in real-world situations is currently beyond our scope of knowledge and technology. Thus, the common but generalized forms of anxiety remain elusive to observational strategies, and the discriminative validity of existing self-report measures is poor. Progress has occurred in diagnostic systems but the validity of these remains controversial.

Social learning, cognitive, interpersonal, and biological models of etiology all seem to have some explanatory power but their relative and interactive importance is unknown as most research has considered them in isolation. Perhaps the most salient progress that has occurred over in the late twentieth century is the development and evaluation of cognitive-behavioral and family treatments. These appear to be highly efficacious with a broad range of clinically referred anxious children. The efficacy of drug treatment with any of the common childhood anxiety disorders remains a speculative issue. The broader community effectiveness and social validity of existing treatments remains unknown; however, there is some evidence that social learning therapies may have the potential to be used as early and preventive interventions in school settings.

5.13.7 REFERENCES

Achenbach, T. M., & Edelbrock, C. (1983). *Manual for the child behaviour checklist and revised child behaviour profile* (2nd ed.). Department of Psychiatry, University of Vermont.

Ainsworth, M. D. S. (1989). Attachments beyond infancy. *American Psychologist, 44,* 709–716.

Ainsworth, M. D. S., Blehar, M. C., Waters, E., & Wall, S. (1978). *Patterns of attachment: A psychological study of the strange situation.* Hillsdale, NJ: Erlbaum.

Allen, A. J., Leonard, H, & Swedo, S. E. (1995). Current knowledge of medications for the treatment of childhood anxiety disorders. *Journal of the American Academy of Child and Adolescent Psychiatry, 34,* 976–986.

American Psychiatric Association (1987). *Diagnostic and statistical manual of mental disorders* (3rd ed. rev.). Washington, DC: Author.

American Psychiatric Association (1994). *Diagnostic and statistical manual of mental disorders* (4th ed.). Washington, DC: Author.

Anderson, J. C., Williams, S., McGee, R, & Silva, P. A. (1987). DSM-III disorders in preadolescent children: Prevalence in a large sample from the general population. *Archives of General Psychiatry, 44,* 69–76.

Barnes, G. G. (1985). Systems theory and family theory. In M. Rutter & L. Hersor (Eds.), *Child and adolescent psychiatry: Modern approaches* (2nd ed., pp. 216–229) Oxford: Blackwell.

Barrett, P. M. (1995, July). *Group treatment of anxious children.* Paper presented at the Fifth World Congress of Cognitive and Behavioral Therapies, Copenhagen, Denmark.

Barrett, P. M., Dadds, M. R., & Rapee, R. M. (1996). Family treatment of childhood anxiety: A controlled trial. *Journal of Consulting and Clinical Psychology, 64,* 333–342.

Barrett, P. M., Rapee, R. M., Dadds, M. R., & Ryan, S. (1996). Family enhancement of cognitive styles in anxious and aggressive children: The FEAR effect. *Journal of Abnormal Child Psychology, 24,* 187–203.

Barrios, B. A., & Hartmann, D. P. (1988). Fears and anxieties. In E. J. Mash & L. G. Terdal (Eds.), *Behavioral assessment of childhood disorders* (2nd ed., pp. 196–26). New York: Guilford Press.

Bauer, D. H. (1976). An exploratory study of developmental changes in children's fears. *Journal of Child Psychology and Psychiatry, 17,* 69–74.

Beidel, D. C. (1991). Social phobia and overanxious disorder in school-age children. *Journal of the American Academy of Child and Adolescent Psychiatry, 30,* 545–552.

Berney, T., Kolvin, I., Bhate, S. R., Garside, R. F., Jeans, J., Kay, B., & Scarth, L. (1981). School phobia: A therapeutic trial with clomipramine and short-term outcome. *British Journal of Psychiatry, 138,* 110–118.

Bernstein, G. A. (1994). Psychopharmacological interventions. In T. H. Ollendick, N. J. King, & W. Yule (Eds.), *International handbook of phobic and anxiety disorders in children and adolescents* (pp. 439–452). New York: Plenum.

Bernstein, G. A., & Borchardt, C. M. (1991). Anxiety disorders of childhood and adolescence: A critical review: *Journal of the American Academy of Child and Adolescent Psychiatry, 30,* 519–532.

Bernstein, G. A., & Garfinkel, B. D. (1986). School phobia: The overlap of affective and anxiety disorders. *Journal of the American Academy of Child Psychiatry, 25,* 235–241.

Bernstein, G. A., Garfinkel, B. D., & Borchardt, C. M. (1990). Comparative studies of pharmacotherapy for school refusal. *Journal of the American Academy of Child and Adolescent Psychiatry, 29,* 773–781.

Biederman, J. (1987). Clonazepam in the treatment of prepubertal children with panic-like symptoms. *Journal of Clinical Psychiatry, 48,* 38–42.

Biederman, J. (1991). Psychopharcology. In J. M. Wiener (Ed.), *Textbook of child and adolescent psychiatry* (pp. 545–570). Washington, DC: American Psychiatric Press.

Biederman, J., Rosenbaum, J. F., Hirshfeld, D. R., Faraone, S. V., Bolduc, E. A., Gersten, M., Meminger, S. R., Kagan, J., Snidman, N., & Reznick, S. (1990). Psychiatric correlates of behavioral inhibition in young children with and without psychiatric disorders. *Archives of General Psychiatry, 47,* 21–26.

Birmaher, B., Waterman, G. S., Ryan, N., Cully, M., Balach, L., Ingram, J., & Brodsky, M. (1994). Fluoxetine for childhood anxiety disorders. *Journal of the American Academy of Child and Adolescent Psychiatry, 33,* 993–999.

Blagg, N. R., & Yule, W. (1984). The behavioral treatment of school refusal: A comparative study. *Behavior Research and Therapy, 22,* 119–127.

Borkovec, T. D., Weerts, T. C., & Bernstein, D. C. (1977). Assessment of anxiety. In A. R. Ciminero, K. S. Calhoun, & H. E. Adams (Eds.), *Handbook of behavioral assessment* (pp. 367–428). New York: Wiley.

Bowlby, J. (1969). *Attachment and Loss: Vol. 2. Separation, anxiety and anger.* New York: Basic Books.

Bowlby, J. (1973). *Attachment and loss.* (Vol. 2). New York: Basic Books.

Brady, E. U., & Kendall, P. C. (1992). Comorbidity of anxiety and depression in children and adolescents. *Psychological Bulletin, 111,* 244–255.

Brewin, C. R. (1987). *Cognitive foundations of clinical psychology.* London: Erlbaum.

Butler, G., & Mathews, A. (1983). Cognitive processes in anxiety. *Advances in Behaviour Research and Therapy, 5,* 51–62.

Clement, P. W., & Miller, D. C. V.(1967). Group play therapy and tangible reinforcers used to modify the behavior of eight year old boys. *Behavior Research and Therapy, 5,* 301–312.

Cobham, V. E., & Dadds, M. R. (1995, July). *Group treatment of anxious children: The role of parental anxiety.* Paper presented at the Fifth World Congress of Cognitive and Behavioral Therapies, Copenhagen., Denmark.

Coffey, B. J. (1990). Anxiolytics for children and adolescents: Traditional and new drugs. *Journal of Child and Adolescent Psychopharmacology, 1,* 57–83.

Costello, E. J. (1989). Child psychiatric disorders and their correlates: A primary care pediatric sample. *Journal of American Academy of Child and Adolescent Psychiatry, 28,* 851–855.

Cowan, P. A., Cohn, D. A., Pape-Cowan, C. P., & Pearson, J. L. (1996). Parent's attachment histories and children's externalizing and internalizing behaviors. *Journal of Consulting and Clinical Psychology, 64,* 53–63.

Croake, J. W. (1969). Fears of children. *Human Development, 12,* 239–247.

Croake, J. W., & Knox, F. H. (1973). The changing nature of children's fears. *Child Study Journal, 3,* 91–105.

Dadds, M. R., Barrett, P. M., Rapee, R. M., & Ryan, S. (1996). Family process and child anxiety and aggression: An observational analysis. *Journal of Abnormal Child Psychology, 24,* 715–734.

Dadds, M. R., & Powell, M. B. (1991). The relationship of interparental conflict and marital adjustment to aggression, anxiety and immaturity in aggressive and nonclinic children. *Journal of Abnormal Child Psychology, 19,* 553–567.

Dadds, M. R., Rapee, R. M., & Barrett, P. M. (1994). Behavioral observation. In T. H. Ollendick, N. J. King & W. Yule (Eds.), *International handbook of phobic and anxiety disorders in children and adolescents* (pp. 349–364). New York: Plenum.

Dadds, M. R., Spence, S. H., Holland, D., Barrett, P. M., & Laurens, K. (1997). Early intervention and prevention of anxiety disorders: A controlled trial. *Journal of Consulting and Clinical Psychology, 65,* 627–635.

Davey, G. C. L. (1992). Classical conditioning and the acquisition of human fears and phobias: A review and synthesis of the literature. *Advances in Behavior Research and Therapy, 14,* 29–66.

DeKlyen, M. (1996). Disruptive behavior disorder and intergenerational attachment patterns. *Journal of Consulting and Clinical Psychology, 64,* 357–365.

Dumas, J. E., LaFreniere, P. J., & Serketich, W. J. (1995). "Balance of power": A transactional analysis of control in mother–child dyads involving socially competent, aggressive, and anxious children. *Journal of Abnormal Psychology, 104,* 104–113.

Edelbrock, C. (1985, June). Teachers' perceptions of childhood anxiety and school adjustment. Paper presented at a conference for "Anxiety Disorders in Children: Implications for School Adjustment," Cape Cod, MA.

Ekman, P. (1980). *The face of man.* New York: Garland.

Emery, R. E. (1982). Interparental conflict and the children of divorce and discord. *Psychological Bulletin, 92,* 310–330.

Famularo, R., Kinscherf, R., & Fenton, T. (1988). Propranolol treatment for childhood post-traumatic stress disorder, acute type: A pilot study. *American Journal of Diseases in Children, 142,* 1244–1247.

Foa, E. B., & Kozak, M. J. (1986). Emotional processing of fear: Exposure to corrective information. *Psychological Bulletin, 99,* 20–35.

Fonseca, A. C. (1993). Fears in children and adolescents: A study on the Portuguese population. *Revista Portuguesa de Pedagogia, 27,* 75–92.

Fox, J. E., & Houston, B. K. (1981). Efficacy of self instructional training for reducing children's anxiety in evaluation situations. *Behavior Research & Therapy, 19,* 509–515.

Fox, J. E., & Houston, B. K. (1983). Distinguishing between cognitive and somatic trait and state anxiety in children. *Journal of Personality and Social Psychology, 45,* 862–870.

Francis, G., Last, C. G., & Strauss, C. C. (1992). Avoidant disorder and social phobia in children and adolescents. *Journal of the American Academy of Child and Adolescent Psychiatry, 31,* 1086–1089.

Freeman, B. J., Roy, R. R., & Hemmick, S. (1976). Extinction of a phobia of physical examination in a 7-year-old mentally retarded boy. *Behavior Research & Therapy, 14,* 63–64.

Freud, S. (1909). Analysis of a phobia in a five-year-old boy. *Standard Edition, 10,* 3–149. London: Hogarth Press, 1955.

Giebenhain, J. E., & O'Dell, S. L. (1984). Evaluation of a parent training manual for reducing children's fears of the dark. *Journal of Applied Behavior Analysis, 17,* 121–125.

Gittelman, R. (1984). Anxiety disorders in children. In L. Grinspoon (Ed.), *Psychiatry update* (Vol. III, pp. 410–418). Washington, DC: American Psychiatric Association.

Gittelman-Klein, R. (1988). Childhood anxiety disorders. In C. J. Kestenbaum & D. T. Williams (Eds.), *Handbook of clinical assessment of children and adolescents* (Vol. 2). New York: NYU Press.

Gittelman-Klein, R., & Klein, D. F. (1971). Controlled imipramine treatment of school phobia. *Archives of General Psychiatry, 25,* 204–207.

Gittelman-Klein, R., & Klein, D. F. (1973). School phobia: Diagnostic considerations in the light of imipramine effects. *Journal of Nervous Mental Disorders, 156,* 199–215.

Glennon, B., & Weisz, J. R. (1978). An observational approach to assessment of anxiety in young children. *Journal of Consulting and Clinical Psychology, 46,* 1246–1257.

Goodyer, I. N. (1990). Family relationships, life events and childhood psychopathology. *Journal of Child Psychology and Psychiatry and Allied Disciplines, 31* (1), 161–192.

Graae, F., Milner, J., Rizzotto, L., & Klein, R. G. (1994). Clonazepam in childhood anxiety disorders. *Journal of the American Academy of Child and Adolescent Psychiatry, 33,* 372–376.

Gray, J. (1988). The neuropsychological basis of anxiety. In C. Last & M. Hersen (Eds.), *Handbook of anxiety disorders.* New York: Pergamon.

Graziano, A. M., De Giovanni, I. S., & Garcia, K. A. (1979). Behavioral treatment of children's fears: A review. *Psychological Bulletin, 86,* 804–830.

Graziano, A. M., & Mooney, K. C. (1980). Family self-control instructions for children's night time fear reduction. *Journal of Consulting and Clinical Psychology, 48,* 206–213.

Green, S. M., Loeber, R., & Lahey, B. B. (1992). Child psychopathology and deviant family hierarchies. *Journal of Child and Family Studies, 1,* 341–350.

Haley, J. (1976). *Problem-solving therapy.* San Francisco: Jossey-Bass.

Harlow, H., & Harlow, M. (1962). Social deprivation in monkeys. *Scientific American, 207,* 136–146.

Heard, P. M., Dadds, M. R., & Conrad, P. (1992). Assessment and treatment of simple phobias in children: Effects on family and marital relationships. *Behavior Change, 9,* 73–82.

Hershberg, S. G., Carlson, G. A., Cantwell, D. P., & Strober, M. (1982). Anxiety and depressive disorders in psychiatrically disturbed children. *Journal of Clinical Psychiatry, 43,* 358–361.

Hetherington, E. M., & Martin, B. (1979). Family interaction. In H. C. Quay & J. S. Werry (Eds.), *Psychopathological disorders of childhood* (pp. 30–82). New York: Wiley.

Hirshfeld, D. R., Rosenbaum, J. F., Biederman, J., Bolduc, E. A., Faraone, S. V., Snidman, N., Reznick, J. S., & Kagan, J. (1992). Stable behavioral inhibition and its association with anxiety disorder. *Journal of the American Academy of Child and Adolescent Psychiatry, 31,* 103–111.

Jay, S. M., & Elliott, C. (1984). Behavioral observation scales for measuring children's distress: The effects of increased methodological rigor. *Journal of Consulting and Clinical Psychology, 52,* 1106–1107.

Jay, S. M., Ozolins, M., Elliott, C., & Caldwell, S. (1983). Assessment of children's distress during painful medical procedures. *Journal of Health Psychology, 2,* 133–147.

Jersild, A. T., & Holmes, F. B. (1935). *Children's fears.* New York: Teachers' College, Columbia University.

Kagan, J., Reznick, J. S., & Snidman, N. (1988). Biological bases of childhood shyness. *Science, 240,* 167–171.

Kashani, J. H., Dandoy, A. C., & Orvaschel, H. (1991). Current perspectives on anxiety disorders in children and adolescents: An overview. *Comprehensive Psychiatry, 32,* 481–495.

Kashani, J. H., & Orvaschel, H. (1988). Anxiety disorders in mid adolescence: A community sample. *American Journal of Psychiatry, 145,* 960–964.

Kashani, J. H., & Orvaschel, H. (1990). A community study of anxiety in children and adolescents. *American Journal of Psychiatry, 147,* 313–318.

Katz, E. R., Kellerman, J., & Siegel, S. E. (1980). Behavioral distress in children with cancer undergoing medical procedures: Developmental considerations. *Journal of Consulting and Clinical Psychology, 48,* 356–365.

Kazdin, A. E. (1985). Recent advances in child behavior therapy. In S. I. Pfeiffer (Ed.), *Clinical child psychology:*

Introduction to theory, research and practice. Orlando, FL: Grune & Stratton.

Keller, M. B., Lavori, P., Wunder, J., Beardslee, W. R., Schwarts, C. E., & Roth, J. (1992). Chronic course of anxiety disorders in children and adolescents. *Journal of the American Academy of Child and Adolescent Psychiatry, 31,* 595–599.

Kelley, C. K. (1976). Play desensitization of fear of darkness in preschool children. *Behavior Research & Therapy, 14,* 79–81.

Kendall, P. C. (1990). *Coping cat workbook.* Philadelphia, PA: Department of Psychology, Temple University.

Kendall, P. C. (1994). Treating anxiety disorders in youth: Results of a randomised clinical trial. *Journal of Consulting and Clinical Psychology, 62,* 100–110.

Kendall, P. C., Chansky, T. E., Kane, M. T., Kim, R. S., Kortlander, E., Ronan, K. R., Sessa, F. M., & Siqueland, L. (1992). *Anxiety disorders in youth.* Boston: Allyn & Bacon.

Kendall, P. C., Flannery-Schroeder, E., Panichelli-Mindel, S. M., Southam-Gerow, M., Henin, A., & Warman, M. (in press). Treatment of anxiety disorders in youth: A second randomized clinical trial. *Journal of Consulting and Clinical Psychology.*

Kendall, P. C., & Southam-Gerow, M. A. (1996). Long-term follow-up of a cognitive-behavioral therapy for anxiety-disordered youth. *Journal of Consulting and Clinical Psychology, 64,* 724–730.

King, N. J., Hamilton, D. J., & Ollendick, T. H. (1988). *Children's phobias: A behavioral perspective.* Chichester, UK: Wiley.

King, N. J., Hamilton, D. J., & Murphy, G. C. (1983). The prevention of children's maladaptive fears. *Child and Family Behvaiour Therapy, 5,* 43–57.

King, N. J., & Ollendick, T. H. (1989). School refusal: Graduated and rapid behavioral treatment strategies. *Australian and New Zealand Journal of Psychiatry, 23,* 213–223.

King, N. J., Ollier, K., Iacuone, R., Schuster, S., Bays, K., Gullone, E., & Ollendick, T. H. (1989). Fears of children and adolescents: A cross-sectional Australian study using the revised Fear Survey Schedule for Children. *Journal of Child Psychology and Psychiatry, 30,* 775–784.

Klein, D. F. (1964). Delineation of two-drug responsive anxiety syndromes. *Psychopharmacologia, 5,* 397–408.

Klein, R. G. (1991). Parent–child agreement in clinical assessment of anxiety and other psychopathology: A review. *Journal of Anxiety Disorders, 5,* 187–198.

Klein, R. G., Koplewicz, H. S., & Kanner, A. (1992). Imipramine treatment of children with separation anxiety disorder. *Journal of the American Academy of Child and Adolescent Psychiatry, 31,* 21–28.

Klein, R. G., & Last, C. G. (1989). *Anxiety disorders in children.* London: Sage.

Kohlmann, C. W., Schumacher, A., & Streit, A. (1988). Trait anxiety and parental child rearing behaviour: Support as moderator variable. *Anxiety Research, 1,* 53–64.

Kohut, H. (1971). *The analysis of the self.* New York: International Universities Press.

Kranzler, H. (1988). Use of buspirone in an adolescent with overanxious disorder. *Journal of the American Academy of Child and Adolescent Psychiatry, 27,* 789–790.

Krohne, H. W., & Hock, M. (1991). Relationships between restrictive mother–child interactions and anxiety of the child. *Anxiety Research, 4,* 109–124.

Krohne, H. W., & Hock, M. (1993). Coping dispositions, actual anxiety, and the incidental learning of success- and failure-related stimuli. *Personality and Individual Differences, 15,* 33–41.

Krohne H. W. (1992). Developmental conditions of anxiety and coping. A two process model of child rearing effects.

In K. A. Hagtvet (Ed.), *Advances in test anxiety research* (Vol. 7, pp. 143–155). The Netherlands: Swets & Zeitlinger.

Kutcher, S. P., & MacKenzie, S. (1988). Successful clonazepam treatment of adolescents with panic disorder. *Journal of Clinical Psychopharmacology, 8,* 299–301.

Kutcher, S. P., Reiter, S., Gardner, D. M., & Klein, R. G. (1992). The pharmacotherapy of anxiety disorders in children and adolescents. *Pediatric Clinics of North America, 15,* 41–67.

Lang, P. J., & Lazovic, A. D. (1963). Experimental desensitization of a phobia. *Journal of Abnormal and Social Psychology, 66,* 519–525.

Lang, P. J. (1968). Fear reduction and fear behavior. Problems in treating a construct. In J. M. Schleen (Ed.), *Research in psychotherapy* (pp. 000–000). Washington, DC: American Psychological Association.

Last, C. G. (1988). Anxiety disorders in childhood and adolescence. In C. G. Last & M. Hersen (Eds.), *Handbook of anxiety disorders* (pp. 531–540). New York: Pergamon.

Last, C. G., Hersen, M., Kazdin, A. E., Finkelstein, R., & Strauss, C. C. (1987). Comparison of DSM-III separation anxiety and overanxious disorders: Demographic characteristics and patterns of comorbidity. *Journal of the American Academy of Child and Adolescent Psychiatry, 26,* 527–531.

Le Baron, S., & Zeltzer, L. (1984). Assessment of acute pain and anxiety in children and adolescents by self-reports, observer reports, and a behavior checklist. *Journal of Consulting and Clinical Psychology, 52,* 729–738.

Le Roy, J. B., & Derdeyn, A. (1976). Drawings as a therapeutic medium: The treatment of separation anxiety in a 4 year-old boy. *Child Psychiatry and Human Development, 6,* 155–169.

Lewis, S. A. (1974). A comparison of behavior therapy techniques in the reduction of fearful avoidant behavior. *Behavior Therapy, 5,* 648–655.

McDaniel, K. D. (1986). Pharmacologic treatment of psychiatric and neurodevelopmental disorders in children and adolescents (I). *Clinical Pediatrics, 25,* 65–71.

Mahler, M. (1968). *On human symbiosis and the vicissitudes of individuation.* New York: International Universities Press.

Main, M. (1996). Overview of the field of attachment. *Journal of Consulting and Clinical Psychology, 64,* 237–243.

Marks, I. M. (1969). *Fears and phobias.* New York: Academic Press.

Matson, J. (1981) Assessment and treatment of clinical fears in mentally retarded children. *Journal of Applied Behavior Analysis, 14,* 287–294.

Mattison, R. E. (1992). Anxiety disorders. In S. R. Hooper, G. W. Hynd, & R. E. Mattison (Eds.), *Child psychopathology: Diagnostic criteria and clinical assessment* (pp. 179–202). Hillsdale, NJ:Erlbaum.

McFarlane, J. W., Allen, L., & Honzik, M. P. (1954). *A developmental study of the behavior problems of normal children between 21 months and 14 years.* Berkeley, CA: University of California Press.

McGee, R., Feehan, M., Williams, S., Partridge, F., Silva, P. A., & Kelly, J. (1990). DSM-III disorders in a large sample of adolescents. *Journal of the American Academy of Child and Adolescent Psychiatry, 29,* 611–619.

Meichenbaum, D. H., & Genest, M. (1980). Cognitive behavior modification: an integration of cognitive and behavioral methods. In F. H. Kanfer & A. P. Goldstein, (Eds.), *Helping people change: A textbook of methods.* New York: Pergamon.

Meichenbaum, D. H., & Goodman, J. (1971). Training impulsive children to talk to themselves: A normal range of developing self-control. *Journal of Abnormal Psychology, 77*, 115–126.

Melamed, B. & Siegel, L. (1975). Reduction of anxiety in children facing hospitalization and surgery by use of filmed modeling. *Journal of Consulting and Clinical Psychology, 46*, 1357–1367.

Melamed, B., Yurcheson, R., Fleece, E. L., Hutcherson, S., & Hawes, R. (1978). Effects of film modeling on the reduction of anxiety-related behaviors in individuals varying in level of previous experience in the stress situation. *Journal of Consulting and Clinical Psychology, 46*, 1357–1367.

Messer, S. C., & Beidel, D. C. (1994). Psychosocial correlates of childhood anxiety disorders. *Journal of the American Academy of Child and Adolescent Psychiatry, 33*, 975–983.

Miller, L. C. (1983). Fears and anxiety in children. In C. E. Walker & M. C. Roberts (Eds.), *Handbook of clinical child psychology* (pp. 337–380). New York: Wiley.

Miller, L. C., Barrett, C. L., & Hampe, E. (1974). Phobias of childhood in a prescientific era. In A. Davids (Ed.), *Child personality and psychopathology: Current topics* (Vol. 1., pp. 89–134). New York: Wiley.

Miller, L. C., Barrett, C. L., Hampe, E., & Noble, H. (1972). Factor structure of childhood fears. *Journal of Consulting and Clinical Psychology, 39*, 264–268.

Milos, M. E., & Reiss, S. (1982). Effects of three play conditions on separation anxiety in young children. *Journal of Consulting and Clinical Psychology, 50*, 389–395.

Minuchin, S. (1974). *Families and family therapy*. Cambridge, MA: Harvard University Press.

Morris, R. H., & Kratochwill, T. R. (1983). *Treating children's fears and phobias*. New York: Pergamon.

Mowrer, O. H. (1960). *Learning theory and behavior*. New York: Wiley.

Murphy, C. M., & Bootzin, R. R. (1973). Active and passive participation in the contact desensitization of snake fear in children. *Behavior Therapy, 4*, 203–211.

Neisworth, J. T., Madle, R. A., & Goeke, D. E. (1975). "Errorless" elimination of separation anxiety: A case study. *Journal of Behavior Therapy and Experimental Psychiatry, 6*, 79–82.

Ollendick, T. H. (1983). Reliability and validity of the Revised Fear Survey Schedule for Children (FSSC-R). *Behavior Research & Therapy, 21*, 685–692.

Ollendick, T. H., & Francis, G. (1988). Behavioral assessment and treatment of childhood phobias. *Behavior Modification, 12*, 165–204.

Ollendick, T. H., King, N. J., & Frary, R. B. (1989). Fears in children and adolescents: Reliability and generalizability across gender, age and nationality. *Behavior Research & Therapy, 27*, 19–26.

Ollendick, T. H., Matson, J. L., & Helsel, W. J. (1985). Fears in children and adolescents: Normative data. *Behavior Research and Therapy, 23*, 465–467.

Oosterlaan, J., Prins, P. J. M., & Sergeant, J. (1992). *A Dutch translation of the Fear Survey Schedule for Children*. Paper presented at the SECAP meeting in Saratosa, FL.

Panella, D., & Henggeler, S. W. (1986). Peer interactions of conduct-disordered, anxious-withdrawn, and well-adjusted black adolescents. *Journal of Abnormal Child Psychology, 14*, 1–11.

Paul, G. L. (1996) *Insight versus desensitization in psychotherapy*. Stanford, CA: Stanford University Press.

Perrin, S., & Last, C. G. (1992). Do childhood anxiety measures measure anxiety? *Journal of Abnormal Child Psychology, 20*, 567–578.

Pfeffer, C. R., Lipkins, R., Plutchik, R., & Mizruchi, M. (1988). Normal children at risk for suicidal behavior. A two-year follow-up study. *Journal of the American Academy of Child and Adolescent Psychiatry, 27*, 34–41.

Pfefferbaum, B., Overall, J. E., Boren, H. A., Frankel, L. S., Sullivan, M. P., & Johnson, K. (1987). Alprazolam in the treatment of anticipatory and acute situational anxiety in children with cancer. *Journal of the American Academy of Child and Adolescent Psychiatry, 26*, 532–535.

Puig-Antich, J., Lukens, E., Davies, M., Goetz, D., Brenn-Quattrock, J., & Todak, G. (1985). Psychosocial functioning in prepubertal major depressive disorders: 1. Interpersonal relationships during the depressive episode. *Archives of General Psychiatry, 42*, 511–517.

Rapee, R. M. (1991). Psychological factors involved in generalized anxiety. In R. M. Rapee & D. H. Barlow (Eds.), *Chronic anxiety, generalized disorder, and mixed anxiety-depression* (pp. 76–96). New York: Guilford Press.

Rapee, R. M., & Barlow, D. H. (1992). Generalized anxiety disorder, panic disorder and the phobias. In P. B. Sutker & H. E. Adams (Eds.), *Comprehensive handbook of psychopathology* (2nd ed.). New York: Plenum.

Rapee, R. M., Barrett, P. M., Dadds, M. R., & Evans, L. (1994). Reliability of the DSM-III-R childhood anxiety disorders using a structured interview. *Journal of the American Academy of Child and Adolescent Psychiatry, 33*, 984–992.

Reynolds, C. R., & Paget, K. D. (1981). Factor analysis of the revised children's manifest anxiety scale for blacks, males and females with national innovative sample. *Journal of Consulting and Clinical Psychology, 49*, 352–359.

Riddle, M. A., Hardin, M. T., King, B., Scahill, L., & Woolston, J. L. (1990). Fluoxetine treatment of children and adolescents with Tourette's and obsessive compulsive disorder. Preliminary clinical experience. *Journal of American Academy of Child and Adolescent Psychiatry, 29*, 45–48.

Riddle, M. A., Scahill, L., King, R. A., Hardin, M. T., Anderson, G. M., Ort, S. I., Smith, J. C., Leckman, J. F., & Cohen, D. J. (1992). Double-blind, cross-over trial of fluoxetine and placebo in children and adolescents with obsessive compulsive disorder. *Journal of American Academy of Child and Adolescent Psychiatry, 31*, 1062–1069.

Rosenbaum, J. F., Biederman, J., Bolduc, E. A., Hirshfield, D. R., Faraone, S. V., & Kagan, J. (1992). Comorbidity of parental anxiety disorders as risk for childhood-onset anxiety in inhibited children. *American Journal of Psychiatry, 149*(4), 475–481.

Rosenstein, D. S., & Horowitz, H. A. (1996). Adolescent attachment and psychopathology. *Journal of Consulting and Clinical Psychology, 64*, 244–253.

Rubin, K. H., & Clark, M. L. (1983). Preschool teachers' ratings of behavioral problems: Observational, sociometric, and social-cognitive correlates. *Journal of Abnormal Child Psychology, 11*, 273–286.

Rutter, M., Macdonald, H., LeCouteur, A., Harrington, R., Bolton, P., & Bailey, A. (1990). Genetic factors in child psychiatric disorders-II. Empirical findings. *Journal of Child Psychology and Psychiatry, 31*, 39–83.

Sanderson, W. C., Di Nardo, P. A., Rapee, R. M., & Barlow, D. H. (1990). Syndrome comorbidity in patients diagnosed with a *DSM-III*-revised anxiety disorder. *Journal of Abnormal Psychology, 99*, 308–312.

Sheslow, D. W., Bondy, A. S., & Nelson, R. O. (1982). A comparison of graduated exposure, verbal coping skills, and their combination in the treatment of children's fear of the dark. *Child and Family Behavior Therapy, 4*, 33–45.

Silverman, W. K. (1991). Diagnostic reliability of anxiety disorders in children using structured interviews. *Journal of Anxiety Disorders, 5*, 105–124.

Silverman, W. K. (1992). Taxonomy of anxiety disorders in children. In G. D. Burrows, R. Noyes, & S. M. Roth

(Eds.), *Handbook of anxiety* (Vol. 5, pp. 281–308). Amsterdam: Elsevier.

Silverman, W. K., & Nelles, W. B. (1988). The Anxiety Disorders Interview Schedule for Children. *Journal of the American Academy of Child and Adolescent Psychiatry, 27,* 772–778.

Simeon, J. G., & Ferguson, H. B. (1987). Alprazolam effects in children with anxiety disorders. *Canadian Journal of Psychiatry, 32,* 570–574.

Simeon, J. G., Ferguson, H. B., Knott, V., Roberts, N., Gauthier, B., Dubois, C., & Wiggins, D. (1992). Clinical, cognitive and neurophysiological effects of alprazolam in children and adolescents with overanxious and avoidant disorders. *Journal of the American Academy of Child and Adolescent Psychiatry, 31,* 29–33.

Solyom, L., Silberfeld, M., & Solyom, C. (1976). Maternal overprotection in the aetiology of agoraphobia. *Canadian Psychiatric Association Journal, 21,* 109–113.

Spence, S. H. (1994). Preventative strategies. In T. H. Ollendick, N. J. King, & W. Yule (Eds.), *International handbook of phobic and anxiety disorders in children and adolescents* (pp. 453–474). New York: Plenum.

Spence, S. H. (1996). *The structure of anxiety symptoms amongst children: A confirmatory factor analytic study.* Manuscript submitted for publication.

Stark, K. D., Humphrey, L. L., Crook, K., & Lewis, K. (1990). Perceived family environments of depressed and anxious children. *Journal of Abnormal Child Psychology, 22,* 33–51.

Strauss, C. C., Frame, C. L., & Forehand, R. L. (1987). Psychosocial impairment associated with anxiety in children. *Journal of Clinical Child Psychology, 16,* 235–239.

Strauss, C. C., Lahey, B. B., Frick, P., Frame, C. L., & Hynd, G. W. (1988). Peer social status of children with anxiety disorders. *Journal of Consulting and Clinical Psychology, 56,* 137–141.

Strauss, C. C., Lease, C. A., Last, C. G., & Francis, G. (1988). Overanxious disorder. An examination of developmental differences. *Journal of Abnormal Child Psychology, 16,* 433–443.

Stavrakaki, C., Vargo, B., Roberts, N., & Boodoosing, L. (1987). Concordance among sources of information for ratings of anxiety and depression in children. *Journal of the American Academy of Child and Adolescent Psychiatry, 26,* 733–737.

Suomi, S. J. (1986). Anxiety-like disorders in young nonhuman primates. In R. Gittelman (Ed.), *Anxiety disorders of childhood* (pp. 1–23). New York: Guilford Press.

Suomi, S. J., Seaman, S. F., Lewis, J. K., DeLizio, R. D., &

McKinney, W. T. (1978). Effects of imipramine treatment of separation induced social disorders in rhesus monkeys. *Archives of General Psychiatry, 35,* 321–327.

Target, M., & Fonagy, P. (1994). Efficacy of psychoanalysis for children with emotional disorders. *Journal of American Academy of Child and Adolescent Psychiatry, 33,* 361–371.

Thyer, B., Parrish, R. T., & Curtis, G. C. (1985). Ages of onset of *DSM-III* anxiety disorders. *Comprehensive Psychiatry, 26,* 113–122.

Thyer, B. A., & Sowers-Hoag, K. M. (1988). Behavior therapy for separation anxiety disorder. *Behavior Modification, 12,* 205–233.

Van Hasselt, V. B., Hersen, M., Bellack, A. S., Rosenblum, N. D., & Lamparski, D. (1979). Tripartite assessment of the effects of systematic desensitization in a multiphobic child: An experimental analysis. *Journal of Behavior Therapy and Experimental Psychiatry, 10,* 51–55.

van Ijzendoom, M. H., & Bakermans-Kranenburg, M. J. (1996). Attachment representations in mothers, fathers, adolescents and children: A meta-analytic search for normative data. *Journal of Consulting and Clinical Psychology, 64,* 8–21.

Vasey, M. W. (1993). Development and cognition in childhood anxiety. The example of worry. In T. H. Ollendick & R. Prinz (Eds.), *Advances in clinical child psychology* (Vol. 15, pp. 1–39). New York: Plenum.

Velez, C. N., Johnson, J., & Cohen, P. (1989). A longitudinal analysis of selected risk factors for childhood psychopathology. *Journal of the American Academy of Child and Adolescent Psychiatry, 28,* 861–864.

Werry, J. S. (1991). Overanxious disorder: A review of taxonomic properties. *Journal of the American Academy of Child and Adolescent Psychiatry, 30,* 533–544.

Werry, J. S. (1994). Diagnostic and classification issues. In T. H. Ollendick, N. J. King, & W. Yule (Eds.), *International handbook of phobic and anxiety disorders in children and adolescents* (pp. 21–42). New York: Plenum.

Wine, J. D. (1979). Test anxiety and evaluation threat: Children's behavior in the classroom. *Journal of Abnormal Child Psychology, 7,* 45–59.

Wolpe, J. (1958). *Psychotherapy by reciprocal inhibition.* Stanford, CA: Stanford University Press.

World Health Organization (1992). *The ICD-10 classification of mental and behavioral disorders: Clinical descriptions and diagnostic guidelines.* Geneva: Author.

Yule, W., Udwin, O., & Murdoch, K. (1990). The Jupiter sinking: Effects on children's fears, depression and anxiety. *Journal of Child Psychology and Psychiatry, 31,* 1052–1061.

5.14
Specific Phobias

GOLDA S. GINSBURG
University of Baltimore, MD, USA
and
WENDY K. SILVERMAN
Florida International University, Miami, FL, USA

5.14.1 DEFINITION AND PHENOMONOLOGY

A specific phobia (SP) is a persistent and excessive fear in the presence of, or in anticipation of, a circumscribed object or event (*DSM*; American Psychiatric Association, 1994). Unlike a "normal" nonclinical fear, an SP usually leads to extreme avoidance of the fear-provoking object or event, resulting in severe distress and interference in the daily functioning of children and their families. For example, children with an SP of dogs may not leave their home to avoid a possible encounter with a dog; children with an SP of sleeping alone in the dark may insist that their parents sleep along with them; children with an SP of medical procedures (such as injections) may refuse to go to doctors' appointments or to hospitals. Also, in contrast to children's normal fears, SPs are usually out of proportion to reality and do not dissipate by reassurance, reason, or information.

In referring to phenomonology, it has become common to focus on the three-response system: behavioral, cognitive, and physiological (e.g., Lang, 1977). In terms of the behavioral system, avoidance is most common, and, as noted, typically children go to great lengths to avoid the feared object or situation. Additional behavioral manifestations include tantruming, crying, or "freezing up" when faced with the feared object or event. In terms of the cognitive system, often children report catastrophic beliefs that involve feared outcomes, particularly of physical or personal injury (e.g., "the dog will bite me," "I'll get hit by lightening"). Finally, in terms of the physiological system, manifestations include somatic complaints (e.g., stomach aches, headaches), accelerated heart rate, sweating, shakiness, and muscle tension (Last, 1991). A vasovagal fainting response occurs in a majority of children with phobias of blood-injection-injury (American Psychiatric Association, 1994; Page, 1994).

5.14.1.1 Developmental Variations

Most of what is known about developmental variations is based on research of nonpathological fears using nonclinic samples of children. Findings from this research generally show that the number and intensity of children's fears decrease with age (e.g., Eme & Schmidt, 1978; Ollendick, King, & Frary, 1989). For example, in Ollendick et al. (1989), self-ratings of fear, among a school sample of 1185 children (aged 7–16 years) residing in the US and Australia, indicated that children in the youngest age group (aged 7–10 years) reported a greater number of fears (mean number = 17) compared

to children in the middle (aged 11–13 years; mean number = 13) or oldest age group (aged 14–16 years; mean number = 12). Children in the youngest group also reported a higher intensity of fears as reflected by their total fear score (mean = 138.83) compared with children in the middle (mean = 133.44) and oldest age group (mean = 129.46) (Ollendick et al., 1989).

In addition to the number and intensity of fears, research findings suggest developmental variations in the content of children's fears in nonclinical samples (e.g., Bauer, 1976; Bell-Dolan, Last, & Strauss, 1990; McGee, Feehan, Williams, & Anderson, 1992; Ollendick et al., 1989). Earlier reviews of this literature (e.g., Morris & Kratochwill, 1983; Ollendick & Francis, 1988; Silverman & Nelles, 1990) indicated that loss of support, loud noises, and unfamiliar people predominate in infancy; imaginary creatures, small animals, and the dark predominate in the middle childhood years; and achievement/performance, social-evaluation, and bodily injury predominate in early and late adolescence.

Longitudinal investigations corroborate these patterns. For instance, McGee et al. (1992), in a study of community children (*N* = 925) assessed at age 11 and again at age 15 (using structured diagnostic interview and parent ratings), found that the content of children's fears changed over time. At age 11, children's fears were likely to be of the dark, heights, or animals; at age 15, the fears were likely to be of social and agoraphobic situations.

Although research using clinic samples of children with anxiety disorders is sparse (e.g., Last, Perrin, Hersen, & Kazdin, 1992; Strauss & Last, 1993), extant findings suggest similar developmental patterns in the content of childrens' fears. For instance, children with a primary diagnosis of social phobia (SOP; social-evaluation/performance fears) tend to be older than children with a primary diagnosis of separation anxiety disorder (SAD) or SP (animals, dark) (see Section 5.14.2).

5.14.1.2 Gender Variations

Research on gender variations using clinic samples has been conducted primarily with respect to prevalence rates (see Section 5.14.5). Research on gender variations in children's fears using nonclinic populations, and using self-, parent-, teacher-, and peer-ratings, shows that girls report more fears, and obtain higher fear ratings from others, than do boys (both frequency and intensity) (e.g., Croake, 1969; Ollendick, 1983; Ollendick & King, 1994; Ollendick, Yang, Dong, Xia, & Lin, 1995; Ollendick, Yule, & Ollier, 1991; Silverman &

Nelles, 1988b). One common explanation is that gender role expectations or attributions may be operating. That is, it is more acceptable for girls than for boys to act "feminine," which includes admitting to fears or behaving in a fearful manner (Maccoby, 1980). Consistent with this notion is the finding that children of both genders tend to ascribe more fear to girls than to boys (Ollendick et al., 1995; Silverman & Nelles, 1988b).

Although a positive relation between "femininity" and a negative relation between "masculinity" (as measured by self-report measures) and fear/anxiety have been found in adult populations (Carey, Dusek, & Spector, 1988; Dillon, Wolf, & Katz, 1988), these hypotheses have not been investigated directly in children. However, preliminary findings from a study on gender and children's fears (Ginsburg & Silverman, 1997) suggest that self-ratings of fear may indeed be associated with gender role orientation. Based on a clinic sample of children ($N = 92$; mean age = 10.3 years) diagnosed with a primary *DSM-III-R* anxiety disorder, a significant negative correlation ($r = -0.21$; $p < 0.05$) was found between children's total scores on the FSSC-R and self-ratings of masculinity on the Children's Sex Role Inventory (Boldizar, 1991).

5.14.1.3 Race and Cultural Variations

Studies of children's fears using nonclinic samples suggest that fears (as measured by child self-rated fear surveys) may be more frequent and intense in American minority groups, such as African-Americans, than in Caucasians (Lapouse & Monk, 1959; Nalven, 1970; Neal & Turner, 1991). Reviews of these studies also suggest that level of fearfulness as well as the presence of specific fears may vary by culture (see Fonesca, Yule & Erol, 1994). For example, a study by Ollendick, Yang, King, Dong, and Akande (1996) examined fears (using the FSSC-R) of 1200 children, (aged 7–17 years), from the US, Australia, China, and Nigeria (300 children from each country), and found several differences in number, level, and content, as well as differences in developmental and gender patterns across countries. One finding, for instance, was that Nigerian children reported more and higher levels of fear compared to their American, Australian, or Chinese counterparts, who did not differ from each other. Moreover, girls and boys in Nigeria reported similar levels of fear; girls in each of the other countries reported higher levels than boys. Finally, the Nigerian children were more likely to report intense fears associated with physical danger (e.g., snakes,

guns, getting shock from electricity); the American and Australian children reported more intense fears of personal safety (e.g., burglars, getting lost). In explaining these cultural variations in fears, Ollendick et al. (1996) point to cultural differences in socialization practices. That is, countries such as Nigeria tend to emphasize socialization practices such as inhibition, compliance, and obedience (and thus children with more fear), and countries such as the US and Australia do not have this emphasis.

Despite these cultural variations, several studies have found similarities in the types of objects and situations feared by children across cultures. For example, in comparing the top 10 fears endorsed on the FSSC-R by children from five different countries (Portugal, UK, Turkey, Australia, and US), seven of the fears were the same across countries (Fonesca et al., 1994). These included: fears of being hit by a car or truck; not being able to breathe; bomb attacks; fire/being burned; burglars; falling from a height; and serious illness. Similarly, in the Ollendick et al. (1996) study cited above, the most common intense fears (i.e., the 10 fears rated "a lot" with the greatest frequency) across countries showed considerable overlap, and reflected fears of danger and/or death (e.g., not being able to breath, being hit by a car or truck, bombing attacks, failing from high places, death/dead people) and failure and/or criticism (e.g., failing a test, having parents argue, and getting poor grades).

Taken all together, the results from cross-cultural studies using nonclinic samples of children suggest that although certain types of fears appear to be culturally meaningful or specific, there also appear to be certain types of fears that are experienced uniformly by children across various cultures. Further research on the specific nature of the socialization practices (e.g., parenting practices) that influence the development of childhood fears across cultures awaits further systematic study.

In terms of racial/cultural variations using clinic samples of youth with anxiety disorders, findings, although sparse, suggest that youth with SP may be more alike than different. For instance, Last and Perrin (1993) compared the sociodemographic background, clinical characteristics, and life-time prevalence rates of *DSM-III-R* anxiety disorders (not only SP) of African-American ($N = 30$) and White children ($N = 139$) aged 5–17 years who presented to a childhood anxiety specialty clinic. Relevant to SP, Last and Perrin found that although the African-American children scored higher than the White children on the FSSC-R, the difference did not reach statistical significance.

Ginsburg and Silverman (1996) compared various characteristics of Hispanic ($N = 90$) and Caucasian children ($N = 143$) who presented to a childhood anxiety specialty clinic. Similar to the findings of Last and Perrin (1993), the children were more similar than different on the variables examined. One significant difference relevant to SP, however, was that the Hispanic parents rated their children as having more fears than did the parents of Caucasian children (using a parent version of the FSSC-R).

In sum, as far as we know, only two studies have examined systematically race and cultural variations of fears in clinic samples that included children with SP (Ginsburg & Silverman, 1996; Last & Perrin, 1993). Although both studies found more similarities than differences between the samples studied, further research is needed before firm conclusions are drawn.

5.14.2 ONSET AND STABILITY

Research has shown that the onset of many SPs occurs during childhood or adolescence (e.g., Ost, 1985, 1987; Ost & Hugdahl, 1983; D. V. Sheehan, K. E. Sheehan, & Minichiello, 1981; Thyer, Parrish, Curtis, Nesse, & Cameron, 1985), and that some SPs are stable over time. For example, one of the most extensive studies on the onset of SP, based on the retrospective reports of adult patients with SP ($N = 370$), reported that the average age of onset for animal phobia was seven, age nine for blood phobia, and age 12 for dental phobia (Ost, 1987).

Other studies, using retrospective reports of adult patients with SP have found similar patterns with respect to age of onset. For instance, Marks and Gelder (1966) found that the onset of phobias of darkness, insects, and blood-injury began before age seven; the onset of animal phobias was somewhat earlier, age 4.4 years. Liddell and Lyons (1978) found that the age of onset for blood phobia was 8.8 years, 10.8 years for dental phobia, and 11.9 years for thunderstorm phobias.

Another way to glean information about the onset and stability of SP in children is to examine the ages in which children present for treatment for SP and to assess the disorder's duration. Last et al. (1992) examined sociodemographic and clinical characteristics of youth ($N = 188$; aged 6–18 years) referred to a child anxiety specialty clinic and reported on developmental variations in primary *DSM-III-R* anxiety diagnoses. The average age at intake for children with a primary diagnosis of SOP ($N = 61$) was found to be 14.4 years, 10.3 years for SAD ($N = 84$), and 12.1 years for SP ($N = 80$). With respect to age of onset, the ages

were 11.3 years for SOP, 7.5 years for SAD, and 8.4 years for SP.

Strauss and Last (1993), in a comparison of clinical characteristics of children who presented to a childhood anxiety clinic with primary diagnoses of either SP or SOP (aged 4–17 years), found that of the children with SP (N = 38; mean age = 11.1 years) the mean age of onset was 7.8 years and the average duration of the children's SP was 3.3 years.

In examining the average age at intake for children who presented to our research clinic, the Child Anxiety and Phobia Program at Florida International University, Miami, it was found also that the average age of the children ($N = 340$; aged 5–18 years) with primary *DSM-III-R* anxiety diagnoses varied. For instance, the average age of children with SAD ($n = 51$) was 8.7 years, 11.7 years for SOP ($n = 42$), and 9.9 years for SP ($n = 143$).

Finally, results obtained from longitudinal studies are yet another way to glean information about onset and stability of SP in children. Perhaps the most widely cited study is that of Agras, Chapin, and Oliveau (1972). They followed a community sample of 30 untreated phobic individuals (10 children under the age of 20 years and 20 adults) over a five-year period. After five years, 100% of the children were viewed as "improved" compared to 43% of the adults. Although the conclusion drawn by Agras et al. was that many phobic conditions improve without treatment, particularly in children, a reinterpretation of these data (Ollendick, 1979) revealed that the improved children were not symptom-free, and most continued to exhibit symptoms of sufficient intensity to be rated between "no disability" and "maximum disability" at the follow-up assessment. Ollendick's reinterpretation thus suggested that some types of phobias persist over time for a proportion of youngsters.

Another study conducted by Milne et al. (1995) examined the frequency of clinical phobias (SP, SOP, and agoraphobia (AG) combined) and subclinical fears in a community sample of youth over a one-year period as part of a large, two-stage epidemiological study on adolescent depression. In the first stage of the study (screening stage), a depressive symptom questionnaire was administered to a large community sample ($N = 3283$; 80% were White and the majority were 7th-graders). In the second stage (diagnostic stage), a selected sample of youth and their mothers ($N = 487$) were assessed with a structured diagnostic interview. These stages were repeated annually for up to three years, the number of children assessed at all three time periods was 112. Relevant here is the finding that of the 112 youth, 11% (with any type of phobia; $n = 12$) continued to meet diagnosis for that same type of phobia one year later.

5.14.3 DIAGNOSIS

A summary of the criteria for an SP diagnosis using the *DSM-IV* (APA, 1994) and *ICD-10* (World Health Organization, 1992) systems are presented in Table 1. In both systems, a diagnosis of SP is assigned when children display a persistent, recurrent, and/or excessive fear toward an object or event. Exposure to the phobic stimulus generally provokes an immediate anxiety reaction, often manifested in children as crying, having tantrums, freezing, or clinging. Generally, the phobic situation is avoided or experienced with severe distress. A key factor in assigning a diagnosis of SP is that the symptoms must impair functioning significantly.

Differences in the *ICD-10* and *DSM-IV* pertain to their views about the classification of the phobia as an adult or child disorder (based on whether the fear is developmentally age-appropriate), about the persistence of symptoms, and the classification of phobia subtypes. Specifically, according to *ICD-10*, phobias may be classified as either of one of two disorders, "phobic anxiety disorder of childhood" (under the broader category, "Emotional Disorders with Onset Specific to Childhood") or "phobic anxiety disorder" (under the broader category, "Neurotic, Stress-related, and Somatoform Disorders"), generally used for adults. The criteria for the childhood-onset disorder requires that the fears be age-appropriate but excessive and impairing. In cases in which fears are not age-specific, the adult disorder is assigned to that child as a diagnosis. In contrast, *DSM-IV* has only one classification for phobias, and fears need not be age-appropriate to be assigned the diagnosis. For *ICD-10*, duration is

Table 1 Diagnostic criteria for specific phobias in children.

DSM-IV

   A. A marked, persistent fear that is excessive or unreasonable, prompted by the presence or anticipation of an object or situation (e.g., flying, heights, animals)

   B. Exposure to the feared object or situation usually provokes an immediate anxiety response. In children this may be expressed by crying, tantrums, freezing, or clinging

   C. A recognition that the fear is excessive or unreasonable (this feature may be absent in children)

   D. The feared object or situation(s) is avoided or endured with intense anxiety or distress

   E. The avoidance or distress toward the feared object or situation significantly interferes with the person's normal routine, occupational (or academic) functioning, or social activities or relationships, or causes marked distress

   F. Fear is present for at least six months for individuals under age 18 years

   G. The individual does not meet criteria for another mental disorder that better accounts for their anxiety, panic attacks, or phobic avoidance associated with the specific object or situation (e.g., obsessive compulsive disorder, separation anxiety disorder)

ICD–10 (includes both child and adult descriptions)

   A. Phobic anxiety disorders. Disorders in which anxiety is evoked only, or predominantly, in well-defined situations that are not currently dangerous. Consequently, these situations are avoided or endured with dread. The patient's concern may be focused on individual symptoms like palpitations or feeling faint and is often associated with fears of dying, losing control, or going mad. Contemplating entry to the phobic situation usually generates anticipatory anxiety

   B. Specific (isolated) phobias. Phobias that are restricted to highly specific situations such as proximity to particular animals, heights, thunder, darkness, flying, closed spaces, etc. Types of specific phobias are classified as: acrophobia, animal phobia, claustrophobia, simple phobia

   C. Phobic anxiety disorder specific to childhood. Fears displayed during childhood, that arise in a majority of children, but that are abnormal in degree. Fears displayed in childhood that are not a normal part of psychosocial development (e.g., agoraphobia) are coded under the adult categories

   D. Excludes generalized anxiety disorder and when associated with conduct disorders not part of the diagnostic criteria; for *DSM-IV*, the children's symptoms must be continuous for six months to receive a diagnosis. Finally, *ICD-10* childhood onset does not specify subtypes of SP; *ICD-10* adult-onset phobia subtypes include: acrophobia, animal phobia, claustrophobia, simple phobia. The subtypes of *DSM-IV* are: animal (e.g., cats, dogs, insects); natural environment (e.g., storms, heights, water); blood-injection-injury (e.g., seeing blood, needles); situational (e.g., public transportation, elevators, flying); and other (e.g., loud noises, costume characters).

5.14.3.1 Differential Diagnosis

A diagnosis of SP should only be given once other anxiety conditions have been ruled out. For example, according to the *DSM*, a diagnosis of SP is assigned only when the fear is not restricted to situations that involve separation (as in SAD), social-evaluation and embarrassment (as in SOP), dirt/contamination (as in obsessive compulsive disorder, OCD), or fears of having a panic attack and/or being unable to escape (as in panic with or without AG). It is also essential that the fear not be a part of a larger reaction to a traumatic event, as in post-traumatic stress disorder, or a more pervasive pattern of anxiety, as in generalized anxiety disorder (GAD).

Finally, although children who refuse to attend school are often labeled as having a "school phobia," research has revealed that these children refuse school for a myriad of reasons (Bernstein & Garfinkel, 1986; Burke & Silverman, 1987; Kearney & Silverman, 1997) which may or may not be related to having SP. For instance, a child may refuse to attend school because of fears of speaking in class (SOP), being away from a parent (SAD), or hearing the bell ring (SP, situational subtype). Thus, to derive a differential diagnosis for children who present with school refusal, it is important to carefully assess the specific reasons for the school refusal.

5.14.3.2 Comorbidity

Clinic and community studies indicate that up to one-half of all children present with more than one comorbid disorder (see Caron & Rutter, 1991 for a review). Several studies examining the comorbid patterns among samples of clinic-referred children with anxiety disorders have been conducted (e.g., Last, Strauss, & Francis, 1987; Last et al., 1992; Strauss & Last, 1993). Last et al. (1987) examined the comorbid *DSM-III* diagnoses of

a sample of 73 children (aged 5–18 years) with primary diagnoses of SAD ($n = 24$), over-anxious disorder (OAD; $n = 11$), SP ($n = 11$), and major depression ($n = 11$). Findings with respect to SP indicated that 64% of the children in the SP group had a comorbid diagnosis. The most common comorbid anxiety disorder was SAD (39%).

In a subsequent study, Last et al. (1992) examined comorbid lifetime history diagnoses in children with anxiety disorders ($N = 188$; aged 5–18 years). Relevant to SP were the findings that 60 of the 80 children (75%) with a primary diagnosis of SP had a lifetime history of any anxiety diagnosis; 32.5% had a history of any depressive disorder; and 22.5% had a history of any disruptive disorder. The most common additional anxiety disorder was again SAD ($n = 31$; 38.8%).

Hammond-Laurence and Silverman (1997) examined current rates of comorbid diagnoses in a large sample of children referred to an anxiety specialty clinic ($n = 356$; aged 6–17 years. With respect to SP, the findings indicated that this was the most common diagnosis of the sample and, typically, children with a primary diagnosis of SP met criteria for a secondary diagnosis of another SP (29%) or SAD (18%). Also of interest is the finding that children with only one anxiety disorder tended to be rated lower (on average) in clinical severity relative to children with multiple disorders, indicating that there is "clinical significance" to having multiple comorbid disorders.

Although the high comorbid rates reported in the studies just cited could be due in part to the Berkson effects, that is, both the Last et al. (1987, 1992) and the Hammond-Laurence and Silverman (1997) studies were conducted at anxiety specialty clinics that attract the most severely anxious youth, these findings are in accord with the growing body of literature concerned with comorbidity (Caron & Rutter, 1991). However, a great deal more work is needed to understand the meaning and implications of comorbidity, not only in terms of clinical presentation, but also in terms of prognosis and treatment.

5.14.4 ETIOLOGY

5.14.4.1 Biological

Evidence for the role of biological factors is based largely on findings from family aggregate and twin studies (e.g., Burglass, Clarke, Henderson, Kreitman, & Presley, 1977; Davey, Forster, & Mayhew, 1993; Fyer et al., 1990; Fyer, Mannuzza, Chapman, Martin, & Klein, 1995; Kendler, Neale, Kessler, Heath, & Eaves,

1992; Last, Hersen, Kazdin, Orvaschel, & Perrin, 1991; Moran & Andrews, 1985; Noyes et al., 1986; Reich & Yates, 1988; Solyom, Beck, Solyom, & Hugel, 1974; Torgersen, 1979). Not all of these studies focused exclusively on SP, but examined various types of phobic and anxiety disorders. Overall, however, these studies provide support for a positive familial contribution to these disorders.

A representative study that focused on SP was conducted by Fyer et al. (1990). In this study, the probands of adults diagnosed with SP ($N = 49$) were assessed, including all their first-degree relatives, using the Schedule for Affective Disorders and Schizophrenia (SADS; Endicott & Spitzer, 1978). First-degree relatives of a normal proband group ($N = 119$) served as the control group. The results indicated that relatives of individuals with SP evidenced a higher rate of SP themselves (31%) compared with relatives of those in the comparison group (11%). In addition, 15% of the children whose parents had SP, compared to 8% of children whose parents did not have SP, evidenced SP.

Another study by the same research group (Fyer et al., 1995) compared the familial aggregation of three different types of phobic disorders: SP ($N = 15$), SOP ($N = 39$), and panic with AG ($N = 49$). All participants were of European descent, with one living first-degree relative, and were recruited from on-going studies that were being conducted at two different anxiety disorders research clinics. None of the participants who comprised each of the three phobic disorder groups had comorbid diagnoses (present or lifetime). The control participants, who were recruited from a randomly selected patient acquaintance list, were 77 "not ill" individuals, that is, no past or current psychiatric diagnoses. *DSM-III-R* diagnoses were assessed using a combination of a direct interview (i.e., SADS-Lifetime Anxiety Version) and family informants' reports.

The results indicated that relatives of individuals in the SP group had significantly higher rates of SP (31%) than the relatives of individuals in the control group (9%). Interestingly, the rates of SP in the relatives of individuals with panic/AG (10%) and SOP (13%) did not differ significantly from the rates found in the relatives of individuals in the control group (9%). In interpreting these results, Fyer et al. (1995) suggested that there may be an "existence of separable, etiologically discrete syndromes within the group of cases identified by each of the three *DSM-III-R* criteria sets" (p. 572). However, the authors caution that this notion may apply to "pure" diagnostic cases (i.e., those with no present or life-time comorbid diagnoses). Also not clear is

whether it applies to each subtype of SP (e.g., if relatives of blood phobics were more at risk for blood phobias than for dog phobias) as this issue was not examined due to limited sample sizes. In addition, although the findings provide evidence for some type of familial risk for SP, what is not clear is whether this familial risk is due to shared genes, common family environmental factors, or an interaction of the two (Foley & Hay, 1992; Silverman, Cerny, & Nelles, 1988).

Additional evidence of a biological contribution comes from twin studies (e.g., Abe, Oda, Ikenaga, & Yamada, 1993; Kendler et al., 1992; Slater & Shields, 1969; Stevenson, Batten, & Cherner, 1992; Torgersen, 1979; Young, Fenton, & Lader, 1971). For example, in one of the largest studies examining genetic and common familial environmental influences in the etiology of phobic disorders (AG, SOP, and SP), Kendler et al. administered diagnostic and clinical interviews to 2163 adult female twins recruited from a population-based twin registry. Findings relevant here indicated that concordance rates of animal phobia for monozygotic and dizygotic twins were 25.9% and 11.0%, respectively. Concordance rates for situational phobia for monozygotic and dizygotic twins were 22.2% and 23.7%, respectively. According to Kendler et al., such findings provide support for the contribution of genetic factors in the etiology of SP, with a higher contribution of familial environmental factors operating for situational phobias.

Another avenue for investigating biological contributions to SP has been in the area of behavioral inhibition. Behavioral inhibition (BI) refers to the temperament of approximately 10–20% of Caucasian infants who are predisposed to being irritable, shy, and fearful as toddlers, and cautious, quiet, and introverted as school-aged children (e.g., Biederman et al., 1990, 1993a, 1993b; Hirshfeld et al., 1992; Kagan, Reznick, & Gibbons, 1989; Kagan, Reznick, & Snidman, 1987). Although studies generally support a positive association between anxiety disorders and BI in children, it is premature to conclude that BI is linked uniquely with SP, or with any other specific anxiety disorder.

With this caveat in mind, emerging evidence from this line of research suggests that BI in infancy may be a risk factor for phobic disorders (e.g., Biederman et al., 1990, 1993a, 1993b). For example, a study conducted by Biederman et al. (1990) used a structured interview (DICA-parent version) to examine the prevalence of *DSM-III-R* internalizing disorders (i.e., major depression, SAD, OAD, avoidant disorder [AVD], phobic disorders, and OCD) as well as externalizing disorders (i.e., oppositional defiant, conduct, attention deficit disorder, encopresis, enuresis) in three different cohorts of children. The first cohort, examined cross-sectionally, was the at-risk group and comprised offspring of parents with psychiatric diagnoses. Children in this cohort were classified as either inhibited ($N = 18$; mean age = 5.9 years) or uninhibited ($N = 12$; mean age = 4.9 years). The second cohort (Kagan's original cohort; Kagan, Reznick, & Snidman, 1987, 1988) was an epidemiologically derived sample of children who, at age 21 months, had been classified as either inhibited ($N = 22$) or uninhibited ($N = 19$). The mean age of the children at the time of the reassessment was 8 years. The third cohort of children had no medical or psychiatric disorders ($N = 20$; mean age = 7.8 years) and was obtained from primary pediatric care referrals.

Most relevant here are the findings that were found with the children in Kagan's original cohort. Specifically, the findings indicated that the inhibited compared with the uninhibited children had significantly higher rates of phobic disorders (31.8% vs. 5.3%, respectively). Inhibited compared with uninhibited children also had higher rates of OAD, SAD, and AVD, but this finding was not statistically significant. In exploratory analyses of the specific fears of the children who met criteria for a phobic disorder ($n = 9$), the results indicated that the average number of fears per child was 3.4, and that the most common fears were: standing up and speaking in front of class ($n = 5$); animals or bugs ($n = 5$); strangers ($n = 4$); the dark ($n = 4$); being called on in class ($n = 3$); crowds ($n = 3$); elevators ($n = 2$); and physicians ($n = 2$).

In a review of the research literature on BI and anxiety disorders, Turner, Beidel, and Wolff (1996) concluded that children with stable BI have higher rates of anxiety disorders (any type) and phobias compared with uninhibited children. With respect to phobias, BI appears to be associated most closely with those phobias that are social or social-evaluative in nature. Turner et al. also pointed out that although the research suggests that BI is neither necessary nor sufficient for developing an anxiety/phobic disorder, its presence may serve to increase children's vulnerability to anxiety disorders, including SP.

5.14.4.2 Psychosocial Factors

The emphasis that may be placed on specific psychosocial factors is likely to be influenced in part by the theoretical model or orientation to which the researcher or practitioner ascribes

(e.g., psychoanalytic, behavioral, cognitive, familial). These models are summarized briefly below.

5.14.4.2.1 Psychoanalytic

According to the psychoanalytic perspective (Freud, 1909/1955), phobias develop in response to unconscious forbidden sexual or aggressive impulses. The anxiety experienced by these impulses are "defended" against via displacement of these feelings on to less threatening objects or situations. Hence, in Freud's famous case of Little Hans, Hans' phobia of horses was attributed to his attempt to defend against or avoid anxiety aroused by his sexual desire for his mother and his wish to do away with his father, the competitor. The child defended against the anxiety of these impulses by displacing his feelings on to an external object that can be avoided (i.e., horses). It has been difficult to verify empirically the psycho-analytic conceptualization of SP because of the unconscious nature of the main, hypothesized processes, namely, displacement. Moreover, subsequent analysis of this case by Wolpe and Rachman (1960) revealed no direct evidence for Hans' wish to sleep with his mother, for his hatred or fear of his father, nor for the supposed relation between horses and Hans' father.

5.14.4.2.2 Behavioral

Behavioral perspectives emphasize the role of conditioning (classical, operant, and vicarious) in the acquisition of phobias. For instance, case reports, such as Little Peter (Jones, 1924a; 1924b) and Little Albert (Watson & Rayner, 1920), demonstrated how a child could acquire a phobia of a previously neutral stimulus (e.g., a rat) by contiguous pairing with an aversive event. Empirical and case reports have supported both direct (classical conditioning) and indirect (vicarious exposure) conditioning models (e.g., Liddell & Lyons, 1978; Merckelbach, De Ruiter, Van De Hout, & Hoekstra, 1989).

Subsequent research has extended initial, conditioning theory to "neoconditioning" theory, reflected by the writings of Rescorla (1988) and Davey (1992). In Rescorla's and Davey's reformulation of conditioning, the emphasis is not on contiguous pairing of stimuli but on one's expectancy that the conditioned stimulus predicts the unconditioned stimulus and by one's evaluation of the unconditioned stimulus. According to this reformulation, learning that a stimulus predicts another occurs separately from learning that the predicted stimulus is aversive. For example, by often playing near a neighbor's house in which a big dog sits in the yard, a child may learn that the house is associated with the presence of a big dog. If the child is later bitten by a dog in some other location, the child may come to fear the neighbor's house because it reliably predicts a stimulus (a dog) that has acquired aversive properties. Reiss (1991), similarly, delineated a neoconditioning theory, one that also emphasizes a cognitive expectancy account that involves certain individual personality differences, such as anxiety sensitivity.

Also representing an important extension of conditioning theory was Mowrer's (1939) two-factor model which postulated Pavlovian conditioning in the initial acquisition of fear, and operant conditioning in the maintenance of fear in that fear serves as an acquired source of motivation or drive, (i.e., behaviors that reduced fear are reinforced). The adequacy of Mowrer's two-factor model in explaining the persistence of phobic fear and avoidant behavior has been questioned, however, because many individuals with phobias can confront the phobic stimulus without either covert avoidance or a subsequent aversive unconditioned stimulus (Menzies & Clarke, 1995). That is, according to Mowrer, this should lead to reductions in fear and avoidant behavior, but this does not always occur (Clarke & Jackson, 1983). Modified conditioning explanations consequently have been developed to account for this, such as the partial irreversibility of fear account (Solomon & Wynne, 1954), the preparedness account (Seligman, 1970, 1971), the incubation account (Eysenck, 1979), the safety signal account (Rachman, 1983), and the serial conditioned stimulus account (Stampfl, 1991).

Yet another way to conceptualize phobia acquisition (or reacquisition) is the notion of dishabituation of formerly mastered fears. More specifically, this is the notion that fears are not unlearned but are tempered or assuaged via habituation or extinction in certain contexts. Bouton (1991) reviewed evidence in support of this view, suggesting that extinction of fear responses do not involve unlearning of previously learned associations; rather, it involves learning to discriminate contexts in which the conditioned stimulus–unconditioned stimulus relationship exists from contexts in which the relationship does not exist. Hence, from this perspective, reinstatement of children's fears can occur when children are reexposed to fearful stimuli in situations that are not associated with safety.

Rachman (1977) espoused the importance of additional pathways in "indirect" fear acquisition, namely, vicarious exposure and the transmission of information or instruction. Support for these pathways has been provided

in the subclinical fears of adults (e.g., Hekmat, 1987; Murray & Foote, 1979; Ost, 1985; Rimm, Janda, Lancaster, Nahl, & Dittmar, 1977), and in the fears of nonclinic referred children (Milgrom, Mancle, King, & Weinstein, 1995; Ollendick, King & Hamilton, 1991).

Taken all together, empirical support for the various conditioning reformulations and extensions have been uneven across laboratories, samples, disorders, and so on. This unevenness helped, in part, to spur the "cognitive revolution" that occurred in behavioral psychology in the 1970s. This perspective is discussed next.

5.14.4.2.3 Cognitive

Maladaptive cognitions and cognitive processes are believed to play an important role in the etiology and/or maintenance of SP. It is unclear, however, whether such cognitive activity is the cause or consequence of the fear response. Also unclear is how cognitions and/or cognitive processes vary with development. In contrast to the research literature on cognitive explanations of SP in adults, literature on this issue in children is sparse. Moreover, the extant studies are based on either nonclinic samples of children with different types of fears, or on clinic samples of children with different types of anxiety disorders. Nevertheless, these studies provide some useful information which may shed light on the role of cognitions and cognitive processes in children with SP.

In terms of cognitions, Kendall and colleagues (e.g., Kendall & Chansky, 1991) have suggested a heuristic distinction between cognitive deficiencies (i.e., a lack of cognitive activity such as problem solving, planning, or perspective taking) and cognitive distortions (i.e., cognitive activity that is characterized by misperceptions, exaggerations, or overattending to environmental threat). Children with excessive fear and anxiety are hypothesized to present with the latter. In support of this hypothesis, early research on the cognitive activity of highly anxious children indicated that these children are more likely than their nonanxious counterparts to engage in cognitive distortions, such as thoughts that focus on negative evaluations or unfavorable social comparisons (e.g., Francis, 1988; Prins, 1985; 1986; Zatz & Chassin, 1985).

Prins (1986), for example, examined children's self-speech and self-regulation during a fear-provoking task. Forty-four children (aged 8–12 years) with varying levels of fear of water were asked to perform three tasks in a pool that provoked differential levels of fear (e.g., jumping or diving from a low board, diving from a high board). The children were classified into three groups (high, moderate, and low anxious) based on their performance during a regular swimming lesson at school, observed by the researchers. Children's self-statements (positive, neutral, negative) were assessed via interviews immediately following each task. Relevant here were the findings that the children in the high anxious group engaged in significantly more negative self-statements (e.g., "I'll fall hard," "It will go wrong," "Last time I fell on my belly,") relative to the children in the moderate and low anxious groups. Interestingly, however, no differences were observed among the groups in the frequency of positive or neutral self-statements.

In a study using adolescents recruited from high schools, King, Mietz, Tinney, and Ollendick (1995) compared the cognitions of adolescents who were low and high in test anxiety. Classification of low ($N = 25$; mean age = 15.6 years) and high ($N = 22$; mean age = 15.75 years) test anxiety was based on the adolescents' scores (i.e., the bottom and top 5%) on the Test Anxiety Scale for Children (TASC; Sarason, Davidson, Lighthall, Waite, & Ruebush, 1960). The two groups were compared on psychiatric diagnoses, levels of fear, anxiety, depression, and cognitions. Cognitions were assessed after a brief math and language test using the Children's Cognitive Assessment Questionnaire (CCAQ; Zatz & Chassin, 1983, 1985). The CCAQ has 50 statements about different types of thoughts: on-task, off-task, positive and negative self-evaluations, and coping self-statements. Findings with respect to diagnoses indicated that of the high test anxious youth that were interviewed ($n = 18$), 61% had an anxiety or phobic disorder (four youth had SP) compared to 2% of children in the low anxious group. With respect to cognitions, the adolescents in the high test anxiety group reported more off-task thoughts (e.g., "I wish this were over"), more negative self-evaluations (e.g., "I'm doing poorly on this"), more coping thoughts (e.g., "try to relax"), and fewer positive self-evaluations (e.g., "I do well on tests like this") than the adolescents in the low test anxious group. According to King et al., these results are consistent with the notion that nonnegative thinking may be related more strongly to adjustment than positive thinking (i.e., Kendall's notion of the "power of non-negative thinking"). Clinically, the implications are that it might be important to teach children with high test anxiety to control their off-task and negative self-talk rather than teaching the development of coping self-statements.

There is also a growing body of research on the factors that influence the thinking of anxious children. Some of these studies have included subsamples of youth with SP (Barrett, Rapee, Dadds, & Ryan, 1996), while some have not specified the specific types of anxiety disorders comprising the samples (e.g., Chorpita, Albano, & Barlow, 1996). Some of the factors that have been examined include: cognitive interpretive style (Barrett et al. 1996; Chorpita et al., 1996); causal attribution (Bell-Dolan & Wessler, 1994); and attentional bias (e.g., Vasey, Daleiden, Williams, & Brown, 1995). For example, in Barrett et al.'s study on children's cognitive interpretive style, children (aged 7–14 years) with anxiety disorders ($N = 152$; 27 had SP) were presented with several ambiguous situations and were asked to provide interpretations of the situations and to problem-solve a plan of action. One-half of the situations were social in nature (e.g., "You are going to school and a group of children are following you ... ") and the other half were physical (e.g., "On the way to school you feel funny in your tummy ... "). The comparison groups were nonclinic-referred children ($n = 26$) and clinic-referred children with *DSM-III-R* diagnoses of Oppositional Defiant Disorder (ODD; $n = 27$). The results indicated that the children with anxiety disorders perceived more threat in the ambiguous situations than the nonclinic children, but less threat relative to children with ODD. In addition, relative to both comparison groups, the children with anxiety disorders generated more avoidant plans as solutions to these situations. A closer examination of the responses of children with different primary anxiety diagnoses indicated that children with SP and OAD gave more threat interpretations to the physical situations than children with SAD. Moreover, children with SP gave more avoidant solutions to physical situations than children with any other type of anxiety disorder.

In terms of attentional bias, Martin, Horder, and Jones (1992) compared the response time for naming the colors of written words using a modified Stroop task of nonclinical school children (aged 6–13 years) with and without fears of spiders. Fearfulness was based on children's affirmative or negative responses to both of two questions: (i) whether the child liked spiders and (ii) whether the child would pick up a spider. All children completed a Stroop task that included spider-related and neutral words. The children with fears of spiders were found to be slower than the children without fears of spiders in their naming the color of spider-related words (e.g., web, crawl, hairy), supporting the notion of attentional bias in fearful children. Vasey et al. (1995) found similar results when they examined modified Stroop test performance using a sample of children (aged 9–14 years) with and without anxiety disorders ($N = 12$ in each group), supporting the hypothesis that children with anxiety disorders exhibit an attentional bias toward emotionally threatening stimuli. Vasey et al. further discuss how anxious children's narrowing of attention (i.e., hyperattention) may increase a child's focus on danger and threat stimuli, increase the encoding of threatening material, and thus maintain or increase levels of fear and anxiety.

In sum, empirical support is beginning to accumulate for the role of cognitions and certain cognitive processes in the etiology and/or maintenance of anxiety disorders. However, few studies have focused exclusively on the role of cognitions and cognitive processes in clinic samples of children diagnosed specifically with SP. This issue thus awaits further investigation.

5.14.4.2.4 Family

Familial contributions are also believed to play an important role in the development of SP. As noted in section 5.14.4.1, considerable evidence has documented that anxiety/fear "run in families." Specifically, findings from top-down studies generally reveal that children whose parents have an anxiety disorder are at risk of developing an anxiety disorder themselves (e.g., Silverman, Cerny, Nelles, & Burke, 1988; Turner, Beidel, & Costello, 1987; Weissman, Leckman, Merikangas, Gammon, & Prusoff, 1984). However, the specific mechanisms of transmission remain unclear. Two processes, parental modeling and parental child management (e.g., use of rewards and punishments) of fearful/avoidant behavior, have received the most attention by researchers. It is noted, however, that most of the studies conducted have not used clinic samples of children with SP. Most have used clinic samples of children with different types of anxiety disorders or nonclinic samples of children with different types of fears.

In terms of parental modeling, Milgrom et al. (1995) examined parental modeling as part of a larger study on origins of childhood dental fears. Children ($N = 895$; aged 5–11 years) recruited from public schools during dental exams, and their mothers or female guardians, were interviewed and administered several questionnaires to assess direct conditioning, parental modeling, and control variables (e.g., socioeconomic status (SES)). Most relevant here are the findings that among the parental modeling variables, maternal level of dental fear and maternal oral health were significant predictors of dental fears in the children, even

after controlling for gender, age, and other sociodemographic variables.

Although not containing children with SP, another study conducted by Muris, Steerneman, Merckelbach, and Meesters (1996) provided further evidence for an association between parental modeling, particularly by mothers, and levels of child fear. These authors made use of the notion of "social referencing" in interpreting their findings: that is, children's tendencies to "look to" their parents, particularly their mothers, for emotional information as a way to appraise the dangers of a situation (Muris et al., 1996).

In discussing the contribution of parental modeling to child fear and anxiety problems, Silverman et al. (1988) suggested that it is not parental fear *per se* that is critical, but the extent to which parental fear is associated with parental avoidant behavior. Capps, Sigman, Sena, Henker, and Whalen (1996) provided evidence for this notion in a study in which they compared 16 offspring (aged 8–14 years) of parents with AG with 16 offspring of non-psychiatric parents who were matched on age, gender, SES, and ethnicity. No significant correlation was found between parents' and children's self-ratings of fearfulness. However, the number of situations avoided by parents with AG was correlated significantly with the children's anxiety symptom scores, assessed via a structured interview.

In addition to parental modeling, research suggests that certain types of parental child management approaches may be associated with child fear and anxiety problems (e.g., Bush, Melamed, Sheras, & Greenbaum, 1986; Zabin & Melamed, 1980). For example, in Zabin and Melamed (1980), parents completed a questionnaire in which they endorsed the child management approach (e.g., positive reinforcement, punishment) that they used most often to encourage their child to deal with various fearful situations (e.g., getting a haircut, going to the dentist). Parental scores on this questionnaire were correlated with several indices of child trait anxiety (based on child and parent ratings) and state anxiety (based on child, parent, observer, and physiological measures) during their hospitalization for a fearful pediatric procedure.

Although measures of parent discipline varied in the strength of their relation to each of the child anxiety measures, and at each assessment period, overall, the patterns of results revealed that parental disciplinary techniques were associated with measures of child anxiety. More specifically, children whose parents endorsed using positive reinforcement and modeling of nonfearful behavior displayed low levels of child anxious behaviors (based on observer, child, and physiological measures). In contrast, children whose parents endorsed using punishment, physical force, or reinforcement of dependency displayed high levels of anxious behaviors (based on observer, parent, child, and physiological measures). Research findings obtained via direct observations of parent–child interactions of clinic samples of children corroborate this link between parental modeling as well as certain types of parental child management approaches and children's fear/anxiety problems (Barrett et al., 1996; Chorpita et al., 1996; Dadds, Barrett, Rapee, & Ryan, 1996). As noted, however, these studies contain too few children with SP (or the numbers are unspecified) to draw firm conclusions about the role of the family and family processes in the development of this particular disorder in children.

5.14.5 EPIDEMIOLOGY

Estimates of SP in childhood vary depending on the methodology used. Some of these methodological differences include variations in the informant (child, parent, both), the assessment method (structured vs. unstructured interviews), the sample (clinic or community), the age and gender of the participants, and whether an impairment index was included as part of the definition. Despite these differences, epidemiological studies provide a clearer picture than ever before of the prevalence of SP.

Table 2 presents findings from community studies, which have estimated rates of SP as ranging between 2 and 9% (e.g., Anderson, Williams, McGee, & Silva, 1987; Bird et al., 1988; Costello et al., 1988; Fergusson, Harwood, & Lynskey, 1993; McGee et al., 1990). The rate of SP among children who present for treatment has been estimated as being approximately 7% of referrals at outpatient community mental health clinics (Graziano & DeGiovanni, 1979; Silverman & Kearney, 1992), and approximately 30–35% of referrals at outpatient child anxiety specialty clinics (e.g., Last et al., 1987, 1992).

5.14.5.1 Prevalence of Phobia Subtypes

Information on the prevalence of each of the subtypes of SP among children is based largely on studies of youth who present to child anxiety specialty clinics. For example, in Strauss and Last's (1993) study, described earlier, in which the clinical characteristics of children with SOP and SP were compared, the most common subtypes of phobias of the 38 children (mean age 11.1 years) with a primary diagnosis of SP were:

darkness 29%, school 24%, dogs 16%, other animals 8%, heights 8%, insects 8%, elevators 5%, and 3% for swimming, needles, drains, taxidermy.

In the Ginsburg and Silverman (1996) study, also described earlier, the most common subtypes of phobias were the same for the Hispanic and Caucasian children, namely, darkness/sleeping alone and small animals (i.e., dogs and cats). Silverman and Kearney (1992), in their survey of practicing psychologists, found that the most common types of fears treated were those relating to separation from caregivers, school, social situations, tests, and the dark.

5.14.5.2 Sociodemographic Risk Factors

Information detailing sociodemographic risk factors for SP is sparse. In this section, findings from community- and clinic-based studies are summarized briefly. These studies have tended to focus on SES, race, and gender.

5.14.5.2.1 Socioeconomic status

Most of what is known about SES as a risk factor for SP is based on samples of children who present at anxiety disorders specialty clinics. For example, in the Strauss and Last (1993) study in which the sociodemographic and clinical characteristics of children with SOP and SP were compared, Hollinghead index was used to assess SES. Of the subsample of children with SP, 22% were classified as levels I (major professionals) and II (medium business, minor professional, technical), 59% were classified as levels III (skilled craftsmen, clerical, and sales workers) and IV (machine operators and semiskilled workers) and 19% were classified as level V (unskilled workers, menial service workers). Last et al. (1992), in their comparison of the sociodemographic and clinical characteristics of a large sample of children with anxiety disorders ($N = 188$), found that most of the children with SP ($n = 80$) came from middle- to upper-class families.

In another study, annual family income was obtained for a sample (ages 6–17 years; mean age 10.1 years) of Caucasian ($N = 143$) and Hispanic ($N = 99$) families of youth with anxiety disorders (Ginsburg & Silverman, 1996). Of the Caucasian families, 8.5% had incomes of $15 000 or less, 22.6% had incomes of $15 000–30 000, and 68.9% had incomes over $30 000. Among the Hispanics, 29.2% had incomes of $15 000 or less, 28.1% had incomes of $15 000–30 000, and 42.7% had incomes over $30 000.

Table 2 Prevalence of specific phobias in epidemiological studies.

Study	N	Age	M:F ratio	Rate of SP
Anderson et al. (1987)	792	11	1:1.7	2.4
McGee et al. (1990)	943	15	1:2.9	3.6
Bird et al. (1988)	777	4–16		2.6
Costello et al. (1988)	789	7–11	1:2.0	9.2
Fergusson et al. (1993)	961	15		5.1
Kashani et al. (1987)	150	14–16	G > B	4.7
Kashani and Orvaschel (1990)	210	8,12,17	1:6	3.3

Source: Anderson (1994) and Silverman and Ginsburg (1998).

5.14.5.2.2 Racial/ethnic variations

Rates of SP and other psychiatric disorders were assessed in a community sample of youth in Puerto Rico using a multistage assessment procedure consisting of the parent and teacher versions of the Child Behavior Checklist (CBCL; Achenbach & Edelbrock, 1983) at the first stage (for screening), and a structured diagnostic interview at the second stage (for diagnosing) (Bird et al., 1988). As can be seen from Table 2, prevalence rates for SP in Puerto Rican youth (2.6%) were similar to those found in Caucasian youth.

Similar rates of SP in samples of African-American and White children (Last & Perrin, 1993) and in samples of Hispanic and White children (Ginsburg & Silverman, 1996), obtained from child anxiety specialty clinics, have also been reported. Specifically, Last and Perrin (1993) found that SP was among the "top" two primary diagnoses in both of their groups, both at intake (26.7% for African-Americans and 18.0% for Whites) and for lifetime prevalence (50% for African-Americans and 40.3% for Whites). Ginsburg and Silverman (1996) found SP to be the top primary diagnosis at intake in both of their groups, with a rate of 38.4% for Hispanics and 47.6% for Whites.

5.14.5.2.3 Gender

With respect to gender, several epidemiological studies have found rates of SP to be higher in girls than boys (see Table 2). This is consistent with the studies on nonclinical fears. In contrast, studies examining rates of SP in clinic samples of children generally have found rates of SP to be equal for boys and girls (Ginsburg & Silverman, 1996; Last & Perrin, 1993).

5.14.6 ASSESSMENT

The most widely used methods for assessing children's cognitive/subjective, behavioral, and physiological response systems (Lang, 1977) are summarized in this section. Choosing the "best" assessment procedure depends largely on the specific goal or desired outcome (e.g., self-rating scales may be best for screening, interview schedules for diagnosing) (Silverman & Kurtines, 1996). A protypical approach to assessment involves eliciting information from multiple perspectives (child, parent, teacher) and examining each of the three response systems. It is noted, however, that manifestations of fear/anxiety measured by these three systems do not necessarily covary (i.e., desynchrony).

5.14.6.1 Cognitive/Subjective

The most commonly used strategies to assess the cognitive/subjective system include clinical interviews, self-report questionnaires, and self-monitoring procedures, although these strategies may also be used to assess the behavioral (e.g., "do you try as hard as you can to stay away from dogs?") and physiological response systems (e.g., "does your heart beat fast when you see a dog?").

Clinical interviews are characterized as either unstructured (or nonstandardized) or structured (or standardized) (Richardson, Dohrenwend, & Klein, 1965). In the unstructured interview, the specific questions and the sequence of the questions asked vary depending on the interviewees' responses and on the interviewers' subjective judgements and training. Structured interviews contain a set of questions that are asked of all respondents in the same sequence (see Silverman, 1991, 1994, for reviews). Because of problems with the reliability of diagnoses derived from unstructured interviews (Edelbrock & Costello, 1984), the use of structured and semistructured interview schedules has increased through the years. Of the structured interviews available (e.g., the Schedule for Affective Disorders and Schizophrenia in School-Age Children; Puig-Antich & Chambers, 1978, the Diagnostic Interview for

Children and Adolescents; Herjanic & Reich, 1982, the Diagnostic Interview Schedule for Children; Costello, Edelbrock, Dulcan, Kalas, & Klaric, 1984), only the Anxiety Disorders Interview Schedule for Children (ADIS-C/P; Silverman & Nelles, 1988a; Silverman & Albano, 1996) was designed specifically for use with children with SPs and other anxiety disorders. Its utility for diagnosing SPs in youth has been studied extensively (Rapee, Barrett, Dadds, & Evans, 1994; Silverman & Eisen, 1992; Silverman & Nelles, 1988a; Silverman & Rabian, 1995), and have yielded excellent reliability coefficients (Kappa coefficients ranging from 0.84 to 1.0, depending on the reliability paradigm used (i.e., interrater, test–retest).

To assess the presence of SP, the ADIS-C/P contains a list of objects/events (e.g., dark, dogs, needles) to which the child/parent is instructed to rate the child's degree of fear and avoidance using a Feelings Thermometer. The Feelings Thermometer is useful in that it simplifies the rating task for children and removes some of the variability attributed to language skills that occur when young children respond to questionnaires (Barrios, Hartmann, & Shigetomei, 1981). In addition to fear ratings, the ADIS-C/P provides for an assessment of degree of interference by obtaining such ratings from the child and parent alike, also using a modified Feelings Thermometer. Additional sections of the ADIS-C/P contain questions addressing onset, course, and etiology of each specific phobia.

Another frequently used method for assessing the cognitive/subjective system are self-rating scales. The most widely used scale for assessing fears in children is the Revised Fear Survey Schedule for Children (FSSC-R; Ollendick, 1983). This measure provides information on the number, severity, and types of fears that children experience in 80 different situations. Factor analysis has revealed five factors including: (i) fear of the unknown, (ii) fear of failure and criticism, (iii) fear of minor injury and small animals, (iv) fear of danger and death, and (v) medical fears (Ollendick, 1983).

Other self-rating scales have been developed to assess a broad range of children's fears, including the Louisville Fear Survey (Miller, Barrett, Hampe, & Noble, 1972) and the Children's Fear Survey Schedule (Ryall & Dietiker, 1979). In addition, self-rating scales have been developed to assess children's specific fears, such as dental procedures (Children's Fear Survey Schedule; Melamed & Lumley, 1988), darkness (Nighttime Coping Response Inventory and Nighttime Fear Inventory; Mooney, 1985), medical procedures/hospital (Fears Schedule; Bradlyn, 1982), snakes (Snake Attitude Measure; Kornhaber & Schroeder, 1975), and tests (Test Anxiety Scale for Children; Sarason et al., 1960).

Despite the ease in administration and scoring of children's self-rating scales, as well as their apparent face validity, their utility in providing differential diagnoses, particularly of SP, awaits further study. Last, Francis and Strauss (1989), used the FSSC-R to compare the fears of 111 children (aged 5–18 years; mean age not provided) who presented at a childhood anxiety clinic and who met *DSM-III-R* criteria for a range of anxiety disorders. Specifically, 44 children had a primary diagnosis of SAD, 33 had a primary diagnosis of OAD, and 34 had a primary diagnosis of either SOP or SP (combined together as a "phobic group," with the most common subtype being school-related phobias). No differences were found across these diagnostic groups in either their total FSSC-R scores or their factor scores. Interestingly, however, differences among the groups were observed with respect to the total number of intense fears endorsed (i.e., number of items that children rated "a lot"), with the phobic group endorsing the least. Comparisons of the frequency of certain individual FSSC-R items indicated that children in the phobic group were more likely to endorse the school item than children in the OAD group, but were not different from children in the SAD group. Also, less than one-half of the children in the phobic group endorsed "a lot" of fear on the school item, despite the primary reason for being classified in the phobic group was based on reports of school-related fears obtained during a structured interview.

In another study, Perrin and Last (1992) examined the FSSC-R as well as other self-report measures of anxiety using a sample of 213 boys (aged 5–17 years); 105 with primary diagnoses of anxiety disorders (22 with SP), 56 with primary diagnoses of Attention Deficit Hyperactivity Disorder (ADHD), and 49 with no psychiatric diagnoses. With respect to children's fears, there were no differences among the three groups on the total or five subscale scores of the FSSC-R. There were also no significant differences in the FSSC-R scores of the boys with anxiety disorders who were also school refusers with the scores of the boys with ADHD as well as the normal controls.

In summary, although self-rating scales such as the FSSC-R are used widely, questions remain about their discriminative ability between youth with SP and normal controls as well as among various diagnostic groups. However, there may be some utility in a qualitative analysis of the individual items endorsed.

Another way to assess children's cognitive/ subjective systems is via self-monitoring procedures. Self-monitoring requires that children self-observe and systematically record the occurrence of their fearful thoughts and behaviors. Self-monitoring data also provide information about the antecedents and consequences of fearful reactions as well as the severity and frequency of these reactions. In the authors' work, children engage in self-monitoring via a "daily diary." This requires the children to keep a record of the situations in which fear/anxiety was experienced, whether they confronted or avoided the situation, accompanying cognitions, and a rating of fear.

A more structured procedure described by Beidel, Neal, and Lederer (1991) requires children to mark on a checklist whether certain events occurred and whether they experienced certain feelings. In a community sample of elementary school children involved in an investigation of test-anxiety, Beidel et al. (1991) examined the reliability of the children's self-monitoring, and also compared the frequency and severity of anxiety-producing events during a two-week period for a text-anxious ($n = 17$) and nontest-anxious ($n = 17$) subsample. Compliance was also evaluated. As Beidel et al. point out, assessing reliability for an event-orient assessment procedure is difficult as events are variable and fluctuating. Not surprisingly, therefore, the resulting reliability coefficient (based on an n of 13) was relatively modest and not significant ($r = 0.50$). As preliminary support for validity, however, the test-anxious children reported significantly more emotional distress and more negative behaviors (e.g., crying, somatic complaints) than the nontest-anxious children. Compliance was found to be mixed, with 56% of the test-anxious children completing the forms on 10 of the 14 days, and with the percentage of children completing the forms for all 14 days dropping to 31%.

Similar types of analyses of self-monitoring assessment data using clinic samples of children with SP need to be done. In addition, reactivity effects and whether self-monitoring data are sensitive in showing clinical change from pre- to post-treatment warrant investigation. Methods to increase children's compliance with and accuracy of self-monitoring should also be studied.

5.14.6.2 Behavioral

Behavioral observation procedures provide useful information about the frequency and severity of symptoms/behaviors and their antecedents and consequences. In working with children with SP, the types of symptoms/ behaviors that might be identified/assessed may be classified as (i) verbal behavior, such as rate of speech, positive/negative self-references, verbal social skills, etc., and (ii) overt behavior, such as head/gaze aversions, head nods, posture, eye contact, etc. Although there are a number of ways to observe these behaviors, the most frequent ways are on the basis of discrete response occurrences (i.e., response rate or frequency) or the amount of time that the response occurs (i.e., response duration).

Several observational coding procedures have been developed for assessing fear and anxiety in children. These coding procedures were developed to record discrete child behaviors in specific anxiety-provoking settings, such as in dental, medical, or child–parent separation settings (e.g., Glennon & Weisz, 1978; Melamed & Siegel, 1975). Such behavior observation coding schemes can be adapted for use with children with SP. They can also be adapted for use in analogous situations, which might be more feasible for clinicians.

Unfortunately, however, the psychometric properties of behavioral observation procedures in analogous situations have been insufficiently studied. An exception is a study conducted by Hamilton and King (1991) who examined the temporal stability of an analogous observation procedure using 14 children (aged 2–11 years; mean age not provided) with an SP of dogs. The analogous procedure comprised a series of 14 performance tests. Each test required the child to engage in increasingly more difficult interactions with a dog. Two test administrations were conducted seven days apart, prior to treatment. High test–retest reliability was obtained ($r = 0.97$), with 10 of the 14 children obtaining identical approach scores and with the other four children obtaining increased approach scores, (i.e., they displayed less avoidant behavior from Time 1 to Time 2). These results provide support for the temporal stability of approach scores obtained on analogous observation procedures. However, because of the small sample employed in this study and the wide age range, replication of this study would be worthwhile. Additional questions worth examining in the future include the role of differential levels of initial fear, the specific instructions employed (e.g., high demand vs. low demand), and children's developmental level.

5.14.6.3 Physiological

The most common strategies used to assess the physiological system typically involve measuring children's heart rate, blood pressure, and electrodermal activity (e.g., finger or palm sweat; see King, Hamilton, & Ollendick, 1988). These measurements are usually taken before, during, and after child exposure to the feared object or event. There is a paucity of data on the utility of these measures using samples of children with anxiety disorders, including SP. This is likely due to difficulties involved in using these procedures, including children's frequent movements, children's fears of the test instrumentation (e.g., the electrodes may shock them), and the instruments' sensitivity to nonanxiety influences (e.g., lighting, temperature, noise, novelty). There are also difficulties involved in the interpretive process with children, particularly as they relate to developmental level. For example, in relation to tonic heart rate in children, both heart rate and heart rate variability decrease with age (Shinebourne, 1974). Normative data for psychophysiological measurement with children are also lacking (Venables, 1981).

Despite these difficulties, evidence does suggest that psychophysiological assessment may be a reliable strategy for the assessment of children's anxious symptoms (e.g., Beidel, 1991; Beidel, Fink, & Turner, 1996; Murphy, Alpert, Wiley, & Somes, 1988). Unfortunately, however, the utility of psychophysiological assessments in clinical outcome studies of SP remains to be demonstrated adequately. In a treatment outcome study of childhood SP (described below), the results pertaining to heart rate tended to be uneven, similar to what has been reported in single case-design studies (e.g., Van Hasselt, Hersen, Bellack, Rosenblum, & Lamparski, 1979).

5.14.7 TREATMENT

The research literature shows that the one procedure that is essential to include in a fear or anxiety treatment program, if it is to be successful, is "exposure" (i.e., having the child confront or approach the feared object or event (see Barlow, 1988, for various accounts as to why exposure may work). Exposure may be live (*in vivo*) or imaginal, and with children is generally conducted in a gradual fashion.

The studies reviewed in this section often include an exposure component along with additional cognitive and behavioral strategies. Before discussing this literature, however, several methodological limitations that characterize most of the early studies conducted in this area are worth noting. First, the majority of the treatment outcome studies did not use controlled experimental procedures, clinic referred samples, structured diagnostic proce-

dures, multimethod–multisource assessment procedures, or systematic follow-ups (Silverman & Rabian, 1993). In addition, research has insufficiently addressed the relative efficacy of one treatment strategy over another (e.g., cognitive vs. behavioral) or one format over another (e.g., individual vs. group). There has also been very limited research conducted on potential predictors of treatment outcome (e.g., comorbidity, parental anxiety symptoms, treatment duration). Also absent is any type of conceptual framework to help guide clinicians' and researchers' thinking in how to go about developing and implementing intervention approaches for children with SP. With these limitations in mind, a brief overview is presented of the major cognitive and behavioral strategies that have been used in the treatment of childhood SP. A "transfer of control" model is then presented which might serve as a useful framework for developing and implementing psychosocial interventions for children with SP.

The most commonly used cognitive and behavioral procedures that have been used to treat child SP include: systematic desensitization, flooding, modeling, contingency management, relaxation training, and self-control. Descriptions of each of these strategies, along with evidence supporting their effectiveness, have been presented elsewhere (e.g., see King et al., 1988; Silverman & Eisen, 1993), and will not be detailed here.

Among these strategies, contingency management, modeling, and self-control have received the most attention and appear to be the most promising (Morris & Kratochwill, 1983). Briefly, contingency management, based on the principles of operant conditioning, stresses the importance of the causal relation between stimuli and behavior (Morris & Kratochwill, 1983), and relies on the therapist and the parents to rearrange the environment to ensure that positive consequences follow a child's exposure to the fearful stimulus, and to ensure that positive consequences (e.g., attention) do not follow avoidant behavior. Modeling involves the child learning to be less fearful or anxious by observing others handle the fearful object or event. The models observed by the child may be actual, or "live" models, or they may be observed on films or videotapes, or "symbolic" models. Finally, self-control stresses the important contribution of cognitive processes to behavior change and involves the child directly regulating her or his own behavior by applying specific thinking styles when confronted with the fearful stimulus.

All of the above strategies (i.e., contingency management, modeling, self-control), alone or in combination with other strategies, have been found to be effective in treating children who display a wide range of fears including those related to: nighttime (Graziano, Mooney, Huber, & Ignasiak, 1979; Graziano & Mooney, 1980; King, Cranstoun, & Josephs, 1989); darkness (Giebenhain & O'Dell, 1984; Heard, Dadds, & Conrad, 1992; Jackson & King, 1981; Kanfer, Karoly, & Newman, 1975); loud noises (Tasto, 1969; Wish, Hasazi, & Jurgela, 1973; Yule, Sacks, & Hersov, 1974); public speaking (Cradock, Cotler, & Jason, 1978; Fox & Houston, 1981); heights (Croghan & Musante, 1975; Holmes, 1936; Ritter, 1968); animals (Bandura, Blanchard, & Ritter, 1969; Glasscock & MacLean, 1990; Obler & Terwilliger, 1970; Sreenivasan, Manocha, & Jain, 1979); water (Lewis, 1974; Menzies & Clarke, 1993; Ultee, Griffioen, & Schellekens, 1982); menstruation (Shaw, 1990); telephones (Babbitt & Parrish, 1991); newspapers (Goldberg & Weisenberg, 1992); bowel movements (Eisen & Silverman, 1991); needles (Rainwater et al., 1988); medical procedures (Heard et al., 1992; Peterson & Shigetomi, 1981); dental procedures (Krochak, Slovin, Rubin, & Kaplan, 1988; Siegel & Peterson, 1980); traveling in cars (Stedman & Murphy, 1984; Thankachan, Mishra, & Kumaraiah, 1992); and illness/diseases (Hagopian, Weist, & Ollendick, 1990).

In an early controlled group treatment study that focused on treating childhood phobia, Miller et al. (1972) randomly assigned phobic children ($N = 67$; aged 6–15 years) (67% had a primary fear of school) to one of three treatment conditions: reciprocal inhibition ($n = 21$), play therapy ($n = 23$), and a waitlist control ($n = 23$). Treatment was provided three times a week for eight weeks. Outcomes, based on parent and clinician reports, revealed no significant differences between the two treatment conditions, but children in both treatment conditions improved relative to the children in the waitlist control. Moreover, an examination of children in both active treatments revealed that younger children (aged 6–10 years) appeared to evidence significantly greater improvements relative to older children (aged 11–15 years) in both conditions.

Menzies and Clarke (1993) compared three fear-reduction strategies for children ($N = 48$; aged 3–8) with water phobia. Children were assigned randomly to one of four groups: (i) *in vivo* exposure plus vicarious exposure (watching a model), (ii) vicarious exposure only, (iii) *in vivo* exposure only, and (iv) assessed only. All children received three treatment sessions and assessments were based on the following: behavioral tasks in water (children asked to engage in different tasks of varying difficulty level such as stepping into a pool, putting their

face under water, etc.); self-ratings of water fears; and a combined observer and clinician rating of the children's overall reactions to the phobic situation while the child was engaged in completing tasks in the pool. On all measures, the results revealed that the children in both exposure groups (groups i and iii) improved relative to the assessed only and vicarious only (groups ii and iv). No differences were found between the exposure groups (group i and iii).

The authors, in collaboration with others at the Child and Family Psychology Social Research Center, completed a controlled clinical trials study for children with phobic disorders. This study compared the relative effectiveness of an exposure-based contingency management (CM) treatment, an exposure-based self-control (SC) treatment, and an education-support (ES) comparison condition in which exposure was discussed but was not directly prescribed (such as through CM or SC procedures). A total of 99 children (aged 6–16 years; mean age = 9.9 years) and their parents participated in the study. Fifty-two were boys and 47 were girls. All children met criteria for a primary *DSM-III-R* diagnosis for phobic disorder, including SP ($n = 82$), SOP ($n = 10$), or AG ($n = 7$), based on a structured interview administered separately to the child and parent.

Each of the 99 children and their parents were assigned randomly to one of the three conditions. There were 37 children in the CM condition, 40 in the SC condition, and 22 in ES. Each condition was a 10-week treatment program in which the children and parents were seen in separate treatment sessions with the therapist, followed by a brief conjoint meeting. Results indicated that all the procedures that were used to facilitate the occurrence of exposure, the CM condition, the SC condition, as well as the ES condition, produced effective therapeutic change on all of the main outcome measures (child, parent, and clinicians), including the indices of clinically significant change (i.e., percentage of children who no longer met diagnostic criteria). More impressively, these gains were maintained at three, six and 12 months follow-up. The findings are discussed within the context of the transfer of control model, described in Section 5.14.7.1.

5.14.7.1 Transfer of Control Model

According to the transfer of control model, the therapist is viewed as an expert consultant who possesses knowledge of the skills and methods necessary to produce long-term child therapeutic change. Effective change involves a gradual transfer of the knowledge, skills, and methods from the therapist to the parent to the child (Silverman & Kurtines, 1996). In treating children with SP, the focus of treatment is on controlling the occurrence and successful implementation of exposure to the feared object or situation. Based on findings from our treatment outcome study, it is believed that there are several strategies that might be used to facilitate an adequate transfer of control. These include a more parent-focused treatment, such as CM; a more child-focused treatment, such as SC; a combination (CM followed by SC); a less prescribed strategy, such as ES; a group treatment strategy (Ginsburg, Silverman, & Kurtines, 1995a), and even, perhaps, a format that involves a more thorough and systematic intervention on the child and parent relationship or to what is referred to as "dyadic treatment" (Ginsburg, Silverman, & Kurtines, 1995b). The task ahead for clinicians and researchers is to delineate the particular pathway (and thus, treatment strategy or format) that might be most useful for a child with SP and their family.

5.14.8 CASE STUDY

5.14.8.1 Presenting Problem

Jody, a 12-year-old Caucasian boy, was presented by his mother because of his extreme reactions to thunderstorms. She described that on cloudy or rainy days her son would repeatedly ask questions about the weather, watch only the weather channel on TV or listen to the weather radio, report somatic complaints, and generally appear tense and nervous. During thunderstorms, (a common occurrence in South Florida), Jody would scream, cry, and run and hide in his closet. In addition, Jody would refuse to go outside (e.g., to the mailbox, car, mall, etc.) and refused to sleep alone in his room. Although Jody's mother reported that he was always a worrier, his reactions to thunderstorms (and apprehensions about other natural disasters such as tornadoes) had increased dramatically within the past year and were significantly interfering with his and the family's functioning.

5.14.8.2 Assessment and Diagnosis

Jody and his mother were administered respective child and parent versions of the ADIS-C and ADIS-P. Jody also completed several self-rating scales, and he was administered an *in vivo* behavioral task during which time his heart rate was monitored. As noted above, Jody's mother reported that his fearful and avoidant behavior was interfering with

various aspects of his and the family's life. For instance, his school performance had begun to decline because he was having difficulty concentrating in school when storms were approaching. Socially, Jody's fears prevented him from going on outings (e.g., fishing, camping) and he had begun to run off the playing field during his little league games if he saw lightning or heard thunder. At home, Jody's fear often prevented the family from completing errands or attending activities if a storm was approaching.

Based on Jody and his mother's responses to the interviews, Jody was assigned a diagnosis of SP, natural environment subtype. On the ADIS-C/P, both Jody and his mother reported that his fear of thunderstorms was a "7" on the 8-point fear thermometer. His scores on the questionnaires were also elevated. Jody's *in vivo* behavioral exposure test, which required him to walk outside with the therapist during an afternoon thunderstorm for five minutes, was terminated because he became too upset.

5.14.8.3 Treatment

Jody was enrolled in a 10-week exposure-based treatment program in which parent and child were seen individually and then briefly together. The program, based on the transfer of control model, involved first teaching Jody's mother the principles of contingency management and then teaching both Jody and his mother child self-control strategies. These strategies were then applied in gradual exposure tasks that involved Jody gradually approaching going outside during storms.

Exposure tasks were both imaginal and *in vivo* and were based on a hierarchy that varied how close to being outside Jody would get during thunderstorms. Initial *in vivo* steps on the hierarchy, during which Jody remained outside of the closet but inside the house during a storm, were successful, but as the exposures became more difficult, requiring him to go outside, Jody was unable to complete the exposures and explained to the therapist that storms were just too unpredictable. In discussing these difficulties with Jody's mother, she indicated that she felt Jody's fears were not totally irrational. Many Florida residents had lost their homes during Hurricane Andrew in 1992 and there had been recent incidents of tornadoes in the news.

To deal with these concerns, subsequent treatment sessions addressed some of the common obstacles encountered with treating SP. For instance, emphasis was placed on reviewing with Jody's mother the importance of parental modeling of courageous behavior. In part, this was accomplished by discussing common parental "protective behaviors" and her own fears related to hurricanes. In addition, Jody and his mother were helped to think of alternative ways of handling their fears, including specific steps they could take so that they could be maximally prepared for hurricanes. This included obtaining accurate information about hurricane preparedness and warnings (e.g., that although hurricanes are uncontrollable, there is usually plenty of advance warning and time to prepare). This approach helped to empower the family and enabled them to have an "action plan" if Jody's worst fears were to materialize (e.g., that a hurricane was forecast). All of these methods were helpful and subsequent contracts were successfully carried out, including the one that required him to go fishing with his grandfather on a rainy day.

In the final phase of the transfer of control, wherein self-control strategies were used (including self-reward to replace parental rewards), Jody practiced examining the specific cognitions which played a role in maintaining his fear (e.g., "the hurricane will blow my house away"). Jody learned to recognize when he was afraid or worried, to employ more adaptive coping thoughts and behaviors, and to praise himself for doing so.

5.14.8.4 Post-treatment and Follow-up

At post-treatment assessment, readministration of the relevant sections of the ADIS-C and ADIS-P revealed that Jody no longer met criteria for SP and there was no longer any interference in his daily functioning. In addition, his scores on the questionnaires decreased markedly and Jody was able to do the behavioral exposure test. These gains were maintained at three and 12-month follow-up assessments.

5.14.9 SUMMARY

This chapter presented an overview of what is known about specific phobias in children, beginning with a discussion about phenomenology, including variations which may be associated with age, gender, and race/ethnicity. Information about the onset and stability, diagnostic criteria, and issues related to differential diagnosis was presented. Thinking about etiology, both biological and psychosocial perspectives, was presented next. This was followed by a summary of the epidemiological data which indicate an average prevalence rate of about 2-9% (based primarily on Caucasian community samples). The chapter discussed assessment and treatment procedures that have been found useful for working with children with specific phobias, including the evolving transfer of control model as a possible framework to help guide clinicians' and researchers' thinking in how to develop and implement interventions. A case study was presented to illustrate the issues discussed.

5.14.10 REFERENCES

Abe, K., Oda, N., Ikenaga, K., & Yamada, T. (1993). Twin study on night terrors, fears and some physiological and behavioral characteristics in childhood. *Psychiatric Genetics, 3*, 39–43.

Achenbach, T. M., & Edelbrock, C. (1983). *Manual for the Child Behavior Checklist and Revised Child Behavior Profile.* Burlington, VT: University of Vermont, Department of Psychiatry.

Agras, W. S., Chapin, H. N., & Oliveau, D. C. (1972). The natural history of phobia. *Archives of General Psychiatry, 26*, 315–317.

American Psychiatric Association. (1994). *Diagnostic and statistical manual of mental disorders* (4th ed.). Washington, DC: American Psychiatric Press.

Anderson, J. (1994). Epidemiological issues. In T. H. Ollendick, N. J. King, & W. Yule (Eds.), *International handbook of phobic and anxiety disorders in children and adolescents* (pp. 43–66). New York: Plenum.

Anderson, J. C., Williams, S., McGee, R., & Silva, P. A. (1987). DSM-III disorders in preadolescent children. *Archives of General Psychiatry, 44*, 69–76.

Babbitt, R. L., & Parrish, J. M. (1991). Phone phobia, phact or phantasy? An operant approach to a child's disruptive behavior induced by telephone usage. *Journal of Behavior Therapy and Experimental Psychiatry, 22*, 123–129.

Bandura, A., Blanchard, E. B., & Ritter, B. (1969). Relative efficacy of desensitization and modeling approaches for inducing behavioral affective and attitudinal changes. *Journal of Personality and Social Psychology, 13*, 179–199.

Barlow, D. H. (1988). *Anxiety and its disorders: The nature and treatment of anxiety and panic.* New York: Guilford Press.

Barrett, P. M., Rapee, R. M., Dadds, M. M., & Ryan, S. M. (1996). Family enhancement of cognitive style in anxious and aggressive children. *Journal of Abnormal Child Psychology, 24*, 187–203.

Barrios, B. A., Hartmann, D. P., & Shigetomi, C. (1981). Fears and anxieties in children. In E. J. Mash & L. G. Terdal (Eds.), *Behavioral assessment of childhood disorders* (pp. 259–304). New York: Guilford Press.

Bauer, D. H. (1976). An exploratory study of developmental changes in children's fears. *Journal of Child Psychology and Psychiatry, 17*, 69–74.

Beidel, D. C. (1991). Social phobia and overanxious disorder in school-age children. *Journal of the American Academy of Child and Adolescent Psychiatry, 3*, 545–552.

Beidel, D. C., Neal, A. M., & Lederer, A. S. (1991). The feasibility and validity of a daily diary for the assessment of anxiety in children. *Behavior Therapy, 22*, 505–517.

Beidel, D. C., Fink, C. M., & Turner, S. M. (1996). Stability of anxious symptomatology in children. *Journal of Abnormal Child Psychology, 24*, 257–270.

Bell-Dolan, D. J., Last, C. G., & Strauss, C. C. (1990). Symptoms of anxiety disorders in normal children. *Journal of the American Academy of Child and Adolescent Psychiatry, 29*, 759–765.

Bell-Dolan, D. J., & Wessler, A. E. (1994). Attributional

style of anxious children: Extensions from cognitive theory and research on adult anxiety. *Journal of Anxiety Disorders, 8,* 79–96.

Bernstein, G. A., & Garfinkel, B. D. (1986). School phobia: The overlap of affective and anxiety disorders. *Journal of the American Academy of Child and Adolescent Psychiatry, 25,* 235–241.

Biederman, J., Rosenbaum, J. F., Bolduc-Murphy, E. A., Faraone, S. V., Chaloff, J., Hirshfeld, D. R., & Kagan, J. (1993a). A three-year follow-up of children with and without behavioral inhibition. *Journal of the American Academy of Child and Adolescent Psychiatry, 32,* 814–821.

Biederman, J., Rosenbaum, J. F., Bolduc-Murphy, E. A., Faraone, S. V., Chaloff, J., Hirshfeld, D. R., & Kagan, J. (1993b). Behavioral inhibition as a temperamental risk factor for anxiety disorders. *Child and Adolescent Psychiatric Clinics of North America, 2,* 667–684.

Biederman, J., Rosenbaum, J. F., Hirshfeld, D. R., Faraone, V., Bolduc, E., Gersten, M., Meminger, S., & Reznick, S. (1990). Psychiatric correlates of behavioral inhibition in young children of parents with and without psychiatric disorders. *Archives of General Psychiatry, 47,* 21–26.

Bird, H. R., Canino, G., Rubio-Stipec, M., Gould, M. S., Ribera J., Sesman, M., Woodbury, M., Huertas-Goldman, S., Pagan, A., Sanches-Lacay, A., & Moscoso, M. (1988). Estimates of the prevalence of childhood maladjustment in a community survey in Puerto Rico. *Archives of General Psychiatry, 45,* 1120–1126.

Boldizar, J. P. (1991). Assessing sex typing and androgyny in children: The Children's Sex Role Inventory. *Developmental Psychology, 27,* 505–515.

Bouton, M. E. (1991). Sources of relapse after extinction in Pavlovian and instrumental learning. *Clinical Psychology Review, 11,* 123–140.

Bradlyn, A. S. (1982). *The effects of a videotape preparation package in reducing children's arousal and increasing cooperation during cardiac catheterization.* Unpublished doctoral dissertation, University of Mississippi.

Burglass, D., Clarke, J., Henderson, A. S., Kreitman, M., & Presley, A. S. (1977). A study of agoraphobic housewives. *Psychological Medicine, 7,* 73–86.

Burke, A. E., & Silverman, W. K. (1987). The prescriptive treatment of school refusal. *Clinical Psychology Review, 29,* 570–574.

Bush, J. P., Melamed, B. G., Sheras, P. L., & Greenbaum, P. E. (1986). Mother-child patterns of coping with anticipatory medical stress. *Health Psychology, 5,* 137–157.

Capps, L., Sigman, R., Sena, B., Henker, B., & Whalen, C. (1996). Fear, anxiety and perceived control in children of agoraphobic parents. *Journal of Child Psychology and Psychiatry and Allied Disciplines, 37,* 445–452.

Carey, M. P., Dusek, J. B., & Spector, I. P. (1988). Sex roles, gender, and fears: A brief report. *Phobia Practice and Research Journal, 1,* 114–120.

Caron, C., & Rutter, M. (1991). Comorbidity in child psychopathology: Concepts, issues, and research. *Journal of Child Psychology and Psychiatry, 32,* 1063–1080.

Chorpita, B. F., Albano, A. M., & Barlow, D. H. (1996). Cognitive processing in children: Relationship to anxiety and family influences. *Journal of Clinical Child Psychology, 25,* 170–176.

Clarke, J. C., & Jackson, J. A. (1983). *Hypnosis and behavior therapy: The treatment of anxiety and phobias.* New York: Springer.

Costello, E. J., Costello, A. J., Edelbrock, C. S., Burns, B. J., Dulcan, M. J., Brent, D., & Janiszewski, S. (1988). DSM-III disorders in pediatric primary care: Prevalence and risk factors. *Archives of General Psychology, 45,* 1107–1116.

Costello, A. J., Edelbrock, C. S., Dulcan, M. K., Kalas, R.,

& Klaric, S. H. (1984). *Report to NIMH on the NIMH diagnostic interview schedule for children (DISC).* Washington, DC: National Institute of Mental Health.

Cradock, C., Cotler, S., & Jason, L. A. (1978). Primary prevention: Immunization of children for speech anxiety. *Cognitive Therapy and Research, 2,* 389–396.

Croake, J. W. (1969). Fears of children. *Human Development, 12,* 239–247.

Croghan, L. M., & Musante, G. J. (1975). The elimination of a boy's high building phobia by in vivo desensitization and game playing. *Journal of Behavior Therapy and Experimental Psychiatry, 6,* 87–88.

Dadds, M. R., Barrett, P. M., Rapee, R. M., & Ryan, S. (1996). Family process and child anxiety and aggression: An observational analysis. *Journal of Abnormal Child Psychology, 24,* 715–734.

Davey, G. C. L. (1992). Classical conditioning and the acquisition of human fears and phobias: A review and synthesis of the literature. *Advances in Behaviour Research and Therapy, 14,* 29–66.

Davey, G. C. L., Forster, L., & Mayhew, G. (1993). Familial resemblances in disgust sensitivity and animal phobias. *Behaviour Research and Therapy, 31,* 41–50.

Dillon, K. M., Wolf, E., & Katz, H. (1988). Sex roles, gender, and fear. *The Journal of Psychology, 119,* 355–359.

Edelbrock, C. S., & Costello, A. (1984). Structured psychiatric interviews for children and adolescents. In G. Goldstein & M. Hersen (Eds.), *Handbook of psychological assessment,* (pp. 276–290). New York: Pergamon.

Eisen, A. R., & Silverman, W. K. (1991). Treatment of an adolescent with bowel movement phobia using self-control therapy. *Journal of Behavior Therapy and Experimental Psychiatry, 22,* 45–51.

Eme, R., & Schmidt, D. (1978). The stability of children's fears. *Child Development, 49,* 1277–1279.

Endicott, J., & Spitzer, R. L. (1978). A diagnostic interview: The schedule for affective disorders and schizophrenia. *Archives of General Psychiatry, 35,* 837–844.

Eysenck, H. J. (1979). The conditioning model of neurosis. *Behavioral and Brain Sciences, 2,* 155–199.

Fergusson, D. M., Horwood, L. J., & Lynskey, M. T. (1993). Prevalence and comorbidity of DSM-III-R diagnoses in a birth cohort of 15-year-old. *Journal of the American Academy of Child and Adolescent Psychiatry, 32,* 1127–1134.

Foley, D., & Hay, D. A. (1992). Genetics and the nature of anxiety disorders. In G. F. Burrows, M. Roth, & R. Noyes, Jr. (Eds.), *Handbook of anxiety: Contemporary issues and prospects for research in anxiety disorders* (pp. 21–56). Amsterdam: Elsevier.

Fonesca, A. C., Yule, W., & Erol, N. (1994). Cross-cultural issues. In T. H. Ollendick, N. J. King, & W. Yule (Eds.), *International handbook of phobic and anxiety disorders in children and adolescents* (pp. 67–84). New York: Plenum.

Fox, J. E., & Houston, B. K. (1981). Efficacy of self-instructional training for reducing children's anxiety in an evaluative situation. *Behaviour Research and Therapy, 19,* 509–515.

Francis, G. (1988). Assessing cognitions in anxious children. *Behavior Modification, 12,* 267–280.

Freud, S. (1909/1955). Analysis of a phobia in a five-year-old boy. In J. Strachey (Ed. and Trans.), *Standard edition of the complete psychological works of Sigmund Freud* (Vol. 10, pp. 3–149). London: Hogarth Press.

Fyer, A. J., Mannuzza, T. F., Chapman, L. M., Martin, L. Y., & Klein, D. F. (1995). Specificity in familial aggregation of phobic disorders. *Archives of General Psychiatry, 52,* 564–573.

Fyer, A. J., Mannuzza, S., Gallops, M. P., Martin, L. Y.,

Aaronson, C., Gorman, J. M., Liebowitz, M. R., & Klein, D. F. (1990). Familial transmission of simple phobias and fears. *Archives of General Psychiatry, 47,* 252–256.

Giebenhain, J. E., & O'Dell, S. L. (1984). Evaluation of a parent-training manual for reducing children's fear of the dark. *Journal of Applied Behavioral Analysis, 17,* 121–125.

Ginsburg, G. S., & Silverman, W. K. (1996). Phobic and anxiety disorders in Hispanic and Caucasian children. *Journal of Anxiety Disorders, 10,* 517–528.

Ginsburg, G. S., & Silverman, W. K. (1997). *Gender role orientation and fears in youth with anxiety disorders.* Unpublished manuscript.

Ginsburg, G. S., Silverman, W. K., & Kurtines, W. M. (1995a). Cognitive-behavioral group therapy. In A. R. Eisen, C. A. Kearney, & C. E. Schaefer (Eds.), *Clinical handbook of anxiety disorders in children* (pp. 521–549). Northwale, NJ: Jason Aronson.

Ginsburg, G. S., Silverman, W. K., & Kurtines, W. M. (1995b). Family involvement in treating children with anxiety and phobic disorders: A look ahead. *Clinical Psychology Review, 15,* 457–473.

Glasscock, S. E., & MacLean, W. E. (1990). Use of contact desensitization and shaping in the treatment of dog phobia and generalized fear of the outdoors. *Journal of Clinical Child Psychology, 19,* 169–172.

Glennon, B., & Weisz, J. R. (1978). An observational approach to the assessment of anxiety in young children. *Journal of Consulting and Clinical Psychology, 46,* 1246–1257.

Goldberg, J., & Weisenberg, M. (1992). The case of a newspaper phobia in a 9-year-old child. *Journal of Behavior Therapy and Experimental Psychiatry, 23,* 125–131.

Graziano, A. M., & DeGiovanni, I. S. (1979). The clinical significance of childhood phobias: A note on the proportion of child-clinical referrals for the treatment of children's fears. *Behaviour Research and Therapy, 17,* 161–162.

Graziano, A. M., & Mooney, K. C. (1980). Family self-control instruction for children's nighttime fear reduction. *Journal of Consulting and Clinical Psychology, 48,* 206–213.

Graziano, A. M., Mooney, K. C., Huber, C., & Ignasiak, D. (1979). Self-control instructions for children's fear-reduction. *Journal of Behavior Therapy and Experimental Psychiatry, 10,* 221–227.

Hagopian, L. P., Weist, M. D., & Ollendick, T. H. (1990). Cognitive-behavior therapy with an 11-year-old girl fearful of AIDS infection, other diseases, and poisoning: A case study. *Journal of Anxiety Disorders, 4,* 257–265.

Hamilton, D. I., & King, N. J. (1991). Reliability of a behavioral avoidance test for the assessment of dog phobic children. *Psychological Reports, 69,* 18.

Hammond-Laurence, K., & Silverman, W. K. (1997). *Comorbidity among childhood psychiatric disorders in clinic- referred children and adolescents with anxiety disorders.* Manuscript submitted for publication.

Heard, P. M., Dadds, M. R., & Conrad, P. (1992). Assessment and treatment of simple phobias in children: Effects on family and marital relationships. *Behaviour Change, 9,* 73–82.

Hekmat, H. (1987). Origins and development of human fear reactions. *Journal of Anxiety Disorders, 1,* 197–218.

Herjanic, B., & Reich, W. (1982). Development of a structured psychiatric interview for children: Agreement between child and parent on individual symptoms. *Journal of Abnormal Child Psychiatry, 10,* 307–324.

Hirshfeld, D. R., Rosenbaum, J. F., Biederman, J., Bolduc, E. A., Faraone, S. V., Snidman, N., Reznick, J. S., & Kagan, J. (1992). Stable behavioral inhibition and its association with anxiety disorder. *Journal of the Amer-ican Academy of Child and Adolescent Psychiatry, 31,* 103–111.

Holmes, F. B. (1936). An experimental investigation of a method of overcoming children's fears. *Child Development, 7,* 6–30.

Jackson, H. J., & King, N. J. (1981). The emotive imagery treatment of a child's trauma-induced phobia. *Journal of Behavior Therapy and Experimental Psychiatry, 12,* 325–328.

Jones, M. C. (1924a). The elimination of children's fears. *Journal of Experimental Psychology, 1,* 383–390.

Jones, M. C. (1924b). A laboratory study of fear: The case of Peter. *Pedagogical Seminar, 31,* 308–315.

Kagan, J., Reznick, J. S., & Gibbons, J. (1989). Inhibited and uninhibited types of children. *Child Development, 60,* 838–845.

Kagan, J., Reznick, J. S., & Snidman, N. (1987). The physiology and psychology of behavioral inhibition. *Child Development, 58,* 1459–1473.

Kagan, J., Reznick, J. S., & Snidman, N. (1988). Biological bases of childhood shyness. *Science, 240,* 167–171.

Kanfer, F. H., Karoly, P., & Newman, A. (1975). Reduction of children's fear of the dark by confidence-related and situation threat-related verbal cues. *Journal of Consulting and Clinical Psychology, 43,* 251–258.

Kashani, J. H., Beck, N. C., Hoeper, E. W., Fallahi, C., Corcoran, C. M., McAllister, J. A., Rosenberg, T. K., & Reid, J. C. (1987). Psychiatric disorders in a community sample of adolescents. *American Journal of Psychiatry, 144,* 584–589.

Kashani, J. H., & Orvaschel, H. (1990). A community study of anxiety in children and adolescents. *American Journal of Psychiatry, 147,* 313–318.

Kearney, C. A., & Silverman, W. K. (1997). The evolution and reconciliation of taxonomic strategies for school refusal behavior. *Clinical Psychology: Science and Practice, 3,* 339–354.

Kendall, P. C., & Chansky, T. E. (1991). Considering cognition in anxiety-disordered children. *Journal of Anxiety Disorders, 5,* 167–185.

Kendler, K. S., Neale, M. C., Kessler, R. C., Heath, A. C., & Eaves, L. J. (1992). The genetic epidemiology of phobias in women. *Archives of General Psychiatry, 49,* 273–281.

King, N. J., Cranstoun, F., & Josephs, A. (1989). Emotive imagery and children's night-time fears: A multiple baseline design evaluation. *Journal of Behavior Therapy and Experimental Psychiatry, 20,* 125–135.

King, N. J., Hamilton, D. I., & Ollendick, T. H. (1988). *Children's phobias: A behavioral perspective.* New York: Wiley.

King, N. J., Mietz, A., Tinney, L., & Ollendick, T. H. (1995). Psychopathology and cognition in adolescents experiencing severe test anxiety. *Journal of Clinical Child Psychology, 24,* 49–54.

Kornhaber, R. C., & Schroeder, H. E. (1975). Importance of model similarity on extinction of avoidance behavior in children. *Journal of Consulting and Clinical Psychology, 43,* 601–607.

Krochak, M., Slovin, M., Rubin, J. G., & Kaplan, A. (1988). Treatment of dental phobia: A report of two cases. *Phobia Practice and Research Journal, 1,* 64–72.

Lang, P. J. (1977). Imagery in therapy: An information processing analysis of fear. *Behavior Therapy, 8,* 862–886.

Lapouse, R., & Monk, M. A. (1959). Fear and worries in a representative sample of children. *American Journal of Orthopsychiatry, 29,* 803–815.

Last, G. C. (1991). Somatic complaints in anxiety disordered children. *Journal of Anxiety Disorders, 5,* 125–138.

Last, C. G., Francis, G., & Strauss, C. C. (1989). Assessing fears in anxiety-disordered children with the Revised

Fear Survey Schedule for Children (FSSC-R). *Journal of Clinical Child Psychology, 18,* 137–141.

Last, C. G., Hersen, M., Kazdin, A., Orvaschel, H., & Perrin, S. (1991). Anxiety disorders and their families. *Archives of General Psychiatry, 48,* 928–934.

Last, C. G., & Perrin, S. (1993). Anxiety disorders in African-American and White children. *Journal of Abnormal Child Psychology, 2,* 153–164.

Last, C. G., Perrin, S., Hersen, M., & Kazdin, A. E. (1992). DSM-III-R anxiety disorders in children: Sociodemographic and clinical characteristics. *Journal of the American Academy of Child and Adolescent Psychiatry, 31,* 1070–1076.

Last, C. G., Strauss, C. C., & Francis, G. (1987). Comorbidity among childhood anxiety disorders. *Journal of Nervous and Mental Disease, 175,* 726–730.

Lewis, S. (1974). A comparison of behavior therapy techniques in the reduction of fearful avoidant behavior. *Behavior Therapy, 5,* 648–655.

Liddell, A., & Lyons, M. (1978). Thunderstorm phobias. *Behaviour Research and Therapy, 16,* 306–308.

Maccoby, E. E. (1980). *Social development: Psychological growth and the parent-child relationship.* New York: Harcourt Brace Jovanovich.

Marks, I. M., & Gelder, M. G. (1966). Different onset ages in varieties of phobia. *American Journal of Psychiatry, 123,* 218–221.

Martin, M., Horder, P., & Jones, G. (1992). Integral bias in naming of phobia-related words. *Cognition and Emotion, 6,* 479–486.

McGee, R., Feehan, M., Williams, S., & Anderson, J. (1992). DSM-III disorders from age 11 to age 15 years. *Journal of the American Academy of Child and Adolescent Psychiatry, 31,* 50–59.

McGee, R., Feehan, M., Williams, S., Partridge, F., Silva, P. A. & Kelly, J. (1990). DSM-III disorders in a large sample of adolescents. *Journal of the American Academy of Child and Adolescent Psychiatry, 29,* 611–619.

Melamed, B. G., & Lumley, M. A. (1988). Dental subscale of the Children's Fear Survey Schedule. In M. Hersen & A. S. Bellack (Eds.), *Dictionary of behavioural assessment techniques* (p. 171). Oxford: Pergamon.

Melamed, B. G., & Siegel, L. J. (1975). Reduction of anxiety in children facing hospitalization and surgery by use of filmed modeling. *Journal of Consulting and Clinical Psychology, 43,* 511–521.

Menzies, R. G., & Clarke, J. C. (1993). A comparison of in vivo and vicarious exposure in the treatment of childhood water phobia. *Behaviour Research and Therapy, 31,* 9–15.

Menzies, R. G., & Clarke, J. C. (1995). The etiology of phobias: A nonassociative account. *Clinical Psychology Review, 15,* 23–48.

Merckelbach, H., De Ruiter, C., Van De Hout, M. A., & Hoekstra, R. (1989). Conditioning experiences and phobias. *Behaviour Research and Therapy, 27,* 657–662.

Milgrom, P., Mancle, L., King, B., & Weinstein, P. (1995). Origins of childhood dental fear. *Behavior Research Therapy, 33,* 313–319.

Miller, L. C., Barrett, C. L., Hampe, E., & Noble, H. (1972). Comparison of reciprocal inhibition, psychotherapy, and waiting list control for phobic children. *Journal of Abnormal Psychology, 79,* 269–279.

Milne, J. M., Garrison, C. Z., Addy, C. L., McKeown, R. E., Jackson, K. L., Cuffe, S. P., & Waller, J. L. (1995). Frequency of phobic disorder in a community sample of young adolescents. *Journal of the American Academy of Child and Adolescent Psychiatry, 34,* 1202–1211.

Mooney, K. C. (1985). Children's nighttime fears: Ratings of content and coping behaviors. *Cognitive Therapy and Research, 9,* 309–319.

Moran, C., & Andrews, G. (1985). The familial occurrence of agoraphobia. *British Journal of Psychiatry, 146,* 262–267.

Morris, R. J., & Kratochwill, T. R. (1983). *Treating children's fears and phobias: A behavioral approach.* New York: Pergamon.

Mowrer, O. H. (1939). A stimulus-response theory of anxiety and its role as reinforcing agent. *Psychological Review, 46,* 553–565.

Muris, P., Steerneman, P., Merckelbach, H., & Meesters, C. (1996). The role of parental fearfulness and modeling in children's fear. *Behaviour Research and Therapy, 34,* 265–268.

Murphy, J. K., Alpert, B. S., Willey, E. S., & Somes, G. S. (1988). Cardiovascular reactivity to psychological stress in healthy children. *Psychophysiology, 25,* 144–152.

Murray, E. J., & Foote, F. (1979). The origins of fear of snakes. *Behaviour Research and Therapy, 17,* 489–493.

Nalven, F. B. (1970). Manifest fears and worries of ghetto versus middle class suburban children. *Psychological Reports, 27,* 285–286.

Neal, A. M., & Turner, S. M. (1991). Anxiety disorders research with African-Americans: Current status. *Psychological Bulletin, 109,* 400–410.

Noyes, R., Crowe, R. R., Harris, E. L., Hamra, B. J., McChesney, C. M., & Chaudhry, D. R. (1986). Relationship between panic disorder and agoraphobia. *Archives of General Psychiatry, 43,* 227–232.

Obler, M., & Terwilliger, R. F. (1970). Pilot study on the effectiveness of systematic desensitization with neurologically impaired children with phobic disorders. *Journal of Consulting and Clinical Psychology, 2,* 314–318.

Ollendick, T. H. (1979). Fear reduction techniques with children. In M. Hersen, R. M. Eisler, & P. M. Miller (Eds.), *Progress in behavior modification* (Vol. 8, pp. 127–168). New York: Academic Press.

Ollendick, T. H. (1983). Reliability and validity of the revised Fear Survey Schedule for Children (FSSC-R). *Behaviour Research and Therapy, 21,* 395–399.

Ollendick, T. H., & Francis, G. (1988). Behavioral assessment and treatment of childhood phobias. *Behavior Modification, 12,* 165–204.

Ollendick, T. H., & King, N. J. (1994). Diagnosis, assessment, and treatment of internalizing problems in children: The role of longitudinal data. *Journal of Consulting and Clinical Psychology, 62,* 918–927.

Ollendick, T. H., King, N. J., & Frary, R. B. (1989). Fears in children and adolescents: Reliability and generalizability across gender, age and nationality. *Behaviour Research and Therapy, 27,* 19–26.

Ollendick, T. H., King, N. J., & Hamilton, D. I. (1991). Origins of childhood fears: An evaluation of Rachman's theory of fear acquisition. *Behaviour Research and Therapy, 29,* 117–123.

Ollendick, T. H., Yang, B., Dong, Q., Xia, Y., & Lin, L. (1995). Perceptions of fear in other children and adolescents: The role of gender and friendship status. *Journal of Abnormal Child Psychology, 23,* 439–452.

Ollendick, T. H., Yang, B., King, N. J., Dong, Q., & Akande, A. (1996). Fears in American, Australian, Chinese, and Nigerian children and adolescents: A cross-cultural study. *Journal of Child Psychology and Psychiatry and Allied Disciplines, 37,* 213–220.

Ollendick, T. H., Yule, W., & Ollier, K. (1991). Fears in British children and their relationship to manifest anxiety and depression. *Journal of Child Psychology and Psychiatry and Allied Disciplines, 32,* 321–331.

Ost, L. G. (1985). Ways of acquiring phobias and outcome of behavioral treatments. *Behaviour Research and Therapy, 23,* 683–689.

Ost, L. G. (1987). Age of onset in different phobias. *Journal of Abnormal Psychology, 96,* 123–145.

Ost, L. G., & Hugdahl, K. (1983). Acquisition of agoraphobia, mode of onset and anxiety response patterns. *Behaviour Research and Therapy, 21,* 623–631.

Page, A. C. (1994). Blood-injury phobia. *Clinical Psychology Review, 14,* 443–461.

Perrin, S., & Last, C. G. (1992). Do childhood anxiety measures measure anxiety? *Journal of Abnormal Child Psychology, 20,* 567–578.

Peterson, L., & Shigetomi, C. (1981). The use of coping techniques to minimize anxiety in hospitalized children. *Behavior Therapy, 12,* 1–14.

Prins, P. J. M. (1985). Self-speech and self regulation of high and low anxious children in the dental situation: An interview study. *Behaviour Research and Therapy, 23,* 641–650.

Prins, P. J. M. (1986). Children's self-speech and self-regulation during a fear-provoking behavioral test. *Behaviour Research and Therapy, 24,* 181–191.

Puig-Antich, J., & Chambers, W. (1978). *The Schedule for Affective Disorders and Schizophrenia for School-Aged Children.* New York: New York State Psychiatric Institute.

Rachman, S. (1977). The conditioning theory of fear acquisition: A critical examination. *Behaviour Research and Therapy, 15,* 375–387.

Rachman, S. (1983). Irrational thinking, with special reference to cognitive therapy. *Advanced Behaviour Research and Therapy, 5,* 63–68.

Rainwater, N., Sweet, A. A., Elliott, L., Bowers, M., McNeil, J., & Stump, N. (1988). Systematic desensitization in the treatment of needle phobias for children with diabetes. *Child and Family Behavior Therapy, 10,* 19–31.

Rapee, R. M., Barret, P. M., Dadds, M. R., & Evans, L. (1994). Reliability of the *DSM-III-R* childhood anxiety disorders using structured interview: Interrater and parent-child agreement. *Journal of the American Academy of Child and Adolescent Psychiatry, 33,* 984–992.

Reich, J., & Yates, W. (1988). Family history of psychiatric disorders in social phobia. *Comprehensive Psychiatry, 29,* 72–75.

Reiss, S. (1991). Expectancy model of fear, anxiety and panic. *Clinical Psychology Review, 11,* 141–154.

Rescorla, R. A. (1988). Pavlovian conditioning: It's not what you think it is. *American Psychologist, 43,* 151–160.

Richardson, S. A., Dohrenwend, B. S., & Klein, D. (1965). *Interviewing: Its forms and functions.* New York: Basic Books.

Rimm, D. C., Janda, H. L., Lancaster, D. W., Nahl, M., & Dittmar, K. (1977). An exploratory investigation of the origin and maintenance of phobias. *Behaviour Research and Therapy, 15,* 231–238.

Ritter, B. (1968). The group desensitization of children's snake phobias using vicarious and contact desensitization procedures. *Behaviour Research and Therapy, 6,* 1–6.

Ryall, M. R., & Dietiker, K. E. (1979). Reliability and clinical validity of the Children's Fear Survey Schedule. *Journal of Behavior Therapy and Experimental Psychiatry, 19,* 303–310.

Sarason, S. B., Davidson, K. S., Lighthall, F. F., Waite, R. R., & Ruebush, B. K. (1960). *Anxiety in elementary school children.* New York: Wiley.

Seligman, M. E. P. (1970). On the generality of the laws of learning. *Psychological Review, 77,* 406–418.

Seligman, M. E. P. (1971). Phobias and preparedness. *Behavior Therapy, 2,* 307–320.

Shaw, J. (1990). Menstruation phobia treated by cognitive correction: A case report. *Journal of Behavior Therapy and Experimental Psychiatry, 21,* 49–51.

Sheehan, D. V., Sheehan, K. E., & Minichiello, W. E. (1981). Age of onset of phobic disorders: A reevaluation. *Comprehensive Psychiatry, 22,* 544–553.

Shinebourne, E. A. (1974). Growth and development of the cardiovascular system. In J. A. Davis & J. Dobbing (Eds.), *Scientific foundations of pediatrics* (pp. 198–213). London: Heinemann.

Siegel, L. J., & Peterson, L. (1980). Stress reduction in young dental patients through coping skills and sensory information. *Journal of Consulting and Clinical Psychology, 48,* 785–787.

Silverman, W. K. (1991). Diagnostic reliability of anxiety disorders in children using structured interviews. *Journal of Anxiety Disorders, 5,* 105–124.

Silverman, W. K. (1994). Structured diagnostic interviews. In T. H. Ollendick, N. J. King, & W. Yule (Eds.), *International handbook of phobic and anxiety disorders in children and adolescents* (pp. 293–315). New York: Plenum.

Silverman, W. K. & Albano, A. M. (1996). *The Anxiety Disorders Interview Schedule for Children–IV (Child and Parent Versions).* San Antonio, TX: Psychological Corporation.

Silverman, W. K., Cerny, J. A., & Nelles, W. B. (1988). The familial influence in anxiety disorders: Studies on the offspring of parents with anxiety disorders. In B. B. Lahey & A. E. Kazdin (Eds.), *Advances in clinical child psychology* (Vol. II, pp. 223–248). New York: Plenum.

Silverman, W. K., Cerny, J. A., Nelles, W. B., & Burke, A. E. (1988). Behavior problems in children of parents with anxiety disorders. *Journal of the American Academy of Child and Adolescent Psychiatry, 27,* 779–784.

Silverman, W. K., & Eisen, A. R. (1992). Age differences in the reliability of parent and child reports of child anxious symptomatology using a structured interview. *Journal of American Academy of Child and Adolescent Psychiatry, 31,* 117–124.

Silverman, W. K., & Eisen, A. R. (1993). Phobic disorders. In R. T. Ammerman, C. G. Last, & M. Hersen (Eds.), *Handbook of prescriptive treatments for children and adolescents* (pp. 17–197). Boston: Allyn & Bacon.

Silverman, W. K., & Ginsburg, G. S. (1998). Anxiety disorders. In T. H. Ollendick & M. Hersen (Eds.), *Handbook of child psychopathology* (3rd ed.), New York: Plenum.

Silverman, W. K., & Kearney, C. A. (1992). Listening to our clinical partners: Informing researchers about children's fears and phobias. *Journal of Behavior Therapy and Experimental Psychiatry, 23,* 71–76.

Silverman, W. K., & Kurtines, W. K. (1996). *Anxiety and phobic disorders: A pragmatic approach.* New York: Plenum.

Silverman, W. K., & Nelles, W. B. (1988a). The Anxiety Disorders Interview Schedule for Children. *Journal of the American Academy of Child and Adolescent Psychiatry, 27,* 772–778.

Silverman, W. K., & Nelles, W. B. (1988b). The influence of gender on children's ratings of fear in self and same-aged peers. *Journal of Genetic Psychology, 149,* 17–22.

Silverman, W. K., & Nelles, W. B. (1990). Simple phobia in childhood. In M. Hersen & C. G. Last (Eds.), *Handbook of child and adult psychopathology: A longitudinal perspective* (pp. 183–196). New York: Pergamon.

Silverman, W. K., & Rabian, B. (1993). Simple phobias. *Child and Adolescent Psychiatric Clinics of North America, 2,* 603–622.

Silverman, W. K., & Rabian, B. (1995). Test-retest reliability of the DSM-III-R anxiety childhood disorders symptoms using the Anxiety Disorders Interview Schedule for Children. *Journal of Anxiety Disorders, 9,* 1–12.

Slater, E., & Shields, J. (1969). Genetical aspects of anxiety. In M. J. Lader (Ed.), *Studies of anxiety* (pp. 62–71). London: Royal Medico-Psychological Association.

Solomon, R. L., & Wynne, L. C. (1954). Traumatic avoidance learning: The principles of anxiety conservation and partial irreversibility. *Psychological Review, 61,* 358–385.

Solyom, L., Beck, P., Solyom, C., & Hugel, R. (1974). Some etiological factors in phobic neurosis. *Canadian Psychiatric Association Journal, 19,* 69–78.

Sreenivasan, V., Manocha, S. N., & Jain, V. K. (1979). Treatment of severe dog phobia in childhood by flooding: A case report. *Journal of Child Psychology and Psychiatry, 20*, 255–260.

Stampfl, T. G. (1991). Analysis of aversive events in human psychopathology: Fear and avoidance. In M. R. Denny (Ed.), *Fear, avoidance, and phobias: A fundamental analysis.* Hillsdale, NJ: Lawrence Erlbaum Associates.

Stedman, J. M., & Murphy, J. (1984). Dealing with specific child phobias during the course of family therapy: An alternative to systematic desensitization. *Family Therapy, 11*, 55–60.

Stevenson, J., Batten, N., & Cherner, M. (1992). Fears and fearfulness in children and adolescents: A genetic analysis of twin data. *Journal of Child Psychology and Psychiatry and Allied Disciplines, 33*, 977–985.

Strauss, C. C., & Last, C. G. (1993). Social and simple phobias in children. *Journal of Anxiety Disorders, 2*, 141–152.

Tasto, D. L. (1969). Systematic desensitization, muscle relaxation and visual imagery in the counterconditioning of a four-year-old phobic child. *Behaviour Research & Therapy, 7*, 409–411.

Thankachan, M. V., Mishra, H., & Kumaraiah, V. (1992). Behavioral intervention with phobic children. *Nimhans Journal, 10*, 95–99.

Thyer, B. A., Parrish, R. T., Curtis, G. C., Nesse, R. M., & Cameron, O. G. (1985). Ages of onset of DSM-III anxiety disorders. *Comprehensive Psychiatry, 26*, 113–122.

Torgersen, S. (1979). The nature and origin of common phobic fears. *British Journal of Psychiatry, 134*, 343–351.

Turner, S. M., Beidel, D. C., & Costello, A. (1987). Psychopathology in the offspring of anxiety disorders patients. *Journal of Consulting and Clinical Psychology, 55*, 229–235.

Turner, S. M., Beidel, D. C., & Wolff, P. L. (1996). Is behavioral inhibition related to the anxiety disorders? *Clinical Psychology Review, 16*, 157–172.

Ultee, C. A., Griffioen, D., & Schellekens, J. (1982). The reduction of anxiety in children: A comparison of the effects of systematic desensitization *in vitro* and systematic desensitization *in vivo*. *Behaviour Research and Therapy, 20*, 61–67.

Van Hasselt, V. B., Hersen, M., Bellack, A. S., Rosenblum, N. D. & Lamparski, D. (1979). Tripartite assessment of the effects of systematic desensitization in a multi-phobic child: An experimental analysis. *Journal of Behavior Therapy and Experimental Psychiatry, 10*, 51–55.

Vasey, M. W., Daleiden, E. L., Williams, L. L., & Brown, L. (1995). Biased attention in childhood anxiety disorders: A preliminary study. *Journal of Abnormal Child Psychology, 23*, 267–279.

Venables, P. H. (1981). Automatic reactivity. In M. Rutter (Ed.), *Scientific foundations of developmental psychiatry* (pp. 165–175) Baltimore: University Park Press.

Watson, J. B., & Rayner, R. (1920). Conditioned emotional reactions. *Journal of Experimental Psychology, 3*, 1–14.

Weissman, M. M., Leckman, J. F., Gammon, G. D., Merikangas, K. R., & Prusoff, B. A. (1984). Depression and anxiety disorders in parents and children. *Archives of General Psychiatry, 41*, 845–852.

Wish, P. A., Hasazi, J. E., & Jurgela, A. R. (1973). Automated direct deconditioning of a childhood phobia. *Journal of Behavior Therapy and Experimental Psychiatry, 4*, 279–283.

Wolpe, J., & Rachman, S. (1960). Psychoanalytic evidence: A critique based on Freud's case of Little Hans. *Journal of Nervous and Mental Disease, 131*, 135–147.

World Health Organization (1992). *International classification of mental and behavioral disorders, clinical descriptions and diagnostic guidelines* (10th ed.). Geneva: WHO.

Young, J. P. R., Fenton, G. W., & Lader, M. J. (1971). The inheritance of neurotic traits: A twin study of the Middlesex Hospital Questionnaire. *British Journal of Psychiatry, 119*, 393–398.

Yule, W., Sacks, B., & Hersov, L. (1974). Successful flooding treatment of noise phobia in an eleven-year-old boy. *Journal of Behavior Therapy and Experimental Psychiatry, 5*, 209–211.

Zabin, M. A., & Melamed, B. G. (1980). Relationship between parental discipline and children's ability to cope with stress. *Journal of Behavioral Assessment, 2*, 17–38.

Zatz, S., & Chassin, L. (1983). Cognitions of test-anxious children. *Journal of Consulting and Clinical Psychology, 51*, 524–534.

Zatz, S., & Chassin, L. (1985). Cognitions of test-anxious children under naturalistic test-taking conditions. *Journal of Consulting and Clinical Psychology, 53*, 393–401.

5.15
Obsessive-compulsive Disorder

DEREK BOLTON

Institute of Psychiatry, London, UK

5.15.1 INTRODUCTION

The development of the current conception and classification of what we know as "obsessive-compulsive disorder" (OCD) has been full of controversy. While this fact in itself is not extraordinary in the area of psychopathology, it is remarkable that many of the historical controversies are still alive and some are even kicking. The disorder has proved particularly difficult to define and classify. This has to do with the fact that it involves, or is associated with, various functions and dysfunctions of mind and behavior. It evidently involves the intellect, with thoughts or doubts at or beyond the border of sanity; it frequently involves the emotions, particularly fear and melancholia; it typically involves an apparent impairment of the power of the will, with distressing thoughts and actions persisting against the person's wishes; the behavioral aspects of the disorder are in some cases akin to complex tics, or even to motor movements induced by brain seizure. The development of the current concept of OCD reflects all the various possibilities which this complex phenomenology opens up. Many early psychopathologists tackled the problem, including, for example, Esquirol, Morel, Dagonet, du Saulle, and Ball, in France, Krafft-Ebbing, Westphal, and Wille, in Germany, and Mickle, Tuke, and Jackson, in Britain (Berrios, 1995). During the nineteenth century particularly, what we now know as OCD was alternatively conceived as a disorder of intellect, volition, or emotions, and classified variously along with psychoses, neurologically based motor disorders, and anxiety disorders. The conception of OCD as primarily a disorder of the emotions, and its classification along with typical anxiety disorders, were consolidated during the early twentieth century and were embraced by the major nosological systems, where they remain today enshrined in the most recent editions, *DSM-IV* (American Psychiatric Association, 1994) and *ICD-10* (World Health Organization, 1988). The conception of OCD as an anxiety disorder was consistent with and reinforced by psychoanalytic theory, and it is equally well-suited to behavioral and cognitive behavioral theorizing.

However, major controversies have appeared, or more accurately reappeared, concerning the nature and appropriate classification of OCD. There has been a resurgence of interest in the notion of a spectrum of OCDs within which typical OCD is one kind of case, but which includes conditions other than anxiety disorders. Further, there is a view which has assumed something of the status of an orthodoxy, particularly in the United States, to the effect that the primary dysfunction in OCD is more to do with motor control than with emotional conflict, and that both motor and psychological aspects of the disorder probably cannot be understood in terms of psychological principles, whether psychoanalytic or cognitive-behavioral, since they are due to an hypothesized structural or biochemical neural lesion.

Notwithstanding theoretical uncertainty, progress on the treatment front has been substantial. OCD had been found to be refractory to psychiatric treatments, though some cases showed reasonably good response to psychosurgery, and also resistant to psychoanalysis (Rachman & Hodgson, 1980). The first studies of the course of the disorder showed reasonably good recovery in as little as a third of cases. The position was transformed, however, in the late 1970s and early 1980s, with the development of two new forms of treatment: behavior therapy—specifically exposure with response–prevention—and pharmacotherapy using agents which specifically inhibited uptake of the neurotransmitter serotonin. Trials of these two new forms of treatment, separately or in combination, found good outcome in up to two-thirds of cases. There is thus reason now to be fairly optimistic about prognosis. There is, on the other hand, ample scope for more improvement in a number of areas: in cases where the person has insufficient motivation for behavioral treatment, where there is poor response to treatment, and where there is subsequent serious relapse. In other words the current forms of treatment constantly come up against their limitations, and this requires not only continuing attention to therapeutic details and refinements, but also continuing work on the complex and controversial models of the etiology of the disorder.

5.15.2 OBSESSIVE-COMPULSIVE DISORDER

5.15.2.1 Phenomenology

As a young child, Christine used to worry occasionally about germs, afraid that she would infect other people or vice versa. At age 12 following the death of a family friend Christine was very upset and began washing her hands excessively. A few months later she became preoccupied with thoughts about lines which had to be unwoven by retracing her steps, and this inhibited her from going out. Age 13, Christine's paternal grandmother died of cancer, and she began menstruation during the same year. Over this time Christine became increasingly preoccupied with intrusive, distressing thoughts which usually had violent or sexual content. If a sexual or violent thought occurred in her mind, she would feel compelled to return to the place she had just been, or stage in a behavior sequence, and then move forward again without having the thought, which procedure she felt neutralized having the thought in the first place. In practice, this meant that she would take up to several hours to walk a short distance or get dressed. Christine would spend much time telling her mother of her thoughts, or being helped by her mother to restart activity when she got stuck.

John was referred at two and a half years to a child guidance clinic because of parental concern over his failure to socialize with other children, speech delay, and concern about possible mental retardation. He was clingy with his mother and was never able to dress himself fully. Later at school John was reported to be polite, cooperative, and of slightly above average intelligence. However, he was said to be "painfully slow" and a backward reader with barely legible writing. John was socially isolated, teased, and harassed by his peers. Following entry into secondary school John's difficulties worsened, and at age 11 he was admitted for several weeks to an inpatient psychiatric unit. He presented as a prepubertal boy with faint and hesitant speech. He was severely slow in all his personal functions, requiring the nurses to dress, wash, bathe, and help him eat. If left on his own, he took six to eight hours to dress and often stood motionless for long periods of time being distracted by something irrelevant to the task. He was frequently incontinent due to his slowness. He walked with a skipping gait, and had multiple tics and mannerisms such as squinting his eyes, tapping his hands, touching his right cheek with his left hand, licking his lips, and producing repetitive writhing neck movements, and jerking action of his upper limbs. When leaving a room John would repeatedly tap the door to ensure it was closed, he checked his knife and fork for dirt, and turned his head before starting to walk. John was often preoccupied with the correct manner of performing a task, being fearful he would make a mistake and thus feel compelled to return to the beginning of the sequence. He said he did not resist his habits and felt more anxious when prevented from performing them. He used "magical numbers," often having to tap his hands and feet in sixes and sevens.

These two short descriptions of actual cases illustrate some of the variety of phenomenology in children and adolescents suffering from OCD. There are common features, captured in general terms by the standard diagnostic systems, to be discussed below, but within these broad guidelines there are quite wide variations. With children and adolescents, as for adults with OCD, cleaning compulsions, linked to obsessions about contamination, and checking compulsions, linked to fear of more or less well-specified disasters, are most common. Other common compulsive activities include putting things in a set order, pattern or sequence, either physical or mental, touching, and hoarding (Foa & Kozak, 1995; Riddle et al., 1992; Swedo, Rapoport, Leonard, Lenane, & Cheslow, 1989; Thomsen & Mikkelsen, 1991).

Broadly speaking the phenomenology of OCD is fairly constant through the age range from childhood to adulthood, and this is reflected in the fact that the diagnostic criteria apply across the age range. While the form of the disorder remains essentially the same, some variations in content can be seen. These are generally understandable in biological or psychosocial terms. For example, children and adolescents commonly present with compulsive checking of homework, or with persistent, distressing requests for parents to reassure them that they are safe, and while sexual obsessions are common in adults (Foa & Kozak, 1995; Stern & Cobb, 1978), they are uncommon in children.

As to cultural factors, there is a reasonable amount of data on cultural factors affecting normal childhood fears, but there is little in relation to pathological fear, including obsessional anxiety (Fonseca, Yule, & Erol, 1994). Research on cultural factors affecting OCD has been on adults, and generally the findings are that the disorder presents in similar ways in various cultures, though it remains possible that the content of obsessions and the nature of compulsions may be sensitive in some degree to cultural norms and preoccupations. Most attention has focused on the sometimes very striking apparent similarities between OCD and religious beliefs and rituals, but this alongside the fact that within religions it is explicitly acknowledged that observance to the law can go, as it were, over the top, being no longer piety, but eccentricity or sickness, and in any case usually something to be avoided. This kind of picture has been noted in many countries and religions including Judaism (Greenberg, 1984; Suess & Halpern, 1989), Islam (Mahgoub & Abdel-Hafeiz, 1991; Pfeiffer, 1981), Catholicism (Suess & Halpern; 1989), and Hinduism (Chakraborty & Banerji, 1975; Sharma, 1968). There is, on the other hand, so far no evidence that the extent of religious belief or ritual in a culture affects the risk for developing OCD, at least in the sense that studies in a fairly wide variety of cultures converge on similar figures for prevalence of the disorder (see Section 5.15.2.4).

5.15.2.2 Diagnostic Features

The diagnostic criteria for OCD as specified by *DSM-IV* (American Psychiatric Association, 1994) may be summarized as follows. The person must have either or both of *obsessions* or *compulsions*. "Obsessions" are defined as recurrent, intrusive, distressing mental events, which are not just excessive real-life worries, which the person tries to ignore or suppress or neutralize, and which the person regards as the product of their own mind. "Compulsions" are defined as repetitive behaviors or mental acts carried out in response to obsessions, or according to rigid rules, aimed at reducing distress or averting some dreaded event in the absence of a realistic connection between the activities and the intended consequences. *DSM-IV* specifies that at some point these must have been recognized as excessive or unreasonable, but adds that this criterion need not apply in the case of children. As usual in *DSM-IV*, there is an additional criterion that the symptomatology causes marked distress, is time-consuming, or causes impaired functioning. There is a standard rule specifying that the diagnosis should be made only if the disturbance is not due to the direct physiological effects of a substance or a general medical condition. There is also a further rule excluding the diagnosis of OCD if there is another Axis I disorder present and if the content of obsessions or compulsions is restricted to it, for example, preoccupation with food in the presence of an eating disorder; hair-pulling in the presence of trichotillomania;

concern with appearance in the presence of body dysmorphic disorder; preoccupation with having a serious illness in the presence of hypochondriasis; preoccupation with sexual urges in the presence of paraphilia; or guilty ruminations in the presence of major depressive disorder.

This type of exclusion rule is legitimate, and indeed inevitable, as a means of defining precisely the boundaries of a particular diagnostic category, but of course they might be artificial. Such rules cannot preempt the question whether OCD as so defined is a distinct biopsychological entity compared with the other disorders to which it is apparently related. This bears on the question of "obsessive-compulsive spectrum disorders" to be discussed in Section 5.15.2.5.

ICD-10 uses similar diagnostic criteria (World Health Organiztion, 1988, p. 143). It specifies minimum duration of two weeks, and it defines subtypes of predominantly obsessions, predominantly compulsions, mixed obsessions and compulsive acts, other OCDs, and unspecified.

Foa and her colleagues conducted a field trial involving 431 patients diagnosed as having OCD in seven sites with the aim of examining some empirical and conceptual assumptions of the *DSM-III-R* criteria for OCD and making recommendations for *DSM-IV* and comparisons with *ICD-10* (Foa & Kozak, 1995; with author list correction in Foa et al., 1995). Three issues were examined: (i) the requirement that symptoms of OCD be viewed by the patient as excessive or unreasonable, (ii) the presence of mental compulsions in addition to behavioral compulsions, and (iii) validity of *ICD-10* subcategories. Primary measures were the Yale–Brown Obsessive-Compulsive Scale and face-valid questions about fixity of obsessive-compulsive beliefs. A wide range of views about the unreasonableness of obsessional fears was found among 250 participants: 13% were certain that feared consequences of not performing their compulsions would not occur; 27% were mostly certain; 30% were uncertain; 26% were mostly certain that the feared consequence would occur, and 4% were completely certain that it would occur. Eight percent were classified as currently lacking in insight, and 5% had never recognized the senselessness of their symptoms. The investigators noted that the 5% of patients who reported never having had insight, and perhaps also the 25% who were mostly certain that their symptoms were reasonable, would not formally meet *DSM-III-R* criteria for OCD, and inferred that the participating clinicians with extensive experience with OCD were compensating for imperfections in those criteria. It was subse-

quently proposed that the requirement for insight should be de-emphasized in *DSM-IV*, and a specifier "with poor insight" has been included. It was found that almost 80% of the patients reported having both mental and behavioral compulsions, and the *DSM-III-R* wording has been clarified in *DSM-IV* to make it clearer that compulsions can be mental and not just behavioral. The authors note that the identification of mental compulsive rituals is important for at least two reasons. First, it can eliminate confusion between OCD and other disorders involving ruminations, such as generalized anxiety disorder or depression; only individuals with OCD perform mental rituals. Second, behavior therapy uses very different techniques for obsessions on the one hand and mental rituals on the other; prolonged exposure is used for the former, and blocking techniques for the latter. Findings on the validity of the *ICD-10* subcategories of OCD were equivocal.

5.15.2.3 Differential Diagnoses

It would be fair to say that most of the time diagnosis of OCD is relatively straightforward, but there are some crucial and interesting kinds of cases in which differential diagnoses have to be considered, and the following are the most common and important.

(i) Ruminative brooding with depressed content may be part of a depressive syndrome rather than obsessions in the sense of OCD. Mood congruence so far suggests depressive disorder.

(ii) Anxious mental preoccupation may indicate generalized anxiety disorder (GAD) rather than OCD. Here a critical feature is that in GAD, worrying is seen as excessive but realistic, while in OCD mental preoccupation is unrealistic. However, the line may be difficult to draw, for example, over worry about parental health.

(iii) There is a fine line, at least in theory, between obsessions and delusions. Both are unreasonable, and may be bizarre, with the critical difference traditionally being that obsessions as opposed to delusions are recognized as such (Berrios, 1995). However, this condition is absent in many adult patients with OCD (Foa & Kozak, 1995; Stern & Cobb, 1978), and as already indicated *DSM-IV* has dropped it altogether for children. Differential diagnoses of OCD and psychoses specifically in adolescents is discussed by Thomsen (1992).

(iv) Stereotyped, repetitive behaviors of individuals with very low intelligence, tic disorders, or pervasive developmental disorders may resemble the compulsive behaviors characteristic of OCD. Some typical differences in the content of repetitive thoughts in autism and OCD have been reported in adults (McDougle et al., 1995), although content is not relevant to diagnosis. So far as concerns repetitive behaviors, the differences critical to diagnosis are that obsessive-compulsions are carried out in response to obsessions or according to strict rules, they relieve anxiety, and they generate distress.

One or more of these features is absent in nonobsessional, stereotyped, repetitive behaviors associated with autism (Baron-Cohen, 1989), mental retardation (Bodfish et al., 1995; Vitiello, Spreat, & Behar, 1989), and tics (Cath et al., 1992; Miguel et al., 1995a).

Decision as to appropriate diagnosis in these various kinds of cases requires careful investigation of phenomenology and the pattern of symptomatology as a whole. If two sets of diagnostic criteria are satisfied, then both diagnoses can be appropriately given, though this is subject to priority and exclusion rules in particular (versions of) diagnostic systems. Comorbidity is common in OCD, in children and adolescents as in adults. Other psychopathology has been reported in up to three-quarters of child and adolescent cases, with other anxiety disorders and affective disorders being the most common (Flament et al., 1988; Riddle et al., 1990; Swedo, Rapoport, Leonard, Lenane, & Cheslow 1989; Valleni-Basile et al., 1994).

5.15.2.4 Prevalence

Early estimates of the prevalence of childhood and adolescent OCD ranged between 0.2% and 1.2% of hospital clinic populations (Berman, 1942; Hollingsworth, Tanguay, Grossman, & Pabst, 1980; Judd, 1965) while the first community study found a 0.3% prevalence of "mixed obsessional/anxiety disorders" in 10 and 11 year-olds (Rutter, Tizard, & Whitmore, 1970). Community studies in the late 1980s and early 1990s estimated life-time prevalence of the disorder by adolescence at 1.9% (Flament et al., 1988) and 3% (Valleni-Basile et al., 1994; with correction in Garrison et al., 1995). Adult community studies have estimated 2–3% for life-time prevalence of the disorder in the United States (Karno, Golding, Sorenson, & Burnam, 1988; Robins et al., 1984), with comparable estimates in some other countries and cultures including Uganda (Orley & Wing, 1979) and Canada (Bland, Newman, & Orn, 1988), though with a lower estimate (approximately 1%) in Taiwan (Hwu, Yeh, & Chang, 1989).

As to age of onset, OCD can start very early in childhood, with cases of children below six and as young as three years described in the literature (Adams, 1973; Janet, 1903; Rettew, Swedo, Leonard, Lenane, & Rapoport, 1992). Childhood OCD typically onsets between five and eight years of age or during adolescence (Swedo, Leonard, & Rapoport, 1990), and the age of onset is below 25 years and mostly during adolescence in approximately two-thirds of adult cases (Kringlen, 1965; Pollitt, 1957; Rasmussen & Eisen, 1990). Rasmussen and Tsuang (1986) found two peaks of maximal incidence of the disorder, one at 12–14 years and the other at 20–22 years.

The fact that OCD can often have onset in young children is relevant in several ways to a developmental perspective on etiology. The apparent implication is that whatever maturation has to be reached for the disorder to appear, biological or psychological or both, has already been reached relatively early in childhood. At the same time OCD is apparently not a "developmental disorder": it does not obviously involve any specific developmental delay, and moreover, it can have late onset, in teenage or early adulthood, or beyond. It is also noteworthy that childhood obsessive-compulsive symptomatology appears at around the same time as normal childhood magical thinking and behavior (Gesell, Ames, & Ilg, 1974; Harris, 1994), and the two sets of phenomena—the one psychopathological and the other belonging to normal psychological development—have at least some superficial resemblances; both involve irrational beliefs and the carrying out of rituals aimed, for example, at averting feared outcomes. The exact relevance of these superficial resemblances to the nature of OCD remains controversial, however, and it is discussed further along with other developmental issues in Section 5.15.2.5.

5.15.2.5 Etiology

Accompanying the vigorous interest in OCD there has been much research and theorizing about etiology. The research programmes are of various types, described as psychological, neurological, biological, ethological, or as various compounds of these.

"Psychological" models are characterized by appeal to learning processes involving conditioning or the more complicated information-processing envisaged in the newer cognitive psychological paradigm. There have been many psychological models of OCD, critically reviewed by Jakes (1996), and what follows is a partial review of some main points. For the most part the psychological theories involve variations and elaborations on the themes of neurotic anxiety in combination with active but maladaptive anxiety reduction. This approach to the disorder is obviously linked closely to its typical phenomenology and its classification among the anxiety disorders. A significant exception to this approach is the hypothesis that the core psychological process in OCD is a memory dysfunction leading specifically to chronic doubting and checking (Boone, Ananth, Philpott, Kaur, & Djenderedjian, 1991; Reed, 1977; Sher, Frost, & Otto, 1983). Evidence relating to this hypothesis is conflicting (Martin, Wiggs, Altemus, Rubenstein, & Murphy, 1995; Tallis, 1995), but it plays a role in neuropsychological theorizing which is discussed later in this section.

Otherwise most psychological theories of OCD have emphasized anxiety and anxiety reduction. Obsessions are regarded as expressions of extreme and inappropriate anxiety, and compulsions as strategies for reducing it. Questions then immediately arise as to (i) why the person has such excessive anxiety, and (ii) why an apparently nonsensical, repetitive procedure should reduce it. These are the etiological questions formulated from within this conception of OCD. From the beginning of psychological theorizing about anxiety disorder, there was a clear assumption in both the psychoanalytic and conditioning paradigms that excessive anxiety is generated by trauma and resulting conflict among cognitive-affective states. Applied to obsessional neurosis, the implication is that the patient has experienced or is experiencing some form of trauma, the likely candidate being experience of being out of control over highly salient events (Freud, 1913; Rachman & Hodgson, 1980). As to ritualizing, Freud went on to observe that compulsive anxiety-reducing strategies apparently draw on prerational, magical styles of thinking (Freud, 1913). The basic idea is that, in the absence of real control over salient matters (such as illness and death), helplessness and anxiety can be avoided by taking control over something more within one's power, such as the way food is prepared, or counting in a set pattern. Symbolic power to reduce anxiety would be reinforced by real power according to simple principles of operant conditioning. Cognitive-behavioral theorists have envisaged these kinds of mechanisms as being also involved in the generation and maintenance of OCD (Franzblau, Kanadanian, & Rettig, 1995; Pitman, 1987; Rachman & Hodgson, 1980).

It is a relatively weak claim, though one which can be challenged, as will be considered below, that compulsions reduce the anxiety associated with obsessions and are thereby maintained. It is a much stronger and more controversial hypothesis to suppose that, notwithstanding appearances, obsessions signify anxiety which is in some sense realistic, specifically fear of being unable to control biopsychologically salient events. For what are these hypothesized events? Pitman (1993) notes evidence of raised rates of OCD among high-combat-exposed Vietnam veterans and discusses the case of a man without previous psychopathology who under combat stress developed persistent OCD as well as post-traumatic stress disorder. He observes that if one focuses on counting the feet of the war dead—one of the patient's counting compulsions—at least one avoids looking at their faces (Pitman, 1993, p. 106). However, it is plain that such cases are not the rule, that in most cases of OCD there is no obvious trauma which might help explain onset in this kind of way. Often no precipitating event is reported by the person or family, or reported precipitants are common life events (Rettew et al, 1992; Valleni-Basile et al., 1995), although common stressful events typically exacerbate symptoms in children and adolescents (Swedo, Rapoport, Leonard et al., 1989), and in adults (Rasmussen & Tsuang, 1986). Nor is it clear that adverse parenting experiences are implicated in the development of OCD. Speculation that parents of children who develop OCD are overstrict has not been borne out in any clear way (Judd, 1965; Merkel, Pollard, Wiener, & Staebler, 1993; Valleni-Basile et al., 1995). Hibbs et al. (1991) found raised levels of "expressed emotion" in families of children with OCD, but this phenomenon is known to be associated with a variety of disorders.

The upshot of all this is that the best candidates for highly anxiogenic experiences associated with OCD are likely to be in large part intrapsychic, to do with the individual's interpretation of otherwise ordinary events. One possibility which remains popular since Freud is that the person who develops OCD has particular difficulty managing high levels of negative emotion, such as is linked to loss or aggression, and hence feels out of control when faced with these emotions, and distracts from and temporarily remedies this threatening helplessness by obsessions and compulsions. The findings most relevant here have been on the excessive worrying characteristic of generalized anxiety, with indications that worrying can function as a mechanism for avoiding accessing and processing emotionally relevant information, in adults (Borkovec & Inz, 1990) and in children (Keppel-Benson & Ollendick, 1993; Vasey, 1993). It is likely that intrapsychic avoidance in the child would reflect avoidance of similar emotionally relevant material in the family (Bolton, 1995). Insofar as excessive worrying is systematically associated with obsessional symptomatology (Tallis & de Silva, 1992), it is possible that obsessional thinking and behavior may serve a similar function as worrying, serving to avoid negative emotional states (Schut & Castonguay, 1996).

The view of OCD as fundamentally involving anxiety and anxiety reduction, particularly insofar as the anxiety has predominantly intrapsychic origins, can be elaborated in various ways in the cognitive paradigm. Carr (1974) emphasized the unrealistic threat appraisals in the disorder. McFall and Wollersheim (1979) highlighted various kinds of dysfunctional assumptions such as that one should be perfect, that mistakes should result in condemnation, that the self is powerful enough to prevent disasters. This approach explores the important possibility that what is abnormal in OCD is not the manifest symptomatic thoughts, but is rather the sometimes less apparent assumptions behind, or appraisals of, these thoughts. Another approach along these lines proposes that an inflated sense of responsibility plays a critical role in the generation of OCD (Salkovskis, 1985). This model begins with the fact that everyone has normal, unwanted, intrusive thoughts, and supposes that people with OCD place special significance on these thoughts, perhaps because OCD sufferers have an exaggerated sense of responsibility. This leads to feeling responsible for producing the thought, to feeling oneself to be a bad person, and to excessive guilt. It may also prompt the feeling that they must act to prevent a feared disaster. The "neutralizing" action results in recurrence of the thought. Thus, there arises a vicious circle involving unwanted, intrusive thoughts, feelings of responsibility and guilt, attempts to neutralize the thoughts, and hence, inadvertently, their recurrence (Salkovskis, 1985). Feelings of responsibility and guilt might be exacerbated particularly in the absence of a clear distinction between having a negative thought, and carrying out the negative action itself, a blurring which has been called "thought–action fusion" (Rachman, 1993). Because these cognitive approaches implicate self-worth, guilt, and failure, they can account for the high association between OCD and depression (Van Oppen & Arntz, 1994).

The earlier psychological models of OCD were developmental in various ways. Insofar as conditioning theory implied early traumatic experience, it was in a primitive sense developmental. In Freud's developmental stage theory, obsessionality was linked particularly to the so-called anal stage, in which anxiety about a particular kind of aggression was prominent, namely, aggressive being out of control of one's own action and thereby making a mess (Freud, 1908). Freud (1913) also construed the irrationality of OCD as a pathological expression of normal childhood magical thinking, as belonging to a prerational stage of thought which is normally later replaced by rational thought. Research has shown that rational grasp of everyday causal principles is evident from very early on, from infancy, while appeal to magic can play a role in the young child's explanations of apparent violations of these principles (e.g., Harris, 1994). Freud's developmental approach to the irrationality in OCD can, however, survive this shift in emphasis away from "stage theories" of cognitive development. Indeed, the developmental approach might if anything be strengthened by it; the fact that in children (as also in so-called "magical cultures") magical thinking can coexist with and to some extent interact with rational thinking is so far compatible with this same pattern in OCD.

The possible link between OCD and childhood magical thinking is also relevant to the cognitive formulations of OCD discussed above. Cognitive styles involving, for example, exaggerated responsibility and thought–action fusion may have their origins in apparently related ways of thinking and states of mind typical of childhood, specifically in the tendency to overestimate the self's power, alongside a not yet firmed-up distinction between thought and action (Piaget, 1937, 1960; Vygotsky 1934).

It is also possible to link a psychological developmental model of OCD with an ethological model. The possibility of viewing at least some obsessive-compulsive behaviors as displacement behaviors in the sense of ethological theory was proposed some time ago by Holland (1974). Displacement behaviors are fixed action patterns carried out in the absence of a normal releasing stimulus, typically in situations of drive conflict or frustration, while fixed action patterns are innate and adaptive motor acts or sequences normally triggered by a so-called releasing stimulus, and include behavioral routines such as pecking, grooming, hoarding, and digging (Lorenz, 1966, 1981; Tinbergen, 1953). An explanation of why fixed action patterns occur in the absence of a normal releasing stimulus, typically in situations of drive conflict or frustration, may be that they have a physiologically low initiation threshold, but it is likely that they then acquire tension reducing, reinforcing functions (Eibl-Eibesfeld, 1970; Lorenz, 1966). Such a process is of course fundamental in evolution and learning; what starts as random, meaningless (nonfunctional) behavior turns out to produce benefits for the organism, typically drive-reduction, and is maintained, intensified, and shaped because of those properties. It seems plausible to suggest that the performance of displacement behaviors when faced with being unable to do anything else functions as an "illusion of control" for the animal. This points towards the area of the developmental cognitive account, and specifically towards the functional benefits of ritualized thinking and behavior already discussed.

It is possible in this way to piece together a psychological model of OCD which integrates a reasonable amount of both early and contemporary theorizing, and which provides that strong kind of biopsychological developmental model which runs seamlessly through phylogenesis and ontogenesis. This kind of model of OCD—sketched in some more detail in Bolton (1996)—is a reasonably good fit with some of the data but not with others. As already remarked, the basic view of obsessions and compulsions fits well because it is based on typical phenomemology. As is also well known, the core of this kind of psychological formulation of OCD—which emphasizes anxiety and its reduction—can provide a reasonable model for the effectiveness of behavior therapy methods, to be discussed later, which consist of methods of anxiety-reduction and the acquisition of more adaptive coping. None of these superficial good fits with the data are at all conclusive support, however. Other aspects of the psychological model as sketched above are doubtful and at best unproven, including, as discussed above, the hypothesized experience of being out of control over negative salient events, the link between OCD and normal developmental childhood magical thinking (Leonard 1989; Leonard, Goldberger, Rapoport, Cheslow, & Swedo, 1990), and the role of exaggerated sense of responsibility (Bogert, Katz, Amir, & Foa, 1996; Ladouceur et al., 1995; Van Oppen & Arntz, 1994). A further general problem for developmental accounts of any disorder is how to handle late onset, which in the case of OCD can be well into adulthood.

Relatively good or poor fits with the data are common enough in models of psychopathology, but what is particularly interesting in the case of OCD is the appearance of radical questioning about the orthodox way of looking at things. In its sharpest distinction, the alternative view stands on its head the conventional interpretation of the relation between obsessions and compulsions. It regards compulsive behaviors as primary, as triggered by some kind of neurological deficit, either structural or functional (biochemical) or both, and obsessions as being either mental versions of compulsive behaviors, or as *post hoc* rationalizations of—

confabulations about—compulsive behaviors. Versions of this kind of model of OCD have been proposed by Rapoport and her colleagues (Rapoport, 1990; Rapoport, Swedo & Leonard, 1992; Rapoport & Wise 1988), and have been discussed, for example, by Insel and Winslow (Insel, 1988, 1992; Winslow & Insel, 1991). These models propose that the neurological basis of OCD involves cortico-striatal-thalamo-cortical circuitry, consistent with various lines of evidence including functional brain imaging (Baxter et al., 1988; Lucey et al., 1995; Luxenberg et al. 1988; Swedo et al., 1992; McGuire et al., 1994; Rubin, Villanueva-Meyer, Ananth, Trajmar, & Mena, 1992). The models postulate that structural and/or biochemical lesions in these systems may underlie OCD, and they combine the postulate of neural deficit with the ethological approach to compulsive behaviors, regarding them as akin to displacement activities. However, in the context of neurological deficit models the hypothesis is that these behaviors are triggered meaninglessly, in contrast to the suggestion within psychological models that they are regulated by information, and specifically that they function in the reduction of helplessness and anxiety.

Both Insel and Rapoport also refer to the apparently distinct psychological approach to OCD mentioned earlier, which focuses not so much on the ritualistic resolution of anxiety but more on the chronic doubting which characterizes the disorder. They propose that the basal ganglia, as well as regulating displacement/compulsive behaviors, may also be implicated in the resolution of doubt, and hence that lesions in these same structures may lead to the chronic and extreme skepticism characteristic of OCD (Insel, 1988; Rapoport, 1990).

Various kinds of evidence have been cited in support of the view that a neurological deficit underlies OCD. Association between obsessive-compulsive symptomatology and known as cerebral disease has long been known, particularly the case of encephalitis lethargica (von Economo, 1931), though also Sydenham's chorea (Grimshaw, 1964; Swedo, Rapoport, Cheslow et al., 1989), and multiple sclerosis (Miguel et al., 1995b). There is also association between obsessive-compulsive symptomatology and suspected signs of cerebral disorder, specifically tics (Como, 1995; Pauls, Alsobrook, Goodman, Rasmussen, & Leckman, 1995; Santangelo et al., 1994), and it occasionally appears following head injury (Jenike & Brandon, 1988; Max et al., 1995; McKeon, McGuffin, & Robinson, 1984). OCD sometimes responds to psychosurgery (Chiocca & Martuza, 1990; Hay et al., 1993). Further evidence of abnormal neurological involvement in OCD is well-replicated above normal frequency of neurological soft signs, and not so well replicated below normal performance on neuropsychological tasks such as tests of complex spatial and switching ability (Abbruzzese, Ferri, & Scarone, 1995; Alarcon, Libb, & Boll, 1994; Christensen, Kim, Dysken, & Hoover, 1992; Cox, Fedio, & Rapoport, 1989; Denckla 1989; Head, Bolton, & Hymas, 1989; Hollander et al., 1990; Hymas, Lees, Bolton, Epps & Head, 1991; Max et al., 1993). The most direct evidence of abnormal structural neurological involvement OCD is structural abnormalities detected by computed tomography (CT) or magnetic resonance imaging (MRI), though the findings here are conflicting (Hoehn-Saric & Benkelfat, 1994; Peterson, 1995; Robinson et al., 1995).

Apart from the equivocal structural scan results, the evidence for neurological deficit in OCD can be seen to be circumstantial and something of a mixture. Nor is it the case that the various signs of neurological disorder hang together. For example, in the above cited studies, the extent of neurological soft signs typically do not correlate with the extent of impairments on neuropsychological tests. In an interesting study of various commonly accepted signs of organic dysfunction, such as birth complications and neurological signs, in 61 children and adolescents with OCD and a psychiatric control group, Thomsen and Jensen (1991) found that a latent class analysis assigned fewer OCD children than control patients to the "organic" class, and concluded that the disorder did not depend on cerebral disturbance as detected by conventional neuropediatric methods.

As already indicated, there is the possibility of a specific biochemical abnormality in OCD. The disorder is highly selective in its response to psychotropic medication, suggesting a relatively circumscribed underlying neurochemistry. Most medications which are effective in the treatment of anxiety, depression, or psychosis are generally ineffective for OCD. The only drugs shown so far in group studies of various designs to be effective in the treatment of OCD are the potent inhibitors of synaptic uptake of serotonin (SRIs) (Piccinelli, Pini, Bellantuono, & Wilkinson, 1995; Stein, Spadaccini, & Hollander, 1995). The role of serotonergic fibers in mediating specific behavior remains speculative, however, though there is some evidence that serotonin has a prominent role among the brain mechanisms which may modulate aggressive behavior (Insel & Winslow, 1992). It is also notable that SRIs have been shown to be effective in the treatment of anxiety disorders other than OCD, in adults and

in children (Birmaher et al., 1994; Schneier, Chin, Hollander, & Liebowitz, 1992) and this is consistent with the possibility that their effect in OCD is mediated by an effect on anxiety.

In this context a general point can be noted about the links between abnormal neurological function associated with a disorder, such as abnormal biochemistry or regional glucose metabolism, and "neurological deficit." The main point is that the former does not entail the latter. In brief, abnormal neurological function (in the sense of difference from that associated with no psychopathology) is so far quite compatible with the hypothesis that the disorder involves and is best explained in terms of psychological processes (intentionality, learning, information-processing, etc.). There is no legitimate inference from neurochemical or functional imaging findings to "neurological deficit," if this is understood as meaning that psychological processes and explanation have come to end (as they have in epilepsy, for example). There are complicated issues here to do with the logic of explanation of mental order and disorder, discussed in detail in Bolton and Hill (1996).

To summarize, research programs have focused on various aspects of OCD, including basic psychological processes involved, precursors in phylogenesis, models of how these map onto and are realized by neural structures and functions, and cutting across those topics there is apparent disagreement as to whether etiology can be understood in terms of biopsychological principles (such as adaptation to perceived loss of control) or whether the disorder is mainly a matter of a neurological lesion causing meaningless compulsions and confabulating obsessions. It would be fair to conclude that the etiology of OCD remains in fundamental ways uncertain. The traditional model of OCD and its various expressions in the broad cognitive psychological paradigm have a great deal of plausibility and evidence on their side. They do not, however, predict the array of findings which seem to implicate a neurological deficit. On the other hand, neurological deficits have not yet been definitely identified, and the possible interactions with psychological processes and symptomatology remain speculative.

In the background is the question whether OCD as a nosological entity will correspond to a "kind" in terms of psychological, biological, or neurological theories. It is possible from any or all those points of view that, on the one hand, subtypes of OCD may be significantly different, and on the other hand, that OCD may not be fundamentally different from some other disorders. Concerning neurobiological aspects of OCD, Insel and Winslow (1992) conclude that subgrouping based on such symptom types, character style, or comorbid diagnoses will be increasingly important for understanding the results of neuropharmacological and functional imaging studies. In the OCD family studies and genetics literature it has been suggested that a subtype of OCD is defined by association with tic disorders (Leonard et al., 1992; Pauls et al., 1995), and phenomenological differences have been reported (George, Trimble, Ring, Sallee, & Robertson, 1993). It has also been suggested that there may be an infection-triggered, autoimmune subtype of pediatric OCD and Tourette's syndrome (TS) (Allen, Leonard, & Swedo, 1995). As to the question whether the underlying processes in OCD are similar to those in other disorders, there has been an increasing interest in the concept of "OCD spectrum disorders" (Hollander & Wong, 1995; Tynes, White, & Steketee, 1990). Particular interest has focused on comorbidity and possible etiological linkages between OCD and eating disorder (de Silva, 1993; Halmi et al., 1991; Jarry & Vaccarino 1996; Rubenstein, Altmeus, Piggott, Hess, & Murphy, 1995; Solyom, Freeman, & Miles, 1982; Thiel, Broocks, Ohlmeier, Jacoby, & Schussler, 1995). Hollander and Wong (1995) propose an inclusive model which links hypothesized subtypes of OCD to many other kinds of disorders including somatoform disorders, dissociative disorders, eating disorders, schizo-obsessive disorder, tics, neurological disorders, and impulse disorders.

On the basis of studies, the role of genetic determination of OCD also remains unclear. The standard methodology of twin/adoption studies has not been readily applicable to OCD because of its rarity. Alternatively, particularly when the prevalence of the disorder was thought to be much rarer than it now is, discovery of identical twins both of whom had OCD was thought to provide evidence of genetic determination (Woodruff & Pitts, 1964), and there have been many reports of such twins in the literature (reviewed by Carey & Gottesman, 1981; Macdonald, Murray, & Clifford, 1991; and Pauls, Raymond, & Robertson, 1991). Generally, these findings are inconclusive in the absence of control for environmental factors, standardly by comparison with discordant monozygotic twins.

In the absence of sufficient numbers of twins one or both of whom have OCD, an alternative methodology involves investigation of obsessional traits in community sample twins. Such studies have suggested heritability of a general neurosis factor. Clifford, Murray, and Fulker (1984) gave the Leyton Obsessional Inventory (LOI) and the Eysenck Personality Question-

naire (EPQ) to 419 pairs of nonclinic referred twins. Heritability for LOI trait and symptom scales were estimated as 47% and 44%, respectively and comparison with the EPQ suggested a strongly inheritable neurosis factor. This finding was consistent with studies by Young, Fenton, and Lader (1971) and Torgerson (1980). Clifford et al. (1984) also found, however, an independent obsessional trait factor relating to "incompleteness, cleanliness, and checking."

Again in the absence of a direct twin methodology for studying the genetics of OCD, an alternative, weaker approach examines incidence of the disorder in the families of individuals who have it. Family studies of relatives of OCD probands have consistently suggested rates of OCD or "subthreshold" OCD higher than population base rates, ranging between 4% and 35% (Bellodi, Sciuto, Diaferia, Ronchi, & Smeraldi, 1992; Lenane et al., 1990; Leonard et al., 1992; Riddle et al., 1990; Thomsen, 1995b). This large range reflects at least the vagueness or variable use of the notion of "subthreshold" OCD, together with the fact that the base rate of this condition in the community is unknown; furthermore, the absence of nonclinic control groups in these studies is a significant methodological weakness. Another problem is absence of control for anxiety. Two family studies which controlled for anxiety by including an anxious non-OCD group failed to find raised rates of obsessive-compulsive symptomatology in first-degree relatives (Clark & Bolton, 1985; Last, Hersien, Kazdin, Orvaskhel, & Perrin, 1991). OCD family studies by Black and his colleagues bear on both these points. Black, Noyes, Goldstein, and Blum (1992) found that the rates of anxiety disorder were higher among the relatives of the probands with OCD compared with relatives of psychiatrically normal controls, but the rate of OCD was not; though they did find higher rates of subdiagnostic threshold obsessive-compulsive symptomatology in the parents of probands with OCD than in parents of the control subjects. The findings suggested that anxiety disorder diathesis is transmitted in families with OCD but that its expression is variable, and they were interpreted as consistent with the classification of OCD as an anxiety disorder. Subsequent analysis comparing psychiatric disorders in the relatives of probands with OCD and comorbid major depression or GAD suggested that GAD may represent an alternative expression of the genetic factor(s) contributing to OCD (Black, Goldstein, Noyes, & Blum, 1995).

A different line of evidence relating to genetic factors in OCD comes from studies of the disorder in relatives of patients with tics or TS. Several studies have suggested that TS is inherited as an autosomal dominant trait (Comings, Comings, Devor, & Cloninger, 1984; Kidd & Pauls, 1982; Pauls & Leckman, 1986; Price, Kidd, Cohen, Pauls, & Leckman, 1985), and the inclusion of relatives with OCD improves the fit of the single gene solution (Pauls & Leckman, 1986). These results suggest that in TS families, OCD is part of the TS spectrum. This hypothesis is supported also by the finding that rates of obsessive-compulsive symptoms are raised in relatives of patients with TS compared with relatives of patients with TS who do not themselves have TS (Comings, 1994). This suggests that the genes for TS may also carry risk for OCD. Other studies have shown that OCD occurs at similar rates in families of TS probands whether probands have OCD or not (Eapen, Pauls, & Robertson, 1993; Pauls, Towbin, Leckman, Zahner, & Cohen, 1986.)

A further study by the Yale group (Pauls et al., 1995) takes the converse approach, examining tics and TS and obsessive-compulsive symptomatology in first degree relatives of probands with OCD and nonclinical controls. Results concerning obsessive-compulsive symptomatology replicate previous findings of higher rates in relatives, though absence of an anxiety control group is a methodological weakness as noted above. As to rates of tics and TS, there was a higher rate among relatives of OCD probands than controls (4.6% vs. 1.0%), consistent with the findings of Leonard et al. (1992). This suggests a relationship between the two disorders, and that individuals with OCD and tics are more likely to have the form of OCD related to TS. It was also found that relatives were more likely to have tics/TS if the proband did, indicating that OCD and tics/TS are not always related and suggesting that in OCD families, TS is not an alternative expression of etiology responsible for OCD. This linkage may exist, however, in TS families as indicated above. The study found that relatives of early onset OCD cases (< 18 years) were more likely to have both OCD and tics, with greatest risk in case of onset between five and nine years. This suggests that childhood onset OCD may be the more heritable form (associated with tics/TS). Finally, the Yale group study found that rates of TS/tics were higher in relatives of OCD probands with a family history of OCD compared with those without family history, suggesting a nonfamilial form of OCD. Relative methodological weaknesses of this study include its use of family history as opposed to twin methodology, the absence of an anxiety control group, and use of a clinic sample, which may increase comorbidity and severity. On this last point, two studies of early onset OCD in community cohorts have failed to find association between tics and the disorder (Douglass, Moffitt, Dar, McGee, & Silva, 1995; Flament et al., 1988).

In summary, the role of genetic determination of OCD and whether there are genetically distinct subtypes remains unclear. Macdonald, Murray, and Clifford (1991) conclude their review by proposing that studies of obsessional symptomatology in larger community twin samples are needed, and this methodology would also test the validity of the Yale group's findings and hypotheses with a relatively stronger design.

5.15.2.6 Developmental Course

Studies of the course of OCD may be divided into those conducted before, and those after, development in the late 1970s of the two main current treatments, behavior therapy and pharmacotherapy with SRIs. It would be fair to say that this time period coincided roughly with increasing precision in diagnosis and increasing sensitivity of symptom measurement. A number of earlier long-term follow-up studies using various methodologies reported reasonable recovery in something the order of half of the cases (Lewis, 1936; Pollit, 1957; Rudin, 1953), though a subsequent large study indicated a somewhat less optimistic picture, however, with only one-quarter of the patients showing much improvement over the long term (Kringlen, 1965). The more rigorous studies since the 1970s are generally of the course of the disorder under more or less controlled conditions of effective behavioral and/or pharmacological treatments, and these are discussed in Section 5.15.4.

Other aspects of the course of the disorder concern continuity of presentation. While the content of obsessions and compulsions may change within individuals over time (Rettew et al., 1992), there is, as already noted, remarkable constancy in the phenomenology of OCD through the age range from childhood to adulthood. Further, the disorder usually "runs true" in the sense that disorder substitution is not common. This applies in retrospect, considering the past history of adult cases (Zeitlin, 1986), and in prospect, considering the future long-term course of child and adolescent cases (Bolton, Luckie, & Steinberg, 1995; Leonard et al., 1993; Thomsen & Mikkelsen, 1995).

More complicated, and so far hardly addressed questions, concern precursors of the disorder. As outlined above, one kind of current model of OCD postulates that it is fundamentally a neurological disorder, and it raises the question whether there is a neurodevelopmental pathway to it. Assuming that neurological injury is not sustained after birth, the broad possibilities are that there is a genetic abnormality predisposing to the disorder, or there is an early environmental impact on the brain, *in utero*, or in the form of obstetric complications. Neural abnormalities derived in one or more of the above ways, early in development, would be in principle detectable. They may have no manifestations prior to onset, but could show up as precursors of the disorder, or, particularly in the case of genetic predisposition, as risk factors evident not only in cases but also in relatives who may or may not have the disorder. The hypothesis of a neurodevelopmental pathway would be likely to predict that early onset, in childhood and early adolescence, would be associated with more signs of abnormal neurological involvement, with being male rather than female, with poorer treatment response and prognosis, and possibly with greater familial incidence of related symptomatology.

Such evidence as there is tends to be limited or nonsupportive. There is no clear support for the prediction that early onset cases, particularly males, have poorer prognosis (Bolton et al., 1995; Leonard et al., 1993; Thomsen and Mikkelsen, 1995). In addition, as discussed above, on the basis of studies so far the role of genetic determination remains unclear. So far as the author is aware there has been only one large-scale community study which has examined precursors of OCD in a prospective longitudinal design, the study was part of the Dunedin Multidisciplinary Health and Development Study based in the province of Otago, New Zealand (Douglass et al., 1995). Douglass and her colleagues report longitudinal data from birth on individuals with OCD at age 18 in a cohort of 930 people. The one year prevalence rate of OCD at age 18 was found to be 4% ($N = 37$). The majority of OCD cases met criteria for comorbid disorder, most commonly depression, social phobia, and psychoactive substance dependence. To examine correlates and predictors of OCD, the group with OCD ($N = 37$) was compared with three other groups defined as follows: without any psychopathology ("healthy group") ($N = 590$), conduct disorder without OCD ($N = 45$), and a mixed affective/anxiety disorder group (any anxiety disorder except OCD, and/or major depression or dysthymia) ($N = 215$). No significant differences between the four groups were found on measures of a number of factors implicated by current neurological deficit models of OCD,

including measures of perinatal problems/complications, tics (assessed at ages seven, nine, and 11), and various neuropsychological tests of executive functioning (at age 13). The absence of association between OCD and tics/TS in the Dunedin sample replicates the same negative result found by Flament and her colleagues in their US community sample (Flament et al., 1988). Interestingly, the Dunedin OCD group was distinguished in an apparently quite different way, by reporting more anxiety and depression in late childhood and adolescence. The OCD group reported more depressive symptomatology than any other of the three comparison groups at ages 15 and 18, and at age 11 more than the "healthy group." The OCD group also reported significantly more symptoms of anxiety at age 15 than the healthy group, and at age 18 more than any other group. The investigators concluded that depression in early adolescence was a predictor for OCD in young adulthood, and that the OCD cases at age 18 may be cases of severe, persistent, internalizing disorder.

5.15.3 CONCEPTUALIZATION AND CLINICAL FORMULATION

5.15.3.1 Multimodal Assessment

Clinical diagnosis of OCD should be primarily by clinical interview, with special attention paid to issues of differential diagnosis. Clinical mental state assessment should also screen for any comorbidity, such as depression, which may require separate therapeutic attention. A structured diagnostic interview aids reliable diagnosis and differential diagnosis of OCD, and several such interviews applicable to children are available (Silverman, 1991), such as the Diagnostic Interview Schedule for Children, 2nd edition (DISC-2.1, Fisher et al., 1993), and the Anxiety Disorders Interview Schedule for Children and Parents (ADIS-C/P, Silverman & Nelles, 1988). Care should be taken to supplement such interviews if necessary with questions needed to deliver diagnosis using the most recent editions of the standard diagnostic systems.

Following clinical diagnostic interview, scaled measures of symptomatology may be used, to make assessment of symptoms more precise, and to allow for estimation of change. For children and adolescents these include the Leyton Child Obsessional Inventory (Berg, Rapoport, & Flament, 1986). This 44-item inventory measures the number of obsessive symptoms with yes/no responses as well as degree of resistance and interference with daily activities. The inventory has reasonable test-retest reliability and discriminative validity (Berg et al., 1986), and it is sensitive to symptomatic improvement (Flament et al., 1985). The Leyton Child Obsessional Inventory has also been adapted for use in surveys (Berg, Whitaker, Davies, Flament, & Rapoport, 1988; King, Inglis, Jenkins, Myerson, & Ollendick, 1995). Currently widely used with adults is the Yale–Brown Obsessive Compulsive Scale (Y-BOCS), a semistructured interviewer-based measure with reasonable reliability, validity, and sensitivity to change (Goodman et al., 1989a, 1989b; Van Oppen, Emmelkamp, van Balkom, & van Dyck, 1995; Woody, Steketee, & Chambless, 1995). In the interview, common obsessions and compulsions are screened for, and dominant ones selected for detailed assessment including estimates of severity and interference. Evidence that Y-BOCS scores for obsessions and for compulsions in fact correspond to two factors is conflicting (Coles, Amir, & Foa, 1996; McKay, Danyko, Neziroglu, & Yaryura-Tobias, 1995), and correlation between the Y-BOCS and self-report measures of obsessive-compulsive symptomatology has been found to be relatively low (Coles et al., 1996). The Children's Yale–Brown Obsessive Compulsive Scale (CY-BOCS) consists of virtually the same items and format as the adult version, with minor wording modification for younger children (Berg, 1989; Goodman, Price, Rasmussen, Riddle, & Rapoport, unpublished).

The extent of obsessive-compulsive symptomatology can also be assessed using general observational methods such as self-monitoring and monitoring by parents or nurses (Wolff & Wolff, 1991). There has also been interest in behavioral measures of severity of some aspects of obsessive-compulsive symptomatology (Steketee, Chambless, Tran, Worden, & Gillis 1996). A number of self-report measures are available for assessing unwanted, intrusive thoughts, reviewed by Clark and Purdon (1995), though generally they have been used so far with adults rather than with children.

Apart from diagnostic and quantitative assessment of symptomatology, assessment for clinical purposes depends on the model of etiology being used and on the intended methods of treatment.

5.15.3.2 Treatment Foundation

In preparing the child or adolescent and their family for treatment much depends on the treatment which is to be used. There are currently two main treatments: behavior therapy, specifically exposure with response pre-vention, and pharmacotherapy, specifically using serotonin reuptake inhibitors, and the two treatments can be used in combination.

If behavior therapy is to be used, the standard method of introduction is to frame OCD as an anxiety disorder, with compulsions described as methods of reducing anxiety prompted by obsessional thoughts. Behavioral treatment, specifically occurrence of the obsessional thought (perhaps cued by exposure to an appropriate external stimulus) followed by prevention of the compulsion, can then be described as a desensitization process. In this approach to OCD, preparatory assessment in effect proceeds as for any other anxiety disorder, whether treatment is to be with the individual (Kendall et al., 1991) or the family (Bolton, 1994). This preparatory assessment would include functional analysis of the anxiety—in the case of OCD of the obsessions which express it—and of coping strategies, in this case the compulsions, though perhaps also avoidance, including the role played in these by other family members. Preparation for behavioral treatment for OCD for adults is discussed by, for example, Rachman and Hodgson (1980), and Riggs and Foa (1993), and for children/ adolescents by Piacentini, Gitow, Jaffer, Graae, and Whitaker (1994) and Albano, Knox, and Barlow (1995). The model of OCD as an anxiety disorder also recommends investigation of what realistic aspects of the child's life may be a source of anxiety, what coping skills they have, and what coping skills are being modeled by the parents (Bolton, 1994). If pharmacotherapy is to be used, a view of OCD as linked to biochemical neural imbalance would be proposed.

It is possible also to prepare for treatment by framing OCD in terms of what might be called a "medical model" of the disorder. This has become popular following the neurological and in particular the "neurological deficit" models of the disorder, in which obsessions or compulsions or both are regarded as senselessly triggered by abnormal brain activity. Several OCD treatment manuals for children recommend this approach, employing terms like "hiccoughs of the brain' or "brain short circuits" (Foster, 1994; March, Mulle, & Herbel, 1994; Wever & Phillips, 1994). This is clearly compatible with exclusive use of pharmacotherapy but makes less sense when combined with behavioral therapy. Behavior therapy like any other form of psychological therapy presupposes that some aspect of the symptom is operating under psychological principles, and hence can be learned or at least unlearned.

On the other hand, it might be argued that framing OCD in terms of the "medical model" may provide a useful device in the sense of strategic therapy (Haley, 1976). In this connection it is significant that March et al. (1994) cite as a rationale for their treatment introduction a book on therapy using narrative methods (White & Epston, 1990).

5.15.4 TREATMENT

5.15.4.1 Psychosocial Treatments

As already indicated, the standard psychological treatment for OCD at any age is behavioral therapy, specifically exposure with response prevention. Exposure is to feared stimuli, and these are specifically the obsessional thoughts. This exposure may occur naturally, with the passage of time, or in contact with things in daily life, but may for treatment purposes be artificially provoked by exposure to objects of fear, such as objects thought to be contaminated. Obsessional thoughts generate anxiety, and response prevention is then a matter of not carrying out the compulsion which normally serves to reduce it. At first the person's anxiety rises, but eventually it subsides. With repetition and consolidation, the anxiety associated with not performing the compulsion, and eventually the anxiety associated with the obsessional thought itself, attenuates. In psychological theory the process is fundamentally one of extinction or relearning (Foa & Kozak, 1986; Marks & Tobena, 1990; Rachman & Hodgson, 1980).

There are many crucial principles and technical points to be observed when carrying out exposure with response prevention. They are extensively discussed in the adult literature, for example, Foa and Kozak (1986), Rachman and Hogdson (1980), and Riggs and Foa (1993). Behavioral treatment for children and adolescents with OCD follows basically the same principles as for adults, though there are obviously amendments in procedure to achieve age appropriateness, for example, in explaining treatment rationale, in encouraging engagement and motivation, and in obtaining consent and authority for treatment (Albano et al., 1995; Piacentini et al., 1994). Frequently, the child or adolescent with OCD involves one or both parents in obsessive rituals, and in these circumstances a family therapy approach may be required, with response-prevention being a matter of encouraging the parents in kind but firm refusal to join in (Bolton, Collins, & Steinberg, 1983; Lenane, 1989). Evidence has appeared that adults with OCD also commonly involve family members in rituals (Calvocoressi et al., 1995; Freshman, Amir, Katz, & Foa, 1996). This may mean that family therapy is

indicated in these adult cases as well, but this conclusion is not obviously correct given the high effectiveness of individual treatment for adults. The position is probably that family therapy is useful for children with OCD not simply because the family is involved in the symptoms, but more because of issues of parent–child authority and dependency; that, it is to say, for the same reasons that it is frequently best to involve parents in their child's treatment whatever the presenting problem. This implies that for the older adolescent with OCD, individual behavioral therapy requiring their consent, involvement, motivation and effort, may be indicated more than (or at least as well as) family therapy. This kind of age-related indication for individual as opposed to family therapy has been suggested in the case of eating disorders (Russell, Szmukler, Dare, & Eisler, 1987).

Cognitive models of OCD have naturally suggested cognitive therapy approaches. On the basis of their model McFall and Wollersheim (1979) recommended rational emotive therapy (Ellis, 1962). The development of cognitive therapy for depression and anxiety by Beck and his colleagues (Beck, 1976; Beck, Emery, & Greenberg, 1985) has naturally led to applications of this to OCD. As discussed in Section 5.15.2.5, the cognitive formulations of OCD implicate assumptions and styles linked to both anxiety and depression, and accordingly cognitive therapy for OCD is based on methods already established in the treatment of affective and anxiety disorders, such as challenging negative self-appraisals or overestimation of risk or responsibility (Salkovskis & Warwick, 1985; Van Oppen & Arntz, 1994). All the above work has been with adults, and its applicability to children and younger adolescents is not yet clear. It may be expected that the more the therapeutic approach requires facility with abstract or theoretical styles of thinking the more it is likely to exceed the cognitive abilities of the younger child (Durlak, Fuhrman, & Lampman, 1991; Inhelder & Piaget, 1958). The cognitive therapy approaches used with children emphasize identification and modification of maladaptive self-talk, though in the case of treatment of anxiety specifically they include also focus on appraisal of realistic likelihoods of feared outcomes (Kendall, Kane, Howard, & Siqueland, 1989). These methods have been applied to children with OCD. Henin et al. (1996) reported treatment of two girls aged nine and 10 with OCD following cognitive behavioral principles closely modeled on the methods developed by Kendall and his co-workers for treatment of anxiety in children; in the first phase of treatment the child was presented with ways of coping with situations which habitually triggered obsessive-compulsive symptoms, with use of strategies such as modeling and role-play; once the skills were mastered, exposure and response-prevention were implemented.

The kinds of case in which exposure with response-prevention can most readily be used are those in which there are readily accessible behavioral compulsions in response to obsessions. The technique does not apply in cases where the person has obsessions alone, without compulsive responses to prevent. These cases are, however, rare (Foa & Kozak, 1995). But the technique is also difficult where the compulsive responses to obsessions are themselves mental, because the therapist has no straightforward way of helping the patient stop what they are doing. Cases of mental ritualizing are not so rare (Foa & Kozak, 1995). Both kinds of case—obsessions alone, and where compulsions are predominantly mental—can be brought under the heading of obsessive-compulsive "ruminations." Treatment approaches include behavioral methods such as habituation and thought-stopping (Foa, Steketee, & Ozarow, 1985; Rachman, 1985) as well as the cognitive approaches referred to above.

Another kind of presentation of OCD which requires methods other than straightforward exposure with response-prevention is so-called primary obsessional slowness, described by Rachman (1974). Its status as a separate syndrome is questionable, however, and a linked point is that the indicated treatment—prompting, pacing, and shaping—can be construed as a form of response-prevention, since in effect it prevents the patient from maintaining desired order or exactness (Veale, 1993). In general, notwithstanding the variety of obsessive-compulsive symptomatology and the corresponding need for flexibility and innovation in behavioral treatment approaches, all or most of these approaches can plausibly be regarded as variations on the theme of response-prevention, for example, the treatment of hoarding compulsions by encouraging the patient to throw away unnecessary hoarded items (Ball, Baer, & Otto, 1996; Tallis & de Silva, 1992).

5.15.4.2 Pharmacological Treatments

As noted in Section 5.15.2.5, the only drugs shown so far in group studies of various designs to be effective in the treatment of OCD are the serotonin reuptake inhibitors (Piccinelli et al., 1995; Stein et al., 1995). They are effective not only in adults (Montgomery, 1994) but also in children and adolescents with OCD (DeVane &

Sallee, 1996; DeVeaugh-Geiss et al., 1992; Flament et al., 1985; Geller, Biederman, Reed, Spencer, & Wilens, 1995; Leonard et al., 1989; Riddle et al., 1992). In the case of OCD, as for other disorders, pharmacological treatment of children and adolescents should be accompanied by attention to social and family factors (Rapoport, Leonard, Swedo, & Lenane, 1993). In the context of the demonstrated effectiveness of SRIs for OCD, much remains unclear about their mode of action, including the nature of any abnormalities in the serotonergic system of patients prior to treatment, as well as the links between serotonergic activity and psychological functions (Goodman, Price, Woods, & Charney, 1991; Hoehn-Saric, McLeod, Zimmerli, & Hipsley, 1993; Insel & Winslow, 1992; Rauch & Jenike, 1993).

5.15.4.3 Effectiveness of Treatments

Effectiveness of behavior therapy in approximately 60–80% of cases has been shown in a number of studies of adults (Marks, Hodgson, & Rachman, 1975; Rachman & Hodgson, 1980), as has effectiveness of SRIs (Clomipramine Collaborative Study Group, 1991; Fineberg, Bullock, Montgomery, & Montgomery, 1992), and of combinations of the two treatments (Cox, Swinson, Morrison, & Lee, 1993; Marks, Stern, Mawson, Cobb, & McDonald, 1980; Rachman & Hodgson, 1980; Stanley & Turner, 1995). Treatment gains following behavior therapy in adulthood have been shown to maintain in the medium- to long-term (O'Sullivan & Marks, 1990; O'Sullivan, Noshirvani, Marks, Monteior, & Lelliott, 1991), while long-term preservation of gains under pharmacotherapy may require maintenance dosage for several years (Fineberg, Bullock, Montgomery, & Montgomery, 1992; Stanley & Turner, 1995).

While behavior therapy for OCD is highly effective for most people who participate, about 25–30% of patients suitable for this form of treatment do not comply with it (McDonald, Marks, & Blizard, 1988). Among those who do stay in treatment, up to 80% respond well as noted above, but conversely 20% or more do not. In sum, then, about 40–50% of referred people with OCD are not helped by behavior therapy, and it is important to bear this in mind alongside the impressive figures for its effectiveness. Considerable effort has gone into identifying factors associated with poor response to behavioral treatment in adults. These may include over-valued ideation, comorbid personality disorder, and depression, though these and other possibilities have not as yet been consistently confirmed (Basoglu, Lax,

Kasvikis, & Marks, 1988; Buchanan, Ko, & Marks, 1996; Castel et al., 1994; Fals-Stewart & Lucente, 1993; Foa, 1979; Foa, Kozak, Steketee, & McCarthy, 1992; Keijsers, Hoogduin, & Schaap, 1994; O'Sullivan et al., 1991; Reich & Vasile, 1993). The causes of nonacceptance of behavioral treatment have been relatively less explored, but low motivation is apparently involved, both in adults (Hansen, Hoogduin, Schaap, & de Haan, 1992), and in children and adolescents, for example, in the form of comorbid oppositional defiance (Bolton & Turner, 1984; Wever & Rey, in press).

Motivation in the form of determination to change and belief in self-efficacy may be a crucial factor mediating both treatment compliance and effectiveness in OCD. Cognitive techniques have been used with adults to try to enhance motivation for and engagement in behavior therapy (Salkovskis & Warwick, 1985; Tallis, 1995). It is interesting to note in this connection that the two approaches to behavioral treatment for children and adolescents with OCD referred to earlier (March et al., 1994; Wever & Phillips, 1994), as well as framing OCD in terms of the medical model, also both make liberal use of methods reminiscent of treating habit disorders such as smoking where motivation for change is crucial. Such methods typically involve acknowledging the habit as bad, and emphasizing that the person, not the behavior, is in charge. The whole problem of motivation and the person's attitude to their OCD has received relatively little attention so far in the psychological theory of the disorder. A sophisticated approach would be required, such as the highly influential model of motivation for change constructed by Prochaska and DiClemente which has been applied to treatment seeking and compliance including in relation to habitual and addictive behaviors (Prochaska & DiClemente, 1982; Prochaska, DiClemente, & Norcross, 1992).

As noted in Section 5.15.4.1, obsessional ruminations can be treated by behavioral methods such as thought stopping and habituation and by cognitive approaches such as modification of abnormal risk assessment. They are notoriously difficult to treat, however, and reported results using such methods are mixed (Arts, Hoogduin, Schaap, & de Haan, 1993; Foa et al., 1985; Rachman, 1985; Salkovskis & Westbrook, 1989).

Initial case reports of cognitive therapy for OCD in adults tended to be uncontrolled and inconclusive (James & Blackburn, 1995), but several controlled studies have shown cognitive methods to be at least as effective as exposure plus response prevention. In comparisons with rational emotive therapy, Emmelkamp and his co-workers found that the two had similar effects, with no incremental effect when combined (Emmelkamp & Beens, 1991; Emmelkamp, Visser, & Hoekstra, 1988). Van Oppen et al. (1995) compared cognitive therapy with exposure and response prevention. The cognitive therapy was based on the methods of Beck (1976) and Salkovskis (1985) and focused mainly on estimation of catastrophic risk and of personal responsibility. Seventy-one adult patients were randomly assigned to one of the two treatment conditions, and seven subsequently dropped out of each. Both treatments led to significant improvement, with more participants rated as "recovered" in the cognitive therapy group. It has been also suggested that cognitive therapy techniques might be particularly useful, and certainly worth trying, in cases of failure of behavioral treatment (Salkovskis & Warwick, 1985). As to application to children, Henin et al. (1996) have reported cognitive-behavioral treatment of two children with OCD, as already noted (Section 5.15.4.1), and the outcome was successful in both cases. The role of cognitive change in mediating behavioral change during cognitive therapy, with adults or children, is not yet clear, and indeed the same question arises in the case of behavior therapy (Durlak et al., 1991; Ladouceur, Rheaume, & Leger 1996; Van Oppen, Emmelkamp, et al., 1995).

The treatment of obsessional slowness involving prompting, shaping, and pacing is generally effective while the therapist is participating, but generalization and maintenance outside of sessions is poor (Clark, Sugrim, & Bolton, 1982; Veale, 1993).

Returning to the main treatments currently in use, exposure with response prevention and medication with SRIs, broadly similar results have been found for children and adolescents with OCD as for adults. Positive, though generally partial, response to SRIs has been found in the majority of young patients with OCD, though as for adults there tends to be relapse if medication is withdrawn (DeVane & Sallee, 1996; DeVeaugh-Geiss et al., 1992; Flament et al., 1985; Geller et al., 1995; Leonard et al., 1989; Rasmussen, Eisen, & Pato, 1993; Riddle et al., 1992). There is also usually a good response to behavior therapy in this age group. An early study of 15 adolescents treated mainly by exposure with response prevention found complete or near complete symptom relief in 87% of cases (Bolton et al., 1983). Similar results have been obtained in two studies using well-defined behavior therapy programs combined with pharmacological (SRI) treatment, with significant improvement in approximately 80% ($N = 14$) (March et al., 1994) and 68%

($N = 57$) (Wever & Rey, in press) of cases under these combined treatments.

The question of the course of OCD presenting in childhood and adolescence, and the long term effectiveness of treatments, is important clinically and theoretically. Early follow-up studies of clinically referred children and adolescents with OCD indicated poor medium- to long-term outcome. Warren (1965) followed up 15 young people aged 19–24 years who had been admitted to hospital with obsessive-compulsive states when aged 12–17 years. No treatment was specified except for psychosurgery in one case. Five of the 15 young people still had severe obsessional symptomatology at follow up, and a further four were still handicapped by obsessional symptoms. Four of the 15 tended to develop mild symptoms under stress, and the remaining two were considered completely recovered. Hollingsworth, Tanguay, Grossman, and Pabst (1980) evaluated 10 of 17 pediatric outpatients and inpatients with severe obsessional neurosis treated by intensive psychotherapy in all cases, one-and-a-half to 14 years later. Seven of the 10 cases reported continuation of obsessive-compulsive behavior though at less than pretreatment levels.

The findings from these earlier follow-up studies of reasonable recovery in a third or less of cases of pediatric OCD is comparable with other findings. In the first of a pair of studies from the National Institute of Mental Health (NIMH), Flament and her colleagues followed up 27 children and adolescents assessed as having OCD at NIMH between 1977 and 1983, between two and seven (mean 4.4) years later and at age 13–24 (mean 18.8) years (Flament et al., 1990). Of the 27 subjects, 17 (68%) still qualified for diagnosis of OCD at follow-up. Treatment during the follow-up period was described as diverse, sparse, and uncontrolled. A somewhat better prognosis was found in a Danish cohort of 23 children and adolescents followed up for between 18 months and five years after treatment which did not involve a "structured treatment program" but included use of SRIs in about 25% of cases and behavior therapy in all; about 50% of cases still qualified for diagnosis at follow-up (Thomsen & Mikkelsen, 1995). A similar recovery rate in a community sample of adolescents with OCD has been observed over a two-year period (Berg et al., 1989). Leonard and colleagues followed up a second cohort of 54 children and adolescents with OCD seen at NIMH between 1984 and 1988, between two and seven (mean 3.4) years later (Leonard et al., 1993). At follow-up 43% still qualified for diagnosis of OCD. Treatment during the follow-up period was active, in contrast to the cohort seen by Flament

and her colleagues, and included medication in nearly all cases and behavior therapy in a third. The predicted difference in outcome in the two NIMH cohorts was found; improvement to below diagnostic threshold was found in 57% of cases in the Leonard et al. sample, as opposed to 32% of cases in the Flament et al. sample.

Similar results in a smaller cohort over a longer time period were reported by Bolton et al. (1995, 1996). Fourteen young adults treated for the disorder in adolescence, mainly with behavior therapy and family therapy, were followed up between nine and 14 years later: six (43%) were found to satisfy *DSM-III-R* criteria for OCD at long-term follow-up, while eight (57%) were not. Sustained recovery from OCD was associated with normal levels of social functioning, consistent with the pattern found in Thomsen's Danish sample (Thomsen, 1995a). Recovered participants were not currently taking medication, a finding which contrasted with the report of Leonard and her colleagues that, in their sample, high proportions, up to 80%, of various groups of participants who no longer met diagnostic criteria for OCD continued to receive SRI medication. One possibility is that effective behavior therapy during adolescence may obviate the need for long-term maintenance pharmacotherapy.

5.15.5 FUTURE DIRECTIONS FOR RESEARCH AND PRACTICE

It would be fair to say that the enormous research effort which has gone into understanding OCD since the early 1980s has raised as many questions as have been answered about the nature and etiology of the disorder. There is an apparent contrast between the traditional view of OCD as fundamentally an anxiety disorder and what has emerged as a new orthodoxy, that it is fundamentally a motor disorder caused by some form of neurological lesion. No one kind of evidence, let alone a single test, could ever settle this kind of issue, but evidence from a variety of methodologies— as reviewed in this chapter—will continue to accrue until a coherent pattern or number of patterns emerge. The various methodologies exist at several levels, from the cultural to the neurological, and the questions they address are also important in their own right. Key outstanding issues include the nature of and interaction between the psychological processes implicated in the disorder, such as anxiety, magical belief, exaggerated sense of responsibility, and dysfunctional memory. There are outstanding issues concerning the neurological basis of the disorder, such as concerning the role of serotonin, and the site of structural lesions in some cases. Important questions in the genetics of the disorder remain unclear in the absence of a large community twin study.

A substantial question in the background, interweaving with etiological issues, is the extent to which OCD as understood in the 1990s, is in fact a well-defined psychobiological entity. It may turn out that significant subtypes exist within OCD and/or that causal pathways crisscross OCD and associated or related psychopathologies. In the present state of theoretical uncertainty this is a particularly tempting line of enquiry, although as yet attempts to subcategorize OCD in useful, predictive ways have so far been speculative. One possibility specifically interesting in relation to childhood presentations of the disorder is whether there a distinctive neurodevelopmental pathway to and subtype of the disorder, and future research will no doubt cast light on this issue.

From the treatment point of view both pharmacotherapy with SRIs and behavior therapy using exposure with response-prevention have both been shown to be highly effective for many patients in the short- and long-term. Outstanding issues include how to improve outcome in treatment resistant cases, and how to manage relapse effectively. Cognitive therapy may play an increasingly important role in these respects.

5.15.6 SUMMARY

OCD is a relatively common disorder in children and young people, with current estimates suggesting a life-time prevalence by adolescence of around 2%. Comorbidity with other disorders is common, including depression, other anxiety disorders, and tics. Psychological theories of OCD mainly involve variations on the themes of unresolved anxiety in combination with active but maladaptive anxiety reduction, and they can be linked in one direction to phylogenesis in terms of displacement activities and in the other to ontogenesis in terms of styles of cognitive appraisal. An alternative view is that OCD may be a neurological motor disorder, with obsessional thought being like confabulation. Neuro-imaging findings on the neuroanatomical basis of the disorder are fairly consistent, and the specific effectiveness of SRIs indicates a relatively circumscribed neurochemical basis. On the basis of studies so far the role of genetic determination remains unclear. OCD often begins in childhood or adolescence, and a variety of useful assessment measures have been developed for these early onset cases.

Without current, effective treatments the disorder can run a chronic course. Currently indicated treatments are behavior therapy, specifically exposure therapy with response-prevention, and pharmacotherapy with SRIs. Pharmacotherapy is less time-consuming but behavior therapy may protect more against relapse. Cognitive therapy for OCD has been shown to be as effective as behavior therapy with adults, and is just beginning to be applied with children.

5.15.7 REFERENCES

Abbruzzese, M., Ferri, S., & Scarone, S. (1995). Wisconsin Card Sorting Test performance in obsessive-compulsive disorder: No evidence for involvement of dorsolateral prefrontal cortex. *Psychiatry Research, 58*, 37–43.

Adams, P. L., (1973). *Obsessive children*. New York: Penguin.

Alarcon, R. D., Libb, J. W., & Boll, T. J. (1994). Neuropsychological testing in obsessive-compulsive disorder: a clinical review. *Journal of Neuropsychiatry, 6*, 217–228.

Albano, A. M., Knox, L. S., & Barlow, D. H. (1995). Obsessive compulsive disorder. In A. R. Eisen, C. A. Kearney, & C. E. Schaefer (Eds.) *Clinical handbook of anxiety disorders in children and adolescents* (pp. 282–316). Northvale, NJ: Jason Aronson.

Allen, A. J., Leonard, H. L., & Swedo, S. E. (1995). A new infection-triggered, autoimmune subtype of paediatric OCD and Tourette's syndrome. *Journal of the American Academy of Child and Adolescent Psychiatry, 34*, 307–311.

American Psychiatric Association (1994). *Diagnostic and statistical manual of mental disorders* (4th ed.), Washington, DC: American Psychiatric Association.

Arts, W., Hoogduin, K., Schaap, C., & de Haan, E. (1993). Do patients suffering from obsessions alone differ from other obsessive-compulsives? *Behaviour Research and Therapy, 31*, 119–23.

Ball, S. G., Baer, L., & Otto, M. W. (1996). Symptom subtypes of obsessive-compulsive disorder in behavioral treatment studies: a quantitative review. *Behaviour Research and Therapy, 34*, 47–51.

Baron-Cohen, S. (1989). Do autistic children have obsessions and compulsions? *British Journal of Clinical Psychology, 28*, 193–200.

Basoglu, M., Lax, T., Kasvikis Y., & Marks, I. M. (1988). Predictors of improvement in obsessive-compulsive disorder. *Journal of Anxiety Disorders, 2*, 299–317

Baxter, L., Schwartz, J., Mazziotta, J., Phelps, M., Pahl, J., Guze, B., & Fairbanks, L. (1988). Cerebral glucose metabolic rates in nondepressed patients with obsessive-compulsive disorder. *American Journal of Psychiatry, 145*, 1560–1563.

Beck, A. T. (1976). *Cognitive therapy and the emotional disorders*. New York: International Universities Press.

Beck, A. T., Emery, G., & Greenberg, R. L. (1985). *Anxiety disorders and phobias: A cognitive perspective*. New York: Basic Books.

Bellodi, L., Sciuto, G., Diaferia, G., Ronchi, P., & Smeraldi, E. (1992). Psychiatric disorders in the families of patients with obsessive-compulsive disorder. *Psychiatry Research, 42*, 111–120.

Berg, C. Z. (1989). Behavioral assessment techniques for childhood obsessive-compulsive disorder. In J. L. Rapoport (Ed.), *Obsessive–compulsive disorder in children and adolescents* (pp. 41–70). Washington, DC: American Psychiatric Press.

Berg, C. Z., Rapoport, J. L, & Flament, M. (1986). The Leyton Obsessional Inventory Child Version. *Journal of Child Psychology and Psychiatry, 25,* 84–91.

Berg, C. Z., Rapoport, J. L., Whitaker, A., Davies, M., Leonard, H., Swedo, S. E., Braiman, S., & Lenane, M. (1989). Childhood obsessive-compulsive disorder: a two-year prospective follow-up of a community sample. *Journal of the American Academy of Child and Adolescent Psychiatry, 28,* 528–533.

Berg, C. Z., Whitaker, A., Davies, M., Flament, M. F., & Rapoport, J. L. (1988). The survey form of the Leyton Obsessional Inventory–Child Version: norms from an epidemiological study. *Journal of the American Academy of Child and Adolescent Psychiatry, 27,* 759–763.

Berman, L. (1942). Obsessive compulsive neurosis in children. *Journal of Nervous and mental Diseases, 95,* 26–39.

Berrios, G. E. (1995). Obsessive–compulsive disorder. In G. E. Berrios & R. Porter (Eds.), *A history of clinical psychiatry: The origin and history of psychiatric disorders* (pp. 573–592). London: Athlone.

Birmaher, B., Waterman, G., Ryan, N., Cully, M., Balach, L., Ingram, J., & Brodsky, M. (1994). Fluoxetine for childhood anxiety disorders. *Journal of the American Academy of Child and Adolescent Psychiatry, 33,* 993–999.

Black, D. W., Goldstein, R. B., Noyes, R., & Blum, N. (1995). Psychiatric disorders in relatives of probands with obsessive-compulsive disorder and co-morbid major depression or generalized anxiety. *Psychiatric Genetics, 5,* 37–41.

Black, D. W., Noyes, R., Jr., Goldstein, R. B., & Blum, N. (1992). A family study of obsessive-compulsive disorder. *Archives of General Psychiatry, 49,* 362–368.

Bland, R. C., Newman, S. C., & Orn, H. (1988) Life-time prevalence of psychiatric disorders in Edmonton. *Acta Psychiatrica Scandinavica, 77* (Suppl. 338), 24–32.

Bodfish, J. W., Crawford, T. W., Powell, S. B., Parker, D. E., Golden, R. N., & Lewis, M. H. (1995). Compulsions in adults with mental retardation: Prevalence, phenomenology, and comorbidity with stereotypy and self-injury. *American Journal of Mental Retardation, 100,* 183–192.

Bogert, K. V., Katz, K., Amir, N., & Foa, E. B. (1996). Exaggerated responsibility for harm in obsessive--compulsive disorder. Poster presented at the 30th Annual Convention of the Association for the Advancement of Behavior Therapy, New York, November 1996.

Bolton, D. (1994). Family systems interventions. In T. H. Ollendick, W. Yule, & N. King (Eds.), *International handbook of phobic and anxiety disorders of children* (pp. 397–414). New York: Plenum.

Bolton, D. (1995). Self-knowledge, error and disorder. In M. Davies & A. Stone (Eds.), *Mental simulation: Evaluations & applications* (pp. 209–234). Oxford: Blackwell.

Bolton, D. (1996). Annotation: Developmental issues in obsessive-compulsive disorder. *Journal of Child Psychology and Psychiatry, 37,* 131–137.

Bolton, D., Collins, S., & Steinberg, D. (1983). The treatment of obsessive-compulsive disorder in adolescence: A report of fifteen cases. *British Journal of Psychiatry, 142,* 456–464.

Bolton, D., & Hill, J. (1996). *Mind, meaning, and mental disorder: The nature of causal explanation in psychology and psychiatry.* Oxford: Oxford University Press.

Bolton, D., Luckie, M., & Steinberg, D. (1995). Long-term follow-up of obsessive-compulsive disorder treated in adolescence. *Journal of the American Academy of Child and Adolescent Psychiatry, 34,* 1441–1450.

Bolton, D., Luckie, M., & Steinberg, D. (1996). Obsessive-compulsive disorder treated in adolescence: 14 long-term case histories. *Clinical Child Psychology and Psychiatry, 1,* 411–432.

Bolton, D., & Turner, T. (1984). Obsessive–compulsive neurosis with conduct disorder in adolescence: A report of two cases. *Journal of Child Psychology and Pychiatry, 25,* 133–139.

Boone, K., Ananth, J., Philpott, L., Kaur, A., & Djenderedjian, A. (1991) Neuropsychological characteristics of nondrepresed adults with obsessive-compulsive disorder. *Neuropsychiatry, Neuropsychology, and Behavioral Neurology, 4,* 96–109.

Borkovec, T. D., & Inz, J. (1990). The nature of worry in generalized anxiety disorder: a predominance of thought activity. *Behaviour Research and Therapy, 28,* 153–158.

Buchanan, A. W., Ko, S. M., & Marks, I. M. (1996). What predicts improvement and compliance during the behavioral treatment of obsessive-compulsive disorder? *Anxiety, 2,* 22–27.

Calvocoressi, L., Lewis, B., Harris, M., Trufan, S., Goodman, W. K., McDougle, C. J., & Price, L. H. (1995) Family accomodation in obsessive-compulsive disorder. *American Journal of Psychiatry, 152,* 441–443.

Carey, G., & Gottesman, I. (1981). Twin studies of anxiety, phobic, and obsessive disorders. In D. F. Klein & J. Rabkins (Eds.), *Anxiety: new research and changing concepts* (pp. 117–133). New York: Raven Press.

Carr, A. T. (1974). Compulsive neurosis: A review of the literature. *Psychological Bulletin, 81,* 311–318.

Castle, D. J., Deale, A., Marks, I. M., Cutts, F., Chadhoury, Y., & Stewart, A. (1994). Obsessive-compulsive disorder: Prediction of outcome from behavioral psychotherapy. *Acta Psychiatrica Scandinavica, 89,* 393–398.

Cath, D. C., van-de-Wetering, B. J., van-Woerkom, T. C., Hoogduin, C. A., Roos, R. A., & Rooijmans, H. G. (1992). Mental play in Gilles de la Tourette's syndrome and obsessive-compulsive disorder. *British Journal of Psychiatry, 161,* 542–545.

Chakraborty, A., & Banerji, G. (1975). Ritual, a culture-specific neurosis, and obsessional states in Bengali culture. *Indian Journal of Psychiatry, 17,* 211–216.

Chiocca, A. E., & Martuza, R. L. (1990). Neurosurgical therapy of obsessive-compulsive disorder. In M. A. Jenike, L. Baer, & W. E. Minichiello (Eds.), *Obsessive compulsive disorders: Theory and management* (pp. 283–294). Chicago: Yearbook Medical Publishers.

Christensen, K. J., Kim, S. W., Dysken, M. W., & Hoover, K. M. (1992). Neuropsychological performance in obsessive-compulsive disorder. *Biological Psychiatry, 31,* 4–18.

Clark, D. A., & Bolton, D. (1985). Obsessive–compulsive adolescents and their parents: A psychometric study. *Journal of Child Psychology and Psychiatry, 26,* 267–276.

Clark, D. A., & Purdon, C. L. (1995). The assessment of unwanted intrusive thoughts: A review and critique of the literature. *Behaviour Research and Therapy, 33,* 967–976.

Clark, D. A., Sugrim, I., & Bolton, D. (1982). Primary obsessional slowness: A nursing treatment programme with a 13 year old male adolescent. *Behaviour Research and Therapy, 20,* 289–292.

Clifford, C. A., Murray, R. M., & Fulker, D. W. (1984). Genetic and environmental influences on obsessional traits and symptoms. *Psychological Medicine, 14,* 791–800.

Clomipramine Collaborative Study Group (1991). Clomipramine in the treatment of patients with obsessive-compulsive disorder. *Archives of General Psychiatry, 48,* 730–738.

Coles, M. E., Amir, N., & Foa, E. B. (1996). *Factor structure of the Yale–Brown Obsessive–Compulsive Scale (Y-BOCS).* Poster presented at the 30th Annual

Convention of the Association for the Advancement of Behavior Therapy, New York, November 1996.

Coles, M., Bogert, K. V., Krause, M. S., Amir, N., Salkovskis, P., Kozak, M., & Foa, B. (1996). *The Obsessive Compulsive Inventory.* Poster presented at the 30th Annual Convention of the Association for the Advancement of Behavior Therapy, New York, November 1996.

Comings, D. E. (1994). Tourette syndrome: A heriditary neuropsychiatric spectrum disorder. *Annual Clinical Psychiatry, 6,* 235–247.

Comings, D. E., Comings, B. G., Devor, E. J., & Cloninger, C. R. (1984). Detection of a major gene for Gilles de la Tourette syndrome. *American Journal of Human Genetics, 36,* 704–709.

Como, P. G. (1995). Obsessive–compulsive disorder in Tourette's syndrome. In W. J. Weiner & A. E. Lang (Eds.), *Behavioral neurology of movement disorders* (pp. 281–291), *Advances in Neurology, 65.* New York: Raven Press.

Cox, B. J., Swinson, R. P., Morrison, B., & Lee, P. S. (1993). Clomipramine, fluoxetine, and behavior therapy in the treatment of obsessive-compulsive disorder: A meta-analysis. *Journal of Behavior Therapy and Experimental Psychiatry, 24,* 149–153

Cox, C., Fedio, P., & Rapoport, J. L.(1989). Neuropsychological testing of obsessive-compulsive adolescents. In J. L. Rapoport (Ed.), *Obsessive–compulsive disorder in children and adolescents* (pp. 173–85). Washington, DC: American Psychiatric Press.

Denckla, M. (1989). Neurological examination. In J. L. Rapoport (Ed.), *Obsessive–compulsive disorder in children and adolescents* (pp. 107–115). Washington, DC: American Psychiatric Press.

DeVane, C. L., & Sallee, F. R. (1996). Serotonin selective reuptake inhibitors in child and adolescent psychopharmacology: a review of published experience. *Journal of Clinical Psychiatry, 57,* 55–66.

DeVeaugh-Geiss, J., Moroz, G., Biederman, J., Cantwell, D., Fontaine, R., Greist, J., Reichler, R., Katz, R., & Landau, P. (1992). Clomipramine hydrochloride in childhood and adolescent obsessive-compulsive disorder: a multicenter trial. *Journal of the American Academy of Child and Adolescent Psychiatry, 31,* 45–49.

de Silva, P. (1993) Anorexia and obsessive-compulsive disorder. *Neuropsychiatrie de l'Enfance, 41,* 269–272.

Douglass, H. M., Moffitt, T. E., Dar, R., McGee, R., & Silva, P. (1995). Obsessive–compulsive disorder in a birth cohort of 18-year-olds: prevalence and predictors. *Journal of the American Academy of Child and Adolescent Psychiatry, 34,* 1424–1431.

Durlak, J. A., Fuhrman, T., & Lampman, C. (1991). Effectiveness of cognitive-behavior therapy for maladapting children: A meta-analysis. *Psychological Bulletin, 110,* 204–214.

Eapen, V., Pauls, D. L., & Robertson, M. M. (1993). Evidence for autosomal dominant transmission in Tourette's syndrome—United Kingdom Cohort Study. *British Journal of Psychiatry, 162,* 593–596.

Eibl-Eibesfeld, I. (1970). *The biology of behavior* (Trans. E. Klinghammer). New York: Holt, Rinehart and Winston.

Ellis, A. (1962) *Reason and emotion in psychotherapy.* New York: Lyle-Stuart.

Emmelkamp, P., & Beens, H. (1991) Cognitive therapy with obsessive-compulsive disorder: a comparative evaluation. *Behaviour Research and Therapy, 29,* 293–300.

Emmelkamp, P., Visser, S., & Hoekstra, R. (1988). Cognitive therapy vs. exposure *in vivo* in the treatment of obsessive-compulsives. *Cognitive Therapy and Research, 12,* 103–114.

Fals-Stewart, W., & Lucente, S. (1993). An MCMI cluster typology of obsessive-compulsives: A measure of personality characteristics and its relationship to treatment

participation, compliance and outcome in behaviour therapy. *Journal of Psychiatric Ressearch, 27,* 139–154.

Fineberg, N. A., Bullock, T., Montgomery, D. B., & Montgomery, S. A. (1992). Serotonin reuptake inhibitors are the treatment of choice in obsessive-compulsive disorder. *International Clinical Psychopharmacology, 7* (Suppl. 1), 43–47.

Fisher, P. W., Shaffer, D., Piacentini, J. C., Lapkin, J., Kafantaris, V., Leonard, H., & Herzog, D. B. (1993). Sensitivity of the Diagnostic Interview Schedule for Children, 2nd. ed. (DISC-2.1) for specific diagnoses of children and adolescents. *Journal of the American Academy of Child and Adolescent Psychiatry, 32,* 666–673.

Flament, M. F., Koby, E., Rapoport, J. L., Berg, C. J., Zahn, T., Cox, C., Denckla, M., & Lenane, M. (1990). Childhood obsessive-compulsive disorder: a prospective follow-up study. *Journal of Child Psychology and Psychiatry, 31,* 363–380.

Flament, M. F., Rapoport, J. L., Berg, C. Z., Sceery, W., Kilts, C., Mellstrom, B., & Linnoila, M. (1985). Clomipramine treatment of childhood obsessive-compulsive disorder: A double-blind controlled study. *Archives of General Psychiatry, 42,* 977–983.

Flament, M. F., Whitaker, A., Rapoport, J. L., Davies, M., Berg, C. Z., Kalikow, K., Sceery, W., & Shaffer, D. (1988). Obsessive compulsive disorder in adolescence: an epidemiological study. *Journal of the American Academy of Child and Adolescent Psychiatry, 27,* 764–771.

Foa, E. B. (1979). Failures in treating obsessive-compulsives. *Behaviour Research and Therapy, 17,* 169–176.

Foa, E. B., & Kozak, M. J. (1986). Emotional processing of fear: exposure to corrective information. *Psychological Bulletin, 99,* 20–35.

Foa, E. D., & Kozak, M. J. (1995). *DSM-IV field trial:* Obsessive-compulsive disorder. *American Journal of Psychiatry, 152,* 90–96.

Foa, E. D., Kozak, M. J., Goodman, W. K., Hollander, E., Jenike, M. A., & Rasmussen, S. A. (1995). DSM-IV field trial: Obsessive–compulsive disorder. Correction. *American Journal of Psychiatry, 152,* 654.

Foa, E. B., Steketee, G. S., & Ozarow, B. J. (1985). Behavior therapy with obsessive-compulsives: From theory to treatment. In M. Mavissakalian, S. M. Turner, & L. Michelson (Eds.), *Obsessive-compulsive disorder: Psychological and pharmacological treatment* (pp. 49–129). New York: Plenum.

Foa, E. B., Kozak, M. J., Steketee, G. S., & McCarthy, P. R. (1992). Treatment of depressive and obsessive-compulsive symptoms in OCD by imipramine and behaviour therapy. *British Journal of Clinical Psychology, 31,* 279–292.

Fonseca, A. C., Yule, W., & Erol, N. (1994). Cross-cultural issues. In T. H. Ollendick, W. Yule, & N. King (Eds.), *International handbook of phobic and anxiety disorders of children* (pp. 67–44). New York: Plenum.

Foster, C. (1994). *Polly's Magic Games.* Maine: Dilligraff Publications.

Franzblau, S. H., Kanadanian, M., & Rettig, E. (1995). Critique of reductionistic models of obsessive-compulsive disorder: Toward a new explanatory paradigm. *Social Science and Medicine, 41,* 99–112.

Freshman, M. S., Amir, N., Katz, K., & Foa, E. B. (1996). *Family accommodation and rejection in relatives of OCD patients.* Poster presented at the 30th Annual Convention of the Association for the Advancement of Behavior Therapy, New York, November 1996.

Freud, S. (1908). Character and anal eroticism. In J. Strachey (Ed.), *Standard edition of the complete psychological works of Sigmund Freud* (Vol. 9, pp. 169–175). London: Hogarth Press, 1966.

Freud, S. (1913). Totem and taboo. In J. Strachey (Ed.), *Standard edition of the complete psychological works of*

Sigmund Freud, (Vol. 13, pp. 1–62). London: Hogarth Press, 1966.

Garrison, C. Z., Valleni-Basile, L. A., Jackson, K. L., Waller, J. L., McKeown, R. E., Addy, C. L., & Cuffe, S. P. (1995). Frequency of obsessive-compulsive disorder in a community sample of young adolescents: Errata. *Journal of the American Academy of Child and Adolescent Psychiatry, 34,* 128–129.

Geller, D. A., Biederman, J., Reed, E., Spencer, T., & Wilens, T. (1995). Similarities in response to fluoxetine in the treatment of children and adolescents with obsessive-compulsive disorder. *Journal of the American Academy of Child and Adolescent Psychiatry, 34,* 36–44.

Gesell, A., Ames, L., & Ilg, F. (1974). *Infant and child in the culture today.* New York: Harper and Row.

George, M. S., Trimble, M. R., Ring, H. A., Sallee, F. R., & Robertson, M. M. (1993). Obsessions in obsessive-compulsive disorder with and without Gilles de la Tourette's syndrome. *American Journal of Psychiatry, 150,* 93–97.

Goodman, W. K., Price, L. H., Rasmussen, S. A., Mazure, C., Delgado, P., Heninger, G. R., & Charney, D. S. (1989b). The Yale–Brown Obsessive Compulsive Scale (Y-BOCS): Part II. Validity. *Archives of General Psychiatry, 46,* 1012–1016.

Goodman, W. K., Price, L. H., Rasmussen, S. A., Mazure, C., Fleischman, R. L., Hill, C. L., Heninger, G. R., & Charney, D. S. (1989a). The Yale–Brown Obsessive Compulsive Scale (Y-BOCS): Part I. Development, use, and reliability. *Archives of General Psychiatry, 46,* 1006–1011.

Goodman, W. K., Price, L. H., Woods, S. W., & Charney, D. S. (1991). Pharmacologic challenges in obsessive-compulsive disorder. In J. Zohar, T. Insel, & S. Rasmussen (Eds.), *The psychobiology of obsessive-compulsive disorder* (pp. 162–186). New York: Springer.

Greenberg, D. (1984). Are religious compulsions religions or compulsive: A phenomenological study? *American Journal of Psychotherapy, 38,* 524–532.

Grimshaw, L. (1964). Obsessional disorder and neurological illness. *Journal of Neurology, Neurosurgery and Psychiatry, 27,* 229–231.

Haley, J. (1976). *Problem-solving therapy.* San Fransisco: Jossey-Bass.

Halmi, K. A., Eckert, E., Marchi, P., Sampugnaro, V., Apple, R., & Cohen, J. (1991). Comorbidity of psychiatric diagnoses in anorexia nervosa. *Archives of General Psychiatry, 48,* 712–718.

Hansen, A. M., Hoogduin, C. A., Scaap, C. A., & de Haan, E. (1992). Do drop-outs differ from successfully treated obsessive-compulsives? *Behaviour Research and Therapy, 30,* 547–550.

Harris, P. L. (1994). Unexpected, impossible and magical events: children's reactions to causal violations. *British Journal of Developmental Psychology, 12,* 1–7.

Hay, P., Sachdev, P., Cumming, S., Smith, J. S., Lee, T., Kitchener, P., & Matheson, J. (1993). Treatment of obsessive-compuylsive disorder by psychosurgery. *Acta Psychiatrica Scandinavica, 87,* 197–207.

Head, D., Bolton, D., & Hymas, N. (1989). Deficit in cognitive shifting ability in patients with obsessive-compulsive disorder. *Biological Psychiatry, 23,* 323–327.

Henin, A., Kendall, P. C., Flannery-Schroeder, E., Warman, M., Sugarman, A., & Marrs, A. (1996). Cognitive behavioral therapy of OCD in children: A multiple baseline analysis. Poster presented at the 30th Annual Convention of the Association for the Advancement of Behavior Therapy, New York, November 1996.

Hibbs, E. D., Hamburger, S. D., Lenane, M., Rapoport, J. L., Kruesi, M. J. P., Caesar, C. S., & Goldstein, M. J. (1991). Determinants of expressed emotion in families of normal and disturbed children. *Journal of Child Psychology and Psychiatry, 32,* 757–770.

Hoehn-Saric, R., & Benkelfat, C. (1994). Structural and functional brain imaging in obsessive-compulsive disorder. In E. Hollander, J. Zohar, D. Marazziti, & B. Olivier (Eds.), *Current insights in obsessive-compulsive disorder* (pp. 183–211). Chichester, UK: Wiley.

Hoehn-Saric, R., McLeod, D., Zimmerli, W., & Hipsley, P. (1993). Symptoms and physiologic manifestations in obsessive-compulsive patients before and after treatment with clomipramine. *Journal of Clinical Psychiatry, 54,* 272–276.

Holland, H. C. (1974). Displacement activity as a form of abnormal behaviour in animals. In H. R. Beech (Ed.), *Obsessional states* (pp. 161–173). London: Methuen.

Hollander, E., Schiffman, E., Cohen, B., Rivera-Stein, M. A., Rosen, W., Gorman, J. M., Fryer, A. K., Papp, L., & Liebowitz, M. R. (1990). Signs of central nervous system dysfunction in obsessive-compulsive disorder. *Archives of General Psychiatry, 47,* 27–32.

Hollander, E., & Wong, C. M. (1995). Obsessive-compulsive spectrum disorders. *Journal of Clinical Psychiatry, 56,* 3–6.

Hollingsworth, C. E., Tanguay, P. E., Grossman, L., & Pabst, P. (1980). Long-term outcome of obsessive-compulsive disorder in childhood. *Journal of the American Academy of Child and Adolescent Psychiatry, 19,* 134–144.

Hwu, H. G., Yeh, E. K., & Chang, L. Y. (1989). Prevalence of psychiatric disorders in Taiwan. *Acta Psychiatrica Scandinavica, 79,* 136–147.

Hymas, N., Lees, A., Bolton, D., Epps, K., & Head, D. (1991). The neurology of obsessional slowness. *Brain, 114,* 2203–2233.

Inhelder, B., & Piaget, J. (1958). *The growth of logical thinking from childhood to adolesence.* New York: Basic Books.

Insel, T. R. (1988). Obsessive compulsive disorder: neuroethological perspective. *Psychopharmacology Bulletin, 24,* 365–369.

Insel, T. R. (1992). Neurobiology of obsessive-compulsive disorder: a review. *International Clinical Psychopharmacology, 1,* 31–33.

Insel, T. R., & Winslow, J. T. (1992). Neurobiology of obsessive-compulsive disorder. *Psychiatric Clinics of North America, 15,* 813–824.

Jakes, I. (1996). *Theoretical approaches to obsessive-compulsive disorder.* Cambridge: Cambridge University Press.

James, I. A., & Blackburn, I. M. (1995). Cognitive therapy with obsessive-compulsive disorder. *British Journal of Psychiatry, 166,* 444–450.

Janet, P. (1903). *Les obsessions et la psychiasthenie* (Vol. I), Paris: Felix Alan.

Jarry, J. L., & Vaccarino, F. J. (1996). Eating disorder and obsessive-compulsive disorder: neurochemical and phenomonological abnormalities. *Journal of Psychiatry and Neuroscience, 21,* 36–48.

Jenike, M. A., & Brandon, A. D. (1988). Obsessive-compulsive disorder and head trauma: a rare association. *Journal of Anxiety Disorders, 2,* 353–359.

Judd, L. L. (1965). Obsessive compulsive neurosis in children. *Archives of General Psychiatry, 12,* 136–143.

Karno, M., Golding, J. M., Sorenson, S. B., & Burnam, M. A. (1988). The epidemiology of obsessive-compulsive disorder in five US communities. *Archives of General Psychiatry, 45,* 1094–1099.

Keijsers, G., Hoogduin, C., & Schaap, C. (1994). Predictors of treatment outcome in the behavioral treatment of obsessive-compulsive disorder. *British Journal of Psychiatry, 165,* 781–786.

Kendall, P. C., Chansky, T. E., Friedman, M., Kim, R., Kortlander, E., Sessa, F. M., & Siqueland, L. (1991). Treating anxiety disorders in children and adolescents. In P. C. Kendall (Ed.), *Child and adolescent therapy:*

Cognitive-behavioral procedures (pp. 131-164). New York: Guildford Press.

Kendall, P. C., Kane, M., Howard, B., & Siqueland, L. (1989). *Cognitive-behavioral therapy for anxious children: Treatment manual.* Philadelphia: Psychology Department, Temple University.

Keppel-Benson, J. M., & Ollendick, T. H. (1993). Post traumatic stress disorders in children and adolescents. In C. F. Saylor (Ed.), *Children and disasters* (pp. 29-44). New York: Plenum.

Kidd, K. K., & Pauls, D. L. (1982). Genetic hypotheses for Tourette syndrome. In T. N. Chase & A. J. Friedhoff (Eds.), *Gilles de la Tourette syndrome* (pp. 243-249). New York: Raven Press.

King, N., Inglis, S., Jenkins, M., Myerson, N., & Ollendick, T. H. (1995). Test–retest reliability of the survey form of the Leyton Obsessional Inventory–Child Version. *Perceptual Motor Skills, 80,* 1200-1202.

Kringlen, E. (1965). Obsessional neurotics: A long-term follow-up. *British Journal of Psychiatry, 111,* 709-722.

Ladouceur, R., Rheaume, J., & Leger, E. (1996). *Cognitive change during cognitive treatment and behavioral treatment of checking behaviors.* Communication presented at the 30th Annual Convention of the Association for the Advancement of Behavior Therapy, New York, November 1996.

Ladouceur, R., Rheume, J., Freeston, M., Aublet, F., Jean, K., Lachance, S., Langlois, F., & de Pokomandy, K., (1995). Experimental manipulations of responsibility: an analogue test for models of obsessive-compulsive disorder. *Behaviour Research and Therapy, 33,* 937-946.

Last, C. G., Hersen, M., Kazdin, A. E., Orvaschel, H., & Perrin, S. (1991). Anxiety disorders in children and their families. *Archives of General Psychiatry, 48,* 928-934.

Lenane, M. C. (1989). Families and obsessive-compulsive disorder. In J. L. Rapoport (Ed.), *Obsessive–compulsive disorder in children and adolescents* (pp. 237-249). Washington, DC: American Psychiatric Press.

Lenane, M. C., Swedo, S. E., Leonard, H., Pauls, D. L., Sceery, W., & Rapoport, J. L. (1990). Psychiatric disorders in first degree relatives of children and adolescents with obsessive-compulsive disorder. *Journal of American Academy of Child Adolescent Psychiatry, 29,* 407-412.

Leonard, H. L. (1989). Childhood rituals and superstitions: developmental and cultural perspective. In J. L. Rapoport (Ed.), *Obsessive–compulsive disorder in children and adolescents* (pp. 289-309). Washington, DC: American Psychiatric Press.

Leonard, H. L., Goldberger, E. L., Rapoport, J. L., Cheslow, D. L., & Swedo, S. E. (1990). Childhood ruituals: Normal development of obsessive-compulsive symptoms. *Journal of the American Academy of Child and Adolescent Psychiatry, 29,* 17-23.

Leonard, H. L., Lenane, M. C., Swedo, S. E., Rettew, D. C., Gershon, E. S., & Rapoport, J. L. (1992). Tics and Tourette's disorder: A 2 to 7 year follow-up of 54 obsessive-compulsive children. *American Journal of Psychiatry, 149,* 1244-1251.

Leonard, H. L., Swedo, S. E., Lenane, M. C., Rettew, D. C., Hamburger, S. D., Bartko, J., & Rapoport, J. L. (1993). A 2- to 7-year follow-up study of 54 obsessive-compulsive children and adolescents. *Archives of General Psychiatry, 50,* 429-439.

Leonard, H. L., Swedo, S. E., Rapoport, J. L., Koby, E. V., Lenane, M. C., Cheslow, D. L., & Hamburger, S. D. (1989). Treatment of obsessive-compulsive disorder with Clomipramine and Desipramine in children and adolescents. *Archives of General Psychiatry, 46,* 1088-1092.

Lewis, A. (1936). Problems of obsessional illness. *Proceedings of the Royal Society of Medicine, 29,* 325-336.

Lorenz, K. Z. (1966). *On aggression.* New York: Bantam Books.

Lorenz, K. Z. (1981). *The foundations of ethology.* New York: Springer.

Lucey, J. V., Costa, D. C., Blanes, T., Busatto, G. F., Pilowsky, L. S., Takei, N., Marks, I. M., Ell, P. J., & Kerwin, R. W. (1995). Regional cerebral blood flow in obsessive-compulsive disordered patients at rest: differential correlates with obsessive-compulsive and anxious avoidant-dimensions. *British Journal of Psychiatry, 167,* 629-634.

Luxenberg, J., Swedo, S. E., Flament, M., Friedland, R., Rapoport, J. L., & Rapoport, S. (1988). Neuroanatomical abnormalities in obsessive-compulsive disorder detected with quantitative X-ray computed tomography. *American Journal of Psychiatry, 145,* 1089-1093.

Macdonald, A., Murray, R. M., & Clifford, C. A. (1991). The contribution of heredity to obsessional disorder and personality: a review of family and twin study evidence. In K. Kendler, A. M. Tsuang, & M. Lyons (Eds.), *Genetic issues in psychosocial epidemiology* (pp. 191-212). NJ: Rutgers University Press.

Mahgoub, O. M., & Abdel-Hafeiz, H. B. (1991). Patterns of obsessive-compulsive disorder in Eastern Saudi-Arabia. *British Journal of Psychiatry, 158,* 840-842.

March, J. S., Mulle, K., & Herbel, B. (1994). Behavioral psychotherapy for children and adolescents with obsessive-compulsive disorder: An open trial of a new protocol-driven treatment package. *Journal of the American Academy of Child & Adolescent Psychiatry, 33,* 333-341.

Marks, I., Hodgson, R., & Rachman, S. (1975). Treatment of chronic obsessive-compulsive neurosis by in vivo exposure. *British Journal of Psychiatry, 127,* 349-364.

Marks, I. M., Stern, R. S., Mawson, D., Cobb, J., & McDonald, R. (1980). Clomipramine and exposure for obsessive-compulsive rituals. *British Journal of Psychiatry, 136,* 1-25.

Marks, I. M., & Tobena, A. (1990). Learning and unlearning fear: A clinical and evolutionary perspective. *Neuroscience and Biobehavioral Reviews, 14,* 365-384.

Martin, A., Pigott, T. A., Lalonde, F. M., Dalton, I., Dubbert, B., & Murphy, D. L. (1993). Lack of evidence for Huntington's disease-like cognitive dysfunction in obsessive-compulsive disorder. *Biological Psychiatry, 33,* 345-353.

Martin, M., Wiggs, C. L., Altemus, M., Rubenstein, C., & Murphy, D. L. (1995). Working memory as assessed by subject ordered tasks in patients with obsessive-compulsive disorder. *Journal of Clinical Experimental Neuropsychology, 17,* 786-792.

Max, J. E., Smith, W. L., Lindgren, S. D., Robin, D. A., Mattheis, P., Stierwalt, J., & Morrisey, M. (1995). Case study: Obsessive compulsive disorder after severe traumatic head injury in an adolescent. *Journal of the American Academy of Child and Adolescent Psychiatry, 34,* 45-49.

McDonald, R., Marks, I. M., & Blizard, R. (1988). Quality assurance outcome in mental health care: A model for routine use in clinical settings. *Heath Trends, 20,* 111-114.

McDougle, C. J., Kresch, L. E., Goodman, W. K., Naylor, S. T., Volkmar, F. R., Cohen, D. J., & Price, L. H. (1995). A case-controlled study of repetitive thoughts and behaviour in adults with autistic disorder and obsessive-compulsive disorder. *American Journal of Psychiatry, 152,* 772-777.

McFall, M. E., & Wollersheim, J. P. (1979) Obsessive-compulsive neurosis: A cognitive behavioral formulation and approach to treatment. *Cognitive Therapy and Research, 3,* 333-348.

McGuire, P. K., Bench, C., Frith, C. D., Marks, I. M., Frackowiak, R. S. J., & Dolan, R. J. (1994). Functional anatomy of obsessive-compulsive phenomena. *British Journal of Psychiatry, 164,* 459-468.

McKay, D., Danyko, S., Neziroglu, F., & Yaryura-Tobias, J. A. (1995). Factor structure of the Yale–Brown Obsessive–Compulsive Scale: a two dimensional measure. *Behaviour Research and Therapy, 33,* 865–869.

McKeon, J., McGuffin, P., & Robinson, P. (1984). Obsessive–compulsive neurosis following head injury: a report of four cases. *British Journal of Psychiatry, 144,* 190–192.

Merkel, W. T., Pollard, C. A., Wiener, R. L., & Staebler, C. R. (1993). Perceived parental characteristics of patients with obsessive-compulsive disorder, depression, and panic disorder. *Child Psychiatry and Human development, 24,* 49–57.

Miguel, E. C., Coffey, B. J., Baer, L., Savage, C. R., Rauch, S. L., & Jenike, M. A. (1995a). Phenomenology of intentional repetitive behaviours in obsessive-compulsive disorder and Tourette's disorder. *Journal of Clinical Psychiatry, 56,* 246–255.

Miguel, E. C., Stein, M. C., Rauch, S. L., O'Sullivan, R. L., Stern, T. A., & Jenike, M. A. (1995b). Obsessive-compulsive disorder in patients with multiple sclerosis. *Journal of Neuropsychiatry of Clinical Neuroscience, 7,* 507–510.

Montgomery, S. (1994). Pharmacological treatment of obsessive-compulsive disorder. In E. Hollander, J. Zohar, D. Marazziti, & B. Olivier (Eds.), *Current insights in obsessive-compulsive disorder* (pp. 215–225). Chichester, UK: Wiley.

O'Sullivan, G., & Marks, I. (1990). Long-term outcome of phobic and obsessive-compulsive disorders after treatment. In R. Noyes, M. Roth, & G. D. Burrows (Eds.), *Handbook of anxiety, Vol. 4: The treatment of anxiety* (pp. 87–108). Amsterdam: Elsevier Science.

O'Sullivan, G., Noshirvani, H., Marks, I., Monteior, W., & Lelliott, P. (1991). Six year follow-up after exposure and clomipramine therapy for obsessive-compulsive disorder. *Journal of Clinical Psychiatry, 52,* 150–155.

Orley, J., & Wing, J. K., (1979). Psychiatric disorders in two African villages. *Archives of General Psychiatry, 36,* 513–520.

Pauls, D. L., Alsobrook, J. P., Goodman, W., Rasmussen, S., & Leckman, J. F. (1995). A family study of obsessive-compulsive disorder. *American Journal of Psychiatry, 152,* 76–84.

Pauls, D. L., & Leckman, J. (1986). The inheritance of Gilles de la Tourette syndrome and associated behaviors: Evidence for autosomal dominant transmission. *New England Journal of Medicine, 315,* 993–997.

Pauls, D. L., Raymond, C. L., & Robertson, M. (1991). The genetics of obsessive-compulsive disorder: a review. In J. Zohar, T. Insel, & S. Rasmussen (Eds.), *The psychobiology of obsessive-compulsive disorder* (pp. 89–100). New York: Springer.

Pauls, D. L., Towbin, K., Leckman, J., Zahner, G., & Cohen, D. (1986). Gilles de la Tourette syndrome and obsessive-compulsive disorder: Evidence supporting an etiological relationship. *Archives of General Psychiatry, 43,* 1180–1182.

Peterson, B. S. (1995). Neuroimaging in child and adolescent neuropsychiatric disorders. *Journal of the American Academy of Child and Adolescent Psychiatry, 34,* 1560–1576.

Pfeiffer, W. M. (1981). Culture-bound syndromes. In I. Al-Issa (Ed.) *Culture and psychopathology* (pp. 201–218). Baltimore: University Park Press.

Piacentini, J., Gitow, A., Jaffer, M., Graae, M. D., & Whitaker, M. D. (1994). Outpatient behavioral treatment of child and adolescent obsessive-compulsive disorder. *Journal of Anxiety Disorders, 8,* 277–289.

Piaget, J. (1937). *The construction of reality in the child.* Trans. M. Cook. New York: Basic Books, 1954.

Piaget, J. (1960). *The child's conception of physical causality.* London: Routledge and Kegan Paul.

Piccinelli, M., Pini, S., Bellantuono, C., & Wilkinson, G. (1995). Efficacy of drug treatment in obsessive-compulsive disorder: A meta-analytic review. *British Journal of Psychiatry, 166,* 424–443.

Pitman, R. K. (1987). A cybernetic model of obsessive-compulsive psychopathology. *Comprehensive Psychiatry, 28,* 334–343.

Pitman, R. K. (1993). Post-traumatic obsessive-compulsive disorder: A case study. *Comprehensive Psychiatry, 34,* 102–107.

Pollitt, J. (1957). Natural history of obsessional states—a study of 150 cases. *British Medical Journal, 26,* 194–198.

Price, R. A., Kidd, K. K., Cohen, D. J., Pauls, D. L., & Leckman J. F. (1985). A twin study of Tourette syndrome. *Archives of General Psychiatry, 42,* 815–820.

Prochaska, J., & DiClemente, C., (1982). Transtheoretical therapy: toward a more integrative model of change. *Psychotherapy: Theory, Research and Practice, 19,* 276–288.

Prochaska, J., DiClemente, C. & Norcross, J. (1992). In search of how people change: Applications to addictive behaviors. *American Psychologist, 47,* 1102–1114.

Rachman, S. (1974). Primary obsessional slowness. *Behaviour Research and Therapy, 12,* 9–18.

Rachman, S. (1993). Obsessions, responsibility and guilt. *Behaviour Research and Therapy, 31,* 149–154.

Rachman, S. J. (1985). An overview of clinical and research issues in obsessional-compulsive disorders. In M. Mavissakaliah, S. M. Turner, & L. Michelson (Eds.), *Obsessive–compulsive disorder: Psychological and pharmacological treatment* (pp. 1–47). New York: Plenum Press.

Rachman, S., & Hodgson, R. (1980). *Obsessions and compulsions.* Englewood Cliffs, NJ: Prentice-Hall.

Rapoport, J. L. (1990). Obsessive compulsive disorder and basal ganglia dysfunction. *Psychological Medicine, 20,* 465–469.

Rapoport, J. L, Leonard, H. L., Swedo, S. E., & Lenane, M. C. (1993). Obsessive compulsive disorder in children and adolescents: Issues in management. *Journal of Clinical Psychiatry, 54,* 27–29.

Rapoport, J. L., Swedo, S. E., & Leonard, H. L. (1992). Childhood Obsessive compulsive disorder. *Journal of Clinical Psychiatry, 56,* 11–16.

Rapoport, J. L., & Wise, S. (1988). Obsessive–compulsive disorder: Evidence for basal ganglia dysfunction. *Psychopharmacology Bulletin, 24,* 380–384.

Rasmussen, S. A., & Eisen, J. L. (1990). Epidemiology and clinical features of obsessive-compulsive disorder. In M. A. Jenike, L. Baer, & W. E. Minichiello (Eds.), *Obsessive compulsive disorders: Theory and management* (pp. 10–27). Chicago: Yearbook Medical Publishers.

Rasmussen, S. A., Eisen, J. L., & Pato, M. T. (1993). Current issues in the pharmacologic management of obsessive-compulsive disorder. *Journal of Clinical Psychiatry, 54,* 4–9.

Rasmussen, S. A., & Tsuang, M. T. (1986). DSM-III obsessive-compulsive disorder: clinical characteristics and family history. *American Journal of Psychiatry, 143,* 317–322.

Rauch, S. L., & Jenike, M. A. (1993). Neurobiological models of obsessive-compulsive disorder. *Psychosomatics, 34,* 20–32.

Reed, G. F. (1977). Obsessional personality disorder and remembering. *British Journal of Psychiatry, 130,* 184–185.

Reich, J. H., & Vasile, R. G. (1993). Effect of personality disorders on the treatment outcome of axis I conditions: An update. *Journal of Nervous and Mental Diseases, 181,* 475–484.

Rettew, D. C., Swedo, S. E., Leonard, H. L., Lenane, M. C., & Rapoport, J. L. (1992). Obsessions and compulsions across time in 79 children and adolescents with obsessive-compulsive disorder. *Journal of the American Academy of Child and Adolescent Psychiatry, 31,* 1050–1056.

Riddle, M. A., Scahill, L., King, R. A., Hardin, M. T., Anderson, G. M., Ort, S. I., Smith, J. C., Leckman, J. F., & Cohen, D. J. (1992). Double blind crossover trial of fluoxetine and placebo in children and adolescents with obsessive-compulsive disorder: a multicenter trial. *Journal of the American Academy of Child and Adolescent Psychiatry, 31,* 1062–1069.

Riddle, M. A., Scahill, L., King, R., Hardin, M. T., Towbin, K. E., Ort, S. I., Leckman, J. F., & Cohen, D. J. (1990). Obsessive compulsive disorder in children and adolescents: Phenomenology and family history. *Journal of American Academy of Child Adolescent Psychiatry, 29,* 766–772.

Riggs, D. S., & Foa, E. B. (1993). Obsessive compulsive disorder. In D. H. Barlow (Ed.), *Clinical handbook of psychological disorders* (pp. 189–239). New York: Guildford Press.

Robins, L. N., Helzer, J. E., Weissman, M. M., Orvaschel, H., Gruenberg, E., Burke, J. D., & Regier, D. A. (1984). Life-time prevalence of specific psychiatric disorders in three sites. *Archives of General Psychiatry, 41,* 958–967.

Robinson, D., Wu, H., Munne, R. A., Ashtari, M., Alvir, J., Lerner, G., Koreen, A., Cole, K., & Bogerts, B. (1995). Reduced caudate nucleus volume in obsessive-compulsive disorder. *Archives of General Psychiatry, 52,* 393–398.

Rubenstein, C., Altmeus, M., Piggott, T., Hess, A., & Murphy, D. (1995). Symptom overlap between OCD and bulimia nervosa. *Journal of Anxiety Disorders, 9,* 1–9.

Rubin, R. T., Villanueva-Meyer, J., Ananth, J., Trajmar, P. G., & Mena, I. (1992). Regional xenon 133 cerebral blood flow and cerbral technetium ^{99m}Tc-HMPAO uptake in umedicated patients with obsessive-compulsive disorder and matched normal control subjects: determination by high resolution single-photon emission computed tomography. *Archives of General Psychiatry, 49,* 695–702.

Rudin, E. (1953). Ein Beitrag zur Frage der Zwangskrankenheit insebesondere inhrere hereditaren Beziehungen. *Archives Psychiatrische Nervenkrankheit, 91,* 14–54.

Russell, G., Szmukler, G., Dare, C., & Eisler, I. (1987). An evaluation of family therapy in anorexia nervosa and bulimia nervosa. *Archives of General Psychiatry, 44,* 1047–1056.

Rutter, M., Tizard, J., & Whitmore, K. (1970). *Education, health and behaviour.* London: Longmans.

Salkovskis, P. (1985). Obsessional–compulsive problems: cognitive-behavioural analysis. *Behaviour Research and Therapy, 23,* 571–583.

Salkovskis, P., & Warwick, H. (1985). Cognitive therapy of obsessive-compulsive disorder: Treating treatment failures. *Behavioural Psychotherapy, 13,* 243–255.

Salkovskis, P., & Westbrook, D. (1989). Behaviour therapy and obsessional ruminations: Can failure be turned into success? *Behaviour Research and Therapy, 27,* 149–160.

Santangelo, S. L., Pauls, D. L., Goldstein, J. M. Faraone, S. V. Tsuang, M. T., & Leckman, J. F. (1994). Tourette's syndrome: What are the influences of gender and comorbid obsessive-compulsive disorder? *Journal of the American Academy of Child and Adolescent Psychiatry, 33,* 794–804.

Schneier, F. R., Chin, S. J., Hollander, E., & Liebowitz, M. R. (1992). Fluoxetine in social phobia. *Journal of Clinical Psychopharmacology, 12,* 62–64.

Schut, A. J., & Castonguay, L. G. (1996). *Alexithymia in generalized anxiety disorder: The role of compulsive checking behaviors.* Poster presented at the 30th Annual Convention of the Association for the Advancement of Behavior Therapy, New York, November 1996.

Sharma, B. P. (1968). Obsessive–compulsive neurosis in

Nepal. *Transcultural Research Review, 5,* 38–41.

Sher, K., Frost, R., & Otto, R. (1983). Cognitive deficits in compulsive checkers: An exploratory study. *Behaviour Research and Therapy, 21,* 357–363.

Silverman, W. K. (1991). Diagnostic reliability of anxiety disorders in children using structured interviews. *Journal of Anxiety Disorders, 5,* 105–124.

Silverman, W. K., & Nelles, W. B. (1988). The anxiety disorders interview schedule for children. *Journal of American Academy of Child and Adolescent Psychiatry, 27,* 772–778.

Solyom, L., Freeman, R. J., & Miles, J. E. (1982). A comparative psychometric study of anorexia nervosa and obsessive neurosis. *Canadian Journal of Psychiatry, 27,* 282–286.

Stanley, M. A., & Turner, S. M. (1995). Current status of pharmacological and behavioral treatment of obsessive-compulsive disorder. *Behavior Therapy, 26,* 163–186.

Stein, D. J., Spadaccini, E., & Hollander, E. (1995). Meta-analysis of pharmacotherapy trials for obsessive-compulsive disorder. *International Clinical Psychopharmacology, 10,* 11–18.

Steketee, G., Chambless, D. L., Tran, G. Q., Worden, H., & Gillis, M. M. (1996). Behavioral avoidance test for obsessive-compulsive disorder. *Behaviour Research and Therapy, 34,* 73–83.

Stern, R. S., & Cobb, J. P. (1978) Phenomenology of obsessive-compulsive neurosis. *British Journal of Psychiatry, 132,* 233–239.

Suess, L., & Halpern, M. S. (1989). Obsessive–compulsive disorder: a religious perspective. In J. L. Rapoport (Ed.), *Obsessive-compulsive disorder in children and adolescents* (pp. 311–325). Washington, DC: American Psychiatric Press.

Swedo, S. E., Leonard, H. L., & Rapoport, J. L., (1990). Childhood onset obsessive-compulsive disorder. In M. A. Jenike, L. Baer, & W. E. Minichiello (Eds.), *Obsessive-compulsive disorders: theory and management* (pp. 28–38). Chicago: Medcal Yearbook Publishers.

Swedo, S. E., Pietrini, P., Leonard, H. H., Schapiro, M. B., Rettew, D. C., Goldberger, E. L., Rapoport, S. I., Rapoport, J. L., & Grady, C. L. (1992). Cerebral glucose metabolism in childhood-onset obsessive-compulsive disorder. Revisualization during pharmacotherapy. *Archives of General Psychiatry, 49,* 690–694.

Swedo, S. E., Rapoport, J. L., Cheslow, D. L., Leonard, H. L., R. Ayoub, E. M., Hosier, D. M., & Wald, E. (1989). High prevalence of obsessive-compulsive symptoms in patients with Sydenham's chorea. *American Journal of Psychiatry, 146,* 246–249.

Swedo, S. E., Rapoport, J. L., Leonard, H., Lenane, M., & Cheslow, D. (1989). Obsessive–compulsive disorder in children and Adolescents: Clinical phenomenology of 70 consecutive cases. *Archives of General Psychiatry, 46,* 335–341

Tallis, F. (1995). *Understanding obsessions and compulsions.* London: Sheldon Press.

Tallis, F., & de Silva, P. (1992). *Worry and obsessional symptoms: A correlational analysis. Behaviour Research and Therapy, 30,* 103–105.

Thiel, A., Broocks, A., Ohlmeier, M., Jacoby, G., & Schussler, G. (1995). Obsessive–compulsive-disorder among patients with anorexia nervosa and bulimia nervosa. *American Journal of Psychiatry, 152,* 72–75.

Thomsen, P. H. (1992). Obsessive–compulsive disorder in adolescence. Differential diagnostic considerations in relation to schizophrenia and manic-depressive disorder: A comparison of phenomenology and sociodemographic characteristics. *Psychopathology, 25,* 301–310.

Thomsen, P. H. (1995a). Obsessive–compulsive disorder in children and adolescents: A 6-22 year follow-up study of social outcome. *European Child and Adolescent Psychiatry, 4,* 112–122.

Thomsen, P. H. (1995b). Obsessive–compulsive disorder in children and adolescents: A study of parental psychopathology and precipitating events in 20 consecutive Danish cases. *Psychopathology, 28,* 161–167.

Thomsen, P. H., & Jensen, J. (1991). Latent class analysis of organic aspects of obsessive-compulsive disorder in children and adolescents. *Acta Psychiatrica Scandinavica, 84,* 391–395.

Thomsen, P. H., & Mikkelsen, H. U. (1991). Children and adolescents with obsessive-compulsive disorder: the demographic and diagnostic characteristics of 61 Danish patients. *Acta Psychiatrica Scandinavica, 83,* 262–266.

Thomsen, P. H., & Mikkelsen, H. U. (1995). Course of obsessive-compulsive disorder in children and adolescents: A prospective follow-up study of 23 Danish cases. *Journal of the American Academy of Child and Adolescent Psychiatry, 34,* 1432–1440.

Tinbergen, N. (1953). *Social behaviour in animals.* London: Chapman and Hall.

Torgerson, S. (1980). The oral, obsessive and hysterical personality-syndromes: A study of hereditary and environmental factors by means of the twin method. *Archives of General Psychiatry, 37,* 1272–1277.

Tynes, L., White, K., & Steketee, G. (1990). Toward a new nosology of obsessive-compulsive disorder. *Comprehensive Psychiatry, 31,* 465–480.

Valleni-Basile, L. A., Garrison, C. Z., Jackson, K. L., Waller, J. L., Mckeown, R. E., Addy, C. L., & Cuffe, S. P. (1994). Frequency of obsessive-compulsive disorder in a community sample of young adolescents. *Journal of the American Academy of Child and Adolescent Psychiatry, 33,* 782–91.

Valleni-Basile, L. A., Garrison, C. Z., Jackson, K. L., Waller, J. L., McKeown, R. E., Addy, C. L., & Cuffe, S. P. (1995). Family and psychosocial predictors of obsessive-compulsive disorder in a community sample of young adolescents. *Journal of Child and Family Studies, 4,* 193–206.

Van Oppen, P., & Arntz, A. (1994). Cognitive therapy for obsessive-compulsive disorder. *Behaviour Research and Therapy, 32,* 79–87.

Van Oppen, P., de Haan, E., van Balkom, A., Spinhoven, P., Hooghuin, K., & van Dyck, R. (1995). Cognitive therapy and exposure in vivo in the treatment of obsessive-compulsive disorder. *Behaviour Research and Therapy, 33,* 379–390.

Van Oppen, P., Emmelkamp, P., van Balkom, J., & van Dyck, R. (1995). The sensitivity to change of measures for obsessive-compulsive disorder. *Journal of Anxiety Disorders, 9,* 241–248.

Vasey, M. W. (1993). Development and cognition in childhood anxiety: The example of worry. In T. H. Ollendick & R. J. Prinz (Eds.), *Advances in clinical child psychology* (Vol. 15, pp. 1–39). New York: Plenum.

Veale, D. (1993). Classification and treatment of obsessional slowness. *British Journal of Psychiatry, 162,* 198–203.

Vitiello, B., Spreat, S., & Behar, D. (1989). Obsessive-compulsive disorder in mentally retarded patients. *Journal of Nervous and Mental Disease, 177,* 232–236.

von Economo, C. (1931). *Encephalitis lethargica: its sequelae and treatment.* Oxford: Oxford University Press.

Vygotsky, L. (1934). *Thought and Language,* Trans. E. Hanfmann & G. Vakar. Cambridge, MA: MIT Press, 1962.

Warren, W. (1965). A study of psychiatric inpatients and the outcome six or more years later: II. The follow-up study. *Journal of Child Psychology and Psychiatry, 6,* 141–160.

Wever, C., & Phillips, N. (1994). *The secret problem.* Sydney, NSW: Shrink-Rap Press.

Wever, C., & Rey, J. (in press). Outcome of a combined treatment in juvenile obsessive-compulsive disorder. *Australian and New Zealand Journal of Psychiatry.*

White, M., & Epston, D. (1990). *Narrative means to therapeutic ends.* New York: Norton.

Winslow, J. T., & Insel, T. (1991). Neuroethological models of obsessive-compulsive disorder. In J. Zohar, T. Insel, & S. Rasmussen (Eds.), *The psychobiology of obsessive-compulsive disorder* (pp. 208–226). New York: Springer.

Wolff, R. P., & Wolff, L. S. (1991). Assessment and treatment of obsessive-compulsive disorder in children. *Behavior Modification, 15,* 372–393.

Woodruff, R., & Pitts, F. (1964). Monozygotic twins with obsessional illness. *American Journal of Psychiatry, 120,* 1075–1080.

Woody, S. R, Steketee, G., & Chambless, D. L. (1995). Reliability and validity of the Yale–Brown Obsessive–Compulsive Scale. *Behaviour Research and Therapy, 33,* 597–605.

World Health Organization (1988). *Mental, behavioral, and developmental disorders: Clinical descriptives and diagnostic guidelines (ICD-10).* Geneva, Switzerland: World Health Organization, Division of Mental Health.

Young, J., Fenton, F., & Lader, M. (1971). The inheritance of neurotic traits. *British Journal of Psychiatry, 119,* 393–398.

Zeitlin, H. (1986). *The natural history of psychiatric disorder in children.* Oxford: Oxford University Press.

5.16
Post-traumatic Stress Disorder

SEAN G. PERRIN, PATRICK A. SMITH, and WILLIAM YULE
Institute of Psychiatry, London, UK

5.16.1 INTRODUCTION

The period from the 1970s to the 1990s has shown that children react to life-threatening stressors with various forms of distress, anxiety, fears, depression, and bereavement reactions, as well as post-traumatic stress disorder (PTSD). The form of PTSD varies somewhat according to the age of the child and, sadly, the internal distress often goes unrecognized for long periods by parents and teachers. Indeed, one reason for the initial doubt whether PTSD occurred in children at all was that few investigators had asked children directly how they were affected.

Although post-traumatic stress reactions have been known to occur for centuries, our understanding of people's reactions to life-threatening experiences have been advanced in the aftermath of the major wars of the twentieth century. It was not until the persisting problems of Vietnam veterans were better documented that it was realized that three major groups of symptoms exist: distressing recurring recollections of traumatic events, avoidance of trauma-related stimuli, and a range of symptoms associated with increased arousal. These came to be known as PTSD (American Psychiatric Association, 1980).

Since its inclusion in the third edition of the *Diagnostic and statistical manual for mental disorders* (*DSM-III*) (American Psychiatric Association, 1980), PTSD has been the subject of much debate regarding its validity, etiology, placement among the anxiety disorders, and even its status as a "true" mental disorder (Yehuda & McFarlane, 1995). Nowhere has the controversy over the validity of PTSD as a diagnostic entity been greater than in the child trauma literature (Pynoos, 1994). This is due in part to the observation that the reactions commonly observed in traumatized children are so much wider than the narrow confines described under PTSD in the various revisions of the *DSM* and the *International classification of diseases* (*ICD-10*) (World Health Organization, 1992; Yule, 1994). Moreover, some have suggested that children are so resilient that even when they experience an acutely stressful event, they develop, at worst, some sort of transient reaction disorder (Garmezy, 1984; Garmezy & Rutter, 1985).

Despite the controversy, PTSD is a very useful framework for describing and understanding childrens' reactions to a wide range of life-threatening experiences. Research since the mid-1970s suggests that significant and often chronic symptoms of PTSD are found among children following exposure to war (Arroyo & Eth, 1985; Kinzie, Sack, Angell, Manson, & Rath, 1986; Saigh, 1989a, 1991), natural disaster (Earls, Smith, Reich, & Young, 1988; Frederick, 1985a; Galante & Foa, 1986; Goenjian; 1993; Green et al., 1991; Lonigan, Shannon, Finch, Daugherty, & Saylor, 1991; McFarlane, 1987; Milne, 1977; Newman, 1976), manmade and transportation disasters (Handford et al., 1986; Parry-Jones, 1996; Terr, 1979, 1983; Yule; 1992), violence and violent crime (Malmquist, 1986; Pynoos & Eth, 1988; Schwarz & Kowalski, 1991), sexual abuse (Goodwin, 1988; McLeer, Deblinger, Henry, & Orvaschel,

1992; Wolfe, Gentile, & Wolfe; 1989), and serious medical illness (Nir, 1984; Stuber, Nader, Yashuda, Pynoos, & Cohen, 1991). Still, there remain considerable gaps in our understanding of the disorder in children, particularly in regard to its developmental, neurobiological, and physiological manifestations across those of various ages and abilities.

In this chapter, the literature on childhood PTSD is highlighted and reviewed with a view to increasing the reader's understanding of the phenomenology, assessment, and treatment of the disorder. However, an exhaustive review of the issues pertinent to the manifestation of PTSD following specific types of traumas (e.g., war, torture, natural disaster, and sexual assault) is beyond the scope of this chapter. The reader should be aware that significant differences exist in the clinical presentation and treatment of children with specific trauma histories.

5.16.2 PTSD

5.16.2.1 Phenomenology of Stress Reactions in Children and Adolescents

From their experience working with child and adolescent survivors of the "Herald of Free Enterprise" car ferry sinking (Yule & Williams, 1990), the sinking of the cruise ship, "Jupiter" (Yule, 1992; Yule, Udwin, & Murdoch, 1990), war-affected children of the former Yugoslavia (Smith, Yule, Perrin, & Schwarz, 1996), and childhood survivors of serious road traffic accidents in Britain (Perrin, Yule, & Smith, 1996b; Yule, Perrin, & Smith, 1996), Yule and colleagues have noted a number of reactions that are common in children exposed to traumatic events.

Most children are troubled by repetitive, intrusive thoughts about the trauma. Such thoughts can occur at any time, but particularly when the children are otherwise quiet, as when they are trying to fall asleep. At other times, the thoughts and vivid recollections are triggered off by reminders in their environment. Sleep disturbances are very common, particularly within the first few weeks of the event. Fears of the dark, bad dreams, nightmares, and waking through the sleep cycle are widespread. Separation difficulties are frequent, even among teenagers. For the first few days, children may not want to let their parents out of their sight, even reverting to sleeping in the parents' bed. Many children become much more irritable and angry with parents and peers alike.

Although child survivors often experience a pressure to talk about their experiences, paradoxically they also find it very difficult to talk with parents and peers. Often they do not want to upset the adults, and so parents may not be aware of the full extent of their childrens' suffering. Peers may hold back from asking what happened lest they upset the child further; the survivor often takes this as a subtle form of rejection.

Children report a number of cognitive changes. Many experience difficulties in concentration, especially in school work. Others report memory problems, both in mastering new material and in remembering previously learned skills such as reading music. They become very alert to danger in their environment, being adversely affected by reports of other related traumatic events. Survivors often learn that life is quite fragile, particularly if they sustained any permanent form of injury or witnessed the death of another. This can lead to a sense of a foreshortened future, often expressed as a loss of thoughts about the future. Life priorities frequently change in response to trauma, with some feeling that they should live each day to the full and not plan for the future. Others realize that they have been overconcerned with materialistic or petty matters and resolve to rethink their values, frequently taking on the image of themselves as a helper to others. Such ways of thinking may reflect a change in the child's "assumptive world" (cf., Janoff-Bulman, 1992).

Not surprisingly, many children develop fears associated with specific aspects of the traumatic event(s), with phobic levels of avoidance to trauma-related stimuli and reminders. Many experience "survivor guilt" about others dying or being seriously injured, or think they should have done more to help others to survive. Adolescent survivors report significantly high levels of depression, some becoming clinically depressed, having suicidal thoughts, and taking overdoses in the year after a disaster. A significant number become very anxious after the trauma, although the appearance of panic attacks is sometimes considerably delayed.

In summary, children and adolescents surviving a life threatening trauma show a wide range of symptoms which tend to cluster around symptoms of re-experiencing, avoidance of trauma-related cues and emotions, and increased physiological arousal. There may be considerable comorbidity with depression, generalized anxiety, or pathological grief reactions as well.

5.16.2.1.1 Age and gender-related effects of trauma on children

While there have been relatively few systematic studies examining the impact of trauma at different stages of development, there do appear to be important age-related differences in the expression of PTSD (see Lyons, 1987 and Terr, 1991 for reviews). Schwarz and Perry (1994) have suggested that infants and very young children are more sensitive to emotional states and behavior of parental caregivers than to assessments of danger. As such, a trauma to either the child or primary caregiver may result in global dysfunction, apathy and failure to thrive, excessive crying, eating and sleeping, psychophysiological lability, and overstimulation (Schwarz & Perry, 1994).

Among toddlers and preschool children, high levels of dependency (clinginess) and separation anxiety are frequent, with regressive behaviors such as bed-wetting, baby-talk, and thumbsucking also observed. Diarrhea and frequent somatic complaints may be noted, as well as irritability, sleep problems, and fearfulness. Some children may show delays in cognitive and language development (Law & Conway, 1992) and mutism (Eth & Pynoos, 1985). Reenactment of the trauma through play and difficulty with verbal descriptions of the trauma are common. Many preschool children show a loss of interest in activities and hobbies that previously gave them pleasure. Although some have suggested that emotional numbing may be rare in this age group, this may be an artifact of the difficulty researchers have found eliciting evidence of such symptoms in young children (Frederick, 1985a).

In reviewing data from the Buffalo Creek Disaster, Green et al. (1991) noted that preschoolers had fewer PTSD symptoms overall, and in particular avoidance symptoms, than older children. They hypothesized that it may be more difficult to observe avoidant symptoms (as well as dissociation and emotional numbing) in this age group. Consistent with Schwarz and Perry's hypothesis (1994), the preschool child's perception of the dangerousness of the trauma (i.e., life threat) was not correlated with PTSD symptoms, while life threat was positively associated with PTSD symptoms in school-aged children and adolescents (Green et al.).

Relative to preschool children, those of school age may show an increased frequency of trauma-related nightmares, preoccupation with the trauma, vacillation between withdrawal and aggressive outbursts, and avoidant behaviors (Lyons, 1987). Somatic complaints may be less frequent, and this may be related to an increased verbal ability to describe the trauma. Children of this age can begin to appreciate the irreversibility of tragic events and may exhibit more overt signs of depressed mood and hopelessness.

Given that concentration difficulties are characteristic of PTSD (American Psychiatric Association, 1994), one might expect that children's school work would suffer after a traumatic event. However, Martin and Little (1986) found no differences in scholastic attainment across three groups of 9–10 year-old children with varying degrees of exposure, two months after a tornado. The authors speculated that this may have been the result of the community pulling together in the face of the trauma, and because children were relocated to new schools where teachers were instructed to discuss the children's experiences of the tornado (Martin & Little, 1986).

Among adolescents, there is an increased frequency of adult-like PTSD symptoms, problems with compliance and withdrawal, aggressiveness, substance abuse, and increased feelings of guilt. Problems of identity, eating, self-mutilation, and personality may also be noted (Schwarz & Perry, 1994). In contrast to younger children, there is generally an absence of traumatic play. In addition, there is clearer evidence of impaired academic performance post-trauma in adolescents. Girls who survived the sinking of the Jupiter who were above average in performance during the three years before the sinking, plummeted significantly to merely average levels one year after the disaster (Yule, 1992). Two years after the accident, the 16-year old survivors still performed less well in national school exams, although the difference with pretrauma performance was no longer as marked (Tsui, 1990).

With respect to gender, girls consistently score higher across measures of post-traumatic distress, anxiety, and depression than boys in a number of studies, including children exposed to a shipping disaster (Yule, 1992), a hurricane (Lonigan et al., 1991), flood (Green et al., 1991), an earthquake (Pynoos et al., 1993), and war in former Yugoslavia (Smith et al., 1996). One study (Burke, Moccia, Borus, & Burns, 1986) did find boys' distress to be higher than girls five months after a flood; however, this pattern reversed at a follow-up assessment five months later.

5.16.2.1.2 Cultural factors in the expression of PTSD

There has been some debate over the appropriateness of using PTSD to characterize the traumatic reactions of children from non-Western countries (see Eisenberg, 1996 and Summerfield, 1996). Unfortunately, there are few empirical investigations from which to draw firm conclusions. Studies of children's fears more generally suggest that the most common

fears are the same across different countries and cultures (see Fonesca, Yule, & Erol, 1994 for a review). Indeed, the current literature suggests that there are remarkably few psychiatric disorders which are culture-specific (Leff & Bhugura, 1993). However, the question remains whether the traumatic reactions observed in children across different cultures are more similar than different and when such reactions should be considered abnormal or pathological.

Working with a core set of self-report instruments to screen children in exceptionally difficult circumstances, Yule, Pynoos, and others have begun to study this issue more directly. The Impact of Events Scale (IES) (Horowitz, Wilner, & Alvarez, 1979) has been modified for use with children in both civilian and war situations. Examining data from studies of war affected children in Iraq, Kuwait, and the former Yugoslavia, it was found that the IES factor structures obtained from children in Iraq (Dyregrov & Yule, 1995) and Yugoslavia (Perrin, Smith, Schwartz, & Yule 1996a) were identical to that obtained from British children who had survived the Jupiter shipping disaster. In addition, the number of war traumas reported by children from Yugoslavia was positively correlated with levels of distress on translated versions of the IES, Birleson Depression Inventory (Birleson, 1981), and Revised Children's Manifest Anxiety Scale (Reynolds & Richmond, 1978) (Perrin et al., 1996a). Moreover, this battery of instruments proved sensitive to pre–post-treatment changes in Yugoslavian children who participated in cognitive behavioral treatment (Dyregrov & Yule, 1995).

Finally, Pynoos and colleagues observed that child survivors of the Armenian earthquake not only show the classic symptoms of PTSD as measured with structured interview and self-report questionnaires, but also show greatly increased salivary cortisol levels and disturbed basal heart rates (Pynoos et al., 1993). The presence of these physiological markers of hyperarousal, which are presumably less affected by cultural influences than scores on translated self-report inventories, lends considerable support to the argument for PTSD symptoms manifesting across cultures. Of course, assessments and interventions should be culture-sensitive. As suggested by Parry-Jones (1996), labeling clinically significant stress reactions need not be stigmatizing and indeed may ensure that appropriate treatment services are offered.

5.16.2.2 Diagnostic Features

PTSD first entered the diagnostic nomenclature with its appearance in *DSM-III* (American

Psychiatric Association, 1980), appearing in the anxiety disorders section. The criteria were based largely on a then emerging body of research with adult trauma survivors, particularly combat veterans. Under *DSM-III*, PTSD was characterized by: (i) the experience of a traumatic event outside the range of usual human experience; (ii) distressing and recurring recollections of the traumatic event; (iii) numbing of responsiveness and/or reduced involvement with the external world; and (iv) at least two of a variety of symptoms including survivor guilt, sleep disturbances, hyperarousal, avoidance of trauma-related stimuli, and impaired concentration (Lyons, 1987). However, few and vague descriptions of the manifestations of PTSD in children of different ages were noted, owing to the paucity of methodologically sound research available on children's reactions to traumatic events.

The third revised edition of the *DSM* (*DSM-III-R*) (American Psychiatric Association, 1987) was the first to note the occurrence of PTSD in children but the specific criteria remained largely unchanged. Rather, the revisions involved a reorganization of the existing symptoms under re-experiencing, numbing and avoidance, and increased arousal categories (Lyons, 1987). However, there were two exceptions. First, a "sense of a foreshortened future" was added based on research with the children of the Chowchilla bus kidnaping (Lyons, 1987). Second, and unfortunately, "survival guilt" was removed, although this symptom is found frequently in both children and adults presenting with PTSD (Yule, 1994).

Under *DSM-IV* (American Psychiatric Association, 1994), the requirements for meeting a diagnosis of PTSD have changed considerably from its predecessors. The *DSM-IV* criteria for PTSD are as follows:

(i) The person has been exposed to a traumatic event in which both of the following have been present:

(a) The person has experienced, witnessed, or been confronted with an event or events that involve actual or threatened death or serious injury, or a threat to the physical integrity of oneself or others.

(b) The person's response involved intense fear, helplessness, or horror. Note: In children, it may be expressed by disorganized or agitated behavior.

(ii) The traumatic event is persistently re-experienced in at least one of the following ways:

(a) Recurrent and intrusive distressing recollections of the event, including images, thoughts, or perceptions. Note: In young children, repetitive play may occur in which themes or aspects of the trauma are expressed.

(b) Recurrent distressing dreams of the event. Note: In children, there may be frightening dreams without recognizable content.

(c) Acting or feeling as if the traumatic event were recurring (includes a sense of reliving the experience, illusions, hallucinations, and dissociative flashback episodes, including those that occur upon awakening or when intoxicated). Note: In young children, trauma specific re-enactment may occur.

(d) Intense psychological distress at exposure to internal or external cues that symbolize or resemble an aspect of the traumatic event.

(e) Physiological reactivity upon exposure to internal or external cues that symbolize or resemble an aspect of the traumatic event.

(iii) Persistent avoidance of stimuli associated with the trauma and numbing of general responsiveness (not present before the trauma), as indicated by at least three of the following:

(a) Efforts to avoid thoughts, feelings, or conversations associated with the trauma.

(b) Efforts to avoid activities, places, or people that arouse recollections of the trauma.

(c) Inability to recall an important aspect of the trauma.

(d) Markedly diminished interest or participation in significant activities.

(e) Feelings of detachment or estrangement from others.

(f) Restricted range of affect (e.g., unable to have loving feelings).

(g) Sense of a foreshortened future (e.g., does not expect to have a career, marriage, children, or a normal life span).

(iv) Persistent symptoms of increased arousal (not present before the trauma), as indicated by at least two of the following:

(a) Difficulty falling or staying asleep.

(b) Irritability or outbursts of anger.

(c) Difficulty concentrating.

(d) Hypervigilance.

(e) Exaggerated startle response.

(v) Duration of the disturbance (symptoms in (ii), (iii), (iv) are more than one month)

(vi) The disturbance causes clinically significant distress or impairment in social, occupational, or other important areas of functioning.

Specify if:

Acute: If duration of symptoms is less than three months.

Chronic: If duration of symptoms is three months or more.

With delayed onset: Onset of symptoms at least six months after the stressor.

In particular, criterion (i) has been clarified greatly such that more emphasis is placed on the threatening nature of the traumatic event to the person rather than it being outside the range of normal human experience. Also, the ways in which several symptoms manifest themselves in children are defined more clearly. Similar to *DSM-III*, *DSM-IV* notes that children's re-experiencing can be expressed as repetitive and trauma-thematic play, nightmares with/without traumatic content, and re-enactment of the trauma. Interestingly, the fourth edition no longer specifies "loss of previously acquired developmental skills" as a potential avoidance item and this may affect case identification (Ribbe, Lipovsky, & Freedy, 1995).

The inclusion of PTSD among the anxiety disorders in the *DSM* has led to considerable controversy among trauma and anxiety researchers alike (cf., Pynoos, 1994; Saigh, 1989b). While characterized by predominant symptoms of fear, avoidance, and hyperarousal, PTSD differs from the other anxiety disorders in that it requires a "putative" event (i.e., the trauma). Thus, there is an assumed causal relationship between an external event and the onset of the disorder. In this way, PTSD more resembles an adjustment disorder. Indeed, the notion that PTSD is "a normal reaction to an abnormal situation" has led some to question whether it is in fact a psychiatric disorder at all (cf., O'Donohue & Elliot; 1992).

PTSD also differs from the anxiety disorders in other important ways. Foa, Steketee, & Olasov-Rothbaum (1989) observed that trauma giving rise to PTSD violated more of the survivor's safety assumptions than did events leading to other forms of anxiety. Also, there was a much greater likelihood of fear generalization and subjective re-experiencing of the anxiety-eliciting event in PTSD than other anxiety disorders (Foa et al., 1989). Some have suggested that it is this internal, subjective experience of the traumatic event that most seems to set PTSD apart from the other anxiety disorders (Jones & Barlow, 1992; Keppel-Benson & Ollendick; 1993). Others have argued that it is the psychogenic amnesia and numbing of general responsiveness which separate PTSD clearly from anxiety, and places it more appropriately among the dissociative disorders. Still others (Pitman et al., 1990) have pointed out that exposure to trauma cues in combat veterans was just as likely to produce responses of anger and grief than fear, and thus PTSD might arguably be placed among the affective disorders.

To add to the controversy, it is widely recognized that the PTSD criteria, as currently defined, poorly reflect the wide variety of major stress responses reported in the literature. Thus, it can be argued that many seriously traumatized individuals might not meet criteria for PTSD under the *DSM*. As mentioned above, "survivor guilt" and grief reactions have largely

been lost in each subsequent revision since *DSM-III*. Nor is there any mention in *DSM-IV* of the profound sexual, interpersonal, and identity problems often found in survivors of repeated sexual assault.

This has led some to ask whether a spectrum of disorders, including PTSD, should be delineated to capture more accurately the range of traumatic responses seen by clinicians and researchers (Kolb, 1988). In this regard, some have argued for an additional grouping to be recognized—Disorders of Extreme Stress Not Otherwise Specified (DESNOS) (Herman, 1992). The distinction between PTSD and DESNOS is similar to the distinction drawn by Terr (1991) between Type I (characterized by intrusive recollections) and Type II (characterized by denial, numbing, and dissociation) PTSD in children (Yule, 1994).

PTSD is also included in the tenth edition of the *International classification of diseases* (*ICD-10*) (World Health Organization, 1992). However, its inclusion among the adjustment disorders has avoided the controversy surrounding PTSD in the *DSM*. According to *ICD-10*: "[PTSD] arises as a delayed or protracted response to a stressful event or situation ... of an exceptionally threatening or catastrophic nature, which is likely to cause pervasive distress in almost anyone (e.g., natural or man made disaster, combat, serious accident, witnessing the violent death of others, or being a victim of torture, terrorism, rape, or other crime)" (World Health Organization, 1992, p. 147).

ICD-10 lists symptoms similar to those in *DSM-III-R*, but emphasizes the presence of repetitive, intrusive memories characteristic of the disorder rather than the avoidance symptoms. Specifically, the manual states: "A conspicuous emotional detachment, numbing of feeling, and avoidance of stimuli that might arouse recollections of the trauma are often present but *are not essential* for the diagnosis. The autonomic disturbances, mood disorder, and behavioral abnormalities are all contributory to the diagnosis but not of prime importance" (World Health Organization, 1992, p. 148). It is also worth noting that the *ICD-10* states that PTSD should only be diagnosed when it arises within six months of a major trauma, whereas *DSM-IV* allows the diagnosis to be made when onset occurs after six months post-trauma (as noted by the specification Delayed Onset (American Psychiatric Association, 1994).

5.16.2.2.1 Prevalence

Epidemiological investigations of adults in the general population estimate a lifetime prevalence of PTSD between 1 and 9.2% (see Fairbank, Schlenger, Saigh, & Davidson, 1995 for a review of epidemiological investigations of PTSD). The prevalence of PTSD among children in the community is unknown. There have been no epidemiological investigations of the disorder to date. However, there have been several studies of PTSD in children exposed to war, natural disaster, violent crime, and sexual abuse ("at-risk" groups).

Prevalence rates from studies of at-risk children vary widely (from 0 to 100%). This extreme variability is consistent with findings from studies of at-risk adults (Fairbank et al., 1995), and is reflected in the estimates given for at-risk groups in *DSM-IV* (3–58%) (American Psychological Association, 1994). Therefore, the following studies must be interpreted with caution. Specific diagnostic criteria for PTSD were not widely available until 1980. The term "psychic trauma" which included extreme fear reactions, grief, agitation, and depression was more often found in the literature. Also, few, if any, reliable screening instruments for childhood PTSD had been developed which severely undermined reliable estimation of the prevalence of PTSD (Galante & Foa; 1986; Yule & Williams, 1990).

In one of the earliest studies of at-risk children, Terr (1979) noted that the incidence of psychic trauma was 100% among 26 children involved in the Chowchilla bus-kidnaping. This rate was independent of the child's background and developmental history (Terr, 1979). Interestingly, in a separate study, the prevalence of "extreme fright" and psychic trauma was 40% in an age, race, and sex-matched "normal" control group chosen from the same school district as the kidnap victims (Terr, 1983), an unexpectedly high rate among so-called "normal" school-aged children.

Two additional studies provide estimates for PTSD among children exposed to civilian acts of violence. Pynoos et al. (1987) examined the occurrence of PTSD in 159 children one month after an attack by a sniper on their school playground. Seventy-seven percent of the children under direct threat (i.e., those on the playground) had moderate or severe PTSD as measured by the PTSD Reaction Index. Moderate or severe PTSD was also high (67%) among children not exposed to the sniper but at the school on the same day (Pynoos et al.).

More recently, Schwarz and Kowalski (1991) assessed 64 preadolescent school children six months after a shooting spree by a woman in their school. Prevalence rates were presented separately for the three diagnostic categorizations of PTSD under *DSM-III*, *DSM-III-R*, and *DSM-IV*, and the PTSD Reaction Index. Using "conservative" symptom thresholds (i.e., symptoms occurring "much" or "most of the time"), the prevalence of PTSD under *DSM-III* was 16%. By contrast, the prevalence of PTSD under *DSM-III-R* was only 8%, and 9% under *DSM-IV* (Schwarz & Kowalski, 1991). Using "liberal" symptom threshold levels (i.e., symptoms occurring at least "a little of the time"), prevalence rates ranged from 91% under *DSM-III* to 50% for *DSM-III-R*, and 26% for *DSM-IV*. This study underlines the difficulty with comparing PTSD prevalence rates across studies which use different versions of the *DSM*. Arguably, it also points out the risk of not identifying true cases of PTSD when using the subsequent revisions of the criteria under *DSM-III-R* and *DSM-IV*.

Several investigations have examined the prevalence of PTSD among children exposed to war. Kinzie et al. (1986) conducted one of the first investigations using operationally defined diagnostic criteria to study the effects of war on 40 Cambodian refugees living in Oregon. Nearly four years after leaving refugee camps in Cambodia as adolescents, 50% met current *DSM-III* criteria for PTSD based on structured clinical interviews. More severe psychiatric effects were found in those who had been separated from family members (Kinzie et al., 1986). Sack et al. (1994) reported much lower rates (lifetime = 21.5%; current = 18.0%) in 200 Cambodian refugees in the United States. Similarly, in a study of 840 war-affected children from Lebanon, Saigh (1991) observed a much lower rate of current PTSD (32.5%). Interestingly, levels of PTSD were consistent across routes of exposure (direct, observation, and indirect) (Saigh, 1991).

Several studies have investigated the prevalence of traumatic reactions in children following natural and manmade disasters. Handford et al. (1986) found higher than normal anxiety scores on children and adolescents from 35 households 1.5 years after the "Three Mile Island" nuclear disaster. None of the children, however, met criteria for a diagnosis of PTSD based on structured interviews. Similarly, Earls et al. (1988), using structured diagnostic interviews, found no cases of PTSD in 32 children and adolescents one year after a flash flood, although many met several criteria for the disorder.

By contrast, McFarlane, Policansky, and Irwin (1987) found a high frequency of PTSD symptom clusters (94%) obtained from parent and teacher versions of the Rutter Scales in 808 children two months after large-scale brushfires in Australia. Similarly, Milgram, Toubiana, Klingman, Raviv, and Goldstein (1988) observed a 40% prevalence rate for PTSD in children one month after a bus accident. Bradburn (1991) reported prevalence rates of 27% for moderate PTSD and 36% for mild PTSD in 22 children aged 10–12 years, some 6–8 months after the San Francisco earthquake. Of 179 children aged 2–15 years who were examined two years after the Buffalo Creek disaster, 37% received probable PTSD diagnoses based on retrospective examination of records (Greene et al., 1991).

A number of large-scale investigations of PTSD in children were conducted following Hurricane Hugo which struck South Carolina in 1989. Based on self-report data, Lonigan et al. (1991) reported PTSD prevalence rates of 5.06% in a no-exposure group, 10.35% in a mild, 15.54% in a moderate, and 28.95% in a high-exposure group of hurricane survivors. The overall prevalence rate for PTSD in the sample was 5% ($n = 5687$) nearly three months after the hurricane (Shannon, Lonigan, Finch, & Taylor, 1994). Similarly, Garrison, Weinrich, Hardin, Weinrich, and Wang (1993) reported current prevalence rates ranging from 1.5 to 6.2% one year after the hurricane in 11–17 year-olds.

From the above studies it can be seen that reliable estimation of the prevalence of PTSD in children and adolescents is extremely difficult, particularly from data collected before the operationalizing of PTSD in *DSM*. Moreover, there is considerable variability in prevalence estimates depending upon the age of the child, time since the trauma, assessment methods used, and under which version of *DSM* caseness was established.

5.16.2.2.2 Etiology

In contrast to most of the phenomenological classifications in *DSM-IV* (American Psychiatric Association, 1994) and *ICD-10* (World Health Organization, 1992), PTSD is one of the few psychiatric disorders which specifies an etiological agent. However, *DSM-IV* also recognizes that, at worst, only slightly more than half (58%) of those exposed to a trauma go on to develop PTSD (American Psychiatric Association, 1994). Thus, while trauma may be a necessary agent in the development of PTSD, it is clearly not a sufficient one (Yehuda & McFarlane, 1995). It is with this background that etiological theories have emerged to explain the development of PTSD since the early 1980s. A complete review of the etiological theories of PTSD is beyond the scope of this chapter and the interested reader should consult Foa et al. (1989) and Friedman, Charney, and Deutch (1995) for details. This chapter focuses on three

models which have received considerable attention from researchers and for which there is limited empirical support or ongoing investigation. However, it should be noted that none of the etiological models put forward to date can explain adequately the full range of symptoms seen in PTSD (Yehuda & McFarlane, 1995).

5.16.2.2.3 A learning theory account of PTSD

Numerous researchers have proposed the use of Mowrer's (1960) two-factor learning theory to explain the development of PTSD (see Foa et al., 1989 for a review). Mowrer's is a conditioning model, incorporating elements of both Pavlovian and operant conditioning. As applied to PTSD, the traumatic event is an unconditioned stimulus that elicits certain involuntary responses: (i) orientation to the threat cue; (ii) autonomic arousal; (iii) fear; and (iv) the behavioral "flight or fight' response (Southwick, Bremner, Krystal, & Charney, 1994). Because of their proximity to the threatening event (the unconditioned stimulus (UCS)), previously neutral stimuli become conditioned stimuli (CS), capable of eliciting the same involuntary responses (conditioned response (CR)) as the trauma itself. For example, a child struck while crossing the street by a yellow taxicab (UCS) becomes overwhelmed with fear and intrusive thoughts of the accident (CR) upon any subsequent exposure to yellow taxicabs (CS).

Under normal conditions, repeated exposure to yellow cabs (CS) without being involved in an accident (UCS) should lead to extinction of the conditioned anxiety response (CR). However, with PTSD (Keane, Zimmering, & Caddell, 1985), this extinction fails to occur because the traumatized individual is negatively reinforced (i.e., their anxiety goes down) for avoiding the CS (e.g., yellow cabs). In addition, other previously neutral stimuli associated with the CS, such as the color yellow itself, may also elicit the conditioned anxiety response through the process of stimulus generalization. Finally, the CS themselves may go on to condition other nontrauma-related stimuli (higher order conditioning). Thus, traumatized persons may find themselves confronted with a wide array of anxiety-eliciting cues in their environment that cause persistent hyperarousal, intrusive recall of the traumatic event, and behavioral avoidance of the conditioned cues (Keane et al., 1985).

5.16.2.2.4 An emotional processing model

Observations from work on experimentally conditioned neuroses have led to the development of an emotional processing account of

PTSD derived from Lang's (1985) information processing theory of anxiety which, in contrast to conditioning models, takes into account subjective appraisals of the traumatic event in the development of PTSD. According to the emotional processing model (Foa & Kozak, 1986), traumatic events lead to the development of fear structures in memory that act to prevent further traumatization. These fear structures contain information about the objective characteristics of the trauma, the individual's responses to the trauma, and their subjective appraisal of the dangerousness and meaningfulness of the event (Foa & Kozak, 1986). Activation of this fear structure leads to increases in arousal, reexperiencing, and avoidant behaviors.

The meaning the individual attaches to the trauma, and their responses to it, are as important as the objective characteristics of the trauma. Specifically, the emotional processing model postulates that traumatic events can lead to changes in one's fundamental assumptions about safety and self-efficacy. This in turn leads to the development of new assumptions which attach increased threat value to a variety of previously neutral or even safety-signaling cues (Foa & Kozak, 1986). Consequently, many stimuli in the environment can now activate the fear structure, making it more readily accessible in memory than other potentially adaptive emotion networks, and diverting attentional resources from other nontrauma-related cues.

Ultimately, the fear structure can only be consolidated into long-term memory when corrective information (both cognitive and affective) is incorporated to develop a new information structure (Foa & Kozak, 1986). Foa et al. (1989) suggest that *in vivo* and imaginal exposure provide the type of corrective feedback necessary for consolidation of the fear structure. Specifically, increased contact with feared stimuli leads to habituation of the anxiety response, which they argue is a form of corrective feedback, as well as changes in the individual's beliefs about the likelihood of being retraumatized in the presence of neutral cues and safety signals.

5.16.2.2.5 A neurobiological model of PTSD

Numerous interrelated brain systems are activated during stressful events and have been implicated in the development of PTSD (see Friedman et al., 1995 for a review). The relationships among these systems are complex and poorly understood (Southwick et al., 1994). Given the complex interrelationships among brain systems, it is extremely unlikely that any

one-to-one correspondence exists between PTSD symptoms and particular neurotransmitters or hormones (Southwick et al., 1994). Still, three systems have received considerable attention: the noradrenergic system, the hypothalamic pituitary (HPA) axis, and the endogenous opiates. These systems assist our understanding of the phenomenology of PTSD and have important implications for pharmacological treatment of the disorder (Sutherland & Davidson, 1994).

First, it has been suggested that these persistent symptoms of arousal reflect sympathetic nervous system dysregulation resulting from changes in the noradrenergic system (Southwick et al., 1994). During stressful events, central and peripheral levels of the neurotransmitter norepinephrine (NE) are increased leading to increases in heart rate and blood pressure and the experience of fear. These increases appear to serve an adaptive function as they arouse the individual and activate centers of the brain important to orienting to external stimuli, selective attention, and memory encoding of the event. However, repeated or uncontrollable stress may lead to chronic elevations in NE and alterations in NE receptors in the locus coereleus, resulting in the persistent physiological arousal seen in PTSD. There is an emerging body of evidence suggesting that veterans with PTSD have increased levels of NE and changes in noradrenergic receptivity compared with veterans without PTSD and veterans with other disorders (see Southwick et al., 1994 for a review). In addition to its effects on arousal, Pitman (1989) has suggested high states of NE-mediated arousal may "supercondition" traumatic events in memory, leading to persistent re-experiencing symptoms.

Second, there is increasing evidence that chronic or uncontrollable stress produces changes in activity of the corticotropin-releasing factor (CRF) and the hypothalamic-pituitary-adrenal (HPA) axis. The HPA system is known to play an important role in the stress response: releasing cortisol and adrenocorticotropic hormone (ACTH) assists in energy metabolism and tissue repair. Glucocorticoids exert negative feedback on the HPA axis to help maintain these hormones at nontoxic levels. Additionally, it appears that the NE and HPA systems stimulate each other, primarily through the action of CRF, leading to a mutually reinforcing feedback loop (Southwick et al., 1994).

Again, there is evidence that exposure to repeated or uncontrollable stress appears to cause the HPA system to become highly sensitized, leading to greater fluctuation in cortisol levels over a 24 h period (Southwick et al., 1994). A number of studies with combat veterans (see Southwick et al., 1994 and Yehuda & McFarlane, 1995 for a review) have found decreased levels of urinary cortisol in those with PTSD compared with psychiatric and normal controls, as well as changes in the number and receptivity of glucocorticoid receptors in the brain. Interestingly, Southwick et al. (1994) note that in animal studies, chronic elevation of glucocorticoids has been associated with damage to the hippocampal region and learning deficits, which may help explain the short-term memory impairments found in patients with PTSD.

Third, endogenous opiates are also released during periods of acute stress, leading to increased pain thresholds which may allow the individual to survive life-threatening events (Southwick et al., 1994). Again, however, it has been hypothesized that exposure to chronic and uncontrollable stress leads to increased sensitization of the opioid system such that lower levels of stress continue to produce the analgesic response (Maier, 1986). This response has been shown in Vietnam veterans during exposure to trauma-related cues (van der Kolk, Greenberg, Orr, & Pittman, 1989) and may contribute to development of avoidance and numbing symptoms (Southwick et al., 1994). Moreover, it has been suggested that the heightened sensitivity of the opioid system may play a role in intrusive recall of the trauma through its effects on NE and the consolidation of memory (McGaugh, 1990).

While other areas of the central nervous system are certainly involved in the pathogenesis of PTSD, the above findings are pertinent. First, dysregulation of the HPA and noradrenergic systems may explain why individuals with PTSD frequently suffer from chronic levels of hyperarousal, hyper-reactivity to trauma-related stimuli, emotional numbing, and difficulties with concentration and memory (including intrusive imagery) (Southwick et al., 1994). Second, these findings further our understanding of why not all individuals develop PTSD. Rather than viewing PTSD as a normal reaction to an abnormal event, it may be a complex psychological and biological response to trauma involving the phenotypic expression of vulnerabilities to the disorder (Yehuda & McFarlane, 1995). Finally, the ability to distinguish individuals with and without PTSD based on the role of HPA and noradrenergic dysregulation provides further evidence of the validity of the disorder, and has significant implications for the assessment and treatment of PTSD in both adults and children.

5.16.2.2.6 Characteristics of the trauma and other risk factors for PTSD

Regarding the trauma itself, revisions to Criterion A under *DSM-IV* aim to provide a tighter objective definition of the event, and recent research with children has concerned the relationship between the objective characteristics of the stressor and subsequent symptoms. A number of studies have reported the presence of a dose–response relationship among children involved in a sniper attack on a school (Pynoos et al., 1987), a shipping accident (Yule et al., 1990), an earthquake (Pynoos et al., 1993), a hurricane (Lonigan et al., 1991), and during war (Kuterovac, Dyregrov, & Stuvland, 1994). Similarly, attention to refining the descriptions of the nature of children's traumatic experiences has led to a more precise identification of the specific features of traumatic events which are associated with risk of PTSD. For example, exposure to direct life threat, witnessing mutilating injury or grotesque death (especially of family members or friends), and hearing unanswered screams for help were associated with more severe pathology among children and adolescents after a shipping disaster (Yule & Williams, 1990) and an earthquake (Pynoos et al., 1993).

The relationship between trauma and response has been described in detail by Terr (1991) who distinguishes between Type I and Type II traumatic events. Type I traumas are single, sudden, severe, acute stressors (e.g., natural disasters). By contrast, Type II traumas, such as childhood sexual or physical assault, are typically repeated, chronic, and expected. Terr (1991) suggests that Type I traumas are more likely to result in classic PTSD symptoms, whereas children exposed to Type II traumas are more likely to show characterological problems. While this distinction is of potential clinical relevance, it has yet to be empirically investigated and should not be overly applied. Indeed, traumatic events experienced during war are often repeated and chronic, but the associated psychopathology contains a high prevalence of classic PTSD symptoms (Kuterovac et al., 1994).

It is recognized, however, that stressors cannot be completely defined in objective terms (Rachman, 1980), and there is increasing interest in cognitive threat appraisal and attributional processes among children and adolescents (Joseph, Brewin, Yule, & Williams, 1991, 1993). The revised diagnostic criteria for the defining stressor in *DSM-IV* now include immediate responses of intense fear, helplessness, or horror (or disorganized or agitated behavior in children) in the face of actual or threatened life threat or injury to self or others (American Psychiatric Association, 1994). This stands in important contrast to previous formulations in which the stressor was seen as one that would cause significant distress to almost anyone.

There is evidence that attributional processes can mediate symptoms in child survivors. In young survivors of a shipping accident, Joseph, Brewin, Yule, and Williams (1993) found that more internal and controllable attributions were associated with intrusive thoughts and depressive feelings one year after the accident. Yule et al. (1990) have presented some evidence of a subjective dose–response relationship in survivors of the same accident. Children who had wanted to go on the cruise but had not obtained places were far less badly affected than those who went on the trip, but more badly affected than those who had never wanted to go.

Whatever the nature of the traumatic event and the child's appraisal of it, there are clearly a number of risk and protective factors which influence the development of disorder in children. Girls have been found to be more vulnerable than boys in a number of studies including a shipping disaster (Yule, 1992), a hurricane (Lonigan et al., 1991), and an earthquake (Pynoos et al., 1993) across a variety of self-report measures. Interestingly, Burke et al. (1986) found boys' distress to be higher than girls' five months after a flood, but reported that 10 months after the flood, girls showed more distress.

Age has been thought to be a factor in the development of PTSD. However, following the earthquake in Armenia, age was not found to correlate with Stress Reaction Index scores (Pynoos et al., 1993). Keppel-Benson and Ollendick (1993) argued that younger children may be protected from strong emotional reactions because of their limited cognitive capacity, particularly their awareness of threats of harm. Preliminary evidence of this hypothesis was found by Green et al. (1991) who noted that preschoolers' perceptions of threat were unrelated to symptomatology following the Buffalo Creek disaster. However, there are insufficient studies to determine whether children of different ages are at different risk of developing PTSD.

Studies of premorbid risk factors in children are also very limited. As yet, no studies have investigated systematically pretrauma abuse histories, psychological functioning, or familial psychiatric history in relation to the child's subsequent risk of PTSD. However, regarding premorbid ability and academic attainment, Yule and Udwin (1991) found that among survivors of the Jupiter shipping accident, an increased risk of PTSD was associated with low pretrauma attainment at school.

In addition to pretrauma risk factors, events and processes following exposure have been shown to influence development of the disorder. Family reactions to a disaster may be important moderating factors in the development of childhood PTSD. Studying families after the Australian bushfires, McFarlane (1987) found that parents' adjustment was an important determinant of the adjustment of their children: families who found it difficult to share their immediate reactions had more trouble with long-term adjustment. Equally important, the child's reaction to the fires affected the family's adjustment, demonstrating the reciprocal interactions among family members.

Pynoos (1994) argues that there are many interacting critical factors which play a role in the progression from traumatic exposure to subsequent psychopathology. These include social structures, community organization, family functioning, and the individual stressful challenges to the child. Pynoos' (1994) developmental model provides a useful framework for understanding this pathway, and implicates potential areas for prevention and treatment.

5.16.2.2.7 Developmental course

Being explicitly developmental, Pynoos' (1994) model (see above) provides a useful framework for understanding the course of post-trauma reactions in children. Nevertheless, there are very few systematic studies which have examined the long-term effects of exposure to traumatic events on children.

Two months after the Australian bushfires, children who had been exposed were rated as less disturbed on Rutter's screening scales than a nonexposed comparison group studied elsewhere (McFarlane et al., 1987). However, by eight months, both parents and teachers reported significant increases in the numbers of children at high risk of psychiatric disorder, and these high rates were maintained at 26 months. Around a third of this sample was still preoccupied with the event more than two years later (McFarlane et al., 1987).

Fourteen months after a school sniper attack in Los Angeles, Nader, Pynoos, Fairbanks, and Frederick (1991) found that the majority of children felt afraid when they thought about the attack, and most were specifically afraid of recurrence. In her follow-up of child survivors of a bus hijacking, Terr (1979, 1983) found very few children who were fear free some five years after the event. Thus it appears that fear may be a long-lasting consequence of traumatic events in children.

Assessing Cambodian refugees who had emigrated to America four years earlier as adolescents, Kinzie et al. (1986) found a range of intrusive and avoidance phenomena (50% of the sample suffered from PTSD), but also major depressive disorder. Prolonged depressive symptoms were found in this sample of adolescents and young adults who had been exposed to massive and repeated trauma.

Results from a six to seven-year follow-up of survivors of the Jupiter shipping accident (Yule & Udwin, 1991; Boyle et al., 1995) revealed soberingly high rates of psychiatric disorder. Preliminary results from a cohort of 98 survivors showed that of the 51% who met criteria for PTSD at some time since the disaster, 60% had PTSD which lasted for up to two years, with a further 18% having PTSD for five years. Rates of other disorder, including panic, separation anxiety, OCD, substance abuse, dysthymia, and hypomania, were also elevated compared with a control group. Thus, a range of symptoms may persist over several years. Children do improve over time, however. After a school bus crash, high levels of acute stress reactions during the first week dropped markedly over the following nine months, although initial levels of distress predicted later ones (Milgram et al., 1988).

Evidence from the Jupiter follow up (Boyle et al., 1995) and other studies suggest that the severity of the stressor may be one of the most important factors in determining the severity of later pathology. However, while Kinzie et al. (1986) found no direct relationship between extent and type of exposure and psychiatric diagnosis four years later among Cambodian refugees, their current living situation showed a strong relationship to diagnosis. McFarlane's (1987) data show family factors to be an important variable moderating outcome. It seems that the course of post-traumatic stress symptoms such as intrusive re-experiencing and avoidance of feelings follow a different time course than symptoms of depression and anxiety, both of which increase after the first six months postdisaster. Clearly, there will be a complex interaction over time of factors which influence the course and chronicity of stress reactions (Pynoos, 1994) and further research is needed to delineate these factors.

5.16.3 CONCEPTUALIZATION AND CLINICAL FORMULATION

5.16.3.1 Multimodal Assessment

As stated above, PTSD is a cluster of symptoms overlapping several domains of functioning. As such, the interview should be geared towards assessing all aspects of client functioning. This can be accomplished through a direct interview with the child as well as the family and teachers, self-report inventories and diaries, and psychophysiological recording. In addition, the therapist should try to gather all available information possible about the exact nature of the trauma from other witnesses, news reports, and police/rescue personnel. Finally, establishing the nature and extent of impairment through review of available medical and school reports is important. Experience has shown that these additional sources of information are important to help the interviewer understand the sequence of events during the trauma and often reveal symptoms that either are not readily admitted or remembered by the child and his or her family.

5.16.3.1.1 Interviewing the child

Pynoos and Eth (1986) have developed a technique for interviewing young children shortly after the witness of a traumatic or violent event, although it has broad applicability to all types of direct and indirect trauma experienced by children. The interview is broken down into three components: opening, trauma, and closure. "Opening" refers to the establishment of a focused but free discussion of the traumatic event. This is accomplished by: (i) communicating to the child that the interviewer has experience with talking to children about their traumatic experiences; (ii) giving the child pencil and paper and asking them to "draw whatever you would like but something you can tell a story about"; and (iii) encouraging the child to elaborate further (verbally or through drawing) on the story.

During the second stage of the interview, aspects of the child's drawing are linked explicitly to some aspect of the traumatic event by the therapist to facilitate emotional release. For example, the therapist might say, "I bet you wish that your father could have been saved in the end like the clown." Once the therapist has judged that the child is ready to proceed emotionally, he or she may say, "Now is a good time to tell what happened and what you saw." The child is supported in their focus on the traumatic event by asking them to draw the traumatic event, focusing and describing the sensory aspects of the event, the worst moment, any violence or mutilation, and how they coped with these experiences. Pynoos and Eth (1986) have also suggested that the child be encouraged to describe any plans or thoughts they had or have about ways in which they could have remedied the situation, feelings of blame, the desire for retaliation and fears of counter-retaliation, and feelings of control. Then the therapist inquires about previous traumas, recent dreams that may be remembered, their concerns about the future, and current stresses.

In the third and final stage of the interview, the process of termination is begun. This is accomplished by having the child review and summarize the session, normalizing the child's reactions to the traumatic event, and linking the trauma to the original drawing or story (Pynoos & Eth, 1986). In addition, the therapist may discuss with the child information they have about the expected course of the disorder. This is done by helping them identify potentially fear-eliciting, trauma-related stimuli and their potential reactions to these stimuli outside the session. To bolster the child's self-esteem, the therapist may remark on the child's courage during the event and in retelling the story during the interview. Finally, the child is asked to describe what was helpful or disturbing about the interview process and the therapist expresses his or her respect for the child's views and the privilege of having shared the interview experience with them. While the above interview technique does not specifically include any standardized assessment of PTSD symptomatology, it has proven useful in raising awareness of the sensitive nature of the trauma interview and the importance of therapist skill in obtaining accurate information.

5.16.3.1.2 Childhood measures of post-traumatic distress

Since the mid-1980s, a variety of interview techniques and instruments have been developed to assess PTSD in children directly. The majority have been adapted from semi-structured psychiatric interviews or self-report questionnaires originally developed with adults. In addition, several pre-existing measures, originally designed to assess childhood anxiety, fear, depression, and behavioral disturbance have been applied to the study of childhood PTSD. This section will introduce the reader to some of the more widely used instruments. Readers interested in a more comprehensive review of the available measures of childhood PTSD and their psychometric properties are referred to Nader (1996) and McNally (1991).

Perhaps the most widely used measure of PTSD symptomatology is the IES (Horowitz et al., 1979). It assesses the cardinal symptoms of PTSD (intrusion and avoidance), and has been used with children aged eight years and over (Yule & Udwin, 1991; Yule & Williams, 1990). It has proven particularly useful in the assessment of post-traumatic stress when used in conjunction with measures of childhood anxi-

ety, fear, and depression (Stallard & Law, 1993; Yule & Udwin, 1991). Such measures include the Birleson Depression Inventory (Birleson, 1981), the Children's Manifest Anxiety Scale (Reynolds & Richmond, 1978), and the Fear Survey Schedule for Children (Ollendick, 1983). However, it should be noted that factor analyses suggest that some items of the IES are misunderstood by children and should be replaced (Yule et al., 1990).

Another widely used measure of childhood PTSD is the Children's Post Traumatic Stress Reaction Index (CPTS-R) (Frederick, 1985b). In a number of major studies of child trauma (Nader et al., 1991; Pynoos et al., 1987, 1993; Pynoos & Nader, 1988), the CPTS-R has been shown to have good internal consistency and to relate well to clinical judgement of PTSD severity (Yule & Udwin, 1991). Saigh's (1989) Children's Posttraumatic Stress Disorder Inventory is a structured inventory designed to explore *DSM-III* PTSD symptoms and has good psychometric properties. Finally, the Children's Impact of Traumatic Events Scale-Revised (CITES-R) (Wolfe, Gentile, Sas, & Wolfe, 1991) was developed to assess the impact of sexual abuse on children.

There are a number of semistructured interviews based directly on *DSM* criteria available that allow the interviewer to diagnose PTSD in the child. These include: the Clinician Administered PTSD Scale for Children (CAPS-C; Nader, Kriegler, Keane, Blake, & Pynoos, 1994); the Diagnostic Interview Schedule for Children (DISC; Shaffer et al., 1996); and the Diagnostic Interview for Children and Adolescents Revised (DICA; Reich, Shakya, & Taibelson, 1991). All require the interviewer to be trained in the administration of the scale, and have been shown to possess adequate validity and reliability (cf., Nader, 1995).

Unfortunately there has been a dearth of standardized approaches to the assessment of stress reactions in children less than eight years of age. While children between three and eight years can often give adequate verbal responses to questions from standardized measures used with older children, there is a need to develop measures particularly suited for young children. This is particularly important in light of the legal implication of PTSD interviews and emerging data on suggestibility in children.

Still, it has been argued that the rush to develop semi-structured interviews to elicit and quantify PTSD in children is somewhat misguided in that they simply rephrase *DSM* criteria into questionnaire format (Yule, 1994). As discussed above, many of the *DSM* criteria are irrelevant to children, and thus semistructured interviews may have only limited validity in assessing the complete range of traumatic reactions observed in traumatized children. Moreover, it should be recognized that the interview is itself both a potentially threatening and therapeutic experience, requiring considerable skill and sensitivity on the part of the interviewer, and a firm understanding of child development. The establishment of rapport and a safe environment in which the child can discuss painful and angry feelings are very important to acquiring accurate information. The use of semistructured interviews and self-report questionnaires must always be placed within this context.

Finally, physiological measures such as galvanic skin response, heart rate, and respiration may prove useful in the assessment of PTSD, although they have received limited attention in the childhood PTSD literature (Finch & Daugherty, 1993).

5.16.3.1.3 Interviewing the parent

While the importance of interviewing children directly has been clearly established (Nader & Pynoos, 1989; Reich & Earls, 1987; Terr, 1979), children may not report the full range of PTSD symptoms (Nader & Fairbanks, 1994). Thus, a comprehensive psychiatric assessment should include a direct interview with the parents or primary caregivers. Most of the semistructured diagnostic interviews available include both child and parent versions which allow the interviewer to cover all symptoms systematically with parents and child. This is particularly important where the symptom may be of a particularly embarrassing nature, as with enuresis, thumb-sucking, and crying, or where the child may be unaware of their behavior, as in "clinging" or sleep disturbances.

Beyond a comprehensive coverage of the child's developmental history and current symptom state, it is important to establish the time-line of events leading up to, including, and following the trauma as this may help the therapist in assessing the child's accuracy of recall (Nader, 1995). Young children (less than eight years of age) are prone to time distortions because of age-appropriate levels of cognitive maturation. However, even older children may confuse the sequence of events because of extreme emotional arousal and chaos experienced during the traumatic event.

5.16.3.1.4 Discrepancies in parent and child reports

Children often minimize the extent and severity of their own disruptive behaviors, whereas parents often overemphasize these

symptoms while remaining unaware of particular fears or negative emotions (Nader & Pynoos, 1989). An additional problem with parental reports is that parents may be inclined to minimize the effect of a trauma on their child and thus under-report symptoms (Sternberg et al., 1993). This may occur as a function of the parents' own abhorrence to the trauma and its recall. It is important then that the therapist be attentive to the parents' emotional state and level of arousal when recalling the trauma.

5.16.3.2 Treatment Formulation

From the above outline of multimodal assessment, it follows that treatment formulation will draw on a number of sources. Conventionally, treatment planning will be based on an assessment of current difficulties, the child's (and his or her family's) premorbid functioning, and currently available resources. Additionally, in trauma work, the kind of intervention offered will depend on how recently the traumatic event occurred.

Where children are seen within days or weeks after the traumatic event, the aim of intervention is to facilitate recovery rather than to treat symptoms. In general, recovery will be facilitated by retelling the facts of the incident, expressing feelings associated with it, normalizing reactions, educating and informing about the expected course, and by the enhancement of coping strategies (see Section 5.16.4.1.2 and Pynoos & Eth 1986). Nevertheless, effective intervention at this stage will depend also on a thorough assessment of the child's living situation and available resources. Work with carers is necessary to assist them to help their children, especially when they have themselves been directly involved in the incident. Practical issues of social welfare may arise, for instance, in cases where there is ongoing community violence, or where the child has suffered a parental bereavement. Here, multidisciplinary work is required so that as secure and safe an environment as possible is available to the child in the immediate aftermath and short term following the incident.

Treatment formulation will differ when children are referred months to years after the event. A comprehensive pretrauma history from the child's carers will help in understanding the child's usual reactions to stress and their ways of coping: whether current symptomatology is in part a function of prior temperament; what changes in behavior the traumatic event precipitated; and in setting appropriate treatment goals. Considering the child's developmental level will allow one to assess which if any of the presenting complaints are normal age-appropriate behaviors (e.g., separation anxiety), as well as guiding the choice of treatment strategies. Given the important mediating role of parental reactions and fears (McFarlane, 1987), assessment of all family members is usually necessary, both to determine whether adults or siblings also require intervention, and to advise carers on management of their children. Since the severity of the trauma is an important factor in determining the severity of later pathology (Yule, 1994), assessing the extent and type of exposure is necessary, and to address multiple episodes within a single traumatic event (Pynoos & Nader, 1993).

Treatment goals will differ according to the pattern of presenting problems, but common goals normally will include helping the child to understand the nature and effects of trauma, facilitating his or her ability to think and talk about the event without debilitating anxiety, and reducing the intensity and frequency of intrusive, avoidant, and hyperarousal symptoms (Ribbe et al., 1995). Prioritizing goals will be done collaboratively with the child and their carers, and will address those symptoms that are impacting most severely on the child's day-to-day functioning.

Common to most treatment approaches is the notion that the traumatic event requires adequate emotional processing (Rachman, 1980), and at the core of most psychosocial treatment methods is imaginal exposure to the event to facilitate such processing (see below). Also, given the range of reactions to critical incidents, a flexible approach to treatment is called for by which the child's coping strategies to deal with distressing symptoms are developed and enhanced. To take a common example of symptom management, sleep hygiene techniques can often be therapeutically beneficial while addressing the central trauma. While clinicians must be alerted to their own avoidance of the most difficult aspects of the child's experience, prioritizing areas of particular difficulty with the child and then bolstering coping strategies may increase a sense of mastery and self-efficacy while reducing feelings of helplessness and victimization.

Children with PTSD may present with other Axis I comorbidity and chronic pain reactions resulting from injury, and in this case, treatment formulation will be modified accordingly. In traumatic bereavement, Dyregrov (1991) recommends that the traumatic nature of the death needs to be addressed before grieving can proceed.

Given the cascade of events that may follow a traumatic incident, treatment formulation will also address secondary adversities, with the aim of preventing further complications. Often, these may be traumatic reminders, ongoing legal processes, and anniversaries. It is common, for example, that academic attainment drops following exposure (e.g., Yule, 1994), and this in turn may potentially impact on the child's functioning in other areas and later into adulthood. Therefore, a comprehensive treatment plan may include "pulsed intervention" at times of expected stress such as changing schools and anniversaries (e.g., James, 1989).

5.16.4 TREATMENT

While there is a growing number of single case studies and detailed clinical descriptions of treating traumatized children, there are as yet no randomized controlled outcome trials. In the main, however, treatment approaches are broadly cognitive behavioral: the guiding principle is that exposure to trauma-related cues and memories in tolerable doses is needed to reduce PTSD symptoms. Professionals can help by creating a relatively safe environment in which such recounting can take place. Given the nature of many traumatic events, early intervention is often best done in groups and through existing structures such as schools. Work has also focused on contingency planning and disaster management using a public health approach which involves community resources. There is little available evidence for the effectiveness of pharmacological treatment of PTSD in children.

5.16.4.1 Psychosocial Approaches

5.16.4.1.1 *Preventative measures and contingency planning*

Traumatic events are by their nature unexpected and uncontrollable. Nevertheless, it is well recognized that much can be done to alleviate distress in children if the unexpected is planned for. Outside the family, school is a primary source of social support for children, and a number of authors (Klingman, 1993; Pynoos & Nader, 1988; Yule & Gold; 1993) have provided guidelines for how schools can plan to help child survivors of catastrophes. Particular emphasis is placed on schools and mental health professionals working together.

Planning for disasters will not prevent them from happening, but by anticipating many of the actions needed, schools may reduce the impact of critical incidents. Thus, Yule and Gold (1993) recommend a number of short-, medium-, and long-term tasks for school staff to be alerted to. School staff should be made aware of the likely psychological effects of disasters on children, parents, and teachers before disaster strikes through liaison with local child mental health services. In the event of a traumatic incident, immediate action should include ensuring that correct information can get into and out of the school, ensuring that several staff have access to next-of-kin lists, setting up strategies to deal with enquiries, informing parents about what has happened with care and sensitivity and reuniting parents and children, nominating a press officer to deal with the media, informing staff and pupils in an appropriate and careful way, attempting to stick to normal routines as much as possible, and planning for attendance at funerals.

School staff should be briefed about what has happened, and after contacting relevant outside agencies, debriefing meetings can be set up for directly involved staff and children. Procedures for monitoring both staff and children should be set up, and strategies for allowing young people who want to express their feelings about the situation should be activated.

In the medium term, it will be important for children who remain at home or in hospital to be contacted, and arrangements made either for their return to school or for alternative teaching. Affected staff and children may continue to need support, and this will be achieved more easily if ground rules for working with outside agencies have been set up beforehand. Close liaison with parents at this stage will be necessary.

In the longer term, introducing strategies to continue to monitor vulnerable pupils and staff is useful, to decide how to mark anniversaries, and to be aware that legal processes and media attention may bring back distressing memories and cause temporary upsets within the school. Schools should not have to deal with such enormously difficult issues such as death and bereavement for the first time following a crisis, and it is recommended that schools plan the curriculum to work with rites of passage as a matter of course.

Both Klingman (1993) and Yule and Gold (1993) advise that classroom interventions by teachers can be effective in defusing and normalizing emotions, not least by addressing rumors and myths about the disaster. Classroom interventions will include monitoring for high-risk children, since in themselves, they are no substitute for individual, group, or family interventions when needed (Pynoos & Nader, 1993).

5.16.4.1.2 Debriefing and crisis intervention

When schools are prepared for the unexpected, they are in an optimal position to provide early crisis intervention, with support from mental health professionals. Pynoos and Nader (1993) describe a number of "psychological first aid" strategies for common symptoms which can help to normalize the recovery process. They point out that these must be developmentally appropriate and provide a number of examples of techniques or strategies for use by teachers in schools.

A more widely used technique is Critical Incident Stress Debriefing (CISD) (Mitchell, 1983; Mitchell & Everly, 1993). Developed initially for use with emergency service personnel, debriefing has been adapted and used successfully with children following disasters (Dyregrov, 1991). Within a few days of an incident, the survivors are brought together in a group with an outside leader. During the introductory phase, the leader sets the ground rules for the meeting, emphasizing that they are there to share feelings and help each other and that what goes on in the meeting is private. The information should not be used to tease other children. No one has to talk, although all are encouraged to do so. The leader clarifies the facts of what actually happened in the incident. This allows for clarifications of any misunderstandings about how the traumatic event unfolded. They are asked about what they thought when they realized something was wrong, and this leads naturally to discussions of how they felt and their current emotional reactions. In this way, children share the various reactions they have experienced and usually learn that others have felt similarly. The leader labels their responses as normal (understandable) reactions to an abnormal situation.

Many children are relieved to learn that they are not the only ones experiencing strange feelings, that there is an explanation and that they are not going mad or crazy. The leader summarizes the information arising in the group, elicits and reinforces the existing coping strategies of the children, and educates them in what simple steps they can take to control some of their reactions. They are also told of other help available should their distress persist. The aim of debriefing is to facilitate the recovery process rather than to treat existing symptoms. The combination of normalizing reactions and teaching basic coping strategies can do much to enhance children's sense of mastery and control over their feelings. There is promising evidence from two studies which report reductions in distress among children following debriefing meetings.

Following the sinking in Athens of the cruise ship "Jupiter," which was carrying a party of British school children, Yule and Udwin (1991) described how they carried out a debriefing session with 24 survivors 10 days after the event. The debriefing meeting was carried out at school with the involvement of the survivors' teachers. As part of the meeting, the girls completed a screening battery consisting of the IES (Horowitz et al., 1979), the Birleson Depression Inventory (Birleson, 1981), and the revised Children's Manifest Anxiety Scale (Reynolds & Richmond, 1978). The girls were rescreened between 5 and 10 months later, and results were compared with the same self-report measures from a group of 15 girls from a different school who did not participate in any debriefing (Yule, 1992). The debriefing group showed significantly lower IES scores, and this effect was strongest for intrusive thoughts. The debriefing group also showed significantly reduced fears (Fear Survey Schedule) (Ollendick, Yule, & Ollier, 1991) compared with the control group. Scores on the depression and anxiety measures were slightly but not significantly lower. While these results are promising, some girls in the debriefing group went on to receive group treatment, making it impossible to isolate the effects of debriefing from subsequent therapy.

More convincing evidence is reported by Stallard and Law (1993), who carried out debriefing sessions with a group of seven young survivors of a minibus accident. The two debriefing meetings were carried out one week apart in school, and six months after the accident. The same screening battery as above was used before the first session, and children were subsequently rescreened three months later. Significant reductions were found in the group scores on all measures (PTSD, depression, and anxiety). Although no control data were obtained, given the stability of the scores in the six months before intervention, the authors argue that the improvement was related to the intervention.

Following a recent spate of well-publicized traumatic incidents involving school children, the call for debriefing and crisis counseling for all survivors is increasing. Although the available evidence is promising, there are no controlled studies demonstrating the efficacy of debriefing in reducing later distress. Given the debate about the usefulness of CISD among adults (Meichenbaum, 1994; Mitchell, 1996), there is a clear need for further evaluation of its efficacy with children. It is not known, for example, whether all survivors benefit, nor indeed when best to offer such debriefing.

5.16.4.1.3 Group treatment

Where critical incidents involve relatively large numbers of children, it makes sense to direct some therapeutic support through naturally existing groupings that are present in communities and schools. As with debriefing, the aims of such therapeutic groups will be to share experiences and feelings, to boost children's sense of mastery and control, and to share ways of solving common problems. Pynoos and Nader (1993) point out that providing a forum for the expression of feelings is not sufficient for groups: this may only renew feelings of anxiety unless a constructive, therapeutic approach is taken. A variety of approaches to group treatment have been described following earthquakes (Galante & Foa, 1986; Goenjian, 1993), a school sniper attack (Gillis, 1993), and shipping disasters (Yule & Udwin, 1991; Yule & Williams, 1990).

After a devastating earthquake in Italy in 1980, Galante and Foa (1986) carried out a group treatment program with 62 children from the most severely affected village. They describe a relatively structured approach, holding roughly monthly meetings throughout the academic year. Sessions lasted for an hour and each group consisted of four children from the same grade. Sessions focused on communicating about feelings (particularly about the earthquake), discussion and normalization of fear reactions, "active discharge of feelings about the earthquake," focusing on the future and rebuilding of their village, and sharing active coping strategies. Pre- and postgroup evaluation using the Rutter Children's Behaviour Questionnaire for Teachers (Rutter, 1967; Zimmerman-Tansella, Minghetti, Tacconi, & Tansella, 1978) showed a significant reduction in distress which compared favorably with children from other villages where children did not receive such support. Additionally, frequency counts were taken during sessions of repeating earthquake stories and the expression of related and unrelated fears. It is interesting that after an initial rise in these scores in the first few groups, they showed a dramatic decline only after a session where children looked to the future and were engaged in play to rebuild the village and provide safer housing.

A somewhat less structured approach was described by Yule and Williams (1990) with child and adult survivors of the Herald of Free Enterprise shipping disaster. Groups were open to any survivor to attend and met initially at monthly intervals over about a year, tailing off to every six to eight weeks thereafter. The children seemed to appreciate the opportunity to share their feelings with others without having to explain everything to outsiders. They took advantage of the cognitive behavioral problem solving approach by which efforts were made to help them identify things they were finding difficult and to use the resources of the group to develop solutions. The therapist working with the children also acted as a go-between with the parents' group. Yule and Williams (1990) suggested that an important part of group work with children following a disaster is that they have time together without the pressure of having to talk about the trauma.

Gillis (1993) worked with children following a school sniper attack. In small groups, both structured and more open-ended elements were used, including role play and re-enactment of the shooting. Gillis emphasizes that when groups are less structured, setting clear limits is important, for if behavior is out of control, it is likely to result in an increase in the children's anxiety. He found that running separate groups for boys and girls was better because of the different reactions they had to the attack, boys showing more externalizing reaction, and girls more internalizing ones. Groups comprised children of the same level of maturity, and Gillis suggests that it is optimal to work with groups of six to eight children.

It is notable that while the group treatment approaches reported above are well described and appear promising, there are no controlled studies providing evidence for the efficacy of such groups. There is a consensus that group interventions will be effective for some, but not all, children. However, one function of therapeutic groups is to screen for high-risk children who may need individual therapy. More generally, children whose problems persist despite group help should be treated individually.

5.16.4.1.4 Individual treatment

Broadly-based cognitive behavioral treatment methods aim to help survivors make sense of what has happened and to master feelings of anxiety and helplessness after a traumatic incident. Most survivors recognize that eventually they must "face up to the traumatic event." The problem for the clinician is how to help the survivor remember and re-experience the event and the emotions that it engenders so that the distress can be mastered rather than magnified. This will depend foremost on the establishment of a safe and trusting environment in which the traumatic event can be remembered and discussed. Therapists must be prepared to ask children about the most difficult aspects of the traumatic experience, but at the same time ensure that exposure to traumatic memories is paced so that the child does not experience overwhelming anxiety. For many children, talking directly about the traumatic event may be too difficult and other means of accessing traumatic memories must be found.

Asking children to draw their experiences often assists in the recall of both the event and the accompanying emotions. Pynoos and Eth (1986) provide a detailed account of how drawings may be used, not as projective techniques, but as a means of communicating about the experience (see Section 5.16.3.1.1). In younger children, play may be used similarly. Misch, Phillips, Evans, and Berekowitz (1993) gave children models and dolls representing the various components of the traumatic event which the children then used to answer questions about their experience.

At the core of cognitive-behavioral treatments with children is the use of imaginal and *in vivo* exposure techniques within a safe therapeutic environment. Results of controlled trials with adults generally support the use of exposure therapy for PTSD (e.g., Boudewyns & Hyer, 1990; Cooper & Clum, 1990; Keane, Fairbank, & Caddell, 1989), but trials of these techniques are still needed with children. Nevertheless, single case studies with children have shown very promising results.

Saigh (1987a) was the first to show that, as Rachman (1980) had predicted, longer exposure sessions than normal are needed if desensitization is to occur. He employed flooding techniques to treat a 14-year-old Lebanese boy who met criteria for PTSD after having been abducted and tortured. The imaginal flooding process consisted of 10 min of deep muscle relaxation, followed by 60 min of therapeutic stimulation during which the boy was instructed to imagine the particular details of four anxiety-evoking scenes. SUDS ratings were elicited at two min intervals during the aversive scene presentations. After seven flooding sessions, SUD levels decreased appreciably. Post-treatment and at four months follow-up, there were clinically significant treatment gains in self-reported anxiety (STAI; Spielberger, Gorsuch, & Luschene, 1970), depression (BDI; Beck, Rush, Shaw, & Emery, 1979), and misconduct, and virtually no arousal to the anxiety provoking scenes. The boy could complete all activities of a Behavioral Avoidance Test (BAT) involving a 10 min walk to the place where he had been kidnapped. The efficacy of such procedures was confirmed in a series of clinical replications involving multiple baselines across traumatic scenes (Saigh 1987b, 1989a, 1989b); and Saigh (1992) subsequently has summarized a five-stage intervention process involving education, imagery training, relaxation training, the presentation of anxiety provoking scenes, and debriefing.

Yule (1992) has described a different approach in the treatment of a 16-year-old boy who had survived a shipping accident two years earlier. The boy was asked to imagine and describe accurately what he had observed, heard, felt, smelled, and thought during the accident. The session was audiotaped and the boy went on to listen to the tape at home between sessions. Following treatment, significant clinical gains were observed on the standardized measures of anxiety and depression, and on the IES. After treatment, the boy could travel on a boat again for the first time in two years.

Therapeutic exposure under supportive circumstances seems to deal well with intrusion symptoms and behavioral avoidance. However, a flexible treatment approach which uses additional techniques to treat other common reactions such as sleep disturbance, separation anxiety, anger and conduct problems, prolonged grief reactions, generalized anxiety, and depression will be necessary.

Sleep disturbance is a common problem among children who have lived through traumatic experiences. A careful analysis will reveal whether the problem is one of getting off to sleep or in waking due to trauma-related nightmares. In the former case, implementing relaxation routines before bed and masking thoughts with music may help. In the latter, there are now positive cognitive behavioral techniques for alleviating nightmares, including dream restructuring approaches. In younger children, post-traumatic regressive behavior may include night time enuresis, and this may be treated using star charts and enuresis alarm techniques while addressing the central trauma.

Given the nature of traumatic events, children are frequently bereaved as a consequence. Pynoos and Nader (1988) emphasize the need to help children to distinguish their trauma-related responses from those related to grief, and suggest that where several children are bereaved, small groups can be beneficial in the initial stages. Dyregrov's (1993) account of the distinguishing features of traumatic bereavement implies that the traumatic nature of the death and post-trauma reactions need to be addressed before grieving can begin. Black (1993) uses a variety of techniques, including the use of drawings and play in her work with children who have been bereaved because of one parent killing another. Importantly, she also describes how family work—including that with new carers—is necessary in cases where a child has lost a parent.

Guilt, self-blame, helplessness, and vulnerability are common themes among older children and adolescents who have survived traumatic events. While these may be related to depressive features, they are often seen to have a different quality to them. Children may talk of omens, relating perhaps to a search for meaning as well as being related to issues of culpability. In work with younger children, it is important that any misunderstandings about the causes of the event are clarified, while with older children, cognitive restructuring may be used to counter misattributions of predictability, causality, and responsibility. Janoff-Bulman's (1985) work with adults about the shattering of key assumptions regarding self-invulnerability, life meaningfulness, and world justice are useful here.

Pynoos' (1994) developmental framework for understanding trauma reactions has a number of implications for therapeutic intervention. The model suggests that the interaction over time of many critical factors (including the complexity of the traumatic experience and the interactions of traumatic reminders, secondary stress, post-traumatic distress, and development) play a role in the progression from traumatic exposure to psychopathology. Each of these factors can be seen as a potential focus for intervention. Similarly, James (1989) describes the use of early intervention with subsequent "pulsed intervention" over time using multifaceted treatment approaches.

Finally, the most recent addition to the armamentarium of individual treatment techniques for PTSD is Eye Movement Desensitization and Reprocessing (EMDR) (Shapiro, 1989). The technique employs dual-attention tasks, most notably saccadic eye movements, to facilitate accelerated processing of traumatic memories and is fully described elsewhere (Shapiro, 1995). There is considerable controversy about the efficacy of the procedure in adults with PTSD, and no controlled trials with children. Some authors have described how EMDR can be adapted successfully and used with children (e.g., Greenwald, 1994). Cocco and Sharpe (1993) report the successful use of an auditory variant of EMDR with a 4-year-old boy diagnosed as suffering from PTSD following a violent robbery. Further research is clearly needed, but given the poor understanding of the rationale behind EMDR and the lack of any convincing evidence for its efficacy in work with children, the procedure should be used with care until outcome evaluation data and reliable protocols are available.

5.16.4.1.5 Community approaches

Following large-scale disasters, whole communities may be affected and this clearly requires a different kind of approach. The type of intervention will depend, broadly, on the nature of the disaster and the kind of community affected.

Early intervention is designed to help reduce levels of distress that may later lead to psychopathology and will allow for screening of vulnerable individuals. Often, the needs of the community will be for short-term therapeutic assistance rather than a traditional mental health service. Therefore, and because of the chaos that ensues following mass disaster, outreach services are recommended in the first place. Joyner and Swenson (1993) provide an account of Project Hugo, implemented after Hurricane Hugo struck South Carolina in 1989. Outreach teams of counselors quickly provided support and information to thousands of affected people. Telephone hotlines were set up, and fliers and information booklets produced. Joyner and Swenson stress the need for networking among emergency and support teams, as well as for building on the existing pastoral resources of the community (i.e., churches or schools).

Concentrating on the needs of children after the Australian bushfires, McFarlane (1991) has described how a preventative outreach program was implemented through schools using workbooks for pupils. The workbooks provided information about the bushfires as well as exercises designed to label and normalize common reactions, and to help children develop coping strategies with help from parents and teachers.

Where pre-existing community resources are either scarce or completely devastated by the disaster, the needs are different, and a modified approach is needed. Pynoos et al. (1993) characterized the psychological effects on children of the Armenian earthquakes of 1988 as severe, pervasive, and chronic. In this case, it was not possible to set up telephone hotlines or draft in teams of counselors from elsewhere: following an evaluation of existing services and a pilot screening of children, the emphasis here was on training local therapists to carry out brief psychotherapy and behavioral therapy (Goenjian, 1993). Therapists were selected carefully before training, and worked in pairs or teams such that they could support each other. Makeshift clinics were set up, and group and individual therapy, which included play, drawing, and storytelling, was implemented wherever possible including parents and teachers. Two therapeutic booklets, one for adults and one for children, were prepared and distributed. Importantly, considerable attention was paid to helping manage the stress of community leaders and the newly trained carers, themselves also affected by the devastation.

The trend in the twentieth century for war increasingly to affect civilians (particularly women and children) directly (UNICEF; 1996) has led to attempts by international relief agencies to meet the psychological needs of children in areas of recent and ongoing conflict (Kuterovac et al., 1994; Macksoud, Dyregrov, & Raundalen, 1993; Smith & Yule, 1995). The emphasis has been on rebuilding scarce local resources by training health workers, teachers, religious leaders, and others to deliver services at a variety of levels. Useful manuals that can be used by teachers and others in recognizing the signs of traumatic stress and providing initial treatment have been written after conflicts in Mozambique (Raundalen, Dyregrov, & Gronvold-Bugge, 1990; Richman, 1991, 1993), Lebanon (Macksoud et al., 1993), and Sri Lanka (Nikapota & Samarasinghe, 1993), but it should be noted that none of these has yet been evaluated in the field.

5.16.4.2 Pharmacological Approaches

There is little available data on the pharmacological treatment of PTSD in children and adolescents. It has barely been studied, and usually as an adjunct to psychosocial treatments (Terr, 1996). Still, it is being increasingly recognized as part of a multidimensional treatment approach to PTSD in adults (Sutherland & Davidson, 1994). As discussed above, PTSD is a disorder of various symptoms including severe anxiety, dissociation and disorganization, depression, and anger, and with potential underlying neurobiological mechanisms. As such, pharmacological treatment in children cannot be ruled out.

A variety of pharmacological agents have been used in the treatment of adults with PTSD to varying degrees of success including: tricyclic antidepressants (TCAs); monoamine oxidase inhibitors (MAOIs; phenelzine); selective serotenergic reuptake inhibitors (SSRIs; fluoxetine, sertraline, and fluvoxamine); anticonvulsant agents (carbamazepine and valproic acid); benzodiazepines (aprazolam, clonazepam, lorazepam); clonidine; and beta-blockers (propranolol). While inferring from adult studies that such agents would be appropriate with children or effective is not possible, a brief discussion on this topic is instructive. In several controlled trials with adult PTSD patients (Davidson et al., 1990; Frank, Kosten, Giller, & Dan, 1988; Shestatzky, Greenberg, & Lerer, 1988), drugs with serotonergic action (TCAs, MAOIs, and SSRIs) have achieved the most positive effects with the best results achieved after longer treatment trials (Sutherland & Davidson, 1994). TCAs and SSRIs are often prescribed for children with severe anxiety and depressive reactions and their potential use with children and adolescents with PTSD should be explored.

Again, as discussed above, many of the symptoms of PTSD have been hypothesized to result from excessive activity of the central adregeneric system, leading some clinicians to use adrenergic blocking agents such as propranolol and clonidine (Sutherland & Davidson, 1994). In one of the few studies to directly approach this issue in children, Kinzie and Leung (1989) found that clonidine (a centrally acting drug sometimes used for treatment of Tourette's syndrome) may help children who have significant avoidant symptoms, startle responses, or trauma-related depression. Pynoos and Nader (1993) note preliminary results suggesting that clonidine may reduce persistent arousal in children. In an uncontrolled, nonblind study, Famularo, Küscheff, & Fenton, (1988) found that propranolol (a β-blocking agent) relieved the arousal symptoms of children who were exposed to sexual assault. The results of these studies are consistent with previous trials of clonidine and propranolol in adult combat veterans (see Kolb, Burris, & Griffith, 1984).

While carefully controlled drug-treatment trials in children and adolescents with PTSD are awaited, use of pharmacological agents shows some promise. While many psychologists express an appropriate level of caution (if not aversion) when considering referral of children for pharmacological treatment, the presence of chronic and severely debilitating symptoms of PTSD in a child may require thoughtful consideration of pharmacotherapy.

Still, some precautions are worth mentioning here. First, Lundin (1994) has suggested that drugs be chosen carefully so that they do not undermine the individual's capacity for working through the trauma. Thus, he suggests that making regular use of benzodiazepines is generally inadvisable. Second, the issue of comorbid diagnoses should be evaluated thoroughly as some agents may be useful for targeting particular PTSD symptoms but may affect certain comorbid conditions. Finally, as noted by Sutherland and Davidson (1994) in their review of the literature, response to pharmacotherapy in PTSD may be relatively slow, perhaps reflecting underlying structural changes in the brain, and trials of eight weeks or longer may be necessary to achieve the maximum benefits.

5.16.4.3 Efficacy

There have been no randomized, controlled treatment trials for PTSD in children, and no long-term treatment follow up studies. However, regarding debriefing, Yule (1992) observed that children who attended debriefing meetings fared better on a range of outcome measures than children who were not offered such help. Inferences drawn from this study must be limited, however, since the debriefing group also received additional treatment. Stallard and Law's (1993) uncontrolled trial of debriefing showed significant improvements on standardized self-report measures in a small group of young children involved in a road traffic accident.

Galante and Foa's (1986) evaluation of structured group therapy showed significant teacher-rated improvements on the Rutter Questionnaire (Rutter, 1967) in children from one earthquake-affected village. By comparison, in only one out of five affected villages where therapeutic groups were not held did children improve significantly. Concerning individual therapy, Saigh's series (1987a, 1987b, 1989a, 1989b) of single case multiple baseline across traumatic scene studies is promising for behaviorally based exposure treatments. In an uncontrolled trial of individual cognitive behavior therapy with 19 sexually abused and traumatized children, Deblinger, McLeer, & Henry (1990) found that all symptoms showed some improvement: each major category of PTSD symptoms improved, and although some children were still symptomatic, none met criteria post-treatment.

5.16.5 FUTURE DIRECTIONS FOR RESEARCH AND PRACTICE

The study of post-traumatic stress reactions in children remains wide open with regard to areas in need of additional research. Five main areas appear particularly important for the area of child traumatic stress: (i) descriptive studies of young people's reactions across trauma types and age/developmental stages; (ii) neurobiological correlates of PTSD; (iii) neuropsychological and physiological assessment of PTSD; (iv) follow-up studies of children with PTSD; and (v) response to psychological and pharmacological treatment.

The paucity of data available looking at post-traumatic reactions at different age levels has been highlighted. While PTSD can be diagnosed even in very young children, it is inaccurate to assume that PTSD, as currently defined, is sufficient to capture the breadth of children's post-traumatic reactions. Additional research using age-appropriate measures and standardized behavioral observation methods are needed. Furthermore, children's post-traumatic perceptions of the trauma, themselves, and their world have yet to be evaluated in any systematic fashion. The adaptation of belief scales based on the work of Janoff-Bulman (1992) to children may be useful in this regard.

The neurobiological models of PTSD have not been rigorously tested in children. Studies employing the hormonal, neuronal, and brain-imaging techniques used with adults need to be developed for use with children and adolescents. Similarly, psychophysiological measures have only been used in the 1990s with children, however, with promising findings (cf., Pynoos et al., 1993). Additional studies employing salivary cortisol tests and ambulatory measures of hyperarousal may be of particular use in this regard. Moreover, studies using neuropsychological measures developed with children to increase our understanding of the memory and concentration impairments associated with PTSD in children are needed.

Finally, and perhaps most important, is the need for long-term follow-up and treatment studies of PTSD in children and adolescents. Studies employing both referred and nonreferred children with PTSD and carefully selected control groups are necessary before any firm conclusions about the chronicity of PTSD, and the effectiveness of currently available treatments, can be reached.

5.16.6 SUMMARY

In this chapter the literature on the nature and treatment of PTSD in children and adolescents has been highlighted. This literature is growing but clearly lags behind its adult counterpart. However, current research supports the conclusion that children and adolescents exposed to severe and life-threatening traumas can develop PTSD as well as other disorders.

While PTSD as a diagnostic category has significant limitations for capturing all the effects of trauma in both children and adults, it has proved a useful guideline for both clinical and research purposes. In particular, there is an emerging body of work suggesting that across cultures and traumatic events, children exhibit similar types of stress reactions, which may reflect post-traumatic changes in the central nervous system as well as emotional and cognitive disturbances. Unfortunately, our understanding of the effects of trauma at different ages and their chronicity remains poor, and like other areas of child psychopathology, controlled treatment-outcome studies of childhood PTSD are desperately needed.

5.16.7 REFERENCES

American Psychiatric Association (1980). *Diagnostic and Statistical Manual of Mental Disorders* (3rd ed.). Washington, DC: American Psychiatric Association.
American Psychiatric Association (1987). *Diagnostic and Statistical Manual of Mental Disorders* (3rd ed. Rev.). Washington, DC: American Psychiatric Association.
American Psychiatric Association (1994). *Diagnostic and Statistical Manual of Mental Disorders* (4th ed.). Washington, DC: American Psychiatric Association.
Arroyo, W., & Eth, S. (1985). Children traumatized by Central American warfare. In S. Eth & R. S. Pynoos (Eds.), *Posttraumatic stress disorder in children*. Washington, DC: American Psychiatric Press.
Beck, A. T., Rush, A. J., Shaw, B. F., & Emery, G. (1979). *Cognitive therapy of depression*, New York: Guilford Press.
Birleson, P. (1981). The validity of depressive disorder in childhood and the development of a self-rating scale: A research report. *Journal of Child Psychology and Psychiatry, 22*, 73–88.
Black, D. (1993). When father kills mother. In G. Forrest (Ed.), *ACPP Occasional Papers*, Number 8. London: Association for Child Psychology and Psychiatry.
Boudewyns, P. A., & Hyer, L. (1990). Physiologic response to combat memories and preliminary treatment outcome in Vietnam veteran PTSD patients treated with direct therapeutic exposure. *Behavior Therapy, 21*, 63–87.
Boyle, S., Bolton, D., Nurrish, J., O'Ryan, D., Udwin, O., & Yule, W. (1995). *The Jupiter sinking follow up: Predicting psychopathology in adolescence following trauma*. Paper presented at International Society for Traumatic Stress Studies Annual Meeting (November), Boston, MA.
Bradburn, L. S. (1991). After the earth shook: children's stress symptoms 6–8 months after a disaster. *Advances in Behavioural Research & Therapy, 13*, 173–179.
Burke, J., Moccia, P., Borus, J., & Burns, B. (1986). Emotional distress in fifth grade children ten months after a natural disaster. *Journal of the American Academy of Child and Adolescent Psychiatry, 25*, 536–541.
Cocco, N., & Sharpe, L. (1993). An auditory variant of eye movement desensitization in a case of childhood post-traumatic stress disorder. *Journal of Behavior Therapy and Experimental Psychiatry, 24*, 373–377.
Cooper, N. A., & Clum, G. A. (1990). Imaginal flooding as a supplementary treatment for PTSD in combat veterans: a controlled study. *Behaviour Therapy, 20*, 381–391.
Davidson, J. R. T., Kudler, H. S., Smith, R., Mahoney, S. L., Lipper, S., Hammett, E., Saunders, W. B., & Cavenar, J. O. (1990). Treatment of posttraumatic stress disorder with amitriptyline and placebo. *Archives of General Psychiatry, 47*, 259–266.
Deblinger, E., McLeer, S. V., & Henry, D. (1990). Cognitive behavioral treatment for sexually abused children suffering posttraumatic stress: Preliminary findings. *Journal of the American Academy of Child and Adolescent Psychiatry, 19*, 747–752.
Dyregrov, A. (1991). *Grief in children: A handbook for adults*. London: Jessica Kingsley.
Dyregrov, A. (1993). The interplay of trauma and grief. In G. Forrest (Ed.), *ACPP Occasional Papers*, Number 8.
Dyregrov, A., & Yule, W. (1995, May). *Screening measures: The development of the UNICEF screening battery*. Paper presented at The Fourth European Conference on Traumatic Stress, Paris.
Earls, F., Smith, E., Reich, W., & Jung, K. G. (1988). Investigating psychopathological consequences of disaster in children: A pilot study incorporating a structured diagnostic approach. *Journal of the American Academy of Child and Adolescent Psychiatry, 27*, 90–95.
Eisenberg, C. (1996, August). *Mental health of people and*

the effects of war on children. Plenary paper presented at the Tenth World Congress of Psychiatry, Madrid, Spain.

Eth, S., & Pynoos, R. S. (1985). Psychiatric interventions with children traumatized by violence. In D.H. Schetky & E. P. Benedek (Eds.), *Emerging issues in child psychiatry and the law* (pp. 285–309). New York: Brunner/Mazel.

Fairbank, J. A., Schlenger, W. E., Saigh, P. A., & Davidson, J. R. T. (1995). An epidemiologic profile or post-traumatic stress disorder: Prevalence, comorbidity, and risk factors. In M. J. Friedman, D. S. Charney, & A. Y. Deutch (Eds.), *Neurobiological and clinical consequences of stress: From normal adaptation to PTSD* (pp. 415–427). Philadelphia: Lippincott-Raven.

Famularo, R., Kinscherff, R, & Fenton, T. (1988). Propranolol treatment for childhood posttraumatic stress disorder, acute type. *American Journal of the Disordered Child, 142,* 144–1247.

Finch, A. J., & Daugherty, T. K. (1993). Issues in the assessment of posttraumatic stress disorder in children. In C. F. Saylor (Ed.), *Children and disasters: Issues in clinical child psychology* (pp. 45–66). New York: Plenum.

Foa, E. B., & Kozak, M. J. (1986). Emotional processing of fear: Exposure to corrective information. *Psychological Bulletin, 99,* 220–35.

Foa, E. B., Steketee, G., & Olasov-Rothbaum, B. (1989). Behavioral/cognitive conceptualizations of post-traumatic stress disorder. *Behavior Therapy, 20,* 155–176.

Fonseca, A. C., Yule, W., & Erol, N. (1994). Cross-cultural studies of children's fears. In T. H. Ollendick, N. King, & W. Yule (Eds.), *International handbook of phobic and anxiety disorders in children and adolescents* (pp. 67–84). New York: Plenum.

(1988). A randomized clinical trial of phenelzine and imipramine for post traumatic stress disorders. *American Journal Psychiatry, 145,* 1289–1291.

Frederick, C. (1985a). Children traumatized by catastrophic situations. In S. Eth & R. S. Pynoos (Eds.), *Posttraumatic stress disorder in children* (pp. 73–99). Washington, DC: American Psychiatric Press.

Frederick, C. (1985b). Selected foci in the spectrum of post traumatic stress disorders. In L. J. Murphy (Ed.), *Perspectives on disaster recovery* (pp. 110–130). East Norwalk, CT: Appleton-Century-Crofts.

Freidman, M. J., Charney, D. S., & Deutch, A. Y. (1995). *Neurobiological and clinical consequences of stress: From normal adaptation to post-traumatic stress disorder.* Philadelphia: Lippincott-Raven.

Galante, R., & Foa, D. (1986). An epidemiological study of psychic trauma and treatment effectiveness after a natural disaster. *Journal American Academy of Child Psychiatry, 25,* 357–363.

Garrison, C. Z., Weinrich, M. W., Hardin, S. B., Weinrich, S., & Wang, L. (1993). Post-traumatic stress disorder in adolescents after a hurricane. *American Journal of Epidemiology, 138,* 52–53.

Garmezy, N. (1984). Stress-resistant children: The search for protective factors. In J. Stevenson (Ed.), *Recent research in developmental psychology. Journal of Child Psychology and Psychiatry* (Suppl. 4, pp. 213–233). Oxford: Pergamon.

Garmezy, N., & Rutter, M. (1985). Acute reactions to stress. In M. Rutter & L. Hersov (Eds.), *Child and adolescent psychiatry: Modern approaches* (2nd ed., pp. 152–176). Oxford: Blackwell Scientific Publications.

Gillis, H. M. (1993). Individual and small-group psychotherapy for children involved in trauma and disaster. In C. F. Saylor (Ed.), *Children and disasters* (pp. 165–186). New York: Plenum.

Goenjian, A. (1993). A mental health relief programme in Armenia after the 1988 earthquake. *British Journal of Psychiatry, 163,* 230–239.

Goodwin, J. (1988). Post traumatic symptoms in abused children. *Journal of Traumatic Stress, 4,* 475–488.

Green, B. L., Korol, M., Grace, M. C., Vary, M. G., Leonard, A. C., Glesser, G. C., & Smithson-Cohen, S. (1991). Children and disaster: Age, gender, and parental effects on PTSD symptoms. *Journal of the American Academy of Child and Adolescent Psychiatry, 30,* 945–951.

Greenwald, R. (1994). Applying eye movement desensitization and reprocessing (EMDR) to the treatment of traumatized children: Five case studies. *Anxiety Disorders Practice Journal, 1,* 83–97.

Handford, H. A., Mayes, S. O., Mattison, R. E., Humphrey, F. J., Bagnato, S., Bixler, E. O., & Kales, J. D. (1986). Child and parent reaction to the TMI nuclear accident. *Journal of American Academy of Child Psychiatry, 25,* 346–355.

Herman, J. L. (1992). Complex PTSD: A syndrome in survivors of prolonged and repeated trauma. *Journal of Traumatic Stress, 5,* 377–391.

Horowitz, M. J., Wilner, N., & Alvarez, W. (1979). Impact of event scale: A measure of subjective stress. *Psychosomatic Medicine, 41,* 209–218.

James, B. (1989). *Treating traumatized children: New insights and creative interventions.* Lexington, MA: Lexington Books.

Janoff-Bulman, R. (1992). *Shattered assumptions: Towards a new psychology of trauma.* New York: Free Press.

Jones, J. C., & Barlow, D. H. (1992). A new model for posttraumatic stress disorder: Implications for the future. In P. A. Saigh (Ed.), *Post-traumatic stress disorder: A behavioral approach to assessment and treatment* (pp. 147–165). New York: Macmillan.

Joseph, S. A., Brewin, C. R., Yule, W., & Williams, R. (1991). Causal attributions and psychiatric symptoms in survivors of the Herald of Free Enterprise disaster. *British Journal of Psychiatry, 159,* 542–546.

Joseph, S. A., Brewin, C., Yule, W., & Williams, R. (1993). Causal attributions and psychiatric symptoms in adolescent survivors of disaster. *Journal of Child Psychology Psychiatry, 34,* 247–253.

Joyner, C. D., & Swenson, C. C. (1993). Community level intervention after a disaster. In C. F. Saylor (Ed.), *Children and Disasters* (pp. 211–239). New York: Plenum.

Keane, T. M., Fairbank, J. A., & Caddell, J. M. (1989). Implosive (flooding) therapy reduces symptoms of PTSD in Vietnam combat veterans. *Behavior Therapy, 20,* 245–260.

Keane, T. M., Zimmering, R. T., & Caddell, J. M. (1985). A behavioral formulation of PTSD in Vietnam veterans. *The Behavior Therapist, 8,* 9–12.

Keppel-Benson, J. M., & Ollendick, T. H. (1993). Posttraumatic stress disorders in children and adolescents. In C. F. Saylor (Ed.), *Children and disasters* (pp. 29–43). New York: Plenum.

Kinzie, J. D., & Leung, P. (1989). Clonidine in Cambodian patients with posttraumatic stress disorder. *Journal of Nervous and Mental Diseases, 177,* 546–550.

Kinzie, J. D., Sack, W. H., Angell, R. H., Manson, S., & Rath, B. (1986). The psychiatric effects of massive trauma on Cambodian children: I. The children. *Journal of the American Academy of Child and Adolescent Psychiatry, 25,* 370–376.

Klingman, A. (1993). School-based intervention following a disaster. In C. F. Saylor (Ed.), *Children and disasters* (pp. 187–210). New York: Plenum.

Kolb, L. C. (1988). A critical survey of hypotheses regarding PTSD in light of recent research. *Journal of Traumatic Stress, 3,* 291–304.

Kolb, L. C., Burris, B., & Griffith, S. (1984). Propranolol and Clonidine in the treatment of the chronic posttraumatic stress disorders of war. In B. Van der Kolk (Ed.), *Posttraumatic stress disorder: Psychological and biologi-*

cal sequelae (pp. 97–107). Washington, DC: American Psychiatric Association.

Kuterovac, G., Dyregrov, A., & Stuvland, R. (1994). Children in war: A silent majority under stress. *British Journal of Medical Psychology, 67,* 363–375.

Lang, P. J. (1985). The cognitive psychophysiology of emotion: Fear and anxiety. In A. H. Turner & J. Maser (Eds.), *Anxiety and the anxiety disorders* (pp. 131–170). Hillsdale, NJ: Lawrence Erlbaum Associates.

Law, J., & Conway, J. (1992). Effect of abuse and neglect on children's speech and language. *Developmental Medicine and Child Neurology, 34,* 943–948.

Leff, J., & Bhugra, D. (1993). *Principles of social psychiatry.* Oxford: Blackwell.

Lonigan, C. J., Shannon, M. P., Finch, A. J., Daugherty, T. K., & Saylor, C. M. (1991). Children's reactions to a natural disaster: Symptom severity and degree of exposure. *Advances in Behaviour Research and Therapy, 13,* 135–154.

Lundin, T. (1994). The treatment of acute trauma: Posttraumatic stress disorder prevention. In D. A. Tomb (Ed.), *Posttraumatic Stress Disorder: Psychiatric Clinicas of North America* (Vol. 17, pp. 385–392). Washington, DC: American Psychiatric Association.

Lyons, J. L. (1987). Posttraumatic stress disorder in children and adolescents: A review of the literature. *Developmental and Behavioral Pediatrics, 8,* 349–356.

Macksoud, M. S., Dyregrov, A., & Raundalen, M. (1993). Traumatic war experiences and their effects on children. In J. P. Wilson & B. Raphael (Eds.), *International handbook of traumatic stress syndromes* (pp. 625–633). New York: Plenum.

Maier, S. F. (1986). Stressor controllability and stress induced analgesia. *Annals of the New York Academy of Science, 467,* 55–72.

Malmquist, C. P. (1986). Children who witness parental murder: Posttraumatic aspects. *Journal of the American Academy of Child and Adolescent Psychiatry, 25,* 320–325.

Martin, S., & Little, B. (1986). The effects of a natural disaster on the academic abilities and social behavior of school children. *British Columbian Journal of Special Education, 10,* 167–182.

McFarlane, A. C. (1987). Family functioning and over-protection following a natural disaster: The longitudinal effects of post-traumatic morbidity. *Australia and New Zealand Journal of Psychiatry, 21,* 210–218.

McFarlane, A. C. (1994). Helping victims of disasters. In J. R. Freedy & S. E. Hobfoll (Eds.), *Traumatic stress: From theory to practice* (pp. 287–314). New York: Plenum.

McFarlane, A. C., Policansky, S., & Irwin, C. P. (1987). A longitudinal study of the psychological morbidity in children due to a natural disaster. *Psychological Medicine, 17,* 727–738.

McGaugh, J. L. (1990). Significance and remembrance: The role of neuromodulatory systems. *Psychological Science, 1,* 15–25.

McLeer, S. V., Deblinger, E., Henry, D., & Orvaschel, H. (1992). Sexually abused children at high risk for post-traumatic stress disorder. *Journal of the American Academy of Child and Adolescent Psychiatry, 31,* 875–879.

McNally, R. J. (1991). Assessment of posttraumatic stress disorder in children. *Psychological Assessment, 3,* 531–537.

Meichenbaum, D. (1994). *A clinical handbook/practical therapist manual for assessing and treating adults with post-traumatic stress disorder (PTSD).* Ontario: Institute Press.

Milgram, N. A., Toubiana, Y., Klingman, A., Raviv, A., & Goldstein, I. (1988). Situational exposure and personal loss in children's acute and chronic reactions to a school bus disaster. *Journal of Traumatic Stress, 1,* 339–532.

Milne, G. (1977). Cyclone Tracy II: The effects of Darwin on Children. *Australian Psychologist, 12,* 55–62.

Misch, P., Phillips, M., Evans, P., & Berekowitz, M. (1993). Trauma in preschool children: A clinical account. *Association of Child Psychology and Psychiatry: Occasional Papers, 8,* 11–18.

Mitchell, J. T. (1983). When disaster strikes: The critical incident stress debriefing process. *Journal of Emergency Medicine, 8,* 36–39.

Mitchell, J. T. (1996, March). *Critical Incident Stress Management: Current status and future directions.* Paper presented at the annual meeting of the European Society for Traumatic Stress Studies conference, Sheffield, UK.

Mitchell, J. T., & Everly, G. S. (1993). *Critical incident stress debriefing: An operations manual for the prevention of trauma among emergency service and disaster workers.* Baltimore, MD: Chevron Publishing.

Mowrer, O. H. (1960). *Learning theory and behavior.* New York: Wiley.

Nader, K. O. (1995). Assessing traumatic experiences in children. In J. P. Wilson & T. M. Keane (Eds.), *Assessing psychological trauma and PTSD: A handbook for practioners* (pp. 217–244). New York: Guilford Press.

Nader, K. O., & Fairbanks, L. (1994). The suppression of reexperiencing: Impulse control and somatic symptoms in children following traumatic exposure. *Anxiety, Stress, and Coping: An International Journal, 7,* 229–239.

Nader, K. O., Kriegler, J., Keane, T., Blake, D., & Pynoos, R. S. (1994). *Clinician Administered PTSD Scale: Child and Adolescent Version (CAPS-C).* White River Junction, VT: National Center for PTSD.

Nader, K. O., & Pynoos, R. S. (1989). *Child posttraumatic stress disorder inventory: Parent Interview.* Unpublished manuscript, University of California, Los Angeles.

Nader, K. O., Pynoos, R. S., Fairbanks, L., & Frederick, C. (1991). Childhood PTSD reactions one year after a sniper attack. *American Journal of Psychiatry, 147,* 1526–1530.

Newman, C. J. (1976) Children of disasters: Clinical observations at Buffalo Creek. *American Journal of Psychiatry, 133,* 306-312.

Nikapota, A., & Samarasinghe, D. (1993). *Training manual for helping children in situations of armed conflict.* Colombo, Sri Lanka: UNICEF.

Nir, Y. (1984). Post traumatic stress disorder in children with cancer. In S. Eth & R. S. Pynoos (Eds.), *Post traumatic stress disorder in children* (pp. 121–132). Washington, DC: American Psychiatric Press.

O'Donohue, W., & Elliot, A. (1992). The current status of posttraumatic stress disorder as a diagnostic category: Problems and proposals. *Journal of Traumatic Stress, 5,* 421–439.

Ollendick, T. H. (1983). Reliability and validity of the Revised Fear Survey Schedule for Children (FSSC-R). *Behaviour Research & Therapy, 21,* 685–692.

Ollendick, T. H., Yule, W., & Ollier, K. (1991). Fears in British children and its relationship to manifest anxiety and depression. *Journal of Child Psychology and Psychiatry, 32,* 321–331.

Parry-Jones, W. (1996, August). *Planning treatment programmes for traumatised school children.* Paper presented at ACPP 3rd European Conference, Glasgow, Scotland.

Perrin, S., Smith, P., Schwartz, D., & Yule, W. (1996a, November). *Self-report of stress reactions: A cross-cultural validation study.* Paper presented at the 12th Annual Convention of the International Society for Traumatic Stress Studies, San Francisco.

Perrin, S., Yule, W., & Smith, P. (1996b, November). *Post traumatic stress in children as a function of sibling and parental exposure to the trauma.* Paper presented at the 12th Annual Convention of the International Society for Traumatic Stress Studies, San Francisco.

Pitman, R. (1989). Posttraumatic stress disorder, hormones, and memory. *Biological Psychiatry*, *226*, 221–223.

Pitman, R., Orr, S., Forgue, D. F., Altman, B., de Jong, J. B., & Herz, L. R. (1990). Psychophysiologic responses to combat imagery of Vietnam veterans with posttraumatic stress disorder versus other anxiety disorders. *Journal of Abnormal Psychology*, *99*, 49–54.

Pynoos, R. S. (1994). In R. S. Pynoos (Ed.), *Posttraumatic stress disorder: A clinical review*. Lutherville, MD: Sidran Press.

Pynoos, R. S., & Eth, S. (1986). Witness to violence: The child interview. *Journal of the American Academy of Child and Adolescent Psychiatry*, *25*, 306–319.

Pynoos, R. S., Frederick, C., Nader, K. O., Arroyo, W., Steinberg, A., Eth, S., Nunez, F., & Fairbanks, L. A. (1987). Life threat and posttraumatic stress in school-age children. *Archives of General Psychiatry*, *44*, 1057–1063.

Pynoos, R. S., Goenjian, A., Karakashian, M., Tashjian, M., Manjikian, R., Manoukian, G., Steinberg, A. M., & Fairbanks, L. A. (1993). Posttraumatic stress reactions in children after the 1988 Armenian earthquake. *British Journal of Psychiatry*, *163*, 239–247.

Pynoos, R. S., & Nader, K. O. (1988). Psychological first aid and treatment approaches for children exposed to community violence: Research implications. *Journal of Traumatic Stress*, *1*, 243–267.

Pynoos, R. S., & Nader, K. O. (1993). Issues in the treatment of posttraumatic stress in children and adolescents. In J. Wilson & B. Raphael (Eds.), *International handbook of traumatic stress syndromes* (pp. 535–549). New York: Plenum.

Rachman, S. (1980). Emotional processing. *Behaviour Research and Therapy*, *18*, 51–60.

Raundalen, M., Dyregrov, A., & Gronvold Bugge, R. (1990). *Reaching children through teachers: Helping the war traumatized child: A manual*. Maputo: Red Cross.

Reich, W., & Earls, F. (1987). Rules for making diagnosis on the basis of multiple sources of information: Preliminary strategies. *Abnormal Child Psychology*, *15*(4), 601–606.

Reich, W., Shakya, J. J., & Taibelson, C. (1991). *Diagnostic Interview for Children and Adolescents (DICA)*. St. Louis, MO: Washington University.

Reynolds, C. R., & Richmond, B. O. (1978). What I think and feel: A revised measure of children's manifest anxiety. *Journal of Abnormal Child Psychology*, *6*, 271–280.

Ribbe, D. P., Lipovsky, J. A., & Freedy, J. R. (1995). Posttraumatic Stress Disorder. In A. R. Eisen, C. A. Kearny, & C. E. Schaefer (Eds.), *Clinical handbook of anxiety disorders in children and adolescents* (pp. 317–356). Northvale, NJ: Jason Aronson.

Richman, N. (1991). *Helping children in difficult circumstances: A teacher's manual*. London: Save the Children.

Richman, N. (1993). *Communicating with children: Helping children in distress*. London: Save the Children.

Rutter, M. (1967). A children's behaviour questionnaire for completion by teachers: Preliminary findings. *Journal of Child Psychology and Psychiatry*, *8*, 1–11.

Sack, W. H., McSharry, S., Clarke, G. N., Kinney, R., Seeley, M. S., & Lewinsohn, P. (1994). The Khmer Adolescent Project: I. Epidemiologic findings in two generations of Cambodian refugees. *Journal of Nervous and Mental Diseases*, *182*, 387–395.

Saigh, P. A. (1987a). *In-vitro* flooding of an adolescent's posttraumatic stress disorder. *Journal of Clinical Child Psychology*, *16*, 147–150.

Saigh, P. A. (1987b). *In-vitro* flooding of a childhood posttraumatic stress disorder. *School Psychology Review*, *16*, 203–211.

Saigh, P. A. (1989a). The use of *in-vitro* flooding in the treatment of a traumatized adolescent. *Journal of Behavioural and Developmental Paediatrics*, *10*, 17–21.

Saigh, P. A. (1989b). The validity of *DSM-III* posttraumatic stress disorder classification as applied to children. *Journal of Abnormal Psychology*, *198*, 189–192.

Saigh, P. A. (1991). The development of posttraumatic stress disorder following four different types of traumatization. *Behaviour Research and Therapy*, *29*, 213–216.

Saigh, P. A. (1992). The behavioral treatment of child and adolescent posttraumatic stress disorder. *Advances in Behaviour Research and Therapy*, *14*, 247–275.

Shaffer, D., Fisher, P., Dulcan, M., & Davies, M. (1996). The NIMH Diagnostic Interview Schedule for Children (DISC-2.3): Description, acceptability, prevalences, and performance in the MECA study. *Journal of the American Academy of Child and Adolescent Psychiatry*, *35*(7), 865–877.

Shannon, M. P., Lonigan, C. J., Finch, A. J., & Taylor, C. M. (1994). Children exposed to disaster. I: Epidemiology of posttraumatic symptoms and symptom profiles. *Journal of the American Academy of Child and Adolescent Psychiatry*, *33*, 80–93.

Shapiro, F. (1989). Eye movement desensitization: a new treatment for post traumatic stress disorder. *Journal of Behaviour Therapy and Experimental Psychiatry*, *20*, 211–217.

Shapiro, F. (1995). *Eye movement desensitization and reprocessing: Basic principles protocols and procedures*. New York: Guilford Press.

Schestazky, M. Greenberg, D., & Lerer, B. (1988). A controlled trial of phenelzine in posttraumatic stress disorder. *Psychiatry Research*, *24*, 149–155.

Schwarz, E. D., & Kowalski, J. M. (1991). Posttraumatic stress disorder after a school shooting: Effects of symptom threshold selection and diagnosis by *DSM-III, DSM-III-R*, or proposed *DSM-IV*. *American Journal of Psychiatry*, *148*, 592–597.

Schwarz, E. D., & Perry, B. D. (1994). The post-traumatic response in children and adolescents. *Psychiatric Clinics of North America*, *17*, 311–326.

Smith, P., & Yule, W. (1995, May). *The Mostar Programme*. Paper presented at the fourth annual European Conference on Traumatic Stress, Paris, France.

Smith, P., Yule, W., Perrin, S., & Schwartz, D. (1996). *Maternal reactions and child distress following the war in Bosnia*. Paper presented at the 12th Annual Convention of the International Society for Traumatic Stress Studies (November), San Francisco.

Southwick, S. M., Bremner, D., Krystal, J. H., & Charney, D. S. (1994). Psychobiologic research in post-traumatic stress disorder. *Psychiatric Clinics of North America*, *17*, 251–264.

Spielberger, C. D., Gorsuch, R. L., & Luschene, R. E. (1970). *Manual for the State-Trait Anxiety Inventory*. Palo Alto, CA: Consulting Psychologists Press.

Stallard, P., & Law, F. (1993). Screening and psychological debriefing of adolescent survivors of life threatening events. *British Journal of Psychiatry*, *163*, 660–665.

Sternberg, K. J., Lamb, M. E., Greenbaum, C., Cichetti, D., Dawud, S., Cortes, R. M., Krispin, O., & Lorey, F. (1993). Effects of domestic violence on children's behavior problems and depression. *Developmental Psychology*, *29*, 44–52.

Stuber, M. L., Nader, K. O., Yashuda, P., Pynoos, R. S., & Cohen, S. (1991). Stress response after pediatric bone marrow transplantation: Preliminary results of a prospective longitudinal study. *Journal of the American Academy of Child and Adolescent Psychiatry*, *30*, 952–959.

Summerfield, D. (1996). *The impact of war and atrocity on civilian populations: Basic principles for NGO interventions and a critique of psychosocial trauma projects* (Paper 14). London: Overseas Development Institute Network.

Sutherland, S. M., & Davidson, R. T. (1994). Pharmacotherapy for post-traumatic stress disorder. *Psychiatric Clinics of North America, 17*, 409–423.

Terr, L. C. (1979). The children of Chowchilla. *Psychoanalytic Study of the Child, 34*, 547–623.

Terr, L. C. (1983). Chowchilla revisited: The effects of psychic trauma four years after a schoolbus kidnapping. *American Journal of Psychiatry, 140*, 1543–1550.

Terr, L. C. (1991). Childhood traumas: An outline and overview. *American Journal of Psychiatry, 148*, 10–20.

Terr, L. C. (1996). Acute responses to external events and posttraumatic stress disorder. In M. Lewis (Ed.), *Child and adolescent psychiatry: A comprehensive textbook* (pp. 753–763). Baltimore, MD: Williams & Wilkins.

Tsui, E. P. (1990). *The "Jupiter" sinking disaster: Effects on teenager's school performance.* Unpublished master's dissertation, Institute of Psychiatry, University of London.

UNICEF (1996). *Annual state of the world's children report.* New York: United Nations Childrens Relief Fund.

Van der Kolk, B. A., Greenberg, M. S., Orr, S. P., Pittman, R. K. (1989). Endogenous opioids, stress induced analgesia, and posttraumatic stress disorders. *Psychopharmacology Bulletin, 25*, 417–421.

Wolfe, V. V., Gentile, C., Sas, L., & Wolfe, D. A. (1991). Children's Impact of Traumatic Events Scale: A measure of post-sexual abuse PTSD symptoms. *Behavioral Assessment, 13*, 359–338.

Wolfe, V. V., Gentile, C., & Wolfe, D. A. (1989). The impact of sexual abuse on children: A PTSD formulation. *Behavior Therapy, 20*, 215–228.

World Health Organization (1992). *International classification of diseases: 10th edition.* Geneva: WHO.

Yehuda, R., Boisoneau, D., Lowry, M. T., & Giller, E. L. (1993). Relationship between lymphocyte glucocorticoid receptor number and urinary-free cortisol excretion in mood, anxiety, and psychotic disorder. *Biological Psychiatry, 34*, 18–25.

Yehuda, R., Kahana, B., Binder-Byrnes, K., Southwick, S. M., Mason, J. W., & Giller, E. L. (1995). Low urinary cortisol excretion in Holocaust survivors with posttraumatic stress disorder. *American Journal of Psychiatry, 152*, 982–986.

Yehuda, R., & McFarlane, A. C. (1995). Conflict between current knowledge about posttraumatic stress disorder and its original conceptual basis. *American Journal of Psychiatry, 152*, 1705–1713.

Yule, W. (1992). Post traumatic stress disorder in child survivors of shipping disasters: The sinking of the "Jupiter." *Psychotherapy and Psychosomatics, 57*, 200–205.

Yule, W. (1994). Post traumatic stress disorders. In M. Rutter, E. Taylor, & L. Hersov (Eds.), *Child and adolescent psychiatry: Modern approaches* (3rd ed., pp. 392–406). Oxford: Blackwells.

Yule, W., & Gold, A. (1993). *Wise before the event: Coping with crises in schools.* London: Calouste Gulbenkian Foundation.

Yule, W., Perrin, S., & Smith, P. (1996, August). *The effects on pre-school children of catastrophic events.* Paper presented at the Third European Conference of The Association for Child Psychology and Psychiatry, Glasgow, Scotland.

Yule, W., & Udwin, O. (1991). Screening child survivors for post-traumatic stress disorders: Experiences from the "Jupiter" sinking. *British Journal of Clinical Psychology, 30*, 131–138.

Yule, W., Udwin, O., & Murdoch, K. (1990). The "Jupiter" sinking: Effects on children's fears, depression and anxiety. *Journal of Child Psychology and Psychiatry, 31*, 1051–1061.

Yule, W., & Williams, R. (1990). Post traumatic stress reactions in children. *Journal of Traumatic Stress, 3*, 279–295.

Zimmerman-Tansella, C. H., Minghetti, S., Tacconi, A., & Tansella, M. (1978). The children's behavioural questionnaire for completion by teachers in an Italian sample: Preliminary results. *Journal of Child Psychology and Psychiatry, 19*, 167–173.

5.17
Depression

WILLIAM M. REYNOLDS
University of British Columbia, Vancouver, BC, Canada

5.17.1 INTRODUCTION

It can be estimated that depression affects onwards of two million children and adolescents in the USA and Canada. As an internalizing disorder in young people it is a source of intense misery and distress to those affected. By its nature, depression is often a silent disorder that generally affects few persons other than the depressed youngster. Because of its internalizing nature, we may view depression as an insidious psychological disturbance in young people. Thus, for some youngsters depression may be inconspicuous yet have deleterious effects on the child.

Depression is a disorder and disturbance of mood that has been described from ancient times with continued efforts to clarify the nature of this aspect of the human condition. Although we no longer ascribe the etiology of depression, or melancholia, to the function of bodily humors such as black bile or "perturbations of the soul" (Jackson, 1986), there are many commonalties between ancient and contemporary descriptions of the phenomenology of depression. In the early part of the twentieth century, a number of psychoanalysts sought to explain depression in light of the prominent analytic theories of the time, as seen in the work of Karl Abraham, Sigmund Freud, Sandor Rado and, somewhat later, Melanie Klein. Although not specific to depression, of particular note is the pioneer work of Adolf Meyer, whose formulations of psychopathology may be seen as approximating a biopsychosocial perspective.

More recently, the study of depression has encompassed many diverse fields of scientific inquiry. Psychology and psychiatry are those fields that typically come to mind, but a wide-ranging review of the fields that have examined depression include: biochemistry, genetics, social work, nursing, counseling, business, epidemiology, pharmacology, neurology, pediatrics, general medicine, biology, zoology, sociology, education, physiology, endocrinology, and other disciplines. There are well over 1000 research and clinical articles on depression in children and adolescents that have been published in English language journals, with hundreds of new studies appearing each year. The range of investigations and domains covers a vast spectrum of the biopsychosocial sciences, from research on the activity of killer cells in depressed adolescents and the relationship between killer cell activity and severity of self-reported depression to studies of maternal attachment behavior and depressive affect in preschool children.

As described in this chapter, the wide range of scientific disciplines that have focused on depression in children and adolescents supports an integrated perspective for the understanding of this disorder in young people. This perspective may be illustrated by a biopsychosocial model of depression. The biopsychosocial model provides a platform or framework for exploring the nature and enhancing our understanding of depression by examining the complex interplay between the biological endowment and characteristics of the individual, the person's psychological competence, and the psychosocial stressors that may affect the individual. The biopsychosocial perspective is not unique to the study of depression and has been applied to a wide range of human conditions and problems.

5.17.1.1 Depression as an Internalizing Disorder

In the conceptualization of psychopathology in children and adolescents, a predominant theme over the past two decades has been the differentiation of disorders as a function of their general phenotypic expression. This has lead to the categorization of disorders as primarily internalizing or externalizing, based on their general symptom manifestation (Reynolds, 1992a). Internalizing disorders are those that tend to be composed of relative covert symptoms, many of which are cognitive, internal to the youngster, or relatively difficult to observe. Externalizing disorders are overt, highly observable either directly or indirectly (such as in the outcome of certain antisocial behaviors), and typically expressed as behavioral excess.

Depression and depressive (mood) disorders in children and adolescents may be viewed as internalizing disorders. Depression as a psychological disorder is replete with symptom characteristics that are internal to the individual. These features include symptoms of cognitive, emotional, behavioral, and physiological impairment or dysfunction. Depression is more than just a low or dysphoric mood such as feeling sad, blue, or down in the dumps. Depression typically affects multiple areas of individual functioning, including behavioral, emotional, somatic, and cognitive domains. Depressive disorders represent serious forms of psychopathology of childhood and adolescence, given that some depressive episodes may lead to potentially life-threatening or negative outcomes. Previous notions of "adolescent turmoil" or the perspective of the adolescent who is "just going through a moody stage" are no longer viable conceptualizations (Offer & Schonert-Reichl, 1992). This is amply evident when one considers the large numbers of depressed and suicidal youth, a significant number of whom do not survive to adulthood or do so with significantly reduced psychosocial competence or functioning.

Overt behavior problems in youngsters have typically been characterized by disorders of behavioral excesses, and as such are often viewed as externalizing problems. Externalizing disorders, such as conduct disorders and attention-deficit hyperactivity disorder, represent classes of disorders that frequently come to the attention of classroom teachers or parents. Symptoms of these disorders are typically represented by behavioral excesses that interfere with normal classroom behavior or social interactions. Contrary to this, internalizing disorders such as depression are often undetected due to the more covert nature of their symptoms. For instance, feelings of subjective misery, hopelessness, fatigue, anhedonia, difficulty sleeping, and other symptoms of depression may not be readily observable, particularly in youngsters who may be characterized as shy or somewhat withdrawn. Depression differs from other behavior disorders of childhood and adolescence in its comorbidity with suicidal risk.

5.17.1.2 Depression as a Problem in Children and Adolescents

Depression in children and adolescents, within the scope of current nomenclature and systems of classification, is considered to be a mood disorder similar in many respects to this disorder in adults. From another perspective, depression in children and adolescents may be considered as significant perturbation of mood.

A depressed youngster may experience a range of symptoms, some of which may be overt, such as irritability or distinctly sad appearance, and others may be covert, as illustrated by feelings of low self-worth, hopelessness, suicidal thoughts, and guilt. In young people, depression represents a negative psychological state, that may be characterized as one of intense, subjective misery, despondency, and in some youngsters, irritability. Depression in children and adolescents can cause significant impairment in daily functioning and personal and social involvement (Puig-Antich et al., 1985). Children who are depressed are often withdrawn from the world around them, finding little pleasure in positive events or settings. Treats and previously fun activities are no longer desirable or sufficient to lighten their spirits. In young children, this affective state may be characterized as being moody or distant from others and slow to respond to social interactions with peers and family. Adolescents who are depressed often feel alone, helpless, and frustrated with friends and family who do not seem to understand them. Although this may characterize a great many adolescents, the depth and quality of these characteristics in depressed adolescents, and in particular, their lack of positive response to previously reinforcing events or activities generally distinguishes depression in adolescents from more normative trials and tribulations associated with the normative course of adolescence.

Some children and adolescents who are depressed also manifest suicidal thoughts and behaviors. This is particularly problematic and in some cases leads to death or physically disabling outcomes. Epidemiological data suggests that suicidal behaviors are a serious problem among children and adolescents (Reynolds & Mazza, 1994). Although some youngsters who demonstrate suicidal thoughts and behaviors do not manifest clinical levels of depression, the majority of suicidal youngsters are depressed, with many who view suicide as a way of ending their intense psychological distress.

Depression can take a variety of courses and chronicity, with relapse and recurrence relatively common over the lifespan (Keller, 1994; Kovacs, 1996a). Kovacs and colleagues, in a noteworthy longitudinal study of depression in children, found that for some youngsters, particularly those with a dysthymic disorder, their depression may last for many years, and in some children represents a precursor or risk factor for other psychiatric disorders (Kovacs, 1985; 1996b; Kovacs, Feinberg, Crouse-Novak, Paulauskas, Pollock, & Finkelstein, 1984a). Similarly, in a retrospective study of children who attended the Maudsley Hospital in London, UK, Harrington, Fudge, Rutter, Pickles, and Hill (1990) investigated the adult psychiatric status of 52 participants who initially demonstrated a significant number of depressive symptoms and 52 matched nonpsychiatric controls. They found that 40% of the childhood depressed group met Research Diagnostic Criteria (Spitzer, Endicott, & Robins, 1978) for depression within five years of entering adulthood, with 58% demonstrating a history of an affective disorder at the time of follow-up compared to 25% of the control sample. These investigations suggest that depression in children and adolescents may have long-term negative consequences.

Wamboldt (1994) examined the nature of medical and psychiatric disorders reported in child and adolescent patients seen at nine medical-psychiatric settings that are considered Type III or IV (moderate to severe medical and psychiatric problem treatment) child and adolescent medical-psychiatric units in the USA. With regard to psychiatric disorders, Wamboldt found a greater prevalence of internalizing disorders than externalizing disorders, with 32% of the patients demonstrating mood disorders, primarily depression. These data are based on a sample of 768 youngsters admitted during 1991 and who manifested both medical and psychiatric problems.

A number of studies suggest what appears to be a secular trend in the age of onset of depressive disorders in children and adolescents, with first episodes of depression found in increasingly younger children (Kovacs & Gatsonis, 1994; Lewinsohn, Rohde, Seeley, & Fisher, 1993). This is a significant point of concern and buttresses the need to recognize depression in young people at early stages and provide intervention or prevention.

5.17.1.3 Contemporary Interest

Contemporary interest in the study of depression in children and adolescents began in the late 1970s and early 1980s. Prior to this, the predominant perspectives in the literature were that depression in children was: nonexistent, masked, or expressed in symptoms that were significantly different from those found in depressed adults (Reynolds, 1985). Depression in children was also conceptualized by the construct of depressive equivalents (Glaser, 1967; Hollon, 1970). In this manner, depression in children was inferred by overt, negative behaviors such as acting-out, aggression, hyperactivity, and delinquency, as well as psychosomatic and hypochondriacal disorders (Lesse,

1981). Some exceptions to these perspectives were postulated (e.g., Sandler & Jaffe, 1965) although for a number of reasons, did not significantly influence the existing status of depression in childhood (Bemporad, 1994).

Early research and clinical interest in depression in children and adolescents also focused on bipolar disorder. This was generally seen as an early onset of a typically adult disorder. The extreme nature of symptoms in manic depressive illness and mania, and the similarity between symptoms of these disorders in children and adolescents to those found in adults, led to a number of clinical reports (e.g., Beres & Alpert, 1940; Campbell, 1952). Carlson (1994) notes that Kraepelin in 1921 was one of the first to describe manic depressive illness in a child. However, research reports on manic depressive illness in children and adolescents are scarce before the 1970s.

In the 1970s, a small but significant number of clinical and research reports appeared that suggested the importance of studying depression in young people. An important article that shed light on the existence of depression in childhood was published in 1970 by Pozanaski and Zrull who described clinical cases gleaned from the outpatient files of the Children's Psychiatric Hospital at the University of Michigan Medical Center from the years 1964 to 1968. Based upon an examination of records of 1788 children, 98 cases were identified that showed significant evidence of depression, with 14 cases providing sufficient file data for in-depth examination and reporting. Children ranged in age from 3 to 12 years. Primary symptoms of depression in these youngsters included: sad, unhappy, depressed appearance; withdrawal; expressed feelings of rejection and being unloved; and autoerotic behavior. Poor self-image and self-worth were predominant as a depressive symptom.

Weinberg and his colleagues are frequently associated with the development of the first contemporary diagnostic criteria for depression in children (Ling, Oftedal, & Weinberg, 1970; Weinberg, Rutman, Sullivan, Penick, & Dietz, 1973). The Weinberg criteria were an outcome of the observation of depressive symptoms in children that were phenomenologically similar to symptoms of the disorder as specified for adults. An examination of the symptoms and criteria delineated by Weinberg et al. (1973) shows a great deal of communality with contemporary diagnostic formulations. In the late 1970s, Petti (1978) developed the Bellevue Index of Depression (BID), a semistructured clinical interview of depression designed for use with children based on Weinberg symptomatology.

In the early 1980s researchers also began to test the viability of unique conceptualizations of depression in childhood. Christ, Adler, Isacoff, and Gershansky (1981) investigated the concept of masked depression by examining clinical records of over 10 000 psychiatrically hospitalized children and adolescents. They compared diagnoses of depression (psychotic and neurotic) with: symptoms of depression (suicidal behavior, sleep disturbance, appetite changes, fatigue, etc.) specified by contemporary classification systems; and hypothesized masked features of depression as indicated by serious aggression and misbehavior. The authors found that youngsters with a diagnosis of a depressive disorder demonstrated greater numbers of contemporary symptoms of depression, while masked features were negatively related to this diagnosis, and occurred at a lower frequency in depressed youngsters as compared to youngsters with other psychopathology.

Around this time period, a number of reports began to emerge as to the clinical use of adult antidepressant medications with children. Antidepressant medications were relatively new but, within 10 years of early reports with adults, Frommer (1967) described the use of antidepressants with children. Additional reports by Kuhn and Kuhn (1971) and Stack (1971), among others, soon followed.

In 1980, the American Psychiatric Association (APA) published the third edition of the *Diagnostic and statistical manual of mental disorders* (*DSM-III*; APA 1980). Depressive (mood) disorders where listed in the adult disorders section, differential symptom criteria and duration specifications for major depression and dysthymic disorder, respectively were provided for these disorders in children and adolescents as compared to the disorders in adults. The publication of *DSM-III*, as well as research findings such as those by Christ et al. (1981), led to a focus on symptoms of depression in children and adolescents as similar in many regards to adults.

The acceptance of the largely adult specifications for depression in the *DSM* is not universal nor, as suggested by Nurcombe and colleagues (Nurcombe, 1994; Nurcombe et al., 1989), strongly supported by research evidence. Nurcombe (1994) examined the validity of major depression as a diagnosis in children and adolescents using as criteria: natural history, psychobiological markers, genetic studies, response to treatment, and construct validity. The last was based on multivariate analyses of various checklists and measures. As presented, much of the evidence is mixed, suggesting that depressive disorders in children may not be as currently defined by *DSM* with more work

needed for the presentation of diagnostic validity of the disorder.

Based on diagnostic and epidemiological surveys of children and adolescents it is evident that depression is a significant problem among youngsters (Reynolds & Johnston, 1994). Epidemiological studies suggest that between 3% and 5% of children and 7–10% of adolescents manifest clinical levels of depression (Fleming & Offord, 1990; Lewinsohn, Hops, Roberts, Seeley, & Andrews, 1993; Poznanski & Mokros, 1994; Whitaker et al., 1990), with lifetime rates in young people significantly higher (Lewinsohn et al., 1993). These data, and the general undertreatment of depression in children and adolescents (Keller, Lavori, Beardslee, Wunder, & Ryan, 1991) point to the critical need for study, identification, and treatment of depression in young people.

5.17.2 BIOPSYCHOSOCIAL MODEL OF DEPRESSION IN CHILDREN AND ADOLESCENTS

In psychiatry, the biopsychosocial perspective represents a shift from a biomedical model, with its focus primarily on the biology of disease or disorders, to one of integration of psychological and dynamic characteristics, social and environmental forces, and biological bases. The biopsychosocial model is useful for the study and understanding of depression in children and adolescents, as well as adults. The biopsychosocial perspective has also been applied to numerous other aspects of human behavior and disorders (Paris, 1994; Shalev, 1993).

The psychobiological approach to the study of human behavior and problems has a long history (Dewsbury, 1991), and is illustrated in its earlier presentation by the integrated, commonsense perspective of Adolf Meyer. Meyer's perspective of psychiatric disturbance as due in part to, or exacerbated by environmental causes, can be viewed as a precursor to the current biopsychosocial perspective. Meyer's integrated approach to psychiatry, which he called psychobiology (Meyer, 1957), was also interactive, in that psychiatric illness was viewed as an interaction (or reaction) between the psychobiological and life stressors. Likewise, the biobehavioral model of depression proposed by Akiskal (1979) is consistent with this perspective and integrates biological, psychosocial, developmental, and environmental stressors as a basis for the development of depression.

The biopsychosocial model for the provision of general medical services was espoused by

Engel (1978, 1980). Presented as a systems approach in which the person does not exist in isolation, the biopsychosocial model was proposed in part to deal with the general over-reliance of physicians on the biomedical model in which the focus was on disease with limited concern about the patient as a person. In this manner, the biopsychosocial model or perspective is similar in its general focus to the approach of Meyer in psychiatry, and provides a useful heuristic for developing an understanding of depression in children and adolescents.

The biopsychosocial perspective, although not extensively practiced, has been a relatively popular concept within the psychiatric treatment literature because it suggests an integrated systems approach for therapy. Karasu (1990) in his comparison and integration of models of psychotherapy (dynamic, cognitive, and interpersonal) for depression, has provided suggestions for the indication of pharmacotherapy, psychotherapy, or their combination for the treatment of this disorder. The combinatory approach to treatment conforms to the "biopsychological perspective" of childhood depression described by Kashani and Cantwell (1983).

The basic applications of this perspective are not new to the study of depression in children and adolescents. Lewis and Lewis (1979) described a psychobiological perspective on depression that recognized psychoanalytic, genetic, and biochemical bases for the development and subsequent treatment of depression in children. Vasile et al. (1987) described a "biopsychosocial approach" for treating persons with depression that implements a consultation model for the evaluation and recommendation of psychological, pharmacological, or combined therapies. Although specific to adults, this integrative and evaluative approach appears useful for the treatment of depressed children and adolescents.

The biopsychosocial model of depression delineated by Reynolds (1997a) and briefly described below provides a perspective for understanding depression in children and adolescents as well as a framework for intervention and the provision of services. Within this model, biological, as well as psychosocial, factors play a role in child and adolescent depression. In some cases, there is a greater emphasis exerted by either the biological or psychosocial, indicating a primary modality for treatment of the disorder. However, the interactive nature of the model suggests that multimodal treatments may show the greatest efficacy, both in initial treatment gains and potential reduction of reoccurrence.

5.17.2.1 Tripartite Model

The biopsychosocial perspective on depression in children and adolescents may be represented as a tripartite dynamic model (Reynolds, 1997a). This model is illustrated in Figure 1. Similar to the model of reciprocal determinism postulated by Bandura (1978) for understanding human behavior, the biopsychosocial prospective (described below) considers reciprocal pathways. The strength of these pathways in the pathogenesis, maintenance, or exacerbation of depression or depressive disorders may vary as function of developmental level, individual strengths and deficits within each domain, nature of the reciprocal interactions, and the nature of the depressive outcome.

In the model, biological, psychological, and social–environmental attributes and influences are closely intertwined with intersecting pathways unique to each individual. Given the myriad combinations and interactions, the untangling of these main effects, interactions, and reciprocal paths for an individual is well beyond the scope of current science and practice. However, it is likely that, with sufficient scrutiny, major sources and some level of interactions across the three primary domains can be investigated to gain insight into the nature, potential etiology, exacerbating and maintaining factors, and the possible course and outcome of the individual's affective status.

Two aspects that are not depicted, yet which are critical, are that this model is dynamic and developmental. There is evidence to infer that depression in children is, in a number of respects, different from depression in adults, although there are probably more communalities than differences. There is also the likelihood that some differences are not specific to diagnostic symptomatology, but in its internal structure. Likewise, there are a number of possible developmental trajectories that may relate to differences in the nature as well as expression of depression in youngsters as compared to adults. It may be that biological components of depression become more pronounced as the human organism matures. This may be most evident in findings from neuroendocrine research that has focused on the relationship between hypothalamic–pituitary–adrenal axis function and depression in children (Puig-Antich et al., 1989). Overall, research examining neurobiological correlates in depressed children compared to adults has been mixed (Emslie, Weinberg, Kennard, & Kowatch, 1994).

The psychological domain includes cognitive and behavioral competencies and deficits that are linked to the ontogenesis of depression. As

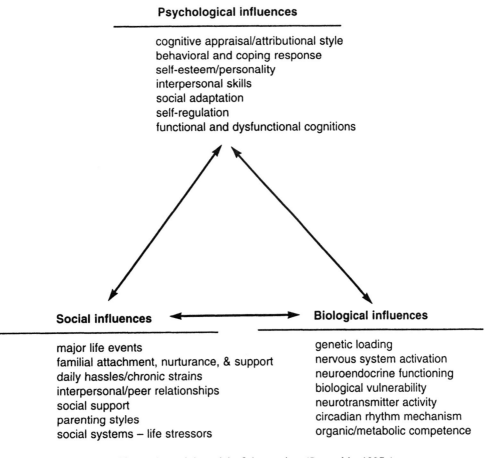

Figure 1 Biopsychosocial model of depression (Reynolds, 1997a).

models of depression suggest, these components do not act in isolation, but are set in motion by the experience of socio-environmental factors, such as stress, nurturance, and attachment, along with a biological propensity or interaction. However, the cognitive and behavioral/coping functioning of the individual will determine to some extent the impact of the social system (i.e., interpersonal stressors, minor/major life event, etc.) on affective competence and biological/neuroendocrine response/interaction. Likewise, dysfunctional cognitions and behavioral response can be a function of neuroendocrine influences (Wright & Thase, 1992).

Magnusson (1985) has described an interactional paradigm for examining aspects of human functioning that integrates psychology and biology as important person factors in examining person by environment interactions and is consistent with the biopsychosocial perspective. As such, a longitudinal approach is needed to understand the mechanism of human behavior. In this regard, development plays a critical role in the biopsychosocial perspective and can be considered to be an

important component of psychology, biology, and the social domain. Magnusson and colleagues (Magnusson & Torestad, 1993; Stattin & Magnusson, 1989) have delineated this interactional approach with a major focus on the developmental and biological nature of person, and in particular adolescent and environment interactions, cumulating in the description of a holistic, dynamic model of personality. This approach also has utility for the study and understanding of depression in young people.

5.17.2.2 Biopsychosocial Domains and Interactions

The biopsychosocial model presented in Figure 1 is a simplified representation of the primary domains and their potential interactions. In reality, the level of interactions of both direct and indirect effects of individual components within and between domains is, in most situations, quite complex and, given the potential numbers and measurability of these variables, is beyond the scope of most research investigations. Remschmidt (1992) notes that the interactions between biological and psychosocial variables that influence the development of psychopathology in children and adolescents may be multiplicative as well as additive.

It is important to recognize that both strengths and weaknesses may be present within each domain. Thus, a youngster may show a deficit in the interpersonal skills domain as a psychological influence, or may demonstrate competence in interpersonal skills that may reduce vulnerability for depression. In a similar vein, personality may enhance psychological resilience or act as a factor that exacerbates biological or social–environmental events. Likewise, biological competence may provide a protective factor for adverse or stressful major life events.

Within the scope of this chapter it is not possible to provide delineation of the main effects of factors associated with the biological, psychological, and social–environmental domains, and the researched interactions between these domains and depression in children and adolescents. Research shows that all three domains play a role in the manifestation of depression in children and adolescents. Described below are a few examples of each domain of the model.

5.17.2.2.1 Biological influences

Biological bases of depressive disorders have been extensively examined in adults and to a more limited extent children and adolescents (Emslie et al. 1994). Domains of inquiry range from brain neurochemistry, such as serotonin mechanism, adrenal-hyper-cortical functioning and activity, and sleep architecture to genetics. Also included in this research domain is the study of antidepressants. For example, a great deal of research in psychiatry has focused on serotonergic mechanisms, specifically the role of serotonin (5-HT) in the regulation of psychological and biological functioning. This research has had a major impact on the development of new classes of pharmacological agents for the treatment of depression, such as antidepressant medications that are selective in their serotonin reuptake properties. These latter agents include such drugs as fluoxetine (Prozac), sertraline (Zoloft), and paroxetine (Paxil). Within the model, biology affects as well as interacts with psychosocial factors to increase vulnerability for the development of maladaptive psychological processes and adaptation.

Likewise, a great deal of interest and research has focused the hypothalamic–pituitary–adrenocortical (HPA) axis as a biological focal point in the environmental stress–depressive response pathway. A number of biological systems and factors, such as prolactin, growth hormone, melatonin metabolism, sleep, and neurotransmitter activity have been linked as of potential etiological relevance to depression (Leibenluft, Fiero, & Rubinow, 1994). There is also evidence to suggest a genetic loading for various depressive disorders, such as major depression and bipolar disorder, with bipolar disorder having the greater genetic component (Herdman, Gough, Liskowski, & Hall, 1995).

5.17.2.2.2 Psychological influences

The domain of psychological influences may best be described as the psychological characteristics, both strengths and weaknesses, as well as vulnerabilities that make up the youngster's emotional and mental health competence. In Figure 1 a number of individual characteristics are listed to provide a general description of this domain. In reality, there are many other psychological influences, some of which are well defined by research and theory, and others that are less well defined or understood. These factors may be either protective or risk factors.

A number of cognitive and behavioral processes are particularly relevant to the understanding of the development of depression. Some of these components are linked to theories of depression. For example, the role of self-regulation (Kanfer, 1970) as it relates to problems in self-control (self-monitoring, self-evaluation, self-reinforcement) has been postulated by Rehm (1977) as model of depression. Problems or deficits in cognitive appraisal, maladaptive behavioral response to reinforcement, dysfunctional cognitions, and erroneous attributional style have been identified by various contemporary theories and models as linked to the development of depression (Abramson, Seligman, & Teasdale, 1978; Beck, 1967; Ellis, 1962; Lewinsohn, 1975).

5.17.2.2.3 Social influences

The social component represents the social–environmental domain and by its nature includes a very wide range of influences. Included here are: stressful events, including major negative life events as well as daily hassles and chronic strains; parental influences, including attachment, nurturance, marital discord, support, and parenting style; social support; peer and interpersonal relationships; and a host of social and environmental influences such as exposure to violence, victimization, maltreatment, social disadvantage, peer and social pressures, and school and work stress among others.

As an example, parental nurturance is a broad domain that includes parenting behavior such as the nature and use of discipline (e.g., consistent/inconsistent, reasonable/harsh, etc.); communication style; over/under controlling; parental warmth; and other behaviors, characteristics, and competencies. Straus and Kantor (1994), in a retrospective study of adults queried as to having received corporal punishment during their teen years, found that corporal punishment was significantly related to increased risk for depression, even when controlling for factors such as socioeconomic status (SES), gender, age, and parental marital violence. Oakley-Browne et al. (1995) also found that adverse parenting in childhood had an increased risk for depression in adulthood. It is also important to note that, during adolescence, there is often a transition in the relationship that youngsters have with parents and peers, with peers becoming increasingly important as a source for support and attitude development.

5.17.2.3 Summary

In the biopsychosocial model, the three primary domains (biology, psychology, and social) interact to produce depression in persons. The nature, course, severity, treatment viability, and other characteristics of depression in young people as well as adults is a function of the nature of the interactions and the domain-specific characteristics and vulnerabilities. This model is also reciprocal, in that factors within the domains may interact as well as affect other domains in a reciprocal manner.

For example, some psychosocial stressors have been noted to be responsible for suppressed T-lymphocyte function (Brosschot et al., 1994; Syvalahti, 1987) and a host of hormonal changes. Such abnormalities in immune function and endocrine changes can increase vulnerability to depression. In adolescents, major negative life events have been linked to reduced immune function and neuroendocrine changes (Birmaher et al., 1994).

As the interactional approach may suggest, it is virtually impossible to separate out the variances associated with any one domain, given the potential complexities of the interactions within as well as between domains. However, researchers are beginning to recognize the multivariate nature of these domains as a basis for the study of depression. In a study examining the prediction of major depression in a sample of 1360 women (680 pairs of twins), Kendler, Kessler, Neale, Heath, and Eaves (1993) examined the main effects (both direct and indirect) of a number of biological (e.g.,

genetic), social (e.g., stressful life events), and psychological (e.g., neuroticism) factors.

The biopsychosocial model suggests there are multiple pathways to the development of depression in children and adolescents. From this perspective, psychological, social and biological models have validity but are individually insufficient to explain the range of etiologies associated with depression.

5.17.3 DIAGNOSTIC FORMULATIONS OF DEPRESSION IN CHILDREN AND ADOLESCENTS

The diagnosis of depression involves the evaluation and comparison of the characteristics and duration of an individual's symptoms with criteria and classification rules for one or more disorders. In this manner, diagnosis constitutes an assessment or measurement procedure. Thus, measurement error, or the reliability of the diagnosis is an important consideration. Sources of potential measurement error in making a diagnosis include error due to the informant, the diagnostic instrument (e.g., clinical interview), the diagnostician, as well as the classification system. In some respects, a diagnosis may be viewed as a hypothesis that represents "the clinician's best judgment" (Rush, 1990, p. 5) of the individual's condition. Research suggests that the diagnosis of psychopathology and, more specifically, depressive disorders in children is not perfect (APA, 1980; Vitiello, Malone, Buschle, Delaney, & Behar, 1990). For the evaluation of depression in children and adolescents, diagnosis is one method with the outcome being a characterization of specific disorder or disorders based on a formal classification scheme. Other measurement procedures, such as the assessment of severity of depressive symptoms, either by clinical interview or self-report without comparison to a classification system, are often used in clinical and research applications with children and adolescents. The latter may be viewed as providing a focus on the assessment of depression as a syndrome rather than delineating categorically distinct depressive disorders. As noted by Nurcombe (1994), the perspective of depression as a syndrome is postulated on the specifications of symptoms and signs that are predominated by dysphoric mood.

The classification systems currently used in formulating psychiatric diagnoses are continually being refined. In this sense, such systems are not static, immutable, or complete in their description of inclusion and exclusion criteria for specific disorders. This iterative process is exemplified by ongoing revisions in the *DSM* by the APA and the *International statistical classification of diseases and related health problems (ICD)* by the World Health Organization (WHO, 1992). These are the primary but not the only systems or approaches to the classification of depressive disorders. It is also important to recognize that depressive symptoms may occur in a number of medical and neurological conditions (Klerman, 1987; Rush, 1990) that need to be considered in the diagnosis of a depressive disorder. Several systems that have been used to diagnose depression in children and adolescents are described below.

5.17.3.1 Systems and Approaches in the Diagnosis of Depression

There are a number of classification systems that have been developed or provide for the diagnosis of depressive disorders in children and adolescents. Most of the current systems are based on a taxonomic approach for the differentiation of type and subtypes of depressive disorders based on particular clusters of symptoms and symptom duration. In North America the primary system used for the classification of depressive disorders in children, adolescents, and adults is the *DSM-IV* (APA, 1994). The *DSM-IV* criteria for depression in children and adolescents are described in a later section.

For certain research applications, the Research Diagnostic Criteria (RDC), developed by Spitzer et al. (1978) is used for the diagnosis of depressive subtypes. The RDC provides greater specificity of subtypes of depression and may be evaluated using a formal diagnostic clinical interview, the Schedule for Affective Disorders and Schizophrenia (SADS; Endicott & Spitzer, 1978) for adults as well as adolescents, and the kiddie SADS for children (K-SADS; Puig-Antich & Chambers, 1978), which has also been used for adolescents (e.g., Lewinsohn, Rohde, & Seeley, 1995). These interview schedules are specific to the RDC in the diagnoses they provide, although research investigators have developed algorithms for deriving *DSM* diagnoses from SADS interviews.

As noted earlier, Poznanski and Zrull (1970) using a chart-review method, provided descriptions of clinical symptoms constituting depression in children. As such, these symptoms were viewed as a basis for the diagnosis of depression in youngsters, with the general premise being that depression as a disorder did manifest itself in childhood (Poznanski, Krahenbuhl, & Zrull, 1976, Poznanski & Zrull, 1970). Later, Poznanski and her colleagues (Poznanski, 1982; Poznanski, Mokros, Grossman, & Freeman,

1985) reformulated their clinical description of symptomatology for depression in children, and developed a clinical interview for the assessment of depression in children (Poznanski, Cook, & Carroll, 1979; Poznanski et al., 1984).

In the early 1970s, Weinberg and colleagues proposed a set of criteria for depression in children (Weinberg et al. 1973) with Weinberg and Brumback (1976) providing diagnostic criteria for mania in children. The Weinberg criteria for depression include (i) the presence of both dysphoric mood and self-deprecatory thoughts; (ii) two or more of: aggressive behavior, sleep disturbance, change in school performance, diminished socialization, change in attitude toward school, somatic complaints, loss of usually energy, and change in appetite and/or weight; and (iii) symptoms need to be present for more than one month and represent a change in the child's usual behavior. Although the Weinberg criteria are rarely used today, they are noteworthy for their early impact as well as their similarity to symptom specifications for current *DSM-IV* criteria for depressive disorders in young people.

5.17.3.2 *Diagnostic and Statistical Manual of Mental Disorders*

Depressive disorders in the *DSM-IV* fall under the category of mood disorders, and include major depression, bipolar disorders, cyclothymic disorder, and dysthymic disorder as primary mood disorders. Disorders are differentiated by specific clusters of symptoms, age of onset, and the duration of symptoms. Disorders that are most likely to be found in school-aged youngsters are major depression and dysthymia, although adjustment disorder with depressed mood is also diagnostically relevant. Bipolar disorders also demonstrate an onset during adolescence in a significant number of individuals who develop this disorder (Loranger & Levine, 1978; McGlashan, 1988). The depressive disorders subsumed under the domain of mood disorders in the *DSM-IV* and their associated course and subtype specifiers are presented in Table 1. It should also be noted that diagnostic categories of: mood disorder due to medical condition; substance-induced mood disorder; and mood disorder not otherwise specified may also be diagnosed in children and adolescents.

5.17.3.2.1 *Major depressive disorder*

Major depressive disorder (MDD) in *DSM-IV* is presented as a relatively severe, acute form of depression. Major depressive disorder may be classified as a single episode or recurrent, the

Table 1 *DSM-IV* Mood Disorders in Children and Adolescents.

Major depressive disorder
   single episode[1-6]
   recurrent[1-8]
Dysthymic disorder (early onset)[2]
Depressive disorder not otherwise specified (NOS)
Bipolar disorder I
   single manic episode[3,4,6]
   most recent episode depressed[1-9]
   most recent episode hypomanic[7-9]
   most recent episode manic[3,4,6-9]
   most recent episode mixed[3,4,6-9]
   most recent episode unspecified[7-9]
Bipolar disorder II
   hypomanic[7-9]
   depressed[1-9]
Cyclothymic disorder
   May also include:
     [1] with melancholic features
     [2] with atypical features
     [3] with catatonic features
     [4] with postpartum onset
     [5] chronic
     [6] severity/psychotic/remission specifiers
   course specifiers:
     [7] with seasonal pattern
     [8] with rapid cycling
     [9] with/without interepisode recovery

latter specifying a history of previous MDD episode(s). As a disorder, MDD is defined by the following criteria and symptomatology: the presence of five of the following symptoms, one of which is either dysphoric or irritable mood, or loss of interest or pleasure in all or almost all activities. The other symptoms include: sleep problems as manifested by insomnia or hypersomnia; complaints or other evidence of diminished ability to think, make decisions, or difficulty concentrating; loss of energy or general fatigue; eating problems as manifested by decreased or increased appetite or significant weight loss or gain (in young children failure to make expected weight gains is symptomatic); psychomotor retardation or agitation; suicidal or morbid ideation, death wishes, or suicide attempts; and feelings of self-reproach, worthlessness, or excessive or inappropriate guilt (which may be delusional). Symptoms need to be present nearly every day for a period of at least two weeks. Exclusion criteria are also specified that preclude a number of other pathologies, such as organic mental disorder and other etiologies (i.e., a normal response to bereavement) as concomitant problems, for a diagnosis of major depression. The *DSM-IV* provides information to assist the clinician in a differential diagnosis of major depression, as opposed to several conditions that may include significant depressive symptoms.

As shown in Table 1, major depression may be specified as a single episode (without a history of manic or hypomanic episode) or recurrent, the latter describing a history of two or more major depressive episodes separated by at least two months of normal functioning. There is also a range of additional features that may characterize the nature of the depressive episode, including: with melancholic features, catatonic features, atypical features, postpartum onset (adolescents), and indications of the severity (mild, moderate, severe), with or without psychotic features, and in partial or full remission. A seasonal pattern, often referred to as seasonal affective disorder, may be indicated.

5.17.3.2.2 Dysthymic disorder

In the *DSM-IV* dysthymic disorder represents a relatively chronic depressive disorder that is typically less severe in symptom distress than major depression, but typically of greater duration. Diagnostic criteria for dysthymic disorder in children and adolescents includes a depressed or irritable mood for most of the day, and manifested most of the time over a period of at least one year, although there may be periods of up to two months during which symptoms are not present. In addition to symptoms of depressed or irritable mood, at least two of the following symptoms must be present when depressed: appetite loss or gain, insomnia or hypersomnia, fatigue or low energy level, low self-esteem, difficulty concentrating or problems making decisions, and feelings of hopelessness. Exclusion criteria include: showing no evidence of major depressive episode during the initial year of the disorder; never having a manic or hypomanic episode; and not being superimposed on a chronic psychosis, or due to or maintained by an organic factor. Diagnostic criteria for dysthymia in children and adolescents differ from those for adults for whom symptoms of this disorder must be present for two years for a diagnosis.

5.17.3.2.3 Bipolar disorder

Bipolar disorder is a severe and typically long-term psychiatric condition that often represents a diagnostic challenge for clinicians. A number of researchers have noted the difficulties in this diagnosis as well as the propensity for misdiagnosis (Carlson, 1994; Joyce, 1984; Weller, Weller, Tucker, & Fristad, 1986). The essential feature of bipolar disorder is the occurrence of one or more episodes of mania or hypomania, typically with a history of one or more major depressive episodes. The *DSM-IV* delineates two forms of bipolar disorder, bipolar disorder I and bipolar disorder II, that differ as a function of the level of mania, with bipolar II associated with a hypomanic episode. Table 1 provides a description of the types of episodes of mania and depression associated with bipolar disorders. Of note is the mixed episode in which criteria for a manic episode and major depressive episode are present nearly every day with the youngster rapidly cycling between disorders. As noted in Table 1, bipolar disorder may also conform to a seasonal pattern.

The manic episode, which may last from one week to several months, is characterized by a clear-cut period of mood elevation, irritability, or expansiveness. In addition, three (or four if the manic episode is characterized by irritability) of the following symptoms must be present, including: grandiosity or inflated self-esteem, reduced need for sleep, more or excessively talkative, flights of ideas or perception that thoughts are racing, very distractible, increased time spent on goal-directed activities or psychomotor agitation, and overinvolvement in pleasurable, potentially risk-taking activities. Lastly, the overall clinical picture is sufficiently severe to cause impairment in functioning or require hospitalization. A somewhat milder variant that does not include the latter criteria of significant impairment in functioning nor delusions, is specified as a hypomanic episode.

5.17.3.2.4 Cyclothymic disorder

Cyclothymic disorder is a chronic mood disorder, symptomatically similar to bipolar disorder but of less severity. Cyclothymic disorder is analogous to dysthymic disorder in that depressive symptoms are not sufficient for a diagnosis of major depression, and the symptoms must be present for one year with periods of up to two months in which symptoms are not present. During the course of the disorder, there are numerous hypomanic episodes and periods of depressed mood or loss of interest or pleasure.

5.17.3.3 Alternatives to *DSM*: Clinical Severity, Subsyndromal Depression, and Depressive Symptoms

There have been a number of suggestions that criteria for *DSM* depressive disorders are too stringent and results in an underestimate of persons with significant levels of depressive symptoms. Thus, a person may show a level of depressive symptoms that is not sufficient to meet criteria for a *DSM* disorder yet, by its symptom severity level, may be considered clinically relevant and a valid target for intervention. Bland (1994) noted the problem of threshold in the use of *DSM*-specific criteria for diagnosis, in that a certain number of symptoms are required for a diagnosis and the patient who falls one symptom short of this does not receive a diagnosis, even when presenting symptoms are severe.

Gotlib, Lewinsohn, and Seeley (1995) found that youngsters who had clinically significant levels of depressive symptoms but did not meet criteria for major depression were twice as likely to develop a psychiatric disorder as compared to a nondepressed group, and also demonstrated significantly poorer psychosocial functioning than the nonsymptomatic group. Youngsters with clinically significant depressive symptoms were similar in psychosocial functioning to a comparison group of youngsters with major depression. These results suggest the clinical importance of attending to youngsters who may not meet criteria for major depression yet show significant levels of depressive symptomatology.

Judd, Rapoport, Paulus, and Brown (1994) examined depressive symptom data from the National Institute of Mental Health epidemiological catchment area (ECA) study and developed a clinical condition that they described as "subsyndromal symptomatic depression." Similarly, Horwath, Johnson, Klerman, and Weissman (1994) focused on ECA incidence data specific to persons who developed an episode of major depression over a one year interval between interviews. They found that persons with prior symptoms of depression or a dysthymic disorder were at relative risk for depression, with 50% of individuals who developed a major depressive episode demonstrating a history of depressive symptoms. The authors highlight the clinical importance of depressive symptoms by noting that "if depressive symptoms could be identified and treated before major depression first developed, many first onset cases of major depression could potentially be prevented" (p. 333), and that "measures designed to identify this group prior to the onset of major depression may represent an important step in primary prevention" (p. 333). Although the data from Judd et al. (1994) and Horwath et al. (1994) is specific to adults, it can be generalized to children and adolescents. Toward this end, a multiple-gate assessment procedure has been presented by Reynolds (1986a) for the identification of children and adolescents with significant clinical levels of depressive symptomatology.

In the diagnostic classification of mood disorders in the WHO *ICD-10*, a depressive episode may be classified as a severe depressive episode or a mild depressive episode, the latter different from dysthymia. However, in the worldwide field trials of the *ICD-10*, relative low interrater agreement was found for the mild depressive episode (code F31.1) as well as dysthymia (F34.1) (Sartorius et al. 1993). Sartorius et al. suggest that clinicians had difficulty distinguishing between dysthymia and mild depressive episode and recurrent mild depressive disorder (F33.1), as well as generalized anxiety disorder (F41.1), mixed anxiety and depressive disorder (F41.2) and adjustment disorder (F43.2). It is also useful to note that although interrater reliability for these disorders was low for the worldwide field trials, interrater agreement was even lower for field trials in the USA and Canada (Regier, Kaelber, Roper, Rae, & Sartorius, 1994). Although these data are based on adult samples, it does demonstrate that our diagnostic formulations of depressive disorders are still in a state of evolution.

5.17.4 ASSESSMENT OF DEPRESSION IN CHILDREN AND ADOLESCENTS

Assessment is a procedure basic to the identification of depression in children and adolescents for clinical purposes, as well as for use in the study of biological, social, and psychological characteristics; sequaele; outcome; determination of treatment efficacy; and other research applications. There are two primary categories of assessment measures: those designed for obtaining a diagnosis, and measures developed to evaluate the severity of depressive symptomatology. Although diagnostic measures may provide severity scores, their primary utilization is as diagnostic tools. In general clinical practice and in a multitude of research applications, the assessment of depression in children and adolescents is typically accomplished using self-report severity measures or clinical interviews, the latter including diagnostic measures and severity measures. Reports by significant others such as parents, teachers, and peers have been used to a limited extent and are not discussed in this chapter. Readers interested in assessment of depression via reports of others, as well as the issue of informant variability, are directed to Clarizio (1994) and Kazdin (1994).

There are several characteristics of depression that support the use of self-report assessment procedures, given linguistic and metacognitive competence in the child. Depression as an internalizing disorder includes primary symptoms that are internal to the youngster and are not easily observable. Cognitive symptoms of guilt, self-deprecation, suicidal ideation, hopelessness, and feelings of worthlessness are depressive symptoms that are subjective to the child. Some vegetative symptoms such as insomnia, appetite loss, and other problems are sometimes difficult for others to observe and may go undetected by parents and significant others.

This chapter presents information on several self-report measures of depression for children and adolescents. Although a number of structured and semistructured clinical interviews exist, the application of these interviews is generally limited to various research investigations. The primary tools used in the clinical assessment of depression in children and adolescents in clinical and school settings are self-report measures. Diagnostic interviews are briefly noted below and several semistructured clinical interviews that provide for the assessment of the severity of depressive symptomatology in children and adolescents are described.

The manner in which we assess depression in youngsters guides how we organize our perspective of depressive phenomena. For the determination of depression according to formal classification criteria that includes both inclusion and exclusion components, the standard practice in research investigations has been the use of diagnostic clinical interviews. Structured clinical interviews are typically formulated to evaluate all symptoms, their duration, and potential exclusion criteria as specified by a formal set of diagnostic criteria. In this manner, the K-SADS (Puig-Antich & Chambers, 1978) was designed to provide diagnostic information on disorders in youngsters according to the RDC (Spitzer et al., 1978). Likewise, *DSM* criteria for psychiatric disorders are assessed by other interviews such as the Child Assessment Schedule (Hodges, Kline, Stern, Cytryn, & McKnew, 1982), Diagnostic Interview for Children and Adolescents-Revised (Reich & Welner, 1988), and the Diagnostic Interview Schedule for Children-Revised (Shaffer et al., 1993); see Hodges' (1994) and Reynolds' (1992b) reviews of these and other clinical interview measures.

Self-report severity measures typically evaluate a range of depressive symptoms with the assessment format specific to the depth of symptom expression (e.g., frequency of occurrence, severity, etc.). Most of these measures generally provide a total score that may be compared to a derived cutoff score. In this manner, many severity measures of depression allow for the evaluation of a clinical level of depressive symptomatology, assuming an adequate coverage of the symptom domain (Reynolds, 1994). Using the nomenclature of Compas, Ey, and Grant (1993), single-scale self-report depression measures assess depressed mood in youngsters, and self-report measures that are components of a comprehensive assessment measure or that were developed to assess all symptoms of classification system specified depressive disorders allow for the assessment of depressive syndromes. Thus, self-report scales are not designed as diagnostic measures.

Limitations on the use of self-report are primarily developmental. Linguistic competence, including reading and comprehension ability, are important considerations when using self-report measures. These task demands suggest that most youngsters aged eight years and above who do not have learning problems can respond to self-report measures that include language at a third-grade reading level. To avoid confounding with reading, it is recommended that measures be read to youngsters below 10 years of age. Likewise, it is important to consider metacognitive demands of the measure. Thus, task demands go beyond reading to include the ability to recognize one's emotional and behavioral characteristics as they apply to a specified time-frame and evaluate the frequency, severity, or nature of these characteristics.

The ability of the youngster to self-monitor their behavior and emotions as well as self-evaluate these facets is a requirement of most measures. There are a number of additional developmental aspects specific to assessment of depression in children that are of primary concern to the assessment of young children rather than adolescents and address both the reliability and validity of measures of depression in youngsters. Many of these issues are generic to the use of self-report methods with children and are described in more detail elsewhere (Reynolds, 1992b).

As a function of the limitations noted above, there are few self-report measures that can be used with children below the age of eight years, although there is some research to suggest that self-report measures of depression can be used with children as young as ages 5 or 6 years. (Ialongo, Edelsohn, Werthamer-Larsson, Crockett, & Kellam, 1993). For children aged six and above, clinical interviews, such as the Children's Depression Rating Scale-Revised (CDRS-R; Poznanski et al. 1984) may be used, although some youngster's metacognitive ability for emotions may limit their response. Thus, for young children, parent reports using clinical

interviews are a primary source of information, with parent's reports also of value for school-age children, assuming reliable and valid reporting on the part of the parent.

5.17.4.1 Self-report Measures of Depression for Children and Adolescents

Since the mid-1970s, a number of self-report measures have been developed for the assessment of depression in children and adolescents, with some researchers and clinicians using measures designed for use with adults. The use of self-report questionnaires for the assessment of depressive symptomatology in young people has witnessed a rapid growth in research and clinical applications. From a few reports in the early 1980s, to the routine use of self-report depression measures in a wide range of child and adolescent mental health disciplines, self-report measures provide a simple and direct method for the evaluation of the clinical severity of depressive symptoms in children and adolescents. Table 2 lists the more common self-report measures used in North America. These measures are among the most frequently used self-report scales for the assessment of depressive symptomatology in children and adolescents (Archer, Maruish, Imhof, & Piotrowski, 1991). A brief description of several of these measures is provided below. More information on these and other self-report measures of depression in children and adolescent is given by Reynolds (1994).

5.17.4.1.1 Children's Depression Inventory

The Children's Depression Inventory (CDI; Kovacs, 1979, 1992) as described by Kovacs and Beck 1977) was originally developed as a downward revision of the Beck Depression Inventory (BDI; Beck, Ward, Mendelson, Mock, & Erbaugh, 1961). The CDI is one of the most frequently used research measures of depression in children and consists of 27 items, each evaluating a symptom of depression or related affect. Items are presented as three statements of varying symptom severity. Several of the items may be confusing to some children (e.g., I do not do what I am told most of the time).

The CDI manual (Kovacs, 1992) presents normative data based on a sample of 1266 children and young adolescents from an unspecified number of schools in Florida. Data appear to be a subsample of youngsters from a previously published study by Finch, Saylor, and Edwards (1985). Data on the race or ethnicity of the standardization sample is not

Table 2 Description of self-report measures of depression used with children and adolescents in North America.

Measure/authors	Development target population	Number of items	Response format	Manual available
Children's Depression Inventory Kovacs (1979, 1992)	children/adolescents	27	3-alternative	Yes
Children's Depression Scale Lang and Tisher (1987)	children/adolescents	66	card sort	Yes
Reynolds Child Depression Scale Reynolds (1989)	children	30	Likert 4-point	Yes
Reynolds Adolescent Depression Scale Reynolds (1986b)	adolescents	30	Likert 4-point	Yes
Beck Depression Inventory Beck, Ward, Mendelsohn, Mock, and Erbaugh (1961)	adults	21	4-alternative	Yes[a]

[a] The manual for the Beck depression inventory is specific to the use and characteristics of the BDI with adults.

reported, and data is provided for children in grades 2 through 8. Norms are not provided for high school students. Although not indicated in the manual, the normative sample data was based on an oral administration of the CDI as indicated in the original article by Finch et al. (1985). The CDI manual has been reviewed by Reynolds (1994).

The psychometric characteristics of the CDI have been reported in many studies. Researchers typically report internal consistency reliability coefficients in the low to upper 0.80s (Cole & Carpentieri, 1990; Kovacs, 1983; Reynolds, Anderson, & Bartell, 1985; Smucker, Craighead, Craighead, and Green, 1986) and test–retest reliability coefficients ranging from 0.38 to 0.87 (Finch, Saylor, Edwards, & McIntosh, 1987; Kovacs, 1980/1981, 1983; Nelson & Politano, 1990; Saylor, Finch, Spirito, & Bennett, 1984; Smucker et. al., 1986; Weiss et al., 1991). The variability in test–retest reliability is in part a function of the time interval between assessments and the sample characteristics.

One line of research has examined the utility of the CDI in distinguishing between depressed and nondepressed youngsters (e.g., Curry & Craighead, 1990; Fristad, Weller, Weller, Teare, & Preskorn, 1988; Moretti, Fine, Haley, & Marriage, 1985; Saylor et al., 1984). The results of these studies are mixed and tend to show a lack of diagnostic efficacy.

Although not designed as a diagnostic measure the CDI is useful in assessing the severity of depressive symptomatology. One question that has emerged is whether a particular cutoff score can represent a clinically relevant level of depressive symptoms on the CDI. A cutoff score of between 17 and 19

appears to be appropriate, given the score distributions for the CDI found with various school-based and clinical samples of children. In samples of school-based or nondepressed youngsters a mean CDI score of 8–10, and a standard deviation of 7–8 points is typically reported (Cole, 1991; Cole & Carpentieri, 1990; Craighead, Curry, & Ilardi, 1995; Finch et al., 1985; Ollendick, Yule, & Ollier, 1991; Smucker et al., 1986; Saylor et al., 1984). In large samples of nonreferred children a score of 19 identifies approximately 10% of the sample.

5.17.4.1.2 Reynolds Child Depression Scale

The Reynolds Child Depression Scale (RCDS; Reynolds, 1989) is a 30-item self-report measure designed for use with children aged 8–13. On the RCDS 29 items are rated as to the frequency of their occurrence during the past two weeks using a four-point "almost never" to "all the time" response format. Items are worded to evaluate current symptom status (e.g., item 8: I feel like crying; item 14: I feel like hurting myself). Seven items are reverse keyed (e.g., item 25: I feel like having fun) with a negative response indicative of depressive symptom status. Item 30 consists of five smiley-type faces ranging from sad to happy, that the child completes by placing an X over the face that indicates how he or she feels and represents an evaluation of dysphoric mood.

The RCDS has been used in a number of descriptive and intervention studies of depression in children (e.g., Bartell & Reynolds, 1986; Huebner, Scott, & Alderman, 1993; Rawson, 1992; Reynolds et al., 1985; Reynolds & Graves, 1989; Roseby & Deutsch, 1985; Smoller & Brosgole, 1993). The manual for the RCDS provides normative information on over 1600 children representing heterogeneous ethnic and socioeconomic backgrounds, along with procedures for administration, scoring and interpretation, and data on reliability and validity. The internal consistency reliability of the RCDS with the standardization sample was 0.90. Internal consistency reliability of the RCDS with samples of normal and depressed youngsters have ranged from 0.87 to 0.92 (Bartell & Reynolds, 1986; Crowley & Emerson, 1996; Reynolds, 1989; Reynolds et al., 1985; Reynolds & Graves, 1989). Reynolds and Graves (1989) report a test–retest reliability coefficient of 0.85 for the RCDS using a four-week interval between testing with an ethnically diverse sample of 220 children from grades 3 through 6, and a mean difference in RCDS scores between the two assessments of less than two points.

Validity data for the RCDS have been reported in the form of high correlations with other self-report and clinical interview measures of childhood depression, as well as content validity, factor analysis, discriminant validity, and clinical utility (Reynolds, 1989). Researchers have reported correlations between the RCDS and the CDI ranging from 0.70 to 0.79 across several studies (e.g., Bartell & Reynolds, 1986; Crowley & Emerson, 1996; Reynolds, 1989; Reynolds et al., 1985). Reynolds (1989) reports a correlation between the RCDS and CDRS-R of 0.76. Using the CDRS-R cutoff score to provide a base rate for a clinical level of depression, Reynolds (1989) reported a specificity rate of 97%, sensitivity of 73%, a Yule's Y of 0.81 ($P < 0.0001$) and a phi coefficient of 0.73 ($P < 0.0001$) for the RCDS cutoff score with a sample of 82 children. A number of studies (e.g., Rawson & Tabb, 1993; Stark, Reynolds, & Kaslow, 1987) have shown the RCDS to be sensitive to treatment outcome as a measure of depression.

5.17.4.1.3 Children's Depression Scale

The Children's Depression Scale (CDS; Tisher & Lang, 1983) was developed in Australia and uses a modified card-sort response format with its 66 items individually listed on cards and the child sorting the cards into one of five boxes labeled: very wrong, wrong, don't know/not sure, right, and very right. The CDS evaluates two broad factors, with 18 items comprising a "positive affective experience" (P score) subscale, and the remaining 48 items a depression subscale (D score). The positive affect scale includes one subscale of eight items (pleasure and enjoyment), with the remaining items on the P scale described as

miscellaneous (Lang & Tisher, 1987). The depression subscale includes five subscales, (affective response, social problems, self-esteem, sickness and death, guilt, and pleasure and enjoyment) along with nine additional miscellaneous items. A manual by Lang and Tisher (1987) for use in North America was published with norms based on 37 normal children from Australia. There is also an adult-respondent form of the CDS (Tisher, 1995).

Several studies have described the psychometric characteristics of the CDS. Tisher, Lang-Takac, and Lang (1992) report on a test–retest study by Tonkin and Hudson (1981) who found a one week test–retest reliability coefficient of 0.74 for the CDS with a sample of 60 children. Internal consistency reliability has been found to be high, ranging from 0.92 to 0.94 (e.g., Bath & Middleton, 1985; Kazdin, 1987). Kazdin (1987) with a clinical sample of 185 children, reported correlations of 0.48 and 0.51 between child report on the CDS D scale and scores on the CDI and a modified form of the BID interview, respectively.

The CDS appears to be a reliable child self-report measure, although the number of items and format make administration and scoring a bit cumbersome. The lack of sufficient normative data is a limitation for the clinical use of this measure.

5.17.4.1.4 Reynolds Adolescent Depression Scale

The Reynolds Adolescent Depression Scale (RADS; Reynolds, 1986b) is designed to evaluate the severity of depressive symptoms in adolescents aged 12–18. The RADS consists of 30 items written to reflect symptoms delineated by the *DSM-III* (APA, 1980) for major depression and dysthymic disorder, as well as additional symptoms delineated by the RDC. Items on the RADS require a third-grade reading level. Although written at the time *DSM-III* was in effect, there have been few changes in symptoms and criteria for depressive disorders between *DSM-III*, *DSM-III-R* (APA, 1987), and *DSM-IV* (APA, 1994). Items on the RADS evaluate a range of symptom domains, including somatic, motivational, cognitive, mood, and vegetative components of depression.

The RADS was normed on an ethnically diverse sample of 2460 adolescents ages 12–19 years. The RADS norms appear to be relatively robust, with similar mean scores reported in a number of other studies of school-based youngsters in the USA and Canada (Dalley, Bolocofsky, Alcorn, & Baker, 1992; Reynolds & Miller, 1989; Schonert-Reichl, 1994; Weist,

Proescher, Freedman, Paskewitz, & Flaherty, 1995). The RADS has been used as a measure of depressive symptomatology in numerous studies with school-based and clinical samples of adolescents (Adams & Adams, 1993; Adams, Overholser, & Spirito, 1994; Brand, King, Olson, Ghaziuddin, & Naylor, 1996; King et al., 1996; King, Hovey et al., 1997; King, Radpour, Naylor, Segal, & Jouriles, 1995; King, Raskin, Gdowski, Butkus, & Opipari, 1990; King, Segal et al., 1995; King, Segal, Naylor, & Evans, 1993; Licitra-Kleckler & Waas, 1993; Nieminen & Matson, 1989; Sadowski & Kelley, 1993; Wurzbacher, Evans, & Moore, 1991).

The reliability of the RADS is generally reported as high, ranging from 0.91 to 0.96 with samples of normal and depressed adolescents ranging in size from 62 to 2120 (Dalley et al., 1992; Reynolds, 1987, 1990; Reynolds & Coats, 1982; Reynolds & Miller, 1989; Schonert-Reichl, 1994). Test–retest reliability based on a sample of 104 adolescents who were tested with a six week interval between testings was 0.80. A 12 week test–retest reliability coefficient of 0.79 was also found for the RADS with a sample of 415 high school students (Reynolds, 1987). More recently, Reynolds and Mazza (in press) reported a test–retest reliability coefficient of 0.87 in a sample of 89 young adolescents from an inner-city school with an average retest interval of three weeks.

The validity of the RADS has been shown in relationships with other depression scales and measures of related constructs. The RADS has demonstrated strong correlations with other self-report measures of depression, including the BDI (Beck et al., 1961), and Center for Epidemiological Studies depression scale (Radloff, 1977) ($r = 0.71–0.89$). Kahn, Kehle, and Jenson (1987) in a study of 349 adolescents found a correlation of 0.75 between the RADS and CDI. Shain, Naylor, and Alessi (1990) in a sample of 45 adolescent inpatients with major depression, reported a correlation coefficient of 0.87 between the RADS and CDI.

Criterion-related validity of the RADS has been shown using semistructured clinical interviews of depression. In a study of 111 adolescents, Reynolds (1987) reported a correlation of 0.83 between the RADS and the Hamilton Depression Rating Scale (HDRS; Hamilton, 1967). In their study of adolescents with major depression, Shain et al. (1990) reported a correlation of 0.73 between the RADS and the HDRS. Reynolds and Mazza (in press) found a correlation of 0.76 between the RADS and HDRS. Overall, in studies of clinical samples of adolescents, investigators have reported strong evidence for criterion-related validity for the RADS with diagnostic and semistructured clinical interview measures of depression (King, Katz et al., 1997; Reinecke & Schultz, 1995).

The RADS uses a cutoff score to describe a clinical level of depressive symptom severity. The RADS cutoff score has been validated in several studies, using both HDRS scores as well as formal diagnosis based on the SADS as criterion measures (Reynolds, 1987). Using the RADS cutoff score of 77 and a HDRS cutoff of 15 with a subsample of 32 adolescents from a psychiatric center, Carey, Kelley, and Carey (1991) reported that 78.1% were correctly classified using the cutoff scores on these two measures.

In a study of adolescents with major depression and an age and sex matched normal control group, Shain et al. (1991) found significant differences in RADS scores between youngsters with major depression ($M = 85.5$) and normal controls ($M = 45.5$) $t = 9.02$, $p < 0.0001$. Reynolds and Mazza (in press) reported a hit rate of 94% and a kappa coefficient of 0.71 using the RADS cutoff score in comparison to a clinical cutoff score of 16 on the HDRS. The RADS has demonstrated clinical efficacy in its use in a number of adolescent depression treatment studies (Hains, 1992; Kahn, Kehle, Jenson, & Clark, 1990; Reynolds & Coats, 1986).

5.17.4.1.5 Beck Depression Inventory

The BDI (Beck et al., 1961) was developed for adults and consists of 21 items, each consisting of four statements of varying degrees of symptom severity. A number of investigators have used the BDI with adolescents, although the reading requirements and format of the scale present difficulty for some youngsters. Users of the BDI often apply cutoff scores used with adults to adolescents without adequate validation.

Internal consistency reliability of the BDI with adolescents has been reported in the 0.70s to 0.80s (Kashani, Sherman, Parker, & Reid, 1990; Reynolds & Coats, 1982; Roberts, Lewinsohn, & Seeley, 1991; Strober, Green, & Carlson, 1981). Strober et al. (1981) reported a five-day test–retest reliability of 0.69 in a sample of 78 psychiatric inpatient adolescents, similar to the short-term test–retest reliability of 0.67 reported by Roberts et al. (1991) with a large sample of school-based youngsters. In a study of 37 older adolescents, Kutcher & Marton (1989) found a one-week test–retest reliability coefficient of 0.83. Overall, the reliability of the BDI with adolescents is lower than that found in other self-report measures of depression developed specifically for youngsters.

Validity evidence for the BDI has been mixed in clinical and school-based samples. Barrera and Garrison-Jones (1988) with a sample of hospitalized psychiatric patients ($n = 65$) and school-based adolescents ($n = 49$) reported reasonable sensitivity and specificity in the school sample but poor results for the psychiatric sample. Kashani et al. (1990) noted a relatively low sensitivity rate (48%) using the BDI cutoff score of 16 in a sample of 100 clinic referred adolescents. Roberts et al. (1991) in a study of 1704 adolescents who completed the BDI as well as a diagnostic interview, found a correlation of 0.50 between the BDI and a 14-item form of the HDRS, which is relatively low, with low kappa coefficients for the BDI in identifying cases of major depression ($\kappa = 0.14$) and dysthymia ($\kappa = 0.03$). The somewhat lower reliability, adult language and comprehension demands, and issues of validity of the BDI cutoff score with adolescents are issues that should be recognized in the use of the BDI with adolescents.

5.17.4.2 Clinical Interview Severity Measures of Depression

A number of diagnostic and severity interview measures have been developed for the evaluation of depression in children and adolescents. As noted earlier, diagnostic measures that assess the wide range of psychopathology found in young people will not be discussed in this chapter. Described below are two semistructured clinical interviews that evaluate the severity of depressive symptoms, in youngsters. These measures, the CDRS-R (Poznanski et al., 1984) and the HDRS (Hamilton, 1967) have been used in research and treatment outcome applications.

5.17.4.2.1 Children's Depression Rating Scale-Revised

The CDRS-R (Poznanski et al. 1984) was originally developed in 1979 (Poznanski et al., 1979) and is a semistructured clinical interview measure of the severity of symptoms of depression designed for use with children aged 6–12. The CDRS-R consists of 17 items, each representing a depressive symptom, and rated on a 1 (normal) to 7 (severe) scale. On the CDRS-R, 14 of the items are presented in an interview format, and three items (depressed affect, tempo of language, and hypoactivity) are observational. The CDRS-R requires 20–30 minutes to administer.

Poznanski and her colleagues (Poznanski et al., 1979; Poznanski, Cook, Carroll, & Corzo,

1983; Poznanski, Carroll, Banegas, Cook, & Grossman, 1982) have reported acceptable levels of reliability and evidence of validity of the CDRS in differentiating RDC-diagnosed youngsters. Poznanski, Freeman, & Mokros (1985) recommends a score of 40 and above on the CDRS-R as a clinical cutoff for depression in children. Using a cutoff score of 44, Jensen, Burke, and Garfinkel (1988) reported sensitivity of 50% and specificity of 79% for a diagnosis of major depression in a sample of 35 youngsters aged 8–18, 12 of whom had a diagnosis of major depression. Heiligenstein and Jabobsen (1988) modified the CDRS-R with the removal of somatic items for the evaluation of depression in medically ill youngsters. The CDRS and CDRS-R have been used as severity measures in research on depression in children and adolescents (e.g., Mokros, Poznanski, Grossman, & Freeman, 1987; Shain et al., 1990; Weller, Weller, Fristad, Cantwell, & Preskorn, 1986), and the CDRS-R was used as an outcome measure in treatment studies of depression in children by Liddle and Spence (1990) and Stark et al. (1987).

5.17.4.2.2 Hamilton Depression Rating Scale

The HDRS (Hamilton, 1960, 1967) is a clinical interview measure of the severity of depressive symptoms and one of the most frequently used outcome measures in psychiatric studies of depression in adults. There are several versions of the HDRS, the most popular being the 17 item form. Items are evaluated by the clinician as to their severity with higher scores indicative of greater depressive pathology. Two items that assess psychomotor retardation and psychomotor agitation, are observational. Items on the HDRS are scored from 0 to 4 or 0 to 2 depending on the symptom assessed, with high scores indicating greater symptom pathology. Researchers have utilized a number of cutoff scores to delineate a clinical level of depressive symptomatology, with such scores typically ranging from 15 to 20.

There are a number of caveats to the use of the HDRS. It should be noted that a number of contemporary symptoms of depression are not evident on the HDRS (e.g., low self-esteem, self-deprecation, etc.). Likewise, several items dealing with loss of insight, hypocondriasis, and several anxiety items are tangentially related to depression. Nevertheless, as a severity measure of depression, the HDRS, with minor adjustments for age differences, works quite well with adolescents.

Research using the HDRS has included both clinical and nonclinical samples of adolescents

(Alessi, McManus, Grapentine, & Brickman, 1984; King, Naylor, Hill, Shain, & Greden, 1993; King, Segal et al., 1995; King et al., 1996; Reynolds, 1987; Shain et al., 1990). Reynolds (1987) found an internal consistency reliability of 0.91 for the HDRS with a sample of 111 school-based adolescents, and Reynolds and Mazza (in press) reported a reliability of 0.85 with young adolescents. Robbins, Alessi, Colfer, and Yanchyshyn (1985) obtained an interrater reliability of 0.90 with a sample of adolescent psychiatric inpatients. King, Naylor, Segal, Evans, & Shain (1993) reported an interrater reliability of 0.97 in a sample of 30 depressed and nondepressed adolescents.

5.17.4.3 Assessment Summary

A number of interviews and rating scales developed for the assessment of depression in children and adolescents have been described. A positive outcome since the mid-1980s in the study of depression in children and adolescents has been the development of diverse methodologies and procedures for the assessment of this disorder in youngsters. Although the role of child self-report in the evaluation process has been stressed, the availability of other rich sources of information can only serve to increase our perspectives regarding the mental health of children and adolescents. An examination of measures for the evaluation of depression in youngsters indicates that there is no one right or correct measure. Rather, there are different measures designed for different assessment purposes. Furthermore, the variance in sources of information about a youngster's depression, although disconcerting to researchers and scientists who often seek parsimony among measures of the same construct, may suggest that there is also no one right or correct source of information. The issue of differences in reports among sources of information, or informant variability is a complex issue that has developmental as well as psychometric underpinnings. Additional information on this issue as it relates to the assessment of depression in children and adolescents is given by Kazdin (1994).

It is recommended that the evaluation of depression in a child, particularly a young child, involves multiple assessment measures and, where possible, multiple assessment methods (e.g., self-report, clinical interview, reports by significant others). Waller and Rush (1983) have provided an interesting approach to assessment and diagnosis of depression in children which incorporates formal psychological assessment, medical procedures, and response to treatment for distinguishing primary depression, organic affective syndrome, and situational depression in children. As found in numerous research studies, disagreements occur across methods and measures. In such cases, a close examination of the specific assessment information is warranted, with the clinician deciding how best to combine these data. In the above discussion of depression assessment measures, there is an evident gap in procedures for the evaluation of depression in children below the age of 6 or 7 years.

5.17.5 PSYCHOLOGICAL TREATMENT OF DEPRESSION IN CHILDREN AND ADOLESCENTS

It is evident that depression is a serious psychological disturbance that is experienced by a very large number of children and adolescents. Surveys and studies of service utilization suggest that most of these youngsters do not receive treatment of any type (Keller et al., 1991). The high prevalence rate combined with the potential range of long-term negative consequences (e.g., Kovacs, 1996b) supports the need and requirement for effective treatment procedures. Treatment approaches for depression in children and adolescents are, for the most part, modifications or direct applications of procedures developed for use with adults. Depressed youngsters represent a particularly vulnerable population. Unlike children and adolescents with externalizing problems, such as conduct disorder, for whom treatment may be viewed by the youngster as undesirable or even punitive, depressed youngsters often see treatment as a potential avenue to reduce or alleviate their severe distress.

The empirical evidence for the efficacy of contemporary psychological treatments for depression in children and adolescents is limited to fewer than a dozen studies that have been conducted since 1980. Thus, for practical purposes, our evidence for the use of contemporary psychotherapies for the treatment of depression in youngsters is predicated on the results of these investigations. The use of psychoanalytically based treatments has a somewhat longer history, although there is limited empirical evidence to support therapeutic efficacy.

5.17.5.1 Range of Therapeutic Approaches

There are a multitude of treatment modalities across the two primary domains of psychological and somatic approaches. The latter include the use of antidepressant medications, such as tricyclics, monoamine oxidase inhibitors, specific serotonin reuptake inhibitors, and lithium carbonate. These procedures have generated a body of empirical research that allows for the evaluation of their clinical efficacy although, as in the case with psychotherapy, the number of studies is small in comparison to research with adults.

As noted, there have been fewer than a dozen empirical demonstrations of the efficacy of psychological treatments designed for the amelioration of affective disorders and depressive symptoms in children and adolescents. The small number of experimental studies on the psychological treatment of depression in children and adolescents is perplexing, particularly given the large number of empirical outcome studies on the treatment of depression in adults. However, a similar situation exists with regard to the number of pharmacological interventions for depression in young people in comparison to the large number of studies of antidepressant efficacy with adults.

A brief overview of control-group studies of psychotherapy for the treatment of depression in children and adolescents is presented in this chapter. Case reports, including single-subject designs, have been reported and been reviewed previously (Reynolds, 1992b).

5.17.5.2 Control-group Investigations

For the demonstration of clinical efficacy and generalizability, control-group experimental treatment studies that provide data on the efficacy of psychological treatments for depression in children and adolescents are of significance. The majority of the published empirical, control group investigations have utilized a range of cognitive-behavioral procedures, and have typically compared youngsters receiving such treatment with groups of youngster who receive another potentially active treatment, therapeutic support, and/or are assigned to a wait-list condition and do not receive treatment during the period of study. A number of contemporary psychotherapy investigations for depression in children and adolescents are briefly described below and summarized in Tables 3 and 4. In the majority of controlled group investigations reported below, structured therapy manuals have been developed that provide evidence for the combination of specific treatment components.

In addition to studies reported in peer-reviewed publications, a number of investigators have provided partial descriptions of treatment outcome studies within books or chapters in books. Results of a cognitive-behavioral intervention for depression with children were described in Stark (1990) and in a chapter by Stark, Rouse, and Livingston

(1991) who reported on treatment outcome with 24 children who were randomly assigned to a cognitive-behavioral (self-control, social skills, relaxation training, and cognitive restructuring) or traditional counseling intervention (therapeutic discussion and support). Family therapy, consistent with treatment components of each condition was also provided. Treatments consists of 24–26 sessions of 45–50 minutes over a $3^1/_2$ month period administered in small groups of four youngsters to a group. Both conditions showed significant decreases in depressive symptomatology in participants at posttreatment with treatment gains maintained at a seven month follow-up. On one outcome measure, the cognitive-behavioral group was superior to the counseling condition, although this difference was not found at follow-up. Actual test score means for the groups at various assessment points were not provided by the authors.

5.17.5.3 Psychotherapy Treatment Studies with Children

One of the first control group treatment studies for depression in children was reported by Butler, Miezitis, Friedman, and Cole (1980) who compared a role play condition that emphasized role play, social skills and social problem solving and a cognitive restructuring treatment based in part on rational-emotive therapy. Control groups consisted of an attention and waitlist condition. Participants were a school-based sample of 54 moderately depressed fifth and sixth grade children. The active treatments and attention condition consisted of 10 one-hour sessions conducted in small groups of six or seven children. A pretest–post-test design was used, although the authors did not conduct a follow-up evaluation to determine the maintenance of treatment gains. Multiple outcome measures were used, with the CDI the only measure of depression. At the post-test, significant decreases in CDI scores were found for the two active treatment conditions, as well as for the waitlist control group. The attention group remained relatively unchanged in their self-reported level of depressive symptomatology.

The results of the Butler et al. (1980) investigation were somewhat mixed. Although decreases were found for the two active treatments, the level of mean CDI scores for these groups at post-test (14 and 16 points) may be considered elevated. Likewise, the decrease in scores seen in the waitlist, but not the attention placebo control is puzzling. A significant methodological problem was the failure to include a follow-up assessment in the research design. In this sense, the extent to

Table 3 Summary of controlled group psychological interventions for depression in children and adolescents.

Study	Treatment groups	Sample size	Sessions Number	Sessions Duration	Depression measures	Outcome posttest	Follow-up length	Follow-up outcome
Butler et al. (1980)	cognitive-restructuring (CR)	14	10	60 min	CDI	[PR=CR=WL]>AC		
	role-play (RP)	14						
	attention control (AC)	13						
	waitlist control (WL)	13						
Reynolds and Coats (1986)	cognitive-behavioral (CB)	9	10	50 min	RADS	[CB=RT]>WL	5 weeks	CB=RT=WL
	relaxation training (RT)	11			BDI	[CB=RT]>WL		[CB=RT]>WL
	waitlist control (WL)	10			BID	[CB=RT]>WL		[CB=RT]>WL
Stark, Reynolds, and Kaslow (1987)	cognitive-behavioral (CB)	9	12	50 min	CDI	PS=CB, CB>WL	8 weeks[b]	CB=PS
	problem solving (PS)	10			RCDS	[CB=PS]>WL		CB=PS
	waitlist control (WL)	9			CDRS-R			CB>PS
Kahn et al. (1990)	cognitive-behavioral (CB)	17	12	50 min	RADS	[CB, RT, SM]>WL	4 weeks	[CB=RT=SM]
	relaxation training (RT)	17	12	50 min	CDI	[CB, RT, SM]>WL		
	self-modeling (SM)[a]	17	12	12 min	BID	RT=CB, SM CB, SM>WL		
	Waitlist control (WL)	17						
Lewinsohn et al., (1990)	cognitive-behavioral (CB)	21	14	120 min	BDI	[CB=CBP]>WL	4 weeks[c]	CB=CBP
	CB + parent (CBP)	19	14	120 min	CES-D	[CB=CBP]>WL		CB=CBP
	waitlist control (WL)	19			CBCL-D	CBP>CB, CBP=WL		CB=WL, CBP>CB
Liddle and Spence (1990)	cognitive-behavioral (CB)	11	8	60 min	CDI	CB=AC=WL	12 weeks	CB=AC=WL
	attention control (AC)	10	8	60 min	CDRS-R			
	waitlist control (WL)	10						
Marcotte and Baron (1990)	rational-emotive (RET)	12	12	60 min	BDI	RET=WL	8 weeks	RET>WL
	waitlist control (WL)	13						
Fine et al. (1991)	social skills (SS)	30	12	50 min	CDI	TS>SS[d]	9 months	TS=SS
	therapeutic support (TS)	36			K-SADS	TS>SS		TS=SS
Haines (1992)	cognitive-behavioral (CB)	9	9[e]	40 min	RADS	[CB=RT]>WL	11 weeks	CB=RT
	relaxation training (RT)	8						
	waitlist control (WL)	8						

[a] The self-modeling treatment was individually administered. [b] Follow-up assessment was for CB and PS groups. WL group received treatment following posttesting. [c] Follow-up assessment also completed at 6, 12, and 24 months. [d] P < 0.10. [e] Sessions included three group and six individual sessions.

Table 4 Summary of noncontrolled group psychological interventions for depression in children and adolescents.

Study	Treatment groups	Sample size	Sessions Number	Sessions Duration	Depression measures	Outcome postest	Follow-up length	Follow-up outcome
Mufson et al. (1994)	interpersonal (IPT-A)	11	12	45 min	BDI	$t = 7.03$***		
					HDRS	$t = 9.16$***		
Belsher et al. (1995)	cognitive therapy (CT)[a]	15	12	variable	BDI	$t = 6.51$***	10 weeks[b]	gain
								maintenance
					IDS-C	$t = 5.96$***		gain
								maintenance

>[a] Approximately 40% of participants also received medication. [b] Second follow-up conducted at approximately 20 weeks.
*** $P < 0.001$.

which the groups maintained treatment gains and evaluation of treatment generalization is unknown. This study is noteworthy in that it appears to be the first published experimental group intervention for depression in children, and it used an attention control condition.

Stark et al. (1987) compared a cognitive-behavioral treatment that was largely predicated on self-control and attribution retraining components, and a behavioral problem-solving treatment that utilized components of interpersonal problem-solving, increased engagement in pleasant activities, and self-monitoring to a waiting list control condition. Participants at post-testing were 28 moderately depressed children, aged 9–12. Assessment measures included the RCDS, CDI, and CDRS-R along with measures of related domains. The intervention was school-based and consisted of 12 50-minute sessions administered in small groups over a five-week period.

At post-testing, both active treatments demonstrated significant improvement in depressive symptomatology while the difference for the waiting list control group was non-significant. An eight-week follow-up showed a general maintenance of the treatment effects, with some children in the self-control condition showing continued improvement from post-test to follow-up. Children in the waiting list condition were treated after the post-test and were not included in the between-group comparisons at follow-up. Results indicated that the treatments were reasonably effective, with 88% of the children in the self-control group and 67% of those in the behavioral group reporting nondepressed levels of depressive symptomatology at the follow-up assessment. On the basis of this study and further development of active components, Stark (1990) has provided a more comprehensive treatment program for depression in children that is expanded in its scope, content, and duration.

In a study conducted in Australia, Liddle and Spence (1990) compared social competence training (SCT) intervention that included cognitive and behavioral treatment components, to an attention placebo control group, and a waiting list control group with a sample of 31 children aged 7–11. The authors indicated that children were identified based on a multiple-source multiple-stage screening procedure recommended by Reynolds et al. (1985). Children were selected from the population of regular class youngsters attending two Catholic schools in Sydney, Australia, and for whom parental permission for assessment was provided. Children were administered the CDI, which was read to younger-age children and those with reading problems. A cutoff score of 19 was used to select children for the second stage of the assessment procedure. Of the 380 children tested, 70 (18.4%) obtained a score of 19 or higher on the CDI. Two weeks following the initial screening, the CDRS-R was individually administered to the 70 youngsters. Using a cutoff score of 40 on the CDRS-R, 33 children were identified as demonstrating a clinical level of depression.

Of the 33 children identified, permission from parents for child participation in treatment was obtained for 31 youngsters. It is interesting to note that there were 10 girls and 21 boys, suggesting a gender difference of 2 to 1, with boys demonstrating a higher rate of depression, assuming that there was minimal difference in the proportion of males and females in the total sample. The mean age of the sample was 9.2 years (SD = 1.15). For the total treatment sample the mean CDI score was 21.32, with a mean of 42.03 on the CDRS-R, suggesting a moderate to severely depressed sample. Participants were randomly assigned to either a SCT condition (*n* = 11), an attention placebo control (APC) (*n* = 10), or a waiting list control group (*n* = 10).

Treatment for the SCT and APC consisted of eight one-hour sessions administered once a week to youngsters in groups of 4–6 children. The waiting list group did not receive any treatment and were evaluated at pretest, post-test, and at a three month follow-up evaluation. The SCT intervention focused on teaching social skills, interpersonal problem solving, and included components of cognitive restructuring. Self-monitoring of negative thoughts was also included. There appear to be similarities between treatment components of the SCT program and the behavioral problem-solving intervention developed by Stark et al. (1987). The attention/placebo control consisted of teaching drama to participants and appears to be more of an attention control condition rather than a placebo treatment.

At post-testing, all groups showed a modest decrease in CDI scores with no difference in treatment efficacy between groups. Unfortunately the CDI was the only depression measure used to evaluate treatment effects. Similar findings were reported for the follow-up assessment. Overall, the SCT intervention failed to produce meaningful treatment effects beyond those found in the attention and waitlist control conditions. This is an interesting study that appears to be the first to include younger children (i.e., age seven years and above). The lack of clinical efficacy is somewhat unexpected given previous studies and may be in part a function of the younger age of participants.

5.17.5.4 Psychotherapy Treatment Studies with Adolescents

In the first published control group treatment study for depression in adolescents, Reynolds and Coats (1986) compared a cognitive-behavioral treatment, a relaxation training group, and a waiting list control group with a sample of 30 moderately to severely depressed high school students. The two active treatment conditions were administered in 10 50-minute sessions twice a week for a five-week period. A follow-up assessment was conducted after four weeks from the end of treatment. Assessment measures included the RADS, BDI, and BID, along with measures of related constructs (e.g., anxiety, self-esteem). A school-based screening procedure was used to identify participants with the pretest representing a second assessment point. Both active therapies were presented in a structured format, with detailed treatment manuals established for each condition. The cognitive-behavioral therapy used procedures found in similar treatments of depression in adults, with modifications made for developmental and situational (e.g., home, school, peer-group, etc.) differences of adolescents. Components included teaching self-control procedures (i.e., self-monitoring, self-evaluation, and self-reinforcement), cognitive restructuring consistent with aspects of Beck's (1967, 1976) cognitive therapy, and procedures for increasing involvement in pleasant activities (Lewinsohn, Munoz, Youngren, & Zeiss, 1978). The relaxation training condition involved training in progressive relaxation procedures, along with guided imagery procedures. Both treatments were matched for therapist time and amount of homework assignments.

At post-testing, significant treatment gains for both active treatment conditions were found and maintained at the four week follow-up evaluation. Significant decreases in depression were reported by youngsters in the cognitive-behavioral and relaxation groups at post-test, with minimal change in the waiting list youngsters. Therapeutic effects of the interventions on participants' self-concept and level of anxiety were also reported by Reynolds and Coats (1986), with the relaxation training condition demonstrating the greatest reduction in self-reported anxiety.

Several of the treatment conditions of the Reynolds and Coats (1986) study were replicated by Kahn, Kehle, Jenson, and Clark (1990) who reported a treatment outcome study with 68 moderately depressed young adolescents. Treatment conditions for depression included cognitive-behavioral, relaxation training, and a self-modeling, along with a waitlist control group. The cognitive-behavioral treatment included pleasant activity scheduling and other behavioral components consistent with the approach of Lewinsohn et al. (1978), along with cognitive restructuring, self-control, and social skills training. The relaxation training group was similar to that of Reynolds and Coats (1986). Cognitive-behavioral and relaxation treatments were group administered in 12 50-minute sessions. The self-modeling treatment was individual with each youngster developing a three-minute videotape of themselves modeling nondepressive behaviors (e.g., smiling, positive verbalizations, and appropriate eye contact). Outcome measures included the RADS, CDI, and BID.

The authors reported significant treatment gains for the three active therapy conditions at post-testing and at a four week follow-up. The greatest therapeutic gains at post-testing and follow-up were found for the cognitive-behavioral and relaxation training conditions. The results of this investigation are consistent with Reynolds and Coats (1986), and suggest treatment generalizability as well as the efficacy of these procedures with young adolescents.

Lewinsohn, Clarke, Hops, and Andrews (1990) reported on the downward extension of the coping with depression course (Lewinsohn et al., 1978), a multimodal psychoeducational intervention for unipolar depression (Clarke & Lewinsohn, 1989). The sample consisted of 59 adolescents who met *DSM-III* criteria for major depression or RDC criteria for current minor or intermittent depressive disorder. Treatment conditions included: cognitive-behavior therapy group administered to adolescents only and consisting of 14 two hour sessions over a seven week period; the same cognitive-behavioral treatment administered to another group of adolescents along with group-training for parents (seven two-hour sessions) of these adolescents; and a waitlist control group.

The cognitive-behavioral intervention utilized a social learning approach to the treatment of depression, and included: pleasant activities scheduling; social skills training; cognitive restructuring; relaxation training; and a component focusing on communication, negotiation, and conflict resolution skills. The parent training included discussion of the components and skills taught to the adolescents and training in negotiation, communication and conflict-resolution skills.

Treatment outcome was reported for post-treatment, and follow-up assessments at 1, 6, 12 and 24 months. The waitlist condition was only available at post-testing. At post-testing, both active treatments demonstrated significant change as compared to the waitlist group, but were not significantly different from each other in their treatment efficacy. Treatment gains were maintained with a trend toward further improvement at follow-up assessments. The lack of the waitlist group as a comparison condition following post-treatment limited the long-term generalization of follow-up results.

In one of the few experimental studies conducted in a psychiatric setting, Fine, Forth, Gilbert, and Haley (1991) compared a social skills training group with a therapeutic support group for the treatment of depression in a group of 66 adolescent outpatients with a *DSM-III-R* diagnosis of major depression or dysthymia. The social skills condition consisted of self-monitoring of self and other's feelings, assertiveness training, conversation skills, social problem solving and conflict resolution. The therapeutic support treatment was designed as a therapeutic and supportive milieu for discussing problems and enhancing self-concept and self-worth. Outcome data (CDI and others measures) were reported for 47 youngsters who completed eight or more of the 12 treatment sessions. Within-group (pretest to post-test) differences indicated significant improvement for both treatments on a 12 item symptom scale derived from the K-SADS, with only the therapeutic support group showing significant post-test change on the CDI. Between-group analyses indicated the therapeutic support condition was superior on the K-SADS, with no difference between groups on the CDI. At a nine month follow-up there were no differences between groups on the outcome measures.

The results of this study are mixed. The social skills group showed minimal change in self-reported depressive symptoms on the CDI (pretest $M = 20.3$, post-test $M = 18.4$). On the K-SADS change from clinical to nonclinical levels was found in 50% of the therapeutic support group and 40% of the social skills group. This study suggests that social skills training alone may have limited therapeutic benefits. The superiority of the therapeutic support group suggests the potential utility of more interpersonal problem-solving therapies with adolescents.

In a study of 25 adolescent boys, 15–16 years of age, seeking training in stress management, Hains (1992) examined, in comparison to a waitlist control group, the efficacy of: a cognitive-behavioral intervention for stress inoculation based on the work of Meichenbaum (1985); an anxiety management procedure predicated on the work of Suinn (1986) with a strong relaxation training component. Although the focus of the study was on anxiety and stress management, depressive symptoma-

tology was also examined at pretest, post-test, and follow-up. Interventions incorporated both group (three sessions) and individual (six sessions) therapy, with an 11 week follow-up conducted for the two active treatment conditions. Because of the selection criteria, group means on the RADS of participants suggested mild levels of depressive symptomatology, below means reported in other investigations (e.g., Kahn et al., 1990; Reynolds & Coats, 1986). However, given the small number of studies reported in the literature, this investigation is of interest, although it may be viewed as treating a subclinical level of depression. At post-testing, significant treatment gains on the RADS were found for the two active conditions in comparison for the waitlist group, with treatment groups maintaining treatment gains at follow-up.

In a study conducted in Canada with francophone youngsters, a cognitive therapy for depression was compared to a waiting list control group in a study of 25 depressed adolescents conducted by Marcotte and Baron (1993). The authors used a cognitive treatment package based on the rational-emotive model of depression. The treatment was administered in 12 60-minute sessions over a six week period. Participants were ages 14–17 years and were identified by the three-stage school-based screening procedure suggested by Reynolds (1986a). Significant treatment gains were found on the BDI in the cognitive group in comparison to the waitlist condition at post-test and at eight week follow-up.

As noted earlier, there have been several open trial studies of psychotherapies for the treatment of depression in adolescents. Although not described in detail in this chapter they are noted and present promising evidence for treatment efficacy. These studies are listed in Table 4. The study by Mufson et al. (1994) was based on a modification of the interpersonal psychotherapy of Klerman and Weissman (Klerman & Weissman, 1982). The modification of this intervention for adolescents was originally described by Moreau, Mufson, Weissman, and Klerman (1991) and more fully in Mufson, Moreau, Weissman, and Klerman (1993). Significant posttreatment gains in depressive symptomatology scores were found on the BDI and the HDRS.

A noncontrol group treatment study using cognitive therapy for depression in adolescents was reported by Belsher et al. (1995) with 15 adolescents who met criteria for *DMS-III-R* major depression. The authors reported significant reduction in depressive symptomatology at post-testing and two follow-ups (10 and 20 weeks) on the BDI and a clinician rating form of the Inventory of Depressive Symptomatology (Rush et al., 1986). It is also noteworthy that, similar to Mufson et al. (1993), the authors and colleagues have presented a more detailed description of their cognitive therapy for depression in adolescents in a book (Wilkes, Belsher, Rush, & Frank, 1994).

In both of the open trials noted above, significant reductions in depressive symptomatology were reported. However, as has been found in controlled group investigations, it is not uncommon to find symptom reduction also to occur in waitlist or control conditions, such that the primary focus is the demonstration of greater clinical efficacy of the active condition in comparison to control conditions. The same design issues apply to the evaluation of pharmacotherapies.

A significant finding from the majority of studies was the relative treatment efficacy of cognitive-behavioral therapies for the treatment of depression, with promising results reported for interpersonal psychotherapy. It is also noteworthy that treatment effectiveness was reported across therapies based on between 10 and 15 sessions, with treatment gains maintained at follow-up for most studies. This suggests that brief, structured contemporary psychotherapies are potentially efficacious for the treatment of depression in children and adolescents. Given what is known regarding the clinical efficacy of pharmacotherapies, contemporary psychotherapies should be considered as a general first line of treatment unless clinical data shows strong support for antidepressant treatment. For example, in a descriptive study of melancholic and nonmelancholic subtype adolescent psychiatric inpatients with major depression who were "significantly incapacitated by their symptoms," Robbins, Alessi, and Colfer (1989, p. 100) found that 68% of youngsters with nonmelancholic major depression responded to an intensive six week, broad-based psychosocial treatment without the use of medication. Adolescent inpatients with melancholic type major depression showed minimal response to psychotherapy, although 26% of these youngsters did show significant improvement with psychotherapy alone.

Given the lack of significant side-effects and the slow, but growing literature to suggest efficacy, contemporary psychotherapies for depression in children and adolescents need to be integrated into the standard of practice for the treatment of affective disorders in young people. It is also useful to note that in a study of treatment acceptability for interventions for depression in children, Tarnowski, Simonian, Bekeny, and Park (1992) found that mothers view psychological interventions to be significantly more acceptable than pharmacological, with cognitive-behavioral and behavioral interventions found somewhat more acceptable than social skills interventions. At this point, it appears that there is sufficient evidence to support the use of cognitive-behavioral procedures for the treatment of depression by clinicians. Based on the evidence of studies cited above, it does not appear that interventions with social skills enhancement or training are particularly useful as a stand-alone treatment. Further empirical study of interpersonal psychotherapy and other procedures should be undertaken to provide clinicians with a range of tested psychotherapeutic treatment approaches. Lastly, the efficacy of relaxation training has been noted in several studies, with its inclusion as a component noted in others, suggests that this approach may be viable for treating depression in some youngsters.

5.17.6 PHARMACOTHERAPY FOR DEPRESSION IN CHILDREN AND ADOLESCENTS

The use of medications for the treatment of mood disorders in children and adolescents has a long history compared to the application of psychotherapy. An examination of the pharmacological literature suggests that most empirical investigations of antidepressant medications for the treatment of depression (as well as a host of other disorders such as obsessive compulsive disorder [OCD], enuresis, school phobia, anxiety problems, etc.) have been conducted with children, with few investigations that focus on the treatment of depressed adolescents.

It is important to recognize that the administration of antidepressant medications does not result in a cure of the depression. Antidepressant drugs will show therapeutic effects in some youngsters; however, typically the symptoms of depression will return if the treatment is discontinued during the course of the depressive illness (Johnston & Fruehling, 1994).

The research on the efficacy of antidepressants with children and adolescents is growing as newer drugs and classes of antidepressants are placed on the market. Rather than review each of the dozen or so controlled studies of antidepressant therapy with children and adolescents, this chapter provides a brief review of the general findings and some of the issues inherent in the use of pharmacological agents with children and adolescents. It should be noted that in addition to pharmacotherapy, reports of electroconvulsive therapy (Bertagnoli

& Borchard, 1990) and light/phototherapy for seasonal affective disorder (seasonal pattern) (Sonis, Yellin, Garfinkel, & Hoberman, 1987) with depressed youngsters have been published. Light therapy has also been suggested as an adjunct in the treatment of depressive symptoms in bipolar disorder in adolescents (Papatheodorou & Kutcher, 1995). This chapter does not review studies of pharmacotherapy for treatment of bipolar disorder in children and adolescents. For bipolar disorder, lithium is one of the more commonly used drugs along with carbamazepine. The treatment of bipolar disorder in youngsters as well as adults is a difficult undertaking and frequently involves the testing of various drugs, singly and in combination. Data from research and clinical studies suggest that pharmacological agents used with adults for the treatment of bipolar disorder work about as effectively with young people (Carlson, 1994).

5.17.6.1 Pharmacotherapy for Depression in Children and Adolescents

A large number of case reports and a limited number of experimental studies have been published examining the efficacy of tricyclic antidepressants (TCAs), monoamine oxidase inhibitors, selective serotonin reuptake inhibitors (SSRIs), and other drugs for the treatment of unipolar depression, and lithium carbonate and other compounds for the treatment of bipolar disorder in children and adolescents. Pharmacotherapy of depression in children and adolescents is somewhat controversial due to the limited treatment response over placebo reported in numerous double-blind clinical trials. Reviews of the pharmacological studies for depression in young people can be found in Alessi, Naylor, Ghaziuddin, and Zubieta (1994), Jensen, Ryan, and Prien (1992), and Johnston and Fruehling (1994).

Since the mid-1980s, a number of newer antidepressants have appeared on the market with demonstrated efficacy for adults. Of particular note have been the SSRIs including fluoxetine, fluvoxamine, sertraline, and paroxetine. There have been reports of fluoxetine use with youngsters (e.g., Dech & Budow, 1991; Naylor & Grossman, 1991), although at the time of this chapter the author could not find published controlled group outcome studies using these agents for depression in youngsters. Initial research with fluoxetine by Riddle, Hardin, King, Seahill, & Woolston (1990), with a sample of 10 youngsters with Tourette's syndrome and OCD, found mixed results specific to treatment of obsessive compulsive symptoms. Significant agitation was noted as a

response to fluoxetine in four of the 10 participants, but there were minimal adverse biological side-effects. The latter may be expected, given the general lack of anticholinergic and antihistaminic side-effects with fluoxetine. Riddle et al. (1989) also reported a case of a fluoxetine overdose in an adolescent. Open trials of SSRIs have been reported by Apter et al. (1994), Boulos, Kutcher, Gardner, and Young (1992), and others. Initial reports suggest significant clinical efficacy for fluoxetine, even with youngsters who previous failed to respond to TCAs (Boulos et al., 1992).

By far, the majority of published, control group investigations of antidepressants for the treatment of depression in children and adolescents has utilized tricyclic antidepressants such as imipramine, amitriptyline, nortriptyline, and desipramine. Researcher reports on TCAs for the treatment of depression in children began to appear in the late 1960s and early 1970s (Frommer, 1967; Kuhn & Kuhn 1971; Ling et al., 1970; Weinberg et al., 1973). Stack (1971) reported on 490 depressed children, including 116 preschool children, treated with antidepressants, most of which were TCAs.

A general finding across controlled antidepressant treatment studies of depression in children and adolescents has been the lack of superiority of medications over placebo control conditions. Rationales for this lack of treatment efficacy have ranged from invalidity of the diagnosis of depression in children using current classification systems to errors in design methodology and insufficient sample size (Conners, 1992; Jensen et al., 1992). With regard to the latter, most of the published studies utilized relatively small sample treatment groups, such that power to detect a significant difference is often compromised. However, in a recent study by Kutcher et al. (1994) of desipramine for major depression in adolescents, 60 adolescents were studied after using a placebo washout phase prior to treatment. In this well-controlled investigation, antidepressant and placebo groups did not differ across a wide range of outcome measures including psychometric as well as laboratory assessments. A similar finding was reported by Kye et al. (1996) in a controlled study of amitriptyline for major depression in 31 adolescents (22 completers) with major depression, using a two-week placebo-washout period.

5.17.6.2 Summary of Pharmacological Interventions

The overriding conclusion from the majority of double-blind placebo-controlled studies is that the scientific data indicates antidepressants are not significantly more effective than placebo conditions in the treatment of unipolar depression in children and adolescents (Ambrosini, Bianchi, Rabinovich, & Elia, 1993; Elliot, 1992; Johnston & Fruehling, 1994). This has caused clinical and research dissonance, given the large number of youngsters who are treated with antidepressants by clinicians who report individual clinical efficacy (Fisher & Fisher, 1996). Johnston and Fruehling (1994) provided a comprehensive review of studies of antidepressant medications for the treatment of depression in children and adolescents up to that time. These authors note the overwhelming use of antidepressants in clinical practice and the lack of scientific evidence to support efficacy. With so many clinicians using these agents, Johnston and Fruehling (1994) suggest that clinicians may be seeing a level of clinical usefulness not evident in the drug studies. They also recommend that for most youngsters with depression "antidepressant medication should not be the 'first-line' treatment." The dilemma of scientific evidence and clinical use of antidepressants has been debated (Eisenberg, 1996; Fisher & Fisher, 1996). It is evident that the jury is out as to whether antidepressants can be recommended for use with young people. This supports the need for further study of psychosocial interventions as well as the examination of the utility of combined pharmacotherapy–psychotherapy treatments for depressed young people. The evaluation of pharmacological treatments for depression in children and adolescents is complex, and the issue of side-effects, although not dealt with in this review, is significant and a major consideration in the use of antidepressant medication.

Lastly, as noted earlier, several case reports and an open trial have examined the combined efficacy of pharmacotherapy and psychotherapy. Given that psychotherapy is often seen as an important component of treatment along with antidepressant medications, there needs to be greater focus on the clinical outcome of combined pharmacotherapy and psychotherapy with depressed children and adolescents. The combinatory approach to treatment, that is, the use of both pharmacotherapy and psychotherapy, is consistent with the biopsychological perspective of childhood depression. The biopsychosocial approach suggested by Vasile et al. (1987) makes use of a consultation model for the recommendation of psychological, pharmacological, or combined therapies. This integrative and evaluative approach appears useful for the treatment of depressed children and adolescents.

5.17.7 COMORBIDITY OF DEPRESSION AND OTHER PSYCHOPATHOLOGY IN CHILDREN AND ADOLESCENTS

The study of the coexistence of other psychopathology along with depression in children, adolescents, and adults has emerged as a significant field of inquiry (Anderson & McGee, 1994; Caron & Rutter, 1991; Kendall & Clarkin, 1992). Comorbidity is a term originally used in medicine to describe the existence of a distinct, separate disease or disorder that is present during the course of a primary disorder or disease that is the focus of attention.

In the study of psychiatric disorders in children and adolescents, the finding of comorbidity is becoming increasingly evident. In a study of 476 new admissions by adolescents (mean age 15.6 years) to inpatient and outpatient settings in 29 clinical settings in 21 states, multiple diagnoses (two or more clinical disorders) at intake were found in 67% of the sample, with three or more concurrent disorders found in 26% of the sample (Reynolds, 1997b). Pfeffer and Plutchik (1989) in a study of comorbidity in children, found an average of 2.38 diagnoses in a sample of 106 inpatients and a mean of 2.35 diagnoses in a sample of 101 outpatients. The authors found 39 children with a primary diagnosis of major depression, only three (7.6%) of whom did not have a coexisting *DSM-III* Axis I or Axis II disorder. The most frequent comorbid disorder was dysthymic disorder (56.4%), followed by borderline personality disorder (46.2%), specific developmental disorder (38.5%), and conduct disorder (28.2%).

Alessi and Magen (1988), in a study of 160 child psychiatric inpatients, found that 48 (30%) children had three or more Axis I disorders. A higher rate of co-occurrence of three or more disorders was found among the 25 youngsters with a depressive disorder (52%) compared to the 135 children in the nondepressed psychiatric group (26%). The depressed youngsters included 16 children with major depression (MDD) and nine children with dysthymic disorder. Although the comorbidity of other Axis 1 and several Axis II disorders did not differ in proportion to that found in children with other diagnoses, there were some differences in comorbidity between youngsters with major depression and dysthymic disorder. Nearly 89% of dysthymic children also manifested an anxiety disorder, as compared to 25% of MDD children. The children with major depression also demonstrated a similar frequency of comorbidity with attention deficit disorder and conduct disorder. The high comorbidity between dysthymic disorder and anxiety disorders suggests that there may be some degree of nosological similarity between these forms of psychopathology.

The comorbidity with major depression was examined by Mitchell, McCauley, Burke, and Moss (1988) separately for children ($n = 45$) and adolescents ($n = 50$) who were seen in a clinical setting. Diagnoses were based on RDC using the K-SADS. The most frequent comorbid disorder in both children and adolescents was separation anxiety (42% and 44%, respectively). Conduct disorder was comorbid in 16% of children and 14% of adolescents. However, unlike separation anxiety that did not show significant gender differences in its presentation, conduct disorders were only present in preadolescent boys, whereas in adolescents, a somewhat greater proportion of girls (17%) than boys (10%) had conduct disorder comorbid with major depression.

One of the most noteworthy investigations of psychopathology comorbidity in adolescents is a study conducted by Lewinsohn and colleagues (Lewinsohn et al., 1995; Rohde, Lewinsohn, & Seeley, 1991) in a western Oregon community. This study used diagnostic methods to evaluate a community sample of adolescents for *DSM-III-R* psychiatric disorders, incorporating two assessment periods approximately 14 months apart. Rohde et al. (1991) examined prevalence of current and lifetime depression and comorbidity in a sample of 1710 adolescents. There were 50 adolescents with a current diagnosis of major depression and 347 with lifetime prevalence of depression. There were 21 (42.0%) of the depressed youngsters who demonstrated one or more additional psychiatric disorders, with anxiety disorders (18%), disruptive behaviors (conduct disorder and oppositional defiant disorder) (8%), substance use (14%), and eating disorders (4%) present. For the lifetime estimates of comorbidity, 42.9% of adolescents with a lifetime diagnosis of major depression also had experienced one or more additional psychiatric disorders. In their 1995 (Lewinsohn et al., 1995) report on a sample of 1507 youngsters aged 14 to 18, there were 342 with a lifetime diagnosis of major depression. Of these adolescents, there were 67 with comorbid anxiety disorders, 78 with substance abuse disorder, and 36 with disruptive behavior. It should be noted that the authors did not include cases with other comorbid disorders, such as eating disorders and schizophrenia. Of the group with major depression, 205 youngsters did not demonstrate other psychopathology. Lewinsohn et al. (1995) examined the proportion of youngsters who were receiving treatment by the number of diagnoses. Of youngsters with

a psychiatric diagnosis without comorbidity (i.e., pure cases) 24.8% were receiving treatment. There was a significant increase in the proportion of adolescents receiving treatment as a function of comorbidity (50.4% for two disorders and 65.9% for three or more disorders).

Another major study of comorbidity in children with depressive disorders is the longitudinal investigation of Kovacs and colleagues (Kovacs, 1990; Kovacs et al., 1984a, 1984b; Kovacs, Akiskal, Gatsonis, & Perrone, 1994; Kovacs, Gatsonis, Paulauskas, & Richards, 1989; Kovacs, Paulauskas, Gatsonis, & Richards, 1988) who studied a cohort of 104 children aged 8–13 presenting diagnoses of major depressive disorder ($n = 46$), dysthymic disorder ($n = 23$), combined major depressive disorder and dysthymic disorder (double depression; $n = 16$), and adjustment disorder with depressed mood. In this cohort, significant comorbid conduct and anxiety disorders were also noted.

5.17.7.1 Comorbidity and Biological Communalities

The mechanisms for comorbidity are probably quite complex, and are beginning to be hypothesized. For instance, Lam, Solyom, and Tompkins (1991) found similarities in seasonal symptom variation among bulimic patients to those found among persons with seasonal affective disorder and hypothesized that there may be a common neurobiological abnormality, possibly involving serotonergic dysfunction. Genetic predisposition has also been noted as a potential explanation for some patterns of comorbidity. Walters et al. (1992), using evidence from twin studies suggests that there may be a partial shared common genetic basis for bulimia nervosa and major depression. Mufson, Weissman, and Warner (1992) examined comorbid depression and anxiety in children of parents with major depression, major depression and panic disorder, and other disorders, finding evidence for familial transmission. Similarly, Paul (1988), in examining the comorbidity between anxiety disorders and depression and a range of biological aspects of these disorders, suggests that anxiety and depression may represent different phenotypes of a common neurobiological substrate.

5.17.7.2 The Range of Disorders Comorbid with Depression

Case reports have illustrated a wide-range of disorders that may co-occur with depression in children and adolescents, including: trichotillo-mania (Naylor & Grossman, 1991; Weller, Weller, & Carr, 1989); autism (Komoto, Usui, & Hirata, 1984); borderline personality disorder (Stone, 1981); and conversion symptom (Weller & Weller, 1983), the latter obscuring the depressive disorder.

Most research on the comorbidity of depression and other psychiatric disorders in children and adolescents has been based on clinical samples with a few noteworthy community-based studies, such as that of Lewinsohn and colleagues (1995). In the study of depression and its comorbidity, a particularly ubiquitous relationship with anxiety disorders has been evident and generated a tremendous amount of research and debate (Brady & Kendall, 1992; Kendall, Kortlander, Chansky, & Brady, 1992; King, Gullone, & Ollendick, 1990; Weissman, 1990). In addition to anxiety disorders, researchers have reported comorbidity of depression in youngsters with attention deficit disorder (Alessi & Magen, 1988; Biederman, Munir et al., 1987; Jensen et al., 1988), conduct disorders (Alessi & Magen, 1988; Kovacs, Paulauskas, et al., 1988; Puig-Antich, 1982), substance abuse (De Milio, 1989; Levy & Deykin, 1989), and eating disorders (Alessi, Krahn, Brehm, & Wittekindt, 1989).

5.17.7.3 Comorbidity with Other Internalizing Disorders and Problems

Depressive disorders, by their symptom definitions, share a number of features with other disorders such as eating disorders and anxiety disorders. By its definition, comorbidity refers to a different case as may occur when a relationship between two disorders is found as a function of shared symptoms alone. However, it may be that certain disorders also share various precursors or etiological factors that result in an increased risk for their co-occurrence. The disorders presented below were selected in large part as a function of the research literature. It is evident that other disorders may also show some level of comorbidity, but by their nature or incidence/prevalence have not been a major focus of study.

5.17.7.3.1 Anxiety disorders

Anxiety disorders represent a major domain of psychopathology and a wide range of clinical disorders. One of the earliest reports of childhood depression and other psychopathology focused on the relationship between school phobia and childhood depression. Agras (1959) described seven children aged 6–12 years who demonstrated school phobia, six of whom

showed significant depressive symptoms. It is interesting to note that the comorbidity of depression and symptoms of anxiety was viewed by Agras (1959, p. 534) as similar "phenomen-ologically to the depressive disorders of adults."

School refusal or school phobia has continued to be linked or found comorbid with depression (Bernstein & Garfinkel, 1986; Naylor, Staskowski, Kenney, & King, 1994). In a study of 35 children with school phobia, Waldron, Shrier, Stone, and Tobin (1975) found that a significantly greater number of these youngsters manifested depression (56%) than a comparison group of children diagnosed as having other neuroses (26%). With a matched sample of 28 inpatient and 28 out-patient youngsters who were evaluated as school refusers, Borchardt, Giesler, Bernstein, and Crosby (1994) found a diagnosis of major depression in 85.7% of the inpatients and 46.4% of the outpatients, the only comorbid diagnosis that was significantly different in proportions between the two groups.

In a study of the comorbidity of depressive disorders with anxiety disorders, Kovacs, Gatsonis et al. (1989) reported that 41% of their sample of 104 youngsters with major depression and/or dysthymic disorder had an anxiety disorder at the initial (index) study episode of depression, with separation anxiety and overanxious disorder the most frequent comorbid diagnoses. In 19 of 30 participants with major depression the anxiety disorder predated the onset of depression. Strauss, Last, Hersen, and Kazdin (1988) found that 28% of 106 children and adolescents with a *DSM-III* diagnosis of an anxiety disorder had a concomitant diagnosis of major depression.

5.17.7.3.2 Eating disorders

A great deal of discussion and research has focused on the comorbidity and relationship between depression and eating disorders (Swift, Andrews, & Barklage, 1986). Rastam (1992) in a study comparing 51 adolescents with anorexia nervosa to a matched control group of school-based adolescents found that 69% of the former also met criteria for major depression or dysthymic disorder, compared to 10% of the school-based comparison group. They did not find clear evidence to suggest that depression was an antecedent of anorexia. Smith and Steiner (1992) found comorbid major depression in 53% of a sample of adolescent girls seen in an eating disorders clinic. In a six year follow-up of 23 anorexic youngsters, Smith, Feldman, Nasserbakht, and Steiner (1993) found a lifetime prevalence of major depression in 86.9% of the sample.

A significant study of comorbidity was presented by Herzog, Keller, Sacks, Yeh, and Lavori (1992) with 229 females seen in a treatment setting with anorexia nervosa ($n = 41$), bulimia nervosa ($n = 98$) and mixed anorexia nervosa and bulimia nervosa ($n = 90$) using RDC criteria for diagnosis. They found that major depression was the most common comorbid disorder. For the total sample, at least one affective disorder was found in 63% of the cases, with 41% (94 cases) manifesting major depression. Patients with both anorexia and bulimia demonstrated the highest rate of comorbidity with major depression (53%) in comparison to the other eating disorder groups, and 76% of this mixed group had at least one affective disorder. It is also of interest that the mixed group was younger in age than the other groups at onset of the eating disorder ($M = 17.5$, versus 19.1 for anorexia and 18.8 for bulimia).

In a school-based sample of 3287 adolescents in France, Ledoux, Choquet, and Manfredi (1993) found a relatively high rate of depressive symptom endorsement among youngsters who engaged in binge eating (20.2%) compared to non-binge eaters (6.3%) $\chi^2 = 45.06, p < 0.001$. There was also a gender difference, with a higher proportion of binge-eating girls reporting high levels of depressive symptoms (26.6%) compared to binge-eating boys (10.6%).

In addition to clinic and school-based studies, case studies have also reported comorbidity between eating disorders and depression. In a somewhat unique case report, Alessi et al. (1989) reported on a case of a nine-year-old girl with anorexia nervosa and major depression. The child was hospitalized for 10 weeks and received psychotherapy. Significant decreases in scores on the CDRS-R (from 76 at intake to 20 at week nine of treatment) and increases in weight from 52.5 pounds to 70 pounds at discharge were reported with the youngster maintaining this weight for two weeks. Although this case is considered rare, it does show that comorbidity of these disorders may have an early onset in some youngsters.

5.17.7.4 Comorbidity with Externalizing Disorders and Problem Behaviors

The comorbidity of depression with externalizing disorders is a significant area of research, with questions as to why such diverse forms of psychological disorders co-occur and what underlying mechanism may be responsible for this outcome. Such questions remain to be answered. For the present, the comorbidity of depression and conduct disorders, substance abuse, and attention-deficit hyperactivity disorder (ADHD) are examined.

5.17.7.4.1 Conduct disorder

There is a substantial literature base on the coexistence of depression and conduct disorder, the latter sometimes operationalized as juvenile delinquency. In the early 1970s, a number of investigators were identifying depression among adolescents seen in clinical settings for delinquent youth (e.g., Weinberg & van Den Dungen, 1971). Some of the studies discussed below were based on youngsters adjudicated as delinquent, the majority of whom we may assume meet criteria for conduct disorder, although this may not apply to all youngsters.

In a study using RDC diagnosis of depression in a sample of juvenile delinquents, Chiles, Miller, and Cox (1980) found 28 (23%) of a sample of 120 adolescents met criteria for major depression. Somewhat lower rates were reported by Alessi et al. (1984) who found 15.5% of a sample of 71 incarcerated juvenile offenders had a RDC diagnosis of major depressive episode and another 15.5% had a diagnosis of minor depressive disorder. An additional 8.5% were diagnosed having a major depressive disorder in remission. Kovacs, Paulauskas, Gatsonis, and Richards (1988) found that in their sample of 104 children, 17 (16%) had a comorbid conduct disorder at the time of the study initial (index) depressive episode, with another seven youngsters who received a diagnosis of conduct disorder during the course of the study and after remission of the index episode of depression. There were no differences in proportion of comorbidity between types of depressive disorders.

Kutcher, Marton, and Korenblum (1989) reported on the psychiatric morbidity of adolescents admitted to an inpatient psychiatric unit. After excluding four youngsters with conduct disorder without comorbid Axis I disorders, the authors found 26 of the remaining 96 adolescents had a conduct disorder comorbid with other Axis I disorders. Comorbid disorders to the conduct disorder included depression (five cases), bipolar disorder (eight cases), psychotic disorders (seven cases) and other disorders (six cases).

Within the same domain of disruptive behaviors, researchers have also found oppositional defiant disorder (ODD) comorbid with depression. Wenning, Nathan, and King (1993) found that 14 of 28 children (aged 6–13) seen in a clinical setting who had a diagnosis of ODD also met criteria for dysthymia. None of the children had episodes of major depression. The authors, in a retrospective examination of intake diagnoses, indicated that only one of the 14 children with ODD and dysthymia were so diagnosed at intake. The remaining 13 children were found to also have had dysthymia at intake, that had been overlooked and only identified by interviews with therapists who were given the opportunity to review *DSM-III-R* mood disorder criteria.

In a study of 56 child and adolescent psychiatric inpatients with major depressive disorder, Meller and Borchardt (1996) found 41% with comorbid conduct disorder. An examination of symptoms that differentiated between depression only and comorbid groups indicated that anxious mood was present to a greater extent in youngsters with depression only.

5.17.7.4.2 Attention deficit hyperactivity disorder

The coexistence of hyperactivity and depression in children has been noted since the 1970s, with a wide range in rates of comorbidity (Biederman, Newcorn, & Sprich, 1991). Brumback and Weinberg (1977) studied 223 children aged 6–12 years who were referred to an educational diagnostic center. Using Weinberg criteria for the diagnosis of depression, 136 children were depressed with 86 (63%) of these children also demonstrating hyperactivity. The authors noted that for some of the youngsters with depression and hyperactivity, their hyperactivity was somewhat episodic with depression, worsening during depressive episodes and decreasing as depression remitted.

Weinberg and Emslie (1991) described the diagnostic status of 100 children and adolescents referred to a pediatric neurology clinical setting, finding a diagnosis of ADHD in 63 youngsters. Of these 63 youngsters, 46 (73%) also had a diagnosis of depression, with the majority of these youngsters ($n = 40$) also manifesting developmental-specific learning disorders. The authors also noted that in a group of 65 children recently referred to their clinical setting who had a *DSM-III-R* diagnosis of major depression, 21 (32%) also had a diagnosis of ADHD, with the ADHD preceding the depressive disorders in all cases. Similarly, Biederman et al. (1994) in a study of 140 boys found major depression comorbid in 39 (27.9%) youngsters.

ADHD has also been noted in adolescents with bipolar disorder, with West, McElroy, Strakowski, Keck, and McConville (1995) finding eight (57%) of 14 bipolar patients with *DSM-III-R* mania or hypermania demonstrating a comorbid ADHD. In all cases, the ADHD predated the onset of bipolar disorder, by an average of six years. The prior presentation of ADHD and the time between onset of disorders is consistent with ADHD typically identified in childhood, and bipolar disorder often emerging during adolescence.

5.17.7.4.3 Substance abuse

When studying comorbidity in adolescents, a relatively common finding is the coexistence of substance abuse and psychiatric illness. Depressive disorders are among the most studied disorders comorbid with substance abuse (e.g., Bukstein, Brent, & Kaminer, 1989), although conduct disorders and substance abuse tend to show higher rates of comorbidity (Kaminer, Tarter, Bukstein, & Kabene, 1992). The study of substance abuse and depression in young people is a very important domain of research as well as clinical attention. Substance abuse is a major problem in adolescents. In the study of psychopathology accompanying substance abuse, depression and conduct disorders appear to be the most concomitant disorders (Kaminer, 1991).

As noted, there have been numerous reports of depressive disorders concurrent with substance abuse. Kashani, Keller, Solomon, Reid, and Mazzola (1985) reported on 16 cases of double depression as well as another 12 youngsters with either major depressive disorder or dysthymic disorder in a sample of 100 adolescents with substance abuse disorders. The comorbidity of affective disorders and other psychiatric disorders in an inpatient psychiatric sample of 156 adolescents aged 13–18 with substance abuse was examined by Bukstein, Glancy, and Kaminer (1992) who found an affective disorder in 51.3% of the sample, second to conduct disorder which was found in 70.5% of the youngsters. Of the mood disorders identified, 30.7% demonstrated major depression, 5.1% dysthymia, 7.7% bipolar, and there were 9.0% of the sample who were comorbid with adjustment disorder with depressed mood. A significant number (22 of the 48) of the youngsters with major depression and substance abuse also had an additional diagnosis of conduct disorder. Overall, nearly 27% of the sample of substance abusers also had concurrent diagnoses of conduct disorder and an affective disorder. In determining the timing of the onset of disorders, in the major depression–substance abuse only group, the substance abuse preceded the onset of major depression by one year.

In a study of 52 inpatient adolescent substance abusers, Hovens, Cantwell, and Kiriakos (1994) found major depression and dysthymia present in 25% and 33% of youngsters, respectively. Of particular interest was the examination of the temporal sequence of substance abuse and psychiatric disorders. The authors found that substance abuse preceded the cases with major depression by about $3^1/_2$ years. A different picture was evident for youngsters with dysthymia, with dysthymia emerging prior to the onset of substance abuse in approximately 53% of the cases.

Stowell and Estroff (1992) examine the discharge diagnosis of 226 consecutive adolescent admissions (aged 12–18 years) to two inpatient treatment settings for substance abuse problems. Mood disorders were found in 61% of substance abusers, with 18% comorbid with major depression, 34% dysthymia, 9% bipolar, and 12% double depression with both major depression and dysthymia. Based on self-report data, the authors suggested that depression preceded the regular use of substances in 68% of the sample. However, this is not to suggest a causal pathway. Stowell and Estroff also noted that significant psychosocial stressors—such as sexual and physical abuse, parental substance abuse, divorce and separation, death of family members or close friends, and other stressors—may be contributory factors. In such cases, substance abuse became greater after such psychosocial stressors and exacerbated depressive symptoms.

Similar rates of depression among substance abusers were reported by Deykin, Buka, and Zeena (1992) with a sample of 223 chemically dependent adolescents in a residential treatment setting. They found 24.7% of the sample met *DSM-III-R* criteria for major depression, with a significantly higher proportion of females (48.2%) compared to males (16.9%) with major depression. With regard to temporal order of onset, 35.2% of those with depression developed chemical dependence following the depression, with chemical dependence preceding depression in 43.1% of the sample and occurring at the same time in 21.6% of the sample of comorbid youngsters. Other investigators studying youngsters with substance abuse have reported rates of major depression of 35% (DeMilio, 1989) with presence of any affective disorder noted as high as 78% (McKay, Murphy, Maisto, & Rivinus, 1992).

5.17.7.5 Diagnostic Overshadowing

A significant issue in the study of comorbidity is that of diagnostic overshadowing. In the Wenning et al (1993) investigation, the majority (93%) of the children with comorbid ODD and depression were not identified as being depressed as well as oppositional at intake.

Likewise, other externalizing disorders such as ADHD may mask a depressive disorder or, as Weinberg and Emslie (1991) suggest, children referred for ADHD may not be systematically evaluated for the presence of additional psychopathology. A similar recommendation was made by McClellan, Rubert, Reichter, and Sylvester (1990) who found that a significant number of children who had an anxiety or depressive disorder also demonstrated attention deficit disorder (ADD). These authors suggested that clinicians evaluating children referred for ADD should consider the potential for a comorbid or primary affective disorder.

The above are useful examples of diagnostic overshadowing. Such cases may most frequently occur when an internalizing disorder such as depression is masked (in an overt sense) by the extremes and behavioral excesses found in most externalizing disorders.

5.17.7.6 Comorbidity Summary

The extensive findings of comorbidity among children and adolescents with psychiatric disorders, including depressive disorders, has important implications for our understanding of depressive disorders in young people, as well as approaches to identification, treatment, and prevention.

It is evident that when we study comorbidity within select clinical samples, such as in groups of youngsters referred to an eating disorders clinic or substance abusers in a chemical dependency treatment setting, rates of comorbidity will differ from those found in large-sample studies of depressed youngsters. Furthermore, data regarding comorbidity based on clinic samples may be biased and represent somewhat inflated values as a function of increased treatment seeking due to greater distress caused by two or more disorders, increased likelihood of referral, and other selection biases (du Fort, Newman, & Bland, 1993). Likewise, certain types of comorbidity may be seen to a greater extent in treatment and other clinical settings. For instance, depression comorbid with externalizing disorders, such as conduct disorder, ADHD, or substance abuse, is at increased risk for referral or identification by others. To more accurately understand the comorbidity between two disorders, data from large, representative samples drawn from the general population are needed.

A question in the study of comorbidity is that of the temporal relationship between disorders. That is, do consistent findings suggest that one disorder commonly predates another, and if so, does this indicate a predisposition of one disorder to another? As described in this chapter, a few studies have examined this by investigating the onset of disorders. For the most part, findings suggest that in the cases of certain comorbid disorders that may develop during certain developmental periods, there is little evidence to suggest that the initial disorder is a precursor to the emergence of the second disorder. For instance in the case of bipolar disorder with comorbid ADHD, the ADHD which typically is diagnosed in childhood predates the onset of bipolar disorder which tends to emerge during adolescence and young adulthood. For other disorders, the onset in reference to the index episode of depression may occur prior, during, or subsequent to the depressive episode.

From the above studies, it is quite clear that many youngsters with depression also manifest other forms of psychopathology, both of internalizing and externalizing phenomenology. Toward understanding the nature of comorbidity, investigators have begun to examine the course and potential causal pathways of depression and comorbid psychopathology (Capaldi, 1991; Caron & Rutter, 1991; Loeber, Russo, Stouthamer-Loeber, & Lahey, 1994).

The examination of the coexistence of other psychopathology and depression in children and adolescents is important for a number of reasons. As Alessi and Magen (1988) noted, the existence of multiple disorders may in some individuals lead to the development of a depressive disorder. Likewise, the co-occurrence may create an increased stress response with psychological and biological interactions. Clearly the biopsychosocial approach is critical when examining comorbidity.

5.17.8 SUMMARY AND CONCLUSIONS

In this chapter a biopsychosocial perspective was presented as a framework for understanding some of the complexities inherent in our knowledge of depression in children and adolescents. The biopsychosocial model provides a scaffold for examining the features, correlates, and etiologies of depression in young people. In this regard, it can be seen and understood that depression in children and adolescents is a complex interaction of social and environmental factors, predispositions, cognitive and behavioral skills and competencies, biological vulnerability factors, and other individual difference variables.

The importance for understanding the nature, identification, and treatment of depression in children and adolescents is best understood by the basic fact that depressed youngsters feel intense psychological distress and misery. Depressed children and adolescents face daily impairments in psychological functioning and often perceive that there is no hope for improvement. Research suggests that for many depressed youngsters, the long-term outcome is poor, with the likely development of more severe pathology in adulthood (Harrington, 1996; Kovacs, 1996a, 1996b).

The past two decades have provided professionals with a remarkable amount of information on depression as an internalizing disorder in children and adolescents. This has resulted in the development of measures that are now used by clinicians for the identification of depressed youngsters, as well as the publication of empirically tested treatment manuals for the provision of psychotherapy. Advances in the understanding of psychobiological correlates of depression in children and adolescents, and advances in pharmacological interventions also provide insight into the basic nature of this disorder in young people. Of domains in which basic and applied research needs to be conducted, the understanding of the developmental nature of depression in children remains an area of critical importance. Research and theoretical descriptions on the developmental nature of depression in children have begun to appear. However, there are numerous questions specific to the expression and syndromal description of depression in children and adolescents that still need to be answered.

Likewise, we are just beginning to understand the course of depression, although much of this is based on a few well-conceived and executed studies. However, given the heterogeneity of depressive disorders and the myriad etiological and interactive variables that come into play, we will require extensive investigation across numerous samples to determine how depressive disorders, both syndromal and subsyndromal, affect children and adolescents.

5.17.9 REFERENCES

Abramson, L. Y., Seligman, M. E. P., & Teasdale, J. D. (1978). Learned helplessness in humans: Critique and reformulation. *Journal of Abnormal Psychology, 87,* 49–74.

Adams, D. M., Overholser, J. C., & Spirito, A. (1994). Stressful life events associated with adolescent suicide attempts. *Canadian Journal of Psychiatry, 39,* 43–48.

Adams, J., & Adams, M. (1993). Effects of a negative life event and negative perceived problem-solving alternatives on depression in adolescents: A prospective study. *Journal of Child Psychology and Psychiatry, 34,* 743–747.

Agras, S. (1959). The relationship of school phobia to childhood depression. *American Journal of Psychiatry, 116,* 533–536.

Akiskal, H. S. (1979). A biobehavioral approach to

depression. In R. A. Depue (Ed.), *The psychobiology of the depressive disorders* (pp. 409–437). New York: Academic Press.

Alessi, N. E., Krahn, D., Brehm, D., & Wittekindt, J. (1989). Prepubertal anorexia nervosa and major depressive disorder. *Journal of the American Academy of Child and Adolescent Psychiatry, 28,* 380–384.

Alessi, N. E., & Magen, J. (1988). Comorbidity of other psychiatric disturbances in depressed psychiatrically hospitalized children. *American Journal of Psychiatry, 145,* 1582–1584.

Alessi, N. E., McManus, M., Grapentine, W. L., & Brickman, A. (1984). The characterization of depressive disorders in serious juvenile offenders. *Journal of Affective Disorders, 6,* 9–17.

Alessi, N., Naylor, M. W., Ghaziuddin, M., & Zubieta, J. K. (1994). Update on lithium carbonate therapy in children and adolescents. *Journal of the American Academy of Child and Adolescent Psychiatry, 33,* 291–304.

Ambrosini, P. J., Bianchi, M. D., Rabinovich, H., & Elia, J. (1993). Antidepressant treatments in children and adolescents: 1. Affective disorders. *Journal of the American Academy of Child and Adolescent Psychiatry, 32,* 1–5.

American Psychiatric Association (1980). *Diagnostic and statistical manual of mental disorders* (3rd ed.). Washington, DC: Author.

American Psychiatric Association (1987). *Diagnostic and statistical manual of mental disorders* (3rd ed. Rev.). Washington, DC: Author.

American Psychiatric Association (1994). *Diagnostic and statistical manual of mental disorders* (4th ed.). Washington, DC: Author.

Anderson, J. C., & McGee, R. (1994). Comorbidity of depression in children and adolescents. In W. M. Reynolds and H. F. Johnston (Eds.), *Handbook of depression in children and adolescents* (pp. 581–601). New York: Plenum.

Apter, A., Ratzoni, G., King, R. A., Weizman, A., Iancu, I., Binder, M., & Riddle, M. A. (1994). Fluvoxamine open-label treatment of adolescent inpatients with obsessive-compulsive disorder or depression. *Journal of the American Academy of Child and Adolescent Psychiatry, 33,* 342–348.

Archer, R. P., Maruish, M., Imhof, E., & Piotrowski, C. (1991). Psychological test usage with adolescent clients: 1990 survey findings. *Professional Psychology: Research and Practice, 22,* 247–252.

Bandura, A. (1978). The self-system in reciprocal determinism. *American Psychologist, 33,* 344–358.

Barrera, M., & Garrison-Jones, C. V. (1988). Properties of the Beck Depression Inventory as a screening instrument for adolescent depression. *Journal of Abnormal Child Psychology, 16,* 263–273.

Bartell, N. P. & Reynolds, W. M. (1986) Depression and self-esteem in academically gifted and nongifted children: A comparison study. *Journal of School Psychology, 24,* 55–61.

Bath, H. I., & Middleton, M. R. (1985). The Children's Depression Scale: Psychometric properties and factor structure. *Australian Journal of Psychology, 37,* 81–88.

Beck, A. T. (1967) *Depression: Causes and treatment.* Philadelphia: University of Pennsylvania Press.

Beck, A. T. (1976). *Cognitive therapy and the emotional disorders.* New York: International Universities Press.

Beck, A. T., Ward, C., Mendelson, M., Mock, J., & Erbaugh, J. (1961) An inventory for measuring depression. *Archives of General Psychiatry, 4,* 561–571.

Belsher, G., Wilkes, T. C. R., & Rush, A. J. (1995). An open, multisite pilot study of cognitive therapy for depressed adolescents. *Journal of Psychotherapy Practice and Research, 4,* 52–66.

Bemporad, J. R. (1994). Dynamic and interpersonal theories of depression. In W. M. Reynolds & H. F. Johnston (Eds.), *Handbook of depression in children and adolescents* (pp. 81–95). New York: Plenum.

Beres, D., & Alpert, A. (1940). Analysis of a prolonged hypomanic episode in a five-year-old child. *American Journal of Orthopsychiatry, 10,* 794–800.

Bernstein, G. A., & Garfinkel, B. D. (1986). School phobia: The overlap of affective and anxiety disorders. *Journal of the American Academy of Child and Adolescent Psychiatry, 25,* 235–241.

Bertagnoli, M. W., & Borchardt, C. M. (1990). A review of ECT for children and adolescents. *Journal of the American Academy of Child and Adolescent Psychiatry, 29,* 302–307.

Biederman, J., Munir, K., Knee, D., Armentano, M., Autor, S., Waternaux, C., & Tsuang, M. (1987). High rate of affective disorders in probands with attention deficit disorder and in their relatives: A controlled family study. *American Journal of Psychiatry, 144,* 330–333.

Biederman, J., Lapey, K. A., Milberger, S., Faraone, S. V., Reed, E. D., & Seidman, L. J. (1994). Motor preference, major depression and psychosocial dysfunction among children with attention deficit hyperactivity disorder. *Journal of Psychiatric Research, 28,* 171–184.

Biederman, J., Newcorn, J., & Sprich, S. (1991). Comorbidity of attention deficit hyperactivity disorder with conduct, depressive, anxiety, and other disorders. *American Journal of Psychiatry, 148,* 564–577.

Birmaher, B., Rabin, B. S., Garcia, M. R., Jain, U., Whiteside, T. L., Williamson, D. E., Al-Shabbout, M., Nelson, B. C., Dahl, R. E., & Ryan, N. D. (1994). Cellular immunity in depressed, conduct disorder, and normal adolescents: Role of adverse life events. *Journal of the American Academy of Child and Adolescent Psychiatry, 33,* 671–678.

Bland, R. C. (1994). Introduction. *Acta Psychiatrica Scandinavica, (Suppl. 376),* 5–6.

Borchardt, C. M., Giesler, J., Bernstein, G. A., & Crosby, R. D. (1994). A comparison of inpatient and outpatient school refusers. *Child Psychiatry and Human Development, 24,* 255–264.

Boulos, C., Kutcher, S., Gardner, D., & Young, E. (1992). An open naturalistic trial of fluoxetine in adolescents and young adults with treatment-resistant major depression. *Journal of Child and Adolescent Psychopharmacology, 2,* 103–111,

Brady, E. U., & Kendall, P. C. (1992). Comorbidity of anxiety and depression in children and adolescents. *Psychological Bulletin, 111,* 244–255.

Brand, E. F., King, C. A., Olson, E., Ghaziuddin, N., & Naylor, M. (1996). Depressed adolescents with a history of sexual abuse: Diagnostic comorbidity and suicidality. *Journal of the American Academy of Child and Adolescent Psychiatry, 35,* 34–41.

Brosschot, J. F., Benschop, R. J., Godaert, G. L. R., Olff, M., De Smet, M., Heijnen, C. J., & Ballieux, R. E. (1994). Influence of life stress on immunological reactivity to mild psychological stress. *Psychosomatic Medicine, 56,* 216–224.

Brumback, R. A., & Weinberg, W. A., (1977). Relationship of hyperactivity and depression in children. *Perceptual and Motor Skills, 45,* 247–251.

Bukstein, O. G., Brent, D. A., & Kaminer, Y. (1989). Comorbidity of substance abuse and other psychiatric disorders in adolescents. *American Journal of Psychiatry, 146,* 1131–1141.

Bukstein, O. G., Glancy, L. J., & Kaminer, Y. (1992). Patterns of affective comorbidity in a clinical population of dually diagnosed adolescent substance abusers. *Journal of the American Academy of Child and Adolescent Psychiatry, 31,* 1041–1045.

Butler, L., Miezitis, S., Friedman, R., & Cole, E. (1980).

The effect of two school-based intervention programs on depressive symptoms in preadolescents. *American Educational Research Journal, 17,* 111–119.

Campbell, J. D. (1952). Manic depressive psychosis in children: Report of 18 cases. *Journal of Nervous and Mental Disease, 116,* 424–439.

Capaldi, D. M. (1991). Co-occurrence of conduct problems and depressive symptoms in early adolescent boys: I. Familial factors and general adjustment at grade 6. *Development and Psychopathology, 3,* 277–300.

Carey, T. C., Kelley, M. L., & Carey, M. P. (1991, August). *The relation of cognitions, emotions and behavior to depressive symptomatology.* Paper presented at the Annual Meeting, American Psychological Association, San Francisco.

Carlson, G. A. (1994). Adolescent bipolar disorder: Phenomenology and treatment implications. In W. M. Reynolds & H. F. Johnston (Eds.), *Handbook of depression in children and adolescents* (pp. 41–60). New York: Plenum.

Caron, C., & Rutter, M. (1991). Comorbidity in child psychopathology: Concepts, issues, and research strategies. *Journal of Child Psychology and Psychiatry, 32,* 1063–1080.

Chiles, J. A., Miller, M. L., & Cox, G. B. (1980). Depression in an adolescent delinquent population. *Archives of General Psychiatry, 37,* 1179–1184.

Christ, A. E., Adler, A. G., Isacoff, M., & Gershansky, I. S. (1981). Depression: Symptoms versus diagnosis in 10,412 hospitalized children and adolescents (1957–1977). *American Journal of Psychotherapy, 35,* 400–412.

Clarizio, H. F. (1994). Assessment of depression in children and adolescents by parents, teachers, and peers. In W. M. Reynolds & H. F. Johnston (Eds.), *Handbook of depression in children and adolescents* (pp. 235–248). New York: Plenum.

Clarke, G., & Lewinsohn, P. M. (1989). The coping with depression course: A group psychoeducational intervention for unipolar depression. *Behaviour Change, 6,* 54–69.

Cole, D. A. (1991). Preliminary support for a competency-based model of depression in children. *Journal of Abnormal Psychology, 100,* 181–190.

Cole, D. A., & Carpentieri, S. (1990). Social status and the comorbidity of child depression and conduct disorders. *Journal of Consulting and Clinical Psychology, 58,* 748–757.

Compas, B. E., Ey, S., & Grant, K. E. (1993). Taxonomy, assessment, and diagnosis of depression during adolescence. *Psychological Bulletin, 114,* 323–344.

Conners, C. K. (1992). Methodology of antidepressant drug trials for treating depression in adolescents. *Journal of Child and Adolescent Psychopharmacology, 2,* 11–22.

Craighead, W. E., Curry, J. F., & Ilardi, S. S. (1995). Relationship of Children's Depression Inventory factors to major depression among adolescents. *Psychological Assessment. 7,* 171–176.

Crowley, S. L., & Emerson, E. N. (1996). Discriminant validity of self-reported anxiety and depression in children: Negative affectivity or independent constructs? *Journal of Clinical Child Psychology, 25,* 139–146.

Curry, J. F., & Craighead, W. E. (1990). Attributional style in clinically depressed and conduct disordered adolescents. *Journal of Consulting and Clinical Psychology, 58,* 109–115.

Dalley, M. B., Bolocofsky, D. N., Alcorn, M. B., & Baker, C. (1992). Depressive symptomatology, attributional style, dysfunctional attitude, and social competency in adolescents with and without learning disabilities. *School Psychology Review, 21,* 444–458.

Dech, B., & Budow, L. (1991). The use of fluoxetine in an adolescent with Prader–Willi Syndrome. *Journal of the American Academy of Child and Adolescent Psychiatry, 30,* 298–302.

DeMilio, L. (1989). Psychiatric syndromes in adolescent substance abusers. *American Journal of Psychiatry, 146,* 1212–1214.

Dewsbury, D. A. (1991). "Psychobiology". *American Psychologist, 46,* 198–205.

Deykin, E. Y., Buka, S. L., Zeena, T. H. (1992). Depressive illness among chemically dependent adolescents. *American Journal of Psychiatry, 149,* 1341–1347.

du Fort, G. G., Newman, S. C., & Bland, R. C. (1993). Psychiatric comorbidity and treatment seeking: Sources of selection bias in the study of clinical populations. *Journal of Nervous and Mental Disease, 181,* 467–474.

Eisenberg, L. (1996). Commentary: What should doctors do in the face of negative evidence? *Journal of Nervous and Mental Disease, 184,* 103–105.

Elliott, G. R. (1992). Dilemmas for clinicians and researchers using antidepressants to treat adolescents with depression. *Journal of Child and Adolescent Psychopharmacology, 2,* 7–9.

Ellis, A. (1962). *Reason and emotion in psychotherapy.* New York: Lyle Stuart.

Emslie, G. J., Weinberg, W. A., Kennard, B. D., Kowatch, R. A. (1994). Neurobiological aspects of depression in children and adolescents. In W. M. Reynolds & H. F. Johnston (Eds.), *Handbook of depression in children and adolescents* (pp. 143–165). New York: Plenum.

Endicott, J., & Spitzer, R. L. (1978) A diagnostic interview: The schedule for affective disorders and schizophrenia. *Archives of General Psychiatry, 35,* 837–844.

Engel, G. L. (1978). The biopsychosocial model and the education of health professionals. *Annals of the New York Academy of Science, 310,* 169–181.

Engel, G. L. (1980). The clinical application of the biopsychosocial model. *American Journal of Psychiatry, 137,* 535–544.

Finch, A. J., Saylor, C. F., & Edwards, G. L. (1985). Children's Depression Inventory: Sex and grade norms for normal children. *Journal of Consulting and Clinical Psychology, 53,* 424–425.

Finch, A. J., Saylor, C. F., Edwards, G. L., & McIntosh, J. A. (1987). Children's Depression Inventory: Reliability over repeated administrations. *Journal of Clinical Child Psychology, 16,* 339–341.

Fine, S., Forth, A., Gilbert, M., & Haley, G. (1991). Group therapy for adolescent depressive disorder: A comparison of social skills and therapeutic support. *Journal of the American Academy of Child Psychiatry, 30,* 79–85.

Fisher, R. L., & Fisher, S. (1996). Antidepressants for children: Is scientific support necessary? *Journal of Nervous and Mental Disease, 184,* 99–102.

Fleming, J. E., & Offord, D. R. (1990). Epidemiology of childhood depressive disorders: A critical review. *Journal of the American Academy of Child and Adolescent Psychiatry, 29,* 571–580.

Frommer, E. A. (1967). Treatment of childhood depression with antidepressant drugs. *British Medical Journal, 1,* 729–732.

Glaser, K. (1967) Masked depression in children and adolescents. *American Journal of Psychotherapy, 21,* 565–574.

Gotlib, I. H., Lewinsohn, P. M., & Seeley, J. R. (1995). Symptoms versus a diagnosis of depression: Differences in psychosocial functioning. *Journal of Consulting and Clinical Psychology, 63,* 90–100.

Hains, A. A. (1992). Comparison of cognitive-behavioral stress management techniques with adolescent boys. *Journal of Counseling and Development, 70,* 600–605.

Hamilton, M. (1960). A rating scale for depression. *Journal of Neurology, Neurosurgery, and Psychiatry, 23,* 56–62.

Hamilton, M. (1967). Development of a rating scale for primary depressive illness. *British Journal of Social and Clinical Psychology, 6,* 278–296.

Harrington, R. C. (1996). Adult outcomes of childhood

and adolescent depression: Influences on the risk for adult depression. *Psychiatric Annals, 26,* 320–325.

Harrington, R., Fudge, H., Rutter, M., Pickles, A., & Hill, J. (1990). Adult outcomes of childhood and adolescent depression: I. Psychiatric status. *Archives of General Psychiatry, 47,* 465–473.

Heiligenstein, E., & Jacobsen, P. B. (1988). Differentiating depression in medically ill children and adolescents. *Journal of the American Academy of Child and Adolescent Psychiatry, 27,* 716–719.

Herdman, R. C., Gough, M., Liskowski, D. R., & Hall, L. L. (1995). *New developments in the biology of mental disorders.* Piscataway, NJ: Research & Education Association.

Herzog, D. B., Keller, M. D., Sacks, N. R., Yeh, C. J., & Lavori, P. W. (1992). Psychiatric comorbidity in treatment-seeking anorexics and bulimics. *Journal of the American Academy of Child and Adolescent Psychiatry, 31,* 810–818.

Hodges, K. (1994). Evaluation of depression in children and adolescents using diagnostic clinical interviews. In W. M. Reynolds & H. F. Johnston (Eds.), *Handbook of depression in children and adolescents* (pp. 183–208). New York: Plenum.

Hodges, K., Kline, J., Stern, L., Cytryn, L., & McKnew, D. (1982). The development of a child assessment interview for research and clinical use. *Journal of Abnormal Child Psychology, 10,* 173–189.

Hollon, T. H. (1970). Poor school performance as a symptom of masked depression in children and adolescents. *American Journal of Psychotherapy, 24,* 258–263.

Horwath, E., Johnson, J., Klerman, G. L., & Weissman, M. M. (1994). What are the public health implications of subclinical depressive symptoms? *Psychiatric Quarterly, 65,* 323–337.

Hovens, J. G., Cantwell, D. P., & Kiriakos, R. (1994). Psychiatric comorbidity in hospitalized adolescent substance abusers. *Journal of the American Academy of Child and Adolescent Psychiatry, 33,* 476–483.

Huebner, E. Scott, & Alderman, G. L. (1993). Convergent and discriminant validation of a children's life satisfaction scale: Its relationship to self- and teacher-reported psychological problems and school functioning. *Social Indicators Research, 30,* 71–82.

Ialongo, N., Edelsohn, G., Werthamer-Larsson, L., Crockett, L., & Kellam, S. (1993). Are self-reported depressive symptoms in first-grade children developmentally transient phenomena? A further look. *Development and Psychopathology, 5,* 433–457.

Jackson, S. W. (1986). *Melancholia and depression: From Hippocratic times to modern times.* New Haven, CT: Yale University Press.

Jensen, J. B., Burke, N., & Garfinkel, B. D. (1988). Depression and symptoms of attention deficit disorder with hyperactivity. *Journal of the American Academy of Child and Adolescent Psychiatry, 27,* 742–747.

Jensen, P. S., Ryan, N. D., & Prien, R. (1992). Psychopharmacology of child and adolescent major depression: Present status and future directions. *Journal of Child and Adolescent Psychopharmacology, 2,* 31–45

Johnston, H. F., & Fruehling, J. J. (1994). Pharmacotherapy for depression in children and adolescents. In W. M. Reynolds & H. F. Johnston (Eds.), *Handbook of depression in children and adolescents* (pp. 365–397). New York: Plenum.

Joyce, P. R. (1984). Age of onset in bipolar affective disorder and misdiagnosis as schizophrenia. *Psychological Medicine, 14,* 145–149.

Judd, L. L., Rapoport, M. H., Paulus, M. P., & Brown, J. L. (1994). Subsyndromal symptomatic depression: A new mood disorder. *Journal of Clinical Psychiatry, 55*(Suppl 4), 18–28.

Kahn, J. S., Kehle, T. J., & Jenson, W. R. (1987, April). *Depression among middle schools students: Descriptive and correlational analyses.* Paper presented at the Annual Meeting, National Association of School Psychologists, New Orleans, LA.

Kahn, J. S., Kehle, T. J., Jenson, W. R., & Clark, E. (1990). Comparison of cognitive-behavioral, relaxation, and self-modeling interventions for depression among middle-school students. *School Psychology Review, 19,* 196–211.

Kaminer, Y. (1991). The magnitude of concurrent psychiatric disorders in hospitalized substance abusing adolescents. *Child Psychiatry and Human Development, 22,* 89–95.

Kaminer, Y., Tarter, R. E., Bukstein, O. G., & Kabene, M. (1992). Comparison between treatment completers and noncompleters among dually diagnosed substance-abusing adolescents. *Journal of the American Academy of Child and Adolescent Psychiatry, 31,* 1046–1049.

Kanfer, F. H. (1970). Self-regulation: Research, issues, and speculations. In C. Neuringer & J. L. Michael (Eds.), *Behavior modification in clinical psychology* (pp. 178–220). New York: Appleton-Century-Crofts.

Karasu, T. B. (1990). Toward a clinical model of psychotherapy for depression, II: An integrative and selective treatment approach. *American Journal of Psychiatry, 147,* 269–278.

Kashani, J. H., & Cantwell, D. P. (1983). Etiology and treatment of childhood depression: A Biopsychological perspective. *Comprehensive Psychiatry, 24,* 476–486.

Kashani, J. H., Keller, M. B., Solomon, N., Reid, J. C., & Mazzola, D. (1985) Double depression in adolescent substance users. *Journal of Affective Disorders, 8,* 153–157.

Kashani, J. H., Sherman, D. D., Parker, D. R., & Reid, J. C. (1990). Utility of the Beck Depression Inventory with clinic-referred adolescents. *Journal of the American Academy of Child and Adolescent Psychiatry, 29,* 278–282.

Kazdin, A. E. (1987). Children's Depression Scale: Validation with child psychiatric inpatients. *Journal of Child Psychology and Psychiatry, 28,* 29–41.

Kazdin, A. E. (1994). Informant variability in the assessment of childhood depression. In W. M. Reynolds & H. F. Johnston (Eds.), *Handbook of depression in children and adolescents* (pp. 249–271). New York: Plenum.

Keller, M. B. (1994). Depression: A long-term illness. *British Journal of Psychiatry, 165*(Suppl. 26), 9–15.

Keller, M. B., Lavori, P. W., Beardslee, W. R., Wunder, J., & Ryan, N. (1991). Depression in children and adolescents: New data on "undertreatment" and a literature review on the efficacy of available treatments. *Journal of Affective Disorders, 21,* 163–171.

Kendall, P. C., & Clarkin, J. F. (1992). Introduction to special section: Comorbidity and treatment implications. *Journal of Consulting and Clinical Psychology, 60,* 833–834.

Kendall, P. C., Kortlander, E., Chansky, T. E., & Brady, E. U. (1992). Comorbidity of anxiety and depression in youth: Treatment implications. *Journal of Consulting and Clinical Psychology, 60,* 869–880.

Kendler, K. S., Kessler, R. C., Neale, M. C., Heath, A. C., & Eaves, L. J. (1993). The prediction of major depression in women: Toward an integrated etiological model. *American Journal of Psychiatry, 150,* 1139–1148.

King, C. A., Ghaziuddin, N., McGovern, L., Brand, E., Hill, E., & Naylor, M. (1996). Predictors of comorbid alcohol and substance abuse in depressed adolescents. *Journal of the American Academy of Child and Adolescent Psychiatry, 35,* 743–751.

King, C. A., Hovey, J. D., Brand, E., Wilson, R. & Ghaziuddin, N. (1997). Suicidal adolescents post-hospitalization: Parent and family impacts on treatment follow-through. *Journal of the American Academy of*

Child and Adolescent Psychiatry, 36, 85–93.

King, C. A., Katz, S. H., Ghaziuddin, N., Brand, E., Hill, E., & McGovern, L. (1997). Diagnosis and assessment of depression and suicidality using the NIMH Diagnostic Interview Schedule for Children (DISC-2.3). *Journal of Abnormal Child Psychology, 25,* 173–181.

King, C. A., Naylor, M. W., Hill, E. M., Shain, B. N., & Greden, J. F. (1993). Dysthymia characteristics of heavy alcohol use in depressed adolescents. *Biological Psychiatry, 33,* 210–212.

King, C. A., Naylor, M. W., Segal, H. G., Evans, T., & Shain, B. N. (1993). Global self-worth, specific self-perceptions of competence, and depression in adolescents. *Journal of the American Academy of Child and Adolescent Psychiatry, 32,* 745–752.

King, C. A., Radpour, L., Naylor, M. W., Segal, H. G., & Jouriles, E. N. (1995). Parents' marital functioning and adolescent psychopathology. *Journal of Consulting and Clinical Psychology, 63,* 749–753.

King, C. A., Raskin, A., Gdowski, C. L., Butkus, M., & Opipari, L. (1990). Psychosocial factors associated with urban adolescent female suicide attempts. *Journal of the American Academy of Child and Adolescent Psychiatry, 29,* 289–294.

King, C. A., Segal, H., Kaminski, K., Naylor, M. W., Ghaziuddin, N., & Radpour, L. (1995). A prospective study of adolescent suicidal behavior following hospitalization. *Suicide and Life-Threatening Behavior, 25,* 327–338.

King, C. A., Segal, H. G., Naylor, M., & Evans, T. (1993). Family functioning and suicidal behavior in adolescent inpatients with mood disorders. *Journal of the American Academy of Child and Adolescent Psychiatry, 32,* 1198–1206.

King, N. J., Gullone, E., & Ollendick, T. H. (1990). Childhood anxiety disorders and depression: Phenomenology, comorbidity, and intervention issues. *Scandinavian Journal of Behaviour Therapy, 19,* 59–70.

Klerman, G. L. (1987). Depression associated with medical and neurological diseases, drugs, and alcohol. In A. J. Marsella, R. M. A. Hirschfeld & M. M. Katz (Eds.), *The measurement of depression* (pp. 20–29). New York: Guilford.

Klerman, G. L., & Weissman, M. M. (1982). Interpersonal psychotherapy: Theory and research. In A. J. Rush (Ed.), *Short-term psychotherapies for depression: Behavioral, interpersonal, cognitive, and psychodynamic approaches* (pp. 88–106). New York: Guilford.

Komoto, J., Usui, S., & Hirata, J. (1984). Infantile autism and affective disorder. *Journal of Autism and Developmental Disorders, 14,* 81–84.

Kovacs, M. (1979). *Children's Depression Inventory,* University of Pittsburgh School of Medicine, PA: Author.

Kovacs, M. (1980/1981). Rating scales to assess depression in school-aged children. *Acta Paedopsychiatrica, 46,* 305–315.

Kovacs, M. (1983). *The Children's Depression Inventory: A self-rating scale for school-aged youngsters.* Unpublished manuscript.

Kovacs, M. (1985). The natural history and course of depressive disorders in childhood. *Psychiatric Annals, 15,* 387–389.

Kovacs, M. (1990). Comorbid anxiety disorders in childhood-onset depression. In J. D. Maser & C. R. Cloninger (Eds.), *Comorbidity of mood and anxiety disorders* (pp. 271–281). Washington DC: American Psychiatric Press.

Kovacs, M. (1992). *Children's Depression Inventory manual.* North Tonawanda, NY: Multi-Health Systems.

Kovacs, M. (1996a). Presentation and course of major depressive disorder during childhood and later years of the life span. *Journal of the American Academy of Child and Adolescent Psychiatry, 35,* 705–715.

Kovacs, M. (1996b). The course of childhood-onset depressive disorders. *Psychiatric Annals, 26,* 326–330.

Kovacs, M., Akiskal, H. S., Gatsonis, C., & Perrone, P. L. (1994). Childhood-onset dysthymic disorder. Clinical features and prospective naturalistic outcome. *Archives of General Psychiatry, 51,* 365–374.

Kovacs, M., & Beck, A. T. (1977). An empirical-clinical approach toward a definition of childhood depression. In J. G. Schulterbrandt & A. Raskin (Eds.) *Depression in childhood: Diagnosis, treatment and conceptual models,* (pp. 1–25). New York: Raven Press.

Kovacs, M., Feinberg, T. L., Crouse-Novak, M., Paulauskas, S. L., Pollock, M., & Finkelstein, R. (1984a). Depressive disorders in childhood: II. A longitudinal study of the risk for a subsequent major depression. *Archives of General Psychiatry, 41,* 643–649.

Kovacs, M., Feinberg, T. L., Crouse-Novak, M., Paulauskas, S. L., & Finkelstein, R. (1984b). Depressive disorders in childhood: I. A longitudinal prospective study of characteristics and recovery. *Archives of General Psychiatry, 41,* 229–237.

Kovacs, M., & Gatsonis, C. (1994). Secular trends in age at onset of major depressive disorder in a clinical sample of children. *Journal of Psychiatric Research, 28,* 319–329.

Kovacs, M., Gatsonis, C., Paulauskas, S. L., & Richards, C. (1989). Depressive disorders in childhood, IV: A longitudinal study of comorbidity with and risk for anxiety disorders. *Archives of General Psychiatry, 46,* 776–782.

Kovacs, M., Paulauskas, S. L., Gatsonis, C., & Richards, C. (1988). Depressive disorders in childhood: III. A longitudinal study of comorbidity with and risk for conduct disorders. *Journal of Affective Disorders, 15,* 205–217.

Kuhn, V. & Kuhn, R. (1971). Drug therapy for depression in children. Indications and methods. In A. Annell (Ed.), *Depressive states in childhood and adolescence* (pp. 455–459). Stockholm, Sweden: Almqvist & Wiksell.

Kutcher, S., Boulos, C., Ward, B., Marton, P., Simeon, J., Ferguson, H. B., Szalai, J., Katic, M., Roberts, N., Dubois, C., & Reed, K. (1994). Response to desipramine treatment in adolescent depression: A fixed-dose, placebo-controlled trial. *Journal of the American Academy of Child and Adolescent Psychiatry, 33,* 686–694.

Kutcher, S. P., & Marton, P. (1989). Utility of the Beck Depression Inventory with psychiatrically disturbed adolescent outpatients. *Canadian Journal of Psychiatry, 34,* 107–109.

Kutcher, S. P., & Marton, P., & Korenblum, M. (1989). Relationship between psychiatric illness and conduct disorder in adolescents. *Canadian Journal Psychiatry, 34,* 526–529.

Kye, C. H., Waterman, G. S., Ryan, N. D., Birmaher, B., Williamson, D. E., Iyengar, S., & Dachille, S. (1996). A randomized, controlled trial of amitriptyline in the acute treatment of adolescent major depression. *Journal of the American Academy of Child and Adolescent Psychiatry, 35,* 1139–1144.

Lam, R. W., Solyom, L., & Tompkins, A. (1991). Seasonal mood symptoms in bulimia nervosa and seasonal affective disorder. *Comprehensive Psychiatry, 32,* 552–558.

Lang, M., & Tisher, M. (1987). *Children's Depression Scale (CDS) (9–16 years) manual* (North American Edition). Palo Alto, CA: Consulting Psychologists Press.

Ledoux, S., Choquet, M., & Manfredi, R. (1993). Associated factors for self-reported binge eating among male and female adolescents. *Journal of Adolescence, 16,* 75–91.

Leibenluft, E., Fiero, P. L., & Rubinow, D. R. (1994). Effects of the menstrual cycle on dependent variables in mood disorder research. *Archives of General Psychiatry, 51,* 761–781.

Lesse, S. (1981). Hypochondriacal and psychosomatic disorders masking depression in adolescents. *American Journal of Psychotherapy, 35*, 356–367.

Levy, J. C., & Deykin, E. Y. (1989). Suicidality, depression, and substance abuse in adolescence. *American Journal of Psychiatry, 146*, 1462–1467.

Lewinsohn, P. M. (1975). The behavioral study and treatment of depression. In M. Hersen, R. M. Eisler, & P. M. Miller (Eds.), *Progress in behavior modification* (pp. 19–64). New York: Academic Press.

Lewinsohn, P. M., Clarke, G. N., Hops, H., & Andrews, J. (1990). Cognitive-behavioral treatment for depressed adolescents. *Behavior Therapy, 21*, 385–401.

Lewinsohn, P. M., Hops, H., Roberts, R. E., Seeley, J. R., & Andrews, J. (1993). Adolescent psychopathology: I. Prevalence and incidence of depression and other DSM-III-R disorders in high school students. *Journal of Abnormal Psychology, 102*, 133–144.

Lewinsohn, P. M., Munoz, R. F., Youngren, M. A., & Zeiss, A. M. (1978). *Control your depression.* Englewood Cliffs, NJ: Prentice-Hall.

Lewinsohn, P. M., Rohde, P., & Seeley, J. R. (1995). Adolescent psychopathology: III. The clinical consequences of comorbidity. *Journal of the American Academy of Child and Adolescent Psychiatry, 34*, 510–519.

Lewinsohn, P. M., Rohde, P., Seeley, J. R., & Fisher, S. A. (1993). Age-cohort changes in the lifetime occurrence of depression and other mental disorders. *Journal of Abnormal Psychology, 102*, 110–120.

Lewis, M., & Lewis, D. O. (1979). A psychobiological view of depression in childhood. In A. French & I. Berlin (Eds.), *Depression in children and adolescents* (pp. 29–45). New York: Human Sciences Press.

Licitra-Kleckler, D. M., & Waas, G. A. (1993). Perceived social support among high-stress adolescents: The role of peers and family. *Journal of Adolescent Research, 8*, 381–402.

Liddle, B., & Spence, S. H. (1990). Cognitive-behaviour therapy with depressed primary school children: A cautionary note. *Behavioural Psychotherapy, 19*, 85–102.

Ling, W., Oftedal, G., & Weinberg, W. (1970). Depressive illness in childhood presenting as severe headache. *American Journal of Diseases in Children, 120*, 122–124.

Loeber, R., Russo, M. F., Stouthamer-Loeber, M., & Lahey, B. B. (1994). Internalizing problems and their relation to the development of disruptive behaviors in adolescence. *Journal of Research on Adolescence, 4*, 615–637.

Loranger, A. W., & Levine, P. M (1978). Age at onset of bipolar affective illness. *Archives of General Psychiatry, 35*, 1345–1348.

Magnusson, D. (1985). Implications of an interactional paradigm for research on human development. *International Journal of Behavioral Development, 8*, 115–137.

Magnusson, D., & Torestad, B. (1993). A holistic view of personality: A model revisited. *Annual Review of Psychology, 44*, 427–452.

Marcotte, D., & Baron, p. (1993). L'efficacité d'une stratégie d'intervention émotivo-rationnelle auprès, d'adolescents dépressifs de milieu scolaire. *Revue Canadienne de Counseling, 27*, 77–92.

McClellan, J. M., Rubert, M. P, Reichler, R. J., & Sylvester, C. E. (1990). Attention deficit disorder in children at risk for anxiety and depression. *Journal of the American Academy of Child and Adolescent Psychiatry, 29*, 534–539.

McGlashan, T. H. (1988). Adolescent versus adult onset of mania. *American Journal of Psychiatry, 145*, 221–223.

McKay, J. R., Murphy, R. T., Maisto, S. A., & Rivinus, T. R. (1992). Characteristics of adolescent psychiatric patients who engage in problematic behavior while intoxicated. *Journal of the American Academy of Child and Adolescent Psychiatry, 31*, 1031–1035.

Meichenbaum, D. (1985). *Stress inoculation training.* New York: Pergamon.

Meller, W. H., & Borchardt, C. M. (1996). Comorbidity of major depression and conduct disorder. *Journal of Affective Disorders, 39*, 123–126.

Meyer, A. (1957). *Psychobiology.* Springfield, IL: Charles Thomas.

Mitchell, J., McCauley, E., Burke, P., & Moss, S. J. (1988). Phenomenology of depression in children and adolescents. *Journal of the American Academy of Child and Adolescent Psychiatry, 27*, 12–20.

Mokros, H. B., Poznanski, E., Grossman, J. A., & Freeman, L. N. (1987). A comparison of child and parent ratings of depression for normal and clinically referred children. *Journal of Child Psychology and Psychiatry, 28*, 613–627.

Moreau, D., Mufson, L., Weissman, M. M., & Klerman, G. L. (1991). Interpersonal psychotherapy for adolescent depression: Description of modification and preliminary application. *Journal of the American Academy of Child and Adolescent Psychiatry, 30*, 642–651.

Moretti, M. M., Fine, S., Haley, G., & Marriage, K. (1985). Childhood and adolescent depression: Child-report versus parent-report information. *Journal of the American Academy of Child Psychiatry, 24*, 298–302.

Mufson, L., Moreau, D., Weissman, M. M., Wickramaratne, P., Martin, J., & Samoilov, A. (1994). The modification of interpersonal psychotherapy with depressed adolescents (IPT-A): Phase I and Phase II studies. *Journal of the American Academy of Child and Adolescent Psychiatry, 33*, 695–705.

Mufson, L., Moreau, D., Weissman, M. M., & Klerman, G. L. (1993). *Interpersonal psychotherapy for depressed adolescents.* New York: Guilford Press.

Mufson, L., Weissman, M. M., & Warner, V. (1992). Depression and anxiety in parents and children: A direct interview study. *Journal of Anxiety Disorders, 6*, 1–13.

Naylor, M. W., & Grossman, M (1991). Trichotillomania and depression (letter to the Editor). *Journal of the American Academy of Child and Adolescent Psychiatry, 30*, 155–156.

Naylor, M. W., Staskowski, M., Kenney, M. C., & King, C. A. (1994). Language disorders and learning disabilities in school-refusing adolescents. *Journal of the American Academy of Child and Adolescent Psychiatry, 33*, 1331–1337.

Nelson, W. M., & Politano, P. M. (1990). Children's Depression Inventory: Stability over repeated administrations in psychiatric inpatient children. *Journal of Clinical Child Psychology, 19*, 254–256.

Nieminen, G. S., & Matson, J. L. (1989). Depressive problems in conduct-disordered adolescents. *Journal of School Psychology, 27*, 175–186.

Nurcombe, B. (1994). The validity of the diagnosis of major depression in childhood and adolescence. In W. M. Reynolds & H. F. Johnston (Eds.), *Handbook of depression in children and adolescents* (pp. 61–77). New York: Plenum.

Nurcombe, B., Seifer, R., Scioli, A., Tramontana, M. G., Grapentine, W. L., & Beauchesne, H. C. (1989). Is major depressive disorder in adolescence a distinct diagnostic entity? *Journal of the American Academy of Child and Adolescent Psychiatry, 28*, 333–342.

Oakley-Browne, M. A., Joyce, P. R., Wells, J. E., Bushnell, J. A., & Hornblow, A. R. (1995). Adverse parenting and other childhood experience as risk factors for depression in women aged 18–44 years. *Journal of Affective Disorders, 34*, 13–23.

Offer, D., & Schonert-Reichl, K. A. (1992). Debunking the myths of adolescence: Findings from recent research. *Journal of the American Academy of Child and Adolescent Psychiatry, 31*, 1003–1014.

Ollendick, T. H., Yule, W., & Ollier, K. (1991). Fears in British children and their relationship to manifest anxiety and depression. *Journal of Child Psychology and Psychiatry, 32*, 321–331.

Papatheodorou, G., & Kutcher, S. (1995). The effect of adjunctive light therapy on ameliorating breakthrough depressive symptoms in adolescent-onset bipolar disorder. *Journal of Psychiatry and Neuroscience, 20*, 226–232.

Paris, J. (1994). The etiology of borderline personality disorder: A biopsychosocial approach. *Psychiatry, 57*, 316–325.

Paul, S. M. (1988). Anxiety and depression: A common neurobiological substrate? *Journal of Clinical Psychiatry, 49*(Suppl. 10), 13–16.

Petti, T. A. (1978). Depression in hospitalized child psychiatry patients: Approaches to measuring depression. *Journal of the American Academy of Child Psychiatry, 17*, 49–59.

Pfeffer, C. R., & Plutchik, R. (1989). Co-occurrence of psychiatric disorders in child psychiatric patients and nonpatients: A circumplex model. *Comprehensive Psychiatry, 30*, 275–282.

Poznanski, E. O. (1982). The clinical phenomenology of childhood depression. *American Journal of Orthopsychiatry, 52*, 308–313.

Poznanski, E. O., Carroll, B. J., Banegas, M. C., Cook, S. C., & Grossman, J. A. (1982). The dexamethasone suppression test in prepubertal depressed children. *American Journal of Psychiatry, 139*, 321–324.

Poznanski, E. O., Cook, S. C., & Carroll, B. J. (1979). A depression rating scale for children. *Pediatrics, 64*, 442–450.

Poznanski, E. O., Cook, S. C., Carroll, B. J., & Corzo, H. (1983). Use of the Children's Depression Rating Scale in an inpatient psychiatric population. *Journal of Clinical Psychiatry, 44*, 200–203.

Poznanski, E. O., Freeman, L. N., & Mokros, H. B. (1985). Children's Depression Rating Scale–Revised. *Psychopharmacology Bulletin, 21*, 979–989.

Poznanski, E. O., Grossman, J. A., Buchsbaum, Y., Banegas, M., Freeman, L., & Gibbons, R. (1984). Preliminary studies of the reliability and validity of the Children's Depression Rating Scale. *Journal of the American Academy of Child Psychiatry, 23*, 191–197.

Poznanski, E. O., Krahenbuhl, V., & Zrull, J. P. (1976). Childhood depression: A longitudinal perspective. *Journal of the American Academy of Child Psychiatry, 15*, 491–501.

Poznanski, E. O., & Mokros, H. B. (1994). Phenomenology and epidemiology of mood disorders in children and adolescents. In W. M. Reynolds & H. F. Johnston (Eds.), *Handbook of depression in children and adolescents* (pp. 19–39). New York: Plenum.

Poznanski, E., Mokros, H. B., Grossman, J., & Freeman, L. N. (1985). Diagnostic criteria in childhood depression. *American Journal of Psychiatry, 142*, 1168–1173.

Poznanski, E., & Zrull, J. P. (1970). Childhood depression: Clinical characteristics of overtly depressed children. *Archives of General Psychiatry, 23*, 8–15.

Puig-Antich, J. (1982). Major depression and conduct disorder in prepuberty. *Journal of the American Academy of Child Psychiatry, 21*, 118–128.

Puig-Antich, J., & Chambers, W. (1978). *The Schedule for Affective Disorders and Schizophrenia for School-age Children (Kiddie-SADS)*. New York: New York State Psychiatric Institute.

Puig-Antich, J., Dahl, R., Ryan, N., Novacenko, H., Goetz, D., Goetz, R. M., Twomey, J., & Klepper, T. (1989). Cortisol secretion in prepubertal children with major depressive disorder: Episode and recovery. *Archives of General Psychiatry, 46*, 801–809.

Puig-Antich, J., Lukens, E., Davies, M., Goetz, D.,

Brennan-Quattrock, J., & Todak, G. (1985). Psychosocial functioning in prepubertal children with major depressive disorders, I. Interpersonal relationships during the depressive episode. *Archives of General Psychiatry, 42*, 500–507.

Radloff, L. S. (1977) The CES-D Scale: A self-report scale for research in the general population. *Applied Psychological Measurement, 1*, 385–401.

Rastam, M. (1992). Anorexia nervosa in 51 Swedish adolescents: Premorbid problems and comorbidity. *Journal of the American Academy of Child and Adolescent Psychiatry, 31*, 819–829.

Rawson, H. E. (1992). The interrelationship of measures of manifest anxiety, self-esteem, locus of control, and depression in children with behavior problems. *Journal of Psychoeducational Assessment, 10*, 319–329.

Rawson, H. E., & Tabb, B. A. (1993). The effects of therapeutic intervention on childhood depression. *Child and Adolescent Social Work Journal, 10*, 39–52.

Regier, D. A., Kaelber, C. T., Roper, M. T., Rae, D. S., & Sartorius, N. (1994). The ICD-10 clinical field trial for mental and behavioral disorders: Results in Canada and the United States. *American Journal of Psychiatry, 151*, 1340–1350.

Rehm, L. P. (1977). A self-control model of depression. *Behavior Therapy, 8*, 787–804.

Reich, W., & Welner, Z. (1988). *Revised version of the Diagnostic Interview for Children and Adolescents (DICA-R)*. St. Louis, MO: Washington University School of Medicine.

Reinecke, M. A., & Schultz, T. M. (1995). Comparison of self-report and clinician ratings of depression among outpatient adolescents. *Depression, 3*, 139–145.

Remschmidt, H. (1992). The interaction of biological and psychosocial influences in developmental psychopathology. In H. Remschmidt & M. H. Schmidt (Eds.), *Developmental psychopathology* (pp. 17–25). Lewiston, NY: Hogrefe & Hubner.

Reynolds, W. M. (1985). Depression in childhood and adolescence: Diagnosis, assessment, intervention strategies and research. In T. R. Kratochwill (Ed.), *Advances in school psychology.* (Vol., 4. pp. 133–189). Hillsdale, NJ Lawrence Erlbaum.

Reynolds, W. M. (1986a). A model for the screening and identification of depressed children and adolescents in school settings. *Professional School Psychology, 1*, 117–129.

Reynolds, W. M. (1986b). *Reynolds Adolescent Depression Scale*. Odessa, FL: Psychological Assessment Resources.

Reynolds, W. M. (1987) *Reynolds Adolescent Depression Scale: Professional Manual*. Odessa, FL: Psychological Assessment Resources.

Reynolds, W. M. (1989) *Reynolds Child Depression Scale: Professional Manual*. Odessa, FL: Psychological Assessment Resources.

Reynolds, W. M. (1990). Development of a semi-structured clinical interview for suicidal behaviors in adolescents. *Psychological Assessment: A Journal of Consulting and Clinical Psychology, 2*, 382–390.

Reynolds, W. M. (1992a). The study of internalizing disorders in children and adolescents. In W. M. Reynolds (Ed.), *Internalizing disorders in children and adolescents* (pp. 1–18). New York: Wiley.

Reynolds, W. M. (1992b). Depression in children and adolescents. In W. M. Reynolds (Ed.), *Internalizing disorders in children and adolescents* (pp. 149–253). New York: Wiley.

Reynolds, W. M. (1994). Assessment of depression in children and adolescents by self-report questionnaires. In W. M. Reynolds & H. F. Johnston (Eds.), *Handbook of depression in children and adolescents* (pp. 209–234). New York: Plenum.

Reynolds, W. M. (1997a). *A biopsychosocial model of*

depression in children and adolescents. Unpublished manuscript.

Reynolds, W. M. (1997b). *Comorbidity of psychiatric disorders at intake among adolescents seen in inpatient and outpatient clinical settings.* Unpublished manuscript.

Reynolds, W. M., Anderson, G. & Bartell, N. (1985). Measuring depression in children: A multimethod assessment investigation. *Journal of Abnormal Child Psychology, 13,* 513–526.

Reynolds, W. M. & Coats, K. I. (1982, July). *Depression in adolescents: Incidence, depth and correlates.* Paper presented at the 10th International Congress of the International Association for Child and Adolescent Psychiatry, Dublin, Ireland.

Reynolds, W. M. & Coats, K. I. (1986). A comparison of cognitive-behavioral therapy and relaxation training for the treatment of depression in adolescents. *Journal of Consulting and Clinical Psychology, 54,* 653–660.

Reynolds, W. M. & Graves, A. (1989). Reliability of children's reports of depressive symptomatology. *Journal of Abnormal Child Psychology, 17,* 647–655.

Reynolds, W. M., & Johnston, H. F. (1994). The nature and study of depression in children and adolescents. In W. M. Reynolds & H. F. Johnston (Eds.), *Handbook of depression in children and adolescents* (pp. 3–17). New York: Plenum.

Reynolds, W. M. & Mazza, J. J. (1994). Suicide and suicidal behaviors in children and adolescents. In W. M. Reynolds & H. F. Johnston (Eds.), *Handbook of depression in children and adolescents* (pp. 525–580). New York: Plenum.

Reynolds, W. M., & Mazza, J. J. (in press). Reliability and validity of the Reynolds Adolescent Depression Scale with young adolescents. *Journal of School Psychology.*

Reynolds, W. M., & Miller, K. L. (1989). Assessment of adolescents' learned helplessness in achievement situations. *Journal of Personality Assessment, 53,* 211–228.

Riddle, M. A., Brown, N., Dzubinski, D, Jetmalani, A. J., Law, Y. & Woolston, J. L. (1989). Fluoxetine overdose in an adolescent. *Journal of the American Academy of Child and Adolescent Psychiatry, 28,* 587–588.

Riddle, M. A., Hardin, M. T., King, R., Scahill, L., & Woolston, J. L. (1990). Fluoxetine treatment of children and adolescents with Tourette's and obsessive compulsive disorders: Preliminary clinical experience. *Journal of the American Academy of Child and Adolescent Psychiatry, 29,* 45–48.

Robbins, D. R., Alessi, N. E., Colfer, M. V. (1989). Treatment of adolescents with major depression: Implications of the DST and the melancholic clinical subtype. *Journal of Affective Disorders, 17,* 99–104.

Robbins, D. R., Alessi, N. E., Colfer, M. V., & Yanchyshyn, G. W. (1985). Use of the Hamilton Rating Scale for Depression and the Carroll Self-Rating Scale in adolescents. *Psychiatry Research, 14,* 123–129.

Roberts, R. E., Lewinsohn, P. M., & Seeley, J. R. (1991). Screening for adolescent depression: A comparison of depression scales. *Journal of the American Academy of Child and Adolescent Psychiatry, 30,* 58–66.

Rohde, P., Lewinsohn, P. M., & Seeley, J. R. (1991). Comorbidity of unipolar depression: II. Comorbidity with other mental disorders in adolescents and adults. *Journal of Abnormal Psychology, 100,* 214–222.

Roseby, V. & Deutsch, R. (1985). Children of separation and divorce: Effects of a social role-taking group intervention on fourth and fifth graders. *Journal of Clinical Child Psychology, 14,* 55–60.

Rush, A. J. (1990). Problems associated with the diagnosis of depression. *Journal of Clinical Psychiatry, 51*(Suppl.), 15–22.

Rush, A. J., Giles, D. E., Schlesser, M. A., Fulton., C. L., Weissenberger, J., & Burns, C. (1986). The Inventory of

Depressive Symptoms (IDC): Preliminary findings. *Psychiatry Research, 18,* 65–87.

Sadowski, C., & Kelley, M. L. (1993). Social problem solving in suicidal adolescents. *Journal of Consulting and Clinical Psychology, 61,* 121–127.

Sandler, J., & Jaffee, N. G. (1965). Notes on childhood depression. *International Journal of Psychoanalysis, 46,* 88–96.

Sartorius, N., Kaelber, C. T., Cooper, J. E., Roper, M. T., Rae, D. S., Gulbinat, W., Ustun, T. B., & Regier, D. A. (1993). Progress toward achieving a common language in psychiatry: Results from the field trial of the clinical guidelines accompanying the WHO classification of mental and behavioral disorders in ICD-10. *Archives of General Psychiatry, 50,* 115–124.

Saylor, C. F., Finch, A J., Spirito, A., & Bennett, B. (1984). The Children's Depression Inventory: A systematic evaluation of psychometric properties. *Journal of Consulting and Clinical Psychology, 52,* 955–967.

Schonert-Reichl, K. A. (1994). Gender differences in depressive symptomatology and egocentrism in adolescence. *Journal of Early Adolescence, 14,* 49–64.

Shaffer, D., Schwab-Stone, M., Fisher, P., Cohen, P., Piacentini, J., Davies, M., Conners, C. K., & Reiger, D. (1993). The Diagnostic Interview Schedule for Children-Revised Version (DISC-R): I. Preparation, field testing, interrater reliability, and acceptability. *Journal of the American Academy of Child and Adolescent Psychiatry, 32,* 643–650.

Shain, B. N., Kronfol, Z., Naylor, M., Goel, K., Evans, T., & Schaefer, S. (1991). Natural killer cell activity in adolescents with major depression. *Biological Psychiatry, 29,* 481–484.

Shain, B. N., Naylor, M., & Alessi, N. (1990). Comparison of self-rated and clinician-rated measures of depression in adolescents. *American Journal of Psychiatry, 147,* 793–795.

Shalev, A. Y. (1993). Post-traumatic stress disorder: A biopsychosocial perspective. *Israeli Journal of Psychiatry and Related Sciences, 30,* 102–109.

Smith, C., Feldman, S., Nasserbakht, A., & Steiner, H. (1993). Psychological characteristics and *DSM-III-R* diagnosis at 6-year follow-up of adolescent anorexia nervosa. *Journal of the American Academy of Child and Adolescent Psychiatry, 32,* 1237–1245.

Smith, C., & Steiner, H. (1992). Psychopathology in anorexia nervosa and depression. *Journal of the American Academy of Child and Adolescent Psychiatry, 31,* 841–843.

Smoller, A. S., & Brosgole, L. (1993). Visual and auditory affect recognition in depressed and nondepressed latency aged children. *International Journal of Neuroscience, 70,* 29–38.

Smucker, M. R., Craighead, W. E., Craighead, L. W., & Green, B. J. (1986). Normative and reliability data for the Children's Depression Inventory. *Journal of Abnormal Child Psychology, 14,* 25–39.

Sonis, W. A., Yellin, A. M., Garfinkel, B. D., & Hoberman, H. H. (1987). The antidepressant effect of light in seasonal affective disorder of childhood and adolescence. *Psychopharmacology Bulletin, 23,* 360–363.

Spitzer, R. L., Endicott, J., & Robins, E. (1978). Research diagnostic criteria: Rationale and reliability. *Archives of General Psychiatry, 35,* 773–782.

Stack, J. J. (1971). Chemotherapy in childhood depression. In A. Annell (Ed.), *Depressive states in childhood and adolescence* (pp. 460–466). Stockholm, Sweden: Almqvist & Wiksell.

Stark, K. D. (1990). *Childhood depression: School-based intervention.* New York: Guilford Press.

Stark, K. D., Reynolds, W. M., & Kaslow, N. J. (1987). A comparison of the relative efficacy of self-control therapy and behavioral problem-solving therapy for depression in children. *Journal of Abnormal Child Psychology, 15*, 91–113.

Stark, K. D., Rouse, L. W., & Livingston, R. (1991). Treatment of depression during childhood and adolescence: Cognitive behavioral procedures for the individual and family. In P. C. Kendall (Ed.), *Child and adolescent therapy: Cognitive-behavioral procedures* (pp. 165–206). New York: Guilford Press.

Stattin, H., & Magnusson, D. (1989). Social transition in adolescence: A biosocial perspective. In A. de Ribaupierre (Ed.), *Transition mechanisms in child development: The longitudinal perspective* (pp. 147–190). Cambridge, UK: Cambridge University Press.

Stone, M. H. (1981). Depression in borderline adolescents. *American Journal of Psychotherapy, 35*, 383–399.

Stowell, R. J. A., & Estroff, T. W. (1992). Psychiatric disorders in substance-abusing adolescent inpatients: A pilot study. *Journal of the American Academy of Child and Adolescent Psychiatry, 31*, 1036–1040.

Straus, M. A., & Kantor, G. K. (1994). Corporal punishment of adolescents by parents: A risk factor in the epidemiology of depression, suicide, alcohol abuse, child abuse, and wife beating. *Adolescence, 29*, 534–561.

Strauss, C. C., Last, C. G., Hersen, M., & Kazdin, A. E. (1988). Association between anxiety and depression in children and adolescents with anxiety disorders. *Journal of Abnormal Child Psychology, 16*, 57–68.

Strober, M., Green, J., & Carlson, G. (1981). Utility of the Beck Depression Inventory with psychiatrically hospitalized adolescents. *Journal of Consulting and Clinical Psychology, 49*, 482–483.

Suinn, R. M. (1986). *Anxiety management training manual.* Fort Collins, CO: Rocky Mountain Behavioral Science Institute.

Swift, W. J., Andrews, D., & Barklage, N. E. (1986). The relationship between affective disorders and eating disorders: A review of the literature. *American Journal of Psychiatry, 143*, 290–299.

Syvalahti, E. (1987). Endocrine and immune adaptation in stress. *Annals of Clinical Research, 19*, 70–77.

Tarnowski, K. J., Simonian, S. J., Bekeny, P., & Park, A. (1992). Acceptability of interventions for childhood depression. *Behavior Modification, 16*, 103–117.

Tisher, M. (1995). Teacher's assessments of prepubertal childhood depression. *Australian Journal of Psychology, 47*, 93–96.

Tisher, M., & Lang, M. (1983). The Children's Depression Scale: Review and further developments. In D. P. Cantwell & G. A. Carlson (Eds.), *Affective disorders in childhood and adolescents—An update* (pp. 181–203). Jamaica, NY: Spectrum Publications.

Tisher, M., Lang-Takac, E., & Lang, M. (1992). The Children's Depression Scale: Review of Australian and overseas experience. *Australian Journal of Psychology, 44*, 27–35.

Tonkin, G., & Hudson, A. (1981). The Children's Depression Scale: Some further psychometric data. *Australian Council for Educational Research Bulletin for Psychologists, 30*, 11–18

Vasile, R. G., Samson, J. A., Bemporad, J., Bloomingdale, K. L., Creasey, D., Fenton, B. T., Gudeman, J. E., & Schildkraut, J. J. (1987). A biopsychosocial approach to treating patients with affective disorders. *American Journal of Psychiatry, 144*, 341–344.

Vitiello, B., Malone, R., Buschle, P. R., Delaney, M. A., & Behar, D. (1990). Reliability of DSM-III diagnoses of hospitalized children. *Hospital and Community Psychiatry, 41*, 63–67.

Waldron, S., Shrier, D. K., Stone, B., & Tobin, F. (1975). School phobia and other childhood neuroses: A systematic study of the children and their families. *American Journal of Psychiatry, 132*, 802–808.

Waller, D. A., & Rush, A. J. (1983). Differentiating primary affective disease, organic affective syndromes, and situational depression on a pediatric service. *Journal of the American Academy of Child Psychiatry, 22*, 52–58.

Walters, E. E., Neale, M. C., Eaves, L. J., Heath, A. C., Kessler, R. C., & Kendler, K. S. (1992). Bulimia nervosa and major depression: A study of common genetic and environmental factors. *Psychological Medicine, 22*, 617–622.

Wamboldt, M. Z. (1994). Current status of child and adolescent medical-psychiatric units. *Psychosomatics, 35*, 434–444.

Weinberg, J., & van den Dungen, M. (1971). Depression and delinquency in adolescence. In A. Annell (Eds.), *Depressive states in childhood and adolescence* (pp. 296–302). Stockholm, Sweden: Almqvist & Wiksell.

Weinberg, W. A., & Brumback, R. A. (1976). Mania in childhood: Case studies and literature review. *American Journal of Diseases in Children, 130*, 380–385.

Weinberg, W. A., & Emslie, G. J. (1991). Attention deficit hyperactivity disorder: The differential diagnosis. *Journal of Child Neurology, 6*(Suppl.), S23–S36.

Weinberg, W. A., Rutman, J., Sullivan, L., Penick, E. C., & Dietz, S. G. (1973). Depression in children referred to an educational diagnostic center: Diagnosis and treatment. *Journal of Pediatrics, 83*, 1065–1072.

Weiss, B., Weisz, J. R., Politano, M., Carey, M., Nelson, W. M., & Finch, A. J. (1991). Developmental differences in the factor structure of the Children's Depression Inventory. *Psychological Assessment: A Journal of Consulting and Clinical Psychology, 3*, 38–45.

Weissman, M. M. (1990). Evidence for comorbidity of anxiety and depression: Family and genetic studies of children. In J. D. Maser & C. R. Cloninger (Eds.), *Comorbidity of mood and anxiety disorders* (pp. 349–365). Washington, DC: American Psychiatric Press.

Weist, M. D., Proescher, E. L, Freedman, A. H., Paskewitz, D. A., & Flaherty, L. T. (1995). School-based health services for urban adolescents: Psychosocial characteristics of clinic users or nonusers. *Journal of Youth and Adolescence, 24*, 251–265.

Weller, E. B., & Weller, R. A., (1983). Case report of conversion symptom associated with major depressive disorder in a child. *American Journal of Psychiatry, 140*, 1079–1080.

Weller, R. A., & Weller, E. B. (1986). Tricyclic antidepressants in prepubertal depressed children: Review of the literature. *Hillside Journal of Clinical Psychiatry, 8*, 46–55.

Weller, E. B., Weller, R. A., & Carr, S. (1989). Imipramine treatment of trichotillomania and coexisting depression in a seven-year-old. *Journal of the American Academy of Child and Adolescent Psychiatry, 28*, 952–953.

Weller, R. A., Weller, E. B., Fristad, M. A., Cantwell, M. L., & Preskorn, S. H. (1986). Dexamethasone suppression test and clinical outcome in prepubertal depressed children. *American Journal of Psychiatry, 143*, 1469–1470.

Weller, R. A., Weller, E. B., Tucker, S. G., & Fristad, M. A. (1986). Mania in prepubertal children: Has it been underdiagnosed? *Journal of Affective Disorders, 11*, 151–154.

Wenning, K., Nathan, P., & King, S. (1993). Mood disorders in children with oppositional defiant disorder: A pilot study. *American Journal of Orthopsychiatry, 63*, 295–299.

West, S. A., McElroy, S. L., Strakowski, S. M., Keck, P. E., & McConville, B. J. (1995). Attention deficit hyperactivity disorder in adolescent mania. *American Journal of Psychiatry, 152*, 271–273.

Whitaker, A., Johnson, J., Shaffer, D., Rapoport, J. L., Kalikow, K., Walsh, B. T., Davies, M., Braiman, S., & Dolinsky, A. (1990). Uncommon troubles in young people: Prevalence estimates of selected psychiatric disorders in a nonreferred adolescent population. *Archives of General Psychiatry, 47*, 487–496.

Wilkes, T. C. R., Belsher, G., Rush, A. J., & Frank, E. (1994). *Cognitive therapy for depressed adolescents.* New York: Guilford Press.

World Health Organization (1992). *International statistical classification of diseases and related health problems* (10th Rev.). Geneva, Switzerland: Author.

Wright, J. H., & Thase, M. E. (1992). Cognitive and biological therapies: A synthesis. *Psychiatric Annals, 22*, 451–458.

Wurzbacher, K. V., Evans, E. D., & Moore, E. J. (1991). Effects of alternative street school on youth involved in prostitution. *Journal of Adolescent Health, 12*, 549–554.

5.18
Suicide and Suicide Attempts During Adolescence

ANTHONY SPIRITO and DEIDRE DONALDSON
Rhode Island Hospital and Brown University School of Medicine, Providence, RI, USA

5.18.1 INTRODUCTION

Although suicide is rare in childhood, the rates of adolescent (15–19 year-olds) suicide almost tripled from 1950 to 1980. From 1980 to 1992, the rate increased by another 28.3%, from 8.5 to 10.9 per 100 000 (Centers for Disease Control [CDC], 1995a). The sharp rise in adolescent suicide is of significant concern. Beyond the emotional toll on the survivors and the tragic loss of a life so young, there are also considerable economic costs related to suicide. It has been estimated that each youth suicide results in approximately $432 000 worth of lost economic productivity (Weinstein & Saturno, 1989). Suicide attempts that do not result in death are also a significant public health problem. They occur at a very high rate (7–10% of adolescents report that they have attempted suicide) and a significant number (approximately 2–3%) of suicide attempters receive costly medical care following their attempts (CDC, 1995a).

This chapter summarizes many of the factors that contribute to adolescent suicide and suicide attempts. Adolescent suicide completers and attempters form separate, but overlapping groups. Thus, it is necessary to describe both. The first portion of this chapter discusses factors associated with completed and attempted suicide. The second portion of the chapter describes the clinical evaluation of suicide attempters. A bio-psychosocial model is utilized to synthesize the multiple factors that may affect outcome among suicide attempters. Understanding these factors also aids in the development of comprehensive and effective treatment plans for this high-risk group of adolescents. The final section discusses treatments for adolescents with suicidal ideation and adolescents who have attempted suicide.

5.18.2 PHENOMENOLOGY

Suicidal behavior includes both thoughts and actions. For some adolescents, a suicide attempt is the result of an impulsive act in the face of significant stress. For others, suicide attempts follow a course from passive suicidal ideation, to serious consideration of suicide as an option, followed by active planning. Suicidal thoughts may vary in frequency, intensity, and duration. The time course prior to a suicide attempt can be quite variable, ranging from many months of suicidal ideation to only several days or even hours. A suicide attempt may hold a particular meaning for either an individual or family; for example, it may be an indirect way of communicating distress or a way to receive attention within a family. Completed suicides may occur in adolescents who did not actually want to die but rather made an impulsive attempt using lethal means. Thus, the psychological characteristics associated with adolescent suicidality vary significantly, and no one pattern of psychopathology adequately describes adolescents who experience suicidal ideation, make a suicide attempt, or complete suicide.

5.18.3 DIAGNOSTIC FEATURES

Suicide and attempted suicide are not psychiatric disorders, but rather, symptoms of emotional distress which may be associated with certain psychiatric disorders such as depression. Consequently, there are no true diagnostic criteria. However, there is a great deal of confusion in the literature regarding what constitutes a "true" suicide attempt, and even suicidal ideation. What degree of ideation is necessary before a clinician or researcher considers an adolescent a suicide ideator? Similarly, does there have to be a certain level of suicidal intent or sufficient medical lethality for a suicide attempt to be considered a "true" suicide attempt? A variety of terms have been used to describe suicidal behavior. Standard nomenclature for suicidal behavior does not currently exist, which makes it difficult to interpret empirical findings. Reference to terms such as self-injury, self-mutilation, parasuicide, and suicide threats is common, and the term "suicidal gesture" is used in clinical notes and sometimes in research reports. The latter term typically refers to a suicide attempt of low medical lethality. This chapter uses the terms "completed suicide," "attempted suicide" and "suicidal ideation."

Several characteristics of a suicide attempt are pertinent to determining its severity. These include the intensity of suicidal ideation prior to the attempt, method of attempt, the precipitant of the attempt, and suicidal intent accompanying the attempt.

5.18.3.1 Ideation

The degree of suicidal ideation accompanying an attempt may be a marker of the seriousness of a suicide attempt. Spirito, Overholser, and Vinnick (1995) found that more than half of a sample of 203 adolescent suicide attempters demonstrated clinically significant levels of ideation on the Suicide Ideation Questionnaires (Reynolds, 1987): 13.8% of the sample scored in the 99th percentile and 43.3% scored in the 95th percentile or above. However, a significant number of adolescents did not report very high levels of suicide ideation, suggesting either an impulsive attempt or denial of their suicidal state.

5.18.3.2 Method of Attempt

The method of attempting suicide is not typically a useful indication of severity because the large majority of adolescents attempt suicide by drug overdose (Spirito, Brown, Overholser, & Fritz, 1989). Compared to adults, adolescents have limited access to other more lethal means of suicide which may account for the over-representation of overdoses. Because of the availability of medical care in most Western nations, overdoses are rarely fatal. The potential for a medically serious suicide attempt increases when prescription drugs are available, regardless of whether or not the drugs have been prescribed for the adolescent or another family member. Suicide attempts by other means, for example, hanging or firearms, often warrant greater concern and consideration by clinicians. However, clinicians should not minimize the seriousness of suicide attempts by overdose before investigating other associated features of the suicide attempt.

5.18.3.3 Precipitant of the Attempt

The precipitant of a suicide attempt is another important factor which seems to be comparable across nations. In the United States, stress related to parents, school, friends, and boyfriend/girlfriend relationships are the most common precipitants (Spirito, Overholser & Stark, 1989). In Britain, very similar findings have been reported (Hawton & Fagg, 1992). It is, therefore, important for clinicians not to minimize a suicide attempt because the precipitating problem is a common everyday event. Adolescents should be interviewed regarding the precipitant to the suicide attempt in order to thoroughly understand the significance of the particular stressor in the adolescent's life.

5.18.3.4 Intent

The intent of a suicide attempt appears to be important in terms of understanding differences in the severity of suicide attempts. Spirito et al. (1995) reported that only a minority of suicide attempters report extensive planning (4%), writing a suicide note (14%), or performed final acts in anticipation of their death prior to the attempt as assessed using the Suicide Intent Scale (Beck, Schuyler, & Herman, 1974). Many adolescents expect their attempt to cause their death (31%) and a significant number are ambivalent or sorry to have survived their attempt (57%).

A factor analysis of the Suicide Intent Scale revealed three aspects of suicidal intent specific to adolescent suicide attempters (Spirito, Sterling, Donaldson, & Arrigan, 1996). One factor, labeled Expected Outcome, included items that address the expectations, purpose, seriousness, and lethality, as well as ambivalence about living following a suicide attempt. A second factor, Isolation Behaviors, consisted of isolation at the time of the attempt, timing of attempt, precautions against discovery, and acting to gain help. A third factor, Planning Activities, included items about degree of premeditation, planning, and final acts. The findings of the factor analysis suggest that it may be more useful, when evaluating adolescent suicide attempters, to examine subjective factors, particularly Expected Outcome, and selected objective factors, such as those found in the Planning Activities factor, rather than the overall level of suicidal intent.

The distinction between impulsive, unplanned attempts, and planned attempts is important in assessing the seriousness of suicide attempts. Brent (1987) found that a group of suicide attempters with high levels of hopelessness had made premeditated and highly lethal attempts compared to the unplanned and impulsive attempts made by adolescents who did not report high levels of hopelessness. In a general hospital sample, Brown, Overholser, Spirito, and Fritz (1991) found that about one-third of the suicide attempts could be classified as planned and two-thirds could be described as impulsive. Those adolescents who planned a suicide attempt were more hopeless and depressed and experienced greater suicidal ideation than the other impulsive attempters. Slap, Vorters, Chaudhuri, and Centor (1989) found that a lack of impulse control differentiated adolescent suicide attempters from a group of nonpsychiatrically hospitalized adolescents. There also appear to be gender differences in impulsivity in that male adolescent suicide attempters are more often described as displaying impulsive behavior than female suicide attempters (Marks & Haller, 1977). Because impulsivity does not characterize every adolescent suicide attempter, it can be used as a variable to classify a subgroup of these attempters.

5.18.4 PREVALENCE

Internationally, the youth suicide rate varies but is consistently one of the highest causes of death during adolescence. Diekstra and Golbinat (1993) reviewed statistics on suicide rates reported to the World Health Organization's (WHO) mortality data bank. The countries with the highest youth (15–24 years) suicide rates included Sri Lanka (62.3 per 100 000 in 1986), Finland (25.1 per 100 000 in 1991), Switzerland and Austria (16.2 per 100 000 in 1991), and Canada (15.0 per 100 000 in 1990). Suicide is the third leading cause of death among youth age 15–24 years old in the United States (National Center for Health Statistics [NCHS], 1993). The absolute number of deaths by suicide among adolescents in the US is fairly small (usually between 2000 and 2500 adolescents per year).

The statistics on suicide rates have generally been considered to be an underestimate of the true incidence due to misclassification of deaths that might be suicides (e.g., single car crashes, as well as failure to report deaths as suicides due to social stigma). The magnitude of the discrepancy between actual suicide rates and the reported statistics has been a subject of considerable debate (Males, 1991). The reporting of a suicide is related to several factors including whether mental illness preceded the death, who certifies the death, and the means of death (e.g., single car crash vs. gunshot wound). If there has been a true increase in the rate of adolescent suicide, as many suggest, one reason may be that adolescents from larger birth cohorts appear to be at higher risk for suicide than those in smaller cohorts (Holinger & Offer, 1987). This may reflect the fact that fewer opportunities and increased competition are more evident in larger cohorts than smaller ones, and may result in hopelessness and eventual suicide.

Systematic data collection of suicide attempt rates is rare. Estimates of adolescent suicide attempts in the United States range from approximately 8% in a study conducted in Oregon (Lewinsohn, Rhode, & Seeley, 1993) to 8.6% in a national survey of a representative sample of students in grades 9–12 collected by the Centers for Disease Control (1995a) using the Youth Risk Behavior Surveillance System. Based on 1988 data, Holinger (1990) estimated that over 15 000 adolescents between the ages of 10 and 19 attempted suicide and received medical attention. Several studies have attempted to calculate rates of suicide attempts seen in emergency departments. A rate of 140 per 100 000 was calculated based on suicide attempts in a suburban Chicago area (Christoffel, Marcus, Sagerman, & Bennett, 1988), while a rate of 316.8 per 100 000 was calculated in a suburban county of Atlanta (Birkhead, Galvin, Meehan, O'Carroll, & Mercy, 1993). Diekstra (1993) estimates a lifetime prevalence of attempted suicide for adolescents in the international community ranging from 2% to

20%. Because of the manner in which these statistics are collected, and because there is no central registry of suicide attempts, it is difficult to compare rates across countries, and changes in the rates over time are also difficult to interpret.

The WHO/EURO multicenter study collected data on attempted suicide in 15 European centers (Platt et al., 1992). Suicide attempt rates ranged from 72 per 100 000 in Leiden to 426 per 100 000 in Helsinki for men between the ages of 15 and 24 years. For women between the ages of 15 and 24 years, the rates ranged from 112 per 100 000 in Guipuzeon to 763 per 100 000 in Pontoise. The overall European rate for 15 to 19 year-old males was 106 per 100 000 and 323 per 100 000 for 15 to 19 year-old females. The highest adolescent rate was 911 per 100 000 in Pontoise followed by 791 per 100 000 in Szeged.

As regards suicide ideation, females report much higher rates than males in most countries of the world. Data collected in 1993 using the Youth Risk Behavior Surveillance Survey in the United States supported these findings (CDC, 1995b). Across all racial and ethnic groups, females reported more suicidal ideation than males.

5.18.5 ETIOLOGY: RISK FACTORS

There is no definitive underlying cause for suicide. However, there are a number of demographic (e.g., gender and race), psychiatric (e.g., certain mental disorders such as depression and conduct disorder; prior suicide attempts), biological (e.g., dysfunction of the serotoninergic system), and socio-environmental (access to lethal methods, e.g., firearms; exposure to suicidal behavior) factors which increase the risk of suicide. These risk factors will be reviewed in turn.

5.18.5.1 Gender

In all age groups, females attempt suicide more often than males, but males complete suicide more often than females. According to Centers for Disease Control data collected in the United States in 1992 (1995a), the suicide rate for adolescent males was 18.4 per 100 000 compared to a rate of 3.7 per 100 000 for adolescent females. Diekstra (1993) examined the suicide rates in 19 countries between 1970 and 1986. The rate for men increased across all age groups with a mean increase of 70% in the suicide rates in adolescents and young adults. For young women the increase was closer to 40%. One potential reason for the difference in suicide rates between males and females may be method preference. Males are more likely to use highly lethal suicide attempt methods whereas females are more likely to use less lethal methods, particularly drug overdoses (Sigurdson, Staley, Matas, Hildahl, & Squair, 1994). Although some drug overdoses can be lethal in high doses, most suicide attempts by drug overdose are reversible if brought to medical attention within a reasonable amount of time. In India and in Southeast Asia, where medical care is not always readily available, the majority of suicides are committed by women by overdose (Shaffer, 1988).

The difference in suicide methods between males and females has been linked to stereotypic sex role behavior. That is, men tend to delay expressing their distress and during this period of delay, find more lethal methods for suicide attempts, while females express their affect in a more immediate and sometimes impulsive fashion. There is some evidence to support this contention. When male adolescent suicide attempters were compared to female adolescent suicide attempters on measures of depression, hopelessness, suicidal ideation, and suicidal intent, the only differences between sexes were that males reported more final acts in anticipation of death and a greater degree of planning than the female attempters (Spirito et al., 1993).

5.18.5.2 Race

In the United States, adult Caucasians commit suicide more frequently than adult African-Americans, typically at a 3:1 ratio (NCHS, 1993). However, since the mid-1960s the suicide rate for adult African-American males has nearly tripled, and has doubled for adult African-American females. This increase has also been noted in adolescents, particularly males. For African-American adolescent males, the rate increased from 5.5 per 100 000 in 1980 to 14.8 per 100 000 in 1992, an increase of 164%. The suicide rate rose from 1.6 per 100 000 in 1987 to 1.9 per 100 000 in 1992 for African-American adolescent females, an increase of 19% (CDC, 1995a).

These differences in suicide rates by race have not been well studied. Gibbs and Hines (1989) hypothesized that there are protective factors in the African-American population, such as strong maternal family ties or church and fraternal organizations that increase social support and cohesion, thus decreasing the rate of suicide. Others note that African-American males die by other violent means besides suicide more frequently than whites, which may account for the larger rates of suicide in Caucasians than African-Americans (Gibbs &

Hines, 1989). The dramatic increase in the 1980s of African-American adolescent suicide rates has led some to speculate that if culture is a protective factor, the rates of suicide may be equalizing because social factors which promote deculturalization exist (Shaffer, Gould, & Hicks, 1994).

Hispanic youth have lower rates of suicide than Caucasians, although suicide was the third leading cause of death for Hispanic youth in 1990 (NCHS, 1993). Gender differences in suicidal behaviors seem to be less prominent among Hispanic teenagers (Spirito et al., 1993).

Very high rates of suicide have been estimated among Native American adolescents (26.3 per 100 000) (US Congress, Office of Technology Assessment, 1990). This is due, at least in part, to the much larger proportion of adolescents and young adults among Native Americans than Caucasians. In addition, the suicide rates vary greatly among different tribes (McIntosh, 1983–84). One troubling example of the problem of suicide among Native American adolescents is the Zuni tribe. The suicide rate among Zuni adolescents rose steadily from 5.6 per 100 000 in 1957 to 32.2 per 100 000 in 1989.

5.18.5.3 Psychiatric Disorders

Certain psychiatric disorders are common among adolescents who complete suicide. Approximately 90% of adolescents in the New York City area who completed suicide in one study had a prior psychiatric diagnosis (Shaffer et al., 1996). These findings are comparable to those reported previously in Pittsburgh (Brent et al., 1988) and in Finland (Marttunen, Aro, Henriksson, & Lonnqvist, 1991). The most common psychiatric diagnosis in the New York City study (Shaffer et al., 1996) was Mood Disorder, occurring at a rate (61%) somewhat higher than that reported in the Finnish national study (51%) and in Pittsburgh (49%). Bipolar disorder was uncommon in both the Finnish study and the New York City study. In the New York City study, there was also a much higher percentage of Disruptive Behavior Disorders among the adolescents than the Finnish national study.

Bipolar Disorder, Affective Disorder with co-morbidity (especially Attention Deficit Disorder, Substance Abuse, and Conduct Disorder), a lack of previous mental health treatment, and availability of firearms in the home differentiated 27 adolescents who had committed suicide from 56 psychiatric inpatients who had seriously considered or attempted suicide (Brent et al., 1988). Blumenthal and Kupfer

(1986) believe that the coexistence of the antisocial and depressive symptoms are a particularly high risk combination for adolescent suicide. A high rate of substance use in the male adolescents who completed suicide was found in the New York City study (Shaffer et al., 1996), where approximately 60% of the male adolescent suicide victims had one of the following risk factors: prior suicide attempt, mood disorder, and substance/alcohol use. Depression and substance abuse were the most common risk factors in Canadian youths age 15 to 24 years old (Sigurdson et al., 1994). Alcohol plays a prominent role in suicides among Alaskan natives (Hlady & Middaugh, 1988) and is particularly prevalent in tribes which have high adolescent suicide rates.

Some adolescents evidence no psychiatric disorder prior to suicide completion (Apter et al., 1993). These adolescents have been described as perfectionistic and rigid (Apter et al.), and more likely to have prior suicidal behavior, legal, or disciplinary problems, and family psychopathology (Brent, Perper, Moritz, Baugher, et al., 1993). Thus, it seems likely that pathology exists in this group, but is more covert and/or denied by the family.

There is limited research regarding personality characteristics and disorders among suicidal adolescents. In Finland, 32% of adolescents in a sample of completed suicides were diagnosed with a personality disorder (Marttunen et al., 1991). Antisocial Personality Disorder among males and Borderline Personality among both males and females were the most common diagnoses reported. One-third of 58 suicides between the ages of 15 to 19 years old in Sweden were diagnosed with Borderline Personality Disorder by psychological autopsy methods (Runeson & Beskow, 1991).

Psychiatric disorders have also been investigated among suicide attempters and ideators. There has been interest in determining whether adolescent suicide attempters have a higher rate of Borderline Personality Disorder than other adolescents. However, there have only been a few studies in this area using adolescent samples. Pfeffer, Newcorn, Kaplan, Mizruchi, and Plutchik (1988) examined factors associated with suicidal behavior in a chart review of the clinical diagnoses of 200 consecutively admitted adolescent psychiatric inpatients and found a positive association between suicidal behavior in adolescent females and Borderline Personality Disorder. Brent et al. (1993) reported on increased evidence of borderline personality disorder or traits among psychiatrically hospitalized suicide attempters compared to psychiatric controls who had never been suicidal.

Depression has also been implicated in suicidal ideation and attempts (Garrison, Jackson, Addy, McKeown, & Waller, 1991). Mood disorders, particularly depression, may be precursors to different types of suicidal behavior. However, it appears that other related difficulties (e.g., substance abuse or conduct problems), are often seen in combination with depressed mood. Substance use is also related to suicide attempts (Pfeffer et al., 1988) and is considered a risk factor for both attempted and completed suicide because it can affect multiple domains of functioning, (i.e., affective, cognitive, social, and behavioral; Shaffer, 1988). For example, alcohol may lower inhibition and lead to more impulsive and dangerous behaviors that result in death. When combined with depressed mood, substance abuse significantly increases the risk of suicide in vulnerable groups.

5.18.5.4 Prior Suicide Attempts

One of the best predictors of completed suicide is a previous suicide attempt (Spirito, Brown, et al., 1989; Diekstra, 1989). In their review of the literature, Shaffer and colleagues (1988) concluded that in approximately 20% of all suicides completed by male adolescents and 33% of all suicides completed by females, a history of a prior suicide attempt is evident. Among adolescents, male suicide attempters are much more likely than females to eventually complete suicide (Goldacre & Hawton, 1985; Otto, 1972). A previous attempt by active means, such as hanging or shooting, has also been found to be predictive of later completed suicide (Otto, 1972). In addition, it has been estimated that adolescents who attempted suicide are 8.1 times more likely to reattempt suicide than those who have never made a suicide attempt (Lewinsohn et al., 1993).

5.18.5.5 Biological Factors

The endocrine and neurotransmitter systems have been the major focus of research to determine whether biological correlates of suicide exist. Most of this research has been conducted with adults and is quite complex and methodologically complicated. Findings have been based on postmortem tissue analyses, brain chemistry, cerebrospinal fluid, and neuroendocrine correlates. Major findings are available in detailed reviews (Rifai, Reynolds, & Mann, 1992; Roy, 1994) and are briefly outlined in this chapter.

Serotonin is the major neurotransmitter that has been linked to suicidal behavior. Low levels of serotonin (5-HIAA) and 5-hydroxytrypto-phan (5-HTP) have been reported among suicide attempters and found to be related to impulsivity and aggressive behavior in both depressed and non-depressed samples (Roy, 1994; Traskman-Bandz et al., 1993). Seroto-nergic changes appear to be most strongly related to impulsive aggression and violent suicides (Mann et al., 1992). In another study (Nordstrom et al., 1994), low CSF levels of 5-HIAA were related to increased suicide risk following attempted suicide in depressed patients.

Several studies report that suicidal behavior is associated with low CSF concentrations of the dopamine metabolite, HVA. However, these findings seem to be applicable to depressed patients only. In a five year follow-up study (Roy, DeJong, & Linnoila, 1989), dopaminergic activity was shown to be related to repeat suicide attempts among depressed patients. The mechanism by which serotonin levels affect suicidal behavior is unknown, but environ-mental factors and other variables are most likely involved because many individuals with low CSF concentrations do not attempt suicide.

Although more research is needed to clarify the differential roles of various receptor sites and their relation to suicide, reduced serotonin levels are related to repeat suicide attempts, impulse control, and aggression in depressed and nondepressed samples. It also appears that the reduced activity of serotonin may be related to a higher risk of death by suicide following an unsuccessful suicide attempt. Although this area has promise, a lumbar puncture is necessary to gather a specimen of CSF, which limits its applicability to clinical care. There is a serotonin metabolite level that can be measured by urine sample, which may ultimately provide useful information regarding suicide risk. However, at present biological factors are not routinely assessed when evaluating suicidal behavior.

5.18.5.6 Method of Suicide: Firearms

In the United States, suicides are most commonly completed by using firearms (Hol-inger, 1990). In 1992, 64.9% of all suicides among people less than 25 years old were by firearms (CDC, 1995a). Hanging was the second most common suicide method. For 15–19 year-olds, the rate of suicide by firearms increased 81% between 1980 and 1992, probably reflect-ing greater access to firearms by adolescents. Guns have been shown to be twice as prevalent in the homes of adolescents who complete suicide compared to adolescents who either

attempt suicide or have other psychiatric disorders (Brent et al., 1991). However, the method of storing guns has no effect on suicide (Brent et al., 1991). When firearms are available in the home, suicidal adolescents will actively kill themselves at a rate 75 times higher than when firearms are not available at home (Brent et al.). The most common method of attempting suicide among adolescents is by drug overdose. Estimates range between 75% and 95% of subjects across a number of studies conducted in the United States (Spirito, Brown, 1989) and Britain (Hawton & Fagg, 1992).

5.18.5.7 Exposure

Another potential risk factor for completed suicide is previous exposure to suicidal behavior in the family or in the peer group. Shaffi, Carrigan, Whittinghill, and Derrick (1985) found that adolescents who complete suicide are significantly more likely to have been exposed to suicidal behavior in parents, rela-tives, or friends. The risk of completing suicide increases with having a family member who has committed suicide. Higher rates of suicide and suicide attempts have been noted in the relatives of suicide completers compared to community controls (Brent et al., 1994).

Not only does exposure lead to increased risk of completed suicide, but the risk of attempting suicide increases significantly if there is a family history of suicide attempts (Sorenson & Rutter, 1991). Adolescents who report that a peer attempted or completed suicide display higher levels of depression and more frequent suicidal behavior themselves than those with no such exposure (Hazell & Lewin, 1993). However, Brent, Perper, Moritz, Baugher et al. (1993) examined the psychiatric sequelae of the suicide of a peer and found that suicide attempt rates did not differ between those exposed and those unexposed. The exposed group demonstrated more suicidal ideation and depression than the unexposed group. At three-year follow-up, the exposed group had an increased incidence of depression, anxiety, and Post-traumatic Stress Disorder compared to the unexposed group, but the two groups did not differ on suicidal behavior (Brent, Moritz, Bridge, Perper, & Canobbio, 1996).

The findings with respect to familial cluster-ing of suicide and suicide attempts indicate that a genetically linked biological mechanism such as the serotonergic system may be involved. Alternatively, exposure may allow suicidal behavior to be modeled by family members who attempt or complete suicide. There are a number of studies (discussed in Section 5.18.7.7) in which family dysfunction increases the risk of suicidal behavior. Studies designed to differentiate the role of genetic and/or psychological mechanisms have yet to be conducted.

Adolescents may also be exposed to suicide indirectly via television or the news media. Several studies have demonstrated that a prominent report of a suicide in the media leads to an increase in suicides, particularly among young people, for one to two weeks following the news coverage (Shaffer, 1988; Phillips & Carstensen, 1986). In addition, exposure to a violent death, regardless of the means (e.g., homicide or car crash) increases the likelihood of subsequent suicides among youth in the community. It has been found that victims of high social status, deaths motivated by revenge, and failure of the media to report a victim's prior psychiatric disturbance increase the risk of imitation (Davidson, 1989; Davidson & Gould, 1989). Consequently, the Centers for Disease Control (1988) have developed guidelines for the media on reporting suicides.

There is also conflicting data regarding the relationship between fictional suicide stories and subsequent imitative suicides. Gould and Shaffer (1986) found increased suicide rates among adolescents in the New York City area two weeks before and two weeks after four television movies about suicide were broadcast. However, when the same movies were shown in California and Pennsylvania, albeit by only one station, which limited the audience and the impact, the findings were not replicated (Phillips & Paight, 1987).

5.18.6 DEVELOPMENTAL COURSE

The rates of suicide vary across development. Although rare, suicide rates among children 10 to 14 years old in the United States have been estimated to be on the rise, increasing two and a half times between 1970 and 1986, from 0.6 to 1.5 per 100 000 (US Bureau of the Census, 1990). As stated previously, the rate for adolescents increased from 8.5 to 10.9 per 100 000 between 1980 and 1992 (CDC, 1995a). Various investigators have emphasized the need to examine developmental risks and protective factors for suicide. Characteristic of this approach is an emphasis on the relation between suicidal behavior and developmental factors, for example, sociocognitive functioning, as opposed to chronological age. The range of developmental skills within a particular age group may vary greatly or fluctuate as a function of emotional distress (Jacobson et al., 1995).

Up to 1997, limited empirical work has examined suicide from a developmental per-

spective. However, McDowell and Stillion (1994) delineated several commonalities and differences in suicide across the lifespan. The commonalities include biological, psychological, cognitive, and environmental factors. With respect to biological factors, the serotonin hypothesis and gender differences described have been shown to transcend all ages (McDowell & Stillion, 1994). Psychological factors such as depression, low self-esteem, and hopelessness also contribute to suicide across the life span. Cognitive factors related to suicide across development include depressogenic thought patterns, such as cognitive rigidity, all-or-none thinking, and overgeneralization. In addition, perfectionism has been found to be a risk factor regardless of age (Hewitt, Flett, & Turnball-Donovan, 1992; Hewitt, Newton, Flett, & Callander, 1997). Regarding environmental factors, exit events (e.g., parental divorce), all types of abuse, and family stressors have been found to play a role in suicide for both children and adults, as has the presence of a means for completing suicide. Moreover, the precipitants of suicidal acts in young children (Pfeffer, Conte, Plutchik, & Jerrett, 1980) and adolescents (Spirito et al., 1989) are similar.

McDowell and Stillion (1994) also outlined suicide risk factors unique to young children and to adolescents. Risk factors for children younger than 15 years of age include impulsivity, a sense of inferiority, the expendable child syndrome, an immature view of death, and extreme levels of persistent family turbulence. With respect to impulsivity, suicidal behavior in young children has been found to be more violent and impulsive; for example, jumping or running out in front of a car (Joffe & Offord, 1983). Pfeffer et al. (1980) reported that jumping was the most common means of attempt among 6 to 12 year-old outpatient psychiatry patients. A sense of inferiority was used by McDowell and Stillion (1994) to refer to the Eriksonian concept of industry, or the need to develop confidence and positive self-regard. This concept is relevant to the findings in the literature regarding the relation between suicide and low self-esteem (e.g., Stillion, McDowell, & Shamblin, cited in McDowell & Stillion, 1994). The "expendable child syndrome" is a concept that refers to children whose parents communicate low regard and even hostility toward them to the extent that children believe they are expendable, which is related to the wish to die.

Concrete operational thinking, common in latency-aged children, has implications for the meaning and understanding of suicide in young children. Carlson et al. (1987) reported that although children between 8 and 12 years of age contemplate suicide, they have difficulty conceiving of the circumstances that might lead one to commit suicide and plan to carry it out. Similarly, young children's understanding of death, causality, and reversibility have important implications for suicidal behavior in this group (Jacobson et al., 1995). In addition, family problems have long been reported to be a more important factor for younger than older suicidal children because of the dependence of younger children on adult caregivers for survival (Otto, 1972). A particular family factor identified as a risk factor for children under 12 years of age is the presence of suicidal behavior in their parents (Pfeffer et al., 1980). With respect to suicide attempts, attempters younger than 14 years of age have been found to be more likely to leave a suicide note prior to an attempt and use hanging vs. ingestion as a means to attempt suicide (Garfinkel, Froese, & Hood, 1982).

Risk factors specific to adolescent suicide include the adolescent's mood state, the inability to develop a sense of identity, egocentrism, risk-taking behaviors, and social isolation (McDowell & Stillion, 1994). As discussed earlier, psychiatric diagnoses, particularly depression, conduct disorder, and substance abuse, are significant risk factors for suicide during adolescence. In addition, adolescents who have no sense of identity may not have the necessary level of self-competence to cope with the stressors that confront them during this period. Self-esteem has been found to be inversely related to suicidal ideation and behavior in both adolescent psychiatric patients and normal high school controls (Overholser, Adams, Lehnert, & Brinkman, 1995). Similarly, cognitive changes characterized by a renewed period of egocentrism may increase feelings of self-consciousness and consequently overgeneralization, such as that reported in depressive cognition patterns.

It has been suggested that a sense of invulnerability characterizes adolescents, and this has been hypothesized to lead to increased risk taking. Empirical studies of the relation between risk-taking behaviors and suicide have not yet been reported. Some studies have examined the role of interpersonal relationships and suicidal behavior. Peer relationship difficulties are one of the most common precipitants of suicide attempts in adolescence (Spirito et al., 1989), and suicidal adolescents have been found to be socially isolated and have poor peer relationships (King, Raskin, Gadowski, Butkus, & Opipari, 1990; Spirito et al. 1989). Adolescents are also more likely than younger children to mutilate themselves and make a planful suicide attempt (McDowell & Stillion, 1994).

5.18.7 CONCEPTUALIZATION AND CLINICAL FORMULATION OF ATTEMPTED SUICIDE

There is no standardized treatment for adolescent suicide ideators and attempters. Consequently, it is important to perform a comprehensive assessment in order to target in treatment those deficit areas that may trigger further survival behavior.

5.18.7.1 Multimodal Assessment

There are a number of important factors to consider when evaluating an adolescent who has just attempted suicide. One assessment model can be seen in Figure 1. This conceptual model is similar to a number of other models that have been hypothesized in the literature, and is based on the assumption that suicidal individuals display cognitive, behavioral, and emotional deficits which increase their risk of suicidal behavior at times of increased stress. Both the adolescent and his/her parents/guardians should be interviewed to complete the assessment.

Only one assessment model to date has been tested empirically. Based on epidemiologic data collected with a large sample of high school students, Lewinsohn, Rohde, and Seeley (1996) postulated a model which includes the constructs of psychopathology, environmental factors, interpersonal problems, and physical illness which affect cognitions/coping, leading to suicidal behavior. Using structural equation modeling, psychopathology had the strongest (0.34) direct effect on suicidal behavior. Physical health and environmental factors had small, but statistically significant, direct effects. All four constructs had statistically significant indirect effects on suicidal behavior via cognitive/coping style. Cognitive/coping style also had a direct effect on suicidal behavior (0.20). Tests of this model with clinical populations would be a useful contribution to the literature.

Assessment of the suicide attempter at the time of the attempt is critical in formulating an adequate treatment plan. Assessment should be conducted with both the adolescent and family members. Suicidal ideation preceding the attempt, as well as the reasons for the suicide attempt, must be investigated. The first goal of this evaluation is to determine whether the adolescent requires a psychiatric admission, usually based on continued suicidal ideation, a major psychiatric disorder that cannot be treated initially as an outpatient, or psychological or family factors that may place the adolescent at continued risk for immediate self-harm or a reattempt. The following areas are particularly important to assess: suicidal intent

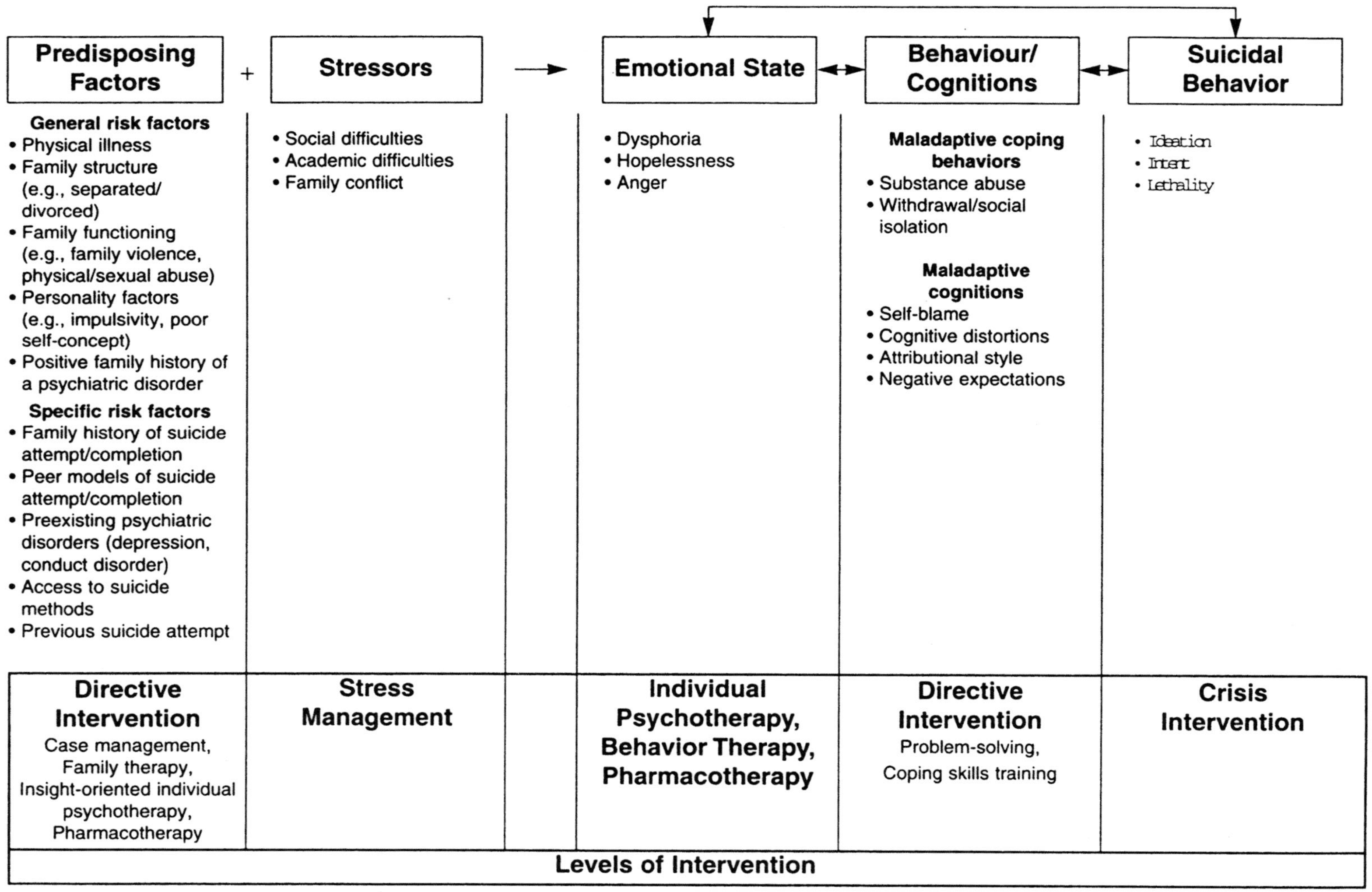

Predisposing Factors + **Stressors** → **Emotional State** ↔ **Behaviour/ Cognitions** ↔ **Suicidal Behavior**

Predisposing Factors

General risk factors
- Physical illness
- Family structure (e.g., separated/divorced)
- Family functioning (e.g., family violence, physical/sexual abuse)
- Personality factors (e.g., impulsivity, poor self-concept)
- Positive family history of a psychiatric disorder

Specific risk factors
- Family history of suicide attempt/completion
- Peer models of suicide attempt/completion
- Preexisting psychiatric disorders (depression, conduct disorder)
- Access to suicide methods
- Previous suicide attempt

Stressors
- Social difficulties
- Academic difficulties
- Family conflict

Emotional State
- Dysphoria
- Hopelessness
- Anger

Behaviour/Cognitions

Maladaptive coping behaviors
- Substance abuse
- Withdrawal/social isolation

Maladaptive cognitions
- Self-blame
- Cognitive distortions
- Attributional style
- Negative expectations

Suicidal Behavior
- Ideation
- Intent
- Lethality

Levels of Intervention

Directive Intervention
Case management, Family therapy, Insight-oriented individual psychotherapy, Pharmacotherapy

Stress Management

Individual Psychotherapy, Behavior Therapy, Pharmacotherapy

Directive Intervention
Problem-solving, Coping skills training

Crisis Intervention

Figure 1 An assessment model (*Adolescent Health Problems* (p.103), by Wallarden and Siegel, 1995, New York: Guilford Press. Copyright 1995 by Guilford Press. Reprinted with permission).

or reason for the suicide attempt; current coexisting stressors; preexisting psychiatric disorders; family history, particularly of suicidal behavior; previous suicidal behavior; self-stated coping strategies and social support; an evaluation of the risk of an immediate reattempt; and attitudes of the adolescent and family towards further mental health treatment (Hawton, 1986). These factors are elaborated on in the following sections.

5.18.7.2 Attempt Characteristics

The intent of the suicide attempt maybe the most important characteristic of the attempt to assess in clinical formation. Data from adolescents (Spirito et al., 1989) suggest that two aspects of suicidal intent, making plans prior to a suicide attempt and expected negative outcome, are the most important factors in determining high risk adolescents.

5.18.7.3 Emotional State

An adolescent's mental status at the time of the attempt, as well as premorbid psychological factors (particularly depression, hopelessness, and anger) are important to assess, both in terms of their individual impact and their contribution to a diagnosis of a specific psychiatric disorder. Depressed mood has been implicated in many studies of adolescent suicide attempters. Spirito et al. (1989) reviewed the literature and found very high rates of depressed affect among attempters, ranging from 30% to 82%, across studies in psychiatric inpatients, outpatients, and emergency department settings. The lowest rates were found in suicide attempters who were medically hospitalized.

Hopelessness may contribute to suicidal ideation and behavior above and beyond depression. Hopelessness refers to a negative attitude about future events, including a global expectation of negative future occurrences. Spirito, Williams, Stark, and Hart (1988) found higher levels of hopelessness among adolescent suicide attempters than among either nonsuicidal adolescents in an outpatient psychiatric clinic or normal control subjects. In a separate study, Spirito, Overholser, and Hart (1991) found higher levels of hopelessness in adolescent suicide attempters than in nonsuicidal psychiatrically hospitalized adolescents. Some studies (e.g., Robbins & Alessi, 1985) have reported that hopelessness among adolescents is associated with the number of suicidal gestures, the seriousness of suicidal intent, and the medical lethality of a suicide attempt. Hopelessness has also been shown to have a stronger relationship

to suicidal behavior than other factors, such as family dysfunction (Levy, Jurkovic, & Spirito, 1995). Gender effects on hopelessness (i.e., females report greater levels of hopelessness than males) have also been reported (Cole, 1989; Spirito, 1991). However, several studies have found comparable levels of hopelessness among adolescent suicide attempters and depressed adolescents (Brent, Kolko, Allan, & Brown, 1990; deWilde, Kienhorst, Diekstra, & Wolters, 1993).

Another important variable related to adolescent suicide attempts is anger. Anger has been shown to be more strongly related to suicidal ideation and behavior than depression (Cairns, Peterson, & Neckerman, 1988; Choquet & Menke, 1989). Repressed anger has also been shown to be highly correlated with hopelessness (Brown et al., 1991). When compared to normal adolescents, suicide attempters report an increased incidence of experiencing anger as well as higher levels of internalized anger (Lehnert, Overholser, & Spirito, 1994). Many adolescents report significant anger prior to their attempt (Hawton, O'Grady, Osborn, & Cole, 1982; Withers & Kaplan, 1987). These angry feelings may be expressed via verbal outbursts, but at other times the anger is repressed. Anger has also been associated with the seriousness of the suicide attempt (Gispert, Wheeler, Marsh, & Davis, 1985). In several studies, the strongest predictor of future suicidal tendencies and suicide reattempts was the level of anger at the time of the initial attempt (Myers, McCauley, Calderon, & Treder, 1991). At times, the anger and irritability so prominent in adolescent suicide attempters may be a symptom of depressive illness. At other times, anger and irritability may also be indicative of a conduct disorder. Indeed, a large proportion of childhood suicide attempters have been shown to exhibit assaultive and aggressive behavior independent of depression (Pfeffer, Plutchik, & Mizruchi, 1983). Thus, the origin of the aggressive and angry feelings must be differentiated on an individual basis.

5.18.7.4 Cognitive Variables

A negative attributional style (i.e., likelihood of attributing undesirable events to oneself or others, to unstable factors, or to global causes) has been found to be related to suicidal behavior in adults. Evidence in adolescents is more limited. The results of two studies of adolescents showed that suicide attempters were more likely than the nonsuicidal psychiatric patients to attribute good events to global causes and negative events to stable aspects of the environment (Rotheram-Borus, Trautmen, Dopkins, & Shrout, 1990; Spirito, Overholser et al., 1991). Although further study is needed, these data suggest that a maladaptive attributional style may be more related to overall level of psychopathology than specifically to suicidal behavior among adolescents.

Another cognitive factor which has been seen studied in suicidal adolescents is problem solving. Problem-solving deficits are important to investigate because the data have direct implications for the types of interventions that may be appropriate for this high-risk group. Female adolescent suicide attempters have been distinguished from nonsuicidal psychiatrically disturbed adolescents by their poorer interpersonal problem-solving ability and maladaptive attributional style (Rotheram-Borus et al., 1990). Sadowski and Kelley (1993) found that suicide attempters reported poor problem-solving orientation as well as less adequate problem-solving skills in general, than a comparison group of psychiatric patients and normal high school students. In addition, these adolescent suicide attempters reported less cognitive responding and deficits in initiating the problem-solving process than the other groups when confronted with problem situations. Suicidal children have also been found to use fewer active cognitive coping strategies than controls (Asarnow, Carlson, & Guthrie, 1987). Orbach, Rosenheim, and Mary (1987) compared psychiatrically hospitalized children with suicidal ideation and behavior to children with chronic medical illnesses and normal controls on the ability to generate alternative solutions to situations involving life and death. The suicidal children generated fewer alternatives than the normal or the chronically ill children. Among the suicidal children, those most attracted to death were least capable of generating effective alternative solutions. In a study comparing inpatient suicide attempters to controls, there was no difference in their ability to generate solutions to standardized personal problems (Wilson et al., 1995). However, when asked about how they coped with their most recent severe stressor, suicide attempters reportedly used fewer coping strategies and more maladaptive coping strategies than the controls.

Perfectionism is another cognitive characteristic which has been investigated in regard to adolescent suicidal behavior. Both self-oriented and socially prescribed perfectionism were found to be positively related to hopelessness in adolescent psychiatric inpatients (Hewitt et al., 1997). However, only the relation between socially prescribed perfectionism and suicidal ideation attained significance. Moreover, only socially prescribed perfectionism contributed

unique variance to suicidal ideation when the effects of age, gender, self-oriented perfectionism, and hopelessness were controlled.

In summary, cognitive deficits such as poor problem solving and cognitive distortions appear more frequently in a significant portion of adolescent suicide attempters compared to non-suicidal adolescents. It is unclear whether these are temporary deficits evident at the time of acute stress, or more enduring characteristics. In either case, it is important for clinicians to identify and intervene in these deficit areas when they present.

5.18.7.5 Maladaptive Coping Strategies

Social isolation and avoidance behavior are maladaptive coping strategies reported by adolescent suicide attempters. More adolescent suicide attempters report using social withdrawal when faced with a problem than normal control subjects (Spirito Overkolser, et al., 1989). However, the use of social withdrawal among adolescent suicide attempters is similar to that found among nonsuicidal psychiatrically hospitalized adolescents (Spirito, Francis, Overholser, & Frank, 1996). Both groups reported using social withdrawal as a maladaptive coping strategy. These findings suggest that it is important for clinicians to address avoidance behavior. For example, adolescents who attempt suicide maybe similar to nonsuicidal adolescents in the sense that they attempt to use a number of coping strategies prior to the suicide attempt. However, they may use more maladaptive cognitive strategies and at a certain point, withdraw from social contact, which may increase the risk of a suicide attempt. This may be a sequence effect; adolescent suicide attempters may initially use adaptive coping strategies, then move on to maladaptive strategies, and finally withdraw prior to an attempt.

Attachment behavior has also been investigated as a precursor to social withdrawal. In a sample of both inpatient and outpatient adolescent psychiatric patients, 86% had attachment-related trauma when they were young (Adam, Sheldon-Keller, & West, 1996). These traumatic family experiences, including separation and abuse, may affect the development of attachment behavior, which may be a mediating mechanism for suicidal behavior, especially among female adolescents (Adam et al., 1996).

Substance use and abuse can be considered another maladaptive coping behavior. Studies in the US report significant rates of substance abuse ranging from 23% to as high as 42% among adolescent suicide attempters (Spirito,

Brown et al., 1989). Work by Hawton & Fagg (1992), found elevated rates (39% males, 21% females) of consumption of alcohol a few hours before the attempt among British suicide attempters, but rates were not as high as typical rates reported in the US. In a large survey of high school students, alcohol use was associated with an increased suicide attempt rate, particularly among Caucasian adolescents (Adcock, Nagy, & Simpson, 1991). For Caucasian adolescents, the suicide attempt risks increased from 9% to 27% while among African-Americans it increased from 10% to 21%. Substance use, if it is of a chronic nature, can lead to significant psychosocial problems which eventually result in a suicide attempt. If substance use precedes a suicide attempt, it may interfere with problem solving and thus be a proximal factor to the suicide attempt.

5.18.7.6 Physical and Sexual Abuse

A history of physical or sexual abuse has been associated with suicidal behaviors in a number of studies. In a survey of almost 4000 predominantly white adolescents in a suburban/rural area, attempted suicide was reported by 4.7% of the physically-abused students, 5.1% of the sexually-abused students, and 9.2% of students who reported both physical and sexual abuse (Hibbard, Ingersoll, & Orr, 1990). Garnefski, Dieskta, and de Heus (1992) compared a sample of predominantly Caucasian high school students with a history of suicidal behavior to high school students with no such history. Of the female attempters, 51% reported a history of physical abuse and 32% had experienced sexual abuse. Of the females who did not attempt suicide, 24% reported a history of physical abuse and 7% reported sexual abuse. Of the male attempters, 22% had experienced sexual abuse compared to 2% of the non-attempters. This study did not include truant or dropout students, who may have an even higher incidence of physical and sexual abuse. A comparison of adolescent suicide attempters with depressed and nondepressed adolescents with no history of suicide attempts revealed that suicidal adolescents were more likely to report a history of sexual abuse (33%) than depressed (21%) or nondepressed adolescents (5%) who had not attempted suicide (deWilde et al., 1992). More depressed individuals (29%) reported physical abuse than suicide attempters (23%) or nondepressed adolescents (7%).

Deykin, Alpert, and McNamara (1985) examined adolescent suicide attempters who were identified following an emergency department visit and a matched comparison group of adolescents treated for medical conditions unrelated to suicide attempts. The suicide attempters were three to six times more likely than the comparison group to have had contact with state social services departments for an abuse-related incident. No information regarding reasons for social service involvement was available. The relationships between prior physical or sexual abuse and subsequent health-risk behaviors and suicide attempts were examined in a nonclinical sample of 600 high school students (Riggs, Alario, & McHorney, 1990). Those students who were victims of previous sexual maltreatment were three times more likely to have attempted suicide and those students with a history of physical maltreatment were five times more likely than those without a history of maltreatment.

Psychiatrically-hospitalized adolescents categorized as attempters, ideators, or nonsuicidal (i.e., those admitted for reasons other than suicide attempts and with no current suicide ideation) have been studied as to the effects of abuse (Shaunesey, Cohen, Plummer, & Berman, 1993). Females were more likely than males to have histories of both types of abuse, or sexual abuse alone, and females with past sexual abuse had a higher frequency of suicide attempts than females with no history of sexual abuse. In addition, adolescents with a high frequency of abuse (i.e., 10 or more events) had made significantly more suicide attempts.

5.18.7.7 Family Functioning

A number of studies have shown higher rates of family disturbance in suicide attempters compared to psychiatric controls (Mitchell & Rosenthal, 1992) and the severity of suicidal intent has been related to the degree of family dysfunction (Brent et al., 1990). Suicidal psychiatric inpatient adolescents and suicidal high school students report more distress and family dysfunction than nonsuicidal high school students (Adams, Overholser, & Lehnert, 1994). In a sample of high school students, family dysfunction influenced suicidal behavior indirectly through depression (Martin, Rozanes, Pearce, & Allison, 1995). In a large study of high school students, adolescents who reported a history of a suicide attempt also reported more frequent stresses related to their parents and more physical abuse, runaways, and family disruption than those who had not had previous attempts (Wagner, Cole, & Schwartzman, 1995).

Stressful life events as triggers of suicidal behavior have been of interest to many clinicians and researchers. Adams, Overholser, and Spirito (1994) examined both intrafamilial and extrafamilial life events. Hospitalized adolescent suicide attempters reported the loss of a family member due to death or divorce more often than high school controls (Adams, Overholser, & Spirito, 1994). Adolescent suicide attempters also reported a greater number of "exit events" such as parental divorce and chronic life stressors compared to nonsuicidal adolescents. Suicidal ideation was directly related to stressful life events among the female suicide attempters. The number of exit events was positively related to hopelessness and suicidal ideation among adolescent females. Although suicide risk seems to increase when elevated levels of stressful events exist, a high degree of family cohesion may mediate the effects of these stressful events (Rubenstein, Heeren, Housman, Rubin, & Stechler, 1989).

5.18.8 PSYCHOSOCIAL TREATMENTS

Treatment for adolescent suicidal behavior is quite varied and there is no one standard treatment approach for this group. A number of clinical articles have addressed the treatment of suicide ideators, focusing mainly on the management of the acute suicidal episode with little emphasis on ongoing treatment. A limited number of articles have been written on the treatment of adolescents following a suicide attempt. The majority of this work has also focused on short-term management of the adolescent following the suicidal crisis. Finally, interventions that focus on adolescents that have psychiatric disorders common to suicidal behavior, such as depression (e. g., Lewinsohn, Clarke, Hops, & Andrews, 1990), might also be considered as treatment approaches for adolescent suicidal behavior.

5.18.8.1 Suicide Ideators

Fremouw, de Perczel, and Ellis (1990) have outlined in great detail the principles for managing a suicide ideator. In particular, four principles are advocated: therapeutic activism, restoring hope, delaying of suicidal impulses, and environmental interventions. In regard to therapeutic activism, increasing the availability of the therapist during the suicidal crisis, working directly with the adolescent on problem solving and, when necessary, directing the adolescent and parents in how to manage a suicidal crisis are recommended (Fremouw et al., 1990). By actively working with the adolescent on how to solve problems and by taking one problem at time and generating solutions, the therapist can help to restore hope in what appears to be a hopeless situation. With

adolescents, there are often acute conflicts with a family member, particularly parents. It is important for the therapist to actively assist in resolving the conflicts among family members at least for the short term and emphasize that the adolescent can make it through the current stress no matter how painful it seems. Environmental interventions are often necessary, such as working with the family on coping with adolescent suicidal behavior. It is important to involve parents in actively monitoring the adolescent's behavior. At the same time, removing pills and/or firearms from the home is very important. Finally, prior to the completion of a session, it is important for the therapist to work with the adolescent and their family on structuring the time between sessions to minimize the possibility of repeat attempts.

One particularly helpful problem-solving technique in managing suicide ideators has been described by Schneidman (1985). When confronted with a suicidal client, Schneidman suggests that the therapist and the patient write down a list of what might be done in the situation, including committing suicide. Then the therapist asks the patient to rank order the options from the most difficult and fatal (i.e., suicide) to the least difficult solutions. The therapist then begins to discuss the least difficult and painful solutions until the adolescent and the therapist find a solution, even a partial solution, that is acceptable to the adolescent. Schneidman contends that this approach has a calming effect on the adolescent because the therapist is helping to outline alternatives that the adolescent, due to cognitive restriction, was unable to generate. By discussing various options and their pros and the cons, progress is made because suicide is no longer the only solution.

5.18.8.2 Suicide Attempters

Adolescent suicide attempters have a significantly higher reattempt rate and risk of eventual completed suicide than adolescents who have not previously attempted suicide (Lewinsohn, Rohde, & Seeley, 1994). In 1997, there are no standard interventions for adolescent suicide attempters. Rather, intervention is typically developed on an individual basis, according to the symptoms occurring at the time of the suicide attempt.

The large majority of adolescents who attempt suicide can be treated effectively as outpatients. However, treatment noncompliance is particularly problematic among adolescent suicide attempters. Spirito et al. (1992) followed adolescent suicide attempters for three months after they were evaluated in an emergency department and discharged to outpatient care and found that 18% never attended an outpatient appointment, 11% went only once, 3% went twice, and 23% only went to three or four sessions. Even more striking are the results obtained by Trautman, Stewart, and Morishima (1993) indicating that adolescent suicide attempters drop out of outpatient psychotherapy at a much faster rate than nonsuicidal adolescents. Suicide attempters attended a median of three sessions before dropout, while nonsuicidal adolescents attended approximately 11 sessions.

This high rate of dropout of adolescent suicide attempters from psychotherapy suggests that clinicians who are evaluating adolescents immediately after a suicide attempt should take certain steps to ensure that outpatient therapy is accomplished following discharge. These include setting a specific date and time for the follow-up appointment; thoroughly explaining the reasons for continued outpatient care; explaining why therapy is important in the long run; and reviewing the likely goals and length of outpatient therapy (Jellinek, 1978). The adolescent's and their parents'/guardians' expectations for therapy should also be reviewed. Where resistance or hesitancy is noted, the clinician should address these problems. For example, if there is concern that the parents will not be able to get the adolescent to attend therapy, then problem-solving steps and potential alternatives to ensure the adolescent receives therapy should be reviewed with parents. In order to enhance compliance, it is preferable to discuss brief treatment (e.g., four sessions) with the option of continuation based on progress during that time. Asking adolescents and their parents to attend four treatment sessions before making a decision about further ongoing psychotherapy may be the most realistic approach to enhancing treatment compliance. Setting a specific time limit on psychotherapy has been shown to be more useful in ensuring treatment attendance than more open-ended treatment contracts (Sledge, Moras, Hartley, & Levine, 1990). As a final step, prior to discharge after a suicide attempt, the clinician might generate several potential stressors and ask how the adolescent would cope with those stressors if they were encountered. A directive, problem-solving approach will help the adolescent, particularly when discharged into a stressful situation. This type of "emergency plan" should focus on practical steps the adolescent should take if any suicidal feelings reemerge.

In developing a treatment plan for adolescent suicide attempters, therapists must rely on guidelines derived from either theoretical considerations or clinical care. Empirically-based guidelines specifically for suicide attempters are not available. In the initial therapy sessions with someone who has recently attempted suicide, a crisis intervention plan needs to be activated. The therapist must be continuously available, limit access to suicide methods, reestablish a no-suicide agreement if necessary, and ensure that the adolescent is not socially isolated, either from peers or from family. While managing the crisis using these guidelines, the therapist must also try to understand the reasons for the suicidal behavior and establish a working alliance with the adolescent in order to both reduce the risk of further suicidal behavior and maintain the adolescent in treatment (Berman & Jobes, 1991). Adolescents should be prepared, for example via role playing, for situations that may arise in the future that may elicit suicidal feelings. This approach can help prepare them for difficult circumstances as well as reduce the possibility of relapse.

The exact nature of treatment will vary according to the adolescent's presenting problems, the training and theoretical orientation of the therapist, and the adolescent's reactions to therapy. In general, however, there are a number of principles of psychotherapy with suicidal clients which should be observed no matter what the specific nature of treatment. In addition to those described above, these principles include maintaining an empathic but objective view of the suicidal adolescent, thoroughly understanding the motives of the suicidal behavior, continual reassessment and modification of hopelessness, assessment and modification of cognitive rigidity which impairs problem-solving, and education of the adolescent's family regarding suicide and suicidal behavior (Blumenthal & Kupfer, 1986). Once the crisis has passed, the feelings of depression and hopelessness associated with the suicidal behavior may begin to be addressed. The therapist can move from understanding the emotions that accompanied this suicidal behavior to specific problem-solving techniques that help to generate more effective ways of coping with life stressors as well as additional suicidal feelings that may arise in the future. In addition, after a short course of treatment, occasional booster sessions to help suicidal adolescents have some continuing contact with a therapist and review coping skills may be helpful in preventing additional suicidal behavior.

Although empirical data does not exist, several specific treatment modalities have been suggested for use with suicide attempters. First, cognitive therapy has been suggested as a possible treatment of choice for suicide attempters because it is highly structured and systematic. The cognitive distortions often evident in adolescent suicide attempters can be addressed directly using such a treatment approach. One goal of treatment is to help the adolescent become more aware of the relationships between their thoughts, emotions, and behaviors. Adolescents can begin to monitor their thoughts that lead to depressive cognitions and begin to challenge the validity of negative thought patterns (Bedrosian & Epstein, 1984). A number of cognitive techniques specifically useful for suicidal persons have been described (Freeman & Reinecke, 1993). These include reattribution of blame for the suicide precipitants, "decatastrophizing" (re-evaluating whether the adolescent is overestimating the "catastrophic" nature of their problems), making a list of pros and cons in regards to the circumstances precipitating the suicidal behavior, listing options and alternatives, "scaling" the severity of the events (e.g., from one to 100) to prevent the adolescent from conceptualizing everything as "black and white," and thought stopping.

One cognitive approach advocated by numerous clinicians as being helpful for suicidal patients is problem solving. As discussed above, therapy with suicidal adolescents often involves active teaching of new coping skills. Problem-solving therapy can help teach adolescents new ways of conceptualizing their problems and generating alternatives, because these adolescents often are unable to generate alternatives on their own. A description of the problem-solving approach with adolescent suicide attempters can be found in Brent and Kolko (1990). One focus of problem-solving is on interpersonal areas. Adolescents may at times use suicide attempts in a coercive manner for interpersonal gain. Thus, interpersonal problem solving to improve peer and family relationships can be effective. One behavioral approach to complement problem-solving efforts is to use social skills training for those adolescents who are particularly deficient in basic social skills which affect their peer relationships. Group therapy has been suggested as a potentially useful modality for treating adolescent suicide attempters. The group format can be helpful in teaching social skills and problem-solving skills as well as in reducing isolation and stigma associated with suicidal behavior.

Family therapy is often advocated as a means to deal with the intense conflict within families which can lead to maladaptive actions, including suicidal behavior (Richman, 1979). Family therapy itself helps to shift focus away from the individual adolescent, which in turn allows conflictual issues which have contributed to the development of the suicidal behavior to be investigated (Richman, 1979). Family therapy

programs emphasizing communication and problem-solving skills that have been used with other high-risk adolescents (e.g., Robin, 1981) are applicable to work with families of adolescent suicide attempters. A six session cognitive-behavioral family therapy approach for adolescent suicide attempters has been described by Rotheram-Borus, Piacentini, Miller, Graae, and Castro-Blanco (1994). This treatment approach is very structured and includes a number of activities designed to create a positive atmosphere among family members, teach problem-solving strategies to all family members, shift the emphasis of the family to a concept of difficult situations as opposed to difficult family members (i.e., the adolescent), and enhance the confidence of the family members in mental health treatment. A number of cognitive techniques such as restructuring and reframing are used in this treatment approach as well as behavioral contracting, therapist modeling, and role playing. Outcome data are still being collected on this promising treatment approach.

5.18.8.3 Secondary Prevention of Suicidal Behavior in High-risk Groups

Another approach to reducing suicidal behavior is to study well-defined groups that are known to be at higher risk for suicide. These groups, such as runaways, Native Americans, adolescents who come from families with a history of suicidal behavior, adolescents who have been diagnosed with major depression, and surviving friends of adolescents who have completed suicide, often have significantly higher rates of suicidal behavior in their immediate or more distant history compared to other adolescents. Thus, interventions designed to help the overall functioning of high-risk groups may also have an effect on suicidal behavior. Unfortunately, few studies have specifically observed the effects of interventions on suicidal behavior. Rotheram-Borus and Bradley (1991) reported on an intervention with suicidal runaways seen in community shelters that resulted in reduced rates of suicide attempts when compared to the agency rate prior to implementation of the program.

Intervention programs specifically tailored for Native Americans must be based on an understanding of the cultural values and social factors that affect suicidal behaviors. For example, an intervention for Native American adolescents who attempted suicide and were living at a boarding school has been described (Ward, 1984). Tribal elders conducted group discussions about leadership in an attempt to reduce suicidal behavior. Interventions have also been conducted with Native Americans who have been incarcerated, in residential alcohol treatment programs, or school dropouts. However, these programs have not been empirically evaluated nor was suicidal behavior a specific outcome measure.

There have been several empirical treatment trials for other psychiatric disorders relevant to suicidal youth (e.g., depressed, substance abusing, and conduct disordered youth). However, suicidal behavior has not been typically examined at follow-up. It is important for researchers conducting interventions in these areas to investigate the effects of the interventions on suicidal behavior. Another area of treatment research that may have relevance for the treatment of adolescent suicidal behavior is cognitive-behavioral treatment of Borderline Personality Disorder. Among suicide attempters, especially adults, self-injury is common. Conversely, individuals diagnosed with Borderline Personality Disorder very often display suicidal behavior. Thus, for adolescent suicide attempters who demonstrate repetitive suicidal behaviors, treatment approaches advocated for Borderline Personality Disorder may be useful. However, these interventions have yet to be tested with adolescent populations.

5.18.8.4 Primary Prevention of Suicidal Behavior

Suicide awareness programs have been advocated as a way to help adolescents become more sensitive to identifying a peer in suicidal crisis and helping the suicidal teen get the professional assistance that is needed. Thus, these programs may promote effective coping strategies in adolescents. Despite their intuitive appeal, the efficacy of these suicide prevention programs is, at best, modest. Shaffer et al. (1990) studied the effects of three different school-based prevention programs and found a significant increase in the proportion of students who admitted to personal difficulties, suicidal thoughts, or the need for professional help. A study of a 14-hour experiential program in Israel (Orbach & Bar-Joseph, 1992) reported a mild reduction of suicidal feelings and hopelessness. Girls seemed to benefit more than boys, and those students with greater suicidal tendencies improved more than their peers. Other studies suggest that knowledge may improve from such educational efforts, but that attitudes about suicide and behavior are largely unaffected immediately following the education (Shaffer et al., 1990; Spirito, Overholser, Ashworth, Morgan, & Benedict-Drew,

1988) and at 18-month follow-up (Vieland, Whittle, Garland, Hicks, & Shaffer, 1991). Kalafat and Elias (1994) did find a positive change in attitudes towards help-seeking and intervening with trusted peers. However, suicide awareness programs may be viewed most negatively by adolescents who have made a prior suicide attempt (Shaffer, Garland, Underwood, & Whittle, 1987). Another intervention program helped high-risk students but was no more effective than an assessment-only condition (Shaffer et al., 1987).

To be most helpful, specific programs targeting particular groups of adolescents (e.g., males vs. females, attempters vs. non-attempters, depressed vs. nondepressed) may need to be developed (Overholser, Hemstreet, Spirito, & Vyse, 1989). Alternatively, prevention programs that focus on general mental health interventions such as social skills training, problem solving, crisis management, and anger control may be more beneficial than programs focusing only on suicide (Berman & Jobes, 1991). Shaffer et al. (1988) reviewed the literature and found that only a minority of school-based programs were designed to improve teenagers' coping skills by training in stress management. For adolescents with no psychiatric disorders, the examination of maladaptive methods used when faced with difficult life situations and establishment of programs to improve problem-solving and coping skills may be helpful (Hawton, 1986).

5.18.9 PSYCHOPHARMACOLOGY

Psychotropic medication should be considered as a possible treatment modality for all adolescent suicidal behavior. At times, medication is clearly indicated for a particular psychiatric disorder such as major depression or bipolar affective disorder. At other times, medications may be helpful in reducing acute symptomology which, in turn, may improve the adolescent's acceptance and receptivity to other psychotherapies (Berman & Jobes, 1991). Of course, prescribing medications for suicidal adolescents requires careful monitoring, particularly for those adolescents thought to be at higher risk for reattempts. However, there have not been specific drug trials that have examined effects of medication on the functioning of suicide attempters.

5.18.10 EFFICACY/EFFECTIVENESS OF TREATMENTS

There have been several empirical treatment studies examining different therapy approaches with adult suicide attempters. Outpatient therapy and outreach following a suicide attempt have been found to result in fewer reattempts (Welu, 1977). Other studies have not found differences in reattempts after outreach programs (Gibbons, Butler, Urwin, & Gibbons, 1978). Lieberman and Eckman (1981) compared behavior therapy to insight-oriented psychotherapy in adult psychiatric inpatients following a suicide attempt. There was no difference in the reattempt rate between the two groups, although the behavior therapy group had significantly less suicide ideation and fewer suicide threats. In a 1990 study, cognitive-behavioral treatment was found to be slightly superior to standard care in reducing repeat attempts during a 6-month treatment course of adult suicide attempters (Salkovkis, Atha, & Storer, 1990). A similar treatment protocol found a reduction in hopelessness at follow-up, but no differences between groups that received a cognitive-behavioral treatment and nondirective treatment on suicidal ideation and intention at follow-up (Patsiokas & Clum, 1985).

There have been very few empirical trials of treatment with adolescent suicide attempters. Deykin, Hsieh, Joshi, and McNamara (1986) conducted randomized outreach intervention with adolescent suicide attempters after they had been seen in an emergency department. Social work follow-up with the families was offered to help the adolescents keep their follow-up appointments, to provide support, and explore additional services for the adolescents. The suicide attempters in the experimental group were twice as likely as controls to comply with recommendations for other services. In addition, they had fewer visits in the emergency department for suicidal behavior and follow-up. However, there was no difference in repeat suicide attempts after adjusting for prior history of suicidal behavior. The use of group therapy with adolescents with a history of suicidal behavior has also been described. Ross and Motto (1984) conducted a 35 session group over a 40-week period. The goals of the group treatment included providing a peer and professional support system, teaching ways to deal with stress and dysphoria, improving self-image, and teaching group members how to befriend others. At two-year follow-up, none of the 14 members of the group contacted had made further suicide attempts.

5.18.11 FUTURE DIRECTIONS FOR RESEARCH AND PRACTICE

The significant international differences in adolescent suicide rates are not fully understood and need to be investigated further. Attempted suicide in adolescence is a much more frequent phenomena than completed suicide, but the epidemiologic knowledge base on attempted suicide is quite limited, both nationally and internationally. The World Health Organization is attempting to establish a more systematic data collection method regarding suicide attempts, and similar systems have been advocated by the Centers for Disease Control. Greater knowledge of the epidemiology of attempted suicide is important because it offers the potential to reach adolescents demonstrating suicidal behavior early in the spectrum of suicidality, and thus potentially having a greater effect on future lethal suicidal behavior.

The risk factors for completed suicide have been investigated fairly well. One area that deserves more attention is the influence of family and peers on adolescent suicidal behavior. A greater understanding in this area may lead to more primary prevention strategies and a subsequent reduction in suicide and suicidal behavior. As reviewed above, it is clear that the majority of adolescents who complete suicide have a diagnosable psychiatric disorder. The mental health field is in the early stages of its development of well-tested and effective treatment programs for the major psychiatric disorders related to adolescent suicidal behaviors, such as depression and substance use. Both psychosocial and psychopharmacologic treatments used for these psychiatric disorders are adopted from adult studies. As the mental health field advances and conducts more empirical research specifically looking at child and adolescent psychiatric disorders, the benefits of learning how to treat these disorders effectively will undoubtedly apply not only to the major symptoms of the disorder, but also to the associated symptoms such as suicidality.

Specific interventions designed to reduce adolescent suicidal behavior are few and far between. Although suicide attempters are a high-risk group in need of treatment, treatment proves particularly difficult with this population. Not only is treatment compliance a problem, but there is no such thing as standard psychotherapeutic care for a suicide attempter. This is probably due to the heterogeneous nature of the suicide attempters in this population. However, it would appear that future research should focus on testing at least some minimum guidelines for the treatment of suicide attempters in the months following a suicide attempt.

Secondary prevention of suicidal behavior is another area where clinical research is important. Intervention programs that might be tested in future research include services for populations at high risk for suicide, such as runaways, depressed adolescents, friends of adolescents who have completed suicide, and adolescents in families with a strong history of suicidal behavior. Primary prevention programs aimed at improving self-esteem and problem-solving skills in schools have the potential to improve mental health and possibly reduce the onset of suicidal behavior.

It is clear that approaches to both intervention and prevention of suicidal behavior among adolescents must incorporate a number of different perspectives. Such multi-pronged approaches will be necessary to advance clinical treatment and research in this area. Collaboration between researchers and clinicians in the field of adolescent suicidal behavior may improve our understanding of suicidal behavior and the interaction of environmental, psychological, and biological factors that need to be addressed in these adolescents.

5.18.12 SUMMARY

This chapter has provided an overview of the factors which contribute to both completed suicide in adolescence and/or attempted suicide in adolescence. Females attempt suicide much more frequently than males, while males complete suicide much more frequently than females. Caucasians attempt and complete suicide more often than members of other races. The most common psychiatric disorders implicated in suicide are depression, conduct disorder, and substance abuse. Comorbidity is often evident. Adolescents who have made a prior suicide attempt are at much greater risk for eventual completed suicide than those adolescents without a prior attempt. Use of a firearm in a suicide attempt greatly increases the risk of completing suicide. Prior exposure to suicidal behavior also increases the risk of suicidal behavior.

For adolescents who attempt suicide, a model for comprehensive assessment was presented. This model includes emotional (anger, depression, and hopelessness), cognitive (attributional style, problem solving, and perfectionism), and family factors. Treatments for suicidal behavior are in their infancy. Efficacy of the existing treatments has not been established. Interventions that focus on problem solving and affect management appear promising and in need of future research.

5.18.13 REFERENCES

Adam, K., Sheldon-Keller, A., & West, M. (1996). Attachment, organization and history of suicidal behavior in clinical adolescents. *Journal of Consulting and Clinical Psychology, 64*, 264–272.

Adams, D., Overholser, J., & Spirito, A. (1994). Stressful life events related to adolescent suicide attempts. *Canadian Journal of Psychiatry, 39*, 43–48.

Adams, D., Overholser, J., & Lehnert, R. (1994). Perceived family functioning and adolescent suicidal behavior. *Journal of the American Academy of Child and Adolescent Psychiatry, 33*, 498–507.

Adcock, A., Nagy, S., & Simpson, J. (1991). Selected risk factors in adolescent suicide attempts. *Adolescence, 26*, 818–828.

Apter, A., Bleich, A., King, R., Kron, S., Fluch, A., Kotter, M., & Cohen, D. J. (1993). Death without warning? A clinical postmortem study of suicide in 43 Israeli adolescent males. *Archives of General Psychiatry, 50*, 138–142.

Asarnow, J., Carlson, G., & Guthrie, D. (1987). Coping strategies, self-perceptions, hopelessness, and perceived family environments in depressed and suicidal children. *Journal of Consulting and Clinical Psychology, 53*, 361–366.

Beck, A. T., Schuyler, D., & Herman, I. (1974). Development of suicidal intent scales. In A. T. Beck, H. L. P. Resnik, & D. J. Lettiere (Eds.), *The prediction of suicide* (pp. 45–56). Philadelphia: Charles Press.

Bedrosian, R., & Epstein, N. (1984). Cognitive therapy of depressed and suicidal adolescents. In H. Sucak, A. Ford, & N. Rushforth (Eds.), *Suicide in the young* (pp. 345–366). Boston: L. John Wright.

Berman, A. L., & Jobes, P. A. (1991). The treatment of the suicidal adolescent. *Adolescent suicide. Assessment and intervention* (pp. 163–225). Washington, DC: American Psychological Association.

Birkhead, G., Galvin, V., Meehan, P., O'Carroll, P., & Mercy, J. (1993). The emergency department in the surveillance of attempted suicide: Findings and methodological considerations. *Public Health Reports, 108*, 323–331.

Blumenthal, S. J., & Kupfer, D. J. (1986). Generalizable treatment strategies for suicidal behavior. *Annals of the New York Academy of Science, 487*, 327–340.

Brent, D. (1987). Correlates of the medical lethality of suicide attempts in children and adolescents. *Journal of the American Academy of Child and Adolescent Psychiatry, 26*, 87–89.

Brent, D., & Kolko, D. (1990). The assessment and treatment of children and adolescents at risk for suicide. In S. Blumenthal & D. Kupfer (Eds.), *Suicide over the life cycle: Risk factors, assessment, and treatment of suicidal patients* (pp. 253–302). Washington, DC: American Psychiatric Press.

Brent, D., Kolko, D., Allan, N., & Brown, R. (1990). Suicidality in affectively disordered adolescent inpatients. *Journal of the American Academy of Child and Adolescent Psychiatry, 29*, 586–593.

Brent, D., Moritz, G., Bridge, J., Perper, J., & Canobbio, R. (1996). Long-term impact of exposure to suicide: A three-year controlled follow-up. *Journal of the American Academy of Child and Adolescent Psychiatry, 35*, 646–653.

Brent, D., Perper, J., Allman, C., Moritz, G., Wartella, M., & Zelenak, J. (1991). The presence and availability of firearms in the homes of adolescent suicides: A case-control study. *Journal of the American Medical Association, 266*, 2989–2995.

Brent, P. A., Perper, J. A., Goldstein, C. E., Kolko, D. J., Allan, M. J., Allman, C. J., & Zelenak, J. P. (1988). Risk factors for adolescent suicide: A comparison of adolescent suicide victims with suicidal inpatients. *Archives of General Psychiatry, 45*, 581–588.

Brent, P. A., Perper, J. A., Moritz, G., Allman, C., Shweers, J., Roth, C., Balach, L., Canobbio, R., & Liotus, L. (1993). Psychiatric sequelae to the loss of an adolescent peer to suicide. *Journal of the American Academy of Child and Adolescent Psychiatry, 32,* 509–517.

Brent, P. A., Perper, J., Moritz, G., Baugher, N., & Allman, C. (1993). Suicide in adolescents with no apparent psychopathology. *Journal of the American Academy of Child and Adolescent Psychiatry, 32,* 494–500.

Brent, D., Peyser, J., Moritz, G., Liotus, L., Shweers, J., & Roth, C. (1994). Suicide in affectively ill adolescents: A case-control study. *Acta Psychiatrica Scandinavica, 89,* 52–58.

Brown, L., Overholser, J., Spirito, A., & Fritz, G. (1991). The correlates of planning in adolescent suicide attempts. *Journal of the American Academy of Child and Adolescent Psychiatry, 30,* 95–99.

Cairns, R. B., Peterson, G., & Neckerman, H. J. (1988). Suicidal behavior in aggressive adolescents. *Journal of Clinical Child Psychology, 17,* 298–309.

Carlson, G. A., Asarnow, J. R., & Orbach, I. (1987). Developmental aspects of suicidal behavior in children. *Journal of the American Academy of Child and Adolescent Psychiatry, 26*(2), 186–192.

Centers for Disease Control. (1988) CDC recommendation for a community plan for the prevention and containment of suicide attempts. *Morbidity and Mortality Weekly Report, 37* (Suppl. 5–6), 1–12.

Centers for Disease Control (1995a). Suicide among children, adolescents, and young adults—United States, 1980–1992. *Morbidity and Mortality Weekly Report, 44,* 289–291.

Centers for Disease Control. (1995b). Youth Risk Behavior Surveillance—United States, 1993. *Morbidity and Mortality Weekly Reports, 44,* SS-1.

Choquet, M., & Menke, H. (1989). Suicidal thoughts during early adolescence: Prevalence, associated troubles and help-seeking behavior. *Acta Psychiatrica Scandinavia, 81,* 170–177.

Christoffel, K. K., Marcus, D., Sagerman, S., & Bennett, S. (1988). Adolescent suicide and suicide attempts: A population study. *Pediatric Emergency Care, 4,* 32–40.

Cole, D. A. (1989). Psychopathology of adolescent suicide: hopelessness, coping beliefs, and depression. *Journal of Abnormal Psychology, 98,* 248–255.

Davidson, L. (1989). Suicide clusters and youth. In C. Pfeffer (Ed.), *Suicide among youth: Perspectives on risk and prevention* (pp. 83–99). Washington, DC: American Psychiatric Press.

Davidson, L., & Gould, M. S. (1989). Contagion as a risk factor for youth suicide. *Report of the Secretary's Task Force on Youth Suicide: Vol. 2. Risk factors for youth suicide* (DHHS Publication No. (ADM) 89-1622, pp. 88–109). Washington, DC: US Government Printing Office.

deWilde, E., Kienhorst, C., Diekstra, R., & Wolters, W. (1992). The relationship between adolescent suicidal behavior and life events in childhood and adolescence. *American Journal of Psychiatry, 149,* 45–51.

deWilde, E., Kienhorst, C., Diekstra, R., & Wolters, W. (1993). The specificity of psychological characteristics of adolescent suicide attempters. *Journal of the American Academy of Child and Adolescent Psychiatry, 32,* 51–59.

Deykin, E. Y., Alpert, J. J., & McNamara, J. J. (1985). A pilot study of the effect of exposure to child abuse or neglect on adolescent suicial behavior. *American Journal of Psychiatry, 142,* 1299–1303.

Diekstra, R. F. (1989). Suicidal behavior in adolescents and young adults: The international picture. *Crisis, 10,* 16–35.

Diekstra, R. F. (1993). The epidemiology of suicide and parasuicide. *Acta Psychiatrica Scandinavia, 371*(Suppl.), 9–20.

Diekstra, R. F., & Golbinat, W. (1993). The epidemilogy of suicidal behavior: A review of three continents. *World Health Statistics Quarterly, 46,* 52–68.

Eggert, L., Thompson, E., Herting, J., & Nicholas, L. (1995). Reducing suicide potential among high-risk youth: Tests of a school-based prevention program. *Suicide and Life-Threatening Behavior, 25,* 276–296.

Freeman, A., & Reinecke, M. (1993). *Cognitive therapy of suicidal behavior: A manual for treatment.* New York: Springer.

Fremouw, W., de Perczel, M., & Ellis, T. (1990). *Suicide risk: Assessment and response guidelines.* New York: Pergamon.

Garfinkel, B. D., Froese, A., & Hood, J. (1982). Suicide attempts in children and adolescents. *American Journal of Psychiatry, 139,* 1257–1261.

Garnefski, N., Dieksta, R. F., & de Heus, P. (1992). A population-based survey of the characteristics of high school students with and without a history of suicidal behavior. *Acta Psychiatria Scandinavica, 86,* 189–196.

Garrison, C., Jackson, K., Addy, C., McKeown, R., & Waller, J. (1991). Suicidal behaviors in young adolescents. *American Journal of Epidemiology, 133,* 1005–1014.

Gibbons, J. S., Butler, J., Urwin, P., & Gibbons, M. (1978). Evaluation of a social work service for self-poisoning patients. *British Journal of Psychiatry, 133,* 11–118.

Gibbs, J. T., & Hines, A. M. (1989). Factors related to sex differences in suicidal behavior among black youth: Implications for intervention and research. *Journal of Adolescent Research, 4,* 152–172.

Gispert, M., Wheeler, K., Marsh, L., & Davis, M. S. (1985). Suicidal adolescents: Factors in evaluation. *Adolescence, 20,* 753–762.

Goldacre, M., & Hawton, K. (1985). Repetition of self-poisoning and subsequent death in adolescents who take overdoses. *British Journal of Psychiatry, 146,* 395–398.

Gould, M. S., & Shaffer, D. (1986). The impact of suicide in television movies: Evidence of imitation. *New England Journal of Medicine, 315,* 690–694.

Hawton, K. (1986). *Suicide and attempted suicide among children and adolescents.* Beverly Hills, CA: Sage.

Hawton, K., & Fagg, J. (1992). Deliberate self-poisoning and self-injury in adolescents: A study of characteristics and trends in Oxford, 1976–1989. *British Journal of Psychiatry, 161,* 816–823.

Hawton, K., O'Grady, J., Osborn, M., & Cole, D. (1982). Adolescents who take overdoses: Their characteristics, problems, and contacts with helping agencies. *British Journal of Psychiatry, 140,* 118–123.

Hazell, P., & Lewin, T. (1993). Friends of adolescent suicide attempters and completers. *Journal of the American Academy of Child and Adolescent Psychiatry, 32,* 76–81.

Hewitt, P. L., Flett, G. L., & Turnball-Donovan W. (1992). Perfectionism and suicide potential. *British Journal of Clinical Psychology, 31,* 181–190.

Hewitt, P. L., Newton, J., Flett, G. L., & Callander, L. (1997). Perfectionism and suicide ideation in adolescent psychiatric patients. *Journal of Adnormal Child Psychology, 25,* 95–101.

Hibbard, R. A., Ingersoll, G. M., & Orr, D. P. (1990). Behavioral risk, emotional risk, and child abuse among adolescents in a nonclinical setting. *Pediatrics, 86,* 896–901.

Hlady, W. G., & Middaugh, J. P. (1988) Suicides in Alaska: Firearms and alcohol. *American Journal of Public Health, 78,* 179–180.

Holinger, P. C. (1990). The causes, impact, and preventability of childhood injuries in the United States. *American Journal of Diseases of Children, 144,* 670–676.

Holinger, P. C., & Offer, D. (1987). Suicide and homicide in the United States: An epidemiologic study of violent death, population changes, and the potential for prediction. *American Journal of Psychiatry, 144,* 215–219.

Jacobson, L., Rabinowitz, I., Popper, M., Solomon, R., Sokol, M., & Pfeffer, C. (1995). Interviewing prepubertal children about suicidal ideation and behavior. In M. E. Hertzig & E. A. Farber (Eds.), *Annual progress in child psychiatry and development* (pp. 295–321). New York: Brunner/Mazel.

Jellinek, M. (1978). Referrals from a psychiatric emergency room. Relationship of compliance to demographic and interview variables. *American Journal of Psychiatry, 135,* 209–213.

Joffe, R. T., & Offord, D. R. (1983). Suicidal behavior in childhood. *Canadian Journal of Psychiatry, 28,* 57–63.

Kalafat, J., & Elias, M. (1994). An evaluation of school-based suicide awareness intervention. *Suicide and Life-Threatening Behavior, 24,* 224–233.

King, C., Raskin, A., Gadowski, C., Butkus, M., & Opipari, L. (1990). Psychosocial factors associated with urban adolescent female suicide attempts. *Journal of the American Academy of Child and Adolescent Psychiatry, 29,* 289–294.

Lehnert, R., Overholser, J., & Spirito, A. (1994). Internalized and externalized anger in adolescent suicide attempters. *Journal of Adolescent Researcher, 9,* 105–119.

Levy, S., Jurkovic, G., & Spirito, A. (1995). A multisystem analysis of adolescent suicide attempts. *Journal of Abnormal Child Psychology, 23,* 221–234.

Lewinsohn, P., Clarke, G., Hops, H., & Andrews, J. (1990). Cognitive-behavioral treatment for depressed adolescents. *Behavior Therapy, 21,* 385–401.

Lewinsohn, P., Rohde, P., & Seeley, J. (1993). Psychosocial characteristics of adolescents with a history of suicide attempt. *Journal of the American Academy of Child and Adolescent Psychiatry, 32,* 60–68.

Lewinsohn, P., Rohde, P., & Seeley, J. (1994). Psychosocial risk factors for future adolescent suicide attempts. *Journal of Consulting & Clinical Psychology, 62,* 297–305.

Lewinsohn, P., Rohde, P., & Seeley, J. (1996). Adolescent suicidal ideation and attempts: Prevalance, risk factors, and clinical implications. *Clinical Psychology: Sense and Practice, 3,* 25–46.

Lieberman, R., & Eckman, T. (1981). Behavior therapy vs. insight oriented therapy for repeated suicide attempters. *Archives of General Psychiatry, 38,* 1126–1130.

Males, M. (1991). Teen suicide and changing cause of death certification, 1953–1987. *Suicide and Life-Threatening Behavior, 21,* 245–259.

Mann, J., McBride, P., Brown, R., Linnoila, M., Leon, A., Demeo, M., Mieczkowski, T., Mysers, J., & Stanley, M. (1992). Relationship between central and perceptual serotonin indexes in depressed and suicidal psychiatric inpatients. *Archives of General Psychiatry, 49,* 442–446.

Marks, P. A., & Haller, D. L. (1977). Now I lay me down for keeps: A study of adolescent suicide attempts. *Journal of Clinical Psychology, 33,* 390–400.

Martin, G., Rozanes, P., Pearce, C., & Allison., S. (1995). Adolescent suicide, depression, and family dysfunction. *Acta Psychiatrica Scandinavica, 92,* 336–344.

Marttunen, M., Aro, H., Henriksson, M., & Lonnqvist, T. (1991). Mental disorders in adolescent suicide. *Archives of General Psychiatry, 48,* 834–839.

McDowell, E., & Stillion, J. (1994). Suicide across the phases of life. In G. G. Noam & S. Borst (Eds.), *Children, Youth, and Suicide: Developmental Perspective* (pp. 7–22). San Francisco: Jossey-Bass.

McIntosh, J. (1983–84). Suicide among Native Americans: Further tribal data and considerations. *Journal of Death and Dying, 14,* 215–229.

Mitchell, M., & Rosenthal, D. (1992). Suicidal adolescents: Family dynamics and the effects of lethality and hopelessness. *Journal of Youth and Adolescence, 21,* 23–33.

Myers, K., MacCauley, E., Calderon, R., & Treder, R. (1991). The 3-year longitudinal course of suicidality and predictive factors for subsequent suicidality in youths with major depressive disorder. *Journal of the American Academy of Child and Adolescent Psychiatry, 30,* 804–810.

National Center for Health Statistics. (1993). Advance report of final mortality statistics, 1990. *Monthly Vital Statistics Report, 41, 7,* 1–44.

Nordstrom, P., Samuelsson, M., Asberg, M., Traksman-Bendz, L., Aberg-Wistedt, A., Nordin, C., & Bertilson, L. (1994). CSF 5-HIAA predicts suicide risk after attempted suicide. *Suicide and Life-Threatening Behavior, 24,* 1–9.

Orbach, I., & Bar-Joseph, H. (1992). The impact of a suicide prevention program for adolescents on suicidal tendencies, hopelessness, ego identity, and coping. *Suicide and Life-Threatening Behavior, 23,* 120–129.

Orbach, I., Rosenheim, E., & Mary, E. (1987). Some aspects of cognitive funcitoning in suicidal children. *Journal of the American Academy of Child and Adolescent Psychiatry, 26,* 181–185.

Overholser, J., Adams, D., Lehnert, K., & Brinkman, D. (1995). Self-esteem deficits and suicidal tendencies among adolescents. *Journal of the American Academy of Child and Adolescent Psychiatry, 34,* 919–928.

Overholser, J. C., Hemstreet, A., Spirito, A., & Vyse, S. (1989). Suicide awareness programs in the schools. Effects of gender and personal experience. *Journal of the American Academy of Child and Adolescent Psychiatry, 28,* 925–930.

Otto, U. (1972). Suicidal acts by children and adolescents. *Acta Pediatrica Scandinavica, 232*(Suppl.), 7–123.

Patsiokas, A., & Clum, G. (1985). Effects of psychotherapeutic strategies in the treatment of suicide attempters. *Psychotherapy, 22,* 281–290.

Pfeffer, C., Conte, H., Plutchik, R., & Jerrett, I. (1980). Suicidal behavior in latency-age children: An outpatient population. *Journal of the American Academy of Child Psychiatry, 19,* 703–710.

Pfeffer, C., Newcorn, J., Kaplan, G., Mizruchi, M., & Plutchik, R. (1988). Suicidal behavior in adolescent psychiatric inpatients. *Journal of the American Academy of Child Psychiatry, 27,* 357–361.

Pfeffer, C. R., Plutchik, R. L., & Mizrucki, M. S. (1983). Suicidal and assaultive behavior in children: Classification, measurement, and interrelations. *American Journal of Psychiatry, 140,* 154–157.

Philips, D. P., & Carstensen, L. L. (1986). Clustering of teenage suicides after television news about suicides. *New England Journal of Medicine, 315,* 685–689.

Philips, D. P., & Paight, D. (1987). The impact of televised movies about suicide; A replicative study. *New England Journal of Medicine, 317,* 809–811.

Platt, S., Bille-Brahe, U., Kerkhof, A., Schmidtke, A., Bjerke, T., Crepet, P., DeLeu, D., Haring, C., Lonnqvist, J., Michel, K., Philippe, A., Pommereau. X., Querejeta, I., Salander-Renberg, E., Temesuary, B., Wasserman, D., & Sampaio-Fario, J. (1992). Parasuicide in Europe: The WHO/EURO multicentre study on parasuicide. I. Introduction and preliminary analysis for 1989. *Acta Psychiatrica Scandinavica, 85,* 97–104.

Reynolds, W. (1987). *Suicide Ideation Questionnaire.* Odessa, FL: Psychological Assesment Resources.

Richman, J. (1979). The family therapy of attempted suicide. *Family Process, 18,* 131–142.

Rifai, A., Reynolds, C., & Mann, J. J. (1992). Biology of elderly suicide. *Suicide and Life-Threatening Behavior, 22,* 48–61.

Riggs, S., Alario, A. J., & McHorney, C. (1990). Health risk behaviors and attempted suicide in adolescents who report prior maltreatment. *Journal of Pediatrics, 116,* 815–820.

Robin, A. L. (1981). A controlled evaluation of problem-solving communication training with parent–adolescent. *Behavior Therapy, 12,* 593–609.

Robbins, D., & Alessi, M. (1985). Depressive symptoms and suicidal behavior in adolescents. *American Journal of Psychiatry, 142,* 588–592.

Ross, C., & Motto, J. (1984). Group counseling for suicidal adolescents. In H. Sudak, A. Ford, & N. Rushforth (Eds.), *Suicide in the young.* Littleton, MA: John Wright PSG.

Rotheram-Borus, M. J., & Bradley, J. (1991). Triage model for suicidal runaways. *American Journal of Orthopsychiatry, 61,* 122–127.

Rotheram-Borus, M. J., Piacentini, J., Miller, S., Graae, F., & Castro-Blanco, D. (1994). Brief cognitive behavioral treatment for adolescent suicide attempters and their families. *Journal of the American Academy of Child and Adolescent Psychiatry, 33,* 508–517.

Rotheram-Borus, M. J., Trautman, P., Dopkins, S., & Shrout, P. (1990). Cognitive style and pleasant activities among female adolescent suicide attempters. *Journal of Consulting and Clinical Psychology, 58,* 553–561.

Roy, A. (1994). Recent biological studies on suicide. *Suicide & Life-Threatening Behavior, 24,* 10–14.

Roy, A., DeJong, J., & Linnoila, M. (1989). Cerebrospinal fluid momoamine metabolites and suicidal behavior in depressed patients. *Archives of General Psychiatry, 46,* 609–612.

Rubenstein, J. L., Heeren, T., Housman, D., Rubin, C., & Stechler, G. (1989). Suicidal behavior in "normal" adolescents: Risk and protective factors. *American Journal of Orthopsychiatry, 59*(1), 59–71.

Runeson, B., & Beskow, J. (1991). Borderline personality disorder in youth Swedish suicides. *Journal of Nervous and Mental Disease, 179,* 153–156.

Sadowski, C., & Kelley, M. L. (1993). Social problem solving in suicidal adolescents. *Journal of Consulting and Clinical Psychology, 61*(1), 121–127.

Salkovkis, P., Atha, C., & Storer, D. (1990). Cognitive-behavioral problem-solving in the treatment of petients who repeatedly attempt suicide. *British Journal of Psychiatry, 157,* 871–876.

Schneidman, E. (1985). *Definition of suicide.* New York: Wiley.

Shaffer, D. (1988). The epidemiology of teen suicide: An examination of risk factors. *Journal of Clinical Psychiatry, 49,* 36–41.

Shaffer, D., Garland, A., Gould, M., Fisher, P., & Trautman, P. (1988). Preventing teenage suicide: A critical review. *Journal of the American Academy of Child and Adolescent Psychiatry, 27,* 675–687.

Shaffer, D., Garland, A., Underwood, M., & Whittle, B. (1987). *An evaluation of three youth suicide prevention programs in New Jersey.* Report prepared for the New Jersey State Department of Health and Human Services.

Shaffer, D., Gould, M. Fisher, P., Trautman, P., Moreau, D., Kleinman, M., & Flory, M. (1996). Psychiatric diagnosis in child and adolescent suicide. *Archives of General Psychiatry, 53,* 339–348.

Shaffer, D., Gould, M., & Hicks, R. (1994). Worsening suicide rate in black teenagers. *American Journal of Psychiatry, 131,* 1810–1812.

Shaffer, D., Vieland, V., Garland, A., Rojas, M., Underwood, M., & Busner, C. (1990). Adolescent suicide attempters: Response to suicide prevention programs. *Journal of the American Medical Association, 264,* 3151–3155.

Shaffi, M., Carrigan, S., Whittinghill, J., & Derrick, A. (1985). Psychological autopsy of completed suicide in children and adolescents. *American Journal of Psychiatry, 142,* 1061–1064.

Shaunesey, K., Cohen, J. L., Plummer, B., & Berman, A. (1993). Suicidality in hospitalized adolescents: Relation-

ship to prior abuse. *American Journal of Orthopsychiatry, 63,* 113–119.

Sigurdson, E., Staley, D., Matas, M., Hildahl, K., & Squair, K. (1994). A five year review of youth suicide in Manitoba. *Canadian Journal of Psychiatry, 39,* 397–403.

Slap, G. B., Vorters, D. F., Chaudhuri, S., & Centor, R. M. (1989). Risk factors for attempted suicide during adolescence. *Pediatrics, 84,* 762–772.

Sledge, W., Moras, K., Hartley, D., & Levine, M. (1990). Effect of time-limited psychotherapy on patient dropout rates. *American Journal of Psychiatry, 147,* 1341–1347.

Snyder, R. (1981). The first offender program: Children and our future. In I. N. Berlin (Ed.), *The International Year of the Child, 1979–1980.* Albuquerque, NM: University of New Mexico Press.

Sorenson, S. B., & Rutter, C. M. (1991). Transgenerational patterns of suicide attempt. *Journal of Consulting and Clinical Psychology, 59,* 861–866.

Spirito, A., Bond, A., Kurkjian, J., Devost, L., Bosworth, T., & Brown, L. (1993). Gender differences among adolescent suicide attempters. *Crisis: International Journal of Suicide and Crisis Studies, 62,* 464–468.

Spirito, A., Brown, J., Overholser, J., & Fritz, G. (1989). Attempted suicide in adolescence. A review and critique of the literature. *Clinical Psychology Review, 9,* 335–363.

Spirito, A., Francis, G., Overholser, J., & Frank, N. (1996). Coping, depression, and adolescent suicide attempts. *Journal of Clinical Child Psychology, 25,* 147–155.

Spirito, A., Overholser, J., Ashworth, S., Morgan, J., & Benedict-Drew, C. (1988). Evaluation of a suicide awareness curriculum for high school students. *Journal of the American Academy of Child and Adolescent Psychiatry, 27,* 705–711.

Spirito, A., Overholser, J., & Hart, K. (1991). Cognitive characteristics of adolescent suicide attempters. *Journal of the American Academy of Child and Adolescent Psychiatry, 30,* 604–608.

Spirito, A., Overholser, J., & Stark, L. (1989). Common problems and coping strategies, II: Findings with adolescent suicide attempters. *Journal of Abnormal Child Psychology, 17,* 213–221.

Spirito, A., Overholser, J., & Vinnick, L. (1995). Adolescent Suicide Attempters in General Hospitals: Psychological Evaluation and Disposition Handling. In J. L. Wallander & L. J. Siegel (Eds.), *Adolescent Health Problems: Behavioral Perspectives* (pp. 97–116). New York: Guilford Press.

Spirito, A., Plummer, B., Gispert, M., Levy, S., Kurkjian, J., Lewander, W., Hagberg, S., & Devost, L. (1992). Adolescent suicide attempts: Outcomes at follow-up. *American Journal of Orthopsychiatry, 62,* 464–468.

Spirito, A., Sterling, C., Donaldson, D., & Arrigan, M. (1996). Factor analysis of the Suicide Intent Scale with adolescent suicide attempters. *Journal of Personality Assessment, 67,* 90–101.

Spirito, A., Williams, C., Stark, L. J., & Hart, K. (1988). The Hopelessness Scale for Children: Psychometric properties and clinical utility with normal and emotionally disturbed adolescents. *Journal of Abnormal Child Psychology, 16,* 445–458.

Traskman-Bandz, L., Alling, C., Alsen, M., Regnell, G., Simonsson, P., & Ohman, R. (1993). The role of monomines in suicidal behavior. *Acta Psychiatrica Scandinavica Suppl. 371,* 45–47.

Trautman, P. D., Stewart, N., & Morishima, A. (1993). Are adolescent suicide attempters noncompliant with out-patient care? *Journal of the American Academy of Child and Adolescent Psychiatry, 32,* 89–94.

US Bureau of the Census (1990). *Statistical Abstract of the United States: 1989* (110th ed.) Washington, DC: Government Printing Office.

US Congress, Office of Technology Assessment. (1990).

Indian adolescent mental health (OTA-H 446). Washington, DC: Government Printing Office.

Vieland, V., Whittle, B., Garland, A., Hicks, R., & Shaffer, D. (1991). The impact of curriculum based suicide prevention programs for teenagers: An 18-month follow-up. *Journal of the American Academy of Child and Adolescent Psychiatry, 30,* 811–815.

Wagner, B., Cole, R., & Schwartzman, P. (1995). Psychosocial correlates of suicide attempts among junior and senior high school youth. *Suicide and Life-Threatening Behavior, 25,* 358–372.

Ward, J. A. (1984). Preventive implications of a Native Indian mental health program: Focus on suicide and violent death. *Journal of Preventive Psychiatry, 2,* 371–385.

Weinstein, M. C., & Saturno, P. J. (1989). Economic impact of youth suicide and suicide attempts. *Report of the Secretary's Task Force of Youth Suicide: Vol. 4. Strategies for the prevention of youth suicide* (DHHS Publication No. (ADM) 89–1624, pp. 82–93). Washington, DC: Government Printing Office.

Welu, T. C. (1977). A follow-up program for suicide attempters. *Suicide and Life-Threatening Behavior, 7,* 17–30.

Wilson, K., Seltzer, J., Bergman, J., Kral, M., Inayatullah, M., & Elliott, C. (1995). Problem-solving, stress, and coping in adolescent suicide attempters. *Suicide and Life-Threatening Behavior, 25,* 241–252.

Withers, L. E., & Kaplan, D. W. (1987). Adolescents who attempt suicide. A retrospective clinical chart review of hospitalized patients. *Professional Psychology: Research and Practice, 18,* 391–393.

5.19

Attention-deficit Hyperactivity Disorder in Children and Adolescents

C. KEITH CONNERS
Duke University Medical Center, Durham, NC, USA
and
DREW ERHARDT
Pepperdine University, Malibu, CA, USA

5.19.1 INTRODUCTION

The childhood disorder now known as attention-deficit hyperactivity disorder (ADHD) has a long and controversial history. A number of milestones are commonly cited in the evolution of the concept in its present form. The behavioral symptoms of inattention, impulsive behavior, and hyperactivity have remained fairly constant across many decades, although the interpretation of their origins and meaning has shifted with changes in the scientific paradigms of human behavior (Table 1).

At the end of the nineteenth century, mental afflictions were commonly divided into "moral" and physical causes. The attribution of moral carried different connotations from its usage today, meaning the impairment of judgment or restraint in the face of overwhelming stimulation, rather than mere unethical or immoral behavior. External and internal stimuli, including excesses of emotion and pain, were considered moral causes as opposed to purely physical causes. Because of their intensity they could overwhelm efforts to restrain impulse and thus prevent acting in acceptable ways. Thus, an influential text of the day stated that, "Every impression on the sensorium, through the external senses, and every passion in excess, may become a moral cause of insanity" (Burrows, 1828, p. 9).

Twenty years before Still (1902) provided his account of the impulsive, hyperactive child suffering from lapses in moral restraint, James provided a penetrating analysis of behavioral inhibition (James, 1890). Although his discussion of attention is deservedly well-known, few realize that James anticipated the modern linkage of attentional processes with behavioral inhibition and discharge of impulse into motor behavior. In adopting the traditional notion of a "moral" aspect of behavioral self-control, James argued that every overt action involves a hesitation requiring effortful attention to an "idea" that provides the impetus to action. A failure to restrain action is the consequence of a failure to hold the idea of a desired action in the focus of attention. This failure of attention is therefore the ultimate basis of an explosive and impulsive behavior pattern: "There is a normal type of character, for example, in which impulses seem to discharge so promptly into movements that inhibitions get no time to arise" (p. 537). Thus, James's influential opus established behavioral inhibition as exclusively a mental, as opposed to a physical, process—a process which linked impulsivity with inattention.

This was the prevailing paradigm when the physician Still (1902) provided an account of 20 youngsters whom he described as suffering from a defect of moral control. His clinical description of impulsive, inattentive, and overactive children anticipated much of what is now described as ADHD, although it also included features we would currently include under conduct, antisocial, or oppositional categories. These lapses in self-restraint did not discount the role of genetic and constitutional factors in the individual which might alter the threshold for succumbing to stimulation.

A shift of paradigms to a physical basis for behavioral disinhibition began three decades later. The catastrophic medical phenomena of the world wars, the pandemic of influenza and von Economo's encephalitis, along with the growing awareness of the long-term consequences of "reproductive casualties," provided the impetus to a more medical paradigm—specifically a neurological one—for explaining the deviant behavioral excesses and cognitive limitations of children. Although neuroanatomy was well-developed at this time, the neurological paradigms were largely those of a static system involving cortical inhibition over

Table 1 Some historical landmarks in the evolution of ADHD.

Author/event	Contribution
James (1890)	Linking of defects in voluntary inhibition of action to attentional phenomena: "Effort of attention is thus the essential phenomenon of will" (p. 562)
Still (1902)	Accurate clinical description of a syndrome of involving loss of "volitional inhibition" and "moral control"
Postencephalitis, in 1920	A syndrome described by numerous authors, involving emotional instability, irritability, lying, thieving, impaired memory and attention, poor motor control and general hyperactivity, and requiring milieu, cognitive, and behavioral therapies
Kahn and Cohen (1934)	Described the hyperkinetic syndrome as one of "organic-drivenness" due to brain-stem defects or (later) disinhibition due to cortical damage
Bradley (1937)	Administered benzedrine to a heterogeneous group of hospitalized hyperkinetic and behaviorally disordered children, noting an immediate calming effect on disinhibited behavior as well as an increased zest for learning
Goldstein (1942)	Based on observations of after effects of brain injuries in war, he called attention to many behavior patterns which were commonly considered "functional" as really being due to an "organic" etiology
Strauss and Lehtinen (1947)	Description of a brain damage syndrome with characteristic perceptual, motor, and emotional characteristics
Laufer, Denhoff, and Solomons (1957)	Comprehensive clinical description of a "hyperkinetic impulse disorder," with experiments implicating diencephalic (thalamic) mechanisms
Pasamanick and Knobloch (1959)	Described a "continuum of reproductive casualty" which was responsible for a syndrome of minimal cerebral damage in infancy
Clements and Peters (1962)	A classic paper describing the concept of minimal brain dysfunction, later formalized by Clements (1966) in a consensus statement, and linked to attentional dysfunctions by others from the Arkansas group (Dykman, Ackerman, Clements, & Peters, 1971)
American Psychiatric Association (1980)	Formalization of a diagnostic category whose core disorder is attentional in nature, and in which separate subtypes are evident involving hyperactivity, impulsivity, and inattention

more primitive appetitive systems. Organic explanations of behavior were largely based on a conception of the brain along strict localization of functions within separate structures. But Goldstein's (1942) studies of penetrating head wounds and war injuries broadened the range of behavioral phenomena from localized motor impairments to subtle disturbances of cognitive function such as "concrete thinking." These early postwar writings provided a way of understanding subtle behavioral disturbances as organically based phenomena linked to specific types of brain damage. "Organicity" came to mean a style of behavior as much as a statement of etiology.

During this same period, a very different paradigm was provided by Gestalt psychology, with its focus on the role of perceptual phenomena such as visual illusions. Here the emphasis was on the way the brain organizes sensory input and regulates output according to certain principles involving goodness of fit and whole–part relationships among sensory ele-

ments. Motor acts reflected control by organized perceptual structures. Werner, Strauss, and their colleagues applied these paradigms to the plentiful cases of children with identifiable neurological conditions such as cerebral palsy, providing an impetus to the perceptual-motor re-education programs initiated by Cruikshank and others in the early and mid-1940s (Kessler (1980) gives a good account of this period).

These studies of relatively extreme medical phenomena gradually filtered into thinking about behaviors that were not readily explained by obvious neurological antecedents. Eventually, however, it became clear that the paradigm of neurological damage had to be abandoned because many cases of apparently organic behavior had no identifiable neurological insults. But the notion lingered on that the perceptual, motor, and learning features associated with known brain damage were indicators of underlying brain dysfunction, but dysfunction that was minimal compared to the usual neurological catastrophes. The concept of minimal brain dysfunction (MBD) was the immediate progenitor of current descriptive classifications of the disruptive behavior disorders, including ADHD. In the definitive conference paper describing the syndrome of MBD, Clements (1966) proposed that:

> The term "minimal brain dysfunction syndrome" refers ... to children of near average, average, or above average intelligence with certain learning or behavioral disabilities ranging from mild to severe which are associated with deviations of function of the central nervous system. [The disabilities may be shown by] various combinations of impairment in perception, conceptualization, language, memory and *control of attention, impulse, or motor function* [italics added]. (pp. 9–10)

This concept incorporates much of the language and thinking of the previous 70 years, in which learning and behavioral disabilities were linked to the central nervous system through characteristic perceptual, cognitive, and motor patterns, and highlights the role of control of attention, impulse and motor function.

It is generally believed that the term MBD was eventually replaced for lack of direct evidence regarding brain dysfunction (Barkley, 1996). In fact, the concept received considerable support. The prospective perinatal collaborative study by the National Institute of Neurological Diseases and Blindness of 56 000 children followed from birth, demonstrated that symptoms of overactivity and learning disabilities were clearly predictable from adverse perinatal events, including maternal smoking and alcohol use (Nichols & Chen, 1981). As fundamental neuroscience has advanced, there has been unexpected further support for the concept of MBD. As noted by Rapoport and Castellanos (1996), "Since the publication of *DSM-III-R* in 1987 ... a number of anatomic MRI studies ... have in fact documented minimal but significant brain anatomical deviations—ironically, minimal brain dysfunction now takes on new meaning!" (p. 267).

However, the boundaries of the MBD concept were simply too large, allowing as it did for various combinations of impairment across many types of behavior. Anticipating the integrative review by Douglas and Peters (1978), the Arkansas group (Clements & Peters, 1962; Dykman, Ackerman, Clements, & Peters, 1971) began to narrow the core processes to attention. At the same time, the second edition of the *Diagnostic and statistical manual of mental disorders* (*DSM-II*) defined the hyperkinetic reaction of childhood as a disorder "characterized by overactivity, restlessness, distractibility,

and short attention span." (American Psychiatric Association, 1968, p. 50.) This definition is etiological in that it characterizes the syndrome as a reaction, in keeping with then-prevailing psychoanalytic doctrine. Between the introduction in 1980 of *DSM-III* and of *DSM-IV* in 1994, opinion vacillated regarding the centrality of attention and hyperactivity/impulsivity in the syndrome, but etiological explanations were no longer included as necessary in a system which attempts to be purely descriptive.

This brief review highlights the evolutionary nature of the ADHD concept, and its dependence upon the prevailing scientific paradigms used to explain behavior and mental functioning. Evolution of the concept has proceeded from the mentalistic formulations of the nineteenth century, to the organic concepts of the early twentieth century, and finally to a purely behavioral and descriptive formulation. This chapter depicts the current state of the art with respect to assessment, diagnosis, and treatment, and points to the clinical and research goals which are yet to be achieved in understanding the disorder and its treatment.

5.19.2 PHENOMENOLOGY

5.19.2.1 Core Features

Despite great variation with respect to diagnostic labels, etiologic theories, and conceptions of primary deficits, clinical descriptions of children with the neurobehavioral syndrome now referred to as ADHD have been remarkably stable. The doggerel verse used to describe *Fidgety Phil* in 1863 by the German pediatrician Heinrich Hoffman might today be replaced by a downloaded video clip of a hyperactive child, but the symptoms depicted by any medium will include some combination of developmentally inappropriate levels of inattention, impulsivity, and overactivity that emerge early in life and persist with time and across situations. Indeed, despite comprising a heterogeneous set of behavioral and cognitive problems, it has been parsimonious to consider the symptoms of ADHD as emerging from deficient regulation in three areas: attention, response inhibition, and activity level. This familiar tripartite division of core features has not always been supported by factor analytic studies of parent and teacher behavior ratings, from which two rather than three stable dimensions consistently emerge (Hinshaw, 1994). One factor comprises inattention, cognitive impulsivity and, in some instances, restlessness, whereas the other is formed by behavioral impulsivity and motoric overactivity (Bauermeister, Alegria, Bird, Rubio-Stipec, & Canino, 1992; Lahey et al.,

1988). However, in a study of a national normative sample, confirmatory factor analysis was used to demonstrate that a three-factor model was the best fit to the 18 *DSM-IV* symptoms (Conners, Parker, & Sitarenios, 1996). Nevertheless, the high correlation of the impulsivity and hyperactivity factors justifies their lumping together for practical purposes. Hence, the current diagnostic system employed in the USA (discussed below) defines inattention and hyperactivity–impulsivity as the core broad dimensions of ADHD.

It has long been recognized that the core features of ADHD, however partitioned, do not represent unitary constructs and precise specification of symptoms is lacking. The following are brief discussions of the heterogeneity and phenomenology of these features.

5.19.2.1.1 Inattention

Although coordinated in function, multiple dimensions of attention have been identified and evidence is emerging that each type reflects a separate underlying neural network (Mesulam, 1990; Posner, 1988; Voeller, 1991 (review)). Components of attention most consistently described include (i) arousal or alertness, (ii) selective or focused attention (the ability to attend to particular stimuli while ignoring competing, irrelevant stimuli), (iii) attentional capacity or span of apprehension (the amount of information to which the child can attend at one time), and (iv) sustained attention or vigilance (the persistence of focus over time). Clinically, children with ADHD may show fairly specific attentional problems, but more often have attentional difficulties that are multifaceted. Common manifestations include an inability to remain engaged in schoolwork, chores (and, in some instances, games), high rates of off-task behavior, seeming to be in another world when being spoken to, difficulties recalling and following through on instructions with multiple steps, poor task completion, distractibility by stimuli that are more appealing than the task at hand, and a disregard for details that often leads to careless mistakes.

Laboratory evidence compiled by Douglas in the 1980s (Douglas, 1983) led to the predominant view that poor sustained attention or vigilance represented the core deficit in children with ADHD. Indeed, the frequency with which these children drift off-task and fail to persist with effortful activities of low inherent interest suggests a vigilance decrement. However, results of laboratory studies aimed at illuminating this attention deficit have been conflicting. Whereas some investigations reveal deficient vigilance in ADHD samples (e.g., Seidel &

Joschko, 1990), many have failed to support a sustained attention deficit (e.g., Schachar, Logan, Wachsmuth, & Chajczyk, 1988; Sergeant & Scholten, 1985; van der Meere, Wekking, & Sergeant, 1991). Part of the problem is that the vigilance decrement is an age-related phenomenon which is much less evident in older children and adolescents (Seidel & Joschko, 1990). In light of such findings, some have argued that the clinical phenomena commonly interpreted as a sustained attention deficit actually reflect a problem with the preparation, regulation, speed, and consistent execution of motor output (Barkley, 1995b; van der Meere, van Baal, & Sergeant, 1989). Barkley (1994) has reframed attentional problems in children with ADHD as deficits in goal-directed persistence, meaning that the persistence of their effortful behavior is highly dependent on the nature of the task context (e.g., intrinsic interest or novelty) and on immediately available reinforcement rather than being shaped by distal rewards and future goals. Clearly, the nature and primacy of attentional problems in ADHD remain elusive. Contributing to this state of affairs is the complex intertwining of cognitive, motivational, affective, and behavioral variables, along with varying task parameters, in the responses regarded as reflecting attention, both in the laboratory and the natural environment.

5.19.2.1.2 Hyperactivity

Characteristic symptoms in the hyperactive domain vary in both nature and degree. Features ranging from excessive talking and noise-making, to an inability to remain seated, are regarded as reflecting hyperactivity. The category encompasses both the child who taps his feet, fidgets, and manipulates objects when seated, to the whirling dervish who blazes chaotically through space with a driven, accelerated quality. Common to many of the symptoms in this domain is that they lack direction or purpose and are extraneous to the task at hand. As with inattentive symptoms, there is significant situational variability in hyperactivity (Luk, 1985), suggesting a deficient capacity to regulate activity levels to different setting or task demands (Routh, 1978). Thus, the child who stands out so painfully in the structured classroom setting may be far less distinguishable from peers on the playground. Despite the modulation of hyperactive symptoms by environmental factors, it is noteworthy that youngsters with ADHD generally exhibit greater levels of motor activity than comparison children throughout the day, including during sleep (Porrino et al., 1983). Moreover, whereas certain measures of inattention have not been found to distinguish children with ADHD from those with other psychiatric conditions, hyperactivity may represent a more specific marker of the disorder (Halperin, Matier, Bedi, Sharma, & Newcorn, 1992; Roberts, 1990).

5.19.2.1.3 Impulsivity

Although current *DSM* criteria in the impulsivity domain are limited to blurting out answers prematurely, difficulty waiting one's turn, and interrupting or intruding upon others, other impulsive features are commonly observed in children with ADHD, including engaging in physically dangerous activities without considering the possible consequences, deficient inhibition of intense emotional responses, and a hasty, careless response style when working on tedious or cognitively demanding tasks (Brown & Quay, 1977). A proclivity towards impulsive acts may also underlie the higher than average accident rate seen among youngsters with ADHD (Hartsough & Lambert, 1985; Szatmari, Offord, & Boyle, 1989a).

As with inattention and hyperactivity, the category of impulsivity is often conceptualized in an overly inclusive manner which makes it difficult to operationalize. Convergent validity is problematic as various measures of impulsivity (e.g., continuous performance tests, matching familiar figure tests, and parent or teacher ratings) tend to correlate poorly with one another (Milich & Kramer, 1984). There does, however, appear to be justification for distinguishing cognitive and behavioral aspects of impulsivity as they appear to be distinct factors (Taylor, 1994), with differing diagnostic and predictive significance. For example, measures of cognitive impulsivity have been found to distinguish ADHD from psychiatric comparison children (Halperin et al., 1992). In a longitudinal study of 400 boys conducted by White et al. (1994), both cognitive and behavioral impulsivity predicted academic achievement problems, but only the latter was associated with increased risk for antisocial behavior.

In contrast to prior conceptualizations of the disorder that identified hyperactivity or inattention as primary deficits, Barkley (1994) has argued that an impaired capacity to inhibit or delay responding is at the core of ADHD. This theory contends that the chief and associated features of ADHD can be regarded as secondary to poor inhibitory control. For instance, the capacity to inhibit responses is said to permit self-regulation which, in turn, limits task-

irrelevant motor activity and makes persistence in the face of boredom, fatigue, or competing stimuli possible. Thus, Barkley reverses the causal direction of the relationship between impulsivity and inattention as interpreted by James.

5.19.2.2 Associated Features and Comorbidity

The phenotypic heterogeneity of ADHD is a product not only of the variegated nature of its core symptoms, but also multiple associated clinical features and co-occurring psychiatric conditions. The most common secondary features among children with ADHD include academic underachievement, noncompliant and aggressive behavior, family discord, and poor peer relationships. Adequate functioning in these domains has significance for mastering many critical developmental tasks (Richters et al., 1995). Conversely, poor functioning in these areas is highly predictive of later maladjustment (Hinshaw, 1994), making these secondary features of ADHD particularly pernicious. The following are brief comments regarding the particular difficulties experienced in these domains by children with ADHD.

The symptoms of ADHD typically compromise a child's ability to meet academic as well as behavioral demands at school. An overwhelming majority of children with the disorder demonstrate academic performance problems relative to their classmates (Cantwell & Baker, 1991), as indexed by lower rates of on-task behavior (Abikoff, Gittelman-Klein, & Klein, 1977) and academic task completion (Pfiffner & Barkley, 1990), and by higher rates of academic underachievement, placement in special education services, grade retention, and dropping out of school (Barkley, DuPaul, & McMurray, 1990; Barkley, Fischer, Edelbrock, & Smallish, 1990; Hinshaw, 1992b). Learning disabilities are highly correlated with externalizing or disruptive behavior disorders in general, but the relationship appears to be strongest with ADHD (DuPaul & Stoner, 1994; Hinshaw, 1992b). Although prevalence estimates of learning disorders among youngsters with ADHD vary widely, most recent estimates employing conservative criteria for defining learning disorders range from 10% to 25% (Hinshaw, 1992a; Semrud-Clikeman et al., 1992). Despite their far above chance co-occurrence and complex bidirectional influences, consensus has emerged that ADHD and learning disabilities represent distinct disorders (Shaywitz, Fletcher, & Shaywitz, 1995).

Children with ADHD commonly manifest a variety of externalizing features. These typically involve willful noncompliance or defiance in response to adult directives or rules, disruption of ongoing activities, argumentativeness, temper outbursts, verbal hostility, and physical aggression (Loney & Milich, 1982). Such behaviors are often of sufficient severity and duration to warrant a diagnosis of oppositional defiant disorder (ODD), which pertains to recurrent, age-inappropriate patterns of negative, defiant, and hostile behaviors, often accompanied by an irritable mood (American Psychiatric Association, 1994). Recurrent patterns of the more serious antisocial behaviors (e.g., stealing, property destruction, aggression towards persons or animals, deceit, truancy) that comprise conduct disorder (CD) (American Psychiatric Association, 1994) are less common than ODD features but still co-occur with ADHD at rates that far exceed chance. The rates of ODD or CD found in ADHD samples have ranged from 30% to over 50% (Anderson, Williams, McGee, & Silva, 1987; Beiderman, Newcorn, & Sprich, 1991). Despite the high degree of overlap between ADHD and both ODD and CD, research, examining group differences in variables including environmental background, family psychiatric history, cognitive impairments, family interactions, and course, supports the partial independence of these syndromes (Abikoff & Klein, 1992; Hinshaw, 1987). Moreover, those ADHD children with comorbid CD may represent a qualitatively distinct subgroup from ADHD youngsters without a comorbid disruptive behavior disorder (Hinshaw, 1994).

The intra- and extrafamilial interpersonal functioning of ADHD children is frequently disturbed. Elevated rates of negative and conflictual parent–child interactions characterize families with an ADHD child (Barkley, Karlsson, & Pollard, 1985; Mash & Johnston, 1982). In addition, these families are marked by higher levels of parental stress and psychopathology and lower levels of marital harmony and self-perceived parenting competence than those found in families without a disturbed child, although some of these findings apply to ADHD children with comorbid ODD or CD (Anastopoulos, Guevremont, Sheton, & Du-Paul, 1992; Anderson, Hinshaw, & Simmel, 1994; Johnston, 1996; Schachar & Wachsmuth, 1990). The interactions of ADHD children with their teachers, like those with parents, are often characterized by lower than average rates of positive exchanges and higher rates of commands and negativity (Pfiffner & Barkley, 1990). Although the child and parent characteristics are bidirectional in their effects, it is worth emphasizing that many negative parent characteristics disappear with corrective intervention with the child, an important therapeutic point in reducing the guilt of parents prone to blame themselves for the appearance of the child's behavioral symptoms.

Peer relationships are also typically disrupted as children with ADHD have difficulties initiating and maintaining friendships (Guevremont, 1990). In fact, studies employing sociometric measures with ADHD samples have consistently revealed them to be poorly accepted or actively rejected by peers at much higher rates than normal children and children with other psychiatric disorders (Asarnow, 1988; Milich & Landau, 1982; Whalen & Henker, 1992). Rather than arising from deficient prosocial skill deficits, the social failure experienced by ADHD children appears to relate most strongly to their interpersonally noxious behaviors (e.g., aggression, noncompliance, disruption, and intrusiveness), affective dysregulation, and impaired capacity to modulate their social responses to shifting environmental demands. Moreover, the peer rejection suffered by children with ADHD emerges after very brief periods of interaction (Erhardt & Hinshaw, 1994; Pelham & Bender, 1982), is stable over time, and represents a robust predictor of a variety of adverse long-term outcomes (e.g., academic failure, school dropout, criminality or psychopathology) (Parker & Asher, 1987).

With respect to formal psychiatric diagnoses, ADHD is most commonly comorbid with ODD, CD, and learning disorders (see previous discussion). However, other disorders also co-occur with ADHD at above-chance levels. Indeed, it is more common for ADHD to present with one or more comorbid conditions than in the absence of another diagnosis (Newcorn & Halperin, 1994). These include anxiety disorders, which may occur in 25% or more of children with ADHD (Biederman et al., 1991), expressive language disorders (Hamlett, Pelligrini, & Conners, 1987; Zentall, 1989), Tourette's and other tic disorders (Cohen & Leckman, 1994), and motor coordination deficits (Barkley, 1990). The evidence with respect to co-occurring mood disorders is mixed, with some studies finding substantially elevated prevalence rates (Biederman, et al., 1991) and others reporting no significantly enhanced risk for affective illness in ADHD samples (Gittleman, Mannuzza, Shenker, & Bonagura, 1985; Lahey et al., 1988). Consideration of comorbid conditions is critical as they may have important implications for etiology, severity, course, and response to both pharmacologic and psychosocial treatments (March, Wells, & Conners, 1995a; Newcorn & Halperin, 1994).

5.19.2.3 Variations Related to Gender and Development

5.19.2.3.1 Gender

The expression, associated features, and course of ADHD in females is receiving increasing attention. However, research in this area remains scarce and what exists is plagued by small sample sizes which limit statistical power and preclude definitive conclusions regarding gender differences. The following comments on what is currently known have been culled from Arnold's (1996) summary of the findings emerging from a conference convened in late 1994 by the Child and Adolescent Disorders Branch of the National Institute of Mental Health to review the literature on gender differences in ADHD.

A preponderance of available evidence suggests a basic similarity between males and females with respect to the qualitative expression of the disorder; quantitatively, however, females with ADHD may, on average, show less hyperactive–impulsive behavior and less inattention than do their male counterparts. It is important to bear in mind that similar gender differences with respect to these behaviors exist in the normal population (Achenbach & Edelbrock, 1983; Goyette, Conners, & Ulrich, 1978), which raises the thorny issue of whether gender-based norms for establishing deviance should be incorporated into diagnostic thresholds. Diagnostically, the Predominantly Inattentive subtype of ADHD appears to be overrepresented in females compared to the Combined subtype (Lahey et al., 1994). Gender differences have emerged for comorbid conditions, as males with ADHD exhibit a higher rate of antisocial-spectrum difficulties, including aggression, oppositional-defiant behavior, and conduct disorder symptoms. Although some data suggest more severe intellectual, learning, and language deficits in females with ADHD, findings related to these variables are few and sufficiently mixed that conclusions would be premature. Sex-based differences in response to psychostimulant medications do not appear to exist. Insufficient evidence exists to address whether the outcomes of males and females with ADHD differ, although the greater severity of core symptoms and higher levels of associated antisocial problems may presage a more negative outcome for males. Concerns continue to be raised that females with ADHD represent an underdiagnosed and underserved population.

5.19.2.3.2 Developmental variation

The diagnosis of ADHD and the delineation of a coherent clinical picture of the disorder across the life-span are complicated by the developmental nature of the constituent behaviors. Many preschool-aged children are highly active and exhibit both inattentive and impulsive behaviors. Yet it is often difficult to distinguish normal variation in such behaviors that will dissipate as development proceeds, from the initial expression of a pathological syndrome that is likely to be chronic, impairing, and deserving of treatment (Campbell, 1990). Nevertheless, early onset behavior problems prove to be chronic and serious in a proportion of children who show such difficulties, particularly when a constellation of overactive, inattentive, impulsive, and defiant behaviors are fairly severe, persist for a year or longer, and are accompanied by negative parenting practices and family adversity (Campbell, 1990, 1995; Richman, Stevenson, & Graham, 1982). As discussed later in this chapter, it is now well-established that symptom patterns of sufficient severity and duration to warrant a diagnosis of ADHD in early childhood tend to persist at least into adolescence in a substantial majority of cases (Weiss & Hechtman, 1993).

Another way in which ADHD represents a developmental disorder is that its expression typically varies with age. Despite a trend toward overall symptom reduction with maturity (Barkley, 1990), both core and associated symptoms tend to be present in each age group, but with an altered topography. March et al. (1995a) summarize how ADHD symptoms manifest at different ages; Weiss & Hechtman (1993) provide a detailed discussion. For example, hyperactivity declines with age and minor extraneous motor behaviors (e.g., fidgeting or tapping) or an internal sense of restlessness may replace the excessive running and climbing of early and middle childhood (American Psychiatric Association, 1994). Some researchers have failed to find similar developmental declines in inattentive symptoms (Hart, Lahey, Loeber, Applegate, & Frick, 1995; Parker, Sitarenios, & Conners, 1996). Changes in symptom patterns are likely to reflect not only physiological maturation but also shifting social ecologies and environmental demands (Whalen & Henker, 1980). During adolescence, increased demands to manage multiple classes, to complete multistaged projects within a certain timeframe, and to structure one's own time, tend to increase the salience of organizational and executive functioning deficits in ADHD (Wender, 1995). Conversely, many symptoms may become less notable once individuals escape the unique demands of school and exercise greater freedom to determine working and living environments which provide a better match for their particular profile of strengths and deficits.

5.19.3 DIAGNOSIS

As part of the comprehensive assessment process described later in this chapter, the clinician will typically determine whether a child satisfies official diagnostic criteria for ADHD. Although limited in scope and utility, arriving at an accurate categorical diagnosis does represent a legitimate part of the assessment process as it serves a number of important functions. These include providing a common language for communication among professionals for both research and clinical purposes, conveying useful information on likely associated features, course, and treatment response and, on a more pragmatic level, facilitating the payment for clinical services by insurers and managed care providers (Volkmar, 1991).

The evolution of diagnostic systems for ADHD has been both incited and accompanied by constant debate regarding definitional boundaries, labels, and primary symptoms. The frequent changes in classification schemes and marked differences between those used in the USA and Europe have obstructed progress in our understanding of the disorder because they have compromised the legitimacy of cross-study comparisons. As noted by Hinshaw (1994), the ultimate aim of any categorical diagnostic scheme is to identify subgroups of individuals who are homogeneous with respect to presentation, pathogenesis, family history, course, and treatment response. Although this still represents a distal goal with respect to psychiatric nosology, progress is evident in the increasing reliance on empirical field trials of prospective criteria along with expert consultation to inform diagnostic systems (Lahey et al., 1994).

One by-product of such progress is the growing rapprochement between the two major taxonomies for psychopathology: the *DSM-IV* in the USA (American Psychiatric Association, 1994) and the *International statistical classification of diseases and related health problems, tenth revision (ICD-10)* (World Health Organization, 1992a). Conceptually, these diagnostic systems are quite similar in that the behavioral symptoms each lists as comprising ADHD are identical or show only minor variations in wording. The *DSM-IV* criteria for ADHD are listed in Table 2.

In addition to their overlap in symptom content, both criteria sets stipulate that symptoms be present to developmentally inappropriate degrees, persistent for at least six months, pervasive across settings, emergent before (*DSM-IV*) or by (*ICD-10*) the age of seven, and associated with significant impairment in social, academic, or occupational functioning (although significant distress can substitute for impairment in *ICD-10*). Despite their gradual convergence, significant differences remain between the diagnostic approaches to ADHD contained in *DSM-IV* and *ICD-10*. The *DSM-IV* system, drawing upon the results of factor analytic studies and extensive field trials (e.g., Bauermeister et al., 1992; Lahey et al., 1984, 1988), groups symptoms into the two dimensions of inattention and hyperactivity–impulsivity and defines three diagnostic subtypes on the basis of an individual's profile on these dimensions. Specifically, "ADHD Combined Type" requires at least six of the nine symptoms in both the inattention and hyperactive–impulsive domains, whereas the "ADHD, Predominantly Inattentive Type" and the "ADHD, Predominantly Hyperactive-impulsive Type" each require six or more symptoms in one problem area but fewer than six symptoms in the other domain.

The distinction of an inattentive subtype of ADHD (which is also commonly referred to as "attention deficit disorder without hyperactivity") is well supported by factor and cluster analytic studies and by data showing that family history and comorbid symptom patterns in such a subgroup diverge from those found in other children who are diagnosed with ADHD (Cantwell & Baker, 1992; Goodyear & Hynd, 1992). However, the validity of the unprecedented predominantly hyperactive–impulsive subgroup is less well established. This subtype has been found to apply disproportionately to children below school age (Lahey et al., 1994) who have had little opportunity to exhibit inattentive symptoms which become most evident in demanding, structured environments (e.g., careless errors, disorganization, or poor task completion). Thus, some suggest that the predominantly hyperactive–impulsive group may represent a developmental precursor of "ADHD, combined type" rather than a distinct subtype (Barkley, 1995a). Nonetheless, the *DSM-IV* criteria for ADHD is generally regarded to be an improvement over its predecessors, yielding diagnoses that are more reliable and more clearly associated with functional impairment (McBurnett, Lahey, & Pfiffner, 1993).

In *ICD-10*, the term "hyperkinetic disorder" is adopted rather than ADHD, and inattention, hyperactivity, and impulsivity are listed as separate problem areas, with diagnosis requiring symptoms in all three domains. However, inattention and hyperactivity are regarded as cardinal features and are emphasized over impulsive symptoms (World Health Organization, 1992b). Thus, the diagnosis of "hyperkinetic disorder" requires the presence of six of

Table 2   *DSM-IV* diagnostic criteria for attention-deficit hyperactivity disorder.

A.   Either (1) or (2):

(1)   Six (or more) of the following symptoms of **inattention** have persisted for at least six months to a degree that is maladaptive and inconsistent with development level:

Inattention

  (a)   often fails to give close attention to details or makes careless mistakes in schoolwork, work, or other activities

  (b)   often has difficulty sustaining attention in tasks or play activities

  (c)   often does not seem to listen when spoken to directly

  (d)   often does not follow through on instructions and fails to finish schoolwork, chores, or duties in the workplace (not due to oppositional behavior or failure to understand instructions)

  (e)   often has difficulty organizing tasks and activities

  (f)   often avoids, dislikes, or is reluctant to engage in tasks that require sustained mental effort (such as schoolwork or homework)

  (g)   often loses things necessary for tasks or activities (e.g., toys, school assignments, pencils, books, or tools)

  (h)   is often easily distracted by extraneous stimuli

  (i)   is often forgetful in daily activities

(2)   Six (or more) of the following symptoms of **hyperactivity–impulsivity** have persisted for at least six months to a degree that is maladaptive and inconsistent with developmental level:

Hyperactivity

  (a)   often fidgets with hands or feet or squirms in seat

  (b)   often leaves seat in classroom or in other situations in which remaining seated is expected

  (c)   often runs about or climbs excessively in situations in which it is inappropriate (in adolescents or adults, may be limited to subjective feelings of restlessness)

  (d)   often has difficulty playing or engaging in leisure activities quietly

  (e)   is often on the go or often acts as if driven by a motor

  (f)   often talks excessively

Impulsivity

  (g)   often blurts out answers before questions have been completed

  (h)   often has difficulty awaiting turn

  (i)   often interrupts or intrudes on others (e.g., butts into conversations or games)

B.   Some hyperactive–impulsive or inattentive symptoms that cause impairment were present before age seven years

C.   Some impairment from the symptoms is present in two or more settings (e.g., at school/work and at home)

D.   There must be clear evidence of clinically significant impairment in social, academic, or occupational functioning

E.   The symptoms do not occur exclusively during the course of a pervasive developmental disorder, schizophrenia, or other psychotic disorder and are not better accounted for by another mental disorder (e.g., mood disorder, anxiety disorder, dissociative disorder, or a personality disorder)

Code based on type:

314.01 Attention-Deficit Hyperactivity Disorder, Combined Type: if both criteria A1 and A2 are met for the past six months

314.00 Attention-Deficit Hyperactivity Disorder, Predominantly Inattentive Type: if criterion A1 is met but criterion A2 is not met for the past six months

314.01 Attention-Deficit Hyperactivity Disorder, Predominantly Hyperactive–Impulsive Type: if criterion A2 is met but criterion A1 is not met for the past six months

nine symptoms of inattention, three of five hyperactive features, and one of four impulsivity symptoms. Of note is the fact that the item pertaining to excessive talking, which is grouped with the hyperactivity features in *DSM-IV*, is placed among the impulsivity items in *ICD-10*.

Other differences between the *DSM-IV*, and *ICD-10* systems pertain to subtyping, exclusionary criteria, and comorbidity. For example, *ICD-10* regards the predominantly inattentive and predominantly hyperactive–impulsive subtypes of ADHD, recognized by *DSM-IV*, to be subthreshold conditions for which separate diagnostic codes are not provided. Rather, the primary division within the *ICD-10* hyperkinetic disorders is between "disturbance of activity and attention," which corresponds closely to the *DSM-IV* ADHD, combined type, and "hyperkinetic conduct disorder," a mixed category that is applied when the criteria for both hyperkinetic disorder and conduct disorder are met.

The existence of the hyperkinetic conduct disorder diagnosis in *ICD-10* illustrates one difference in the way in which the two nosologies manage the comorbidity so common to ADHD. As discussed by Taylor (1994), *DSM-IV* represents a multiple diagnosis scheme in which comorbid diagnoses are readily assigned if the criteria for each is met, provided that the symptoms of one disorder are not better accounted for by a coexisting condition. Contrasting with this approach is the single diagnosis scheme adopted by *ICD-10*. Although multiple diagnoses are permitted, the system steers the diagnostician towards choosing a single disorder on the basis of the best available match between the child's presentation and the prototypic descriptions offered in *ICD-10*. Supporting this more conservative approach to multiple diagnoses is the inclusion in *ICD-10* of precedence rules (e.g., depressive and anxiety disorders generally take precedence over hyperkinetic disorders) and listing of exclusionary criteria which are more restrictive than those found in *DSM-IV*. One limitation common to both classification schemes is the developmental insensitivity of both the symptoms listed and the diagnostic thresholds (Barkley, 1995a; Hinshaw, 1994). Thus, preschool children and adults are judged by the same items and diagnosed using the same cutpoints, despite the changing topography and severity of symptoms with maturation. Taylor (1994) provides a more detailed consideration of the *DSM* vs. *ICD* approach to diagnosing ADHD.

Regardless of which classification scheme is used, a number of additional factors complicate the clinical judgment involved in assigning an ADHD diagnosis and create the potential for both overdiagnosis and misclassification. First, many of the symptoms occur frequently in nondisordered youngsters and reflect normal developmental variation rather than an underlying pathology. Second, the heterogeneous presentation of ADHD children and the variability in performance and symptom expression within a given child as a function of time, task, and setting variables can make the disorder an elusive target. Third, many of the symptoms are not specific to ADHD but can be associated with other forms of psychopathology (e.g., anxious or depressive disorders) and with adverse environmental circumstances (e.g., chaotic families, ineffectual classrooms, or psychosocial stressors). These potential pitfalls in diagnosing ADHD place a premium on the clinician's assessment of the developmentally deviant and impairing nature of presenting symptoms, reliance on a comprehensive multimodal, cross-informant assessment battery, and command of child psychopathology to aid in differential diagnosis.

Detailed differential diagnosis is especially important in ADHD due to both the frequent co-occurrence of ADHD with other disorders (as discussed above) and to the potential for other syndromes to produce symptoms that overlap with the behavioral criteria for ADHD. Examples of the potential clinical implications of differential diagnosis include the markedly different patterns of impairment and outcomes that typify ADHD with and without conduct disorder (Hinshaw, 1992a; Walker, Lahey, Hynd, & Frame, 1987), the divergent treatment plans indicated for ADHD, learning disorders, and their combination (DuPaul & Stoner, 1994), and the less favorable stimulant response among ADHD children with comorbid anxious disorders (Pliszka, 1989). Although a detailed discussion of differential diagnosis in ADHD is beyond the scope of this chapter (see Barkley, 1990; Sharma, Matier, & Halperin, 1994), the process typically requires a thorough knowledge of the full spectrum of childhood disorders and reference factors such as age and type (acute versus insidious) of onset, course (episodic versus chronic), symptom pervasiveness, family psychiatric history, and the child's environmental context (e.g., psychosocial stressors, family relations, and school climate).

5.19.4 PREVALENCE

The reported prevalence of any disorder is strongly affected by many variables, including the definition of "caseness," sampling methods, the sampling frame, age, and comorbidity. These factors probably account for the range of prevalence of 2–6.3% in recent studies of

ADHD (Szatmari, Offord, & Boyle, 1989b), and 20% or more in some older studies.

5.19.4.1 Caseness Criteria

Slight differences in symptom criteria can markedly affect recorded prevalence of the disorder. When the *DSM* shifted from the hyperactivity–impulsivity–inattention criteria of *DSM-III* to the single list of 14 symptoms of *DSM-III-R*, ADHD became 14.4% more prevalent than attention deficit disorder/hyperactivity (Lahey, Loeber, Stouthamer, Christ, 1990). It had been observed for some time that English clinicians tended to record far fewer cases of their *ICD-9* equivalent of attention deficit disorder (ADD) (hyperkinetic disorder), than their American counterparts. The causes of this unequal prevalence of hyperactivity in the UK and the USA were investigated by British and American clinicians and research panels using both *ICD-9* and *DSM-III* criteria. Although there was poor clinician reliability, the specially trained research panels reliably found that *ICD-9* generated fewer diagnoses of hyperkinetic syndrome than did *DSM-III* for attention deficit disorder with hyperactivity. This difference was greatest for UK clinicians, and both the diagnostic scheme and clinician training contributed significant variance to the difference in reported rates (Prendergast et al., 1988). When using standard rating scales, the mean hyperactivity score of English school-children is actually higher than their American peers (Taylor & Sandberg, 1984).

Questionnaires can yield any prevalence rate, depending upon the choice of cutoff score. But other factors affect prevalence obtained by ratings. The format of questionnaires used for assessing hyperactivity or ADHD can have an impact on the obtained prevalence rates. In a study of 2000 Australian and English school-children, a rate of 5.6% was found using the Conners teacher rating scale, 7.5% using a scale which compared behavior to a normal standard, and 8.9% using a scale with yes–no format. When all three scales were required for inclusion, the rate dropped to 3.5%, whereas the rate for identification by any one of the three scales rose to 12% (Holborrow, Berry, & Elkins, 1984).

The symptom informant has a strong effect on recorded prevalence. One of the largest studies, carried out on 5000 children in the Bay area of San Francisco, demonstrated that hyperactivity varied from 1% to 12% depending upon whether one, two, or three "system definers" of parent, teacher, and clinician made the diagnosis (Lambert, Sandoval, & Sassone, 1978). One study, using a structured diagnostic interview with mid-Western nine-year-olds and a parent, found a rate of 3.5% by child report, 12% by parent report, and 1.7% when both were required (Shekim et al., 1985).

5.19.4.2 National and Cultural Factors

In identifying the setting and task parameters which affect the expression of ADHD symptoms, researchers have been sensitive to context in a narrow sense. However, less attention has been paid to the impact of broader contextual issues such as culture, socioeconomic status, and ethnicity, on the expression, course, treatment response, and outcome of ADHD. The behavioral features that comprise ADHD appear in diverse cultures, although reported prevalence rates vary (Bhatia, Nigam, Bohra, & Malik, 1991; Szatmari et al., 1989b; Tao, 1992). Such variation may reflect true differences in prevalence but is more often thought to arise from differences with respect to assessment procedures, classification systems, standards for demarcating normal from disordered behavior, and culturally biased perceptions of behaviors (American Psychiatric Association, 1994; Chandra, 1993; Reid, 1995; Taylor, 1989). Although some studies have suggested a lack of uniformity in the rates of ADHD-related behaviors across socioeconomic and ethnic lines (e.g. Goyette, et al., 1978; Stevens, 1981; Waechter, Anderson, Juarez, Langsdorf, & Madrigal, 1979), findings in this area have been mixed.

Cross-national studies have been too few and methodologically different to warrant firm findings, but some evidence suggests that both the rates of the disorder and its definition may vary as a function of child-rearing values and gender roles in different cultures. A rating scale study of 344 second through fourth graders in Italian schools showed a markedly higher rate of hyperactivity in Italian boys (20%) than comparable US norms. The rate for girls was only 3%. Although Italian children exhibited rates of hyperactive behaviors similar to those of children in New Zealand, Spain, and portions of the USA, factor structures of the ratings for boys and girls were different, suggesting the need for separate factor analyses for males and females in cross-national research. Hyperactivity and conduct problems, in fact, were separate factors for girls, whereas such behaviors were subsumed under a single factor for boys. There were also important similarities and differences with the factor structures for boys and girls in Italy and Spain. These differences were interpreted as reflecting differences in the cultural acceptability of certain behaviors in Italy and Spain (O'Leary, Vivian, & Nisi, 1985). Notable cultural and ethnic differences in prevalence have been reported for Mexican and African-American studies of hyperactivity and ADD (Juarez, Madrigal, & Anderson, 1981; Lansdorf, 1979; Solis & Solis, 1988; Waechter et al., 1979). A teacher rating scale study was carried out in 2770 Chinese children from elementary schools in urban, suburban, and mountain communities. Prevalence rates of hyperactivity varied from 3.1% in urban areas, to 7.8% in suburban, and 7% in mountain communities (Yu, Yu, & Xiao, 1985). The suburban rates are closely comparable to the rate of 8.76% found in comparably aged recent Chinese immigrants (Yao, Solanto, & Wender, 1988). The marked regional differences contrast with relatively minor regional effects in national surveys within the USA (Achenbach, Conners, Quay, Verhulst, & Howell, 1989; Achenbach, Howell, Quay, & Conners, 1991) perhaps reflecting a greater range of regional differences in economic and social circumstances in the Chinese sample.

5.19.4.3 Comorbidity

Community-based studies show that many of the socioeconomic, gender, and family dysfunction factors associated with ADHD disappear when influences of comorbidity are statistically controlled (Szatmari et al., 1989a). Children of parents with diagnoses of panic disorder, major depressive disorder, or no diagnosis show marked differences in the rates of diagnosed attention-deficit disorders. The comorbidity of ADD and anxiety and/or depressive disorders was examined in 163 7–17-year-old offspring of parents with panic, depression, or no diagnoses. Diagnoses of ADD by self-report, parent report, and best-estimate consensus were all higher in the offspring of affected parents. Much higher rates of ADHD were reported when anxiety and/or depression were present in the child as well (McClellan, Rubert, Reichler, & Sylvester, 1990).

5.19.4.4 Developmental Factors

A major problem with categorical diagnostic schemes such as *DSM* is that fixed numbers of symptoms are required, and the normative rate of symptoms may change with age. For this reason, authoritative sources recommend supplementing *DSM* categorical criteria with norm-based symptom criteria (Barkley, 1990). The problem of syndromal definition is further complicated by differences in age trends for hyperactive–impulsive symptoms and inattention symptoms. Biological parents of hyperactive–impulsive children, compared with adoptive parents, show clear evidence of

inattention but no hyperactivity–impulsivity, suggesting that the familial or genetic trait of hyperactivity-impulsivity tends to disappear in adolescence or adulthood (Alberts, Firestone, & Goodman, 1986). This finding is consistent with long-term follow-up studies which also suggest age-related changes in symptomatology (Hechtman, 1989; Weiss & Hechtman, 1986).

Although there is little doubt regarding age-related changes in the level of symptomatology, a more important issue is whether the syndromal structure is similar across ages. If not, then one could reasonably argue that a different appellation, such as "residual state," might be needed instead of the same diagnostic label that is used in childhood. In a recent study of a large national sample, both parents and teachers rated the 18 *DSM-IV* symptoms on a four-point Likert scale (not at all, just a little, pretty much, very much). Three different models of the factor structure were tested: a single linear factor; a hyperactivity–impulsivity and inattention two-factor model; and a hyperactivity–impulsivity-inattention three-factor model. For both parents and teachers the three-factor model provided the best fit to the data across all age groups (3–17 years), using stringent goodness-of-fit criteria. However, for practical purposes the two-factor model is probably sufficient, given a high correlation between the hyperactivity and impulsivity item clusters (Conners et al., 1996). This study clearly showed strong age-related declines in hyperactivity–impulsivity, whereas inattention tended to remain constant across the age groups. This cross-sectional study replicates a similar finding from the study of 7–12-year-old males with ADHD diagnoses followed longitudinally over a four year period (Hart et al., 1995).

5.19.5 ETIOLOGY AND RISK FACTORS

Modern concepts of disease emphasize that diseases are best conceptualized as a product of accumulated risks. There are many pathogens that require certain factors in the host before the disease will manifest itself. There are many protective factors, both biological and social, that operate in the host to ward off disease. Various contributing factors, such as genetic influences, neonatal and perinatal insults to the brain, normal variability of temperament patterns, and environmental risks and protective factors, interact in complex ways to produce the final behavioral outcome in a child. Considerable research demonstrates that many psychological and psychosocial phenomena are the result of biological risks (Rutter & Casaer, 1991). This concept is important because it frames the nature of research questions—

instead of asking: What is the cause of ADHD? with its implicit assumption of a single etiological pathway, it directs researchers to ask: What are the various combinations of risks and protections that produce the syndrome of ADHD?

The concept of risk factors is important for prevention, assessment, and treatment. Some environmental risks can be eliminated altogether, such as eliminating air-borne lead or other pollutants, preventing maternal smoking or drinking during pregnancy, or providing adequate nutrition to the developing brain. An understanding of biological risks is also important in the assessment and treatment process because knowledge regarding biological sources of ADHD helps parents by ameliorating guilt, develops rapport during assessment, and promotes positive attitudes towards the child and the family by minimizing blame and scapegoating. The role of biological risks in producing the syndrome has been important in gaining acceptance for school-based interventions for ADHD as one of the legitimate handicapping conditions.

Protective factors can offset or ameliorate the impact of risks, even when those risks are at the severe end of the spectrum (Werner & Smith, 1967; Werner et al., 1968). Good parenting, achievement orientation and the value of effort, socioeconomic advantage, educational opportunity, good diets, antistress techniques, and positive lifestyles, can all minimize otherwise disastrous effects of biological and environmental risks. The most important protective factors are social, parental, and educational. These form the basis of therapeutic efforts with ADHD children.

Among the most important risk factors for ADHD are various comorbid conditions that may occur along with ADHD. These conditions—anxiety, aggression, oppositionality, depression—may occur as genetically linked risks, secondary consequences, or simply as independently occurring processes. Some conditions, such as low self-esteem and demoralization, are almost inevitable secondary consequences of ADHD itself. Demoralization, depression, and anxiety frequently become part of the adolescent and adult picture of the disorder as the result of cumulative insults to self-esteem and failure in social and educational settings.

5.19.5.1 Genetic Risk Factors

Although no single marker for genetic transmission of ADHD has been found, comprehensive review of the neurobiological literature strongly suggests genetic and biolo-

gical explanation for the syndrome (Zametkin, 1989). Overviews of the literature on genetic, biochemical, neurobehavioral, and neuroanatomical correlates of ADHD suggest that motor-regulatory systems involving subcortical and frontal systems are associated with ADHD. These studies also suggest a possible genetic basis because they implicate deficiencies in several neurotransmitters and because family studies show some concordance between affected parents and their children (Hynd, Hern, Voeller, & Marshall, 1991; McMahon, 1981).

Controlled case studies provide strong suggestions of genetic influences on hyperactivity and disruptive behavior (Heffron, Martin, & Welsh, 1984). Furthermore, more recent research applying powerful multiple regression techniques strongly suggests that ADHD is highly heritable (Gillis, Gilger, Pennington, & DeFries, 1992), with heritability estimates of 0.87–0.98. These estimates were similar to more recent data from hyperactive twins studied in London. Data from mixed-sex pairs did not support a two-threshold genetic explanation for the male excess of hyperactivity. The link between adverse family factors and hyperactivity was weak (Stevenson, 1992). Evidence suggests that only some forms of ADHD may be genetic, with the milder (situational) types showing less genetic influence and more association with antisocial behavior. These findings cast doubt on the validity of combining situational and pervasive hyperactivity into a single diagnostic category of ADHD, and also support a frequent finding that antisocial behaviour carries a different genetic pattern than ADHD (Goodman & Stevenson, 1989a, 1989b).

Family-genetic studies show that there are a number of associated risks shared with ADD, including conduct disorders, anxiety, depression, antisocial behavior, alcoholism, maternal personality disorders, and proneness to substance abuse in the first-degree relatives of ADHD (Cantwell, 1988). Relatives of ADD probands have a higher morbidity risk for ADD, antisocial disorders, and mood disorders than relatives of psychiatric and normal controls. The increased risk for ADD, however, cannot be accounted for by gender or generation of relative, the age of proband, social class, or the intactness of the family (Biederman, Faraone, Keenan, Knee, & Tsuang, 1990). Similar risks are found in ADHD girls as found in boys (Faraone, Biederman, Keenan, & Tsuang, 1991a). There are particularly high risks for offspring of parents with conduct, oppositional, or antisocial disorders (Faraone, Biederman, Keenan & Tsuang, 1991b). Further evidence of the genetic link to behavior problems comes from studies using parent ratings rather than diagnoses (O'Connor, Foch, Sherry, & Plomin, 1980). A classical twin analysis compared intraclass correlations for 54 pairs of identical twins and 38 pairs of same-sex fraternal twins, using a revised form of a parent symptom rating questionnaire (Conners, 1970). For seven of eight factor scales, correlations were significantly greater for the identical than for the fraternal twins. The identical twin correlations were similar to the test–retest reliabilities of the scales, suggesting that nearly all of the reliable variance for these behavioral problems was shared by identical twins.

There is a surprising link between familial ADHD and anxiety disorders (Biederman, Faraone, Keenan, Steingard, & Tsuang, 1991). Risk of anxiety disorders was twice as high in relatives of ADD when accompanied by an anxiety disorder than in those of ADD without anxiety disorder; there was also a tendency for relatives who had ADD to have a greater risk for anxiety disorders than relatives without ADD. Similar findings hold for affective disorders (Biederman, Newcorn, & Sprich, 1991). Some genetic risks may involve specific influences upon the early development of the fetus, as evidenced by the incidence of dysmorphology in the first-degree relatives of ADHD (Deutsch, Matthysse, Swanson, & Farkas, 1990). These studies suggest genetic heterogeneity for the disorder, and the possible value of dividing the disorder into more than one biological subtype.

Comorbidity of ADHD and learning disorders is high, with estimates ranging from 20% to 50%. It is not yet clear whether ADHD and reading disorders (RD) are genetically related or independent. Monozygotic and dizygotic twin pairs, in which at least one member of each pair was RD, were assessed for ADHD. Trends in the data and subtype analyses suggest that in some cases RD and ADHD may occur together because of a shared genetic etiology, and that a genetically mediated comorbid subtype may exist (Gilger, Pennington, & DeFries, 1992). Moreover, the specific type of learning disorder may be genetically determined, with phonological coding (i.e., sound-based reading) showing high heritability, while orthographic coding (i.e., visually based reading) shows no heritability. Phonological coding was substantially lower for most ADHD children with reading disabilities, indicating a developmental deficit in phonological coding rather than an equal developmental lag across all component reading skills (Olson, Rack, Conners, DeFries, & Fulker, 1991; Olson, Wise, Conners, & Rack, 1990; Olson, Wise, Conners, Rack, & Fulker, 1989).

5.19.5.2 Medical and Environmental Risk Factors

Medical factors are sometimes important because of their intertwined relationship to parenting variables and other aspects of social development. For example, low birthweight influences not only physical and cognitive competencies, but the behavior of mothers towards the child (Landry, Chapieski, Richardson, Palmer, & Hall, 1990). In a similar study (Lewis & Bendersky, 1989), independent impacts of severe intraventricular hemorrhage, other common medical complications of prematurity, and socioeconomic status, on the development in the second year of life were moderated by both the socioeconomic circumstances and the degree of medical complications.

Medical services are highly overused by ADHD children and families, even though mental health services are underused by ADHD children (Offord et al., 1987; Szatmari et al., 1989a). One reason may be that ADHD children have more actual psychosocial events leading to medical care than normal children. In one study they had more than twice as many actual medical and psychosocial events involving significant threat to the child. The causal direction of some of these risks is uncertain since many of the events may reflect the impulsivity and risk-taking behaviors of the children, and adverse environmental variables may be correlated through their relationship with comorbid conditions (Jensen, Shervette, Xenakis, & Bain, 1988).

5.19.5.3 Metabolic and Nutritional Factors

Metabolic and nutritional explanations of hyperkinesis have been around at least since 1929 when a report described a 12-year-old boy who,

> had been termed by psychiatrists and psychologists a "nervous hyperkinetic child." To use his own words, "I have to keep on going and be doing something ... " His diet was meager in meats and vegetables and rich in candy and cookies. This inadequacy of diet allied with hyperkinesis suggested the treatment. (Seham & Seham, 1929, p. 1)

Although comprehensive reviews of the role of nutrients, food additives, and sugar generally indicate a somewhat limited basis for inferring relationship to the etiology of ADHD (Milich, Wolraich, & Lindgren, 1986; Wolraich, Wilson, & White, 1995), current evidence suggests a complex intertwining of nutritional variables, such as sugar intake, exposure to environmental toxins, and other risk factors. Consider, for example, the role of cadmium and zinc. Cadmium is frequently inhaled from sidestream smoke by children (i.e., secondary smoke from smoking adults in the near environment). A large study of hair cadmium on the eastern shore of Maryland (Thatcher, McAlaster, Lester, & Cantor, 1984) found that children with high cadmium levels had lower IQ and poorer reading ability than those with low cadmium levels. However, this effect did not hold for children who regularly ate whole-wheat bread. Statistical controls ruled out demographic variables as causes. This unlikely phenomenon was found to depend upon the intake of zinc in the wheat kernel. The cadmium effect was inversely related to the levels of zinc measured in the children. The authors concluded that dietary zinc protects against the toxic effects of cadmium. Dietary intake of carbohydrate was also inversely related to the levels of zinc, a replicated finding in several studies for both micronutrients and vitamins (see below for further discussion of dietary risk factors). Thus, excess dietary sugar was found to have an important negative effect via its impact upon intake of needed dietary zinc. Even with socioeconomic status (SES) and other background factors controlled statistically, a multiple regression indicated that 20% of variance in reading level was accounted for by the combination of cadmium and the dietary factors.

5.19.5.4 Lead

The Centers for Disease Control (CDC) have published a major revision of their 1985 statement on prevention of lead poisoning in children (CDC, 1991). New evidence supports DHHS Secretary Louis Sullivan's assertion that lead is the number one environmental health threat to American children [Letters to the Editor, 1992]. The evidence linking low levels of lead exposure (10 µg or more per deciliter of whole blood), and a constellation of neurotoxic and other adverse effects in young children, is compelling. One study found that each 10 µg dl^{-1} increase in lead lowered IQ by eight points. The importance of lead as a subtyping factor in hyperactive children has been somewhat controversial, but considerable evidence suggests a relationship (David, Hoffman, Sverd, & Clark, 1977). Lead becomes especially important as the range of sociodemographic factors is increased and the risks of exposure are greater. Living in a crowded, urban neighborhood with high lead levels in older houses close to the increased lead deposition from automobile fumes, in combination with lower levels of nutrients such as calcium and iron, combines multiple risks.

Calcium and iron protect against lead assimilation into the brain and gut, but are more likely to be absent from the child's diet if mothers (especially single mothers) start them earlier on cow's milk in order to return to work. Since the iron in cow's milk is less assimilable than breast milk, socioeconomic and nutritional risks interact. This form of complex interaction among risk factors may be the rule rather than the exception, making specific etiological or causal factors in ADHD difficult to disentangle.

5.19.5.5 Vitamins and General Nutrition

Several studies suggest a complex path relating hyperactivity, inattention, and cognitive function to nutritional status. Benton and Roberts (1988) reported that taking a vitamin and mineral supplement over an eight month period increased the nonverbal intelligence of 12-year-old British schoolchildren. The study was a well-designed double-blind placebo-controlled trial. This trial attracted considerable attention, and several replication studies appeared. A large study involving 615 US schoolchildren was carried out over a 12 month period of supplementation. The tablets contained either placebo or vitamins and minerals at 50%, 100%, and 200% of the US recommended daily allowance. Significant improvement in nonverbal intelligence was found for the 100% supplementation group compared with placebo. Equally important is the replicated finding of decline in performance IQ in the placebo-treated group (Benton & Buts, 1990). The cause of the apparent increase in nonverbal IQ with supplementation, and decline with the passage of time, is unclear.

Benton and Cook (1991) reported a study of 47 six-year-old children with a randomized double-blind procedure aimed at finding the nutritional and behavioral factors responsible. They found a 7.6 point IQ gain in the supplement group compared with a decline of 1.7 points in the placebo controls. Nutritional analyses revealed a strong positive relationship ($r = 0.55$, $P < 0.004$) between the amount of sugar in the diet and the change in IQ scores for three different IQ tests. The authors interpreted the findings to mean that high sugar intake is associated with vitamin deficiencies, which in turn result in lower IQ test results, mediated by effects upon attention and distractibility during testing. Supplementation is therefore more effective in children with the worst diets, that is, those who ingest excessive levels of carbohydrates and sugar. The argument was supported by direct observation by trained observers blind to the experimental conditions, showing that fidgeting and frustratibility during IQ testing showed a significant improvement in the supplemented group but not the placebo group.

The fact of excess sugar intake among children presenting for clinical services is indisputable. Its interpretation, however, is problematical. Dietary factors (e.g., high carbohydrate intake) may account for poor nutrition, but might also represent some correlated effect from social class or family characteristics. For example, the fact that children in the lowest quartile of attention are in the highest quartile of refined sugar intake was found to be related to parental license in giving access to the refrigerator (Prinz & Riddle, 1986). Available evidence of this type does not make it possible to determine (i) whether parents who are poor limit-setters produce uncontrolled children whose diets simply reflect another area in which the children lack self-control, or (ii) whether lack of dietary control leads to poor nutrition and thence poor cognitive and behavioral control.

These issues assume particular importance in patients from lower income groups since it is well known that poorer education and lower income are associated with poorer dietary status. We believe that there is a subgroup of ADHD children who are defined by the facts that they come from the lower part of the SES distribution. They routinely have poor dietary intake of vitamins and micronutrients; have relatively high carbohydrate to protein intake, and are lower in performance IQ than equivalent SES patients with good nutritional status. Nutritionally defined subgroups within the lower SES category may be an important predictor of developmental course and stimulant treatment response.

5.19.5.6 Temperament as a Risk Factor for ADHD

It has long been suspected that normal variations in temperament can dispose to later problems of ADHD. Certain extremes of normal temperament might become disorders when they conflict with parental styles or environmental requirements, despite being normal biological variations. There is little doubt that activity level is highly heritable and is normally distributed in the population (Conners & Kronsberg, 1985). In one study, Boudreault and Thivierge (1986) examined the relationship between temperament and externalizing- or internalizing-type behavior problems in school in 295 male and 301 female seven-year-olds. A temperament questionnaire was filled out by parents and the Conners Teacher Questionnaire was completed by teachers twice over a four week interval. The results indicated that a temperamental pattern of high activity and high approach with new stimuli predisposed boys to present externalizing behavior problems in school, whereas the temperamental traits of low adaptability or withdrawal with new stimuli predisposed girls to internalizing behavior problems in school. Others report relationships between parent ratings of adjustment problems and early temperament (Brody, Stoneman, & Burke, 1988). Long-term follow-up studies suggest that the adult outcome of ADHD may be related to early temperament styles (Hechtman, 1991). Predictions of long-term outcome based upon early temperament holds up in follow-up studies of epidemiological samples (Lambert, 1988).

One novel hypothesis considers vigilant attention as a temperamental trait. Weinberg and Brumback. (1990) suggest that the trait of vigilance has behaviors which overlap those of attention deficit–hyperactivity disorder. Vigilance is the state of being watchful, awake, and alert. Motor restlessness (fidgeting and moving about, yawning and stretching, talkativeness, or a combination of these) may be a method to improve alertness when sitting or standing still or when involved in tasks requiring continuous mental performance. In order to stay awake when prevented from being active, persons with lowered vigilance will stare off, daydream, show minor hyperactivity, and finally may fall asleep. They will also complain of boredom and monotony and usually avoid or lose interest in structured or repetitive activities. This trait is viewed as a dominantly inherited condition with onset in early childhood and worsening with age. Persons with this "primary disorder of vigilance" are described as having a remarkably kind and caring temperament. This description could be seen as simply another way of viewing ADHD; however, casting it as an inherited temperament trait has heuristic value since it shifts the search for etiology to extremes of normal temperament variation, rather than to a pathological process.

Short sleep durations and high ADHD symptom ratings appear to be features of children with a difficult temperament or high motor activity when awake and asleep. Thus, some children with colic (which is a common finding in the early history of ADHD children), may represent an extreme of a normal temperament trait (Weissbluth, 1983, 1984).

5.19.5.7 Overview of Etiology and Risk Factors

It seems obvious that many different genetic, medical, temperamental and environmental risks can produce symptoms indistinguishable from ADHD. If extreme enough, virtually any single factor can, by itself, lead to the syndrome. However, it is seldom the case that single risk factors occur; rather, it is not uncommon to see family-genetic, medical, and other risks occur in combination. Development is transactional, so that risk factors create effects which then become a part of the ADHD picture; this new picture then leads to further complications, and so on. The high risks associated with maternal smoking or alcohol use (Nichols & Chen, 1981) are themselves linked to certain family psychiatric disorders as well as to the family environment of the mother and the toxic smoking environment of the child. In our view, then, the task of assessment in ADHD must focus on the understanding of the past and present risks, protective factors, and their interaction. The task of treatment is to maximize the protective factors while applying available remedies aimed at the biological substrata of behavior.

5.19.6 DEVELOPMENTAL COURSE AND OUTCOME

Results of longitudinal studies reported in the 1980s and early 1990s dramatically altered the prevailing view of ADHD as a disorder with symptoms that remit following puberty. In contrast to this putative benign course, these prospective investigations have revealed ADHD to be a typically chronic condition, marked by the persistence of symptoms into adolescence and often into adult life for the majority of children diagnosed with the disorder (Klein & Mannuzza, 1991; Weiss & Hecthman, 1993).

More than two-thirds of adolescents who were diagnosed with ADHD (by whatever label) in childhood continue to meet diagnostic criteria for the disorder, although the manifestations of the syndrome are likely to change over time, as discussed above (Barkley et al., 1990; Gittelman et al., 1985; Hart et al., 1995). Beyond the continuity of ADHD features, this group is characterized by rates of academic underachievement, school failure, low self-esteem, peer rejection, substance abuse, delinquency, and family disharmony that exceed those found among control subjects (Barkley et al., 1990; Faigel, Sznajderman, Tishby, Turel & Pinus, 1995; Fischer, Barkley, Edelbrock, & Smallish, 1990; Gittelman et al., 1985).

This pattern of persistent symptoms and heightened risk for negative outcomes across a broad spectrum of functional domains also appears to apply to at least half of the adults who received ADHD diagnoses as children. Investigations of this population are fewer and

results more variable than for adolescents. Nevertheless, the emerging literature indicates the persistence of impairing ADHD symptomatology in a majority of cases along with generally lower levels of educational and occupational attainment and higher levels of job instability, substance abuse, antisocial behavior, and psychological distress than found in matched control groups (Barkley, Murphy, & Kwasnik, 1996; Biederman et al., 1995; Mannuzza, Gittelman-Klein, Bessler, Malloy, & LaPadula, 1993; Weiss & Hecthman, 1993). However, a number of carefully conducted studies have not found elevated rates of mood or anxiety disorders in adults with histories of ADHD (Gittelman et al., 1985; Mannuzza et al., 1993).

Despite this sobering outcome for many children with ADHD, it is important to note that a substantial proportion do indeed experience symptom remission and develop into well-adjusted, productive adults. Weiss and Hechtman (1993) estimate that up to one-third or more of children with ADHD may become indistinguishable from normal controls during adulthood. Thus, the heterogeneity that characterizes so many aspects of ADHD also applies to its course and outcome. Predictors of outcome, however, defy easy identification and are likely to involve complex interactions between a host of child, family, and ecological variables. The confounding of various predictors in many ADHD children can lead to misleading conclusions. For example, evidence suggests that the aforementioned link between childhood ADHD and later substance abuse is indirect; ADHD behaviors only increase the risk for substance abuse when they are accompanied by antisocial behavior patterns in childhood and it is the antisocial behavior rather than the early ADHD that predicts substance abuse (Lynskey & Fergusson, 1995). Similarly, aggression or other signs of conduct disorder may mediate the association between ADHD and later criminality and antisocial spectrum disorders (Hinshaw, 1994; Klein & Mannuzza, 1991). Clearly, the links between childhood externalizing symptoms and a variety of outcomes may be highly specific yet difficult to elucidate in the context of complex, multivariate causal chains.

5.19.7 CONCEPTUALIZATION AND CLINICAL FORMULATION

5.19.7.1 Multimodal Assessment

There has been no dearth of assessment research in ADHD. A recent synthesis of this literature commissioned by the Office of Special Education evaluated over 1300 references

(McKinney, Montague, & Hocutt; 1993). Along with many others (Angold, 1989; Barkley, Fischer, Newby, & Breen, 1988; Luiselli, 1991; McConaughy, 1993a; Morris & Collier, 1987; Ostrom & Jenson, 1988; Schaughency & Rothlind, 1991a), the authors of this synthesis assert that ADHD assessment should involve multiple informants, rely upon multiple technologies (ratings, interviews, direct observations, laboratory measures, and self-reports), cover multiple domains (home, school, peers, intra- and interpersonal functioning), and allow for a functional analysis that specifies treatment needs.

The major problem with these multilevel assessments is how to integrate information across informants and domains in such a way that the needs of both diagnosis and treatment formulation are served. Achenbach and colleagues made an attempt to formalize such a system using a multiaxial, cross-informant typology (Achenbach, 1992; McConaughy, 1993a). That approach has spawned vigorous debate (Macmann, Barnett, & Lopez, 1993; Martens, 1993; McConaughy, 1993b) and empirical validation has not yet occurred. In general, a best-estimate diagnosis is recommended by most authors, though rules for decision making and integration of information are usually left unspecified.

Experienced clinicians typically recommend a comprehensive evaluation that includes (i) a history of pregnancy, delivery, and developmental milestones from infancy; (ii) a family history of psychiatric disorders; (iii) assessment of specific symptoms, including their severity and frequency, situational specificity, and duration; (iv) an educational assessment which covers both academic functioning and classroom behavior; (v) intrapsychic processes, including self-image and sense of efficacy with family, peers, and school; (v) child and family interaction patterns and family structure; and (vii) neurological status when indicated by other evidence (Weiss & Hechtman, 1993). Although such an elaborate process provides a wealth of data, it does little to set boundaries around the disorder or to specify which treatments, in which combinations should be given; and it provides no clear operational methods for determining when treatment works.

Concerns about operational measures and lack of norms regarding attentional processes, and lack of consensual diagnostic criteria have prompted some to caution school psychologists against the diagnostic enterprise altogether (Ostrom & Jenson, 1988). They argue that there is a lack of a consensual definition of the disorder; that empirical research and theory have not isolated the particular attentional processes in question; and that there are no adequately normed measures of attentional processes alleged to cause the disorder. Instead, they recommend identification of the pattern of strengths and weaknesses, direct observations in the classroom with a normal control (response discrepancy), and a multigating approach (teacher identification, selection of the most severe cases, followed by school psychologist's evaluation of on-task behavior in the classroom and positive and negative social interactions at recess). This represents a more practical approach within schools and is responsive to treatment needs. However, from a broader perspective, this approach ignores the chronic long-term nature of ADHD, the role of medical treatment needs, and the treatments relating to home environment and social processes outside the school. It makes the assumption that all that is going on with these children is available to the naked eye, and that neurocognitive processes can be readily managed by strictly behavioral means. Throwing away everything we have learned about the biosocial nature of this disorder seems a heavy price to pay for the clarity of a strictly behavioral approach.

McKinney et al. (1993) were also disappointed at the paucity of studies assessing educationally relevant variables that specify how inattention, impulsivity, and overactivity impair learning on specific instructional tasks and in different educational settings. In response to this challenge, DuPaul and Stoner (1994) recommend a five-stage process of school-based assessment which starts with a teacher complaint involving one or more of the three main symptom categories (inattention, impulsivity, or overactivity): (i) use of normed teacher ratings of ADHD symptoms, followed by a multimethod assessment involving parent and teacher interviews; (ii) review of school records; (iii) behavior rating scales; (iv) observations of inclass behavior; and (v) academic performance data. A diagnostic formulation is made based on the number of ADHD symptoms, their deviance from age and gender norms, age of onset and chronicity, pervasiveness across situations, degree of functional impairment, and the presence of other disorders. A treatment plan is then developed which takes into account the severity of the symptoms, a functional analysis of behavior, the presence of associated disorders, response to prior treatment, and community-based resources. This is then followed by periodic collection of assessment data and a revision of the plan as necessary.

This approach is comprehensive, incorporates most current knowledge regarding ADHD, and reflects state-of-the-art clinical practice. However, it is both costly and potentially burdensome for the school system to undertake and inevitably extend services into the broader mental health system. An unanswered question is whether a straightforward approach which starts with the teacher's complaint, observes the behavior in the classroom, and immediately applies behavioral interventions without a broader diagnostic process involving labeling works as well as the more comprehensive five-stage process outlined by DuPaul and Stoner. Here, the assessment would be limited strictly to procedures which impact upon intervention, such as rates of deviant behaviors or academic functioning using curriculum-based measurement. An example is an eight-year-old boy with ADHD who attended regular third grade classes at his local elementary school. During academic instruction, he frequently displayed disruptive behaviors that rarely occurred during the rest of the school day. A brief functional analysis showed that disruptive behaviors were maintained by escape from task demands. Curriculum-based assessment revealed that disruptive behavior occurred most frequently during specific seating and grouping arrangements. Finally the effectiveness of an intervention derived from the assessments showed an immediate reduction in disruptive behavior and an increase in appropriate behavior that lasted throughout the data collection period (Umbreit, 1995).

Schaughency and Rothlind (1991b) also recommend a multimethod approach to assessment directed at answering four questions: Does the child meet *DSM* diagnostic criteria? Does an alternative diagnosis or conceptualization account for his or her difficulties (differential diagnosis)? Does the child display the behaviors to a developmentally inappropriate extent? Do these behaviors impair the child's functioning in school, social relationships, and/or in the home? They suggest a structured diagnostic interview with multiple informants to answer the first and second questions (along with IQ and achievement data, if needed), and information on developmental course and onset; behavior rating scales with multiple informants to answer the third question; and sociometrics and archival data (referrals, grades, classroom performance, etc.) to answer the final question. They recommend a best-estimate diagnostic approach, and also agree that we do not yet know what aspects of attention are disordered or how to measure them. They argue that the better performance of ADHD children in structured situations limits the utility of structured tasks for assessment. Their recommendations seem appropriate for younger children, but omits self-report information which is

necessary in older children and adolescents (Conners & Wells, 1985). Self-report becomes increasingly important as children get older and develop more comorbid internalizing symptomatology. Their suggestion of using a lay interviewer instrument such as the Diagnostic Interview for Children and Adolescents or Diagnostic Interview Schedule for Children has the major disadvantage that these instruments significantly overdiagnose psychiatric disorders. This would be likely to significantly overburden the already-strained resources of the schools. The use of sociometrics (Hops & Lewin, 1984), although ecologically valid, has enormous practical problems, not the least of which is the necessity of getting informed consent from parents of both the peers and the target child.

Although multimethod/multisource information could theoretically prevent some of the excesses of diagnosis which occur with single-instrument methods, the question of whether the limited incremental validity and costs of these approaches (Homatidis & Konstantareas, 1981) can be justified in school settings and managed-care environments remains to be seen. In any case, most would agree that assessment for diagnosis, and assessment for treatment, although overlapping, are not the same thing and therefore require complementary methods. Structured interviews provide information needed to determine the diagnosis, but provide little guidance regarding target behaviors or modes of intervention. To address the latter, specific classroom behavior and academic problems must be identified, along with the nature of the home environment, particularly with regard to parenting practices and skills. If more extended contact is impossible, as often happens for either economic or geographic reasons, one provides parents with a list of resources which includes information regarding token management systems, self-monitoring' skills, behavior contracting, schools and the law, books, legal resources, classroom modifications which work with most ADHD children, resources for parenting skills training, and parent support groups.

Our own clinical practice in a university medical school setting typically proceeds by collecting as much "free" information ahead of time for which the client is not billed, including a biographical history filled out by parents, parent and teacher rating scales which are computer-scored and analyzed (Conners, 1989); a developmental history and temperament scale (Conners & March, 1993); a multidimensional anxiety scale (March, Sullivan, & Conners, 1996); and a child depression scale (Kovacs' Child Depression Inventory, 1993). Office interviews are then conducted with the parents using a semistructured *DSM-IV* interview for ADHD, ODD, and CD if screening questions indicate that the latter is relevant (Conners, Erhardt, & Sparrow, in press); and an interview regarding family-genetic, medical, temperamental, and environmental risk factors (Conners, in press). While this interview is being carried out, computerized testing is usually conducted, including a continuous performance test (Conners, 1994a, 1994b; Conners, March, Fiore, & Butcher, 1994). This process takes 1–2 hours of clinical time. A separate session is usually held to provide feedback and initiate treatment plans. Whether or not the child meets any criteria for a *DSM* disorder, specific behaviors or academic problems which triggered the referral must be assessed and treated. Sometimes this amounts to simple reassurance in overanxious parents; but often the nonpharmacologic interventions will be the same in these very mild cases as that for someone meeting full diagnostic criteria. Some authors argue that diagnosis is therefore a waste of time (Ostrom & Jenson, 1988).

5.19.7.2 Treatment Formulation

The heterogeneity of the ADHD population with respect to presenting symptoms and comorbid conditions dictates that intervention strategies be individually tailored and based on results of a comprehensive clinical assessment. Indeed, despite its methodological shortcomings, the multimodal treatment study conducted by Satterfield and colleagues suggests that long-term, highly individualized treatment plans devised on the basis of detailed assessments may improve long-term outcome for ADHD youngsters (Satterfield, Satterfield, & Schell, 1987). As emphasized by Mash and Terdel (1988), assessment and treatment should be highly integrated and mutually informing clinical activities. Formulations regarding the contexts within which interventions need to occur (e.g., home, school, or peer group) and the nature of those interventions (e.g., pharmacologic, behavioral, or pedagogic) should develop during the course of the evaluation. After intervention has begun, formal periodic assessments should take place as a means of monitoring the child's status relative to the baseline evaluation in order to inform decisions about the need to modify, add, or terminate treatments. For example, an intensification of school-based behavioral programs may be indicated on the basis of an assessment documenting an increase in teacher-reported classroom misbehavior.

The selections of specific treatments for ADHD children cannot at present be informed by any known cure, certain or simple etiology, or any consensus regarding the underlying nature of the disorder. Thus, clinicians must rely whenever possible on interventions with empirically validated efficacy for the primary treatment targets identified through the comprehensive assessment. Hence psychostimulant medications and behavior therapy delivered through parents, teachers, or direct contingency management approaches are the likely cornerstones of treatment programs for ADHD. The need for adjunctive interventions to complement these core treatment components should be anticipated for many children with ADHD. Moreover, clinicians should endeavor to clearly delineate the relevant targets for each treatment. For example, improved attention to tasks may be identified as a target of pharmacotherapy, whereas reduced oppositionality may represent a goal of parent training. The specific foci of treatment should reflect the chief presenting concerns of the parents and/or child and the deficits or problem areas uncovered by the assessment, with particular emphasis on those features that are most impairing to current functioning and most highly associated with poor prognosis. Thus, reducing aggressive behavior or redressing academic deficits may be prioritized as treatment goals despite such problems representing associated rather than primary features of ADHD.

Common to each planned treatment component should be programmatic efforts to promote generalization of gains across behaviors, settings, and time (Conners et al., 1994). Extending the duration of treatments (e.g., years versus months), which is consistent with the chronic nature of ADHD, may contribute to temporal generalization. Improved generalization may also result from incorporating significant others into treatment (e.g., parents, teachers, or peers), using diverse training experiences, and providing booster sessions.

Decisions related to the sequencing and cessation of various pharmacologic and psychosocial treatment components are complex and cannot as of yet be informed by a body of evidence from controlled studies. Ultimately, such decisions must be made on the basis of clinical judgment, following consideration of relevant factors such as symptom severity, age and developmental level of the child, comorbid symptoms or conditions, the palatability of various treatments to the child and family, and the extent of available resources, both within the family and the community. Some argue that behavioral interventions should always be initiated prior to medications (Hoza, Vallano,

& Pelham, 1995) but the demonstrated short-term efficacy of stimulant treatment in conjunction with its low cost and ease of administration relative to psychosocial interventions may provide some justification for introducing pharmacotherapy as the initial treatment component. Moreover, a favorable stimulant response may enhance the efficacy of subsequent interventions, although this has yet to be demonstrated empirically.

A final point related to treatment planning involves the coordination of clinical services. The adequate treatment of children with ADHD is typically a complex and lengthy process, the many facets of which are unlikely to be within any given practitioner's scope of competence. It is thus necessary for the individual clinician to be familiar with community resources that may be of benefit to ADHD children and their families and to establish the relationships with professionals from other disciplines that are necessary to develop coordinated, multimodal treatment plans.

5.19.8 TREATMENT

Two primary goals should guide the selection and implementation of interventions for children with ADHD: (i) optimizing current functioning across behavioral, academic, family, and social domains by reducing the severity and impact of core and associated symptoms; and (ii) prevention of the adverse outcomes known to result for many of these youngsters by intensively targeting those problem areas (such as aggression and other antisocial behaviors, academic underachievement or failure, family dysfunction, or peer rejection) most strongly associated with poor prognosis. In the light of these overarching goals and the multifaceted problems experienced by most children with ADHD, consensus has emerged that no single treatment is likely to be sufficient for addressing the acute and chronic clinical needs of this population. Clinical and research efforts have moved towards the identification of multimodal treatment packages with the hope that active components will interact in a complementary or synergistic fashion to maximize therapeutic effects (Abikoff & Hechtman, 1996; March, Wells, & Conners, 1995b; Pelham & Murphy, 1986; Richters et al., 1995).

5.19.8.1 Psychosocial Interventions

Despite the well-established short-term clinical efficacy of psychostimulant medications (March, Erhardt, Johnston, & Conners, 1995; Swanson et al., 1993), alternative or adjunctive

psychosocial interventions are invariably required for one or more of the following reasons: (i) medications are not an option for a minority of children with ADHD due to nonresponse, intolerable side effects, or parent refusal; (ii) gains achieved by medication often fail to normalize functioning in the short term and have yet to be associated with long-term benefits; (iii) many associated symptoms of ADHD (e.g., academic skill deficits or family disharmony) are not appropriate targets for pharmacotherapy (as reflected in the adage "pills don't teach skills"); (iv) the restriction of stimulant-related benefits to times when the child is actively medicated often results in a need for other interventions to be in place during evenings, weekends, and vacations; and (v) the use of combination treatments may permit lower intensities or dosages of each component (e.g., lower medication dosages resulting from the presence of concurrent contingency management programs).

Prior to discussing a selection of the wide range of psychosocial treatments which have been applied to children with ADHD, we wish to highlight that behaviorally oriented interventions enacted through parents, teachers, or direct contingency management programs in the classroom represent the most widely applied and empirically supported psychosocial interventions for ADHD (Hinshaw & Erhardt, 1993; Pelham & Hinshaw, 1992). Although less common and less efficacious with ADHD populations, cognitive-behavioral interventions, social skill training programs, and individual child treatment also warrant comment due to their potential utility as adjunctive components in multimodal treatment packages. There are a number of additional interventions with limited or no established efficacy for ADHD populations, including dietary management, electroencephalographic biofeedback, relaxation training, ocular exercises, chiropractic methods, megavitamins, and sensory integration training.

5.19.8.1.1 Parent-based interventions

Following their successful application to children with oppositionality, aggression, and other conduct problems (Wells, 1995), parent training (PT) approaches were extended to ADHD populations in the early 1980s and have emerged as the most prevalent psychosocial treatment for the disorder. Two objectives which characterize PT programs for ADHD are educating parents about the disorder and teaching a comprehensive set of behavior management skills so that parents may act as change agents to reduce negative behavior and promote adaptive functioning in the natural environment. Efforts are also geared towards improving the general family emotional climate and altering coercive parent–child interactions which may contribute to the exacerbation of ADHD symptoms and oppositional behavior (Barkley, 1990; Campbell, 1990).

Detailed, session by session descriptions of PT programs are available (Anastopoulos & Barkley, 1990; Barkley, 1987; Hembree-Kigin & McNeil, 1995; McMahon & Forehand, in press; Newby, Fischer, & Roman, 1991). Despite some variation in format, duration, and content, PT programs for ADHD generally rely heavily on therapist modeling, behavior rehearsal (e.g., role playing), and homework and include the following components: (i) psychoeducation on ADHD; (ii) introduction to social learning theory and general behavior management principles; (iii) positive reinforcement skills (e.g., positive attending, "catch your child being good," promoting independent play, or effective ignoring); (iv) effective commands; (v) point or token economy systems; (vi) nonphysical punishment procedures (e.g., response cost or time out); and (vii) managing behavior outside of the home. (A valuable augmentation to the psychoeducational component of PT is parent involvement in an organization designed to support and provide information to families with children with ADHD and related disorders (e.g., Children and Adults with Attention Deficit Disorders).) Innovative additions to some recent PT programs have included stress and mood management for parents, interventions to enhance marital functioning, academic support skills for the home, inputs to improve peer functioning, and training parents to advocate effectively for their child at school (Wells, in press). Specialized interventions incorporating aspects of behavioral, cognitive, and family systems approaches have been developed for families with ADHD adolescents (Robin & Foster, 1989) and found to yield improvements to family functioning (Anastopoulos, Barkley, & Shelton, 1996).

Controlled studies of PT have found it to reduce primary and associated symptoms of ADHD and to have favorable effects on parenting stress and parenting self-esteem (Anastopoulos et al., 1996; Anastopoulos, Shelton, DuPaul, & Guevremont, 1993; Wells, in press). Despite their documented efficacy for ADHD, PT approaches do not appear to achieve the same magnitude of behavioral effects as pharmacotherapy, typically fail to normalize functioning, and place high demands on parents that can reduce compliance and maintenance of treatment effects (Hinshaw, 1994; Pelham & Hinshaw, 1992).

5.19.8.1.2 School-based interventions

Some form of classroom intervention is almost invariably indicated for children with ADHD due to the adverse impact of inattentive, overactive, impulsive, and associated symptoms on learning, performance of acquired skills, and adherence to class rules and routines. School-based treatment for ADHD children may comprise both academic (e.g., tutors or special education services) and behavioral interventions. The former (DuPaul & Stoner, 1994) are not reviewed here but are often indicated due to scholastic skill deficits and possible comorbid learning disorders. Rather, we focus on behavioral interventions designed to improve the child's ability to meet both comportment and academic demands at school.

A host of classroom interventions for ADHD address antecedents of behavior by making modifications to the classroom environment, materials, and instructional techniques in an effort to create a "prosthetic" environment that helps to minimize the impact of ADHD symptoms (Abramowitz, 1994; Pfiffner & O'Leary, 1993). Beneficial changes to classroom structure may involve establishing clear and salient class rules, arranging seating so that the child is distanced from likely distracters and surrounded by well-behaved peers, instituting highly consistent routines (e.g., for turning in completed homework), and insisting that students use a daily assignment book. Students with ADHD often show higher rates of on-task behavior and task completion through the use of timers, assignments that are shortened or divided into smaller parts, checklists outlining the steps involved in a task, and alternative response methods (e.g., oral reports and videotapes). Moreover, the effectiveness of instructional methods is likely to be enhanced when they incorporate higher levels of activity, stimulation, and novelty than is typical for most classrooms.

Another group of school-based treatments for ADHD focuses on manipulating the consequences of behavior. In direct contingency management approaches, a behavior therapist establishes formal reinforcement systems with clear guidelines for behaviors that both earn and lose tokens, which may subsequently be exchanged for tangible reinforcers (e.g., access to a rewarding classroom computer). Numerous studies have documented the effectiveness of such methods for improving both academic productivity and classroom behavior (Ayllon & Rosenbaum, 1977; Hinshaw & Erhardt, 1993; Pelham & Hinshaw, 1992).

More common, however, are models in which therapists consult with teachers in order to educate them about ADHD and teach effective instructional and behavior management strategies. Much of the content in such interventions parallels that found in PT, albeit with adaptations to ensure applicability to the school environment. Thus, teachers learn to make positive attention contingent upon desirable behavior, issue effective commands and reprimands, provide high rates of prompts and feedback, establish token economies specifying individual or group-based contingencies, use response cost and time out as punishments, and enact many of the antecedent modifications discussed above. Teachers, like parents, are encouraged to provide a high ratio of positive to negative consequences but also cautioned that prudent negative consequences, such as response cost and time out, are often essential components of behavioral programs for youngsters with ADHD (Abramowitz, 1994). Detailed discussions of these and additional school-based interventions for students with ADHD, including daily report cards (DRC), behavior contracts, self-monitoring and self-reinforcement, study and organizational skill training, and group-based contingencies can be found in DuPaul and Stoner (1994), Parker (1992), and Pfiffner and O'Leary (1993). Additionally, Burcham, Carlson, and Milich (1993) review key features of educational practices for ADHD judged to be most promising in a project of the US Department of Education.

DRC systems merit comment because they represent a widely used and highly effective intervention wherein daily rewards are issued or withheld by parents at home contingent upon the child's behavior at school. DRC systems begin with teachers and parents collaboratively identifying behavioral and academic goals which are tailored to the unique needs of the child (e.g., "follows teacher instructions promptly," "completes and turns in homework," and "remains seated when required"). Next teachers complete a brief checklist (or DRC) at predetermined times throughout the school day that indicates whether the child met his/her goals. The DRC is sent home with the child daily and parents either provide or withhold rewards depending on the child's performance. When used alone or in combination with classroom reinforcement programs, the home–school contingencies enacted through a DRC represent a powerful means of improving both academic performance and classroom behavior (Abramowitz, 1994). Additional advantages include their low cost, ease and brevity of use, incorporation of more potent reinforcers than may be available at school, and provision of regular communication between teachers and parents.

Despite the significant benefits associated with the implementation of these behavioral school interventions in research protocols (Abikoff & Gittelman, 1984; Abramowitz, 1994), they continue to be underutilized in clinical practice. Obstacles to implementation include inadequately funded school systems, lack of training among both school and mental-health personnel to provide behavioral consultation to teachers, and demands on teachers' time which limits the practicality of some interventions (DuPaul & Stoner, 1994; Reid, Vasa, Maag, & Wright, 1994). Efforts to improve the ease of implementation and palatability for such interventions need to receive high priority in light of the typically unmet needs of students with ADHD and the legal rights of these children to adjunctive educational services (Davila, Williams, & MacDonald, 1991).

5.19.8.1.3 Child-based interventions

(i) Cognitive-behavioral methods

The prospect of addressing ADHD with cognitive-behavioral (CB) interventions initially inspired much enthusiasm due to the theoretical appeal of matching the disorder with a treatment approach designed to foster planful self-regulation. Investigations of many types of CB procedures, including verbal self-instructions, problem solving strategies, attribution retraining, self-evaluation, self-reinforcement, and anger control training, have emerged since the mid-1970s. As concluded in earlier reviews (Abikoff, 1991; Hinshaw & Erhardt, 1991), this line of research has generally failed to yield strong support for the application of CB methods to ADHD populations, particularly with respect to the much hoped for generalization of treatment gains across time and settings. Results for procedures based on self-instructional training methods have been particularly dismal.

Nonetheless, some positive outcomes have been found for anger management training and for procedures where the child is taught to monitor, evaluate, and reinforce themselves with respect to particular target behaviors (Hinshaw & Erhardt, 1991). Anger-coping programs, which are typically conducted in a group format, focus on teaching children to recognize their unique anger cues, to develop cognitive or behavioral plans for coping with anger adaptively, and to practice implementing those plans under realistic, provocative circumstances, such as being taunted by peers. However, at least two preconditions need to be met in order for these or any other cognitive intervention to yield clinically significant and generalized gains in ADHD youngsters: (i) key adults in the child's life (parents and teachers) must be taught to model, prompt, and reinforce targeted skills; and (ii) extrinsic reinforcement programs must be initiated to reward the child for the display of cognitive skills. Another rarely mentioned but useful application of a CB approach for this population involves employing cognitive restructuring methods to challenge and modify maladaptive beliefs about ADHD held by parents and teachers which may hinder their implementation of other treatments. Braswell and Bloomquist (1991) offer a detailed description of the clinical applications of CB procedures with ADHD children.

(ii) Social skill training

Despite the often glaring social failures of youngsters with ADHD, traditional social skill training programs, emphasizing the acquisition of prosocial behaviors, do not appear to be generally effective in improving the peer functioning of this population (DuPaul & Stoner, 1994; Whalen & Henker, 1992). This may well relate to the fact that youngsters with ADHD, as a group, do not appear to be deficient in the targeted social skills *per se*, but rather show problems in skill performance in natural social settings along with elevated rates of socially noxious behaviors.

Hinshaw (1992c) notes the broad array of potential foci for interventions designed to improve the social competence of children with ADHD, including decreasing negative behaviors known to be associated with poor peer status (e.g., aggression), teaching deficient social skills, enhancing self-monitoring of social behavior, altering social goals (e.g., emphasizing affiliation over dominance), teaching social problem-solving skills, promoting more accurate social information processing, and improving academic performance. He argues that meaningful and durable change in the social arena is only likely to result from multifaceted, individually tailored interventions that are delivered in naturalistic settings over long periods of time in combination with pharmacologic treatments and behavioral reinforcement programs.

Guevremont (1990) has developed a program for enhancing peer functioning that is more comprehensive than those typically employed. The approach combines social and CB skill training with programming to promote generalization and strategic peer involvement. Also promising are the multipush efforts to address peer problems contained in the intensive summer day camp treatment programs developed by Pelham (Pelham & Hoza, 1996). In addition to behavioral instruction of specific social skills (e.g., communication and conflict resolution), children are taught anger management strategies, trained in sports and game skills, and continuously reinforced for the display of appropriate social behavior in highly naturalistic classroom and playground settings. Moreover, a "buddy system" encourages the development of dyadic friendships, which may buffer some of the consequences of being unpopular in the larger peer group.

(iii) Psychotherapy

There is no compelling evidence to support the use of individual psychotherapy to address the core symptoms of ADHD (Hinshaw, 1994). Nevertheless, the experience of repeated failures across domains and frequent negative feedback from both adults and peers can lead to low self-esteem, demoralization, and negative self-image in many children with ADHD. Such problems do represent legitimate foci of expressive and CB psychotherapies which thus should be considered as adjunctive treatments for some youths with ADHD. Indeed, the multimodal treatment study conducted by Abikoff and Hecthman (1996) included a psychotherapy component for which a specific manual was developed. Greenfield, Gottlieb, and Weiss (1992) discuss some of the indications, challenges, and adaptations associated with conducting individual psychotherapy with children with ADHD.

5.19.8.2 Pharmacologic Interventions

Stimulant drugs such as Ritalin (methylphenidate) or dexedrine (dextroamphetamine) have been well-documented in their ability to bring about almost instantaneous behavioral changes in a wide array of symptomatic behaviors in ADHD. It is this remarkable alteration of behaviors, usually impervious to ordinary blandishments by parents and teachers, that helped make ADHD one of the most researched disorders in the behavioral sciences (as well as controversial in the public sphere). Contrary to popular belief, however, the pharmacologic treatment of ADHD is not a simple matter. It is true that a few drugs are highly efficacious against a wide array of symptoms, and have few side effects or adverse long-term consequences. But there are many variables that affect results in individual cases, and the deceptive ease of use of these medicines often leads to casual management without concern for the overall treatment needs of the child and family. Detailed examination of pharmacologic strategies with

ADHD shows that physicians must engage in a complex algorithm for deciding which drug to use, at what dose, and in what form (Greenhill et al., in press). Comprehensive reviews of efficacy and safety of stimulant drugs with ADHD are available (Swanson, McBurnett, Christian, & Wigal, 1995), and the interrelationship among genetics, neuroimaging and the neuropharmacology of ADHD have been well-described (Ernst & Zametkin, 1995). Here, we will focus on the essential clinical phenomena that need to be understood as part of a comprehensive treatment approach to ADHD. Important variables to consider are patient selection, choice of drugs, dose–response, time–action, side effects, and measurement issues.

5.19.8.2.1 Patient selection

Several meta-analyses of drug studies are in agreement in showing that stimulant drugs are most efficacious for symptoms of hyperactivity and other externalizing behavior problems, and somewhat less so for cognitive and achievement problems (Kavale, 1982; Ottenbacher & Cooper, 1983; Thurber & Walker, 1983). The effect sizes in those studies are very large—about one standard deviation for behavioral symptoms, and about half that for cognitive and academic problems. Although it is generally thought that the stimulants are specifically indicated only for hyperactivity, comprehensive reviews show that in addition to the primary symptoms of motor restlessness, concentration, effortful attention to tasks, and self-regulation; stimulants also improve general deportment and compliance, reduce verbal and physical aggression, decrease negative social behaviors, and improve academic productivity and accuracy (Swanson, et al. 1995). Comorbid anxiety may reduce the level of effect from stimulants (Pliszka, 1989) and be better treated with antidepressants such as imipramine (Pliszka, 1987). The fact that normal children also show improved function with stimulants warns against the misconception that the response to stimulants is diagnostic (Rapoport et al., 1980).

5.19.8.2.2 Choice of drugs

There are three stimulants approved by the Food and Drug Administration to treat ADHD patients of all ages: dextroamphetamine (Dexedrine, manufactured by SmithKline-Beachem), methylphenidate (Ritalin, manufactured by CIBA-Geigy), and magnesium pemoline (Cylert, manufactured by Abbot Laboratories). Dextroamphetamine and methylphenidate are structurally related to the catecholamines,

dopamine and norepinephrine, whereas pemoline exerts its action primarily through dopaminergic mechanisms (Greenhill, 1992). As noted in recent reviews (March, Erhardt, et al., 1995, March, Wells, & Conners, 1995b), these compounds tend to increase central nervous system (CNS) activity in some but not all brain regions. They increase the activity of striatum and connections between orbitofrontal and limbic regions, while having an inhibitory effect on the neocortex. Stimulants act by enhancing the release of catecholamines into the synaptic cleft, decreasing their reuptake and slowing down their degradation by inhibiting monoamine oxidase. Direct postsynaptic agonist activity is also postulated for dextroamphetamine and methylphenidate. Although catacholaminergic mechanisms are undoubtedly involved in the mechanism of action in ADHD—perhaps by favorably altering the processes by which the CNS allocates attentional resources and/or decides stimulus salience—the exact processes by which these compounds work remain uncertain (Zametkin & Rapoport, 1987).

5.19.8.2.3 Dose–response and time–action

Two essential aspects of stimulant treatment are constructing a dose–response curve and analyzing time–action effects. The former refers to the relationship between dose of drug and the presence of benefits and adverse effects. Establishing these relationships depends on understanding the relationship between the timing of administration, onset of response, point of maximum responsiveness, and loss or offset of drug effect. Empirical evidence suggests that dose and response are independent of body weight and that there is wide intersubject variability in response to the same dose (Rapport & Kelly, 1991). The time–action curve for attentional functioning is somewhat different from that of motor behavior (Solanto & Conners, 1982). Departures from a linear dose–response pattern are common, with some children showing a threshold effect (no response below a threshold level) and others a quadratic response (linear at lower doses and degradation at higher doses). Clinically then, each child requires an individually constructed dose–response curve, taking into consideration the time–action effects of the drug at each dose before making dosage adjustments (Erhardt & Conners, 1995). When titration is accomplished in the traditional open fashion, one starts with the lowest possible dose, working upward every 5–7 days until benefits are maximized or the patient shows prohibitive side effects.

Sprague and Sleator (1977) first suggested that the dose of methylphenidate required to achieve optimal effect for social behavior is higher than the dose required for cognitive function. They found that a high dose in a demanding memory task actually lowered performance below that of the placebo condition. Although there have been several failures to replicate findings of curvilinear dose–response effects with effortful cognitive tasks, some well-designed studies nevertheless continue to find that key attentional and academic measures show a quadratic relationship of dose and effect (Rapport, DuPaul, Stoner, & Jones, 1986). More recent reviews express concern regarding "cognitive toxicity" of high doses, particularly when the laboratory or academic task is difficult or complex (Aman & Rojahn, 1992; Swanson, Cantwell, Lerner, McBurnett, & Hanna, 1991). Interestingly, some studies (Rapport & Kelly, 1991) find that higher doses of stimulants are more effective as the task becomes more complex and demanding. Rapport and Kelly summarized a large number of cognitive tasks used in drug studies and reported that (i) in 100% of the studies the higher dose was better than the lower dose, and (ii) those judged more complex responded, in general, better to the higher dose (though individual group curves sometimes show curvilinear effects). In any case, the findings generally support the proposition that each child requires an individualized assessment in order to define the appropriate dose for the particular target behavior in question, whether behavioral or cognitive.

Dextroamphetamine is usually started at 2.5–5 mg a day and gradually increased in 2.5–5 mg increments; methylphenidate is usually started at 5 mg twice a day and then titrated in 5 mg per dose increments every 4–7 days. Peak behavioral effects are noted 1–3 hours after ingestion and dissipate in 3–6 hours for both methylphenidate and dextroamphetamine. Pemoline is usually started at 37.5 mg each morning and titrated in 18.75 mg increments to maximum clinical effectiveness. Most children respond at a total daily dose of 56.5–75 mg. Although stepped-dose open-label trials of stimulants are the rule in clinical practice, double-blind placebo-controlled titration trials, using parent and teacher ratings and objective measures of performance and academic productivity, can be very helpful in distinguishing a true drug effect from a placebo response and in establishing the best dose for an individual child.

Clinical experience suggests that sustained-release methylphenidate is variably absorbed and shows variable behavioral effects, whereas the dextroamphetamine spansule may show a more even pattern of bioavailability. However, since both tablet and sustained release stimulants are swiftly absorbed after oral administration, it is not surprising that controlled studies show no benefit for sustained release methylphenidate over the standard formulation (Pelham et al., 1987). The sustained release preparations are often helpful when the standard preparation dissipates too rapidly, or when there is stigma associated with going to the teacher or nurse for a midday dose.

5.19.8.2.4 Side effects

Frequent stimulant-related side effects and their management are summarized in Table 3. Since many side effects diminish after several weeks of treatment, patience during stepped-dose titration is important in handling mild to moderate side effects, such as mild anorexia or sleep disturbance. Sometimes gastrointestinal difficulties can be ameliorated by administration of stimulants before, during, or after meals, depending on the child. (In the child on pemoline, prominent gastrointestinal side effects, including but not limited to anorexia, should prompt consideration of pemoline-induced hepatitis since, though rare—less than 1%—it requires drug discontinuation.) Insomnia can sometimes be avoided by reducing the last dose or by earlier administration. Exacerbation of ADHD symptoms and/or irritable dysphoric mood during stimulant offset (stimulant rebound) is uncommon but can be disruptive, especially near the end of the day during homework periods. Rebound requires adjusting the dose or perhaps switching to a sustained release preparation or to a different stimulant.

Stimulants do not appear to adversely influence ultimate growth and height in most children, although a minority of children may be affected either because of calorie restriction or direct effects on growth hormone. Thus, routine drug holidays are not indicated; when necessary, periods off medication may bring about a rebound in growth rate. Caution is in order when using stimulants in children with a personal or family history of hallucinations or thought disorder, especially since attentional abnormalities are common in children at risk for schizophrenia. Close monitoring of blood pressure and pulse is not mandatory with stimulant treatment unless there is a pre-existing cardiovascular disorder, such as tachyarrhythmias or hypertension. Because of the potential for transaminitis (an elevation of liver function enzymes), pemoline requires liver function test

Table 3 Side effects of stimulant drugs.

Side effect	Possible management strategies
For all side effects	Unless severe, allow 7–10 days for tolerance to develop. Evaluate dose–response relations Evaluate time–action effects and then adjust dosing intervals or switch to a sustained-release preparation Evaluate for concurrent conditions, including comorbidities and environmental stressors Consider switching stimulant drugs
Anorexia/dyspepsia	Administer before, during, or after meals If on pemoline, consider drug-induced hepatitis
Dysphoric mood/emotional construction	Reduce dose or switch to a long-acting preparation Consider comorbidity requiring alternative or adjunctive treatment Switch stimulants
Insomnia/nightmares	Omit or reduce last dose Administer medication earlier in the day If taking sustained-release preparation, switch to tablet drug Consider adding a sedating antihistamine or clonidine at bedtime only
Tics	Firmly establish correlation between tics and pharmacotherapy by examining dose–response relationships, including a no medication condition If tics are very mild or abate after 7–10 days on medication, reconsider risks and benefits of continued stimulant treatment and renew informed consent Switch stimulants Consider nonstimulant treatment, eg clonidine or a tricyclic antidepressant (TCA) If tic disorder and ADHD are severe, consider combining stimulant with a high-potency neuroleptic
Dizziness	Monitor blood pressure and pulse Encourage adequate hydration If associated only with peak effects, change to a sustained-release preparation Switch stimulants, especially to pemoline
Weight loss	Give drug after breakfast and after lunch Implement calorie enhancement strategies, especially a scheduled fourth meal before bedtime Brief drug holidays
Slowed growth	Apply weight loss remedies Weekend and vacation (longer) drug holidays Consider another stimulant or a nonstimulant drug
True rebound	Switch to sustained-release preparation or to pemoline Combine long- and short-acting preparations Consider combined psychostimulant (at a lower dose) with a TCA or switching to bupropion
Psychosis	Discontinue stimulant treatment Assess for comorbid thought disorder Consider alternative treatments

In J. Jefferson & J. Geist (Eds.) *Psychopharmacology clinic of North America*, Pharmacology therapy of attention-deficit hyperactivity disorder by March et al., 1996, New York, Saunders. Copyright 1996 by The Journal of Practical Psychiatry and Behavioral Health. Reprinted with permission.

at baseline and every six months and should be discontinued if double-normal transaminases arise.

One of the major decisions in initiating drug therapy is which stimulant to prescribe in individual cases. In an early study, Millichap and Fowler (1967) randomly assigned 75 6–12-year-old children to dextroamphetamine, methylphenidate, or a placebo and found no differences between the two drugs on 11 behavioral laboratory measures or clinical rating measures. Although for every side effect examined dextroamphetamine had a higher frequency and severity, neither drug had a medically significant frequency of intolerable side effects requiring drug discontinuation. An early review of nine studies by Millichap and Fowler (1967) showed 84% efficacy for methylphenidate compared with 69% for dextroamphetamine, whereas Barkley's (1977) review of 14 methylphenidate and 15 dextroamphetamine studies found approximately equal efficacy with about 70% improvement rate for both stimulants (Arnold, Heustis, & Smeltzer, 1978). Although reasonably consistent, these results are all between-subject effects. Several studies which compare crossovers of the stimulants within subjects, show approximately equal efficacy overall, but not always for the same subjects (Pelham, et al., 1990; Winsberg, Press, Bialer, & Kupietz, 1974). Using a wide variety of social, academic, and behavioral measures, Pelham et al. (1990) also found that dextroamphetamine and methylphenidate were generally equivalent but that some subjects responded better to one drug than to the other. When dosages are raised to their maximum without side effects, the two stimulants are quite comparable in efficacy, but some children who respond to one do not respond to the other (Elia, Borcherding, Rapoport, & Keysor, 1991; Sallee, Stiller, & Perel, 1992). These studies imply that in clinical practice one should try alternative medications within the same class before going on to other classes of drugs. Pemoline shows comparable efficacy to the other stimulants but has had a perhaps unjustified reputation as being prone to produce toxic liver effects (Conners & Taylor, 1980; Conners, Taylor, Meo, Kurtz, & Fournier, 1972; Knights & Viets, 1975; Pelham et al., 1990), and should be considered along with other stimulants as a first-line drug for ADHD (March, Johnston, & Conners, 1996). Antidepressant drugs represent another class of drugs whose efficacy is satisfactory, but which carry higher risks for serious cardiovascular side effects (Gickling & Thompson, 1985; Ross, Poidevant, & Miner, 1995).

5.19.8.2.5 Measurement of drug treatment effects

Parent and teacher ratings have been the most widely used methods for assessing stimulant drug effects, and are considered an essential aspect of treatment monitoring. However, the considerations of dose and time–action effects described above suggests that multilevel assessment of drug effects is likely to be necessary in an optimal treatment regimen. Relying on behavioral ratings alone may jeopardize the cognitive function of the child if dosage is titrated upwards without regard to possible adverse effects on more subtle attentional and learning processes. Curriculum-based measurement uses the rate of learning in standard reading, spelling, or arithmetic tasks, using brief timed samples of performance. These methods have been successfully used in assessing and measuring treatment progress of ADHD children (Atkins & Pelham, 1991; Atkins, Pelham, & Licht, 1985). A number of classroom-based measures of academic productivity have been described which show good discriminative ability in differentiating ADHD children from controls. These methods appear to be sensitive to drug treatment and are certainly more ecologically valid than conventional standardized tests of academic function which tend to be insensitive to treatment (Balthazor, Wagner, & Pelham, 1991; Pelham, 1986; Pelham, Bender, Caddell, Booth, & Moorer, 1985; Pelham et al., 1987).

5.19.9 FUTURE DIRECTIONS FOR RESEARCH AND PRACTICE

5.19.9.1 Future of Assessments of ADHD

Considerable advances have been made in our understanding of both the processes of attention and inhibition (Conners, March, Erhardt, Butcher, & Epstein, 1995). As yet, however, these newer approaches have not been accompanied by methods that are easily transported from the laboratory to the clinic. Nevertheless, computerized tests based upon neurocognitive models are likely to be available for use once adequate normative studies and validity studies are undertaken. These new approaches will be necessary to meet the justified criticisms of those who argue that the core features of ADHD have never been adequately operationalized. Equally important as assessments at the level of microprocesses of attention and inhibition, are larger family, social, and developmental issues, which at present are poorly assessed. Until assessments have an adequate treatment target, however, they had, perhaps, better be left alone.

5.19.9.2 System Issues in Treatment

One of the most common failings of physicians in medication management is the failure to insist upon the other treatments which are known to be important for the long-term success of ADHD. The overprescription of stimulant drugs, though undoubtedly magnified by public hysteria and the media, represents a real problem. At the same time, practitioners in schools and clinics often fail to provide physicians with the support they need in terms of feedback regarding the effect of dosage and drug changes both in the home and school setting. This problem represents failure of communication across professional boundaries, failure to develop a *modus vivendi* between professional disciplines, and a lack of rational distribution of assessment and treatment resources. We have the sad fact of teachers referring children for medication because they cannot be managed in the classroom, partly because the school system itself is bogged down in meetings and assessments required by law, with few resources left to address immediate behavioral concerns in the classroom, and partly because school psychologists and other professionals have little training in actual intervention strategies, but have plenty of training in modes of assessment which are both outmoded, time consuming, and inappropriate for the school setting.

Underprescription of stimulants is also a problem. There are many children who go unrecognized as having a legitimate disorder with profound consequences for their own and their family's development. This represents a failure of programs for screening with tools that can identify the threshold for administration of drugs, as well as an inadequate understanding by the public of the importance of early recognition and intervention.

5.19.9.3 Research Issues in ADHD

The current diagnostic criteria are based entirely upon observable symptoms or behaviors directed at the two concepts of overactivity–impulsivity and inattention. Yet there is clear evidence that activity and attention are both multidimensional concepts. Activity that involves motor overflow and fidgeting is quite different from activity that is disrupted because action schemas, both short- and long-term, flounder due to lapses of working memory or lack of meaningful goals. The loss of attention due to lack of arousal is clearly different than that involving a highly aroused, overly vigilant state in which every stimulus has excitatory value and salience. The brain is too complex and subtly geared to the richness of the environmental transactions it must make to have one activity center or attention center, yet our assessments and treatments appear to be predicated on nineteenth-century concepts of the way the brain works. If there are several different circuits involved in alerting to, switching to, and sustaining focus on things, biology dictates that if it can go wrong, at some point it will, for some of the people some of the time. Therefore, we can expect there to be several different types of attention disorder.

As James (1890) so presciently observed, the key to behavioral inhibition is closely related to attention, yet our criteria make no distinction between disinhibition in the classroom due to the inattention of the poor reader faced with an impossible task, and disinhibition which comes from an extremely low threshold for detecting movement in peripheral vision. The major research task, then, in our opinion is the resolution of the heterogeneous syndrome we now call ADHD into subtypes based on a clear understanding of the underlying brain mechanisms which regulate attentional and inhibitory states. Subtypes based solely on overt symptom criteria leave us at a stage of nosology comparable to that when medicine included fever as a major class of disorder. (A fuller discussion of the relationship between neuro-cognitive models and ADHD is given by Conners et al., 1995.)

5.19.10 SUMMARY

ADHD has evolved from nineteenth-century concepts of impairment of will, to an organically based neurological condition, to a behavioral syndrome of uncertain etiology. Despite limitations in knowledge about the etiology of the condition, considerable agreement regarding the clinical features, developmental course, response to treatment, and adult outcome have accumulated, allowing reasonable preventive, ameliorative, and therapeutic interventions. The core features of inattention and hyperactivity–impulsivity are readily identified using clinical interview, rating scales, and developmental history. The presence of several comorbid symptoms, including conduct disturbance, oppositional behavior, learning disorders, anxiety, and depression, complicates assessment and enlarges the boundaries of treatment needs for most ADHD children beyond the core symptoms themselves. ADHD appears to encompass a spectrum that runs from near-normal to very severe, posing difficult problems of determining a level of functional impairment that warrants diagnosis and intervention. This leads to broad variations in estimates of prevalence. There is still uncertainty as to whether inattention and hyperactivity are part of the same disorder, or two separate disorders. The fact that many different risk factors may lead to ADHD, including genetic, medical, environmental, temperamental, metabolic, and nutritional variables, suggests that ADHD may have several subtypes depending upon the pattern of insults to the developing brain. Protective factors enter in as variables that can reduce impairment below the threshold level of expression required for diagnosis. It is relatively clear that in the absence of intervention and protective factors such as high IQ or good family circumstances, untreated ADHD results in an adult condition of considerable consequence in terms of overall adjustment, vocational and academic accomplishment, and productive lifestyle.

Except for relatively mild versions of ADHD, multimodal treatment is almost always indicated. The sequence, degree, and length of these treatments may vary as a function of developmental level, emergent secondary symptoms such as problems in peer relationships, and parental and community resources. Most treatment packages will include a consideration of medication, school interventions for both behavior and academic competence, and interventions with the parents as the main therapeutic vehicles. Child-based interventions, such as cognitive therapy and psychotherapy, will be less useful, although these can sometimes be quite helpful in individual cases. The use of behaviorally based strategies such as token systems, contracting, and self-monitoring will prove to be more helpful. Pharmacologic management is also a multimodal therapy in the sense that all elements of the social system—school, child, parent, and physician—need to be involved for successful implementation of this adjunct to the total treatment package.

Future research with ADHD will probably focus upon continued efforts to identify the particular nature of the anatomic, neurochemical, and molecular bases of the disorder, with more precise assessment tools being linked to better understanding of the brain-related processes involved. The resolution of ADHD into more specific subtypes, identifiable by behavioral methodologies, would seem to be a particularly important clinical goal. On the treatment side, ongoing studies of the relative merits of single and combined therapies should elucidate which treatment strategies are effective, although such findings will ultimately require developmental level-specific versions to be useful.

5.19.11 REFERENCES

Abikoff, H. (1991). Cognitive training in ADHD children: Less to it than meets the eye. *Journal of Learning Disabilities, 24,* 205–209.

Abikoff, H., & Gittelman, R. (1984). Does behavior therapy normalize the classroom behavior of hyperactive children? *Archives of General Psychiatry, 41,* 449–454.

Abikoff, H., Gittelman-Klein, R., & Klein, D. (1977). Validation of a classroom observation code for hyperactive children. *Journal of Consulting and Clinical Psychology, 45,* 772–783.

Abikoff, H., & Hechtman, L. (1996). Multimodal therapy and stimulants in the treatment of children with attention deficit hyperactivity disorder. In E. D. Hibbs & P. S. Jensen (Eds.), *Psychosocial treatments for child and adolescent disorders: Empirically-based strategies for clinical practice* (pp. 341–369). Washington, DC: American Psychological Association.

Abikoff, H., & Klein, R. G. (1992). Attention-deficit hyperactivity and conduct disorder: Comorbidity and implications for treatment. *Journal of Consulting and Clinical Psychology, 60,* 881–892.

Abramowitz, A. J. (1994). Classroom interventions for disruptive behavior disorders. *Child and Adolescent Clinics of North America, 3,* 343–360.

Achenbach, T. (1992). New developments in multiaxial empirically based assessment of child and adolescent psychopathology. In J. Rosen & P. McReynolds (Eds.), *Advances in psychological assessment* (Vol. 8, pp. 75–102). New York: Plenum.

Achenbach, T. M., Conners, C. K., Quay, H. C., Verhulst, F. C., & Howell, C. T. (1989). Replication of empirically derived syndromes as a basis for taxonomy of child/adolescent psychopathology. *Journal of Abnormal Child Psychology, 17*(3), 299–323.

Achenbach, T. M., & Edelbrock, C. S. (1983). *Manual for the Child Behavior Profile and Child Behavior Checklist.* Burlington, VT: Author.

Achenbach, T. M., Howell, C. T., Quay, H. C., & Conners, C. K. (1991). National survey of problems and competencies among four- to sixteen-year-olds: Parents' reports for normative and clinical samples. *Monographs of the Society For Research In Child Development, 56*(3), 1–131.

Alberts, C. J., Firestone, P., & Goodman, J. T. (1986). Attention and impulsivity characteristics of the biological and adoptive parents of hyperactive and normal control children. *American Journal of Orthopsychiatry, 56*(3), 413–423.

Aman, M. G., & Rojahn, J. (1992). Pharmacological intervention. In N. N. Singh & I. L. Beale (Eds.), *Learning disabilities: Nature, theory, and treatment* (pp. 478–525). New York: Springer-Verlag.

American Psychiatric Association (1968). *Diagnostic and statistical manual of mental disorders* (2nd ed.). Washington, DC: Author.

American Psychiatric Association (1980). *Diagnostic and statistical manual of mental disorders* (3rd ed.). Washington, DC: Author.

American Psychiatric Association (1994). *Diagnostic and statistical manual of mental disorders* (4th ed.). Washington, DC: Author.

Anastopoulos, A. D., & Barkley, R. A. (1990). Counseling and training parents. In R. A. Barkley, *Attention deficit hyperactivity disorder: A handbook for diagnosis and treatment* (pp. 397–431). New York: Guilford Press.

Anastopoulos, A. D., Barkley, R. A., & Shelton, T. L. (1996). Family-based treatment: Psychosocial intervention for children and adolescents with attention deficit hyperactivity disorder. In E. D. Hibbs & P. S. Jensen (Eds.), *Psychosocial treatments for child and adolescent disorders: Empirically-based strategies for clinical practice* (pp. 267–284). Washington, DC: American Psychological Association.

Anastopoulos, A. D., Guevremont, D. C., Shelton, T. L., & DuPaul, G. J. (1992). Parenting stress among families of children with attention deficit hyperactivity disorder. *Journal of Abnormal Child Psychology, 20,* 503–520.

Anastopoulos, A. D., Shelton, T. L., DuPaul, G. J., & Guevremont, D. C. (1993). Parent training for attention deficit hyperactivity disorder: Its impact on parent functioning. *Journal of Abnormal Child Psychology, 21,* 581–596.

Anderson, C. A., Hinshaw, S. P., & Simmel, C. (1994). Mother–child interactions in ADHD and comparison boys: Relationships with overt and covert externalizing behavior. *Journal of Abnormal Child Psychology, 22,* 247–265.

Anderson, J. C., Williams, S., McGee, R., & Silva, P. A. (1987). DSM-III disorders in preadolescent children: prevalence in a large sample from the general population. *Archives of General Psychiatry, 44,* 69–76.

Angold, A. (1989). Structured assessments of psychopathology in children and adolescents. In C. Thompson (Ed.), *The instruments of psychiatric research.* New York: Wiley.

Arnold, L. E. (1996). Sex differences in ADHD: Conference summary. *Journal of Abnormal Child Psychology, 24,* 555–569.

Arnold, L. E. Heustis, R., & Smeltzer, D. J. (1978). Methylphenidate versus dextroamphetamine versus caffeine in minimal brain dysfunction. *Archives of General Psychiatry, 35,* 463–473.

Asarnow, J. R. (1988). Peer status and social competence in child psychiatric inpatients: A comparison of children with depressive, externalizing, and concurrent depressive and externalizing disorders. *Journal of Abnormal Child Psychology, 16,* 151–162.

Atkins, M. S., & Pelham, W. E. (1991). School-based assessment of attention deficit hyperactivity disorder. *Journal of Learning Disabilities, 24,* 197–204.

Atkins, M. S., Pelham, W. E., & Licht, M. H. (1985). A comparison of objective classroom measures and teacher ratings of attention deficit disorder. *Journal of Abnormal Child Psychology, 13,* 155–167.

Ayllon, T., & Rosenbaum, M. (1977). The behavioral treatment of disruption and hyperactivity in school settings. In B. Lahey & A. Kazdin (Eds.), *Advances in clinical child psychology* (Vol. 1, pp. 83–118). New York: Plenum.

Balthazor, M. J., Wagner, R. K., & Pelham, W. E. (1991). The specificity of the effects of stimulant medication on classroom learning-related measures of cognitive processing for attention deficit disorder children. *Journal of Abnormal Child Psychology, 19,* 35–52.

Barkley, R. (1977). A review of stimulant drug research with hyperactive children. *Journal of Child Psychology and Psychiatry, 18,* 137–165.

Barkley, R. A. (1987). *Defiant children: A clinician's manual for parent training.* New York: Guilford Press.

Barkley, R. A. (1990). *Attention deficit hyperactivity disorder: A handbook for diagnosis and treatment.* New York: Guilford Press.

Barkley, R. A. (1994). Impaired delayed responding: A unified theory of attention deficit hyperactivity disorder. In D. K. Routh (Ed.), *Disruptive behavior disorders in childhood* (pp. 11–58). New York: Plenum.

Barkley, R. A. (1996). Attention-deficit hyperactivity disorder. In E. J. Mash & R. A. Barkley (Eds.), *Child psychopathology* (pp. 63–112). New York: Guilford Press.

Barkley, R. A., DuPaul, G. J., & McMurray, M. B. (1990). A comprehensive evaluation of attention deficit disorder with and without hyperactivity as defined by research criteria. *Journal of Consulting and Clinical Psychology, 58,* 775–789.

Barkley, R. A., Fischer, M., Edelbrock, C. S., Smallish, L. (1990). The adolescent outcome of hyperactive children diagnosed by research criteria: I. An 8-year prospective follow-up study. *Journal of the American Academy of Child & Adolescent Psychiatry, 29,* 546–557.

Barkley, R. A., Fischer, M., Newby, R. F., & Breen, M. J. (1988). Development of a multimethod clinical protocol for assessing stimulant drug response in children with attention deficit disorder. *Journal of Clinical Child Psychology, 17*(1), 14–24.

Barkley, R. A., Karlsson, J., & Pollard, S. (1985). Effects of age on the mother–child interactions of hyperactive children. *Journal of Abnormal Child Psychology, 13,* 631–638.

Barkley, R. A., Murphy, K., & Kwasnik, D. (1996). Psychological adjustment and adaptive impairments in young adults with ADHD. *Journal of Attention Disorders, 1,* 41–54.

Bauermeister, J. J., Alegeria, M., Bird, H., Rubio-Stipec, M., & Canino, G. (1992). Are attentional-hyperactivity deficits unidimensional or multidimensional syndromes? Empirical findings from a community survey. *Journal of the American Academy of Child and Adolescent Psychiatry, 31,* 423–431.

Benton, D., & Buts, J. (1990). Vitamin/mineral supplementation and intelligence. *The Lancet,* 1158–1160.

Benton, D., & Cook, R. (1991). Vitamin and mineral supplements improve the intelligence scores and concentration of six-year-old children. *Personality and Individual Differences, 12,* 1151–1158.

Benton, D., & Roberts, G. (1988). Effect of vitamin and mineral supplementation on intelligence of a sample of schoolchildren. *The Lancet,* 140–143.

Bhatia, M. S., Nigam, V. R., Bohra, N., & Malik, S. C. (1991). Attention deficit disorder with hyperactivity among pediatric outpatients. *Journal of Child Psychology and Psychiatry, 32,* 297–306.

Biederman, J., Faraone, S. V., Keenan, K., Knee, D., & Tsuang, M. T. (1990). Family-genetic and psychosocial risk factors in DSM-III: Attention deficit disorder. *Journal of the American Academy of Child and Adolescent Psychiatry, 29,* 526–533.

Biederman, J., Faraone, S. V., Keenan, K., Steingard, R., & Tsuang, M. T. (1991). Familial association between attention deficit disorder and anxiety disorders. *American Journal of Psychiatry, 148,* 251–256.

Biederman, J., Newcorn, J., & Sprich, S. (1991). Comorbidity of attention deficit hyperactivity disorder with conduct, depressive, anxiety, and other disorders. *American Journal of Psychiatry, 148,* 564–577.

Biederman, J., Wilens, T., Mick, E., Milberger, S., Spencer, T. J., & Faraone, S. V. (1995). Psychoactive substance use disorders in adults with attention deficit hyperactivity disorder (ADHD): Effects of ADHD and psychiatric comorbidity. *American Journal of Psychiatry, 152,* 1652–1658.

Boudreault, M., & Thivierge, J. (1986). The impact of temperament in a school setting: An epidemiological study. Special Issue: Canadian Academy of Child Psychiatry: A Canadian perspective. *Canadian Journal of Psychiatry, 31*(6), 499–504.

Bradley, C. (1937). The behavior of children receiving benzedrine. *American Journal of Psychiatry, 94,* 577–585.

Braswell, L., & Bloomquist, M. (1991). *Cognitive-behavioral therapy with ADHD children: Child, family, and school intervention.* New York: Guilford Press.

Brody, G. H., Stoneman, Z., & Burke, M. (1988). Child temperament and parental perceptions of individual child adjustment: an intrafamilial analysis. *American Journal of Orthopsychiatry, 58,* 532–542.

Brown, R. T., & Quay, L. C. (1977). Reflection-impulsivity of normal and behavior disordered children. *Journal of Abnormal Child Psychology, 5,* 457–462.

Burcham, B., Carlson, L., & Milich, R. (1993). Promising school-based practices for students with attention deficit disorder. *Exceptional Children, 60,* 174–180.

Burrows, G. M. (1828). *Commentaries on the causes, forms, symptoms and treatment, moral and medical, of insanity.* London: Thomas and George Underwood.

Campbell, S. B. (1990). *Behavior problems in preschool children: Clinical and developmental issues.* New York: Guilford Press.

Campbell, S. B. (1995). Behavior problems in preschool children: A review of recent research. *Journal of Child Psychology and Psychiatry, 36,* 113–149.

Cantwell, D. P. (1988). Families with attention deficit disordered children and others at risk. *Journal of Chemical Dependency Treatment, 1*(2), 163–186.

Cantwell, D. P., & Baker, L. (1991). Association between attention-deficit hyperactivity disorder and learning disorders. *Journal of Learning Disabilities, 24,* 88–95.

Cantwell, D. P., & Baker, L. (1992). Attention deficit disorder with and without hyperactivity: A review and comparison of matched groups. *Journal of the American Academy of Child and Adolescent Psychiatry, 31,* 432–438.

Centers for Disease Control. (1991). *Preventing lead poisoning in children.* Atlanta, GA: Author.

Chandra, P. S. (1993). Cross-cultural psychiatry and children with defiant behaviors. *American Journal of Psychiatry, 150,* 1279–1280.

Clements, S. (1966). Minimal brain dysfunction in children—terminology and identification. *National Institute of Neurological Diseases and Blindness Monograph No. 3.* Bethesda, MD: US Public Health Service.

Clements, S., & Peters, J. (1962). Minimal brain dysfunctions in the school-age child. *Archives of General Psychiatry, 6,* 185–197.

Cohen, D. J., & Leckman, J. F. (1994). Developmental psychopathology and neurobiology of Tourette's syndrome. *Journal of the American Academy of Child and Adolescent Psychiatry, 33,* 2–15.

Conners, C. K. (1970). Symptom patterns in hyperkinetic, neurotic, and normal children. *Child Development, 41,* 667–682.

Conners, C. K. (1972). Symposium: behavior modification by drugs. II. Psychological effects of stimulant drugs in children with minimal brain dysfunction. *Pediatrics, 49,* 702–708.

Conners, C. K. (1989). *Manual for Conners' Rating Scales.* North Tonawanda, NY: Multi-Health Systems.

Conners, C. K. (1994a). *The Conners Continuous Performance Test.* Toronto, Canada: Multi-Health Systems.

Conners, C. K. (1994b). *The continuous performance test (CPT): Use as a diagnostic tool and measure of treatment outcome.* Paper presented at the Annual Meeting of the American Psychological Association, Los Angeles, CA.

Conners, C. K. (in press). *Risk-factors checklist for ADHD.* Toronto, Canada: Multi-Health Systems.

Conners, C., Erhardt, D., & Sparrow, E. (in press). *CADDI: A structured interview for ADHD and other externalizing disorders.*

Conners, C. K., & Kronsberg, S. (1985). Measuring activity level in children. *Psychopharmacology Bulletin, 21,* 893–897.

Conners, C., & March, J. (1993). *Developmental history form for ADHD and related disorders.* Toronto, Canada: Multi-Health Systems.

Conners, C. K., March, J. S., Erhardt, D., Butcher, T., & Epstein, J. (1995). Assessment of attention deficit disorders (ADHD): Conceptual issues and future trends. *Journal of Psychoeducational Assessment.* Monograph series, Advances in psychoeducational assessment, 185–204.

Conners, C. K., March, J. S., Fiore, C., & Butcher, T. (1994). *Information processing deficits in ADHD: Effect of stimulus rate and methylphenidate.* Paper presented at the Annual Meeting of the American College of Neuropsychopharmacology, Honolulu, HI.

Conners, C. K., Parker, J., & Sitarenios, G. (1996). Parent and teacher ratings of DSM-IV ADHD symptoms: A test of the subtype model. Submitted.

Conners, C. K., & Taylor, E. (1980). Pemoline, methylphenidate, and placebo in children with minimal brain dysfunction. *Archives of General Psychiatry, 37,* 922–930.

Conners, C. K., Taylor, E., Meo, G., Kurtz, M. A., & Fournier, M. (1972). Magnesium pemoline and dextroamphetamine: a controlled study in children with minimal brain dysfunction. *Psychopharmacologia, 26*(4), 321–336.

Conners, C. K., & Wells, K. C. (1985). ADD-H Adolescent Self-Report Scale. *Psychopharmacology Bulletin, 21*(4), 921–922.

Conners, C. K., Wells, K. C., Erhardt, D., March, J. S., Schulte, A., Osborne, S., Fiore, C., & Butcher, A. T. (1994). Multimodality therapies: Methodologic issues in research and practice. *Child and Adolescent Psychiatric Clinics of North America: Disruptive Disorders, 3,* 361–377.

David, O., Hoffman, S., Sverd, J., & Clark, J. (1977). Lead and hyperactivity: Lead levels among hyperactive children. *Journal of Abnormal Child Psychology, 5,* 405–416.

Davila, R. R., Williams, M. L., & MacDonald, J. T. (1991). *Clarification of policy to address the needs of children with attention deficit hyperactivity disorders within general and/or special education* (memo). Washington, DC: US Department of Education.

Deutsch, C. K., Matthysse, S., Swanson, J. M., & Farkas, L. G. (1990). Genetic latent structure analysis of dysmorphology in attention deficit disorder. *Journal of the American Academy of Child and Adolescent Psychiatry, 29,* 189–194.

Douglas, V. I. (1983). Attention and cognitive problems. In M. Rutter (Ed.), *Developmental neuropsychiatry* (pp. 280–329). New York: Guilford Press.

Douglas, V., & Peters, K. (1978). Toward a clearer definition of the attentional deficit of hyperactive children. In G. Hale & M. Lewis (Eds.), *Attention and the development of cognitive skills* (pp. 173–248). New York: Plenum.

DuPaul, G. J., & Stoner, G. (1994). *ADHD in the schools: Assessment and intervention strategies.* New York: Guilford Press.

Dykman, R., Ackerman, P., Clements, S., & Peters, J. (1971). Specific learning disabilities: An attentional deficit syndrome. In H. Myklebust (Ed.), *Progress in learning disabilities* (Vol. 2, pp. 56–94). New York: Grune and Stratton.

Elia, J., Borcherding, B. G., Rapoport, J. L., & Keysor, C. S. (1991). Methylphenidate and dextroamphetamine treatments of hyperactivity: Are there true nonresponders? *Psychiatry Research, 36,* 141–155.

Erhardt, D., & Conners, C. K. (1995). Methodological and assessment issues in pediatric psychopharmacology. In J. M. Wiener (Ed.), *Diagnosis and psychopharmacology of childhood and adolescent disorders* (pp. 97–147). New York: Wiley.

Erhardt, D., & Hinshaw, S. P. (1994). Initial sociometric impressions of attention-deficit hyperactivity disorder and comparison boys: Predictions from social behaviors and from nonbehavioral variables. *Journal of Consulting and Clinical Psychology, 62,* 833–842.

Ernst, M., & Zametkin, A. (1995). The interface of genetics, neuroimaging and neurochemistry in attention-deficit hyperactivity disorder. In F. E. Bloom & D. J. Kupfer (Eds.), *Psychopharmacology: The fourth generation of progress* (pp. 1643–1652). New York: Raven.

Faigel, H. C., Sznajderman, S., Tishby, O., Turel, M., & Pinus, U. (1995). Attention deficit disorder during adolescence: A review. *Journal of Adolescent Health, 16,* 174–184.

Faraone, S. V., Biederman, J., Keenan, K., & Tsuang, M. T. (1991a). A family-genetic study of girls with *DSM-III* attention deficit disorder. *American Journal of Psychiatry, 148,* 112–117.

Faraone, S. V., Biederman, J., Keenan, K., & Tsuang, M. T. (1991b). Separation of DSM-III attention deficit disorder and conduct disorder: Evidence from a family-genetic study of American child psychiatric patients. *Psychological Medicine, 21,* 109–121.

Fischer, M., Barkley, R. A., Edelbrock, C. S., Smallish, L. (1990) The adolescent outcome of hyperactive children diagnosed by research criteria: II. Academic, attentional, and neuropsychological status. *Journal of Consulting and Clinical Psychology, 58,* 580–588.

Gickling, E. E., & Thompson, V. P. (1985). A personal view of curriculum-based assessment. Special Issue: Curriculum-based assessment. *Exceptional Children, 52,* 205–218.

Gilger, J. W., Pennington, B. F., & DeFries, J. C. (1992). A twin study of the etiology of comorbidity: attention-deficit hyperactivity disorder and dyslexia. *Journal of the American Academy of Child and Adolescent Psychiatry, 31,* 343–348.

Gillis, J. J., Gilger, J. W., Pennington, B. F., & DeFries, J. C. (1992). Attention deficit disorder in reading disabled twins: Evidence for a genetic etiology. *Journal of Abnormal Child Psychology, 20,* 303–315.

Gittelman, R., Mannuzza, S., Shenker, R., & Bonagura, N. (1985). Hyperactive boys almost grown up. *Archives of General Psychiatry, 42,* 937–947.

Goldstein, K. (1942). *After-effects of brain injuries in war.* New York: Grune and Stratton.

Goodman, R., & Stevenson, J. (1989a). A twin study of hyperactivity: I. An examination of hyperactivity scores and categories derived from Rutter teacher and parent questionnaires. *Journal of Child Psychology and Psychiatry and Allied Disciplines, 30,* 671–689.

Goodman, R., & Stevenson, J. (1989b). A twin study of hyperactivity: II. The aetiological role of genes, family relationships and perinatal adversity. *Journal of Child Psychology & Psychiatry & Allied Disciplines, 30,* 691–709.

Goodyear, P., & Hynd, G. W. (1992). Attention-deficit disorder with (ADD/H) and without (ADD/WO) hyperactivity: Behavioral and neuropsychological differentiation. *Journal of Clinical Child Psychology, 21,* 273–305.

Goyette, C. H., Conners, C. K., & Ulrich, R. F. (1978). Normative data on Revised Conners Parent and Teacher Rating Scales. *Journal of Abnormal Child Psychology, 6,* 221–236.

Greenfield, B., Gottlieb, S., & Weiss, G. (1992). Psychosocial interventions: Individual psychotherapy with child, and family and parent counseling. *Child and Adolescent Psychiatric Clinics of North America, 1,* 481–503.

Greenhill, L. (1992). Pharmacologic treatment of attention deficit hyperactivity disorder. In D. Shaffer (Ed.), *The psychiatric clinics of North America: Pediatric psychopharmacology* (pp. 1–27). Philadelphia, PA: Saunders.

Greenhill, L., Abikoff, H., Arnold, E., Conners, C., Wells, K., Elliott, G., Hechtman, L., Hinshaw, S., Hoza, B., Jensen, P., March, J., Newcorn, J., Pelham, W., Severe, J., Swanson, J., & Vitiello, B. (1996). Medication treatment strategies in the MTA study: Relevance to

clinicians and researchers. *Journal of the American Academy of Child and Adolescent Psychiatry, 35,* 1304–1313.

Guevremont, D. C. (1990). Social skills and peer relationship training. In R. A. Barkley, *Attention-deficit hyperactivity disorder: A handbook for diagnosis and treatment* (pp. 540–572). New York: Guilford Press.

Halperin, J. M., Matier, K., Bedi, G., Sharma, V., & Newcorn, J. H. (1992). Specificity of inattention, impulsivity, and hyperactivity to the diagnosis of attention-deficit hyperactivity disorder. *Journal of the American Academy of Child and Adolescent Psychiatry, 31,* 190–196.

Hamlett, K. W., Pellegrini, D. S., & Conners, C. K. (1987). An investigation of executive processes in the problem-solving of attention deficit disorder-hyperactive children. *Journal of Pediatric Psychology, 12,* 227–240.

Hart, E. L., Lahey, B. B., Loeber, R., Applegate, B., & Frick, P. J. (1995). Developmental change in attention-deficit hyperactivity disorder in boys: a four-year longitudinal study. *Journal of Abnormal Child Psychology. 23*(6), 729–749.

Hartsough, C. S., & Lambert, N. M. (1985). Medical factors in hyperactive and normal children: Prenatal, developmental, and health history findings. *American Journal of Orthopsychiatry, 55,* 190–210.

Hechtman, L. (1989). Attention-deficit hyperactivity disorder in adolescence and adulthood: An updated follow-up. *Psychiatric Annals, 19,* 597–603.

Hechtman, L. (1991). Resilience and vulnerability in long term outcome of attention deficit hyperactive disorder. Special issue: Child and adolescent psychiatry. *Canadian Journal of Psychiatry, 36,* 415–421.

Heffron, W. A., Martin, C. A., & Welsh, R. J. (1984). Attention deficit disorder in three pairs of monozygotic twins: A case report. *Journal of the American Academy of Child Psychiatry, 23,* 299–301.

Hembree-Kigin, T. L., & McNeil, C. B. (1995). *Parent–child interaction therapy.* New York: Plenum.

Hinshaw, S. P. (1987). On the distinction between attentional deficits/hyperactivity and conduct problems/aggression in child psychopathology. *Psychological Bulletin, 101,* 443–463.

Hinshaw, S. P. (1992a). Academic underachievement, attentional deficits, and aggression: Comorbidity and implications for intervention. *Journal of Consulting and Clinical Psychology, 60,* 893–903.

Hinshaw, S. P. (1992b). Externalizing behavior problems and academic underachievement in childhood and adolescence: Causal relationships and underlying mechanisms. *Psychological Bulletin, 111,* 127–155.

Hinshaw, S. P. (1992c). Intervention for social competence and social skill. *Child and Adolescent Clinics of North America, 2,* 539–552.

Hinshaw, S. P. (1994). *Attention deficits and hyperactivity in children.* Thousand Oaks, CA: Sage.

Hinshaw, S. P., & Erhardt, D. (1991). Attention-deficit hyperactivity disorder. In P. C. Kendall (Ed.), *Child and adolescent therapy: Cognitive-behavioral procedures* (pp. 98–128). New York: Guilford Press.

Hinshaw, S. P., & Erhardt, D. (1993). Behavioral treatment. In V. B. Van Hasselt & M. Hersen (Eds.), *Handbook of behavior therapy and pharmacotherapy for children: A comparative analysis* (pp. 233–250). Needham Heights, MA: Allyn & Bacon.

Holborow, P. L., Berry, P., & Elkins, J. (1984). Prevalence of hyperkinesis: A comparison of three rating scales. *Journal of Learning Disabilities, 17,* 411–417.

Homatidis, S., & Konstantareas, M. M. (1981). Assessment of hyperactivity: Isolating measures of high discriminant ability. *Journal of Consulting and Clinical Psychology, 49,* 533–541.

Hops, H., & Lewin, L. (1984). Peer sociometric forms. In T.

Ollendick & M. Hersen (Eds.), *Child behavioral assessment: Principles and procedures* (pp. 124–147). New York: Pergamon.

Hoza, B., Vallano, G., & Pelham, W. E. (1995). Attention-deficit hyperactivity disorder. In R. T. Ammerman & M. Hersen (Eds.), *Handbook of child therapy in the psychiatric setting* (pp. 181–198). New York: Wiley.

Hynd, G. W., Hern, K. L., Voeller, K. K., & Marshall, R. M. (1991). Neurobiological basis of attention-deficit hyperactivity disorder (ADHD). *School Psychology Review, 20*, 174–186.

James, W. (1890). *The principles of psychology.* New York: Gryphon Editions.

Jensen, P. S., Shervette, R. E., Xenakis, S. N., & Bain, M. W. (1988). Psychosocial and medical histories of stimulant-treated children. *Journal of the American Academy of Child and Adolescent Psychiatry, 27*, 798–801.

Johnston, C. (1996). Parent characteristics and parent-child interactions in families of nonproblem children and ADHD children with higher and lower levels of oppositional-defiant behavior. *Journal of Abnormal Child Psychology, 24*, 85–104.

Juarez, L. J., Madrigal, J., & Anderson, R. P. (1981). Social and cultural aspects of behavior disorders among minority children: Reflections upon contemporary literature. *Spanish Speaking Mental Health Research Center Monographs 8.*

Kahn, E., & Cohen, L. (1934). Organic drivenness: A brain stem syndrome and an experience. *New England Journal of Medicine, 210*, 748–756.

Kavale, K. (1982). The efficacy of stimulant drug treatment for hyperactivity: A meta-analysis. *Journal of Learning Disabilities, 15*, 280–289.

Kessler, J. W. (1980). History of minimal brain dysfunction. In H. E. Rie & E. D. Rie (Eds.), *Handbook of minimal brain dysfunctions: A critical view* (pp. 18–52). New York: Wiley.

Klein, R. G., & Mannuzza, S. (1991). Long-term outcome of hyperactive children: A review. *Journal of the American Academy of Child and Adolescent Psychiatry, 30*, 383–387.

Knights, R. M., & Viets, C. A. (1975). Effects of pemoline on hyperactive boys. *Pharmacology, Biochemistry and Behavior, 3*, 1107–1114.

Kovacs, M. (1993). *The Children's Depression Inventory (CDI).* Toronto, Canada: Multi-Health Systems.

Lahey, B. B., Applegate, B., McBurnett, K., Biederman, J., Greenhill, L., Hynd, G. W., Barkley, R. A., Newcorn, J., Jensen, P., Richters, J., Garfinkel, B., Kerdyk, L., Frick, P. J., Ollendick, T., Perez, D., Hart, E. L., Waldman, I., & Shaffer, D. (1994). DSM-IV field trials for attention deficit hyperactivity disorder in children and adolescents. *American Journal of Psychiatry, 151*, 1673–1685.

Lahey, B. B., Loeber, R., Stouthamer-Loeber, M., & Christ, M. A. (1990). Comparison of *DSM-III* and *DSM-III-R* diagnoses for prepubertal children: Changes in prevalence and validity. *Journal of the American Academy of Child and Adolescent Psychiatry, 29*(4), 620–626.

Lahey, B. B., Pelham, W. E., Schaughency, E. A., Atkins, M. S., Murphy, H. A., Hynd, G. W., Russo, M., Hartdagen, S., & Lorys-Vernon, A. (1988). Dimensions and types of attention deficit disorder with hyperactivity in children: A factor analytic and cluster analytic approach. *Journal of the American Academy of Child and Adolescent Psychiatry, 27*, 330–335.

Lambert, N. M. (1988). Adolescent outcomes for hyperactive children: Perspectives on general and specific patterns of childhood risk for adolescent educational, social, and mental health problems. *American Psychologist, 43*, 786–799.

Lambert, N. M., Sandoval, J. H., & Sassone, D. M. (1978). Prevalence estimates of hyperactivity in school children. *Pediatric Annals, 7*, 68–86.

Landry, S. H., Chapieski, M. L., Richardson, M. A., Palmer, J., & Hall, S. (1990). The social competence of children born prematurely: effects of medical complications and parent behaviors. *Child Development, 61*, 1605–1616.

Lansdorf, R. (1979). Ethnicity, social class, and perception of hyperactivity. *Psychology in the Schools, 16*, 293–298.

Laufer, M., Denhoff, E., & Solomons, G. (1957). Hyperkinetic impulse disorder in children's behavior problems. *Psychosomatic Medicine, 19*, 39–49.

Letters to the Editor. (1992). *Science, 256*, 294–295.

Lewis, M., & Bendersky, M. (1989). Cognitive and motor differences among low birth weight infants: impact of intraventricular hemorrhage, medical risk and social class. *Pediatrics, 83*, 187–192.

Loney, J., & Milich, R. (1982). Hyperactivity, inattention, and aggression in clinical practice. In M. Wolraich & D. K. Routh (Eds.), *Advances in developmental and behavioral pediatrics* (Vol. 2, pp. 113–147). Greenwich, CT: JAI Press.

Luk, S. (1985). Direct observation studies of hyperactive behaviors. *Journal of the American Academy of Child Psychiatry, 24*, 338–344.

Lynskey, M. T., & Fergusson, D. M. (1995). Childhood conduct problems, attention deficit behaviors, and adolescent alcohol, tobacco, and illicit drug use. *Journal of Abnormal Child Psychology, 23*, 281–302.

Macmann, G., Barnett, D., & Lopez, E. (1993). The child behavior checklist/4-18 and related materials: Reliability and validity of syndromal assessment. *School Psychology Review, 22*, 308–312.

Mannuzza, S., Gittelman-Klein, R., Bessler, A., Malloy, P., & LaPadula, M. (1993). Adult outcome of hyperactive boys: Educational achievement occupational rank, and psychiatric status. *Archives of General Psychiatry, 50*, 565–576.

March, J. S., Erhardt, D., Johnston, H., & Conners, C. K. (1995). Pharmacotherapy of attention-deficit hyperactivity disorder. In J. W. Jefferson & J. H. Greist (Eds.), *The psychiatric clinics of North America: Annual of drug therapy.* Philadelphia: Saunders.

March, J. S., Johnston, H., & Conners, C. K., (1996). Pharmacotherapy of attention-deficit hyperactivity disorder. In J. Jefferson & J. Greist (Eds.), *Psychopharmacology Clinic of North America.* New York: Saunders.

March, J. S., Sullivan, K., & Conners, C. K. (1996). The Multidimensional Anxiety Scale for Children (MASC): Reliability and validity. *Journal of Abnormal Child Psychology,* submitted.

March, J. S., Wells, K., & Conners, C. K. (1995a). Attention-deficit/hyperactivity disorder: Part I. Assessment and diagnosis. *Journal of Practical Psychiatry and Behavioral Health, 1*, 219–228.

March, J. S., Wells, K., & Conners, C. K. (1995b). Attention-deficit/hyperactivity disorder: Part II. Treatment strategies. *Journal of Practical Psychiatry and Behavioral Health, 2*, 23–32.

Martens, B. (1993). Social labeling, precision of measurement, and problem solving: Key issues in the assessment of children's emotional problems. *School Psychology Review, 22*, 308–312.

Mash, E. J., & Johnston, C. (1982). A comparison of the mother–child interactions of younger and older hyperactive and normal children. *Child Development, 53*, 1371–1381.

Mash, E. J., & Terdel, L. G. (1988). Behavioral assessment of child and family disturbance. In E. J. Mash & L. G. Terdel (Eds.), *Behavioral assessment of childhood disorders* (2nd ed., pp. 3–69). New York: Guilford Press.

McBurnett, K., Lahey, B. B., & Pfifner, L. J., (1993).

Diagnosis of attention deficit disorders in DSM-IV: Scientific basis and implications for education. *Exceptional Children, 60,* 108–117.

McClellan, J. M., Rubert, M. P., Reichler, R. J., & Sylvester, C. E. (1990). Attention deficit disorder in children at risk for anxiety and depression. *Journal of the American Academy of Child and Adolescent Psychiatry, 29,* 534–539.

McCaughy, S. (1993a). Advances in empirically-based assessment of children's behavioral and emotional problems. *School Psychological Review, 22,* 285–307

McConaughy, S. (1993b). Responses to commentaries on advances in empirically based asessment. *School Psychology Review, 22,* 334–342.

McKinney, J., Montague, M., & Hocutt, A. (1993). *Synthesis of research on the assessment and identification of students with attention deficit disorder.* Washington, DC: Office of Special Education Programs, Office of Special Education and Rehabilitative Services, US Department of Education.

McMahon, R. (1981). Biological factors in childhood hyperkinesis: A review of genetic and biochemical hypotheses. *Journal of the American Academy of Child and Adolescent Psychiatry, 37,* 12–21.

McMahon, R., & Forehand, R. (in press). *Helping the noncompliant child: A clinician's guide to parent training.* New York: Guilford Press.

Mesulam, M. M. (1990). Large-scale neurocognitive networks and distributed processing for attention, language, and memory. *Annals of Neurology, 28,* 597–613.

Milich, R., & Kramer, J. (1984). Reflections on impulsivity: An empirical investigation of impulsivity as a construct. In K. Gadow & I. Bialer (Eds.), *Advances in learning and behavioral disabilities* (Vol. 3, pp. 57–94). Greenwich, CT: JAI Press.

Milich, R., & Landau, S. (1982). Socialization and peer relations in hyperactive children. In K. D. Gadow & I. Bialer (Eds.), *Advances in learning and behavioral disabilities* (Vol. 1, pp. 283–339). Greenwich, CT: JAI Press.

Milich, R., Wolraich, M., & Lindgren, S. (1986). Sugar and hyperactivity: A critical review of empirical findings. *Clinical Psychology Review, 6,* 493–513.

Millichap, J., & Fowler, G. W. (1967). Treatment of "minimal brain dysfunction" syndrome. *Pediatric Clinics of North America, 14,* 767–777.

Morris, R. J., & Collier, S. J. (1987). Assessment of attention deficit disorder and hyperactivity. In C. L. Frame & J. L. Matson (Eds.), *Handbook of assessment in childhood psychopathology: Applied issues in differential diagnosis and treatment evaluation. Applied clinical psychology.*

Newby, R. F., Fischer, M., & Roman, M. A. (1991). Parent training for families of children with attention deficit-hyperactivity disorder. *School Psychology Review, 20,* 252–265.

Newcorn, J. H., & Halperin, J. M. (1994). Comorbidity among disruptive behavior disorders: Impact on severity, impairment, and response to treatment. *Child and Adolescent Psychiatric Clinics of North America, 3,* 227–252.

Nichols, P. L., & Chen, T. C. (1981). *Minimal brain dysfunction: A prospective study.* Hillsdale, NJ: Erlbaum.

O'Connor, M., Foch, T., Sherry, T., & Plomin, R. (1980). A twin study of specific behavioral problems of socialization as viewed by parents. *Journal of Abnormal Child Psychology, 8*(2), 189–199.

Offord, D. R., Boyle, M. H., Szatmari, P., Rae-Grant, N. I., Links, P. S., Cadman, D. T., Byles, J. A., Crawford, J. W., Blum, H. M., & Byrne, C. (1987). Ontario Child Health Study: II. Six-month prevalence of disorder and rates of service utilization. *Archives of General Psychiatry, 44,* 832–836.

O'Leary, K. D., Vivian, D., & Nisi, A. (1985). Hyperactivity in Italy. *Journal of Abnormal Child Psychology, 13,* 485–500.

Olson, R. K., Rack, J. P., Conners, F. A., DeFries, J. C., & Fulker, D. W. (1991). Genetic etiology of individual differences in reading disability. In L. V. Feogans, E. J. Short, & L. J. Meltzer (Eds.), *Subtypes of learning disabilities: Theoretical perspectives and research* (pp. 113–135). Hillsdale, NJ: Erlbaum.

Olson, R., Wise, B., Conners, F. A., & Rack, J. (1990). Organization, heritability, and remediation of component word recognition and language skills in disabled readers. In T. H. Carr & B. A. Levy, (Eds.), *Reading and its development: Component skills approaches* (pp. 261–322). San Diego, CA: Academic Press.

Olson, R., Wise, B., Conners, F. A., Rack, J., & Fulker, D. W. (1989). Specific deficits in component reading and language skills: Genetic and environmental influences. *Journal of Learning Disabilities, 22,* 339–348.

Ostrom, N. N., & Jenson, W. R. (1988). Assessment of attention deficits in children. *Professional School Psychology, 3*(4), 253–269.

Ottenbacher, J., & Cooper, H. (1983). Drug treatment of hyperactivity in children. *Developmental Medicine and Child Neurology, 25,* 358–366.

Parker, H. C. (1992). *The ADD hyperactivity handbook for schools.* Plantation, FL: Impact.

Parker, J. D. A., Sitarenios, G., & Conners, C. K. (1996). Abbreviated Conners' Rating Scales revisited: A confirmatory factor analytic study. *Journal of Attention Disorders, 1,* 55–62.

Parker, J. G., & Asher, S. R. (1987). Peer relations and later personal adjustment: Are low-accepted children at risk? *Psychological Bulletin, 102,* 357–389.

Pasamanick, B., & Knobloch, H. (1959). Syndrome of minimal cerebral damage in infancy. *Journal of the American Medical Association, 170,* 1384–1387.

Pelham, W. E. (1986). The effects of psychostimulant drugs on learning and academic achievement in children with attention-deficit disorders and learning disabilities, In J. K. Torgesen & B. Wong (Eds.), *Psychological and Educational Perspectives on Learning Disabilities* (pp. 259–295). New York: Academic Press.

Pelham, W. E., & Bender, M. E. (1982). Peer relationships in hyperactive children: Description and treatment. In K. Gadow & I. Bialer (Eds.), *Advances in learning and behavioral disabilities* (Vol. 1, pp. 365–436). Greenwich, CT: JAI Press.

Pelham, W. E., Bender, M., Caddell, J., Booth, S., & Moorer, S. (1985), The dose–response effects of methylphenidate on classroom academic and social behavior in children with attention deficit disorder. *Archives of General Psychiatry. 42*(10), 948–952.

Pelham, W. E., Greenslade, K. E., Vodde-Hamilton, M., Murphy, D. A., Greenstein, J. J., Gnagy, E. M., Guthrie, K. J., Hoover, M. D., & Dahl, R. E. (1990). Relative efficacy of long-acting stimulants on children with attention deficit–hyperactivity disorder: A comparison of standard methylphenidate, sustained-release methylphenidate, sustained-release dextroamphetamine, and pemoline. *Pediatrics, 86*(22), 226–237.

Pelham, W. E., & Hinshaw, S. P. (1992). Behavioral intervention for ADHD. In S. M. Turner, K. S., Calhoun, & H. E. Adams (Eds.), *Handbook of clinical behavior therapy* (2nd ed., pp. 259–283). New York: Wiley.

Pelham, W. E., & Hoza, B. (1996). Intensive treatment: A summer treatment program for children with ADHD. In E. D. Hibbs & P. S. Jensen (Eds.), *Psychosocial treatments for child and adolescent disorders: Empirically-based strategies for clinical practice,* (pp. 311–340). Washington, DC: American Psychological Association.

Pelham, W. E., & Murphy, H. A. (1986). Behavioral and

pharmacological treatment of attention deficit and conduct disorders. In M. Hersen (Ed.), *Pharmacological and behavioral treatment: An integrative approach* (pp. 108–148). New York: Wiley.

Pelham, W. E., Sturges, J., Hoza, J., Schmidt, C., Bijlsma, J. J., Milich, R., & Moorer, S. (1987). Sustained release and standard methylphenidate effects on cognitive and social behavior in children with attention deficit disorder. *Pediatrics, 80,* 491–501.

Pfiffner, L. J., & Barkley, R. A. (1990). Educational placement and classroom management. In R. A. Barkley, *Attention-deficit hyperactivity disorder: A handbook for diagnosis and treatment* (pp. 498–539). New York: Guilford Press.

Pfiffner, L. J., & O'Leary, S. G. (1993). School-based psychological treatments. In J. L. Matson (Ed.), *Handbook of hyperactivity in children* (pp. 234–255). Boston: Allyn & Bacon.

Pliszka, S. R. (1987). Tricyclic antidepressants in the treatment of children with attention deficit disorder. *Journal of the American Academy of Child and Adolescent Psychiatry, 26,* 127–132.

Pliszka, S. R. (1989). Effect of anxiety on cognition, behavior, and stimulant response in ADHD. *Journal of the American Academy of Child and Adolescent Psychiatry, 28,* 882–887.

Porrino, L. J., Rapoport, J. L., Behar, D., Sceery, W., Ismond, D. R., & Bunney, W. E. (1983). A naturalistic assessment of the motor activity of hyperactive boys: I. Comparison with normal controls. *Archives of General Psychiatry, 40,* 681–687.

Posner, M. (1988). Structures and function of selective attention. In M. Dennis, E. Kaplan, M. Posner, D. Stein, & R. Thompson (Eds.), *Clinical neuropsychology and brain function: Research, measurement, and practice* (pp. 169–201). Washington, DC: American Psychological Association.

Prendergast, M., Taylor, E., Rapoport, J. L., Bartko, J., Donnelly, M., Zametkin, A., Ahearn, M., Dunn, G., Wieleberg, H. (1988). The diagnosis of childhood hyperactivity: A US–UK cross-national study of *DSM-III* and *ICD-9. Journal of Child Psychology and Psychiatry and Allied Disciplines. 29*(3), 289–300

Prinz, R., & Riddle, D. (1986). Association between nutrition and behavior in five-year old children. *Nutrition Reviews, 44,* 151–158.

Rapoport, J. L., Buchsbaum, M. S., Weingartner, H., Zahn, T. P., Ludlow, C., & Mikkelsen, E. J. (1980). Dextroamphetamine. Its cognitive and behavioral effects in normal and hyperactive boys and normal men. *Archives of General Psychiatry, 37,* 933–943.

Rapoport, J., & Castellanos, X. (1996). Attention-deficit/ hyperactivity disorder. In J. M. Weiner (Ed.), *Diagnosis and psychopharmacology of childhood and adolescent disorders* (2nd ed., pp. 265–292). New York: Wiley.

Rapport, M. D., DuPaul, G. J., Stoner, G., & Jones, J. T. (1986). Comparing classroom and clinic measures of attention deficit disorder: Differential, idiosyncratic, and dose–response effects of methylphenidate. *Journal of Consulting and Clinical Psychology, 54,* 334–341.

Rapport, M. D., & Kelly, K. L. (1991). Psychostimulant effects on learning and cognitive function: Findings and implications for children with attention deficit hyperactivity disorder. *Clinical Psychology Review, 11,* 61–92.

Reid, R. (1995). Assessment of ADHD with culturally different groups: The use of behavioral rating scales. *School Psychology Review, 24,* 537–560.

Reid, R., Vasa, S. F., Maag, J. W., & Wright, G. (1994). An analysis of teachers' perceptions of attention deficit-hyperactivity disorder. *Journal of Research and Development in Education, 27,* 195–202.

Richman, N., Stevenson, J., & Graham, P. (1982).

Preschool to school: A behavioral study. London: Academic Press.

Richters, J. E., Arnold, L. E., Jensen, P. S., Abikoff, H., Conners, C. K., Greenhill, L. L., Hechtman, L., Hinshaw, S. P., Pelham W. E., & Swanson, J. M. (1995). NIMH collaborative multisite multimodal treatment study of children with ADHD: I. Background and rationale. *Journal of the American Academy of Child and Adolescent Psychiatry, 34,* 987–1000.

Roberts, M. A. (1990). A behavioral observation method for differentiating hyperactive and aggressive boys. *Journal of Abnormal Child Psychology, 18,* 131–142.

Robin, A. L., & Foster, S. L. (1989). *Negotiating parent-adolescent conflict.* New York: Guilford Press.

Ross, P. A., Poidevant, J. M., & Miner, C. U. (1995). Curriculum-based assessment of writing fluency in children with attention-deficit hyperactivity disorder and normal children. *Reading & Writing Quarterly: Overcoming Learning Difficulties, 11,* 201–208.

Routh, D. K. (1978). Hyperactivity. In P. Magrab (Ed.), *Psychological management of pediatric problems* (pp. 3–48). Baltimore: University Park Press.

Rutter, M., & Casaer, P. (1991). *Biological risk factors for psychosocial disorders.* New York: Cambridge University Press.

Sallee, F. R., Stiller, R. L., & Perel, J. M. (1992). Pharmacodynamics of pemoline in attention deficit disorder with hyperactivity. *The Journal of the Academy of Child and Adolescent Psychiatry, 31,* 244–251.

Satterfield, J. H., Satterfield, B. T., & Schell, A. M. (1987). Therapeutic interventions to prevent delinquency in hyperactive boys. *Journal of the American Academy of Child and Adolescent Psychiatry, 26,* 56–64.

Schachar, R., Logan, G., Wachsmuth, R., & Chajczyk, D. (1988). Attaining and maintaining preparation: A comparison of attention in hyperactive, normal, and disturbed control children. *Journal of Abnormal Child Psychology, 16,* 361–378.

Schachar, R., & Wachsmuth, R. (1990). Hyperactivity and parental psychopathology. *Journal of Child Psychology and Psychiatry, 31,* 381–392.

Schaughency, E. A., & Rothlind, J. (1991). Assessment and classification of attention deficit hyperactive disorders. *School Psychology Review, 20*(2), 187-202.

Seham, M., & Seham, G. (1929). The relation between malnutrition and nervousness. *American Journal of Diseases of Children, 37*(1), 1–5.

Seidel, W. T., & Joschko, M. (1990). Evidence of difficulties in sustained attention in children with ADDH. *Journal of Abnormal Child Psychology, 18,* 217–229.

Semrud-Clikeman, M., Biederman, J., Sprich-Buckminster, S., Lehman, B. K., Faraone, S. V., & Norman, D. (1992). Comorbidity between ADHD and learning disability: A review and report in a clinically referred sample. *Journal of the American Academy of Child and Adolescent Psychiatry, 31,* 439–448.

Sergeant, J., & Scholten, C. A. (1985). On resource strategy limitations in hyperactivity: Cognitive impulsivity reconsidered. *Journal of Child Psychology and Psychiatry, 26,* 97–109.

Sharma, V., Matier, K., & Halperin, J. M. (1994). Disruptive behavior disorders: Assessment and differential diagnosis. *Child and Adolescent Psychiatric Clinics of North America, 3,* 253–270.

Shaywitz, B. A., Fletcher, J. M., & Shaywitz, S. E. (1995). Defining and classifying learning disabilities and Attention-Deficit/Hyperactivity Disorder. *Journal of Child Neurology, 10*(Suppl. 1), S50–S57.

Shekim, W. O., Kashani, J., Beck, N., Cantwell, D. P., Martin, J., Rosenberg, J., & Costello, A. (1985). The prevalence of attention deficit disorders in a rural midwestern community sample of nine-year-old children.

Journal of the American Academy of Child Psychiatry, 24(6), 765–770.

Solanto, M. V., & Connors, C. K. (1982). A dose–response and time–action analysis of autonomic and behavioral effects of methylphenidate in attention deficit disorder with hyperactivity. *Psychophysiology, 19*(6), 658–667.

Solis, C. R. P., & Solis, C. V. P. (1988). Estimacion del grado de actividad de los escolares segun los padres y maestras, y su relacion con la impulsividad cognoscitiva. (Estimation of the activity level of schoolchildren according to parents and teachers, and its relation with cognitive impulsivity.). *Salud Mental, 11*, 30–39.

Sprague, R. L., & Sleator, E. K. (1977). Methylphenidate in hyperkinetic children: Differences in dose effects on learning and social behavior. *Science, 198*, 1274–1276.

Stevens, G. (1981). Bias in the attribution of hyperkinetic behavior as a function of ethnic identification and socioeconomic status. *Psychology in the Schools, 18*, 99–106.

Stevenson, J. (1992). Evidence for a genetic etiology in hyperactivity in children. *Behavior Genetics, 22*(3), 337–344.

Still, G. (1902). Some abnormal psychical conditions in children. *Lancet, 1*, 1008–1012, 1077–1082, 1163–1168.

Strauss, A., & Lehtinen, L. (1947). *Psychopathology and education of the brain-injured child.* New York: Grune and Stratton.

Swanson, J. M., Cantwell, D., Lerner, M., McBurnett, K., & Hanna, G. (1991). Effects of stimulant medication on learning in children with ADHD. *Journal of Learning Disabilities, 24*, 219–230.

Swanson, J. M., McBurnett, K., Christian, D. L., & Wigal, T. (1995). Stimulant medications and the treatment of children with ADHD. *Advances in Clinical Child Psychology, 17*, 265–322.

Swanson, J. M., McBurnett, K., Wigal, T., Pfiffner, L., Lerner, M. A., Williams, L., Christian, D. L., Tamm, L., Willcutt, E., Crowley, K., Clevenger, W., Khouzam, N., Woo, C., Crinella, F. M., & Fisher, T. D. (1993). Effect of stimulant medication on children with attention deficit disorder: A review of reviews. *Exceptional Children, 60*, 154–162.

Szatmari, P., Offord, D. R., & Boyle, M. H. (1989a). Correlates, associated impairments and patterns of service utilization of children with attention deficit disorder: Findings from the Ontario Child Health Study. *Journal of Child Psychology and Psychiatry and Allied Disciplines, 30*, 205–217.

Szatmari, P., Offord, D. R., & Boyle, M. H. (1989b). Ontario Child Health Study: Prevalence of attention deficit disorder with hyperactivity. *Journal of Child Psychology and Psychiatry and Allied Disciplines, 30*, 219–230.

Tao, K. T., (1992). Hyperactivity and attention deficit disorder syndromes in China. *Journal of the American Academy of Child and Adolescent Psychiatry, 31*, 1165–1166.

Taylor, E. (1989). On the epidemiology of hyperactivity. In T. Sagnolden & T. Archer (Eds), *Attention deficit disorder: Clinical and basic research* (pp. 31–52). Hillsdale, NJ: Erlbaum.

Taylor, E. (1994). Similarities and differences in *DSM-IV* and *ICD-10* diagnostic criteria. *Child and Adolescent Clinics of North America, 3*, 209–226.

Taylor, E., & Sandberg, S. (1984). Hyperactive behavior in English schoolchildren: A questionnaire survey. *Journal of Abnormal Child Psychology, 12*, 143–155.

Thatcher, R., McAlaster, R., Lester, M., & Cantor, D. (1984). Comparisons among EEG, hair minerals and diet predictions of reading performance in children. *Annals of the New York Academy of Sciences, 425*, 421–423.

Thurber, S., & Walker, C. (1983). Medication and

hyperactivity: A meta-analysis. *The Journal of General Psychology, 108*, 79–86.

Umbreit, J. (1995). Functional assessment and intervention in a regular classroom setting for the disruptive behavior of a student with attention deficit hyperactivity disorder. *Behavioral Disorders, 20*(4), 267–278.

van der Meere, J., van Baal, M., & Sergeant, J. (1989). The additive factor method: A differential diagnostic tool in hyperactivity and learning disability. *Journal of Abnormal Child Psychology, 17*, 409–422.

van der Meere, J., Wekking, E., & Sergeant, J. (1991). Sustained attention and pervasive hyperactivity. *Journal of Child Psychology and Psychiatry, 32*, 275–284.

Voeller, K. K. S. (1991). What can neurological models of attention, intention, and arousal tell us about attention-deficit hyperactivity disorder? *Journal of Neuropsychiatry, 3*, 209–216.

Volkmar, F. R. (1991). Classification in child and adolescent psychiatry: Principles and issues. In M. Lewis (Ed.), *Child and adolescent psychiatry: A comprehensive textbook* (pp. 415–421). Baltimore: Williams & Wilkins.

Waechter, D., Anderson, R. P., Juarez, L. J., Langsdorf, R., & Madrigal, J. F. (1979). Ethnic group, hyperkinesis, and modes of behavior. *Psychology in the Schools, 16*, 435–439.

Walker, J. L., Lahey, B. B., Hynd, G. W., & Frame, C. L. (1987). Comparison of specific patterns of antisocial behavior in children with conduct disorder with or without coexisting hyperactivity. *Journal of Consulting and Clinical Psychology, 55*, 910–913.

Weinberg, W. A., & Brumback, R. A. (1990). Primary disorder of vigilance: A novel explanation of inattentiveness, daydreaming, boredom, restlessness, and sleepiness. *Journal of Pediatrics, 116*, 720–725.

Weiss, G., & Hechtman, L. T. (1986). *Hyperactive children grown up.* New York: Guilford Press.

Weiss, G. & Hechtman, L. T. (1993). *Hyperactive children grown up: ADHD in children, adolescents, and adults* (2nd ed.). New York: Guilford Press.

Weissbluth, M. L. K. (1983). Sleep patterns, attention span, and infant temperament. *Journal of Developmental and Behavioral Pediatrics, 4*, 34–36.

Weissbluth, M. (1984). Sleep duration, temperament, and Conners' ratings of three-year-old children. *Journal of Developmental and Behavioral Pediatrics, 5*, 120–123.

Wells, K. C. (1995). Parent management training. In G. P. Sholevar (Ed.), *Conduct disorders in children and adolescence* (pp. 213–236). Washington, DC: American Psychiatric Press.

Wells, K. C. (in press). Adaptations for specific populations. In R. McMahon & R. Forehand (Eds.), *Helping the noncompliant child: A clinician's guide to parent training.* New York: Guilford Press.

Wender, E. H. (1995). Attention deficit hyperactivity disorders in adolescence. *Developmental and Behavioral Pediatrics, 16*, 192–195.

Werner, E., Bierman, J., French, F., Simonian, K., Connor, A. Smith, R., & Campbell, M. (1968). Reproductive and environmental casualties: A report on the 10-year follow-up of the children of the Kauai pregnancy study. *Pediatrics, 42*, 112–127.

Werner, E., & Smith, R. (1967). *Kauai's children come of age.* Honolulu, HI: University of Hawaii Press.

Whalen, C. K., & Henker, B. (1980). *Hyperactive children: The social ecology of identification and treatment.* New York: Academic Press.

Whalen, C. K., & Henker, B. (1992). The social profile of attention-deficit hyperactivity disorder: Five fundamental facets. *Child and Adolescent Psychiatric Clinics of North America, 1*, 395–410.

White, J. L., Moffitt, T. E., Caspi, A., Bartusch, D. J., Needles, D. J., & Stouthamer-Loeber, M. (1994). Measuring impulsivity and examining its relation to delinquency. *Journal of Abnormal Psychology, 103,* 192–205.

Winsberg, B., Press, M., Bialer, I., & Kupietz, S. (1974). Dextroamphetamine and methylphenidate in the treatment of hyperactive/aggressive children. *Pediatrics, 53,* 236–241.

Wolraich, M. L., Wilson, D. B., & White, J. W. (1995). The effect of sugar on behavior or cognition in children. *Journal of the American Medical Association, 274,* 1617–1621.

World Health Organization (1992a). *International statistical classification of diseases and related health problems* (10th revision). Geneva, Switzerland: Author.

World Health Organization. (1992b). *The ICD-10 classification of mental and behavioural disorders: Clinical descriptions and diagnostic guidelines.* Geneva, Switzerland: Author.

Yao, K. N., Solanto, M. V., & Wender, E. H. (1988). Prevalence of hyperactivity among newly immigrated Chinese–American children. *Journal of Developmental and Behavioral Pediatrics, 9,* 367–373.

Yu, C. S., Yu, F. W., & Xiao, L. Y. (1985). An epidemiological investigation of minimal brain dysfunction in six elementary schools in Beijing. *Journal of Child Psychology and Psychiatry and Allied Disciplines, 26*(5), 777–787.

Zametkin, A. J. (1989). The neurobiology of attention-deficit hyperactivity disorder: A synopsis. *Psychiatric Annals, 19,* 584–586.

Zametkin, A. J., & Rapport, J. L. (1987). Noradrenergic hypothesis of attention deficit with hyperactivity: A critical review. In H. Y. Meltzer (Ed.), *Psychopharmacology: The third generation of progress* (pp. 837–842). New York: Raven.

Zentall, S. S. (1989). Production deficiencies in elicited language but not in the spontaneous verbalizations of hyperactive children. *Journal of Abnormal Child Psychology, 16,* 657–673.

5.20
Conduct Disorders

RONALD J. PRINZ
University of South Carolina, Columbia, SC, USA

5.20.1 INTRODUCTION

The constellation of conduct disorders in children and adolescents presents a major challenge for society. Conduct disorders account for about half of all youth referrals for mental health services, tend to remain stable or worsen over time, and often cross generations (Costello, 1989; Loeber, 1990). Youth exhibiting various forms of conduct disorders victimize others, disrupt their families, fail at school, commit crimes in the community, and abuse alcohol and other drugs. In some cases, conduct disordered behaviors persist throughout the individual's life. These disorders inflict untold psychological, social, and economic costs on youth, families, victims, and communities, in the form of remedial education, law enforcement, heavy utilization of outpatient and inpatient mental health services, physical and emotional harm to others, property destruction, substance abuse, teen parenthood, school dropout, and adult criminality (Robins, 1981).

5.20.2 CONDUCT DISORDERS

5.20.2.1 Phenomenology

Conduct disorders are characterized by a recurring and persistent pattern of antisocial behavior involving the violation of others' basic rights and major societal norms or rules. The term which used to be singular is now plural in recognition of the multiplicity of profiles exhibited by youth with a conduct disorder. Some youth manifest conduct disorder in terms of overt aggressive and hostile acts towards others, while other youth show a pattern of covert, deceitful acts (e.g., stealing, lying, truancy) without accompanying interpersonal aggression, and still others show a combination of these two patterns of antisocial behavior. For some youth, conduct problems begin around school entry, and for others these problems do not emerge until the start of puberty. Conduct disorder can be found in youth with poorly developed relationships with peers and in youth who have well-developed social networks albeit with deviant peers. In sum, although many of these youth have in common some aspects of antisocial functioning, there is considerable variation in terms of expression, age of onset, and social relations.

Developmental context is important in considering whether aggressive or otherwise antisocial behaviors constitute a conduct disorder. It is common for preschool-age children to engage in some behaviors that bear some resemblance to features of conduct disorder. For example, many four-year olds on at least a sporadic basis take things that do not belong to them, lie to get their way, and display tantrum outbursts that include hitting others or destroying property. Engaging in these behaviors occasionally at age four is sufficiently common to be considered a usual aspect of development. The same behaviors at age ten are developmentally out of step with agemates and are more likely to be indicative of the conduct-disorder constellation. Similarly but at the other end of childhood, the developmental norms of adolescence need to be considered. Adolescence is a period of development marked by rebelliousness punctuated by some acting out behavior. Occasional rule or law breaking, such as skipping school or writing graffiti in a public place, is sufficiently commonplace to be considered almost normative developmentally in adolescence. To distinguish between normative misconduct and antisocial disorder, the frequency and seriousness of the behaviors need to be considered. A competing consideration is that conduct problems including serious misdeeds might be increasing among adolescents to the point that such acts are becoming almost normative in frequency (Coie & Jacobs, 1993).

5.20.2.2 Diagnostic Considerations

In the *Diagnostic and statistical manual of mental disorders* (*DSM-IV*; American Psychiatric Association, 1994), Conduct disorder (CD) falls within a larger domain called attention-deficit and disruptive behavior disorders. CD shares this domain with somewhat related diagnoses of oppositional defiant disorder (ODD) and attention-deficit hyperactivity disorder (ADHD). The *DSM-IV* diagnosis of CD requires the presence of three or more manifestations of repeated and persistent antisocial

behavior over a 12-month period before age 18, with the behavioral disturbances resulting in significant impairment in social, academic, or job functioning.

Specifically, the three (or more) manifestations of antisocial behavior can be any of 15 criteria that are distributed across four domains: aggression towards people or animals, destruction of property, deceitfulness or theft, and serious violations of rules. Aggression includes bullying or threatening, fighting, use of dangerous weapons, physical cruelty to people or animals, confrontational theft, and coercive sexual activity. Property destruction includes vandalism or firesetting. Deceitfulness or theft includes breaking and entering, lying to obtain goods or favors or to avoid obligations, and nonconfrontive theft. Serious violations of rules includes staying out late even against parental prohibitions (beginning before age 13), running away, and school truancy.

A major departure by *DSM-IV* over previous versions is the specification of two CD types based on age at onset. *DSM-IV* distinguishes between childhood and adolescent onset. Childhood-onset CD begins prior to age 10 and requires at least one of the criterion manifestations of antisocial behavior before that age. Adolescent-onset CD begins in adolescence but also requires that none of the criterion manifestations occurred prior to age 10. The distinction between early vs. later onset is consistent with differing developmental patterns that have emerged in longitudinal and etiological research.

The *ICD-10* classification system (World Health Organization, 1992) also references conduct disorders in children and adolescence but uses an organizing scheme different from that found in *DSM-IV*. The core definition of conduct disorder in the two systems is essentially the same. However, instead of making the distinction between early and later onset, *ICD-10* identifies different subtypes. According to *ICD-10*, CD can be confined to the family context, which means that antisocial and aggressive behavior is confined primarily to interactions with family members. The unsocialized and socialized types of CD, which were present in earlier *DSM* versions, are part of *ICD-10* and distinguish between youth who have seriously disturbed relationships with other children and youth who are well integrated into their peer group. *ICD-10* categorizes ODD as one type of conduct disorder, whereas *DSM-IV* treats ODD as a category distinct from CD. However, both systems define ODD as the presence of markedly defiant, disobedient, and noxious behavior without the more severe aggressive or antisocial acts that violate the law or others' rights. Furthermore, both systems note that ODD is typically seen in children below the age of 9 or 10 and can be a precursor to CD in some children at a young age.

5.20.2.3 Prevalence

Estimates for the prevalence of CD have varied considerably. Costello (1989) reported that CDs affect approximately 5–8% of the general child population. Kazdin's (1995) review of prevalence indicated that the estimated rate of conduct disorders in children aged 4–18 has ranged from 2% to 6%. *DSM-IV* (American Psychiatric Association, 1994) reported that CD rates for youth under age 18 range from 6% to 16% for males and from 2% to 9% for females, although the basis or source of these estimates is not provided.

It is unclear specifically what has accounted for the wide variation in prevalence estimates. The actual obtained rate, however, can be greatly influenced by the threshold criteria for each of the symptom categories. For example, the symptom category pertaining to initiation of physical fights can be stretched or contracted depending on the frequency and intensity one requires for the fighting criterion. Kazdin (1995) noted that adolescents in the general population report very high rates of theft, assault, and vandalism, which implies that prevalence rates of CD diagnosis based on adolescent self-report could be quite high. In other words, the source of diagnostic information could significantly affect estimate of prevalence. The high variation in prevalence estimates could also reflect different time periods and sampling methods. Finally, there is some evidence to suggest that CD is becoming more prevalent in females over time (Loeber, 1990; Viemero, 1992) while not becoming less prevalent in males. Nonetheless, it is clear that CD is a highly prevalent problem that will not go away on its own.

5.20.2.4 Etiology

Much of the etiological work related to CD has focused on the study of risk factors, and to a lesser extent protective factors, that may impinge on the development of antisocial behavior. A number of significant clusters of risk factors have emerged over many years of research via longitudinal and cross-sectional studies. Some of the main categories of risk for CD include temperament, familial factors, school and peer factors, and sociological factors.

Although there is tremendous variability in developmental outcome, toddlers who show difficult temperaments are at heightened risk of developing conduct problems at school entry which might escalate over time (Campbell, 1991; Campbell, Breaux, Ewing, & Szumowski, 1986). Young children who exhibit greater impulsivity, emotional lability, and irritability than their agemates often face adverse environmental reactions if their behavioral style persists through early childhood. Given that most toddlers exhibit occasional outbursts and impatience, useful delineation of this risk factor emphasizes the frequent, chronic, and persistent nature of temperament difficulties.

Temperament difficulties do not typically persist or escalate independent of environmental context. Here is where familial risk factors may operate to potentiate temperamental risk. It is reasonable to hypothesize that parenting difficulties and family adversity exacerbate the adverse impact of child temperament difficulties, and that child temperament difficulties also add to parental and familial stress (Bates, Bayles, Bennett, Ridge, & Brown, 1991; Campbell et al., 1986; Dumas, 1992; Loeber & Stouthamer-Loeber, 1986; Moffitt, 1990; Offord, Boyle, & Racine, 1991). Such a transactional perspective does not preclude the possibility that there are multiple pathways to conduct disorder. For example, at the extreme ends of the spectrum, in children who do not exhibit early temperament difficulties, marked parenting problems such as severe child abuse can still lead to the development of conduct disorder. Conversely, for children showing intense difficulties with early temperament, positive parenting may not be sufficient to prevent the emergence of conduct disorder. However, any adequate etiological model for conduct disorder also must account for what happens to the many children between those two extremes.

A strong body of evidence exists supporting the contention that parenting difficulties during early and middle childhood significantly influence the development of early conduct problems (Patterson, 1982; Patterson, Reid, & Dishion, 1992; Wahler & Dumas, 1987). Relevant parenting dimensions include poor discipline (Farrington & West, 1981; McCord, 1988; Patterson et al., 1992), lack of positive parental response (Loeber & Stouthamer-Loeber, 1986; Wadsworth, 1980), and coercive family process (Patterson, 1982). Other risk factors in the family context, which may disrupt parenting and contribute to risk for CD, include alcohol and illicit drug abuse by caregivers (West & Prinz, 1987), parental social insularity and social disadvantage (Dumas, 1986; Wahler & Dumas, 1987), parental criminality and psychopathology (Offord, 1982; Robins, 1981), and marital discord (Offord & Boyle, 1986; Rutter & Giller, 1983).

Children already showing disruptive and inattentive behaviors in class tend to develop learning difficulties as well (Moffitt, 1990, 1993a, 1993b), which adds to their frustration. Learning difficulties plus the aversive responses from teachers provoked by aggressive and disruptive behaviors help to create negative school experiences that accelerate conduct problems (Campbell, 1991; Hawkins & Lishner, 1987; Hawkins & Weis, 1985; Hirschi, 1969; Walker & Buckley, 1973). Academic difficulties in elementary school and school failure leading to truancy and dropout during adolescence are both potential contributors to the development of serious antisocial behavior (Loeber, 1990). In addition, there is some evidence that certain school environments, such as those that are disorganized with large classes and nonrewarding practices, can exacerbate antisocial behavior (Rutter, Maughan, Mortimore, Ouston, & Smith, 1979; Rutter et al., 1974).

Disturbed relations with peers is another common source of risk, in the form of rejection by mainstream peers followed by attraction to deviant peer groups (Dishion, Patterson, Stoolmiller, & Skinner, 1991; Elliott, Huizinga, & Ageton, 1985; Snyder, Dishion, & Patterson, 1986; West & Farrington, 1977). A common assertion in the literature is that peers exert a strong influence that can promote antisocial behavior including substance abuse (Dishion & Andrews, 1995; Elliott et al., 1985). However, there is some disagreement about whether the peer influence is a primary causal variable or just a concomitant outcome. For example, Block, Block, and Keyes (1988) demonstrated that early family socialization practices exert a more cause influence than peer variables, particularly on substance abuse. On the other hand, adolescent-onset CD seems to be more closely tied to exposure to deviant peer influences than childhood-onset CD (Capaldi & Patterson, 1994).

Another perspective on possible etiological mechanisms derives from a social information processing framework. Specifically, Dodge and others have identified deficiencies in critical social-cognitive skills that are related to aggressive tendencies (Crick & Dodge, 1994; Dodge, 1985; Dodge, Bates, & Pettit, 1990; Dodge, Pettit, McClaskey, & Brown, 1986). Key features include an attributional bias towards presuming hostile intent in others (Dodge & Frame, 1982; Lochman, 1987), failure to attend to relevant social cues (Dodge et al., 1990), low skill level in social problem-solving (Asarnow & Callan, 1985; Lochman, Lampron, & Rabiner, 1989), and a tendency to view aggression as

leading to positive outcomes (Perry, Perry, & Rasmussen, 1986; Dodge et al., 1986).

Yet another category of etiological theory about CD derives from a set of approaches inadequately identified as sociological in nature. A number of researchers from different perspectives have recognized that the larger social context, including neighborhood, economic stratum, community, and cultural reference group, has some connection to the development and desistance of antisocial patterns of behavior in children and adolescents. For example, social interactionists such as Patterson, Wahler, and their colleagues have demonstrated how high levels of family adversity associated with economic disadvantage exert indirect effects on youth antisocial behavior via disrupted parenting and related consequences (Capaldi & Patterson, 1994; Wahler & Hann, 1987). Others have shown how community and peer influences coalesce to impact youth behavior (Sampson & Groves, 1989), how exposure to community violence can increase youth antisocial behavior and other adjustment problems (Richters & Martinez, 1993), and how forces of prejudice and racism manifesting in exclusion from the mainstream, threats to self-identity, and demoralizing conditions of hopeless poverty can induce expressions of anger and outrage taking the form of antisocial acts (Boyd-Franklin, 1989; McLoyd, 1990; Ogbu, 1988).

5.20.2.5 Developmental Course

For childhood-onset CD, children who ultimately develop the disorder show prodromal signs at school entry or even earlier. The early starters often exhibit pronounced cross-situational aggressive behavior between ages four and eight (Dumas, 1992; Loeber, 1988, 1990; Loeber & LeBlanc, 1990; Patterson, DeBaryshe, & Ramsey, 1989), which is quite likely to meet the criteria for a diagnosis of ODD. Early aggression is predictive not only of later delinquency (Loeber, 1990) but also subsequent substance abuse (Hawkins, Catalano, & Miller, 1992). Oppositional-aggressive behavior interacts with parenting difficulties to place such children at further risk as they enter school (Patterson et al., 1992). During the early years of elementary school, children at risk for early-onset CD experience learning difficulties (Offord & Waters, 1983; Rutter & Giller, 1983), particularly in reading and language-related skills (Moffitt, 1993a, 1993b). Such children often engage in high rates of inappropriate classroom behavior that includes ignoring teacher instructions, hitting classmates, disrupting class, and destroying property (Prinz, Connor, & Wilson, 1981). Aversive reactions from teachers (Campbell, 1991; Walker & Buckley, 1973) and rejection from peers (Bierman, 1986; Cantrell & Prinz, 1985; Dodge, 1989; Parker & Asher, 1987) often further escalate the children's conduct problems and set the stage for full-blown CD.

Adolescent-onset CD has a somewhat different developmental course. Unlike youth with childhood-onset CD, the late starters develop at least minimal social skills and adequate peer relations, do not show antisocial behavior problems in early elementary school, and seem to acquire delinquent tendencies more from a deviant peer group than from coercive family interactions (Patterson et al., 1989, 1992). Late starters are not necessarily free from family problems, and their antisocial behavior can precipitate family difficulties (or aggravate existing ones). It is presumed that in comparison with early starters, late starters are more likely to desist by early adulthood with respect to delinquent behavior (Patterson et al., 1992).

5.20.3 CONCEPTUALIZATION AND CLINICAL FORMULATION

5.20.3.1 Multimodal Assessment

Appraisal of core CD symptomatology is a significant facet of assessment. For younger children, the main sources of information about conduct problems are parents and teachers via behavioral rating scales. Direct observation of child behavior in social settings (e.g., home, classroom, playground) can also provide useful data about interactive style, particularly with respect to interpersonal aggression. Structured diagnostic interviews of the caregiver have potential utility with younger and older children. For older children, youth report via self-report instruments (behavioral rating scales, behavioral incident checklists) and structured diagnostic interviews add breadth to the assessment of conduct problems.

Several rating scales have acceptable psychometric properties and adequate coverage of content pertinent to conduct disorder. The Child Behavior Checklist, a 113-item instrument, covers youth ranging from 2–16 years of age and has versions for parent, teacher, and youth report (Achenbach & Edelbrock, 1983). The Conners Parent and Teacher Rating Scales are a collection of instruments varying in length and specificity which are particularly useful for assessing comorbid ADHD as well as nuances of conduct problems and antisocial behavior (Conners, 1969, 1970, 1973; Goyette, Conners, & Ulrich, 1978). The Eyberg Child Behavior

Inventory, a 36-item instrument designed specifically to assess aspects of conduct and oppositional problems in youth aged 2–16 years, is particularly useful for pinpointing problem areas and assessing treatment effects (Eyberg, 1992; Eyberg & Robinson, 1983; Eyberg & Ross, 1978).

Some intervention programs rely on direct observation, either in the home or in a clinic analogue setting, as a basis for characterizing the specific nature of the problems and for driving treatment implementation (Patterson, 1982; Sanders, Dadds, & Bor, 1989). With younger children, such observations may involve family tasks that involve free play by children and transition tasks that place demands on them. With older children, the observation tasks tend to take the form of problem-discussion tasks for families to attempt. In general, observation seems to be particularly useful for assessing key family processes and other interpersonal interactions (e.g., playground interactions) that might bear on the maintenance of CD, rather than for trying to establish rates and extent of conduct problems.

A major challenge in assessing conduct problems is the variability in types of symptoms that youth with CD can exhibit. While most of the younger children early-onset CD group exhibit demonstrative aggression towards others in public settings, the older youth are more variable. Some adolescents who clearly qualify for a CD diagnosis exhibit little or no overt aggression towards others but instead commit covert acts such as vandalism, cruelty to animals, or nonconfrontational theft. Others only commit aggressive acts in specific circumstances, such as in coercive sexual encounters. The implication of this variability is that there is no single constellation of symptoms to monitor for all youth with CD.

5.20.3.2 Treatment Formulation

Treatment strategies for CD differ somewhat for pre-adolescents vs. adolescents, and the distinction is not simply between early-onset vs. later-onset CD. By definition, pre-adolescent children exhibiting CD symptomatology belong to the early-onset group. However, adolescents in treatment for CD may have either early-onset or later-onset histories but this difference may not manifest in behavioral differences during adolescence. Consequently, CD treatment for CD may vary as a function of severity and setting constraints rather than onset history.

Historically, treatment for CD focused on intrapsychic approaches including play therapy and individual psychotherapy with children, which have met with less recent acceptance in the absence of evidence for efficacy or promise (Kazdin, 1987). Current treatment focuses much more on the social contexts in which children misbehave, namely in the family, in school, and with peers. Much of the current treatment for CD is predicated on the assumption that children with conduct problems need a concentrated regimen of accelerated positive socialization. Treatment strategies emanating from this assumption enlist parents, teachers, and even peers as therapeutic agents. Essentially, the more ecologically oriented interventions attempt to restructure the youth's social environment to shape and reinforce positive behaviors and limit antisocial behavior.

An alternative formulation focuses on the internal cognitive set characteristic of youth who engage in high rates of antisocial behavior. The proponents of the cognitive approach argue that changes in the social environment, in the absence of addressing beliefs and attitudes that lead to antisocial behavior, will not produce lasting positive gains.

5.20.4 TREATMENT

5.20.4.1 Psychosocial Treatments

One of the most common and well-researched psychosocial treatments for pre-adolescent youth with CD is parent training in behavioral management skills. Although there are several variants of parent training (Miller & Prinz, 1990), most approaches have in common a core set of principles and goals: (i) Parent trainers help parents pinpoint, and then monitor, specific positive and negative behaviors that they want to change. (ii) Positive reinforcement, which is a central construct in parent training, is emphasized as more important than punishment. (iii) Parents are encouraged to replace corporal punishment with time-out from reinforcement for the younger children or loss of privileges for the older ones. (iv) The principle of shaping is promoted as a strategy for starting with children's existing behavioral repertoires and expanding their capabilities. (v) Systematic attending and ignoring are key parenting skills that are particularly effective with younger children. (vi) Many of the parent training programs emphasize positive communications by parents to motivate children and strengthen family relationships. (vii) Programs attempt to increase the probability of positive parental attention for child prosocial behaviors (e.g., cooperation, calm talking, appropriate play behavior, sharing, complying with adult requests, staying out of fights) and to assist parents in coping more effectively with child antisocial, aggressive, and noncompliant behaviors.

Parent training is administered in group or individual format (or some combination of both). There are advantages and disadvantages to each format. With the group approach, parents receive support and modeling from other parents, they get to benefit from hearing other parents' questions and the group leader's responses, and the process is more cost efficient. Disadvantages of the group format include: (i) a fixed program that does not permit individual variation in content or pacing, (ii) fewer opportunities to handle each parent's concerns and difficulties, and (iii) inflexibility with respect to scheduling (or rescheduling). The individual format (i.e., therapist works with one family at a time) has a number of advantages: (i) a functional analysis of the particular family can be conducted; (ii) the pace, content, and relative emphasis in therapy can be tailored to the family's needs; (iii) crises can be handled more readily; and (iv) the therapist develops a closer relationship with youth and family that can sustain engagement in treatment. Conversely, therapy with individual families does not engender the same level of social support and normalizing of experiences that the group approach affords.

With adolescents, family-based treatment approaches tend to take the form of family therapy over parent training, with some exceptions (see Patterson, Chamberlain, & Reid, 1982). In contrast to parent training in which the therapist works primarily with the parents, family therapy involves at least the parent(s) and adolescent plus other members of the household such as siblings and extended family. Some of the more prominent family therapy approaches include structural family therapy (Minuchin, 1974; Minuchin & Fishman, 1982; Minuchin, Montalvo, Guerney, Rosman, & Schumer, 1967), functional family therapy (Alexander & Parsons, 1982; Barton & Alexander, 1981; Jameson & Alexander, 1994), and behavioral family therapy (Miller & Prinz, 1990; Tolan & Mitchell, 1989). Although adopting somewhat varied tactics, these three therapy approaches share in common the recognition that youth antisocial behavior is bound up to some degree in family interactions. Furthermore, these approaches all attempt to help families attain their goals and improve relationships and communication within the family.

A relatively new treatment approach has emerged called "multisystemic therapy," which is a hybrid of traditional family therapy and behavior therapy with a strong emphasis on ecological context (Henggeler & Borduin, 1990).

In multisystemic therapy, the therapist works with the family and the youth in the home and elsewhere to alter systemic processes known to be related to antisocial behavior. Multisystemic therapists address parental discipline, family communication and affect, peer associations, school issues, and other potentially significant domains in the larger contexts in which the youth operates.

In addition to interventions that focus primarily on larger contexts such as school and home, there are also youth-focused approaches that involve therapists working one-on-one or in small groups with children or adolescents. The youth-focused approaches arise primarily out of the social-skills and cognitive-behavioral areas (Dush, Hirt, & Schroeder, 1989; Kazdin, 1987; Michelson, 1987). Youth-focused treatments for CD include social skills training, problem-solving training, self-control training, anger management, or some combination of these. Social-skills approaches typically include individual and group reinforcement, coaching and shaping of specific interpersonal behaviors, positive group activities, friendship skills, and listening/speaking skills (Bierman, 1989; Bierman, Miller, & Staub, 1987; Michelson, Sugai, Wood, & Kazdin, 1983; Prinz, Blechman, & Dumas, 1994). Other approaches have combined interpersonal problem-solving and self-instruction (self-talk) in an effort to alter the cognitive bases assumed to underlie conduct problems (e.g., Kazdin, Bass, Siegel, & Thomas, 1989; Kazdin, Esveldt-Dawson, French, & Unis, 1987). Lochman and colleagues have focused on a cognitive-behavioral variant, primarily with young adolescents, that has focused on strategies for anger management (Lochman, 1992; Lochman, Burch, Curry, & Lampron, 1984; Lochman & Curry, 1986).

5.20.4.2 Pharmacological Treatments

Several psychoactive medications have been tried with children or adults who exhibit various forms of aggressive behavior. For example: (i) methylphenidate, D-amphetamine, pemoline citrate, and clonidine have been used with youth with comorbid CD and ADHD (Hinshaw, 1991; Hinshaw, Heller, & McHale, 1992); (i) diphenhydramine, clonazepam, and buspirone have been used with children showing CD combined with anxiety; (iii) fluoxetine, imipramine, desipramine, nortriptyline, and bupropion have been used for comorbid CD and depression; and (iv) lithium carbonate, neuroleptics, propranolol, carbamazepine, antidepressants, and buspirone have

been used to address aggressive symptomatology (including self-injurious behavior) in individuals with CD (Campbell & Spencer, 1988; Zavodnick, 1994). However, evidence has not yet emerged in support of pharmacological treatment for the general population of youth with conduct disorder (Stewart, Myers, Burket, & Lyles, 1990). Zavodnick recommends medication primarily as an adjunct to behavioral and parent management treatments, particularly when conduct disorder co-occurs with a diagnosable disorder such as ADHD or depression.

CD and associated problems such as substance abuse, criminality, risky sexual behavior, and school failure are complex constellations of behaviors that are embedded in social contexts. Pharmacological treatment is predicated on an assumption of biological determination (or at least biological influence) that runs orthogonal to a social-contextual analysis. It is not clear at the present time that pharmacological treatment should be the primary approach of choice for many youth whose patterns of antisocial behavior are extricably connected to family, peer, school, and community influences.

5.20.4.3 Efficacy/Effectiveness of Treatments

Social-learning-based parent training for families with a conduct-problem child or young adolescent has met with some success by focusing on parental monitoring and supervision, discipline (e.g., compliance training, timeout, elimination of coercive parenting methods), and quality of parent–child interaction (Dumas, 1989; Kazdin, 1987; Miller & Prinz, 1990). A number of studies conducted by Patterson and colleagues have demonstrated that the majority of children exhibiting pronounced aggressive behavior and related conduct problems respond favorably to systematic parent training interventions (Fleischman, 1981; Patterson, 1974, 1982; Patterson, Chamberlain, & Reid, 1982; Patterson & Fleischman, 1979). Webster-Stratton and her colleagues also found that parenting training, primarily in group-administered formats, produced significant gains for conduct problems in preadolescents over untreated controls that were maintained at one-year follow-up (Webster-Stratton, 1984; Webster-Stratton, Hollinsworth, & Kolpacoff, 1989; Webster-Stratton, Kolpacoff, & Hollinsworth, 1988).

Parent-training investigators have acknowledged that optimum results are not always obtained and that there are obstacles to intervention (Hawkins, Catalano, Morrison, et al., 1992; Kazdin, 1987; Miller & Prinz, 1990).

One challenge is the difficulty in producing lasting changes in families with severe socioeconomic disadvantage and social isolation (Dumas, 1984; Dumas & Wahler, 1983; Patterson & Fleischman, 1979). Another problem is keeping families in treatment without premature attrition, or for that matter getting families into treatment to begin with (McMahon, Forehand, Griest, & Wells, 1981; Miller & Prinz, 1990; Prinz & Miller, 1994). In view of these kinds of difficulties, there is growing support for home-based family interventions (Fraser, Pecora, & Haapala, 1991; Henggeler, Melton, & Smith, 1992; Tharp, 1991) as a way of addressing the needs of culturally and economically diverse populations, avoiding the perceived stigma of clinic-administered treatments, and overcoming the practical obstacles of transportation, childcare, and management of appointments.

Multisystemic therapy (MST; Henggeler & Borduin, 1990) has shown promise with youthful offenders, a most challenging population. Henggeler et al. (1986) compared MST with usual community treatment for juvenile offenders and their families and found that MST was associated with a decrease in reported conduct and related adjustment problems and an improvement in quality of family interaction. Mann, Borduin, Henggeler, and Blaske (1990) randomly assigned chronic juvenile offenders either to MST or individual counseling and found that the youth participating in MST showed significantly lower recidivism over a four-year period (22% vs. 71%). Similar results were reported by Borduin, Henggeler, Blaske, and Stein (1990) in a study applying MST to adolescent sexual offenders. Henggeler, Melton, and Smith (1992) found that MST proved superior to incarceration with respect to subsequent behavior of serious juvenile offenders.

Child cognitive-behavioral therapies have led to at least short-term benefits in observed classroom behavior, academic performance, and teacher/parent reports of aggression and social adjustment (Dush, Hirt, & Schroeder, 1989). Two notable studies targeted truly antisocial samples and evaluated long-term impact (Kazdin, Bass, Siegel, & Thomas, 1989; Lochman, 1992). Kazdin et al. (1989) found that interpersonal problem-solving led to major improvements (immediate and at one-year follow-up) in prosocial behavior and in reductions of aggressive behavior at home and school but cautioned that child-focused intervention may not be sufficient for sustained, clinically significant improvement. Lochman (1992) found that a school-based cognitive-behavioral intervention had significant effects at three-year follow-up in terms lower rates of

substance use (alcohol and marijuana) and higher rates of self-esteem in mid-adolescence, compared with untreated peers. However, the intervention had only limited effects on the adolescents' general level of conduct problems, causing Lochman (1992) to suggest that family intervention may be crucial to use in combination with youth-focused interventions.

Social skills interventions have also shown some degree of promise. Michelson et al. (1983) found that a social-skills training program with children aged 8–12 years who had conduct problems produced one-year maintenance of improved social adjustment. Bierman (Bierman, 1989; Bierman, Miller, & Staub, 1987) tested a 10 session social skills training with aggressive-rejected children aged 7–10 years using heterogeneous training groups composed of high-risk and competent children, individual and group reinforcement, coaching and shaping of specific interpersonal behaviors, and enjoyable group activities. Bierman et al. (1987) reported a reduction in antisocial behavior and some improvement in peer acceptance at one-year follow-up. Prinz et al. (1994) evaluated a peer coping-skills intervention that focused on enhancing speaking and listening skills for handling social challenges in small heterogeneous groups (i.e., equal proportions of children with high-risk and socially competent status in the same group). Children aged 7–9 years with high rates of aggressive behavior who received the peer coping-skills program made significant improvement over controls at post-intervention and next-school-year follow-up in terms of a reduced level of aggressive behavior and greater communication effectiveness as judged by teachers (Prinz et al., 1994). Of additional interest is that inclusion of socially competent children without aggressive profiles did not result in iatrogenic effects on those children and actually produced significant gains in communication effectiveness (over socially competent children who did not receive the peer intervention).

5.20.5 FUTURE DIRECTIONS FOR RESEARCH AND PRACTICE

From a treatment perspective, one of the most challenging aspects of conduct disorder work has to do with engaging youth and families in the treatment process and maintaining engagement and full participation. Youth with antisocial behavior problems tend to come from families where many of the adults in the household are antisocial themselves and somewhat reticent to participating in treatment. Motivating caregivers to participate meaningfully in the treatment process is as yet an unsolved problem. In a free society, we cannot realistically force youth or parents to participate in treatment. The challenge is to find strategies for motivating and supporting prosocial treatment participation.

A related issue concerns matching of interventions and treatment strategies with particular youth and families. Although subgroups of youth with conduct disorder have been identified, these subgroups are not sufficiently specific or useful to match with treatment strategies. Treatment for conduct disorders often fails, and there are many contributing factors to such failure that need to be studied in order to arrive at clusters of characteristics and circumstances under which one strategy might be more successful than another. Cultural, familial, developmental, and topographical (i.e., type of conduct problems) variables may all play a role.

The future treatment strategies for conduct disorders that have the greatest likelihood for success will probably look like this. (i) Multiple participants, including parents, siblings, teachers, peers, and targeted youth, will contribute to the breadth of interventions. (ii) Interventions will begin early in the trajectory of antisocial behavior. (iii) Greater emphasis will be placed on preventive interventions before children enter the judicial system or are expelled from school. (iv) Interventions will be longer (sometimes lasting for several years), with phases of periodic maintenance and booster contacts. (v) Service delivery systems will rely more heavily on ecologically oriented models that include home visits, neighborhood programs, and family-support approaches.

5.20.6 SUMMARY

The conduct disorders are characterized by a recurring and persistent pattern of antisocial behavior and violation of major societal norms. Antisocial behaviors typically fall into four domains: aggression towards others, destruction of property, theft and other deceit, and serious rule violations (e.g., chronic school truancy). *DSM-IV* distinguishes between childhood and adolescent onset of conduct disorder. Childhood-onset conduct disorder that persists throughout adolescence is associated with greater severity and long-term adverse consequences (e.g., adult criminality, higher rate of violence) than is found with adolescent-onset conduct disorder. Etiological factors include parenting difficulties during early and middle childhood, other familial factors, early temperamental difficulties, school effects, and disturbed peer relations. Assessment methods for conduct disorder include direct observation with younger children, diagnostic interview schedules with youth or caregivers, and rating scales with parent, teacher, or youth informants. The more promising treatment approaches include social-learning-based approaches to parent training and family intervention, an ecological family approach called multisystemic therapy, and child cognitive-behavioral therapies that include social skills interventions, interpersonal problem-solving, and cognitive attributional retraining. Psychopharmacological intervention may be helpful primarily as an adjunctive treatment for youth who have comorbid ADHD or depression. Future research will need to address the challenge of motivating youth and families in treatment and in developing better strategies for matching approaches and incentives to individual cases.

5.20.7 REFERENCES

Achenbach, T. M., & Edelbrock, C. S. (1983). *Manual for the Child Behavior Checklist and Revised Child Behavior Profile*. Burlington, University of Vermont, Department of Psychiatry.

Alexander, J. F., & Parsons, B. V. (1982). *Functional family therapy: Principles and procedures*. Carmel, CA: Brooks/Cole.

American Psychiatric Association (1994). *Diagnostic and statistical manual of mental disorders* (4th ed.). Washington, DC: American Psychiatric Association.

Asarnow, J. R., & Callan, J. W. (1985). Boys with peer adjustment problems: Social cognitive processes. *Journal of Consulting and Clinical Psychology, 53*, 80–87.

Barton, C., & Alexander, J. F. (1981). Functional family therapy. In A. S. Gurman & D. P. Kniskern (Eds.), *Handbook of family therapy* (pp. 403–443). New York: Brunner/Mazel.

Bates, J. E., Bayles, K., Bennett, D. S., Ridge, B., & Brown, M. M. (1991). Origins of externalizing behavior problems at eight years of age. In D. J. Pepler & K. H. Rubin (Eds.), *The development and treatment of childhood aggression* (pp. 93–119). Hillsdale, NJ: Erlbaum.

Bierman, K. (1986). The relationship of social aggression and peer rejection in middle childhood. In R. J. Prinz (Ed.), *Advances in behavioral assessment of children and families* (pp. 51–178). Greenwich, CT: JAI Press.

Bierman, K. (1989). Improving the peer relationships of rejected children. In B. B. Lahey & A. E. Kazdin (Eds.), *Advances in clinical child psychology* (Vol. 12, pp. 53–84). New York: Plenum.

Bierman, K., Miller, C. M., & Staub, S. (1987). Improving the social behavior and peer acceptance of rejected boys: Effects of social skill training. *Journal of Consulting and Clinical Psychology, 55*, 194–200.

Block, J., Block, J. H., & Keyes, S. (1988). Longitudinally foretelling drug usage in adolescence: Early childhood peer and environmental precursors. *Child Development, 59*, 336–355.

Borduin, C. M., Henggeler, S. W., Blaske, D. M., & Stein, R. (1990). Multisystemic treatment of adolescent sexual offenders. *International Journal of Offender Therapy and Comparative Criminology, 34*, 105–113.

Boyd-Franklin, N. (1989). *Black families in therapy: A*

multisystems approach. New York: Guilford Press.

Campbell, M., & Spencer, E. K. (1988). Psychopharmacology in child and adolescent psychiatry: A review of the past five years. *Journal of the American Academy of Child and Adolescent Psychiatry, 27,* 267–279.

Campbell, S. B. (1991). Longitudinal studies of active and aggressive preschoolers: Individual differences in early behavior and outcome. In D. Cicchetti & S. L. Toth (Eds.), *Rochester Symposium on Developmental Psychopathology, Vol. 2: Internalizing and externalizing expressions of dysfunction* (pp. 57–90). Hillsdale, NJ: Erlbaum.

Campbell, S. B., Breaux, A. M., Ewing, L. J., & Szumowski, E. K. (1986). Correlates and predictors of hyperactivity and aggression: A longitudinal study of parent-referred problem preschoolers. *Journal of Abnormal Child Psychology, 14,* 217–234.

Cantrell, V. L. & Prinz, R. J. (1985). Multiple perspectives of rejected, neglected, and accepted children: Relationship between sociometric status and behavioral characteristics. *Journal of Consulting and Clinical Psychology, 53,* 884–889.

Capaldi, D. M., & Patterson, G. R. (1994). Interrelated influences of contextual factors on antisocial behavior in childhood and adolescence for males. In D. C. Fowles, P. Sutker, & S. H. Goodman (Eds.), *Progress in experimental personality and psychopathology research* (pp. 165–198). New York: Springer.

Coie, J. D., & Jacobs, M. R. (1993). The role of social context in the prevention of conduct disorder. *Development and Psychopathology, 5,* 263–275.

Conners, C. K. (1969). A teacher rating scale for use in drug studies with children. *American Journal of Psychiatry, 126,* 884–888.

Conners, C. K. (1970). Symptom patterns in hyperkinetic, neurotic, and normal children. *Child Development, 41,* 667–682.

Conners, C. K. (1973). Rating scales for use in drug studies with children. *Psychopharmacological Bulletin, 9,* 24–84.

Costello, E. J. (1989). Developments in child psychiatric epidemiology. *Journal of the American Academy of Child and Adolescent Psychiatry, 28,* 836–841.

Crick, N. R., & Dodge, K. A. (1994). A review and reformulation of social information processing mechanisms in children's social adjustment. *Psychological Bulletin, 115,* 74–101.

Dishion, T. J., & Andrews, D. W. (1995). Preventing escalation in problem behaviors with high-risk young adolescents: Immediate and 1-year outcomes. *Journal of Consulting and Clinical Psychology, 63,* 538–548.

Dishion, T. J., Patterson, G. R., Stoolmiller, M., & Skinner, M. L. (1991). Family, school, and behavioral antecedents to early adolescent involvement with antisocial peers. *Developmental Psychology, 27,* 172–180.

Dodge, K. A. (1985). Attributional bias in aggressive children. In P. C. Kendall (Ed.), *Advances in cognitive-behavioral research and therapy* (Vol. 4, pp. 75–110). Hillsdale, NJ: Erlbaum.

Dodge, K. A. (1989). Enhancing social relationships. In E. J. Mash & R. J. Barkley (Eds.), *Behavioral treatment of childhood disorders* (pp. 222–244). New York: Guilford Press.

Dodge, K. A., Bates, J. E., & Pettit, G. S. (1990). *Mechanisms in the cycle of violence. Science, 250,* 1678–1683.

Dodge, K. A., & Frame, C. L. (1982). Social cognitive biases and deficits in aggressive boys. *Child Development, 53,* 620–635.

Dodge, K. A., Pettit, G. S., McClaskey, C. L., & Brown, M. (1986). Social competence in children. *Monographs of the Society for Research in Child Development, 51* (2, Serial No. 213).

Dumas, J. E. (1984). Child, adult-interactional, and socioeconomic setting events as predictors of parent training outcome. *Education and Treatment of Children, 7,* 351–364.

Dumas, J. E. (1986). Indirect influence of maternal social contacts on mother–child interactions: A setting event analysis. *Journal of Abnormal Child Psychology, 14,* 205–216.

Dumas, J. E. (1989). Treating antisocial behavior in children: Child and family approaches. *Clinical Psychology Review, 9,* 197–222.

Dumas, J. E. (1992). Conduct disorder. In S. M. Turner, K. S. Calhoun, & H. E. Adams (eds.), *Handbook of clinical behavior therapy* (2nd ed., pp. 285–316). New York: Wiley.

Dumas, J. E., & Wahler, R. G. (1983). Predictors of treatment outcome in parent training: Mother insularity and socioeconomic disadvantage. *Behavioral Assessment, 5,* 301–313.

Dush, D. M., Hirt, M. L., & Schroeder, H. E. (1989). Self-statement modification in the treatment of child behavior disorders: A meta-analysis. *Psychological Bulletin, 106,* 97–106.

Elliott, D. S., Huizinga, D., & Ageton, S. (1985). *Explaining delinquency and drug use.* Beverly Hills, CA: Sage.

Eyberg, S. M. (1992). Assessing therapy outcome with preschool children: Progress and problems. *Journal of Clinical Child Psychology, 221,* 306–311.

Eyberg, S. M., & Robinson, E. A. (1983). Conduct problem behavior: Standardization of a behavioral rating scale with adolescents. *Journal of Clinical Child Psychology, 12,* 347–354.

Eyberg, S. M., & Ross, A. W. (1978). Assessment of child behavior problems: The validation of a new inventory. *Journal of Clinical Child Psychology, 7,* 113–116.

Farrington, D. P., & West, D. J. (1981). The Cambridge study in delinquent development (United Kingdom). In S. A. Mednick & A. E. Baert (Eds). *Prospective longitudinal research: An empirical basis for the primary prevention of psychosocial disorders* (pp. 183–201). New York: Oxford University Press.

Fleischman, M. J. (1981). A replication of Patterson's "Intervention for boys with conduct problems." *Journal of Consulting and Clinical Psychology, 49,* 342–351.

Fraser, M. W., Pecora, P. J., & Haapala, D. A. (1991). *Families in crisis: The impact of intensive family preservation services.* Hawthorne, NY: Aldine de Gruyter.

Goyette, C. H., Conners, C. K., & Ulrich, R. F. (1978). Normative data on revised Conners Parent and Teacher Rating Scales. *Journal of Abnormal Child Psychology, 12,* 421–436.

Hawkins, J. D., Catalano, R. F., & Miller, J. Y. (1992). Risk and protective factors for alcohol and other drug problems in adolescence and early adulthood: Implications for substance abuse prevention. *Psychological Bulletin, 112,* 64–105.

Hawkins, J. D., Catalano, R. F., Morrison, D. M., O'Donnell, J., Abbott, R. D., & Day, L. E. (1992). The Seattle Social Development Project: Effects of the first four years on protective factors and problem behaviors. In J. McCord & R. Tremblay (Eds.), *The prevention of antisocial behavior in children* (pp. 139–161). New York: Guilford Press.

Hawkins, J. D., & Lishner, D. (1987). Etiology and prevention of antisocial behavior in children and adolescents. In D. H. Crowell, I. M. Evans, & C. R. O'Donnell (Eds.), *Childhood aggression and violence: Sources of influence, prevention, and control* (pp. 263–282). New York: Plenum.

Hawkins, J. D., & Weis, J. G. (1985). The social development model: An integrated approach to delinquency prevention. *Journal of Primary Prevention, 6,* 73–97.

Henggeler, S. W., & Borduin, C. M. (1990). *Family therapy and beyond: A multisystemic approach to treating the behavior problems of children and adolescents.* Pacific Grove, CA: Brooks/Cole.

Henggeler, S. W., Melton, G. K., & Smith, L. (1992). Multisystematic treatment of juvenile offenders: An effective alternative to incarceration. *Journal of Consulting and Clinical Psychology, 60,* 953–961.

Henggeler, S. W., Rodick, J. D., Borduin, C. M., Hanson, C. L., Watson, S. M., & Urey, J. R. (1986). Multisystemic treatment of juvenile offenders: Effects on adolescent behavior and family interaction. *Developmental Psychology, 22,* 132–141.

Hinshaw, S. P. (1991). Stimulant medication and the treatment of aggression in children with attentional deficits. *Journal of Clinical Child Psychology, 20,* 301–312.

Hinshaw, S. P., Heller, T., & McHale, J. P. (1992). Covert antisocial behavior in boys with attention-deficit hyperactivity disorder: External validation and effects of methylphenidate. *Journal of Consulting and Clinical Psychology, 60,* 274–281.

Hirschi, T. (1969). *Causes of delinquency.* Berkeley, CA: University of California Press.

Jameson, P. B., & Alexander, J. F. (1994). Implications of a developmental family systems model for clinical practice. In L. L'Abate (Ed.), *Handbook of developmental family psychology and psychopathology* (pp. 392–411). New York: Wiley

Kazdin, A. E. (1987) Treatment of antisocial behavior in children: Current status and future directions. *Psychological Bulletin, 102,* 187–203.

Kazdin, A. E. (1995). *Conduct disorders in childhood and adolescence.* Thousand Oaks, CA: Sage.

Kazdin, A. E., Bass, D., Siegel, T., & Thomas, C. (1989). Cognitive-behavioral therapy and relationship therapy in the treatment of children referred for antisocial behavior. *Journal of Consulting and Clinical Psychology, 57,* 522–536.

Kazdin, A. E., Esveldt-Dawson, K., French, N. H., & Unis, A. S. (1987). Problem-solving skills training and relationship therapy in the treatment of antisocial child behavior. *Journal of Consulting and Clinical Psychology, 55,* 76–85.

Lochman, J. E. (1987). Self and peer perceptions and attributional biases of aggressive and nonaggressive boys in dyadic interactions. *Journal of Consulting and Clinical Psychology, 55,* 404–410.

Lochman, J. E. (1992). Cognitive-behavioral intervention with aggressive boys: Three-year follow-up and preventive effects. *Journal of Consulting and Clinical Psychology, 60,* 426–432.

Lochman, J. E., Burch, P. R., Curry, J. F., & Lampron, L. B. (1984). Treatment and generalization effects of cognitive-behavioral and goal-setting interventions with aggressive boys. *Journal of Consulting and Clinical Psychology, 52,* 915–916.

Lochman, J. E., & Curry, J. F. (1986). Effects of social problem-solving training and self-instruction training with aggressive boys. *Journal of Clinical Child Psychology, 15,* 159–164.

Lochman, J. E., Lampron, L. B., & Rabiner, D. L. (1989). Format differences and salience effects in assessment of social problem-solving skills of aggressive and nonaggressive boys. *Journal of Abnormal Child Psychology, 18,* 230–236.

Loeber, R. (1988). The natural history of juvenile conduct problems, delinquency, and associated substance use: Evidence for developmental progressions. In B. B. Lahey & A. E. Kazdin (Eds.), *Advances in clinical child psychology* (Vol. 11, pp. 73–124). New York: Plenum.

Loeber, R. (1990). Development and risk factors of juvenile antisocial behavior and delinquency. *Clinical Psychology Review, 10,* 1–42.

Loeber, R., & LeBlanc, M. (1990). Toward a developmental criminology. In M. Tonry & N. Morris (Eds.), *Crime and justice* (Vol. 12, pp. 375–473). Chicago: University of Chicago Press.

Loeber, R., & Stouthamer-Loeber, M. (1986). Family factors as correlates and predictors of juvenile conduct problems and delinquency. In N. Morris & M. Tonry (Eds.), *Crime and justice: An annual review of research* (Vol. 7, pp. 29–149). Chicago: University of Chicago Press.

Mann, B. J., Borduin, C. M., Henggeler, S. W., & Blaske, D. M. (1990). An investigation of systemic conceptualizations of parent–child coalitions and symptom change. *Journal of Consulting and Clinical Psychology, 58,* 336–344.

McCord, J. (1988). Parental behavior in the cycle of aggression. *Psychiatry, 51,* 14–23.

McLoyd, V. C. (1990). The impact of economic hardship on Black families and children: Psychological distress, parenting, and socioemotional development. *Child Development, 61,* 311–346.

McMahon, R. J., Forehand, R., Griest, D. L., & Wells, K. C. (1981). Who drops out of therapy during parent behavioral training? *Behavioral Counseling Quarterly, 1,* 79–85.

Michelson, L. (1987). Cognitive-behavioral strategies in prevention and treatment of antisocial disorders in children/adolescents. In J. D. Burchard & S. N. Burchard (Eds.), *Prevention of delinquent behavior* (pp. 190–219). Beverly Hills, CA: Sage.

Michelson, L., Sugai, D., Wood, R., & Kazdin, A. E. (1983). Comparative outcome study of behavioral social skills training, cognitive problem-solving, and Rogerian treatments for child psychiatric outpatients: Process, outcome, and generalization effects. *Behavior Research and Therapy, 21,* 545–556.

Miller, G. E., & Prinz, R. J. (1990). Enhancement of social learning family interventions for childhood conduct disorder. *Psychological Bulletin, 108,* 291–307.

Minuchin, S. (1974). *Families and family therapy.* Cambridge, MA: Harvard University Press.

Minuchin, S., & Fishman, H. (1982). *Techniques of family therapy.* Cambridge, MA: Harvard University Press.

Minuchin, S., Montalvo, B., Guerney, B., Rosman, B., & Schumer, F. (1967). *Families of the slums.* New York: Basic Books.

Moffitt, T. E. (1990). Juvenile delinquency and attention deficit disorder: Boys' developmental trajectories from age 3 to age 15. *Child Development, 61,* 893–910.

Moffitt, T. E. (1993a). Adolescence-limited and life-course-persistent antisocial behavior: A developmental taxonomy. *Psychological Review, 100,* 674–701.

Moffitt, T. E. (1993b). The neuropsychology of conduct disorder. *Development and Psychopathology, 5,* 135–151.

Offord, D. R. (1982). Family backgrounds of male and female delinquents. In J. Gunn & D. P. Farrington (Eds.) *Delinquency and the criminal justice system* (pp. 120–131). New York: Wiley.

Offord, D. R., & Boyle, M. H. (1986). Problems in setting up and executing large-scale psychiatric epidemiological studies. *Psychiatric Developments, 3,* 257–272.

Offord, D. R., Boyle, M. C., & Racine, Y. A. (1991). The epidemiology of antisocial behavior in childhood and adolescence. In D. J. Pepler & K. H. Rubin (Eds.), *The development and treatment of childhood aggression* (pp. 31–54). Hillsdale, NJ: Erlbaum.

Offord, D. R. & Waters, B. G. (1983). Socialization and its failure. In M. D. Levine, W. B. Carey, A. C. Crocker, & R. T. Gross (Eds.), *Developmental-behavioral pediatrics* (pp. 244–259). Philadelphia: Saunders.

Ogbu, J. U. (1988). Cultural diversity and human development. In D. T. Slaughter (Ed.), *Black children and poverty: A developmental perspective* (pp. 11–28). San Francisco: Jossey Bass.

Parker, J. G., & Asher, S. R. (1987). Peer relations and later personal adjustment: Are low-accepted children at risk? *Psychological Bulletin, 102,* 357–389.

Patterson, G. R. (1974). Interventions for boys with conduct problems: Multiple settings, treatments, and criteria. *Journal of Consulting and Clinical Psychology, 42,* 471–481.

Patterson, G. R. (1982). *Coercive family process.* Eugene, OR: Castalia.

Patterson, G. R., Chamberlain, P., & Reid, J. B. (1982). A comparative evaluation of parent training procedures. *Behavior Therapy, 13,* 638–650.

Patterson, G. R., DeBaryshe, B. D., & Ramsey, E. (1989). A developmental perspective on antisocial behavior. *American Psychologist, 44,* 329–335.

Patterson, G. R., & Fleischman, M. J. (1979). Maintenance of treatment effects: Some considerations concerning family systems and follow-up data. *Behavior Therapy, 10,* 168–185.

Patterson, G. R., Reid, J. B., & Dishion, T. J. (1992). *A social interactional approach: IV. Antisocial boys.* Eugene, OR: Castalia.

Perry, D. G., Perry, L. C., & Rasmussen, P. (1986). Cognitive social learning mediators of aggression. *Child Development, 57,* 700–711.

Prinz, R. J., Blechman, E. A., & Dumas, J. E. (1994). An evaluation of peer coping-skills training for childhood aggression. *Journal of Clinical Child Psychology, 23,* 193–203.

Prinz, R. J., Connor, P. A., & Wilson C. C. (1981). Hyperactive and aggressive behaviors in childhood: Intertwined dimensions. *Journal of Abnormal Child Psychology, 9,* 191–202.

Prinz, R. J., & Miller, G. E. (1994). Family-based treatment for childhood antisocial behavior: Experimental influences on dropout and engagement. *Journal of Consulting and Clinical Psychology, 62,* 645–650.

Richters, J. E., & Martinez, P. E. (1993). Violent communities, family choices, and children's chances: An algorithm for improving the odds. *Development and Psychopathology, 5,* 609–627.

Robins, L. N. (1981). Epidemiological approaches to natural history research: Children's antisocial disorders. *Journal of the American Academy of Child Psychiatry, 20,* 566–580.

Rutter, M., & Giller, H. (1983). *Juvenile delinquency: Trends and perspectives.* New York: Penguin.

Rutter, M., Maughan, B., Mortimore, P., Ouston, J., & Smith, A. (1979). *Fifteen thousand hours: Secondary schools and their effects on children.* Cambridge, MA: Harvard University Press.

Rutter, M., Yule, B., Quinton, D., Rowlands, O., Yule, W., & Berger, M. (1974). Attainment and adjustment in two geographical areas: III—Some factors accounting for area differences. *British Journal of Psychiatry, 125,* 520–533.

Sampson, R. J., & Groves, W. B. (1989). Community structure and crime: Testing social-disorganization theory. *American Journal of Sociology, 94,* 774–802.

Sanders, M. R., Dadds, M. R., & Bor, W. (1989). A contextual analysis of oppositional child behavior and maternal aversive behavior in families of conduct disordered children. *Journal of Clinical Child Psychology, 18,* 72–83.

Snyder, J., Dishion, T. J., & Patterson, G. R. (1986). Determinants and consequences of associating with deviant peers. *Journal of Early Adolescence, 6,* 29–43.

Stewart, J. T., Myers, W. C., Burket, R. C., & Lyles, W. B. (1990). A review of the psychopharmacology of aggression in children and adolescents. *Journal of the American Academy of Child and Adolescent Psychiatry, 29,* 269–277.

Tharp, R. G. (1991). Cultural diversity and treatment of children. *Journal of Consulting and Clinical Psychology, 59,* 799–812.

Tolan, P. H., & Mitchell, M. E. (1989). Families and the therapy of antisocial and delinquent behavior. *Journal of Psychotherapy and the Family, 6,* 29–48.

Viemero, V. (1992). Changes in patterns of aggression among Finnish girls over a decade. In F. Bjorkqvist & P. Niemela (Eds.), *Of mice and women: Aspects of female aggression* (pp. 99–106). San Diego, CA: Academic Press.

Wadsworth, M. E. J. (1980). Early life events and later behavioral outcomes in a British longitudinal study. In S. B. Sells, K. Crandell, M. Roff, J. S. Strauss, & W. Pollin (eds.), *Human functioning in longitudinal perspective* (pp. 168–180). Baltimore: Williams & Wilkins.

Wahler, R. G., & Dumas, J. E. (1987). Stimulus class determinants of mother–child coercive interchanges in multidistressed families: Assessment and intervention. In J. D. Burchard & S. N. Burchard (Eds.), *Prevention of delinquent behavior* (pp. 190–219). Beverly Hills, CA: Sage.

Wahler, R. G., & Hann, D. M. (1987). An interbehavioral approach to clinical child psychology: Toward an understanding of troubled families. In D. H. Ruben & D. J. Delprato (Eds.), *New ideas in therapy: Introduction to an interdisciplinary approach (pp. 53–78).* New York: Greenwood Press.

Walker, H. M. & Buckley, N. K. (1973). Teacher attention to appropriate and inappropriate classroom behavior: An individual case study. *Focus on Exceptional Children, 5,* 5–11.

Webster-Stratton, C. (1984). Randomized trial of two parent-training programs for families with conduct-disordered children. *Journal of Consulting and Clinical Psychology, 52,* 666–678.

Webster-Stratton, C., Hollinsworth, T., & Kolpacoff, M. (1989). The long-term effectiveness and clinical significance of three cost-effective training programs for families with conduct-problem children. *Journal of Consulting and Clinical Psychology, 57,* 550–553.

Webster-Stratton, C., Kolpacoff, M., & Hollinsworth, T. (1988). Self-administered videotape therapy for families with conduct problem children: Comparison with two cost-effective treatments and a control group. *Journal of Consulting and Clinical Psychology, 56,* 558–566.

West, D. J., & Farrington, D. P. (1977). *The delinquent way of life.* London: Heinemann.

West, M. O., & Prinz, R. J. (1987). Parent alcoholism and childhood psychopathology. *Psychological Bulletin, 102,* 204–218.

World Health Organization (1992). *The ICD-10 classification of mental and behavioural disorders.* Geneva, Switzerland: Author.

Zavodnick, J. M. (1994). Pharmacotherapy. In G. P. Sholevar (Ed.), *Conduct disorders in children and adolescents* (pp. 269–298). Washington, DC: American Psychiatric Press.

5.21
Substance Abuse Disorders

HOLLY B. WALDRON

The University of New Mexico, Albuquerque, NM, USA

5.21.1 INTRODUCTION

Only a half century ago the use of alcohol and other drugs among adolescents was quite rare, with the number of youth reporting ever drinking or using drugs estimated at one in five and frequent drinking or drug use essentially nonexistent (McCarthy & Douglass, 1949; Prosser, 1954). Over the years drinking and drug use have escalated sharply, to proportions many consider epidemic (Johnston, O'Malley, & Bachman, 1993). Similar increases in problems associated with alcohol and other illicit drug use have also been observed, including premature school drop out, crime, injuries and fatalities due to accidents and violence, sexual promiscuity and risk for sexually transmitted diseases, and teen pregnancy.

Although substance use and related problems have received greater attention in mental health fields in recent years, researchers and clinicians continue to struggle with fundamental conceptual and empirical issues. Some of the most perplexing issues include the complex and varied factors influencing the development of the disorders, the heterogeneous presentation of substance abuse disorders, the similarities and differences between adolescent and adult abuse, and the comorbidity of substance abuse with other disorders among adolescents, complicating diagnosis, assessment, and treatment.

This chapter provides an overview of adolescent substance abuse disorders, highlighting the challenges facing researchers and clinicians. The chapter is divided into three main sections focusing on (i) the nature of substance abuse disorders, (ii) methods for assessing adolescent substance use, and (iii) intervention approaches employed and the evidence for treatment effectiveness. Recommendations for further study of adolescent substance abuse disorders are also presented.

5.21.2 SUBSTANCE ABUSE DISORDERS

5.21.2.1 Phenomenology

Considerable ambiguity exists regarding the definition of substance abuse. A major obstacle in defining the concept of abuse is the array of terms such as recreational, experimental, problematic, pathological, risky, harmful, occasional, episodic, regular, light, moderate, and heavy use, employed to characterize substance use (Kaminer, 1994). On one point, however, theorists generally agree: substance abuse is not a unitary concept, but a complex phenomenon with heterogenous patterning and multiple determinants.

A unique characteristic of substance abuse disorders, unlike other mental disorders, is that they vary depending on factors such as the immediate social environment or the availability of substances. Moreover, classification depends on the presence of a "willing host [the abuser] who is an active participant in generating these disorders" (Newcomb, 1995, p. 7). Yet, substance use is a covert behavior not easily seen by parents, teachers, or other health professionals whose suspicion of use can be low. Failure to detect signs of use, in the absence of valid, reliable, practical definitions for the disorders, contributes to substance abuse being a commonly missed or misdiagnosed problem and hampers clinical efforts to identify adolescents in need of assessment, preventive care, and treatment. In addition, these problems have probably slowed research effort on prevalence, history, genetics, and treatment outcome (Bukstein, 1995).

5.21.2.1.1 Problems in defining abuse

The peak reporting of substance use occurred at the end of the 1970s and early 1980s when as many as 90% of high school seniors reported some alcohol use and nearly 50% marijuana use. Moreover, the majority of substance-involved youth do not develop substance abuse problems and do not go on to abuse as adults, with most drug use dropping sharply after age 21 (Blane, 1976; Kandel & Logan, 1984). In light of high rates of involvement, together with evidence for the discontinuity of use from youth into adulthood, the reality of normative adolescent substance use cannot be ignored. Some researchers have even suggested that, to a degree, drug use has developmental, adaptational utility for adolescents (Labouvie, 1986; Shedler & Block, 1990). Adolescents may use alcohol and other drugs to assert independence from their parents, identify with peers, or oppose societal norms and values, all part of the normal exploration of identity issues.

At the other extreme, any level of substance use by adolescents could be considered pathological. Use, or even possession, of alcohol and other drugs by underage youth constitutes illegal behavior in the USA and is often accompanied by truancy, curfew violations, shoplifting, and a host of other problem behaviors (Donovan & Jessor, 1985). Substance use also increases exposure to risky situations such as driving while intoxicated, engaging in sexual behavior that increases risk for AIDS, and engaging in violent exchanges (Farrell, Danish, & Howard, 1992; FeCaces, Stinson, & Hartford, 1991). Further, substance use can interfere with crucial developmental tasks, such as prosocial identity formation, interpersonal and educational skill acquisition, and family and work responsibility assumption (Baumrind, 1985; Bentler, 1992).

Certainly, diagnosing the vast majority of teenagers with a substance abuse disorder is problematic and a definition by which to identify adolescents abusing substances and in need of treatment is critical. Baumrind (1985) argued that drug abuse should be defined empirically, using frequency and problem consequences as determinants. Similarly, Pandina (1986) offered an operational definition on the basis of intensity (quantity and/or frequency) of use, presence of criteria-based symptoms, and negative consequences. However, no clear cut-offs have been established for quantity and frequency. The substance-related symptoms exhibited by adolescents have rarely been the focus of investigation and, as a result, are still poorly understood (Blum, 1987; Filstead, Parrella, & Conlin, 1988; Stewart & Brown, 1995). And even when a pattern of negative consequences is present, whether they result from substance use or stem from other preexisting or cooccurring factors such as another psychiatric disorder is often unclear (Bukstein, 1995).

Some have argued that substance abuse reflects only one aspect of a syndrome of problem behavior (Jessor & Jessor, 1977) or of general deviance (McGee & Newcomb, 1992). From such a perspective, substance abuse is not conceptualized as a disorder, but as a cluster of norm-violating attitudes and activities such as unconventionality, criminal behavior, and low academic orientation (Donovan & Jessor, 1985; McGee & Newcomb, 1992). Thus, a definition of substance abuse may need to address the broader context of problems intrinsically related to drug and alcohol use.

The widely varied patterning of use among adolescents must also be taken into account in any definition of substance abuse. Types of drugs used should certainly be considered. Alcohol, marijuana, stimulants, cocaine, opioids, sedatives, hallucinogenics, inhalants, and even anabolic steroids (for athletic enhancement) are all potential agents of abuse with specific pharmacologic effects. In addition, the number of drugs used and the combinations of drugs, age of the user, quantity and frequency of use of each substance, negative consequences stemming from use, presence of related problems, and developmental progression of use may all be factors that bear on the distinction between nonproblem use and abuse.

Tolerance, for example, develops rapidly to the euphoric effects of stimulants. With the larger doses of stimulants necessary to reproduce the euphoria, the potential for negative side effects increases and toxic overdose can be fatal. By contrast, tolerance develops more slowly to alcohol and the toxicity of marijuana is generally low. Thus, a consumption of one or two beers or smoking marijuana with friends on the weekend might not be considered abuse for a 17-year-old high school senior, whereas snorting crystal methadrine (i.e., crack) at the same rate might be judged more serious. On the other hand, an 11-year-old drinking one or two drinks or smoking marijuana with any regularity would probably be considered for treatment of substance abuse, given the quantity/frequency of use at such an early age of onset and the potential for rapid developmental progression of drug use.

5.21.2.1.2 Adult vs. adolescent use

Although most conceptualizations of adolescent abuse have been based on adult theories, models, and findings, the appropriateness of this approach has long been questioned and evidence is accumulating that adolescent use differs from adult use in important ways. Some differences are probably due to the restricted age range of the adolescent period. Adolescents have typically been experiencing substance problems for a shorter length of time (Brown, Mott, & Myers, 1990) and have had less time to exhibit deterioration in role functioning (Blum, 1987). Compared to adults, adolescents have also encountered fewer and different serious consequences related to their use, including physical evidence of dependence (Filstead, 1982; Filstead et al., 1988; Vingilis & Smart, 1981).

The patterning of use also appears to differ for adults and adolescents. For example, White and Labouvie (1989) found that adolescents drink less frequently than adults and consume less alcohol overall, but consume larger amounts at one time. Given the smaller body size and weaker tolerance of many youth, teens who drink can experience dangerous physical effects and alcohol-related problems at a lower level of consumption than adults. Brown et al. (1990) reported that 70–98% of adolescents in treatment abuse multiple substances, whereas reports of adult polysubstance use have been considerably lower. Also, the types and patterns of withdrawal symptoms among adolescents appear unique (Brown, Vik, & Creamer, 1989; Martin, Kaczynski, Maisto, Bukstein, & Moss, in press; Stewart & Brown, 1995). Adolescents also have a higher likelihood of certain negative social consequences, given their position of dependence and lower status in family and social systems (Barnes, 1984; White & Labouvie, 1989).

However, researchers have also noted similarities between adolescents and adults with respect to the pharmacologic effects of drugs, reasons for use, and the settings in which use occurs (Barnes, 1981). Also, similarities have been found with respect to patterns of problem drinking, including psychological dependence, binge drinking, and social consequences of drinking (Andersson & Magnusson, 1988; Hughes, Power, & Francis, 1992).

The question of whether adolescent abuse is a distinct category from adult abuse may be intertwined with the issues of nonproblem use versus abuse. Some researchers have found greater continuity from the adolescent period into adulthood for particular typologies of early-onset problem drinking (Babor et al., 1992). However, the majority of adolescents do not fit the severe category. All along the continuum of quantity/frequency and negative consequences of use there are adolescents who still appear to "mature out" of problem use when they reach adulthood (Blum, 1987; Winters & Henly, 1988). As evidence accumulates, we may yet be able to identify different levels or forms of use among adolescents, such as nonproblem use, problem use with relatively good prognosis for spontaneous remission, and problem use that persists into adulthood.

5.21.2.1.3 Comorbidity

Substance abuse disorders in adolescents are widely held to have a high prevalence of comorbidity with other psychological disorders. The most common disorder coexisting with adolescent substance involvement is conduct disorder. DeMilio (1989) found that 42% of adolescents presenting for treatment of substance abuse also met criteria for conduct disorder; Bukstein, Glancy, and Kaminer (1992) found 62% of adolescents receiving inpatient treatment were dually diagnosed. The interactive effects of conduct disorder and substance use and abuse are not well understood, but evidence indicates that dual diagnosis increases the likelihood of continued behavioral disturbance and substance use. Although attention deficit hyperactivity disorder (ADHD) has been hypothesized as a comorbid condition, Alterman and Tarter (1986) concluded that the apparent relationship between substance abuse and ADHD was an artifact of the high coincidence of ADHD and conduct disorder. This finding has been confirmed by Barkley and his colleagues who found that adolescents with only ADHD used substances no more frequently than normals (Barkley, Fischer, Edelbrock, & Smallish, 1990).

Affective disorders, anxiety, and bulimia also commonly coexist with adolescent substance abuse. For example, DeMilio (1989) reported a dual diagnosis of major depressive disorder for 35% of a treatment sample; Bukstein et al. (1992) found 30% in an inpatient setting. Studies examining the coexistence of anxiety and other disorders with substance abuse have been more common with adults but, like depression, the pattern of the relationship is probably similar for adolescents. Possible mechanisms for the connection between mood and substance abuse disorders are the depressive pharmacological effects of some drugs and the negative social consequences, such as school failure and peer rejection, experienced by adolescents using alcohol and other drugs. Similarly, the actual or expected pharmacologic effects of substances in reducing anxiety is an obvious explanation for the comorbidity with anxiety disorders. The relationship between substance abuse and bulimia is less clear, and the high comorbidity between bulimia and mood disorders may account for some of the comorbidity between bulimia and substance abuse.

The comorbidity issue adds a level of complexity to understanding substance abuse. Research examining adolescent substance abuse disorders often specifically excludes adolescents with dual diagnoses in order to limit potential confounds. However, even when the coexistence of disorders is the question of interest, the lack of valid, reliable definitions of substance abuse and other disorders of childhood and adolescence has hampered investigations. Moreover, the concept of comorbidity is inherently fraught with problems such as identifying comorbid disorders using sets of symptoms which result from the same underlying cause. For example, Crowley and Riggs (1995) observed that adolescents dually diagnosed with substance abuse and conduct disorders epitomize the general deviance syndrome, in which substance use and other deviant behaviors are viewed as stemming from common causes. Whether substance abuse is primary or occurs secondary to another disorder, and how the interaction of coexisting disorders influence the onset, identification, course, and treatment of substance abuse, problems remain in question.

5.21.2.2 Diagnostic Features

Formal diagnostic classification systems for substance use disorders have primarily evolved since the mid-1970s and have been developed exclusively for adults, with no distinction made between adolescent and adult users. The first criteria-based classifications appeared in the third edition of the *Diagnostic and statistical manual of mental disorders* (*DSM-III*; American Psychiatric Association, 1980), which identified two categories of substance use disorders: substance abuse and substance dependence. Substance abuse was defined as pathological use associated with impairment of social or occupational functioning with a one-month duration, and dependence as the presence of tolerance or withdrawal and either pathological use or impairment in social or occupational functioning due to such use. Prior to the third edition, the *DSM* viewed substance use problems such as alcoholism and drug dependence as subsets of sociopathic personality disturbance. The designation of a separate category for substance use disorders in *DSM-III* differentiated substance use from antisocial behavior more generally and recognized the importance of research on the nature of the disorders (Nathan, 1991).

A number of serious limitations of *DSM-III* were noted, however, including the insensitivity of the criteria in addressing heterogeneity of problems, the lack of theoretical and empirical basis for some criteria, and inconsistencies across criteria in various substance categories (cf. Nathan, 1991; Rounsaville, 1987). In addition, the reliance on tolerance or withdrawal for the dependence diagnosis determined that, in most cases, adolescents could only be diagnosed as abusers, since they rarely exhibit many of the tolerance or withdrawal symptoms for alcohol or other drugs (Hughes et al., 1992; Vingilis & Smart, 1981).

The *DSM-III-R* (American Psychiatric Association, 1987) was designed to correspond more closely to the *International classification of disease, ninth edition* (*ICD-9*), which had effected a conceptual shift in classifying substance use disorders. In keeping with the conceptual shift, the definition of dependence was expanded to include clinically significant behaviors, cognitions, and symptoms indicative of use and no single symptom was required for a diagnosis of dependence. Marked tolerance and withdrawal symptoms remained in the list of criteria, but other criteria—such as spending large amounts of time on activities to acquire substances, symptoms of intoxication when expected to fulfill major role obligations at work, school, or home, and giving up important activities because of substance use—made it easier for adolescents to be diagnosed with dependence. The changes also allowed for more variability in patterns of use.

By default, abuse was diagnosed when sufficient criteria for dependence were not met. Thus, abuse was conceptualized as a milder or predependence stage in the cluster of disorders. However, some research suggests that abuse and dependence disorders have distinct courses (Hasin, Grant, & Endicott, 1990), questioning the notion of a presumed continuum of severity.

The revision of the system for *DSM-IV* (American Psychiatric Association, 1994) was intended to reflect empirical research more closely and to increase compatibility with the *ICD-10* system. Accordingly, three essential changes were made to the classification of dependence: the criteria regarding the inability to fulfill major role obligations and the criteria for duration were dropped, and subtypes of tolerance and withdrawal symptoms were added. However, adolescents with substance use problems commonly experience difficulty in meeting role obligations. With regard to educational expectations, truancy, attending classes while under the influence of alcohol or drugs, school failure, and premature dropout are common. Similarly, failures to meet role obligations are frequently observed in family contexts. Thus, the elimination of the role obligation criterion will probably reduce the number of adolescents who are diagnosed as dependent.

The criteria for substance abuse in *DSM-IV* were expanded, requiring the presence of clinically significant impairment or distress, including the failure to fulfill major role obligations and recurrent substance-related legal problems, as part of the maladaptive pattern of substance use. The addition of the role obligation criteria to this category could facilitate diagnostic classification. Nevertheless, adolescents who show a maladaptive pattern of use must now also exhibit at least minimal impairment or distress. This moves classification of abuse away from a topographical definition of substance use, such as quantity, frequency, or patterning of use, toward a definition based on dysfunction associated with use, and essentially raises the bar for adolescents to meet criteria, since adolescent behaviors tend to be more detectable than distress resulting from the behaviors.

The most disturbing aspect of the evolution of classification systems for substance use is the complete lack of evidence either to support or reject the applicability of the systems with adolescents. To illustrate, consider the nature of the prevailing diagnostic systems. The *DSM* and *ICD* systems are categorical rather than dimensional, classifying substance abuse on the basis of clustering of symptoms as opposed to viewing symptoms as occurring along a continuum. Within these systems, then, it is possible for adolescents to exhibit high quantity and frequency of use, yet not meet criteria for a substance abuse disorder if they manage to avoid negative consequences or other signs of impairment considered part of the discrete cluster of symptoms that currently define abuse. The confirmation of the reliability and validity of the current approach for adolescents or, alternatively, the formulation of an age-specific substance abuse definition and diagnostic criteria appropriate for adolescents could play a key role in the development and evaluation of prevention and treatment programs.

5.21.2.3 Prevalence

5.21.2.3.1 Substance abuse disorders

The epidemiology of substance abuse disorders in adolescents has rarely been investigated, with the vast majority of research focused on prevalence of substance use more generally. Moreover, comparison across studies has been impeded by factors such as nonuniform definitions of abuse, the particular diagnostic system employed, and the type and age of sample selected. Using the *DSM-III* system, for example, Kashani et al. (1987) found a prevalence of 5.3% for alcohol abuse or dependence disorders and a 3.3% for drug abuse or dependence disorders in a community sample of 15-year-olds. Deykin, Levy, and Wells (1986), using the same system, found a prevalence rate of 8.2% for alcohol disorders and 9.4% for drug disorders in a young college population ranging from 16 to 19 years of age. Also focusing on older youth, aged 17–19 years, but using the *DSM-IIIR*, Reinherz, Giaconia, Lefkowitz, Pakiz, and Frost (1993) found a prevalence of 34% for alcohol abuse disorders and 9.8% for drug abuse disorders. Although the rates of alcohol disorders seem particularly high in this study, Cohen et al. (1993) examined two age groups, 14- to 16-year olds, and 17- to 20-year olds, with reported rates of 4.1% and 3.1% for younger boys and girls, respectively, and 20.3% and 8.9% for older boys and girls, respectively. The estimates vary widely and more uniformity in methodology is needed for developing a foundation of empirical work before any conclusions about epidemiology of substance abuse disorders in adolescents can be drawn.

5.21.2.3.2 Substance use survey data

Compared to substance abuse disorders, prevalence of substance use among adolescents has been much more intensively studied. Data are regularly obtained through two national surveys, the National Household Survey on Drug Abuse, a federal project studying illegal drug use in the USA by adults and adolescents

since 1971, and the University of Michigan Monitoring the Future project, which focuses on high school seniors. These surveys have revealed a general pattern of increasing substance use among adolescents through the late 1970s and early 1980s, followed by marked declines through 1991. The senior survey data (Johnston et al., 1993), for example, shows that peak lifetime use of alcohol (i.e., having ever used) among high school seniors was 93.2% in 1980, but use in the past month declined from 72.1% in 1978 to 54.0% in 1991. Binge drinking (i.e., having an episode of five or more drinks on one occasion in the past two weeks) among seniors peaked in 1981 at 41.4%, but had dropped to 29.8% by 1991, and daily drinking peaked in 1979 at 6.9%, but had dropped to 3.6% by 1991. Similarly, lifetime use of marijuana peaked in 1980 at 60.3%, with highest daily use in 1978 at 10.7% and lowest use reported for 1991 at 2.0%. Stimulant and cocaine use peaked later, with peak past year stimulant use at 20.3% in 1982 and cocaine use at 13.1% in 1985. The percentage of past month stimulant use dropped from 10.7 in 1982 to 3.7 in 1990, and cocaine use dropped from 6.7 in 1985 to 1.9 in 1990. Other drugs use patterns have shown similar patterns of peak and decline, although it is interesting to note that lifetime prevalence of alcohol use has not shown the same sharp declines as for other drugs.

Recent survey data suggest that drug use may be on the rise again. According to the National Household Survey (Substance Abuse and Mental Health Services Administration [SAMHSA], 1996), the rate of past month illicit drug use among adolescents aged 12–17 years increased from 8.2% to 10.9% between 1994 and 1995, a rate which has doubled since 1992. Past month use of alcohol in 12- to 17-year-olds had fallen from 25.2% in 1988 to 15.7% in 1992, and was up to 21.6% and 21.1% in 1994 and 1995, respectively. Significant increases were also reported for past month marijuana use, from 6% in 1994 to 8.2% in 1995, continuing an upward trend since 1992. Similarly, between 1994 and 1995, cocaine use increased from 0.3% to 0.8% and hallucinogen use increased from 1.1% to 1.7%.

Tobacco use appears to be on the rise as well. The Youth Risk Behavior Survey reported current cigarette use among students in grades 9–12 increasing from 27.5% in 1991 to 34.8% in 1995 (Centers for Disease Control and Prevention, 1996). These findings are consistent with the Monitoring the Future project, which reported rates of smoking by 10th and 12th graders increasing, respectively, from 20.8% and 28.3% in 1991 to 27.9% and 33.5% in 1995. These rates are alarming when considering that roughly 11% of students reportedly smoke a half-pack per day or more (Johnston et al., 1993) and this percentage may be rising as well.

The rate of first use of marijuana, cocaine and crack, inhalants, and other substances, including adolescent alcohol use, has also risen sharply in the same period. First use has shown utility in predicting prevalence rates several years later. Increases in this index now could indicate continuing rise in prevalence for several years.

5.21.2.3.3 Prevalence by age, gender, race, and ethnicity

In general, prevalence rates for the use of alcohol and other substances increase with age. In 1993, for example, the Monitoring the Future project found that past month drinking to the point of intoxication was 28.9% for 12th graders, 19.8% for 10th graders, and 7.8% for 8th graders. Similarly, use of marijuana was 10.9% among 10th graders, but only 5.1% among eighth graders. Inhalant use is one exception, with past month use reported at 3.3% for 10th graders and 5.4% for eighth graders, based on 1994 data. This exception may result from the decreased availability of drugs in junior high and middle schools, compared to high schools, leaving glue or paint cans more readily available for getting high. Despite lower rates overall, trajectories of use for the younger age groups suggests there is reason for concern. That is, during the same period of time the senior survey revealed declines in cocaine, alcohol, and other drug use among seniors, use of these same substances increased among eighth graders.

Comparisons for gender have consistently shown that males tend to use alcohol and drugs in higher proportions than females, especially at higher levels of use (Johnston et al., 1993). The exceptions are sedatives, stimulants, and smoking tobacco, where rates are similar for males and females (Johnston et al., 1993; SAMHSA, 1996). Also, the fall and rise in prevalence rates over time appear to have been the same for male and female adolescents (SAMHSA, 1996).

According to Bachman et al., (1991), Native American adolescents had the highest prevalence of use for cigarettes, alcohol, and most other drugs; Anglo/European Americans (i.e., non-hispanic whites) had higher rates of use than Hispanic Americans, African-Americans, or Asian-Americans. However, National Household Survey data for 1994–1995 revealed no ethnicity differences in smoking (SAMHSA, 1996). With respect to changes in rates over time, during the period of overall declining use (i.e., through 1992) rates of use among non-

hispanic whites showed dramatic declines, whereas rates for black and for Hispanic youth remained relatively steady. Prevalence rates across culture and race should continue to receive careful scrutiny. If these patterns hold, research will be needed to understand the mechanisms by which substance use became entrenched in these groups and to examine the necessity of developing treatment programs individually tailored to the needs of particular groups.

5.21.2.4 Etiology

5.21.2.4.1 Risk and protective factors

Although a broad spectrum of factors has been associated with the initiation and maintenance of substance use, no single etiological theory or model adequately accounts for the marked heterogeneity of patterns of substance abuse disorders. A number of researchers have adopted a risk factor perspective as a way to understand the multiple determinants and antecedents of drug use and abuse, including biological, cultural and societal, interpersonal, and intrapersonal factors (Hawkins, Catalano, & Miller, 1992). Although biological influences such as genetic, physiological, and biochemical factors have been shown to affect susceptibility to drug use, these factors have not accounted for large proportions of the variance. Because substance abuse is a complex phenomenon, any single-factor biological cause or theory is unlikely (Bukstein, 1995). Within the broad cultural and social context, substance use can be influenced by factors such as poverty, the existence of laws and social norms favorable toward substance use, and the general availability of alcohol and drugs. Intrapersonal influences include a wide range of individual cognitive and behavioral factors (e.g., positive attitudes toward drug use), aggression and other disruptive behavior problems, and low commitment to education. General findings on interpersonal factors have included familial influences such as: parent and sibling use, parent attitudes toward use, parenting practices, poor communication and parent–adolescent conflict, and parent–child bonding. In addition, poor peer relationships or having friends who use drugs increase the risk for use.

Researchers have also identified a variety of protective factors across the cultural/social, interpersonal, and intrapersonal domains that influence the likelihood of substance use initiation or reduce level of drug use. These factors may moderate the relationship between risk factors and use/abuse, or may have a direct effect on reducing drug involvement (Newcomb, 1995). Sanctions against drug use, family support, self-acceptance, and religiosity are but a few of the protective factors that have been identified (cf Hawkins et al., 1992).

The factors influencing substance abuse are likely to be interdependent and bidirectional. For example, Dishion, Patterson, and Reid (1988) found that parental drug use had both a direct effect, believed to result from modeling and opportunities for use, and an indirect effect, resulting from impaired parental control when parents were under the influence of drugs or alcohol. Similarly, findings of increased stress, increased conflict, highly charged negative affect, lack of openness, and poor cohesion in families, as well as the tendency of adolescents to seek support in relationships outside the family, may all have reciprocal influence. One model suggests that adolescents may not directly imitate their parents' use of specific drugs, but they may be exposed to observing that drug use is one method of coping with psychological stress (Kandel, Kessler, & Margulies, 1978). Effective problem solving may, in turn, attenuate drug use by providing an alternative for coping with stressful life events and family disturbance. Examining another aspect of influence, Duncan, Duncan, and Hops (1994) found that the largest effects of family cohesion on adolescent substance use occur in middle and later adolescence. Taking their results together with other research (Dishion et al., 1988; Patterson, Reid, & Dishion, 1992), they suggested that family influence may vary in a curvilinear fashion over time, with a low point in early adolescence when peer influences peak. Such research begins to tease apart the complex interactions among risk and protective factors associated with substance abuse and holds promise for much needed model development for adolescent substance abuse.

Although the mechanism by which risk and protective factors exert causal influence is poorly understood, Bry, McKeon, and Pandina (1982) found evidence that substance abuse derives from the sheer number of risk factors rather than the presence of any one factor or particular set of factors. These findings have been corroborated by Newcomb and his associates who also found that exposure to more risk factors was not only correlated with use, but predicted increasing drug use over time, providing support for a multiple etiological pathway model of drug use (McGee & Newcomb, 1992; Newcomb, Maddahian, & Bentler, 1986). The risk and protective factor model is a useful one for predicting youth who may develop substance abuse problems and for identifying specific targets for intervention. A limitation of the risk and protective factor model is that, in the absence of longitudinal

research, we cannot distinguish between etiological factors, through which we may discover avenues of control, and factors which are merely antecedents or correlates of abuse and have common causes.

5.21.2.4.2 Theory development

Within the substance abuse literature, conceptual models are abundant (Lettieri, Sayers, & Pearson, 1980). In addition to the risk or vulnerability model, models proposed to explain the development of substance abuse disorders range from biological to spiritual and from intrapersonal to sociocultural. Two quite narrow models are the educational model, which views abuse as resulting from a lack of accurate information, and the disease model, which views abuse as irreversible and requires total abstinence to manage the disease. Although these perspectives may not be incompatible with other models, they fail to account for much of what is currently known about the correlates of abuse.

More comprehensive theories can be organized within the broader framework of intrapersonal, cognitive, learning, conventionality/ social attachment, and interactional models (Petraitis, Flay, & Miller, 1995). Intrapersonal perspectives place more emphasis on characteristics of adolescents themselves, including personality traits, affective states, and/or behavioral skills, in the etiology of substance use. Although the self-medication hypothesis has been articulated in cognitive-behavioral frameworks as well, the role of substance use as a coping mechanism is an example of an intrapersonal (psychodynamic) perspective. Low self-esteem and self-derogation are also central intrapersonal constructs in theories of etiology.

Cognitive theories focus on the role of adolescents' perceptions of use in decision making related to the initiation and continuation of substance abuse. Attitudes, normative beliefs, and substance use expectancies, as well as self-efficacy, influence the evaluation of the benefits of use (e.g., peer approval) and the costs of use (e.g., health dangers) in decision making.

Operant learning perspectives view substance use in the context of the antecedents and consequences surrounding the behavior. In the presence of stress, for example, substance use may result in tension reduction, regulation of negative affect, or social enhancement, any of which may serve to reinforce use and thereby increase the likelihood that substance use will recur in the future. The social learning model is expanded to allow for cognitively mediated learning through observation and imitation of models (e.g., parents, siblings, or peers) who use substances and it includes self-efficacy beliefs and coping as key concepts.

The conventionality/social attachment approaches stem from sociological theories of control which argue that strong commitment to society, families, schools, and religions inhibits the expression of deviant impulses that all individuals share. Substance use, then, is but one manifestation of a broader cluster of unconventional or problem behaviors which develops in the context of weak conventional bonds, and are maintained through social learning and contingencies in the environment.

Family models view problems such as substance abuse as maladaptive behaviors expressed by one or more family members, but reflecting dysfunction in the system as a whole. The behavior may be viewed as serving an important function in the family, allowing the family to cope with internal or external stressors or maintain other processes that have become established in the organization of the system.

Integrative theories are increasingly complex, but account for more of the findings in the research literature (Petraitis et al., 1995). For example, family interaction theory (Brook, Brook, Gordon, Whiteman, & Cohen, 1990) incorporates family factors, social learning, and intrapersonal characteristics known to affect substance use. Problem-behavior theory (Jessor & Jessor, 1977) emphasizes unconventionality, but also incorporates cognitive, intrapersonal, social learning concepts and accounts for substance abuse and a variety of other deviant behaviors such as juvenile delinquency, poor school performance, and precocious sexual activity.

Flay and Petraitis have attempted to organize the array of theories focusing on substance use etiology into one comprehensive macromodel (Flay & Petraitis, 1994; Petraitis et al., 1995). Their model of triadic influence assumes that health-related behaviors such as substance use are most immediately controlled by decisions or intentions that are a function of three streams of influence: (i) cultural–environmental factors which influence attitudes, (ii) social situation-contextual factors which influence social learning and normative beliefs, and (iii) intrapersonal factors which influence self-efficacy. These streams have different origins and flow through causal factors which are organized into levels ranging from very proximal to distal to ultimate. The stream of influence, independently and in interaction with one another, are recognized as having both direct and indirect effects on behavior (Flay & Petraitis, 1994). This work highlights the complementarity of existing theories and may provide a useful structure for

identifying gaps in our knowledge base with respect to etiology.

5.21.2.5 Developmental Course

One avenue which may hold promise for differentiating nonproblem use from more serious substance involvement is research examining the developmental trajectory associated with initiation and progression of use. Before substance use becomes problematic, adolescents pass through a stage during which they are not committed to continuing use and have not integrated substance use as a regular part of life (Clayton, 1992). Typically, adolescents who become abusers follow a relatively invariant sequence for drug use, beginning with alcohol and/or cigarette use, followed by marijuana, and then other hard drugs. This progression from "soft" to "hard" drug use, the "gateway" phenomenon (Kandel, 1975), has been confirmed in a number of studies (Andrews, Hops, Ary, Lichtenstein, & Tildesley, 1991; Kandel, Yamaguchi, & Chen, 1992; Welte & Barnes, 1985). Moreover, Ellickson, Hays, and Bell (1992) found that weekly alcohol use followed marijuana use and preceded use of all other illicit drugs, and that weekly smoking formed a distinct stage between initial use of pills and other hard drugs.

According to Kandel et al. (1978), different factors may predominate each stage of use or predicting the progression to other stages. Their findings suggested that parent modeling may have greater influence on the use of alcohol and tobacco, whereas peers may have greater influence on marijuana use. The use of other illicit drugs was more related to family relationship disturbance and general psychology dysfunction. Thus, although dysfunctional use of drugs can be generally characterized by increasing quantities and varieties of drugs used, understanding substance abuse disorders may involve not only identifying the types and number of substances adolescents have used and the quantity and frequency of use, but also the sequencing or patterning of use, as well as the factors predominating each stage. As Dishion et al. (1988) noted, different models may be required to explain the variations in patterning and progression of use.

5.21.3 CONCEPTUALIZATION AND CLINICAL FORMULATION

5.21.3.1 Multimodal Assessment

Assessment approaches range from narrow inquiry into substance use behavior to broad, multifaceted approaches which address use patterns, problem consequences, other aspects of use (e.g., drug use expectancies, normative beliefs, or readiness to change), and functioning across multiple domains (e.g., school, family, or leisure time). The purpose of the assessment, or the question the assessment is intended to answer, should determine the type of information obtained, how the information is obtained, and who provides the information. A self-report screening instrument summarizing substance use quantity and frequency may be sufficient to determine need for further evaluation among youth at risk for substance abuse problems. However, more comprehensive approaches are often used in establishing a diagnosis, evaluating treatment needs (i.e., inpatient or detoxification), developing a treatment formulation, or evaluating treatment effectiveness.

The main source of information is usually the adolescent, although collateral information is often obtained from parents or others in the social environment (i.e., teachers, siblings, or peers). Methods for assessing substance abuse include interviewing, questionnaires, checklists, rating scales, and physiological measures (e.g., urine toxicology screens). Observational measures are sometimes used to examine particular aspects of adolescent functioning, such as family and peer interactions (Hops, Tildesley, Lichtenstein, Ary, & Sherman; 1990), and self-monitoring has been used with adults (Sobell & Sobell, 1995).

In general, assessment of adolescents requires some recognition of the cognitive developmental level of the adolescent, attention to issues of engagement in the process and the need for establishing rapport, and careful consideration of issues of confidentiality. Although the validity of self-report of use has been questioned, adult studies have shown that direct self-report measures have high sensitivity in detecting substance use problems, and compare favorably to biomedical measures such as blood and urine tests (Sobell & Sobell, 1995). Similarly, some support has been found for adolescents (Bailey, Flewelling, & Rachal, 1992; Needle, McCubbin, Lorence, & Hochhauser, 1983), but more systematic examination is needed to address this issue in adolescent populations (Winters & Stinchfield, 1995).

5.21.3.1.1 Methods for assessing substance use

Almost all measures of substance use behavior focus on some type of direct self-report of frequency (e.g., how many days per month use occurred) and intensity of use (e.g., number of drinks consumed). The majority of adolescents referred for treatment use multiple substances, necessitating inquiry about the quantity/frequency of use of each specific drug type. Two general approaches to assessing frequency and quantity of substance use have been described: quantity/frequency self-report questionnaires and calendar-based interviewing methods. Many self-report instruments measuring use of alcohol and other substances provide summaries of use behavior or are scaled in a way that precludes detailed assessment of use (e.g., 0 times per week, 1–2 times per week, 3 times or more per week). As a result, such measures fail to capture the patterning of use with any degree of precision that would allow for the calculation of peak blood alcohol concentration, a potentially important indicator of dangerous or even life-threatening alcohol use. Summary measures have also been shown to produce significantly lower estimates of use (Sobell & Sobell, 1995) and may also fail to detect reductions in use among very heavy users who, for example, could decrease their use from daily to three times per week.

An alternative method is the time line follow back procedure (Sobell & Sobell, 1995), a structured interview technique that samples a specific time period, using a monthly calendar and memory anchor points to reconstruct daily consumption during the period of interest. A number of studies have compared the methods, including quantity/frequency measures and time line follow back, finding generally similar estimates. In principle, the time line follow back may offer the most sensitive assessment for adolescents, having the advantage of assessing the widely variable drinking patterns that often characterize teen drinking and that might not be modeled adequately by the averaging approaches (Leccese & Waldron, 1994). In a recent study, initial evidence for the internal reliability and convergent validity of the time line method for adolescent drinkers was found (Waldron, 1996). Moreover, a group of adolescents who were classified as nonproblem drinkers on the basis of the *Adolescent Drinking Index* (Harrell & Wirtz, 1989), a standardized alcohol screening instrument, were identified with substantial amounts of binge drinking. Of 67 nonabstaining youth who scored below the cut-off on the standardized instrument, half were reporting peak blood alcohol concentrations between 0.10 and 0.48 ($M = 0.11$), levels which suggest these youth may have been good candidates for harm reduction interventions. These findings support the use of time line follow back with adolescents and point to one direction for future research.

Urine toxicology screens and other biomedical markers can be valuable for corroborating self-report (O'Farrell & Maisto, 1987). When multiple measures, such as self-report, urinalyses, and collateral reports attained by interviewing parents or peers, converge to give the same results, there is greater confidence in the validity of measures. Another useful aspect of biomedical tests is the potential for a "bogus pipeline" effect, creating the impression that there is an accurate check on self-report and thereby increasing honesty in descriptions of one's substance use (Miller, Westerberg, & Waldron, 1995).

5.21.3.1.2 Diagnosis

Several interview instruments have been designed specifically to determine whether an individual meets currently established criteria for disorders of substance abuse and substance dependence according to a specific taxonomic system. The *Adolescent Diagnostic Interview* (Winters & Henly, 1993) is one such system which covers *DSM-III-R* symptoms of psychoactive substance use disorders and thereby assumes the applicability of adult syndromes to adolescents. This structured interview explores the adolescent's drug use history and signs of abuse or dependence for several drug categories, and also covers levels of functioning and psychosocial stressors. Diagnosis, as a binary (present vs. absent) process, represents a gross indicator of problem use with limited utility when used in isolation or as an outcome measure in treatment research. As a treatment issue, however, adolescents whose use is prolonged and heavy without periods of abstinence must be assessed for dependence, since physiological withdrawal may require specific medical or psychological interventions (Kaminer, 1994).

5.21.3.1.3 Screening instruments

Screening instruments are designed to identify the potential presence of a particular problem. As such, they are typically used as a preliminary step in assessment, as a way of determining if further, more comprehensive assessment is necessary. As noted in the discussion of time line follow back, one limitation of screening instruments is their reliance on cut-off scores for decision making. With lower cut-off points, instruments can inappropriately identify adolescents as needing more extensive assessment or intervention, whereas higher cut-off can fail to identify adolescents who are in need of additional services. Moreover, the reduction of a continuously distributed variable to a binary classification probably sacrifices predictive power. Conversely, screening instruments are characteristically easy and inexpensive to administer and are especially useful in settings where large numbers of adolescents must be screened in a short period of time, such as within the juvenile justice system, adolescent medicine units, or general mental health agencies serving adolescents with varied presenting problems. Table 1 presents screening instruments and basic information about each.

5.21.3.1.4 Comprehensive assessment instruments

In addition to assessing substance use behavior, comprehensive assessments also take into account the consequences of substance use, the contexts within which use occurs, the functions which the use serves in the adolescent's life, and the co-occurrence of other problem behaviors. As noted above, many other classes of variables have been found to be related in complex ways to level of substance use, including age, comorbid disorders, peer factors, personality factors, biological and genetic factors, family functioning, and level of social skills. The existence of these relationships suggests that a comprehensive assessment of adolescent substance use could be enriched by information in these areas as well. More comprehensive assessment procedures usually allow for the examination of adolescents' scores along a continuum or along several continua. These instruments are designed to be given after a screening instrument or other process indicates the need for further assessment of alcohol and drug use. Table 2 displays the main characteristics of six comprehensive adolescent assessment instruments.

5.21.3.1.5 Other substance-related questionnaires

To the extent that substance abuse is multiply determined and is associated with diverse problem behaviors presumably generated by common causes, broad, multidimensional assessment is vital. Newcomb and Bentler (1989) maintained that any focus on substance use, in isolation from the associated antecedents, concurrent events, or consequences constituting the more general problem-behavior syndrome of which substance abuse is a part, will be distorted. A number of other instruments have been used to assess various aspects of alcohol and drug use in adolescents. Among them are measures of alcohol, use attitudes toward alcohol, unconventionality of behavior, and expectancies about alcohol and other drugs (cf Leccese & Waldron; 1994; Winters & Stinchfield, 1995). These instruments can be combined with other measures to assess specific concerns the clinician may have in the formulation of the treatment plan or may be used for research purposes.

Table 1 Characteristics of screening instruments.

Instrument	Administration method	Items	Time to administer	Psychometrics	Information provided
Drug and Alcohol Problem Quick Screen (DAP; Schwartz & Wirtz, 1990)	Self-report	30	10	Limited validity data	Cut-off for substance use risk; indicates the need for further assessment
Drug Use Screening Inventory (DUSI; Tarter & Hegedus, 1991)	Self-report or computer administered	149	20	Adequate content validity	Functioning measured across 10 domains; absolute problem density, overall problem index, and relative problem density scores
Perceived Benefit of Drinking Scale (Petchers & Singer, 1987)	Self-report	5	1	Adequate internal consistency and divergent validity	Scale scores reflect frequency, intoxication, and problems related to substance use
Personal Experience Screening Questionnaire (PESQ; Winters, 1992)	Self-report	40	10	High internal consistency, adequate discriminant and predictive validity	Indicates the need for further assessment
Problem Oriented Screening Instrument (POSIT; Rahdert, 1991)	Self-report	139	30–45	None reported	Functioning measured across 10 domains, "red-flag" items signal the need for further assessment
Teen Health Advisor (Paperny, Aono, Lehman, Hammer, & Riusser, 1990)	Computer administered	32–62	10	None reported	High-risk behavior evaluation and advice or referral information across several domains
Substance Abuse Subtle Screening Inventory-Adolescent (SASSI-A; Miller, 1990)	Self-report	81	20	Limited validity data, no reported reliability data	Face valid alcohol, face valid other drug, obvious attributes, subtle attributes, defensiveness (two scales), and two experimental scales

Table 2 Characteristics of comprehensive assessment instruments.

Instrument	Administration method	Items	Time to administer	Psychometrics	Information provided
Adolescent Diagnostic Interview (ADI; Winters & Henley, 1993)	Structured or computerized interview	varies	45–60	Adequate interrater, test–retest reliability, and criterion-related validity	*DSM-III-R* substance use disorders, functioning across several domains, psychosocial stressors, and screens for memory and orientation
Adolescent Drug Abuse Diagnosis (ADAD; Friedman & Utada, 1989)	Structured interview	150	45–60	High interrater, test–retest reliability, adequate concurrent, convergent, and discriminant validity	Problem severity ratings and need for treatment across nine domains
Adolescent Problem Severity Index (APSI; Metzger, Kushner, & McLellan, 1991)	Semistructured or computerized interview	varies	45–60	None reported	Composite score (number of risk factors) and severity rating (need for treatment) across seven domains
Adolescent Self Assessment Profile (ASAP; Wanberg, 1991)	Self-report	203	45–60	Adequate internal consistency	Profile of adjustment, functioning, and substance use across multiple domains
Personal Experience Inventory (PEI; Winters & Henley, 1989)	Self-report, computer administered	276	45–60	Adequate internal consistency, test–retest reliability, concurrent, discriminant and predictive validity	Substance use frequency and severity, personal and environmental risk factors, problem screening and faking
Teen Addiction Severity Index (T-ASI; Kaminer, Bukstein, & Tarter, 1991)	Semistructured interview	134	30–45	Adequate interrator reliability	Problem severity and need for treatment across seven domains rated by both client and interviewer

5.21.3.2 Treatment Formulation

How assessment findings should be used in treatment planning has seldom been addressed in the literature. The National Institute on Drug Abuse has developed the Adolescent Assessment/Referral System which advocates an assessment battery approach for identifying potential problems across multiple domains, including substance use, diagnosis, family functioning, and psychological functioning. Using this system, treatment planning determining whether the individual needed substance abuse treatment, family therapy, or other interventions is guided on the problem areas identified in the assessment. The Drug Use Screening Inventory (Tarter, 1990) represents a single, brief screening instrument that provides an assessment across 10 domains of functioning. This instrument was developed as a treatment formulation instrument yielding assessment findings that lead directly to treatment planning. However, evaluations of the effectiveness of assessment systems for treatment formulation and subsequent adolescent treatment outcomes have not been studied.

More often, treatment formulation is guided by the therapeutic orientation of agency or treatment provider. In addition to assessing the topography of substance use and related behaviors for the purpose of evaluating change brought about by intervention, behavioral treatment models might include a functional analysis of the behavior which is incorporated into treatment (e.g., modifying contingencies in the environment on the basis of the functional analysis). Family treatment models may include standardized family assessment instruments and measures of family interaction, but, for treatment formulation, most often conduct assessments of family functioning in an ongoing fashion in the context of family therapy sessions (Alexander, Barton, Waldron, & Mas, 1983).

Some obvious circumstances, such as evaluating the need for medical supervision of detoxification or inpatient treatment for suicidal substance abusers, influence treatment matching for adolescents. Beyond such examples, however, strategies for matching adolescents to treatments on the basis of assessment findings are premature (Project MATCH, 1997). Identifying environmental treatments for medical problems with quite different etiology (e.g., dietary restriction for phenylketonuria) may apply to substance abuse as well, challenging how we think about treatment formulation. And, as Henly and Winters (1989) noted, a variety of paths have been found leading to substance involvement and a variety of paths may also lead out. Given our

current level of understanding of substance abuse disorders, treatment formulation should be determined on the basis of what has been shown empirically to work (Wagner & Kassel, 1995).

5.21.4 TREATMENT

5.21.4.1 Psychosocial Treatments

Psychosocial treatment models for substance abuse include the broadest spectrum of approaches in settings ranging from inpatient intervention to street-based harm reduction programs (e.g., needle exchange), from residential living to outpatient primary-care interventions, and from juvenile detention to school- and community-based preventive services provided for secondary and tertiary care. Inpatient programs typically provide a detailed admission assessment, psychosocial evaluation, exploration of chemical use history and assessment of educational, legal, and psychological status (Wheeler & Malmquist, 1987). Program components include group therapy, lectures, work assignments, a therapeutic milieu, attendance at support meetings, family therapy, and recreational activities. Therapeutic communities, used for adolescents with more severe drug abuse, have similar orientations to inpatient treatment but are longer term, with an average length of stay of 6–9 months. Outpatient treatment can include intensive day-treatment programs, services provided by individual, group, and family therapists, and education-based interventions usually offered in larger contexts.

5.21.4.1.1 Traditional and 12-step models

Modalities of treatment offered across the range of settings have included individual, family based, and group therapies based on a wide variety of orientations such as traditional 12-step philosophies, cognitive-behavioral, family, and educational models as well as recreation therapies and vocational counseling. Inpatient and residential treatment programs have traditionally used a milieu approach, a multimodal treatment often including an education component, individual, group, and family therapy, recreational activities. In many clinical settings, approaches to adolescent treatment for substance use problems are based on the philosophy and principles of Alcoholics Anonymous and/or Narcotics Anonymous (AA/NA; Wheeler & Malmquist, 1987). The philosophy holds that individuals cannot effect change on their own. Rather, individuals must recognize a higher spiritual power to attain a healthy (and abstinent) lifestyle, drawing upon resources from within and support from others and following the 12-step process for recovery.

5.21.4.1.2 Cognitive-behavioral models

Behavioral and cognitive-behavioral approaches have been the focus of many preventive intervention programs (Gilchrist & Schinke, 1985; Pentz, 1985) and are increasingly being used to treat adolescent substance abuse (Turner, Liddle, & Dakof 1996; Waldron & Slesnick, 1997). These approaches, based on principles of learning, often incorporate a stress-coping model of substance abuse and focus on teaching adolescents appropriate skills to avoid substance use. Treatment components may include self-monitoring, social skills training (e.g., problem solving or assertiveness), mood regulation (e.g., relaxation training, anger management, or modifying cognitive distortions), and relapse prevention (e.g., drug and alcohol refusal skills). Modeling, behavior rehearsal, feedback, and homework assignments are characteristic of treatment techniques.

5.21.4.1.3 Family therapy models

Family therapy has been a widely accepted treatment for substance abuse, frequently implemented with adolescent abusers (Stanton & Shadish, 1997; Waldron, 1997). Family systems models view substance abuse as a reflection of relationship dysfunction, and treatment is aimed at restructuring the interactional patterns associated with the abuse, theoretically making the abuse unnecessary in the maintenance of system functioning (Stanton & Todd, 1982). Techniques focus on developing the therapeutic relationship, helping family members understand the interrelatedness of their behaviors and the symptomatic behavior in a way consistent with family change (e.g., reframing), and restructuring or shifting family interaction patterns and establishing new behaviors.

Behavioral family models emphasize training parents in contingency management aimed to increase prosocial behaviors incompatible with substance use and decrease substance use behavior. Communication and conflict-resolution skills training are commonly used to enhance families' behavioral repertoires and allow them to resolve problems independently. The increased positive interactions they experience when putting such skills to use are presumed to reinforce the likelihood that the new behaviors will become established patterns.

5.21.4.2 Pharmacological Treatments

5.21.4.2.1 Pharmacotherapy for substance abuse

Mechanisms for pharmacological treatments of substance abuse include treatments which make drug use aversive, provide an alternative substitute for the drug, block the reinforcing effects of the drug, or relieve drug craving or withdrawal (Kaminer, 1994). However, these approaches are rarely used with adolescents because of the particular topography of substance use among adolescents and the potential problems associated with improper use of pharmacological treatments, as well as a host of other practical and ethical considerations. For example, disulfiram (Antabuse) causes intense nausea and other adverse effects when combined with alcohol and is typically used with regular, heavy drinkers who are motivated to achieve abstinence. Noncompliance (i.e., drinking while taking disulfiram) can be medically dangerous. Because adolescents tend to drink more impulsively, consuming alcohol in episodic binges, the potential for noncompliance and subsequent medical complications is high. Thus, apart from the general ethical considerations concerning aversion therapies with adolescents and issues related to consent for treatment, disulfiram would be inappropriate for use with adolescents.

Nevertheless, no pharmacological evidence suggests that adolescents should be treated differently than adults. No specific contraindications exist for nicotine gum or patch, heroin substitutes such as l-acetyl-methadol and buprenorphine, methylphenidate or other stimulants for cocaine abuse with adolescents (Kaminer, 1994). Substitution of methadone for heroin use may also be helpful in eliminating craving or blocking the euphoric effects of the drug in heroin-addicted adolescents for whom detoxification is contra-indicated (e.g., pregnant teens who abuse heroin). Although access to methadone programs for adolescents is more difficult than for adults, methadone may also reduce harm among adolescent heroin users by eliminating the danger of contracting AIDS from contaminated needles (Kaminer, 1994).

5.21.4.2.2 Pharmacotherapy for dual diagnosis

The most common pharmacotherapy for adolescent substance abusers is the use of psychoactive medications to treat symptoms or disorders coexisting with the abuse. For example, adolescents with a dual diagnosis of substance abuse disorder and major depressive disorder may be treated with antidepressants such as imipramine, amitriptyline, or other tricyclics, or with sertraline or other serotonin reuptake inhibitors. Obviously, in the presence of suicide risk, the cardiotoxicity of any medications less cardiotoxic must be considered. By the same token, use of medications with addictive properties such as benzodiazepines, which may be used for adolescents diagnosed with anxiety disorders, would not be appropriate for adolescents with comorbid substance abuse disorder.

In general, Bukstein (1995) has advised against the use of pharmacological agents for substance-abusing adolescents without significant coexisting psychopathology. The main issue with pharmacotherapy for adolescent substance use problems is lack of any empirical attention. In a rare study, Kaminer (1992) reported on the facilitation of cocaine abstinence in adolescent using tricyclic antidepressant desipramine, with six-month follow-up findings confirming continued abstinence. Future research is needed to validate pharmacological treatments.

5.21.4.3 Efficacy and Effectiveness of Psychosocial Treatments

Compared to the number and variety of treatment approaches implemented in clinical settings for adolescent substance abuse, remarkably little research has examined treatment effectiveness. Prior to 1980, most of the evidence was based on findings from several large-scale studies examining treatment outcomes across different modalities. Rush (1979), for example, found a number of patient characteristics (i.e., older onset, being in school or having a job, absence of other behavioral disturbance, mono-drug use) were associated with better outcomes for 2938 adolescents in primarily in outpatient settings, but that treatment variables such as length of treatment were not. The Drug Abuse Reporting Program (Sells & Simpson, 1979), another large-scale study, compared outcomes for 5405 adolescents in four treatment settings: methadone maintenance, therapeutic community, outpatient, and detoxification. Reductions in substance use were found during treatment, although at follow-up only decreases in opiate use were observed. Another large scale study, the Treatment Outcome Prospective Study (Hubbard, Cavanaugh, Craddock, & Rachal, 1985), evaluated treatment outcomes for 240 adolescents participating in residential or outpatient programs. Although reduced substance use was found for both settings, residential treatment clients fared better than outpatient clients. Unfortunately, no control or comparison groups were included in these studies.

5.21.4.3.1 Traditional interventions

One study (Amini, Zilberg, Burke, & Salasnek, 1982), has compared a psychodynamically oriented inpatient drug treatment with an outpatient probation service intervention in a sample of 74 substance abusing adolescents. Subjects were randomly assigned to treatment condition and both groups showed significant decreases in drug use. No between-group differences were found. A number of other studies, however, have examined treatments based on AA/NA philosophy. Friedman, Schwartz, & Utada (1989) evaluated the outcome of a day treatment intervention program using a pre/post design. The program used a modified version of the AA 12 steps, daily meetings, guided group interaction and group therapy, ration-emotive and reality therapy approaches. The mean number of months for follow-up evaluation was 14.6. Of 222 participants, with a mean age of 16.6 years, 85% reported less drug use than when they started in the program. Another pre/post only study was conducted by Alford, Koehler, & Leonard (1991), who examined the effectiveness of AA/NA programs. They evaluated outcomes for 157 substance abusing adolescents treated in an inpatient setting and found that 71% of male treatment completers and 79% of female completers were abstinent six months following discharge. After two years, abstinence among males had dropped to 40%, among females to 61%. Grenier (1985) compared outcome of a residential treatment program based on AA principles with a waiting list control group. The treatment group showed significantly greater abstinence (65.5% vs. 14.3%) two years after treatment.

Multimodal programs have also been examined. Feldman (1983) found significant reductions in substance use for 71 black and Latino adolescents who participated in an intervention consisting of recreational activities, counseling, family intervention, and legal services. Barrett, Simpson, and Lehman (1988) evaluated four community-based drug abuse intervention programs providing individual, group, and family therapy, recreational and community service activities, and substance abuse education. Three months after intake, significant improvements for all problem behaviors were revealed, but no differences were found between programs. Braukmann et al. (1985) compared delinquent adolescents in Teaching Family group homes with living in a treatment-as-usual group home and an untreated group. The Teaching Family group homes, applying skills training, self-government, motivation, relationship development and youth advocacy, showed significant during-treatment decreases in substance use. However, these decreases did not persist at 12-month follow-up.

5.21.4.3.2 Behavioral outpatient interventions

Davidge and Forman (1988) reviewed eight case studies published between 1967 and 1985 which provided limited support for behavior therapy with adolescent substance abusers. These studies were limited by small sample sizes, lack of control or comparison conditions and, in many cases, only anecdotal reporting of substance use behavior. Two of the cases, however, used urine analysis to validate self-report of substance use, lending more strength to study claims. These cases used contingency contracting with the adolescent and parents, focusing on school, work, and relationships (Cook & Petersen, 1985; Fredericksen, Jenkins, & Carr, 1976). The adolescents in both cases had drastically reduced substance use or remained abstinent at post-treatment and at follow-up through one year in one case and three years in the other.

In other behavioral investigations, Duehn (1978) evaluated the effectiveness of aversive conditioning for adolescents with severe drug-use histories. At 6- and 18-month follow-up, completed abstinence was reported for six of the seven youth who had participated in the 14 week covert sensitization training program. DeJong and Henrich (1980) conducted a two year follow-up study of 89 young addicts in a behavior modification program who attended a rehabilitation center for at least seven days. They reported that one-third of the total sample remained drug free. In a set of two studies using a pre/post design, Iverson and colleagues (Iverson, Jurs, Johnson, & Rohen, 1978; Iverson & Roberts, 1980) conducted a community education-based program for parents and adolescents and found significant reductions in drug use at post-treatment and six-month follow-up.

Using a between-groups design, Smith (1983) compared an eight-session school-based group treatment, focusing on skills training in the areas of problem solving, social skills, and self-monitoring, with a no treatment control condition for adolescent marijuana users. Self-reported use was reduced and academic and peer functioning was enhanced for the youth in the treatment. In a residential treatment setting, Hawkins, Catalano, and Miller (1992) found improved role play performance involving avoidance of drug use and interpersonal problem solving in an applied behavioral social skills training intervention in adolescents in a residential treatment center.

For both traditional and behavioral interventions, wide variation with respect to control groups, random assignment, outcome measures, and number and latency of follow-up assessments can be seen. However, none of the studies comparing across two or more intervention conditions found evidence that any treatment approach examined was better than any other. In their review of nonfamily-based treatments, Catalano, Hawkins, Wells, Miller, & Brewer (1990–91) addressed the limitations of these studies and could only conclude that some treatment is better than no treatment. In the absence of more randomized clinical trials including appropriate alternative comparison conditions, no more definitive conclusions can be made. Several federally funded controlled trials of promising treatment approaches are currently underway and are likely to improve the knowledge base with respect to empirically validated treatments for adolescent substance abuse.

5.21.4.3.3 Family-based interventions

In the last decade or so, considerable advances have been made in evaluating the effectiveness of family treatments for adolescent substance abuse, with a dozen or more controlled trials completed or underway (Stanton & Shadish, 1997; Waldron, 1997). Much of the impetus for these advances stemmed from the early controlled studies of family therapy conducted by Szapocznik and his colleagues. Scopetta, King, Szapocznik, and Tillman (1979) investigated whether family interventions need to be ecologically focused, involving multiple systems, or whether intervention within the conjoint family context is sufficient. Although both groups showed improved outcomes following treatment, no differences were found between the two interventions. In another set of studies, Szapocznik, Kurtines, Foote, Perez-Vidal, and Hervis (1983, 1986) compared two variations of structural family systems therapy, conjoint family therapy and one-person family therapy, examining whether family therapy outcome varies on the basis of who participates in the sessions. Families in both intervention conditions showed significant improvement at the end of therapy. Moreover, compared to conjoint therapy, one-person family therapy led to slightly greater improvement for some outcome measures. These studies were limited by small sample sizes, high attrition, inadequate substance use measurement, and the absence of a nonfamily comparison condition. However, like other early outcome studies, the findings of pre/post changes were promising.

Other randomized trials comparing systems family therapy to alternative family-based interventions have also been conducted. Friedman (1989) found pre/post differences comparing the effectiveness of Functional Family Therapy (Alexander & Parsons, 1982) to a parenting skills group intervention. Although no between-group differences were found, 93% of the families in family therapy engaged in treatment compared to only 67% of the parenting group families. In a reanalysis of these data which included treatment dropouts as failures, Stanton and Shadish (1997) reported that a significant difference between the two groups emerged, highlighting the importance of considering differential attrition in conducting treatment outcome research. Lewis, Piercy, Sprenkle, and Trepper (1990) also evaluated an integrative family therapy model, comparing Purdue Brief Family Therapy, to a didactic, family-oriented parenting skills intervention. Both interventions were found to significantly reduce drug use at post-treatment. However, a greater percentage of youth receiving family therapy decreased their use, compared to the parenting group intervention. No follow-up data were reported.

A number of randomized trials have included nonfamily comparison interventions in their designs. Joanning, Thomas, Quinn, and Mullen (1992) compared a family systems intervention to two comparison conditions, a family drug education intervention and adolescent group therapy. The results at post-treatment revealed that family therapy was most effective in decreasing problem behaviors and drug use, with 54% of youth in family therapy abstinent, compared to 29% in the family education condition and 17% in the group therapy condition. Using a more complex ecological intervention, Henggeler et al. (1991) conducted two studies, comparing multisystemic family therapy to individual therapy in the first study and to a treatment-as-usual juvenile probation supervision intervention in the second. As had been found in treating delinquents, multisystemic family therapy produced significantly better outcomes at post-test. Liddle et al. (1993) compared a multisystemic, multidimensional family therapy to two alternative treatments: adolescent group therapy and a family education group. All three conditions were associated with reduced substance use, with greatest and most consistent improvement in the family therapy condition, in which youth decreased their use from daily to about once a week for alcohol and marijuana, with 30% abstinent. Group therapy also showed gradual decline in drug use from pretreatment to follow-up, not apparent at post-treatment, and the

authors suggested that the effect may have resulted from the delay between adolescents putting newly acquired skills into use and deriving benefit from implementing them.

Two behavioral family therapy trials have also been conducted. Azrin, Donohue, Besalel, Kogan, and Acierno (1994) compared behavioral family therapy to a process-oriented, nondirective (supportive) adolescent group therapy intervention. Compared to the supportive group intervention, behavioral family therapy produced greater reductions in substance use and improvements in other areas of functioning. In another behavioral family therapy evaluation, Krinsley and Bry (1997) examined the impact of a school-based behavioral family therapy intervention compared to a school-based intervention only condition. Relative to pretreatment, students who participated in family therapy showed greater reductions than students in the school intervention alone during the 15 months following treatment. The differences between groups appeared even greater over time, illustrating the importance of conducting follow-up assessments.

In the first controlled study of its kind, Turner, Liddle, and Dakof (1996) recently reported results of a randomized clinical trial comparing cognitive-behavior therapy and multisystemic family therapy for adolescent substance abuse to a treatment-as-usual condition. The cognitive-behavioral and family interventions both included individual and conjoint family sessions. The cognitive-behavioral condition included self-monitoring, communication and problem-solving skills training, contingency contracting, and substance refusal skills, while the family condition was a multidimensional family intervention (Liddle et al., 1993). Preliminary results indicated that both of the experimental treatments produce greater reductions in substance use relative to treatment-as-usual. However, some findings suggest that although there were no differences between the two active conditions through six month follow-up, the cognitive-behavioral treatment appeared more effective through a 12 month follow-up. However, data analysis is incomplete and no conclusions can be drawn until the final results are examined.

Taken together, the results of controlled clinical trials evaluating family-based interventions suggest that family therapy is an effective treatment for adolescents substance abuse. Only one study (Henggeler et al., 1991) reported finding no differences between family therapy and a nonfamily intervention. Every study demonstrated significant reductions in substance use from pre- to post-treatment. In seven of eight studies comparing family therapy to a nonfamily-based intervention, youth receiving family therapy showed greater reductions in substance use than those receiving adolescent group therapy (Azrin et al., 1994; Joanning et al., 1992; Liddle et al., 1993), family education (Joanning et al., 1992; Liddle et al., 1993), and individual therapy, individual tracking through schools, or juvenile justice systems (Henggeler et al., 1991; Krinsley & Bry, 1997). When compared to parenting skills training programs, family therapy fared better in the Lewis et al. (1990) study and in the Friedman (1989) study when dropouts were included in analysis. Stanton and Shadish (1997) give effect sizes in the their meta-analysis of family therapy outcome studies.

5.21.4.3.4 Treatment engagement and retention

Treatment retention in alcohol and drug abuse populations is a widely recognized problem. Adolescents are at even greater risk for dropping out of treatment, compared with adults, because they are less motivated to change, do not perceive treatment as suitable for themselves, and are more likely to be in treatment because of external pressures (Jainchill, Bhattacharya, & Yagelka, 1995). Kaminer and Frances (1991) prospectively compared treatment noncompleters with completers between the ages of 13 and 18, in an inpatient dual disorder substance abuse treatment program designed specifically for adolescents, hypothesizing that treatments which simultaneously address psychiatric issues would improve treatment outcome. Fifty adolescents completed treatment, 14 did not. Involuntary admission, past treatment, and parental psychopathology had no impact on dropout. A trend towards a higher prevalence of mood disorder and adjustment disorder was found in treatment completers. In contrast, the treatment dropout group had a higher prevalence of conduct disorder. Jainchill et al. (1995) also examined factors related to treatment retention in two residential treatment centers, comparing clients age 17 and under with clients 18 to 20 years old. They found that older clients felt more motivated and ready for treatment and perceived treatment to be more suitable for them. The most consistent predictor of treatment retention was age.

A recent research project evaluating the effectiveness of residential treatment for adolescent substance abuse has received funding through the National Institute on Drug Abuse (Jainchill et al., 1995). Data collection has been completed for 938 adolescents, but follow-up data are not yet available. However, several variables correlated significantly with retention.

Consistent with Kaminer and Francis (1991), antisocial lifestyle and poorer psychological functioning may predict early dropout. Other predictors, consistent with Jainchill et al. (1995), included measures of self-esteem, motivation and readiness for change, environmental risk factors, and the interviewer's impressions of the client's likelihood of staying in the program.

Recognizing the problem of engaging drug abusers and their families in treatment, Szapocznik and his colleagues turned their research efforts toward evaluating ways to enhance patient retention in family therapy. In one study, Szapocznik et al. (1988) compared their family systems therapy in combination with an intensive engagement intervention to family systems therapy alone (with engagement as usual). The results were quite pronounced: 93% of the substance abusers and their families in the intensive engagement condition completed intake compared to 47% of the engagement as usual group. Once engaged in treatment, there were no further attrition differences between the groups.

In the second study, Santisteban et al. (1996) replicated the findings of the first study, and even with stricter criteria for treatment engagement they found 81% of the substance abusers and their families in the intensive engagement condition completing intake compared to 60% in the comparison conditions. Moreover, they found that ethnicity was associated with a differential engagement rate in the intensive condition: 97% of the non-Cuban Hispanics in the intensive condition were engaged vs. 64% of the Cuban Hispanics, allowing them to explore further the role of ethnicity in family therapy process. Taken together, motivational issues and their role in retention and recovery should continue as a focus study.

5.21.5 FUTURE DIRECTIONS FOR RESEARCH AND PRACTICE

Research on adolescent substance abuse has been characterized by disparate definitions of abuse, wide variations in subject sampling strategies, and little systematic attention to heterogeneity among adolescents with substance abuse disorders. Such methodological problems may represent primary sources for inconsistency of findings and noncomparability across studies. However, important advances in assessing adolescent substance use have been made in recent years, with the development of a variety of instruments specifically designed for adolescents (Winters & Stinchfield, 1995). Establishing the psychometric properties of these instruments and developing more uniform assessment procedures for research and practice is needed to facilitate the development of treatment formulation procedures and facilitate treatment effectiveness comparisons. Greater collaboration among researchers in this field would also improve comparisons across studies and could yield greater convergence and consistency of findings.

Research is also needed to evaluate assessment strategies more sensitive to patterning of use over time. Some research has shown, for example, that family factors relate more powerfully to stage of substance use than to frequency of use (Brook, Whiteman, & Gordon, 1982). Also, using latent growth modeling to detect similarities and differences in developmental trajectories for substance use, Duncan et al. (1994) found that family cohesion may be more central in delaying escalation of cigarette use than escalation of other substances. With a more detailed and precise assessment of quantity, frequency, and patterning of use, researchers may be able to evaluate the effectiveness and efficacy of family therapies in more sensitive or meaningful ways. For example, forestalling adolescents' progression through the drug use sequence or initiating their return back through the gateway may reflect treatment effectiveness better than overall amount or frequency of use.

Liddle et al. (1993) have attempted to develop a developmentally sensitive treatment model for families of adolescent substance abusers. With respect to gender, different models may also be needed, with girls' substance abuse perhaps best understood in the context of factors such as reasons for using, negative and positive consequences, and expectancies related to use, or family relationships. Considerably more attention has been given to examining the influence of ethnicity on therapy process and outcome (Santisteban et al., 1996; Szapocznik et al., 1988). However, broad-based culturally sensitive treatment models have yet to be developed. Future research should focus on examining the components of treatment models, evaluating the importance of the adolescent development, gender, and ethnicity in relation to treatment effectiveness.

Treatment effectiveness studies have lagged far behind other areas of adolescent substance abuse. Moreover, the vast majority of studies conducted have been plagued with methodological problems. In addition to design and substance use assessment issues, at least half of the studies did not include follow-up assessment, a critical limitation given that several studies conducting follow-up assessments found that patterns of substance use reductions changed over time (Krinsley & Bry, 1997; Liddle et al., 1993; Szapocznik et al.,

1983, 1986) and different conclusions could be drawn about treatment effectiveness on the basis of point in time of measurement. Moreover, differential attrition across conditions may have created confounds in interpreting the results of the outcome studies (Snow, Tebes, & Arthur, 1992; Stanton & Shadish, 1997). Some research has also revealed differential dropout rates in substance abusers with dual diagnoses. Thus, comorbid conditions may play a role in the course of treatment as well. More effort needs to be exerted to follow treatment dropouts and examine patterns of outcome related to client heterogeneity.

None of the studies reviewed reported examining therapy process variables which may have been associated with change. Within the broader psychotherapy literature, therapy process and outcome research has shown great promise in isolating therapist, client, and interactional mediators of outcome. The equivocal findings in the clinical trials for adolescent substance abuse highlight the need for incorporating a process perspective in this area of endeavor as well.

A number of family-based clinical trials compared two or more interventions to one another. However, no clear pattern emerged for the superiority of one treatment model over another. Few studies indicated use of a treatment manual, and fewer still used actual adherence ratings to ensure that the components described were actually being delivered. It is possible that no differences on the basis of theoretical model were found because, despite what techniques and procedures treatment researchers say are being implemented, therapists engaged in essentially the same behaviors across models. Alternatively, therapists may have been true to their models, but the effects of common factors present across all interventions such as therapist empathy or warmth and/or treatment expectancies or motivation may have been critical mediators of change.

Creating a motivational context for change represents a major phase of treatment presumed to produce higher engagement and retention rates in some models of family therapy (Alexander & Parsons, 1982). Similarly, Miller and Rollnick (1991) have developed a motivational enhancement approach that has been shown to be effective as an add-on to traditional treatments and as a stand-alone brief intervention for adult problem drinkers. The central feature of this intervention, like the motivational phase of family therapy, is the nonblaming, nonjudgmental stance taken by the therapist. This focus is wholly consistent with the observation of Stanton and Shadish that a nonconfrontational, nonblaming perspective appears to be essential in the treatment of families with substance abusing members and this component of therapy process merits close examination in future treatment studies with adolescents.

5.21.6 SUMMARY

The lack of uniform definition of substance abuse in adolescents has impeded all areas of research including epidemiology, etiology, diagnosis, assessment, treatment development, and treatment outcome evaluation. Studies of risk and protective factors have identified a variety of correlates of abuse that facilitate prediction of who may develop problems or be appropriate candidates for prevention or intervention. The appearance of well-designed clinical trials evaluating interventions in recent years begins to address the issue of optimal treatment strategies for adolescent substance abuse. Research efforts have led to the identification of several treatment approaches that appear to reduce adolescent substance use, relative to no treatment or alternative treatment comparisons. Family therapy, in particular, has engendered substantial empirical support. However, the mechanisms associated with treatment effectiveness have yet to be examined. Researchers need to channel more efforts into prospective model building, incorporating empirical work from the broader substance abuse literature and relying on more uniform, comprehensive, detailed measurement of use. Moreover, psychotherapy process research is needed to examine aspects of the change process associated with better outcomes.

5.21.7 REFERENCES

Alexander, J. F., Barton, C., Waldron, H. B., & Mas, C. H. (1983). Beyond the technology of family therapy: The anatomy of intervention model. In K. D. Craig & R. J. McMahon (Eds.), *Advances in clinical behavior therapy* (pp. 48–73). New York: Brunner/Mazel.

Alexander, J. F., & Parsons, B. V. (1982). *Functional family therapy*. Monterey, CA: Brooks/Cole.

Alford, G. S., Koehler, R. A., & Leonard, J. (1991). Alcoholics Anonymous–Narcotics Anonymous model inpatient treatment of chemically dependent adolescents: A 2-year outcome study. *Journal of Studies on Alcohol, 52*, 118–126.

Alterman, A. I., & Tarter, R. E. (1986). An examination of selected topologies: Hyperactivity, familial and antisocial alcoholism. In M. Galanter (Ed.), *Recent developments in alcoholism* (Vol. 4, pp. 169–189). New York: Plenum.

American Psychiatric Association (1980). *Diagnostic and statistical manual of mental disorders* (3rd ed.). Washington, DC: Author.

American Psychiatric Association (1987). *Diagnostic and statistical manual of mental disorders* (3rd ed. Rev.). Washington, DC: Author.

American Psychiatric Association (1994). *Diagnostic and Statistical Manual of Mental Disorders* (4th ed.). Washington, DC: Author.

Amini, F., Zilberg, N. J, Burke, E. L., & Salasnek, S. (1982). A controlled study of inpatient vs. outpatient treatment of delinquent drug abuse adolescents: One year results. *Comprehensive Psychiatry, 23*, 436–444.

Andersson, T., & Magnusson, D. (1988). Drinking habits and alcohol abuse among young men: A prospective longitudinal study. *Journal of Studies on Alcohol, 49*, 245–252.

Andrews, J. A., Hops, H., Ary, D., Lichtenstein, E., & Tildesley, E. (1991). The construction, validation, and use of a Guttman scale of adolescent substance use: An investigation of family relationships. *Journal of Drug Issues, 21*, 557–572.

Azrin, N. H., Donohue, B., Besalel, V. A., Kogan, E. S., & Acierno, R. (1994). Youth drug abuse treatment: A controlled outcome study. *Journal of Child and Adolescent Substance Abuse, 3*, 1–16.

Babor, T. F., Hofmann, M., DelBoca, F. K., Hesselbrock, V., Meyer, R. E., Dolinsky, Z. S., & Rounsaville, B. (1992). Types of alcoholics. I. Evidence for an empirically derived typology based on indicators of vulnerability and severity. *Archives of General Psychiatry, 49*, 599–608.

Bachman, J. G., Wallace, J. M., O'Malley, P. M., Johnston, L. D., Kurth, C. L., & Neighbors, H. W. (1991). Racial/ethnic differences in smoking, drinking and illicit drug use among American high school seniors, 1976–89. *American Journal of Public Health, 81*, 372–377.

Bailey, S. L., Flewelling, R. L., & Rachal, J. V. (1992). The characterization of inconsistencies in self-reports of alcohol and marijuana use in a longitudinal study of adolescents. *Journal of Studies on Alcohol, 53*, 636–657.

Barkley, R. A., Fischer, M., Edelbrock, C. S., & Smallish, L. (1990). The adolescent outcome of hyperactive children diagnosed by research criteria: I. An 8-year prospective follow-up study. *Journal of the American Academy of Child and Adolescent Psychiatry, 29*, 546–557.

Barnes, G. M. (1981). Drinking among adolescents: A subcultural phenomenon or a model of adult behaviors? *Adolescence, 16*(61), 211–229.

Barnes, G. M. (1984). Adolescent alcohol abuse and other problem behaviors: Their relationships and common parental influences. *Journal of Youth and Adolescence, 13*, 329–348.

Barrett, M. E., Simpson, D. D., & Lehman, W. E. K. (1988). Behavioral changes of adolescents in drug abuse intervention programs. *Journal of Clinical Psychology, 44*, 461–473.

Baumrind, D. (1985). Familial antecedents of adolescent drug use: A developmental perspective. In C. L. Jones and R. J. Battjes (Eds.), *Etiology of drug abuse: Implications for prevention,* (pp. 13–44). Rockville, MD: National Institutes of Health.

Bentler, P. M. (1992). Etiologies and consequences of adolescent drug use: Implications for prevention. *Journal of Addictive Diseases, 11*, 47–61.

Blane, H. (1976). Middle-aged alcoholics and young drinkers. In H. Blane & M. Chafetz (Eds.), *Youth, alcohol and social policy* (pp. 5–38). New York: Plenum.

Blum, R. W. (1987). Adolescent substance abuse: Diagnostic and treatment issues. *Pediatric Clinics of North America, 34*, 523–531.

Braukmann, C. J., Bedlington, M. M., Belden, B. D., Braukmann, B. P. D., Husted, J. J., Ramp, K. K., & Wolf, M. M. (1985). Effects of a community-based group-home treatment program on male juvenile offenders use and abuse of drugs and alcohol. *American Journal of Drug and Alcohol Abuse, 11*, 249–278.

Brook, J. S., Brook, D. W., Gordon, A. S., Whiteman, M.,

& Cohen, P. (1990). The psychosocial etiology of adolescent drug use: A family interactional approach. *Genetic, Social, and General Psychology Monographs, 116*, 111–267.

Brook, J. S., Whiteman, M., & Gordon, A. S. (1982). Qualitative and quantitative aspects of adolescent drug use: Interplay of personality, family, and peer correlates. *Psychological Reports, 51*, 1151–1163.

Brown, S. A., Mott, M. A., & Myers, M. G. (1990). Adolescent alcohol and drug treatment outcome. In R. R. Watson (Ed.), *Drug and Alcohol Abuse Prevention, Drug and Alcohol Abuse Prevention, Drug and Alcohol Abuse Reviews* (pp. 373–403). Clifton, NJ: Humana.

Brown, S. A., Vik, P. W., & Creamer, V. A. (1989). Characteristics of relapse following adolescent substance abuse treatment. *Addictive Behaviors, 14*, 291–300.

Bry, B. H., McKeon, P., & Pandina, R. J. (1982). Extent of drug use as a function of number of risk factors. *Journal of Abnormal Psychology, 91*, 273–279.

Bukstein, O. G. (1995). *Adolescent substance abuse: Assessment, prevention, and treatment.* New York: Wiley.

Bukstein, O. G., Glancy, L. G., & Kaminer, Y. (1992). Patterns of affective comorbidity in a clinical population of dually diagnosed adolescent substance abusers. *Journal of the American Academy of Child and Adolescent Psychiatry, 31*, 1041–1045.

Catalano, R. F., Hawkins, J. D., Wells, E. A., Miller, J., & Brewer, D. (1990–91). Evaluation of the effectiveness of adolescent drug abuse treatment, assessment of risks for relapse, and promising approaches for relapse prevention. *The International Journal of the Addictions, 25*, 1085–1140.

Centers for Disease Control and Prevention. (1996). Tobacco use and sources of cigarettes among high school students—United States, 1995. *Morbidity and Mortality Weekly Report, 45*(20).

Clayton, R. R. (1992). Transitions in drug use: Risk and protective factors. In M. Glantz & R. Pickens (Eds.), *Vulnerability to drug abuse* (pp. 15–51). Washington, DC: American Psychological Association.

Cohen, P., Cohen, J., Kasen, S., Velez, C. M., Hartmark, C., Johnson, J., Rojas, M., Brook, J., & Streuning, E. L. (1993). An epidemiological study of disorders in late childhood and adolescence. I. Age and gender-specific prevalence. *Journal of Child Psychology and Psychiatry, 34, 851–867.*

Cook, P. S., & Petersen, D. (1985). Individualizing adolescent drug abuse treatment. In A. S. Friedman & G. Beschner (Eds.), *Treatment services for adolescent substance abusers* (pp. 164–177). Rockville, MD: National Institutes of Health.

Crowley, T. J., & Riggs, P. D. (1995). Adolescent substance use disorder with conduct disorder and comorbid conditions. In E. Rahdert & D. Czechowicz (Eds.), *Adolescent drug abuse: Clinical assessment and therapeutic interventions,* (pp. 49–111). Rockville, MD: National Institutes of Health.

Davidge, A. M., & Forman, S. G. (1988). Psychological treatment of adolescent substance abusers: A review. *Children and Youth Services Review, 10*, 43–55.

DeJong, R., & Henrich, G. (1980). Follow-up results of a behavior modification program for juvenile drug addicts. *Addictive Behaviors, 5*, 49–57.

DeLeon, G. (1984, April). *Adolescent substance abusers in the therapeutic community: Treatment outcomes.* Paper presented at the Research Conference on Juvenile Offenders with Serious Alcohol, Drug Abuse, and Mental Health Problems.

Deykin, E., Levy, J. C., & Wells, V. (1986). Adolescent depression, alcohol and drug abuse. *American Journal of Public Health, 76*, 178–182.

DiMileo, L. (1989). Psychiatric syndromes in adolescent substance abusers. *American Journal of Psychiatry, 146*, 1212–1214.

Dishion, T. J., Patterson, G. R., & Reid, J. R. (1988). Parent and peer factors associated with drug sampling in early adolescence: Implications for treatment. In E. R. Rahdert & J. Grabowski (Eds.), *Adolescent drug abuse: Analyses of treatment research* (pp. 69–93). Rockville, MD: National Institutes of Health.

Donovan, J. E., & Jessor, R. (1985). Structure of problem behavior in adolescence and young adulthood. *Journal of Consulting and Clinical Psychology, 56*, 890–904.

Duehn, W. D. (1978). Covert sensitization in group treatment of adolescent drug abusers. *International Journal of the Addictions, 13*, 485–491.

Duncan, T. E., Duncan, S. C., & Hops, H. (1994). The effects of family cohesiveness and peer encouragement on the development of adolescent alcohol use: A cohort-sequential approach to the analysis of longitudinal data. *Journal of Studies on Alcohol, 55*, 588–599.

Ellickson, P. L., Hays, R. D., & Bell, R. M. (1992). Stepping through the drug use sequence: Longitudinal scalogram analysis of initiation and regular use. *Journal of Abnormal Psychology, 101*, 441–451.

Farrell, A. D., Danish, S. J., & Howard, C. W. (1992). Relationship between drug use and other problem behaviors in urban adolescents. *Journal of Consulting and Clinical Psychology, 60*, 705–712.

FeCaces, M., Stinson, F. S., & Hartford, T. C. (1991). Alcohol use and physically risky behavior among adolescents. *Alcohol Health and Research World, 15*, 228–233.

Feldman, H. W. (1983, November). *A summary of the Youth Environment Study Final Reports.* State of California, Department of Alcohol and Drug Programs, Sacramento, CA.

Filstead, W. F. (1982). Adolescence and alcohol. In E. M. Pattison & E. Kaufman (Eds.), *Encyclopedic handbook of alcoholism*, (pp. 156–178). New York: Gardner.

Filstead, W. F., Parrella, D. P., & Conlin, J. M. (1988). Alcohol use and dependency in youth: Examining DSM-III diagnostic criteria. *Drugs & Society, 3*, 145–170.

Flay, B. R., & Petraitis, J. (1994). The theory of triadic influence: A new theory of health behavior with implications for preventive interventions. *Advances in Medical Sociology, 4*, 19–44.

Frederiksen, L., Jenkins, J., & Carr, C. (1976). Indirect modification of adolescent drug abuse using contingency contracting. *Journal of Behavior Therapy and Experimental Psychiatry, 7*, 377–378.

Friedman, A. S. (1989). Family therapy vs. parent groups: Effects on adolescent drug abusers. *The American Journal of Family Therapy, 17*, 335–347.

Friedman, A. S., Schwartz, R., & Utada, A. (1989). Outcome of a unique youth drug abuse program: A follow-up study of clients of Straight, Inc. *Journal of Substance Abuse Treatment, 6*, 259–268.

Friedman, A. S., & Utada, A. (1989). A method for diagnosing and planning the treatment of adolescent drug abusers: The Adolescent Drug Abuse Diagnosis (ADAD) insrument. *Journal of Drug Education, 19*(4), 285–312.

Gilchrist, L. D., Schinke, S. P. (1985). Preventing substance abuse with children and adolescents. *Journal of Consulting and Clinical Psychology, 53*, 121–135.

Grenier, C. (1985). Treatment effectiveness in an adolescent chemical dependency treatment program: A quasi-experimental design. *International Journal of the Addictions, 20*, 381–391.

Harrell, A. V., & Wirtz, P. W. (1989). *Adolescent Drinking Index Test and Manual.* Odessa, FL: Psychological Assessment Resources.

Hasin, D. S., Grant, B. F., & Endicott, J. (1990). The

natural history of alcohol abuse: Implications for definitions of alcohol use disorders. *American Journal of Psychiatry, 147,* 1537–1541.

Hawkins, J. D., Catalano, R. F., & Miller, J. Y. (1992). Risk and protective factors for alcohol and other drug problems in adolescence and early adulthood: Implications for substance abuse prevention. *Psychological Bulletin, 112,* 64–105.

Henggeler, S. W., Borduin, C. M., Melton, G. B., Mann, B. J., Smith, L. A., Hall, J. A., Cone, L., & Fucci, B. R. (1991). Effects of multisystemic therapy on drug use and abuse in serious juvenile offenders: A progress report from two outcome studies. *Family Dynamics of Addition Quarterly, 1,* 40–51.

Henly, G. A., & Winters, K. C. (1989). Development of psychosocial scales of the assessment of adolescents involved with alcohol and drugs. *International Journal of the Addictions, 24,* 973–1001.

Hops, H., Tildesley, E., Lichtenstein, E., Ary, D., & Sherman, L. (1990). Parent-adolescent problem-solving interactions and drug use. *American Journal of Drug and Alcohol Abuse, 16,* 239–258.

Hubbard, R. L., Cavanaugh, E. R., Craddock, S. G., & Rachal, J. V. (1985). Characteristics, behaviors, and outcomes for youth in the TOPS. In A. S. Friedman & G. M. Beschner (Eds.), *Treatment services for adolescent substance abusers* (pp. 49–65). Rockville, MD: National Institutes of Health.

Hughes, S. O., Power, T. G., & Francis, D. J. (1992). Defining patterns of drinking in adolescence: A cluster analytic approach. *Journal of Studies on Alcohol, 53,* 40–47.

Iverson, D. C., Jurs, S., Johnson, L., & Rohen, R. (1978). The effect of an education intervention program for juvenile drug abusers and their parents. *Journal of Drug Education, 8,* 101–111.

Iverson, D. C., & Roberts, T. E. (1980). The juvenile intervention program: Results of the process, impact, and outcome evaluation. *Journal of Drug Education, 10,* 289–301.

Jainchill, N., Bhattacharya, G., & Yagelka, J. (1995). Therapeutic communities for adolescents. In E. Rahdert & D. Czechowicz (Eds.), *Adolescent drug abuse: Clinical assessment and therapeutic interventions* (pp. 190–217). Rockville, MD: National Institutes of Health.

Jessor, R., & Jessor, S. (1977). *Problem behavior and psychosocial development: A longitudinal study of youth.* New York: Academic Press.

Joanning, H., Thomas, F., Quinn, W., & Mullen, R. (1992). Treating adolescent drug abuse: A comparison of family systems therapy, group therapy, and family drug education. *Journal of Marital and Family Therapy, 18,* 345–356.

Johnston, L. D., O'Malley, P. M., Bachman, J. G. (1993). *National survey results on drug use from the Monitoring the Future Study, 1975–1992.* Rockville, MD: National Institutes of Health.

Kaminer, Y. (1992). Desipramine facilitation of cocaine abstinence in an adolescent. *Journal of the American Academy of Child and Adolescent Psychiatry, 31,* 312–317.

Kaminer, Y. (1994). *Adolescent substance abuse: A comprehensive guide to theory and practice.* New York: Plenum.

Kaminer, Y., Bukstein, O., & Tarter, R. E. (1991). The Teen-Addiction Severity Index: Rationale and reliability. *International Journal of the Addictions, 26*(2), 219–226.

Kaminer, Y., & Frances, R. J. (1991). Inpatient treatment of adolescents with psychiatric and substance abuse disorder. *Hospital and Community Psychiatry, 42,* 894–896.

Kandel, D. B. (1975). Stages in adolescent involvement in drug use. *Science, 190,* 912–914.

Kandel, D. B., Kessler, R. C., & Margulies, R. S. (1978). Antecedents of adolescent initiation into stages of drug use: A developmental analysis. *Journal of Youth and Adolescence, 7,* 13–40.

Kandel, D. B., & Logan, J. A. (1984). Patterns of drug use from adolescence to young adulthood: I. Periods of risk for initiation, continued use, and discontinuation. *American Journal of Public Health, 74,* 660–666.

Kandel, D. B., Yamaguchi, K., & Chen, K. (1992). Stages of progression in drug involvement from adolescence to adulthood: Further evidence for the gateway theory. *Journal of Studies on Alcohol, 53,* 447–457.

Kashani, J. H., Beck, N. C., Hoeper, E. W., Fallahi, C., Corcoran, C. M. McAllister, J. A., Rosenberg, T. K., & Reid, J. C. (1987). Psychiatric disorders in a community sample of adolescents. *American Journal of Psychiatry, 144,* 584–589.

Krinsley, K. E., & Bry, B. H. (1997). *Decreasing school failure and early substance use in high risk adolescents through co-ordinated behavioral family and school intervention.* Manuscript submitted for publication.

Labouvie, E. W. (1986). The coping function of adolescent alcohol and drug use. In R. K. Silbereisen, K. Eyferth, & G. Rudinger (Eds.), *Development as action in context: Problem behavior and normal youth development* (pp. 227–240). New York: Springer-Verlag.

Leccese, M., & Waldron, H. B. (1994). Assessing adolescent substance abuse: A critique of current measurement instruments. *Journal of Substance Abuse Treatment, 11,* 553–563.

Lettieri, D., Sayers, M., & Pearson, H. (Eds.) (1980). *Theories on drug abuse: Selected contemporary perspectives.* Rockville, MD: National Institutes of Health.

Lewis, R. A., Piercy, F. P., Sprenkle, D. H., & Trepper, T. S. (1990). Family-based interventions for helping drug-abusing adolescents. *Journal of Adolescent Research, 5,* 82–95.

Liddle, H. A., Dakof, G. A., Parker, K., Barrett, K., Diamond, G. S., Garcia, R., & Palmer, R. (1993). *Effectiveness of family therapy vs. multi-family therapy and group therapy: Results of the Adolescents and Families Project—A randomized clinical trial.* Paper presented at the Annual Meeting of the Society for Psychotherapy Research, Pittsburgh, PA.

Martin, C. S., Kaczynski, N. A., Maisto, S. A., Bukstein, O. G., & Moss, H. B. (in press). Patterns of alcohol abuse and dependence symptoms in adolescent drinkers. *Journal of Studies on Alcohol.*

McCarthy, R. G., & Douglass, E. M. (1949). *Alcohol and social responsibility.* New York: Thomas Y, Crowell C, and Yale Plan Clinic.

McCrady, B. S., Noel, N. E., Abrams, D. B., Stout, R. L., Newlson, H. F., & Hay, W. M. (1986). Comparative effectiveness of three types of spouse involvement in outpatient behavioral alcoholism treatment. *Journal of Studies on Alcohol, 47,* 459–467.

McGee, L., & Newcomb, M. D. (1992). General deviance syndrome: Expanded hierarchical evaluations at four ages from early adolescence to adulthood. *Journal of Consulting and Clinical Psychology, 60,* 766–776.

Metzger, D. S., Kushner, H., & McLellan, A. T. (1991). *Adolescent Problem Severity Index Administration Manual.* Philadelphia, PA: Biomedical Computer Research Institute.

Miller, G. (1990). *Substance Abuse Subtle Screening Inventory-Adolescent (SASSI-A).* Bloomington, IN: SASSI Institute.

Miller, W. R., & Rollnick, S. (1991). *Motivational interviewing.* New York: Guilford Press.

Miller, W. R., Westerberg, V., & Waldron, H. B. (1995). In R. K. Hester & W. R. Miller (Eds.), *Handbook of alcoholism treatment approaches: Effective alternatives* (2nd ed., pp. 17–53). New York: Allyn & Bacon.

Nathan, P. E. (1991). Substance use disorders in DSM-IV. *Journal of Abnormal Psychology, 100,* 356–361.

Needle, R., McCubbin, H., Lorence, J., & Hochhauser, M. (1983). Reliability and validity of adolescent self-reported drug use in a family-based study: A methodological report. *International Journal of Addition, 18,* 901–912.

Newcomb, M. D. (1995). Identifying high-risk youth: Prevalence and patterns of adolescent drug abuse. In E. Rahdert & D. Czechowicz (Eds.), *Adolescent drug abuse: Clinical assessment and therapeutic interventions,* (pp. 7–37). Rockville, MD: National Institutes of Health.

Newcomb, M. D., & Bentley, P. M. (1989). Substance abuse and abuse among children and teenagers. *American Psychologist, 44,* 242–248.

Newcomb, M. D., Maddahian, E., & Bentler, P. M. (1986). Risk factors for drug use among adolescents: Concurrent and longitudinal analyses. *American Journal of Public Health, 76,* 525–531.

O'Farrell, T. J. & Maisto, S. A. (1987). The utility of self report and biological measures of alcohol consumption in alcoholism treatment outcome studies. *Advances in Behaviour Research and Therapy, 9,* 91–125.

Pandina, R. J. (1986). Methods, problems, and trends in studies of adolescent drinking practices. *Annals of Behavioral Medicine, 8,* 20–26.

Paperny, D. M., Aono, J. Y., Lehman, R. M., Hammar, S. L., & Riusser, J. (1990). Computer-assisted detection and intervention in adolescent high-risk health behaviors. *Journal of Pediatrics, 116,* 456–462.

Patterson, G. R., Reid, J. B., & Dishion, T. J. (1992). *Antisocial boys.* Eugene, OR: Castalia.

Pentz, M. A. (1985). Social competence skills and self-efficacy as determinants of substance use in adoelscents. In S. Shiffman & T. A. Wills (Eds.), *Coping and substance use* (pp. 117–142). New York: Academic Press.

Petchers, M. K., & Singer, M. I. (1987). Perceived Benefit of Drinking Scale: Approach to screening for adolescent alcohol abuse. *Journal of Pediatrics, 110,* 977–981.

Petraitis, J., & Flay, B. R., & Miller, T. Q. (1995). Reviewing theories of adolescent substance use: Organizing pieces in the puzzle. *Psychological Bulletin, 117,* 67–86.

Project MATCH (1997). Matching alcoholism treatments to client heterogeneity: Project MATCH posttreatment drinking outcomes. *Journal of Studies on Alcohol, 58,* 7–29.

Prosser, W. L. (1954). The narcotic problem. *UCLA Law Review, 1,* 405–546.

Rahdert, E. R. (Ed.) (1991). *The Adolescent Assessment/ Referral System Manual.* Rockville, MD: US Department of Health and Human Services.

Reinherz, H. Z., Giaconia, R. M., Lefkowitz, E. S., Pakiz, B., & Frost, A. K. (1993). Prevalence of psychiatric disorders in a community population of older adolescents. *Journal of the American Academy of Child and Adolescent Psychiatry, 32,* 369–377.

Rounsaville, B. J. (1987). An evaluation of the DSM-III substance-use disorders. In G. Tischler (Ed.), *Treatment and classification in psychiatry* (pp. 175–194). New York: Cambridge University Press.

Rush, T. V. (1979). Predicting treatment outcomes for juvenile and young-adult clients in the Pennsylvania substance-abuse system. In G. M. Beschner (Ed.) *Youth drug abuse: Problems, issues and treatments* (pp. 629–656). Lexington, MA: Lexington Books.

Santisteban, D. A., Szapocznik, J., Perez-Vidal, A., Kurtines, W. M., Murray, E. J., & LaPerriere, A. (1996). Efficacy of interventions for engaging youth/ families into treatment and some factors that may contribute to differential effectiveness. *Journal of Family Psychology, 10,* 35–44.

Schwartz, R. H., & Wirtz, P. W. (1990). Potential substance abuse detection among adolescent patients using the drug and alcohol (DAP) quick screen, a 30-item questionnaire. *Clinical Pediatrics, 29*(1), 38–43.

Scopetta, M. A., King, O. E., Szapocznik, J., & Tillman, W. (1979). *Ecological structural family therapy with Cuban immigrant families.* Report to the National Institute on Drug Abuse: Grant #H81DA 01696.

Sells, S. B., & Simpson, D. D. (1979). Evaluation of treatment outcome for youths in the Drug Abuse Reporting Program (DARP): A followup study. In G. M. Beschner (Ed.) *Youth drug abuse: Problems, issues and treatments* (pp. 571–628). Lexington, MA: Lexington Books.

Shedler, J., & Block, J. (1990). Adolescent drug use and psychological health: A longitudinal inquiry. *American Psychologist, 45,* 612–630.

Smith, T. E. (1983). Reducing adolescent's marijuana abuse. *Social Work in Health Care, 9,* 33–44.

Snow, D. L., Tebes, J. K., & Arthur, M. W. (1992). Panel attrition and external validity in adolescent substance use research. *Journal of Consulting and Clinical Psychology, 60,* 804–807.

Sobell, L. C., & Sobell, M. B. (1995). Alcohol consumption measures. In J. P. Allen & M. Columbus (Eds.), *Assessing alcohol problems: A guide for clinicians and researchers* (pp. 55–74). Rockville, MD: National Institutes of Health.

Stanton, M. D., & Shadish, W. R. (1997). Outcome attrition and family/couples treatment for drug abuse: A meta-analysis and review of the controlled, comparative studies. *Psychological Bulletin, 122,* 170–191.

Stanton, M. D., & Todd, T. C. (1982). *The family therapy of drug abuse and addiction.* New York: Guilford.

Stewart, D. G., & Brown, S. A. (1995). Withdrawal and dependency symptoms among adolescent alcohol and drug abusers. *Addiction, 90,* 627–635.

Substance Abuse and Mental Health Services Administration. (1996). *Preliminary estimates from the 1995 National Household Survey on Drug Abuse.* Washington, DC: US Government Printing Office.

Szapocznik, J., Kurtines, W. M., Foote, F. H., Perez-Vidal, A., & Hervis, O. (1983). Conjoint versus one-person family therapy: Some evidence for the effectiveness of conducting family therapy through one person. *Journal of Consulting and Clinical Psychology, 51,* 889–899.

Szapocznik, J., Kurtines, W. M., Foote, F. H., Perez-Vidal, A., & Hervis, O. (1986). Conjoint versus one-person family therapy: Further evidence for the effectiveness of conducting family therapy through one person with drug-abusing adolescents. *Journal of Consulting and Clinical Psychology, 54,* 395–397.

Szapocznik, J., Perez-Vidal, A., Brickman, A. L., Foote, F. H., Santisteban, D., Hervis, O, & Kurtines, W. M. (1988). Engaging adolescent drug abusers and their families in treatment: A strategic structural systems approach. *Journal of Consulting and Clinical Psychology, 56,* 552–557.

Tarter, R. E. (1990). Evaluation and treatment of adolescent substance abuse: A decision tree method. *American Journal of Drug and Alcohol Abuse, 16,* 1–46.

Tarter, R. E., & Hegedus, A. M. (1991). The Drug Use Screening Inventory: Its application in the evaluation and treatment of alcohol and other drug abuse. *Alcohol Health and Research World, 15*(1), 65–75.

Turner, R. M., Liddle, H., & Dakof, G. (1996, November). *Experimental evaluation of cognitive-behavior therapy for adolescent substance abuse.* Paper presented at the annual meeting of the Association for Advancement of Behavior Therapy, New York.

Vingilis, E., & Smart, R. G. (1981). Physical dependence on alcohol in youth. In Y. Israel, F. B. Gleser, & H. Kalant (Eds.), *Research advances in alcohol and drug problems* (Vol. 6, pp. 197–215). New York: Plenum.

Wagner, E. F., & Kassel, J. D. (1995). Substance use and abuse. In R. T. Ammerman, & M. Hersen (Eds.), *Handbook of child behavior therapy in the psychiatric setting* (pp. 367–388). New York: Wiley.

Waldron, H. B. (1996, November). *Developments in substance abuse assessment with adolescents.* Paper presented at the annual meeting of the Association for Advancement of Behavior Therapy, New York.

Waldron, H. B. (1997). Adolescent substance abuse and family therapy outcome: A review of randomized trials. In T. H. Ollendick & R. J. Prinz (Eds.), *Advances in clinical child psychology* (Vol. 19, pp. 199–234). New York: Plenum.

Waldron, H. B., & Slesnick, N. (1997, November).

Wanberg, K. W. (1991). *Adolescent Self-Assessment Profile.* Arvada, CO: Center for Alcohol/Drug Abuse Research and Evaluation.

Welte, J. W., & Barnes, G. M. (1985). Alcohol: The gateway to other drug use among secondary-school students. *Journal of Youth and Adolescence, 14,* 487–498.

Wheeler, K., & Malmquist, J. (1987). Treatment approaches in adolescent chemical dependency. *Chemical Dependency, 34,* 437–447.

White, H. R., & Labouvie, E. W. (1989). Towards the assessment of adolescent problem drinking. *Journal of Studies on Alcohol, 50,* 30–37.

Winters, K. C. (1992). Development of an adolescent alcohol and other drug abuse screening scale: Personal Experience Screening Questionnaire. *Addictive Behaviors, 17,* 479–490.

Winters, K. C., & Henly, G. A. (1988). Assessing adolescents who misuse chemicals: The Chemical Dependency Assessment Project. In E. R. Rahdert & J. Gradowski (Eds.), *Adolescent drug abuse: Analyses of treatment research* (pp. 4–18). Rockville, MD: National Institutes of Health.

Winters, K. C., & Henly, G. A. (1989). *Personal Experience Inventory Test and Manual.* Los Angeles, CA: Western Psychological Services.

Winters, K. C., & Henly, G. A. (1993). *Adolescent diagnostic interview schedule and manual.* Los Angeles: Western Psychological Services.

Winters, K. C., & Stinchfield, R. D. (1995). Current issues and future needs in the assessment of adolescent drug abuse. In E. Rahdert & D. Czechowicz (Eds.), *Adolescent drug abuse: Clinical assessment and therapeutic interventions* (pp. 146–171). Rockville, MD: National Institutes of Health.

5.22
Elimination Disorders

C. EUGENE WALKER
University of Oklahoma Health Sciences Center, Oklahoma City, OK, USA

5.22.1 INTRODUCTION

Toilet training is a ritual of considerable interest and concern to parents in all cultures, primitive and advanced (Hindley, Filliozat, Klackenberg, Nicolet-Meister, & Sand, 1965; Whiting & Child, 1964). Over the years, toilet training has been high on the list of concerns of parents with respect to the care of their young children (Ilg & Ames, 1962; Mesibov, Schroeder, & Wesson, 1977; Seim, 1989). It has generally ranked second or third in the list of concerns expressed by parents. The only area to consistently outrank toilet training has been the area of discipline and negative behavior in children.

Perusal of parents magazines and bookshelves with titles of interest to parents indicates a continuing and sustained interest in this area. Most parents spend a significant amount of time and effort in the process of toilet training and regard it as an important accomplishment when the process is complete. In many cultures the process is begun shortly after birth, even though physiological evidence would suggest that children do not have sufficient maturity or control of the muscles and nerves involved to be successful until approximately two years of age.

Although it may be argued that parents are, more concerned about this process than they need be, proper toilet training does serve numerous functions. Most obviously, parents wish to have their children toilet trained as early as possible in order to avoid the unpleasant task of changing diapers and sheets. Almost equal in importance, however, is the idea held by many parents that early completion of toilet training indicates that they are good parents and that their child is superior. Beyond this, the importance of proper toileting to good hygiene and prevention of illness should be noted. Finally, many personality theorists point to the importance of toilet training as an early experience in the socialization of the child (Lieberman, 1972). Parents regard the achievement of toilet training as evidence of a major step in their child's progress towards independence and that their child is normal.

For children, toilet training is the first major developmental challenge they face that is more important to others than to them. The child suddenly discovers that his or her ability to control what was once an involuntary internal process is a matter of extreme interest, as well as social significance, to others, and that failures in this area merit the displeasure of parents and peers alike. Freud saw this process as fundamental to the child's development of respect for authority and social mores.

In spite of the importance parents ascribe to toilet training, they may take widely different views about how to accomplish the process. Some parents take the attitude that it is not necessary to directly toilet train children. Their view being that when the time comes, the child will naturally develop (presumably by example of other family members) the idea that he or she should care for eliminative processes and do so on his or her own. Others, however, believe that children will not learn unless they as parents take an active role in the process. As a result, a great deal of time and energy is invested.

One of the most elaborate procedures for toilet training has been outlined in the book *Toilet training in less than a day* by Azrin and Foxx (1976). In this very ingenious approach to toilet training, the child is first helped to toilet train a doll of the type that wets when squeezed. The child and the parent make a game of training the doll. The doll is given fluid after which the parent and child squeeze the doll to produce wetting accidents. If the wetting takes place in an area designated as the toilet, the doll is praised. If the doll wets in the pants, it is scolded mildly. The child helps the doll check the pants and go to the toilet properly. During the time the child is training the doll, the child is given large quantities of favorite beverages to drink in order to produce a full bladder and the need to urinate. Having trained the doll, the parent and child begin a game in which the child does what was demonstrated on the doll. Dry pants' inspections are made every five minutes and a reward of praise or a small treat is given if the pants are dry. Every 15 minutes the child participates in a potty trial in which an effort is made to urinate, whether the child actually has an urge to do so or not. Azrin and Foxx recommend that a child's potty chair be used for these trials since it is easier for the child to mount and sit on such a chair. In addition, they suggest using the type of potty chair that plays a tune when the child urinates. This alerts the parent and child to the fact that urination is occurring and serves as an added incentive to the child. Eventually, on one of the potty trials, the child will be able to urinate. The parent praises the child for this accomplishment and gives the child a small reward. The child is then encouraged to return to the potty chair at any time he or she feels a need to urinate.

At the beginning of the training, the parent assumes a major part of the responsibility by directing the child in the activities prescribed by the training program. The parent begins to fade involvement by reducing direct involvement until the parent is providing only minimal prompts and reminders that the pants should be dry and that the child should go to the potty if necessary. As the child begins to assume responsibility for the process, the potty practice trials are stopped and checks are made for dry pants every 15 minutes. However, if an accident occurs during this time, the parent shows mild verbal displeasure, has the child feel the wet pants, and then instructs the child to carry out a series of "positive practice trials." These trials are carried out by first having the child start from the place in the house where the accident occurred, walk rapidly to the toilet, remove clothing, and sit on the toilet. The child then does this same procedure starting from other points in the house until a total of 10 trials are completed. The child then cleans himself or herself and is given fresh clothing. The parent reminds the child that pants should be kept dry and wetting should be done in the toilet. This procedure continues for several hours (it can generally be accomplished in a long morning or afternoon if the parent and child are not distracted by other family members or other duties) until the child is using the toilet appropriately and independently while maintaining dry pants. Should accidents occur, following the treatment, these are handled by additional positive practice trials.

A couple of other features of this program are also interesting. First, parents are encouraged to give the child a written certificate at the end of the training to mark the accomplishment. Second, a list of friends and relatives, whom the child admires, is developed. During the training, the parent mentions various individuals from this list as individuals who will be happy when the child has learned and who wish the child success. After the child is successful in the training, the child is permitted to call some individuals from the list to report the accomplishment and receive positive feedback. According to Azrin and Foxx, this method is highly successful and most children can be trained in less than four hours. However, it should be pointed out that some studies of this method (Butler, 1976; Matson & Ollendick, 1977) have reported that most parents do better with this training if they have professional consultation in addition to the book.

A much simpler approach to toilet training was developed by the pediatrician Brazelton (1962) who has made numerous other contributions to our knowledge and understanding of the care of children. Brazelton developed this approach over 30 years ago but it is very sound advice and still has much use today. He recommends that the pediatrician begin a discussion of toilet training with the parents at the nine month visit. He notes that it is about this time that grandparents, friends, and relatives begin to put subtle pressure on the

parents to see that the child is toilet trained. At this time, Brazelton simply discusses with the parents their attitudes about toilet training, attempts to reduce their anxiety, and encourages them to approach this in a relaxed, unpressured manner. He recommends that toilet training not begin at nine months. At around the age of 18 months, the first attempt is made to train the child.

The training begins by obtaining a small potty chair of the size used by children and identifying this as the child's own chair. An association is also made between this chair and the parents larger toilet chair. The parent then has the child sit on the chair with clothes on so that the chair will not feel cold or unfamiliar at the first sitting. The parent reads to the child and gives the child a small treat such as a cookie while the child sits on the chair. The child is not coerced and is free to leave the chair when they wish. After a week or so of getting the child familiar with sitting on the chair, the child is encouraged to sit on the chair without clothes or diapers. When the child is comfortable doing this, he or she is taken to the chair after a diaper has been soiled. The diaper is changed on the seat and the dirty diaper is dropped in to the pot under the child. The parent points out to the child that this is the eventual function of the chair. After doing this several times over a period of days, all diapers and pants are removed from the child for short periods of time when the parent thinks the child is likely to need to use the toilet. The toilet chair is placed in the room or play area near the child and the child is encouraged to use the potty chair. When the child follows through and uses the chair, the parent expresses approval and encourages the child to do this in the future. At this point, the child can be dressed in loose fitting training pants and taught to remove the training pants in order to use the potty chair when needed.

Nap and night training are not attempted until well after the child has mastered daytime control and shows an interest in staying clean and dry. This may coincide with achievement of daytime control or it may be as much as a year or two later. When the child shows an interest in having a dry bed, the parent can offer to help by waking him or her before the parent goes to bed so that the child can empty the bladder. In some cases, the parent may also have to wake the child a little earlier in the morning for toileting. The potty chair is placed beside the bed (Brazelton suggests painting the pot with luminous paint as an added incentive) and the child is encouraged to use the potty chair at any time during the night if needed. Brazelton stresses that these procedures should be carried out in a positive and supportive manner with the child. Where there are failures or problems, the parent is urged to stop the process and reassure the child that he or she is not bad for the failure. Optimism is expressed about success at some future time. Brazelton reported extremely good success with this method and, as a result, it has been widely used by pediatricians for many years.

The timing of toilet training is particularly important. As Walker (1978) has pointed out, toilet training is accomplished relatively easily when the child is ready to learn that skill. On the other hand, almost no amount of effort will produce the desired result if the child has not matured sufficiently and is not ready. Walker recommends attempting procedures similar to those outlined by Brazelton for a period of a week or two, when the child appears to be ready. If the learning takes place relatively effortlessly and with little power struggle, the process is complete and has been successful. However, if the child does not appear to be learning and if conflict is beginning to develop around the process, it is best to cease the training and to make another attempt after a period of about 3–6 months. This process is attempted every 3–6 months until the child is successful. It is extremely unwise to get into bitter power struggles and excessive conflict with the child over the process of toilet training. The disruption of the parent–child relationship is a much more serious problem than toilet training itself.

Signs of readiness that may be employed to determine when the first attempt at toilet training can be made have been outlined by Azrin and Foxx (1976). They suggest that the child be evaluated for physical readiness (does the child have enough finger and hand co-ordination to pick up objects easily and does the child walk easily from room to room without assistance) and instructional readiness (can the child point to the nose, eyes, mouth, or hair; can he or she follow directions to sit down on a chair, stand up, walk with you to a particular place, imitate you in a simple task such as playing patty cake, bring you a familiar object, and place one familiar object with another, for example, put the doll in the truck). A child is considered ready for toilet training when able to accomplish both physical readiness tasks and at least eight out of 10 instructional readiness tasks. Most children achieve this at around 20 months of age.

Brazelton suggests use of similar indices of physical maturation sufficient for toilet training and discusses what he calls "psychologic readiness," which is associated with a desire to control the impulses to defecate and urinate. This desire for control is derived from environmental influences including a secure and gratifying relationship with the parents, resulting in a desire to please them, a wish to identify with and imitate parents and other important adult figures, and the wish to develop autonomy and mastery of the primitive impulses to urinate and defecate. Physical and psychological readiness, according to Brazelton, is achieved by most children at around 18–30 months of age.

There is significant variation in readiness among children, due to the fact that children mature at different rates and often show growth spurts. In general, boys mature more slowly than girls. Individual differences as well as sex differences in developmental rates should be taken into account and children should not be hurried or rushed when they are not ready. Some of the claims of parents who assert that they have trained their children from birth or that their children achieved toilet training skill well before the age of two years should be taken with a grain of salt. Reports of early training are more likely situations in which it is the parent who has been trained to anticipate the child's elimination and to place the child on a potty chair. There is also an understandable exaggeration by parents of their child's accomplishments.

All of the above notwithstanding, the average age at which toilet training is completed varies somewhat from one culture to another. In some countries, there is considerable effort expended to toilet train and children appear to accomplish this goal at a somewhat younger age. Other cultures, which take a more relaxed approach, have statistics which indicate that successful toilet training occurs later in life. The same can be said for socioeconomic levels within a culture. Individuals of higher socioeconomic status generally spend a great deal more effort at toilet training their children and report younger ages for achievement than do individuals of lower socioeconomic status. Unfortunately, precise data on the amount of variability are not available. Therefore, although it is possible to influence the age of toilet training to an extent, by aggressive involvement with the child, the process can only be influenced within certain limits and it is questionable whether the stress and conflict involved are worth it. For example, Whiting and Child (1964), in their classic cross-cultural study of the effects of child rearing on personality, noted that of 22 societies compared there was a wide range of attitudes and expectations regarding toilet training. At one extreme are the Tamala of Madagascar where bowel training begins between the ages of two and three months and the child is expected to be continent by the age of six months. The other extreme is represented by the Dena of Africa where toilet training is not even begun until the child is almost five years of age. Most societies studied began toilet training somewhere between the ages 1.5 and 2.5 years. Those favoring early training found it necessary to use frequent and severe punishment. American culture tends to be mid-range in terms of the age at which toilet training is begun and in the severity of the measures used in training. In the early part of this century, relatively severe and early training practices were the mode. Currently, following the suggestions of Brazelton and Spock, more gentle and gradual approaches are endorsed by most parents.

Given the interest and concern of many parents in the toilet training process, it is not surprising that failures in this process result in numerous requests for professional help. Pediatricians, psychologists, and others who provide health care for children are frequently consulted for advice in treating children who are enuretic (unable to control the process of urination) or encopretic (unable to control bowel function). These two topics and certain related disorders will be considered in the remainder of this chapter.

5.22.2 ENURESIS

5.22.2.1 Phenomenonology

Children who experience difficulty with controlling urine have a number of personal and emotional reactions to this difficultly. First, they are often teased and ridiculed by their peers when the peers learn about it either by seeing a daytime accident or hearing about one that occurred at night. The child's parents generally show considerable anxiety about the fact that their child has not learned to control urine and, as a result, there is often a great deal of displeasure and even disgust directed toward the child. This frequently results in parent–child conflict and, in extreme cases, can even result in child abuse. For a child, it is often a mystery that all of a sudden so many people should be so concerned about a process that was virtually ignored previously. Thus, a two- or three-year-old child who is being toilet trained by the parents may wonder why there has been such a change in attitude and rules regarding this behavior. If bedwetting accidents continue into later childhood years, or if a child who has been dry for a while begins to wet again, he or she may be similarly mystified as to what is happening and why there should be so much social disgrace attached to it. Generally, the child feels that this process is uncontrollable and does not understand why people consider it a fault. Biology is on the side of the young child, at

least, because the process of urination begins as a reflex in the infant and then must be controlled by the child as he or she develops. Nevertheless, the parental disapproval, peer ridicule, and seeming inability of the child to do anything about the problem results in considerable anxiety and loss of self esteem. George Orwell expressed this very well in his autobiography. He was a student at an English boarding school and records:

> It was looked upon as a disgusting crime which the child committed on purpose and for which the proper cure was a beating. For my part I did not need to be told it was a crime. Night after night I prayed with a fervor never previously attained in my prayers, "please God, do not let me wet my bed! Oh, please God, do not let me wet my bed!", but it made remarkably little difference. Some nights the thing happened, others not. There was no volition about it, no consciousness. You did not properly speaking *do* the deed: you merely woke up in the morning and found that the sheets were wringing wet. (Orwell, 1970 p. 379)

Orwell did eventually receive two severe beatings for this behavior at the hands of the principal of his school. After these beatings, he did not wet the bed again but the emotional scars remained.

In addition to the significant emotional consequences surrounding the problem of enuresis and the misguided attempts to correct it, there are other social consequences. For example, children often cannot participate in overnight parties, camping trips, and similar events due to the fact that they would possibly wet the bed. There are also significant problems when staying in hotels or motels or visiting relatives and friends, should the child wet the bed. As a result, children are often left out of significant activities because of their "problem."

DeGraaf, a chemical engineer, has described his frustrating experiences with enuresis and unsuccessful treatment in a paper entitled "Forty years of being treated for nocturnal enuresis" (1992). Eventually, desmopressin acetate (DDAVP) solved the problem in his case. Studies have demonstrated improvement in social relationships and self esteem following successful treatment of enuresis (Moffatt, 1989; Moffatt, Kato, & Pless, 1987).

5.22.2.2 Diagnostic Features

The 10th edition of the *International Classification of Diseases* (ICD-10) (World Health Organization [WHO], 1992a) contains the category "non-organic enuresis" (F 98.0) which is described as involuntary voiding of urine during the day or night which is abnormal in relation to the individual's mental age and not due to any organic or structural cause. This condition may have been present from birth (primary enuresis) or may develop following a period during which the child previously acquired bladder control (secondary enuresis). There may or may not be widespread emotional or behavioral disorder associated with this condition. The volume on *Clinical Description and Diagnostic Guidelines* discusses the possible relationship between the two and concludes that there is no simple way to decide if emotional problems result from, cause, or simply coexist with enuresis. The clinician is instructed to make a judgement in his or her own opinion for each case as to what constitutes the main problem. This same volume amplifies the age criteria by stating that there is no clear cut off, but generally the diagnosis would not be made unless the child has reached a chronological age of five years and a mental age of four years. The descriptors employed in this definition are rather vague and very general (the volume on research diagnostic criteria, 1993, is more precise and fairly similar to the American Psychiatric Association's *DSM-IV* [1994]). The *DSM-IV Diagnostic and statistical manual of mental disorders* contains the diagnostic category "307.6 Enuresis" (not due to a general medical condition). This diagnosis is defined much more precisely than that in *ICD-10* in that it requires: (i) there be repeated voiding of urine into bed or clothes, either involuntary or intentional; (ii) the behavior must be clinically significant in the sense that it is either of a frequency of at least twice a week for three consecutive months or the presence of the wetting causes significant distress or impairment in social, academic, or other important areas of functioning; (iii) the child is chronologically or developmentally at least five years of age; and (iv) the disorder is not due to a physiological effect from a substance (such as a medication) or from any general organic medical condition. In the *DSM-IV* system the diagnostician is instructed to specify the type which can be nocturnal only, diurnal only, or nocturnal and diurnal (*ICD-10* permits this but does not require it). The essence of both of these diagnoses revolves around the concept that, in the absence of organic disorder, the child is not controlling the process of urination when he or she should be able to do so (approximately five years of age) and is experiencing distress or impairment of functioning as a result of this condition. It is interesting to note that *ICD-10* mentions primary and secondary enuresis, whereas *DSM-IV* currently makes no mention of that distinction; however, *DSM-IV* is explicit

about the need to specify whether wetting is day (diurnal) or night (nocturnal) or both. The decision by the writers of *DSM-IV* to specify "clinically significant" as a part of the definition is admirable, but their choice is certainly problematic at times. The requirement that wetting be at least twice a week for at least three consecutive months; or causing distress or impairment in important areas of functioning is a case of comparing apples with oranges. To start with, the frequencies chosen are fairly arbitrary and overly specific, while the term "distress or impairment" is overly vague. Strictly speaking, if the child wet only once (rather than twice) in any given week during the three month period, the child would not qualify as enuretic. On the other hand, if the child wet only once in a similar period but did so under circumstances that were very embarrassing or upsetting, the child could be diagnosed as enuretic.

5.22.2.3 Prevalence

There have been numerous studies of the prevalence of enuresis and the results vary quite widely from one source to another. The major reasons for these discrepencies appear to be differences in the definition of enuresis, differences in populations studied, sampling variations, and methods of data collection. In spite of somewhat conflicting results, there does appear to be some consensus regarding the rate of enuresis.

Physiologically, all children wet during the day and night at birth. By definition, enuresis is not diagnosed until the age of five. Although *DSM-IV* states that the rate for enuresis at age five is 7% for males and 3% for females, the most commonly reported estimate is that approximately 15–20% of five-year-old children are enuretic (Fergusson, Hons, Horwood, & Shannon, 1986; Oppel, Harper, & Rider, 1968). Rates steadily decline until, by the midteens, only approximately 1–2% of males and less than 1% of females would be diagnosable as enuretic. The spontaneous annual remission rate has been estimated at approximately 15% (deJonge, 1973; Forsythe & Redmond, 1974). In some instances, enuresis continues into adulthood. Studies of military recruits suggest that there is a 1–2% prevalence in young adult males (Plag, 1964). Boys are more likely to have problems with enuresis than girls. Some reports suggest that boys may be twice as likely to be involved as girls; however, these data frequently come from clinic-referred patients, and the higher rate of referral of boys for behavior problems may bias these statistics.

Studies in the community at large show some higher incidence in males but not remarkably higher (Fergusson et al., 1986; McGee, Makinson, Williams, Simpson, & Silva 1984; Oppel et al., 1968). Given that girls mature more rapidly than boys, a slightly higher rate in boys would be expected.

Diurnal enuresis is considerably less prevalent than nocturnal enuresis. For example, Hjalmas (1992a) found that only 3.1% of seven-year-old boys and 2.1% of seven-year-old girls experienced day wetting at least once per week. No doubt due to the fact that it is much less common, considerably less is known about diurnal enuresis. Some have speculated that diurnal enuresis may be more common in females than in males; that it may be more likely to occur in children who show signs of emotional disturbance; and may be more difficult to treat, especially if it occurs in older children (deJonge, 1973; Lovibond & Coote, 1970; Shaffer, 1973). Some clinicians are of the opinion that bedwetting in older teenagers and adults may frequently be related to prior child abuse, especially sexually abuse. Although only a small percentage of night-time wetters also wet during the day, a significant percentage (possibly as much as 50–60%) of those with daytime wetting problems also wet the bed at night (Hallgren, 1956). With respect to the primary vs. secondary distinction regarding enuresis, approximately 85% of all cases are considered primary. There is a tendency, as would be expected, for this to decrease with age. Secondary enuresis generally appears between the years of five and eight (APA, 1994). Enuresis is more prevalent in lower socioeconomic levels and in families where the mother has less education (Bakwin & Bakwin, 1972; MacKeith, Meadow, & Turner, 1973). Although there has not been sufficient research to clarify the reason for this, it is no doubt related to different attitudes regarding hygiene in general and toilet training in particular.

5.22.2.4 Etiology

There are three basic approaches to understanding the etiology of enuresis: biological factors, emotional factors, and learning. Each of these areas is briefly examined to determine what it can contribute to the overall understanding of the etiology of this problem.

5.22.2.4.1 *Biological factors*

It should be emphasized that urinary incontinence can be caused by numerous organic factors, ranging from anomalies of the nervous system, the bladder, or other structures of the urinary system to various types of bladder infections to secondary effects from chronic disease or other illnesses. However enuresis is by definition a functional disorder and, therefore, not the result of organic factors. Enuresis is functional urinary incontinence. Although specific organic pathology is explicitly ruled out of consideration with respect to the etiology of enuresis, various approaches to understanding the etiology presuppose some sort of general biological or physiological process underlying the problem. A wide range of factors have been proposed in this realm. Two that have a reasonable amount of support from the research literature are genetics and developmental delay. It has long been known that enuresis runs in families and tends to show the same general trends that are characteristic of disorders that are genetically determined (Bakwin, 1961; Elian, 1991; Fergusson et al., 1986).

Although there is fairly general support for the notion of a genetic influence in enuresis, there is very little sophisticated genetic research on this problem and no specific mechanism or gene has been determined to explain the inheritance of enuresis. For example, it is not possible to predict the inheritance of enuresis for specific individuals within a family. The most that can be said is that it runs in families.

Numerous clinicians and researchers over the years have suspected some sort of developmental delay as the basis for enuresis. Developmental delay is a very vague and nonspecific concept. In the present instance, it would no doubt refer to some delay in neurological development. Some studies have indicated that children who are enuretic are slow in achieving certain developmental milestones (MacKeith, 1972) but other studies have failed to replicate such findings. Developmental delays, when noted, are generally mild and it is questionable whether they would be sufficient to account for the presence of a condition such as enuresis, especially since physiologically the ability should be in place by 2–5 years of age.

Closely related to the developmental delay hypothesis has been the idea that a mild form of organic brain pathology may be involved in enuresis. The usual suspect is some sort of epileptic seizure during the night. Although it is true that individuals who have epileptic seizures often lose control of their urine, the majority of enuretic children do not suffer diagnosable seizure disorders and careful research has failed to produce significant pathology in terms of electroencephalograms (EEGs) in enuretic children (Mikkelsen, Brown, Minichiello, Millican, & Rapoport, 1982; Salmon, Taylor, & Lee, 1973).

A great deal of interest has centered recently on the possibility that the antidiuretic hormone (ADH) may be the cause of enuresis for some children. George, Messerli, and Genest (1975) have noted a circadian rhythm variation in the excretion of the ADH vasopressin in normal subjects in which there was an increase in secretion during the night. Other studies indicated that this increase did not occur in enuretic children (e.g., Rittig, Knudsun, Norgaard, Pedersen, & Djurhuus, 1989). Enuretic children with lower levels of ADH have been shown to produce larger quantities of dilute urine than normal children with the consequence that the probability of bed wetting is increased. However, later research has failed to confirm the earlier findings of a relatively direct path from low ADH levels to increased production of urine, polyuria and bedwetting (Evans & Meadow, 1992; Watanabe, Kawauchi, Kitamori, & Azuma, 1994). This approach seems to have some merit; however, considerably more research is needed before it will be fully understood.

Another possible factor of a biological nature in producing enuresis is what has been referred to as low functional bladder capacity. A child with low functional bladder capacity feels the need to urinate with lower amounts of urine present in the bladder than other children, and consequently voids smaller quantities of urine more frequently. Some investigators have reported smaller functional bladder capacity in enuretic children and have speculated that this limited bladder capacity results in night time wetting (Starfield, 1967; Zaleski, Gerrard, & Shokeir, 1973). However, there is evidence that the functional bladder capacities for enuretics and nonenuretics show considerable overlap (Rutter, 1973) and increases in functional bladder capacity have not been shown to be reliably related to improvement in enuretic children (Starfield & Mellits, 1968).

In addition, sleep disorder may be a biological factor involved in some cases of enuresis. Certainly, parents who present their children for treatment of enuresis almost uniformly report that their child is an exceedingly deep sleeper. Unfortunately, studies that have attempted to measure depth of sleep of bed wetters have failed to show consistent results (Mikkelsen et al., 1980). Although it is plausible to assume that some sort of sleep disorder is related to enuresis, no firm conclusion can be drawn until further research is done. Somewhat related to the sleep etiology of enuresis are various reports that have appeared in the literature, suggesting that sleep apnea may be related to the problem. For example, Weider and Hauri (1985), as well as Timms (1989), have reported

that use of surgery or mechanical devices designed to improve breathing while asleep have resulted in reduction or cessation of bedwetting in a small number of children where this was a problem. Unfortunately, these reports, to date, are all anecdotal and lacking in scientific control. Even if further research were to substantiate this, it would account for only a small proportion of the total number of cases of enuresis.

Finally, food allergies have occasionally been implicated as a biological factor contributing to enuresis (e.g., Egger, Carter, Soothill, & Wilson, 1992). The idea that diet or food allergies may play some part in production of enuresis is certainly intriguing. Various foods are known to affect numerous other body systems; however, research demonstrating a link between food allergies or diet and enuresis, as well as an explanatory mechanism, is currently lacking. Clearly, more research is needed in this area. Should such factors be determined, they may be useful as a first approach to treatment for some cases and as a supplementary approach in others. Since most individuals overcome enuresis by treatment or spontaneous remission without any significant change in diet, it is almost certainly not primarily due to dietary factors.

5.22.2.4.2 Emotional factors

The idea that emotional factors may play a major role in the development of enuresis has a long history. In fact, in previous years many mental health workers were convinced that enuresis was synonymous with some sort of emotional disorder or neurotic conflict. Enuresis was often thought to be related to depression and that wetting was a type of "weeping through the bladder" (Imhof, 1956) or that it might be associated with some sort of sexual conflict in which the urination was symbolic of ejaculation or lubrication (Fenichel, 1946). Others thought that anger might be the major emotional factor and that the wetting was a type of passive aggressiveness against the mother (Soloman & Patch, 1969). Inappropriate or severe toilet training efforts were often implicated. It was frequently noted that a significant amount of family dysfunction, conflict, and other forms of pathology were present in cases where a child was enuretic. Clinicians and researchers thought they saw certain personality characteristics in enuretic children, most commonly immaturity. However, careful research has failed to support any of these notions. Most of these ideas appear to have resulted from a bias in referral patterns to mental health professionals vs. pediatricians. Most enuretic children are treated by pediatricians. Those who show signs of emotional disturbance are generally referred to mental health professionals. As a result, mental health professionals and their literature developed around the idea that some form of emotional disturbance was involved. Studies comparing large unselected samples of enuretic children vs. nonenuretic children failed to find significant relationships between emotional disturbance and enuresis, or to determine any enuretic personality profile (Cullen, 1966; Tapia, Jekel, & Domke, 1960).

The following points appear to be supported by the bulk of the literature and summarize the relationship between emotional disturbance and enuresis. First, the majority of enuretic children are not emotionally disturbed. Second, most emotionally disturbed children are not enuretic. Third, there is, however, a higher incidence of enuresis among emotionally disturbed children than there is among the general population. This area of overlap is relatively modest but has led to considerable misunderstanding. There is no specific diagnosis, emotional condition, or personality pattern associated with enuresis. Although clinical folklore suggests that secondary enuresis is more likely than primary enuresis to be associated with emotional disturbance, research has failed to confirm this (Fritz & Anders, 1979; Cho, 1984). Although data are minimal and somewhat conflicting, there may be a slight increase in the likelihood that emotional disturbance will be present along with enuresis if the enuretic is female, older, and if daytime wetting is present (Moilanen, Jarvelin, Vikevainen-Tervonen, & Huttunen, 1987; Rutter, Tizard, & Whitmore, 1970: Wagner, Smith, & Norris, 1988). Basically, enuresis and emotional disturbance must be thought of as separate categories, which can overlap. The overlap may be accounted for by the fact that emotional distress inhibits learning the necessary skills to control urine, or the distraction of emotional problems may result in a loss of performance of effective urine control techniques that were previously learned. The conflict and rejection suffered by enuretic children may also create emotional distress. At any rate, in most circumstances, the connection between the two is incidental rather than inherent.

5.22.2.4.3 *Learning factors*

The third and probably most useful explanation for the etiology of enuresis has to do with learning principles. This approach assumes that enuresis is a learning problem. The basic rationale of the approach is as follows. At birth, the process of urination is essentially reflexive. When a sufficient amount of urine has collected in the bladder, the bladder reflexively empties. Through experience, individuals learn to delay and inhibit this reflex for relatively long periods of time. However, even adults are often acutely aware of the fact that urination is basically reflexive and that they may not be able to inhibit this reflex indefinitely. At these times, finding a toilet facility is essential. During their developmental years, children are attempting to master the basic learning task of controlling this reflexive behavior. Enuretic children may be regarded as children who are experiencing difficulty in learning this behavior.

Children master many different tasks at different rates, and therefore it is not unexpected that some children will be delayed in developing this skill. That boys have more trouble with this than girls fits with the fact that males mature physically more slowly than females. Genetic factors, neurological factors such as developmental delay, and other biological factors may well play a part in predisposing the enuretic child to have difficulty learning this skill. The learning approach can also readily incorporate many features of the theory of an emotional basis for the etiology of enuresis. It is well known that emotionality interferes with learning or disrupts performance based on previous learning. Emotional distress may, thus, result in enuresis or delay the learning of control. In addition, family dysfunction or laxity in toilet training as well as conflict regarding failures in this respect could readily be seen as contributing to poor achievement. Ineffective or inappropriate toilet training methods would also be expected to result in poor learning. Thus, a learning theory explanation of the problem of enuresis fits best with the facts and encompasses all known information effectively. It also leads to effective treatment strategies, as described later in this chapter.

5.22.2.5 Developmental Course

The developmental course of enuresis is relatively easily described. Urinary incontinence is 100% at birth and steadily declines by approximately 15% per year until midteens when it reaches a level of around 1–2% which continues through adulthood. Most children achieve urinary continence between the ages of three and five with girls achieving this task somewhat more easily than boys. Those who do not learn urinary continence by age five or who lose this ability following a period of continence, are labeled enuretic.

5.22.2.6 Conceptualization and Clinical Formulation

5.22.2.6.1 Multimodal assessment

The assessment of enuretic children has been discussed in detail elsewhere (Walker & Shaw, 1988). The first step should always be a physical examination by a competent physician. Since enuresis is defined as a functional problem, the possibility of organic disease or etiology should be ruled out with care. Typically, a pediatrician or family physician would be able to accomplish this by relatively simple and noninvasive procedures involving an examination of the external genitalia, medical history, and urine analysis. Should a medical condition be diagnosed, this should be treated first. Frequently, after the medical condition is resolved, enuresis continues and may require further treatment. The family physician or pediatrician may do more extensive tests or, on rare occasions, refer the patient to a urologist for further testing. Medical tests that are sometimes, but rarely, required involve x ray, urodynamic testing, uroflowmetry, electromyography, cystometrography, urethral pressure profilimetry, and cystoscopy, for example. These tests are described in considerable detail by Maizels, Gandhi, Keating, and Rosenbaum (1993). In the majority of cases where a child is wetting, explanation for the problem will not reside in organic pathology. Nevertheless, when a medically diagnosable and treatable condition is present that should be tended to first.

Once general medical pathology has been ruled out or corrected, an in-depth psychological assessment is in order. This should begin with a careful history taken by interview that will include aspects of a typical intake interview to determine whether or not psychopathology of any sort is present in the child. Should there be suggestions of psychopathology, these should be explored through standard psychological testing and other assessment procedures. In some instances, where there is significant psychopathology, it is clinically advisable to treat the more serious pathology rather than attempting to treat enuresis in the presence of such pathology. The presence of severe pathology interferes with the treatment of enuresis and makes the outcome problematic. It is important to keep this in mind because practitioners who treat enuretic children often receive referrals from physicians that ostensibly are for the purpose of enuresis but, upon examination, reveal severe personal and/or family pathology that is the real reason for referral. Many physicians prefer to avoid confrontation with patients regarding their emotional difficulties and use enuresis as a token for referral.

If severe psychopathology is not present, treatment for enuresis may be undertaken. In cases where there is mild to moderate psychopathology present, a decision will need to be made as to whether the enuresis should be tackled early on or later in treatment. Often, achievement of success in control of urine enhances self-esteem and encourages progress of the child in other treatment. On the other hand, control of urine may not be possible until other problems are dealt with successfully.

Specific to the problem of enuresis, there should be a complete functional analysis including such things as onset of the problem, frequency, amount of urine expelled, number of times the child uses the bathroom during the day, whether or not urgency is present, reaction of the child and others in the family to the problem, discussion of past attempts at treatment (and their success or failure), family history of enuresis, effects on the child's functioning (especially socialization), power struggles that may be going on in the family regarding the problem, motivation of the child and family to overcome the problem, sleeping arrangements and habits of the child and the family, times at which the wetting accidents occur (day or night), whether or not child abuse (physical or sexual) has occurred, and other factors unique to the child that may play a part in the problem. Following this evaluation, the clinician may find it useful to use a scale developed by Morgan and Young (1975) which is designed to evaluate parental reactions to enuresis. In addition to a careful assessment of the motivation to participate in treatment of the problem, the clinician should carefully evaluate the acceptability of the various approaches to treatment that are described later in this chapter. Since there are a wide variety of approaches to the treatment of enuresis, it is wise to involve the parents and child in the selection of the treatment options.

5.22.2.6.2 Treatment formulation

As noted in the section on etiology, there is a wide range of possible factors that appear to have some relationship to enuresis. These factors involve everything from organic illness through biological/physiological predisposing factors through emotional difficulties to learning problems. Formulation of the case when dealing with an enuretic child will involve careful consideration of all possibilities and blending those factors that appear relevant into a treatment conceptualization and strategy. Depending on the particular blend of factors present, different treatment strategies may be expected to have more or less success and may be more or less acceptable to the child and family. As noted earlier, the general framework of a behavioral or learning theory approach has been found most useful by the majority of clinicians and readily incorporates factors from the other two major approaches to etiology. Thus, an overall strategy of viewing the problem as a failure to learn or to achieve competence in performing the task of controlling urine is clinically useful. The clinician can see his or her role as serving as consultant/coach to the child and family as they work on a resolution of the problem.

5.22.2.7 Treatment

Over the centuries, hundreds of different treatments have been attempted for the problem of enuresis. Glicklich (1951) has reviewed the history of the treatment of enuresis in what is now a classic article. From this review, we know that enuresis has been considered a problem since at least 1515 BC, when a medical text of that era recommended juniper berries, cypress, and beer as medication for enuresis. In subsequent times, numerous concoctions were prepared for the treatment of enuresis. Frequently, these concoctions were ground-up organs or tissue from animals such as the flesh of a hedgehog, the claws of a goat, or the trachea of a cock. At other times, they involved ingestion of a wide variety of chemicals, some of which may actually have been dangerous. Likewise, various substances were injected or applied to the sacral area. These applications and injections were theorized to stimulate the nerves in this area, thus producing continence. One of the more barbaric treatments involved burning blisters in the area. It was thought that the blistering would stimulate the sacral nerves. Cauterization of the opening of the urethra with silver nitrate was employed because it was thought that making this portion of the urethra more tender to the passage of urine would force the child to retain the urine. Occasionally, attempts were even made to seal the opening to the urethra with some substance during the night to prevent the passage of urine. Some thought that the warmth from the bed on the sacral nerves might cause bedwetting, or that the position of lying on the back was conducive to wetting. As a result, there were a number of instruments such as spikes or knotted ropes that were wrapped around the child to prevent the child from lying on their back during sleep.

Various other kinds of rotation of the body at different angles (such as elevating the feet, pelvis, or genitals) were also thought to be beneficial in preventing bedwetting. An apparatus popular during the nineteenth century involved insertion into the rectum of a metallic bung shaped like an elongated olive or small hens egg. Soldered to this bung was a piece of metal that simultaneously exerted pressure on the perineum and the coccygeal region of the spine. Whether a child could sleep comfortably with this device in place is open to serious question; however, it did appear to cut down on bedwetting. Various primitive tribes have employed a variety of measures for the treatment of enuresis, most involving punishment or ridicule. For example, one West African tribe pours a mixture of water and ashes on the head of the child. The child is then driven out into the street while other children of the village clap their hands and run after him or her singing "urine everywhere, urine everywhere." The Navajo indians were known to use a treatment during which the child stood naked with his or her legs spread over the burning nest of a Phoebe. This was thought to help because birds don't wet their nest. Mowrer and Mowrer (1938), in their classic article on the development of the pad-and-bell technique for treatment of enuresis, noted that the following treatments had been employed from time to time:

> innumerable drugs and hormones; special diets (including fresh fruit, caviar, and bacilli); restriction of fluids; voluntary exercises in urinary control; injections of physiological saline, sterile water, paraffin, and other inert substances; real and sham operations; passage of a bougie; public application of cantharides plasters; cauterization of the neck of the bladder; spinal punctures; tonsillectomy; circumcision, clitoridotomy, etc.; high-frequency mechanical vibration and electrical stimulation of various parts of the body; massage; bladder and rectal irrigations; Roentgen and other forms of irradiation; chemical neutralization of the urine; sealing or constriction of the urinary orifice; hydrotherapy; local freezing of the external genitalia with ice or chloratyl; elevation of the foot of the patients bed; sleeping on the back; not sleeping on the back; and use of a hard mattress.

Although some of these treatments may be around in one form or another today, most of them are completely without merit and are no longer used. In fact, some are dangerous. The admonition in the hippocratic oath to, "first do no harm," is very applicable to the case of enuresis. One must seriously consider the advantage of eliminating wet clothes or sheets, as opposed to the danger or risk of a treatment contemplated. Whether the danger is the possibility of physical harm to the child or emotional harm and disruption of the parent–child bond, the potential benefits of treatment may not warrant the risk. This is especially true for younger children since time is a definite ally in elimination of enuresis.

5.22.2.7.1 Psychosocial treatments

(i) Support and encouragement

Most books providing advice to parents and most textbooks for clinicians working with children suggest that the initial attempt to deal with enuresis involves talking with the child in an effort to give the child support and encouragement in his or her attempt to overcome the problem. Often, this will involve a brief medical examination so that the child can be reassured that there is nothing physically wrong or dangerous. The parents are advised to avoid conflict or punishment and to praise the child or provide some reward for success. This is often coupled with restriction of fluids, elimination of any drinks containing caffeine (coffee, tea, cola, soft drinks, etc.), and emptying the bladder just before retiring.

(ii) Periodic awaking

A number of different attempts have been made to use waking the child at night as a means of preventing bedwetting (Creer & Davis, 1975; Young, 1964). The simplest form of this intervention is for the parent to wake the child before the parent goes to bed, so that the child can urinate one more time before attempting to sleep till morning. In other versions, parents attempt to determine the time at which the child wets. The child is then woken 30 minutes prior to the anticipated time of the wetting. Over a period of time the waking time is moved in increments closer and closer to the actual bedtime of the child until the last voiding coincides with going to bed. Other versions employ the opposite strategy if the wetting typically occurs just before getting up in the morning. In these cases, the child is woken earlier than normal and prior to the wetting. The waking time is then gradually made later and later until it coincides with the normal time for getting up in the morning. Generally, waking is left up to the parents. However, some clinicians, especially with older children, employ an alarm clock which the child uses to wake up with.

(iii) Retention control and sphincter exercises

As noted earlier in this chapter, many children who have bedwetting problems appear to have a small functional bladder capacity. These children are noted to urinate frequently during the day and to have a great deal of urgency when they need to urinate (Sorotzkin, 1984; Starfield, 1967). The length of time the child is in bed and asleep exceeds the functional capacity of their bladder, resulting in bedwetting.

Consideration of this led to the development of two approaches to treatment that involve exercises (Miller, 1973). The first exercise involves urine retention. The child is instructed to go to the bathroom and to prepare to urinate, but retain urine as long as possible before beginning the urination process. The child is then encouraged to hold the urine longer each time the urge to urinate occurs. Eventually the child develops control to the point where it is measured in minutes. At this time, the child is allowed to leave the bathroom area and return at a later time to void. A delay of between 30 and 45 minutes is generally encouraged between the first urge to urinate and actual voiding. The approach is based on the rationale that urine retention exercises will increase the tolerance of the bladder for larger and larger volumes of urine.

Sphincter control exercises involve having the child start and stop the stream of urine once urination has begun. The sphincter control exercises are based on the rationale that these exercises increase the voluntary control of the sphincter, thus enabling the child to prevent urination.

(iv) Psychotherapy and family therapy

Use of psychotherapy and/or family therapy for the treatment of enuresis is based on the concept that some personality problem or family dysfunction may be the cause of the problem. As indicated earlier in this chapter there is little empirical evidence to support this position. Nevertheless, individual psychotherapy, family therapy, neurolinguistic reprogramming and use of metaphors have appeared in the literature as possible treatments (Crowley & Mills, 1986; Protinsky & Dillard, 1983; Rydzinski & Kaplan, 1985; Selig, 1982; Wood, 1988).

(v) Hypnosis

A variety of case reports and studies have appeared in the literature employing hypnosis in the treatment of enuresis (Banerjee, Srivastav, & Palan, 1993; Collison, 1970; Kohen, Olness, Corwell, & Heimel, 1980). Following hypnotic induction, the child is encouraged to visualize the urinary system and is given suggestions about holding back urine while asleep, or waking to use the toilet if not able to hold the urine back.

(vi) Cognitive interventions

With the increased interest in cognitive approaches to psychotherapy, attempts have been made to develop treatment programs for enuresis based on cognitive interventions. One such approach (Ronen & Wozner, 1995; Ronen, Wozner, & Rahav, 1992) involves four steps: modification of maladaptive concepts, understanding the enuresis process, increasing bladder control, and developing self-control. This appears to be a well designed protocol involving concepts common in a number of approaches to cognitive therapy. In addition, the bladder control phase involves retention control exercises.

(vii) Pad-and-bell treatment

Treatment of enuresis using a urine alarm was discovered by accident in the early part of the twentieth century by a German physician named Pfaunder. Pfaunder was working in a children's institution where the staff were instructed to change diapers promptly for children who were wet, in order to prevent skin irritation and infection. Pfaunder developed a device that was arranged so that when the child wet, a bell rang to signal to the staff that changing of the diaper was needed.

Pfaunder and the staff at the home were surprised to discover that under these conditions the number of wetting episodes decreased and in many cases ceased (Lovibond & Coote, 1970). Later, Mowrer and Mowrer (1938) experimented with variations of this procedure and demonstrated that it was highly effective in eliminating bedwetting in children. Following the work by the Mowrers, numerous devices were marketed that involved placing a pad in the bed of the child that was connected to a bell and/ or light.

When the child urinated on to the pad, this completed an electrical circuit resulting in the ringing of a bell and/or turning on of a light to wake the child to go to the toilet.

Thousands of simple units of this sort were sold through the medical aids sections of major department store catalogs. In addition, numerous companies marketed devices through newspaper, magazine, and door-to-door sales efforts. Currently, a variety of simplified devices are available on the market that accomplish the same thing. These simplified devices involve sewing a small electrode into the undergarments of the child which responds when wet and activates a buzzer that is attached via a velcro strip to the shoulder of the child's pajamas or which is worn as a wristwatch. The buzzer wakes the child.

(viii) Multiple intervention package programs

A number of books and protocols have appeared in the literature that incorporate multiple components in the treatment of enuresis. These often involve such components as retention control and sphincter exercises, support and encouragement, pad-and-bell, positive practice, rewards, and periodic waking. Two of the most widely known and more carefully researched programs of this sort are dry-bed training (Azrin, Sneed, & Foxx, 1973) and full-spectrum home training (Houts, Liebert, & Padawer, 1983). An excellent description of the latter is available in *Bedwetting: A guide for parents and children* (Houts & Liebert, 1984). These programs are elaborate and require considerable training and supervision of the parents in order to complete them. Some work best when the treatment is carried out by trained assistants.

5.22.2.7.2 Pharmacological treatments

Although virtually every medication or chemical in existence has been administered to children in attempt to control bedwetting, there are currently only three medications that are used with any frequency (Miller, Atkin, & Moody, 1992). The most commonly prescribed medication is imipramine (Tofranil). The exact mechanism by which this medication is helpful in the treatment of enuresis is not clearly understood. A second medication often used is oxybutynin chloride (Ditropan). This drug reduces spasms of the bladder and appears to make the bladder less sensitive, resulting in an increase in functional bladder capacity. The third medication that has aroused a great deal of interest is desmopressin acetate (DDAVP). This medication is a synthetic form of vasopressin, which is a hormone that stimulates the kidneys to concentrate urine. Concentration of the urine reduces the amount of urine produced during the night, and appears to thereby enable some individuals to sleep through the night without bedwetting.

5.22.2.7.3 Other treatments

A wide variety of other approaches to treatment of enuresis have been employed and advocated at one time or another. For example, acupuncture has been used (Huo, 1988; Tuzuner, Kecik, Ozdemir, & Canakei, 1990; Xu, 1991). Chiropractic physicians have recommended spinal manipulations designed to reduce pressure on various nerves in order to prevent bedwetting (Gemmell & Jacobson, 1989). Dietary restrictions and manipulations have been attempted (Egger et al., 1992). Various surgical procedures, including dental surgery, have also been used (Timms, 1989; Weider & Hauri, 1985).

5.22.2.8 Effectiveness of Treatments

Since there is a spontaneous remission rate of approximately 15% each year and since virtually all people are able to control urination by the teenage years, it is often difficult to know whether a particular treatment has been successful or not. There have been thousands of studies in this area, however, and the following conclusions are justified. First, there is no doubt that the most effective form of treatment is the pad-and-bell (Djurhuus, Norgaard, Hjalmas, & Wille, 1992; Forsythe & Butler, 1989; Scott, Barclay, & Houts, 1992). Application of the pad-and-bell generally results in cessation of bedwetting for between 75% and 90% of cases over an 8–12 week period. Unfortunately, relapse rates are substantial and can be as high as 40% (Doleys, 1977). Reapplication of the procedure upon relapse is generally successful and in less time than the original course of treatment. Occasionally a third or fourth application may be necessary. Two other approaches that have been suggested to deal with the relapse problem are the use of overlearning (Young & Morgan, 1972) and intermittent schedules of reinforcement (Finley, Rainwater, & Johnson, 1982).

The various medications that have been employed have had only modest success. Although medications result in some improvement in most children, they often do not produce total cessation of the wetting and relapse rates are exceedingly high when medications are withdrawn. This, coupled with the ongoing expense and possibly dangerous side effects of the medications, makes these not the treatment of first choice except for short term interventions (Maizels et al., 1993; Thompson & Rey, 1995).

Other than a few anecdotal and case reports, psychotherapy and family therapy have not been shown to have significant effectiveness for enuresis (DeLeon & Mandell, 1966). The initial reports on cognitive psychotherapy indicate that this approach may have a higher success rate than more traditional approaches to psychotherapy (Ronen et al., 1992). Hypnosis has been shown to be effective when properly employed (Olness, 1975). Retention control and sphincter exercises initially showed good results but later research failed to confirm earlier findings (Doleys, Schwartz, & Ciminero, 1981; Harris & Purohit, 1977). Nevertheless, there is still interest in this approach and the sound physiological rationale would suggest that, properly employed, this treatment might be effective. Such approaches as restricting fluids, support and encouragement, awakening schedules, and so forth, are modestly effective with relatively simple cases. However, they are not sufficient for more difficult cases. Numerous reports have made excessive claims for the effectiveness of diet, acupuncture, chiropractic manipulation and so forth. Additional and more sophisticated research is needed on these approaches.

Probably the most effective approaches available are the multiple component programs by Azrin and Foxx, and Houts and his colleagues (Walker, 1995). These have much to recommend them in terms of careful research and demonstrated effectiveness. Their main drawback is the elaborate procedures required by the protocols and the amount of training, supervision, and effort required for successful execution of these programs. Some researchers doubt that the increase in efficiency of these programs over the simple use of a pad-and-bell justifies the amount of effort required.

5.22.2.9 Future Directions for Research and Practice

Walker (1995) has outlined a research agenda for enuresis. Given the amount of interest in this problem and the many centuries of effort to correct it, it is surprising how little is actually known about the process of developing urinary continence. There is currently very excellent and basic research underway in the UK by Fielding, (e.g. Fielding, 1982; Fielding, Berg, & Bell, 1978) and numerous excellent studies in Sweden and Denmark (Djrhuus, Norgaard, & Ritting, 1992; Hansson, 1992; Hellstrom, Hanson, Hansson, Hjalmas, & Jodal, 1990; Hjalmas, 1992b; Norgaard, Hansen, Nielsen, Rittig, & Djurhuus, 1989).

Walker (1995) notes that the various subtypes of enuresis have not been carefully evaluated with respect to etiology and treatment. Thus, we know that there is primary and secondary enuresis, diurnal and nocturnal enuresis, regular and intermittent enuresis, and so forth but we do not clearly understand the differences between these and whether there are treatment implications based on these differences.

Walker also notes that the most effective treatment which has been clearly demonstrated for several decades is some variation of the pad-and-bell. However, this is the least frequently employed treatment. This would appear to be an interesting research area in the sociology of science and medicine.

The third area Walker has outlined has to do with relapse rates for treatment of enuresis. All forms of treatment appear to have significant problems with relapse. More research is needed to develop ways of dealing with this problem.

Fourth, the relationship between bladder capacity and continence should be explored for possible treatment implications. Not all children who wet have small functional bladder capacity and, surprisingly, increases in functional capacity have not been shown to be directly related to improvement following treatment. Why this is so is not understood.

Fifth, the relationship between sleep and sleep patterns is not clearly understood with respect to enuresis. Although it is very expensive and time consuming to do research in this area, more work is indicated.

Sixth, the relative contributions of the components of the various package programs should be carefully evaluated with respect to their necessity. The package programs are successful but extremely elaborate and might be simplified with clarifying research.

Finally, more research is needed on the effects of diet on the etiology and management of enuresis. The same could be said of some of the alternative treatments, such as acupuncture and chiropractic manipulation. In some cases these are not known to be effective or ineffective because data are lacking. In particular, the cognitive and self-control approaches are deserving of more research.

5.22.3 ENCOPRESIS

5.22.3.1 Phenomenonology

The experience of the encopretic child is even more distressing than that of the enuretic child. This is for several reasons. First, the soiling accidents are more messy and more unpleasant in odor than are urination accidents. In addition, soiling accidents occur almost exclusively during the day, whereas wetting accidents are more likely to occur at night in one's own bedroom. As a result, the encopretic child lives in considerable terror that at any time he or she may have an accident that will result in an odoriferous mess as well as a great deal of embarrassment and ostracism by others.

The distress is heightened even more because, as discussed later in this chapter, the child generally is unable to control the encopretic episodes. They occur with very little warning and can not be managed successfully by the child without treatment. The child is frequently ridiculed by peers and referred to as "stinky" or some similar, even more derogatory, nickname. There is considerable conflict between parent and child because parents generally regard failure to control the bowels as a lack of motivation or slovenliness. Sometimes they even think it is an outright affront to the parents competence and authority. The percep-

tion, by the child, that all of his or her peers appear to be able to control bowels and that he or she is the only one unable to do so, makes the child feel considerably alienated from humanity and to feel totally incompetent at even basic life processes. This results in a significant lowering of self esteem and a feeling of defeatism. Many of these children feel that if they cannot control a simple thing such as bowel movements, so that they do not offend others around them, how can they control anything, be competent, or achieve in any area. Often, they are mystified as to why they cannot control their bowels and why others become so upset with them when the accidents occur.

In his book, *Worry: How to kick the serenity habit in 98 easy steps*, Robert Morley (1981) humorously notes that his worry in this area began with the requirement in the British school he attended that he and all the other students "write their name in the school register each morning after bowel evacuation."

Beyond these factors, bowel movements tend to be painful for children with encopresis; there is frequently irritation in the anal region from the fecal material; and the day-to-day living of the child may be marked by abdominal pain, gas, and other intestinal discomfort. Occasionally they are frightened by blood in the feces when hard stools scratch the colon and anus. One result of this is that these children often use denial and refuse to acknowledge that there is a problem. A second is that they may become aggressive and hostile toward those around them as a defense for the rejection that they feel from others. Children also frequently resort to subterfuge in hiding their soiled underclothes to avoid conflict with their parents.

James Roosevelt has provided an interesting insight into the problem of encopresis in his autobiographical writing:

> When I first got to Groton I had led so sheltered a life and was so shy that I was afraid to ask where the bathroom was. Hard as it may be to believe, I did what had to be done in my pants or in the bushes. My soiled pants were stuffed in a box, which I buried in the bushes. I suppose I was surrounded by foul smells. Holding back as long as I could, I started to suffer pains. Not knowing the cause, school officials suspected homesickness (well, I was homesick; at home I know where the bathrooms were) and asked my parents to take me home for a few days to ease my adjustment. (1976, pp. 60–61)

5.22.3.2 Diagnostic Features

DSM-IV defines encopresis as the repeated passage of feces into inappropriate places at least once per month for at least three months in a child who is chronologically four years of age (or developmentally the equivalent), in which the behavior is not due to the physiological effects of some substance such as a laxative or a medical illness. The soiling can be involuntary or intentional and the diagnostician has to determine whether or not constipation is present. When constipation is present the condition is referred to as overflow incontinence. The description of encopresis in *DSM-IV* is in very close agreement with the research data and clinical experience of those working in the field. Fecal incontinence is a general term that refers to a lack of control over bowel movements, whatever the cause. Encopresis is a term reserved for cases in which there is no organic basis other than constipation. Indicating that there is no organic basis other than constipation may be splitting hairs a bit; however, constipation is present in the vast majority of encopretic children and contributes to the problem, although it does not signal any serious medical disorder or illness. The constipation is generally behavioral in origin, involving diet and toilet habits. The requirement that the child be four years of age would seem to be unnecessary. Should a child become constipated at any age with resultant encopresis, it would appear to be a significant clinical problem worthy of treatment. This, of course, should be distinguished from the normal soiling or lack of toilet training in very young children (e.g., before the age of two). The *ICD-10* description of nonorganic encopresis describes the condition as repeated voluntary or involuntary passage of feces usually of normal or near normal consistency in places not appropriate for that purpose. *ICD-10* also notes that the condition may be a continuation of normal infantile incontinence beyond the age when bowel control should have developed; it may involve a loss of continence following successful toilet training; or, it may be a deliberate act of defecation in spite of the fact that the child is capable of bowel control. *ICD-10* notes that the symptom may be singular and isolated, or it may be a part of a wider disorder especially an emotional disorder or conduct disorder. The *ICD-10* description notes the possibility that constipation may be present but does not emphasize this as much as *DSM-IV*, and leans rather heavily toward the idea that an emotional disorder may be associated in many cases. Unfortunately, there is little evidence that emotional disturbance plays a major role in encopresis and considerable evidence that the great majority of the cases do involve constipation.

The discussion of encopresis in *ICD-10* also has other problems. For example, describing the feces as usually normal or near normal consistency does not square with the facts. Typically, a large number of the "accidents" consist of stains and rather pasty deposits or streaks on the underwear of these children caused by seepage around the impacted feces in the colon. These accidents are punctuated by large bowel movements of unusual diameter and/or by small, hard stools resembling rocks. Abnormal stools are the result of constipation.

5.22.3.3 Prevalence

As was the case with enuresis, estimates of the prevalence of encopresis vary widely, in large part due to differences in definition employed, populations studied, and methods of gathering data. There are currently no reliable data that indicate the differential rate of various forms of encopresis, such as retentive vs. nonretentive, primary vs. secondary, and so forth. By definition, functional encopresis does not begin before the age of four years. Overall estimates of the occurrence of encopresis range from 1.5–7.5% of children (Doleys et al., 1981). Some of the lower estimates that have been reported in the literature may be due to the fact that many parents are reluctant to discuss or report this problem with respect to their children. Clinicians in pediatric and mental health settings note that parents do not generally volunteer this information and it is obtained only by careful questioning (Walker, 1978). Boys are approximately four to five times more likely to be encopretic than girls (Bellmon, 1966; Rutter et al., 1970). Approximately 30% of encopretics are also found to be enuretic (Levine, 1975).

5.22.3.4 Etiology

Following an extensive review of the literature, Walker (1978) identified three subtypes of encopresis. First, he noted that there are children who can be described as "manipulative soilers." Children of this category soil when it is to their benefit to do so. Thus, some children soil if there is an examination to be given in school that they wish to avoid. The soiling makes it necessary for their parent to come to school and take them home for cleaning. On occasion, soiling appears to be related to anger or desire to distress the parent and represents a form of oppositional behavior. Or, there may be other environmental reasons that determine when the soiling occurs. Both *DSM-IV* and *ICD-10* note that soiling is sometimes intentional.

A second category of soiling is a form of diarrhea or loose bowels caused by excessive stress and expressed through the colon. A possibly related disorder to this is recurrent abdominal pain which may include diarrhea and is thought to be a precursor of irritable bowel syndrome in adults.

The third category is retentive encopresis based on chronic constipation. This is by far the most common etiology of encopresis. It is estimated that 80–90% of the cases fall into this category (Fitzgerald, 1975; Levine, 1975). As with enuresis, there are three general conceptualizations within which the etiology of encopresis may be considered: biological, emotional, and learning.

5.22.3.4.1 Biological factors

As the most common underlying feature of encopresis is constipation, it is quite likely that there are some underlying biological or physiological factors involved. First, some people have a higher constitutional likelihood for developing constipation; this is no doubt genetic (Petti & Davidson, 1991). Likewise, many individuals appear to be genetically predisposed to develop diarrhea under stress. It has also been speculated that some sort of subtle developmental delay may be involved in the development of encopresis (Bellmon, 1996).

5.22.3.4.2 Emotional factors

Early literature on encopresis often assumed a psychodynamic origin for this problem. The symptom was sometimes thought to be a result of an unconscious conflict, anger, depression, or some similar emotional factor. Encopretic children were frequently considered to have a particular personality, possibly involving immaturity, passive aggressiveness, anger, insecurity, anal fixation, anxiety, or low self esteem (Bemporad, Kresch, Asnes, & Wilson, 1978; Hoag, Norriss, Himeno, & Jacobs, 1971). Mothers were often depicted as rigid and masochistic, whereas fathers were thought to be weak, unaffectional, and uninvolved (Bemporad et al., 1978).

Other theories suggested that overly harsh or early attempts at toilet training may be the cause for encopresis (e.g. Hushka, 1942). Although there may be some merit to the idea that emotional factors play a role in the development of encopresis, most studies have failed to indicate such a connection (Fritz & Armbrust, 1982; Levine, 1975). It is probable that if such factors are involved, they are a secondary contributing factor rather than the major factor in most instances.

5.22.3.4.3 Learning factors

The third general rubric under which the development of encopresis can be understood

has to do with learning theory. Obviously, manipulative soiling would follow a reinforcement model. If soiling is successful at manipulating the environment and results in reward for the child, the child will use this behavior in the future under appropriate circumstances. Likewise, chronic diarrhea and irritable bowel syndrome may be understood as symptoms of stress and anxiety which have been conditioned to selected stimuli. Finally, as noted, the most common form of encopresis is based on constipation. The development of constipation is based on behavioral factors such as poor dietary choices, failure to establish good toilet habits, withholding of stools, and similar behaviors which result in constipation.

It is likely that any of the three general categories outlined above (biological, emotional, and learning) may be instrumental in the development of encopresis. In many cases they may all be present to some degree or another. In other cases, one or more may be predominant and the main source of the problem. The most general and all encompassing of the three is the learning formulation because it readily incorporates the others and presents a complete description.

5.22.3.5 Developmental Course

The developmental course of encopresis is relatively simple to describe. At birth, fecal continence does not exist. The bowel reflexively empties when sufficient material is present and when the nerve endings in the rectum are stimulated by the presence of a full bowel. As the child develops, it becomes possible for toilet training to occur and most children develop bowel control relatively easily, prior to urinary control. Problems with encopresis tend to develop after control has been obtained and are generally based, as noted, on constipation which develops in the child. With or without treatment, most cases of encopresis cease by the midteen years. Encopresis persisting into adulthood does occur (Rex, Fitzgerald, & Goulet, 1992) but is rare. The reasons for this are not understood. That is, why would encopresis be a common childhood problem but disappear with or without treatment in the late teens? Whether this is related to improved toileting habits or bodily changes in the adult is not fully understood.

5.22.3.6 Conceptualization and Clinical Formulation

5.22.3.6.1 Multimodal assessment

The assessment of the encopretic child must begin with a medical examination. Typically, the physician will obtain a thorough medical history and do a basic physical examination including a rectal examination and palpation of the intestine for presence of fecal mass. The physician will also generally test for blood in the stool and, given the fact that females often have urinary tract infections if they are encopretic, may perform a urine analysis in females. There are a number of more invasive procedures, such as anorectal manometry, fecal studies, rectal biopsies, and barium enemas, which may be needed depending on what the physician obtains in the history and the initial examination. In the vast majority of cases these tests are not necessary. The basic physical examination can be performed by any competent physician familiar with child health. More advanced testing should be done by a pediatric gastro-enterologist or other specialist. There are some organic pathologies that occur frequently enough that they must be ruled out before behavioral treatment is attempted. These include Hirschprung's disease (in which a segment of the colon has reduced, or a total absence of, neuralinnervation), congenital hypothyroidism, and pathology of the colon and surrounding structures such as anal stenosis, fissures, and so forth.

Psychological assessment must be broad and multifaceted (Walker & Shaw, 1988). First, there should be a screening assessment of the child's mental and emotional status. If significant psychopathology exists or significant family dysfunction is present, it may be necessary and advisable to deal with these prior to attempting treatment of the encopresis. Encopresis protocols tend to be relatively rigorous and demanding in terms of the amount of effort and the precision with which things must be done. If the child or the family is sufficiently disturbed that they are unlikely to be successful with the protocol, it is not appropriate to add the stress of this approach to the already existing stress. The existing difficulties should be dealt with followed by treatment for the encopresis. Should there be evidence of current psychopathology, standard psychological testing and assessment instruments may be needed to evaluate further the mental and emotional condition of the child or the degree of family disorganization.

The examination should include a thorough clinical interview of the parent and the child to determine the basic characteristics of the soiling in terms of frequency, timing, size of stools, staining of underwear, passage of blood during bowel movements, and other characteristics of toilet habits. In addition, the clinician would be interested in the manner and time at which toilet training progressed and whether or not the child

ever achieved control of the bowel. The reaction of the child and the family to the problem and its effect on their interactions, as well as the motivation of each for treatment should be carefully assessed. The clinician should discuss, with the family, previous attempts to deal with the problem and their success or failure. Since diet is often involved in the development of constipation, there should be some exploration of eating habits. The ability and willingness of both the parents and the child to follow a carefully specified protocol are crucial to the success of treatment of encopresis. This should be thoroughly explored and emphasized in the assessment process.

Since the amount of conflict between parent and child regarding soiling is often significant and the family may be dysfunctional, the possibility of child abuse must be considered (Boon, 1991). The abuse may be physical, sexual, or psychological in nature. It is important to emphasize that the majority of children who are encopretic have not been abused (Clayden, 1988). However, in some cases where there has been abuse, the child will soil seemingly as a "cry for help." It is also possible in some cases, where there may be repeated anal rape, for there to be sufficient damage to the anus and musculature in that area that soiling results. This is not a frequent occurrence but is possible. It is important for the clinician to be alert to the possibility of child abuse in cases of encopresis, but it is equally important for the clinician to realize that abuse in these cases is definitely the exception, not the rule.

5.22.3.6.2 Treatment formulation

As noted in the previous section, there appear to be three basic types of conditions that result in soiling (Walker, 1978). One is the manipulative soiler who is using the soiling as an effort to manipulate the environment. This type of case would require a formulation involving family structure and dynamics.

The second category is the child who responds to stress with incontinence. Formulation in these instances will involve an assessment of the internal and external stressors that the child is experiencing in order to plan behavioral as well as other forms of psychotherapy to reduce stress, improve coping, and promote insight or self understanding. Environmental changes may also be required to reduce sources of stress. The overall formulation in these cases will include attempts to improve coping skills of the patient and to simultaneously reduce external stressors such that the problem will be resolved.

The most common etiology for soiling is constipation. The case formulation in these instances involves an evaluation of the factors that led to the constipation and an assessment of the willingness and ability of the child and family to follow the prescribed protocol. The way in which constipation contributes to the problem of encopresis must be understood. There are a number of circumstances through which a child can become constipated. Most of these have to do with diet and toileting behavior. For example, a diet that is lacking in roughage and/or that contains significant amounts of dairy products tends to lead to constipation. Likewise, withholding stools (which children at play often do when they do not wish to interrupt their play) can lead to encopresis. In addition, some individuals appear to have a physiological tendency to become constipated more easily than others. This is probably genetic in origin. There is some suggestion in the literature that certain emotional reactions such as depression may reduce motility of the intestine and eventually produce constipation. The amount of liquid consumed and the amount of dehydration that children experience while playing in warm weather may also be a factor. Lack of exercise is known to be associated with constipation. A number of other factors might also be mentioned, but the main point is that there can be many reasons for the child to become constipated. Unfortunately, when the child becomes constipated, this is frequently not observed by either the child or the parent. The child simply does not take notice of it and the parent assumes that the child has used the toilet at some time when they were not around. Whereas wetting accidents are readily observable, constipation in the early stages is not. Eventually the constipation becomes chronic and results in severe impaction in the colon. This severe impaction and chronic constipation result in stretching the colon which is referred to as psychogenic megacolon. When the colon is stretched and impacted, it ceases to function normally. The peristalic movement that moves material through the intestine and expels it through the anus is muted and unable to perform the task of evacuating the bowel. With this impaction, there is chronic pressure on the anus which results in a loss of the sensation that the child needs to evacuate. Thus, these children frequently report that they do not have the urge to evacuate. Another consequence of chronic impaction is that the liquid material in the intestine that has been emptied from the stomach makes its way only to the point of impaction and is not able to proceed further. As a result, it remains there in a pool. As the child plays or moves around, the wall of the intestine is momentarily separated from the impacted feces allowing a small space through which the liquid material in the pool seeps gradually around the impacted mass and eventually leaks out the anus. This results in the staining of underwear that is very common with encopretic children and which they claim not to be able to predict.

Encopretic children are correct when they say that they did not know it was happening until it was too late, because there was no sensation of contraction and evacuation. The seepage is a passive process. Material simply leaks out the anus without the child having any warning or control over it. In addition to the staining, large bowel movements occur in the clothing or in the toilet when significant amounts of the impacted material are expelled under pressure. These can be extremely embarrassing and upsetting to a child when they happen in public, and at home they are occasionally even large enough that the plumbing facilities cannot accommodate the diameter of the stools. When this happens stools have to be broken into smaller pieces in order to be flushed down the toilet.

These facts are a major part of the formulation and should be communicated to the parents. That is, they should be made aware of the fact that the child has an enlarged colon which is simply not functioning properly and cannot be controlled in the normal way. They should further be informed that the child has lost the sensation of needing to defecate and that the seepage and staining that occurs happens without warning to the child because it is a passive process. Explaining this to the parents often reduces their anger and their disgust because they previously believed that the child was simply defying their authority and refusing to try.

5.22.3.7 Treatment

5.22.3.7.1 Psychosocial treatments

Depending on the formulation of the case, treatment will vary. In cases of manipulative or intentional soiling, the most appropriate treatment would appear to be behavioral psychotherapy to assist the child in coping more effectively with the environment without inappropriate manipulative behavior (Keat, 1979; Walker, Hedberg, Clement, & Wright, 1981). Family therapy may also be very effective in dealing with behavior within the family system that is causing or supporting use of manipulation via soiling (Henggeler & Borduin, 1990).

In cases where diarrhea may be the origin of the soiling, psychotherapy, especially behaviorally oriented psychotherapy, may be helpful in reducing stress and increasing coping skills (Cohen & Reed, 1968; Hedberg, 1973). Anxiety reducing and antidiarrheal medications may also be used (Angelides & Fitzgerald, 1981).

Since the majority of cases of encopresis are based on constipation, the remainder of the remarks in this section are devoted to treatment of this form of encopresis. There have been occasional reports of the treatment of such children with traditional psychotherapy (McTaggert & Scott, 1959; Pinkerton, 1958) as well as family therapy and related approaches (Knights & Pandey, 1990; Margolies & Gilstein, 1983–1984; Wells & Hinkle, 1990; White, 1984).

Numerous case studies and research reports based on adequate samples have reported on the treatment of encopresis using behavioral strategies (Doleys, 1989; Houts & Abramson, 1990; Liebert & Fischel, 1990). Most of these approaches deal with a combination of behavioral principles based on reinforcement and/or punishment along with dietary changes, toileting skills development, changes in toilet habits, and often use of laxatives or enemas for cleansing the colon (Wright & Walker, 1977). Although there is wide variation in the exact components employed in these treatment approaches, a typical approach might involve cleansing the colon via laxatives on the first day of the treatment program, changing the child's diet to make it high in fiber content, and providing rewards for successful toileting attempts as well as for having clean underwear at the end of the day.

Several reports can be found in the literature on the use of biofeedback for bowel control problems (e.g., Whitehead, 1992). Biofeedback procedures are frequently used to assess the functioning of sphincters in children experiencing problems with encopresis. In addition, biofeedback equipment may be used to train a child in proper control of the muscles employed in elimination. Three components are generally employed in these programs: exercise of external sphincter muscles, training in discrimination of rectal sensations, and training in synchronization of the internal and external sphincter muscles so that proper elimination can occur (Latimer, Campbell, & Kasperski, 1984).

There have been reports of the use of hypnosis in the treatment of encopresis. Most of the reports (Olness, 1976; Tilton, 1980) indicate that suggestions are given to the child about the nature of the activity of the colon and of the child's ability to control the process. Finally, there have been attempts to use acupuncture and related procedures in the treatment of encopresis (An et al., 1986).

5.22.3.7.2 *Pharmacological treatments*

The typical treatment by physicians for constipation-based encopresis involves a regime in which the bowel is evacuated and thoroughly cleared. This is done through enemas and laxatives. The regime is then continued for a period of weeks or months, following which the laxative is either abruptly ceased or phased out. Most commonly, mineral oil (1–3 teaspoons, 2–3 times a day) is employed as the laxative (Abrahamian & Lloyd-Still 1984; Behrman, Vaughan, & Nelson, 1987; Levine, Carey, Crocker, & Gross, 1983). The rationale for this treatment is that the severe impaction has produced psychogenic megacolon, thus compromising the functioning of the colon. Treatment begins with a thorough evacuation of the bowel which is generally readily accomplished by laxatives and enemas; however, there have been occasions when impacted material had to be manually removed prior to beginning treatment. Next, daily use of mineral oil as a laxative produces regularity of bowel movements and produces stools that are easily passed. Maintaining a clear colon over a period of time allows the colon to shrink back to its normal shape, re-establish muscle tone, and begin more normal peristalic movement. When the laxative regime is removed, regular bowel movements frequently continue.

5.22.3.8 Effectiveness of Treatments

Medical and behavioral treatments are the most effective treatments for encopresis. In most reports it is found that 80% or more of children become continent with medical protocols employing mineral oil or other laxatives (Levine & Bakow, 1976; Sondheimer & Gervaise, 1982). Unfortunately, there is a significant rate of relapse following these treatments. Abrahamian and Lloyd-Still (1984) did a five-year follow-up study of their patients and found that 47% were completely symptom free, while another 36% found it necessary to use laxatives intermittently to control the symptoms.

Stark, Spirito, Lewis, and Hart (1990) found that mineral oil oriented programs were unsuccessful with a substantial number of children, especially those with behavioral problems. Referral to a psychologist for treatment in these cases appears to be warranted (Stark, Owens-Stively, Spirito, Lewis, & Guevremont, 1990).

Behavioral treatments for encopresis have been reported by a large number of people in both case studies and controlled research. Very high success rates have been reported for these programs (Doleys, 1989; Houts & Abramson, 1990; Liebert & Fischel, 1990; Walker, 1995).

Although follow-up studies have not been as frequent or as extensive as might be wished, the behaviorally oriented programs do not seem to have as bad a record of relapse as do those based solely on mineral oil or laxatives. The difference may be the greater emphasis on skills development in terms of bowel control, toilet habits, and related areas that are included in the behaviorally oriented programs. Most of the behaviorally oriented programs include laxatives and dietary manipulation, but add a significant dimension of behavioral psychotherapy and habit change.

Biofeedback training is sometimes helpful in bowel training and remediation of encopresis. It is particularly helpful in cases where an organic problem underlies the difficulty or in cases where simple behavioral programs are not effective due to underlying organic or physiological impairments (Whitehead, 1992). For example, biofeedback training has been found to be effective with patients following rectal surgery that impaired the functioning of the anal sphincters. It does not appear to improve success rates in the more routine and uncomplicated cases, however (Loening-Baucke, 1995).

Although there have been intriguing reports about the effectiveness of hypnosis and family therapy in the treatment of encopresis, there is not sufficient data to indicate that these are likely to be successful as a primary or singular treatment for the disorder. They would appear to be effective as adjuncts to an overall treatment program involving laxatives, diet manipulation, and careful toilet training. The same could be said for traditional psychotherapy (Achenbach & Lewis, 1971; Berg & Jones, 1964). Evidence for acupuncture and other related approaches is simply not sufficient to determine whether they are effective or not. It is, however, unlikely that they are.

5.22.3.9 Future Directions for Research and Practice

Walker (1995) proposed a research agenda for encopresis. He noted that, compared to enuresis, relatively little research is done on encopresis. Thus, there is a need for more information on virtually every point regarding encopresis. There is a need for considerably more research on the effects of diet and different foods on the process of digestion and elimination. For example, are there foods that are likely to produce constipation other than dairy products? Additionally, are there foods that promote regularity beyond the simple effects of fiber content?

The information on encopresis related to deliberate or manipulative soiling is very limited. Given the nature of this problem, it is difficult to get a group of patients together at one time for study. However, single case study methods and small group studies can be done and there is a need for considerably more work regarding children with encopresis of this sort. Likewise, whereas there is a considerable amount of information about the effects of stress producing diarrhea, there is relatively little known about precise treatments for this.

Areas involving associated features of encopresis need much more delineation, such as socioeconomic factors, ethnic factors, possible genetic influences, emotional status, and family status of encopretic children. None of these are well understood and better understanding might prove valuable in terms of planning treatment.

Wide variability in the size, composition, odor, and color of stools produced by encopretic as well as normal children have been noted. More information about the relationship between these variables and the function of the colon would be valuable.

With respect to various programs that have successfully employed a combination of laxatives, enemas, diet manipulation, and behavioral training, there has been very little research on the importance of the different components in the package and of possible variations in the components based on presenting symptoms, developmental age, or other factors related to the child.

There are a number of cases, that every clinician in this area has encountered, that seem to be resistant to all efforts employed by a variety of professionals. Careful study of some of these cases on an inpatient basis might reveal the source of the recalcitrance.

Finally, there are a number of related problems to encopresis that have little or no research to date, such as smearing of faces, coprophagia, and coprophilia.

Increased sophistication in treatment protocols can be accomplished only as more data are accumulated in the areas outlined above. Were more information available, it should readily be possible to treat children in a shorter amount of time, with fewer relapses and fewer failures.

5.22.4 SUMMARY

Toilet training is an area of great interest and concern to parents. Parents often regard the development of bowel and bladder control in their children as an important developmental milestone for the child and an affirmation of the parents' competence. Unfortunately, more emphasis is often placed on this process than is warranted. Experts generally recommend assessing the readiness of the child for toilet training and then employing a gentle and patient approach based on encouragement and support. Beginning the process at too early an age and employing excessively harsh approaches can often be harmful to the child.

Failure to achieve proper control of the process of urination is referred to as enuresis. Failure in bowel control is termed encopresis. Both enuresis and encopresis are, by definition, functional disorders of incontinence. Thus, organic bases such as specific disease processes must be ruled out prior to a diagnosis of enuresis or encopresis. A variety of biological and emotional factors have been proposed as causitive or contributing factors to the development of enuresis. However, the disorder can best be understood within the framework of learning theory. Development of urinary continence is a process that involves learning to inhibit reflexive emptying of the bladder, and of emptying the bladder at the appropriate time and place. Biological and emotional factors may inhibit the learning process or interfere with performance of skills already learned; however, they are best regarded as contributory factors. The most successful treatments are use of the pad-and-bell (which appears to be effective due to conditioning) and a variety of package programs which employ the pad-and-bell along with other learning and training experiences for the child. Psychotherapy and a variety of other approaches to the treatment of enuresis have not proved sufficiently successful to be regarded as useful. Medication is successful in some cases but has not been demonstrated to be as effective as learning approaches to the treatment of enuresis and suffers from the problem of side effects as well as the ongoing expense of the treatment.

Although numerous biological and emotional factors have been suggested as causes of encopresis, the most common cause is related to constipation and the resultant psychogenic megacolon. Effective treatment requires thorough evacuation of the bowel which permits the tissue to return to its normal shape, tone, and function. Along with restoration of normal functioning of the tissue, retraining of toilet functions is required. Numerous protocols are in the literature both in the pediatric medical literature and in the psychological literature which describe treatment for encopresis. These involve the use of laxatives or enemas for evacuation of the colon, dietary changes to enhance bowel function, and retraining of toileting skills. These programs have been found to be highly effective. Psychotherapy and other forms of treatment are generally ineffective for treatment of encopresis.

5.22.5 REFERENCES

Abrahamian, F. P., & Lloyd-Still, J. D. (1984). Chronic constipation in childhood: A longitudinal study of 186 patients. *Journal of Pediatric Gastroenterology and Nutrition, 3,* 460–467.

Achenbach, T. M., & Lewis, M. (1971). A proposed model for clinical research and its application for encopresis and enuresis. *Journal of the American Academy of Child Psychiatry, 10,* 535–554.

American Psychiatric Association. (1994). *Diagnostic and statistical manual of mental disorders* (4th ed.). Washington, DC: Author.

An, X. C., Zhoo, H. S., Li, X. C., Tang, Y. Y., Sun, J., Liu, J., Yi, J. Q., Yu, Y. X., Zhang, G. C., & Hao, G. (1986). Acupuncture treatment for disturbances in urination and defecation from sacral cryptorachischisis. *Journal of Traditional Chinese Medicine, 6*(2), 95–98.

Angelides, A., & Fitzgerald, J. F. (1981). Pharmacologic advances in the treatment of gastrointestinal diseases. *Pediatric Clinics of North America, 28,* 95–112.

Azrin, N. H., & Foxx, R. M. (1976). *Toilet training in less than a day.* New York: Pocket Books.

Azrin, N. H., Sneed, T. J., & Foxx, R. M. (1973). Dry bed: A rapid method of eliminating bedwetting (enuresis) of the retarded. *Behaviour Research and Therapy, 11,* 427–434.

Bakwin, H. (1961). Enuresis in children. *Journal of Pediatrics, 58,* 806–819.

Bakwin, H., & Bakwin, R. M. (1972). *Behavior disorders in children.* Philadelphia: Saunders.

Banerjee, S., Srivastav, A., & Palan, B. M. (1993, October). Hypnosis and self-hypnosis in the management of nocturnal enuresis: A comparative study with imipramine therapy. *American Journal of Clinical Hypnosis, 36*(2), 113–119.

Behrman, R. E., Vaughan, V. C., & Nelson, W. E. (1987). *Textbook of pediatrics* (13th ed.). Philadelphia: Saunders.

Bellmon, M. (1966). Studies on encopresis. *Acta Paediatrica Scandinavica, 170*(Suppl.), 1–137.

Bemporad, J. R., Kresch, R. A., Asnes, R., & Wilson, A. (1978). Chronic neurotic encopresis as a paradigm of a multifactorial psychiatric disorder. *Journal of Nervous and Mental Disease, 166,* 472–479.

Berg, I., & Jones, K. V. (1964). Functional faecal incontinence in children. *Archives of Disease in Childhood, 39,* 465–472.

Boon, F. (1991, May). Encopresis and sexual assault. *Journal of the American Academy of Child Adolescent Psychiatry, 30*(3), 509–510.

Brazelton, T. B. (1962). A child-oriented approach to toilet training. *Pediatrics, 29,* 121–128.

Butler, J. F. (1976). The toilet training success of parents after reading "Toilet Training in Less Than A Day." *Behavior Therapy, 7,* 185–191.

Cho, S. C. (1984). Clinical study on childhood enuresis. *Seoul Journal of Medicine, 25,* 599–608.

Clayden, G. S. (1988). Reflex anal dilatation associated with severe chronic constipation in children. *Archives of Disease in Childhood, 63,* 832–836.

Cohen, S. I., & Read, J. L. (1968). The treatment of "nervous diarrhea" and other conditioned autonomic disorders by desensitization. *British Journal of Psychiatry, 114,* 1275–1280.

Collison, D. L. (1970). Hypnotherapy in the management of nocturnal enuresis. *Medical Journal of Australia, 1,* 52–54.

Creer, T. L., & Davis, M. H. (1975). Using a staggered-wakening procedure with enuretic children in an institutional setting. *Journal of Behavior Therapy and Experimental Psychiatry, 6,* 23–25.

Crowley, R. J., & Mills, J. C. (1986). The nature and construction of therapeutic metaphors for children. *British Journal of Experimental and Clinical Hypnosis, 3*(2), 69–76.

Cullen, K. J. (1966). Clinical observations concerning behavior disorders in children. *Medical Journal of Australia, 1,* 712–715.

DeGraaf, M. J. M. (1992, October 17). 40 years of being treated for nocturnal enuresis. *The Lancet, 340,* 957–958.

deJonge, G. A. (1973). Epidemiology of enuresis: A survey of the literature. In I. Kolvin, R. C. MacKeith, & S. R. Meadow (Eds.), *Bladder control and enuresis.* Philadelphia: Lippincott.

DeLeon, G., & Mandell, W. (1966). A comparison of conditioning and psychotherapy in the treatment of functional enuresis. *Journal of Clinical Psychology, 22,* 326–330.

Djurhuus, J. C., Norgaard, J. P., Hjalmas, K., & Wille, S. (Eds.) (1992). Nocturnal enuresis. *Scandinavian Journal of Urology and Nephrology, 143*(Suppl.), 3–29.

Djurhuus, J. C., Norgaard, J. P., & Ritting, S. (1992). Monosymptomatic bedwetting. *Scandinavian Journal of Urology and Nephrology, 141*(Suppl.), 7–17.

Doleys, D. M. (1977). Behavioral treatments for nocturnal enuresis in children: A review of the recent literature. *Psychological Bulletin, 84*(1), 30–54.

Doleys, D. M. (1989). Enuresis and encopresis. In T. H. Ollendick & M. Hersen (Eds.), *Handbook of child psychopathology* (2nd ed., pp. 291–314). New York: Plenum.

Doleys, D. M., Schwartz, M. S., & Ciminero, A. R. (1981). Elimination problems: Enuresis and encopresis. In E. J. Mash & L. G. Terdal (Eds.), *Behavioral assessment of childhood disorders* (pp. 679–710). New York: Guilford Press.

Egger, J., Carter, C. H., Soothill, J. F., & Wilson, J. (1992). Effect of diet treatment on enuresis in children with migraine or hyperkinetic behavior. *Clinical Pediatrics, 31*(5), 302–307.

Elian, M. (1991). Treating bed wetting. *British Medical Journal, 302*(6778), 729.

Evans, J. H. C., & Meadow, S. R. (1992). Desmopressin for bed wetting: Length of treatment, vasopressin secretion, and response. *Archives of Disease in Childhood, 67,* 184–188.

Fenichel, O. (1946). *The psychoanalytictic theory of neurosis.* London: Routledge & Kegan Paul.

Fergusson, D. M., Hons, B. A., Horwood, L. J., & Shannon, F. T. (1986). Factors related to the age of attainment of nocturnal bladder control: An eight year longitudinal study. *Pediatrics, 78*(5), 884–890.

Fielding, D. (1982). An analysis of the behavior of day- and night-wetting children: Towards a model of micturition control. *Behaviour Research and Therapy, 20,* 49–60.

Fielding, D. M., Berg, I., & Bell, S. (1978). An observational study of postures and limb movements of children who wet by day and at night. *Developmental Medicine and Child Neurology, 20,* 453–461.

Finley, W. W., Rainwater, A. J., & Johnson, G. (1982). Effect of varying alarm schedules on acquisition and relapse parameters in the conditioning treatment of enuresis. *Behaviour Research and Therapy, 20,* 69–80.

Fitzgerald, J. F. (1975). Encopresis, soiling, constipation: What's to be done? *Pediatrics, 56,* 348–349.

Forsythe, W. I., & Butler, R. J. (1989). Fifty years of enuretic alarms. *Archives of Disease in Childhood, 64,* 879–885.

Forsythe, W. I., & Redmond, A. (1974). Enuresis and spontaneous cure rate: Study of 1129 enuretics. *Archives of Disease in Childhood, 49,* 259–263.

Fritz, G. K., & Anders, T. F. (1979). Enuresis: The clinical application of an etiologically-based classification system. *Child Psychiatry of Human Development, 10,* 103–113.

Fritz, G. K., & Armbrust, J. (1982). Enuresis and encopresis. *Pediatric Clinics of North America, 5,* 283–296.

Gemmell, H. A., & Jacobson, B. H. (1989). Chiropractic management of enuresis: Time-series descriptive design. *Journal of Manipulative and Physiological Therapeutics, 12*(5), 386–389.

Glicklich, L. B. (1951). An historical account of enuresis. *Pediatrics, 8,* 859–876.

George, C. P, Messerli, F. H., Genest, J. et al. (1975). Diurnal variation of plasma vasopressin in man. *Journal of Clinical Endocrinology Metabolism, 41,* 332–338.

Hallgren, B. (1956). Enuresis: I. A study with reference to morbidity, risk and symptomatology. II. A study with reference to certain physical, mental and social factors possibly associated with enuresis. *Acta Psychiatrica Scandinavica, 31,* 379–436.

Hansson, S. (1992). Urinary incontinence in children and associated problems. *Scandinavian Journal of Urology and Nephrology, 141*(Suppl.), 47–54.

Harris, L. S., & Purohit, A. P. (1977). Bladder training and enuresis: A controlled trial. *Behaviour Research and Therapy, 15,* 485–490.

Hedberg, A. G. (1973). The treatment of chronic diarrhea by systematic desensitization: A case report. *Journal of Behavior Therapy and Experimental Psychiatry, 4,* 67–68.

Hellstrom, A. L., Hanson, E., Hansson, S., Hjalmas, K., & Jodal, U. (1990). Micturition habits and incontinence in 7-year-old Swedish school entrants. *European Journal of Pediatrics, 149,* 434–437.

Henggeler, S. W., & Borduin, C. M. (1990). *Family therapy and beyond.* Pacific Grove, CA: Brooks/Cole.

Hindley, C. B., Filliozat, A. M., Klackenberg, G., Nicolet-Meister, D., & Sand, E. A. (1965). Some differences in infant feeding and elimination training in five European longitudinal samples. *Journal of Child Psychology and Psychiatry, 6,* 179–201.

Hjalmas, K. (1992a). Functional daytime incontinence: Definitions and epidemiology. *Scandinavian Journal of Urology and Nephrology, 141*(Suppl.), 39–44.

Hjalmas, K. (1992b). Urinary incontinence in children: Suggestions for definitions and terminology. *Scandinavian Journal of Urology and Nephrology, 141* (Suppl.), 1–6.

Hoag, J. M., Norriss, N. G., Himeno, E. T., & Jacobs, J. (1971). The encopretic child and his family. *Journal of the American Academy of Child Psychiatry, 10,* 242–256.

Houts, A. C., & Abramson, H. (1990). Assessment and treatment for functional childhood enuresis and encopresis: Toward a partnership between health psychologists and physicians. In S. B. Morgan & T. M. Okwumabua (Eds.), *Child and adolescent disorders: Developmental and health psychology perspectives* (pp. 47–103). Hillsdale, NJ: Erlbaum.

Houts, A. C., & Liebert, R. M. (1984). *Bedwetting: A guide for parents and children.* Springfield, IL: Charles C. Thomas.

Houts, A. C., Liebert, R. M., & Padawer, W. (1983). A delivery system for the treatment of primary enuresis. *Journal of Abnormal Psychology, 11,* 513–520.

Huo, J. S. (1988). Treatment of 11 cases of chronic enuresis by acupuncture and massage. *Journal of Traditional Chinese Medicine, 8*(3), 195–196.

Hushka, M. (1942). The child's response to coercive bowel training. *Psychosomatic Medicine, 4,* 301–308.

Imhof, B. (1956). Bettwasser in der erziehungsberatung. *Heilpaedagogische Werkblaetter, 25,* 122–127.

Ilg, F. L., & Ames, L. B. (1962). *Parents ask.* New York: Harper & Brothers.

Keat, D. B. (1979). *Multimodal therapy with children.* Elmsford, NY: Pergamon.

Knights, B., & Pandey, S. K. (1990). Paradoxical approach to the management of faecal incontinence in normal children. *Archives of Disease in Childhood, 65*(6), 598–600.

Kohen, D., Olness, K., Corwell, S., & Heimel, A. (1980, November). *Five hundred pediatric behavioral problems treated with hypnotherapy.* Paper presented at the annual meeting of the American Society of Clinical Hypnosis, Minneapolis, MN.

Latimer, P. R., Campbell, D., & Kasperski, J. (1984). A components analysis of biofeedback in the treatment of fecal incontinence. *Biofeedback and Self Regulation, 9,* 311–324.

Levine, M. D. (1975). Children with encopresis: A descriptive analysis. *Pediatrics, 56*(3), 412–416.

Levine, M. D., & Bakow, H. (1976). Children with encopresis: A study of treatment outcome. *Pediatrics, 58,* 845–852.

Levine, M. D., Carey, W. B., Crocker, A. C., & Gross, R. T. (1983). *Developmental—behavioral pediatrics.* Philadelphia: Saunders.

Lieberman, L. (1972). The changing ideology of socialization: Toilet training, mass media, and society. *International Journal of Contemporary Sociology, 9*(4), 188–199.

Liebert, R. M., & Fischel, J. E. (1990). The elimination disorders—enuresis and encopresis. In M. Lewis & S. M. Miller (Eds.), *Handbook of developmental psychopathology: Perspective in developmental psychology* (pp. 421–429). New York: Plenum.

Loening-Baucke, V. (1995, July). Biofeedback treatment for chronic constipation and encopresis in childhood: Long-term outcome. *Pediatrics, 96*(1), 105–110.

Lovibond, S. H., & Coote, M. A. (1970). Enuresis. In C.G. Costello (Ed.), *Symptoms of psychopathology: A handbook* (pp. 373–396). New York: Wiley.

MacKeith, R. C. (1972). Is maturation delay a frequent factor in the origins of primary nocturnal enuresis? *Developmental Medicine and Child Neurology, 14,* 217–223.

MacKeith, R. C., Meadow, R., & Turner, R. K. (1973). How children become dry. In I. Kolvin, R. C. MacKeith, & S. R. Meadow (Eds.), *Bladder control and enuresis* (pp. 3–21). Philadelphia: Lippincott.

Maizels, M., Gandhi, K., Keating, B., & Rosenbaum, D. (1993, November/December). Diagnosis and treatment for children who cannot control urination. *Current Problems in Pediatrics, 23,* 402–450.

Margolies, R., & Gilstein, K. W. (1983–1984). A systems approach to the treatment of chronic encopresis. *International Journal of Psychiatry in Medicine, 13,* 141–152.

Matson, J. L., & Ollendick, T. H. (1977). Issues in toilet training normal children. *Behavioral Therapy, 8,* 549–553.

McGee, R., Makinson, T., Williams, S., Simpson, A., & Silva, P. A. (1984). A longitudinal study of enuresis from five to nine years. *Australian Paediatric Journal, 20,* 39–42

McTaggert, A., & Scott, M. (1959). A review of twelve cases of encopresis. *Journal of Pediatrics, 54,* 762–768.

Mesibov, G. B., Schroeder, C. S., & Wesson, L. (1977). Parental concerns about their children. *Journal of Pediatric Psychology, 2,* 13–17.

Mikkelsen, E. J., Brown, G. L., Minichiello, M. D., Millican, F. K., & Rapoport, J. L. (1982). Neurologic status in hyperactive, enuretic, encopretic and normal boys. *Journal of the American Academy of Child Psychiatry, 21,* 75–81.

Mikkelsen, E. J., Rapoport, J. L., Nee, L., Gruenau, C.,

Mendelson, W., & Gillin, J. C. (1980). Childhood enuresis: I. Sleep patterns and psychopathology. *Archives of General Psychiatry, 37,* 1139–1144.

Miller, P. M. (1973). An experimental analysis of retention control training in the treatment of nocturnal enuresis in two institutionalized adolescents. *Behavior Therapy, 4,* 288–294.

Miller, K., Atkin, B., & Moody, M. L. (1992). Drug therapy for nocturnal enuresis: Current treatment recommendations. *Practical Therapeutics, 44*(1), 47–56.

Moffatt, M. E. K. (1989). Nocturnal enuresis: Psychologic implications of treatment and nontreatment. *The Journal of Pediatrics, 114*(4), 697–704.

Moffatt, M. E. K., Kato, C., & Pless, I. B. (1987). Improvements in self-concept after treatment of nocturnal enuresis: Randomized controlled trial. *The Journal of Pediatrics, 110*(4), 647–652.

Moilanen, I., Jarvelin, M. R., Vikevainen-Tervonen, L., & Huttunen, N. P. (1987). Personality and family characteristics of enuretic children. *Psychiatria Fennica, 18,* 53–61.

Morgan, R. T. T., & Young, G. C. (1975). Case histories and shorter communications. *Behaviour Research and Therapy, 13,* 197–199.

Morley, R. (1981). *Worry: How to kick the serenity habit in 98 easy steps.* New York: G. P. Putnam's Sons.

Mowrer, O. H., & Mowrer, W. M. (1938). Enuresis: A method for its study and treatment. *American Journal of Orthopsychiatry, 8,* 436–459.

Norgaard, J. P., Hansen, J. H., Nielsen, J. B., Rittig, S., & Djurhuus, J. C. (1989). Nocturnal studies in enuresis: A polygraphic study of sleep EEG and bladder activity. *Scandinavian Journal of Urology and Nephrology, 125*(Suppl.), 73–78.

Olness, K. (1975). The use of self-hypnosis in the treatment of childhood nocturnal enuresis. *Clinical Pediatrics, 14,* 273–279.

Olness, K. (1976). Autohypnosis in functional megacolon in children. *American Journal of Clinical Hypnosis, 19,* 28–32.

Oppel, W. C., Harper, P. A., & Rider, R. V. (1968). The age of attaining bladder control. *Pediatrics, 42,* 614–626.

Orwell, G. (1970). Such, such were the joys. In S. Orwell & I. Angus (Eds.), *The collected essays, journalism and letters of George Orwell: Vol. 4 In front of your nose, 1945–1950* (p. 379). Washington, DC: Penguin.

Petti, M. J., & Davidson, M. (1991). Idiopathic constipation. In W. A. Walker, P. R. Durie, J. R. Hamilton, J. H. Walker-Smith, & J. B. Watkins (Eds.), *Pediatric gastrointestinal disease: Vol. 1 Pathophysiology, diagnosis, management* (pp. 818–829). Philadelphia: Decker.

Pinkerton, P. (1958). Psychogenic megacolon in children: The implications of bowel negativism. *Archives of Disease in Childhood, 33,* 371–380.

Plag, J. A. (1964). *The problem of enuresis in the naval service.* US Navy Medical Neuropsychiatric Research Unit, Report 64–3. Washington, DC: US Government Printing Office.

Protinsky, H., & Dillard, C. (1983). Enuresis: A family therapy model. *Psychotherapy: Theory, Research and Practice, 22*(1), 81–89.

Rex, D. K., Fitzgerald, J. F., & Goulet, R. J. (1992). Chronic constipation with encopresis persisting beyond 15 years of age. *Diseases of the Colon and Rectum, 35*(3), 242–244.

Rittig, S., Knudsen, U. B., Norgaard, J. P., Pedersen, E. B., & Djurhuus, J. C. (1989). Abnormal diurnal rhythm of plasma vasopressin and urinary output in patients with enuresis. *American Journal of Physiology, 256,* F664–F671.

Ronen, T., & Wozner, Y. (1995). A self-control intervention package for the treatment of primary nocturnal enuresis. *Child & Family Behavior Therapy, 17*(1), 1–21.

Ronen, T., Wozner, Y., & Rahav, G. (1992). Cognitive intervention in enuresis. *Child & Family Behavior Therapy, 14*(2), 1–14.

Roosevelt, J. (1976). *My parents: A differing view*. Chicago: Playboy Press.

Rutter, M. (1973). Indication for research. In I. Kolvin, E. C. MacKeith, & S. R. Meadow (Eds.), *Bladder control and enuresis*. Philadelphia: Lippincott.

Rutter, M., Tizard, J., & Whitmore, K. (1970). *Education, health and behaviour*. London: Longmans, Green.

Rydzinski, J. W., & Kaplan, S. L. (1985). A wolf in sheep's clothing? Simultaneous use of structural family therapy and behavior modification in a case of encopresis and enuresis. *Hillside Journal of Clinical Psychiatry, 7*(1), 71–81.

Salmon, M. A., Taylor, D. C., & Lee, D. (1973). On the EEG in enuresis. In I. Kolvin, R. C. MacKeith, & S. R. Meadow (Eds.), *Bladder control and enuresis*. Philadelphia: Lippincott.

Scott, M. A., Barclay, D. R., & Houts, A. C. (1992). Childhood enuresis: Etiology, assessment, and current behavioral treatment. In M. Hersen, R. M. Eisler, & P. M. Miller (Eds.), *Progress in behavior modification* (Vol. 28, pp. 83–117). Pacific Grove: CA: Sycamore.

Seim, H. C. (1989). Toilet training in first children. *Journal of Family Practice, 29*, 633–636.

Selig, A. L. (1982). Treating nocturnal enuresis in one session of family therapy: A case study. *Journal of Clinical Child Psychology, 11*(3), 234–237.

Shaffer, D. (1973). The association between enuresis and emotional disorder: A review of the literature. In I. Kolvin, R. C. MacKeith, & S. R. Meadow, (Eds.), *Bladder control and enuresis*. Philadelphia: Lippincott.

Solomon, P., & Patch, V. D. (1969). *Handbook of psychiatry*. Los Altos, CA: Lange.

Sondheimer, J. M., & Gervaise, E. P. (1982). Lubricant versus laxative in the treatment of chronic functional constipation of children: A comparative study. *Journal of Pediatric Gastroenterology and Nutrition, 1*(2), 223–226.

Sorotzkin, B. (1984). Nocturnal enuresis: Current perspectives. *Clinical Psychology Review, 4*, 293–315.

Starfield, B. (1967). Functional bladder capacity in enuretic and nonenuretic children. *Journal of Pediatrics, 70*, 777–781.

Starfield, B., & Mellits, E. D. (1968). Increase in functional bladder capacity and improvements in enuresis. *Journal of Pediatrics, 72*, 483–487.

Stark, L. J., Owens-Stively, J., Spirito, A., Lewis, A., & Guevremont, D. (1990). Group behavioral treatment of retentive encopresis. *Journal of Pediatric Psychology, 15*(5), 659–671.

Stark, L. J., Spirito, A., Lewis, A. V., & Hart, K. J. (1990). Encopresis: Behavioral parameters associated with children who fail medical management. *Child Psychiatry and Human Development, 20*(3), 169–179.

Tapia, F., Jekel, J., & Domke, H. R. (1960). Enuresis: An emotional symptom? *Journal of Nervous and Mental Disease, 130*, 61–66.

Thompson, S., & Rey, J. M. (1995). Functional enuresis: Desmopressin the answer? *Journal of the American Academy of Child Adolescent Psychiatry, 34*(3), 266–271.

Tilton, P. (1980). Hypnotic treatment of a child with thumbsucking, enuresis and encopresis. *American Journal of Clinical Hypnosis, 22*, 238–240.

Timms, D. J. (1989). Rapid maxillary expansion in the treatment of nocturnal enuresis. *Angle Orthodontist, 60*(3), 229–239.

Tuzuner, F., Kecik, Y., Ozdemir, S., & Canakei, N. (1990). Electro-acupuncture in the treatment of enuresis nocturna. *Acupuncture and Electro-Therapeutics Research International Journal, 14*, 211–215.

Wagner, W. G., Smith, D., & Norris, W. R. (1988). The psychological adjustment of enuretic children: A comparison of two types. *Journal of Pediatric Psychology, 13*(1), 33–38.

Walker, C. E. (1978). Toilet training, enuresis, and encopresis. In P. Magrab (Ed.), *Psychological management of pediatric problems* (Vol. 1, pp. 129–189). Baltimore: University Park Press.

Walker, C. E. (1995). Elimination disorders: Enuresis and encopresis. In M. C. Roberts (Ed.), *Handbook of pediatric psychology* (2nd ed.). New York: Guilford.

Walker, C. E., Hedberg, A. G., Clement, P. W., & Wright, L. (1981). *Clinical procedures for behavior therapy*. Englewood Cliffs, NJ: Prentice-Hall.

Walker, C. E., & Shaw, W. (1988). Assessment of eating and elimination disorders. In P. Karoly (Ed.), *Handbook of child health assessment* (pp. 434–469). New York: Wiley.

Watanabe, H., Kawauchi, A., Kitamori, T., & Azuma, Y. (1994). Treatment system for nocturnal enuresis according to an original classification system. *European Urology, 25*, 43–50.

Weider, D. J., & Hauri, P. J. (1985). Nocturnal enuresis in children with upper airway obstruction. *International Journal of Pediatric Otorhinolaryngology, 9*, 173–182.

Wells, M. E., & Hinkle, J. S. (1990). Elimination of childhood encopresis: A family systems approach. *Journal of Mental Health Counseling, 12*(4), 520–526.

White, M. (1984). Pseudo-encopresis: From avalanche to victory, from vicious to virtuous cycles. *Family Systems Medicine, 2*(2), 150–160.

Whitehead, W. E. (1992). Biofeedback treatment of gastrointestinal disorders. *Biofeedback and Self-Regulation, 17*(1), 59–76.

Whiting, J. W. M., & Child, I. L. (1964). *Child training and personality: A cross-cultural study*. New Haven, CT: Yale University Press.

Wood, A. (1988). King tiger and the roaring tummies: A novel way of helping young children and their families change. *Journal of Family Therapy, 10*, 49–63.

World Health Organization. (1992). *The ICD-10 classification of mental and behavioural disorders: Clinical description and diagnostic guidelines*. Geneva, Switzerland: Author.

Wright, L., & Walker, C. E. (1977). Treatment of the child with psychogenic encopresis: An effective program of therapy. *Clinical Pediatrics, 16*, 1042–1045.

Xu, B. (1991). 302 cases of enuresis treated with acupuncture. *Journal of Traditional Chinese Medicine, 11*(2), 121–122.

Young, G. C. (1964). A staggered-wakening procedure in the treatment of enuresis. *Medical Officer, 111*, 142–143.

Young, G. C., & Morgan, R. T. T. (1972). Overlearning in the conditioning treatment of enuresis: A longterm follow-up study. *Behaviour Research and Therapy, 10*, 419–420.

Zaleski, A., Gerrard, J. W., & Shokeir, M. H. K. (1973). Nocturnal enuresis: The importance of a small bladder capacity. In I. Kolvin, R. C. MacKeith, & S. R. Meadow (Eds.), *Bladder control and enuresis*. Philadelphia: Lippincott.

5.23
Eating Disorders

DAVID M. GARNER
Toledo Center for Eating Disorders, Bowling Green State University, and University of Toledo, OH, USA
and
LINDA E. MYERHOLTZ
Bowling Green State University, OH, USA

5.23.1 INTRODUCTION

Although eating disorders have been recognized as part of psychiatric nomenclature for many years, it has only been in since the mid-1980s that they have commanded interest in mainstream psychology. Undoubtedly, among the factors responsible for the growing attention shown by researchers and clinicians alike is that eating disorders provide a prototypic model of the complex interaction between cultural, somatic, and psychological factors in the expression of disturbed functioning. The varied psychological features associated with eating disorders contribute to their heterogeneity on presentation. Finally, potentially serious physical and psychological sequelae must be addressed in the understanding and the treatment of the eating disorders. These factors, as well as the apparent increasing prevalence of eating disorders among adolescent and young adult women, have led to a rapid acceleration in theoretical formulations and research bearing on pathogenesis and treatment. Since the mid-1970s there has been divergence in etiological formulations as well as convergence of opinion regarding the utility of certain practical intervention principles. In spite of these advancements, current knowledge has yet to yield conclusive support for any one theoretical viewpoint or treatment modality.

The aims of this chapter are to review diagnostic features, some of the more popular models for understanding eating disorders, and to provide an overview of the major approaches to treatment that derive from different theoretical models.

5.23.2 DIAGNOSTIC AND DEFINING FEATURES

5.23.2.1 Phenomonology

A key feature of anorexia nervosa and bulimia nervosa is a persistent overconcern with body size and shape indicated by behavior such as prolonged fasting, strenuous exercise, and self-induced vomiting aimed at decreasing body weight and fat. In anorexia nervosa, the over-concern has been described variously as a relentless pursuit of thinness (Bruch, 1973), a morbid fear of fatness (Russell, 1970), and a weight phobia (Crisp, 1970). The term "bulimia nervosa" was proposed by Russell (1979) to define a syndrome in which the patient suffers from powerful and intractable urges to overeat leading to bouts of binge eating followed by extreme efforts to control weight through self-induced vomiting, laxative abuse, fasting, vigorous exercise, and other behaviors with similar intent. Bulimia nervosa shares many features in common with anorexia nervosa, however, the patient is not emaciated.

There is general agreement that eating disorder symptoms have psychological and developmental significance. Both individual and family theorists have emphasized that eating disorders often represent a developmental struggle for autonomy, independence, and individuality. These normal development hurdles become flashpoints in adolescence, when the vulnerable individual, parents, or entire family are forced to deal with emergent developmental realities. However, the phenomonology of eating disorders cannot be fully appreciated outside the context of cultural values. There has been intense pressure on women to diet in order to conform to ultra-slender role models for feminine beauty (Garner, 1997; Garner & Garfinkel, 1980). Unfortunately, very few women will ever achieve the admired physical form through restrictive dieting, largely owing to biological limits to achieving permanent weight loss. Nevertheless, constructs such as competence, control, attractiveness, self-worth, and self-discipline have continued to be associated with dieting and weight control in our culture. The consequence of the conflict between cultural imperatives and biological realities has been widespread dissatisfaction with body shape and weight that has even affected young girls yet to cross the pubertal threshold (Edlund, Halvarsson, & Sjödén, 1995).

Another aspect of the phenomonology of anorexia nervosa is the "ego-syntonic" nature of certain symptoms such as pathological dieting and other extreme weight controlling behaviors. In contrast to patients with other psychological disorders such as depression or anxiety, most anorexia nervosa patients actively embrace their eating disorder symptoms. It is not uncommon for patients to actually strive for and then cling to an "anorexic identity" due to the disorder's associations with celebrity status and socially desirable traits. The resistance to change seen in anorexia nervosa has obvious implications for treatment and has been a major focus of therapeutic strategies recommended for this disorder (Garner, Vitousek, & Pike, 1997).

5.23.2.2 Diagnosis

The prevailing diagnostic systems, the *Diagnostic and statistical manual of mental disorders, fourth edition* (*DSM-IV*; American Psychiatric Association [APA], 1994) and the *International Classification of Diseases, 10th revision* (World Health Organization, 1992), formally define as well as distinguish the two major eating disorders, anorexia nervosa and bulimia nervosa. By drawing the boundaries for these eating disorders, the current *DSM-IV* diagnostic criteria have substantial implications for clinical care and research.

5.23.2.2.1 Anorexia nervosa

The requirements for diagnosis of anorexia nervosa according to the *DSM-IV* are summarized as follows: (i) refusal to maintain a body weight over a minimally normal weight for age and height (e.g., weight loss leading to maintenance of a body weight less than 85% of that

expected or failure to make expected weight gain during a period of growth); (ii) intense fear of gaining weight or becoming fat, even though underweight; (iii) disturbance in the way that body weight, size, or shape is experienced; (iv) amenorrhea in females (absence of at least three consecutive menstrual cycles).

The *DSM-IV* divides anorexia nervosa into two diagnostic subtypes: (i) restricting type and (ii) binge eating/purging type. The restricting type is defined by rigid restriction of food intake without bingeing or purging, whereas the binge eating/purging type is defined by stringent attempts to limit intake punctuated by episodes of binge eating as well as self-induced vomiting and/or laxative abuse. This diverges from earlier conventions in which anorexia nervosa was subdivided simply on the basis of the presence or absence of binge eating (Casper, Eckert, Halmi, Goldberg, & Davis, 1980; Garfinkel, Moldofsky, & Garner, 1980). Patients who regularly engage in bulimic episodes report greater impulsivity, social/sexual dysfunction, substance abuse, general impulse control problems, family dysfunction, and depression as part of a general picture of more conspicuous emotional disturbance compared to patients with the restricting subtype of anorexia nervosa (Garner, Garfinkel, & O'Shaughnessy, 1985; Garner, Garner, & Rosen, 1993; Herzog, Keller, Sacks, Yeh, & Lavori, 1992; Laessle, Wittchen, Fichter, & Pirke, 1989; Rosen, Murkofsky, Steckler, & Skolnick, 1989). In contrast, restricting anorexia nervosa patients have been described as overly compliant but at the same time obstinate, perfectionistic, obsessive-compulsive, shy, introverted, interpersonally sensitive, and stoical (Casper, 1990, Hsu, Kaye, & Weltzin, 1993; Strober, 1983).

5.23.2.2.2 Bulimia nervosa

The criteria for the diagnosis of bulimia nervosa according to the *DSM-IV* are summarized as follows: (i) recurrent episodes of binge eating (a sense of lack of control over eating a large amount of food in a discrete period of time); (ii) recurrent inappropriate compensatory behavior in order to prevent weight gain (i.e., vomiting, abuse of laxatives, diuretics or other medications, fasting or excessive exercise); (iii) a minimum average of two episodes of binge eating and inappropriate compensatory behaviors per week for the past three months; (iv) self-evaluation unduly influenced by body shape and weight; and (v) the disturbance does not occur exclusively during episodes of anorexia nervosa. Bulimia nervosa patients are further subdivided into purging and nonpurging types based on the regular use of self-induced vomiting, laxatives, or diuretics (APA, 1994).

5.23.2.2.3 Eating disorders not otherwise specified

The *DSM-IV* delineates a large and heterogeneous diagnostic category, "eating disorder, not otherwise specified" (EDNOS), for individuals with clinically significant eating disorders but who fail to meet all of the diagnostic criteria for anorexia nervosa or bulimia nervosa. Unfortunately, the term "not otherwise specified" could be interpreted as connoting eating problems of minor clinical significance. This assumption is incorrect since the clinical picture for many individuals with EDNOS can be every bit as complicated and serious as the two main eating disorders (Walsh & Garner, 1997). The binge eating disorder is a specific example of an EDNOS included in the current *DSM-IV*. This term applies to individuals who share a number of characteristics of individuals with bulimia nervosa, but who do not regularly engage in the inappropriate compensatory behaviors, such as self-induced vomiting, required for the diagnosis of bulimia nervosa. In order to qualify for this diagnosis, binge eating must occur, on average, at least twice a week for a six-month period. Although there is merit in adopting the binge eating disorder into the diagnostic nomenclature, it is critical to remain aware of the fact that binge eating and associated psychological symptoms, particularly in the obese, may be attributed to standard weight loss treatments (cf. Garner & Wooley, 1991). Other examples of EDNOS have received less attention but are of clear clinical importance. Terms such as "bulimia," "compulsive eating," "normal weight bulimia," often used to describe eating disorders, do not appear in the *DSM-IV*.

5.23.2.2.4 Relationship between different eating disorders

There is extraordinary variability within each of the diagnostic subgroups in terms of demographic, clinical, and psychological variables (Welch, Hall, & Renner, 1990). Patients with anorexia nervosa and bulimia nervosa have been observed to move between diagnostic categories at different points in time (Russell, 1979). For example, patients move between the two subtypes of anorexia nervosa (restricting and binge eating/purging types); however, the tendency is for restricters to move toward bulimia (and purging) more often than bulimic anorexics move to an exclusively abstaining mode (Garner et al., 1993; Hsu, 1988; Kreipe, Churchill, & Strauss, 1989).

Even though distinctions between diagnostic subgroups have been emphasized in the research literature, it is important to recognize that the different diagnostic subgroups tend to share many features in common. For example, even though anorexia nervosa patients are differentiated into "restricter" and "binge eating/ purging" subtypes, it must be remembered that virtually all eating disorder patients "restrict their food intake," "diet" and probably "fast" for abnormally long periods of time. Some do this in association with binge eating, some with vomiting, and/or purgation, and some with neither of these symptoms. For some this occurs at a statistically "normal" body weight (bulimia nervosa) and for others it occurs well over the body weight norms (e.g., binge-eating disorder). Figure 1 characterizes the relationship between bingeing, purging, and restricting in subgroups of eating disorder patients at different body weights.

5.23.2.2.5 Differential diagnosis

Patients without anorexia nervosa, bulimia nervosa, or some variant can superficially resemble patients with an eating disorder diagnosis. Patients with a severe affective disorder can display marked weight loss (due to loss of appetite) or hyperphagia. Schizophrenia can present with an aversion to eating and occasionally binge eating or purging. Vomiting and weight loss also can be associated with what has been described as a conversion disorder (Garfinkel, Kaplan, Garner, & Darby, 1983). A range of physical illnesses producing weight loss (e.g., inflammatory bowel disease, chronic hepatitis, Addison's disease, Crohn's disease, undiagnosis cystic fibrosis, diabetes mellitus, hyperthyroidism, tuberculosis, malignancies, malabsorption diseases, or other wasting diseases) should be ruled out as the primary diagnosis (Powers, 1997).

5.23.3 EPIDEMIOLOGY

5.23.3.1 Incidence and Prevalence

Incidence rates are defined as the number of new cases in the population per year, whereas prevalence rates refers to the actual number of cases in the population at a certain point in time. Prevalence studies have been the most common and have often been conducted on high-risk populations such as college students and athletes. There are serious limitations to estimates of the incidence and prevalence of eating disorders, because most have been derived exclusively from self-report instruments and on samples that may not reflect important

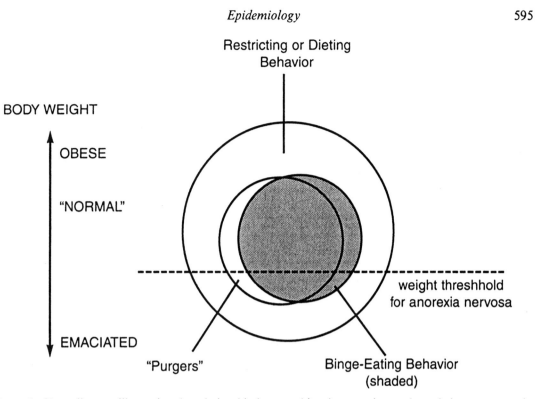

Figure 1 Venn diagram illustrating the relationship between bingeing, purging, and restricting symptoms in eating disorder patients at different body weights. Purging and bingeing are overlaping sets of symptoms that characterize subgroups of patients at different points along the weight spectrum. Anorexia nervosa patients fall below a critical weight threshold (adapted with permission from Garner, Garner, & Rosen, 1993).

demographic differences in base rates. In general, estimates based exclusively on questionnaires yield much higher rates of eating disorders.

Estimates of incidence based on detected cases in primary care practices yielded rates of 8.1 per 100 000 persons per year for anorexia nervosa and 11.5 for bulimia nervosa (Hoek et al., 1995). The most sophisticated prevalence studies using strict diagnostic criteria report rates of about 0.3% for anorexia nervosa and about 1% for bulimia nervosa among young females in the community (Fairburn & Beglin, 1990; Hoek, 1993). This compares to surveys using questionnaires that find that as many as 19% of female students report bulimic symptoms. Prevalence studies of higher risk samples indicate that serious eating disorders occur in as many as 4% of female high school and college students (cf. Fairburn & Beglin, 1990). Suspected cases of clinical eating disorders or subclinical variants are even more common among groups exposed to heightened pressures to diet or maintain a thin shape. Research has confirmed a high incidence of actual or suspected cases among samples of ballet students and professional dancers, wrestlers, swimmers, skaters, and gymnasts (cf. Garner & Rosen, 1991).

5.23.3.2 Gender Considerations

Epidemiological studies have consistently found that eating disorders are more common among women than men; in clinical samples, only 5–10% of patients are men (Hoek et al., 1995). Studies in the USA suggest the incidence of anorexia nervosa among males may be as little as 0.02% per year and the prevalence of current bulimia nervosa in men is between 0.1% and 0.5%. The differences in gender rates for the eating disorders are generally attributed to cultural factors (Garner & Garfinkel, 1980); however, biological and psychodynamic factors may also play a role (Scott, 1986). Eating disorders are less common in men, but when they occur, they have a clinical picture very similar to that observed in women (Andersen, 1990; Olivardia, Pope, Mangweth, & Hudson, 1995).

5.23.3.3 Developmental Considerations

From the earliest descriptions, there has been agreement that anorexia nervosa is a disorder primarily of adolescence and that the core psychopathology often relates to conflicts that emerge with pubertal changes in body shape.

Theander (1996) reviewed the topic of age at onset and concluded that the average age of onset is usually found to be about 17 years of age with about 30% of cases with an onset at 14 years or younger. Selection bias yields younger age at onset in pediatric treatment facilities. Theander (1996) summarizes the distribution of age at onset as follows: (i) there are occasional patients with an early age of onset (7–10 years of age); (ii) the number of cases rises steeply at ages 11 and 12; (iii) most patients develop in the teenage, 13–19; (iv) there is a gradual decline in onset from 20 to 30 years; and (v) there are fewer cases with an onset after 30 years of age. Some have found that age of onset tends to be a bit younger for males than females; however, this point remains controversial (Theander, 1996).

The age of onset of anorexia nervosa is paralleled by data on body dissatisfaction and dieting in nonclinical populations, again supporting developmental vulnerability. Feeling fat and restricting food intake are common among schoolchildren 7–13 years of age (Davies & Furnham, 1986; Edlund et al., 1995; Maloney, McGuire, & Daniels, 1988; Wardle & Beales, 1986). Dieting to lose weight and fear of fatness are common in girls as young as seven years old; these attitudes and behaviors escalate significantly during adolescence, particularly among those at the heavier end of the weight spectrum (Edlund et al.). In a study of 1410 students in grades 9 through 12 (mean age 16.5 years) Timmerman, Wells, and Chen (1990) reported that 2% of the girls and 0.14% of the boys met all of the diagnostic criteria for bulimia nervosa ascertained through an anonymous self-report instrument. Severe dieting because of a fear of fatness has been shown to lead to short-stature syndrome and delayed puberty in a subgroup of young children (Puglifse, Lifshitz, Grad, Fort, & Marks-Katz, 1983). In 1990, 44% of female high school students were trying to lose weight compared to 15% of male students (Serdula et al., 1993). An additional 26% of female students and 15% of male students were trying to keep from gaining more weight. It has been shown that the risk of developing an eating disorder is eight times higher in dieting compared to nondieting 15-year-old girls (Patton, Johnson-Sabine, Wood, Mann, & Wakeling, 1990). Although there are case reports of anorexia nervosa in young children (Fosson, Knibbs, Bryant-Waugh, & Lask; 1987), the consensus is that it is very rare in this age group (Jaffe & Singer, 1989; Lask & Bryant-Waugh, 1997). Similarly, though probably rarely, cases of anorexia nervosa also have been observed at the other end of the age spectrum (Kellett, Trimble, & Thorley, 1976).

5.23.3.4 Have Eating Disorders Changed Over Time?

Anorexia nervosa was once believed to be restricted to the higher socioeconomic classes; however, there is evidence that it has become more common in middle and lower socioeconomic groups (Gowers & McMahon, 1989). According to Russell (1985, 1997), the most dramatic evidence for a transformation in the psychopathology of anorexia nervosa is the increased appearance of binge eating, both in anorexia nervosa and eating disorder patients who are not emaciated. However, the actual extent to which binge eating has become more common in anorexia nervosa is unclear owing to the fact that the symptom may have been identified less reliably in earlier reports (Garner, 1993).

Casper (1983) suggested another shift in the psychopathology of eating disorders over the past several decades whereby "ascetic motives" for weight loss have become less prominent, replaced by the "drive for thinness" as the most common motivational theme. The theme of asceticism was common in early writings on anorexia nervosa (cf. Bell, 1985; Rampling, 1985) and is expressed in the conceptions of dieting as purification, thinness as virtue, and fasting as an act of penitence. Nevertheless, there is a subgroup of eating disordered patients who seem to be motivated by belief in the virtue of oral self-restraint (Garner & Bemis, 1982, 1985; Garner et al., 1997). Evidence suggests that "oral self-restraint" may be part of a more general theme of renunciation of physical gratification (Haimes & Katz, 1988). This is supported by findings that anorexia nervosa patients have elevated scores on the Asceticism subscale of the Eating Disorder Inventory (Garner, 1991), a subscale designed to identify the tendency to seek virtue through the pursuit of spiritual ideals, such as self-discipline, self-denial, self-restraint, self-sacrifice, and control of bodily urges.

5.23.4 COMORBIDITY

Since the earliest descriptions of anorexia nervosa there has been considerable controversy as to whether eating disorders represent discrete psychological entities or are simply manifestations of other illnesses (cf. Beumont, Al-Alami, & Touyz, 1987). Anorexia nervosa and bulimia nervosa each have been considered variants of affective disorder, obsessive-compulsive disorder, or borderline personality disorder. Traits such as hostility, somatization, social maladjustment, physical anhedonia, affective rigidity, interpersonal sensitivity, anxiety, poor self-esteem, external locus of control, and confused sex-role identity have been observed repeatedly in eating disorder patients (Beumont, George, & Smart, 1976; Garfinkel & Garner, 1982; Garner et al., 1993; Johnson & Connors, 1987; Rastam, Gillberg, & Gillberg, 1995; Strober, 1981; Swift & Wonderlich, 1988; Williamson, 1990). Although there is general acceptance that eating disorders are best considered as discrete clinical entities there is growing interest in psychological features that may define meaningful subgroups of eating-disordered patients.

5.23.4.1 Depression

Depression has been described as a common theme in eating disorders, but its precise role is controversial. Pope and Hudson (1988) originally argued that bulimia nervosa is a variant of depression based on evidence that eating disorder patients exhibit: (i) a high prevalence of depression, (ii) a family history of depression, (iii) biological markers of depression, and (iv) a positive response to antidepressant medications. Detractors from this view provide alternative interpretations for these associations and contend that the nature of bulimia nervosa as a variant of depression is "simplistic and theoretically limiting" (Strober & Katz, 1988). Although depression may play an important predisposing role in eating disorders, current evidence fails to support the proposition that eating disorders are simply depressive equivalents (Cooper & Fairburn, 1986; Hinz & Williamson, 1987; Laessle, Kittl, Fichter, Wittchen, & Pirke, 1987; Wilson & Lindholm, 1987). This said, the evidence is overwhelming that depression is one of the most common experiences of those with eating disorders, and to minimize the significance of this experience would be misleading. Moreover, bulimia nervosa patients with a history of affective disorder or substance abuse disorder report significantly more suicide attempts, social impairment, and previous treatment, both before and after the onset of the eating disorder (Hatsukami, Mitchell, Eckert, & Pyle, 1986). Hatsukami et al. (1986) found no suicide attempts among the group of patients with bulimia alone; however, 26.5% of those with concurrent affective disorder and 32.4% with substance abuse had attempted suicide. Bulimia nervosa patients with a history of substance abuse also report a high incidence of stealing, perhaps suggesting a more general problem with impulsivity.

Some studies indicate that depressive states of varying intensities foreshadow the development of anorexia nervosa with lifetime prevalence rates of major depressive illness ranging between 25% and 80% across different samples (Herzog, Keller, Sacks, Yeh, & Lavori, 1992). Halmi et al. (1991) found a lifetime prevalence of 68% for major depression in a sample of severely ill anorexia nervosa patients. Depression can be secondary to starvation and coexisting complications since improved mood often follows nutritional rehabilitation (Eckert, Halmi, Marchi, & Cohen, 1987). One population study found that depression typically did not precede the eating disorder, although it did correlate with onset (Rastam, 1992). In a six-year follow-up, Rastam et al. (1995) found that affective disorders were common throughout the follow-up period, but tended to follow the course of the disorder rather than to precede or postdate it. Thus, a history of affective disorder may be a foreboding complication for a subgroup of eating-disordered patients who may be particularly resistant to treatment efforts. Unfortunately, this subgroup of patients does not seem to respond more favorably to antidepressant therapy than those without a history of mood disorder (Brotman, Herzog, & Woods, 1984).

5.23.4.2 Anxiety

A lifetime prevalence of social phobia has been identified in more than 25% of anorexia nervosa patients (Halmi et al., 1991). The most common anxiety symptoms documented in anorexia nervosa are obsessive-compulsive (OC) in nature (Halmi et al., 1991; Rastam, 1992; Rastam et al., 1995; Rottenberg, 1988; Thiel, Broocks, Ohlmeier, Jacoby, & Schußler, 1995). In reviewing comorbidity in anorexia nervosa, Rothenberg (1988) found OC symptoms reported in anywhere between 11% and 83% of patient samples, either during the active phase of the disorder or after weight restoration. In a sample of 93 women with either anorexia or bulimia nervosa, Thiel et al. (1995) found that 37% met diagnostic criteria for OC disorder. These patients with concomitant OC disorder also had higher mean scores on five of eight Eating Disorder Inventory subscale scores. Rastam et al. followed a sample of anorexia nervosa patients six years after onset and found a high rate of OC disorder and that underlying personality disorders tended to predict poor outcome. A common diathesis between eating disorders and OC disorder is suggested by the finding that 11% of 151 women presenting with OC disorder had a history of anorexia nervosa (Kasvikis, Isakiris, Marks, Basoglu, & Noshirvani, 1986).

5.23.4.3 Personality Disorders

Since the mid-1980s, there has been intense interest in the relationship between eating disorders and personality disorders. A number of reports have indicated that almost two-thirds of eating-disordered patients receive a concurrent diagnosis of a personality disorder, with borderline personality disorder being reported as particularly common (Bulik, Sullivan, Joyce, & Carter, 1995; Cooper et al., 1988; Gillberg, Rastam, & Gillberg, 1995; Johnson, Tobin, & Dennis, 1990; Levin & Hyler, 1986; Piran, Lerner, Garfinkel, Kennedy, & Brouilette, 1988). Levin and Hyler (1986) assessed 24 bulimia nervosa patients and found that 15 (63%) met diagnostic criteria for personality disorder, with six (25%) fulfilling the diagnosis for borderline personality disorder. Similarly, Bulik et al. (1995) found at least one personality disorder in 63% of a sample of 76 women with bulimia nervosa. Fifty-one percent of the personality disorders were in cluster C (specifically, avoidant, OC, or dependent personality disorders), 41% in cluster B (particularly, borderline or histrionic), and 33% in cluster A (paranoid, schizoid, or schizotypal). In an earlier evaluation of 35 patients with eating disorders, Gartner, Marcus, Halmi, and Loranger (1989) found that 57% met the *DSM-III-R* diagnostic criteria for at least one form of personality disorder, with borderline, self-defeating, and avoidant being the most common. Two or more Axis II diagnostic criteria were met by 40% of the patients, and 17% fulfilled all of the criteria for 5–7 personality disorder diagnoses. Wonderlich, Swift, Slotnick, and Goodman (1990) interviewed 46 eating-disordered patients and reported that 72% met criteria for at least one personality disorder. OC personality disorder was common among restricting anorexic patients. Histrionic and borderline personality disorder diagnoses were common among bulimic groups. Johnson et al. (1990) followed patients one year after an initial assessment and found that those who initially scored above a threshold on the self-report Borderline Syndrome Index had a worse prognosis in terms of eating behavior and general psychiatric symptoms. Gillberg et al. (1995) found that OC and avoidant personality disorders were particularly common in a study comparing 51 anorexia nervosa patients with an age-matched community sample.

Arguing that borderline assessment measures are confounded by certain eating symptoms, Pope and Hudson (1989) have challenged the interpretation that borderline personality disorder is over-represented among eating disorders. For example, bulimic eating patterns may be used to satisfy the *DSM-III-R* poor impulse control criterion for borderline personality disorder, making the association between disorders tautological. Nevertheless, the tendency toward poor impulse regulation has been identified as a negative prognostic sign in eating disorders (e.g., Hatsukami et al., 1986; Sohlberg, Norring, Holmgren, & Rosmark, 1989). Results from research on the incidence and prevalence of personality disorders in anorexia nervosa are inconsistent. Some studies indicate remarkably high rates, with avoidant personality disorder occurring in as many as 33% of anorexic restricters and borderline personality disorder occurring in almost 40% of anorexic bulimic patients (Piran et al., 1988). Other studies suggest that personality disorders are relatively uncommon in anorexia nervosa (Herzog et al., 1992; Pope & Hudson, 1989). Impulse control problems, such as self-mutilation, suicide attempts, and stealing, are reported in a subgroup of anorexia nervosa patients, particularly those with purging and/or bulimic symptoms (Fahy & Eisler, 1993; Garner et al., 1993). While personality disturbances are not uniform in eating disorders, their presence suggests meaningful subtypes that may be relevant to treatment planning and prognosis.

5.23.4.4 Sexual Abuse

There has been considerable interest and controversy regarding the role of sexual abuse as a risk factor for the development of eating disorders. Clinical accounts and the observation in some studies of a high incidence of sexual abuse in eating disorder patient samples (Oppenheimer, Howells, Palmer, & Chaloner, 1985) were followed by further clinical reports and numerous empirical studies yielding conflicting findings (Fallon & Wonderlich, 1997). Fallon and Wonderlich summarized the literature and concluded that: (i) childhood sexual abuse appears to be positively associated with bulimia nervosa; (ii) there is less evidence for this association in anorexia nervosa; (iii) childhood sexual abuse does not appear to be a specific risk factor for eating disorders (i.e., it is no higher for eating disorders than in psychiatric controls); (iv) childhood sexual abuse does appear to be associated with greater levels of comorbidity among those with eating disorders, however, there is not strong evidence that it predicts a more severe eating disorder; and (v) a more complex approach to the definition of sexual abuse has led to better prediction of later disturbances in eating. It is indisputable that a significant subgroup of women from some clinical eating disorder samples have a history of sexual abuse and that careful assessment and treatment is important in the process of dealing with resulting feelings of shame, distrust, and anger (Fallon & Wonderlich, 1997).

5.23.5 ETIOLOGY

A complete understanding of anorexia nervosa and bulimia nervosa must account for factors that predispose individuals to each of the eating disorders. Theory should be able to delineate the variety of developmental experiences that interact with these factors to initiate symptom expression as well as account for the maintaining variables (biological, psychological, and interpersonal) and the key variations in the symptom picture. Although current models are unable to specify all of these elements in precise detail, research and clinical observations since the mid-1970s have improved the understanding of eating disorders, which in turn, has led to more sophisticated treatment recommendations.

In the latter half of the twentieth century single-factor causal theories have been replaced by the view that eating disorders are "multi-determined" (Garfinkel & Garner, 1982; Garner, 1993; Garner & Garfinkel, 1980). The symptom patterns represent final common pathways resulting from the interplay of three broad classes of predisposing factors shown in Figure 2. The role of cultural, individual (psychological and biological), and familial causal factors are presumed to combine with each other in different ways leading to the development of eating disorders. The precipitants are less clearly understood except that dieting is invariably an early element. Perhaps the most practical advancements in treatment have come from increased awareness of the perpetuating effects of starvation with its psychological, emotional, and physical consequences (Figure 2).

5.23.5.1 Genetic Contributions

The evidence for genetic vulnerability to anorexia nervosa comes from approximately 100 twin pairs culled from selected twin case report summaries and from twin studies (Garfinkel & Garner, 1982; Holland, Sicotte, & Treasure, 1988). These reports indicate concordance rates of more than 50% for monozygotic twin pairs compared to less than 10% for dizygotic twins. This is in contrast to one study of 11 twin pairs (5 monozygotic) where none of the co-twins was found to be concordant for anorexia nervosa (Waters, Beaumont, Touyz, & Kennedy, 1990). Strober,

Lampert, Morrell, Burroughs, and Jacobs (1990) found first degree relatives of eating disorder patients have a greater risk of having anorexia nervosa. Monozygotic twins have a concordance rate of about 50% compared to about 10% for dizygotic twin pairs (Holland et al., 1988). These studies suggest that there may be a genetic component to the transmission of anorexia nervosa; however, it is not at all clear what is inherited. Is it the specific disorder, a particular personality trait associated with the disorder, or a general vulnerability to psychiatric disturbance? Moreover, the concordance data on twins reared together does not conclusively distinguish between genetic and environmental transmission (Holland et al.).

5.23.5.2 Developmental Theory

Defined in broad terms, many theories have offered developmental explanations of eating disorders. Some formulations have emphasized intrapsychic mediation and others have highlighted interactional factors. Together they have provided a rich understanding of a range of psychological themes that may account for both anorexia nervosa and bulimia nervosa.

Many of the early psychodynamic writings on eating disorders emphasized anorexia nervosa as a rejection of adult femininity. This theme was refined and extended by Crisp (1965) who contends that the central psychopathology of both anorexia nervosa and bulimia nervosa is related to fears of the psychological and biological experiences associated with adult weight. According to this view, starvation becomes the mechanism for avoiding psychobiological maturity because it results in a return to prepubertal appearance and hormonal status. This regression is thought to provide relief from adolescent turmoil and conflicts within the family. Moreover, patients report experiencing themselves as younger following extreme weight loss, and this may be due to the reversal of mature adolescent hormonal profiles that form the biological substrata for psychological experience (Crisp, 1980).

Other developmental theorists have attributed eating disorders to various types of parenting failure. Bruch (1973) and Selvini-Palazzoli (1974) provided a developmental paradigm in which the mother superimposes her own inaccurate perceptions of the child's needs on the child. Such invalidation of the child's experiences results in an arrest of cognitive development and is manifest in debilitating feelings of ineffectiveness that are later evident in adolescent struggles for autonomy and control of the body. Bruch (1973) postulated

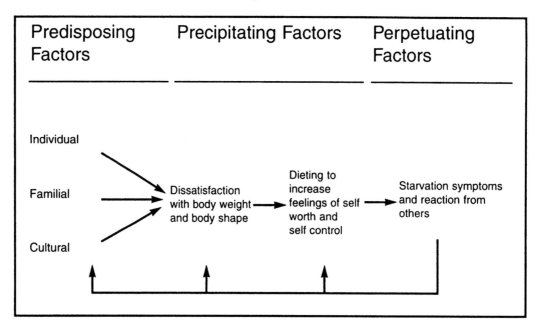

Figure 2 Eating disorders as multidetermined disorders. ("Pathogenesis of anorexia nervosa," by D. M. Garner, 1993, *The Lancet, 341*, p. 1632. Copyright 1993 by *The Lancet*. Reprinted with permission.)

that these early parenting failures lead to fundamental deficits in self-awareness, including the way that the body is perceived and experienced.

A similar view is expressed by theorists working from an object relations model to account for eating disorders (Johnson & Connors, 1987; Masterson, 1977; Stern, 1986; Sugarman, Quinlan, & Devenis, 1982). According to this view, normal development is characterized by the process of separation–individuation, a state achieved by consistent interactions with a primary caretaker who is highly responsive to the needs of the child. Success is reflected by the child's progressive internalization of the ability to accurately recognize, respond, and regulate internal needs and impulses without contact with the immediate caregiver. Accordingly, the different personality structures of eating disordered patients reflect developmental arrest at particular phases of the process of separation–individuation. The eating disorder symptoms are an attempt to cope with needs stemming from incomplete self-development or an interruption of the separation–individuation process.

The self-psychology perspective of Kohut (1971) has also been used to account for eating disorders as a reflection of developmental arrest in the separation–individuation process (Casper, 1983; Goodsitt, 1985; Swift & Letven, 1984). According to this conceptual scheme, the eating disordered patient's lack of a cohesive sense of self is the direct result of the primary

caregiver's failure to provide essential functions during development. These include mirroring, tension regulation, and integration. The obsessive concern about eating and repeated bouts of bingeing and vomiting serve organizing and tension-regulation functions in the attempt to modulate basic deficits in "self-structures." These symptoms become an organizing event in one's life and provide intense stimulation that numb the anguish and emptiness that pervade the eating disordered patient's experience. There is growing empirical evidence to support the clinical view that intense separation distress is common among eating disorders and that many patients demonstrate marked separation anxiety in response to severely as well as mildly stressful situations (Armstrong & Roth, 1989).

Others have emphasized the motivation for binge eating as an attempt to escape negative aspects of self-awareness (cf. Heatherton & Baumeister, 1991). According to this view, the binge eater experiences negative self-evaluations and concerns about perceived negative evaluations from others that are accompanied by anxiety and depression. Binge eating provides a means of avoiding this unpleasant state of negative self-awareness through the narrowing of attention to one facet of the immediate environment.

Strober (1991) has drawn together developmental theory, psychobiology, and personality genetics in offering a valuable understanding of the adaptive mechanisms behind the range of symptoms seen in eating disorder patients. He integrates modern psychoanalytic concepts of development with constructs indicating that: (i) individual differences may be expected in the internal regulators of arousability or temperament that organize self-experiences, and (ii) heritable personality traits, and their presumed biological substrata, set limits within which behavior patterns are expressed. Strober accounts for the differences in traits seen in subgroups of eating disorder patients by incorporating Cloninger's (1989) concept of three bipolar, and primarily genetically determined, dimensions of personality that appear to account for remarkable consistency over time in both normal and psychopathological behavior.

5.23.5.3 Familial Factors

Some of the earliest descriptions of anorexia nervosa emphasized the role of the family in the development of the disorder (cf. Garfinkel & Garner, 1982). The possible role of the family in the development of anorexia nervosa and bulimia nervosa has been described by writers from a range of theoretical orientations (Bruch, 1973; Dare & Eisler, 1997; Garfinkel & Garner, 1982; Humphrey, 1989; Minuchin, Rosman, & Baker, 1978; Root, Fallon, & Friedrich, 1985; Schwartz, Barrett, & Saba, 1985; Selvini-Palazzoli, 1974; Vandereycken, Kog, & Vanderlinden, 1989). A major advancement in family therapy with eating disorders was the formulation of the structural approach of Minuchin et al. (1978). They identified a number of characteristics of the interactions encountered in eating disordered families, including enmeshment, overprotectiveness, rigidity, and poor conflict resolution. The systemic model was applied to eating disorders by Selvini-Palazzoli (1974) and overlaps considerably with the structural model. The systemic approach holds that the identified patient serves an essential homeostatic or stabilizing role within the family. A second generation of family theorists have integrated and greatly elaborated earlier approaches providing very specific advice regarding the treatment of bulimia nervosa (Root et al., 1985; Schwartz et al., 1985; Vandereycken et al., 1989).

Regardless of their orientation, most individual and family theorists have emphasized that anorexia nervosa often represents a developmental struggle for autonomy, independence, and individuality. These issues are very likely to surface in adolescence, when the vulnerable individual, parents, or entire family are forced to deal with emergent developmental realities.

In the only controlled trial examining the efficacy of family therapy for anorexia nervosa, Russell, Szmukler, Dare, and Eisler (1987) found that family therapy was superior to individual therapy for younger patients. This study, as well as clinical experience, suggests that family therapy should be routinely employed as the treatment of choice for young eating disorder patients.

5.23.5.4 The Addiction Model

The term compulsive overeating is somewhat problematical since the *DSM-III-R* diagnostic criteria for OC disorder specifically excludes those who meet an eating disorder diagnosis. Nevertheless, the suggestion that binge eating is compulsive behavior and a form of substance abuse has intuitive appeal on a number of grounds. Studies have shown both that substance abuse and poor impulse regulation are common features in bulimia nervosa (Garner, Rockert, et al., 1985; Garner et al., 1993; Hatsukami, Owen, Pyle, & Mitchell, 1982). Moreover, bulimia nervosa shares several features with addictive disorders that have been summarized by Bemis (1985) as: (i) "loss of control, (ii) preoccupation with the abused substance, (iii) use of the abused substance to cope with stress and negative feelings, (iv) secrecy about the behavior, and maintenance of the addictive behavior despite the aversive consequences" (p. 415).

The addiction model is the framework for Overeaters Anonymous (OA), one of the most popular self-help programs for bulimia nervosa and for other commercial eating disorder programs patterned after the OA or "12-step" approach to chemical dependency. Malenbaum, Herzog, Eisenthal, and Wyshak (1988) have described many of the benefits of OA, including group support, "sponsorship" by someone who has achieved some measure of success, and the clear guiding philosophy originally applied to alcoholism in Alcoholics Anonymous. OA programs are aimed at achieving abstinence from compulsive overeating which is achieved, in part, by adhering to several behavioral axioms. Participants are usually advised to eat nothing beyond three meals a day, on the basis of the premise that certain foods are "addicting" and will trigger bouts of compulsive overeating (Malenbaum et al., 1988).

Although there are parallels between eating disorders and chemical dependency, there are serious theoretical and practical limitations to the comparison. Bemis (1985), and more recently Wilson (1991, 1993), have provided a thorough analysis of the topic, and only the

salient points will be reviewed. The most
obvious flaw in the application of the addiction
model to overeating is that abstinence from food
(unlike abstinence from alcohol) is obviously
unrealistic, and recommending "controlled
eating" is analogous to recommending controlled drinking, which is antithetical to the
abstinence model applied to substance abuse
(Bemis, 1985; Garner, 1985; Malenbaum et al.,
1988; Wilson, 1991, 1993). The parallel breaks
down further in trying to understand the nature
of the compulsive overeater's addiction. Empirical evidence is lacking for the assertion that
specific foods are addicting. Moreover, the OA
explanation of compulsive overeating is completely inconsistent with the far more parsimonious understanding of binge eating, food
preoccupations and food cravings as biological
adaptations to chronic undernutrition (Garner,
1997; Garner, Rockert, et al., 1985; Wardle,
1987). Thus, to the degree that OA programs
encourage "control" by avoiding certain foods
while not deviating from three small meals a day
(Garner, 1985), they may inadvertently collude
with the bulimia nervosa patient's restrictive
eating patterns. Unfortunately, these programs
also reinforce the fear that normal eating will
result in inordinate weight gain. Moreover,
encouraging participants to avoid "forbidden
foods" is inconsistent with the evidence from the
treatment literature on the effectiveness of
incorporating these foods into a daily eating
plan (Rosen & Leitenberg, 1985).

While strongly encouraging abstinence from
bingeing or vomiting is consistent with recommendations of other treatment approaches, the
relative intolerance for "slips" in some abstinence oriented eating disorder programs may
exacerbate the harsh, self-critical, and dichot-
omous thinking patterns that are already
prominent among these patients (Bemis,
1985). The OA model also has been criticized
for presenting compulsive overeating as an
"incurable illness," a characterization that
contradicts the growing literature on treatment
success. Finally, whereas some patients find the
spiritual orientation of the OA approach
appealing, others may find it incompatible with
their religious or moral beliefs. In Wilson's
(1991) review of the addiction model of eating
disorders, he decisively concludes that: (i) it does
not address the core clinical features of eating
disorders, (ii) it fails to account for the effects of
dieting on behavior, and (iii) it may seriously
undermine the effectiveness of treatment. Despite these criticisms, it is important to acknowledge that many find the OA model useful and
effective. Clearly what is needed is research
extending the one uncontrolled report in the
literature (Malenbaum et al., 1988).

5.23.5.5 Cultural Factors

A complete understanding of eating disorders
requires attention to the cultural forces selectively impinging on young girls and women in
modern times. One of the most pernicious has
been the intense pressure to diet and to engage in
strict weight control in order to meet unrealistic
standards for thinness (Garner & Garfinkel,
1980; Garner, Garfinkel, Schwartz, & Thompson, 1980). Young women today are totally
immersed in the cultural admiration of a
physical form for women that has little to do
with the actual shape of most women in our
society. The disconcerting result is a norm in
which women report being dissatisfied with
their shapes and to feeling guilty about eating
even reasonable amounts of food. It has been
increasingly recognized that dieting can play a
direct role in causing a range of symptoms such
as binge eating and mood disturbances (Garner,
1997; Garner, Rockert, et al., 1985; Polivy &
Herman, 1985; Striegel-Moore, Silberstein, &
Rodin, 1986). The values surrounding slender-
ness have become sufficiently embedded in our
cultural value system that many of the symptoms required for eating disorders are not
viewed as unusual or abnormal by members of
the general public (Huon, Brown, & Morris,
1988). There is even some evidence that eating
disorders may have developed a positive social
stereotype and, in some instances, may be
spread by social contagion (Bruch, 1985;
Chiodo & Latimer, 1983). Recognition of the
impact of cultural factors on norms related to
dieting and weight control has led to the
conclusion that eating disorders may develop
in those without underlying personality disturbances or family dysfunction, although
secondary disruption in both of these areas
may be present by the time the person presents
for an assessment (Garner, 1997). Much of
current psychological theorizing related to
eating disorders may be criticized for not
accounting for these cultural factors or, when
they are mentioned, not specifying the details of
how they must be integrated into the understanding of the psychology of the disorder.

5.23.6 MULTIMODAL ASSESSMENT

Descriptive refinements along with advances
in the areas of diagnosis, pathogenesis, and
treatment have resulted in tremendous improvements in the technology of assessment
(Crowther & Sherwood, 1997). While there is
no universally accepted assessment protocol for
eating disorders, there is a consensus on the
value of a multimodal assessment approach
based on the conceptualization of eating

disorders as multidetermined and heterogeneous in nature.

The targets for assessment of the eating disorder patient can be divided into two main areas. First is specific psychopathology and behavioral patterns that define the core features of the disorders. Symptoms such as binge eating, extreme weight control behaviors, and stereotypic attitudes toward weight or shape fall into this category. Second is psychopathology not necessarily specific to eating disorder patients, but that has particular theoretical or clinical relevance. Examples include psychological features such as low self-esteem, perfectionism, fears of psychobiological maturity, poor impulse control, and reactions to sexual abuse. There are also more general associated features such as depression, anxiety and poor social functioning which are important aspects of the psychopathology.

5.23.6.1 Targets of Assessment

5.23.6.1.1 Body weight history

Athough body weight is not "psychopathology" *per se*, it is obviously a fundamental aspect of eating disorders. Determining the patient's current body weight and weight history provide essential diagnostic information. This information serves as a basis for exploring the central psychopathology of eating disorders which is the meaning body weight and shape has to the patient. Since amenorrhea is required for anorexia nervosa, menstrual history should be determined within the context of the weight history.

5.23.6.1.2 Binge eating

Binge eating is a key symptom in bulimia nervosa and binge eating disorder. It occurs in about 50% of cases presenting with anorexia nervosa. Thus, determining the presence or absence of binge eating is critical to diagnosis and treatment planning. The *DSM-IV* defines binge eating as having two main characteristics: (i) consumption of a large amount of food, and (ii) the experience of loss of control. Despite the definitional requirements, research has indicated a significant minority of eating disorder patients describe binges involving relatively small amounts of food. Moreover, in some cases there is no real loss of control. Thus, until there is agreement on the significance of size of binge episodes, it is recommended that assessments follow the system proposed in the eating disorder examination (below) for dividing episodes of overeating into four types based on amount of food eaten (large or small) and

loss of control (present or absent). It is important to determine age of onset, frequency, and duration of binge eating episodes. Likewise, circumstances surrounding binge episodes (settings, times of day, social context, thoughts, and emotions) should be ascertained.

5.23.6.1.3 Extreme weight losing behaviors

The intensity of the dieting efforts and the types of weight losing behaviors employed can reflect psychopathology. A dieting history should pinpoint when dieting first began and its course over time. Information should be gathered regarding extreme weight control behaviors including self-induced vomiting, laxative and diuretic abuse, use of diet pills or other drugs to control appetite, use of emetics, chewing and spitting food out before swallowing, prolonged fasting, and excessive exercise. Diabetic patients may manipulate insulin levels and patients taking thyroid replacement hormone may alter their dosage to control body weight. Establishing the frequency (as well as the number of symptom free days) for vomiting, laxative abuse, and other extreme weight control behaviors is essential in determining the severity of the disorder and the need for medical consultation.

5.23.6.1.4 Psychopathology related to weight or shape

The psychopathology related to weight or shape has been described in various ways over the years including a drive for thinness, fear of fatness, shape and weight dissatisfaction, body size misperception, body image disturbance, and fears associated with physical maturity. Dissatisfaction with overall body shape and disparagement directed toward specific bodily regions are common in eating disorders and should be a focus of assessment. Some patients may actually overestimate their body size. Although research has shown that this is not unique to eating disorder patients, it may have clinical importance, particularly for emaciated patients. A critical psychopathological feature in anorexia nervosa and bulimia nervosa is that patients must be more than merely dissatisfied with their body; they rely on weight or shape as the predominant or even the sole criterion for judging their self-worth. This criterion has been made mandatory for a diagnosis of the two main eating disorders according to the *DSM-IV*. In anorexia nervosa, there is often a denial of the seriousness of a current low weight as well as intense fear of weight gain.

5.23.6.1.5 General psychopathology relevant to eating disorders

Eating disorder patients have been described as suffering from ineffectiveness feelings, low self-esteem, lack of autonomy, obsessionality, interpersonal sensitivity, introversion, poor relationship skills, social anxiety, dependence, perfectionism, fears of psychobiological maturity, poor impulse control, external locus of control, conflict avoidance, developmental pathology, failure in separation–individuation, vulnerability to substance abuse, interoceptive deficits, and idiosyncratic or dysfunctional thinking patterns. Complete psychological assessment should include these areas as well as evaluation of stable personality features, overall psychological distress, depression, anxiety, family functioning, history of sexual abuse, social and vocational adaptation, all of which may be relevant to the development and maintenance of these syndromes.

5.23.6.1.6 Psychopathology secondary to starvation

It may not be apparent from the initial assessment whether psychological distress, cognitive impairment, and behavioral symptoms signal fundamental emotional disturbance or are secondary elaborations resulting from weight loss and chaotic dietary patterns. Symptoms such as poor concentration, lability of mood, depressive features, obsessional thinking, irritability, difficulties with decision making, impulsivity, and social withdrawal have been identified in normal subjects undergoing semistarvation (Garner, 1997). Thus, these symptoms may reflect secondary effects of weight suppression rather than primary psychopathogy in eating disorder patients.

5.23.6.2 Assessment Methods

Various approaches to information gathering have been developed for eating disorders including clinical interviews, self-report measures, self-monitoring, direct behavioral observation, symptom checklists, clinical rating scales, the stroop test, and standardized test meals. The most commonly used methods are semistructured clinical interviews and self-report measures.

5.23.6.2.1 Clinical interview

Clinical interviews have been the primary method for gathering information on eating disorders. The Eating Disorder Examination (EDE, Cooper & Fairburn, 1987) is the most well validated and has generated a large body of research. It is an investigator based semi-structured interview for assessing psychopathology specific to eating disorders and is the current interview method of choice. Responses are organized on four subscales (restraint, eating concern, shape concern, and weight concern). The EDE can be used to arrive at a diagnosis, it has proven sensitive to treatment effects, and it defines different forms of overeating based upon amount of food eaten (large vs. small) and presence or absence of loss of control. The EDE has the advantages of allowing a more fine-grained appraisal of the specific psychopathology of eating disorders and permitting investigator probes to clarify the meaning behind responses to questions. Disadvantages of the interview include the fact that it takes an hour or more to administer, it requires a trained interviewer, and it is not suitable when anonymity or group administration are required.

5.23.6.2.2 Self-report measures

Various self-report instruments have been introduced to measure eating disorder symptoms. The two most widely used in clinical and research settings are the Eating Attitudes Test (EAT) and the Eating Disorder Inventory (EDI). The EAT is a widely used, standardized, self-report measure of eating disorder symptoms (Garner, 1997). A factor analysis of the original 40-item version resulted in a brief, 26-item measure of global eating disorder symptoms. The EDI is a standardized, multiscale instrument with a much broader focus (Garner, 1991). It comprises three subscales tapping attitudes and behaviors concerning eating, weight, and shape (drive for thinness, bulimia, body dissatisfaction) plus subscales assessing more general psychological traits or organizing constructs clinically relevant to eating disorders (ineffectiveness, perfection, interpersonal distrust, interoceptive awareness, maturity fears). The EDI-2 (Garner, 1991) added three new subscales to the original instrument (asceticism, impulse regulation, and social insecurity). The EAT and EDI have good psychometric properties and are sensitive to treatment effects. The EDI provides a psychological profile that can be useful in clinical situations.

Self-report measures have the advantages of being relatively economical, brief, easily administered and objectively scored. They are not susceptible to bias from interviewer–subject interactions and can be administered anonymously. The major disadvantage of self-report measures is that they are less accurate than interview methods, particularly when assessing ambiguous behaviors such as binge eating. They need to be supplemented by symptom frequency data derived by interview or a symptom checklist. Under some circumstances, symptom data gathered using self-report symptom checklist (e.g., Eating Disorder Symptom Checklist; Garner, 1991) can provide information pertinent to a diagnostic formulation. The different methods for assessing psychopathology in eating disorders have different aims, strengths, and weaknesses. The strategy adopted should be guided by the aims of the assessment and, whenever possible, convergent methods should be employed.

5.23.7 CLINICAL DECISION MAKING IN TREATMENT

The number of psychotherapeutic options available in treating eating disorders has expanded remarkably since the mid-1980s. The major approaches to psychotherapy have been well articulated along with a growing list of alternative forms of treatment (Garner & Garfinkel, 1997). The aim of the following section is to briefly review the major treatment options for eating disorders within the context of a decision-making paradigm for integration and sequencing of these treatments.

5.23.7.1 Integration and Sequencing of Treatments

The wisdom of considering integration of different psychotherapeutic procedures is increasingly evident with the demonstrated effectiveness of different forms of treatment (Garner & Needleman, 1997). The notion of applying different treatments to different eating disorder patients is not new and has formed the basis for multidimensional approaches to psychotherapy (Garner, Garfinkel, & Bemis, 1982). However, there has been more recent interest in "stepped-care," "decision-tree," or "integration" models which rely on set rules for the delivery of the various treatment options (Agras, 1993; Fairburn, Agras, & Wilson, 1992; Fairburn & Peveler, 1990; Garner, Garfinkel, & Irvine, 1986; Garner & Needleman, 1997; Tiller, Schmidt, & Treasure, 1993). These overlapping concepts of treatment delivery share the value system of nonallegiance to a single theoretical orientation; however, they have somewhat different points of emphasis.

Figure 3 illustrates a tentative decision-making paradigm for sequencing and integration of treatments for people with eating disorders. The various treatment options are represented by the boxes with sharp corners

(hospitalization, family therapy, self-help, individual therapy, etc.) as well as questions that need to be addressed (boxes with curved corners) related to symptom areas, patient characteristics, or response to previous treatments in determining the treatment to be offered. It does not include all treatment alternatives but concentrates on those for which there is good clinical and/or empirical support. With this schematic in mind, the major approaches to treatment will be reviewed along with the clinical criteria for their integration and sequencing.

5.23.7.2 Hospitalization and Day Treatment

Hospitalization may be considered in the treatment of eating disorders in order to meet at least two different objectives: (i) simple medical stabilization, and (ii) a strategic step aimed at the recovery process (Garner & Sackeyfio, 1993). When aimed at simple medical stabilization in treating physical complications, hospitalization is a medical priority that does not require the commitment by the patient to recover from the eating disorder. This contrasts with hospitalization intended as an important step in the process of recovery from an eating disorder (Andersen, Bowers, & Evans, 1997). As part of recovery, hospitalization not only addresses the physical aspects of the disorder but also targets the psychological problems that maintain it. This requires every effort to enlist the patient's commitment to actively participate in every stage of the treatment process.

There are several general guidelines for hospitalization including: (i) weight restoration or interruption of steady weight loss in patients who are emaciated, (ii) interruption of bingeing, vomiting, and/or laxative abuse that pose medical risks or complications, (iii) evaluation and treatment of other potentially serious physical complications, and (iv) management of associated conditions such as severe depression, risk of self-harm, or substance abuse. On rare occasions, hospitalization may be required to "disengage" a patient from a social system that both contributes to the maintenance of the disorder and disrupts outpatient treatment. Thus, as indicated above (guideline (ii)), the first major treatment consideration is whether or not the eating disorder patient is in sufficient medical danger to require hospitalization. If a careful evaluation of the patient's prior treatment and current motivation for treatment leads to the conclusion that they are clearly unresponsive to psychological treatment, then it is appropriate to consider hospitalization for medical stabilization only and referral to out-

606 Eating Disorders

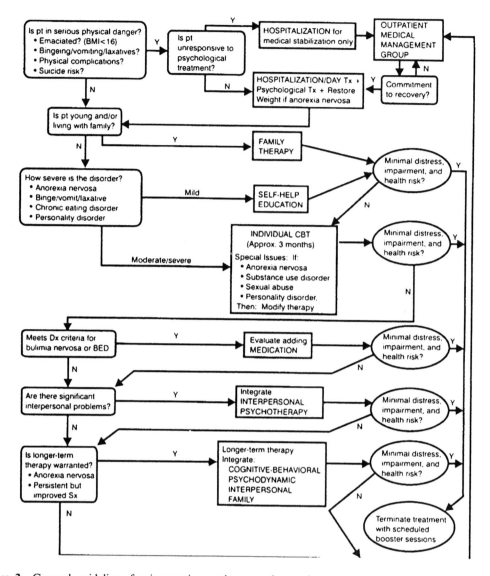

Figure 3 General guidelines for integration and sequencing major treatment options for eating disorder patients. Begin in the upper left corner with the question "is the patient in serious physical danger?" Further criteria for decision making, including symptom areas, patient characteristics, or response to previous treatments, are indicated by boxes with rounded corners (mostly on the left side of the figure). The treatment options are represented by boxes with sharp corners (hospitalization, family therapy, self-help, individual therapy, etc.). The figure does not delineate all treatment alternatives or all considerations for decision making. However, it does include the main interventions for which there is good clinical and/or empirical support and key variables to consider in determining the most appropriate type and intensity of treatment. (*Handbook of Treatment of Eating Disorders* (pp. 50–66), by D. M. Garner and L. Needleman, 1997, New York: Guilford Press. Copyright 1997 by Guilford Press. Reprinted with permission.)

patient medical maintenance discussed below. More typically there is reason for optimism about recovery from the eating disorder. In these cases, hospitalization can usually be brief, again aimed at medical stabilization, but with the addition of psychological counseling and followed by referral to outpatient psychotherapy. The most common exception to brief hospitalization is the emaciated anorexia nervosa patient for whom longer hospitalization is usually required to make steady headway in the

renourishment process. It is generally pointless to negotiate with patients or insurance carriers around the duration of hospitalization required for weight restoration, since the time needed is relatively straightforward and easy to calculate. It is the number of weeks or months required to reach at least 90% of expected weight, gaining at a rate of about three pounds a week and assuming optimal compliance with the treatment program. Even though this is a time-consuming and expensive process, it is an economical alternative if it leads to recovery since a chronic eating disorder inflicts heavy price, both in monetary and emotional terms. At the same time, it is legitimate to question the validity or timing of a lengthy hospitalization aimed at renutrition if steady weight gain does not occur.

Another situation in which hospitalization may be necessary is when a patient has had a protracted period of outpatient treatment and is simply unable to make improvement without the structure and containment offered by the inpatient environment. Indefinite outpatient treatment may be fruitless or even deleterious in the sense that it inadvertently colludes with the patient's ambivalence about recovery. It is like years of insight-oriented psychotherapy with an elevator phobic without ever requiring a ride on an elevator. Without some exposure, the therapist cannot ever assist the patient in confronting fears associated with weight restoration. The patient may perceive the recommendation for hospitalization as a threat or as abandonment, but they should be reassured that it is a humane alternative to the tremendous emotional and financial expense of prolonged and unproductive outpatient therapy. Psychotherapy can only achieve modest goals in the presence of the severe limits imposed by dietary chaos or chronic starvation.

Day treatment or partial hospitalization is the preferred alternative to inpatient care for most patients (Kaplan & Olmsted, 1997). This level of care provides structure around meal times plus the possibility for intensive therapy, without requiring the patient to become totally disengaged from the supports and the therapeutic challenges outside of the hospital. Day treatment programs offer the distinct advantage of being more economical than full hospitalization. They can also provide a useful bridge between inpatient and outpatient care. There are various models for day treatment programs which generally share many features with inpatient programs. The major difference is that patients receive the therapeutic services but do not stay overnight. Inpatient treatment is still the preferred modality for patients who are seriously emaciated, require close medical monitoring, fail to progress in partial care, or are at serious risk of self-harm.

5.23.7.3 Outpatient Medical Management

Concluding that a patient is unresponsive to psychological treatment and then referring to an outpatient medical management (Figure 3) requires careful analysis and considerable reflection. However, there are some chronic or recalcitrant patients who have participated in various forms of treatment over the course of years and finally reach the point where they no longer want treatment for their eating disorder or they can agree that further psychotherapy has a very low probability of success. In these circumstances, psychotherapy aimed at recovery can be highly frustrating for the therapist and the patient alike, often leading to termination with inadequate follow-up plans. Patients are then reluctant to seek further assistance when their medical or psychological condition deteriorates. The key is determining if there really has been sufficient exposure to truly adequate treatment since patients can have extensive exposure to poor treatment or therapists who are not knowledgeable about eating disorders. If careful evaluation leads to the conclusion that the patient has had an adequate course of psychotherapy and (i) is not in imminent psychological or medical danger, (ii) is sufficiently symptomatic to suggest ongoing potential medical risk, and (iii) there is no clear rationale for further psychotherapy, then termination from psychotherapy may be very appropriate as long as it is made conditional on the patient agreeing to participate in ongoing "medical management" (Figure 3). Again, the goal of medical management is very different from psychotherapy. Rather than focusing on overcoming the eating disorder, it is aimed at maintaining medical and psychological stability. It can be conducted in an individual or a group format, meeting weekly with medical supervision. Body weight, electrolytes, and vital signs should be checked with appropriate referral to medical specialists, as needed. Patients derive the added benefits of group support and sharing with similarly afflicted patients. In some cases, these groups set the stage for renewed efforts to actively address the eating disorder symptoms.

5.23.7.4 Self-help and Guided Self-help

There are eating disorder patients at the other end of the severity spectrum who have relatively mild symptoms and who may experience marked improvement or complete recovery with self-help or education-based interventions. Self-help organizations for eating disorders have been very popular since the late 1970s (Baker-Enright, Butterfield, & Berkowitz, 1985). From the mid-1980s, there has been a remarkable increase in number of self-help books available for eating disorder patients and their families (Santrock, Minnett, & Campbell, 1994). Interest in testing the efficacy of self-help has been slower to develop, but there are now a number of studies indicating that some forms of self-help or guided self-help may be quite effective with some eating disorders (see Fairburn & Carter, 1997). As indicated in Figure 3 self-help is recommended for patients with less severe eating disorders symptoms. While self-help is not sufficient as the sole treatment for most patients, there is a significant subgroup who benefit from this extremely economical intervention.

5.23.7.5 Psychoeducation

Figure 3 indicates that psychoeducation should be considered for bulimia nervosa patients with milder symptoms. As will be reviewed in a later section, there have been a number of research studies providing empirical support for the utility of educational approaches in the treatment of eating disorders. Education was originally recommended as part of early descriptions of cognitive behavioral treatment for eating disorders based on the premise that certain faulty assumptions evinced by patients were maintained, at least in part, by misinformation (e.g., Garner & Bemis, 1982). One early psychoeducational primer (Garner, Rockert et al., 1985) emphasized the conflict between the cultural pressures on women to diet and biological compensatory mechanisms which tend to defend a "set point" for body weight. The primer has been updated (Garner, 1997) and provides background for challenging society's harsh standards for women to be thin, education regarding the biology of weight regulation, recommendations for establishing regular eating patterns, and methods for interrupting bingeing and purging. There seems to be general agreement on the utility of incorporating psychoeducation into most treatment approaches for eating disorders. For people with mild eating disorder symptoms (Figure 3), guided self-help or educational groups should be considered as an economical and potentially effective option before proceeding to more costly interventions.

5.23.7.6 Family Therapy

Family therapy is the initial treatment choice for patients who are young and/or living at home (Figure 3). Family therapy should also be regarded as a desirable adjunct to individual therapy with older patients living outside of the home, particularly when family conflicts predominate. For young patients, there are practical as well as theoretical reasons for recommending family therapy. From a strictly practical point of view, the patient shares her home with her parents or guardians who are responsible for her well-being. Parents have the potential to provide powerful directives in support of therapeutic goals. Regardless of theoretical orientation of treatment, family members need assistance in dealing with a young eating disordered patient.

Family therapists have argued convincingly that eating disorders may reflect certain conflicts, dysfunctional roles, or problematic interactional patterns within the family (Dare & Eisler, 1997; Minuchin et al., 1978; Selvini-Palazzoli, 1974). The following are some of the more common problematic themes.

(i) Denial regarding the seriousness of the eating disorder may be manifest by the identified patient and/or the parents. Both the patient and parents may need assistance in accurately labeling the eating disorder which involves neither minimizing or exaggerating the significance of certain symptomatic behaviors.

(ii) Particularly with younger patients, parents may need help in developing an effective parenting style. Guilt and fear may have prohibited them from being firm and effective in establishing guidelines for behavior consistent with recovery. Parents should be encouraged to maintain usual expectations in areas unrelated to food and eating (bedtime, chores, language, treatment of siblings) except when unrealistic parental expectations are directly contributing to the problem. Treatment recommendations should be consistent with the family's value system and appropriate to the developmental stage of the child.

(iii) Parents may need assistance in accepting the patient's need for autonomy and self-expression through traits, interests, and values that may deviate from expectations within the family.

(iv) Under certain circumstances, parental attitudes about weight, shape, thinness, or "fitness" may be inappropriate. Inappropriate family eating patterns, beliefs about food or eating rituals should be identified, and practical interventions need to be designed that address areas of potential conflicts.

(v) An eating disorder can deflect members of the family away from potentially threatening developmental expectations emergent in the transition to puberty. It can function as a maladaptive solution to the adolescent's struggle to achieve autonomy in a family where any move toward independence is perceived as a threat to family unity. It can also become a powerful diversion enabling the parents and the child to avoid major sources of conflict.

(vi) The identified patient's symptoms may be functional within a disturbed family context and the meaning systems that underlie the resulting interactional patterns need to be identified and corrected. Problematic family interactional patterns need to be addressed such as "enmeshment," overprotectiveness, inadequate mechanisms for resolving conflicts, and inappropriate parent–child allegiances that undermine the marital relationship (Minuchin et al., 1978).

Even when family therapy is not the primary mode of treatment, it may be appropriate to integrate family therapy into the longer-term treatment plan. It can be a valuable adjunct to individual therapy in addressing trauma, such as sexual abuse, within the family (Andersen, 1985; Crisp, 1970; Garner et al., 1982; Wooley & Lewis, 1989).

5.23.7.7 Cognitive Behavioral Therapy

Cognitive behavioral therapy (CBT) has become the standard treatment for bulimia nervosa and forms the theoretical base for much of the treatment of anorexia nervosa. The empirical support for CBT in the treatment of eating disorders will be summarized in a later section. As indicated in Figure 3, CBT should be considered the treatment of choice for patients whose age does not mandate family therapy, and whose symptoms are moderate to severe.

The CBT for bulimia nervosa developed by Fairburn and colleagues (Fairburn, 1985; Fairburn, Marcus, & Wilson, 1993) has the following major points of emphasis: (i) self-monitoring of food intake, bingeing, and purging episodes as well as thoughts and feelings which trigger these episodes; (ii) regular weighing; (iii) specific recommendations such as the introduction of avoided foods and meal planning designed to normalize eating behavior and curb restrictive dieting; (iv) cognitive restructuring directed at habitual reasoning errors and underlying assumptions that are relevant to the development and the maintenance of the eating disorder; and (v) relapse prevention.

CBT is also effective in stabilizing the eating patterns of obese individuals who experience recurrent episodes of binge eating (Agras et al., 1992; Telch Agras, Rossiter, Wilfley, & Kenarely, 1990; Wilfley et al., 1993). The results with binge-eating disorder patients are promising; however, the long-term effectiveness of CBT with this group remains unclear.

In the case of anorexia nervosa, CBT has been recommended largely on clinical grounds (Garner, 1986, 1988; Garner & Bemis, 1982; 1985; Garner & Rosen, 1990; Garner et al., 1997; Vitousek & Orimoto, 1993). Case studies and preliminary research provide some grounds

for optimism (Channon, DeSilva, Hemsley, & Perkins, 1989; Cooper & Fairburn, 1984); however, current data are insufficient to warrant meaningful conclusions regarding effectiveness.

There are many areas of overlap between the versions of CBT offered for anorexia and bulimia nervosa; however, there are also important differences that have implications for clinical care (Garner et al., 1997). A major focus for both disorders is the patient's underlying assumption that "weight, shape, or thinness can serve as the sole or predominant referent for inferring personal value or self-worth" (Garner & Bemis, 1982, p. 142). Fear of body-weight gain is a central theme for both anorexia and bulimia nervosa; however, most bulimia nervosa patients can be reassured that treatment will probably result in little weight gain. In contrast, in anorexia nervosa, therapeutic strategies must be aimed at actual weight gain in the face of the implacable wish to maintain a low weight. Establishing a sound and collaborative therapeutic relationship is particularly important in anorexia nervosa since it becomes a fulcrum for gradually helping the patient to relinquish the myriad of ego-syntonic symptoms. As indicated on Figure 3, CBT is modified for anorexia nervosa. It is typically longer in duration and the targets for cognitive interventions are broad, encompassing a wider range of personal and interpersonal subject domains than typical for bulimia nervosa (Garner et al., 1997). This is to address the marked deficits impeding normal psychosocial functioning in many of these patients. Thus, cognitive interventions are aimed not only at beliefs that maintain extreme dieting and chronic weight suppression but also at fundamental assumptions associated with interpersonal conflicts, feelings of ineffectiveness, struggles with autonomy, and fears associated with psychosocial development (Garner & Bemis, 1982; Garner & Rosen, 1990; Garner et al., 1997; Vitousek & Orimoto, 1993; Vitousek & Ewald, 1993). Components of interpersonal therapy and family therapy are often integrated into longer-term CBT for anorexia nervosa (see Figure 3). In the subset of anorexia nervosa patients who do not engage in binge eating, and those who show no obvious serious physical complications, there may be extraordinary resistance to complying with the therapeutic objectives of weight gain. However, as long as there is gradual improvement in symptoms (Figure 3), outpatient therapy is recommended; however, if the patient's condition deteriorates, hospitalization must be considered. Outpatient medical management (groups) should be considered if there is a protracted therapeutic impasse. This often takes the form of apparent psychological insights that invariably fail to translate into symptomatic change.

5.23.7.8 Interpersonal Therapy

Since the mid-1980s, the prevailing view was that CBT's effectiveness with eating disorders was tied to cognitive and behavioral methods aimed specifically at overconcern about weight and shape which are responsible for restrictive dieting and extreme weight controlling behaviors. Changing these attitudes presumably relaxed restrictive dieting and relieved the biological tension created by chronic attempts to suppress body weight. However, a series of studies using interpersonal psychotherapy (IPT), adapted to bulimia nervosa, has prompted re-examination of earlier speculations regarding the specific mechanisms of action in the treatment of binge eating (Fairburn et al., 1995). This is because IPT does not directly focus on eating problems. IPT was originally proposed by Klerman, Weissman, Rounsaville, and Chevron (1984) as a short-term treatment for depression. The IPT treatment process is divided into three stages (Fairburn, 1997). The first stage involves the identification of the interpersonal problems that led to the development and maintenance of the eating problems. The second stage consists of a therapeutic contract for working on these interpersonal problems. The final stage addresses issues related to termination. Fairburn et al. (1991) found IPT somewhat less effective than CBT at the end of treatment; however, patients who received IPT gradually improved during the follow-up period so that after one year, both treatments were equally effective (Fairburn et al., 1993). These findings are maintained over the longer term with patients recieving CBT or interpersonal therapy doing significantly better than those receiving behavior therapy (Fairburn et al., 1995). This pattern of improvement during follow-up was not found in a study of another very different form of interpersonally oriented therapy, supportive-expressive therapy (Garner et al., 1993). These findings suggest that the IPT used by Fairburn et al. contains specific therapeutic ingredients that facilitate change. Further support for the effectiveness of IPT comes from Wilfley et al. (1993) in a study of nonpurging bulimic patients, many of whom presented with obesity. They found both CBT and IPT equally effective in reducing binge eating assessed both at the end of treatment and at one year follow-up.

The evidence that certain interpersonal therapies are as effective with binge eating as CBT has implications for the decision process illustrated in Figure 3. It could be argued that there should be no priority for either IPT or CBT as the initial treatment of choice for bulimia nervosa since both treatments are equally effective in the long-term. Certainly, a therapist well trained in one of the interpersonal therapies described by Fairburn and colleagues should not be encouraged to abandon this form of treatment in favor of CBT. However, we are still inclined to recommend CBT as the preferred initial treatment at this time since it has been shown to have a more rapid effect on symptoms. Moreover, the efficacy of IPT for bulimia nervosa has been demonstrated in just one center compared to many studies in support of CBT. If the findings from the Oxford trials are replicated in other centers, then IPT may become another "standard" initial treatment for bulimia nervosa. At this time, there is no empirical basis for suggesting that IPT should be differentially applied to patients on the basis of premorbid features such as interpersonal conflicts. However, integrating IPT into treatment should be considered for bulimia nervosa patients who fail to respond favorably to an initial course of CBT when interpersonal conflicts predominate according to Figure 3. The IPT orientation should also be a leading candidate for integration into longer term psychotherapy for anorexia nervosa patients or for others with persistent symptoms.

5.23.7.9 Psychodynamic Therapy

There have been no controlled comparisons between longer-term psychodynamic psychotherapy and other forms of treatment; however, dynamically oriented treatments have been well articulated for eating disorders and may be recommended on clinical grounds when other short-term treatments are ineffective (Figure 3). Psychodynamic treatment for eating disorders may be roughly divided into two schools of thought. The first presumes eating disorders do not require fundamental modifications to orthodox dynamic interventions since neither the symptoms nor the disorders represent a unique underlying process. The second conceptualization implies that eating disorders are distinctive in that they require major modifications to traditional dynamic therapy in order to meet the special psychological needs of the patient. There has been considerable movement among dynamically oriented writers toward integrating psychodynamic therapy with active symptom management principles in the treatment of both anorexia nervosa and bulimia nervosa (Bruch, 1973; Casper, 1982; Crisp, 1980, 1997; Goodsitt, 1985, 1997; Stern,

1986; Strober, 1997; Strober & Yager, 1985). However, there are still some who espouse a traditional interpretive framework (Lerner, 1993; Sands, 1992; Sugarman, 1991). At this time, we recommend the integration of longer-term dynamically oriented therapy be considered as an alternative to long-term CBT for patients who fail less expensive approaches.

A new generation of feminist therapists deviate from the traditional views by incorporating the growing literature on the psychology of women into dynamic formulations regarding the etiology and treatment of eating disorders (Fallon, Katzman, & Wooley, 1994; Fallon & Wonderlick, 1997; Katzman, 1994; Kearney-Cooke & Striegel-Moore, 1997; Perlick & Silverstein, 1994; Steiner-Adair, 1994; Striegel-Moore, 1994). They have highlighted the importance of addressing issues such as sexual abuse and other forms of victimization in the development, maintenance, and treatment of eating disorders. Even though controlled studies are lacking at this time, the highly evolved conceptual framework presented by these dynamic-feminist treatment approaches warrants their consideration when abuse is identified during the course of assessment or treatment (Figure 3). At this time, the therapist's orientation, rather than the special needs of the patient, probably determine the decision to apply feminist therapy for eating disorders. However, many of the views articulated by feminist therapists have influenced the applications of other forms of therapy. There are some eating disorder patients, because of the nature of their predisposing and perpetuating factors, who should receive feminist therapy as the treatment of choice.

5.23.7.10 Pharmacotherapy

Figure 3 indicates medication should be considered for patients with bulimia nervosa or binge-eating disorder who fail an initial trial of cognitive behavioral therapy but is generally not indicated for anorexia nervosa. There have been many well-controlled trials since the mid-1980s indicating the effectiveness of some antidepressant medications for bulimia nervosa and the research evidence will be reviewed in detail in a later section. However, in reviewing the research in the field, Raymond et al. (1994) have suggested that medication should not be "the primary mode of therapy with patients with bulimia nervosa" (p. 241). This conclusion is based on the following observations: (i) psychological interventions have been shown to be very effective, (ii) there are high drop-out rates reported in most medication studies, (iii) there are risks of drug side effects, and (iv) data

suggest high relapse rates with drug discontinuation. Based on a multisite collaborative study (Fluoxetine Bulimia Nervosa Collaborative Study Group [FBNC], 1992), fluoxetine hydrochloride (Prozac) is currently the first choice for the treatment of bulimia nervosa (daily dosages of 60 mg were generally superior to 20 mg) and probably should be used at least as an adjunct to psychotherapy in many cases failing in a course of adequate psychological treatment. Tricyclic antidepressants may be an alternative for some patients failing a course of fluoxetine, but side effects, high drop-out rates, and greater lethality with overdose may be a source of concern when treating some patients (Leitenberg et al., 1994; Mitchell et al., 1990). Similarly, monoamine oxidase inhibitors (MAOIs) may be useful in a small minority of patients who fail using fluoxetine and tricyclics. There is some evidence that patients who fail on one tricyclic may benefit from changing to an alternative medication (Mitchell, Raymond, & Specker, 1993). Alternatively, the specific decision to not prescribe medication may be therapeutic in some cases (Raymond et al., 1994).

There is still little evidence for change in the early recommendations that pharmacotherapy has a very limited value with emaciated anorexia nervosa patients and should never be the sole treatment modality (Garfinkel & Garner, 1982). Occasionally patients may benefit from medication to deal with overwhelming anxiety, severe depression or intolerable gastric discomfort after meals, but this only applies to a small minority of patients (Andersen, 1985; Garfinkel & Garner, 1982; Garfinkel & Walsh, 1997).

Thus, in the decision-tree approach for treating eating disorders, antidepressant medication should be considered as an adjunct or possibly an alternative for bulimia nervosa patients who fail to respond to psychosocial therapies or for those whose affective symptoms are clearly impeding progress in other forms of treatment. Drug treatments have generally not proven effective for anorexia nervosa.

5.23.8 PSYCHOLOGICAL TREATMENT RESEARCH

5.23.8.1 Treatment Research on Anorexia Nervosa

Evaluation of treatment response would be aided by an understanding of the natural history of the disorder. While there are no studies of the actual natural history of anorexia nervosa, Theander (1985) has provided an estimate from a long-term follow-up study of 94 patients seen in the early 1960s and thus, probably received treatment that was quite crude compared to modern methods. The patients were evaluated in 1966 (after a mean observation time of 15 years since the onset of the disorder) and again in 1984 (after a mean observation time of 33 years). Table 1 presents outcome status for the sample five, 15, and 33 years after the onset of the disorder and indicates an aggregation over time of patients into the recovered and deceased categories. Of the patients who died, one-third committed suicide and two-thirds died of complications from their disorder. The data in Table 1 dramatically illustrate that the evaluation of outcome in anorexia nervosa varies depending on when the assessment is performed and that, after many years of illness, patients tend either to improve or to die.

Since 1953 there have been more than 60 follow-up studies of anorexia nervosa (Eckert, Halmi, Marchi, Grove, & Cosby, 1995; Fichter & Quadflieg, 1995; Steinhausen, Rauss-Mason, & Seidel, 1991); however, there are few controlled trials comparing different treatment approaches. There is considerable variation in the outcomes reported across these follow-up reports which could be expected given differences among methodologies and treatment settings.

The major outcome criteria used in these follow-up studies have been diagnosis, weight, menses, eating behavior, general psychological functioning, and psychosexual status. Usually a global outcome (good, moderate, poor, death) is derived from some composite of these variables. The mortality rates have varied from 0% to 22%, with over half of the studies reporting deaths in 4% or fewer patients (Garfinkel & Garner, 1982; Herzog, Keller, Lavoni, & Ott, 1987; Sullivan, 1995). The mortality rates for anorexia nervosa are two times higher than for any other psychiatric disorder and more than 12 times higher than all-cause mortality for females. Although the definition of "recovery" has been ambiguous, between 12% and 87% of patients appear to be free of eating disorder

symptoms at follow-up (Hsu, 1996). Consistent with the report by Theander (1985), studies of relatively brief follow-up find fewer patients who are recovered or deceased, with most patients congregating in the moderate to poor outcome. More patients recover and the number of deaths increase as the follow-up is extended.

Some patients can be considered fully recovered at follow-up while others who recover in terms of weight and eating remain disturbed in other areas of functioning. Casper (1990) reported that about 25% of patients classified as having a good outcome in an 8–10-year follow-up were still weight preoccupied and depressed. In a study of 60 anorexia nervosa patients followed 5–14 years after presenting for treatment, Toner, Garfinkel, and Garner (1986) found that 38% were asymptomatic, 27% improved, 27% unchanged, and 8% deceased. While a significant proportion of the sample met *DSM-III* criteria for affective (34%) or anxiety disorders (47%) in the year prior to follow-up, those in the asymptomatic group had scores equivalent to noneating disorder controls on most measures of psychosocial functioning. Rastam et al. (1995) followed a sample of anorexia nervosa patients six years after onset and found that most cases no longer met criteria for the original eating disorder, but many developed bulimia nervosa or atypical eating disorders. In a 12-year follow-up study of 69 hospitalized anorexia nervosa patients, Herzog, Schellberg, and Deter (1997) found that 50% of patients did not improve until more than six years after the first inpatient treatment.

One of the most striking observations regarding outcome is the relatively good prognosis for pediatric compared with older samples. In a summary of pediatric studies, Garfinkel and Garner (1982) indicated that the outcome status of patients in follow-up studies conducted before 1974 were quite similar to that reported in the literature on older adolescents and adults. However, later pediatric outcome studies indicate a very positive prognosis with recovery rates of between 76% and 87% (Cantwell, Sturzenburger, Burroughs, Salkin, & Green, 1977; Goetz, Succop, Reinhart, & Miller, 1977; Martin, 1985; Minuchin et al., 1978; Silverman, 1974). Steinhausen and Glanville (1983) present somewhat less optimistic findings from a 9.4-year follow-up of patients presenting between the ages of 11 and 17. They report that only 30% of their sample could be considered symptom free at follow-up. Similarly, only 50% of the early onset cases ($N = 18$) followed by Hawley (1985) after a mean of 8.7 years were classified as having a good outcome. Theander (1996) reviewed the literature on early onset anorexia nervosa and

Table 1 Long-term outcome in anorexia nervosa.

	Years after onset of the disorder		
Outcome status	5 years (%)	15 years (%)	33 years (%)
Good	55	63	76
Intermediate	19	17	1
Poor	18	7	6
Death	8	13	18

Source: Theander (1985), adapted by permission.

found that there are relatively more boys among patients with extremely early onset. He also reported that early onset predicted better outcome, but long-term outcome is unfavorable for many early onset cases.

Follow-up reports indicating that early age of onset confers a positive prognosis (cf. Garfinkel & Garner, 1982; Herzog, Keller, & Lavori, 1988) as well as the variable, but generally positive, outcome in a number of pediatric samples has led to the interest in family therapy in research studies on anorexia nervosa. In the first controlled trial examining two forms of treatment, Russell et al. (1987) compared family and individual supportive therapy for both anorexia nervosa and bulimia nervosa. It was concluded that family therapy was superior for patients whose disorder was not chronic and that had begun before the age of 19. A somewhat more tentative finding was that individual therapy yielded better results with older patients.

In another study of family treatment, Robin, Siegel, and Moye (1995) randomly assigned 22 adolescent anorexia nervosa patients to 16 months of either behavioral family systems therapy or ego-oriented individual therapy and found that both treatments had a positive effect on body mass index, menstruation, and family interactional patterns. There was no consistent pattern of differential treatment effects; however, the relatively small sample size used in the comparison makes it difficult to detect treatment differences.

Although family intervention was not the object of the study, Crisp et al. (1991) provided collateral evidence for the utility of family intervention in a controlled study in which 90 anorexia nervosa patients were randomly assigned to one of three types of treatment (or referral back to the community). The three treatment conditions were: (i) intensive inpatient treatment followed by 12 sessions of outpatient therapy, (ii) 12 outpatient individual and family psychotherapy sessions, and (iii) 10 outpatient group psychotherapy sessions (both for patients and parents separately). All three active treatments were accompanied by dietary counseling aimed at gradual weight restoration. Outcome was assessed at the end of treatment and at one-year follow-up. Of the 20 control group patients referred back to the community, 14 received some form of treatment and six were untreated. At one year, there were no significant differences between the three active treatment conditions in weight gain, return of menses, or important aspects of psychosocial functioning. Surprisingly, although the inpatient treatment was more intensive (several months of inpatient care followed by 12 outpatient sessions),

presumably much more costly, and delivered as the treatment of choice by Crisp and colleagues for years, it was no more successful than the strictly outpatient approaches. In terms of weight gain at follow-up, inpatient treatment was not superior to the controls. Moreover, the inpatient treatment had a much higher rate of noncompliance (40%) compared to the outpatient conditions (10–15%). A two-year follow-up of this same sample (Gowers, Norton, Halek, & Crisp, 1994) indicated that the positive outcome with the outpatient treatment package was sustained. Thus, the results of this major study challenge the assumption that "more treatment is better" and that inpatient treatment is the treatment of choice for anorexia nervosa.

More evidence for the efficacy of less intensive treatment comes from a study by Treasure et al. (1995) in which 30 anorexia nervosa patients were randomly assigned to either cognitive analytical therapy (CAT) or educational behavioral therapy. At one year, both of these outpatient treatments led to significant weight gain. Patients assigned to the CAT reported significantly greater subjective improvement; however, there were no treatment group differences in other outcome parameters. All these findings are summarized in Table 2.

The relatively small number of carefully controlled trials of treatments for anorexia nervosa may relate, in part, to the protracted, complicated, and variable course in the treatment of the disorder. Many cases require one or more periods of hospitalization at various points during a lengthy and fluctuating recovery process. Since this may require numerous transitions between inpatient and outpatient treatment staff over an extended period of time in response to the patient's changing nutritional status, it is difficult to design a rigorously controlled study protocol suitable for the range of patients presenting for treatment.

5.23.8.2 Treatment Research on Bulimia Nervosa

In contrast to the paucity of controlled trials with anorexia nervosa, there have been more than 25 controlled studies evaluating the efficacy of different treatment approaches to bulimia nervosa (for reviews see Garfinkel & Walsh, 1997; Garner, Fairburn, & Davis, 1987; Mitchell, Raymond, & Specker, 1993). The majority of these studies have involved comparing different forms of treatment or identifying active ingredients within the more successful treatment packages (primarily cognitive-behavioral) using a dismantling approach. Most

Table 2 Comparative treatment studies for anorexia nervosa.

Investigator	Orientation/groups	N	Format/duration[a] (weeks)	Dropouts (%)	Pretreatment BMI	Follow-up BMI	Mean weight gain post-treatment (kg)	Mean weight gain at follow-up (kg)	Duration of follow-up
Growers et al. (1994)	Individual and family behavioral/dynamic	20	I & F (40)	10	15.5 (1.4)	19.0 (2.0)–12 mos.	?	?	12 months
	"No treatment" control[b]	20		?	15.8 (1.7)	20.0 (2.8)–24 mos.	?	12.0 (8.4)	24 months
						17.0 (2.8)–12 mos.	?	?	
Robin et al. (1995)	Behavioral family systems	11	F (54–80)	?	15.0 (1.4)	17.8 (3.2)–24 mos.	?	5.2 (6.3)	12 months
						20.1 (1.1)	5.1 (1.6)	5.0 (1.6)	
	Ego-oriented therapy	11	I (54–80)	?	16.3 (2.8)	19.0 (1.4)	2.7 (2.2)	2.6 (2.2)	
Treasure et al. (1995)	Education behavioral	16	I (20)	38	15.0 (1.0)	17.2 (3.2)	?	5.6 (4.5)	12 months
	Cognitive analytic	14	I (20)	29	15.6 (2.1)	18.2 (2.1)	?	6.9 (4.6)	12 months

? = not reported
[a] F = Family; I = Individual.   [b] Some participants may have been in treatment elsewhere.

treatment packages have been between 10 and 18 weeks in duration, delivered in either a group or an individual format (cf. Garner et al., 1987; McKisack & Waller, 1997). It is evident from these and other studies that treatment can lead to statistically and clinically significant reductions in bingeing, vomiting, and other associated symptoms.

A number of comparative treatment studies of bulimia nervosa that provide very encouraging findings are summarized in Table 3 (see Mitchell et al., 1993 for earlier studies). It is evident from this that CBT, as well as certain other forms of treatment with which it has been compared, lead to marked reductions in bingeing and vomiting. In a long-term prospective follow-up of 91 eating disorder patients from two randomized controlled trials involving CBT, behavior therapy (BT), and focal interpersonal therapy (FIT), Fairburn et al. (1995) found that those received BT did poorly while bulimia nervosa patients who received CBT or FIT did markedly better. Compared to subjects in the BT condition, those in the FIT were twice as likely to be in remission (defined as no longer meeting a *DSM-IV* diagnosis for an eating disorder) and those in the CBT condition were more than three times as likely to be in remission. Similarly, about half of the patients who received CBT or FIT were completely abstinent from all key behavioral symptoms such as binge eating, vomiting, and laxative and diuretic abuse compared to 18% of those receiving BT.

Agras and colleagues (1992, 1994) compared desipramine, CBT, and their combination (with the drug withdrawn at either 16 or 24 weeks) and found that the combined drug and CBT treatment was superior to the other conditions as long as the medication was continued for at least 24 weeks. The finding that the combined treatment was more effective than 16 and 24 weeks of medication alone suggests that the CBT may be important in preventing relapse once medication is withdrawn. In the 1994 follow-up study, both the CBT and the combined 24-week treatment were superior in reducing binge eating to desipramine given for 16 weeks. This study supports earlier research indicating that medication alone is not the most effective treatment for bulimia nervosa but, contrary to an earlier study (Mitchell et al., 1990), it provides important data suggesting that antidepressant therapy may add significantly to the effects of CBT.

There have been a number of empirical studies of the effectiveness of educational and self-help treatments in bulimia nervosa. Educationally-oriented treatment seems to have remarkable impact on behavior for some patients, although the overall treatment results are not as potent as some of the more intensive CBT interventions (Connors, Johnson, & Stuckey, 1984; Huon & Brown, 1985; Wolchik, Weiss, & Katzman, 1986). Ordman and Kirschenbaum (1985) compared CBT to a "brief intervention wait-list" that consisted of just three assessment sessions and minimal intervention. A study comparing the presentation of this educational material in a group "classroom" format (five 90-minute sessions during a one-month period) with individual CBT indicated, for the least symptomatic 25–45% of patients in the sample, both treatments were equally effective on important measures of outcome (Olmsted, Davis, Garner, Eagle, & Rockert, 1991). Nutritional counselling or nutritional management (Beaumont, O'Connor, Touyz, & Williams, 1987) overlaps with the psychoeducational approach described above. Laessle et al. (1991) compared nutritional management (NM) with stress management and found both treatments led to marked improvement in eating symptoms and general psychopathology at the end of treatment and at a 12-month follow-up. However, NM produced a significantly more rapid reduction in binge eating, greater abstinence rates, and greater improvements on some measures of psychopathology.

Huon (1985) was the first to test the effectiveness of a self-help program. Binge eating subjects were recruited from a woman's magazine article and 32% who followed a self-help manual were symptom free at six-month follow-up compared to only 7% of a comparison group. Two later studies have shown short-term benefits of following a self-help manual but neither presented follow-up data (Schmidt et al., 1993; Treasure et al., 1994). In contrast to "pure" self-help, Cooper, Coker, and Fleming (1995) have shown that self-help, supervised by a professional, can be sufficient for some patients. At a four- to six-month follow-up of 82 patients, 16 (20%) had dropped out of the program, and 22 (33%) of those remaining had not binged or vomited over the past month (Cooper et al., 1995). Thus, while self-help is not sufficient as the sole treatment for most patients, there is a significant subgroup who benefit from this extremely economical intervention.

While there has been overall optimism regarding the efficacy of CBT, it again must be emphasized that improvement also has been observed with other forms of treatment. Significant reductions in bingeing and vomiting, as well as associated symptoms, have been found with nondirective (Kirkley, Schneider, Agras, & Bachman, 1985), short-term focal (Fairburn,

Table 3 Comparative treatment studies for bulimia nervosa

Investigator	Orientation/groups	N	Format/duration[a] (weeks)	Dropouts (%)	Reduction pre- to post-treatment %		Abstinent at last week of treatment %		Abstinent at follow-up %		Duration of follow-up
					Binge	Vomit	Binge	Vomit	Binge	Vomit	
Agras et al. (1992)	Cognitive-behavioral	23	I (24)	4	82	83	50	48	55	?	32 weeks
	Desipramine	12	(16)	?	39	43	35	33	?	?	
	Desipramine	12	(24)	?	?	?	?	?	42	?	
	Cognitive-behavioral and desipramine	12	I (16 meds, 24 CBT)	17	?	83	81	65	64	?	
	Cognitive-behavioral and desipramine	12	I (24 meds, 24 CBT)	?	?	?	?	?	70	?	1 & 3 mos.
Wolf and Crowther (1992)	Behaviour therapy	15	G (8)	0	(only report biweekly mean frequencies)						
	Cognitive-behavioral	15	G (8)	0							
	Wait list control	11	NA	9							
Fairburn et al. (1993)	Cognitive-behavioral	25	I (18)	20	?	?	44 (binge & vomit)		36 (binge & vomit)		12 months
	Interpersonal therapy	25	I (18)	32	?	?	35 (b & v)		44 (b & v)		
	Behavior therapy	25	I (18)	48	?	?	26 (b & v)		20 (b & v)		
Gamer et al. (1993)	Cognitive-behavioral	30	I (18)	17	73	82	?	36	–		NA
	Supportive-expressive	30	I (18)	69	62	?	12	–	–		
Thackewray et al. (1993)	Cognitive-behavioral	Total N – 47	I (8)	Total – 17	?		92 (b & v)		69 (b & v)		6 months
	Behavior therapy		I (8)		?		100 (b & v)		38 (b & v)		
	Attention placebo		I (8)		?		69 (b & v)		15 (b & v)		
Agras et al. (1994)[b]	Cognitive-behavioral	23	I (24)	1	?	?			54 (b & v)		12 months
	Desipramine	12	(16)	1	?	?			18 (b & v)		
	Desipramine	12	(24)	3	?	?			67 (b & v)		
	Cognitive-behavioral and desipramine	12	I (16 meds, 24 CBT)	2					40 (b & v)		
	Cognitive-behavioral and desipramine	12	I (24 meds, 24 CBT)	3					78 (b & v)		
Leitenberg et al. (1994)	Cognitive-behavioral	7	I (20)	14	?	?	?	71	?	57	6 months
	Desipramine	7	(20)	57	?	?	?	0	?	0	
	Cognitive-behavioral and desipramine	7	I (20)	29	?	?	?	29	?	29	

Table 3 (continued)

Investigator	Orientation/groups	N	Format/duration[a] (weeks)	Dropouts (%)	Reduction pre- to post-treatment % Binge	Vomit	Abstinent at last week of treatment % Binge	Vomit	Abstinent at follow-up % Binge	Vomit	Duration of follow-up
Treasure et al. (1994)	Cognitive-behavioral	21	I (8)	33	?	?	35	29			
	Self-care manual	41	S (8)	34	?	?	31	24			
	Wait list control	19		42	?	?	17	15			
Cooper and Steere (1995)	Cognitive-behavioral	15	I (18)	13	78	83	46	54	50	50	12 months
	Exposure w/response prevention	16	I (18)	13	79	91	50	43	15	8	
Fairburn et al. (1995)[c]	Cognitive-behavioral	35	I (18)	?					50 (b & v)		M = 5.8 years
	Behavioral	22	I (18)	?					18 (b & v)		
	Focal interpersonal	32	I (18)	?					52 (b & v)		
Jager et al. (1996)	Analytic inpatient	37	IP	14	?	?	34 (b & v)		66 (b & v)		38 months
	Systemic outpatient	46	I (?)	21	?	?	26 (b & v)		44 (b & v)		
Treasure et al. (1996)	Cognitive-behavioral	55	I (16)	27	?	?	30 (b & v)		41 (b & v)		18 months
	Self-care manual and cognitive-behavioral (if needed following self-care)	55	S (8) & I (8)[d]	16	?	?	30 (b & v)		40 (b & v)		

? = not reported

[a] G = group; I = individuals; S = self-care manual; IP = inpatient.   [b] Reports on follow-up of Agras et al. (1992).   [c] Report of follow-up from Fairburn et al. (1986, 1991).   [d] Additional cognitive-behavioral therapy needed for 39 of 55 participants, median sessions = 3.

Kirk, O'Connor, & Cooper 1986; Fairburn et al., 1995), and supportive–expressive therapy (Garner et al., 1993). Understanding the active ingredients of some of these treatments is impeded by the fact that some included techniques such as self-monitoring, meal planning, education regarding the untoward effects of dieting, and behavioral contracting, which are generally considered as more conceptually aligned with CBT. Thus, it remains unclear whether the observed changes in behavior are attributed to the "psychological" components of the treatment or to the dietary management. In a comparison of bulimia nervosa treatment studies using dietary management with those that did not, Laessle, Zoett, and Pirke (1987) concluded that dietary management was associated with superior results. Further support for this hypothesis comes from a study indicating very poor outcome with a 12-week psychodynamically oriented group program that did not incorporate dietary management (Frommer, Ames, Gibson, & Davis, 1987). Nevertheless, there have been two studies of treatments for bulimia nervosa that did not emphasize dietary management (Fairburn et al., 1995; Garner et al., 1993) indicating that dietary management may not be essential for change in eating disorder symptoms.

In summary, a number of carefully controlled studies demonstrated that many patients derive benefit from either individual or group treatment and that CBT tends to perform better than drug and other psychological treatments. Dietary management may enhance the effectiveness of treatments of varying orientations. Since it is evident that not all patients improve with CBT, it is important to consider other treatment options, perhaps sequenced in a systematic manner, as part of a multidimensional model of treatment.

5.23.9 PSYCHOPHARMACOLOGICAL TREATMENT RESEARCH

A wide variety of medications have been tried with eating disorders and while they can play a role in helping some people, they should rarely become the exclusive mode of treatment (Garfinkel & Garner, 1987; Garfinkel & Walsh, 1997; Raymond et al., 1994). According to the decision-tree approach for treating eating disorders (Figure 3), antidepressant medication should be considered as an adjunct or possibly an alternative for bulimia nervosa patients who fail to respond to psychosocial therapies or for those whose affective symptoms are clearly impeding progress in other forms of treatment. Antidepressants have an even more limited role

in the treatment of anorexia nervosa. With this general recommendation in mind, an overview of research on drug treatments will presented.

5.23.9.1 Treatment Research on Anorexia Nervosa

Historically, a variety of medications have been studied for their efficacy in promoting weight gain in women with anorexia nervosa. The rationale for trying many of the medications was based more on clinical observations than on a thorough understanding of the physiological mechanisms involved with this disorder. Unfortunately, we are still at a novice stage in our understanding of the physiological mechanisms that may contribute the development and maintenance of anorexia nervosa. Thus, although many medications have been tried in treating anorexia nervosa, few offer promise.

One class of medications that have been studied in the treatment of anorexia nervosa is antipsychotics. The rationale behind their use was the belief that the disturbed thinking regarding weight and shape, a cardinal feature of this disorder, may be a form of delusional thinking. Also, it was noted that dopamine mediates feeding and often people taking dopamine antagonists will experience weight gain. However, two double blind, placebo-controlled trials utilizing antipsychotic (pimozide and sulpiride) medications showed no statistically significant effects on weight (Vandereycken, 1984; Vandereycken & Pierloot, 1982).

A depressed mood is often associated with anorexia nervosa, and, as mentioned earlier, this is due most often to the effects of starvation. Given this, and that people treated with tricyclic antidepressants often experience an increase in appetite and weight gain, antidepressants have been utilized in treating anorexia nervosa. The results of open trials with antidepressants were promising; however, double-blind placebo-controlled studies yielded mixed results. Lacey and Crisp (1980) and Biederman et al. (1985) did not find significant effects on weight gain with either clomipramine or amitriptyline, respectively. Halmi, Eckert, LaDa, and Cohen (1986), however, did find that patients taking amitriptyline gained weight faster than those on a placebo. Substantial side effects from the amitriptyline were also noted.

One study reports on the effectiveness of lithium in treating anorexia nervosa (Gross et al., 1981). Again, the rationale for trying lithium was based on clinical observations of mood disturbances with anorexia nervosa and the weight gain experienced by many people who are prescribed lithium. The results of this study showed that the group of women with anorexia nervosa prescribed lithium did gain weight at a slightly faster rate, but that this was not statistically significant. Additionally, use of lithium may be problematic with this population due to frequent fluid imbalances if the person is purging.

Cyproheptadine, a serotonin and histamine antagonist, often used to treat allergies, has also been studied for its efficacy in treating anorexia nervosa. Cyproheptadine is a medication that is relatively free of side effects and promotes weight gain in some people who are prescribed it for allergies. Additionally, inhibiting serotonin transmission is believed to stimulate appetite. Thus, three controlled trials using cyproheptadine in treating anorexia nervosa were undertaken in the 1970s and 1980s. Two of the studies showed no significant effect on weight gain over placebo (Goldberg, Halmi, Eckert, Casper, & Davis, 1979; Vigersky & Loriaux, 1977). Halmi et al. (1986), utilizing a higher dosage, found that women with anorexia nervosa treated with cyproheptadine reached their goal weights an average of 10 days faster than those on placebo. This result was true only for the participants with the restricting subtype of anorexia nervosa, however, and the cyproheptadine was actually associated with delayed weight gain in those participants with the binge-purging subtype of anorexia nervosa. Moreover, there is little evidence to suggest that speed of weight gain is positively related to long-term recovery from anorexia nervosa.

Thus, the controlled trials of various medications designed to increase weight gain in women with anorexia nervosa have been generally disappointing. The practice guidelines for treating anorexia nervosa published by the APA (1993), indicate that medications should not be used routinely with this population. If an individual continues to experience mood disturbances following weight restoration, it is recommended that antidepressants be considered. Given that this is a volume that addresses clinical issues in children and adolescents, it should be noted that to date, no controlled trials of any medications reviewed here have been conducted with younger populations.

A more promising lead has been found when the focus is shifted from weight gain to relapse prevention in anorexia nervosa. Kaye, Guirtsman, George, and Ebert (1991) found that 29 of 31 women recovering from anorexia nervosa maintained their weight an average of 11 months when utilizing doses of fluoxetine between 20 and 80 mg daily. In a controlled study, Kaye et al. (1996) found that 63% of weight restored women with anorexia nervosa maintained a healthy body weight and a reduction in core eating disorder pathology for one year while taking fluoxetine. Only 16% of the participants taking a placebo maintained a healthy body weight. Thus, fluoxetine may be a promising agent in helping to prevent relapse in anorexia nervosa. More controlled studies are needed however, before firm conclusions can be drawn about the efficacy of fluoxetine with this population.

In sum, there is still little evidence for change in the early recommendations that pharmacotherapy has a very limited value with emaciated anorexia nervosa patients and should never be the sole treatment approach (Garfinkel & Garner, 1982). Occasionally patients may benefit from medication to deal with overwhelming anxiety, severe depression or intolerable gastric discomfort after meals, but this only applies to a small minority of patients (Andersen, 1985; Garfinkel & Garner, 1982; Garfinkel & Walsh, 1997).

5.23.9.2 Treatment Research on Bulimia Nervosa

In contrast to the lack of efficacy of medications in treating anorexia nervosa, there is some reason for optimism for the role of certain antidepressants in the treatment of bulimia nervosa (Garfinkel & Walsh, 1997; Raymond et al., 1994). The rationale for using antidepressants with bulimia nervosa was derived from several sources. First, as indicated earlier, Hudson and Pope (1988) argued that the efficacy of antidepressants in the treatment of bulimia nervosa suggests that it could be a variation of an affective illness. However, the failure to find any relationship between pretreatment levels of depression and response to medication does not support this view (Horne et al., 1988; Hughes, Wells, Cunningham, & Ilstruys, 1986; Walsh et al., 1988). Additionally, the dosage needed to be effective with bulimia nervosa is often substantially higher than the dosage used to treat mood disturbances (i.e., fluoxetine; FBNC, 1992).

Another more recent argument for pursuing antidepressants in treating bulimia nervosa is based on the hypothesis that dietary restraint may lead to lower levels of serotonin in the central nervous system. Binge eating may be driven by a need to increase brain serotonin (Walsh & Devlin, 1995). However, the merits of boosting serotonin with medication rather than with food is open to debate.

A review of the empirical literature on antidepressant treatment suggests that almost

Eating Disorders

all antidepressants studied have been found to be superior to placebo in reducing binge frequency (Mitchell et al., 1993). Antidepressant therapy also leads to improvement in mood disturbances and reduces preoccupations with weight and shape. Only one controlled study, utilizing the antidepressant amitriptyline, failed to show a significant effect of the drug over placebo (Mitchell & Groat, 1984). Seven studies have been published that examine the efficacy of tricyclics such as imipramine and desipramine (Mitchell et al., 1993). Across these studies mean reduction in binge frequency was 69%. However, mean rate of abstinence from bulimic symptoms was only 24%. Moreover, the relatively high percentage of participants who relapsed while taking antidepressants is a concern (Pyle et al., 1990; Walsh, Hadigan, Devlin, Gladis, & Roose, 1991). For example, Walsh et al. (1991) found that 29% of participants who responded to desipramine during an eight-week trial relapsed during a four-month maintenance phase. Likewise, Pyle et al. (1990) assigned nine responders to a three-month trial of imipramine to either continue the drug treatment ($n = 3$) or to a placebo ($n = 6$). Five of the six participants in the placebo group relapsed and two of the three participants in the imipramine group relapsed. Of the tricyclics, desipramine is recommended as the first medication of choice given its suggested efficacy and minimal anticholineric effects.

There is growing evidence that third-generation antidepressants, selective serotonin reuptake inhibitors (SSRIs), can be effective in treating bulimia nervosa. A multisite collaborative study (FBNC, 1992) indicated that fluoxetine hydrocholride (Prozac) in daily dosages of 60 mg was superior to 20 mg dosages and probably should be used at least as an adjunct to psychotherapy in cases failing a course of adequate psychological treatment. Open studies have been conducted examining the efficacy of other SSRIs. Geretsegger, Greimel, Roed, and Hesselink (1995) conducted an open label study with ipsapirone and reported that 93% of the participants showed greater than a 50% reduction in weekly binges after four weeks of treatment. Mizes, Sloan, Ruderich, Freiheit, and Silverman (1996) found that sertraline yielded a significant reduction in bingeing and purging episodes among seven participants.

Studies that have compared the efficacy of antidepressant treatments to psychotherapeutic interventions have shown that psychotherapy is more effective than drug treatment alone and that participants who received combined drug and psychotherapy interventions may have slightly better outcomes (Agras et al., 1992; Leitenberg et al, 1994; Mitchell et al., 1990;

Walsh et al., 1997). Agras et al. (1992) showed that a combined treatment of CBT and 24 weeks of treatment with desipramine yielded the highest rate of abstinence from bingeing at 32 weeks compared to CBT alone, desipramine alone, and CBT and desipramine treatment for 16 weeks. Likewise, Leitenberg et al. (1994) compared CBT alone, 20 weeks of desipramine treatment, and 20 weeks of combined treatments. There was a high (57%) dropout rate in the desipramine group, thus, the interpretation of the data is limited. However, the percentage of participants abstinent from vomiting at the six-month follow-up was substantially higher for those in the CBT group (57%) than for those in the desipramine group (0%) or in the combined treatment group (29%). Walsh et al. (1997) used a two-stage medication intervention for bulimia nervosa in which fluoxetine was employed if desipramine was either ineffective or poorly tolerated. This approach was compared to a combination of medication and two psychological treatments (cognitive-behavioral and psychodynamic-supportive). The results indicated that the two-stage medication intervention added modestly to the effects of the cognitive-behavioral treatment in reducing binge eating and depression. In addition, cognitive behavioral therapy plus medication was superior to medication alone; however, supportive psychotherapy plus medication was not more effective than medication alone.

MAOIs have been shown to be effective in reducing binge eating. Walsh et al. (1988) reported a 59% reduction in binge frequency in a controlled trial with an MAOI and Kennedy et al. (1988) reported a 22% reduction in binge frequency. However, side effects of MAOIs such as orthostatic hypotension, insomnia, and weight gain may be problematic. Additionally, dietary restrictions involving foods with a high concentration of tyramine or dopamine (aged cheese, beer) are necessary when taking MAOIs because high concentrations of tyramine or dopamine may cause a life threatening rapid increase in blood pressure. Placing people with bulimia nervosa on dietary restrictions is often counter to the therapeutic goals. Thus, it is generally recommended that MAOIs not be utilized as the first trial drug for this population (Kennedy et al., 1988; Walsh et al., 1988).

There have been a number of studies examining the utility of drugs other than antidepressants in the treatment of bulimia nervosa. Several studies of naltrexone, an opioid antagonist, have yielded mixed results. Mitchell, Davis, Goff, and Pyle (1986) reported a 23% decrease in binge size with naloxone. Alger, Schwalberg, Bigaouette, Michaleck, and Howard (1991) conducted a controlled trial with naltrexone and found that it significantly reduced the duration of bingeing episodes but was no better than placebo in reducing frequency of binges. In another controlled trial, naltrexone was no better than placebo in reducing symptoms of bulimia nervosa (Mitchell et al., 1989). Marrazzi, Bacon, Kinzie, and Luby (1995) reported on the results of a double-blind randomized crossover-design trial of naltrexone in treating participants with bulimia nervosa and anorexia nervosa. Out of the 19 participants, 18 showed a greater reduction in bingeing and purging while taking the naltrexone when compared to placebo. Given the mixed results of the above studies, the efficacy of treating bulimia nervosa and perhaps, anorexia nervosa with naltrexone warrants further investigation.

Mood stabilizing drugs such as lithium carbonate have been used in several trials, however, Garfinkel and Walsh (1997) concluded that "there is little evidence that most patients will benefit from their use" (p. 374). Fenfluramine has been studied with bulimia nervosa because of its effects in promoting satiety. An early study by Blouin et al. (1988) produced encouraging findings but a subsequent controlled trial showed no substantial clinical benefit of fenfluramine over placebo (Fahy, Eisler, & Russell, 1993).

5.23.10 FUTURE DIRECTIONS

A major premise in this chapter has been that eating disorders are multidetermined and heterogeneous syndromes resulting from the interplay of biological, psychological, familial, and sociocultural predisposing factors. In this sense, they are probably best understood as final common pathways that appear to have different psychological points of entry. Within this overall context, this chapter has selectively reviewed diagnostic issues, major etiological formulations, and associated psychopathology applied to eating disorders.

From research to date it may be concluded that there has been as much resistance to dispelling the "uniformity myth" applied to eating disorders as has been the case with disorders with a longer or more visible history in the psychological nomenclature. However, research since the mid-1980s has yielded notable advancements in refining the criteria for eating-disordered subgroups and in providing more rigorous research examining psychopathology or psychological topologies associated with diagnostic subtypes. An important direction for future research will be the clearer specification of the relative contribution of particular

biological, psychological, and interpersonal predisposing features considered relevant to eating disorders. It is to be hoped that the extraordinary clinical and research interest in personality disorders, depression, sexual abuse, and addictive behaviors as related to eating disorders will continue to lead to improved understanding. Further research is clearly needed to determine the precise nature and the significance of the observed associations. If past research to date is any indication of future findings, the within-diagnostic-group variability will continue to be as noteworthy as the between-group differences.

It is now evident that certain patients respond relatively quickly to brief interventions, in contrast to others who require more intensive and protracted treatments. Perhaps the most significant goal for future research will be the identification of traits, personality features, or background factors that predict differential response to treatment. Even better would be a taxonomy yielding an accurate match between patient characteristics and treatment type.

Advances in research on psychopathology and treatment efficacy warrant genuine optimism with regard to bulimia nervosa. Less is known about personality and response to treatment for anorexia nervosa because of the relative absence of controlled treatment research with this eating disorder. It is hoped that controlled treatment research will assume a high priority, and that the results will generate the same level of progress as is now evident with bulimia nervosa.

5.23.11 REFERENCES

Agras, W. S. (1993). Short-term psychological treatments for binge eating. In C. G. Fairburn & G. T. Wilson (Eds.), *Binge eating: Nature, assessment, and treatment* (pp. 50–76). New York: Guilford Press.

Agras, W. S., Rossiter E. M., Arnow, B., Schneider, J. A., Telch, C. F., Raeburn, S. D., Bruce, B., Perl, M., & Koran, L. M. (1992) Pharmacologic and cognitive-behavioral treatment for bulimia nervosa: A controlled comparison. *American Journal of Psychiatry, 149,* 82–87.

Agras, W. S., Rossiter, E. M., Arnow, B., Telch, C., Raeburn, S., Bruce, B., & Koran, L. (1994). One year follow up of psychosocial and pharmacologic treatments for bulimia nervosa. *Journal of Clinical Psychiatry, 55,* 179–83.

Alger, S. A., Schwalberg, M. D., Bigaouette, J. M., Michaleck, A. V., & Howard, L. J. (1991). Effect of a tricyclic antidepressant and opiate antagonist on binge-eating in normal weight bulimic and obese, binge-eating subjects. *American Journal of Clinical Nutrition, 53,* 865–871.

American Psychiatric Association (1994). *Diagnostic and statistical manual of mental disorders* (4th ed.) Washington, DC: Author.

Andersen, A. E. (1985). *Practical comprehensive treatment of anorexia nervosa and bulimia.* Baltimore: Johns Hopkins University Press.

Andersen, A. E. (1990). *Males with eating disorders.* New York: Brunner/Mazel.

Andersen, A. E., Bowers, W., & Evans, K. (1997). Inpatient treatment of anorexia nervosa. In D. M. Garner & P. E. Garfinkel (Eds.), *Handbook of treatment for eating disorders* (pp. 327–353). New York: Guilford Press.

Armstrong, J. G., & Roth, D. M. (1989). Attachment and separation difficulties in eating disorders: A preliminary investigation. *International Journal of Eating Disorders, 8,* 141–155.

Baker Enright, A., Butterfield, P., & Berkowitz (1985). Self-help and support groups in the management of eating disorders. In D. M. Garner & P. E. Garfinkel (Eds.), *Handbook of psychotherapy for anorexia nervosa and bulimia* (pp. 491–512), New York: Guilford Press.

Beaumont, P. J. V., Al-Alami, M. S., & Touyz, S. W. (1987). The evolution of the concept of anorexia nervosa. In P. J. V. Beaumont, G. D. Burrows, & R. C. Casper (Eds.), *Handbook of eating disorders: Part 1, Anorexia and bulimia nervosa* (pp. 105–116). New York: Elsevier.

Beaumont, P. J. V., George, G. G. W., & Smart, D. E. (1976). "Dieters" and "vomiters and purgers" in anorexia nervosa. *Psychological Medicine, 6,* 617–622.

Beaumont, P. J. V., O'Connor, M., Touyz, S. W., & Williams, H. (1987). Nutritional counseling in the treatment of anorexia and bulimia nervosa. In P. J. V. Beaumont, G. D. Burrows, & R. C. Casper (Eds.), *Handbook of eating disorders: Part 1: Anorexia and bulimia nervosa.* New York: Elsevier.

Bell, R. (1985). *Holy anorexia.* Chicago: University of Chicago Press.

Bemis, K. M. (1985). "Abstinence" and "nonabstinence" models for the treatment of bulimia. *International Journal of Eating Disorders, 4,* 389–406.

Biederman, J., Herzog, D., Rivinus, T., Harper, G., Ferber, R., Rosenbaum, J., Harmatz, J., Tondorf, R., Orsulack, P., & Schildkraut, J. (1985). Amitriptyline in the treatment of anorexia nervosa. *Journal of Clinical Psychopharmacology, 5,* 10–16.

Blouin, A. G., Blouin, J., Perez, E., Bushnik, T., Zuro, C., & Mulder, E. (1988). Treatment of bulimia with fenfluramine and desipramine. *Journal of Clinical Psychopharmacology, 8,* 261–269.

Brotman, A. W., Herzog, D. B., & Woods, S. W. (1984). Antidepressant treatment of bulimia nervosa: The relationship between bingeing and depressive symptomatology. *Journal of Clinical Psychiatry, 45,* 7–9.

Bruch, H. (1973). *Eating disorders: Obesity, anorexia nervosa and the person within.* New York: Basic Books.

Bruch, H. (1985). Four decades of eating disorders. In D. M. Garner & P. E. Garfinkel (Eds.), *Handbook of psychotherapy for anorexia nervosa and bulimia* (pp. 7–18). New York: Guilford Press.

Bulik, C., Sullivan, P., Joyce, P., & Carter, F. (1995). Temperament character, and personality disorder in bulimia nervosa. *The Journal of Nervous and Mental Disease, 183,* 593–598.

Cantwell, D. P., Sturzenburger, S., Burroughs, J., Salkin, B., & Green, J. K. (1977) Anorexia nervosa: An affective disorder? *Archives of General Psychiatry, 34,* 1087–1093.

Casper, R. C. (1982). Treatment principles in anorexia nervosa. *Adolescent Psychiatry, 10,* 86–100.

Casper, R. C. (1983). On the emergence of bulimia nervosa as a syndrome: A historical view. *International Journal of Eating Disorders, 2,* 3–16.

Casper, R. C. (1990). Personality features of women with good outcome from restricting anorexia nervosa. *Psychosomatic Medicine, 52,* 156–170.

Casper, R. C., Eckert, E. D., Halmi, K. A., Goldberg, S. C., & Davis, J. M. (1980). Bulimia: Its incidence and clinical importance in patients with anorexia nervosa. *Archives of General Psychiatry, 37,* 1030–1034.

Channon, S., DeSilva, P., Hemsley, D., & Perkins, R. (1989). A controlled trial of cognitive-behavioral and behavioral treatment of anorexia nervosa. *Behavior Research and Therapy, 27,* 529–535.

Chiodo, J., & Latimer, P. R. (1983). Vomiting as a learned weight-control technique in bulimia. *Journal of Behavior Therapy and Experimental Psychiatry, 14,* 131–135.

Cloninger, C. R. (1989). A systematic method for clinical description and classification of personality variants. *Archives of General Psychiatry, 44,* 573–588.

Connors, M. E., Johnson, C. L., & Stuckley, M. K. (1984). Treatment of bulimia with brief psychoeducational group therapy. *American Journal of Psychiatry, 141,* 1512–1516.

Cooper, J. L., Morrison, T. L., Bigman, O. L., Abramowitz, S. I., Levin, S., & Krener, P. (1988). Mood changes and affective disorder in the bulimic binge-purge cycle. *International Journal of Eating Disorders, 7,* 469–474.

Cooper, P. J., & Fairburn, C. G. (1984). Cognitive behavioral treatment for anorexia nervosa: Some preliminary findings. *Journal of Psychosomatic Research, 28,* 493–499.

Cooper, Z., & Fairburn, C. G. (1987). The eating disorder examination: A semistructured interview for the assessment of the specific psychopathology of eating disorders. *International Journal of Eating Disorders, 6,* 1–8.

Cooper, Z., Coker, S., & Fleming, C. (1995). An evaluation of the efficacy of cognitive behavioural self-help for bulimia nervosa. *Journal of Psychosomatic Research, 40,* 281–287.

Cooper, P. & Steere, J. (1995). A comparison of two psychological treatments for bulimia nervosa: Implications for models of maintenance. *Behavior Research & Therapy, 33,* 875–885.

Crisp, A. H. (1965). Clinical and therapeutic aspects of anorexia nervosa: Study of 30 cases. *Journal of Psychosomatic Research, 9,* 67–78.

Crisp, A. H. (1970). Anorexia nervosa. "Feeding disorder," nervous malnutrition or weight phobia? *World Review of Nutrition, 12,* 452–504.

Crisp, A. H. (1980). *Anorexia nervosa.* New York: Grune & Stratton.

Crisp, A. H. (1997). Anorexia nervosa as flight from growth: Assessment and treatment based on the model. In D. M. Garner & P. E. Garfinkel (Eds.), *Handbook of treatment for eating disorders* (pp. 248–277). New York: Guilford Press.

Crisp, A. H., Norton, K., Gowers, S., Halek, C., Bowyer, C., Yeldham, D., Levett, G., & Bhat, A. (1991). A controlled study of the effect of therapies aimed at adolescent and family psychopathology in anorexia nervosa. *British Journal of Psychiatry, 159,* 325–333.

Crowther J., & Sherwood N. (1997). Assessment. In D. M. Garner & P. E. Garfinkel (Eds.), *Handbook of treatment for eating disorders* (pp. 34–49). New York: Guilford Press.

Dare, C., & Eisler, I. (1997). Family therapy for anorexia nervosa. In D. M. Garner & P. E. Garfinkel (Eds.), *Handbook of treatment for eating disorders* (pp. 307–326). New York: Guilford Press.

Davies, E., & Furnham, A. (1986). The dieting and body shape concerns of adolescent females. *Journal of Child Psychology and Psychiatry, 3,* 417–428.

Eckert, E. D., Halmi, K. A., Marchi, P., & Cohen, J. (1987). Comparison of bulimic and non-bulimic anorexia nervosa patients during treatment. *Psychological Medicine, 17,* 891–898.

Eckert, E. D., Halmi, K. A., Marchi, P., Grove, W., & Crosby, R. (1995). Ten-year follow-up of anorexia nervosa: Clinical course and outcome. *Psychological Medicine, 25,* 143–156.

Edlund, B., Halvarsson, K., & Sjödén, P. (1995). Eating behaviours, and attitudes to eating, dieting, and body image in a 7-year-old Swedish girl. *European Eating Disorders Review, 3,* 111/1–111/14.

Fahy, T., & Eisler, I. (1993). Impulsivity and eating disorders. *British Journal of Psychiatry, 162,* 193–97.

Fahy, T., Eisler, I., & Russell, G. (1993). A placebo-controlled trial of d-Fenfluramine in bulimia nervosa. *British Journal of Psychiatry, 162,* 597–603.

Fairburn, C. G. (1985). Cognitive-behavioral treatment for bulimia. In D. M. Garner & P. E. Garfinkel (Eds.), *Handbook of psychotherapy for anorexia nervosa and bulimia* (pp. 160–192). New York: Guilford Press.

Fairburn, C. G., (1997). Interpersonal psychotherapy for bulimia nervosa. In D. M. Garner & P. E. Garfinkel (Eds.), *Handbook of treatment for eating disorders* (pp. 278–294). New York: Guilford Press.

Fairburn, C. G., Agras, W. S., & Wilson, G. T. (1992). The research on the treatment of bulimia nervosa: Practical and theoretical implications. *Biology of Feast and Famine,* 317–340.

Fairburn, C. G., & Beglin, S. J. (1990). Studies of the epidemiology of bulimia nervosa. *American Journal of Psychiatry, 147,* 401–408.

Fairburn, C. G., & Carter, J. (1997). Self-help and guided self-help for binge eating problems. In D. M. Garner & P. E. Garfinkel (Eds.), *Handbook of treatment for eating disorders* (pp. 494–500). New York: Guilford Press.

Fairburn, C. G., Jones, R., Peveler, R. C., Carr, S. J., Solomon, R. A., O'Connor, M. E., Burton, J., & Hope, R. A. (1991). Three psychological treatments for bulimia nervosa: A comparative trial. *Archives of General Psychiatry, 48,* 463–469.

Fairburn, C. G., Jones, R., Peveler, R. C., Hope, R. A., & O'Connor, M. E. (1993). Psychotherapy and bulimia nervosa: the longer-term effects of interpersonal psychotherapy, behavior therapy and cognitive behavior therapy. *Archives of General Psychiatry, 50,* 419–428.

Fairburn, C. G., Kirk, J., O'Connor, M. E., & Cooper, P. J. (1986). A comparison of two psychological treatments for bulimia nervosa. *Behaviour Research and Therapy, 24,* 629–643.

Fairburn, C. G., Marcus, M. D., & Wilson, G. T. (1993). Cognitive-behavioral therapy for binge eating and bulimia nervosa. In C. G. Fairburn & G. T. Wilson (Eds.), *Binge eating nature: Assessment and treatment* (361–404). New York: Guilford Press.

Fairburn, C. G., Norman, P. A., Welch, S. L., O'Connor, M. E., Doll, H. A., & Peveler, R. C. (1995). A prospective study of outcome in bulimia nervosa and the long-term effects of three psychological treatments, *Archives of General Psychiatry, 52,* 304–312.

Fairburn, C. G., & Peveler, R. C. (1990). Bulimia nervosa and a stepped care approach to management, *Gut, 31,* 1220–1222.

Fallon, P., Katzman, M. A., & Wooley, S. C. (1994). *Feminist perspectives on eating disorders.* New York: Guilford Press.

Fallon, P., & Wonderlich, S. (1997). Sexual abuse and other forms of trauma. In D. M. Garner & P. E. Garfinkel (Eds.), *Handbook of treatment for eating disorders* (pp. 394–414). New York: Guilford Press.

Fichter, M., & Quadflieg, N. (1995). Comparative studies on the course of eating disorders in adolescence and adults. Is age at onset a predictor of outcome? In H. C. Steinhausen (Ed.), *Eating disorders in adolescence. Anorexia and bulimia nervosa.* Berlin: de Gruyter.

Fluoxetine Bulimia Nervosa Collaborative Study Group (FBNC) (1992). Fluoxetine in the treatment of bulimia nervosa. *Archives of General Psychiatry, 49,* 139–147.

Fosson, A., Knibbs, J., Bryant-Waugh, R., & Lask, B. (1987). Early onset anorexia nervosa. *Archives of Disease in Childhood, 62,* 114–118.

Frommer, M. S., Ames, J. R., Gibson, J. W., & Davis, W.

N. (1987). Patterns of symptom change in the short-term treatment of bulimia. *International Journal of Eating Disorders, 6,* 469–476.

Garfinkel, P. E., & Garner, D. M. (1982). *Anorexia nervosa: A multidimensional perspective.* New York: Brunner/Mazel.

Garfinkel, P. E., & Garner, D. M. (1987). *Psychotropic drug therapies for eating disorders.* Monograph Series. New York: Brunner/Mazel.

Garfinkel, P. E., Moldofsky, H., & Garner, D. M. (1980). The heterogeneity of anorexia nervosa. *Archives of General Psychiatry, 37,* 1036–1040.

Garfinkel, P. E., Kaplan, A. S., Garner, D. M., & Darby, P. L. (1983). The differentiation of vomiting/weight loss as a conversion disorder from anorexia nervosa. *American Journal of Psychiatry, 140,* 1019–1022.

Garfinkel, P. E., & Walsh B. (1997). Drug therapies. In D. M., Garner & P. E. Garfinkel (Eds.), *Handbook of treatment for eating disorders* (pp. 229–247). New York: Guilford Press.

Garner, D. M. (1985). Iatrogenesis in anorexia nervosa and bulimia nervosa. *International Journal of Eating Disorders, 4,* 701–726.

Garner, D. M. (1986) Cognitive therapy for anorexia nervosa. In K. D. Brownell & J. P. Foreyt (Eds.), *Handbook of eating disorders* (pp. 301–327). New York: Basic Books.

Garner, D. M. (1988) Anorexia nervosa. In M. Hersen & C. G. Last (Eds.), *Child behavior therapy casebook* (pp. 263–276). New York: Plenum.

Garner, D. M. (1991). *Eating disorder inventory–2: Professional manual.* Odessa, FL: Psychological Assessment Resources.

Garner, D. M. (1993). Pathogenesis of anorexia nervosa. *The Lancet, 341,* 1631–1635.

Garner, D. M. (1997). Psychoeducational principles in treatment. In D. M. Garner & P. E. Garfinkel (Eds.), *Handbook of treatment for eating disorders* (pp. 145–177). New York: Guilford Press.

Garner, D. M., & Bemis, K. M. (1982). A cognitive-behavioral approach to anorexia nervosa. *Cognitive Therapy and Research, 6,* 123–150.

Garner, D. M., & Bemis, K. M. (1985). Cognitive therapy for anorexia nervosa. In D. M. Garner & P. E. Garfinkel (Eds.), *Handbook of psychotherapy for anorexia nervosa and bulimia* (pp. 107–146). New York: Guilford Press.

Garner, D. M., Fairburn, C. G., & Davis, R. (1987). Cognitive-behavioral treatment of bulimia nervosa: A critical appraisal. *Behavior Modification, 11,* 398–431.

Garner, D. M., & Garfinkel, P. E. (1980). Socio-cultural factors in the development of anorexia nervosa. *Psychological Medicine, 10,* 647–656.

Garner, D. M., & Garfinkel, P. E. (1997). *Handbook of treatment for eating disorders.* New York: Guilford Press.

Garner, D. M., Garfinkel, P. E., & Bemis, K. M. (1982). A multidimensional psychotherapy for anorexia nervosa. *International Journal of Eating Disorders, 1,* 3–46.

Garner, D. M., Garfinkel, P. E., & Irvine, M. J. (1986). Integration and sequencing of treatment approaches for eating disorders. *Psychotherapy and Psychosomatics, 46,* 67–75.

Garner, D. M., Garfinkel, P. E., & O'Shaughnessy, M. (1985). The validity of the distinction between bulimia with and without anorexia nervosa. *American Journal of Psychiatry, 142,* 581–587.

Garner, D. M., Garfinkel, P. E., Schwartz, D. M., & Thompson, M. M. (1980). Cultural expectations of thinness in women. *Psychological Reports, 47,* 483–491.

Garner, D. M., Garner, M. V., & Rosen, L. W. (1993). Anorexia nervosa "restricters" who purge: Implications for subtyping Anorexia nervosa. *International Journal of Eating Disorders, 13,* 171–185.

Garner, D. M., & Needleman, L. (1997). Sequencing and

integration of treatments. In D. M. Garner & P. E. Garfinkel (Eds.), *Handbook of treatment of eating disorders* (pp. 50–66). New York: Guilford Press.

Garner, D. M., Rockert, W., Olmsted, M. P., Johnson, C. L., & Coscina, D. V. (1985). Psychoeducational principles in the treatment of bulimia and anorexia nervosa. In D. M. Garner & P. E. Garfinkel (Eds.), *Handbook of psychotherapy for anorexia nervosa and bulimia* (pp. 513–572). New York: Guilford Press.

Garner, D. M., & Rosen, L. W. (1990). Anorexia nervosa and bulimia nervosa. In A. S. Bellack, M. Hersen, & A. E. Kazdin (Eds.), *International handbook of behavior modification and therapy* (pp. 805–817). New York: Plenum.

Garner, D. M., & Rosen, L. W. (1991). Eating disorders in athletes: Research and recommendations. *Journal of Applied Sports Research, 5,* 100–107.

Garner, D. M., & Sackeyfio, A. H. (1993). Eating disorders. In A. S. Bellack & M. Hersen (Eds.), *Handbook of behavior therapy in the psychiatric setting* (pp. 477–497). New York: Plenum.

Garner, D. M., Vitousek, K. & Pike, K. (1997). Cognitive-behavioral therapy for anorexia nervosa. In D. M. Garner & P. E. Garfinkel (Eds.), *Handbook of treatment for eating disorders* (pp. 94–144). New York: Guilford Press.

Garner, D. M., & Wooley, S. C. (1991). Confronting the failure of behavioral and dietary treatments for obesity. *Clinical Psychology Review, 11,* 729–780.

Gartner, A. F., Marcus, R. N., Halmi, K., & Loranger, A. W. (1989). DSM-III-R personality disorders in patients with eating disorders. *American Journal of Psychiatry, 14,* 1585–1591.

Geretsegger, C., Greimel, K., Roed, I., & Hesselink, J. (1995). Ipsapirone in the treatment of bulimia nervosa: An open pilot study. *International Journal of Eating Disorders, 17,* 359–363.

Gillberg, G., Rastam, M., & Gillberg, C. (1995). Anorexia nervosa 6 years after onset: Part I. Personality disorders. *Comprehensive Psychiatry, 36,* 61–69.

Goetz, P. L., Succop, R. A., Reinhart, J. B., & Miller, A. (1977). Anorexia nervosa in children: A follow-up study. *American Journal of Orthopsychiatry, 47,* 597–603.

Goldberg, S. C., Halmi, K. A., Eckert, E. D., Casper, R. C., & Davis, J. M. (1979). Cyproheptadine in anorexia nervosa. *British Journal of Psychiatry, 134,* 67–70.

Goodsitt, A. (1985). Self psychology and the treatment of anorexia nervosa. In D. M. Garner & P. E. Garfinkel (Eds.), *Handbook of psychotherapy for anorexia nervosa and bulimia* (pp. 55–84). New York: Guilford Press.

Goodsitt, A. (1997). Eating disorders a self psychological perspective. In D. M. Garner & P. E. Garfinkel (Eds.), *Handbook of treatment for eating disorders* (pp. 205–228). New York: Guilford.

Gowers, S., & McMahon, J. B. (1989). Social class and prognosis in anorexia nervosa. *International Journal of Eating Disorders, 8,* 105–110.

Gowers, S., Norton, K., Halek, C., & Crisp, A. (1994). Outcome of outpatient psychotherapy in a random allocation treatment study of anorexia nervosa. *International Journal of Eating Disorders, 15,* 165–177.

Gross, H., Ebert, M., Faden, V., Goldberg, S., Nee, L., & Kaye, W. (1981). A double-blind controlled trial of lithium carbonate in primary anorexia nervosa. *Journal of Clinical Psychopharmacology, 1,* 376–381.

Haimes, A. L., & Katz, J. L. (1988). Sexual and social maturity versus social conformity in restricting anorectic bulimic, and borderline women. *International Journal of Eating Disorders, 7,* 331–341.

Halmi, K. A., Eckert, E., LaDu, T. J., & Cohen, J. (1986). Anorexia nervosa: Treatment efficacy of cyproheptadine and amitriptyline. *Archives of General Psychiatry, 43,* 177–181.

Halmi, K. A., Eckert, E., Marchi, P., Sampugnaro, V., Apple, R., & Cohen, J. (1991). Comorbidity of psychiatric diagnoses in anorexia nervosa. *Archives of General Psychiatry, 48,* 712–718.

Hatsukami, D., Mitchell, J. E., Eckert, E. D., & Pyle, R. (1986). Characteristics of patients with bulimia only, bulimia with affective disorder, and bulimia with substance abuse problems. *Addictive Behaviors, 11,* 399–406.

Hatsukami, D., Owen, P., Pyle, R., & Mitchell, J. (1982). Similarities and differences on the MMPI between women with bulimia and women with alcohol and drug abuse problems. *Addictive Behaviors, 7,* 435–439.

Hawley, R. M. (1985) The outcome of anorexia nervosa in younger subjects. *British Journal of Psychiatry, 146,* 657–660.

Heatherton, T. F., & Baumeister, R. F. (1991). Binge-eating as escape from self-awareness. *Psychological Bulletin, 110,* 86–108.

Herzog, D. B., Keller, M. B., Lavori, P. W., & Ott, I. L. (1987). Social impairment in bulimia. *International Journal of Eating Disorders, 6,* 741–747.

Herzog, D. B., Keller, M. B., & Lavori, P. W. (1988). Outcome in anorexia nervosa and bulimia nervosa: A review of the literature. *Journal of Nervous and Mental Disease, 176,* 131–143.

Herzog, D. B., Keller, M. B., Sacks, N. R., Yeh, C. J., & Lavori, P. W. (1992). Psychiatric morbidity in treatment-seeking anorexics and bulimics. *Journal of the American Academy of Child and Adolescent Psychiatry, 31,* 810–818.

Herzog, W., Schellberg, D., & Deter, H. (1997). First recovery in anorexia nervosa patients in the long-term course: A discrete-time survival analysis. *Journal of Consulting and Clinical Psychology, 65,* 169–177.

Hinz, L. D., & Williamson, D. A. (1987). Bulimia and depression: A review of the affective variant hypothesis. *Psychological Bulletin, 102,* 150–158.

Hoek, H. W. (1993). Review of the epidemiological studies of eating disorders. *International Review of Psychiatry, 5,* 61–74.

Hoek, H. W., Bartelds, A., Bosveld, J., Graff, Y., Limpens, V., Maiwald, M., & Spaij, C. (1995). Impact of urbanization on detection rates of eating disorders. *American Journal of Psychiatry, 152,* 1272–1278.

Holland A. J., Sicotte, N., & Treasure, J. (1988). Anorexia nervosa: Evidence for a genetic basis. *Journal of Psychosomatic Research, 32,* 561–571.

Horne, R. L., Ferguson, J. M., Pope, H. G., Hudson, J. I., Lineberry, C. G., Ascher, J., & Cato, A. (1988). Treatment of bulimia with bupropion: A multicenter controlled trial. *Journal of Clinical Psychiatry, 49,* 262–266.

Hsu, L. K. G. (1988). The outcome of anorexia nervosa: A reappraisal. *Psychological Medicine, 18,* 807–812.

Hsu, L. K. G. (1996). Outcome of early onset anorexia nervosa: What do we know? *Journal of Youth and Adolescence, 25,* 563–568.

Hsu, L. K. G., Kaye, W., & Weltzin, T. (1993). Are the eating disorders related to obsessive compulsive disorder? *International Journal of Eating Disorders, 14,* 305–318.

Hudson, J. I., & Pope, H. G. (1988). Depression and eating disorders. In O. G. Cameron (Ed.), *Presentations of depression.* New York: Wiley.

Hughes, P. L., Wells, L. A., Cunningham, C. J., & Ilstrup, D. M. (1986). Treating bulimia with desipramine: A double-blind placebo-controlled study. *Archives of General Psychiatry, 43,* 182–186.

Humphrey, L. L. (1989). Is there a causal link between disturbed family processes and eating disorders? In W. G. Johnson (Ed.), *Bulimia nervosa: Perspectives on clinical research and therapy.* New York: JAI Press.

Huon, G. F. (1985). An initial validation of a self-help

program for bulimia. *International Journal for Eating Disorders, 4*, 573–588.

Huon, G. F., & Brown, L. B. (1985). Evaluating a group treatment for bulimia. *Journal of Psychiatric Research, 19*, 479–483.

Huon, G. F., & Brown, L., & Morris, S. (1988). Lay beliefs about disordered eating. *International Journal of Eating Disorders, 7*, 239–252.

Jager, B., Liedtke, R., Kunsebeck, H. W., & Lempa, W. (1996). Psychotherapy and bulimia nervosa: Evaluation and long-term follow-up of two conflict-oriented treatment conditions. *Acta Psychiatrica Scandinavica, 93*, 268–278.

Jaffe, A. C., & Singer, L. T. (1989). Atypical eating disorders in young children. *International Journal of Eating Disorders, 8*, 575–582.

Johnson, C. L., & Connors, M. E. (1987). *The etiology and treatment of bulimia nervosa: A biopsychosocial perspective.* New York: Basic Books.

Johnson, C., Tobin, D. L., & Dennis, A. (1990). Differences in treatment outcome between borderline and nonborderline bulimics at one-year follow-up. *International Journal of Eating Disorders, 9*, 617–627.

Kaplan, A., & Olmsted, M. (1997). Partial hospitalization. In D. M. Garner & P. E. Garfinkel (Eds.), *Handbook of treatment for eating disorders* (pp. 354–360). New York: Guilford Press.

Kasvikis, Y. G., Isakiris, F, Marks, I. M., Basoglu, M., & Noshirvani, H. F. (1986). Past history of anorexia nervosa in women with obsessive-compulsive disorder. *International Journal of Eating Disorders, 5*, 1069–1075.

Katzman, M. A. (1994). When reproductive and productive worlds meet: collusion or growth? In P. Fallon, M. A. Katzman, & S. C. Wooley, (Eds.), *Feminist perspectives on eating disorders* (pp. 132–151). New York: Guilford Press.

Kaye, W. H., Gwirtsman, H. E., George, D. T., & Ebert, M. H. (1991). Altered serotonin activity in anorexia nervosa after long-term weight restoration. *Archives of General Psychiatry, 48*, 556–562.

Kaye, W. H., McConaha, C., Nagata, T., Plotnicov, K. H., Sokol, M. S., Weltzin, T. E., Hsu, L. K. G., & La Via, M. C. (1996). Fluoxetine prevents relapse in a majority of patients with anorexia nervosa: A double-blind placebo-controlled study. Presented at the Eating Disorders Research Society Meeting, Pittsburgh, PA.

Kearney-Cooke, A., & Striegel-Moore, R. (1997). The etiology and treatment of body image disturbance. In D. M. Garner & P. E. Garfinkel (Eds.), *Handbook of treatment for eating disorders* (pp. 295–306). New York: Guilford Press.

Kellett, J., Trimble, M., & Thorley, A. (1976). Anorexia nervosa after the menopause. *British Journal of Psychiatry, 128*, 555–558.

Kennedy, S. H., Piran, N., Warsh, J. J., Pendergast, P., Mainprize, E., Whynot, C., & Garfinkel, P. E. (1988). A trial of isocaroxide in the treatment of bulimia nervosa. *Journal of Clinical Psychopharmacology, 8*, 391–396.

Kirkley, B. G., Schneider, J. A., Agras, W. S., & Bachman, J. A. (1985). Comparison of two group treatments for bulimia. *Journal of Consulting and Clinical Psychology, 53*, 43–48.

Klerman, G. L., Weissman, M. M., Rounsaville, B. J., & Chevron, E. (1984). *Interpersonal psychotherapy for depression.* New York: Basic Books.

Kohut, H. (1971). *The restoration of the self.* New York: International Universities Press.

Kreipe, R. E., Churchill, B. H., & Strauss, J. (1989). Long-term outcome of adolescents with anorexia nervosa. *American Journal of Diseases of Children, 143*, 1322–1327.

Lacey, J. H., & Crisp, A. H. (1980). Hunger, food intake and weight: The impact of clomipramine on a refeeding

anorexia nervosa population. *Postgraduate Medical Journal, 56*, 79–85.

Laessle, R. G., Beumont, P. J. V., Butow, P., Lenneris, W., O'Connor, M., Pirke, K. M., Touyz, S. W., & Waadi, S. (1991). A comparison of nutritional management and stress management in the treatment of bulimia nervosa. *British Journal of Psychiatry, 159*, 250–261.

Laessle, R. G., Kittl, S., Fichter, M. M., Wittchen, H. U., & Pirke, K. M. (1987). Major affective disorder in anorexia nervosa and bulimia—a descriptive diagnostic study. *British Journal of Psychiatry, 151*, 785–789.

Laessle, R. G., Waadt, S., & Pirke, K. M. (1987). A structured behaviorally oriented group treatment for bulimia nervosa. *Psychotherapy and Psychosomatics, 48*, 141–145.

Laessle, R. G., Wittchen, H. U., Fichter, M. M., & Pirke, K. M. (1989). The significance of subgroups of bulimia and anorexia nervosa: Lifetime frequency of psychiatric disorders. *International Journal of Eating Disorders, 8*, 569–574.

Lask B., & Bryant-Waugh, R. (1997). Pre-pubertal eating disorders. In D. M. Garner & P. E. Garfinkel (Eds.), *Handbook of treatment for eating disorders* (pp. 476–483). New York: Guilford Press.

Leitenberg, H., Rosen, J. C., Wolf, J., Vara, L. S., Detzer, M. J., & Srebnik, D. (1994). Comparison of cognitive-behavior therapy and desipramine in the treatment of bulimia nervosa. *Behavior Research and Therapy, 32*, 37–45.

Lerner, H. D. (1993). Self-representation in eating disorders: A psychodynamic perspective. In Z. Segal & S. Blatt (Eds.), *The self-in emotional disorders: Cognitive and psychodynamic perspectives* (pp. 267–287). New York: Guilford Press.

Levin, A. P., & Hyler, S. E. (1986). DSM-III personality diagnosis in bulimia. *Comprehensive Psychiatry, 27*, 47–53.

Malenbaum, R., Herzog, D., Eisenthal, S., & Wyshak, G. (1988). Overeaters anonymous: Impact on bulimia. *International Journal of Eating Disorders, 7*, 139–143.

Maloney, M. J., McGuire, J. B., & Daniels, S. R. (1988). Reliability testing of a children's version of the Eating Attitudes Test. *Journal of the American Academy of Child and Adolescent Psychiatry, 27*, 541–543.

Marrazzi, M., Bacon, J., Kinzie, J., & Luby, E. (1995). Naltrexone use in the treatment of anorexia nervosa and bulimia nervosa. *International Clinical Psychopharmacology, 10*, 163–172.

Martin, F. (1985). Treatment and outcome of anorexia nervosa in adolescence: Prospective study and 5 year follow-up. *Journal of Psychiatric Research, 19*, 509–514.

Masterson, J. F. (1977). Primary anorexia nervosa in the borderline adolescent: An object relations view. In P. Harticollis (Ed.), *Borderline personality disorders* (pp. 475–494). New York: International Universities Press.

McKisack, C., & Waller, G. (1997). Factors influencing the outcome of group psychotherapy for bulimia nervosa. *International Journal of Eating Disorders, 22*, 1–13.

Minuchin, S., Rosman, B. L., & Baker, L. (1978). *Psychosomatic families: Anorexia nervosa in context.* Cambridge, MA: Harvard University Press.

Mitchell, J. E., Davis, L., Goff, G., & Pyle, R. (1986). A follow-up study of patients with bulimia. *International Journal of Eating Disorders, 5*, 441–450.

Mitchell, J. E., & Groat, R. (1984). A placebo-controlled, double blind trial of amitriptyline in bulimia. *American Journal of Psychiatry, 140*, 554–558.

Mitchell, J. E., Pyle, R. L., Hatsukami, D., Goff, G., Glotter, D., & Harper, J. (1989). A 2–5 year follow-up study of patients treated for bulimia. *International Journal of Eating Disorders, 8*, 157–165.

Mitchell, J. E., Pyle, R. L., Eckert, E. D., Hatsukami, D.,

Pomeroy, C., & Zimmerman, R. (1990). A comparison study of antidepressants and structured intensive group psychotherapy in the treatment of bulimia nervosa. *Archives of General Psychiatry, 47,* 149–157.

Mitchell, J. E., Raymond, N., & Specker, S. (1993). A review of the controlled trials of pharmachotherapy and psychotherapy in the treatment of bulimia nervosa. *International Journal of Eating Disorders, 14,* 229–247.

Mitchell, J. S., Sloan, D. M., Ruderich, S., Freiheit, S., & Silverman, E. (1996). The efficacy of sertraline in bulimia nervosa patients: A preliminary report. Presented at the Eating Disorders Research Society Meeting, Pittsburgh, PA.

Mizes, J. S., Sloan, D., Ruderich, S., Freiheit, S., & Silverman, E. (1996, November). *The efficacy of sertraline in bulimia nervosa patients: A preliminary report.* Paper presented at the Eating Disorders Research Society Meeting, Pittsburgh, PA.

Olivardia, R., Pope, H., Mangweth, B., & Hudson, J. (1995). Eating disorders in college men. *American Journal of Psychiatry, 152,* 1279–1285.

Olmsted, M. P., Davis, R., Garner, D. M., Eagle, M. & Rockert, W. (1991). Efficacy of brief psychoeducational intervention for bulimia nervosa. *Behavior Research and Therapy, 29,* 71–83.

Oppenheimer, R., Howells, K., Palmer, R. L., & Chaloner, D. A. (1985). Adverse sexual experience in childhood and clinical eating disorders: A preliminary description. *Journal of Psychiatric Research, 19,* 357–361.

Ordman, A. M., & Kirschenbaum, D. S. (1985). Cognitive-behavioral therapy for bulimia: An initial outcome study. *Journal of Consulting and Clinical Psychology, 53,* 305–313.

Patton, G. C., Johnson-Sabine, E., Wood, K., Mann, A. H., & Wakeling, A. (1990). Abnormal eating attitudes in London schoolgirls—A prospective epidemiological study: outcome at 12 month follow-up. *Psychological Medicine, 20,* 383–394.

Perlick, D., & Silverstein, B. (1994). Faces of female discontent: Depression, disordered eating, and changing gender roles. In P. Fallon, M. A. Katzman, & S. C. Wooley (Eds.), *Feminist perspectives on eating disorders* (pp. 77–93). New York: Guilford Press.

Piran, N., Lerner, P., Garfinkel, P. E., Kennedy, S. H., & Brouilette, C. (1988). Personality disorders in anorexia patients. *International Journal of Eating Disorders, 5,* 589–599.

Polivy, J., & Herman, C. P. (1985). Dieting and bingeing: A causal analysis. *American Psychologist, 40,* 193–201.

Pope, H. G., & Hudson, J. I. (1989). Are eating disorders associated with borderline personality disorder? A critical review. *International Journal of Eating Disorders, 8,* 1–9.

Powers, P. (1997). Management of patients with comorbid medical conditions. In D. M. Garner & P. E. Garfinkel (Eds.), *Handbook of treatment for eating disorders* (pp. 424–436). New York: Guilford Press.

Puglifse, M. T., Lifshitz, F., Grad, G., Fort, P., & Marks-Katz, M. (1983). Fear of obesity: A cause of short stature and delayed puberty. *The New England Journal of Medicine, 309,* 513–518.

Pyle, R. L., Mitchell, J. E., Eckert, E. D., Hastsukami, D., Pomeroy, C., & Zimmerman, R. (1990). Maintenance treatment and 6 month outcome for bulimic patients who respond to initial treatment. *American Journal of Psychiatry, 147,* 871–875.

Rampling, D. (1985). Ascetic ideals and anorexia nervosa. *Journal of Psychiatric Research, 19,* 89–94.

Rastam, M. (1992). Anorexia nervosa in 51 Swedish adolescents: Premorbid problems and comorbidity. *Journal of the American Academy of Child & Adolescent Psychiatry, 31,* 819–829.

Rastam, M., Gillberg, C., & Gillberg, C. (1995). Anorexia nervosa 6 years after onset: Part II. comorbid psychiatric problems. *Comprehensive Psychiatry, 36,* 70–76.

Raymond, N. C., Mitchell, J. E., Fallon, P., & Katzman, M. A. (1994). A collaborative approach to the use of medication. In P. Fallon, M. Katzman, & S. C. Wooley (Eds.), *Feminist perspectives on eating disorders* (pp. 231–250). New York: Guilford Press.

Robin, A. L., Siegel, P., & Moye, A. (1995). Family versus therapy for anorexia: Impact on family conflict. *International Journal of Eating Disorders, 17,* 313–322.

Root, M. M. P., Fallon, P., & Friedrich, W. N. (1985). *Bulimia: A systems approach to treatment.* New York: Norton.

Rosen, J. C., & Leitenberg, H. (1985). Exposure plus response prevention treatment of bulimia. In D. M. Garner & P. E. Garfinkel (Eds.), *Handbook of psychotherapy for anorexia nervosa and bulimia* (pp. 193–209). New York: Guilford Press.

Rosen, A. M., Murkofsky, C. A., Steckler, N. M., & Skolnick, N. J. (1989). A comparison of psychological and depressive symptoms among restricting anorexic, bulimic anorexic, and normal-weight bulimic patients. *International Journal of Eating Disorders, 8,* 657–663.

Rothenberg, A. (1988). Differential diagnosis of anorexia nervosa and depressive illness. A review of 11 studies. *Comprehensive Psychiatry, 29,* 427–432.

Russell, G. F. M. (1970). Anorexia nervosa: Its identity as an illness and its treatment. In J. H Price (Ed.), *Modern trends in psychological medicine* (Vol. 2, pp. 131–164). London: Butterworths.

Russell, G. F. M. (1979). Bulimia nervosa: An ominous variant of anorexia nervosa. *Psychological Medicine, 9,* 429–448.

Russell, G. F. M. (1985). The changing nature of anorexia nervosa: An introduction to the conference. *Journal of Psychiatric Research, 19,* 101–109.

Russell, G. F. M. (1997). The history of bulimia nervosa. In D. M. Garner & P. E. Garfinkel (Eds.), *Handbook of treatment for eating disorders* (pp. 11–24). New York: Guilford.

Russell, G. F. M., Szmukler, G. I., Dare, C., & Eisler, I. (1987). An evaluation of family therapy in anorexia nervosa and bulimia nervosa. *Archives of General Psychiatry, 44,* 1047–1056.

Sands, S. (1992). Bulimia dissociation, and empathy: A self-psychological view. In C. Johnson (Ed.), *Psychodynamic treatment of anorexia nervosa and bulimia* (pp. 34–49). New York: Guilford Press.

Santrock, J. W., Minnett, A. M., & Campbell, B. D. (1994). *The authoritative guide to self-help books.* New York: Guildford Press.

Schmidt, U., Jiwany, A., & Treasure, J. (1993). A controlled study of alexithymia in eating disorders. *Comprehensive Psychiatry, 1,* 54–58.

Schwartz, R. C., Barrett, M. J., & Saba, G. (1985). Family therapy for bulimia. In D. M. Garner & P. E. Garfinkel (Eds.) *Handbook of psychotherapy for anorexia nervosa and bulimia,* (pp. 280–307). New York: Guilford.

Scott, D. W. (1986). Anorexia nervosa: A review of possible genetic factors. *International Journal of Eating Disorders, 5,* 1–20.

Selvini-Palazzoli, M. P. (1974). *Self-starvation.* London: Chaucer.

Serdula, M. K., Collins, M. E., Williamson, D. F., Anda, R. F., Pamuk, E. R., & Byers, T. E. (1993). Weight control practices of US adolescents and adults. *Annals of Internal Medicine, 119,* 667–671.

Silverman, J. A. (1974). Anorexia nervosa: Clinical observations in a successful treatment plan. *Journal of Pediatrics, 84,* 68–73.

Sohlberg, S., Norring, C., Holmgren, S., & Rosmark, B. (1989). Impulsivity and long-term prognosis of psychiatric patients with anorexia nervosa/bulimia nervosa.

Journal of Nervous and Mental Disease, 177, 249–258.

Steiner-Adair, C. (1994). The politics of prevention. In P. Fallon, M. A. Katzman, & S. C. Wooley (Eds.), *Feminist perspectives on eating disorders* (pp. 381–394). New York: Guilford Press.

Steinhausen, H. C., & Glanville, K. (1983). A long-term follow-up of adolescent anorexia nervosa. *Acta Psychiatrica Scandinavica, 68,* 1–10.

Steinhausen, C. H., Rauss-Mason, C., & Seidel, R. (1991). Follow-up studies of anorexia nervosa: A review of four decades of outcome research. *Psychological Medicine, 21,* 447–454.

Stern, S. (1986). The dynamics of clinical management in the treatment of anorexia nervosa and bulimia: An organizing theory. *International Journal of Eating Disorders, 5,* 233–254.

Striegel-Moore, R. H. (1994). A feminist agenda for psychological research on eating disorders. In P. Fallon, M. A. Katzman, & S. C. Wooley (Eds.), *Feminist perspective on eating disorders* (pp. 438–454). New York: Guilford Press.

Striegel-Moore, R. H., Silberstein, L. R., & Rodin, J. (1986). Toward an understanding of risk factors in bulimia. *American Pychologist, 41,* 246–263.

Strober, M. (1981). A comparative analysis of personality organization in juvenile anorexia nervosa. *Journal of Youth and Adolescence, 10,* 285–295.

Strober, M. (1983). An empirically derived typology of anorexia nervosa. In P. L. Darby, P. E. Garfinkel, D. M. Garner, & D. V. Coscina (Eds.), *Anorexia nervosa: Recent developments in research* (pp. 185–198). New York: Liss.

Strober, M. (1991). Disorders of the self in anorexia nervosa: An organismic-developmental paradigm. In C. Johnson (Ed.), *Psychodynamic theory and treatment for eating disorders.* New York: Guilford Press.

Strober, M. (1997). Consultation and therapeutic engagement in severe anorexia nervosa. In D. M. Garner & P. E. Garfinkel (Eds.), *Handbook of treatment for eating disorders* (pp. 229–247). New York: Guilford Press.

Strober, M., & Katz, J. L. (1988). Depression in the eating disorders: A review and analysis of descriptive, family, and biological findings. In D. M. Garner & P. E. Garfinkel (Eds.), *Diagnostic issues in anorexia nervosa and bulimia nervosa* (pp. 80–111). New York: Brunner/ Mazel.

Strober, M., Lampert, C., Morrell, W., Burroughs, J., & Jacobs, C. (1990). A controlled family study of anorexia nervosa: Evidence of familial aggregation and lack of shared transmission with affective disorders. *International Journal of Eating Disorders, 9,* 239–53.

Strober, M., & Yager, J. (1985). A developmental perspective on the treatment of anorexia nervosa in adolescents. In D. M. Garner & P. E. Garfinkel (Eds.), *Handbook of psychotherapy for anorexia nervosa and bulimia* (pp. 363–390). New York: Guilford Press.

Sugarman, A. (1991). Bulimia: A displacement from psychological self to body self. In C. Johnson (Ed.), *Psychodynamic treatment of anorexia nervosa and bulimia* (pp. 3–33). New York: Guilford Press.

Sugarman, A., Quinlan, D., & Devenis, L. (1982). Ego boundary disturbance in anorexia: Preliminary findings. *Journal of Personality Assessment, 46,* 455–461.

Sullivan, P. F. (1995). Mortality in anorexia nervosa. *American Journal of Psychiatry, 152,* 1073–1074.

Swift, W. J., & Letven, R. (1984). Bulimia and the basic fault. *Journal of the American Academy of Child and Adolescent Psychiatry, 23,* 489–497.

Swift, W. J., & Wonderlich, S. A. (1988). Personality factors and diagnosis in eating disorders: Traits, disorders, and structures. In D. M. Garner & P. E. Garfinkel (Eds.), *Diagnostic issues in anorexia nervosa*

and bulimia nervosa (pp. 112–165). New York: Brunner/ Mazel.

Telch, C. F., Agras, W. S., Rossiter, E. M., Wilfley, D., & Kenardy, J. (1990). Group cognitive-behavioral treatment for the non-purging bulimic: An initial evaluation. *Journal of Consulting and Clinical Psychology, 58,* 629–635.

Thackwray, D., Smith, M., Bodfish, J., & Meyers, A. (1993). A comparison of behavioral and cognitive-behavioral interventions for bulimia nervosa. *Journal of Consulting & Clinical Psychology, 61,* 639–645.

Theander, S. (1985). Outcome and prognosis in anorexia nervosa and bulimia: Some results of previous investigations, compared with those of a Swedish long-term study. *Journal of Psychiatric Research, 19,* 493–508.

Theander, S. (1996). Anorexia nervosa with an early onset: Selection, gender, outcome, and results of a long-term follow-up study. *Journal of Youth and Adolescence, 25,* 419–429.

Thiel, A., Broocks, A., Ohlmeier, M., Jocoby, G., & Schußler, G. (1995). Obsessive-compulsive disorder among patients with anorexia nervosa and bulimia nervosa. *American Journal of Psychiatry, 152,* 72–75.

Tiller, J., Schmidt, U., & Treasure, J. (1993). Compulsory treatment for anorexia nervosa: Compassion or coercion? *British Journal of Psychiatry, 162,* 679–680.

Timmerman, M. G., Wells, L. A., & Chen, S. (1990). Bulimia nervosa and associated alcohol abuse among secondary school students. *American Academy of Child and Adolescent Psychiatry, 29,* 118–122.

Toner, B. B., Garfinkel, P. E., & Garner, D. M. (1986) Long-term follow-up of anorexia nervosa. *Psychosomatic Medicine, 48,* 520–529.

Treasure, J., Schmidt, U., Troop, N., Tiller, J., Todd, G., Keilen, M., & Dodge, E. (1994). First step in managing bulimia nervosa: Controlled trial of therapeutic manual. *British Medical Journal, 308,* 686–687.

Treasure, J., Todd, G., Brolly, M., Tiller, J., Nehmed, A., & Denman, F. (1995). A pilot study of a randomized trial of cognitive analytical therapy vs. educational behavioral therapy for adult anorexia nervosa. *Behavioural Research and Therapy, 33,* 363–367.

Vandereycken, W. (1984). Neuroleptics in the short-term treatment of anorexia nervosa: A double-blind placebo-controlled study with sulpiride. *British Journal of Psychiatry, 144,* 288–292.

Vandereyecken, W., & Pierloot, R. (1982). Pimozide combined with behavior therapy in the short-term treatment of anorexia nervosa. *Acta Psychiatry Scandinavia, 66,* 445–450

Vandereycken, W., Kog, E., & Vanderlinden, J. (1989). *The family approach to eating disorders.* New York: PMA.

Vigersky, R. A., & Loriaux, D. L. (1977). Anorexia nervosa as a model of hypothalamic dysfunction. In R. Vigersky (Ed.), *Anorexia nervosa* (pp. 109–122). New York: Raven Press.

Vitousek, K. B., & Ewald, L. S. (1993). Self-representation in eating disorders: A cognitive perspective. In: Z. Segal & S. Blatt (Eds.), *The self-in emotional disorders: Cognitive and psychodynamic perspectives* (pp. 221–257). New York: Guilford Press.

Vitousek, K. B., & Rimoto, L. (1993). Cognitive-behavioral models of anorexia nervosa, bulimia nervosa, and obesity. In P. Kendal & K. Dobson (Eds.), *Psychopathology and cognition* (pp. 191–142). New York: Academic Press.

Walsh, B. T., & Devlin, M. J. (1995). Psychopharmacology of anorexia nervosa, bulimia nervosa, and binge eating. In F. Bloom & D. Kupfer (Eds.), *Psychopharmacology: The fourth generation of progress.* New York: Raven Press.

Walsh, B. T., & Garner D.M. (1997). Diagnostic issues. In D. M. Garner & P. E. Garfinkel (Eds.), *Handbook of treatment for eating disorders* (pp. 25–33), New York/London: Guilford Press.

Walsh, B. T., Gladis, M., Roose, S. P., Stewart, J. W., Stetner, F., & Glassman, A. H. (1988). Phenelzine vs. placebo in 50 patients with bulimia. *Archives of General Psychiatry, 45*, 471–475.

Walsh, B. T., Hadigan, C. M., Devlin, M. J. Gladis, M., & Roose, S. P. (1991). Long-term outcome of antidepressant treatment for bulimia nervosa. *American Journal of Psychiatry, 148*, 1206–1212.

Walsh, B. T., Wilson, G. T., Loeb, K. L., Devlin, M. J., Pike, K. M., Roose, S. P., Fleiss, J., & Waternaux, C. (1997). Medication and psychotherapy in the treatment of bulimia nervosa. *American Journal of Psychiatry, 154*, 523–531.

Wardle, J. (1987). Compulsive eating and dietary restraint. *British Journal of Clinical Psychology, 26*, 47–55.

Wardle, J., & Beales, S. (1986). Restraint, body image and food attitudes in children from 12 to 18 years. *Appetite, 7*, 209–217.

Waters, B. G. H., Beaumont, P. J. V., Touyz, S., & Kennedy, M. (1990). Behavioural differences between twin and non-twin female sibling pairs discordant for anorexia nervosa. *International Journal of Eating Disorders, 9*, 265–273.

Welch, G. W., Hall, A., & Renner, R. (1990). Patient subgrouping in anorexia nervosa using psychologically-based classification. *International Journal of Eating Disorders, 9*, 311–322.

Wilfley, D. E., Agras, W. S., Telch, C. F., Rossiter, E. M., Schneider, J. A., Cole, A. G., Stifford, L., & Raeburn, S. D. (1993). Group cognitive-behavioral therapy and group interpersonal psychotherapy for the nonpurging bulimic individual: A controlled comparison. *Journal of Consulting and Clinical Psychology, 2*, 296–305.

Williamson, D.A. (1990). *Assessment of eating disorders: besity, anorexia, and bulimia nervosa.* New York: Pergamon.

Wilson, G.T. (1991). The addiction model of eating disorders: A critical analysis. *Advances in Behaviour Research and Therapy, 13*, 27–72.

Wilson, G. T., & Lindholm, L. (1987). Bulimia nervosa and depression. *International Journal of Eating Disorders, 6*, 725–732.

Wilson, G.T. (1993). Assessment of binge eating. In C. G. Fairburn & G. T. Wilson (Eds.), *Binge eating: Nature assessment, and treatment* (pp. 227–249). New York: Guilford Press.

Wolchik, S. A., Weiss, L., & Katzman, M.A., (1986). An empirically validated, short-termed psychoeducational group treatment program for bulimia. *International Journal of Eating Disorders, 5*, 21–34.

Wolf, E. & Crowther, J. (1992). An evaluation of behavioral and cognitive-behavioral group interventions for the treatment of bulimia nervosa in women. *International Journal of Eating Disorders, 11*, 3–15.

Wonderlich, S. A., Swift, W. J., Slotnick, H. B., & Goodman, S. (1990). DSM-III-R personality disorders in eating-disorder subtypes. *International Journal of Eating Disorders, 9*, 607–616.

Wooley, S. C., & Lewis, K.G. (1989). The missing woman: Intensive family-oriented treatment of bulimia. *Journal of Feminist Family Therapy, 1*, 61–83.

World Health Organization (1992). *The ICD-10 classification of mental and behavioral disorders: Clinical descriptions and diagnostic guidelines* (pp. 176–181). Geneva, Switzerland: Author.

5.24
Sleep Disorders

AVI SADEH and REUT GRUBER
Tel Aviv University, Israel

5.24.1 INTRODUCTION

Sleep or rest appears to be a basic need of every organism. Despite many years of sleep research, many of the fundamental questions such as the function of sleep have only been partially resolved or replaced by more specific questions, such as the function of rapid eye movement (REM) sleep or the influence of daytime naps on functioning.

In the attempt to unveil the function of sleep, research efforts have focused mainly on the effects of sleep deprivation on the individual's mental and physiological functioning. It has been shown that significant and prolonged sleep deprivation can lead to serious cognitive and behavioral deficits and can eventually cause medical complications and even death in extreme cases. The effects of partial sleep deprivation, which is closer to the phenomenology of sleep disorders, have been less striking, but in general the literature suggests that the partially sleep-deprived individual may pay a significant price in behavioral, cognitive, and medical terms (e.g., Babkoff, Caspy, Mikulincer, & Sing, 1991; Bonnet, 1985). Despite the fact that extensive research has been conducted on the effects of sleep deprivation in animals and in adults, only limited research efforts have been focused on children. These studies have demonstrated relationships between sleep disorders and learning and behavior problems in children and adolescents (see Alvarez, Dahlitz, Vignau, & Parkes, 1992; Dahl, 1996; Kahn, Mozin, Rebuffat, Sottiaux, & Muller, 1989; Quine, 1992; Thorpy, Korman, Spielman, & Glovinsky, 1988).

From a clinical perspective, sleep is a very sensitive barometer to the medical and mental well-being of the individual. The most prominent manifestation of the close relationships between sleep and psychopathology and medical disorders is the presence of sleep difficulties or sleep-related complaints as symptoms or even as major diagnostic features of many psychiatric and medical disorders.

The close ties between sleep disorders and psychopathology are best manifested in professional diagnostic systems such as the *DSM-IV* (American Psychiatric Association, 1994). In addition to more than 50 manual pages dedicated to sleep disorders, sleep-related problems are often included in the symptoms or diagnostic criteria of other major affective and anxiety disorders (see Table 1). In addition, it has been demonstrated repeatedly that sleep is very sensitive to psychosocial stressors. Extensive research has documented the vulnerability of the sleep–wake system to various experimental and natural stressors, ranging from sleeping in an unfamiliar setting (i.e., the sleep laboratory) to serious traumatic life events (see Sadeh, 1996, for a recent review).

Table 1 Sleep-related difficulties associated with *DSM-IV* diagnoses of the American Psychiatric Association, 1994.

Mood disorders
Major depressive episode: insomnia or hypersomnia, fatigue and loss of energy, irritable mood in children
Manic episode: decreased need for sleep, and distractibility
These symptoms are manifested in less severe forms of affective disorders.

Anxiety disorders
Generalized anxiety disorder: sleep disturbances (difficulty in falling or staying asleep, or restless unsatisfying sleep), being easily fatigued, irritability and restlessness
Post-traumatic stress disorder: difficulty in falling or staying asleep, difficulty concentrating, hypervigilance, recurrent distressing dreams (nightmares)
Separation anxiety disorder: persistent reluctance or refusal to go to sleep without being near a major attachment object, repeated nightmares involving the theme of separation

Source: American Psychiatric Association (1994).

Disrupted sleep has also been associated with difficult temperament in early childhood (e.g., Carey, 1974; Sadeh, Lavie, & Scher, 1994; Zuckerman, Stevenson, & Baily, 1987). It has also been shown that older children who suffer from sleep problems are more likely to exhibit other behavior problems (Gass & Strauch, 1984; Jenkins, Bax, & Hart, 1980; Richman, Stevenson, & Graham, 1982).

Most of the studies demonstrating strong links between sleep and behavior problems or psychopathology are correlative in nature and therefore preclude a better understanding of the cause-and-effect nature of these relationships (see Dahl, 1996; Sadeh, Hayden, McGuire, Sachs, & Civita, 1994; Sadeh et al., 1995c). This important issue is evident in the case of attention deficit and hyperactivity disorder (ADHD). A number of studies have documented higher rates of sleep problems in children diagnosed with ADHD compared to normal children (see Dahl, 1996). These studies included subjective and objective measures that supported the notion that the sleep of ADHD children is significantly more disturbed or shorter (e.g., Tirosh, Sadeh, Munvez, & Lavie, 1993). Traditionally, clinicians and parents tended to interpret this finding intuitively by attributing the sleep problem to the fact that the child is running in "turbo" mode or is hyperalert, and therefore, cannot stop and initiate sleep or is still hyperactive during sleep. Research supports the competing hypothesis that sleep deprivation in children may lead to behaviors or symptoms associated with ADHD such as inattention, difficulties in concentration and sustaining attention, impulsiveness, and increased activity level (Anders, Carskadon, Dement, & Harvey, 1978; Navelet, Anders, & Guilleminault, 1976). There have been some descriptions of clinical cases of children diagnosed with ADHD that suffered from a major sleep disorder, where treating the underlying sleep disorder led to disappearance of the ADHD symptoms (Dahl, 1996; Dahl, Pelham, & Wierson, 1991).

Sleep disruptions have also been associated with various medical disorders. For example, asthma is considered to be one of the most common illnesses during childhood, affecting 5–15% of children (e.g., Strachan, Anderson, Limb, O'Neill, & Wells, 1994). Asthma is a disorder of the respiratory system which tends to become more dysfunctional during sleep. Indeed, sleep difficulties are very often associated with asthma during childhood, with a survey in 1995 reporting that as many as 61% of asthmatic children suffer from sleep difficulties (Madge et al., 1995).

5.24.2 SLEEP DISORDERS IN CHILDREN

Sleep disorders cover a wide range of phenomena associated with the multiple sleep–wake systems related to the specific mechanisms responsible for consolidated and refreshing sleep, inhibition of behavior during sleep or sleep–wake transitions, control of breathing during sleep, and the timing of sleep ("the biological clock").

A number of diagnostic systems exist for sleep disorders (e.g., American Psychiatric Association, 1994; Diagnostic Classification Steering Committee, 1990; World Health Organization, 1992). These systems vary in their emphasis on phenomenology, etiology, and medical or psychosocial factors. The following description will be based on the *DSM-IV* (American Psychiatric Association, 1994). Due to space limitations, many issues will be only partially addressed or not addressed at all. For additional information, the reader is referred to professional books on children's sleep disorders (Ferber & Kryger, 1995; Guilleminault, 1987; Sheldon, Spire, & Levy, 1992).

The first diagnostic distinction used by *DSM-IV* with regard to sleep disorders is between the dyssomnias and the parasomnias. Dysomnias refers to the disorders of initiating or maintaining sleep and to those related to excessive sleepiness. These disorders include: primary insomnia, primary hypersomnia, narcolepsy, breathing-related sleep disorder, and circadian rhythm sleep disorder. Parasomnias are disorders manifested in unique behaviors or physiologic phenomena occurring during sleep or sleep–wake transitions.

5.24.2.1 Phenomenology

The clinical presentation of various sleep disorders often changes as the child matures, and the involvement of parents as primary observers and reporters changes accordingly.

5.24.2.1.1 Primary insomnia

Primary insomnia is related to disorders in initiating and maintaining sleep (DIMS). This diagnosis covers the most common sleep complaints during childhood and include problems such as difficulty going to bed, difficulty falling asleep, and multiple and/or prolonged night-wakings. This category is equivalent to the *ICD-10* classification of "nonorganic insomnia" (World Health Organization, 1992). The clinical picture is related to the developmental status of the child, as are the source of the referral, the etiology, and the clinical interventions.

During infancy and early childhood, the most common complaints (usually of the parents) are related to the child's incapacity to "sleep through the night" which is manifested in difficulties such as falling asleep without parental involvement, multiple and prolonged night-wakings during which the child usually signals (by crying or calling), and requires parental intervention to resume sleep. In most cases, the child does not exhibit strong manifestations of distress during the day and compensates during daytime napping for the sleepless nights. The parents are often exhausted by their child's sleep difficulties, and in many cases they show signs of distress and tension that may lead to difficulties in their daily functioning and their relationship with the child.

As children mature, during the preschool and school ages, the clinical features of insomnia undergo significant changes. The dominance of night-wakings and difficulties in resuming sleep following nocturnal awakening during early childhood is replaced by sleep onset difficulties, bed refusal, fears, and bedtime struggles. When fears are involved the child often seeks the proximity of the parents during the night and may end up cosleeping with the parents. The child is usually able to address these fears and the subsequent reluctance to go to sleep or difficulties to resume sleep after night-waking. Older children and adolescents may lie in bed for prolonged periods unable to fall asleep or resume sleep. In many cases, the parents are unaware, or are only partially aware of the problem, because the child no longer seeks their attention.

Parental and cultural attitudes, and the different lifestyle of the family, may have a significant influence on whether a specific set of problems or behaviors are considered a sleep problem. For instance, parent–child cosleeping is considered a normal and acceptable practice in many cultures and by many parents. In these families, cosleeping is a habitual sleeping arrangement that meet the needs of the parents and their culture. However, in western societies, cosleeping is usually an unfavored practice that generally represents an attempt to solve a child's sleep problem.

5.24.2.1.2 Primary hypersomnia

Excessive sleepiness is usually manifested by very extended sleep periods and an unusual pressure to sleep during the daytime. This relatively rare cluster of disorders is not fully understood and may be the result of different neurologic or physiologic origins. One recurrent form of the disorder, the Kleine–Levin syndrome has, in addition to the excessive sleep

episodes, other clinical manifestations that may be confused with psychiatric disorders. These behaviors include indiscriminate and inappropriate sexual behavior, compulsive overeating, and in some individuals other symptoms such as depression, confusion, irritability, and hallucinations. The Kleine–Levin syndrome is relatively rare and more prevalent in males (approximately 3:1 ratio). The age at onset is usually middle or late puberty but no prevalence estimates exist for children or adolescents.

ICD-10 specifies nonorganic hypersomnia as a separate classification that is usually associated with other mental disorders such as affective disorders (World Health Organization, 1992).

5.24.2.1.3 Narcolepsy

Unintentional sleep episodes are common phenomena in sleepy or sleep-deprived individuals. However, in narcolepsy, sleep attacks unexpectedly, regardless of the situation and in combination with cataplexy (sudden loss of muscular tone in response to emotional stimuli), hypnogogic hallucination, and loss of muscle tone (paralysis). The disorder is very serious and highly disruptive to normal life. Narcolepsy is associated with excessive daytime sleepiness, difficulty waking in the morning, and in many cases with hyperactivity (Guilleminault, 1987).

5.24.2.1.4 Breathing-related sleep disorder

The maintenance of continuous breathing during wakefulness as well as during sleep is a crucial function of the central nervous system (CNS) and other peripheral systems. During sleep, the breathing system is more vulnerable and more likely to fail than during wakefulness. Failures in breathing during sleep lead to arousals, fragmented, and nonrefreshing sleep. Clinical complaints in children may include excessive sleepiness and low level of arousal, or other symptoms associated with fatigue in children such as irritability and hyperactivity. Observers (usually the parents) may report loud snoring and long episodes of breathing pauses during sleep terminated by a loud and active breathing effort. Most affected children (as well as adults) are unaware of their snoring, breathing difficulties, and sleep fragmentation. Sometimes the child may even be considered a "good sleeper," since they readily go to bed and sleep through the night and for an extended duration. In addition, children with obstructive sleep apnea may experience breathing problems during wakefulness, may be more susceptible to complications in diseases associated with upper airways blockage, and present features such as swallowing difficulties and poor speech articulation.

Breathing-related sleep disorders are further subdivided into obstructive, central, and mixed sleep apnea and other nonapnea disorders. A discussion of these subcategories is beyond the scope of this chapter.

5.24.2.1.5 Circadian rhythm sleep disorder

The evolution of sleep–wake rhythms that favors the dark hours for nocturnal sleep occurs during the first few months of life. "Sleeping through the night" is the expression used to describe this maturational milestone. However, this association between the light–dark and the sleep–wake cycles cannot be taken for granted. Circadian rhythm sleep disorders (CRSD) relate to all the deviations or the incongruity between these basic rhythms. Children with CRSD may experience difficulties falling asleep at normal, age-appropriate evening hours and waking up in the morning, but would be "good sleepers" given the opportunity to go to sleep at very late hours and wake-up later in the morning (delayed sleep phase type, DSPT; Weitzman et al., 1981). Other children may experience the opposite problem, the advanced sleep phase, manifested in difficulty staying awake until normal evening bedtime hours with a tendency to wake up for the day at a very early morning hour. Other possible manifestations include the irregular sleep–wake patterns and the non-24-hour sleep–wake patterns that describe deviations from a regular sleep–wake schedule. These disorders, if not attributed to organic factors, fall under the *ICD-10* category of nonorganic disorder of the sleep–wake schedule (World Health Organization, 1992).

Children and adolescents with CRSD may experience serious problems when forced to adapt to normal social schedules such as early school hours. When they encounter serious difficulties waking up in the morning for the school day they are often considered unmotivated and face disciplinary actions from their parents and school authorities who fail to appreciate the potential biological origin of their problem.

Irregular and non-24-hour sleep–wake patterns are often reported in blind children and in children with pervasive developmental disorders or other neurobehavioral disorders (Lapierre & Dumont, 1995; Okawa et al., 1987; Sadeh, Klitzke, Anders, & Acebo, 1995; Tzischinsky, Skene, Epstein, & Lavie, 1991)

In addition to the above disorders of the biological clock, some externally induced schedule disorders exist. These disorders include the rhythm disturbances associated with the jet-lag phenomenon or with other forced shifts of the sleep–wake schedule. These disorders are usually transient and disappear with time after the normal sleep-wake schedule is reinstated.

5.24.2.1.6 Nightmare disorder

This is the first representative of the heterogeneous group of the parasomnias. The main feature of the nightmare disorder is the repeated occurrence of terrifying dreams that result in the child's awakening. Following the nightmare, the child often exhibits high levels of anxiety that may lead to refusal to go to bed, or to stay alone in the dark. Young children usually respond to their parents' attempts to soothe them but may insist on parental proximity for prolonged periods.

Verbal children may report the content of the dream and it may relate to their daily lives or their normal anxieties such as getting lost or being separated from their parents. Children may also report scary dreams about monsters, evil animals, or other creations of their imagination, or those they were exposed to while watching TV or movies. Other prevalent nightmares are those related to loss of control (e.g., free fall from different places) and a variety of threats of self-injury and death (e.g., drowning). It has been reported that many children refrain from sharing these private negative experiences with their parents and therefore parents may be unaware what their child is experiencing (Terr, 1987). A similar category exists in *ICD-10* (World Health Organization, 1992).

5.24.2.1.7 Sleep terror disorder

The sleep terror disorder is characterized by the repeated occurrence of abrupt awakenings from sleep with a scream or cry that conveys the sense that the child is terrorized. Usually the child continues to yell, cry, and fight during these episodes and is difficult to awaken or comfort. In many cases the child, even with open eyes, does not appear to recognize their parents and may struggle with them as they try to calm the child who also presents signs of autonomic arousal such as tachicardia, rapid breathing, sweating, pupils dilation, increased muscle tone, and flushing of the skin. The child does not remember these events the following morning. If awakened during the episode, the child looks confused and disoriented. Usually the child does not reach full awareness and returns to sleep following the episode. The night terror events commonly last between one and 10 minutes but can be longer if the child is not awakened by their parents. A similar category exists in *ICD-10* (World Health Organization, 1992).

5.24.2.1.8 Sleepwalking disorder

Sleepwalking episodes are common in childhood. The phenomenon may have different manifestations, but typically, the child gets out of bed in the middle of the night and starts wandering around the house. The child may look confused and disoriented but is capable of finding their way around and sometimes performs quite complex activities. Parents may find the child asleep on a different bed in a different room the next morning or may notice the episode while it is occurring and redirect the child to bed to resume normal sleep. Many different behaviors are seen during nightwalking episodes. These behaviors include eating, using the bathroom (sometimes urinating in inappropriate places), talking, or fearful running around. Usually the child has no recollection (or only vague memory) of the sleepwalking episode the following morning. Since these behaviors are highly counterintuitive many parents tend to be alarmed by these events and seek professional help. A similar category exists in *ICD-10* (World Health Organization, 1992).

5.24.2.1.9 Other parasomnias

There are some other unusual behavior patterns that have been associated with sleep and are considered parasomnias. These parasomnias include: REM sleep behavior disorder (activities and behaviors occurring during REM sleep and are associated with vivid dream recall), sleep paralysis (inability to move during sleep–wake transitions), and rhythmical movement disorders, periodic leg movements in sleep, and bruxism (tooth grinding).

5.24.2.2 Diagnostic Features

The diagnostic process of sleep disorders in children should include the following considerations:

(i) the disordered aspect of sleep (e.g., sleep schedule, sleep quality, or related behaviors);

(ii) the primary origin of the disorder (physiologic and organic vs. psychosocial);

(iii) the psychophysiological effects of the disorder (e.g., deteriorated daytime functioning);

(iv) the psychosocial effects of the disorder (e.g., disrupts parent–child relationships);

(v) Other potential external causes (e.g., substance abuse, another medical or psychiatric disorder).

All of the diagnostic systems are based on the principle that a medical origin for the disorder should be excluded (including comorbidity with another major mental disorder) before a psychosocial diagnosis is made. The origins of a number of specific disorders such as circadian rhythm sleep disorders and the parasomnias are not fully understood and therefore such a distinction is not always justified.

5.24.2.2.1 Primary insomnia

The *DSM-IV* diagnostic criteria for primary insomnia are as follows: (i) the predominant complaint is difficulty initiating or maintaining sleep, or nonrestorative sleep, for at least one month; (ii) the sleep disturbance (or associated daytime fatigue) causes clinically significant distress or impairment in social, occupational, or other important areas of functioning; (iii) the sleep disturbance does not occur exclusively during the course of another primary sleep disorder; (iv) the disturbance does not occur exclusively during the course of another mental disorder; and (v) the disturbance is not due to the direct physiological effects of a substance or a general medical condition.

In addition to these standard diagnostic criteria, a differential diagnosis of primary insomnia should exclude the diagnosis of CRSD. Furthermore, difficulties falling asleep at a certain age-appropriate hour may result from the child's anxieties, fears, and other psychosocial factors that would justify the diagnosis of primary insomnia. However, if these difficulties result from the child's biological tendency to fall asleep at a late hour (assuming the child is not experiencing any difficulties), then the child is probably suffering from sleep-phase delay and therefore a diagnosis of CRSD would be warranted.

5.24.2.2.2 Primary hypersomnia

Excessive sleepiness during the day is a normal experience explained by many factors including chronic insufficient sleep or sleep deprivation, transient effects such as jet-lag, and identified sleep disorders such as insomnia or breathing-related disturbances. All these factors must be excluded before considering primary hypersomnia as a diagnosis.

The major *DSM-IV* diagnostic criteria for primary hypersomnia is the predominant complaint of excessive sleepiness for at least one month (or less if recurrent) as evidenced by either prolonged sleep episodes or daytime sleep episodes that occur almost daily. All of the other criteria are similar to those of primary insomnia, with the exception that primary insomnia as well as other primary sleep, mental, and medical disorders must be excluded before reaching a primary hypersomnia diagnosis.

Primary hypersomnia as defined by *DSM-IV* tends to be very rare in general, and particularly so, in children. Most of these disturbances have a late age of onset, usually appearing during adolescence or adulthood. The Kleine–Levin syndrome is distinguished by prolonged sleep episodes and by the clinical manifestation of inappropriate sexual and aggressive behaviors described earlier.

5.24.2.2.3 Narcolepsy

The *DSM-IV* criteria for narcolepsy are as follows: (i) irresistible attacks of sleep that occur daily over at least three months; (ii) the presence of cataplexy (sudden loss of muscle tone, most often in association with intense emotion) and/ or recurrent intrusions of elements of REM sleep into the transition between sleep and wakefulness, as manifested by either hypnopompic or hypnagogic hallucinations or sleep paralysis at the beginning or end of sleep episodes; and (iii) the disturbance is not due to the direct physiologic effects or a substance or another general medical condition.

5.24.2.2.4 Breathing-related sleep disorder

The *DSM-IV* uses only two criteria for breathing-related sleep disorder (BRSD): (i) sleep disruption due to a sleep-related breathing problem; and (ii) the disturbance is not better explained by another mental disorder or by direct physiological effects of a substance. Since the child is usually unaware of having disturbed sleep in BRSD and the parents may also be unaware of the disorder, the first diagnostic signs are very often signs of fatigue, sleepiness and other manifestations of difficulties in arousal level. The full diagnosis of BRSD requires a complete laboratory assessment including monitoring of the breathing system during sleep and a medical examination that includes assessment of the airway (nasal airflow, tonsillar size, mandibular, and facial abnormalities). These assessment procedures can verify the existence of a BRSD, its severity, its subtype (e.g., central vs. obstructive apnea), and the appropriate intervention.

5.24.2.2.5 Circadian rhythm sleep disorder

Like many other species in nature, the human mind is programmed to be alert during daytime hours and to rest or sleep during night time hours. The circadian clock is a very powerful mechanism underlying our behavior and functioning. It includes a nonspecific general clock that controls our rest–activity cycle and multiple clocks that affect various distinct domains of human behavior such as different cognitive functions (Monk, 1994; Montagner, De Roquefeuil, & Djakovic, 1992). The initial step in diagnosing CRSD is the identification of a persistent sleep problem that results from a mismatch between the individual's own circadian sleep-wake pattern and the environmentally appropriate sleep–wake schedule. In addition, *DSM-IV* requires the following requirements: clinically significant stress or a functional impairment and the exclusion of another sleep or mental disorder and any substance effects.

As indicated earlier the major diagnostic issue is differentiating between primary insomnia and CRSD (see Section 5.24.5).

5.24.2.2.6 The parasomnias

Isolated and infrequent episodes of the parasomnias are very common in children. Most forms of these episodes are prevalent during early and middle childhood and become uncommon during adolescence. Therefore, it is difficult to draw the line when these episodes should be considered a disorder. The basic guideline is that a diagnosis of a disorder should be made whenever the phenomenon becomes very frequent, involves violent or dangerous behaviors, or results in significant functional impairment. In addition, if the phenomenon persists from childhood to adolescence it is more likely to warrant a diagnosis.

The main diagnostic criteria for nightmare disorder is repeated awakenings from sleep with recall of terrifying dreams that usually involve threats to survival, security, and self-esteem. Very young children may not be able to produce verbal recall but usually appear oriented and communicative. On awakening from these dreams the child rapidly becomes oriented and alert and usually responds well to parental comfort.

Differential diagnosis from sleep terror disorder is based on these features of dream recall, orientation, and interactive responsiveness which are quite distinguishable from the disorientation and relative unresponsiveness that characterized the sleep terror. In addition, sleep terror disorder is associated with severe autonomic arousal response. Differentiation between sleep terror disorder and epilepsy or REM sleep behavior disorder is based on electroencephalogram (EEG) records and specific stereotyped behaviors.

Sleepwalking disorder is characterized by repeated episodes in which the child rises from bed during sleep and walks about relatively unresponsive to others. It is difficult to awaken the child, and once awake the child is usually amnesic regarding the episode. Another feature is that the child's normal behavior is usually restored shortly after a full awakening from the episode.

Another parasomnia that does not fall under specific *DSM-IV* diagnostic category is that of rhythmical movement disorder. This disorder refers to the very common phenomena of self-soothing behaviors performed by the child during sleep-wake transitions. These behaviors, such as body rocking, head rolling, and banging, are common in young children (more than 50%) and are usually considered normal behavior. But when the phenomenon becomes disruptive or is perceived to be dangerous (e.g., an infant that bangs its head fiercely against the wall), parents often become alarmed and seek professional help.

5.24.2.3 Prevalence

The review of the literature on issues pertaining to prevalence and incidence of sleep problems in children is quite disappointing. The number of solid and systematic studies in this field is very small. In most fields, these studies do not usually involve consensus clinical guidelines or diagnostic criteria, and therefore it is difficult to assess the prevalence rates of these disorders using any systematic diagnostic system. However, the existing surveys provide some sense as to which phenomena are more prevalent than the others and their peak age of onset and time course.

5.24.2.3.1 Primary insomnia

The prevalence of primary insomnia and its etiology appears to change systematically during development and therefore close attention should be given to developmental issues when assessing children presenting with insomnia.

Moore and Ucko (1957) defined a night-waking problem when the child awakened and cried at least once between midnight and 5 a.m. on at least four of seven nights, for at least four consecutive weeks. Using this definition and relying on maternal reports, they reported that at three months of age 70% of the infants "slept" through the night, whereas 83% of the six month olds and 90% of the nine month olds "slept" through the night. Richman (1981) defined sleep problem in one-year-old infants

as either regular sleep onset fussing periods lasting more than 30 min, or night-waking episodes that required parental intervention occurring at least four nights a week. Other surveys using parental reports indicated that 20–30% of the children suffer from these problems during the first three years (e.g., Adair, Bauchner, Philipp, Levenson, & Zuckerman, 1991; Beltramini & Herzig, 1983; Jenkins, et al. 1980; Johnson, 1991; Richman, 1981; Scher et al., 1995; Zuckerman et al., 1987). Research based on objective sleep measures derived from methods like time-lapse video and actigraphy (activity based monitoring) suggests that night wakings are more prevalent than reported by parents (Anders; 1979; Paret, 1983; Sadeh, Lavie, Scher, Tirosh, & Epstein, 1991). For instance, it was found that nonreferred normal young children (9–24 months of age) woke-up twice a night on average in comparison to an average of more than four night-wakings in referred "sleep-disturbed" infants (Sadeh et al., 1991). Most of these infants resumed their sleep without fussing or requiring help and therefore their parents were not even aware of their night-wakings.

In school-age children the prevalence of primary insomnia appears to drop to 1–5% (Gass & Strauch, 1984; Richman et al., 1982). However, there are indications that these problems are underestimated because older children are less likely to alert their parents to their sleep problems (Anders et al., 1978). Kahn et al. (1989) surveyed predadolescents (aged 8–10 years) using parental reports. A prevalence of 43% for a variety of sleep difficulties was reported by the parents. "Poor sleep," a rough equivalent of primary insomnia, was reported in 14% of the children.

In adolescence, chronic or severe sleep difficulties have been self-reported by 11–33.4% of the youth (Bearpark & Michie, 1987; Kirmil-Gray, Eagleston, Gibson, & Thorensen, 1984; Morrison, McGee, & Stanton, 1992; Price, Coates, Thoresen, & Grinstead, 1978). Since these surveys did not use detailed criteria to identify the exact nature of the problems (e.g., difficulty falling asleep due to primary insomnia vs. delayed sleep phase), it is difficult to provide good estimates of primary insomnia in this age group.

5.24.2.3.2 Primary hypersomnia and narcolepsy

Primary hypersomnia and narcolepsy are relatively scarce in young children and tend to appear in adolescence or adulthood. It is estimated that the prevalence of narcolepsy in the general population ranges between 0.04% and 0.09% (Dement, Carskadon, & Ley, 1973).

Narcolepsy is usually diagnosed in late adolescence or in adulthood. In a study of 400 narcoleptic patients, Yoss and Daly (1960) reported that only 4% were younger than 15 years when their diagnosis was made. Retrospective studies suggest that early signs of the disorder may appear earlier in many children. Challamel et al. (1994) reported on the basis of aggregated studies of 235 adult patients that 34% of the patients presented their first narcoleptic symptoms before they were 15 years old and 16% before they were 10 years old. There are, however, claims that professionals often fail to diagnose narcolpsy and therefore the disorder is either underdiagnosed or its diagnosis is seriously delayed (Baird, 1987).

5.24.2.3.3 Breathing-related sleep disorder

The prevalence of BRSD in children is unknown. It is certainly not a rare disorder, but data on prevalence in the general population is lacking.

5.24.2.3.4 Circadian rhythm sleep disorder

The prevalence of CRSD in children has not been established but the awareness of these disorders is growing rapidly. During adolescence when there is a normal tendency to delay the sleep phase the prevalence is estimated as high as 7% for delayed sleep phase type.

5.24.2.3.5 The parasomnias

It is estimated that 10–50% of children aged three to five years have nightmares severe enough to alarm their parents. Since nightmares are such a prevalent experience (at least on a periodic or sporadic basis), it is difficult to estimate how many of these children warrant a diagnosis of nightmare disorder. The prevalence of nightmares in older children has not been established although there are indications that the phenomenon decreases significantly as children grow beyond the preschool years.

The prevalence of night terror disorder is estimated between 1% and 6% in children (Beltramini & Hertzig, 1983; Gass & Strauch, 1984; Kales et al., 1980a; Klackenberg, 1987). It is also estimated that the prevalence of this disorder decreases with age.

Sleepwalking appears to be a prevalent phenomenon during childhood. One study reported that 15% of 5–12-year-olds have had at least one episode. An incidence of 10% for at least two episodes during a year period prior to the study was reported for 3–11-year-old Swiss children (Gass & Strauch, 1984). The peak age

for sleepwalking in this study was 10. In a longitudinal study of 212 children studied between six and 16 years of age, the incidence of sleepwalking was 40%. But when the frequency of the episodes was examined, only 2–3% of the children had experienced at least one episode a month. The prevalence rates peaked at ages 11–12 years (Klackenberg, 1987).

5.24.2.4 Etiology

Sleep as a biobehavioral phenomenon is affected by multiple maturational, physiological, environmental and psychosocial factors. Different sleep disorders vary in their loading on medical and psychosocial factors. Primary insomnia is by definition the disorder that is most likely to originate or be maintained by psychosocial and environmental factors. Primary hypersomia and BRSD are more heavily influenced by medical factors. On the other hand, CRSD and the parasomnias are loaded by a complex matrix of physiological and psychosocial factors that are difficult to untangle.

5.24.2.4.1 Primary insomnia

The timing, duration, and structure of sleep change dramatically during the first year of life. On average, newborns spend close to 18 h in sleep each day. Their sleep is multiphasic and consists of five to six sleep episodes spread throughout the daytime and night-time hours. Significant individual differences in sleep duration exist already during the first few days of life (Sadeh, Dark, & Vohr, 1996). While some newborns sleep close to 22 h a day, others spend only 7–8 h in sleep. In a rapid maturational process during the first year of life, most infants significantly reduce sleep duration and their sleep progressively becomes more consolidated and concentrated during the night. These developmental changes are crucial for the understanding of early childhood insomnia because most of the problems seen in infants and young children could be viewed as a developmental delay. Most infants develop consolidated sleep, sometimes described as "sleeping through the night," toward the end of the first year. This significant shift is very sensitive and can be complicated and compromised by many factors.

Another significant process that occurs during the first year of life is the transition from the parents as the major soothing agents of the infant to a growing self-regulatory self-soothing capacity. This transition is manifested in the parents decreased involvement around bedtime and the child's growing ability to fall asleep without parental presence. Close relationships exist between parental involvement in the soothing processes and the child's difficulty falling asleep and night-waking problems (Adair et al., 1991; Johnson, 1991; Van Tassel, 1985). Many intervention studies show significant improvement or resolution of children's night-waking and difficulty falling asleep when parents are encouraged to withdraw from their active involvement around bedtime (see Section 5.24.4). These findings suggest that the etiology of many of these problems is heavily influenced by parent–child bedtime interactions that either reward the child for activities that are incompatible with self-soothing and consolidated sleep patterns or prevent the pressure to develop more appropriate ones.

Other psychosocial factors such as parental and in particular, maternal psychopathology have also been associated with increased likelihood of sleep problems in the child (e.g., Benoit, Zeanah, Boucher, & Minde, 1992; Guedeney & Kreisler, 1987; Richman, 1981; Scott & Richards, 1990; Seifer, Sameroff, Dickstein, Hayden & Schiller, 1996; Van Tassel, 1985; Zuckerman et al., 1987). In general this literature suggests that maternal depression, sense of incompetence, separation difficulties, and insecure attachment may contribute to or exacerbate sleep problems in early childhood. It has been suggested that these parental attitudes, personality and psychodynamic factors affect sleep through direct bedtime interactions (Sadeh & Anders, 1993).

Trauma, stress, and anxiety are the underlying cause of many forms of primary insomnia (Sadeh, 1996). It has been documented in numerous studies on stress and trauma in children that sleep difficulties are among the most common nonspecific responses to such conditions (see Sadeh, 1996, for a review). In many cases it is possible to link the onset of the disorder, as an immediate or delayed response, to stressful or anxiety provoking events. Often it is difficult to trace back the association and a disorder that originated from stress continues to be maintained by other intervening factors.

In older children, anxieties and fears are probably the most common cause of primary insomnia but the theme of these anxieties may change according to phase-specific issues. For instance, a 3-year-old child may develop nighttime fears and sleep onset difficulties in response to a transition to a new daycare program, while an 11-year-old child may develop anxieties and sleep onset difficulties in response to a growing sexual awareness and anxieties related to

masturbation that are likely to rise when the child is alone in bed.

From a different angle, primary insomnia in children has been associated with the child's personality and psychopathology. Close links between sleep problems and "difficult temperament" and other behavior problems have been documented (see Section 5.24.1). The causal links are difficult to interpret but undoubtedly children with behavior or temperament problems, whatever the source of these difficulties, are more likely to develop sleep disorders. A similar picture exists in adolescence. Sleep problems have been associated with depression, anxiety, and related negative self-perceptions (Dahl, 1996; Kirmil-Gray et al., 1984; Marks & Monroe, 1976; Price et al., 1978).

Beyond the psychosocial and developmental factor in the etiology of primary insomnia, it is important to note that some common physiological factors may underlie the clinical picture. For instance, a number of medical and physiological factors may be involved in the etiology of night-waking problems in infants and young children. Among those identified factors are milk intolerance (Kahn et al., 1989), esophageal reflux (Kahn et al., 1991), atopic eczema (Reid & Lewis-Jones, 1995), and colic.

5.24.2.4.2 Primary hypersomnia and narcolepsy

Little is known about this cluster of relatively rare disturbances. The etiology of these disorders is usually attributed to neurological and hormonal processes. Genetic and hormonal influences have been identified in disorders such as Kleine–Levin and narcolepsy. Some of these processes have been associated with pubertal changes, thus explaining their onset and other phenomena such as the links, in some cases, between the clinical manifestations and the menstrual cycle. The origin of these disorders is organic in nature although most of the underlying neurophysiological mechanisms are still unknown. Insufficient or dysregulated sleep tends to exacerbate the clinical manifestations of these disorders.

5.24.2.4.3 Breathing-related sleep disorder

The most common cause for BRSD in children is airway obstruction due to anatomical and neurological complications. Enlarged tonsils and adenoids are among the prevalent reasons for upper airway blockage. Central sleep apnea is caused by CNS failure to control the breathing process. Full understanding of the various mechanisms involved in this family of disorders is still lacking, however.

5.24.2.4.4 Circadian rhythm sleep disorder

The understanding of the etiology of CRSD has significantly increased since the mid-1970s. Some of the mechanisms involved in mediating between the light–dark cycle and the sleep–wake rhythm have been identified and systematically studied. This new knowledge includes the specific role of the hormone melatonin, which is secreted from the pineal body during darkness, in transferring the external light–dark information into other brain centers controlling the sleep–wake cycle. It is now more clearly understood that the 24-h sleep–wake rhythm requires constant light–dark information and when such information is blocked (e.g., by experimental measures or blindness), the sleep–wake cycle loses its stable organization. This explains why reports on specific CRSD disorders, such as free-running or disorganized sleep–wake rhythms, have mostly been associated with blind adults and children, and more specifically with their different melatonin secretion patterns (e.g., Lewy & Newsome, 1983; Tzischinsky et al., 1991). Another group that has been associated with CRSD is children who suffer from "brain-damage" or psychoneurological, developmental disorders. It is assumed that these children either have dysfunctional neurological systems that fail to control the circadian clock or have difficulties interpreting the environmental cues that are essential for controlling the circadian system.

Delayed sleep phase has mostly been associated with adolescence as adolescents seem to have a natural tendency to delay sleep onset and insufficient sleep (Carskadon & Dement, 1987). It has been suggested that this delay tendency is not only due to the psychosocial influences of adolescence but also associated with pubertal changes (Carskadon, Viera, & Acebo, 1993).

5.24.2.4.5 The parasomnias

Little is known about the etiology of the parasomnias. A number of constitutional or predisposing genetic, developmental, and psychological factors have been suggested as well as factors associated with sleep structure. Anxiety, stress, and insufficient sleep are among the factors that may contribute to or exacerbate these phenomena.

5.24.2.5 Developmental Course

The issue of the persistency and continuity of sleep problems in early childhood is important since the common belief shared by many professionals and parents is that children outgrow these problems and therefore early interventions are not critical. Despite the fact that maturational processes seem to resolve the sleep difficulties in many young children, a number of studies have shown that these problems tend to be very persistent (Kateria, Swanson, & Trevarthin, 1987; Richman et al., 1982; Salzarulo & Chevalier, 1983; Zukerman et al., 1987). For instance, when infants identified as sleep-disturbed at 8 months of age were revisited when they were three years old, 41% of them still suffered from sleep problems (Zuckerman et al.). These studies indicate that many sleep-disturbed children continue to suffer from sleep problems for prolonged periods although the characteristics of their problem may change significantly. Some retrospective studies with adult insomnia patients report that a large proportion of these patients suffered from sleep problems from early childhood, suggesting that these problems are likely to turn into chronic disorders if not treated (Hauri & Olmstead, 1980).

The course of hypersomnia, BRSD, and the parasomnias is very specific to the source of the disorder and the interventions involved. As described earlier, some disorders (the Kleine–Levin syndrome, narcolepsy) tend to appear (or to be diagnosed) in adolescence. In contrast, the parasomnias tend to appear in early childhood and disappear as the child matures, usually prior to or during adolescence.

5.24.3 CONCEPTUALIZATION AND CLINICAL FORMULATION

The assessment and diagnosis of sleep disorders in children should be based on two components: (i) the assessment of sleep schedule, sleep duration, and sleep quality; and (ii) the assessment of daytime functioning and signs of fatigue, sleepiness, and other arousal disorders.

One unique feature of sleep disorders that separates it from many other psychosocial and biobehavioral disorders is that in addition to subjective or parental reports, sleep can be directly measured and quantified by objective measures that have been established by extensive research efforts. However, in clinical practice and clinical research the assessment of common sleep disorders of childhood is still mostly based on subjective reports. This section reviews some of the available objective measurement tools for clinical assessment of sleep disorders. Some of these assessment tools (such as polysomnographic (PSG) studies) are often necessary to identify organic or medical sources for the disorders and are therefore crucial for correct diagnosis and treatment. In many cases, it is also crucial to exclude major psychiatric or developmental disorders when diagnosing sleep disorders.

5.24.3.1 Multimodal Assessment

Since sleep–wake regulation plays such a major role in the arena of emotional regulation and psychopathology (Dahl, 1996), it is imperative for any clinical diagnostic procedure within the context of medical or behavioral disorders to include screening questions regarding the possible existence of sleep or alertness problems. This screening investigation should include questions regarding sleep schedule, sleep quality, known or suspected sleep disorders, and questions regarding daytime sleepiness and fatigue (Dahl & Carskadon, 1995; Ferber, 1995; Sadeh & Anders, 1993).

The assessment of sleep disorders involves a systematic intake interview and, in many cases, medical examination and laboratory or ambulatory monitoring of sleep–wake patterns. In addition, when excessive sleepiness is suspected, it is important to objectively evaluate the level of sleepiness of the child.

5.24.3.1.1 Initial information

Parents or other caregivers are generally the best source of information regarding the child's present sleep problem, its history and etiology, and the associated psychosocial factors. If the child is old enough they may be able to describe the difficulties, particularly when emotional and psychosocial factors play an important role. The preliminary information for screening and evaluating sleep disorders includes the child's sleep patterns (schedule, quantity, and quality), sleep history, bedtime rituals, and other psychosocial factors. In many cases, it is recommended that the parents and/or the child be asked to complete a daily sleep log for one week to provide more detailed information regarding specific issues that are of interest to the clinician and to serve as a baseline assessment for later treatment progress evaluation. It is also important to understand what kind of interventions or efforts have been made already to solve the problem (i.e., self- or professionally-driven attempts) (Dahl & Carskadon, 1995; Ferber, 1995; Sadeh & Anders, 1993).

In assessing primary insomnia, primary hypersomnia, and the parasomnias in infants

and children it is particularly important to evaluate the psychosocial, individual, and family contexts. The assessment should include efforts to identify specific stressors in the child and family's life, given the important role that stress plays in these disorders (Sadeh, 1996).

When there is a suspected or potential physical or medical source for the disorder, a medical examination is required as part of the initial assessment.

5.24.3.1.2 Assessment of sleep

Clinicians interested in sleep disorders have the advantage of being able to measure and quantify the clinical problem objectively in addition to receiving subjective reports of the child or the parents. With infants and children the parents are usually the reporters; however, their ability to report is limited. Parents are mostly aware of their child's sleep problem if the child signals (cries and requires intervention) during the night or, in the case of older children, if they communicate their problem directly to their parents (Sadeh, 1996; Sadeh & Anders, 1993). It has been shown that parents are relatively good reporters of their child sleep–wake schedule, but when it comes to sleep quality (i.e., number or duration of night-wakings), their reports are less accurate and might be adversely affected by various motivational and situational factors (Sadeh, 1996; Sadeh et al., 1991).

The traditional objective and comprehensive method to assess sleep is PSG (e.g. Anders, Emde, & Parmelee, 1971). This method is usually based on a laboratory study (although ambulatory studies have started to gain in popularity in recent years) for a single night. PSG provides information regarding the EEG, the electro-oculogram (eye movements), the electromyogram (muscle tone), and respiratory patterns during sleep. These data enable assessment of sleep structure, sleep stages, and specific disturbances during sleep such as those related to disordered breathing.

A number of ambulatory methods have been developed to assess sleep in the child's natural home environment. These methods include direct observations (Thoman, 1975), time-lapse video recording (Anders & Sostek, 1976), pressure-sensitive mattress recording of motility and respiration (Thoman & Whitney, 1989), and actigraphy–activity monitoring with a wrist-watch like device that has already been adopted for clinical practice (Sadeh, 1994; Sadeh et al., 1991, 1995a). See Table 2 for a description of the advantages and shortcomings of each method.

Table 2 Assessment tools for diagnosis and treatment follow-up in sleep disorders.

Method	Description	Advantages	Limitations
Polysomnography	Laboratory or ambulatory multiple-channel physiologic recording that requires wiring electrodes, post-testing interpretation (Anders et al., 1971)	Provides the most elaborate data. Crucial for diagnosing organic causes for sleep disorders	Expensive, disrupts natural sleep settings, and causes stress. Usually limited to one night
Videosomnography	Time-lapse video enables the monitoring of child's sleep patterns at home (Anders & Sostek, 1976)	Provides information about sleep onset, sleep–wake states, night-wakings, and parental interventions	Requires transportation to the home, and a postmonitoring observer scoring
Sensitive mattress	A system based on a pressure sensitive mattress installed in the child's bed (e.g., Thoman & Whitney, 1989)	Provides useful information about sleep–wake states and respiratory patterns	Requires home installation and a complex postmonitoring analysis
Direct observation	This method is based on trained observers who observe the infant and record his or her sleep–wake states on an ongoing basis. In addition a sensor pad and a strip chart recorder provide respiration data that facilitate state differentiation (e.g., Thoman, 1975)	Provides valuable information on sleep–wake and to some extent on sleep states in infants ("quiet" vs. "active" sleep). Provides information on respiration patterns	May disrupt normal home-setting. Very demanding task for the observers and requires complex postmonitoring analysis. Has only been used with infants
Actigraphy	Actigraphy is based on a small computerized activity monitor attached to the child's wrist or ankle. The activity data is automatically translated to sleep–wake measures that have been validated against polysomnography (Sadeh et al., 1995a)	Enables 24 h continuous nonintrusive measurement of sleep–wake and activity patterns. Cost-effective. Provides information on sleep schedule, night-wakings, and sleep quality	Some artifact may result from the fact that the only channel measured is activity. Sleep disturbances seen in the activity data are difficult to interpret without complementary information
Sleep diary	Parents or child complete a sleep diary that includes bedtimes, sleep onset time, number and timing of night-wakings and other sleep-related events and disruptions (e.g., Douglas & Richman, 1984)	Easy and inexpensive to administer. Provides additional information regarding relevant events associated with sleep (e.g., how the parents intervene)	Limited by the subjective knowledge of the parents or the child. May be biased by a variety of motivational issues. Parents and children may lose interest with prolonged administration
Sleep questionnaires	Parents or child complete a general sleep questionnaire characterizing their sleep problems (e.g., "child wakes up regularly every night")	Easy to administer. Provides general information on sleep difficulties	The subjective components may play a major role since the questions are not anchored to specific nights as in the daily logs

5.24.3.1.3 *Assessment of excessive sleepiness*

As described earlier, fatigue and excessive sleepiness may have different manifestations in children. The primary sign of sleepiness is a tendency or a growing pressure to sleep. Other signs in infants and children include irritability, fussiness, hyperactivity, affective dysregulation, difficulties in attention, and concentration (Dahl, 1996). Many of these signs may be observed directly in the school or the clinical setting or reported by the parents.

The multiple sleep latency test (MSLT) was designed to measure and quantify the pressure to fall asleep in children and adults (Carskadon & Dement, 1982). The basic procedure is to ask the subject to lie in bed with eyes closed and to try to fall asleep. Individuals who fall asleep rapidly (e.g., within 5 minutes) are considered very sleepy. Higher sleep latencies are interpreted as increased alertness. This procedure is repeated a few times during daytime hours. Norms and clinical criteria have been established.

5.24.3.2 Treatment Formulation

Treatment strategy is heavily based on the diagnosis and the clinical interpretation of applicable intervention avenues. For most clinical sleep disorders, pharmacological treatments are available, although the pervasive belief is that whenever possible the use of sleep-related drugs should be avoided, particularly with children. Potent psychosocial treatments are available for many sleep disturbances and they should be considered the treatment of choice.

Although Section 5.24.5 presents psychosocial and medical–pharmacological treatments separately, it is important to remember that this is not the recommended approach, rather, an integrated approach is usually called for. Even when medical treatment is required, motivational and psychological factors of the child and the parents play a major role in their response to treatment and therefore should be evaluated and addressed in the course of treatment.

5.24.4 TREATMENT

This section discusses the different approaches to treatment in children's and adolescents' sleep disorders. Due to the heterogeneous nature and the wide variety of sleep disorders, there are multiple psychosocial and medical therapeutic approaches. The following section reflects an attempt to review this wide range of interventions with a special focus on the psychosocial approaches.

5.24.4.1 Psychosocial Treatments

The psychosocial treatments of sleep disorders in infants and children constitute a relatively well-documented domain of multiple behavioral and psychodynamic approaches. This is particularly true for infants and young children and less so for older children and adolescents. Most of the emphasis is on primary insomnia which is the disorder that responds best to these interventions.

5.24.4.1.1 *Primary insomnia*

The recommended psychological treatment should include both behavioral components aimed at changing the sleep habits of the child and a psychodynamic component enabling the working-through of psychodynamic issues related to sleep difficulties (whenever such issues exist). The main issues in such a brief and focused psychological treatment are usually related to separation, soothing capacities, and limit setting. Therefore, in addition to the benefits of solving the specific sleep disorder, the brief psychological treatment might serve as a vehicle for the parents and child to acquire skills and competencies that may be useful in broader contexts (e.g., self-soothing, limit-setting).

The central hypothesis that underlies most behavioral interventions in early childhood is that sleep problems are the result of habitual, learned parent–child interactional patterns (Sadeh & Anders, 1993). Sadeh & Anders (1993) suggest that one of the key factors in the evolution of sleep problems in childhood is related to soothing skills that are acquired by children during development. The lack of these self-soothing skills is manifested in the case of a 18-month-old boy who cannot fall asleep without being rocked or breast-fed by his mother or by the 10-year-old girl who refuses to sleep in her own bed separated from her parents because of fears associated with sleep, dreaming, or darkness. An additional assumption is that sleep difficulties may be associated with sleep-competitive activities, that have been maintained by a variety of positive and negative reinforcers (Bootzin, 1977; Bootzin & Nicassio, 1978), such as parental reactions that perpetuate the sleep difficulties (Blampied & France, 1993). Hence, the target of the different modes of the behavioral treatment is to break these associations by teaching the child to fall asleep and to maintain sleep with minimal interaction with the parents.

Since the capacity for "sleeping through the night" is acquired by most infants by six months of age, most parents and clinicians prefer to wait for the maturational process to occur during this period. Despite this general attitude, it has been shown that an improvement in sleep patterns may be achieved by behavioral intervention with breast-fed infants as young as eight weeks old (Pinilla & Birch, 1993), or even by prevention programs based on educating expecting parents (in delivery classes) how to help their children develop healthy and mature sleep habits (Wolfson, Lacks, & Futterman, 1992).

According to the "behavioral extinction" approach, parents are instructed to stop attending to the child during the night. They are instructed to ignore the child's crying and protests until the child falls asleep due to exhaustion and lack of reinforcers (Sadeh & Anders, 1993). However, the extinction approach is difficult to implement for most parents since there is usually a postextinction response burst, an increase in the frequency and intensity of the behavior that is likely to accompany the introduction of extinction (Lawton, France, & Blampied, 1991; Rickert & Johnson, 1988). This treatment is difficult for many parents who experience such behavior as abandonment on their part. Therefore, more gradual and less aversive variants of the extinction technique have been recommended.

In the gradual extinction approach, the parental response to the child during falling asleep or night-waking are suspended for constant (Douglas & Richman, 1984) or increasing intervals of time (Ferber, 1995), and parents are advised to decrease their proximity to and involvement with the child during the night. For example, a parent may initially stop rocking the child to sleep, and instead remain close to the child's bed for a while until the child falls asleep. In the next step, the parent would leave the child's bedroom once the child has been put to bed (Sadeh & Anders, 1993).

Another alternative aimed at to make the extinction less aversive for both child and parents is using a combination treatment of sedative medication for the child and extinction (France, Blampied, & Wilkinson, 1991).

The stimulus control therapy attempts to break the association between the sleep environment and wakefulness by teaching the child not to engage in sleep "incompatible" behavior in the bedroom, and to establish the bed and bedroom as cues for sleep (e.g., to be in the bedroom only when drowsy or asleep) (Bootzin & Perlis, 1992).

Another way to break the rewarding association among night-waking, crying, and parental intervention is that of "scheduled awakenings." According to this approach the parents awaken the child prior to the time of the expected spontaneous awakening (McGarr & Hovel, 1980).

Parental cosleeping with the child has been used as an intervention method. According to this method, one parent sleeps in the child's bedroom for a one-week period without having any other interactions with the child throughout the night. This method is based on the assumption that in many cases infant sleep problems are related to the child's separation anxiety. The presence of the parent in the child's room is expected to reassure the child and enable consolidated sleep (Sadeh, 1994).

The methods described above are usually implemented within a standard clinical setup including clinical sessions with a therapist. However, some programs have used only written information and guidelines to the parents as the sole intervention. Written manuals containing instructions for parents without therapist support were found as highly effective in reducing waking during the night as the "conventional" format. The improvement was more gradual than the improvement in the sleep program with therapist involvement, but there was no difference in the final achievements of both groups (Seymour, Brock, During, & Pole, 1989). Adoption of behavioral principles into a group therapy format was not found to be effective (Messer, Lauder, & Humphrey, 1994).

Many studies demonstrate the efficacy of behavioral interventions in treating sleep problems, particularly during early childhood. Generally, the reported success rate range has been between 73% and 90% (e.g., Adair, Zuckerman, Bauchner, Philipp, & Levenson, 1992; Jones & Verduyn, 1983; Richman, Douglas, Hunt, Landsdown, & Levere, 1985; Roberts, 1993; Sadeh, 1994). Moreover, it has been found that a brief behavioral intervention program focused on helping families manage children with sleep disturbances could be generalized to improving daytime mother–child interactions (Minde, Faucon, & Falkner, 1994).

High success rates have been reported for a variety of extinction strategies (e.g., Adair et al., 1992; Adams & Rickert, 1989; Durand & Mindell, 1990; France & Hudson, 1990; Jones & Verduyn, 1983; Pritchard & Appelton, 1988; Richman et al., 1985; Rickert & Johnson, 1988; Sadeh, 1994).

Most of the reports have documented dramatic improvement within a one-week period. The use of extinction is reportedly accompanied by reduction in parental anxiety, and improvement in parental self-esteem, depression, marital satisfaction, and sense of control following extinction-based treatments of sleep disturbance. In addition, an improvement in infant sense of security has also been documented (France et al., 1991). These findings could be used to reassure parents who fear that such a strategy may harm their child. The stimulus control therapy was found to be effective, though its efficacy was measured in combination with other therapeutic components (Weissbluth, 1982). The scheduled awakening strategy proved difficult for parents to follow though it was found to be effective in reducing the number of night-wakings (e.g., McGarr & Hovel, 1980; Ricket & Johnson, 1988; Weissbluth, 1982).

All of the above reported efficacy studies are based on parental reports with their obvious limitations with one exception that has used both parental reports and actigraphic monitoring (Sadeh, 1994). This study documented two processes that occur during these interventions: (i) the infant's sleep becomes more consolidated and less fragmented; and (ii) the children acquire the capacity to soothe themselves back to sleep without parental interventions.

Psychodynamic approaches have also been implemented in treating early childhood primary insomnia. Psychodynamically oriented approaches have been used in order to understand and interpret the meaning of the child's sleep behavior in the context of the child–parent relationship (Daws, 1989). Since many sleep problems in children reflect parent–child interactions, parental anxieties, and psychopathology, these issues become the focus of psychodynamic treatment. The efficacy of the psychodynamic approach is yet to be established empirically, however, we believe that family and psychodynamic issues should be addressed in most cases to facilitate the efficacy of behavioral interventions.

As the child matures, the characteristics of the insomnia progressively resemble those seen at older ages and the insomniac adolescent gradually resembles the insomniac young adult and similar approaches found to be effective with adults can be adopted (Ferber, 1995). These methods include improving sleep hygiene, normalizing sleep schedules, stimulus control, sleep restriction training, biofeedback, cognitive therapy, and dynamic psychotherapy (Ferber, 1995; Morin et al., 1994).

Since little research has been conducted with adolescent subjects, efficacy of the different approaches is based on studies with adult subjects. The findings from different studies and reviews indicate that nonpharmacological interventions produce reliable and durable changes in sleep patterns of patients with chronic insomnia (e.g., Bootzin & Perlis, 1992; Morin et al., 1994). For instance, Morin et al. conducted a meta-analysis of nonpharmacological interventions for insomnia to examine the efficacy of the different treatment approaches. They found that psychological intervention produced a reliable change in sleep latency and in time awake after sleep onset.

5.24.4.1.2 Primary hypersomnia and narcolepsy

In addition to the pharmacological treatments, psychosocial interventions in hypersomnia and narcolepsy focus on two main issues: (i) regulating the sleep–wake schedule and extending sleep to reduce sleepiness (e.g., scheduling daily naps, maintaining strict and regular sleep–wake schedule; and (ii) consulting the child, the parents, and the school system in an effort to optimize the child's social and school adjustment.

Daytime sleep schedules have been found to be effective in reducing somnolence during the day (Billiard, 1976; Roehrs et al., 1986; Rogers & Aldrich, 1993) and in improving cognitive functioning (Mullington & Broughton, 1993). In addition to the difficulties to function due to the excessive sleepiness, narcoleptic children may suffer adjustment problems due to the unique form of their syndrome. Adult narcoleptic patients have been described as depressed and prone to adjustment disorders, anxiety, personality disorders, and alcohol dependency. There are also some indications that most adult narcoleptic patients benefit from psychotherapy and support groups (Alaia, 1992; Zarcone, 1973). The efficacy of such interventions with children and adolescents has not been established, however.

5.24.4.1.3 Breathing-related sleep disorder

The treatment of these disorders is primarily medical. Psychological work with the child and family is often focused on compliance with some of the medical interventions.

5.24.4.1.4 Circadian rhythm sleep disorder

Readjustment of the circadian system requires small, gradual, and consistent changes in bedtime and wake-up time, and requires one to two weeks of stability to realign all the components of the system (Dahl, 1992). This gradual change could be achieved by the combined effect of chronotherapy and light therapy.

The traditionally accepted treatment for delayed sleep phase is chronotherapy (Czeisler et al., 1981). Chronotherapy is a behavioral technique in which bedtime is systematically delayed or advanced, following the child's natural biological tendency (Ferber, 1995). Czeisler et al. reported that chronotherapy was effective in advancing sleep onset and wake-times with no reduction in sleep efficiency in five adult patients. Research focused on treatment in infants and adolescents has yet to be conducted.

In dealing with the adolescent age group, treatment must include behavioral contracts with specifically delineated rules, rewards, consequences, and a measure of monitoring components (Dahl, 1992). The behavioral contract should specify the time of going to sleep and awakening, avoidance of napping during the day, and the amount and timing of exposure to bright light. Parents and child should agree upon the reinforcements for keeping the program. The reinforcements should be given on a weekly basis during follow-up meetings with the therapist. The importance of keeping to the new schedule as strictly as possible, including holidays and weekends, must be emphasized and explained to the child and the parents. It is only after the schedule has been stabilized that there may be a place to negotiate "exceptions" for special occasions (e.g., trips, parties).

The treatment of delayed sleep phase syndrome was found to be effective in adolescents who were cooperative and were not suffering from depression, but was not effective in adolescents who expressed a refusal to go to school (Ferber & Boyle, 1983). In other studies, it was demonstrated that patients who had delayed phase syndrome and significant psychopathology (e.g., depression) responded poorly to treatment (Billiard, Verge, Touchon, Carlander, & Besset, 1993; Lahmeyer & Lilie, 1987). Therefore, it seems that whenever the circadian rhythm disorder is complicated by additional psychopathology, the success of treatment depends on the success of additional psychotherapy and psychiatric treatments.

When there are motivational factors that help perpetuate the problem (e.g., social or academic problems that the child is trying to avoid by staying away from school when tired, or special incentives for the child to stay up late), individual and family psychotherapy is recommended in addition to chronotherapy and light therapy.

5.24.4.1.5 Nightmares, sleep terror, sleepwalking, and other parasomnias

Two components should be considered in the approach to treating specific parasomnias. The first component is that of management aimed at providing protection and safety for the child. This is the most important consideration in coping with sleepwalking or night-terror episodes (Kales et al., 1980b; Kales, Soldatos, &

Kales, 1987). The second component is additional symptomatic treatment in those cases where the arousals are dangerous or disruptive to the child or the family and no obvious precipitant can be identified (Rosen, Mahowald, & Ferber, 1995). When attacks are very frequent, if they persist beyond the age they would normally cease, if they start beyond that age (Stores, 1990), or if they follow a traumatic event (Rosen et al., 1995; Stores, 1990), protection is not enough and there might be a need for additional treatment.

Regarding the management of night terrors and sleepwalking, the recommendations are very practical. It is advisable to remove everything from the bedroom (and house) that could be hazardous. If possible, it is recommended that the bedroom be located on the ground floor of the house. It is important to lock the windows and cover the panes with heavy drapes (Keefauver & Guilleminault, 1995). In addition, it is recommended that sleep deprivation or other circumstances that might cause the child excessive sleep be avoided (Driver & Shapiro, 1993) and that the sleep–wake schedule be made regular (Rosen et al., 1995).

It is important to assure both the parents and the child that the problem is temporary, and that it is neither "abnormal" nor bearing significant consequences for the future (Mahowald & Rosen, 1990). It is also important to recommend that the parents do not discuss the episodes with the child the following day, since such discussion might be stressful for the child (who usually does not remember anything) and it may inadvertently reinforce the behavior. Furthermore, during the night, parents should resist trying to awaken and comfort the child. Waking the child may increase disturbance (Stores, 1990). The most appropriate response is to help the child to settle down when the acute episode subsides or if the child awakens when it ends. In cases in which night terrors occur at a regular and predicted time, it is possible to wake the child before each episode, keep them awake for few minutes, and thus break the cycle of night terror (Stores, 1990).

Another treatment approach is based on relaxation mental imagery. This form of treatment allows the child to utilize self-regulation techniques to control the previously uncontrolled night-time behaviors (Mahowald & Rosen, 1990). This method has been described as effective in treating parasomnias (Driver & Shapiro, 1993; Pesikoff & Davis, 1971).

When treating nightmares there is a special need to address potential sources for the fears (e.g., horror films) and to remove them (Dahl, 1992), simultaneously providing support and comfort to the child (Driver & Shapiro, 1993).

Psychotherapy is indicated with children and in families where significant psychopathology is present.

5.24.4.2 Pharmacological and Other Medical Treatments

Medical interventions play a significant role in treating many sleep disorders. While in some disorders, drugs and other medical interventions are the only available treatment, in other disorders they are too readily used when they should not be considered the treatment of choice.

5.24.4.2.1 Primary insomnia

Most experts in the field believe that medication is not a recommended treatment for insomnia in children. However, in practice high rates of medication use have been reported for infants and children.

The most common hypnotics that have been used for treating insomniac children are niaprazine (Nopron R) and trimeprazine tartrate (Vallergan Forte R) (Navelet, 1996). Sedatives such as chloral hydrate (Adler, 1990), benzodiazepines, and sedatives containing cough medicine have also been used by clinicians (Chavin & Tinson, 1980; Dahl, 1992; Werry & Carlielle, 1983).

Generally, it has been found that in the short-run sleep problems improve with the use of sedatives. However, most of the studies have not differentiated between different types of sleep disorders or ages of the children, and possess methodological deficiencies. For example, Russo, Vymut, and Gurauraj-Allen (1976) found dipheramine HCl to be effective in decreasing sleep latency time and reducing the number of awakenings in children aged 2–12 years who had a variety of sleep difficulties. Besana, Fiocchi, DeBartolomies, Magno, and Donati (1984) found niaprazine to be effective in the treatment of sleep disorders in children aged 2–13 years who had difficulties with onset and maintaining of sleep due to different emotional and medical conditions. However, both studies did not differentiate between different age groups or different sleep disorders. In a different clinical setting, Simonoff and Stores (1987) found tromerazine to be an effective treatment in reducing night-waking. However, their sample consisted of children with severe psychopathology and therefore does not represent the majority of infants with sleep difficulties.

Despite short-term improvement in insomnia as the result of sedative use, studies have shown little or no long-term benefit (Chavin & Tinson,

1980; Jones & Verduyn, 1983; Richman, 1986; Richman et al., 1985; Seymour, 1987). In addition, side effects of using sedatives in children include tolerance effects, withdrawal effects, and the fact that children who are not able to self-comfort behaviorally will often fight sleep despite the sedatives. This could result in increased levels of activity and awareness of the child when he or she is medicated (Dahl, 1992). Moreover, the problem may recur when the medication is stopped.

The use of medication is usually not indicated for insomnia in adolescents unless it is to treat a specific disorder that is related to insomnia. Since the insomnias that seem most likely to occur in adolescents are primarily associated with either psychiatric problems or with a circadian rhythm disorder, it seems important to make a careful diagnosis, and, in cases of psychiatric disorders such as anxiety or depression, the medication should be appropriate in treating both the sleep problem and the affective problem (i.e., by sedatives that provide an anxiolytic or depressant effect the next day; see Nicholson, 1994). When choosing to use sedatives, it is advisable to prescribe relatively small doses that enable the preservation of normal sleep architecture both during ingestion and after withdrawal.

Sleep-inducing medications may have adverse effects such as impaired performance the following day and anterograde amnesia, rebound insomnia when treatment is stopped, dependence, and developed tolerance.

5.24.4.2.2 Primary hypersomnia and narcolepsy

There is little empirical data in the younger narcoleptic population to guide treatment decisions (Dahl, 1992). Hence, the treatment of narcolepsy and cataplexy in children reflects clinical experience with older adult patients (Lawrence & Billiard, 1995).

The goal of the pharmacological treatment is to control the narcoleptic symptoms and to allow the patient full participation in daily activities. Pharmacological treatment usually includes: REM-suppressant medication such as trycyclic antidepressants and clomipramine, desmethylimipramine, or other 5HT2 reuptake inhibitors aimed at dealing with cataplexy and hypnogogic hallucinations, and stimulant medication such as pemoline and methylphenidate, or amphetamines aimed at dealing with daytime sleepiness (Parkes, 1994). The effectiveness of these pharmacological treatments in increasing alertness of narcoleptic patients has been demonstrated in a number of studies (Guillerminault, 1993; Rogers & Aldrich, 1993). However, since narcolepsy is a long-lasting illness, it is important to take into account issues related to tolerance, addiction, and adverse side effects.

It is important to remember that despite medication, most adult narcoleptic patients experience narcoleptic symptoms, especially somnolence, which is very disruptive to functioning during the day (Scumacher, Merritt, & Cohen, 1993). Further research should be conducted to evaluate the efficacy of pharmacological treatments of narcolepsy in children.

5.24.4.2.3 Breathing-related sleep disorder

Optional medical treatments for obstructive sleep apnea syndrome (OSAS) include surgical, mechanical therapy, and medical–pharmacological treatment. The surgical approach includes adenotonsillectomy and tracheostomy that are often used in treating sleep apnea in children and adults. Adenotonsillectom, removing tonsils and adenoids, is a solution for enlarged tonsils and adenoids that have been found to cause obstruction (Stores, 1990; Stradling, Thomas, Warely, Williams, & Feeland, 1990). Tracheostomy is a surgical intervention aiming at enlarging the breathing passway itself by introducing a canula into it. Tracheostomy is indicated for children with severe and/or complicated OSAS in whom other treatment approaches are either not possible or unsuccessful.

Since there are potentially serious complications involved in these surgical procedures, they are recommended only in serious cases (Carrol & Louglin, 1995; Powell; Guilleminault, & Riley, 1994). There is little scientific information and no consensus or guidelines for surgical treatment of childhood OSAS (Carrol & Louglin, 1995). Hence, further research concerning efficacy of this treatment strategy is required.

Nasally applied continuous airway pressure (CPAP) has become the major nonsurgical, long-term form of treatment used in obstructive sleep apnea and it is currently the treatment of choice. The method is based on providing intermittent positive pressure through a nose mask to overcome obstructions and hypoventilation syndromes (Sullivan & Grunstein, 1994). When CPAP treatment is initiated there is an immediate reduction in daytime somnolence. This has been demonstrated using the multiple sleep latency test (Lamphere, Roehrs, & Wittig, 1989). Serious complications of CPAP appear to be rare. Nasal congestion is a side effect of CPAP therapy that can be pharmacologically or, in very rare cases, surgically treated.

CPAP is effective in reducing the severity of obstructive sleep apnea, but it does not lead to a permanent cure (Marcus et al., 1995). CPAP treatment for OSAS was found to be effective in more than 85% of the pediatric patients. Objective measures such as MSLT, before and after one year of treatment, have confirmed its efficacy in adults, indicating that after a year of CPAP treatment sleepiness as measured by the MSLT was significantly raised (Sforza & Lugaresi, 1995).

In contrast with the reported efficacy of the CPAP treatment, the use of medication to treat sleep apnea has been disappointing (Strollo & Rogers, 1996). Nasal decongestants and topical steroids can be used as a short-term solution in cases of OSAS in children.

5.24.4.2.4 Circadian rhythm sleep disorder

Since the architecture of sleep in CRSD has no abnormalities, and because the patients usually have no difficulties with sleep onset given the opportunity to sleep at a less commonly accepted time of day, there is no indication for drug therapy in this disorder.

A relatively new approach to the treatment of sleep problems is the use of melatonin for regulating sleep. Melatonin plays an important role in the induction of sleep in the human organism. The secretion of melatonin is controlled by an endogenous rhythm-generating system in the brain which is synchronized by the light-dark cycle, so that melatonin levels are high during dark hours and low during light hours.

Exogenous melatonin has been found useful in the treatment of sleep disorders in adults (Dahlitz et al., 1991; McFarlane, Cleghorn, Brown, & Streiner, 1991); however, some studies have shown that the results are not maintained when treatment is terminated (Alvarez et al., 1992; Dahlitz et al.). There are relatively few studies examining melatonin therapy for sleep disorder in children.

Melatonin treatment has been found to be effective in treating highly disabled children with severe sleep disorders that have resisted conventional treatment (Jan, Espezel, & Appelton, 1994). In addition, melatonin has been found to be effective in treating blind retarded children with a problematic sleep–wake cycle (Lapierre & Dumont, 1995). However, concerns regarding the safety of using melatonin in prepubertal children have been raised due to the links between melatonin and sexual maturation.

Since the circadian cycle, and hence the sleep–wake cycle, may be shortened or lengthened by exposure to bright light (Regestein & Monk, 1995), early morning exposure to bright light and activity can be an important adjunct to maintaining an early schedule (Dahl, 1992). Exposure to bright light has been shown to be effective in treating circadian rhythm disorders in adult patients (e.g., Lack & Wright, 1993; Lewy, Singer, & Sack, 1985). Guilleminault, McCann, Quera-Salva, and Cetel (1993) reported a positive response in five of 14 mentally retarded and neurologically damaged children with severe sleep disorders.

5.24.4.2.5 *Nightmares, sleep terror, sleepwalking, and other parasomnias*

Drug treatment may be considered if night terrors or sleepwalking occur very frequently, or if the problem interferes with the child participating in normal social interactions. The common drugs for treating parasomnias are diazepam, imipramine, benzodiazepines, and tricyclic antidepressants. For night terrors, both diazepam and imipramine have been shown to be effective. Diazepam is considered the drug of choice because it is associated with fewer side effects (McDaniel, 1987). Benzodiazepines and tricyclic antidepressants have been shown to be useful (Fisher, Kahn, Edwards, & Davis, 1973; Guilleminault, 1994; Kavey, Whyte, Resor, & Gidro-Frank, 1987). Low doses of a benzodiazepine may also be effective (Fisher et al., 1973; Pesikoff & Davis, 1971), but there is a high rate of relapse particularly during times of stress (Driver & Shapiro, 1993).

Combining pharmacological and psychological treatment may be effective: drugs could be used for treating acute current difficulties, and different therapeutic tools could be used for long-term treatment, thus avoiding tolerance and adverse side effects.

5.24.5 FUTURE DIRECTIONS FOR RESEARCH AND PRACTICE

This chapter raises many areas of insufficient knowledge and research efforts. Information on diagnosis, prevalence, time course, and interventions is lacking for many specific sleep disorders. Many of the definitions of the disorders are too vague and rely heavily on subjective interpretations of the child, parents, and clinicians. Despite the fact that a number of objective assessment tools have been established, they have yet to be adopted for clinical research and practice.

Clinical sleep research has mostly focused on two age periods: infancy and adulthood.

There is a significant gap in clinical knowledge on children during school years and the adolescent period. For instance, there are clinical assumptions that school children and adolescents can benefit from relaxation training and other behavioral methods that have demonstrated efficacy with adults; however, this efficacy has not been established for children.

Another area with limited information pertains to the maturational-developmental processes of the sleep–wake system beyond early childhood. Longitudinal research is needed to assess the continuity of sleep problems across the life span effects of early disturbances of the sleep–wake system on other behavioral and neuropsychological systems.

There is a growing body of research indicating that: (i) sleep disturbances are very common in early childhood; (ii) sleep problems in early childhood are persistent; and (iii) brief and focused interventions are effective in treating most of the common sleep problems. This knowledge should be translated to clinical practice by shifting the focus to prevention and early detection and intervention. The study of Wolfson et al. (1992) is a good example of a prevention program and its potential efficacy.

The strong links between sleep problems and psychopathology require special attention. Future experimental and clinical studies should focus on assessing the role of sleep disorders and sleep deprivation in the evolution of psychopathology in children.

We believe that in the near future the current trend of adopting a multidimensional approach in diagnosing and treating sleep disorders will become the prevailing standard of practice. This multidimensional approach will include: (i) objective and subjective assessment of sleep; (ii) assessment of psychosocial factors including psychopathology and stress; (iii) combining behavioral or medical treatment with psychosocial interventions aimed at psychodynamic and family issues associated with the disorder; and (iv) assessing the efficacy of interventions by subjective and objective measures.

5.24.6 SUMMARY

This chapter raises a number of clinical and empirical issues that are fundamental to the diagnosis and treatment of children's sleep disorders.

(i) Sleep disorders are very prevalent during infancy, childhood, and adolescence. Since many studies have not used standard criteria to define specific sleep disorders, and some disorders have been studied mostly in clinical settings, the prevalence of many specific disorders in the general population has not been well established.

(ii) Despite the fact that objective measures of specific disorders like night-waking problems have been established, they have not been incorporated into clinical research and practice which is still heavily based on subjective reports.

(iii) The diagnostic criteria for many specific disorders are still relatively vague with no empirical consensus. Therefore, in clinical research it is difficult to compare studies and in many cases to even identify the specific disorders under investigation.

(iv) Sleep disorders, daytime behavior, and psychopathology are highly inter-related. Screening for sleep problems should be included in any clinical assessment with children. Specific attention should be given to daytime sleepiness and paradoxical signs of fatigue.

(v) When signs of sleepiness and fatigue exist with no "simple" explanation, such as insufficient sleep, a full evaluation is needed, including identification of medical disorders such as breathing-related sleep disorders by means of a full polysomnographic study.

(vi) When a sleep disorder exists in the context of known psychopathology one should not assume that the psychopathology is the cause of the sleep problem. The sleep problem should be thoroughly assessed and treated appropriately. It may be the cause of the associated psychopathology.

(vii) Primary insomnia should be primarily treated by psychosocial interventions. The efficacy of short-term focused interventions has been strongly supported in young children and additional research is needed in the case of older children and adolescents.

(viii) Since stress and other psychosocial factors play an important role in most of the sleep disorders in children, it is important to assess these factors and intervene accordingly, even in those disorders which primarily require medical treatments.

(ix) Psychosocial and psychodynamic issues should always be addressed in the evaluation and treatment phases as underlying powerful factors in the evolution and maintenance of a child's sleep problem.

5.24.7 REFERENCES

Adair, R., Bauchner, H., Philipp, B., Levenson, S., & Zuckerman, B. (1991). Night waking during infancy: Role of parental presence at bedtime. *Pediatrics, 84,* 500–504.

Adair, R., Zuckerman, B., Bauchner, H., Philipp, B., &
Levenson, S. (1992). Reducing night waking in infancy: A primary care intervention. *Pediatrics, 89,* 585–588.

Adams, L. A., & Rickert, V. I. (1989). Reducing bedtime tantrums: comparison between positive routines and graduated extinction. *Pediatrics, 84,* 756–761.

Adler, R. (1990). Common behavioral disturbances. In M. J. Robinson (Ed.), *Practical paediatrics* (2nd ed., pp. 543–549). Singapore: Longman.

Alaia, S. L. (1992). Life effects of narcolepsy: Measures of negative impact, social support and psychological well-being. In M. Goswami, C. P. Pollak, F. L. Cohen, M. J. Thropy, & N. B. Kavey (Ed.), *Psychosocial aspects of narcolepsy* (pp. 1–22). New York: Haworth Press

Alvarez, B., Dahlitz, M. J., Vignau, J., & Parkes, J. D. (1992). The delayed sleep phase syndrome: clinical and investigative findings in 14 subjects. *Journal of Neurology, Neurosurgery and Psychiatry, 55,* 665–670.

American Psychiatric Association. (1994). *Diagnostic and statistical manual of mental disorders* (4th ed.). Washington, DC: American Psychiatric Association.

Anders, T. (1979). Night waking in infants during the first year of life. *Pediatrics, 63,* 860–864.

Anders, T. F., Carskadon, M. A., Dement, W. C., & Harvey, K. (1978). Sleep habits of children and the identification of pathologically sleepy children. *Child Psychiatry and Human Development, 9,* 56–62.

Anders, T. F., Emde, R., & Parmelee, A. A. (1971). *A manual of standardized terminology, techniques and criteria for the scoring of states of sleep and wakefulness in newborn infants.* Los Angeles: UCLA Brain Information Service.

Anders, T. F., & Sostek, A. M. (1976). The use of time-lapse video recording of sleep–wake behavior in human infants. *Psychophysiology, 13,* 155–158.

Babkoff, H., Caspy, T., Mikulinncer, M., & Sing, H. C. (1991). Monotonic and rhythmic influences: a challenge for sleep deprivation research. *Psychological Bulletin, 109,* 411–428.

Baird, W. P. (1987). *Narcolepsy: A non-medical presentation.* San Carlos, CA: American Narcolepsy Association.

Bearpark, H. M., & Michie, P. T. (1987). Prevalence of sleep/wake disturbances in Sydney adolescents. *Sleep Research, 16,* 304.

Beltramini, A., & Hertzig, M. (1983). Sleep and bedtime behavior in preschool-aged children. *Pediatrics, 71,* 153–158.

Benoit, D., Zeanah, C., Boucher, C., & Minde, K. (1992). Sleep disorders in early childhood: Association with insecure maternal attachment. *Journal of the American Academy of Child and Adolescent Psychiatry, 31,* 86–93.

Besana, R., Fiocchi, A., DeBartolomies, L., Magno, F., & Donati, C. (1984). Comparison of Niaprazine and placebo in pediatric behaviour and sleep disorders: double-bind clinical trial. *Current Therapeutic Research, 36,* 58–66.

Billiard, M. (1976). Competition between the two types of sleep, and the recuperative function of REM sleep versus NREM sleep in narcoleptics. In C. Guilleminault, W. C. Dement, & P. Passouant (Eds.), *Narcolepsy* (pp. 77–96). New York: Spectrum.

Billiard, M., Verge, M., Touchon, J., Carlander, B., & Besset, A. (1993). Delayed sleep phase syndrome: subjective and objective data, chronotherapy and follow-up. *Sleep Research, 22,* 172.

Blampied, N. M., & France, K. G. (1993). A behavioral model of infant sleep disturbance. *Journal of Applied Behavior Analysis, 26,* 477–492.

Bonnet, M. H. (1985). Effect of sleep disruption on sleep, performance, and mood. *Sleep, 8,* 11–19.

Bootzin, R. R. (1977). Effects of self-control procedures for insomnia. In R. B. Stuart (Ed.), *Behavioral self-management: strategies, techniques and outcomes* (pp. 176–195). New York: Brunner/Mazel.

Bootzin R. R., & Nicassio, P. M. (1978). Behavioral treatment for insomnia. In M. Hersen, R. M. Eisler, & P. M. Miller (Eds.), *Progress in behavior modification* (Vol. 6, pp. 1–45) New York: Academic Press.

Bootzin R. R., & Perlis M. E. (1992). Nonpharmacologic treatments of insomnia. *Journal of Clinical Psychiatry, 53,* 37–42.

Carey, W. (1974). Night waking and temperament in infancy. *Journal of Pediatrics, 84,* 756–758.

Carrol, J. L., & Louglin, G. M. (1995) Obstructive sleep apnea syndrome in infants and children: diagnosis and management. In R. Ferber & Kryger (Eds.), *Principles and practice of sleep medicine in the child* (pp. 193–216). Philadelphia: W. B. Saunders.

Carskadon, M. A., & Dement, W. C. (1982). The Multiple Sleep Latency Test: What does it measure? *Sleep, 5,* s67–s72.

Carskadon, M. A., & Dement, W. C. (1982). Sleepiness in the normal adolescent. In C. Guilleminault (Ed.), *Sleep and its disorders in children* (pp. 53–66). New York: Raven Press.

Carskadon, M. A., Viera, C., & Acebo, C. (1993). Association between puberty and delayed phase preference. *Sleep, 16,* 258–262.

Challamel, M. J., Mazzola, M. E., Nevsimalova, Cannard, C., Louis, J., & Revol, M. (1994). Narcolepsy in children. *Sleep, 17,* s17–s20.

Chavin, W., & Tinson, S. (1980). The developing child: Children with sleep difficulties. *Health Visitor, 53,* 477–480.

Czeisler, C. A., Richardson, G. S., Coleman, R. M., Zimmerman, J. C., Moore-Ede, M. C., Dement, W. C., & Weitzman, E. D., (1981). Chronotherapy: resetting the circadian clocks of patients with delayed sleep phase insomnia. *Sleep, 4,* 1–21.

Dahl, R. E. (1992). The pharmacologic treatment of sleep disorder. *Psychiatric Clinics of North America, 1,* 161–178.

Dahl, R. E. (1996). The regulation of sleep and arousal: development and psychopathology. *Development and Psychopathology, 8,* 3–27.

Dahl, R. E., & Carskadon, M. A. (1995). Sleep and its disorders in adolescence. In R. Ferber & M. Kryger (Eds.), *Principles and practice of sleep medicine in the child* (pp. 19–27). Philadelphia: W. B. Saunders.

Dahl, R. E., Pelham, W., & Wierson, M. (1991). The role of sleep disturbances in attention deficit disorder symptoms: a case study. *Journal of Pediatric Psychology, 16,* 229–239.

Dahlitz, M. J., Alvarez, B., Vignau, J., English, J., Arendt, J., & Parkes, J. D. (1991). Delayed sleep phase syndrome response to melatonin. *Lancet, 337,* 1121–1124.

Daws, D. (1989), *Through the night; Helping parents and sleepless infants,* London: Free Association Books.

Dement, W. C., Carskadon, M. A., & Ley, R. (1973). The prevalence of narcolepsy II. *Sleep Research, 2,* 147.

Diagnostic Classification Steering Committee (M. J. Thorpy, Chairman) (1990). *International classification of sleep disorders: diagnostic and coding manual* Rochester, MN: American Sleep Disorders Association.

Douglas, J., & Richman, N. (1984). *My child won't sleep.* Harmondsworth, UK: Penguin.

Driver, H. S., & Shapiro, C. M., (1993). ABC of sleep disorders: Parasomnias. *British Medical Journal, 306,* 921–924.

Durand, V. M., & Mindell, J. A. (1990). Behavioral treatment of multiple childhood sleep disorders. *Behavior Modification, 14,* 37–49.

Ferber, R. (1995). Sleeplessness in children. In R. Ferber & M. Kryger (Eds.), *Principles and practice of sleep medicine in the child* (pp. 79–89). Philadelphia: W. B. Saunders.

Ferber, R., & Boyle M. D. (1983). Delayed sleep phase syndrome versus motivated sleep phase delay in adolescents. *Sleep Research, 12,* 239.

Ferber, R., & Kryger, M. (Eds) (1995). *Principles and practice of sleep medicine in the child.* Philadelphia: W.B. Saunders.

Fisher, C., Kahn, E., Edwards, A., & Davis, D. M. (1973). The psychophysiological study of nightmares and night terrors. *Archives of General Psychiatry, 28,* 252–259.

France, K. G., & Hudson, S. M. (1990). Behavior management of infant sleep disturbance. *Journal of Applied Behavioral Analysis, 23,* 91–98.

France, K. G., Blampied, N. M., & Wilkinson, P. W. (1991). Treatment of infant sleep disturbance by trimeprazine in combination with extinction. *Developmental and Behavioral Pediatrics, 5,* 308–314.

Gass, E., & Strauch, I. (1984). The development of sleep behavior between 3 and 11 years. In *Proceedings of the 7th European Sleep Congress.* Munich.

Guedeney, A., & Kreisler, L. (1987). Sleep disorders in the first 18 months of life: Hypothesis on the role of mother–child emotional exchanges. *Infant Mental Health Journal, 8,* 307–318.

Guilleminault, C. (1987). Narcolepsy and its differential diagnosis. In C. Guilleminault (Ed.), *Sleep and its disorders in children* (pp. 181–193). New York: Raven Press.

Guilleminault, C. (1993). *Amphetamines and narcolepsy: use of the Stanford database.*

Guilleminault, C. (1994). *Narcolepsy syndrome.* In M. H. Kryger, T. Roth, & W. C. Dement (Eds.), *Principles and practice of sleep medicine* (2nd ed., pp. 549–561). Philadelphia: W. B. Saunders.

Guilleminault, C., McCann, C. C., Quera-Salva, M., & Cetel, M. (1993). Light therapy as treatment of dyschronosis in brain impaired children. *European Journal of Pediatrics, 152,* 754–759.

Hauri, P., & Olmstead, E. (1980). Childhood-onset insomnia. *Sleep, 3,* 59–65.

Jan, G. E., Espezel, H., & Appleton, R. E. (1994). The treatment of sleep disorders with melatonin. *Developmental Medicine and Child Neurology, 36,* 97–107.

Jenkins, S., Bax, M. & Hart, H. (1980). Behavior problems in preschool children. *Journal of Child Psychology and Psychiatry, 21,* 5–17.

Johnson, M. (1991). Infant and toddler sleep: A telephone survey of parents in one community. *Journal of Developmental and Behavioral Pediatrics, 12,* 108–114.

Jones, D. P. H., & Verduyn, C. M. (1983). Behavioural management of sleep problems. *Archives of Diseases in Childhood, 58,* 442–444.

Kahn, A., Mozin, M., Rebuffat, E., Sottiaux, M., & Muller, M. F. (1989). Milk intolerance in children with persistent sleeplessness: A prospective double-blind crossover evaluation. *Pediatrics, 84,* 595–603.

Kahn, A., Rebuffat, E., Sottiaux, M., Dufour, D., Cadranel, S., & Reiterer, F. (1991). Arousals induced by proximal esophageal reflux in infants. *Sleep, 14,* 39–42.

Kales A., Soldatos C. R., Bixler, E. O., Ladda, R. L., Charney, D. S., Weber, G., & Schweitzer, P. K., (1980a). Hereditary factors in sleep walking and night terrors. *British Journal of Psychiatry, 137,* 111–118.

Kales A., Soldatos C. R., Caldwell, A. B., Kales, J. D., Humphrey, F. J., Charney I. L., & Schweitzer, P. K. (1980b). Somnambulism: clinical characteristics and personality patterns. *Archives of General Psychiatry, 37,* 1406–1410.

Kales, A., Soldatos, C. R., & Kales, J. D. (1987). Sleep disorders: insomnia, sleepwalking, night terrors, nightmares, and enuresis. *Annals of Internal Medicine, 106,* 582–592.

Kateria, S., Swanson, M., & Trevarthin, G. (1987).

Persistence of sleep disturbances in preschool children. *Journal of Pediatrics, 110*, 642–646.

Kavey, N. B., Whyte, J., Resor, S., & Gidro-Frank, S. (1987). Classification and treatment of somnambulism. *Sleep Research, 16*, 368.

Keefauver, S. P., & Guilleminault, C. (1995). Sleep terrors and sleepwalking. In R. Ferber, M. H. Kryger, T. Roth, & W. C. Dement (Eds.), *Principles and practice of sleep medicine in the child* (pp. 567–573). Philadelphia: W. B. Saunders.

Kirmil-Gray, K., Eagleston, J. R., Gibson, E., & Thorensen, C. E. (1984). Sleep disturbances in adolescents: sleep quality, sleep habits, beliefs about sleep, and daytime functioning. *Journal of Youth and Adolescence, 13*, 375–384.

Klackenberg, G. (1987). Incidence of parasomnias in children in a general population. In C. Guilleminault (Ed.), *Sleep and its disorders in children* (pp. 99–113). New York: Raven Press.

Lack, L., & Wright, H. (1993). The effect of evening bright light in delaying the circadian rhythms and lengthening the sleep of early morning awakening insomniacs. *Sleep, 16*, 436–443.

Lahmeyer, H. W., & Lilie, J. K. (1987). Personality affects treatment outcome in phase delay sleep syndrome. *Sleep Research, 16*, 282.

Lamphere, J., Roehrs, T., & Wittig R., (1989). Recovery of alertness after CPAP in apnea, *Chest, 96*, 1364–1367.

Lapierre, O., & Dumont, M. (1995). Melatonin treatment of a non-24-hour sleep–wake cycle in a blind retarded child. *Biological Psychiatry, 38*, 119–122.

Lawrence, W. B., & Billiard, M. (1995). Narcolepsy, Kleine–Levin syndrome, and other causes of sleepiness in children. In R. Ferber & M. Kryger (Eds.), *Principles and practice of sleep medicine in the child* (pp. 125–134). Philadelphia: W. B. Saunders.

Lawton, C., France, K. G., & Blampied, N. M. (1991). Treatment of infant sleep disturbance by graduated extinction. *Child and Family Behavior Therapy, 13*, 39–56.

Lewy, A. J., Singer, C. M., & Sack, R. L. (1985). Treatment of appropriately phase typed sleep disorders using properly timed bright light. *Sleep Research, 14*, 304.

Lewy, A. J., & Newsome, D. A. (1983). Different types of melatonin circadian secretory rhythms in some blind subjects. *Journal of Clinical and Endocrinological Metabolism, 56*, 1103–1107.

Madge, P. J., Nisbet, L., McColl, J. H., Vallance, A., Paton, J. Y., & Beattie, J. O. (1995). Home nebuliser use in children with asthma in two Scottish Health Board Areas. *Scottish Medical Journal, 40*, 141–143.

Mahowald, M. W., & Rosen, G. M. (1990). Parasomnias in children. *Pediatrician, 17*, 21–31.

Marcus, C. L., Ward, S. L., Mallory, G. B., Rosen, C. L., Beckerman, R. C., Weese-Meyer, D. E., Brouillette, R. T., Trang, H. T., & Brooks, L. J. (1995). Use of continuous positive airway pressure as treatment of childhood constructive sleep apnea. *Journal of Pediatrics, 172*, 88–94.

Marks, P. A., & Monroe, J. L. (1976). Correlates of adolescent poor sleepers. *Journal of Abnormal Psychology, 85*, 243–246.

McDaniel, K. D. (1987). Pharmacologic treatment of psychiatric and neurodevelopmental disorders in children and adolescents: I, II, and III. *Annual Progress in Child Psychiatry and Child Development,* 462–493.

McFarlane, J. G., Cleghorn, J. M., Brown, G. M., & Streiner, D. L. (1991). The effects of exogenous melatonin on the total sleep time and daytime alertness of chronic insomniacs: a preliminary study. *Biological Psychiatry, 30*, 371–376.

McGarr, R. J., & Hovel, M. F. (1980). In search of the sandman: Shaping an infant to sleep. *Education and Treatment of Children, 3*, 173–182.

Messer, D. J., Lauder, L., & Humphery, S. (1994). The effectiveness of group therapy in treating children's sleeping problems. *Child: Care, Health and Development, 20*, 267–277.

Minde, K., Faucon, A., & Falkner, S. (1994), Sleep problems in toddlers: effects of treatment on their daytime behavior. *Journal of the American Academy of Child and Adolescent Psychiatry, 33*, 1114–1121.

Monk, T. H. (1994). Circadian rhythms in subjective activation, mood and performance efficiency. In M. H. Kryger, T. Roth, & W. C. Dement (Eds.), *Principles and practice of sleep medicine* (2nd ed., pp. 321–330). Philadelphia: W. B. Saunders.

Montangner, H., De Roquefeuil, G., & Djakovic, M. (1992). Biological, behavioral and intellectual activity rhythms of the child during its development in different education environments. In Y. Touitou & E. Haus (Eds.), *Biological rhythms in clinical and laboratory medicine* (pp. 214–229). Berlin: Springer-Verlag.

Moore, T., & Ucko, L. (1957). Night waking in early infancy, Part 1. *Archives of Disease in Childhood, 32*, 333–342.

Morin, C. M., Culbert, J. P., & Schwartz, M. (1994), Nonpharmacological interventions for insomnia: a meta-analysis of treatment efficacy. *American Journal of Psychiatry, 151*, 1172–1180.

Morrison, D. N., McGee, R., & Stanton, W. R. (1992). Sleep problems in adolescence. *Journal of the American Academy of Child and Adolescent Psychiatry, 31*, 94–99.

Mullington, J., & Broughton, R. (1993). Scheduled naps in the management of daytime sleepiness in narcolepsy-cataplexy. *Sleep, 16*, 444–456.

Navelet, Y. (1996). Insomnia in the child and adolescent. *Sleep, 19*, S23–S28.

Navelet, Y., Anders, T. F., & Guilleminault, C. (1976). Narcolepsy in children. In C. Guilleminault, W. Dement, & P. Passouant (Eds.), *Narcolepsy* (pp. 171–177). New York: Spectrum.

Nicholson A. N., (1994). Hypnotics: clinical pharmacology and therapeutics. In M. H. Kryger., T. Roth., & W. C. Dement (Eds.), *Principles and practice of sleep medicine* (2nd ed., pp 355–363). Philadelphia: Saunders.

Okawa, M., Nanami, T., Wada, S., Shimizu, T., Hishikawa, Y., Sasaki, H., Nagamine, H., & Takahashi, K. (1987). Four congenitally blind children with circadian sleep–wake rhythm disorder. *Sleep, 10*, 101–110.

Paret, I. (1983). Night waking and its relationship to mother-infant interaction in nine-month-old infants. In J. Call, E. Galenson, & R. Tyson (Eds.), *Frontiers of infant psychiatry* (pp. 171–177). New York: Basic Books.

Parkes, D. (1994). Introduction to the mechanism of action of different treatments of narcolepsy. *Sleep, 17*, s93–s966.

Pesikoff, R. D., & Davis, P. C. (1971), Treatment of pavor nocturnus and somnambulism in children. *American Journal of Psychiatry, 128*, 134–137.

Pinilla, T., & Birch, L. L. (1993). Help me make it through the night: behavioral entrainment of breast-fed infants' sleep pattern. *Pediatrics, 91*, 436–444.

Powell, N. B., Guilleminault C., & Riley R. W. (1994). Surgical therapy for obstructive sleep apnea. In M. H. Kryger, T. Roth, & W. C. Dement (Eds.), *Principles and practice of sleep medicine* (2nd ed., pp. 706–721). Philadelphia: W. B. Saunders.

Price, V. A., Coates, T. J., Thoresen, C. E., & Grindstead, O. A. (1978). Prevalence and correlates of poor sleep among adolescents. *American Journal of Disease in Children, 132*, 583–586.

Pritchard, A., & Appleton, P. (1988). Management of sleep problems in pre-school children. *Early Child Development and Care, 34*, 227–240.

Quine, L. (1992). Severity of sleep problems in children with severe learning difficulties: description and correlates. *Journal of Community & Applied Social Psychology, 2,* 247–268.

Regestein, Q. R., & Monk, T. H. (1995). Delayed sleep phase syndrome: a review of its clinical aspects. *American Journal of Psychiatry, 152,* 602–608.

Reid, P., & Lewis-Jones, M. S. (1995). Sleep difficulties and their management in preschoolers with atopic eczema.- *Clinical and Experimental Dermatology, 20,* 38–41.

Richman, N. (1981). A community survey of characteristics of one- to two-year-olds with sleep disruptions. *Journal of the American Academy of Child Psychiatry, 20,* 281–291.

Richman, N. (1986). Recent progress in understanding and treating sleep disorders. *Advances in Developmental and Behavioral Pediatrics, 7,* 45–63.

Richman, N., Douglas, J., Hunt, H., Landsdown, R., & Levere, R (1985). Behavioral methods in the treatment of sleep disorders—a pilot study. *Journal of Child Psychology and Psychiatry, 26,* 581–590.

Richman, N., Stevenson, J., & Graham, P. (1982). *Preschool to school: A behavioral study.* London: Academic Press.

Rickert, V. I., & Johnson, C. M. (1988). Reducing nocturnal awakening and crying episodes in infants and young children: A comparison between scheduled awakening and systematic ignoring. *Pediatrics, 81,* 203–212.

Roberts, S. (1993). Tackling sleep problems through clinically-based approaches. *Health Visitor, 66,* 173–174.

Roehrs, T., Zorick, F., Witting, R., Paxton, C., Sicklesteel, J., & Roth, T. (1986). Alerting effects of naps in patients with narcolepsy. *Sleep, 9,* 194–199.

Rogers, A. E., & Aldrich, M. (1993). The effects of regularly scheduled naps on sleep attacks and excessive daytime sleepiness associated with narcolepsy. *Nursing Research, 42,* 111–117.

Rosen, G., Mahowald, M. W., & Ferber, R. (1995). Sleepwalking, confusional arousals, and sleep terrors in the child. In R. Ferber & M. Kryger (Eds.), *Principles and practice of sleep medicine in the child* (pp. 99–106). Philadelphia: W. B. Saunders.

Russo, R. M., Vymut, J., & Gurauraj-Allen, J. E. A. (1976). The effectiveness of diphenhydramine HCl in pediatric sleep disorders. *The Journal of Clinical Pharmacology, 16,* 284–288.

Sadeh, A. (1994). Assessment of intervention for infant night waking: parental reports and activity-based home monitoring. *Journal of Consulting and Clinical Psychology, 62,* 63–98.

Sadeh, A. (1996). Stress, trauma and sleep in children. *Child and Adolescent Psychiatric Clinics of North America, 5,* 685–700.

Sadeh, A. (1996). Evaluating night-wakings in sleep-disturbed infants: Methodological study of parental reports and actigraphy. *Sleep, 19,* 757–762.

Sadeh, A., & Anders, T. F. (1993). Infant sleep problems: origins, assessment, intervention. *Infant Mental Health Journal, 14,* 17–34.

Sadeh, A., Dark, I., & Vohr, B. R. (1996). Newborns' sleep–wake patterns: The role of maternal, delivery and infant factors. *Early Human Development, 44,* 113–126.

Sadeh, A., Hauri, P., Kripke, D., & Lavie, P. (1995a). The role of actigraphy in sleep medicine. *Sleep, 18,* 288–302.

Sadeh, A., Hayden, R. M., McGuire, J., Sachs, H., & Civita, R. (1994). Somatic, cognitive and emotional characteristics of abused children in a psychiatric hospital. *Child Psychiatry and Human Development, 24,* 191–200.

Sadeh, A., Klitzke, M., Anders, T. F., & Acebo, C. (1995b). Sleep and aggressive behavior in a blind retarded adolescent: A concomitant schedule disorder? *Journal of the American Academy of Child and Adolescent Psychiatry, 34,* 820–824.

Sadeh, A., Lavie, P., & Scher, A. (1994). Maternal perceptions of temperament of sleep-disturbed toddlers. *Early Education and Development, 5,* 311–322.

Sadeh, A., Lavie, P., Scher, A., Tirosh, E., & Epstein, R. (1991). Actigraphic home monitoring of sleep-disturbed and control infants and young children: A new method for pediatric assessment of sleep–wake patterns. *Pediatrics, 87,* 494–499.

Sadeh, A., McGuire, J. P. D., Sachs, H., Seifer, R., Trembley, A., Civita, R., Hayden, R. M. (1995c). Sleep and psychological characteristics of children on a psychiatric inpatient unit. *Journal of the American Academy of Child and Adolescent Psychiatry, 34,* 813–819.

Salzarulo, P., & Chevalier, A. (1983). Sleep problems in children and their relationships with early disturbances of the waking–sleeping rhythms. *Sleep, 6,* 47–51.

Scher, A., Tirosh, E., Jaffe, M., Rubin, L., Sadeh, A., & Lavie, P. (1995). Sleep patterns of infants and young children in Israel. *International Journal of Behavioral Development, 18,* 701–711.

Scott, G., & Richards, M. (1990). Night waking in infants: Effects of providing advice and support for parents. *Journal of Child Psychology and Psychiatry, 31,* 551–567.

Scumacher, A., Merritt, S., & Cohen, F. L. (1993). The relationship between symptom severity and drug effectiveness as perceived by persons with narcolepsy. *Sleep Research, 22,* 263.

Seifer, R., Sameroff, A. J., Dickstein, S., Hayden, L. C., & Schiller, M. (1996). Parental psychopathology and sleep variation in children. *Child and Adolescent Psychiatric Clinics of North America, 5,* 715–727.

Seymour, F. W. (1987). Sleep problems in young children. *New Zealand Medical Journal, 100,* 347–349.

Seymour, F. W., Brock, P., During, M., & Pole, G. (1989), Reducing sleep disruptions in young children: evaluation of therapist-guided and written information approaches: a brief report. *Journal of Child Psychiatry, 30,* 913–918.

Sforza, E., & Lugaresi, E. (1995). Daytime sleepiness and nasal continuous positive airway pressure therapy in obstructive sleep apnea syndrome patients: effects of chronic treatment and 1-night therapy withdrawal. *Sleep, 18,* 195–201.

Sheldon, H. S., Spire, J. P., & Levy, H. B. (1992). *Pediatrics sleep medicine.* Philadelphia: W. B. Saunders.

Simonoff, E. A., & Stores, G., (1987). Controlled trial of trimeprazine tartrate for night waking. *Archives of Disease in Childhood, 62,* 253–257.

Stores, G. (1990). Sleep disorders in children. *British Medical Journal, 301,* 351–352.

Strachan, D. P., Anderson, H. R., Limb, E. S., O'Neill, A., & Wells, N. (1994). A national survey of asthma prevalence, severity, and treatment in Great Britain. *Archives of Diseases in Childhood, 70,* 174–178.

Stradling, J. R., Thomas, G., Warely, A. R. H., Williams, P., & Feeland, A. (1990). Effect of tonsillectomy on nocturnal hypoxaemia, sleep disturbance, and symptoms in snoring children. *Lancet, 335,* 249–253.

Strollo, P. J., & Rogers, R. M. (1996). Current concepts: obstructive sleep apnea. *The New England Journal of Medicine, 11,* 99–104.

Sullivan, C. E., & Grunstein, R. (1994). Continuous positive airway pressure in sleep disordered breathing. In M. H. Kryger, T. Roth & W. C. Dement (Eds.), *Principles and practice of sleep medicine* (2nd ed., pp. 694–705). Philadelphia: Saunders.

Terr, L. C. (1987). Nightmares in children. In C. Guilleminault (Ed.), *Sleep and its disorders in children* (pp. 231–242). New York: Raven Press.

Thoman, E. B. (1975). Sleep and wake behaviors in the

neonates: consistencies and consequences. *Merrill-Palmer Quarterly, 21,* 295–314.

Thoman E. B. & Whitney, M. P. (1989). Sleep states in infants monitored at home: Individual differences, development trends and origins of diurnal activity. *Infant Behavior and Development, 12,* 59–75

Thorpy, M. J., Korman, E., Spielman, A. J., & Glovinsky, P. B. (1988). Delayed sleep phase syndrome in adolescents. *Journal of Adolescents Health Care, 9,* 222–227.

Tirosh, E., Sadeh, A., Munvez, R., & Lavie, P. (1993). Effects of Methylphenidate on sleep in children with attention-deficit hyperactivity disorder. *American Journal of Diseases of Childhood, 147,* 1313–1315.

Tzischinsky, O., Skene, D., Epstein, R., & Lavie, P. (1991). Circadian rhythms in 6-sulfatoxymelatonin and nocturnal sleep in blind children. *Chronobiology International, 8,* 168–175.

Van Tassel, E. B. (1985). The relative influence of child and environmental characteristics on sleep disturbances in the first and second years of life. *Developmental and Behavioral Pediatrics, 6,* 81–86.

Weissbluth, M. (1982). Modification of sleep schedule with reduction of night waking: A case report. *Sleep, 5,* 262–266.

Weitzman, E. D., Czeisler, C. A., Coleman, R. M., Spielman, A. J., Zimmerman, J. C., & Dement, W. C. (1981). Delayed sleep phase syndrome, a chronobiological disorder with sleep-onset insomnia. *Archives of General Psychiatry, 38,* 737–746.

World Health Organization (1992). *International statistical classification of diseases and related health problems (ICD-10)* (10th ed.). Geneva, Switzerland: Author.

Wolfson, A., Lacks, P., & Futterman, A. (1992). Effects of parent training on infant sleeping patterns, parents' stress, and perceived parental competence. *Journal of Consulting and Clinical Psychology, 60,* 41–48.

Werry J. S., & Carlielle, J., (1983). The nuclear family, suburban neurosis, and iatrogenesis in Aukland mothers of young children. *Journal of the American Academy of Child Psychiatry, 22,* 172–179.

Yoss, R., & Daly, D. (1960). Narcolepsy in children. *Pediatrics, 25,* 1025–1033.

Zarcone, V. (1973). Narcolepsy. *New England Journal of Medicine, 188,* 156–166.

Zuckerman, B., Stevenson, J., & Baily, V. (1987). Sleep problems in early childhood: Predictive factors and behavioral correlates. *Pediatrics, 80,* 664–671.

5.25
Somatoform Disorders in Childhood and Adolescence

JUDY GARBER

Vanderbilt University, Nashville, TN, USA

Somatoform Disorders in Childhood and Adolescence

5.25.1 INTRODUCTION

Medically unexplained somatic symptoms are a common problem in adults and there is increasing evidence that these physical symptoms begin during childhood and adolescence (Kellner, 1986; Pilowsky, Bassett, Begg, & Thomas, 1982). Excessive somatic complaints and associated illness behavior can lead to serious developmental problems when accompanied by school absences, academic failure, and withdrawal from normal social activities. Moreover, the search for diagnoses and cures of these persistent physical complaints can place children at risk of unnecessary medical tests and treatments, which can be very expensive for the family, medical profession, and society. During this time of increasing attention to the cost of health care, there is a growing concern about the expenditure of both human and economic resources to deal with pediatric somatization. Several reviews of somatization in children (Campo & Fritsch, 1994; Campo & Garber, in press; Garralda, 1992, 1996; Nemzer, 1996) have highlighted the importance of this area to researchers and clinicians in both the psychiatric and medical communities. This chapter builds on these earlier reviews and further synthesizes the literature on somatoform disorders in children and adolescents.

5.25.2 HISTORY OF SOMATOFORM DISORDERS

The term *somat* is derived from the Greek word meaning body. As early as ancient Greece, the clinical entity of conversion symptoms was recognized. The word hysteria referred to physical symptoms that could not be explained medically. In the past, hysteria was thought to be a disorder in women due to abnormal movement of the uterus, and the term "somatization" was used to describe the belief that some neuroses could be manifested as bodily disorders (Steckel, 1943). Steckel defined somatization as a bodily disorder that arises as the expression of a deep-seated neurosis, "especially as a disease of the conscious" (p. 580). More recently, Lipowski (1988) defined somatization as "a tendency to experience and communicate somatic distress and symptoms unaccounted for by pathological findings, to attribute them to physical illness, and to seek medical help for them" (p. 1359).

Briquet (1859) was one of the first in modern times to observe a condition in which patients complained of multiple chronic, unexplainable physical symptoms. He also was one of the first to describe scientifically the syndrome of "hysteria." In the later 1800s, several physicians including Charcot, Bernheim, and Janet began treating hysterical symptoms with hypnosis. Freud (1896/1962) proposed that painful memories and affect from a traumatic event, typically of a sexual nature, can be "dissociated" from conscious awareness and then "converted" into somatic symptoms that symbolize an aspect of the trauma. Such dissociation and conversion were hypothesized to be the processes underlying hysterical symptoms.

Psychoanalytic theory changed the term hysteria to conversion hysteria, and in 1952 the *Diagnostic and statistical manual* (*DSM-I*) (American Psychiatric Association (APA), 1952) modified the term conversion hysteria to conversion reaction. Dissociative reaction referred to the mental manifestations of hysteria including amnesia, fugue states, and multiple personality. In 1968, *DSM-II* (APA, 1968) relabeled the categories to be "hysterical neurosis, conversion type" and "hysterical neurosis, dissociative type." *DSM-II* also created a category for the chronic multisystem somatoform disorder, and referred to it as "Briquet's syndrome." Separate categories were designated for "conversion disorder" and "dissociative disorder" and only parenthetically retained the term "hysterical neurosis" in *DSM-III* (APA, 1978) and *DSM-III-R* (APA, 1987). Some have questioned, however, whether conversion and dissociative disorders should be categorized separately because it is not unusual for both to occur in the same individual, and both disorders are characterized by psychological dissociation (Nemiah, 1985). *DSM-III* expanded the number of diagnoses under the rubric of somatoform disorders to include Body Dysmorphic Disorder, Hypochondriasis, and Somatoform Pain Disorder in addition to Conversion Disorder and Somatization.

Some of the specific criteria defining the various Somatoform Disorders have changed in *DSM-IV*. For example, whereas in *DSM-III* and *DSM-III-R* Conversion Disorder was broader and included autonomic symptoms (e.g., vomiting, endocrine dysfunction), *DSM-IV* has returned to a narrower set of criteria involving neurological symptoms. Autonomic symptoms that used to be part of the Conversion Disorder criteria in *DSM-III* now fall under the category of "undifferentiated somatoform disorder" or "somatoform disorder not otherwise specified." The separation of autonomic and sensory-motor symptoms in the criteria for defining conversion disorders has been questioned, particularly with regard to children in whom conversion-like disorders are particularly likely to be characterized by a mixture of motor, sensory, and autonomic symptoms (Looff, 1970).

The symptoms defining Somatization Disorder also have undergone several changes. In *DSM-III-R* any 13 symptoms from a list of 35 were required for the diagnosis. In *DSM-IV* a certain number of symptoms are required from each of the four physiological categories. This is more similar to the criteria outlined in *DSM-III*, which required a certain number of symptoms from each of six categories.

Thus, the specific names of the diagnoses that comprise somatoform disorders as well as the criteria that define them have undergone several changes with each new version of the *DSM*. This chapter focuses on somatoform disorders as defined by *DSM-III-R* and *DSM-IV*.

5.25.3 PHENOMENOLOGY

According to the fourth edition of the *Diagnostic and statistical manual of mental disorders* (*DSM-IV*; APA, 1994), "the common feature of Somatoform Disorders is the presence of physical symptoms that suggest a general medical condition ... and are not fully explained by a general medical condition, by the direct effects of a substance, or by another mental disorder" (p. 445). To receive a diagnosis of a somatoform disorder, the symptoms must cause clinically significant distress or impairment in social, occupational (academic), or other areas of functioning. Marital discord and diminished work performance are common. The group of conditions categorized as Somatoform Disorders do not necessarily share a common etiology or mechanism. Rather, they are classified together due to the clinical utility of needing to exclude medical conditions or substances as the cause of the bodily symptoms that comprise the disorders. Although each of the seven diagnoses included under the rubric of somatoform disorders has its own unique set of symptoms and criteria, they share several characteristics in common. Associated features often include depression, anxiety, suicidality, and impulsivity. It is not unusual for substance abuse to develop as a result of medications taken to alleviate the physical discomfort of the medical symptoms. Personality disorders, particularly histrionic, dependent, borderline, and antisocial are not uncommon. There also may be significant academic/occupational and social impairment due to frequent school or work absences and lack of involvement in normal social or extracurricular activities.

The course of somatoform disorders tends to be chronic with exacerbations of symptoms waxing and waning. Prognosis tends to be best when onset is acute, not complicated by personality disorders, associated with an identifiable stressor, and there is an absence of secondary gain as a result of symptom complaining (*DSM-IV;* APA, 1994).

Individuals with somatoform disorders typically take on the "sick role" and engage in illness behavior. Illness behavior is the manner in which individuals perceive and respond to somatic sensations that may or may not signify disease (Mechanic, 1972). Whereas most people pay little attention to such sensations, persons with somatoform disorders tend to interpret even normal sensations as indicating disease, and they respond by excessive complaining of symptoms, seeking medical treatment, and limiting their activities so that it interferes with their occupational/academic or social functioning.

"Exaggerated," "abnormal," or "medically unexplained" illness behavior has been examined extensively in adults (e.g., Pilowsky, 1987; Reesor & Craig, 1988) and is a problem not only for the individual who suffers from distress and impaired functioning, but also for society, which bears the costs associated with lost work days and overutilization of health services. Approximately 50% of physician visits are for complaints for which medical evaluation yields no evidence of disease (Barsky, Wyshak, & Klerman, 1986). Because individuals with somatoform disorders maintain the belief that there is something physically wrong with them, they often undergo many painful, expensive, and unnecessary medical tests and procedures in search of the presumed disease. They are generally not reassured by negative findings and therefore seek out multiple physicians ("doctor shop"), looking for one who will provide them with a medical explanation for their symptoms. They tend to be resistant to suggestions that their symptoms might be associated with psychosocial factors and they often ignore referrals to mental health professionals.

Despite speculation that symptoms of somatoform disorders and associated illness behavior begin in childhood, little is known about childhood forms and precursors of these diagnoses (Parmelee, 1986). Because children typically do not take themselves to the doctor, children with somatoform disorders must first convince their parents of the need to seek medical treatment. It also is not unusual for parents to share the belief that the child's symptoms require medical attention, thereby reinforcing or actually helping to generate the illness behaviors and beliefs in the child.

5.25.4 DIAGNOSTIC FEATURES

In *DSM-IV* (pp. 445–469), the Somatoform Disorders comprise seven distinct diagnoses: Somatization Disorder, Undifferentiated Somatoform Disorder, Conversion Disorder, Pain Disorder, Hypochondriasis, Body Dysmorphic Disorder, and Somatoform Disorder Not Otherwise Specified. Table 1 presents the *ICD-10* disorders that correspond to the somatoform disorders in *DSM-IV*. The criteria that define each of the *DSM-IV* somatoform disorders are the same for children, adolescents, and adults. These criteria are described briefly below.

5.25.4.1 Somatization Disorder

Somatization Disorder is characterized by a pattern of recurrent, multiple somatic complaints that cannot be explained fully by any known general medical condition or the direct effects of a substance. If a medical condition is present, the symptoms or associated dysfunction are in excess of what would be expected given the history or medical findings. The physical complaints must have begun before the age of 30 and have occurred over several years. Somatization disorder rarely is diagnosed in children; it is not uncommon, however, for symptoms to begin in adolescence with menstrual difficulties being one of the earliest symptoms in women. For a diagnosis of somatization disorder, a history of a certain number of symptoms are required in each of four areas: pain, gastrointestinal, sexual/reproductive, and pseudoneurological.

5.25.4.2 Undifferentiated Somatoform Disorder

Undifferentiated Somatoform Disorder is very similar to somatization disorder but fewer symptoms are required. It is defined by one or more medically unexplained, distressing, or impairing somatic complaints that persist for at least six months. Chronic fatigue or weakness of unknown medical origin, sometimes referred to as "Neurasthenia," would be given this diagnosis. Because a shorter duration and fewer symptoms are required, this may be a more appropriate diagnosis for children than somatization disorder.

5.25.4.3 Conversion Disorder

Conversion Disorder involves symptoms or deficits in voluntary motor or sensory functions that suggest a neurological or general medical condition. Conversion symptoms are referred to as "pseudoneurological" and include such problems as paralysis, blindness, and seizures. Because the onset or exacerbation of the symptom or deficit is preceded by conflict or other stressors, conversion disorder is believed to be associated with psychological factors.

5.25.4.4 Pain Disorder

Pain disorder is defined specifically by pain, which causes significant distress or impairment, and is of sufficient severity to warrant clinical attention. According to *DSM-IV*, two types of pain disorder can be identified: Pain Disorder Associated with Psychological Factors, and Pain Disorder Associated with Both Psycholo-

Table 1 Somatoform disorders in *DSM-IV* and *ICD-10*.

DSM-IV somatoform disorders		*ICD-10 somatoform disorders*	
300.81	Somatization disorder	F45.0	Somatization disorder
300.81	Undifferentiated somatoform disorder	F45.1	Undifferentiated somatoform disorder
300.81	Somatoform disorder not otherwise specified	F45.9	Other somatoform disorder
300.11	Conversion disorder	F44	Dissociative (conversion)
		F44.4–44.7	Dissociative disorder of movement and sensation
307.80	Pain disorder associated with psychological factors	F45.4	Persistent somatoform pain disorder
307.89	Pain disorder associated with psychological factors and a general medical condition		
307.7	Hypochondriasis	F45.2	Hypochondriacal disorder
300.7	Body dysmorphic		
		F45.3	Somatoform autonomic dysfunction
		F48	Other neurotic disorders
		F48.0	Neurasthenia

gical Factors and a General Medical Condition. In both subtypes, psychological factors are judged to play an important role in the onset, maintenance, and severity of the disorder. The primary difference is that in the latter diagnosis, both psychological factors and medical factors contribute to the onset and exacerbation of the pain. Several recurrent pain conditions in children would receive this diagnosis (e.g., recurrent abdominal pain, headaches, chest pain).

5.25.4.5 Hypochondriasis

In Hypochondriasis, the individual is preoccupied with fears of having or the belief of already having a serious disease despite medical reassurance to the contrary. The person misinterprets one or more bodily signs or symptoms such as heartburn, shortness of breath, or a minor cough as being indicative of a serious illness. The level of concern is not delusional, however, and the person can acknowledge that the fears may be unwarranted.

5.25.4.6 Body Dysmorphic Disorder

Body Dysmorphic Disorder is the preoccupation with some imagined or slight physical defect in appearance, particularly about flaws of the face or head (e.g., hair, nose, skin, eyes). Individuals often have difficulty controlling their preoccupation with the supposed deformity and may spend hours a day thinking about their "defect." In this respect, Body Dysmorphic Disorder (dysmorphophobia) is similar to obsessive-compulsive disorder (Phillips, McElroy, Keck, Pope, & Hudson, 1993).

5.25.4.7 Somatoform Disorder Not Otherwise Specified

Somatoform Disorder Not Otherwise Specified includes those cases with significant somatoform symptoms that do not meet all of the criteria for one of the somatoform disorders. Examples are when symptoms have been of shorter than the necessary duration (e.g., hypochondriacal symptoms for less than six months) or when the extent of functional impairment is less than clinically significant.

Table 2 summarizes information from *DSM-IV* concerning other characteristics of the five main somatoform disorders including age of onset, sex differences, cultural influences, prevalence, course, and associated features.

5.25.5 DIFFERENTIAL DIAGNOSIS

An important feature of somatoform disorders is that the symptoms are not produced

voluntarily. This is in contrast to Factitious Disorder and Malingering, in which somatic symptoms are intentional and controllable. In the case of Factitious Disorder, symptoms are feigned in order to assume the sick role, whereas in Malingering symptoms are produced for some external incentive such as financial gain or avoidance of responsibilities. Factitious Disorder by proxy refers to situations in which a parent or caretaker produces, feigns, or stimulates disease in a child, with the incentive appearing to be an internal one for the caretaker.

Somatoform disorders also need to be distinguished from Psychological Factors Affecting Physical Conditions (PFAPC). In PFAPC there is a general medical condition that completely accounts for the physical symptoms but that is adversely affected by specific psychological or behavioral factors. These psychological factors tend to negatively influence the course or treatment of the medical condition. A common example of this is when the patient is noncompliant with a treatment regime (e.g., taking insulin for diabetes) due to emotional or behavioral problems.

5.25.6 COMORBIDITY

Comorbidity is defined as the co-occurrence of two or more disorders in the same individual at the same point in time. It is quite common for individuals with somatoform disorders to have other psychiatric problems and diagnoses including anxiety, depression, suicidality, impulsivity, substance abuse, and personality disorders. In an epidemiological study of psychiatric disorders in adults, Swartz, Landerman, and George (1991) reported that all persons with somatization disorder received another diagnosis, most commonly affective disorder, panic disorder, or simple phobia. In a community sample of adolescents, Taylor, Szatmari, Boyle, and Offord (1996) reported that about 42% of the youth who self-reported high rates of somatic complaints had at least one psychiatric diagnosis, most commonly an emotional disorder.

Several studies have found high rates of anxiety and mood symptoms and disorders among children with recurrent abdominal pain (RAP) (Garber, Zeman, & Walker, 1990; Hodges, Kline, Barbero, & Flanery, 1985a; Hodges, Kline, Barbero, & Woodruff, 1985b; Walker, Garber, & Greene, 1993; Wasserman, Whitington, & Rivera, 1988). Garber et al. (1990) conducted careful psychiatric interviews of children with RAP and found that 11 of 13 had an anxiety disorder and five of 13 had a

Table 2 Somatoform disorders (DSM-IV).

Disorder	Somatization	Conversion	Pain	Hypochondriasis	Body dysmorphic
Age	Onset must begin before age 30 Symptoms typically begin by adolescence Rarely diagnosed before puberty	Onset usually in late childhood to early adulthood Onset rarely before age 10 year or after age 35 years In children under 10 years old; gait problems or seizures are most common	Can occur at any age	It can begin at any age, most commonly during early adulthood	Usually begins during adolescence
Gender	More common in women in US Higher rates in men in some cultures (e.g., Greece, Puerto Rico) Sex ratio varies across cultures	More common in females than males (2:1 to 10:1) In women, conversion symptoms may develop into somatization disorder In men, associated with antisocial personality	Both males and females experience pain disorders Women experience more headaches than men Adolescent girls report more abdominal pain than boys	Equally common in males and females	About equal in males and females
Culture	Content of complaints varies with cultures	More common in lower SES, less educated, developing countries Specific symptoms reflect local cultural ideas	Expressions of and responses to pain varies across cultures	Must consider cultural definitions of illness and what "healers" in their culture tell them about their illness	Culture can influence the extent of emphasis on appearance
Prevalence	0.2–2% in women 0.2% in men	1–3% of adult outpatients Ranges from 11/100 000 to 300/100 000	Relatively common about 10–15% of adults have significant back pain About 10–15% of school children have abdominal pain	4–9% of patients in general medical practices	Little is known about its prevalence May be more common than previously thought

Table 2 (continued)

Disorder	Somatization	Conversion	Pain	Hypochondriasis	Body dysmorphic
Course	Chronic, but fluctuating Rarely remits	Onset is generally acute, but may have gradually increasing symptoms Episodes of acute symptoms are brief, but recurrent	Acute pain episodes tend to resolve after a brief duration Chronic pain can persist for years	Usually a chronic course, although symptoms may wax and wane	Onset may be gradual or abrupt Chronic course
Associated features	Functional disorders (e.g., irritable bowel syndrome)	*La belle indifference* Dissociation	With: psychological factors and/or general medical conditions Insomnia	May become homebound May have poor insight about excessiveness of complaints	Excessive grooming behavior and "mirror checking" Seek plastic surgery "Ideas of reference" about the presumed defect Eating disorders

mood disorder. Similarly, Wasserman et al. (1988) reported that 26 of 31 RAP patients had psychiatric disorders, with anxiety being the most common. Walker et al. (1993) reported that children with RAP had significantly higher levels of emotional symptoms than healthy controls, but less than children being evaluated in a psychiatric clinic specifically for emotional problems. Thus, children with RAP clearly have comorbid emotional problems, although their symptoms tend to be less severe than found among children receiving psychiatric treatment for anxiety and depression.

In their review, Bass and Murphy (1995) concluded that somatoform disorders are associated with very high rates of personality disorders and that the illness behavior of persons with somatoform disorders is "a life-style in which the sick role is a model of relating to self and others" (p. 424). They argued, therefore, that it might make more sense to think of the somatoform disorders as Axis II personality disorders rather than as Axis I disorders with comorbid personality disorders.

5.25.7 PREVALENCE

Epidemiological studies indicate that somatization disorder occurs in only 0.05–0.38% of the adult population (Swartz et al., 1991). The diagnosis of somatoform disorders is extremely rare in prepubertal children (Offord et al., 1987), although it has been diagnosed among adolescents. In a study of the six-month prevalence of child psychiatric disorders in a community sample, Offord et al. reported that somatization disorder was so rare among children 4–11-years old ($n = 1442$) that prevalence estimates for that age group could not be obtained reliably. Among adolescents aged 12–16 years, polysymptomatic somatization disorder was identified in 4.5% of boys ($n = 608$) and 10.7% of girls ($n = 624$). Thus, somatization disorder appears to increase with age and is about twice as common in adolescent girls as boys.

Other studies examining prevalence of child psychiatric disorders in pediatric (Costello et al., 1988) and community samples (Bird et al., 1988), however, have failed to report the rates of any of the somatoform disorders. This might be because somatoform disorders are considered to be so rare during childhood that researchers have decided that it was not worth the extra time to interview everyone about these syndromes. In addition, because information about actual medical status is needed to make the diagnoses, it is difficult to obtain this in large epidemiological studies. It is likely that it is for these reasons that somatoform disorders

have been excluded from the various versions of the most frequently used interview in epidemiological studies (i.e., the Diagnostic Interview Schedule for Children, DISC; Costello; Edelbrock, Kalas, Kessler, & Klaric; 1982; Shaffer et al., 1996). Questions about somatoform disorders were not included in either the completed National Institute of Mental Health (NIMH)-funded Methods for the Epidemiology of Child and Adolescent Mental Disorders (MECA) study (Lahey et al., 1996) or the planned NIMH-funded Multi-Site Study of Mental Health Service Use, Need, Outcomes, and Costs in Child and Adolescent Populations (UNOCCAP) study. Therefore, the lifetime incidence and one-year prevalence rates of any of the Somatoform Disorders will remain unknown. A separate study in which both medical and psychiatric symptoms can be assessed in a large epidemiological sample is needed to determine more precisely the incidence and prevalence of somatoform disorders in children and adolescents.

Some children meeting the diagnostic criteria for somatization disorder have been identified in clinical samples (Kriechman, 1987; Livingston & Martin-Connici, 1985), but this is quite unusual. Several investigators have suggested that the *DSM* criteria are inappropriate for children, particularly given the fact that sexual and reproductive symptoms are required (Garber, Walker, & Zeman, 1991; Livingston & Martin-Connici, 1985). Other diagnoses such as undifferentiated somatoform disorder or pain disorder are probably more applicable to children.

In contrast to the finding that diagnosed somatoform disorders are rare in childhood, physical complaints have been shown to be quite common in children and adolescents (Garber et al., 1991; Goodman & McGrath, 1991). In a sample of 540 children in grades three through 12, Garber et al. assessed how frequently children had had each of 36 physical complaints in the preceding two weeks. About half the sample indicated on the Children's Somatization Inventory (CSI; Walker, Garber, & Greene, 1991; Walker & Greene, 1989, 1991a) at least one physical symptom during the prior two weeks; the most commonly reported symptoms were headaches, low energy, sore muscles, and abdominal discomfort. Factor analysis of the CSI revealed four symptom clusters that corresponded to four of the categories that defined somatization disorder in *DSM-III-R*: cardiovascular, gastrointestinal, pain/weakness, and pseudoneurological. About 1% of the sample endorsed at least 13 symptoms, and approximately 15% reported four or more symptoms. This was an important study because it provided information about the rates of self-reported somatic complaints across a wide age range. However, it is limited because independent medical assessments were not conducted to determine whether the reported physical symptoms were the result of actual disease. Thus, the rates of medically unexplained symptoms in children might be lower than that reported in this study.

Taylor et al. (1996) similarly conducted a community study with over 1000 Canadian adolescents (aged 12–16 years) and found the rates of some somatic symptoms and concerns to be quite high. About 50% (44.3–54.4%) of these teens reported that "their health should be better," headaches, worries about health, stomach aches or cramps, and aches and pains. Loss of functions (e.g., ability to swallow, voice, consciousness, hearing, sight) were reported much less frequently (2.9–7.5%). Although the rates of some individual symptoms were high, there did not appear to be a group of teens with extreme scores who might meet the criteria for somatization disorder. The average number of symptoms for those youth who had visited any medical service in the previous six months was 4.9, which is far below the 13 required for a diagnosis of somatization disorder.

Several other studies have found relatively high rates of somatic symptoms and concerns in children. The most common symptom is headaches, which has been reported in 10–30% of children and adolescents (Aro, Paronen, & Aro, 1987; Belmaker, Espinoza, & Pogrund, 1985; Larson, 1991; Oster, 1972; Rutter, Tizard, & Whitmore, 1970). Recurrent abdominal pain also is very common, reported in 10–24% of school-aged children and adolescents (Apley, 1975; Apley & Naish, 1958; Belmaker et al., 1985; Garber et al., 1991; Hyams, Burke, Davis, Rzepski, & Andrulonis, 1996). Other common somatic symptoms in children and adolescents are limb pains or so-called "growing pains" found in 5–20% of children (Apley, 1958; Belmaker et al., 1985; Garber et al., 1991; Larson, 1991; Oster, 1972), chest pain in about 7–15% (Belmaker et al.; Garber et al.), daily fatigue in about 15%, and 33.3–50% of adolescents complaining of fatigue weekly (Belmaker et al.; Larson, 1991), dizziness in about 15% of children (Garber et al.; Larson, 1991), and other gastrointestinal symptoms such as nausea and vomiting (Apley, 1975; Garber et al.; Larson, 1991). Worries about health also are common in children. Orr (1986) found that 40% of children and adolescents endorsed worrying about their health often, and 20% indicated they worried "all the time" about their health.

Pseudoneurological symptoms tend to be reported much less frequently (Garber et al., 1991; Rutter et al., 1970; Stefansson, Messina, & Meyerowitz, 1976). The most commonly reported conversion or pseudoneurological symptoms in children and adolescents are pseudoseizures, fainting, gait abnormalities, and sensory symptoms (Goodyer, 1981; Goodyer & Mitchell, 1989; Grattan-Smith, Fairley, & Procopis, 1988; Lehmkuhl, Blanz, Lehmkuhl, & Braun-Scharm, 1989; Leslie, 1988; Maloney, 1980; Spierings, Poels, Sijben, Gabreels, & Renier, 1990; Steinhausen, Aster, Pfeiffer, & Gobel, 1989; Volkmar, Poll, & Lewis; 1984).

5.25.7.1 Age Effects

Somatoform disorders are rarely diagnosed before puberty, although specific somatic complaints are not uncommon during childhood. For example, the rate of recurrent abdominal pain peaks at about age nine and the rate of headaches peaks about age 12 (Oster, 1972), and even preschoolers have been reported to have somatic symptoms (e.g., stomach aches, vomiting) associated with psychological distress (Prugh, 1983). Pseudoneurological symptoms and diagnosed conversion disorder are extremely rare before age six, but increase with age particularly during adolescence (e.g., Lehmkuhl et al., 1989; Stefansson et al., 1976; Volkmar et al., 1984). Similarly, polysymptomatic complaints become increasingly more common during adolescence (Achenbach, Conners, Quay, Verhulst, & Howell, 1989; Offord et al., 1987). Although all the criteria for somatization disorder are rarely met in childhood, the majority (55%) of adults receiving a diagnosis of somatization disorder report experiencing their first somatic symptoms before age 15, and their symptoms tended not to remit (Swartz et al., 1991). Thus, not all symptoms that comprise somatoform disorders may be present across development, although it is likely that some symptoms and precursors of these disorders can be observed by early adolescence.

5.25.7.2 Sex Differences

Table 2 shows the rates of each of the somatoform disorders in men and women as reported in *DSM-IV*. There are some differences between children and adults in the rates of somatoform disorders in girls vs. boys. Prior to puberty the prevalence of somatization disorders is about equally rare in girls and boys. With the onset of puberty and menarche in girls, there tends to be an increase in the rates of somatic complaints in girls compared to boys (Aro & Taipale, 1987; Belmaker, 1984). There appears to be a decline in symptom reporting among adolescent boys (Garber et al., 1991). Moreover, girls tend to be more consistent than boys in reporting somatic symptoms over time (Rauste-von Wright & von Wright, 1981; Walker & Greene, 1991b).

Pseudoneurological or conversion symptoms have also been found to be more prevalent in females than males, and this begins to become apparent during adolescence (Lehmkuhl et al., 1989; Turgay, 1980; Volkmar et al., 1984). Among prepubertal children, some studies have found the rates of conversion disorder to be about equal for boys and girls (Stevens, 1986), whereas other studies have reported the rates to be higher among girls than boys (Goodyer, 1981; Volkmar et al., 1984).

The greater rate of somatic complaints among adolescent girls than boys could be due to several factors. There may be an actual rise in the number and types of somatic symptoms girls experience during adolescence, particularly due to symptoms associated with their menstrual cycle. It also is possible, however, that the discrepant rates are due to sex differences in reporting tendencies. Girls may be more willing to express their distress to others and might view it as a legitimate means of obtaining social support. Indeed, girls generally seek support from others more than boys (Belle, Burr, & Cooney, 1987), and in particular girls seek care for their physical complaints more than boys (Lewis & Lewis, 1989). Moreover, in a study of children's use of emotion display rules, Zeman and Garber (1996) found that girls reported they would be significantly more likely than boys to express pain. In addition, compared to boys, girls reported that they thought other people would be more accepting and understanding of their expressions of emotions. Thus, boys may be less willing to endorse somatic symptoms because they think others will be less tolerant of such complaints or see it as unmasculine.

These sex differences could have their roots in children's socialization history. For example, Walker and Zeman (1992) found that parents encouraged illness behavior more in girls than in boys. Fuchs and Thelen (1988) found that children reported that their parents reacted differently to the emotional displays of girls vs. boys. In general, parental socialization pressures tend to be perceived by children to be directed toward the masking of distress in boys vs. girls.

Thus, there appear to be sex differences in the rates of somatic complaints and illness behavior in children, and this becomes particularly apparent during adolescence. These differences could be the result of girls actually experiencing more somatic distress than boys, as well as to girls' greater willingness to express this distress to others.

5.25.7.3 Sociocultural Factors

Although it is likely that social, cultural, and ethnic factors might influence the development and expression of somatic complaints (Kirmayer, 1984), there has been little research on this issue in children. Whereas some studies have found an association between somatoform disorders in children and low socioeconomic status (SES), low levels of parental education, or living in a rural area (Aro et al., 1987; Proctor, 1958; Steinhausen et al., 1989), other studies have not found such a relation (Stevenson, Simpson, & Bailey, 1988; Walker & Greene, 1991a). In developing countries, 1.3–5% of child psychiatry outpatients have been found to have conversion disorders (Herman & Simonds, 1975; Proctor, 1958).

It is possible that cultural factors influence the presentation of somatic symptoms and may contribute to the higher incidence of conversion disorder in less-developed countries. Prazar (1987) asserted that less sophisticated individuals are more likely to present with symptoms that are not easily explained physiologically, although he argued that there is no relation between conversion symptoms and SES. In contrast, Taylor et al. (1996) found in a community sample of Canadian adolescents a significant association between poverty and somatic complaints. It is possible, however, in the Taylor et al. study that these somatic symptoms reflected real illnesses due to their less favorable living conditions.

Studies in Turkey (Turgay, 1980) and India (Srinath, Bharat, Girimaji, & Seshadri, 1993) have found conversion symptoms to be a common presentation of psychiatric disorders. For example, Srinath et al. (1993) reported that conversion disorder (mostly pseudoseizures) was diagnosed in 30% of inpatients and 15% of outpatients.

Weisz and colleagues (Weisz et al., 1987; Weisz et al., 1993) have compared the behavioral and emotional problems of children and adolescents in the US vs. Thailand. Weiss et al. (1987) found that among children aged 6–11 years, five of the six differences that were considered to be medium to large effects involved somatic difficulties. Thai children were rated by their parents to be higher on "doesn't eat well," "constipated," "feels dizzy," and "underactive, lacks energy." Thai adolescents also were rated higher on the latter three symptoms (Weisz et al., 1993). However, Thai children were not more likely than American children to have the most common somatic complaints such as headaches and stomach aches. Thai children were rated higher than American children on overcontrolled behaviors. Weisz et al. (1987, 1993) suggested that there probably are more cultural pressures in this Asian society for children to have self-control, emotional restraint, and social inhibition. It could be that such societal demands increase the likelihood of children expressing their distress somatically rather than behaviorally.

5.25.8 ETIOLOGY

Multiple factors have been proposed to explain the etiology of somatoform disorders including genetics, personality, somatic and perceptual sensitivity, family processes, stress and trauma, and emotional communication. Because of the heterogeneity of somatoform disorders, it is likely that different models will explain the specific disorders that comprise this category. It is also likely that a more complex biopsychosocial model that incorporates different aspects of various perspectives will ultimately explain the processes leading to the development of somatoform disorders.

5.25.8.1 Genetics and Personality

Somatization is clearly familial (Edwards, Zeichner, Kuczmierczyk, Boczkowski, 1985; Garber et al., 1990; Kriechman, 1987; Routh & Ernst, 1984; Walker et al., 1991; Wasserman et al., 1988), which is likely due to a combination of genetic and environmental factors. Adoption studies have found somatization disorder to be over five times more common in female first-degree relatives of probands with somatization than in the general population (Cloninger, 1986). Twin studies, on the other hand, have not provided much evidence of a strong genetic contribution to the development of somatization (Gottesman, 1962; Inouye, 1972; Torgensen, 1986), although there might be a genetic factor for somatic anxiety (Kendler, Heath, Martin, & Eaves, 1987).

Cloninger and colleagues (Bohman, Cloninger, von Knorring, & Sigvardsson, 1984; Cloninger, Sigvardsson, von Knorring, & Bohman, 1984; Guze, Cloninger, Martin, & Clayton, 1986) have also found genetic links between somatization disorder and antisocial personality and alcoholism. The biological fathers of adopted-away women who were "high-frequency somatizers" tended to have a history of violent crime (Cloninger, 1986). Cadoret (1978) similarly found that adopted-away daughters of antisocial patients were more likely to suffer medically unexplained somatic symptoms compared to controls. Studies of somatizing children have also found high rates of externalizing disorders among their relatives (Kriechman, 1987; Routh & Ernst, 1984).

Shields (1982) proposed that the personality traits that predispose to somatization may be what is inherited rather than somatization *per se*. Cloninger (1986) suggested that persons with somatization disorder are characterized by distractibility, impulsivity, and failure to habituate to repetitive stimuli. It is possible that these traits contribute to the link between somatization and antisocial personality disorder.

In a study specifically designed to assess personality, Stern, Murphy, and Bass (1993) reported that 72% of somatization patients compared to only 36% of controls had personality disorders, particularly passive-dependent, histrionic, and sensitive-aggressive. Tyler, Fowler-Dixon, and Ferguson (1990) have described a hypochondriacal personality disorder that presumably underlies somatization disorder and includes excessive preoccupation with health, distorted perceptions of minor symptoms, and frequent medical consultations. In children, excessive somatic complaints have been associated with obsessiveness, conscientiousness, hypersensitivity, insecurity, lack of perceived competence, anxiety, and possibly behavioral inhibition (Cunningham et al., 1987; Garralda, 1992; Kagan, Reznick, & Snidman, 1988; Walker et al., 1993). The extent to which these temperamental features during childhood become personality disorders that then predispose individuals to develop adult somatoform disorders needs to be explored further.

5.25.8.2 Somatic and Perceptual Sensitivity

Individuals with somatoform disorders have also been hypothesized to have greater somatic and/or perceptual sensitivity (Barsky & Klerman, 1983; Kellner, 1990). Various forms of normal physiological arousal and bodily changes are associated with somatizing symptoms. For example, contractions of the scalp muscles are observed with headaches (e.g., Fujii, Kachi, & Sobue, 1981; Sainsbury & Gibson, 1954); elevated electromyograph levels in paravertebral muscles can be found in patients with lower back pain (Dolce & Raczynski, 1985; Flor, Turk, & Birbaumer, 1985); contractions of smooth muscle in the alimentary tract are common in abdominal pain patients (Whitehead & Schuster, 1985), and esophageal motility is found in persons with chest pain (Clouse & Lustman, 1983). These normal physiological reactions can develop into more persistent or severe symptoms in several ways. First, somatizers might have a more sensitive physiological system such that they respond more intensely than normals to the same level of physical stimulation. Second, even if their initial response is within the normal range, they might have a more sustained physiological reaction and a slower return to baseline. Third, it is possible that somatizers respond normally physiologically, but simply attend to their symptoms more than others. Finally, somatizers also might misinterpret their normal bodily sensations as indicating a more serious condition than is warranted.

It is likely that individuals differ in their degree of somatic sensitivity, that is, the intensity with which they experience a particular level of somatic stimulation. Moreover, under conditions of stress, high somatic sensitivity will increase the likelihood that symptoms of affective arousal will be translated into somatic symptoms. The existing evidence in children relevant to this hypothesis is mixed. Using a painful cold pressor stimulus, Feuerstein, Barr, Francoeur, Houle, and Rafman (1982) did not find any meaningful differences in the autonomic, subjective, or behavioral responses of children with RAP compared with healthy controls. In contrast, using lower intensity stimulation with an algometer, Alfven (1993) reported that RAP children had significantly lower pressure pain thresholds than well children. Thus, if somatizers are hypersensitive to physical stimulation, this might be particularly apparent at lower levels of stimulation and for some forms of stimulation but not others.

Even if somatizers do not respond more sensitively initially to somatic stimulation, it also might be that they have a more prolonged somatic reaction once exposed. The reasons for this sustained reaction could be either physical or psychological; that is, once aroused it simply might take more time for their physiology to return to baseline, and therefore they experience the symptoms longer. It also is possible, however, that individuals who somatize are more likely to continue to attend to their symptoms, thereby sustaining a higher level of arousal for a longer period of time.

The extent to which individuals attend to normal bodily sensations can be learned. For example, Pennebaker and Skelton (1978) found that the instructions given to subjects could influence whether or not they perceived a bodily sensation. Moreover, habitual attention to somatic symptoms in certain parts of the body

is likely to increase one's perceptions of sensations in that area, (Kellner, 1986). Such attentional variation can lead to either an amplification or minimization of bodily sensations (Barsky, Goodman, Lane, & Cleary, 1988; Mayou, 1976).

Finally, normal physiological reactions are sometimes misinterpreted as reflecting a more serious somatic problem, that is, whereas most individuals normalize common symptoms and attribute them to minor physical variation or environmental factors, individuals who somatize tend to attribute such normal bodily symptoms to much more pathological causes (Robbins & Kirmayer, 1991). This misinterpretation itself could increase the amount of stress experienced by the individual, and thereby lead to a more severe or sustained somatic reaction.

Thus, individuals with somatoform disorders are hypothesized to have an increased somatic and/or perceptual sensitivity. Somatic sensitivity is likely the result of a more severe initial physiological response to stimulation or a more sustained reaction with a slower return to baseline. Perceptual sensitivity is reflected by a normal physiological reaction that receives greater attention or that is misinterpreted as reflecting a more serious somatic problem.

5.25.8.3 Family Processes

The family environment can influence the development of somatization symptoms in children in several ways. Although the specific amount of genetic vs. environmental factors which contribute to the high rates of somatization in relatives of children with somatoform disorders is unclear, the presence of "ill" persons in the family environment can influence the child's psychological development through such processes as modeling and reinforcement (Craig, 1978; Fordyce, 1978; Turkat, 1982). Walker et al. (1993) suggested that the high numbers of potential models of illness behavior in families of children with recurrent abdominal pain provide more opportunities for vicarious learning of such behavior and for the observation of these models receiving reinforcement of their illness behavior (Whitehead, Busch, Heller, & Costa, 1986).

Operant learning can also play a role in the development and maintenance of recurrent pain in children (McGrath, 1987) and in the reduction of symptoms and disability (Sanders et al., 1989; Sank & Biglan, 1974). Positive reinforcement of expressions of pain (Osborne, Hatcher, & Richtsmeier, 1989) and discouragement of adaptive coping responses have been found to be associated with higher rates of illness behavior in children (Dunn-Geier, McGrath, Rourke, Latter, & D'Astous, 1986). Walker et al. (1993) found that children with abdominal pain reported that their parents responded more frequently to their symptom complaints with increased attention and special privileges compared to well children.

Whereas some have reported that parental lack of care and childhood illness significantly predicted adult somatization (Craig, Boardman, Mills, Daly-Jones, & Drake, 1993), others have suggested that parents of somatizing children are overprotective and promote separation fears (Grattan-Smith et al., 1988; Lehmkuhl et al., 1989; Robinson, Alverez, & Dodge, 1990) which can increase children's sense of vulnerability and fragility (Green & Solnit, 1964). The children's somatic symptoms can serve to maintain proximity to important attachment figures (Henderson, 1974; Wooley, Blackwell, & Winget, 1978) and may be the consequence of children's anxiety about being separated from such persons (Garber et al., 1990; Hodges et al., 1985b).

Family system theorists have suggested that psychosomatic symptoms can serve a function within the family system to avoid conflict, particularly between the parents (Minuchin et al., 1975; Minuchin, Rosman, & Baker, 1978; Mullins & Olson, 1990). Disturbed patterns of communication, cohesion, and support have been reported among families of children with somatoform disorders (Maloney, 1980; Walker, McLaughlin, & Greene, 1988; Wasserman et al., 1988), although not necessarily worse than families of children with emotional disorders (Walker et al., 1993). In somatizing families, physical symptoms often become the means of communication of distress, and are the focus of attention rather than the relationship problems that exist among family members (Lask & Fosson, 1989; Maisami & Freeman, 1987).

Wood (1993) proposed a biobehavioral family model that focuses on the mutual influence of individual factors, such as psychophysiologic reactivity, and family patterns, such as parental discord, triangulation, and negative affectivity. She suggested that high levels of individual psychophysiologic reactivity and stressful family patterns will potentiate one another and interact to influence the outcome of disease processes. This model needs to be tested further with regard to children with somatoform disorders in particular.

Thus, socialization processes can contribute to the development of excessive somatic complaints in children (Parmelee, 1986) and the eventual onset of somatoform disorders. Further research is needed in which the actual behaviors of parents in response to their children's somatic complaints is observed. Longitudinal studies are also needed to untangle the direction of causality between parenting behavior and child symptoms. Such studies can serve as a basis for interventions aimed at preventing the development and maintenance of somatization symptoms and disorders.

5.25.8.4 Stress and Trauma

Higher levels of negative life events have been found to be associated with greater frequency of illness episodes and health service utilization (Beautrais, Fergusson, & Shannon, 1982; Boyce et al., 1977; Roghmann & Haggerty, 1973), symptom maintenance, and illness exacerbations (Chase & Jackson, 1981; Perrin, MacLean, & Janco, 1988). Among children with somatization disorders in particular, some studies have found an association with stressful life events (Aro, 1987; Greene, Walker, Hickson, & Thompson, 1985; Hodges et al., 1985a; Pantell & Goodman, 1983; Robinson et al., 1990; Scaloubaca, Slade, & Creed, 1988; Walker & Greene, 1987), whereas other studies have failed to find such a relation (McGrath, Goodman, Firestone, Shipman, & Peters, 1983; Turgay, 1980; Walker & Greene, 1991a; Wasserman et al., 1988). The life-event profiles of children with somatizing disorders have been found to be similar to those of children with psychiatric disorders and different from healthy controls (Hodges et al. ; Scaloubaca et al., 1988; Turgay, 1980), although other studies have reported that children with recurrent pain experience fewer negative life events than children with emotional disorders (Walker et al., 1993). The different results across these studies may be due to differences in the types of psychiatric comparison groups studied and in the types of life events assessed. For example, children with somatizing problems tend to report a greater number of events involving family illness in particular compared to healthy and psychiatric children (Hodges et al.; Walker et al.; Wasserman et al.). There also is some evidence that early loss is linked to somatization and recurrent pain (Mallouh, Abbey, & Gillies, 1995; Wasserman et al.).

It also is possible that stress is a general risk factor that contributes to the onset and maintenance of many types of disorders. The more interesting and important question is what factors in combination with stress make some people vulnerable to one disorder rather than another. That is, what is the particular model in which stress is a part that predicts specific disorders (Garber & Hollon, 1991)? In a prospective study of 197 pediatric patients with chronic abdominal pain, Walker, Garber, and Greene (1994) found that among children who had high levels of negative life events, those who had been reported to be low in social competence had higher levels of somatic complaints one year later compared to children who were high in social competence. In addition, Walker et al. found that among boys who experienced high levels of negative life events, those whose mothers were characterized by high levels of somatic symptoms had higher levels of somatic symptoms a year later. Thus, both social competence and maternal somatic complaints moderated the relation between stress and somatization in pediatric patients. This indicates that a more complex model which includes stress in combination with other psychosocial factors may be needed to explain the onset and maintenance of somatization in children. The extent to which such a model generalizes to normative populations needs to be studied further.

Traumatic life events, particularly physical and sexual abuse, have also been linked to somatization. Early theories suggested that childhood trauma was a factor in most cases of hysteria (Briquet, 1859; Freud, 1896/1962). Despite the general rejection of Freud's "seduction theory," there continues to be an interest in the association between childhood physical and sexual abuse and somatic and conversion symptoms (Green, 1993; Loewenstein, 1990; Morrison, 1989; Rimza, Berg, & Locke, 1988). Pseudoneurological symptoms (e.g., pseudoseizures), genitourinary and gastrointestinal symptoms, in particular, have been observed among victims of sexual abuse (Bowman, 1993; Goodwin, Simms, & Bergman, 1979; Hunter, Kilstrom, & Loda, 1985; Klevan & DeJong, 1990; LaBarbera & Dozier, 1980). Prospective studies of abused children are needed to establish the predictive link between early trauma and subsequent somatoform symptoms and disorders.

5.25.8.5 Emotional Communication

Traditional psychodynamic theory has been particularly prominent in the explanation of conversion disorder. According to this view, an unconscious intrapsychic conflict, wish, or need is "converted" into a somatic symptom, which presumably expresses symbolically some aspect of the conflict while at the same time protecting the person from conscious awareness (Engel, 1962). Critics of this perspective argue that the evidence is limited concerning the symbolic meaning of the symptom and its link to the unconscious.

More modern approaches assert that somatizing is a psychological defense whereby individuals experience and express emotional distress physically rather than acknowledge unpleasant affects, memories, or conflicts (Shapiro & Rosenfeld, 1987; Simon, 1991). Constructs such as alexithymia (Nemiah, 1977; Sifneos, 1973) and the defensive style of "repression" (Weinberger, Schwartz, & Davidson, 1979) have been proposed to explain the association between somatic symptoms and reduced emotional awareness and expression.

Alexithymia is characterized by difficulties in identifying and describing feelings, difficulty distinguishing between feelings and the bodily sensations of emotional arousal, limited imagination and fantasy life, and a concrete and reality-based cognitive style (Taylor, Baglay, Ryan, & Parker, 1990). Adult patients with somatization disorder have been found to have higher scores on a self-report measure of alexithymia compared to patients with other psychiatric disorders (Bagby, Taylor, & Parker, 1994; Taylor et al., 1990), although alexithymia has also been found to be associated with depression, neuroticism, and eating disorders (Bourke, Taylor, Parker, & Bagby, 1992; Cohen, Auld, & Brooker, 1994; Wise & Mann, 1994). More research needs to be conducted regarding the measurement and construct validity of alexithymia in adults, and its particular relation to somatoform disorders. There also has been almost no research on alexithymia in children.

Because young children have limited cognitive and linguistic abilities, it is not unusual to hear them express their emotional distress with physical symptoms. This might be particularly apparent in those families or cultures in which the expression of emotional distress is discouraged, whereas somatic complaints receive acceptance and attention (Escobar, Burnam, & Karno, 1987). Although there is a large developmental literature concerning the emergence of emotional competence in children (e.g., Saarni, 1990), little is known about the emotional development of children with somatoform disorders. Children who somatize might be especially likely to show delays or deviation in their emotional competence, particularly regarding emotional identification and expression; that is, they might be less competent at linking affects with situations, or expressing emotions in certain contexts, particularly those involving negative affect. Thus, although there has been considerable theoretical speculation about the role of affect expression and emotional competence in the development of somatization, the relevant empirical investigations have not yet been conducted.

5.25.9 COURSE AND PROGNOSIS

There have been few systematic longitudinal studies of children and adolescents with somatoform disorders and therefore little is known about their course and prognosis. Studies have varied with regard to the types of patients and disorders studied, the length of the follow-ups, and the specificity vs. generality of the outcomes assessed. In general, acute onset of fewer and transient symptoms tends to have a better prognosis than insidious onset of multiple symptoms that are recurrent or chronic (Ernst, Routh, & Harper, 1984; Grattan-Smith et al., 1988; Robins & O'Neal, 1953), although the findings have not always been consistent with this perspective (Goodyer & Mitchell, 1989; Lehmkuhl et al., 1989).

Several follow-up studies of children and adolescents with RAP have revealed that many (25–50%) of these patients continue to experience somatic complaints as adults (Apley & Hale, 1972; Christensen & Mortensen, 1975; Liebman, 1978; Stickler & Murphy, 1979; Stone & Barbero, 1970; Walker, Garber, Van Slyke, & Greene, 1995). In a five-year follow-up study, Walker et al. (1995) found that children and adolescents originally diagnosed with RAP reported significantly higher levels of abdominal discomfort, other somatic symptoms, and functional disability than formerly healthy controls. Moreover, the former RAP patients had higher levels of internalizing emotional symptoms (e.g., anxiety and depression) and significantly higher levels of mental health service utilization than the healthy comparison group. With regard to pseudoneurologic or conversion symptoms, studies have found that over 50% of patients with such symptoms tend to show significant clinical improvement or recovery, although a subset of children with conversion disorders go on to develop somatization disorder or other psychiatric problems including anxiety and personality disorders (Bangash, Worley, & Kandt, 1988; Goodyer, 1981; Goodyer & Mitchell, 1989; Grattan-Smith et al., 1988; Kotsopolous & Snow, 1986; Lehmkuhl et al., 1989; Leslie, 1988; Maisami & Freeman, 1987; Proctor, 1958; Schneider & Rice, 1979; Spierings et al., 1990; Turgay, 1990; Wyllie et al., 1991). Kotsopoulos and Snow (1986) reported that 40% of 20 children with conversion disorder continued to have somatic or psychiatric symptoms 1–3 years after the initial assessment.

There is also evidence that some children originally diagnosed as having a somatoform disorder (e.g., conversion disorder) were later discovered to have had or to have developed a medical condition that explained their earlier

symptoms (Robins & O'Neil, 1953; Woodbury, De Maso, & Goldman, 1992). Some researchers have argued, however, that early subclinical impairments in medical disorders, such as multiple sclerosis or tumors of the nervous system, might trigger a vulnerable person to develop conversion symptoms (Caplan & Nadelson, 1980; Nemzer, 1996; Rivinus, Jamison, & Graham, 1975). Thus, careful follow-up studies are needed to examine the continuity of somatic symptoms over time and to explore the extent to which diagnoses of somatoform symptoms and disorders were originally or subsequently develop into actual medical conditions.

5.25.10 CONCEPTUALIZATION AND CLINICAL FORMULATION

5.25.10.1 Assessment

There are few standard methods and measures for assessing somatoform disorders in children and adolescents. Comparisons across studies are difficult because different criteria and different instruments containing different lists of symptoms have been used. Assessment and diagnosis of somatoform disorders is especially challenging because independent medical assessments are needed to determine whether the reported physical symptoms are the result of identifiable organic disease and, if there is organic disease, whether there is functional impairment beyond what would be expected. Furthermore, the diagnosis of somatoform disorders is not simply a matter of the absence of medical findings. Rather, clinicians need to conduct a careful assessment to determine whether the patient meets the various symptom criteria for a somatoform disorder as well as for any other psychiatric diagnoses.

Another difficulty in assessing and diagnosing childhood somatoform disorders is that, in contrast to children with most other kinds of psychiatric problems, children with somatoform disorders are typically brought to pediatricians and general practitioners rather than to psychiatrists or psychologists. It is critical that physicians lay the groundwork for possible psychosocial intervention by explaining to the child and family that the routine comprehensive evaluation involves assessing both physical and psychological factors. Presented in this way, physicians can reduce resistance by the patient and family to inquiries about emotional issues that they might view to be private and irrelevant to the medical condition for which they are seeking help.

In addition to conducting a physical examination and obtaining a complete medical history, the pediatrician or family practitioner also should get a psychosocial history, an assessment of any recent stressors, and conduct a thorough mental status examination. Physicians are obviously quite adept at performing the necessary medical evaluations to detect physical illness, however, they often miss the psychiatric symptoms in children (Costello & Edelbrock, 1985). This is partially due to their lack of experience with the methods for evaluating psychiatric symptoms in children. Therefore, it is important for physicians to have screening measures that they can use to identify those patients for whom referral for further psychiatric evaluation might be appropriate.

Several commonly used psychological instruments are available for assessing somatic complaints as well as other emotional and behavioral problems in children. The Child Behavior Checklist (CBCL; Achenbach & Edelbrock, 1983) has versions for parents, teachers, and children to complete. A somatic complaints subscale can be derived from the CBCL. The Personality Inventory for Children (PIC; Wirt, Lachar, Klinedinst, & Seat, 1984), which is a personality questionnaire completed by parents about their children, also contains a somatic complaints subscale. Neither the CBCL nor the PIC, however, can be used to diagnose somatoform disorders (Prichard, Ball, Culbert, & Faust, 1988). This is largely because the extent to which somatic symptoms are the result of an actual organic problem requires an independent medical evaluation. There are also measures that assess somatic complaints in particular. The CSI (Garber et al., 1991; Walker et al., 1991; Walker & Greene, 1989) was developed explicitly to assess symptoms of somatization disorder in children and adolescents. The CSI includes symptoms from the *DSM-III-R* (APA, 1987) criteria for somatization disorder and from the somatization factor of the Hopkins Symptom Checklist (Derogatis, Lipman, Rickels, Uhlenhuth, & Covi, 1974). Children rate the extent to which they have experienced each of 35 symptoms in the last two weeks using a five-point scale ranging from 0 = not at all to 4 = a whole lot. A total score, obtained by summing the ratings, can range from zero to 140. Both test–retest reliability and internal consistency for the CSI have been found to be quite good (Walker et al.). There also is a parent form of the Children's Somatization Inventory (P-CSI) that includes the same symptoms as the CSI and is completed by parents with reference to their children.

A similar questionnaire was developed by Benjamin and Eminson (1992) that measured lifetime prevalence of symptoms in 11–16-year-old British children. They found that somatic and emotional symptoms were correlated, particularly in girls. About 20% of the children reported worries about health that affected their school attendance.

The Ontario Child Health Study used a 17-item list containing questions about the experience of bodily distress, worries and concerns about health, and the experience of having lost faculties for no apparent reason. Items were checked either 0 = never or not true, 1 = sometimes true, or 2 = often or very true. A total "somasick" score can be calculated by adding items marked one or two, yielding a possible total score of 34. Psychometric properties of this scale have not been reported (Taylor et al., 1996).

Thus, when physicians suspect the possibility of a somatoform disorder in children, their assessment should include a thorough physical exam to rule out medical explanations for the child's symptoms, general measures of child behavioral and emotional symptoms (e.g., CBCL), more specific measures of the most likely emotional problems including anxiety and depression (e.g., Children's Depression Inventory, Kovacs, 1980/1981; Revised Children's Manifest Anxiety Scale, RCMAS, Reynolds & Richmond, 1985), specific measures of somatic complaints (e.g., CSI), and an assessment of the extent of impairment and functional disability due to the somatic symptoms (e.g., Functional Disability Inventory, FDI; Walker & Greene, 1991b). Although the physician will still not be able to make a diagnosis of a somatoform disorder on the basis of these instruments, these measures will provide important information to guide decisions about the possible need for further medical and psychological evaluation.

It also is generally considered to be a good idea to obtain information from multiple sources, although there are known problems with lack of agreement across informants (Achenbach, McConaughy, & Howell, 1987). Who is the best source of information regarding children's somatic problems? Because somatic symptoms are primarily subjective, it is crucial to ask the children themselves. Parents and teachers can be useful informants, however, about the onset and duration of children's physical complaints and the extent of impairment associated with these complaints, such as not playing with friends or not doing school work.

Results of studies examining the relation between parent and child report about somatic complaints have differed as a function of the sample used. Taylor et al. (1996) explored in a community sample the extent of agreement between adolescents and their parents' reports about the teens' somatic symptoms using the 17-item questionnaire from the Ontario Child Health Study. They found a high correlation between parents and youth ($r = 0.80$), but little agreement on the endorsement of specific symptoms (all kappas were less than 0.30).

Garber, Van Slyke, and Walker (1997) studied mother–child concordance regarding children's somatic and emotional symptoms in children diagnosed with either a physical, emotional, or no disorder. Whereas well children and their mothers showed a high level of concordance, mothers of children with recurrent abdominal pain reported more child somatic and emotional symptoms than their children. Discordance was in the direction of mothers reporting more symptoms in their children than the children themselves, and this was associated with higher levels of maternal distress. Thus, obtaining reports from multiple sources can provide useful information from different perspectives, although the level of concordance is likely to be low.

Finally, given the presumably unconscious nature of conversion symptoms, they are likely to be particularly difficult to assess. The Dissociative Experiences Scale is a self-rating scale that has been used to measure dissociative symptoms in adults (Bernstein & Putnam, 1986) and children (Putnam, Helmers, & Trickett, in press). When other diagnostic procedures have been exhausted, sodium amytal interviews are sometimes tried. Weller, Weller, and Fristad (1985) described several case studies in which they used amytal interviews with children to remove conversion symptoms and to differentiate between feigned and actual symptoms. Weller et al. (1985) concluded that a properly administered amytal interview can be a safe and effective diagnostic and therapeutic tool with children.

An interesting technique for diagnosing pseudoseizures is video-electroencephalographic monitoring. During a seizure, the patient is simultaneously videotaped and the EEG recorded. If there is no electrical brain activity, the seizure is assumed to be a conversion symptom (Nemzer, 1996).

Thus, the assessment of somatoform disorders in children and adolescents should involve multiple methods including child self-report inventories, parent questionnaires, psychiatric interviews, medical evaluations, family histories, and amytal interviews when appropriate. More research needs to be conducted to determine the best way to integrate the information obtained from these various methods and sources.

5.25.10.2 Treatment Formulation

Because patients with somatoform disorders tend to think of their symptoms as resulting from medical rather than psychological causes, they can be particularly reluctant to seek or accept psychological explanations for their symptoms, and they may be resistant to psychosocial interventions. Therefore, it is important for health-care workers to acknowledge the reality of the patient's physical distress and also to provide reassurance that the symptoms are not severe or life-threatening (Kellner, 1991; Maisami & Freeman, 1987), although too much reassurance should be avoided (Warwick & Salkovskis, 1985).

Routine use of an interdisciplinary team comprised of physicians, nurses, psychologists, and social workers can be especially helpful because it communicates to the patient and family that all aspects of the child's health are being considered, and it can provide a coordinated management approach (Mayou, Bass, & Sharpe, 1995). The treatment team can explain to patients that their physical problems can also have emotional consequences. This is sometimes a good way of introducing the need for psychological assessment and possible psychosocial intervention. At least at first, it is probably not necessary for patients with somatoform disorders to believe that psychological factors played a role in the development or maintenance of their symptoms. After some rapport has been developed with the patient, however, the possible contribution of psychological factors to their symptoms can and should be discussed. Moreover, the diagnosis of a somatoform disorder can be presented as "good news" if it means the absence of a serious medical condition. When a referral is made for mental health services, the child patient and family should be reassured that the pediatrician or family practitioner will continue to be involved in their treatment. Such close liaison can help minimize any sense of abandonment or rejection they might experience.

With regard to the treatment of conversion symptoms, in particular, there is an old controversy among clinicians as to whether it is first necessary to remove the physical symptom and then conduct psychotherapy to deal with the underlying psychopathology, or whether the psychotherapeutic intervention will simultaneously address the symptom and its causes. Various procedures used for removing the symptom include suggestion (Proctor, 1958; Rock, 1971), encouragement (Gold, 1965), and chemical abreaction through the use of medications such as amobarbital (Laybourne & Churchill, 1972). More recent perspectives do not recommend withholding psychotherapy until the symptom is removed. Rather, clinicians now suggest helping the patient and family recognize that the symptom is not life-threatening in order to reduce their anxiety, and thereby make them more open to other treatments (Kellner, 1986; Maisami & Freeman, 1987; Schulman, 1988).

An important goal of any intervention with children and adolescents experiencing somatoform symptoms and disorders is to encourage their return to normal activities and to discourage "sick role" behaviors such as missing school, staying in bed, and avoiding friends. This rehabilitative approach involves a reframing of the child's symptoms and has two important features. First, it emphasizes that patients do not need to wait until their symptom(s) have improved for them to engage in their normal academic and social activities. This teaches them that they can keep going even when they are experiencing symptoms and discomfort. Patients with pseudoneurologic symptoms, particularly motor problems, are sometimes encouraged to do prescribed exercises or to see a physical therapist who can assist them with gradually returning to normal functioning (Dubowitz & Hersov, 1976) and with giving up their symptom while also "saving face" (Bolton & Cohen, 1986).

Second, this approach shifts the responsibility for "cure" from the physician to the patient; that is, the child changes from being a passive recipient of care to becoming an active collaborator in his or her recovery. Rather than looking for attention and rewards for sick role behaviors, the child seeks reinforcement and praise for his or her efforts at overcoming the symptoms and persevering in spite of them.

Another method sometimes used to reduce sick role behaviors is to arrange regular appointments with the physician independent of the child's physical condition. This provides children and their parents with opportunities to meet with their doctor without the child having to be symptomatic. In addition, the physician can use these appointments to reassess whether any medical conditions have developed that could account for their somatoform symptoms.

One additional complication in the treatment of children and adolescents with somatoform disorders is that not only does the child patient need to be convinced of the role of psychological factors, but typically the parents also need to be persuaded. There is often a shared belief among family members of the medical origins of the child's symptoms. Parents often are the primary reinforcers of the child's sick role

behaviors. Therefore, interventions need to target the beliefs and behaviors of parents as well as the children.

Family perspectives about psychosomatic conditions (Minuchin et al., 1975, 1978; Mullins & Olson, 1990) suggest that the child's somatic symptoms serve a function within the family system. Family therapists argue that interventions should not focus on the identified child's symptoms because that distracts the family from the more important family processes that are maintaining the symptom. Minuchin and colleagues recommend that family therapy targets the enmeshment, parental overprotection, and conflict avoidance that often characterize these families. Thus, the basic principles for treating somatoform disorders include acknowledging the patient's physical symptoms while at the same time explaining to both the child and parents the possible contribution of psychological factors to the onset and maintenance of the child's symptoms. A multidisciplinary approach that involves collaboration between the physician and mental health workers is recommended. A primary goal of any intervention is the minimization of sick role behaviors and encouragement of a return to normal activities as soon as possible, although for some children this may need to be a gradual process.

5.25.11 TREATMENT

5.25.11.1 Psychosocial

Psychosocial approaches to the treatment of somatoform disorders in children and adolescents have generally included behavioral and cognitive techniques, psychodynamic psychotherapy, and group and family therapies. The particular technique used depends on the specific symptoms and disorder. Relaxation training (Larsson, 1992; Larsson & Mellin, 1988), hypnosis (Elkins & Carter, 1986), and biofeedback (Klonoff & Moore, 1986; Mizes, 1985) have been used to reduce tension associated with headaches and other pains. Cognitive interventions teach self-monitoring and coping strategies (Sanders, Shepherd, Cleghorn, & Woolford, 1994). Behavioral methods are used to reinforce mastery over symptoms and to reduce secondary gain associated with sick role behaviors (Delameter, Rosenbloom, Conners, & Hertweck, 1983; Mizes, 1985). Psychodynamic approaches aim to help children with conversion disorders to gain insight into unconscious conflicts and to identify how psychological factors can influence the maintenance of symptoms (Goodyer & Taylor, 1985). Some form of parent training, family education, or family therapy can be used to apprise parents of their possible role in the onset and maintenance of their child's somatic symptoms and to improve communication among family members (Mullins & Olson, 1990). For those children with somatoform disorders who are shy, unassertive, and have difficulty expressing negative emotions, interventions that also improve self-esteem, promote assertiveness, and train in emotion expression and regulation techniques can be helpful (Nemzer, 1996).

Reattribution techniques that involve simply making the link for the child and parents between the occurrence of a stressor and the onset of symptoms can sometimes lead to symptom improvement. When such insight is followed by targeted problem-solving such as making appropriate environmental and behavioral changes, symptom reduction may happen rapidly (Wilkinson & Mynors-Wallis, 1994). For example, interventions such as changing a child's classroom or having a conference with the teacher to address the child's specific concerns can eliminate somatic symptoms being used to avoid school.

Although there are many interesting case studies in the literature using a variety of psychosocial approaches for the treatment of specific patients (e.g., Andrasik, Burke, Attanasio, & Rosenblum, 1985; Delameter et al., 1983; Elkins & Carter, 1986; Linton, 1986; Miller & Kratochwill, 1979), there are relatively few controlled trials for the treatment of somatoform disorders in children. These studies have targeted specific somatic complaints, particularly recurrent abdominal pain (Finney, Lemanek, Cataldo, Katz, & Fuqua, 1989; Sanders et al., 1989, 1994) and headaches (Larsson & Mellin, 1988; McGrath et al., 1988; Osterhaus et al., 1993).

Finney and colleagues (Edwards, Finney, & Bonner, 1991; Finney et al., 1989) have examined the efficacy of using several different techniques including self-monitoring, limited parent attention, relaxation training, increased dietary fiber, and required school attendance. Finney et al. found that a group of 16 children who received a brief multicomponent targeted intervention comprising all of these methods had improved pain symptoms and decreased school absences compared to the untreated comparison group ($n = 16$). In addition, the treated group had significantly decreased medical care utilization.

Sanders and colleagues (Sanders et al., 1989, 1994) have conducted two studies examining the efficacy of cognitive-behavioral treatment of recurrent abdominal pain in children. In the first study (Sanders et al., 1989), the treatment program consisted of differential reinforcement of well behavior, cognitive coping skills training, and various generalization enhancement procedures. Although both the treatment and control groups showed a reduction in pain symptoms, the cognitive-behavioral treatment group had a more rapid improvement that generalized to the school setting, and a larger proportion of the treated children were completely pain-free at the three month follow-up.

Their second study (Sanders et al., 1994) compared the efficacy of a cognitive-behavioral family intervention (CBFI) with standard pediatric care (SPC) in 44 children with recurrent abdominal pain aged 7–14 years. Again, children in both treatment conditions showed improvements on pain intensity and pain behavior. The children in the CBFI group, however, also had a higher rate of complete elimination of pain, lower levels of relapse, and lower levels of interference with their activities. Thus, these studies show that some form of intervention typically leads to symptom improvement, although the more extensive treatments have broader and possibly longer-lasting effects on symptoms and functioning.

Efficacy of specific treatments for headaches in children and adolescents has been mixed. Relaxation training has been found to be superior to attention placebo control for the treatment of tension headaches (Larsson & Mellin, 1988) and migraines in adolescents (Larsson, 1992). Osterhaus et al. (1993) found that a combined treatment consisting of relaxation training, temperature biofeedback, and cognitive techniques reduced headache frequency and duration, although not intensity, compared with a waiting list control. Osterhaus et al. suggested that an increase in the ability to relax and a decrease in anxiety contributed to improvement. Helm-Hylkema, Orlebek, Enting, Thijssen, and Ree (1990) used the same training program as that of Osterhaus et al. but in a clinical setting and found that 90% of their young adolescent patients showed significant improvement. McGrath et al. (1988), however, reported that among adolescents attending a pediatric neurology clinic for migraines, relaxation was not found to be more effective than a "placebo" discussion of psychological topics. It could be that their control condition, which involved receiving reassurance and assistance, and attending to psychological factors, was sufficiently effective in reducing migraines among these adolescents. Thus, relaxation procedures show some promise in reducing headaches in children and adolescents, although further research needs to be conducted exploring what might be the effective ingredients of "control" interventions. Although much has been written about how to deal therapeutically with conversion disorders (e.g., Hodgman, 1995; Maisami & Freeman, 1987), there have been few controlled treatment studies in either adults or children. Adult patients who received psychotherapy for pseudoseizures have been found to be significantly improved compared to those who did not undergo treatment (Lesser, Lueders, & Dinner, 1983; Meierkord, Will, Fish, & Shorvon, 1991).

5.25.11.2 Medical Interventions

Treating somatoform disorders with medical interventions such as pharmacology and hospitalization is a complex issue because of the message it sends to the child and family. One concern about using medication is that this might perpetuate the patients' beliefs about the organic etiology of their symptoms. Indeed, some physicians resort to prescribing placebos to avoid the patient's anger about not receiving medical treatment. This could have the negative effect, however, of perpetuating the child's view of him or herself as sickly and in need of medical intervention.

On the other hand, providing some medical intervention helps to validate the reality of patients' physical distress and thereby might increase their willingness to accept other forms of treatment as well; that is, if the physician does not simply dismiss patients' symptoms as being "all in their head," then patients might be more open to a multimodal approach. Moreover, some medical interventions, even if they are over-the-counter remedies, can at least alleviate some of the physical discomfort they are experiencing.

In addition, if a child with a somatoform disorder is experiencing comorbid symptoms such as anxiety or depression, then psychopharmacological treatment aimed at reducing these symptoms might be warranted. If children's somatic symptoms are reduced as a function of psychotropic medication, then this might help to convince them and their parents that psychological factors may be contributing to their physical problems. In adults, antidepressants have been found to reduce somatic symptoms in depressed patients, and anxiolytic medications appear to alleviate somatic symptoms in patients diagnosed with anxiety disorders, such as panic (Kellner, 1991). There have been no controlled treatment studies of the use of antidepressants or antianxiety medications for children or adolescents with somatoform disorders with comorbid emotional disorders. There is some evidence of the efficacy of selective serotonin reuptake inhibitors

(SSRIs) for the treatment of adolescent depression (Emslie, Rush, & Weinberg, in press) and pediatric obsessive compulsive disorder (Riddle et al., 1992), and for the use of medications in the treatment of childhood anxiety disorders (Allen, Leonard, & Swedo, 1995). Given the high rates of anxiety and depressive disorders among children with some forms of recurrent somatic complaints (e.g., Garber et al., 1990; Hodges et al., 1985a; 1985b), such a treatment study might be informative.

Sometimes the patient's lack of improvement with medical treatment can assist in the diagnosis of a somatoform disorder; that is, if the symptoms do not get better with a medication known to be effective for a particular medical condition, then it is less likely that the patient has that condition. Thus, prescribing medication can serve as a diagnostic test as well as a form of treatment.

Are there any conditions under which hospitalization of children with somatoform disorders would be warranted? If the use of outpatient psychotherapy and pharmacological interventions have been found to be ineffective, then pediatric or psychiatric hospitalization may be appropriate. Inpatient hospitalization has been suggested when there is diagnostic uncertainty or marked functional impairment, such as persistent school refusal (Goodyer, 1981; Leslie, 1988). Such treatment can be accomplished best with a multidisciplinary team on a pediatric medical psychiatry inpatient unit (Campo & Raney, 1995). Hospitalization provides an opportunity for careful observation and control of environmental contingencies. Moreover, removal from the environmental conditions that might be producing or exacerbating the symptoms can be informative and therapeutic.

5.25.12 CONCLUSION AND FUTURE DIRECTIONS

The diagnostic criteria that define somatoform disorders have changed with each new edition of the *DSM*. The validity of these criteria for use with children still needs to be investigated. Epidemiological studies are needed that assess the full range of symptoms that comprise these disorders and that test the validity of different symptom cut-offs and combinations.

One of the real challenges for diagnosing somatoform disorders is the necessity of conducting comprehensive medical as well as psychiatric evaluations. Multidisciplinary teams that include medical and psychiatric staff are required for the assessment and treatment of patients with somatoform disorders. These evaluations should include information from multiple sources (i.e., children, parents, teachers) and should use multiple assessment methods including questionnaires, psychiatric interviews, observation, and amytal interviews when relevant. Similarly, interventions typically will require the cooperation of physicians and mental health specialists. Successful treatment is likely to involve individual therapy with the child as well as family therapy that addresses the system maintaining the child's symptoms.

Somatoform disorders are a heterogeneous category of loosely associated syndromes. They share the feature of physical symptoms that are not explained simply by a medical condition. It is likely that multiple factors comprising a biopsychosocial model contribute to the etiology of somatoform disorders. Moreover, it also is likely that a unique, although somewhat overlapping, set of processes underlie each disorder.

There also are age, sex, and cultural differences in somatic complaints and somatoform disorders that need to be studied further. How might the observed sex differences in the rates of somatoform disorder inform us about its etiology? Similarly, how are the different rates and patterns of somatic complaints in different cultures and subcultures explained?

Additional issues for future research concern the comorbidity of somatoform disorders with other internalizing problems. To what extent do other emotional disorders such as anxiety and depression underlie the somatic symptoms that comprise somatoform disorders? What is the extent of somatic symptoms in children with other emotional disorders (McCauley, Carlson, & Calderon, 1991)? How do children diagnosed with emotional disorders with and without somatic symptoms differ with regard to their prognosis, etiology, and treatment response?

Somatoform disorders are important because they drain society's economic and medical resources, strain the family environment, and hinder children's social and academic development. Further research is needed that addresses the assessment, etiology, prognosis, and treatment of each of the different types of somatoform disorders across the lifespan. Early interventions that target high-risk populations can help reduce the cost of these disorders to both individuals and society.

ACKNOWLEDGMENT

This work was supported in part by a grant from the National Institute of Child Health & Human Development (RO 1 HD 23264).

5.25.13 REFERENCES

Achenbach, T. M., Conners, C. K., Quay, H. C., Verhulst, F. C., & Howell, C. T. (1989). Replication of empirically derived syndromes as a basis for taxonomy of child/ adolescent psychopathology. *Journal of Abnormal Child Psychology, 17,* 299–323.
Achenbach, T. M., & Edelbrock, C. S. (1983). *Manual for the Child Behavior Checklist and Revised Child Behavior Profile.* Burlington, VT: University of Vermont.
Achenbach, T. M., McConaughy, S. H., & Howell, C. T. (1987). Child/adolescent behavioral and emotional problems: Implications of cross-informant correlations for situational specificity. *Psychological Bulletin, 101,* 213–232.
Alfven, G. (1993). The pressure pain threshold (PPT) of certain children suffering from recurrent abdominal pain of non-organic origin. *Acta Paediatrica, 82,* 481–483.
Allen, A. J., Leonard, H., & Swedo, S. E. (1995). Current knowledge of medications for the treatment of childhood anxiety disorders. *Journal of the American Academy of Child and Adolescent Psychiatry, 34,* 976–986.
American Psychiatric Association (1952). *Diagnostic and statistical manual of mental disorders.* Washington, DC: American Psychiatric Press.
American Psychiatric Association (1968). *Diagnostic and statistical manual of mental disorders* (2nd ed.). Washington, DC: American Psychiatric Press.
American Psychiatric Association (1978). *Diagnostic and statistical manual of mental disorders* (3rd ed.). Washington, DC: American Psychiatric Press.
American Psychiatric Association (1987). *Diagnostic and statistical manual of mental disorders* (3rd ed. Rev.). Washington, DC: American Psychiatric Press.
American Psychiatric Association (1994). *Diagnostic and statistical manual of mental disorders* (4th ed.). Washington, DC: American Psychiatric Press.
Andrasik, F., Burke, E. J., Attanasio, V., Rosenblum, E. L. (1985). Child, parent and physician reports of a child's headache pain: Relationships prior to and following treatment. *Headache, 25,* 421–425.
Apley, J. (1958). A common denominator in the recurrent pains of childhood. *Proceedings of the Royal Society of Medicine, 51,* 1023–1024.
Apley, J. (1975). *The child with abdominal pain.* Oxford: Blackwell.
Apley, J., & Hale, B. (1973). Children with recurrent abdominal pain: How do they grow up? *British Medical Journal, 3,* 7–9.
Apley, J., & Naish, N. (1958). Recurrent abdominal pains: A field survey of 1000 school children. *Archives of Diseases of Children, 33,* 165–170.
Aro, H. (1987). Life stress and psychosomatic symptoms among 14 to 16-year-old Finnish adolescents. *Psychological Medicine, 17,* 191–201.
Aro, H., Paronen, O., & Aro, S. (1987). Psychosomatic symptoms among 14–16 year old Finnish adolescents. *Social Psychiatry, 22,* 171–176.
Aro, H., & Taipale, V. (1987). The impact of timing of puberty on psychosomatic symptoms among fourteen to sixteen year-old Finnish girls. *Child Development, 58,* 261–268.
Bagby, R. M., Taylor, G. J., & Parker, D. A. (1994). The twenty-item Toronto Alexithymia Scale. *Journal of Psychosomatic Research, 38,* 23–40.
Bangash, I. H., Worley, G., & Kandt, R. S. (1988). Hysterical conversion reactions mimicking neurological disease. *American Journal of Diseases of Childhood, 142,* 1203–1206.
Barsky, A. J., Goodson, J. D., Lane, R. S., & Cleary, P. D. (1988). The amplification of somatic symptoms. *Psychosomatic Medicine, 50,* 510–519.
Barsky, A. J., & Klerman, G. (1983). Overview: Hypo-

chondriasis, bodily complaints, and somatic styles. *American Journal of Psychiatry, 140,* 273–283.

Barsky, A. J., Wyshak, G., & Klerman, G. L., (1986). Psychiatric comorbidity in *DSM-III-R* hypochondriasis. *Archives of Senses Psychiatry, 4,* 101–108.

Bass, C., & Murphy,. M. (1995). Somatoform and personality disorders: Syndromal comorbidity and overlapping developmental pathways. *Journal of Psychosomatic Research, 39,* 403–427.

Beautrais, A., Fergusson, D., & Shannon, F. (1982). Life events and childhood morbidity: A prospective study. *Pediatrics, 70,* 935–940.

Belle, D., Burr, R., & Cooney, J. (1987). Boys and girls as social support theorists. *Sex Roles, 17,* 657–665.

Belmaker, E. (1984). Nonspecific somatic symptoms in early adolescent girls. *Journal of Adolescent Health, 5,* 30–33.

Belmaker, E., Espinoza, R., & Pogrund, R. (1985). Use of medical services by adolescents with non-specific somatic symptoms. *International Journal of Adolescent Medicine and Health, 1,* 150–156.

Benjamin, S., & Eminson, D. M. (1992). Abnormal illness behavior: Childhood experiences and long term consequences. *International Review of Psychiatry, 4,* 55–70.

Bernstein, E., & Putnam, F. W. (1986). Development, reliability and validity of a dissociation scale. *Journal of Nervous and Mental Disorders, 174,* 727–735.

Bird, H. R., Canino, G., Rubio-Stipec, M., Gould, M. S., Ribera, J., Sesman, M., Woodbury, M., Huertas-Goldman, S., Pagan, A., Sanchez-Lacy, A., & Moscoso, M. (1988). Estimates of the prevalence of childhood maladjustment in a community survey in Puerto Rico. *Archives of General Psychiatry, 45,* 1120–1126.

Bohman, M., Cloninger, C. R., von Knorring, A. L., Sigvardsson, S. (1984). An adoption study of somatoform disorders: III. Cross-fostering analysis and genetic relationship to alcoholism and criminality. *Archives of General Psychiatry, 41,* 872–878.

Bolton, J., & Cohen, P. (1986). "Escape with honour": The need for face-saving. *Bulletin of Anna Freud Centre, 9,* 19–33.

Bourke, M. P., Taylor, G. J., Parker, J. D. A., & Bagby, R. M. (1992). Alexithymia in women with anorexia nervosa: A preliminary investigation. *British Journal of Psychiatry, 161,* 240–243.

Bowman, E. S. (1993). Etiology and clinical course of pseudoseizures: Relationship to trauma, depression and dissociation. *Psychosomatics, 34,* 333–342.

Boyce, T. W., Jensen, E. W., Cassel, J. C., Collier, A. M., Smith, A. H., & Ramsey, C. T. (1977). Influence of life events and family routines on childhood respiratory-tract illness. *Pediatrics, 60,* 609–615.

Briquet, P. (1859). *Traite de Hysterie.* Paris: J. B. Balliaere and Fils.

Cadoret, R. J. (1978). Psychopathology in adopted-away offspring of biologic parents with antisocial behavior. *Archives of General Psychiatry, 35,* 176–184.

Campo, J. V., & Fritsch, S. L. (1994). Somatization in children and adolescents. *Journal of the American Academy of Child and Adolescent Psychiatry, 33,* 1223–1235.

Campo, J. V., & Garber, J. (in press). Somatization. In R. T. Ammerman & J. V. Campo (Eds.), *Handbook of pediatric psychology and psychiatry.* Boston: Allyn & Bacon.

Campo, J. V., & Raney, D. (1995). The pediatric medical-psychiatric unit in a psychiatric hospital. *Psychosomatics, 36,* 438–444.

Caplan, L. R., & Nadelson, T. (1980). Multiple sclerosis and hysteria: Lessons learned from their association. *Journal of the American Medical Association, 243,* 2418–2421.

Chase, H. P., & Jackson, G. G. (1981). Stress and sugar control in children with insulin-dependent diabetes mellitus. *Journal of Pediatrics, 98,* 1011–1013.

Christensen, M. F., & Mortensen, O. (1975). Long-term prognosis in children with recurrent abdominal pain. *Archives of Diseases of Childhood, 50,* 110.

Cloninger, C. R. (1986). *Somatoform and dissociative disorders.* Philadelphia: Saunders.

Cloninger, C. R., Sigvardsson, S., von Knorring, A. L., Bohman, M. (1984). An adoption study of somatoform disorders. *Archives of General Psychiatry, 41,* 863–871.

Clouse, R. E., & Lustman, P. J. (1983). Psychiatric illness and contraction abnormalities of the esophagus. *New England Journal of Medicine, 309,* 1337–1342.

Cohen, K., Auld, F., & Brooker, H. (1994). Is alexithymia related to psychosomatic disorder and somatising? *Journal of Psychosomatic Research, 38,* 119–127.

Costello, A., Edelbrock, C. S., Kalas, R., Kessler, M. K., & Klaric, S. (1982). *National Institute of Mental Health Diagnostic Interview Schedule of Children.* Bethesda, MD: National Institutes of Health.

Costello, E. J., & Edelbrock, C. S. (1985). Detection of psychiatric disorders in pediatric primary care: A preliminary report. *Journal of the American Academy of Child Psychiatry, 24,* 771–774.

Costello, E. J., Edelbrock, C., Costello, A. J., Dulcan, M. K., Burns, B. J., & Brent, D. (1988). Psychopathology in pediatric primary care: The hidden morbidity. *Pediatrics, 82,* 415–424.

Craig, K. D. (1978). Social modeling influences on pain. In R. A. Sternbach (Ed.), *The psychology of pain* (pp. 73-109). New York: Raven Press.

Craig, T. K. J., Boardman, A. P., Mills, K., Daly-Jones, O., & Drake, H. (1993). The South London Somatisation Study I: Longitudinal course and the influence of early life experiences. *British Journal of Psychiatry, 163,* 579–588.

Cunningham, S. J., McGrath, P. J., Ferguson, H. B., Humphreys, P., D'Astrous, J., Latter, J., Goodman, J. T., & Firestone, P. (1987). Personality and behavioral characteristics in pediatric migraine. *Headache, 27,* 16–20.

Delameter, A. M., Rosenbloom, N., Conners, K., & Hertweck, L. (1983). The behavioral treatment of hysterical paralysis in a ten-year-old boy: A case study. *Journal of the American Academy of Child Psychiatry, 1,* 73–79.

Derogatis, L. R., Lipman, R. S., Rickels, K. Uhlenhuth, E. H., & Covi, L. (1974). The Hopkins Symptom Checklist. *Behavioral Science, 19,* 1–15.

Dolce, J. J., & Raczynski, J. M. (1985). Neuromuscular activity and electromyography in painful backs: Psychological and biomechanical models in assessment and treatment. *Psychological Bulletin, 97,* 502–520.

Dubowitz, V., & Hersov, L. (1976). Management of children with nonorganic (hysterical) disorders of motor function. *Developmental Medicine and Child Neurology, 18,* 358–368.

Dunn-Geier, J., McGrath, P. J., Rourke, B. P., Latter, J., & D'Astous, D. (1986). Adolescent chronic pain: The ability to cope. *Pain, 26,* 23–32.

Edwards, M. C., Finney, J. W., & Bonner, M. (1991). Matching treatment with recurrent abdominal pain symptoms: An evaluation of dietary fiber and relaxation treatments. *Behavior Therapy, 22,* 257–267.

Edwards, P. W., Zeichner, A., Kuczmierczyk, A. R., & Boczkowski, J. (1985). Familial pain models: The relationship between family history of pain and current pain experience. *Pain, 21,* 379–384.

Elkins, G. R., & Carter, B. D. (1986). Hypnotherapy in the treatment of childhood psychogenic coughing: A case report. *American Journal of Clinical Hypnosis, 29,* 59–63.

Emslie, G., Rush, A. J., & Weinberg, A. W. (in press). A double-blind randomized placebo-controlled trial of fluoxetine in depressed children. *Archives of General Psychiatry.*

Engel, G. L. (1962). *Psychological development in health and disease.* Philadelphia: Saunders.

Ernst, A. R., Routh, D. K., & Harper, D. C. (1984). Abdominal pain in children and symptoms of somatization disorder. *Journal of Pediatric Psychology, 9,* 77–86.

Escobar, J. I., Burnam, A., & Karno, M. (1987). Somatization in the community. *Archives of General Psychiatry, 44,* 713–720.

Feuerstein, M., Barr, R., Francoeur, E., Houle, M., & Rafman, S. (1982). Potential biobehavioral mechanisms of recurrent abdominal pain in children. *Pain, 13,* 287–298.

Finney, J. W., Lemanek, K. L., Cataldo, M. F., Katz, H. P., & Fuqua, R. W. (1989). Pediatric psychology in primary healthcare: Brief targeted therapy for recurrent abdominal pain. *Behavior Therapy, 20,* 283–291.

Flor, H., Turk, D. C., & Birbaumer, N. (1985). Assessment of stress-related psychophysiological reactions in chronic back pain patients. *Journal of Consulting and Clinical Psychology, 53,* 354–364.

Fordyce, W. E. (1978). Learning processes in pain. In R. A. Sternbach (Ed.), *The psychology of pain* (pp. 49–72). New York: Raven Press.

Freud, S. (1896/1962). The ethiology of hysteria. In *Complete psychological works of Sigmund Freud* (pp. 191–221). London: Hogarth.

Fuchs, D., & Thelen, M. H. (1988). Children's expected interpersonal consequences of communicating their affective state and reported likelihood of expression. *Child Development, 59,* 1314–1322.

Fujii, S., Kachi, T., & Sobue, I. (1981). Chronic headache: Its psychosomatic aspect. *Japanese Journal of Psychosomatic Medicine, 21,* 411–419.

Garber, J., & Hollon, S. D. (1991). What can specificity designs say about causality in psychopathology research? *Psychological Bulletin, 110,* 129–136.

Garber, J., Van Slyke, D., & Walker, L. S. (1997). Concordance between mothers' and children's reports of somatic and emotional symptoms in patients with recurrent abdominal pain or psychiatric disorders. Manuscript under review.

Garber, J., Walker, L. S., & Zeman, J. L. (1991). Somatization symptoms in a community sample of children and adolescents: Further validation of the Children's Somatization Inventory. *Psychological Assessment: A Journal of Consulting and Clinical Psychology, 3,* 588–595.

Garber, J., Zeman, J. L., Walker, L. S. (1990). Recurrent abdominal pain in children and adolescents: Psychiatric diagnoses and parental psychopathology. *Journal of the American Academy of Child and Adolescent Psychiatry, 29,* 648–656.

Garralda, M. E. (1992). A selective review of child psychiatric syndromes with a somatic presentation. *British Journal of Psychiatry, 161,* 759–773.

Garralda, M. E. (1996). Somatization in children. *British Journal of Psychiatry,* 13–33.

Gold, S. (1965). Diagnosis and management of hysterical contracture in children. *British Medical Journal, 1,* 21–23.

Goodman, J. E., & McGrath, P. J. (1991). The epidemiology of pain in children and adolescents: A review. *Pain, 46,* 247–264.

Goodwin, J., Simms, M., & Bergman, R. (1979). Hysterical seizures in four adolescent girls. *American Journal of Orthopsychiatry, 49,* 698–703.

Goodyer, I. M. (1981). Hysterical conversion reactions in childhood. *Journal of Child Psychology and Psychiatry, 22,* 179–188.

Goodyer, I. M., & Mitchell, C. (1989). Somatic and emotional disorders in childhood and adolescence.

Journal of Psychosomatic Research, 33, 681–688.

Goodyer, I. M., & Taylor, D. C. (1985). Hysteria. *Archives of Diseases of Childhood, 63,* 680–681.

Gottesman, I. I. (1962). Differential inheritance of the psychoneuroses. *Eugenics Quarterly, 9,* 223–267.

Grattan-Smith, P., Fairley, M., & Procopis, P. (1988). Clinical features of conversion disorder. *Archives of Diseases of Children, 63,* 408–414.

Green, A. (1993). Child sexual abuse: Immediate and long-term effects and intervention. *Journal of the American Academy of Child and Adolescent Psychiatry, 32,* 890–902.

Green, M., & Solnit, A. J. (1964). Reactions to the threatened loss of a child: A vulnerable child syndrome. *Pediatrics, 34,* 58–66.

Greene, J. W., Walker, L. S., Hickman, G., Thompson, J. (1985). Stressful life events and somatic complaints in adolescents. *Pediatrics, 75,* 19–22.

Guze, S. B., Cloninger, C. R., Martin, R. L., Clayton, P. J. (1986). A follow-up and family study of Briquet's syndrome. *British Journal of Psychiatry, 149,* 17–23.

Helm-Hylkema, J. van der, Orlebek, J. F., Enting, L. A., Thijssen, J. H. H., & Ree, J. van (1990). Effects of behavior therapy and plasma B-endorphin in young migraine patients. *Psychoneuroendocrinology, 15,* 39–45.

Henderson, S. (1974). Care eliciting behavior in man. *Journal of Nervous and Mental Diseases, 159,* 172–181.

Herman, R. M., & Simonds, I. F. (1975). Incidence of conversion symptoms in children evaluated psychiatrically. *Modern Medicine, 72,* 597–604.

Hodges, K., Kline, J. J., Barbero, G., & Flanery, R. (1985a). Depressive symptoms in children with recurrent abdominal pain and in their families. *Journal of Pediatrics, 107,* 622–626.

Hodges, K., Kline, J. J., Barbero, G., & Woodruff, C. (1985b). Anxiety in children with recurrent abdominal pain and their parents. *Psychosomatics, 26,* 859–866.

Hodgman, C. H. (1995). Conversion and somatization in pediatrics. *Pediatrics in Review, 16,* 29–34.

Hunter, R. S., Kilstrom, N., & Loda, F. (1985). Sexually abused children: Identifying masked presentations in a medical setting. *Child Abuse and Neglect, 9,* 17–25.

Hyams, J. S., Burke, G., Davis, P. M., Rzepski, B., & Andrulonis, P. A. (1996). Abdominal pain and irritable bowel syndrome in adolescents: A community-based study. *Journal of Pediatrics, 129,* 220–226.

Inouye, E. (1972). Genetic aspects of neurosis. *International Journal of Mental Health, 1,* 176–189.

Kagan, J. Reznick, J. S., & Snidman, N. (1988). Biological bases of childhood shyness. *Science, 240,* 167–171.

Kendler, K. S., Heath, A. C., Martin, N. G., & Eaves, L. J. (1987). Symptoms of anxiety and symptoms of depression. *Archives of General Psychiatry, 44,* 451–457.

Kellner, R. (1986). *Somatization and hypochondriasis.* New York: Praeger.

Kellner, R. (1990). Somatization. *The Journal of Nervous and Mental Disease, 178,* 150–160.

Kellner, R. (1991). *Psychosomatic syndromes and somatic symptoms.* Washington, DC: American Psychiatric Press.

Kirmayer, L. (1984). Culture, affect and somatization. Part 1. *Transcultural Psychiatric Research Review, 21,* 159–188.

Klevan, J. L., & DeJong, A. R. (1990). Urinary tract symptoms and urinary tract infection following sexual abuse. *American Journal of Diseases of Childhood, 144,* 242–244.

Klonoff, E. A., & Moore, D. J. (1986). "Conversion reactions" in adolescents: A biofeedback-based operant approach. *Journal of Behavioral Therapy and Experimental Psychiatry, 17,* 179–184.

Kotsopoulos, S., & Snow, B. (1986). Conversion disorders in children: A study of clinical outcome. *Psychiatric Journal of the University of Ottawa, 11,* 134–139.

Kovacs, M. (1980/1981). Rating scales to assess depression in school-aged children. *Acta Paedopsychiatric, 46,* 305–315.

Kriechman, A. M. (1987). Siblings with somatoform disorders in childhood and adolescence. *Journal of the American Academy of Child and Adolescent Psychiatry, 26,* 226–231.

LaBarbera, J. D., & Dozier, J. E. (1980). Hysterical seizures: The role of sexual exploitation. *Psychosomatics, 21,* 897–903.

Lahey, B. B., Flagg, E. W., Bird, H. R., Schwab-Stone, M. E., Canino, G., Dulcan, M. K., Leaf, P. J., Davies, M., Brogan, D., Bourdon, K., Horwitz, S. M., Rubio-Stipec, M., Freeman, D. H., Lichtman, J. H., Shaffer, D., Goodman, S. H., Narrow, W. E., Weissman, M. M., Kandel, D. B., Jensen, P. S., Richters, J. E., & Regier, D. A. (1996). The NIMH methods for the Epidemiology of Child and Adolescent Mental Disorders (MECA) Study: Background and Methodology. *Journal of the American Academy of Child and Adolescent Psychiatry, 35,* 855–864.

Larson, B. S. (1991). Somatic complaints and their relationship to depressive symptoms in Swedish adolescents. *Journal of Child Psychology and Psychiatry, 32,* 821–832.

Larsson, B. (1992). Behavioral treatment of somatic disorders in children and adolescents. *European Child and Adolescent Psychiatry, 1,* 68–81.

Larsson, B., & Mellin, L. (1988). The psychological treatment of recurrent headache in adolescents—short term outcome and its prediction. *Headache, 28,* 187–195.

Lask, B., & Fosson, A. (1989). *Childhood illness: The psychosomatic approach.* New York: Wiley.

Laybourne, P. C., & Churchill, S. W. (1972). Symptom discouragement in treating hysterical reactions of childhood. *International Journal of Child Psychotherapy, 1,* 111–123.

Lehmkuhl, G., Blanz, G., Lehmkuhl, U., & Braun-Scharm, H. (1989). Conversion disorder: Symptomatology and course in childhood and adolescence. *European Archives of Psychiatry and Neurological Sciences, 238,* 155–160.

Leslie, S. A. (1988). Diagnosis and treatment of hysterical conversion reactions. *Archives of Diseases of Children, 63,* 506–511.

Lesser, R. P., Lueders, H., Dinner, D. S. (1983). Evidence for epilepsy is rare in patients with psychogenic seizures. *Neurology, 33,* 502–504.

Lewis, C. E., & Lewis, M. A. (1989). Educational outcomes and illness behaviors in participants in a child-initiated care system: A 12-year follow-up study. *Pediatrics, 84,* 845–850.

Liebman, W. H. (1978). Recurrent abdominal pain in children: A retrospective survey of 119 patients. *Clinical Pediatrics (Philadelphia), 17,* 149–153.

Linton, S. J. (1986). A case study of the behavioral treatment of chronic stomach pain in a child. *Behavior Change, 3,* 70–73.

Lipowski, Z. J. (1988). Somatization: The concept and its clinical application. *American Journal of Psychiatry, 145,* 1358–1368.

Livingston, R., & Martin-Connici, C. (1985). Multiple somatic complaints and possible somatization disorder in prepubertal children. *Journal of the American Academy of Child Psychiatry, 24,* 603–607.

Loewenstein, R. J. (1990). Somatoform disorders in victims of incest and child abuse. In R. P. Kluft (Ed.). *Incest related syndromes of adult psychopathology* (pp. 76–107). Washington, DC: American Psychiatric Press.

Looff, D. H. (1970). Psychophysiological and conversion reactions in children. *Journal of the American Academy of Child Psychiatry, 9,* 318–331.

Maisami, M., & Freeman, J. M. (1987). Conversion reactions in children as body language: A combined child psychiatry/neurology team approach to the management of functional neurologic disorders in children. *Pediatrics, 80,* 46–52.

Mallouh, S. K., Abbey, S. E., & Gillies, L. A. (1995). The role of loss in treatment outcome of persistent somatization. *General Hospital Psychiatry, 17,* 187–191.

Maloney, M. J. (1980). Diagnosing hysterical conversion reactions in children. *Journal of Pediatrics, 97,* 1016–1020.

Mayou, R. (1976). The nature of bodily symptoms. *British Journal of Psychiatry, 129,* 55–60.

Mayou, R., Bass, C., & Sharpe, M. (1995). *Treatment of functional somatic symptoms.* Oxford: Oxford University Press.

McCauley, E., Carlson, G. A., & Calderon, R. (1991). The role of somatic complaints in the diagnosis of depression in children and adolescents. *Journal of the American Academy of Child and Adolescent Psychiatry, 30,* 631–635.

McGrath, P. J. (1987). The multidimensional assessment and management of recurrent pain syndromes in children. *Behavior Research and Therapy, 25,* 251–262.

McGrath, P. J., Goodman, J. T., Firestone, P., Shipman, R., & Peters, S. (1983). Recurrent abdominal pain: A psychogenic disorder? *Archives of Diseases of Childhood, 58,* 888–890.

McGrath, P. J., Humphreys, P., Goodman, J. T., Keene, D., Firestone, P., Jacob, P., & Cunningham, S. J. (1988). Relaxation prophylaxis for childhood migraine: A randomized placebo-controlled trial. *Developmental Medicine and Child Neurology, 30,* 626–631.

Mechanic, D. (1972). Social psychologic factors affecting the presentation of bodily complaints. *The New England Journal of Medicine, 286,* 1132–1139.

Meierkord, H., Will, B., Fish, D., & Shorvon, S. (1991). The clinical features and prognosis of pseudoseizures diagnosed using video-EEG telemetry. *Neurology, 41,* 1643–1646.

Miller, A. J., & Kratochwill, T. R. (1979). Reduction of frequent stomach complaints by time out. *Behavior Therapy, 10,* 211–218.

Minuchin, S., Baker, L., Rosman, B. L., Liebman, R., Milman, L., & Todd, T. C. (1975). A conceptual model of psychosomatic illness in children. *Archives of General Psychiatry, 32,* 1031–1038.

Minuchin, S., Rosman, B. L., & Baker, L. (1978). *Psychosomatic families: Anorexia nervosa in context.* Cambridge, MA: Harvard University Press.

Mizes, J. S. (1985). The use of contingent reinforcement in the treatment of a conversion disorder: A multiple baseline study. *Journal of Behavior Therapy and Experimental Psychiatry, 16,* 341–345.

Morrison, J. (1989). Childhood sexual histories of women with somatization disorder. *American Journal of Psychiatry, 146,* 239–241.

Mullins, L. L., & Olson, R. A. (1990). Familial factors in the etiology, maintenance, and treatment of somatoform disorders in children. *Family Systems Medicine, 8,* 159–175.

Nemiah, J. C. (1977). Alexithymia: Theoretical considerations. *Psychotherapy and Psychosomatics, 8,* 199–206.

Nemiah, J. C. (1985). Somatoform disorders. In H. I. Kaplan & B. I. Sadock (Eds.), *Comprehensive textbook of psychiatry* (4th ed., pp. 924–942). Baltimore, MD: Williams & Wilkins.

Nemzer, E. D. (1996). Somatoform disorders. In M. Lewis (Ed.). *Child and adolescent psychiatry: A comprehensive textbook* (2nd ed., pp. 693–702). Baltimore, MD: Williams & Wilkins.

Offord, D. R., Boyle, M. H., Szatmari, P., Rae-Grant, N. I., Links, P. S., Cadman, D. T., Byles, J. A., Crawford, J. W., Blum, H. M., Byrne, C., Thomas, H., & Woodward, C. A. (1987). Ontario Child Health Study II.: Six-month prevalence of disorder and rates of service utilization. *Archives of General Psychiatry, 44,* 832–836.

Orr, D. (1986). Adolescence, stress and psychosomatic issues. *Journal of Adolescent Health Care, 7*(Suppl.), 975–1085.

Osborne, R. B., Hatcher, J. W., & Richtsmeier, A. J. (1989). The role of social modeling in unexplained pediatric pain. *Journal of Pediatric Psychology, 14,* 43–61.

Oster, J. (1972). Recurrent abdominal pain, headache, and limb pains in children and adolescents. *Pediatrics, 50,* 429–436.

Osterhaus, S. O. L., Passchier, J., Helm-Hylkema, H. van der, de Jong, K. T., Orlebeke, J. F., de Grauw, A. J. C., Dekker, P. H. (1993). Effects of behavioral psychophysiological treatment of schoolchildren with migraine in a nonclinical setting: Predictors and process variables. *Journal of Pediatric Psychology, 18,* 697–715.

Pantell, R. H., & Goodman, B. W. (1983). Adolescent chest pain: A prospective study. *Pediatrics, 71,* 881–887.

Parmelee, A. H. (1986). Children's illnesses: Their beneficial effects on behavioral development. *Child Development, 57,* 1–10.

Pennebaker, J. W., & Skelton, J. A. (1978). Psychological parameters of physical symptoms. *Personality and Social Psychological Bulletin, 4,* 524–530.

Perrin, J. M., MacLean, W. E., & Janco, R. L. (1988). Does stress affect bleeding in hemophilia? *The American Journal of Pediatric Hematology/Oncology, 10,* 230–235.

Phillips, K. A., McElroy, S. L., Keck, P. E., & Hudson, J. (1993). Body Dysmorphic disorder: 30 cases of imagined ugliness. *American Journal of Psychiatry, 150,* 302–308.

Pilowsky, I. (1987). Abnormal illness behavior and chronic pain. In G. D. Burrows, D. Elton, & G. V. Stanley (Eds.), *Handbook of chronic pain management* (pp. 131–136). New York: Elsevier.

Pilowsky, I., Bassett, D. L., Begg, M. W., Thomas, P. G. (1982). Childhood hospitalization and chronic intractable pain in adults: A controlled retrospective study. *International Journal of Psychiatry and Medicine, 12,* 75–184.

Prazar, G. (1987). Conversion reactions in adolescents. *Pediatric Review, 8,* 279–286.

Prichard, C. T., Ball, I. D., Culbert, I., & Faust, D. (1988). Using the personality inventory for children to identify children with somatoform disorders: MMPI findings revisited. *Journal of Pediatric Psychology, 3,* 237–245.

Proctor, J. T. (1958). Hysteria in childhood. *American Journal of Orthopsychiatry, 28,* 394–407.

Prugh, D. G. (1983). *The psychosocial aspects of pediatrics.* Philadelphia: Lea & Febiger.

Putnam, F. W., Helmers, K., & Trickett, P. K. (in press). Development, reliability and validity of a child dissociative scale. *Child Abuse and Neglect.*

Rauste-von Wright, M., & von Wright, J. (1981). A longitudinal study of psychosomatic symptoms in healthy 11–18 year old girls and boys. *Journal of Psychosomatic Research, 25,* 525–534.

Reesor, K. A., & Craig, K. D. (1988). Medically incongruent chronic back pain: Physical limitations, suffering, and ineffective coping. *Pain, 32,* 35–45.

Reynolds, C. R., & Richmond, B. O. (1985). *The Revised Children's Manifest Anxiety Scale Manual.* New York: Western Psychological Services.

Riddle, M. A., Scahill, L., King, R. A., Hardin, M. T., Anderson, G. M., Ort, S. I., Smith, J. C., Leckman, J. F., & Cohen, D. J. (1992). Double-blind, crossover trial of fluoxetine and placebo in children and adolescents with obsessive compulsive disorder. *Journal of the American Academy of Child and Adolescent Psychiatry, 31,* 1062–1069.

Rimza, M. E., Berg, R. A., Locke, C. (1988). Sexual abuse:

Somatic and emotional reactions. *Child Abuse and Neglect, 12,* 201–208.

Rivinus, T. M., Jamison, D. L., & Graham, P. J. (1975). Childhood organic neurological disease presenting as psychiatric disorder. *Archives of Diseases of Childhood, 40,* 115–119.

Robbins, J. M., & Kirmayer, L. J. (1991). Attributions of common somatic symptoms. *Psychological Medicine, 21,* 1029–1045.

Robins, E., & O'Neal, P. (1953). Clinical features of hysteria in children—with a note on prognosis: A two to seventeen year follow-up study of 41 patients. *Nervous Child, 10,* 246–271.

Robinson, J. O., Alverez, J. H., Dodge, J. A. (1990). Life events and family history in children with recurrent abdominal pain. *Journal of Psychosomatic Research, 34,* 171–181.

Rock, N. (1971). Conversion reactions in childhood: A clinical study on childhood neuroses. *Journal of the American Academy of Child Psychiatry, 10,* 65–3.

Roghmann, K. J., & Haggerty, R. J. (1973). Daily stress, illness, and use of health services in young families. *Pediatric Research, 7,* 520–526.

Routh, D. K., & Ernst, A. R. (1984). Somatization disorder in relatives of children and adolescents with functional abdominal pain. *Journal of Pediatric Psychology, 9,* 427–437.

Rutter, M., Tizard, J., & Whitmore, K. (1970). *Education, health, and behavior.* London: Longman Group.

Saarni, C. (1990). Emotional competence: How emotions and relationships become integrated. In R. Thompson (Ed.), *Socioemotional Development: Nebraska Symposium on Motivation* (pp. 115–181). Lincoln, NE: University of Nebraska Press.

Sainsbury, P., & Gibson, J. G. (1954). Symptoms of anxiety and tension and the accompanying physiological changes in the muscular system. *Journal of Neurological and Neurosurgical Psychiatry, 17,* 216–224.

Sanders, M. R., Rebgetz, M., Morrison, M., Bor, W., Gordon, A., Dadds, M., & Shepherd, R. (1989). Cognitive-behavioral treatment of recurrent nonspecific abdominal pain in children: An analysis of generalization, maintenance, and side effects. *Journal of Consulting and Clinical Psychology, 57,* 294–300.

Sanders, M. R., Shepherd, R. W., Cleghorn, G., & Woolford, H. (1994). The treatment of recurrent abdominal pain in children: A controlled comparison of cognitive-behavioral family intervention and standard pediatric care. *Journal of Consulting and Clinical Psychology, 62,* 306–314.

Sank, L. I., & Biglan, A. (1974). Operant treatment of a case of recurrent abdominal pain in a 10-year old boy. *Behavior Therapy, 5,* 677–681.

Scaloubaca, D., Slade, P., & Creed, R. (1988). Life events and somatization among students. *Journal of Psychosomatic Research, 32,* 221–229.

Schneider, S., & Rice, D. R. (1979). Neurologic manifestations of childhood hysteria. *Journal of Pediatrics, 94,* 153–156.

Schulman, J. L. (1988). Use of a coping approach in the management of children with conversion reactions. *Journal American Academy of Child and Adolescent Psychiatry, 27,* 785–788.

Shaffer, D., Fisher, P., Dulcan, M. K., Davies, M., Piacentini, J., Schwab- Stone, M. E., Lahey, B. B., Bourdon, K., Jensen, P. S., Bird, H. R., Canino, G., & Regier, D. A. (1996). The NIMH Diagnostic Interview Schedule for Children version 2.3 (DISC-2.3): Description, acceptability, prevalence rates, and performance in the MECA study. *Journal of the Academy of Child and Adolescent Psychiatry, 35,* 865–877.

Shapiro, E. G., & Rosenfeld, A. A. (1987). *The somatizing child.* New York: Springer.

Shields, J. (1982). Genetic studies of hysterical disorders. In A. Roy (Ed.), *Hysteria*. New York: Wiley.

Sifneos, P. E. (1973). The prevalence of "alexithymic" characteristics in psychosomatic patients. *Psychotherapy and Psychosomatics, 22*, 255–262.

Simon, G. E. (1991). Somatization and psychiatric disorder. In L. J. Kirmayer & J. M. Robbins (eds.), *Current concepts of somatization research and clinical perspectives*. Washington, DC: American Psychiatric Press.

Spierings, C., Poels, P. J. E., Sijben, N., Gabreels, F. J. M., & Renier, W. O. (1990). Conversion disorders in childhood: A retrospective follow-up study of 84 patients. *Developmental Medicine and Child Neurology, 32*, 865–871.

Srinath, S., Bharat, S., Girimaji, S., Seshadri, S. (1993). Characteristics of a child inpatient population with hysteria in India. *Journal of the American Academy of Child and Adolescent Psychiatry, 32*, 822–825.

Steckel, W. (1943). *The interpretation of dreams*. New York: Liveright.

Stefansson, J. G., Messina, J. S., & Meyerowitz, S. (1976). Hysterical neurosis, conversion type: Clinical and epidemiological considerations. *Acta Psychiatra Scandinavian, 53*, 119–138.

Steinhausen, H. C., Aster, M. V., Pfeiffer, E., & Gobel, D. (1989). Comparative studies of conversion disorders in childhood and adolescence. *Journal of Child Psychology and Psychiatry, 30*, 615–621.

Stern, K., Murphy, M., & Bass, C. (1993). Personality disorders in patients with somatisation disorder: A controlled study. *British Journal of Psychiatry, 163*, 785–789.

Stevens, H. (1986). Is it organic or is it functional, is it hysteria or malingering? *Neuropsychiatry, 9*, 241–254.

Stevenson, J., Simpson, J., & Bailey, V. (1988). Research note: Recurrent headaches and stomachaches in preschool children. *Journal of Child Psychology and Psychiatry, 29*, 897–900.

Stickler, G. B., & Murphy, D. B. (1979). Recurrent abdominal pain. *American Journal of Diseases of Childhood, 133*, 486–489.

Stone, R., & Barbero, G. (1970). Recurrent abdominal pain in childhood. *Pediatrics, 45*, 732–738.

Swartz, M., Landerman, R., & George, L. K. (1991). The diagnosis of somatization disorder. In L. N. Robins & D. A. Regier (Eds.), *Psychiatric disorders in America* (pp. 220–257). New York: Free Press.

Taylor, G. J., Baglay, M., Ryan, D.P., Parker, J. D. A. (1990). Validation of the alexithymia construct: A measurement-based approach. *Canadian Journal of Psychiatry, 35*, 290–297.

Taylor, D. C., Szatmari, P., Boyle, M. H., & Offord, D. R. (1996). Somatization and the vocabulary of everyday bodily experiences and concerns: A communicate study of adolescents. *Journal of the American Academy of Child and Adolescent Psychiatry, 35*, 491–499.

Torgensen, S. (1986). Genetics of somatoform disorders. *Archives of General Psychiatry, 43*, 502–505.

Turgay, A. (1980). Conversion reactions in children. *Psychiatric Journal of the University of Ottawa, 5*, 287–294.

Turgay, A. (1990). Treatment outcome for children and adolescents with conversion disorder. *Canadian Journal of Psychiatry, 35*, 585–589.

Turkat, I. D. (1982). An investigation of parental modeling in the etiology of diabetic illness behavior. *Behavior Research and Therapy, 2*, 547–552.

Tyler, P., Fowler-Dixon, R., & Ferguson, B. (1990). The justification for the diagnosis of hypochondriacal personality disorder. *Journal of Psychosomatic Research, 34*, 637–642.

Volkmar, R. R., Poll, J., & Lewis, M. (1984). Conversion reactions in children and adolescents. *Journal of the American Academy of Child and Adolescent Psychiatry, 23*, 424–430.

Walker, L. S., Garber, J., & Greene, J. W. (1991). Somatization symptoms in pediatric abdominal pain patients: Relation to chronicity of abdominal pain and parent somatization. *Journal of Abnormal Child Psychology, 19*, 379–394.

Walker, L. S., Garber, J., & Greene, J. W. (1993). Psychosocial correlates of recurrent childhood pain: A comparison of pediatric patients with recurrent abdominal pain, organic illness, and psychiatric disorders. *Journal of Abnormal Psychology, 102*, 248–258.

Walker, L. S., Garber, J., & Greene, J. W. (1994). Somatic complaints in pediatric patients: A prospective study of the role of negative life events, child social and academic competence, and parental somatic symptoms. *Journal of Consulting and Clinical Psychology, 62*, 1213–1221.

Walker, L. S., Garber, J., Van Slyke, D., & Greene, J. W. (1995). Long term health outcomes in patients with recurrent abdominal pain. *Journal of Pediatric Psychology, 20*, 233–245.

Walker, L. S., & Greene, J. W. (1987). Negative life events, psychosocial resources, and psychophysiological symptoms in adolescents. *Journal of Clinical Child Psychology, 16*, 29–36.

Walker, L. S., & Greene, J. W. (1989). Children with recurrent abdominal pain and their parents: More somatic complaints, anxiety, and depression than other patient families? *Journal of Pediatric Psychology, 14*, 231–243.

Walker, L. S., & Greene, J. W. (1991a). Negative life events and symptom resolution in pediatric abdominal patients. *Journal of Pediatric Psychology, 16*, 341–360.

Walker, L. S., & Greene, J. W. (1991b). The Functional Disability Inventory: Measuring a neglected dimension of child health status. *Journal of Pediatric Psychology, 16*, 39–58.

Walker, L. S., McLaughlin, F. J., & Greene, J. W. (1988). Functional illness and family functioning: A comparison of healthy and somaticizing adolescents. *Family Process, 27*, 317–325.

Walker, L. S., & Zeman, J. L. (1992). Parental response to child illness behavior. *Journal of Pediatric Psychology, 17*, 49–71.

Warwick, H. M., & Salkovskis, P. M. (1985). Reassurance. *British Medical Journal, 290*, 1028.

Wasserman, A. L., Whitington, P. F., & Rivera, F. P. (1988). Psychogenic basis for abdominal pain in children and adolescents. *Journal of the American Academy of Child and Adolescent Psychiatry, 27*, 179–184.

Weinberger, D. A., Schwartz, G. E., & Davidson, R. G. (1979). Low-anxious, high-anxious, and repressive coping styles: Psychometric patterns and behavioral physiological responses to stress. *Journal of Abnormal Psychology, 88*, 369–380.

Weisz, J. R., Suwanlert, S., Chaiyasit, W., Weiss, B., Achenbach, T. M., & Walter, B. (1987). Epidemiology of behavioral and emotional problems among Thai and American children: Parent reports for ages 6 to 11. *Journal of the American Academy of Child and Adolescent Psychiatry, 26*, 890–897.

Weisz, J. R., Suwanlert, S., Chaiyasit, W., Weiss, B., Achenbach, T. M., & Eastman, K. L. (1993). Behavioral and emotional problems among Thai and American adolescents: Parent reports for ages 12 to 16. *Journal of Abnormal Psychology, 102*, 395–403.

Weller, E. B., Weller, R. A., & Fristad, M. A. (1985). Use of sodium amytal interviews in pre-pubertal children: Indications, procedure and clinical utility. *Journal of the American Academy of Child Psychiatry, 24*, 747–749.

Whitehead, W. E., Busch, C. M., Heller, B. R., & Costa, P. T. (1986). Social learning influences on menstrual symptoms and illness behavior. *Health Psychology, 5,* 13–23.

Whitehead, W. E., & Schuster, M. M. (1985). *Gastrointestinal disorders: Behavioral and physiological basis for treatment.* Orlando, FL: Academic.

Wilkinson, P., & Mynors-Wallis, L. (1994). Problem solving therapy in the treatment of unexplained physical symptoms in primary care: A preliminary study. *Journal of Psychosomatic Research, 38,* 591–598.

Wirt, R. D., Lachar, D., Klinedinst, J. K., & Seat, R. D. (1984). *Multidimensional description of child personality: A manual for the Personality Inventory for Children.* Los Angeles: Western Psychological Services.

Wise, T. N., & Mann, L. S. (1994). The relationship between somatosensory amplification, alexithymia, and neuroticism. *Journal of Psychosomatic Research, 38,* 515–521.

Wood, B. L. (1993). Beyond the "psychosomatic family": A biobehavioral family model of pediatric illness. *Family Process, 32,* 261–278.

Woodbury, M. M., De Maso, D. R., & Goldman, S. J. (1992). An integrated medical and psychiatric approach to conversion symptoms in a four-year-old. *Journal of the American Academy of Child and Adolescent Psychiatry, 31,* 1095–1097.

Wooley, S. C., Blackwell, B., & Windet, C. (1978). A learning theory model of chronic illness behavior: Theory, treatment, and research. *Psychosomatic Medicine, 40,* 379–401.

Wyllie, E., Friedman, D., Luders, H., Morris, H., Rothner, D., Turnbull, J. (1991). Outcome of psychogenic seizures in children and adolescents compared with adults. *Neurology, 41,* 742–744.

Zeman, J., & Garber, J. (1996). Display rules for anger, sadness, and pain: It depends on who is watching. *Child Development, 67,* 957–973.

5.26
Factitious Disorders

JUDITH A. LIBOW
Children's Hospital Oakland, CA, USA

5.26.1 INTRODUCTION

Factitious disorder, simply put, is the intentional simulation of illness through a variety of false pretenses. This includes reporting exaggerated symptoms, fabricating laboratory results, and actually inducing symptoms through physical means such as ingestion of substances, injection, or suffocation. Factitious illnesses often result in numerous expensive and painful, not to mention unnecessary, laboratory tests, hospitalizations, and surgical procedures for the young "patient" before the charade is finally uncovered.

What is not so simple is the identification and understanding of this disorder, which poses serious challenges in differential diagnosis and effective treatment. Much better represented in the adult literature, often as "Munchausen syndrome," factitious disorder in youngsters is certainly known to occur, but has yet to be studied in any systematic manner. There is a very limited literature on factitious disorders in children *per se*, while there is an extensive literature of related disorders, diagnoses, and conditions which may provide intriguing clues to the etiology of this disorder. While this chapter will address factitious illness which involves a child or adolescent as the object of unnecessary medical attention, we will find that the perpetrator can actually be the child him or herself, the parent, the family unit, or a complex pathological collusion between parent and child. The relationships between these different yet similar presentations is still little understood, but poses intriguing clues for fiuture understanding of the development of the many forms of somatization and illness exaggeration throughout the lifespan.

5.26.2 FACTITIOUS DISORDERS

5.26.2.1 Phenomenology

Factitious illnesses have no doubt been observed for as long as there have been healers and physicians. Reports in the medical literature dating back to the early nineteenth century (Gavin, 1838; Jacobi, 1895) indicated a variety of falsely presented medical conditions such as factitious fevers. However, the most systematic and seminal discussion of fabricated illness dates back to the work of Asher (1951) writing in *Lancet*, who first coined the colorful name of "Munchausen's syndrome." This term was used to describe a perplexing type of patient who wandered far and wide seeking medical treatments and hospitalizations for nonexistent or self-induced illnesses. These patients were notorious for dramatic presentations, brief emergency room or surgical stays often ending in early detection and the flight of the patient to the next hospital or city. At the time, Asher reported that the three major organ system presentations involved abdominal, hemorrhagic, and neurologic symptoms. Since Asher's original paper, there have been hundreds of Munchausen syndrome papers in the adult medical literature elaborating on individual or sometimes a series of factitious illness cases involving all manner of factitious presentations, including fevers (Aduan, Fauci, Dale, Herzberg, & Wolff, 1979), rashes (Reich & Gottfried, 1983), and even psychiatric presentations (Hay, 1983; Phillips, Ward, & Ries, 1983; Pope, Jonas, & Jones, 1982).

5.26.2.1.1 *Munchausen syndrome and factitious disorder*

The disorder described by Asher was named after a fascinating man and equally colorful character, the Baron Karl Friedrich Hieronymus von Munchausen, an eighteenth century cavalry officer and mercenary who was renowned for telling elaborate tales of his imaginary adventures, chronicled by his friend Rudolf Erich Raspe (Sakula, 1978). Both men and women from all walks of life have been described as exhibiting the "Munchausen" disorder. The mean age of onset of the disorder is said to be most commonly in the patient's early twenties (Raymond, 1987) and perhaps up to half the cases may begin in adolescence (Plassmann, 1994a). The literature reports that men tend to predominate in the most chronic, "wandering" form of Munchausen syndrome (at a ratio of 2:1) in which multiple physicians, towns, and hospitals are caught up in the patient's relentless charade. Women have been found to predominate (at a 3:1 ratio) in the less dramatic forms of factitious disorder, more likely in episodic or less elaborate impostures (Eisendrath, 1996). However, the methods of self-abuse and the range of false symptoms and organ systems involved have been remarkably extensive and dramatic, confined neither to a single gender, ethnicity, socioeconomic, or age group. Many of these patients are involved in the medical, nursing, or health care professions (Plassmann, 1994b).

Within the factitious disorder (FD) literature are a handful of reports on children or adolescents discovered to have manufactured their own symptoms and illnesses. The reports of young children include a four year old feigning seizures (Croft & Jervis, 1989), a nine, ten, and fourteen year old creating skin lesions (Lovejoy, Marcuse, & Landrigan, 1971; White, Pearson, & Coddington, 1966), several series of children between 11 and 17 years with factitious fevers (Aduan et al., 1979; Herzberg & Wolff, 1972; Wedel, 1971), preadolescents adulterating laboratory specimens (Abe, Shinozima, Okuno, Abe, & Ochi, 1984; Abrol, Heck, Gleckel, & Rosner, 1990), and factitious charges of sexual and physical abuse by a 12 year old (Feldman & Smith, 1996).

Factitious illnesses show increasing sophistication with age, and the adolescent literature includes a patient deliberately ingesting steroids (Witt & Ginsberg-Fellner, 1981), a patient scraping her skin and pouring nutritional supplements down the drain (Sanders, 1995), self-induced chronic joint inflammation and pain in a 15 year old (Paperny, Hicks, & Hammar, 1980), use of a wrist tourniquet for self-induced edema by a 15 year old (Rodriguez-Moreno, Ruiz-Martin, Mateo-Soria, Rozadilla, & Roig-Escofet, 1990), the injection of exogenous egg protein into the bladder (Tojo et al., 1990), and 15 hospitalizations for a wide variety of nonexistent illnesses by an adolescent (Raymond, 1987).

The vast majority of these reports have appeared in the medical rather than the psychiatric literature, with the resultant emphasis more on the unraveling of the medical puzzle than an explication of the etiology or family dynamics. As in the case of adult FDs, it is clear that these cases, particularly with more clever adolescent imposters, can stymie physicians for several years before being discovered as factitious (Abe et al., 1984; Paperny et al., 1980). They generally result in an expensive, destructive process of multiple hospitalizations, laboratory procedures, and surgeries before the fabrication is finally unmasked. The physical and psychological toll on the patient, and the professional/emotional toll on the physicians and the health care system can be enormous (Schreier & Libow, 1993a).

5.26.2.1.2 Factitious disorder by proxy

That the great majority of FDs in children is seen in adolescents is no doubt due to the fact that a certain basic level of medical sophistication is required to create and maintain believable symptoms capable of entrapping physicians successfully. Unfortunately, a substantial number of very young children are also, in fact, victims of fabricated illness—victims of Munchausen by proxy syndrome (MBPS), or factitious disorder by proxy (FDbP). First systematically described and named by British pediatrician Meadow (1977), MBPS involves the use of the child (or less commonly, another adult) as the proxy "patient." The parent or caregiver exaggerates symptoms, or actually induces illness in her child in order to maintain an ongoing relationship with doctors and hospitals (Schreier & Libow, 1993a). The most common methods of inducing illness include poisoning, suffocation, tampering with specimens or intravenous lines, skin adulteration, witholding medication, and false reporting of symptoms. The child manifests the factitious illness, but it is the parent/mother who carries the FDbP diagnosis.

There are currently several hundred cases of FDbP reported in the medical literature, with the vast majority of perpetrators being mothers (Levin & Sheridan, 1995; Schreier & Libow, 1993a) with complex societal and systemic reasons for this gender imbalance. These mothers have been classically described as highly devoted, seemingly very concerned, and medically sophisticated parents, although a subset of these parents have also been noted to be more hostile and demanding (Libow & Schreier, 1986). A review in 1987 by Rosenberg reported on 117 cases in the literature, and found that 24% of the mothers themselves had Munchausen syndrome or at least some elements of FD. Classically, the fathers or partners of the MBPS mother are described as distant, uninvolved, or emotionally disengaged from the family. The child victims can be of any age, gender, or birth order, and sometimes several children in one family are victimized serially or simultaneously. Child victims can be biological children, adoptive, or foster children, and often do not show any obvious signs of attachment problems or physical child abuse. The age of the child victims have ranged from as young as fetuses subjected to prenatal fabrication (Goodlin; 1985; Goss & McDougall, 1992), to infants (Light & Sheridan, 1990; Meadow, 1990), preschoolers (Guandolo, 1985) and latency age (Libow & Schreier, 1986; Palmer & Yoshimura, 1984) as well as adolescent victims (Katz, Mazer, & Litt, 1985). Generally it is the infants and toddlers who are subjected to the most active forms of physical symptom inductions such as suffocation and poisoning (McClure, Davis, Meadow, & Sibert, 1996), while the older children tend to be victims of what have been called the "milder" form of MBPS (Roth, 1990; Warner & Hathaway, 1984). "Doctor shopping" and symptom exaggeration, in which the parent does not actively induce symptoms herself, can also subject the child to unnecessary procedures and medications through exaggerated or false reporting of symptoms (Masterson, Dunworth, & Williams, 1988). Often older children have been noted to engage in either passive or active collusion in such fabrications, confirming their mother's reports to the physicians (Woolcott, Aceto, Rutt, Bloom, & Glick, 1982), failing to report falsehoods (Sanders, 1995), or even participating in inducing symptoms.

Factitious disorder by proxy differs in a number of ways from FD, although there are obvious areas of overlap. Often the "by proxy" deception takes longer to be revealed, because the mothers are more convincing imposters and the fabrications are more sophisticated (Schreier & Libow, 1993a). Some percentage of the proxy victims actually die from the abuse. Rosenberg (1987) calculated that number to be approximately 9% of cases, although that likely represents an overestimation due to the preponderance of more severe cases in the literature she reviewed. Because the proxy cases involve an innocent victim, the morbidity and mortality of the patients is even more distressing, as is the devastating impact of this abuse, once it is revealed, on the treating physicians who are drawn into unintentional participation in the abuse (Schreier & Libow, 1993a).

5.26.2.2 Diagnostic Features/Differential Diagnosis

5.26.2.2.1 Diagnosis of childhood factitious disorder

As in all forms of factitious illness, the first and most important issue in differential diagnosis is the ruling out of bona fide physical illness. No matter how obscure or elusive, the presence of a true medical illness which can account for the presenting symptoms negates the diagnosis of FD, unless the symptoms are exaggerated way out of proportion to what should reasonably be expected. Thus, physicians generally expend considerable effort in attempting to provide the most exhaustive medical workup possible for a patient with mysterious symptoms, including extensive laboratory tests, radiological procedures, biopsies, genetic studies, and hospital observations, and often institute treatments in the hope that responses to treatment might provide clues to diagnosis. In most cases the diagnosis of FD is the last possibility considered, when all else has been ruled out, and when the "illness" fails to fit any usual pattern of symptoms, is physiologically impossible, fails to respond in an expected way to common treatments, and provides other clues as to its inconsistency and its tendency to reoccur only when the patient is not being observed closely. The identification of factitious illness in younger children tends to be easier due to the lack of sophistication of the falsifications, but as with adults, can be greatly complicated when the patient has coexisting, bona fide medical problems such as asthma, or serious iatrogenic illness induced by efforts to treat the original "problem." Livingston (1992) reminds us that several organic disease states have

> vague, strange, and transient symptoms and are easily confused with somatization: systemic lupus, multiple sclerosis, juvenile rheumatoid arthritis, acute intermittent porphyria, partial complex seizures, and inflammatory bowel disease ... it may be that only the longitudinal picture will establish the diagnosis firmly but a reasonable clinical judgment about working diagnosis can often be reached by complete history from multiple sources, thorough mental status exam, a careful probe for the family history, personality patterns and comorbid difficulties known to be associated with somatoform disorders, and ancillary psychological exams for characteristic profiles and findings. (pp. 14–15)

DSM-IV (American Psychiatric Association, 1994) includes "Factitious Disorder" as an Axis I disorder involving three elements, including: (i) the intentional production of physical/psychological signs and symptoms; (ii) the motivation to assume the sick role; and (iii) the absence of external incentives for the behavior. It includes three subcodes based on whether the signs and symptoms are predominantly psychological, predominantly physical, or a combination of physical and psychological in nature. *ICD-9* (Stegman & Aaron, 1996) lists factitious disorders as subcategories of "Hysteria" under "Neurotic Disorders."

There are separate categories for factitious illness with psychological symptoms (300.16) and other and unspecified factitious illness (300.19) which includes factitious physical symptoms. There is a different category for "Munchausen syndrome" or chronic factitious illness with physical symptoms (301.51) in *ICD-9*, coded separately under the "Histrionic personality disorders."

Seemingly quite straightforward, the diagnosis of FD in adults as well as children and adolescents is complicated by its considerable overlap with a number of related disorders which also involve the presentation of physical or psychological symptoms which are unobservable, do not appear to have an organic basis, or have an element of conscious production, unconscious motivation, or secondary gain for the patient. Somatization disorder, malingering, conversion disorder, anxiety disorders, and mood disorders can all be confused with FD, and differential diagnosis is often a challenge. The three most critical variables in differentiating the phenomenon of FD are the following.

(i) *Motivation.* Patients who are motivated to produce factitious symptoms for obvious external gain, such as disability payments, avoidance of military service, or evasion of criminal prosecution, rather than less conscious needs as in FD, are identified as malingerers, a V-Code in *DSM-IV*. Identification of the possible material gain/motivation of the patient requires careful identification of the tangible impact of the patient role on the person's lifestyle, finances, and responsibilities. In the case of children, the differential diagnosis of malingering from somatization and factitious disorder is complicated by the fact that in all cases, the child's creation of illness symptoms is likely to result in reduced school attendance and considerably increased parental involvement. In these cases, a careful psychosocial and family systems evaluation will be critical in sorting out the likely motivation for assuming the sick role, and determining whether fully conscious as opposed to less conscious needs are being gratified. In the case of the FDs, it is proposed that assuming a dependent yet controlling role in relationship to the powerful and caregiving physician is the primary motivation. However, in reality there are often tangible gains for young FD patients—such as missing school or engendering parental sympathy—which can be identified as possible secondary incentives, but not the primary motivators of the behavior.

(ii) *Intentionality.* Probably the most difficult variable to assess in FD is the degree to which the exaggeration or falsification of symptoms is conscious and intentional. Elaborately orchestrated deceptions are much easier to identify as intentional than exaggerated symptom complaints. By definition, FD is intentional, although believed to be compulsively driven, and therefore not entirely under the control of the patient. Patients who present repeatedly with a range of nonexistent medical complaints involving multiple symptoms and organ systems, but who are *not* consciously exaggerating or falsifying symptoms, are diagnosed with somatization disorder. As in FD, somatization can be episodic or chronic, and can pose major difficulties for the physician attempting to treat questionable symptoms with no apparent organic basis. Conversion disorder is diagnosed in the case of more restricted symptoms related to identified stressors (e.g., abdominal pain or "paralysis" following an incest experience). As in factitious disorder, somatization can be episodic or chronic, and can pose major difficulties for the physician atempting to treat questionable symptoms with no apparent organic basis.

(iii) *Chronicity.* There is some confusion about the use of the term "Munchausen syndrome," as it is often used generically to refer to all forms of fabricated illness. In general, presentation of the patient with chronic false symptoms, and a lifestyle centered around repeated wandering from hospital to hospital seeking medical care is classically known as "Munchausen syndrome," while FD is not as chronic, and can involve even a single episode (Folks & Freeman, 1985; Nadelson, 1979).

Munchausen patients have also been described as having poorer employment histories and more antisocial traits (Carney, 1980; Folks & Freeman, 1985; Spiro, 1968). Clearly, the term FD is more appropriate for use with child patients by these criteria. While many authors use both terms interchangably to describe patients who produce their own symptoms, others have attempted to identify differences in the groups in terms of gender distribution (Feldman & Eisendrath, 1996; Folks & Freeman, 1985), age, and degree of compulsivity

(Spiro, 1968). What remains unclear is whether more episodic FD is qualitatively different, or whether the episodic patient eventually becomes the chronic Munchausen patient, given sufficient success over time in the impostering of illness.

What becomes clear is that the differentiation of patient intentionality, motivation, and even frequency of fabrication are not always easy to gauge by the clinician making the diagnosis, suggesting there may be considerable lack of specificity in the actual use of these terms or in the disorders themselves. A number of clinicians have proposed the concept of a continuum or spectrum of related disorders including Aduan et al. (1979), Barsky (1992), Fink (1992), Folks and Freeman (1985), and Nadelson (1979). Cramer, Gershberg, and Stern (1971) remind us that "A volitional factor in the genesis of hysterical symptoms has long been recognized ... " as well as " ... unconscious factors in the genesis of malingering" (p. 576). A number of authors have pointed to the multiple difficulties in differentiating the various "dissimulating disorders" including Jonas and Pope (1985) who remind us that malingering, conversion disorders and FDs have several striking similarities. All typically begin in late adolescence or early adulthood, all appear to have a relatively chronic course, therapeutic approaches appear to be relatively ineffective for all, and the patients all appear to display a similar pattern of psychiatric diagnoses which include histrionic, antisocial, and borderline personality disorders. They even suggest there may be a gender bias in diagnosis, with women tending to receive somatization and conversion disorder diagnoses, while men may tend to be perceived as Munchausen or malingering patients.

Spiro (1968) agrees that hysterical and factitious symptomatology are not always mutually exclusive categories, and he describes a classic Munchausen patient who also suffered occasional conversion abdominal pain. Fink (1992) also points out that while somatization and FD appear to constitute separate entities at any one point in time, the categories may actually merge or overlap over time. That is, his study of 113 patients found that 18% of his "persistent somatizers" were discovered to have intentionally self-induced their diseases, lesions, or illnesses at least once or to have manipulated test results. "The number of patients who had produced factitious objective symptoms were probably underestimated as they were only registered if clear evidence was present" (p. 134). He suggests that we may tend to underdiagnose the number of patients with FD because clear evidence of deliberate fabrication is not always present, and it is so difficult to know whether symptoms are actually consciously produced.

It is possible that this clinician bias towards diagnosing somatization is even stronger when it comes to child patients, as it may be even more psychologically difficult for medical providers to suspect children of deliberate falsifications, and there is less extensive psychosocial history available for assessing possible motivation, intent, etc. Some authors have indicated awareness that some supposed child "somatizers" may in fact be intentionally producing their symptoms (Garralda, 1996; Sanders, 1995). There is often a broad definition of child somatization used in the literature, such as Campo and Fritsch's (1994) use of the term for "medically unexplained physical symptoms" (p. 1223). In the absence of any attention to the issues of motivation or conscious awareness, this broad use of the term "somatization" could easily encompass an unknown percentage of deliberately "ill" children. This remains an issue for which our definitions and diagnostic tools require further refinement.

5.26.2.2.2 Diagnosis of factitious disorder by proxy

DSM-IV (American Psychiatric Association, 1994) includes a second category of factitious disorder, called "Factitious Disorder Not Otherwise Specified." This is supposed to incorporate cases of FDbP, although FDbP itself is included in the *DSM-IV* Appendix as needing additional study and refinement. It is differentiated from the category of "Factitious Disorder" by its definition as "Intentional production or feigning of physical or psychological symptoms *in another person who is under the individual's care.*" Thus, their definition would include the abuse of an elderly person, hospital patient, or another adult. As in FD, the diagnosis requires the motivation to assume the sick role by proxy, the absence of external incentives, and the condition that the behavior is not better accounted for by another mental disorder. Perpetrators may, and often do, also receive additional diagnoses of various personality, somatoform, or mood disorders where appropriate. There is no discrete psychiatric diagnostic category within *ICD-10* for FDbP.

As in FD, the parental behaviors seen in MBPS or FDbP first and foremost must be differentiated from those seen in response to bona fide physical illness. If the medical problem in question is, in fact, due to real physical illness, the diagnosis of FDbP is inaccurate. Krener and Adelman (1988) point out that there are some superficial similarities

between the "pathogenic parents with Munchausen's syndrome by proxy and the parents of chronically ill children" (p. 946). They demonstrate that chronic illness itself may create some features of parental behavior commonly seen in FDbP parents, including extensive medical knowledge, an unusual focus on the child's bodily products, and "inseparable maternal devotion." While there are very few known cases of misdiagnosed FDbP, the potential dangers of wrongly accusing a parent of this form of child abuse and mental disorder are very sobering. One of the few known cases of a misdiagnosis of FDbP involved a mother who was jailed for the murder of her infant son, believed to have poisoned him with ethylene glycol (Chin & Breu, 1991). It was only the illness of a second child, while his mother was in jail and without access to this child, that alerted authorities to the misdiagnosis and eventually allowed for the discovery of the rare genetic disorder that had killed one child and made the other so ill. In the majority of cases, physicians are generally extremely cautious about making the diagnosis, often spending months or years, and sometimes hundreds of thousands of dollars in repeated tests and procedures before acknowledging that FDbP is the only possible explanation of a persistant medical puzzle (Schreier & Libow, 1993a).

What is often confusing to diagnosticians and physicians is that the behavior of the parent with FDbP seems to fall on a continuum that includes a range of both normal and abnormal parent behavior in relation to the health care system. Eminson and Postlewaite (1992) suggest there exists a range of "parents' desire to consult for their child's symptoms" which includes nine points along the spectrum with classical neglect at one extreme and classical MBPS (or FDbP) at the other. They propose that other points along the spectrum include parental carelessness, noncompliance, and "normal" responses to child's symptoms, progressing up the scale to anxious behaviors, exaggeration, and finally, invention of symptoms. It clearly requires patience, expertise, considerable time, and investigation of the family system and the presenting symptoms in order to differentiate the anxious parent, the somatizing parent, or the thought-disordered parent, from the parent with FDbP. As in FD, the central elements of the FDbP diagnosis once again revolve around a persistent search for treatment of an induced or exaggerated illness, the parent's conscious intent to deceive, and an unconscious motivation for a relationship with the medical system rather than more material secondary gain. As Meadow (1984) reminds us, "Unfortunately there is no sharp dividing line between deliberate falsification (malingering for conscious gain) and abnormal illness behaviour in which there is unconscious gain (hysterical behaviour). The end result for the child is the same, and can be both cruel and dangerous, regardless of the origin of the mother's behaviour" (p. 156).

Even more complex is the difficulty of diagnostically sorting out the puzzle of FDs in the case of older children. Beyond the age of toddlerhood, many if not most child victims of FDbP are believed to have at least some level of awareness of the exaggeration or induction of their symptoms by their parents, and some are known to actively participate in verifying "the story" in the case of "doctor shopping" (Woollcott et al. 1982) or actually inducing their symptoms. In fact, the one study of adults victimized by FDbP as children (Libow, 1995) found that many of the victims were fully aware of the deception, but too intimidated or unsure of how to free themselves from this abuse to speak up. Sanders (1995) presents what she calls a "continuum of collusion with Munchausen by proxy syndrome" which includes the categories of the naive child, passive acceptance, active participation, and active harm.

Many studies indicate that some child and adolescent victims of FDbP actively collude in the deceptions with their parents in an effort to protect or maintain a relationship with their parents or continue the "only life they know" (Schreier & Libow, 1993a). What becomes very difficult at this point is to sort out the appropriateness of using the FD diagnosis for the child actively participating in the fabrication as opposed to the status of FDbP victim. It becomes particularly difficult to differentiate the child's possible beliefs and motivations regarding the illness—for example, should the colluding child be considered a somatizer if a parent is responsible for directing the deliberate falsifications?

Other concerns have been raised about the diagnosis of FDbP including those of Morley (1995) and Baldwin (1996) who are concerned about the nonspecificity of many of the criteria for this diagnosis, and the inclusion of other forms of fabrication beyond active induction of illness including false symptom reporting and exaggeration of genuine illness; some feel this may result in overinclusion of too many anxious or overdramatizing parents. Fisher and Mitchell (1995) take issue with the concept of FDbP as a "syndrome" as they feel that perpetrators manifest a wide range of psychopathology and presentations, with many "psychological, psychiatric, and environmental pathways leading to a behaviour of fabricating illness in a child" (p. 533).

5.26.2.3 Prevalence

5.26.2.3.1 Factitious disorder prevalence

Solid, systematic prevalence data on FD does not really exist, due to the significant challenges in assessment of intentionality and motivation, and the surreptitious nature of this disorder (Taylor & Hyler, 1993). Furthermore, since diagnostic criteria for factitious and somatoform conditions have been under revision over the years, epidemiological studies are difficult to conduct (Krener, 1994).

There is actually more prevalence-related literature available on FD in adults, with factitious fever one of the most studied single symptoms. Knockaert, Vanneste, Vanneste, and Bobbaers (1992) found that 3.5% of 199 cases of fever of unknown origin seen at one hospital over a 10 year period were factitious. Their review of four other studies of unexplained fever revealed rates of factitious fever ranging from 2.5% to 4.5%. Herzberg and Wolff (1972) reported that 13 patients in a sample of 200 (or 6.5%) at the National Institutes of Health (NIH) were considered to have factitious fever. A study of fever at Stanford University (Rumans & Vosti, 1978) found that 2.2% of some 500 cases were factitious in origin. Aduan et al. (1979) reported on another study of fever of unknown origin at NIH, involving 343 patients, which identified 9% as factitious (this group included 10 children under 18 years old).

A study that spanned a broader spectrum (Reich & Gottfried, 1983) surveyed 10 years of records on the medical and surgical wards of a Boston hospital, and identified 41 patients with a variety of documented FDs (they do not report prevalence figures) including some adolescents. The most common and serious disorders were infections produced by injection or insertion of contaminants through or into the skin surfaces. They concluded that "factitious disorders are far from rare on hospital wards, at least in tertiary hospitals" (p. 245). Pope et al. (1982) reported on a study of 219 psychiatric patients, which found that 6.4% probably had factitious psychotic symptoms. They suggest that clinicians should be especially suspicious of histrionic and borderline patients who experience "brief dips into psychosis."

A study of 282 patients with heavy utilization of in-patient admissions in Denmark (Fink, 1992) indicated that approximately 20% of the patients had no physical illness or disorder that could adequately explain their multiple admissions. They conducted several comparisons of what they called "persistant somatizers" and "nonsomatizers" and found that 18% of the "persistant somatizers" (defined as having more than six unexplained admissions) had at least one known admission for a factitious illness. It is at least clear that FD in adolescents and adults is not a trivial problem. Unfortunately, similar data does not exist for FD in children. But there are indications that it may not be rare in children, given observations of the high rates of somatization in children (Garralda, 1996) and of conversion symptoms in adolescents (Friedman, 1973) as well as Livingston's (1992) observation that "Mendacious presentations of physical disorder, currently classified either as factitious disorder or as malingering, are also far from rare among young people" (p. 13).

5.26.2.3.2 Factitious disorder by proxy prevalence

The collection of relevant prevalence data on MBPS or FDbP is also confounded by the absence of any national registry on this form of child abuse, and the likelihood that significant numbers of these cases are never identified or are misdiagnosed (Holborow, 1985; Schreier & Libow, 1993b). However, as with FD in adults, there are some intriguing studies which provide suggestive data that can be extrapolated to the larger population.

Some studies have been done on specific types of specialized medical problems in an effort to determine the possible rates of factitious presentations. Light and Sheridan (1990) surveyed 125 infant apnea programs across the United States and reported that 54 cases (2.7 per 1000) were believed to involve parents inducing apnea. Warner and Hathaway (1984) found that about 5% of some 300 parents seen in their allergy clinic appeared to have a "parental obsession" with food allergies that appeared to constitute FDbP. McClure, Davis, Meadow, and Sibert (1996) studied all cases in Ireland in a two year period involving a child protection conference, and identified 55 cases of MBPS out of 128 cases. They reported a combined incidence of MBPS, poisoning, and suffocation of 0.5 per 100 000 children, but admitted that these were likely an underestimate because cases were only identifed if they were reported and a child protection conference was called. They also found large regional differences in patterns of reporting, which also suggested differences in the ability of reporters to effectively recognize or pursue child abuse cases. Similar differences in rates of identified cases were reported by Schreier and Libow (1993b) who surveyed all 880 pediatric neurologists and 388 gastroenterologists in the United States in 1991 to collate data on their MBPS cases. With return rates of 21.8% and 32.4% respectively, these subspecialists reported a total of 273 confirmed cases of

FDbP. As in the McClure study, the significant variability in the number of cases seen by different reporters suggests that there are great differences in the familiarity with and ability to identify these cases and that perhaps a significant number are missed entirely.

5.26.2.4 Etiology

5.26.2.4.1 Origins of factitious disorders

Since there are so few papers on FD in children and adolescents, and even fewer discussions of etiology in childhood cases, the adult literature provides the most useful directions for theory building. However, it must be acknowledged from the outset that all discussions of etiology and treatment are handicapped by the fact that these patients are notoriously resistant to psychotherapeutic intervention, and often flee from the hospital before mental health professionals even have an opportunity to obtain an adequate psychosocial history. However, case studies and theoretical discussions of this disorder provide intriguing ideas about the origins of fabricated illness.

One of the earliest discussions of etiology of chronic FD is offered by Spiro (1968) who points out the parallels between FD and imposture, including the patients' histories of early neglect and deprivation, a desire for mastery over early traumatic experience, and a discrepancy between the patient's self-image and the ego-ideal. He suggests that the patient repeatedly seeks mastery over his/her early experiences of pain and fear by his/her demanding behavior in the guise of being a medical patient, which is coupled with revenge and hostility.

Cramer, Gershberg, and Stern (1971) present four adult Munchausen cases and offer similar observations on their object relationships. In particular, they point to their patients' early experiences with physicians as authority figures who likely began as idealized figures but gradually generated disappointment and eventually, feelings of revenge. They point to their patients' intense wish for closeness and a state of dependency on the physician, paradoxically mixed with feelings of rivalry and desire for control. They describe serious ego disturbances, which are manifested in unstable identifications, primitive defenses and a surge of sadistic wishes against their abandoning parent(s), as represented by the physician. Plassmann (1994a) makes a distinction between the (chronic) Munchausen patient and the (episodic) FD patient, suggesting that the Munchausen patients have a history of infantile-acquired attachment to physicians who are omnipotent, idealized figures, while FD patients have a less idealized relationship with physicians and more of an early fear/interest in their own bodies. He found that many of his FD patients (54%) had been subjected to physical abuse in childhood, which is eventually transformed, often in adolescence, into the patient's destructiveness towards his own body.

Eisendrath (1996) also suggests that childhood experiences of physical or sexual abuse may be significant causes of later FD, generating feelings of guilt in response to sexual excitement or anger. The FD is hypothesized as a possible vehicle for the abuse to be masochistically re-enacted, with the physician serving as the abusing or depriving parent. The use of deception may create a sense of power and superiority in relation to the caregiver. He also suggests that FD may serve as a means for the patient to achieve a greater sense of control and mastery, needed perhaps as a result of childhood traumatic illness. Alternatively, he also proposes a more behavioral theory that FD may have its origins in childhood reinforcement for illness behaviors by eliciting parental attention, support and caring, and an escape from childhood responsibilities. Spiro (1968) describes just such a case in which the earliest memories of a chronic FD patient involved his happy recall of winning his parents' attention during a hospitalization at age four years and a series of later medical complications.

Several authors also highlight the crucial issue of how children learn illness behaviors within the family milieu. Barsky (1992) offers the concept of "amplification" to explain the process by which people learn to interpret their bodily sensations as intense and noxious. While sidestepping the issue of etiology, he suggests the three key elements in this process as bodily hypervigilence to unpleasant bodily sensations, a tendency to focus on weak or infrequent sensations, and the tendency to appraise these sensations as abnormal. The possible contribution of parents in this process is unspecified.

Krener (1994) points more directly to the ways within the family context that children may learn how to experience and communicate their emotional and physical states. "Parents in psychosomatic families may adduce physical symptoms as an explanation of their child's state, behavior, or response, just as they use them to explain their own feelings. Children are more vulnerable than adults to this influence and to developing somatic representations of emotional states, which, like other coping and mastery skills acquired in childhood, involves learning, suggestion, and psychological compliance" (p. 419). It is not difficult to imagine that a child living with a somatizing or even a fabricating parent might come to rely increasingly on somatized explanations and a patient role, eventually coming to participate more actively in convincing physicians to believe in a nonexistent illness.

Unfortunately, the rather limited literature on childhood and adolescent FD is even more restricted in the number of papers which present any detailed early history, parental or family psychosocial background that could shed light on the various theories of the genesis of FD. Many focus almost entirely on the medical presentation (Abe et al., 1984; Abrol et al., 1990; Lovejoy et al., 1971; Paperny et al., 1980; Wedel, 1971). However, a few papers on child FD point to an intriguing link between child and parent preoccupation with illness.

A careful reading of the child FD literature describing family background suggests that some of the mothers play a pivotal role in encouraging or even teaching illness fabrication to the child (Stankler, 1977). Sneed and Bell (1976) describe a 10-year-old boy who presented with abdominal pain, bloody urine, and "kidney stones" which were later found to be ordinary pebbles. The article described the mother as actively involved in the fabrication, reporting "blood" on the stones and describing her own passage of kidney stones years earlier; she "tended to exaggerate physical problems and illnesses for herself, the siblings, and the patient" (p. 127). Her son was described as passive and compliant, and almost completely dependent upon his mother.

Herzberg and Wolff's (1972) report on six children presenting with factitious fever of unknown origin at the NIH also included some fascinating data about the mothers' presentations. The children ranged from 11 to 17 years of age, and were all described as "good, compliant, serious, but lonely" children. The authors felt that four of the mothers had "very troubling chronic illnesses of their own" which appeared highly inconsistent with observations or history. Several of the mothers were actually noted to be involved in the fraudulent reporting of the childrens' temperature elevations; one mother persistently pictured her daughter as suffering from leukemia despite negative findings! The authors observed that the children appeared to be recruited to help the parents with their own inner conflicts. The "sick" children were noted to enjoy increased attention from their parents that might not have otherwise been available as well as a break from demanding schoolwork. Interestingly, two of the six children aspired to be medical doctors!

One of the most elaborate factitious illness presentations (Gilbert, Pierse, & Mitchell, 1987) involved a 13-year-old boy seen over six months time at an otolaryngology clinic with recurrent otalgia, bloody discharge from the ear, and chronic mastoiditis with a cerebrospinal fluid leak. Just as the child was facing a temporal craniotomy, forensic analysis identified the "ear fluid" as beetroot juice, and the boy admitted to placing the material in his ear. A retrospective review of this boy's three-year medical history revealed a long series of nonspecific complaints resulting in 28 outpatient visits, 15 specialist consultations, 4 surgical procedures, 2 endoscopies, 52 blood tests, and 20 x rays. The medical staff wondered if the boy's mother had been coaching him in his fabrications since "It seemed unlikely that a 13-year-old would have the medical sophistication to simulate a cerebrospinal fluid leak or comprehend the significance such a sign would have for the attending surgeons" (p. 232). Also suggestive of FDbP involvement was the mother's domineering style and devoted attendance at bedside, previous health care employment, and efforts to have her son immediately discharged when confronted with the fabrication. Many years earlier, Steinbeck (1961) reported on a 19-year-old girl simulating massive vaginal hemorrhage and hematemesis through concealing blood; her mother was also later found to be an accomplice in her deceptions.

Similar reports of maternal involvement are found in a case described by Croft and Jervis (1989) of a four-year-old, seen over a year's time, with 35 emergency room visits for repeated "fits," trembling, and a "paralyzed" arm which were all being feigned by the child. The boy had a history since age two which included "cyanosis" and episodes of shaking and unconsciousness at age three. The child eventually described how his mother had taught him to simulate his epileptic "fits" by shaking, falling out of his chair, and flickering his eyes, and he reported being rewarded by his mother with food and drink when he performed for her. His "fits" stopped after five months in foster care. Unfortunately, there is no psychosocial history provided for the mother herself.

Perhaps one of the most unusual descriptions of FD collaboration between parent and "child"—in this case a 25-year-old daughter and her 59-year-old mother—is offered by Janofsky (1986). Both mother and daughter were hospitalized together with similar complaints of fevers, nausea, headaches, weakness, etc., and both had long medical histories engaging over 100 physicians. When psychiatric consultations were recommended, both mother and daughter fled the hospital against medical advice. The author suggests that this case of chronic FD in the mother, and a budding FD daughter, would meet the classic criteria of

"folie a deux," or even "folie a famille," given the husband's willing participation as well as the physician son's facilitation of the process!

So it is apparent that FD behavior can involve overt modeling, direct coaching of the child, active collaboration on the part of the parent, and behavioral reinforcement for the child's participation. Many of these parents would no doubt fit the definition of MBPS parents. What becomes increasingly difficult to differentiate diagnostically, and an area of increasingly blurred boundaries, is the distinction between the FDbP parent with a "colluding child," and a childhood FD with a cooperative parent. These cases suggest that at least some percentage of childhood FD cases have their origins in the child's direct exposure to the coaching of a parent with factitious disorder or factitious disorder by proxy.

5.26.2.4.2 Origins of factitious disorder by proxy

As in adult FD, theories of etiology for FDbP are limited by the difficulties in obtaining accurate and detailed psychosocial histories from these reluctant and often court-ordered patients. Spiro's (1968) and Cramer et al.'s (1971) theories of the etiology of FD have many parallels to the origins of FDbP, particularly in terms of histories of early neglect and deprivation, and the mother's enactment of an idealizing/hostile attachment to the physician. The description of a MBPS mother's early background by Wood, Fowlkes, Holden and Castro (1989) is fairly typical. They describe a childhood of early deprivation and humiliation, resulting in marked insecurity, deep resentment of authority figures, and inability to meet the patient's needs through the usual means. In the case of FDbP, the infant or child is hypothesized to serve as a type of "fetish object" in the mother's "perverse" relationship which is focused on reducing anxiety by controlling the physician/authority figure and warding off abandonment (Schreier & Libow, 1993a). While many FDbP mothers appear to have some history of paternal loss or abandonment, others have different, less dramatic types of loss, as in a loss of self- or parental esteem through neglect or traumatic illness, or loss of a father's interest. Interestingly, many mothers with FDbP seem to re-enact these unsatisfying relationships with men in later life by marrying aloof and distant husbands who are often absent and uninvolved in their wives' lives and the children's "illnesses." Somehow, these fathers are allowed to remain aloof and uninvolved by our physicians and health care institutions, who seem to accept their absence or fail to insist on their participation.

In fact, social factors which allow for distortions and inequities in gender roles also appear to play their part in the etiology of FDbP, in that many women grow up in a societal context in which they feel desperately unrecognized, and have few outlets for a sense of power and importance outside of their caretaking roles as mothers. Ironically, the role of "devoted mother" of a chronically ill child is one of the few traditional, socially sanctioned roles for women which also allows them access to an exciting and powerful world of hospitals and health care (Schreier & Libow, 1993a). Others place some responsibility on our medical systems (Donald & Jureidini, 1996; Fialkov, 1984) for the development of MBPS, or on the "medicalization of childhood, clinical and social iatrogenesis and the creation of a society obsessed with health and its concomitant illness" (Baldwin, 1996, p. 161). But while there are interesting theories about these different influences, we know little about the relative contributions of childhood neglect, character disorders, sociocultural influences, and family systems dysfunctions in their eventual evolution into the destructive and often life-threatening behavior of medical abuse.

5.26.2.5 Developmental Course of Factitious Disorders

While addressing a somewhat different population, the literature on the course of somatization disorder in children offers useful directions for our thinking about the course of FD in children. Livingston's (1992) excellent review of somatization in childhood and adolescence found that it tends to have a progressive or chronic course similar to that found in adults. Furthermore, he reported that somatoform syndromes in children that do not yet constitute full somatization disorder may do so over time, and childhood somatizers are unlikely to reach adulthood without developing other kinds of serious psychopathology. His general conclusions were that abdominal and other pains develop first in the early school-age population, followed by neurologic or conversion symptoms during later elementary or adolescent years. The number of symptoms then appears to peak in the female patient's early 20s and decline gradually, although for men the peak appears to be several decades later. Livingston (1993) has also found that children of adults with somatization disorder almost universally develop psychiatric disorders.

Factitious disorder is not ordinarily seen until at least early adolescence in most children due to lack of medical sophistication (Aduan et al., 1979). Children much younger than 12

are very likely to have an active parental ally either engineering or at least encouraging the deception, while adolescent patients might be expected to have some earlier history of medical problems or somatization. Reich and Gottfried's (1983) study of FD provides some data on the early histories of their patients. All of their patients who self-induced their infections began in adolescence although many were not identified until later in adulthood. All of them apparently showed an early interest in medical matters and hypochondriacal preoccupations, although none had histories of serious childhood diseases. Paperny et al. (1980) described the case of a late adolescent whose history of factitious illness spanned the five years between 15 and 20 years of age. He endured 23 hospitalizations and 13 surgical procedures, while functioning as an "excellent student" who worked for a year in an orthopedist's office. An even longer history was available on a 28-year-old FD patient described by Sale and Kalucy (1980) who found that this patient lived with a mother who was ill during most of her childhood, and had infrequent and probably genuine medical visits until age 12. From age 12 through 17 she made frequent use of the gynecology clinic with abdominal pain complaints and engaged in many struggles with her physicians; she manifested features of adult FD from age 17 onwards. Reich, Lazarus, Kelly, & Rogers (1977) provide detailed early history on a 15-year-old boy who simulated an enterovesicular fistula by contaminating his urine with feces and food by retrograde injection of substances into his bladder. They found that his early history included moderately severe asthma, multiple allergies, surgery at age two for hypospadias, and a prolonged episode of unexplained fever at age 12. The authors concluded that the patient's factitious behavior was due to a hypochondriacal anxiety state about his urogenital system, but did not address the question of familial or maternal contributions to his medical history or to his surprising level of medical sophistication at a young age.

Little can be said about the long-term developmental outcome of FD beyond the fact that the illness behavior is likely to continue into adulthood, and may or may not become chronic. All that is available is retrospective data, as neither the young patients actually diagnosed with this disorder nor those whose diagnoses are missed can be studied prospectively.

There is somewhat better developmental data available on child victims of FDbP. It is clear that some percentage of infants subjected to the most severe forms of this abuse will die as a result of suffocation and poisoning (Meadow, 1990) and some will have long-term physical damage (Rosenberg, 1987). Certainly there is known psychological damage to children who endure medical fabrications at the hands of their parents (Bools, Neale, & Meadow, 1993; Roth, 1990). McGuire and Feldman (1989) not only found many severe adverse psychological effects of FDbP on their child victims, but also found that some of their young patients developed conversion symptoms or were starting to manifest FDs themselves.

A fascinating case of a 9 year old being contaminated by human fecal matter by her mother was presented by Palmer and Yoshimura (1984). Their examination of the mother-perpetrator found that the mother herself had an extensive history of FD in adolescence, adult FD later in life (as well as a job as a nurse practitioner), and eventually FDbP using her own daughter! Investigations even earlier into this mother's history revealed that she herself had had an extensive childhood medical history which included an unexplained fracture as an infant, failure to thrive, episodic vomiting, frequent injections for minor complaints, and several questionable procedures done at an early age. The possibility in some families of a multigenerational cycle of MBPS alternating with FD is a fascinating and disturbing one.

A retrospective study of 10 adults who reported themselves as victims of childhood FDbP (Libow, 1995), some as much as 40 years earlier, noted that they experienced serious developmental and emotional problems throughout the lifespan including growth failure, school problems, poor self-esteem, difficulty in relationships, depression, and difficulty separating fantasy from reality. Remarkably, some even reported that their mothers sporadically attempted to continue to abuse them even into adulthood! Thus, unless it is actively stopped by physicians who discover the deception, FDbP may run a chronic course, although the most active forms of induction in the child's early years tend to give way to more indirect forms of illness exaggeration, often gradually drawing the child or adolescent into passive or active cooperation, with increasing risk of physical harm and psychological morbidity.

5.26.3 CONCEPTUALIZATION AND CLINICAL FORMULATION

5.26.3.1 Multimodal Assessment

5.26.3.1.1 The medical puzzle

There are many obstacles to the accurate identification of FDs, starting with the decep-tion on the part of the patient and the lack of an accurate history, the patient's cooperation, or a meaningful medical picture. The episodic and emergency nature of many of the illnesses, the involvement of multiple physicians and institu-tions, and the difficulty for the physician of even contemplating deception on the part of a youngster or a seemingly exemplary parent adds to the challenge of identifying medical deception in a timely way before great harm is done (Guandolo, 1985). Schreier and Libow (1993a) also detail many of the ways in which the susceptible physician is drawn into the patient's imposture and is sometimes blinded to what otherwise appears to be rather obvious and blatant falsification. Often it is the close observation by nursing or ward staff of peculiar family interactions and inappropriate affect on the part of the patient or parent that finally alerts medical staff to take a very different perspective on the intractable medical problem.

In any case, the first step in the assessment of either FD or FDbP is a multidisciplinary team meeting of all involved physicians, social workers, psychologists, specialists, consultants, nurses, and other team members, in order to pool data, share observations, identify discre-pancies, and develop a plan to further pursue investigation of possible deception. While it is often not possible to find direct evidence of fabrication, this is most desirable as it allows for a clear and unambiguous response from the health care team, and possible legal action in the case of child abuse. In the case of childhood factitious disorder, direct evidence can be gathered through such ruses as checking serial numbers on thermometers to identify planted ones (Herzberg & Wolff, 1972), and comparing urine specimens collected under observed and unobserved conditions (Meadow, 1977). In many pediatric hospitals surreptitious video surveillance is now being used under carefully controlled conditions for collecting evidence of medical abuse. Parents have been caught on camera in the act of suffocating as well as poisoning their young children (Samuels, McClaughlin, Jacobson, Poets, & Southall, 1992).

However, in many cases the deception can only be inferred through a careful process of eliminating all other possible medical explana-tions for the child's symptoms. The peculiar, sporadic, physiologically impossible, or unre-sponsive nature of the symptoms may be the major clues available to the alert physician. There are a number of cases of young children in which a direct confrontation has resulted in the child's confession of the fabrication (Abe et al., 1984; Croft & Jervis, 1989; Lovejoy et al., 1971), but in the case of older FD patients or

FDbP parents, there is often flight, denial, and lack of cooperation with treatment. In the case of child victims of serious medical abuse, the separation of the child from the parent often offers the most important diagnostic verification of the fabrication, as the child's condition rapidly improves and symptoms disappear in the absence of the suspected perpetrator. However, there are often legal and ethical obstacles to the separation of suspected victims from their mothers, and even the evidence of child's improvement in the mother's absence is often challenged in court.

5.26.3.1.2 Psychological assessment

If the patient is amenable to a psychological interview, the psychologist can make a significant contribution to the understanding of the patient's dynamics and treatment. Particularly important for these patients is the gathering of a detailed and thorough history, both psychosocial and medical, on the child patient as well as siblings and parents. Nothing can be taken at face value, and all history, particularly of previous illness and dramatic events (such as deaths, fires, car accidents), should be verified through other sources including detailed medical records from other institutions. Many therapists and examiners make the mistake of failing to question and verify *all* important background information provided by FD patients, which only further complicates the understanding of the etiology, dynamics, and personal issues of the patient.

Questions about the patient's motivation, chronicity, and conscious intent to deceive can be fruitfully addressed in psychological interviews and family observations. In particular, an exploration of the patient's relationship to his/her physicians, and the day-to-day impact of the "illness" role on the patient's life may help clarify the function of the deception and the needs being met. An exploration of the patient's current family life, relationships with parents, siblings, and significant others can be useful in clarifying important influences, reinforcers, and models for the sick role. Children are likely to be more candid and less deceptive in their presentation, as they may be less aware of the implications of what they reveal.

Psychological testing instruments can contribute to a comprehensive picture of the patient's functioning, particularly when the examiner uses instruments that are less susceptible to conscious deception. The dissimulation scales of the Minnesota Multiphasic Personality Inventory (MMPI-II) and projective tests such as the Rorschach and the Thematic Apperception Test have been particularly useful in this regard. For example, Aduan et al., (1979) reported psychological test results for five adult FD cases and elicited themes of inhibited expression of anger, affective deprivation, faulty concepts of identity, and difficulty separating self from others. They described FD patients as generally suffering from underlying severe personality disorder " ... characterized by hostility, dependency, imposture and poor impulse control with self-destructive acting-out" (p. 238). A review of psychological test data available on adult FD patients (Schreier & Libow, 1993a) found that identity confusion, and sexual and aggressive impulse control issues were significant; defenses included acting out, projection, somatization, and denial. Only limited and mostly case study test data has been available on child FD patients.

There has also been limited psychological test data presented for child victims of FDbP. Ojeda-Castro (1995) recommends thorough developmental and psychological assessments of child victims to assess for developmental delays due to chronic illness, multiple hospitalizations, or deprived environments. Other important concerns for these children are dependency issues, separation anxiety, issues of bodily integrity, and issues of trust and attachment to caregivers. However, it must be noted that the diagnosis of FD or FDbP cannot be made on the basis of a psychological evaluation alone, as there is no uniform profile of such patients, and many manage to present themselves as fairly "normal."

5.26.3.2 Treatment Formulation

The treatment process begins with the open acknowledgment directly to the patient that his/her caregivers suspect deception. The first (and often the last) phase of treatment is confrontation with the patient and family, when the physicians and health care team reveal their findings and directly address the factitious illness. This confrontation is essentially unavoidable in the case of fabricated illness being actively treated by medical staff, although milder forms of symptom exaggeration can sometimes be addressed more indirectly to help the patient "save face" while referring him/her on to treatment. In the case of illness exaggeration, Richtsmeier and Waters (1984) suggest it is not very useful to directly challenge a "family myth" or explain what is "really going on" if the family is unable to hear it. Instead they recommend developing trust, with the physician continuing to meet with the patient and gradually exploring psychological issues, hopefully eventually resulting in the acceptance of psychological referrals.

The approach selected for the confrontation of the blatantly fabricating patient is critical to the possibility of forming an alliance with the family and maintaining their accessibility for psychotherapeutic treatment. Without a successful confrontation, there is no possibility of ongoing follow-up. A successful confrontation does not necessarily require an admission by the patient, but should at least conclude with an agreement to seek psychological services. Unfortunately, it may not be possible, even with the most carefully chosen team and therapeutic approach, to successfully join with all FD or FDbP patients. In fact, it is very common for cases described in elaborate medical detail in the literature to conclude with the unfortunate fact that the patient was confronted, fled the facility, and was never heard from again (e.g., Rodriguez-Moreno et al., 1990; Witt & Ginsberg-Fellner, 1981). Many of the younger FD patients described in the literature apparently do confess fairly readily to their fabrications when confronted (Abe et al., 1984; Abrol et al., 1990; Croft & Jervis, 1989; Lovejoy et al., 1971; White et al., 1966), which is much less likely in older patients.

Given that denial and flight are common responses to confrontation of adolescents and FDbP perpetrators, practitioners have outlined a number of suggestions for approaching the confrontation to maximize success. Wedel (1971) recommends a "therapeutic confrontation" in which a trusted, supportive social worker is included in the team meeting, which should convey concern and acceptance to decrease the patient's sense of shame and anxiety. Many authors address the need to avoid a punitive, rejecting stance on the part of the medical team, as these feelings are common reactions of health care providers duped into active collusion with unnecessary treatment. Hollender and Hersh (1970) developed an approach which includes the pairing of a confronting physician and a supportive psychiatrist to maximize their success. It is important for the team to include at least one psychiatrist or psychologist, and for an emergency plan to be ready in case the patient becomes actively suicidal (Schreier & Libow, 1993a). If the patient agrees to psychotherapeutic treatment, it is recommended that the contract include the patient's agreement to confine all his/her medical treatment to a single facility or group of physicians familiar with the disorder, to help contain the behavior. In the case of FDbP, this restriction is often built directly into court orders for parent–child reunification.

If the confrontation is successful and the patient remains accessible, the task of treatment remains formidable. Some authors recommend initial psychiatric hospitalization for long-term in-patient care (Plassmann, 1994b) if that is feasible. However, it is much more common for out-patient psychotherapy to be the primary mode of treatment. A combination of behavioral and psychodynamic approaches have been recommended, with an emphasis on exploring the nature of the patient's historical relationships with physicians and authority figures and developing insight into the use of illness in daily life. There is little consensus on successful treatment approaches to the FD patient, and the full range of psychotherapeutic approaches, from behavioral to psychodynamic to family systems, have been utilized, with limited success.

5.26.4 TREATMENT

5.26.4.1 Psychosocial Treatments

5.26.4.1.1 Psychotherapy for factitious disorder

There is virtually no treatment literature available describing psychotherapy for children or adolescents who fabricate illness, and this is especially surprising compared with the considerably more extensive literature on child somatization disorder and its treatment (Campo & Fritsch, 1994; Garralda, 1996). This is partially due to the fact that many of the children fabricating illness make early admissions when confronted. Some of the reports on FD report that younger children, in particular, do not seem to repeat this behavior once confronted, although it is unlikely that many of these patients have been followed prospectively in any systematic way. Suggestions about therapy for these children that have been made, not surprisingly, include the need for involvement of the family system, including Herzberg and Wolff's (1972) recommendation for parental couples therapy to avoid sabotaging the child's treatment. White et al. (1966) suggest that the clinician needs to allay parental concerns about illness, and help the parent(s) minimize secondary gains by insisting the child resume full activity and school responsibilities.

Once again the adult FD literature is more informative on treatment and includes several descriptions of individual therapies. A German psychiatrist, Plassmann (1994c), reviewed approximately 350 papers on the treatment of FD and found that the "vast majority of psychotherapies undertaken do not go beyond an initial phase consisting of several psychiatric interviews" (p. 96). He found that the major issues in successful treatment involved the problem of how to confront the patient, selection of the appropriate setting (in- or out-patient), the establishment of a positive working relationship, and countertransference issues. His review found that the most frequently used therapeutic methods were analytically oriented therapy, hypnosis, psychoanalysis, and group therapy. His paper also described his own psychodynamic treatment of 12 patients, mostly in in-patient or long-term out-patient therapy, which utilized an "approaching phase," an "introjection phase," and a "separation phase."

Most other authors report on only single cases or very small samples. For example, Schoenfeld, Margolin, and Baum (1987) described the long-term treatment of a young adult patient with a combination of dynamic and supportive therapy. They described the value of working with a nurturing female therapist as a "corrective experience," and they used the patient's children to generate treatment motivation. Stone (1977) treated a young woman in an in-patient psychiatric unit, although she checked herself out against medical advice Two male adult FD patients were treated on an in-patient unit in Ireland with a variety of "communication techniques" and the fostering of a highly dependent relationship with the therapist (O'Shea & McGennis, 1982). Fras (1978) described a very supportive, cautious approach to psychotherapy which avoided challenging the patient's denial and resistance too vigorously. A supportive four-month treatment of a patient was described by Jamieson, McKee, and Roback (1979) focused on reinforcing reality-testing, although the patient was apparently still producing symptoms on follow-up. Schreier and Libow (1993a) and Eisendrath and Feder (1996) also report a variety of other approaches that have been used with FD patients including aversive therapy, biofeedback, paradoxical approaches, systems interventions, and behavioral contingencies.

It should be noted that countertransference issues for the therapist working with FD patients can be a significant obstacle to joining with the patient and establishing a positive working relationship. Schreier and Libow (1993a) present two detailed cases narrated directly by the therapists who treated the MBPS mothers which highlighted the therapists' own difficulties even recognizing their patients' manipulations. The patients' efforts at impostering the role of "cooperative patient" apparently sabotaged the therapeutic efforts of even these motivated and well-intentioned therapists.

5.26.4.1.2 *Psychotherapy for factitious disorder by proxy*

As in the treatment of FD, there is no single specific treatment for the parent or adult with FDbP, but instead a variety of psychotherapeutic techniques and approaches, assuming the patient is still amenable for treatment after the initial confrontation. Since few mothers with this disorder immediately acknowledge the problem, most enter therapy guardedly, or under court order. One of the few successful treatment cases was described by Nicol and Eccles (1985) who detailed a one-year treatment of a mother, focused on uncovering and interpreting her fantasies related to her ambivalent relationship with her father and her family culture of exaggerating illness. Lansky and Erickson (1974) described couples work in a family in which the child was being poisoned by the mother with caustic agents and medication.

Palmer and Yoshimura (1984) provided unusually detailed psychosocial histories for both a mother and her child victim of FDbP, and suggested that treatment of such children should be intensive and reality-focused, emphasizing the "gradual removal of pathologic defense mechanisms and on expanding the child's understanding of his or her state of physical health, of the parent's role in the creation of the illness, and of the parent's psychological state" (pp. 507–508). They described the issues of bodily integrity, feelings of helplessness and overly close mother–child interactions that emerged during a play therapy evaluation of their nine-year-old patient.

Suggestions for treatment of very young child victims of factitious illness are offered by Ojeda-Castro (1995), who described a play therapy approach for helping victims resolve issues such as the violation of basic trust, attachment problems, the "incongruous mother image," and the distorted self-image. The sessions begin with thorough cognitive and developmental evaluations of the child, move into regressive play therapy, and gradually work towards joint sessions with the mother, if reunification is anticipated.

One of the more unique, specific approaches to treating children involved in FDbP is offered by Sanders (1995). She proposes a narrative approach to working with families in which children collude in the exaggeration of illness. The goal of the therapist is to challenge the family's "story of illness" and help them develop an "alternative story" and means of coping. Involvement of the parents is considered very important to the success of treatment, and this approach seems mainly useful for more cooperative families.

5.26.4.1.3 *Efficacy of psychosocial treatment*

Unfortunately the difficulty of assessing successful outcome is probably greater in FDs than in most other psychiatric disorders, due to the ever-present risk of deception and the difficulty of accurately verifying the cessation of chronic or compulsive repetition of the behavior. Furthermore, the simple absence of the originally falsified medical symptom(s) may not represent the best outcome measure. As Campo and Fritsch (1994) remind us, "Outcome for patients with troubling somatization early in life may not be as positive when functional and psychiatric status is evaluated at follow-up, as opposed to the presence or absence of the original physical symptom" (p. 1231). That is, a child who stops fabricating an illness after being confronted or even treated in therapy is not necessarily psychologically healthy upon termination of this behavior. Furthermore, one has to questions some "positive" outcomes that have been reported for factitious disorder patients, such as the patient described by Fras (1978) who stopped inducing diabetic problems and started a nursing career, and another (Schoenfeld et al., 1987) who moved from factitious illness to work as a paramedic!

Certain factors do seem to point to better prognosis. The less chronic, more episodic FD patients seem to have a better response to both confrontation and therapy than Munchausen patients. Folks and Freeman (1985) remind us that patients with underlying mood or anxiety disorders have a better prognosis for treatment than those with coexisting personality disorders. We must treat any psychopathology such as depression, conversion symptoms or psychosis, often before the FD itself can be addressed. At the same time, factitious psychological disorders can coexist with factitious physical disorders and must also be ruled out before treatment is derailed.

Above and beyond all of these cautions, it must be noted that the efficacy of treatment approaches for both FD and FDbP is questionable. A handful of papers describe limited success on a case study basis. Even Plassmann's (1994c) report of an intensive treatment study involving 24 patients found that only half the patients even accepted the offer of treatment, and only three of the patients showed a disappearance of factitious symptomatology and marked changes in social competence as a result of treatment.

Reports on the effectiveness of treating mothers with MBPS are equally cautionary. Schreier and Libow's (1993a) review of the literature reports very limited success in the treatment of this disorder, as do McGuire and Feldman (1989), who note little effect of treatment on mothers' insight or medical abuse behavior. They also point out that even if the illness fabrications cease, the child victim may continue to manifest significant psychological problems and may eventually begin to seek inappropriate medical care him or herself. However, the increase in awareness, identification, and treatment of FD cases is beginning to offer some hope for the development of more effective treatments.

5.26.4.2 Pharmacological Treatments

5.26.4.2.1 *Uses of pharmacotherapy*

There are only a handful of reports on the use of pharmacotherapy in the treatment of FDs, and they generally involve treatment of the patient's concurrent mood or anxiety disorders. It has been suggested by Earle and Folks (1986) that antipsychotic medication can be useful for the treatment of brief psychotic episodes in FD patients, just as antidepressants may be appropriate for depressed patients. One apparently successful example in the literature is Schoenfeld et al.'s (1987) use of antianxiety and antidepressant medication in conjunction with dynamic therapy for an FD patient. One of the only known uses of pharmacological agents directly for treatment of FD is described by McDonald et al. (1979) who used sodium amytal ("truth serum") interviews to gather more accurate information from their patients. Unfortunately, they found that it had no real value for treatment itself.

5.26.4.2.2 *Efficacy of pharmacotherapy*

There is no known pharmacotherapy treatment designed specifically for FD or FDbp, although the use of psychoactive medication may be useful in establishing and maintaining the treatment relationship and treating coexisting psychiatric disorders in these patients.

5.26.5 FUTURE DIRECTIONS FOR RESEARCH AND PRACTICE

For a variety of reasons already outlined, the study of FD in children and adolescents is in its very early stages. To begin with, untold numbers of cases of fabricating children and adolescents are likely being misidentified under the broader category of somatizers when their deliberate deceptions are not detected. Thus, there has been a limited pool of actual cases for study and it is likely that only the most blatant or persistant fabrications have been identified. An area ripe for more study is the clarification of the relationship between somatization, malingering, and FD in children, to determine if these represent qualitatively different diagnostic entities or whether there is considerable overlap. Further research may clarify whether there is even a developmental progression from one to the next. Furthermore, we need to better understand the similarities and differences between young people who consciously exaggerate their symptoms and those who actively induce illness; these distinctions are equally important to understand in the mothers who use illness exaggeration and those who engage in the active induction of illness in their children. The establishment of better diagnostic tools for assessing intent, motivation, and conscious deception, and a better program of education for physicians in recognizing the problem would be extremely helpful in collecting better data about these interesting and troubling cases of children who deliberately induce their own illnesses.

Beyond diagnostic considerations, it is clear that our understanding of the etiology and treatment of these disorders is also in its infancy. Earlier and more intensive involvement of pediatric psychologists in the assessment of FD patients, perhaps even before some of the families are confronted and lost to follow-up, would allow for the collection of more detailed psychosocial histories that should include not only the child's detailed medical, developmental, and social history, but the medical and psychosocial histories of mother, father, and all siblings. The intriguing hints in the literature of possible multigenerational replication of FD and FDbP in families can only be fruitfully explored through examination of the family systems and backgrounds of as many family members as possible. In particular, the possible role of mothers with FDbP raising children who themselves later become active fabricators of illness is a fascinating one in our understanding of FD and its genesis in young adults. Further, it suggests that research into the ways that older children may learn to either collude with, or resist, the efforts of a fabricating parent can point directions to effective treatment approaches for victims of MBPS.

One of the suggestions that has been discussed in child abuse and child protection circles is that of developing some type of national registry of FDbP cases, so that better data can be collected on the prevalence, psychosocial histories, and successful and unsuccessful treatment approaches to these cases. Psychological test data is beginning to be collected by individual clinicans working with FDbP parents and by-proxy patients, which, if systematically collected and shared, might help develop profiles useful for clinicians in identifying FD cases. Nation-wide registries might also save our health care systems and child protective services considerable resources, and prevent continued harm to vulnerable children by allowing earlier identification and follow-up of chronic, itinerant FD patients.

5.26.6 SUMMARY

Physicians and clinicians have been sharing their experiences and observations about FDs in the literature for several decades. These simulated illnesses, intentionally exaggerated or induced by the youngster and/or the parent, are often medically treated for long periods of time before finally being discovered as factitious. Physicians are often drawn into believing in these deceptions for many complex reasons, and can unintentionally cause considerable harm to the child through unnecessary treatments, procedures, hospitalizations and the fostering of the child's career as an invalid. While the discovery of fabrications by preadolescent children is generally fairly rapid and tends to result in confession and cessation of the deception, the treatment of factitious illness in adolescents and adults and of factitious illness by proxy is often a difficult, frustrating process complicated by widespread confusion about the diagnosis, and lack of systematic data on etiology and treatment of these disorders. There may be considerably more cases of FD in our health care systems than are commonly recognized, and there appear to be family systems which perpetuate the process of misusing medical resources to meet complex psychological needs, resulting in multiple generations of family somatizers or fabricators. The development of a better research database on family histories, psychological test findings and responses to different treatment approaches could help reduce the serious physical and psychological damage resulting from these forms of self-induced illness, and perhaps prevent some children from progressing to lifetime careers of medical abuse.

5.26.7 REFERENCES

Abe, K., Shinozima, K., Okuno, A., Abe, T., & Ochi, H. (1984). Munchausen's syndrome in children: Bizarre clinical and laboratory features. *Acta Paediatrica Japan, 26,* 539–543.
Abrol, R. P., Heck, A., Gleckel, L., & Rosner, F. (1990). Self-induced hematuria. *Journal of the National Medical Association, 82*(2), 127–128.

Aduan, R. P., Fauci, A. S., Dale, D. C., Herzberg, J. H., & Wolff, S. M. (1979). *Annals of Internal Medicine, 90,* 230–242.

American Psychiatric Association. (1994). *Diagnostic and statistical manual of mental disorders* (4th ed.). Washington, DC: American Psychiatric Association.

Asher, R. (1951). Munchausen's syndrome. *Lancet, 1,* 339–341.

Baldwin, C. (1996). Munchausen syndrome by proxy: problems of definition, diagnosis and treatment. *Health and Social Care in the Community, 4*(3), 159–165.

Barsky, A. J. (1992). Amplification, somatization and the somatoform disorders. *Psychosomatics, 33*(1), 28–34.

Bools, C. N., Neale, B. A., & Meadow, S. R. (1993). Follow up of victims of fabricated illness (Munchausen syndrome by proxy). *Archives of Diseases of Childhood, 69,* 625–630.

Campo, J. V., & Fritsch, S. L. (1994). Somatization in children and adolescents. *Journal of the American Academy of Child and Adolescent Psychiatry, 33*(9), 1223–1235.

Carney, M. W. P. (1980). Artifactual illness to attract medical attention. *British Journal of Psychiatry, 136,* 542–547.

Chin, P., & Breu, G. (1991). The murder that never was. *People Magazine, Dec. 16,* 111–116.

Cramer, B., Gershberg, M. R., & Stern, M. (1971). Munchausen syndrome: Its relationship to malingering, hysteria, and the physician–patient relationship. *Archives of General Psychiatry, 24,* 573–578.

Croft, R. D., & Jervis, M. (1989). Munchausen's syndrome in a 4 year old. *Archives of Disease in Childhood, 64,* 740–741.

Donald, T., & Jureidini, J. (1996). Munchausen syndrome by proxy: Child abuse in the medical system. *Archives of Pediatric and Adolescent Medicine, 150,* 753–758.

Earle, J. R., & Folks, D. G. (1986). Factitious disorder and coexisting depression: a report of successful psychiatric consultation and case management. *General Hospital Psychiatry, 8,* 448–450.

Eisendrath, S. J. (1996). Current overview of factitious physical disorders. In M. D. Feldman & S. J. Eisendrath (Eds.), *The spectrum of factitious disorders* (pp. 21–36). Washington, DC: American Psychiatric Press.

Eisendrath, S. J., & Feder, A. (1996). Management of factitious disorders. In M. D. Feldman & S. J. Eisendrath (Eds.), *The spectrum of factitious disorders* (pp. 195–213). Washington, DC: American Psychiatric Press.

Eminson, D. M., & Postlewaite, R. J. (1992). Factitious illness: recognition and management. *Archives of Disease in Childhood, 67,* 1510–1516.

Feldman, M. D., & Eisendrath, S. J. (Eds.) (1996). *The spectrum of factitious disorders.* Washington, DC: American Psychiatric Press.

Feldman, M. D., & Smith, R. (1996). Personal and interpersonal toll of factitious disorders. In M. D. Feldman & S. J. Eisendrath (Eds.), *The spectrum of factitious disorders,* pp. 175–194. Washington, DC: American Psychiatric Press.

Fialkov, M. J. (1984). Peregrination in the problem pediatric patient. *Clinical Pediatrics, 23,* 571–575.

Fink, P. (1992). Physical complaints and symptoms of somatizing patients. *Journal of Psychosomatic Research, 36*(2), 125–136.

Fisher, G. C., & Mitchell, I. (1995). Is Munchausen syndrome by proxy really a syndrome? *Archives of Disease in Childhood, 72*(6), 530–534.

Folks, D. G, & Freeman, A. M. (1985), Munchausen's syndrome and other factitious illness. *Psychiatric Clinics of North America, 8*(2), 263–278.

Fras, J. (1978). Factitial disease: an update. *Psychosomatics, 19*(2), 119–122.

Friedman, S. B. (1973). Conversion symptoms in adolescents. *Pediatric Clinics of North America, 20*(4), 873–882.

Garralda, M. E. (1996) Somatisation in children. *Journal of Child Psychology and Psychiatry, 37*(1), 13–33.

Gavin, H. (1838). *On feigned and factitious diseases.* Edinburgh: Edinburgh University Press.

Goodlin, R. C. (1985). Pregnant females with Munchausen syndrome. *American Journal of Obstetrics and Gynecology, 153,* 207–210.

Goss, P. W., & McDougall, P. N. (1992). Munchausen syndrome by proxy: a cause of preterm delivery. *Medical Journal of Australia, 157,* 814–817.

Gilbert, R. W., Pierse, P. M., & Mitchell, D. P. (1987). Cryptic otalgia: A case of Munchausen syndrome in a pediatric patient. *Journal of Otolaryngology, 16*(4), 231–233.

Guandolo, V. L. (1985). Munchausen syndrome by proxy: an out-patient challenge. *Pediatrics, 75,* 526–530.

Hay, G. G. (1983). Feigned psychosis: A review of the simulation of mental illness. *British Journal of Psychiatry, 43,* 8–10.

Herzberg, J. H. & Wolff, S. M. (1972) Chronic factitious fever in puberty and adolescence: A diagnostic challenge to the family physician. *Psychiatry in Medicine, 3,* 205–212.

Holborow, P. L. (1985). A variant of Munchausen syndrome by proxy. *Journal of the American Academy of Child Psychiatry, 24*(2), 238.

Hollender, M. D., & Hersh, S. R. (1970). Impossible consultation made possible. *Archives of General Psychiatry, 23,* 343–345.

Jacobi, A. (1895). Hyperthermy in a man up to 148 degrees F. *Transactions of the Association of American Physicians, 10,* 159–191.

Jamieson, R., McKee, E., & Roback, H. (1979). Munchausen's syndrome: an unusual case. *American Journal of Psychotherapy, 33*(4), 616–621.

Janofsky, J. S. (1986). Munchausen syndrome in a mother and daughter: an unusual presentation of folie deux. *Journal of Nervous and Mental Disease, 174*(6), 368–370.

Jonas, J. M., & Pope, H. G., Jr. (1985). The dissimulating disorders: a single diagnostic entity? *Comprehensive Psychiatry, 26,* 58–62.

Katz, R. L., Mazer, C., & Litt, I. F. (1985). Anorexia nervosa by proxy. *The Journal of Pediatrics, 107*(2), 247–248.

Knockaert, D. C., Vanneste, L. J., Vanneste, S. B., & Bobbaers, H. J. (1992). Fever of unknown origin in the 1980s. An update of the diagnostic spectrum. *Archives of Internal Medicine, 152,* 51–55.

Krener, P. (1994). Factitious disorders and the psychosomatic continuum in children. *Current Opinion in Pediatrics, 6,* 418–422.

Krener, P., & Adelman, R. (1988). Parent salvage and parent sabotage in the care of chronically ill children. *American Journal of Diseases of Children, 142,* 945–951.

Lansky, S. B., & Erickson, H. M. (1974). Prevention of child murder. *Journal of the American Academy of Child Psychiatry, 13,* 691–698.

Levin, A. V., & Sheridan, M. S. (1995). *Munchausen syndrome by proxy: Issues in diagnosis and treatment.* New York: Lexington Books.

Libow, J. A. (1995). Munchausen by proxy victims in adulthood: A first look. *Child Abuse and Neglect, 19*(9), 1131–1142.

Libow, J. A., & Schreier, H. A. (1986). Three forms of factitious illness in children: When is it Munchausen syndrome by proxy? *American Journal of Orthopsychiatry, 56,* 602–611.

Light, M. J., & Sheridan, M. S. (1990). Munchausen syndrome by proxy and apnea—A survey of apnea programs. *Clinical Pediatrics, 29*(3), 162–168.

Livingston, R. (1992). Somatization in child, adolescent, and family psychiatry. *Psychiatric Medicine, 10*(3), 13–23.

Livingston, R. (1993). Children of people with somatization disorder. *Journal of the American Academy of Child and Adolescent Psychiatry, 32*(3), 536–544.

Lovejoy, F. H., Marcuse, E. K., & Landrigan, P. J. (1971). Two examples of purpura facititia. *Clinical Pediatrics, 10*(3), 183–184.

Masterson, J., Dunworth, R., & Williams, N. (1988). Extreme illness exaggeration in pediatric patients: A variant of Munchausen by proxy? *American Journal of Orthopsychiatry, 58*(2), 188–195.

McClure, R. J., Davis, P. M., Meadow, S. R., & Sibert, J. R. (1996). Epidemiology of Munchausen syndrome by proxy, non-accidental poisoning, and non-accidental suffocation. *Archives of Disease in Childhood, 75,* 57–61.

McDonald, A., Kline, S. A., & Billings, R. F. (1979). The limits of Munchausen's syndrome. *Canadian Journal of Psychiatry, 24,* 323–328.

McGuire, L. T., & Feldman, K. W. (1989). Psychologic morbidity of children subjected to Munchausen syndrome by proxy. *Pediatrics, 83*(2), 289–292.

Meadow, R. (1977). Munchausen syndrome by proxy. The hinterland of child abuse. *Lancet, 2,* 343–345.

Meadow, R. (1990). Suffocation, recurrent apnea and sudden infant death. *The Journal of Pediatrics, 117,* 351–357.

Meadow, S. R. (1984). Commentary. *Archives of Disease in Childhood, 59,* 156.

Morley, C. J. (1995). Practical concerns about the diagnosis of Munchausen syndrome by proxy. *Archives of Disease in Childhood, 72*(6), 528–530.

Nadelson, T. (1979). The Munchausen spectrum: borderline character features. *General Hospital Psychiatry, 1,* 11–17.

Nichol, A. R., & Eccles, M. (1985). Psychotherapy for Munchausen syndrome by proxy. *Archives of Disease in Childhood, 60,* 344–348.

Ojeda-Castro, M. (1995). Issues in play therapy with victims of Munchausen by proxy syndrome. *Presented at the 103rd Annual Convention of the American Psychological Association,* New York, August, 1995.

O'Shea, B., & McGennis, A. (1982). The psychotherapy of Munchausen's syndrome. *Irish Journal of Psychotherapy, 1,* 17–19.

Palmer, A. J., & Yoshimura, G. J. (1984), Munchausen syndrome by proxy. *Journal of the American Academy of Child Psychiatry, 23*(4), 503–508.

Paperny, D., Hicks, R., & Hammar, S. L. (1980). Munchausen's syndrome. *American Journal of Diseases of Childhood, 134,* 794–795.

Phillips, M. R., Ward, N. G., & Ries, R. K. (1983). Factitious mourning: Painless patienthood. *American Journal of Psychiatry, 140,* 420–425.

Plassmann, R. (1994a). The biography of the factitious-disorder patient. *Psychotherapy Psychosomatics, 62,* 123–128.

Plassmann, R. (1994b). Munchhausen syndromes and factitious diseases. *Psychotherapy Psychosomatics, 62,* 7–26.

Plassmann, R. (1994c). Impatient and outpatient long-term psychotherapy of patients suffering from factitious disorders. *Psychotherapy Psychosomatics, 62,* 96–107.

Pope, H. G., Jonas, J. M., & Jones, B. (1982). Factitious psychosis: phenomenology, family history and long-term outcome of 9 patients. *American Journal of Psychiatry, 139*(11), 1480–1486.

Raymond, C. A. (1987). Munchausen's may occur in younger persons. *Journal of the American Medical Association, 257*(24), 3332.

Reich, P., & Gottfried, L. A. (1983). Factitious disorders in a teaching hospital. *Annals of Internal Medicine, 99,* 240–247.

Reich, P., Lazarus, J. M., Kelly, M. J., & Rogers, M. P. (1977). Factitious feculent urine in an adolescent boy. *Journal of the American Medical Association, 238*(5), 420–421.

Richtsmeier, A. J., Jr., & Waters, D. B. (1984). Somatic symptoms as family myth. *American Journal Diseases of Childhood, 138,* 855–857.

Rodriguez-Moreno, J., Ruiz-Martin, J. M., Mateo-Soria, L., Rozadilla, A., & Roig-Escofet, D. (1990). Munchausen's syndrome simulating reflex sympathetic dystrophy. *Annals of Rheumatic Diseases, 49,* 1010–1012.

Rosenberg, D. (1987). Web of deceit: a literature review of Munchausen syndrome by proxy. *Child Abuse and Neglect, 11,* 547–563.

Roth, D. (1990). How "mild" is mild Munchausen syndrome by proxy? *Israel Journal of Psychiatry and Related Sciences, 27*(3), 160–167.

Rumans, L. W., & Vosti, K. L. (1978). Factitious and fraudulent fever. *American Journal of Medicine, 65,* 745–755.

Sakula, A. (1978). Munchausen: fact and fiction. *Journal of Royal College of Physicians, 12*(3), 286–292.

Sale, I., & Kalucy, R. (1980). An observation on the genesis of Munchausen syndrome. A case report. *Australian and New Zealand Journal of Psychiatry, 14,* 61-64.

Samuels, M. P., McClaughlin, W., Jacobson, R. R., Poets, C. F., & Southall, D. P. (1992). Fourteen cases of imposed upper airway obstruction. *Archives of Disease in Childhood, 67,* 162–170.

Sanders, M. J. (1995). Symptom coaching: Factitious disorder by proxy with older children. *Clinical Psychology Review, 15*(5), 423–442.

Schoenfeld, H., Margolin, J., & Baum, S. (1987). Munchausen syndrome as a suicide equivalent: abolition of syndrome by psychotherapy. *American Journal of Psychotherapy, 41*(4), 604–612.

Schreier, H. A., & Libow, J. A. (1993a). *Hurting for love: Munchausen by proxy syndrome.* New York: Guilford Press.

Schreier, H. A., & Libow, J. A. (1993b). Munchausen by proxy syndrome: diagnosis and prevalence. *American Journal of Orthopsychiatry, 63*(2), 318–321.

Sneed, R. C., & Bell, R. F. (1976). The dauphin of Munchausen: Factitious passage of renal stones in a child. *Pediatrics, 58,* 127–130.

Spiro, H. R. (1968). Chronic factitious illness. Munchausen's syndrome. *Archives of General Psychiatry, 18,* 569–579.

Stankler, L. (1977). Factitious skins lesions in a mother and two sons. *British Journal of Dermatology, 97,* 217–219.

Stegman, M. S., & Aaron, W. S. (Eds.) (1996). *ICD-9-CM Codebook.* Reston, VA: St. Anthony Publishing.

Steinbeck, A. W. (1961). Haemorrhagica histrionica—the bleeding Munchausen syndrome. *Medical Journal of Australia, 48,* 451–456.

Stone, M. H. (1977). Factitious illness. *Bulletin of the Meninger Clinic, 41*(3), 239–254.

Taylor, S., & Hyler, S. E. (1993). Update on factitious disorders. *International Journal of Psychiatric Medicine, 23,* 81–94.

Tojo, A., Nanba, S., Kimura, K., Hirata, Y., Matsuoka, H., Sugimoto, T., Watanabe, N., & Ohkubo, A. (1990). Factitious proteinuria in a young girl. *Clinical Nephrology, 33*(6), 299–302.

Warner, J., & Hathaway, M. J. (1984). Allergic form of Meadow's syndrome (Munchausen by proxy). *Archives of Disease in Childhood, 59,* 151–156.

Wedel, K. R. (1971). A therapeutic confrontation approach to treating patients with factitious illness. *Social Work, 16*(2), 69–73.

White, J. G., Pearson, H. A., & Coddington, R. D. (1966). Purpura factitia: Attracting attention by self-inflicted lesions. *Clinical Pediatrics, 5*(3), 157–160.

Witt, M. E., & Ginsberg-Fellner, F. (1981). Prednisone-induced Munchausen syndrome. *American Journal of Diseases of Childhood, 135,* 852–853.

Wood, P. R., Fowlkes, J., Holden, P., & Castro, D. (1989).

Fever of unknown origin for six years: Munchausen syndrome by proxy. *Journal of Family Practice, 28*(4), 391–395.

Woolcott, P., Aceto, T., Rutt, C., Bloom, M., & Glick, R. (1982). Doctor shopping with the child as proxy patient: A variant of child abuse. *Journal of Pediatrics, 101,* 297–301.

5.27

Schizophrenia in Children and Adolescents

CINDY M. YEE and MARIAN D. SIGMAN
University of California, Los Angeles, CA, USA

5.27.1 INTRODUCTION

Childhood-onset schizophrenia and adolescent-onset schizophrenia are among the most devastating of mental disorders to afflict the young. Fortunately, the incidence of schizophrenia in childhood and early adolescence is quite rare with the onset of schizophrenia typically occurring during late adolescence and early adulthood. In current clinical research and practice, the diagnostic criteria for schizophrenia are the same for children, adolescents, and adults, thereby allowing for developmental effects on the presentation and expression of symptoms. Schizophrenic illness has been identified in children as young as three years of age (Russell, Bott, & Sammons, 1989), although psychotic symptoms do not usually appear or are not detected reliably until a child is at least six or seven years of age (Russell, 1994; Werry, 1996). Schizophrenia in children and adolescents, sometimes referred to as very-early-onset and early-onset schizophrenia, respectively (Werry, 1996), are often treated as distinct disorders although there are conflicting reports about the nature of the differences between the two forms of the between the two forms of the illness (R. F. Asarnow & J. R. Asarnow, 1994).

Some of the earliest observations of childhood- and adolescent-onset schizophrenia date back to Kraepelin's (1883/1915) description of dementia praecox, a form of mental deterioration that involves disturbances of thought and that can occur even in children. Upon observing such symptoms in a group of children, De Sanctis (1906/1973) described the disorder as *dementia praecocissima*. Bleuler (1911/1950) subsequently introduced the term *schizophrenia* to refer to the same condition in children and adults, as identical diagnostic criteria were being used to categorize both groups. By the 1930s, however, all children with profound mental disturbances, including autism and other psychoses, were placed in a general category that was labeled "childhood schizophrenia" (Fish & Ritvo, 1979). This tradition persisted with *DSM-II* (American Psychiatric Association, 1968) and *ICD-8* (World Health Organization, 1967–1969). However, with the introduction of *DSM-III* (American Psychiatric Association, 1980) and *ICD-9* (World Health Organization, 1978), the field returned to the practice of using the same diagnostic criteria for identifying schizophrenia regardless of age. Given the considerable diagnostic heterogeneity that characterized the broad category of childhood schizophrenia from the 1930s until the 1970s, it can be difficult, if not impossible at times, to meaningfully interpret the earlier literature.

The material covered in the present chapter relies on *DSM-III* through *DSM-IV* (American Psychiatric Association, 1994), *ICD-9* (World Health Organization, 1978), and *ICD-10* (World Health Organization, 1992) diagnostic criteria. By necessity, the primary emphasis of this chapter will be on schizophrenia that has been diagnosed before the age of 12 as early adolescent-onset schizophrenia has received relatively less attention in the clinical research literature to date. It should be noted that some variability exists between clinical research sites with regard to the maximum age allowed for receiving a diagnosis of childhood-onset schizophrenia. The National Institute of Mental Health project on childhood-onset schizophrenia, for instance, does not accept patients with an onset of psychosis beyond the age of 12 while the UCLA Childhood-Onset Schizophrenia Research Program has raised the maximum age from 11 to 14 years. Across sites, schizophrenia in childhood is defined by age and not by physical development because there are considerable individual differences in the age at onset of puberty (Werry, McClellan, Andrews, & Ham, 1994).

5.27.2 SCHIZOPHRENIA AND OTHER PSYCHOTIC DISORDERS

5.27.2.1 Phenomenology

Relying upon more recent diagnostic criteria, there have been reasonably consistent findings across studies on the clinical presentation of schizophrenia in children. Moreover, many of the same qualitative symptoms which are found in children can be seen in adult patients diagnosed with schizophrenia. This is not a complete surprise as the same diagnostic criteria are being applied to children and adults, although the possibility remains that there are distinct developmental differences in the expression of schizophrenia (J. R. Asarnow, 1994). It is noteworthy that any similarity in symptomatology has been obtained despite the inherent difficulty in ascertaining complex, internal symptoms in young children and with recognition of the need to distinguish between clinical symptoms, such as delusions, and normal experiences in childhood, such as vivid fantasies (J. R. Asarnow, 1994; Russell, 1994). In the following discussion, some examples of psychotic symptoms in children are provided; additional examples of symptom expression in preadolescence can be found in Russell (1994).

The most common presenting symptom for children, as with adults, is auditory hallucinations. As shown in Table 1, auditory hallucinations have been observed in approximately 80–100% of cases. Command hallucinations, which are hallucinations that involve telling an individual what to do, are perhaps the most frequent and have been noted in over 60% of children with a schizophrenic disorder (McKenna et al., 1994; Russell et al., 1989). Oftentimes, children report that the commands are negative or violent in nature (e.g., "kick the furniture," "hit your mother," "kill the goldfish"). Other auditory hallucinations involve voices that are conversing with one another (e.g., two stuffed animals speaking with one another), are maintaining a running commentary on the child's thoughts or behaviors (e.g., "It was nice that you helped your brother today"), are making persecutory statements (e.g., calling the child names), or are of a religious nature (e.g., the voice of God or the devil calling the child by name).

Visual hallucinations also appear to occur with considerable frequency and have been reported in approximately 40% or more of children diagnosed with schizophrenia, as shown in Table 1. Some visual perceptions may be reported as accessible only to the child (e.g., "The magician does not want anyone else to see him"), whereas other images are assumed

Table 1 Comparison of studies reporting on clinical symptoms in children with schizophrenia.

| Study | N | Age (years) | Hallucinations | | | | Delusions (%) | Thought disorder (%) | Inappropriate or flat affect (%) |
			Auditory (%)	Visual (%)	Tactile (%)	Olfactory (%)			
Green, Padron-Gayol, Hardesty, & Bassiri (1992)	38	5–11	84	47	8		55	100	84
Kolvin (1971); Kolvin, Ounsted Humphrey, & McNay (1971)	33	5–15	81	30			57	60	63
McKenna et al. (1994)	19	8–11[a]	100	79	37	21	95	84	95
Russell, Bott, & Sammons (1989); Russell (1994)	35	4–13[b]	80	37	17	6	63	40	74
Spencer & Campbell (1994)	16	5–11	100	69	25		100	81	81
Volkmar, Cohen, Hoshino, Rende, & Paul (1988); Volkmar (1996)	42[c]	4–11[d]	79	28			86	93	71

[a]Subjects ranged in age from 12 to 16 years when screened for participation in the research study but the onset of psychosis was before age 12. [b]Schizophrenia was diagnosed before the age of 12. [c]The total sample includes children with clinical diagnoses of childhood schizophrenia, psychotic illness with schizophrenic features, and schizophrenia of childhood onset. Upon reclassification with DSM-III criteria, 14 of the 42 children were diagnosed with schizophrenia; the remainder generally appeared to exhibit schizoid disorder. [d]Approximate estimate of age, derived from the mean and standard deviation provided in the report.

to be visible to anyone present ("Can't you see? The branches are turning into snakes and they are going to get us").

Occurring far less frequently, by contrast, are tactile hallucinations (e.g., "I can feel bugs crawling on my legs") and olfactory hallucinations (e.g., "There's a stinky smell that makes me want to throw up"). As can be seen in Table 1, these hallucinations are typically observed in less than one-third of schizophrenic children. There is some evidence to suggest that non-auditory hallucinations may only occur in those children who experience auditory hallucinations (Kolvin et al., 1971; Russell et al., 1989).

As with adults, delusions are also quite common and have been found to occur in 55–100% of children with a schizophrenic disorder (see Table 1). The content of their delusions is varied and might include themes that are persecutory (e.g., someone is trying to harm the child), somatic (e.g., "My arms grow longer every time I go in the swimming pool"), grandiose (e.g., "I have the powers to decide who lives and who dies"), referential (e.g., the rotating emblem at a gas station is sending secret messages to the child), religious (e.g., "I'm not really a boy, I'm an angel that God sent to be on earth"), or bizarre (e.g., a child believes that he is a soccer ball) in nature. With increased age, hallucinations and delusions become more complex and elaborate, and the content reflects the developmental level of the patient. Themes of animals and monsters, for instance, are more prevalent among younger children, whereas sexual themes appear to be less common (Russell et al., 1989).

Another manifestation of schizophrenia is disorganized thinking or formal thought disorder. As shown in Table 1, thought disorder appears to be present in the majority of children diagnosed with schizophrenia and typically has been observed in 80–100% of cases. Signs of thought disorder include loose associations (e.g., "I am 10-years-old. My pen ran out of ink this morning"), illogical thinking ("I hate peanut butter but I love to eat it all the time"), incoherence ("The day to raindrops go"), and poverty of content of speech ("It does. Uh huh. Yes, does"). Obtaining reliable estimates of formal thought disorder in children can be very difficult, however, in view of developmental constraints on cognitive, linguistic, and practical social skills (e.g., Caplan, 1994; Russell, 1994; Werry et al., 1994), which may account for differences in reported rates between studies. Russell et al. (1989), for example, found that only 40% of their cases demonstrated formal thought disorder.

Inappropriate or flat affect are other common symptoms of schizophrenia and typically have been found in over 70% of children with a schizophrenic disorder (see Table 1). Schizophrenic patients may exhibit inappropriate or uncontrollable emotions, such as laughing at a sad story, responding irritably for no apparent reason, or fluctuating rapidly between emotions. Alternatively, children diagnosed with schizophrenia may show no facial expression and speak in a monotone voice.

Grossly disorganized behavior in schizophrenia can include unpredictable agitation (e.g., unprovoked shouting), extreme silliness, and difficulties with such goal-directed behaviors as maintaining personal hygiene. In children diagnosed with schizophrenia, grossly disorganized behavior has been found to varying degrees. McKenna et al. (1994) noted disorganized behavior in 84% of their sample, whereas Russell et al. (1989) detected it in only 40% of their cases. Green, Padron-Gayol, Hardesty, and Bassiri (1992) observed that either grossly disorganized or catatonic behavior was apparent in 32% of their childhood-onset patients. Catatonic motor behaviors involve psychomotor disturbances, ranging from motoric immobility to excited, excessive activity. In general, catatonic behaviors appear to be rare among children. McKenna et al. (1994) reported the highest rate at 37% and Russell (1994) did not find any cases of catatonic behaviors; other studies made no mention of catatonia, suggesting that it was rare or nonexistent in their samples.

Although suicidal ideation or suicide attempts are often present in adults with schizophrenia, rates of their occurrence in children have not been routinely reported in the literature. In a hospitalized sample of 21 childhood-onset schizophrenics, J. R. Asarnow, Tompson, and Goldstein (1994) observed evidence of suicidality in 76% of cases. The authors note that the rate of suicidality in their inpatient sample may be higher than in other samples as suicidal behavior can often precipitate hospitalization.

As Russell (1994) notes, some young children may not experience their psychotic symptoms as being particularly distressing or unusual. Instead, these symptoms may be perceived as indistinguishable from normal experience given their insidious and early onset. As the psychotic symptoms become more intrusive and interfere with attention, however, children may be more likely to become disturbed or frightened and will then describe their symptoms to parents or others. Parents and others who are close to the child initially may not recognize that a child is experiencing hallucinations and may, instead, attribute the child's behavior to daydreaming.

Documentation of the phenomenology of schizophrenic disorder in early adolescence has been relatively sparse in terms of the current number of studies available. Nonetheless, as shown in Table 2, the studies that do report on symptom patterns in adolescent-onset schizophrenia find considerable similarity in the relative proportion of symptom characteristics as compared with those observed in childhood-onset cases. The rates of symptoms noted by Remschmidt, Martin, Schulz, Gutenbrunner, and Fleischhaker (1991) and by Werry, McClellan, and Chard (1991) are somewhat lower than those obtained in children diagnosed with schizophrenia but this may be due in part to methodological differences in ascertaining symptom patterns. In the studies by McKenna et al. (1994), Russell et al. (1989) and Spencer and Campbell (1994), rates for psychotic symptoms were determined through interviews with the children and their families. Green et al. (1992) relied on clinical records, but noted that their charts received extensive documentation as it was understood that they would be reviewed for research purposes. In both studies of adolescents, symptoms were ascertained from reviews of hospital records although Werry et al. also attempted to subsequently interview patients and their families. It is possible, therefore, that reliance upon archival data could account for lower rates of psychotic symptomatology in adolescents than that observed in studies of childhood-onset schizophrenia.

While the constellation of symptoms appears to be similar across children, adolescents, and adults with schizophrenia, considerable heterogeneity exists in symptomatology across patients. To help delineate particular symptom patterns, the concept of positive and negative symptoms has been introduced in the clinical research literature on adults with schizophrenia. The more florid or bizarre symptoms, such as hallucinations and delusions, constitute positive symptoms, whereas deficient or absent behaviors, such as inappropriate affect, unchanging or flat facial expression and minimal speech, are considered negative symptoms. More recently, the concept of "deficit state" has been introduced to focus upon primary and enduring negative symptoms (Carpenter, Heinrichs, & Wagman, 1988). In adult schizophrenic patients, negative symptoms tend to be present early in the illness, are less responsive to treatment than positive symptoms, and are relatively stable over time (Arndt, Andreasen, Flaum, Miller, & Nopoulus, 1995). A predominant pattern of negative symptoms has also been related to poor outcome (e.g., Breier, Schreiber, Dyer, & Pickar, 1991), although

Pogue-Geile and Harrow (1985) point out that the association may be due to the persistence of poor social and occupational functioning.

The distinction between positive and negative symptoms has been applied less frequently to children and adolescents with schizophrenia. Studies in the 1990s have determined that the positive and negative symptom patterns are present in children and adolescents, much as they are in adults (e.g., Maziade et al., 1996; Remschmidt et al., 1991; Remschmidt, Schulz, Martin, Warnke, & Trott, 1994). In examining the course of these two symptom clusters in childhood- and adolescent-onset schizophrenia, Remschmidt et al. (1994) found some suggestion that negative symptoms may occur over a longer period of time than positive symptoms in the period immediately prior to hospitalization, particularly in children.

5.27.2.1.1 A case illustration

Jeremy is an eight-year old whose family moved to the US from England as he was approaching his sixth birthday. His father is a corporate executive and his mother works part-time as a literary agent. He resides with his parents and a 14-year old half-sister from his mother's previous marriage. The pregnancy and delivery were unremarkable and developmental milestones were reached within normal limits. His mother described Jeremy as a bright, active, and inquisitive toddler who needed to be monitored more closely than his sister at this stage to prevent accidents. Family history of psychiatric illness is largely negative with the exception of a paternal aunt who has a fear of heights. Jeremy's father believes that he may have been hyperactive as a child but he was never diagnosed or treated for the disorder; he attributed his behavior to being bored and unchallenged during grade school.

Jeremy started the first grade at a private school shortly after arriving in the US and began to exhibit noncompliant and aggressive behaviors. His teachers and parents initially attributed his behavioral problems to the family's recent move and the transition to a new school. Rather than subside over time, his negative behaviors began to escalate. A behavior management program was implemented by the school and it appeared to be modestly successful. By the end of second grade, however, Jeremy had become increasingly disruptive in the classroom, had begun to destroy other children's property, and was unable to sit still for any length of time. His school performance had declined substantially and he was performing in the low average range. Peer relations were similarly poor. He was referred for a psychiatric

Table 2 Comparison of studies reporting on clinical symptoms in adolescents with schizophrenia.

			Hallucinations						
Study	N	Age (years)	Auditory (%)	Visual (%)	Tactile (%)	Olfactory (%)	Delusions (%)	Thought disorder (%)	Inappropriate or flat affect (%)
Remschmidt, Martin, Schulz, Gutenbrunner, and Fleischhaker (1991)	113	16–20[a]	———————— 23[b] ————————				55	38	37
Werry, McClellan, and Chard (1991)	30[c]	7–17	53	13	13		47		57

[a]Approximate estimate of age, derived from the mean and standard deviation provided in the report.　[b]Not reported by subtype.　[c]Three of the cases were below the age of 12.

evaluation, at which time he was diagnosed with attention-deficit hyperactivity disorder and started on a trial of methylphenidate. The stimulant trial resulted in a further deterioration of behavior whereby Jeremy's behavior became more agitated and unpredictable. This course of medication was discontinued, Jeremy was rediagnosed with chronic adjustment and conduct disorders, and he was referred for psychotherapy.

A psychiatric hospitalization was precipitated when Jeremy attempted to repeatedly stab a classmate with a sharpened pencil and, two days later, tried to choke his sister claiming that she was not his "real sister." Jeremy also had begun to pick at his skin and scabs until he drew blood, discussing the possibility of bleeding to death. On admission, Jeremy was neatly groomed and presented as a friendly but fidgety child with a short attention span. He reported hearing his name whispered but denied any other hallucinatory experiences. When questioned about the violent acts towards his classmate and sister, Jeremy stated that they were not who they seemed to be and that he had to kill the space aliens that had taken over their bodies in order for his real classmate and his real sister to come back to life. Jeremy refused to discuss his own self-injurious behavior and denied any suicidal ideation.

Upon admission to the hospital, physical and neurological exams proved to be normal. The patient made a good adjustment to the hospital environment and initially responded well to the behavior management program that was implemented. After a few days, however, Jeremy began to exhibit increasingly aggressive, chaotic, and disruptive behaviors. In addition, he resumed the practice of picking at his skin. The staff also observed occasional staring spells. An EEG was obtained and although a mild irregularity was observed, the follow-up magnetic resonance image was normal and did not support the possibility of a structural lesion. Jeremy slowly began to disclose psychotic symptoms that included auditory and visual hallucinations. For instance, Jeremy described a wizard appearing and although he could not always see him, the wizard would whisper his name and instruct him to hurt himself because he had disobeyed the rules. By making himself bleed, Jeremy reported that he could make the wizard go away. Jeremy also described seeing daggers that would drop down from the sky. At night, Jeremy was unable to sleep for the entire duration in his own room; he would awaken and attempt to bring a blanket to sleep on the floor next to the nursing station. Jeremy acknowledged that he was afraid but refused to reveal his specific fear, stating that disclosure would

endanger other people. Over time, Jeremy became increasingly disorganized, his social relatedness declined considerably, and he would speak incoherently. He responded extremely well to a trial of risperidone, an atypical antipsychotic medication, that was offered along with supportive psychotherapy and exhibited no psychotic symptoms upon discharge. The total duration of hospitalization was 45 days.

5.27.2.2 Diagnostic Features and Differential Diagnosis

The *DSM-IV* and *ICD-10* definitions of schizophrenia are similar and, as noted, both use the same criteria for children, adolescents, and adults. The primary differences between the two systems is the degree to which diagnostic criteria are specified and the required duration for certain symptomatology, such that the *ICD-10* definition might be more liberal (Werry, 1996). This chapter focuses on *DSM-IV* criteria as this has been the predominant system used in recent studies on childhood-onset and adolescent schizophrenia. Extensive discussions of the similarities and differences between these two diagnostic systems, as well as comparisons with past systems, can be found in J. R. Asarnow (1994) and Werry (1996).

The *DSM-IV* criteria for schizophrenia (see Table 3) requires the presence of psychotic symptoms, accompanied by a deterioration in social and occupational functioning. In children and adolescents, this might be indicated by a failure to achieve the expected level in social development or academic achievement. Psychotic symptoms must be apparent for at least one month while signs of the disorder must persist for at least six months. Duration of symptoms is a particularly critical factor when considering a diagnosis of schizophrenia in children who might otherwise exhibit transient delusions or hallucinations (Rapoport & Ismond, 1996). Finally, symptoms cannot be attributed to another psychiatric disorder, medication, substance use, or a general medical condition. Subtypes of schizophrenia (i.e., paranoid, disorganized, catatonic, undifferentiated, and residual types) can be defined by the pattern of presenting symptoms but this typology appears to be less clearly differentiated in children than it is in adults (Rapoport & Ismond, 1996).

Because certain types of delusions and auditory hallucinations are seen as hallmarks of schizophrenia, they are weighted more heavily when making a diagnosis of schizophrenia. The presence of bizarre delusions or

Table 3 *DSM-IV* diagnostic criteria for schizophrenia.

A. *Characteristic symptoms.* Two (or more) of the following, each present for a significant portion of time during a one-month period (or less if successfully treated):
   (i)   delusions
   (ii) hallucinations
   (iii) disorganized speech (e.g., frequent derailment or incoherence)
   (iv) grossly disorganized or catatonic behavior
   (v)   negative symptoms, that is, affective flattening, alogia, or avolition
   Note: Only one criterion A symptom is required if delusions are bizarre or hallucinations consist of a voice keeping up a running commentary on the person's behavior or thoughts, or two or more voices conversing with each other

B. *Social/occupational dysfunction.* For a significant portion of the time since the onset of the disturbance, one or more major areas of functioning such as work, interpersonal relations, or self-care are markedly below the level achieved prior to the onset (or when the onset is in childhood or adolescence, failure to achieve expected level of interpersonal, academic, or occupational achievement)

C. *Duration.* Continuous signs of the disturbance persist for at least six months. This six-month period must include at least one month of symptoms (or less if successfully treated) that meet criterion A (i.e., active-phase symptoms) and may include periods of prodromal or residual symptoms. During these prodromal or residual periods, the signs of the disturbance may be manifested by only negative symptoms or two or more symptoms listed in criterion A present in an attenuated form (e.g., odd beliefs, unusual perceptual experiences)

D. *Schizoaffective and Mood Disorder exclusion.* Schizoaffective Disorder and Mood Disorder with Psychotic Features have been ruled out because either (i) no Major Depressive, Manic, or Mixed Episodes have occurred concurrently with the active-phase symptoms; or (ii) if mood episodes have occurred during active-phase symptoms, their total duration has been brief relative to the duration of the active and residual periods

E. *Substance/general medical condition exclusion.* The disturbance is not due to the direct physiological effects of a substance (e.g., a drug of abuse, a medication) or a general medical condition

F. *Relationship to a Pervasive Developmental Disorder.* If there is a history of Autistic Disorder or another Pervasive Developmental Disorder, the additional diagnosis of Schizophrenia is made only if prominent delusions or hallucinations are also present for at least a month (or less if successfully treated)

auditory hallucinations involving commenting or conversing voices, therefore, is sufficient to satisfy criterion A, as shown in Table 3. As McKenna et al. (1994) indicate, thought processes may be developmentally immature in the younger patient but are not necessarily indicative of thought disorder or delusions. An adolescent, for instance, might engage in magical thinking which, while age-inappropriate, would not necessarily signify a psychotic disorder. Moreover, hallucinations are not uncommon in young children, and when they are accompanied by disorganized behavior they could lead to a misdiagnosis of schizophrenia. A key consideration, therefore, in making a diagnosis of schizophrenia in children and adolescents is the extent to which psychotic symptoms are pervasive and enduring rather than brief and transient. Disorganized speech is also likely to occur with increased frequency in children and may be indicative of a language deficit or communication disorder rather than schizophrenia (McKenna et al., 1994; Rapoport & Ismond, 1996). As noted by Volkmar and

Schwab-Stone (1996), disorganized speech and grossly disorganized behavior in children may be nonpsychotic, and reliance upon these two characteristic symptoms will likely lead to a misdiagnosis of schizophrenia. Negative symptoms, such as affective flattening, can be difficult to distinguish from the psychomotor retardation that can accompany a mood disorder. Thus, the differential diagnosis of schizophrenia is not only critical but can prove to be a particular challenge in children and adolescents.

A misdiagnosis of childhood-onset schizophrenia, unfortunately, is not an uncommon event. McKenna et al. (1994) at the National Institute of Mental Health (NIMH) received more than 260 referrals from academic centers for children and adolescents with a presumptive diagnosis of childhood-onset schizophrenia. After screening the medical records, 71 children were evaluated at NIMH. Of this sample, fewer than 28% were found to meet diagnostic criteria for schizophrenia while the majority of children were best described by another diagnostic category. Misdiagnosis of schizophrenia is obviously a serious problem as the illness is associated with a relatively poor prognosis and neuroleptic medications that can have grave and potentially irreversible side effects. In addition to false-positives, false-negatives undoubtedly occur with some, as yet unknown, frequency.

One area that can prove to be confusing is the differential diagnosis of schizophrenia from other schizophrenia-spectrum disorders such as schizophreniform disorder, schizoaffective disorder, and schizotypal personality disorder. The primary distinction between schizophrenia and schizophreniform disorder is duration, with the latter requiring the presence of symptoms for less than six months. Schizophreniform disorder, however, is rarely diagnosed in childhood (Rapoport & Ismond, 1996). Schizoaffective disorder involves a concurrent manic or depressive episode during an uninterrupted and active phase of schizophrenic illness. As with adults, differentiating between schizoaffective disorder, mood disorder with psychotic features, and schizophrenia that is accompanied by brief disturbances in mood requires careful documentation of the time course and duration of symptoms. In general, the rate of psychotic symptoms accompanying depression is much higher than in adults, with estimates ranging from 48% in prepubertal depressed children (Chambers, Puig-Antich, Tabrizi, & Davies, 1982) to 31% in an inpatient sample of depressed adolescents (Strober, Lampert, Schmidt, & Morrell, 1993).

Schizotypal personality disorder also presents problems in the differential diagnosis of schizophrenia in children and adolescents. Because the onset of a schizophrenic disorder in children is generally insidious or subacute (J. R. Asarnow & Ben-Meir, 1988; McKenna et al., 1994), it may be difficult to distinguish schizotypal personality disorder from the premorbid phase of schizophrenia. In addition, premorbid schizoid traits have been found to occur with increased frequency among adolescents who subsequently develop schizophrenia (Dalkin, Murphy, Glazebrook, Medley, & Harrison, 1994).

Diagnostic confusion also can arise frequently between schizophrenia and mood disorders. McKenna et al. (1994) found that the majority of children in their sample were misdiagnosed with schizophrenia as a sizable group presented with major depression or bipolar disorder. Rapoport and Ismond (1996) caution that diagnoses such as mood disorder with psychotic features are often overlooked in children and that other depressive disorders also must be considered as well. Of course, many of the same issues must be considered in discriminating between a mood disorder and schizophrenia as when making a differential diagnosis with schizoaffective disorder. Discrimination between the irritability associated with depression and the inappropriate outbursts that can occur with schizophrenia, for instance, is one example of the type of difficulty that may be encountered when evaluating children and adolescents.

With certain anxiety disorders, there may be some similarities in symptom presentation. For instance, the recurrent ruminations and bizarre stereotyped behaviors that are associated with obsessive-compulsive disorder (OCD) could be mistaken for symptoms of schizophrenia. In adult patients, a key diagnostic feature of OCD is that obsessions and compulsions are seen as ego-dystonic or alien and not under the control of the patient. In children with a schizophrenic disorder, psychotic symptoms may seem relatively ego-syntonic and even "normal" given their longstanding presence in the child's life experience (Russell, 1994). Post-traumatic stress disorder also must be ruled out as flashbacks can be confused with the hallucinations that accompany schizophrenia.

The diagnosis of schizophrenia is made separately from the diagnosis of autistic and pervasive developmental disorders (see Table 3). This is specified explicitly in the *DSM-IV* criteria for schizophrenia, probably because of the previous practice of lumping autism and schizophrenia into a single diagnostic group labeled either "childhood schizophrenia" or "childhood psychosis." In fact, the diagnostic criteria for the two disorders are quite different. Autism involves qualitative impairments in both social interaction and communication as well as restricted and stereotyped patterns of behavior and interests. Moreover, delays or abnormal functioning have to occur before the child reaches three years of age, whereas schizophrenia is rarely manifested or detected before six to seven years. Finally, children diagnosed with schizophrenia also tend to have low to normal intellectual functioning, whereas 70–80% of children with autism are also mentally retarded. Diagnostic confusions sometime arise in older, nonretarded children with autism. In some of these children, their preoccupations with stereotyped areas of interest can seem somewhat delusional and some children with autism have communication deficits that include loose associations and illogical thinking. A small number of autistic children develop true hallucinations and delusions (Petty, Ornitz, Michelman, & Zimmerman, 1984) but this tends to be rather infrequent (Volkmar & Cohen, 1991). Asperger's syndrome is a rare form of autism in which the children do not exhibit any communication disorder but do show problems in social interactions and preoccupations with stereotyped interests; these children do not manifest the psychotic symptoms associated with children diagnosed with schizophrenia.

The alternative diagnoses considered thus far are not intended to represent an exhaustive list of candidates. Certainly, numerous other possibilities (e.g., delusional disorder, substance-induced psychotic disorder, psychotic disorder due to a medical condition, degenerative neurological disorders) must be considered along with a diagnosis of schizophrenia (see Rapoport & Ismond, 1996). Even granting that tremendous caution is taken before conferring a diagnosis of schizophrenia on a child, adolescent, or adult, misdiagnoses still can occur with considerable frequency.

Several processes may contribute to diagnostic misclassification of schizophrenia in children and adolescents. One possibility, mentioned earlier, is that it can be difficult to establish the presence of some symptoms, particularly in younger children; symptoms may be overlooked, misinterpreted, or remain uncorroborated. As McKenna et al. (1994) found, schizophrenia also may be applied overinclusively to severely disturbed children who exhibit psychotic symptoms. In their sample, almost one-third of the children did not meet diagnostic criteria for schizophrenia but were best-described as "multidimensionally impaired" (MDI). Such a group of children highlight the continued need to improve upon our current diagnostic classification schemes (Volkmar & Schwab-Stone, 1996). Another factor that may lead to a failure to diagnose schizophrenia is that the characteristic symptoms of the illness may only emerge over time. Children later found to have a schizophrenic disorder, for example, may initially present with significant behavioral problems and receive an attention-deficit or disruptive behavior disorder diagnosis (e.g., Russell, 1994). Still another subset of children may initially present with a disorder, such as psychotic mood disorder (Werry et al., 1994), and only later develop schizophrenia. Finally, as illustrated by Werry et al. (1991), a diagnosis of schizophrenia may precede the onset of a psychiatric disorder such as bipolar disorder.

The diagnostic process is further complicated by the high rate of co-occurrence of other psychiatric disorders with childhood-onset schizophrenia. Russell et al. (1989) determined that 69% of their sample of children with schizophrenia met diagnostic criteria for another psychiatric disorder. Associated diagnoses occurring with the greatest frequency were conduct disorder (29%), atypical depression (26%), dysthymia (11%), and enuresis or encopresis (14%). Among adolescent patients, schizophrenia may coexist with a substance abuse disorder. Werry et al. (1994), for instance, reported a 54% comorbidity rate in their US sample. Although a small number of autistic children have been found to later develop schizophrenia (Petty et al., 1984), there does not appear to be a comorbid association between autism and schizophrenia (Volkmar & Cohen, 1991).

5.27.2.3 Prevalence

The potentially high rate of misdiagnosis of schizophrenia in children and adults is due in part to its rarity. Estimates of the incidence of schizophrenia in childhood range from 0.19 to 1 in 10 000 (Beitchman, 1985; Burd & Kerbeshian, 1987; Gillberg, Wahlstrom, Forsman, Hellgren, & Gillberg, 1986; Häfner & Nowotny, 1995). In adolescence, schizophrenia continues to be rare although it shows a steady increase with each successive year (Gillberg et al., 1986; Häfner & Nowotny, 1995). With the majority of cases of schizophrenia developing during late adolescence and early adulthood, schizophrenia occurs in about 1% of the population across the entire lifespan.

Among childhood-onset schizophrenia cases, there is a consistent sex difference with males exceeding females by a ratio of about 2:1 (Green et al., 1992; Hollis, 1995; Kolvin et al., 1971; Russell et al., 1989; Volkmar et al. 1988). These differences, however, disappear by adolescence where the distribution appears to be equal for both sexes (Hollis, 1995; Remschmidt et al., 1991; Schmidt, Blanz, Dippe, Koppe, & Lay, 1995; Werry et al., 1991). Various suggestions have been offered to explain the apparent influence of age on the sex distribution of schizophrenia in young patients, including the possibility of etiological differences with males showing greater biological vulnerability (J. R. Asarnow, 1994).

5.27.2.4 Etiology

Research examining the relationship between schizophrenia in children and adults has indicated a strong likelihood that the two forms of the disorder are continuous. In addition to the investigations into the phenomenology of childhood-onset schizophrenia described earlier, studies on brain morphology (Frazier et al., 1996), event-related potentials (Strandburg, Marsh, Brown, R. F. Asarnow, & Guthrie, 1994), autonomic responsivity (Zahn et al.,

1997), smooth pursuit eye tracking (Gordon, Frazier et al., 1994), attention and information processing (R. F. Asarnow, Brown, & Strandburg, 1995), and reaction time (Zahn et al., in press) in children have found similar patterns of abnormalities to those observed in adults with schizophrenia. Evidence also exists to suggest that childhood-onset schizophrenia may represent a more homogenous and severe form of the disorder as the genetic loading for schizophrenia, degree of central nervous system dysfunction, and level of environmental insult or stress may be higher in children than in adults with schizophrenia (J. R. Asarnow, 1994; McKenna, Gordon, & Rapoport, 1994).

Additional efforts to understand the etiology of childhood- and adolescent-onset schizophrenias, thus far, are represented largely by the application and extension of theories developed to explain schizophrenia in adults. This research has consistently failed to support the notion that there is a single cause of schizophrenia, and instead, accumulating evidence suggests that schizophrenia is a heterogenous disorder with multiple causes and presentations. Several of the prevailing theories of schizophrenia will be considered.

Considerable evidence indicates genetic contributions to schizophrenia. Results of family and twin studies suggest concordance rates of about 6% in a parent, 9% in a sibling, 13% when one parent is affected, 17% in dizygotic twins, 46% when both parents are affected, and 48% in monozygotic twins (Gottesman, 1991). These findings have been bolstered by the results of adoption studies that demonstrate the genetic influence on schizophrenia although familial environment also appears to play a role (e.g., Kety, Rosenthal, Wender, & Schulsinger, 1976; Tienari et al., 1987). Preliminary findings from the NIMH study on childhood-onset schizophrenia suggests that 13.6% of the children have first-degree relatives with nonaffective psychotic disorders. It is likely, however, that this is an underestimate of a possible genetic influence due to a small sample size and selection bias (Gordon, Frazier et al., 1994). In one child diagnosed with a schizophrenic disorder, there was an apparently balanced translocation involving chromosomes 1 and 7 which, when combined with evidence from other research, suggests a potential gene locus for developmental brain disorders (Gordon, Krasnewich, White, Lenane, & Rapoport, 1994).

Although the evidence for a genetic contribution to schizophrenia is strong, genetic heritability cannot account for all cases of schizophrenia nor does it explain instances whereby the monozygotic twin of a schizophrenic patient fails to develop the illness. Several lines of evidence suggest that other personal and environmental factors may lead to schizophrenia or may influence the outcome of an underlying genetic predisposition. Weinberger (1987) has proposed that schizophrenia is a neurodevelopmental disorder in which a fixed brain lesion or some pathologic condition of the brain occurs early in life. This lesion or brain pathology is likely to involve the dopaminergic neural systems and the prefrontal cortex. Over the normal course of maturation of the neural system, the brain lesion becomes evident with the onset of schizophrenic symptoms. Weinberger suggests that schizophrenia may be rare in children but more common in older adolescents and young adults as maximum dopaminergic activity in the brain does not occur until early adulthood. As for the cause of the lesion, numerous possibilities exist. Mednick, Machon, Huttunen, and Bonett (1988), for instance, have found that maternal exposure to a severe influenza during the second trimester is associated with an elevated frequency of adult schizophrenia in the offspring.

Psychosocial factors also may have a significant impact on the course of schizophrenia. Communication deviance (CD), which refers to an unclear, confusing, and fragmented communication style (Singer & Wynne, 1963), has been found to occur more frequently in the parents of adult schizophrenic patients (e.g., Singer & Wynne, 1965), adolescents at risk of schizophrenia and related disorders (Goldstein, 1987), and children diagnosed with schizophrenia or schizotypal personality disorder (J. R. Asarnow, Goldstein, & Ben-Meir, 1988). The etiological relationship, if any, between CD and schizophrenia is unclear, although it has been suggested that CD may represent an environmental stressor or a biological predisposition to schizophrenia in parents that is reflected in subtle levels of disordered thought or communication (Singer & Wynne, 1965; Miklowitz et al., 1991).

Another psychosocial factor that may contribute to the course of schizophrenia is expressed emotion (EE) or the degree to which critical and emotionally overinvolved attitudes are conveyed to the schizophrenic patient. As reviewed by Goldstein, Strachan, and Wynne (1997), numerous studies have shown that high levels of EE predict relapse among schizophrenic adults. In contrast, the association between EE and schizophrenia in children appears to be less robust although parents of children with schizophrenia or a related condition have been found to be more likely to express harsh criticisms toward their child compared with parents of normal children (J. R. Asarnow et al.,

1994; Hamilton, 1991). On the basis of these data, it is not clear if harsh criticisms arise in response to dealing with a child with a severe mental illness, if some family members of schizophrenic patients tend to express critical comments that contribute to symptoms, or perhaps most likely, if the emotional environment of the family reflects a combination of these factors.

5.27.2.5 Developmental Course

The developmental course of schizophrenia in children and adolescents entails consideration of a broad range of issues, beginning with premorbid adjustment and extending to the prodromal phase, the course of the schizophrenic episode, and subsequent outcome of the disorder that may include relapse. Premorbid adjustment, or the child's level of functioning prior to the onset of schizophrenia, has been found to range from normal to uneven development (Gordon, Frazier et al., 1994). In reviewing the premorbid history of children diagnosed with schizophrenia, several studies have found delays on one or more developmental milestones in approximately one-half of children examined, with the largest and most frequent lags typically occurring in the areas of language and gross motor development (Alaghband-Rad et al., 1995; Hollis, 1995; Watkins, R. F. Asarnow, & Tanguay, 1988). It is clear that a number of childhood-onset schizophrenic patients also experience difficulty with academic performance and school adaptation (J. R. Asarnow et al., 1994; Hollis, 1995). Alaghband-Rad et al. (1995) observed that over half of their sample repeated at least one grade; a substantial proportion had received placements in special education classes and estimates of premorbid IQ tended to be in the low to normal range.

In terms of social development, approximately one-half of patients diagnosed with childhood-onset schizophrenia have been noted to exhibit significant impulsivity and approximately half were viewed as relatively withdrawn and socially impaired (Alaghband-Rad et al., 1995; Hollis, 1995). It is not surprising that when assessed, peer relationships also were quite poor with childhood-onset schizophrenic patients showing significantly greater levels of impairment than children diagnosed with major depressive disorder (J. R. Asarnow et al., 1994).

For some children, the presence of significant developmental delays or disruptive behaviors has been associated with other psychiatric disorders. Approximately one-third of schizophrenic children have a premorbid history marked by at least some feature of pervasive developmental disorder while about one-third have a premorbid history of attentional and hyperactivity problems (Alaghband-Rad et al., 1995; Russell et al., 1994). Overall, Russell (1994) concluded that 86% of their sample had a history of some behavioral or psychiatric disturbance prior to the emergence of psychotic symptoms. There is some evidence to suggest that childhood-onset patients with schizoaffective disorder may tend to have a better premorbid course than children diagnosed with schizophrenia (Eggers, 1989).

The premorbid course for adolescent-onset schizophrenia also appears to be generally poor. In samples obtained in New Zealand and the United States, Werry et al. (1994) observed that 83% of participants exhibited odd, anxious, or disruptive personality styles and that the typical patient had a history of poor adaptive functioning. In comparing the premorbid course between childhood- and adolescent-onset cases, Hollis (1995) found that children with schizophrenia were more likely to have a history of impaired language or speech development. The onset of schizophrenia in early adolescence was more likely to be accompanied by a history of restless and fidgety behavior although there was no significant difference between the two groups in motor development.

The onset of schizophrenia in children is typically gradual and insidious, with an extensive prodromal phase of behavioral disturbance that eventually leads to the emergence of psychotic symptoms. The prodromal period might be characterized by attentional problems, hyperactivity, declines in school performance, poor peer relationships, deterioration in daily functioning (e.g., performing personal hygiene), and social withdrawal (e.g., Green et al., 1992; McKenna et al., 1994; Russell et al., 1989; Watkins et al., 1988). An acute onset of psychotic symptoms appears to be be more characteristic of schizophrenia in adolescents and some adults (e.g., Hollis, 1995; Werry, 1996).

While research into the course of schizophrenia as it occurs in children and early adolescents is quite limited, the available data suggests that many patients will experience recurrent episodes of schizophrenia. J. R. Asarnow et al. (1994) contacted childhood-onset patients one year after discharge from the hospital and found that 89% of their sample continued to meet diagnostic criteria for schizophrenia or schizoaffective disorder rather than some other psychiatric disorder. When the same patients were followed up after 2–7 years, 61% of the sample was diagnosed with schizophrenia while 33% was in remission. Among remitted patients, only one child was free of symptoms two years after their initial hospitalization. Similar rates have been obtained by Eggers (1989) who observed complete remission in 27% of schizophrenic patients included in his study. In comparing children diagnosed with schizophrenia to those with schizoaffective disorder, the rate of remission appears to be comparable although the overall prognosis appears to be better for schizoaffective patients. In both cases, there is evidence to suggest an unremarkable premorbid history is associated with a more favorable outcome (Eggers, 1989).

Among patients diagnosed with adolescent-onset schizophrenia, Werry et al. (1994) similarly found that over 80% continued to experience psychotic episodes two years after follow-up. Schmidt et al. (1995) contacted adolescent-onset patients 1–15 years after the index hospitalization and found that 27% had no further schizophrenic episodes. As with childhood-onset cases, normal premorbid adjustment has been found to be predictive of a good outcome (Werry et al., 1994).

5.27.3 CONCEPTUALIZATION AND CLINICAL FORMULATION

5.27.3.1 Multimodal Assessment

Formulating a diagnosis of schizophrenia in a child or adolescent is obviously a serious proposition given the social stigma, relatively poor prognosis, and potentially irreversible side effects that can accompany antipsychotic medications. As noted earlier, a number of factors may contribute to the misdiagnosis and overdiagnosis of schizophrenia in children and adolescents. Notwithstanding these considerations, care also must be taken to avoid underutilization of this diagnostic category; failure to make a diagnosis of schizophrenia could perpetuate suffering and preclude patients from receiving necessary treatment and appropriate services (McClellan & Werry, 1994). Given the multitude of issues that need to be confronted in considering a diagnosis of schizophrenia in a child or adolescent, a thorough and multimodal assessment is clearly indicated.

Perhaps the first step involved in the diagnostic assessment of schizophrenia in children and adolescents is to obtain a thorough and detailed premorbid history as well as a comprehensive evaluation of the prodromal period and current level of functioning. Development, intellectual functioning, academic achievement, cultural considerations, and family psychiatric history and background are all crucial factors that need to enter into any consideration of possible psychotic symptoms. A challenge inherent to any assessment of schizophrenia in children and adolescents is distinguishing true psychotic manifestations from idiosyncratic thinking and perceptions associated with developmental delays, speech and language disturbances, vivid imaginations, exposure to an extreme traumatic stressor, as well as religious ideation (e.g., McClellan & Werry, 1994; McKenna et al., 1994). A thorough pediatric and neurological evaluation is also indicated to rule out the possibility of an organic psychosis. Results of an investigation by Adams, Kutcher, Antoniw, and Bird (1996) in adolescent-onset schizophrenic patients suggest that current, routine endocrine, and neuroimaging screening tests are of no diagnostic utility unless symptoms suggestive of neurological or endocrinological disorders are present.

Reliance on multiple informants that include the child or adolescent, parents, teachers, caretakers, and other significant individuals is likely to yield the most information and improve diagnostic accuracy. As described above, psychotic symptoms may be initially associated with other psychiatric disorders or they may not be obvious, particularly in younger children. A child, for instance, may initially present with significant behavioral disturbance and receive a diagnosis of conduct disorder or attention-deficit hyperactivity disorder. Months may elapse before the clinical presentation of psychotic symptoms becomes apparent and even then, the disturbances may not present across situations or be evident to all potential informants. Alternatively, some children and adolescents with schizophrenia will require hospitalization because of suicidal, aggressive, or dangerous behavior problems. As illustrated in the case study described earlier, a psychiatric hospitalization may be beneficial when considering a diagnosis of schizophrenia in younger patients as it can provide an excellent opportunity to observe and document a range of behaviors in a controlled setting.

Regardless of whether the evaluation is conducted on an inpatient or outpatient basis, it is critical that the range of symptoms be thoroughly assessed. Reliable and well-validated structured diagnostic interview schedules, such as the Schedule for Affective Disorders and Schizophrenia for School-Age Children-Epidemiologic Version (K-SADS-E; Orvaschel, 1995) and the Diagnostic Interview for Children and Adolescents (DICA; Herjanic & Reich, 1982), are currently available to guide clinicians and clinical researchers through a detailed examination of various diagnoses in children and adolescents. Werry (1996) cautions that structured interviews may be tedious but are clearly warranted given the seriousness of the diagnoses under consideration. Systematic coverage of symptoms is particularly useful when attempting to resolve some of the complexities in distinguishing between disorders. (See McKenna et al. (1994) and McClellan and Werry (1994) for excellent discussions of other key diagnostic issues.)

In addition to diagnostic interviews, a number of rating scales exist for assessing specific schizophrenic symptoms such as thought disorder, negative symptoms, and positive symptoms. These measures include the Kiddie Formal Thought Disorder Rating Scale (K-FTDS) and Story Game (Caplan, Guthrie, Fish, Tanguay, & David-Lando, 1989), Thought Disorder Index (TDI; Arboleda & Holzman, 1985), Scale for the Assessment of Negative Symptoms in Schizophrenia (SANS; Andreasen, 1983), and Scale for the Assessment of Positive Symptoms in Schizophrenia (SAPS; Andreasen, 1984). Although some of these measures have traditionally been used in clinical research settings, they may be appropriate for clinical practice as well. It is important to note that while psychotic symptoms are the hallmark of schizophrenia, most children who report hallucinations are not schizophrenic as they do not present with all of the requisite diagnostic symptoms (McClellan & Werry, 1994). The use of reliable and valid measures of thought disorder that have been found to discriminate between children with schizophrenia, other psychiatric disorders, or no history of psychiatric illness, therefore, can be helpful in ascertaining perceptual, language, and communication disturbances. Moreover, the importance of developmental effects on the K-FTDS and TDI have been demonstrated (Arboleda & Holzman, 1985; Caplan et al., 1989; Caplan, Perdue, Tanguay, & Fish, 1990), so both measures can potentially serve as useful guides in differentiating between age-appropriate and abnormal behaviors.

Finally, children or adolescents who have received an initial diagnosis of schizophrenia will need to be closely monitored and reassessed periodically to determine the course of illness, the impact of treatment, and level of functioning. As demonstrated by McKenna et al. (1994) and Werry et al. (1991), a significant proportion of children and adolescents who are initially diagnosed with schizophrenia are later found to exhibit a different psychotic disturbance, such as bipolar disorder or schizoaffective disorder. Diagnostic reassessment, in some instances, may be complicated by the effects of pharmacological treatments which can lead to a partial, or even, complete remission in symptoms. Over time and with treatment, symptom patterns also are likely to change and influence the patient's

level of functioning accordingly. In some instances, it may be difficult to distinguish between maturational effects and change due to clinical improvement. There also may be marked discrepancies in degree of improvement across domains, such that premorbid levels of functioning may be reached in some areas but not in others. J. R. Asarnow et al. (1994) have demonstrated that there is considerable variability in the course of schizophrenic illness with some children exhibiting deterioration while others show minimal or even substantial improvement over time. Psychoeducational assessment of multiple domains of functioning at multiple points in time, therefore, provides opportunities to determine current strengths and weaknesses for a child and any modifications that might be needed in service provision.

5.27.3.2 Treatment Formulation

A diagnosis of schizophrenia is naturally a devastating event for a child or adolescent and their family members. As with any psychiatric illness, the initial diagnosis may be met with denial or even relief as an explanation has been found for unusual and perhaps frightening behavior. Treatment, therefore, ideally should be oriented not only towards the child but towards addressing the needs of their families as well.

Neuroleptic medication is generally regarded as the cornerstone of treatment for schizophrenia in children, adolescents, and adults. While pharmacological treatment may be considered necessary, it is not sufficient. Various clinical researchers (e.g., Kane, 1987) have recommended that schizophrenia in adults be approached in phases, each with different strategies and goals. The first phase involves the acute presentation of florid psychotic symptoms, and therefore, the necessary emphasis is on the use of antipsychotic drugs to decrease the severity of symptoms. Oftentimes, the child or adolescent will have been admitted to the hospital at this point. Once the acute phase is controlled, there is a stabilization period in which some psychotic symptoms will have improved while others may continue to persist. The third phase is reached once most psychotic symptoms have resolved. During these latter two periods, psychosocial and school-based interventions become critical factors in improving the quality of life, decreasing the likelihood of relapse, and meeting educational needs. When appropriate, rehabilitation programs may help to optimize the social and occupational outcome for many children and adolescents with schizophrenia. Depending upon symptom course and the effectiveness of pharmacologic interventions, residential or day treatment programs may need to be considered.

As with any child who has a debilitating and potentially chronic condition, case management services may be essential to obtaining necessary social services. Access to services can have far-reaching effects. Compliance with neuroleptics, for example, may depend upon the availability of funds for purchasing medication. In general, the burden experienced by family members, who are required to care for a child or adolescent with schizophrenia, can be alleviated to some extent if caregivers can receive guidance on how to access relevant resources. Family psychoeducational programs, which are discussed below, and family advocacy groups may be of substantial benefit to family members of children and adolescents diagnosed with schizophrenia as well as to the patients themselves.

The American Academy of Child and Adolescent Psychiatry (AACAP) has developed a detailed set of practice parameters for the diagnosis and treatment of children and adolescents with schizophrenia (McClellan & Werry, 1994). Although these practice parameters were developed to assist physicians, other clinicians may find the guidelines useful. A number of diagnostic and treatment recommendations are offered that reflect recent research knowledge and advancements in childhood and adolescent-onset schizophrenia.

5.27.4 TREATMENT

5.27.4.1 Psychosocial Treatments

The schizophrenic child or adolescent is likely to face interpersonal, behavioral, and intellectual challenges. Intervention programs, therefore, need to be designed to not only treat the schizophrenic illness but also meet the unique needs of each child.

In light of the earlier discussion on premorbid course, it would be reasonable to expect that many children and adolescents diagnosed with schizophrenia will have exhibited delays in certain areas of functioning, such as language, gross motor, or social development. With the onset of the illness, normal developmental progress may be impeded further. Individualized school programs may need to be developed, therefore, to accommodate the educational needs of a child diagnosed with schizophrenia. Reintegration into the classroom or school may require academic remediation as well as assistance with modifying inappropriate social behaviors and developing suitable social skills. In the classroom, for instance, behavioral interventions may be necessary for minimizing disruptive behaviors and increasing appropriate behaviors.

Social skills training may be helpful in eliminating or reducing the boundary that may exist between a child or adolescent with schizophrenia and his or her peers. With adult patients diagnosed with schizophrenia, skills-focused training leads to more effective interpersonal functioning and improved social adjustment, particularly among patients with a relatively early onset of illness (Marder et al., 1996). The authors speculate that adults with an earlier onset of schizophrenia may have been more socially deficient as they had less time to develop interpersonal skills prior to the onset of their illness, and therefore, may have benefited more from the training program. Such a scenario would argue in favor of implementing social skills training with children and adolescents. To the best of our knowledge, a comprehensive social skills training program has yet to be adapted for children and adolescents with a severe psychiatric disturbance, although an effective program has been developed for adult patients with schizophrenia (Liberman, DeRisi, & Mueser, 1989).

Individual psychotherapy is a traditional mode of treatment for children and adolescents with any psychiatric disturbance. Such approaches typically range from supportive therapies and behavioral or cognitive-behavioral strategies to insight-oriented therapies. AACAP (McClellan & Werry, 1994), however, cautions against the use of insight-oriented therapies, particularly during the acute phases of illness. More recently, psychoeducational family intervention programs have generated considerable interest.

As discussed earlier, there may be an association between the emotional environment of the family and a propensity towards relapse. Current psychoeducational family treatment programs, in contrast to previous techniques, focus on the present and encourage the patient to gradually re-enter the family environment. Family treatment recognizes that intrafamilial processes arise from the complex transactions between family members and patients, who can pose genuine difficulties for their relatives and the resources available to those relatives. Rather than attempt to establish a causal link between families and the patient's illness, treatment is oriented towards assisting patients and their families in the effective management of the illness (Goldstein & Miklowitz, 1995). Although there are various forms of psychoeducationally-oriented family treatment programs, they share certain features that likely contribute to their effectiveness. These include engaging family members early in treatment;

encouraging an open atmosphere rather than attempting to assign fault; educating families about the phenomenology, course, prognosis, etiologic models, and rationale behind different treatments; offering recommendations for coping with the disorder; providing training on improving communication and problem-solving skills; and performing crisis intervention (Goldstein & Miklowitz, 1995). Family intervention can be based in the home or clinic, may involve individual or multiple families, and may include or exclude the patient. As with social skills training, systematic application of psychoeducational family intervention programs appears thus far to have been limited to adult populations.

For some children or adolescents with schizophrenia, a residential treatment center or other out-of-home placement may need to be considered. In a follow-up study of child psychiatric inpatients, J. R. Asarnow, Goldstein, Carlson et al. (1988) found that 57% of children with a schizophrenia spectrum disorder were placed out of the home within 13 months of being discharged from the hospital; the majority were placed in residential treatment centers. The decision to place a child or adolescent out of the home is obviously a complicated issue, around which multiple determining factors may operate. The extent to which long-term therapeutic placements are utilized is likely to depend, in part, on how a patient responds to pharmacological treatment and medication compliance, a topic to which we now turn.

5.27.4.2 Pharmacological Treatments

Children and adolescents diagnosed with schizophrenia have largely received the same medication treatments as adult patients. Pharmacological agents have included conventional neuroleptics such as haloperidol (Haldol), loxapine (Loxitane), thiothixene (Navane), thioridazine (Mellaril), and pimozide (Orap) (Spencer & Campbell, 1994). Treatment with these antipsychotic medications has often been limited by accompanying side effects, such as sedation, weight gain, and extrapyramidal symptoms (EPS) which include dystonia, akinesia, akathisia, and tremor. With conventional neuroleptic treatment of schizophrenia in children and adolescents, there also is the possibility of withdrawal dyskinesia and a potentially irreversible movement disorder, tardive dyskinesia (McClellan & Werry, 1994). More recently, atypical neuroleptic medications such as clozapine (Clozaril) and risperidone (Risperdal) have been introduced. Both of these newer atypical antipsychotic agents appear to be associated with less EPS

(Findling, Grcevich, Lopez, & Schulz, 1996; Kumra et al., 1996). Clozapine, however, has been reserved for treatment-refractory patients as patients treated with this medication must be closely monitored for agranulocytosis and seizures (Kumra et al., 1996).

5.27.4.3 Efficacy of Treatments

As mentioned earlier, it does not appear that a formal social skills training program exists for children and adolescents. In Germany, Remschmidt et al. (1994) have developed a rehabilitation program that was deemed necessary for about 40% of the schizophrenic children and adolescents at their hospital. Results of their study suggest that it was possible to gradually reintegrate most patients back into their families, schools, or professional training programs.

Despite their longstanding tradition, the effectiveness of individual psychotherapies with children and adolescents with schizophrenia has yet to be determined. In schizophrenic adults, results of several controlled trials failed to indicate that individual psychotherapy, either alone or combined with pharmacotherapy, contributed significantly to remission after a psychotic episode or prevention of relapse once the patient had returned to the community (Goldstein, 1989). Psychoeducational family education programs, in contrast, when combined with medication management, have consistently been shown to reduce the likelihood of relapse beyond that associated with medication alone in adult patients. Moreover, there is evidence to suggest that when combined with pharmacologic treatment, family interventions are more effective over a two-year period than individual therapies in delaying relapses and improving social functioning (Goldstein & Miklowitz, 1995). Although there is little reason to doubt that similar effects would not be observed in children and adolescents with schizophrenia, it remains an empirical question as to whether younger patients would obtain similar benefits from family education.

There have been few studies on the effectiveness of neuroleptic medication with children and adolescents; the efficacy of such treatments has been based primarily on extrapolations from double-blind comparison studies conducted with adult schizophrenic patients and case studies involving children and adolescents. In one of the earliest studies utilizing a double-blind and placebo-controlled design, Pool, Bloom, Wielke, Roninger, and Gallant (1976) demonstrated that loxapine and haloperidol were superior to placebo in treating a large sample of adolescents diagnosed with schizophrenia. Spencer and Campbell (1994) similarly found haloperidol to have superior effects over placebo in children with schizophrenia. In a double-blind study comparing an atypical agent with a typical neuroleptic, clozapine was shown to be a more effective form of treatment than haloperidol on all administered measures of psychosis (Kumra et al., 1996). These data are particularly striking as only children who were found to be nonresponsive to at least two typical neuroleptics were included in the study. Results of a case study (Quintana & Keshavan, 1995) and a retrospective chart review study (Findling et al., 1996) suggest that another atypical antipsychotic medication, risperidone, also may be efficacious in the treatment of children and adolescents with schizophrenia.

5.27.5 FUTURE DIRECTIONS FOR RESEARCH AND PRACTICE

With the shift in the late 1970s and 1980s towards greater diagnostic specificity of schizophrenia in childhood and adolescence, a nucleus of clinical research findings began to emerge, supporting the possibility of early-onset forms of schizophrenia. As reviewed in this chapter, a number of similarities were found to exist between child, adolescent, and adult forms of schizophrenia when the same diagnostic criteria were applied. Seeking to determine the degree of continuity with adult schizophrenia was a critical and natural first step. As the fields of childhood- and adolescent-onset schizophrenia mature, however, it will be important to not only continue to extrapolate from the adult research literature and seek similarities and differences between the various forms of schizophrenia but to move towards elucidating a developmental perspective on schizophrenia in children and adolescents. There has been notable movement in this direction, such as the work by Caplan (e.g., Caplan, 1994) on the influence of maturation on communication skills and the assessment of thought disorder.

Because of the many developmental issues that can arise, further progress is needed to assist with diagnostic ambiguities. Overdiagnosis of schizophrenia in children and adolescents is occurring at an alarming rate (McKenna, Gordon, Lenane et al., 1994). Misdiagnoses, such as with attention-deficit hyperactivity disorder, also are not uncommon. As more standardized measures of various aspects of schizophrenia become implemented, diagnostic decisions can become more reliable and valid. Identification of more homogenous samples will also greatly facilitate comparisons of studies conducted by different research groups. In addition, attention needs to be directed to understanding children with psychopathological conditions that appear to fall on the borderline of schizophrenia, such as the MDI group that was identified by McKenna et al. (1994).

The relative youth of the area is underscored by the meager number of longitudinal and long-term follow-up studies. Information from such investigations is crucial to our understanding of schizophrenia in children and adolescents and to its treatment. For instance, it will be important to determine the extent to which course of illness is influenced by stressors in the child's environment as well as protective factors. Information on the long-term course of schizophrenia as child and adolescent patients enter into adulthood will be of considerable utility as patients and their families prepare for the future.

For clinical researchers, childhood-onset schizophrenia provides a unique opportunity to trace the etiologic underpinnings of a rare, but presumably more homogenous form of schizophrenia. The available evidence suggests that childhood- and adolescent-onset schizophrenia are distinct forms of the illness. Accordingly, continued comparisons between these groups will help shed light on the underlying neuropathology as well as the influence of age of onset on neurocognitive and behavioral disturbances in schizophrenia.

Perhaps the most striking deficiency in the literature at present is the relative paucity of research on the efficacy of psychosocial treatments of schizophrenia when diagnosed in children and adolescents. Drawing from the literature on adult schizophrenic patients, it would appear that the development of social skills training programs for children and adolescents, and psychoeducational family intervention programs for their families, are clearly warranted. With such programs in place, multimodal treatment studies could then be conducted to determine the most effective form of treatment for these young patients. As Campbell and colleagues (Campbell & Cueva, 1995; Spencer & Campbell, 1994) have noted, additional research is also needed to assess the use of atypical neuroleptics with younger children and the long-term effects of all antipsychotic medications in children and adolescents with schizophrenia.

Considerable progress has been made in understanding childhood- and adolescent-onset schizophrenias. This is particularly noteworthy in light of the fact that this is a rare and often difficult to diagnose disorder. Further research will assist not only with improving our understanding of schizophrenia but with alleviating the distress and disruptions experienced by children and adolescents diagnosed with schizophrenia and their families.

5.27.6 SUMMARY

Schizophrenia is uncommon in childhood and adolescence, with prevalence estimates ranging from 0.19 to 1 in 10 000. By a ratio of about 2:1, male children are more likely than female children to be diagnosed with schizophrenia. Male and female adolescents, in contrast, are about equally likely to receive this diagnosis. Diagnosis of childhood- and adolescent-onset forms of schizophrenia involves the same criteria as adult forms of the disorder, although developmental variations can complicate diagnostic decision-making. Distinguishing psychotic thought disturbances from idiosyncratic thinking associated with developmental delays, language disturbances, vivid imagination, and stress responses may be difficult but, nonetheless, is essential.

Auditory hallucinations have been noted in approximately 80% of children diagnosed with schizophrenia, along with high rates of visual hallucinations, delusions, formal thought disorder, and inappropriate or flat affect. The presence of pervasive and enduring psychotic symptoms is necessary for making a diagnosis of schizophrenia, and careful documentation of the time course and duration of symptoms is essential for accurate classification. A high rate of misdiagnosis may be quite common (McKenna et al., 1994), with a complex presentation of symptoms and the presence of comorbid conditions often complicating the diagnostic picture. In particular, schizophrenia in children and adolescents is often confused with other schizophrenia-spectrum disorders, major depression, bipolar disorder, and mood disorder with psychotic features. Given the complexity of this disorder and its diagnosis, the use of multiple informants and structured interviews is strongly recommended. Moreover, because change in symptom patterns is common, frequent reassessment is necessary.

With regard to etiology, there appears to be marked continuity between childhood-onset schizophrenia and adult forms of the disorder. Research suggests that childhood-onset schizophrenia is a more homogeneous and severe form of the disorder, in terms of genetic loading, central nervous system dysfunction, and level of environmental insult or stress. As with adult forms of the disorder, theoretical models relating to children and adolescents emphasize the interplay of genetic and environmental factors. However, the adult models may need to be altered to account for biological changes that occur with time. For instance, key aspects of dopaminergic functioning may be low in childhood and increase into early adulthood or, to account for the increased salience of environmental variables, the quality of family communication may prove to be more etiologically significant at different points along the lifespan.

The onset of schizophrenia in children is typically gradual, with an extensive prodromal phase that is marked by attentional problems, hyperactivity, and deterioration in school and social functioning. Acute onset appears to be more common among adolescents and adults. Most children who are eventually diagnosed with schizophrenia have some history of developmental delays, behavioral difficulties, and social impairment; the premorbid course for individuals diagnosed with adolescent-onset schizophrenia is also poor. Recurrence of symptoms is common among childhood- and adolescent-onset cases, although an unremarkable premorbid history may be related to a more favorable outcome.

Treatment of schizophrenia in children and adolescents should be multimodal with pharmacological interventions forming the cornerstone. Conventional neuroleptics as well as atypical antipsychotic agents have been found to be successful in treating children and adolescents with schizophrenia. In adult patients with schizophrenia, their effectiveness in delaying relapses and improving social functioning is significantly improved when combined with a psychoeducational family intervention program. Comparable effects with childhood- and adolescent-onset cases are likely but have not yet been documented. School-based and social skills training interventions may also be beneficial.

In sum, considerable progress has been made in understanding and treating children and adolescents who are diagnosed with schizophrenia. Continued research, particularly involving prospective longitudinal designs, is needed to obtain a better understanding of the presentation, diagnosis, causes, course, and treatment of schizophrenia in children and adolescents.

ACKNOWLEDGMENT

This chapter is dedicated to the memory of Dr. Michael J. Goldstein, colleague, mentor, and friend, who devoted his career to improving our understanding and treatment of schizophrenia through his research and encouragement of young investigators.

5.27.7 REFERENCES

Adams, M., Kutcher, S., Antoniw, E., & Bird, D. (1996). Diagnostic utility of endocrine and neuroimaging screening tests in first-onset adolescent psychosis. *Journal of the American Academy of Child and Adolescent Psychiatry, 35*, 67–73.

Alaghband-Rad, J., McKenna, K., Gordon, C. T., Albus, K. E., Hamburger, S. D., Rumsey, J. M., Frazier, J. A., Lenane, M. C., & Rapoport, J. L. (1995). Childhood-onset schizophrenia: The severity of the premorbid course. *Journal of the American Academy of Child and Adolescent Psychiatry, 34*, 1273–1283.

American Psychiatric Association. (1968). *Diagnostic and statistical manual of mental disorders* (2nd ed.). Washington, DC: American Psychiatric Association.

American Psychiatric Association. (1980). *Diagnostic and statistical manual of mental disorders* (3rd ed.). Washington, DC: American Psychiatric Association.

American Psychiatric Association. (1994). *Diagnostic and statistical manual of mental disorders* (4th ed.). Washington, DC: American Psychiatric Association.

Andreasen, N. C. (1983). *The Scale for the Assessment of Negative Symptoms (SANS)*. Iowa City, IA: University of Iowa.

Andreasen, N. C. (1984). *The Scale for the Assessment of Positive Symptoms (SAPS)*. Iowa City, IA: University of Iowa.

Arboleda, C., & Holzman, P. S. (1985). Thought disorder in children at risk for psychosis. *Archives of General Psychiatry, 42*, 1004–1013.

Arndt, S., Andreasen, N.C., Flaum, M., Miller, D., Nopoulus, P. (1995). A longitudinal study of symptom dimensions in schizophrenia: Prediction and patterns of change. *Archives of General Psychiatry, 52*, 352–360.

Asarnow, J. R. (1994). Annotation: Childhood-onset schizophrenia. *Journal of Child Psychology and Psychiatry, 35*, 1345–1371.

Asarnow, J. R., & Ben-Meir, S. (1988). Children with schizophrenia spectrum and depressive disorders: A comparative study of onset patterns, premorbid adjustment, and severity of dysfunction. *Journal of Child Psychology and Psychiatry, 29*, 477–488.

Asarnow, J. R., Goldstein, M. J., & Ben-Meir, S. (1988). Parental communication deviance in childhood onset schizophrenia spectrum and depressive disorders. *Journal of Child Psychology and Psychiatry, 29*, 825–838.

Asarnow, J. R., Goldstein, M. J., Carlson, G. A., Perdue, S., Bates, S., & Keller, J. (1988). Childhood-onset depressive disorders: A follow-up study of rates of rehospitalization and out-of-home placement among child psychiatric inpatients. *Journal of Affective Disorders, 15*, 245–253.

Asarnow, J. R., Tompson, M. C., & Goldstein, M. J. (1994). Childhood-onset schizophrenia: A follow-up study. *Schizophrenia Bulletin, 20*, 599–617.

Asarnow, R. F., & Asarnow, J. R. (1994). Childhood-onset schizophrenia: Editors' Introduction. *Schizophrenia Bulletin, 20*, 591–597.

Asarnow, R. F., Brown, W., & Strandburg, R. (1995). Children with a schizophrenic disorder: Neurobehavioral studies. *European Archives of Psychiatry and Clinical Neuroscience, 245*, 70–79.

Beitchman, J. H. (1985). Childhood schizophrenia: A review and comparison with adult-onset schizophrenia. *Psychiatric Clinics of North America, 8*, 793–814.

Bleuler, E. (1950). *Dementia Praecox or the group of schizophrenias*. (J. Zinkin, Trans.). New York: International Universities Press (Original work published 1911).

Breier, A., Schreiber, J. L., Dyer, J., & Pickar, D. (1991). National Institute of Mental Health Longitudinal Study of Chronic Schizophrenia: Prognosis and predictors of outcome. *Archives of General Psychiatry, 48*, 239–246.

Burd, L., & Kerbeshian, J. (1987). A North Dakota prevalence study of schizophrenia presenting in childhood. *Journal of the American Academy of Child and Adolescent Psychiatry, 26*, 347–350.

Campbell, M., & Cueva, J. E. (1995). Psychopharmacology in child and adolescent psychiatry: A review of the past seven years, part II. *Journal of the American Academy of Child and Adolescent Psychiatry, 34*, 1262–1272.

Caplan, R. (1994). Thought disorder in childhood. *Journal of the American Academy of Child and Adolescent Psychiatry, 33*, 605–615.

Caplan, R., Guthrie, D., Fish, B., Tanguay, P. E., & David-Lando, G. (1989). The Kiddie Formal Thought Disorder Rating Scale (K-FTDS): Clinical assessment, reliability, and validity. *Journal of the American Academy of Child and Adolescent Psychiatry, 28*, 208–216.

Caplan, R., Perdue, S., Tanguay, P. E., & Fish, B. (1990). Formal thought disorder in childhood-onset schizophrenia and schizotypal personality disorder. *Journal of Child Psychology and Psychiatry, 31*, 169–177.

Carpenter, W. T., Jr., Heinrichs, D. W., & Wagman A. M. I. (1988). Deficit and nondeficit forms of schizophrenia: The concept. *American Journal of Psychiatry, 145*, 578–583.

Chambers, W., Puig-Antich, J., Tabrizi, M., & Davies, M. (1982). Psychotic symptoms in prepubertal major depressive disorder. *Archives of General Psychiatry, 39*, 921–927.

Dalkin, T., Murphy, P., Glazebrook, C., Medley, I., & Harrison, G. (1994). Premorbid personality in first-onset psychosis. *British Journal of Psychiatry, 164*, 202–207.

De Sanctis, S. (1973). On some varieties of dementia praecox (A. J. Gianascol & A. M. Corbiascio, Trans.). In S. A. Szurek & I. N. Perlin (Eds.), *Clinical studies in childhood psychoses: 25 years in collaborative treatment and research* (pp. 31–47). New York: Brunner/Mazel (Original work published 1906).

Eggers, C. (1989). Schizo-affective psychoses in childhood: A follow-up study. *Journal of Autism and Developmental Disorders, 19*, 327–342.

Findling, R. L., Grcevich, S. J., Lopez, I., & Schulz, S. C. (1996). Antipsychotic medications in children and adolescents. *Journal of Clinical Psychiatry, 57* (Suppl. 9), 19–23.

Fish, B., & Ritvo, E. R. (1979). Psychoses of childhood. In J. D. Noshpitz (Ed.), *Basic handbook of child psychiatry: Vol. 2. Disturbances in development* (pp. 249–304). New York: Basic Books.

Frazier, J., Giedd, J. N., Hamburger, S. D., Albus, K. E., Kaysen, D., Vaituzis, A. C., Rajapakse, J. C., Lenane, M. C., McKenna, K., Jacobsen, L. K., Gordon, C. T., Breier, A., & Rapoport, J. L. (1996). Brain anatomic magnetic resonance imaging in childhood-onset schizophrenia. *Archives of General Psychiatry, 53*, 617–624.

Gillberg, C., Wahlstrom, J., Forsman, A., Hellgren, L., & Gillberg, I. C. (1986). Teenage psychoses: Epidemiology, classification and reduced optimality in the pre-, peri- and neonatal periods. *Journal of Child Psychology and Psychiatry, 27*, 87–98.

Goldstein, M. J. (1987). Psychosocial issues. *Schizophrenia Bulletin, 13*, 157–171.

Goldstein, M. J. (1989). Psychosocial treatment of schizophrenia. In S. C. Schulz & C. A. Tamminga (Eds.), *Schizophrenia: Scientific progress* (pp. 318–324). New York: Oxford University Press.

Goldstein, M. J., & Miklowitz, D. J. (1995). The effectiveness of psychoeducational family therapy in the treatment of schizophrenic disorders. *Journal of Marital and Family Therapy, 21*, 361–376.

Goldstein, M. J., Strachan, A. M., & Wynne, L. C. (1997). Relational problems related to a mental disorder or general medical condition. In T. A. Widiger, H. A. Pincus, R. Ross, M. B. First, & W. Davis (Eds.), *DSM-

IV Sourcebook: Volume 3 (pp. 531–567). Washington, DC: American Psychiatric Press.

Gordon, C. T., Frazier, J. A., McKenna, K., Giedd, J., Zametkin, A., Zahn, T., Hommer, D., Hong, W., Kaysen, D., Albus, K. E., & Rapoport, J. L. (1994). Childhood-onset schizophrenia: An NIMH study in progress. *Schizophrenia Bulletin, 20,* 697–712.

Gordon, C. T., Krasnewich, D., White, B., Lenane, M., & Rapoport, J. L. (1994). Brief report: Translocation involving chromosomes 1 and 7 in a boy with childhood-onset schizophrenia. *Journal of Autism and Developmental Disorders, 24,* 537–545.

Gottesman, I. I. (1991). *Schizophrenia genesis: The origins of madness.* New York: Freeman.

Green, W. H., Padron-Gayol, M., Hardesty, A. S., & Bassiri, M. (1992). Schizophrenia with childhood-onset: A phenomenological study of 38 cases. *Journal of the American Academy of Child and Adolescent Psychiatry, 31,* 968–976.

Häfner, H., & Nowotny, B. (1995). Epidemiology of early-onset schizophrenia. *European Archives of Psychiatry and Clinical Neuroscience, 245,* 80–92.

Hamilton, E. B. (1991). *Interactional styles in families of children with depressive disorders, schizophrenia spectrum disorders, and normal controls.* Unpublished doctoral dissertation, University of California, Los Angeles, CA.

Herjanic, B., & Reich, W. (1982). Development of a structured psychiatric interview for children: Agreement between child and parent on individual symptoms. *Journal of Abnormal Child Psychology, 10,* 307–324.

Hollis, C. (1995). Child and adolescent (juvenile onset) schizophrenia: A case control study of premorbid developmental impairments. *British Journal of Psychiatry, 166,* 489–495.

Kane, J. (1987). Treatment of schizophrenia. *Schizophrenia Bulletin, 13,* 171–186.

Kety, S. S., Rosenthal, D., Wender, P. H., & Schulsinger, F. (1976). Studies based on a total sample of adopted individuals and their relatives: Why they were necessary, what they demonstrated and failed to demonstrate. *Schizophrenia Bulletin, 2,* 414–428.

Kolvin, I. (1971). Studies in the childhood psychoses: I. Diagnostic criteria and classification. *British Journal of Psychiatry, 118,* 381–384.

Kolvin, I., Ounsted, C., Humphrey, M., & McNay, A. (1971). Studies in the childhood psychoses: II. The phenomenology of childhood psychoses. *British Journal of Psychiatry, 118,* 385–395.

Kraepelin, E. (1915). *Clinical psychiatry* (A. R. Eiefendorf, Trans.). Delmar, NY: Scholars' Facsimiles and Reprints (Original work published 1883).

Kumra, S., Frazier, J. A., Jacobsen, L. K., McKenna, K., Gordon, C. T., Lenane, M. C., Hamburger, S. D., Smith, A. K., Albus, K. E., Alaghband-Rad, J., & Rapoport, J. (1996). Childhood-onset schizophrenia: A double-blind clozapine-haloperidol comparison. *Archives of General Psychiatry, 53,* 1090–1097.

Liberman, R. P., DeRisi, W. J., & Mueser, K. T. (1989). *Social skills training for psychiatric patients.* New York: Pergamon.

Marder, S. R., Wirshing, W. C., Mintz, J., McKenzie, J., Johnston, K., Eckman, T. A., Lebell, M., Zimmerman, K., & Liberman, R. P. (1996). Two-year outcome of social skills training and group psychotherapy for outpatients with schizophrenia. *American Journal of Psychiatry, 153,* 1585–1597.

Maziade, M., Bouchard, S., Gingras, N., Charron, L., Cardinal, A., Roy, M., Gauthier, B., Tremblay, G., Cote, S., Fournier, C., Boutin, P., Hamel, M., Merette, C., & Martinez, M. (1996). Long-term stability of diagnosis and symptom dimensions in a systematic sample of patients with onset of schizophrenia in childhood and early adolescence. II: Positive/negative

distinction and childhood predictors of adult outcome. *British Journal of Psychiatry, 169,* 371–378.

McClellan, J., & Werry, J. (1994). Practice parameters for the assessment and treatment of children and adolescents with schizophrenia. *Journal of the American Academy of Child and Adolescent Psychiatry, 33,* 616–635.

McKenna, K., Gordon, C. T., Lenane, M., Kaysen, D., Fahey, K., & Rapoport, J. L. (1994). Looking for childhood-onset schizophrenia: The first 71 cases screened. *Journal of the American Academy of Child and Adolescent Psychiatry, 33,* 636–644.

McKenna, K., Gordon, C. T., & Rapoport, J. L. (1994). Childhood-onset schizophrenia: Timely neurobiological research. *Journal of the American Academy of Child and Adolescent Psychiatry, 33,* 771–781.

Mednick, S. A., Machon, R. A., Huttunen, M. O., & Bonett, D. (1988). Adult schizophrenia following prenatal exposure to an influenza epidemic. *Archives of General Psychiatry, 45,* 189–192.

Miklowitz, D. J., Velligan, D. I., Goldstein, M. J., Nuechterlein, K. H., Gitlin, M. J., Ranlett, G., & Doane, J. A. (1991). Communication deviance in families of schizophrenic and manic patients. *Journal of Abnormal Psychology, 100,* 163–173.

Orvaschel, H. (1995). *K-SADS-E* (Fifth revision, *DSM-IV*). Center for Psychological Studies, Nova Southeastern University, Ft. Lauderdale, FL.

Petty, L. K., Ornitz, E., Michelman, J. D., & Zimmerman, E. G. (1984). Autistic children who become schizophrenic. *Archives of General Psychiatry, 41,* 129–135.

Pogue-Geile, M. F., & Harrow, M. (1985). Negative symptoms in schizophrenia: Their longitudinal course and prognostic significance. *Schizophrenia Bulletin, 11,* 427–439.

Pool, D., Bloom, W., Wielke, D. H, Roninger, J. J., & Gallant, D. M. (1976). A controlled evaluation of loxitane in seventy-five adolescent schizophrenic patients. *Current Therapeutic Research, 19,* 99–104.

Quintana, H., & Keshavan, M. (1995). Case study: Risperidone in children and adolescents with schizophrenia. *Journal of the American Academy of Child and Adolescent Psychiatry, 34,* 1292–1296.

Rapoport, J. L., & Ismond, D. R. (1996). *DSM-IV training guide for diagnosis of childhood disorders.* New York: Brunner/Mazel.

Remschmidt, H., Martin, M., Schulz, E., Gutenbrunner, C., & Fleischhaker, C. (1991). The concept of positive and negative schizophrenia in child and adolescent psychiatry. In A. Marneros, N. C. Andreasen, & M. T. Tsuang (Eds.), *Negative versus positive schizophrenia* (pp. 219–242). Berlin: Springer.

Remschmidt, H. E., Schulz, E., Martin, M., Warnke, A., & Trott, G.-E. (1994). Childhood-onset schizophrenia: History of the concept and recent studies. *Schizophrenia Bulletin, 20,* 727–745.

Russell, A. T. (1994). The clinical presentation of childhood-onset schizophrenia. *Schizophrenia Bulletin, 20,* 631–646.

Russell, A. T., Bott, L., & Sammons, C. (1989). The phenomenology of schizophrenia occurring in childhood. *Journal of the American Academy of Child and Adolescent Psychiatry, 28,* 399–407.

Schmidt, M., Blanz, B., Dippe, A., Koppe, T., & Lay, B. (1995). Course of patients diagnosed as having schizophrenia during first episode occurring under age 18 years. *European Archives of Psychiatry and Clinical Neuroscience, 245,* 93–100.

Singer, M. T., & Wynne, L. C. (1963). Differentiating characteristics of parents of childhood schizophrenics, childhood neurotics, and young adult schizophrenics. *American Journal of Psychiatry, 120,* 234–243.

Singer, M. T., & Wynne, L. C. (1965). Thought disorder and family relations of schizophrenics: IV. Results and implications. *Archives of General Psychiatry, 12,* 201–212.

Spencer, E. K., & Campbell, M. (1994). Children with schizophrenia: Diagnosis, phenomenology, and pharmacotherapy. *Schizophrenia Bulletin, 20,* 713–725.

Strandburg, R. J., Marsh, J. T., Brown, W. S., Asarnow, R. F., & Guthrie, D. (1994). Information-processing deficits across childhood- and adult-onset schizophrenia. *Schizophrenia Bulletin, 20,* 685–695.

Strober, M., Lampert, C., Schmidt, S., & Morrell, W. (1993). The course of major depressive disorder in adolescents: Recovery and risk of manic switching in a 24-month prospective, naturalistic follow-up of psychotic and non-psychotic subtypes. *Journal of the American Academy of Child and Adolescent Psychiatry, 32,* 34–42.

Tienari, P., Sorri, A., Lahti, I., Naarala, M., Wahlberg, K., Moring, J., Pohjola, J., & Wynne, L. C. (1987). Genetic and psychosocial factors in schizophrenia: The Finnish Adoptive Family Study. *Schizophrenia Bulletin, 13,* 477–484.

Volkmar, F. R. (1996). Childhood and adolescent psychosis: A review of the past 10 years. *Journal of the American Academy of Child and Adolescent Psychiatry, 35,* 843–851.

Volkmar, F. R., & Cohen, D. J. (1991). Comorbid association of autism and schizophrenia. *American Journal of Psychiatry, 148,* 1705–1707.

Volkmar, F. R., Cohen, D. J., Hoshino, Y., Rende, R. D., & Paul, R. (1988). Phenomenology and classification of the childhood psychoses. *Psychological Medicine, 18,* 191–201.

Volkmar, F. R., & Schwab-Stone, M. (1996). Annotation: Childhood disorders in *DSM-IV. Journal of Child Psychology and Psychiatry, 37,* 779–784.

Watkins, J. M., Asarnow, R. F., & Tanguay, P. E. (1988). Symptom development in childhood onset schizophrenia. *Journal of Child Psychology and Psychiatry, 29,* 865–878.

Weinberger, D. R. (1987). Implications of normal brain development for the pathogenesis of schizophrenia. *Archives of General Psychiatry, 44,* 660–669.

Werry, J. S. (1996). Childhood schizophrenia. In F. R. Volkmar (Ed.), *Psychoses and pervasive developmental disorders in childhood and adolescence* (pp. 1–48). Washington, DC: American Psychiatric Press.

Werry, J. S., McClellan, J. M., Andrews, L. K., & Ham, M. (1994). Clinical features and outcome of child and adolescent schizophrenia. *Schizophrenia Bulletin, 20,* 619–630.

Werry, J. S., McClellan, J. M., & Chard, L. (1991). Childhood and adolescent schizophrenic, bipolar, and schizoaffective disorders: A clinical and outcome study. *Journal of the American Academy of Child and Adolescent Psychiatry, 30,* 457–465.

World Health Organization (1967–69). *Manual of the international statistical classification of diseases, injuries, and causes of death: Based on the recommendation of the World Health Organization Eighth Revision Conference.* Geneva, Switzerland: World Health Organization.

World Health Organization (1978). *Mental disorders: Glossary and guide to their classification in accordance with the ninth revision of the international classification of diseases.* Geneva: World Health Organization.

World Health Organization (1992). *International statistical classification of disease and related health problems* (Vol. 1, 10th revision). Geneva, Switzerland: World Health Organization.

Zahn, T. P., Jacobsen, L. K., Gordon, C. T., McKenna, K., Frazier, J. A., & Rapoport, J. L. (1997). Autonomic nervous system markers of psychopathology in childhood-onset schizophrenia. *Archives of General Psychiatry, 54,* 904–912.

Zahn, T. P., Jacobsen, L. K., Gordon, C. T., McKenna, K., Frazier, J. A., & Rapoport, J. L. (in press). Attention deficits in childhood-onset schizophrenia: Reaction time studies. *Journal of Abnormal Psychology.*

Subject Index

Every effort has been made to index as comprehensively as possible, and to standardize the terms used in the index in line with the following standards:

Thesaurus of Psychological Index Terms, APA, Eighth Edition, for the selection of psychological terms.

Thesaurus of ERIC Descriptors, ERIC, Twelfth Edition, for the selection of education terms not covered by the above.

EMTREE Thesaurus for the selection of medical terms not covered by the above.

IUPAC Recommendations for the nomenclature of chemical terms, with trivial names being employed where normal usage dictates.

In general, the index follows the recommendations laid down in BS ISO 999:1996.

In view of the diverse nature of the terminology employed by the different authors, the reader is advised to search for related entries under the appropriate headings.

The index entries are presented in word-by-word alphabetical sequence. Chemical terms are filed under substituent prefixes, where appropriate, rather than under the parent compound name; this is in line with the presentation given in the *Thesaurus of Psychological Index Terms*.

The index is arranged in set-out style, with a maximum of three levels of heading. Location references refer to page number; major coverage of a subject is indicated by bold, elided page numbers; for example,

> professional licensing, oral examinations **1234–55**
>   and public accountability 266

See cross-references direct the user to the preferred term; for example, character *see* personality

See also cross-references provide the user with guideposts to terms of related interest, from the broader term to the narrower term, and appear at the end of the main heading to which they refer; for example

> credentialing
>   *see also* professional certification; professional licensing; recredentialing

LaVergne, TN USA
04 January 2011
211060LV00002B/26/A